ANDO
ARCHITECT AND ARCHITECTURE

Ando Biography — Architectural Theory, Works, Era and Society + 346 Complete Works, Written by Tadao Ando and Kazukiyo Matsuba, Published by Kajima Institute Publishing Co., Ltd.

安藤忠雄　建築家と建築作品

安藤忠雄　松葉一清　共著　　　　　　　　　　　鹿島出版会

安藤忠雄　建築家と建築作品
目次
・
ANDO ARCHITECT AND ARCHITECTURE
Contents

	緒言	永遠の建築	文:安藤忠雄	006

第I部 安藤忠雄評伝——闘う建築論、作品、時代、社会 文:松葉一清 023

第1章　「わたしの存在感」「情念の基本空間」を求めて　025
都市生活者のアジトとしての住宅

第2章　商業建築に都市の〈公性〉を託す　059
道、広場、都市の文脈

第3章　〈美〉は〈自然〉と融合し、母なる大地に還る　091
国境を超える美術館の挑戦

第4章　「生き続ける近代建築」を目指して　125
建物と建築家の「30年の物語」

第5章　〈無〉は魂の安らぎをもたらす　157
己の精神と向き合う宗教施設

第6章　ランドスケープ、まちづくりへ　183
〈建築〉に始まり、〈建築〉を超える

エピローグ　アンドウは如何にして建築家となりし乎　215

第II部　全346作品録　解説:松葉一清　235

資料　467

安藤忠雄経歴　468
書誌　472
索引　474
著者略歴　480

| | Preface | Timeless Architecture | by Tadao Ando | 006 |

| Part I | Ando Biography — Architectural Theory, Works, Era and Society | by Kazukiyo Matsuba | 023 |

Chapter 1 Quest for "My Presence" and the "Fundamental Space of Pathos" 025
Houses as Hide-outs for Urban Residents

Chapter 2 Expect the City's 'Publicness' in Commercial Buildings 059
Streets, Open Spaces and Urban Context

Chapter 3 'Beauty' Collaborates with 'Nature' to Return to Mother Earth 091
Challenges with Museums Crossing National Borders

Chapter 4 In Pursuit for "Modern Architecture That Will Continue to Exist" 125
"Story for 30 Years" of Buildings and the Architect

Chapter 5 'Nil' Brings Repose of Soul 157
Religious Facilities to Face Own Spirit

Chapter 6 Towards Landscaping and Urban Development 183
Beginning with 'Architecture' and beyond 'Architecture'

Epilogue How ANDO Became an Architect, out of His Memory 215

| Part II | 346 Complete Works | synopsis by Kazukiyo Matsuba | 235 |

Appendix 467

Tadao Ando Career 468
Bibliography 472
Index of Works 477
Author's Profile 480

緒言　永遠の建築
文：安藤忠雄

記憶の中の帝国ホテル

　先月、アメリカでシカゴを訪れた。かつて設計した住宅の横に、集合住宅だったビルを改造してギャラリーをつくるプロジェクトのためだ。仕事の合間に、郊外のオークパークに足を延ばした。文豪ヘミングウェイの故郷として知られるこの街は、近代建築の巨匠フランク・ロイド・ライトが、そのキャリアをスタートした場所でもある。独立後の最初の仕事であるウィンズロー邸から、ライトが42歳までの20年間を過ごした自邸とスタジオ、シカゴ大学そばに建つ代表作ロビー邸まで見て回った。今なお生き生きとして見える、その個性的な空間表現に心奪われながら、スキャンダラスな事件を起こしてこの地を去り、その後も数々の不幸に見舞われ、不遇の時を過ごしながら、70歳代にして落水荘、ジョンソンワックス社をものにし、再び第一線に返り咲くこととなった、偉大なる建築家の激動の人生に思いを馳せた。

　私が初めてライトの建築空間を体験したのは、1950年代末、十代後半の折である。落成披露式の日に関東大震災に見舞われつつ、無傷で建ち残った帝国ホテル──不遇の時代のライトがはるばる日本に来てつくった、この石造りの建築を、大阪から上京した折、偶然に訪れた。まだ建築の道に進むとも考えていない、ライトの名前も知らない時分の訪問だ。歴史や技術を踏まえた見方ができたわけではなかった。だが、大谷石とスクラッチタイルで覆われたエキゾチックな外観、日本の建物のそれとは異なる立体迷宮のごとき内部空間、家具什器に至るまで徹底されたデザインモチーフの展開など、「こんな世界があるのか」と強く衝撃を受けた。

　その後10年経たない内、高度経済成長に浮かれる時代の空気の中で、帝国ホテルもまたあっけなく

Preface Timeless Architecture
by Tadao Ando

Imperial Hotel in My Memory

I visited Chicago in the U.S. last month for a project to renovate an apartment building—which is adjacent to a house I designed before—into a gallery. I made a little side trip to the suburb of Oak Park in my spare time. The village is known as the hometown of literary giant Ernest Hemingway, and was also a place where modern architecture giant Frank Lloyd Wright began his career. I toured around, from Wright's first commission as an independent architect, the William Winslow House, his house and studio where he stayed for 20 years until age 42, to his representative work near the University of Chicago, the Frederick C. Robie House, while being fascinated by the unique spatial expressions, which are still vivid today, and I thought about the tumultuous life of this great architect. Wright left the village after a scandalous incident and spent days of misfortune with numerous troubles, yet he came back to the front line in his 70s by designing Fallingwater and the Johnson Wax Building.

My first experience with one of Wright's architectural spaces was at the end of the 1950s, when I was a late-teen. The Imperial Hotel—hit by the Great Kanto Earthquake on the day of its completion ceremony but surviving undamaged—was a stone-built building designed by Wright in his days of misfortune, while visiting faraway Japan. I happened to visit the Imperial Hotel during a trip from Osaka to Tokyo. It was when I never thought of having a career in architecture, nor had I heard of the name "Wright". I was not able to see the architecture based on history and techniques. Yet, I was majorly shocked to know that there was such a world, with the exotic appearance covered with Oya stones and scratch tiles, the 3-D maze-like interior space unlike Japanese architecture, and through deployment of design motifs including furniture and fixtures.

In less than ten years, the Imperial Hotel was demolished too quickly in the frivolous mood of the

取り壊された。だが、フランク・ロイド・ライトと聞いて、今も心に浮かぶのは、若き日に見た、あの強烈な空間のイメージである。例え建物が消滅しても、私の中で建築は生き続けている。

私の建築の原点──住吉の長屋

　全ての人工物がそうであるように、建築もまた、いつかは風化して潰えるものだ。それに抗おうとする人間の意思の表れが、例えば西欧の連綿と続く石造りの建築思想であり、日本の伊勢の式年遷宮といった稀有の建築システムといえるのかもしれないが──私は、かなうならば、物質それ自体や形式ではなく、記憶として、人々の心の中で永遠に生き続ける建築をつくりたい。その理想に近づくべく、人間の理性の表徴としての幾何学を用い、徹底してモノを削ぎ落した先に見いだせるであろう、無垢の空間を追求する。漠然と広がる世界の中に、ひとつの領域を明示する壁。その内に潜む無地のキャンヴァスのような空洞に光や風といった自然の断片が引き込まれるときに生じる場の彩り、その生命感に人間の魂に訴える力を期待する。

　無論、このような目的意識を最初から明確に持っていたわけではない。大阪で小さな事務所を開き、設計活動を始めたのは1969年。最初の10年は、まず設計の仕事がなかなか得られない、かろうじて見つかっても敷地も狭く、予算も乏しい……といった状況で、その逆境をいかに乗り越え、自分なりの思いを実現できるか──と、建築を職業としていくことで精一杯だった。

　ポツポツと舞い込むのは、小規模な都市住宅と商業施設の設計のみ。いずれも、丹下健三を筆頭とする当時の建築界の最先端からすれば、取るに足らないスケールの仕事だ。だが、それを楔のように一つ一つ街に埋め込んでいくことで、自分なりのキャリアを積み重ねていこうと覚悟を決めた。1972年に自身の建築の意思表明として「都市ゲリラ住居」という文章を書いたが、このタイトルが当時の私の気分をよく表していたように思う。

　がむしゃらに仕事に取り組んでいく中で、1975年に「住吉の長屋」の設計を始めた。低層木造家屋がひしめきあう大阪の下町、その一角に建つ三軒長屋の中央の一軒を建て替える。間口二間、奥行きが八間という規模といい、両隣からの通し梁もろとも解体する工事のリスクといい、予算含めておよそ考えられる最悪の条件の仕事であった。だが、そんな極限の状況下であったからこそ、より深く、真摯に建築と向き合えた。

　「住吉の長屋」は、二層分の高さのコンクリートの構造体を三分割し、その中央を屋根のない中庭と

high economic growth era. Nevertheless, the name of Frank Lloyd Wright still reminds me of the image of the vivid space that I witnessed in my youth. Even though the building does not exist, the architecture continues to persist within my mind.

Starting Point of My Architecture: ROW HOUSE, SUMIYOSHI

Like any artificial products, architecture also weathers and comes to an end at some point. A representation of the human intention to resist such inevitability may include an unbroken line of stone-built architectural ideas in Western Europe, and a rare building system at Ise Jingu Shrine in Japan, in which a new divine palace is built on a regular basis. However, if possible, my desire is the creation of architecture that timelessly survives in the minds of people — as a memory, rather than as a substance itself or a system. In order to approach the ideal architecture, I pursue a pure space that can be found after using geometry as a symbol of human reason, and thoroughly eliminating objects. There is a wall that defines one domain within a vaguely spread out world. Beauty is added to a place when natural segments (such as light and wind) are drawn into a blank canvas-like hollow within the wall. I expect the feeling of vitality to have an appealing power to the human soul.

Of course, I did not have such a clear sense of purpose from the beginning. My design activities began in 1969, when I established a small design office in Osaka. For the first ten years, I struggled to receive commissions. Even when I did have a commission, it was for a small site with limited budget. How to overcome these adverse circumstances and materialize my own thoughts? I strained to keep my architect career.

I only had sparse commissions for small-scale urban houses and commercial facilities. All of them were of no significance in terms of scale, compared with the frontier of the architectural world at that time, led by Kenzo Tange. Nevertheless, I made up my mind to build my unique career by embedding individual designs into a town, as if pounding in a wedge. In 1972, I wrote the manifesto "Urban Guerrilla House" to declare my architectural intentions. I think the title well represents my mood at that time.

While I worked furiously on projects, I began designing Row House, Sumiyoshi in 1975. It was a renovation project of a housing unit, located at the center of a row house with three units in downtown Osaka, packed with low-rise wooden houses. It had almost every worst condition conceivable, such as a size of 3.6m wide and 14.4m long, the high risk of the construction work that demolished the through-beams shared with the neighboring housing units, and the budget. Yet, such worst-case conditions made me confront architecture in a deeper and more sincere manner.

In Row House, Sumiyoshi, the concrete structure with two-story height is divided into three

する構成である。中庭が生活動線を分断するプランは、常識的な感覚からすれば、住みにくいものだろう。実際、完成して建築雑誌などで取り上げられると、内外装ともに打ち放しコンクリートとした仕上げや、不愛想なファサード表現を含め、機能性を軽視し過ぎている、建築家の傲慢だと批判を浴びた。

　だが、ここで問われるべきはこの場所で生活を営むのに本当に必要なものは何か、住まいとは何かという価値観の問題だった。その問いに、私は自然の一部としてある生活こそが住まいの本質であり、自然との対話こそが人間のための空間に最も必要なのだという答えを出した。そして、限られたスペースの中で選択を迫られたとき、無難な便利さよりも、厳しさもやさしさも含めた自然の変化を最大限引き込むことを選んだ。

モダニズムの先へ

　徹底して単純な幾何学形態の内に、複雑多様な空間のシーンを展開させること。あるいは鉄とガラスとコンクリートという現代において最もありふれた素材をもって、どこにもないような個性的な空間をつくりだすこと——「住吉の長屋」の建築プロセスにおける、1ミリの無駄もできない緊張感はまた、私なりの建築のつくり方が確立されるきっかけともなった。

　1970年代当時、建築界は、教条主義的なモダニズムに対する反動で沸いていた。私と同世代の建築を志す若者たちも、鋭いものは皆、ロバート・ヴェンチューリやチャールズ・ムーアなどの言説に反応して、モダニズムからの離脱を時代のテーマと考え始めていた。歴史の引用、脱構築、エコロジー、セルフ・ビルドなど、さまざまなキーワードが次なる建築のイメージとして喧伝された。

　しかし、こうした時代の空気を身体では理解しながら、私は逆に初期の時代のモダニズムに惹かれていた。これは恐らく、私が正当な建築教育を受けることなく、独学で建築を学んだことに起因するのだろう。

　設計活動を始める前、二十代後半の数年間のうちに、私はヨーロッパ、アメリカを中心に世界を巡る旅に出た。充分な予備知識もなく、単に当時知っていた限りの古今の名建築を訪ねる行き当たりばったりの建築行脚であったが、その拙さの分、逆に、素直に建築と出会うことができた。そこで私は、場所によって異なる風土と人間社会の豊かさを知り、同時に"モダニズム"と一つに括られる建築の、実に多様な広がりを目の当たりにした。

　同じモダニズムと言いながら、フィンランドのアルヴァ・アールトの建築と、ル・コルビュジエの建築

parts, and a roofless courtyard is located at the center. Since the courtyard disconnects traffic lines for living, the plan is perhaps inconvenient to live in from a common sense perspective. In fact, when the building was introduced in architectural magazines, it was criticized for its as-cast concrete finish of both interior and exterior, as well as the unfriendly façade expression, since it was considered disregarding of functionality and was regarded as demonstrating the arrogance of the architect.

However, questions regarding the true necessities for living there, and the value of houses should have been asked. As answers to these questions, I came to conclude that a life as a part of nature was the essence of houses, and the most required factor in spaces for humans was conversation with nature. Hence, when I needed to make decisions for the limited space, I chose to maximize incorporation of both severe and gentle changes in nature, rather than just having innocuous convenience.

Beyond Modernism

There were developments of complicated and diversified spatial scenes in thoroughly simple geometric shapes, or the creation of a one-of-a-kind and unique space out of iron, glass, and concrete — the most common materials in modern times. A sense of tension during the construction process of Row House, Sumiyoshi allowed no waste, providing a trigger to establish my own way of making architecture.

In the 1970s, the architectural world was excited over the throwback to the doctrinairism-like modernism. Smart young people of my age who aimed to be architects began to consider that separation from modernism was a theme at that time, in response to statements from Robert Venturi and Charles H. Moore. Various key words, such as citation of history, deconstruction, ecology, and self-build, were disseminated as the image of new architecture.

While my body understood the trends of the era, I was conversely attracted to early modernism. It was perhaps partly due to the fact that I taught myself without receiving a proper architectural education.

Before starting my design activities, I traveled around the world, mainly in Europe and the U.S., for few years in my late 20s. Without enough background knowledge, I simply visited all kinds of old and new, quality architectural works that I knew at that time, during my architectural pilgrimage. Due to my immaturity, I was able to confront architecture in a more straightforward manner. I learned there about different climates of land, and the richness of human society, while witnessing a truly diversified expanse of architecture, which was summarized as "modernism" architecture.

While both are considered as modernism architecture, there are many differences between the architecture of Alvar Aalto in Finland and that of Le Corbusier. Even architectural works of Le Corbusier have completely different spatial natures, such as in the houses of his Purism age, and Notre Dame du

とでは、大きな開きがある。同じル・コルビュジエの建築でも、白の時代の住宅と晩年のロンシャン礼拝堂とでは、全く異質の空間性をはなっている。

　モダニズムとは一体何だったのか、その理想は本当に追求され得たと言えるのか——。初期モダニズムの瑞々しい感性に触れた私は、限界よりも無限の可能性を感じた。そして、モダニズムを否定するのでなく、そこから落ちこぼれたものを拾い合わせていくことで、自分なりに建築の未来を模索していこうと考えた。

　歴史主義や記号論といった知的操作にのみ頼ることなく、ただ目の前にある都市と社会と正面から向き合って、つくっていく。その最も端的な挑戦が、住宅の設計であり、「住吉の長屋」がその最初の成果だった。

都市への挑戦の始まり —— ローズガーデン

　「住吉の長屋」と同時期に設計を進めていた商業施設、神戸北野町での「ローズガーデン」が完成したのは、「住吉」の完成の翌年の、1977年である。今でこそ、商業施設もまた重要な都市建築であるとの認識が、建築界においても当たり前にあるが、経済一辺倒の当時日本の社会においては、評価の対象は空間効率のみ、設計者にできるのは、いかに表層を飾るかというパッケージデザインしかない。商業建築は、建築界からは完全に見捨てられていた。

　だが、公共施設など関わる由もない、都市ゲリラにとっては、商業建築の仕事もまた得難いチャンスであり、商いという人々の日常の営為に深く関わるプログラムを利点ととらえ、仕事に打ち込んだ。そして、北野町の街並みにとけ込むように建つ、レンガの壁に切妻の屋根を持つ建物を設計した。

　既存の街並みに合わせた外装は、1970年代当時、古い街並みを破壊する乱開発の風潮への抵抗であり、これはクライアントの意思でもあった。だが、「ローズガーデン」で私が本当につくりたかったのは、煉瓦壁ではない。力を注いだのは、その壁の向こうの余白の空間だった。

　ときに地上から中空へと回遊する「道」であり、ときにその途中で人々が立ち止まり、ほっと一息つける「よどみ」や「溜り」となる"余白"。いわば建物の中に街路を引き込み、その奥に広場をつくるというアイディアだ。そんなスペースを街のそこここに埋め込んでいくことで、機能性と合理性で埋め尽くされた都市に風穴を開ける——「ローズガーデン」で始めた試みを、その後同じ北野町で関わった7件の商業施設の全てにおいて、しつこく繰り返した。

Haut, Ronchamp in his last years.

What was modernism? Can it be said that its ideal architecture was truly sought? After learning a fresh sense of early modernism, I felt infinite possibilities rather than limitations. I determined to search for the future of architecture in my own manner by picking up things that fell out from modernism, instead of denying modernism.

Without relying solely on intellectual manipulations (such as historicism and semiotics), I would just straightforwardly confront the city and society in front of me, and design. The simplest challenges were the designs of houses, and my first achievement was Row House, Sumiyoshi.

Beginning of the Challenge for Cities: ROSE GARDEN

The commercial facilities Rose Garden in Kitano-cho in Kobe was designed around the same time as Row House, Sumiyoshi. It was completed in 1977, a year after completion of Row House, Sumiyoshi. Although commercial facilities are commonly recognized by today's architectural world as one of the important types of urban architecture, architecture was evaluated only by spatial efficiency at that time in Japanese society, solely focusing on economy. Designers could only make a package design to decorate the surface layers. Commercial facilities were completely abandoned from the architectural world.

Nevertheless, for an urban guerilla who could never participate in public facilities, designing commercial facilities was also a valuable opportunity. I considered the fact that the commercial program was deeply involved in the everyday lives of people as an advantage, and devoted myself to the work. As a result, I designed a brick-wall building with a gabled roof, blending into the townscape of Kitano-cho.

The exterior was designed to fit into the existing townscape, in accordance with the client's intention to resist a trend of overdevelopment in the 1970s involving the destruction of old townscapes. However, brick walls were not what I truly desired to create in Rose Garden. Rather, I focused on void spaces behind the walls.

A "void" sometimes serves as a "path" connecting the ground level to mid-air, or a "stagnant" or "pooling" space for people to occasionally stop and relax. It was an idea like creating a plaza at the back of a street, which was integrated into the building. By embedding such spaces in various locations of the town, I challenged the existing city filled with functionality and rationality. This attempt — initiated in Rose Garden — was persistently repeated in all seven commercial facilities, where I was later involved in the same Kitano-cho.

人々の思いがつくる建築

　自身の目指すべき建築の原型をつかんだ「住吉の長屋」と、建築で都市に挑む手がかりを見出した「ローズガーデン」。この二つの仕事を起点として、今まで走り続けている。

　無我夢中の日々を過ごしているうちに、徐々に仕事の規模も大きくなり、プログラムも多様化、パブリックな施設の計画も手掛けるようになった。設計の自由度が上がれば、その分可能性も広がるから、構想もふくらみ、表現もより大胆になる。だが、その根底にあるヴィジョンは、前述の二つの建物をつくった半世紀前と何ら変わりはない。「住吉の長屋」から「小篠邸」、「城戸崎邸」から「スリランカの住宅」、「モンテレイの住宅」といった国外での特異な状況での仕事に至るまで、あるいは「ローズガーデン」に続く「STEP」、「TIME'S」等の初期の仕事から、「表参道ヒルズ」「東急東横線渋谷駅」といった2000年以降完成の都市施設、あるいは近年の「モンテレイ大学RGSセンター」「上海保利大劇場」といった海外での都市スケールのプロジェクトに至るまで、私の中では全て一本の線でつながっている。

　今改めてそれらの仕事を振り返り思うのは、建築の強度、その存在の強さは、規模の大小、予算や敷地といった与条件の是非にはよらないということだ。例えどんなに小さく、ささやかな仕事であっても、あきらめることなく前を向いて取り組めば、ときに、いかなるビッグ・プロジェクトにも勝る力を、その建築は持ち得る。むしろ逆境にあって、それを乗り越えるべくつくられた建築の方が、より深く社会に息づいているようにも思う。

　「光の教会」は、日本社会が、後にバブル経済と呼ばれる好景気に沸き始めた時、未曽有の建設ラッシュが続く中、その隙間を縫うようにつくられた地域密着型の小規模な教会建築だ。精一杯の浄財を集めて、新たな教会堂をつくろうという信者の熱意と、それに応えるべく、赤字覚悟で工事を引き受けてくれた工務店のビルダーとしての誇りと情熱。彼らの思いを受けて、私が考えたのが階段状に床を掘り下げたワンルームのコンクリートの空間、その正面の壁に十字型の開口を設けただけの建築である。限られた予算のため、外形は単純な箱型にせざるを得なかった。ならば、その箱の中に、いかにして、人々が集い、祈りを捧げるための、神聖な場を生み出すか。1年間余り考えた末に辿り着いたのが、装飾も何もない薄暗闇の中に、十字の光が浮かび上がる、この「光の教会」のアイディアだった。

　建設工事は、紆余曲折がありつつも、工務店の全面的な協力のもとに諸々の困難を打破、建物は1989年7月に完成した。だが、最大の功労者である工務店の社長は、その三か月後、52歳という若さでこの世を去った。工事の後半から、体調は芳しくなかったのを、最後まで現場を守ってくれた。彼の魂

Architecture Created by People's Thoughts

I have continued my journey up until today from my points of origin: Row House, Sumiyoshi, where I grasped the prototype of architecture I should seek, and Rose Garden, where I found a clue for challenging cities by using architecture.

As I worked feverishly, the scale of projects became larger with more varied programs, and I began to plan public facilities. When the degrees of freedom in design increase, possibilities also expand, resulting in a more extensive scheme and more dynamic expressions. However, the underlying vision remains exactly the same as a half century ago, when I made the aforementioned two buildings. In my mind my works form a continuous line: from Row House, Sumiyoshi, Koshino House, and Kidosaki House, to works under peculiar conditions overseas such as House in Sri Lanka and House in Monterrey; and from early works such as Rose Garden followed by Step and Time's, to urban facilities completed after 2000 such as Omotesando Hills and Tokyu Toyoko-Line Shibuya Station, and to overseas urban-scale projects in recent years such as Roberto Garza Sada Center for Arts, Architecture and Design, and Shanghai Poly Theater.

What I think by looking back at these works is that the strength of a building and its sense of presence do not depend on the given conditions such as scale, budget, and site. No matter how small and modest a work may be, a building can occasionally attain a power greater than that of any large-scale project by facing forward and tackling the work without giving up. I rather believe that buildings that were made to overcome adverse conditions are more deeply rooted in society.

Church of the Light is a small, community-based church building. It was built as if to fill the gap during an unprecedented construction boom at the beginning of the buoyant economy in Japan — later called the "bubble economy". Believers keenly collected many donations to build a new church building. The building contractor accepted the job with pride and passion even though taking a loss, in order to respond to the believers' eagerness. In reaction to their desire, I came up with a building with an open concrete space where the floor was dug down in a stair-like manner, and a cross-shaped opening was made on the front wall. Due to the tight budget, there was no choice but to have a simple cubic exterior. The challenge was how to create a sacred place within the box for people to gather and pray. My final idea after about a year of thinking was this design of Church of the Light, where a cross-shaped light appears in a dim-lit space with no decorations.

The construction was full of twists and turns, but thanks to the full cooperation of the contractor, we overcame various challenges and the building was completed in July 1989. The president of the contractor company, who was the key player of the project, passed away three months after the completion, at the

がつくった建築だった。

　事務所スタートから20年余りを経て、自身の取り巻く状況が大きく変わりつつあったとき、このささやかな教会の建築は"何のためにつくるのか、誰のためにつくるのか"という、最も大切な建築の問いを、改めて心に刻んでくれた。教会は今も同じ場所に建って、人々と共に生き続けている。

抽象と具象の重ね合わせ

　1987年、「城戸崎邸」を完成させたときに「抽象と具象の重ね合わせ」という文章を発表した。ここで私は建築を抽象と具象の葛藤としてとらえ、抽象的表現の可能性を示すものとしてアルバースの「正方形礼賛」を、建築の具象性、身体性の象徴としてピラネージの「幻想の牢獄」を挙げた。そして、アルバース的骨格の中にピラネージ的幻想の迷路を潜ませていくことを、自身の建築の一つの命題に、と書いた。

　ちょうど「六甲の集合住宅Ⅱ」の設計が終盤を迎えようとしていた時期だった。急斜面の地形に対し建築の幾何学をいかに扱うか。自身の中で徐々に明確化してきた思考を、整理するためにまとめた文章に過ぎない。だが、はからずもこの文章が、1990年代から徐々に大自然に囲まれた立地の公共施設の設計、国外でのプロジェクトに参加する機会が増えていく中で、〈私〉から〈公〉あるいは〈都市〉から〈地域〉へ、都市ゲリラの先を模索していた私が一歩前へ進むための道標を示していたように思う。

　建築に何ができるのか、そもそも建築とは何なのか──私は、本当の意味での建築の機能とは、人工と自然、個人と社会、現在と過去といった、人間社会にまつわる多様な事象のあいだの関係づくりであると考えている。それらの二項対立の本質が抽象と具象であり、関係づくりとは、そのどちらかを選ぶのではない、対立したまま共存する道を探る"重ね合わせ"の作業だ。この議論を象徴するのが、概念としての建築に対して、具象なるものの集積としてある"場所"というテーマだろう。

　それぞれの場所には、必ずそこにしかない文脈がある。その内容は、土地の歴史や形状、植生から、その中にある既存の構築物、そこから見える風景などさまざまだ。それを注意深く読み取りつつ、新たな建築を加えることによって、場所とそこに息づく共同体の間に新たな関係性、豊かな対話を喚起する。これはポストモダンの一つの潮流であるコンテクスチュアリズムの発想に通じるものだろう。だが、その多くが、既存の文脈との調和、融合を指向するのに対し、私はむしろ、場に刺激をあたえるような、意図的な不連続をこそつくりたいと考える。その不連続、不透明な存在を、幾何学による徹底して明晰明快

young age of 52. He completed the construction task despite his ill health during the latter half of the construction period. He dedicated his soul to the building.

About 20 years had passed since starting my own design office, and the circumstances around me were beginning to change significantly. This small church building reminded me of the most essential questions about architecture: the reason for making it and who is it for. The church still stands at the same location and lives with the people.

Superimposition of Abstraction and Representation

When Kidosaki House was completed in 1987, I published the essay "Superimposition of Abstraction and Representation". I regarded architecture as a conflict of abstractness and concreteness. An example given in the essay of representing the possibilities of abstract expressions was "Homage to the Square" by Josef Albers, and one representing the concreteness / embodiment of architecture was "Prisons" by Giovanni Battista Piranesi. I wrote that one of my architectural propositions would be incorporation of a Piranesi-like imaginary maze into an Albers-like framework.

Around that time, I was about to finish designing Rokko Housing II. How to use architectural geometry for a steeply sloped site? The essay was simply written to organize my thoughts that were gradually becoming clear. However, it appears as if the essay unexpectedly guided my advancement beyond "Urban Guerrilla", from private to public, and from cities to communities, since the 1990s when I was getting more opportunities for participating in designs of public facilities surrounded by nature and overseas projects.

What can be done by architecture? What is architecture to begin with? I believe that the true function of architecture is relationship-building between various elements that are related to human society, such as artificial and natural, individual and society, and present and past. The essence of such binomial oppositions is abstractness and concreteness. Relationship-building does not mean choosing either one; rather, it is a process of "overlapping" them to seek a way for the contrasting elements to coexist. This discussion is perhaps represented by a theme of architecture as a concept versus a "place" as an accumulation of concrete objects.

Each place always has its unique context, consisting of various things such as history, shape, and vegetation of the place, existing structures, and the views from there. By adding new architecture while carefully reading the context, a new relationship is built between the place and existing communities, and rich conversations are evoked. This might have something in common with the ideas of contexturalism, a school of post-modernism. In contrast to most of the ideas that are oriented towards harmony and

な枠組みの中に実現すべく悪戦苦闘する。「住吉の長屋」の中庭、「TIME'S」での高瀬川と「並走する水辺のテラス」、「大阪府立近つ飛鳥博物館」の人工の丘陵としての大階段。いずれもが、予定調和から外れた、合理主義の価値観からすれば非合理な部分をこそ、よりどころとする建築だ。

時をつなぐ建築

　一方で、建築が場所に息づき、風景に溶け込んでいくには、相応の時間がかかる。建築は、完成した時が終わりではない。それがいかに人々に使われ、意図した通り、場所に根付いていくことができるか。ときには、建物が完成した後の時間にも、主体的に関わり、作り手としての責任を果たしていかねば、建築は思う通りには"育たない"。その意味で、1970年代後半から4期にかけて関わった「六甲の集合住宅」プロジェクトや、同じく30余年の間にひとつの島の中に7件の建築をつくった「直島の一連のプロジェクト」、「ローズガーデン」を始めとする「北野町の一連のプロジェクト」や東京調布市での「仙川の一連のプロジェクト」など、ひとつの地域に、継続的に複数の仕事で関わり得た仕事は、私にとって非常に重要な意味を持つ。

　「プンタ・デラ・ドガーナ」を中心とする、イタリアのヴェネチアでの一連のプロジェクトもまた、同様の文脈を持つ仕事だ。ここでは場所性の問題に加えてさらに、古い建物の再生という、いわば過去と現在のあいだの関係づくりが主題としてあった。

　文化とは、歴史や人々の記憶の堆積の上にこそ育まれるものだ。その意味で、過去から現在へと時間を重ね合わせ、未来へとつないでいく再生プロジェクトは、今を生きるものの責務として、あるべき仕事だろう。この新旧の重ね合わせにおいても、意図するのは、安易な迎合ではない、古いものと新しいものが対立的に共存する関係の創出である。

　私が、旧い建物の再生を意識的に考えるようになったのは、1970年代末に「中之島プロジェクトⅠ」を構想した頃からだ。その後、試行錯誤を重ねる中で「中之島プロジェクトⅡ（アーバン・エッグ）」や、「テートギャラリー現代美術館国際設計競技案」などのアイディアが生まれた。いずれも実現は叶わなかったが、前者の新旧が入れ子状に重なる空間構成は、後の「プンタ・デラ・ドガーナ」を中心とする一連の仕事に、後者の新旧が衝突する空間のイメージは、上野の「国立国会図書館　国際子ども図書館」へとつながっている。

　2017年現在も、ヴェネチアの仕事と同じクライアントと、今度はパリで「ブルス・ドゥ・コメルス」

fusion with an existing context, I rather desire to create intentional discontinuity, which will stimulate a place. I struggle to materialize such a discontinuous and opaque existence in a crystal-clear geometric framework. The courtyard of Row House, Sumiyoshi, the waterfront terrace along the Takase River in Time's, and the grand stairs as an artificial hill in Chikatsu-Asuka Historical Museum, Osaka: these architectural works were founded on irrational portions of rationalistic value, outside of a predetermined harmony.

Architecture to Connect Time

Considerable time is needed for a building to live in a place and blend in with the scenery. The time of completion is not the end of a building. How will the building be used by people and take root there in the intended manner? A building never "grows" as an architect expects, unless there are occasional proactive interventions of an architect and fulfilment of the creator's obligations after the completion of the building. In that sense, it was very meaningful for me to have a series of projects that involved continuous multiple projects in the same area. Such examples include: Rokko Housing project that had four stages beginning from the late 1970s, a series of projects in Naoshima that involved seven buildings on an island over about 30 years, a series of projects in Kitano-cho including Rose Garden, and a series of projects in Sengawa in Chofu City, Tokyo.

 The same context was found in a series of projects in Venice, Italy, including Punta della Dogana Contemporary Art Center. In addition to the challenging location issue, there was the main theme of restoration of an old building, or relationship-building between the past and present.

 Cultures are nurtured based on the accumulation of history and people's memories. In this regard, the restoration project — overlapping time from past to present, and connecting it to the future — is a work in which people living in the present time should conduct as an obligation. For this overlap of old and new, I do not intend an easy assentation, but instead a relationship-building where contrasting old and new things coexist.

 I began to be conscious about old building restoration at the end of the 1970s, when I planned Nakanoshima Project I. While utilizing trial and error thereafter, I had ideas for Nakanoshima Project II (Urban Egg Space Strata) and the Tate Gallery of Modern Art, International Design Competition. They were neither materialized. However, the spatial composition of the former with overlapping new and old parts of the building in a nested manner led to a series of projects including Punta della Dogana Contemporary Art Center. The image of collision of old and new spaces in the latter led to The International Library of Children's Literature in Ueno, Tokyo.

という18世紀末に建造された商品取引所を現代美術館として再生するプロジェクトに取り組んでいる。パリの成熟した都市文化の明日のために、この歴史的建造物をいかに力強く生命感に満ちた存在へと再生できるか——大いなる挑戦だ。

終らない闘い

　既存の社会の中に、建築によって新たな関係性を創りだす。これを建築とするならば、1995年の阪神淡路大震災後の被災地で取り組んだ「兵庫グリーンネットワーク」から、瀬戸内の環境再生を目的に始めた「瀬戸内オリーブ基金」、地元大阪のための都市提案プロジェクトのハイライトとして企てた桜の植樹運動「桜の会・平成の通り抜け」、東京湾に浮かぶ88ヘクタールのゴミの埋め立て地を植樹によって海上の森にせんとする「海の森」——などは、ある意味で、私にとって最も大きな建築の仕事であったといえるだろう。

　風景、社会制度の中に入り込んでいって、そこに"刺激"をもたらすような新たな関係性をつくろうとすれば、当然のこと、摩擦や衝突が起こる。建築の原点たる住まいの問題、空間の光と影といった美学上の問題、あるいは都市空間、場所の風土の問題。つくる度にさまざまなテーマに直面し、それらに建築で応えるべく、悪戦苦闘してきた。その全てが挑戦だった。
　だが、それらの挑戦は、決して私一人でなし得た仕事ではない。建築に自らの思いを託し、つくるチャンスを与えてくれるクライアント、私たちが描く画を、技術的努力を尽くして具現化してくれる施工者、そして、産み落とされた建物と付き合い、育ててくれる人々、社会。そうして共に闘ってくれる彼らの存在があって、はじめて私の目指す建築は、建築たり得る。人々と共に闘い、葛藤する時間にこそ、私は生きる喜びを感じる。
　フランク・ロイド・ライトは、91歳でその人生を終えるまで創ることをあきらめず、その死後にグッゲンハイム美術館を完成させた。かなわないまでも、建築家として生きる限り、私も私なりの闘いを続けたい。

Today in 2017, I also work for a restoration project in Paris with the same client as in Venice. A commodity exchange built in the end of the 18th century, called Bourse de Commerce, is going to be renovated into a contemporary museum. How to restore this historical building into a bold existence with vitality, for the future of mature urban culture in Paris? This is a great challenge.

Never-ending Fight

A new relationship is created by architecture in the existing society. If architecture is defined like this, the most significant architectural works for me in a sense were: "Hyogo Green Network" in a disaster-stricken area after the Great Hanshin earthquake in 1995, "Setouchi Olive Foundation" for environmental rehabilitation in Setouchi, the cherry tree planting campaign ASSOCIATION FOR THE HEISEI-ERA ALLEY OF CHERRY BLOSSOMS CAMPAIGN as a highlight of urban proposal project for my hometown of Osaka, and the SEA FOREST tree planting campaign for transforming a 88-hectare landfill site on Tokyo Bay into a forest on the ocean.

Frictions and collisions naturally occur when one enters into a landscape and social system, and tries to create a new relationship that provides "stimulation". For every design I made, I confronted various themes, including a housing problem as an architectural origin, aesthetic problems such as light and shade in a space, issues of urban space, and issues about the climate of the place. I have been struggling to address the themes by using architecture. Everything was challenging.

However, these challenges were never addressed on my own. Architecture that I pursue can only become architecture, because of the existence of people who fight with me: clients who give me opportunities for creation with their passion; contractors who embody our drawings with the best technical effort; and people and society who encounter and raise the resulting building. I feel the joy of life when I fight and struggle together with people.

Frank Lloyd Wright never gave up creating until the end of his life at age 91, and the Guggenheim Museum was completed after he passed away. Even if no match for him, I also desire to continue my own battle, as long as I live as an architect.

第 I 部　安藤忠雄評伝——闘う建築論、作品、時代、社会

文：松葉一清

Part I　Ando Biography — Architectural Theory, Works, Era and Society

by Kazukiyo Matsuba

第1章 「わたしの存在感」「情念の基本空間」を求めて
都市生活者のアジトとしての住宅

Chapter 1　Quest for "My Presence" and the "Fundamental Space of Pathos"
Houses as Hide-outs for Urban Residents

異議申し立ての挫折を超えて

　安藤忠雄が独立した事務所を大阪に構えたのは1969年のことだった。弱冠28歳、日本全国に学生運動が波及し、フォークソングや小劇場演劇など対抗文化が台頭し、異議申し立ての気分がそこかしこに充満していた。若き安藤も1960年代半ばから、大阪を中心に活動した前衛表現者集団「具体」の芸術家たちと交流を深め、その大きなうねりの渦中にいた。しかし、ほどなく都市を包む熱気は醒めていき、眼前に広がったのは、停滞に戸惑う社会の姿だった。

　1970年、大阪、千里丘陵で開催された「日本万国博覧会」は、敗戦後の日本が猛烈な勢いで復興をなし遂げた高度経済成長の「最後の祭り」だった。東京からやってきた丹下健三や黒川紀章らはそこで「未来」を競作したが、空疎さは隠しようもなかった。万博が終わり、農協の団体客が姿を消すと、大阪には急ブレーキがかかった。商業と産業の都を錦の御旗として猛スピードで戦後復興をなしとげた「日本第二の都市」は失速し、市井のひとびとの心には諦念に似た喪失感が浸透しつつあった。「万博のあと」がどうしても描けなかったのである。

　異議申し立ての挫折も失望感を蔓延させた。1968年のパリの「五月革命」に始まる既得権社会への異議申し立ては、わが国では「学生運動」の変質と挫折、内ゲバと呼ばれるメンバー同士の凄惨な殺し合いの露顕で、社会の支持を急速に失った。その傾向は、万博の反動も手伝い、ことに大阪では顕著だった。

　安藤が1973年に打ち出した「都市ゲリラ住居」は、いわば建築家の側から、停滞の打破を宣言するものだった。若かったが、すでに商業建築の領域で先鋭的な感覚の作品を手がけて、知られるようにはなっていた。その活動に期待し、共鳴するひとびとが

1

2

Overcoming Setbacks of Protesting

In 1969, Tadao Ando established an independent office in Osaka, when he was just age 28. At that time, student movements spread throughout Japan, the counterculture (folksongs and small-theater plays) rose, and a mood of protest was everywhere. Amid such tidal wave, since the middle of 1960s, the young Ando had been cultivating personal exchanges with artists from a vanguard expressive group called "Gutai" that was performing activities around Osaka. However, the air of excitement surrounding the city cooled down before long, and what they saw before their eyes was a society bewildered by the backwater.

The "Japan World Exposition 1970" held in the Senri Hills in Osaka, was the "last festival" of rapid economic growth, during which postwar Japan recovered at an amazing rate. Kenzo Tange and Kisho Kurokawa from Tokyo competed for the "future" at the Expo, yet there was no way to cover up emptiness. After the Expo, when a bunch of Nokyo groups had left, Osaka hit the break suddenly. The "second largest city of Japan", which had achieved postwar reconstruction at excessive speed under the banner of a city of commerce and industry, lost its momentum, and a feeling of loss — similar to resignation — was beginning to penetrate into the minds of ordinary citizens. "Post Expo" could not be envisioned by any means.

Setbacks from protests also helped the spread of disappointment. Protesting against a society with vested interests — which began in Paris (the May 1968 events in France) — rapidly fell out of favor with Japanese society, due to the transformation and setbacks of the "student movements", and the exposure of appalling internal strife including the killing of members. Such trends were particularly apparent in Osaka, against a backdrop of backlash from the Expo.

Ando's "Urban Guerrilla House" in 1973 was a manifesto from an architect view to break through from stagnation. Although young, he worked on some edgy projects in the field of commercial architecture, and came to be known. People who have expectations for and sympathize with his activities requested that he design small houses, under the strong will to "continue living in urban areas". In response, the architect came up with three concepts for his "Urban Guerrilla House".

The core idea was setting "individuals" at the center of the logic. Technology development, beginning with the Industrial Revolution in the 18th century, degraded humans into '*homo economicus*'. In the architectural and related domains, the Arts and Crafts Movement by William Morris and Bauhaus attempted to resist the trend but failed. Ando felt that the direction remained lost, and searching continued even in the 1970s. He was concerned that cities might not be able to resist the trend of systemization — a product of modern times — and would be swallowed by a tide of "information revolution" at once.

A shining metallic white image, induced by cities, is homogeneous and cool; however, it is a mere "communal illusion" planted by modern times. An awareness of "houses" — an existence that would not be eroded by it — brought him the concept of "Urban Guerrilla House".

"Urban Guerrilla House" as Self-expression

Houses are an accumulation of illogical ordinary activities. Hence, they are not incorporated into the pattern of an industrialized society from 'upstream', and are detached from 'object' and 'majorities' in that sense. Furthermore, 'residing' and 'living' activities arising from 'individuals' are occupied by grotesquely exposed and naked requirements. Ando hardened his convictions based on his experiences from his childhood: growing up in downtown Osaka and closely watching people's lives. He concluded that houses were shelters that were imagined to completely enclose such 'individual' requirements.

Young Ando thought that the progression of sophisticated "information revolution" at that time would treat 'individuals' as parts and would eliminate a spiritual aspect from 'technologies'. He concluded that the only "fortress" in modern cities to terminate such movement was the houses constructed from 'individuals' as a starting point, and that the rehabilitation of a desire of 'residing' itself would be a human rehabilitation in modern cities.

According to his idea, houses should inevitably include creatural spaces for 'dramatically acquiring life'. The "Urban Guerrilla House" was a guerrilla hide-out as an image, which could only be established at an 'individual' level, instead of from 'upstream'. Therefore, placing 'individuals' at the core of thinking was the highest priority. In addition, he came to conclude that houses must be a "self-expression" based on physical intuition.

都市ゲリラ住居 I–III　1971–1973
guerrilla I–III

1. 「ゲリラI」模型
   Model of "guerrilla I"
2. 「ゲリラII」模型
   Model of "guerrilla II"
3. 「ゲリラIII」模型
   Model of "guerrilla III"

「都市に住み続ける」強固な意思のもとに小住宅の設計を依頼した。建築家はそれに応えて三つの「都市ゲリラ住居」を構想した。

その中心となる考えは「個」を論理の中心に据えることだった。18世紀の産業革命に始まる技術の展開が、人間を〈ホモ・エコノミクス＝経済動物〉に堕落させた。建築とその近傍の領域では、ウィリアム・モリスによるアーツ・アンド・クラフツ運動やバウハウスがその流れに抗しようとしたが挫折の憂き目に遇い、1970年代に至っても方向性は見失われたままで蛇行を続けていると感じた。そして、都市がそうした近代のもたらしたシステム化の流れに抗することができず、迫り来る「情報化」の波に一気に呑み込まれていくのではないかと危惧した。

都市が抱かせるメタリックに光る白色のイメージは、ホモジニアス（均質）でクールだが、近代が植えつけた「共同幻想」にしかすぎず、それに浸食されない存在としての「住居」への気づきが「都市ゲリラ住居」という概念に結びついた。

自己表現としての「都市ゲリラ住居」

住居は、非論理的な日常の行為の集積であり、それゆえ〈上〉からの工業化社会のパターンには組み込まれず、その点で〈もの〉からも〈多数〉からも離脱した存在である。また、〈個〉から発する〈住まう〉〈生活する〉という行為は、グロテスクなほど剥き出しの裸性の要求によって占められている。大阪の下町で育ち、ひとびとの暮らしを目の当たりにしてきた安藤の幼時からの体験が、その確信を深めさせた。住居とは、〈個〉のそれらの要求をすっぽりと包み込むシェルターとしてイメージされるものだと考えた。

当時でも進行しつつあった高度な「情報化」は、〈個〉を部分品として扱い、〈技術〉から魂の側面を抜きにするものだと、若き安藤は考えた。その動きを終わらせる、現代都市における、たったひとつの「砦」が、〈個〉を出発点に構築された住居であり、〈住まう〉という欲求の実現こそが、現代都市の人間的な復権であると位置づけた。

その考えに従うなら、住居は必然的に、動物的な「劇的に生を獲得する」スペースを内包しなければならない。「都市ゲリラ住居」は、イメージとしてのゲリラのアジトであり、それは〈上〉からではなく、あくまでも〈個〉のレベルにおいて成立するものである。よって〈個〉を思考の中心に据えることがなにより重視されるべきである。そしてまた、住居は肉体的な直感を基盤にした「自己表現」でなければならないと考えるに至った。

「ゲリラI」（加藤邸）と命名された小住宅は、大阪市旧・大淀区（現・北区）内の住宅密集地を舞台にしていた。20代のテレビプロデューサー夫妻と生まれたばかりの子ども、ひとりの老親の4人家族のための住宅だった。敷地の中央を中庭状に開放し、そうやっ

3

Chapter 1 Quest for "My Presence" and the "Fundamental Space of Pathos"

住吉の長屋——東邸　1976
row house, sumiyoshi

1. 正面外観
Façade

て生まれた空地に木造平屋切妻屋根の日本間を持つ和風住宅（離れのようだ）と、ヴォールト屋根を持つコンクリートの住棟が向き合った。二つの棟はガラスの回廊で結ばれた。のちに展開する初期の鉄筋コンクリートの都市住宅を思わせる仕立てである。

「ゲリラⅡ」は旭区内のクリーニング店で、1階が店舗、2階が住宅の配置をとり、2階には屋根面を斜めにカットした複数の採光窓が配された。密集地のなかでの自然光確保の工夫である。クリーニング店ゆえに、工業地域から日夜生み出される汚れた作業着が職業的基盤であることも創造への意欲を高めた。計画案の発表時には、アイロンがけをする店内の写真を添えた。「ゲリラⅢ」の「冨島邸」の施主はサラリーマンだった。安藤はこの住宅をのちに取得して、自らの設計事務所として改装を重ね、さまざまな空間の実験的試行の場とした。現在の事務所は、その跡地での新築であり、ゲリラ住居に始まる「冨島邸」は、安藤の活動のひとつの原点となった。

都市住宅の原形の発見

　社会も行き詰まっていたが、建築界もまたモダニズムの専制が揺らぎ、新たな建築像が模索されていた。神格化された丹下健三への批判は、万博を境に高まり、激変する時代を踏まえた建築像が求められた。しかし、そのとき、時代の流れに呼応する〈多様化〉として出現したカプセルなどの新奇なヴォキャブラリーへ参画するのではなく、都市に住み続けたい市井のひとびとが求める「独立住居」を手がけることが「地についた行為」だと安藤は考えた。当時盛んだったコミュニティ論は中途半端で偽善的であり、それより個人の意志に強さを感じ、建築家は彼らの思いを吸い上げて住居を実現することが望ましいとの思いだった。

　そのために「PACKAGED ENVIRONMENT」という概念に思い当たった。三つの住宅を取り巻く環境は密集ゆえにとても厳しかった。モダニズムの住宅でしばしば語られた「ドラマティックな外部環境と内部空間の相互貫入」を空間的なテーマとして追及することは無意味な幻想でしかなく、外部環境は〈嫌悪〉と〈拒絶〉の対象であり、その意思表示としてファサードを捨象し、内部空間を充実したミクロコスモスとする道を選んだ。それが「包み込まれた環境」なのである。

　まさに「住吉の長屋」に結びつく都市住宅の原形の発見だった。

　これらの「都市ゲリラ住居」の模型は、黒く梱包する形で提示された。異様な印象を与えるが、まさに外界からの「ずうずうしく煩わしい干渉」を遮断する意志の表明であり、近代建築が陥っていた通俗的な構成と均質化に対する〈抵抗〉と〈怨念〉を象徴させる意味も込めたのである。

The small house, named GUERRILLA — KATO HOUSE, was a residence for a family of four, a TV producer and his wife in their twenties, a new-born child and an old parent, in a densely built-up area in the former Oyodo Ward (currently Kita Ward), Osaka. The center of the site was open resembling a courtyard, where a Japanese-style one-storied wooden house with a gabled roof and a Japanese-style room (appearing to be a detached house), and an open concrete residential building with a vaulted roof faced each other. A glass corridor connected the two buildings. It was a form that suggests reinforced concrete urban house that would later be developed.

GUERRILLA II was a dry cleaning shop in Asahi Ward. The shop was on the first floor, and the second floor was a residence with multiple windows for light, which cut the roof surface at an angle. It was a device to secure natural light in a densely populated area. Since it was a dry cleaner, its profession was founded on dirty work-clothing produced day and night from industrial areas, and this stimulated Ando's creative urge. At the time of announcing the draft plan, he attached a photo of workers ironing inside the shop. The client of GUERRILLA III — TOMISHIMA HOUSE was a corporate employee. Ando later acquired this house for his design office, repeatedly renovated it and used it as a place for experimental trials of various spaces. The office of today was newly constructed on this site, and TOMISHIMA HOUSE, which originated from the Guerrilla House, became one of the basics of Ando's activities.

Discovery of a Prototype Urban House

While the society came to a dead end, the tyranny of modernism eroded in the architectural world, and new images of architecture were sought. Criticisms of the deified Kenzo Tange arose after the Expo, and an image of architecture based on the rapidly changing times was desired. However, Ando believed that designing "independent houses" — desired by ordinary citizens who wished to continue living in urban areas — would be a "realistic action", rather than engaging in new vocabularies such as 'capsules' that emerged as a form of 'diversification' in response to the trend of that time. He believed that the community theory hotly discussed at that time was incomplete and hypocritical, so it was preferable for architects to find strengths in individual wills, absorb such wills and materialize houses, instead.

This exactly lead to the concept of a 'Packaged Environment'. The environments surrounding the three houses were very harsh due to high densities. The pursuit of the spatial theme of 'mutual intrusion between the dramatic exterior environment and interior spaces' — often discussed in modernist houses — became a meaningless fantasy. The exterior environment was a subject of 'dislike' and 'rejection'. Ando abstracted the façade in order to declare his intention, and chose a way to turn the internal spaces into fulfilling microcosms. This is the 'enclosed environment'.

This was indeed the discovery of the prototype urban house that leads to ROW HOUSE, SUMIYOSHI.

Models of "Urban Guerrilla Houses" were presented in a form wrapped in black. Although it gave an odd impression, it was exactly a declaration of his intension to shut out "shameless and bothersome interferences" from the outside world. He also infused a meaning to symbolize 'resistance' and a 'grudge' against common compositions and homogenization that modern architecture suffered from.

Originated from
ROW HOUSE, SUMIYOSHI

Monthly magazine "Shinkenchiku" is a special magazine for people involved in the architectural area. It is respected for its pioneering spirit as specialized media, which led modern architecture movements rooted in modernism in the 1930s, as well as for being an agora that has consistently provided opportunities for discussion in the architectural world after World War II. The magazine became a place for Ando to present his works, with Row House, Sumiyoshi as a start. The February issue of 1977, including ROW HOUSE, SUMIYOSHI, hit the stores after New Year's in 1977 — a year that opened up a new perspective in the architectural world.

A reinforced concrete-structured row house in the downtown — where the common citizens of Osaka lived — was reconstructed into a house based on the citizens' intensions. The architect had a mission to materialize people's unconscious intensions into an actual space. Everything was developed from there.

Located in Osaka, the row house — as a Japanese-style townhouse — had provided places to live for general people, from before WWII and throughout the rapid economic growth period. However, it barely survived changes in the urban environment and lifestyles. Furthermore, reconstruction was an urgent necessity due to the aging of the wooden structure. For Ando, building an Osaka-style apartment or condominium after demolishment and removal of the row house appeared a tragedy: if carried out, residences would only be animal cages.

Ando believed that row houses must be something different. There was a big picture of life, based on the workplace and the residence. Residents in cities regarded row houses as a training hall for mental and physical training. Lifestyles with self-improvement as urban residents were commonly seen. In contrast, apartments and condominiums were only temporary dwellings, since they were composed of factors that quantify functions. Ando thought that there was a need to newly create a row house as a modern urban residence.

How should the architecture be in particular? Basically speaking, while maintaining the long-retained ordinariness of the row houses, insertion of extraordinary spaces may create a new modern urban residence. Ando attempted to create a plan and spatial composition to renew the row house — which would become a trigger of the new lifestyle for the residents — while preserving the relationship between the residents and spaces, which had been fostered and maintained in the traditional row house.

住吉の長屋　1976
row house, sumiyoshi

2. 居室を結ぶ2階のブリッジ
Bridge on the second floor connects the rooms

3. 屋上から2階ブリッジと寝室を望む
Bridge and bedroom on the second floor viewed from the roof

2

3

ところで、梱包された住宅の内部空間は、外界との接触を最小限に抑えたがために生まれた〈闇〉と、そこに自然光をもたらす〈突出した孔〉とによって構成される。闇に沈潜した住人は、注ぐ光を求めて天空に向かって触手を延ばすのである。それもまた初期に安藤が手がけた一連の鉄筋コンクリートの独立小住宅の基本構成の発見にほかならなかった。

「住吉の長屋」に始まる

建築の領域に関わるひとびとにとって月刊誌「新建築」には特別の思いがある。1930年代のモダニズムに根ざした近代建築運動を牽引した専門メディアとしての先駆性に始まり、第2次世界大戦後は一貫して建築界に議論の場を提供してきたアゴラとしての存在への敬意である。「住吉の長屋」をきっかけに同誌が安藤にとっての作品発表の場となった。「住吉の長屋」を掲載した1977年の2月号は、同年の正月明けに発売された。建築界の新しい視界が開けていく1年が始まった。

大阪の市井のひとびとが暮らす下町の長屋を、彼らの意志を踏まえた場として鉄筋コンクリートで再構築していく。彼らが潜在的に意識していることを、建築家は空間の形で実現していく使命を帯びている。そこからすべてが展開していった。

長屋は大阪にあって、第2次世界大戦以前から高度経済成長期を通して、いわば日本流のタウンハウスとして、一般のひとびとに住居を提供してきた。しかし、都市環境、そして生活様式の変化にさすがに耐えられなくなっていた。また、木造ゆえに老朽化による建替えも差し迫った課題だった。長屋が解体撤去されたあとに、大阪流の文化住宅や分譲集合住宅(マンション)が建つのは悲劇に思えた。それではアニマル・ケージしか住居が用意されなくなるではないか。

長屋はそうではなかったはずだ。そこには職住を踏まえた生活の全体像があった。都市に棲みつくひとびとは、長屋を精神的にも肉体的にも自身を発展させる道場のように位置づけ、都市生活者としての自己研鑽に励む暮らしがどこでも見かけられた。一方、文化住宅やマンションは、機能を数量化したファクターで構成するがゆえに仮住まいの場でしかない。それならば、長屋を、現代の都市住居として新たにつくりだす必要があると安藤は考えた。

具体的にどのような建築にすればよいのか。長屋が長く保持してきた日常性を保ちながらも、そこに非日常的な空間を挿入することで、新たな現代の都市住居となりうるのではないか。伝統的な長屋が育み、維持してきた、棲み手と空間の関係は継承しながら長屋を一新することで、新しい生活の契機となる平面計画、空間構成を目指した。

4

Birth of the Light Garden

The light garden in Row House, Sumiyoshi was born from such thoughts. He subjected centrality, above all, to the light garden. It was supposed to be roughly the size of a small green space like a spot garden that many of traditional row houses had retained behind the buildings, plus some space on the main street side reserved for pot-grown plants. The light garden was created as a place for people to interact with nature in a city — a place that had been fostered by row houses. The nature in a city includes sky, light, wind, and rain. The relationship between the residents of the row house and nature should be preserved, since nature adds expressions to the light garden.

A reinforced concrete-structured box — symbolizing the urban lives of "individuals" — was inserted after cutting away part of the row house. Common sense would suggest that removing the central unit may cause collapse of the structure, since neighboring units in a wooden row house share border walls. However, thanks to the amazing power of youthfulness, the architect and contractors had no fear of doing so. It was fortunate that Row House, Sumiyoshi was materialized without any accident.

On the main street side, the thick and robust concrete wall has an entrance that is an opening but is closed unless necessary, and there are no windows or other elements. The "individual" living space is surrounded by the robust walls. The concrete box as a shelter indeed became a symbol of the strong will to live in a city.

As a result of such an exterior appearance, the interior spatial composition naturally became centripetal. Facing the outdoor light garden, a living room is located on the entrance side, and a dining room and kitchen are located at the back on the first floor. The second floor has extra rooms — assumed to be a bedroom and spare room. A concrete path with Genshouseki (type of slate) connects the separated residential spaces. Outdoor stairs, connected to the path, are arranged as access between the first and second floors.

The light garden is at the center of lifestyle planning in this urban residence, and also plays a centripetal role. As stated earlier, the garden is a space to feel nature. Dramatic effects with natural light on each room via the light garden were envisioned throughout the changing seasons. In that sense, the light garden occupies an important position that is infrangible from ordinary life and becomes the core of a new urban life, yet is still an extraordinary space.

住吉の長屋　1976
row house, sumiyoshi

4. 2階寝室よりブリッジと予備室を見る
   Bridge and the spare room
   viewed from the second floor bedroom
5. 光庭の断面パース
   Cross section perspective of the light garden

住吉の長屋　1976
row house, sumiyoshi

6. (前ページ) 光庭から食堂方向を望む
(previous page) View of the dining room from the light garden

光庭の誕生

　「住吉の長屋」の光庭は、そこから誕生した。なにより求心性を光庭に託した。広さは、伝統的な長屋の多くが保持してきた建物の背後にある坪庭のような小さな緑の空間と、表通りに面した側にとられた鉢物の植物を置く余白とを足しあわせたぐらいを想定した。光庭は、そのようにして長屋の育んできた、都市のなかで自然とひとびとが接する場として設営された。都市のなかの自然とは、空であり、光であり、風であり、雨である。その自然が光庭に表情を与えることによって、長屋での棲み手と自然の関係は継承されるはずだ。

　長屋の一角を切り取った後に、〈個〉がそこで都市生活を送る象徴となる鉄筋コンクリートの箱を挿入した。常識的に考えれば、連続する木造長屋の住戸は境の壁を共有していたから、中央の一軒を切り取ればその時点で構造面で倒壊の恐れがある。若さとは凄いもので、建築家も施工者も恐れを知らず、やってしまった。幸い事故にはならず、「住吉の長屋」は実現にこぎつけた。

　厚く強固なコンクリート壁の表通り側には、開口部でありながら必要がない限り閉ざされている玄関はあっても、窓もなにもない。強固な壁に〈個〉の住空間は囲われている。シェルターであるコンクリートの箱は、まさに都市で暮らす強固な意志を象徴するものとなった。

　外観がそのような形態となったことから、内なる空間構成も自ずと求心的なものとなった。屋外空間の光庭に向き合う形で、1階には玄関側が居間、奥にダイニングキッチンを配した。2階は、それぞれ寝室と子ども部屋を想定した予備室とした。二分された居室空間を結ぶ形で玄昌石を敷いたコンクリートの通路を設け、1、2階の行き来はこの通路につながる屋外の階段を利用する配置となった。

　光庭は、この都市住居で繰り広げられる生活のプランニング上でも中心的な位置を占め、求心的な役割も担う。そこは先に述べたように自然を感知する空間であり、移ろいゆく季節のなかで、光庭を介して各室にもたらされる自然光の演出的な効果が想定された。光庭はその意味では非日常的な空間でありながら、日常の暮らしに切り離せない重要な位置を占め、新しい都市生活の核になりうると期待したのである。

光と闇が綾を織りなす陰翳礼讃

　「住吉の長屋」と同時に発表した「番匠邸」では、光庭に代わり、居間を、生活空間

1

In Praise of Shadows:
Beautiful Patterns of Light and Darkness

In BANSHO HOUSE — announced at the same time as ROW HOUSE, SUMIYOSHI, the living room was designated as the symbolic place of living spaces, instead of the light garden. Ando pursued a unique space in this house by reconsidering the living room as a place for people to gather.

The living room was made as an "individual" realm surrounded by walls. In this enclosed place, the residents cultivate their selves. The task of finding an established place and one's own place in the environment was expected. Stairs to the second floor are at a corner of the living room on the first floor. A line of light from the second floor window comes through via a gap in the stairway. The light provides centrality to the enclosed living room. Light was regarded as a foundation of the residents, resembling a fireplace. In addition, the light comes from one spot, and therefore does not uniformly illuminate the space. Homogenized spaces of modern architecture were denied, and the entangled light and darkness emphasize each other.

A beautiful pattern of light and darkness reminds us of a memory of darkness in Japanese traditional spaces. The one existing here is not a copy of forms in Japanese traditional architecture, rather, it is a preserved image of spaces that are recognized as archetypal scenery. It was assumed that the fullness of life in the living room would extend its area to the kitchen on the first floor and the bedroom on the second floor. Since those rooms are not completely segmented from the living room, it was also expected that the light falling onto the living room would connect them to one another.

The form of BANSHO HOUSE is a combination of a cube and cuboid, intended for breaking the completeness of geometric cubes by displacing compositions. This displacement had an effect to bring about a change to combinations of the living room and other areas in the internal space. In addition, the two geometric shapes are partially buried in the site, representing Ando's opinion in which residents themselves root in the ground and settle there.

番匠邸　1976
bansho house

1. 南側外観
Exterior appearance on the south side

の象徴化された場と位置づけた。居間をひとが集まるという行為の場と捉え直す、この住宅ならではのオリジナリティを目指した。

　居間は壁に囲われた〈個〉の領域として設営された。その閉ざされた場で、棲み手は自我を培養し、環境の中に確固たる自己の場を切り取る作業を期待された。1階に配した居間の一角には2階への階段を設けた。その階段室の空隙を介して、2階の窓から一条の光がもたらされる。この光が囲われた居間に求心性をもたらす。暖炉と同じく、光は生活するひとびとのよりどころとして設えられた。そして、その光は一点から浸入してくるがゆえに、空間を均質に照らしだすことがない。近代建築の均質空間は否定され、光と闇は錯綜することで互いを際立たせるのである。

　光と闇が織りなす綾は、日本の伝統的な空間の闇に対する記憶を呼び覚ます。ここにあるのは日本の伝統建築の形態の複写ではなく、わたしたちが原風景として知覚する空間のイメージの継承に他ならない。居間における生活の膨らみが、1階のキッチン、2階の寝室へと領域を拡大していくことを想定した。それらの各室は、居間と完全には分節されておらず、居間に落ちて来る光が各室を結びつけることも期待した。

　「番匠邸」の形態は立方体と直方体の箱を組み合わせたが、構成をずらすことで、幾何学的なキューブの完結性を崩壊させることを意図した。このずれは内部空間の居間と他の領域の組み合わせにも変化をもたらす効果をあげている。また、二つの幾何立体は敷地のなかに埋もれる配置となっており、大地に棲み手自身が根を下ろして、棲みつく主張を代弁している。

　こうした一連の独立住宅は、大阪のひとびとの都市に棲む意志を目の当たりにして育ったがゆえに実現することが出来た。住宅を発注した棲み手もまた、都市に棲む作法を生まれながらにして身につけていたからこそ、一連の初期の住宅群が生まれ落ちたのである。

　近代建築は、その内部の空間構成に、自然光をどのようにあふれさせ、あるいは制約するかで、禁欲的な美に基づく表現性を担保してきた。それはまさに谷崎潤一郎の『陰翳礼讃』であり、近代建築にひとつの完成形をもたらしたルイス・カーンのいうところの「原風景を建築が提示することによって、ひとはその建築を理解する」とする「形は機能を啓示する（形は機能を連想させる）」の実践に他ならなかった。

　なりふりかまわない都市に棲み続けたいという庶民の欲望を、建築家が吸い上げ、代弁して空間化することによって近代建築の祖形に近づいたのだとするなら、それは実に興味深いいきさつと思えてならない。建築家、施主、そして土地の文脈の幸福な邂逅をそこに見てとることもできるだろう。

Chapter 1 Quest for "My Presence" and the "Fundamental Space of Pathos" 038

番匠邸　1976
bansho house

2. 居間から食堂方向を望む
View of the dining room from the living room

状況に楔す

ふり返ると「新建築」誌で「住吉の長屋」を発表した1977年は、英国の建築評論家チャールズ・ジェンクスが『ポスト・モダニズムの建築言語』（リッツォーリ）を刊行した年にあたる。近代建築批判のバイブルと見なされる同書は、1930年代以来、建築界を支配してきたモダニズムを、容赦なく嘲り、批判し、ポスト・モダンへと建築界が舵を切るきっかけをつくった。折りも折り、「住吉の長屋」の発表は、近代建築の揺らぎのなかで、安藤が自分なりに考えてきたことを、まとめて世に問うきっかけとなった。

安藤は「状況に楔す」と題した論考を、「住吉の長屋」の掲載号に寄稿した。ポスト・モダニズムが市民権を得て、モダニズムを批判することが、むしろ多数派を占めるに至るなかで、自分の立脚点を明らかにしておく意味が、この論考には込められていた。機能主義やインターナショナルスタイルは終局を迎え、建築界には現実から建築を切り離す「知の操作」が蔓延しているなかでの、自身の立脚点の明示だった。

近代は、科学技術を偏重するあまり、人間を解析可能な単純な存在に貶め、本来、近代が目指した「自我の確立」と異なる方向に建築も進んでしまった。しかし、その反動としての「知の操作」がもたらす非日常空間は、あまりにも空間芸術性が高く、このままでは建築は社会から遊離し、日常的な意味を失うのではと案じられた。

一方、「都市住宅」誌の編集長をつとめた植田実氏らが鉄筋コンクリートの住宅作品の発表の場を与えてくれたおかげで、すでに安藤の作品に対する建築界の印象はある程度広まっていた。ただ、それは、あらゆる生活要素を削り落として抽象の空間に到達したという誤解に近いものだった。コンクリート打ち放しの裸形の空間がそう受け取らせたのである。この際、そこも明確に修整しておきたいと考えたのである。

「情念の基本空間」を追い求める

抽象の空間を目指したのではなく、「空間の原形」を追い求めて、そこに至ったのである。一般に抽象の空間は、禁欲の美学に基づく「知の操作」によるのに対し、「空間の原形」は「情念」によってもたらされると安藤は考えた。同時に、長く継続するであろう建築家の創造活動の根底となる「空間の原形」を基本として保有しておくべきだとも考えた。情念を生みの親とする「空間の原形」は、建築家たる自分の「生の証」であり、そこに「わたしの存在感」を託すことができれば空間を享受するひとたちの精神の深層に訴えかけることも可能だろう。それがかなえば、「空間の原形」は、互いの生の叫びで

Driving a Wedge into the Situations

When looking back, the year 1977 — when Ando published Row House, Sumiyoshi in "Shinkenchiku" magazine — was also a year when British architectural critic Charles Alexander Jencks published *"The Language of Post-Modern Architecture"* (Rizzoli). In the book, Jencks mercilessly ridiculed and criticized modernism, which had dominated the architectural world since the 1930s. The book is regarded as a bible of modern architecture criticism, and triggered a change of direction in the architectural world towards postmodernism.

Ando contributed a discussion article, entitled "Driving a Wedge into the Situations", to the magazine with the Row House, Sumiyoshi article. In this article, he gave a meaning to clarifying his own foundation in the climate where post modernism had gained its citizenship and the majority had come to criticize modernism. It was a declaration of his foundation, at a time when functionalism and international styles came to an end, and when "intellectual manipulation" was flourishing in the architectural world to detach architecture from reality.

Meanwhile, an impression of Ando's works had already been established to some extent in the architectural world, since the chief editor of "Urban Housing" magazine, Makoto Ueda, and others provided opportunities to present reinforced concrete-structured houses by Ando. However, it was incorrectly interpreted: an abstract space was achieved by eliminating all factors of life. The as-cast concrete, and naked spaces brought such thoughts. Ando wanted to take this opportunity to clearly correct this misunderstanding.

Pursuit of "Fundamental Space of Pathos"

Ando achieved the idea by seeking the 'prototype of spaces', rather than abstract spaces. Ando thought that abstract spaces were generally brought by "intellectual manipulation" based on stoic aesthetics, while the prototype of spaces was brought by "pathos". At the same time, he thought that the 'prototype of spaces' — a foundation of long-lasting creative activities of an architect — should be kept as a basis. The 'prototype of spaces' born from the pathos was his "proof of living" as an architect. He then would be able to urge people, who would relish the spaces, in the depths of their minds.

The "fundamental space of pathos" is created from shutting off relationships with the outside world by concrete walls, and eliminating articulations based on functions in an internal composition. Light plays an important role in the creation process, and he emphasized that he had focused on light.

It is also associated with regular uses of limited materials (concrete and blocks). Since the materials are naked, wind blowing or light passing through them can be more deeply recognized. Light was consistently regarded as an important factor in spatial presentation. A spatial experience, created with such wind and light, cannot be expected for functionally articulated spaces. Ando thought it would be a trigger to recognize a resident's "internal scenery" in everyday life. This "internal scenery" corresponds to the internal space that the resident originally has. By doing so, he attempted to break the situation where not only the surrounding environment but also the self would become ambiguous. That is, such action would be led by the "fundamental space of pathos", and it became the basic philosophy for a series of reinforced concrete-structured independent houses around this time.

番匠邸　1976
bansho house

3. ルーフガーデンから見た増築のアトリエと中庭
Extended atelier and courtyard viewed from the roof garden

の対話を可能にする有力な媒体になると思った。

「情念の基本空間」は、コンクリートの壁で外部との関係を絶ち、内部構成は機能による分節（アーティキュレート）を排するところから生まれる。その生成に重要な役割を演じるのは光であり、光を重視してきたことを訴えた。

それは常に限定的なマテリアル（コンクリートやブロック）を使ってきたこととも関連している。マテリアルが剥き出しの裸形であり、そうすることで建築家自らが採用した空間構成は一際、明確になる。裸形であるがために、そこを通る風や、射し込む光も、より深く認識できる。光は一貫して空間演出の重要な要素として取り扱った。そうした風や光が演出する空間体験は、機能的に分節された空間には期待できない、棲み手の「内的風景」を暮らしのなかで自覚させる契機になると考えた。この「内的風景」は、棲み手自身がもともと持っている内面空間と対応する。そうすることによって、取り巻く環境のみならず自己まで曖昧になる状態を打破しようと試みた。つまるところ、そうした作用をもたらすのが「情念の基本空間」であり、この時期の鉄筋コンクリート独立住宅の基本理念となった。

現代生活空間の象徴化

次に、この「情念の基本空間」を、建築家は生活空間の象徴化にまで至らさなければならないと考えた。

京の町屋も農家も、象徴化された生活空間を備えており、それが伝統的な木造家屋を歴史や年輪を超えた情念の空間として認識させる。京の町屋でいうとミセノマ、オクがそれであり、農家においては土間が共同体意識を根底から支える作業空間として存在した。そこに生活があったからこそ象徴的な空間になりえたのであり、単に空間が劇的というだけでは空間の象徴化は不可能だっただろう。

「情念の基本空間」は、現代においては、囲われたコンクリートの壁のなかで、風や光が機能の空隙を認識させる点で、非日常的な体験をもたらすものである。しかし、非日常的であるがゆえに、他の日常的な空間を活性化する役割を果たしうると考えた。壁で囲われた個人は、その時点で社会から切り離され、社会への従属から解き放たれている。取り巻く環境と妥協することによる自我の喪失が、「情念の基本空間」では無関係なものになっていく。そうやって、そこは生活空間の象徴化された場になりうるのである。

「住吉の長屋」を例にとるなら、厚い壁に開口部を穿たず、周囲の過酷な都市的環境から擁護された棲み家を構築し、内部の個の領域を確保しようと努めた。そこには現代

双生観──山口邸　1975
soseikan — yamaguchi house

南西側外観
Exterior appearance on the southwest side

立見邸　1974
tatsumi house

正面外観
Façade

都市が個人の居住空間を根絶させてしまうのではという危機認識があった。だからこそ、外部との無防備な連携を絶ち、内部空間を確保し、充実させる必要があると認識した。

もとより内部での生活は個人に根ざしていて、外部とは関連なく、〈個〉の生を展開していく場が求められているからだ。「住吉の長屋」は、壁で周囲とは隔絶された空間に光庭だけがぽっかりと開いて、触れ合えなかったはずの都市の自然としての空が内部空間に取り込まれている。この吹き抜けは非日常的だが、それが居間、台所、寝室などの日常の空間と接することで、日常の生活と光庭に触発された棲み手の情念の混在が実現する。そこに「情念の基本空間」が生活空間の象徴化に至るひとつの道筋を示しえたと安藤は自認する。

「冨島邸」「双生観」「立見邸」「平林邸」の初期の4作において、「情念の基本空間」を探究し、それを踏まえて「住吉の長屋」「番匠邸」では日常生活における空間の意味づけを試みた。それは4戸の住宅を抱える「帝塚山タワープラザ」の広場の空間へと展開していった。

都市は「情念の基本空間」を内包する建築の集合体であるべきだとも考えた。そこには一般解はなじまない。建築は個々に異なる存在であり、個々の都市の住宅は生活を内包している。近代がもたらした都市と社会の不毛の解決を、ひとは普遍解に求めたがるが、そうした状況認識では解決には至らないという確信があった。住民のコミュニティに建築家が一役買うことが、近代都市の行き詰まり解決の処方箋とされたが、それもまた普遍解を求めるものであり、ここまで述べてきたような個人の棲み手を基本の単位とする「情念の基本空間」にはなじまない。

建築は、そして、建築家も近代がもたらした状況を甘受して対症療法に走るのではなく、まさに「状況に楔する」ことが求められていた。その勇気と決意がなければ、モダニズムの専制が過去のものとなってしまった建築界において、創造の持続は望みえないのではないだろうか。棲み手も主体性への決意を求められ、その決意に応える建築をどう創作していくか。ポスト・モダニズムの隆盛を横目に、単なる抽象への固執や回帰では対処しえない時代が始まっていった。

都市は「純白ではないキャンバス」

自らの設計事務所を立ち上げて十年近くになろうとしていた。無我夢中でやってきたわけだが、一瞬、歩をとめて考えることが、このころからできるようになっていた。当時の大阪は、戦前に建てられた木造住宅がまだまだ都心にも残り、それらは老朽化し

Symbolization of Modern Living Space

In the next step, the architect thought that he must achieve symbolization of living spaces from this "fundamental space of pathos".

Machiya in Kyoto and farm houses have symbolized living spaces, which help the traditional wooden houses to be recognized as spaces of pathos beyond history and growth rings. *Misenoma* and *Oku* were such examples of machiya in Kyoto, and a dirt floor in farm houses existed as workspaces to fundamentally support a sense of community. They could be symbolic spaces only because there were people's lives there. Symbolization of spaces would have been impossible if a space was just being dramatic.

In modern days, the "fundamental space of pathos" provides an extraordinary experience, since wind and light make people recognize the gap between functions, surrounded by concrete walls. Due to its extraordinariness, Ando thought it can play a role in stimulating other ordinary spaces. Individuals who are surrounded by walls are detached from the society and released from subordination thereto at this point.

Internal life is originally rooted in individuals in the first place, not related to the external, so places where individuals can live their lives are required. In Row House, Sumiyoshi, the light garden is widely open in a space disconnected from its surroundings by walls, and integrates sky — a connection with nature in cities that could not be accomplished without a garden — into the interior spaces. Although the atrium is extraordinary, it touches the ordinary spaces such as the living room, kitchen, and bedrooms, creating the coexistence of an ordinary life and the residents' pathos induced by the light garden. Ando acknowledges that the "fundamental space of pathos" there could demonstrate one route for symbolizing living spaces.

He explored the "fundamental space of pathos" in his early works: Tomishima House, Soseikan, Tatsumi House, and Hirabayashi House. In Row House, Sumiyoshi and Bansho House, he attempted to create a meaning for spaces in everyday life, based on the above. It then developed into the plaza space in Tezukayama Tower Plaza with four housing units.

He thought that cities should be an aggregation of buildings involving the "fundamental space of pathos". General solutions do not fit there. Individual buildings are different, and individual urban buildings enclose the lives inside. Although people tend to seek for a universal solution to the desolation of cities and society that the modern times provide, he was convinced that such awareness of the situation would bring no resolution. Architects playing a role in resident communities were considered a solution to an impasse in modern cities. However, it is also a pursuit of a universal solution, and does not fit into the "fundamental space of pathos" discussed here, in which individual residents are regarded as basic units.

For architecture as well as architects, "Driving a Wedge into the Situations" was certainly required, instead of simply accepting the conditions brought by modern times and heading towards symptomatic measures. Without such courage and commitment, sustainable creation might not be expected in the architectural world, where the modernist tyranny faded away in the past. The residents are also required to commit to independence, so how should architecture be created to respond to the commitment? Apart from the prosperity of post modernism, it was a beginning of an era, which could not be handled with a simple attachment or recurrence to mere abstract.

1

貫入——平林邸　1976
Interpenetration — hirabayashi house

1. 南側外観
Exterior appearance on the south side

帝塚山タワープラザ　1976
tezukayama tower plaza

1. 西側外観
Exterior appearance on the west side
2. ショップエリアを見下ろす
Downward view of the shop area

て存在が危うくなりつつあった。多くは敷地が小さすぎて、いわゆるマンションにも事務所ビルにも建て替えられず、そのために残ったにすぎなかった。戦前の木造住宅、戦後、急場しのぎに建てられた建物、それらと建て替えられたコンクリート造が、大阪には同居するかたちで混在し、景観は否が応にも猥雑にならざるをえなかった。

そんな大阪を一新したいとは考えなかった。

絵画も建築も美を追い求める点では変わりはないが、絵画が純白のキャンバスに描かれるのに対して、建築はそうではない。安藤は建築家として、戦前から時間を追って建設された建物が重層する大阪をそのまま受け入れ、急速な近代化とそれがもたらす生活の快適さの陰で失われつつあった人間本来の安らぎを、木造の住宅をコンクリートボックスで置き換えることによって実現することに取り組んできた。

そのような視点に基づいて「住吉の長屋」を振り返った。

尺貫法で測るなら元の長屋は間口2間の奥行き8間、それを切りとってコンクリートの箱を挿入した。道路側の外壁面は完全に閉ざし、なかに光庭を開いた。そのため、ただでさえ狭い住宅は極限の空間になった。

それを設計する過程で、真の意味での暮らしの豊かさとはなにかを実感した。ローコストという動かしがたい条件は、基本的なものを見抜く目を養ってくれる。空間に限界もあれば、生活にも大きな制約がある。だから、とにかく不要なものを排除するしかない。そこで精神と体力の限界を知るとき、簡素な生活空間は豊かな場に変わるに違いない。快適さや利便性と交換に失った暮らしの確かな手応えが住宅設計に際しての大きな課題と認識するようになった。

呼吸する素材

建築家のなしうることとはなにか。うわべの飾りは排し、ひとつひとつの素材と葛藤する。おのれの体温を自覚しながら、寸法やプロポーションを知の力を総動員して極めてゆく。そこから「住吉の長屋」は生まれた。空間としては、三分した単純な骨格を基本に、限定した素材をあてて、極小の宇宙をつくりだそうとした。その行為そのものが葛藤であり、闘いでもあった。

光庭は閉塞の空間に、光や風、雨といった自然の感覚をもたらすものであり、それがあるゆえに狭小な住宅は決して閉ざされた場となることはない。光はデッキの下では濃い陰影をそこにもたらし、光庭に面した窓ガラスで反射してコンクリートの壁面を輝かせる。風は素材の表面を撫でるかのように吹き抜けていく。素材はそのような自然の働きかけで呼吸を始める。光こそが美の演出者であり、一方、風や雨は棲み手がそれを

Cities are "Not Pure-White Canvas"

More than ten years had passed following the establishment of his own design office. Thereafter, he worked passionately, but he was able to take a moment to think. In Osaka at that time, there were still quite a few wooden houses built before the war, and those dilapidated ones were in danger of being demolished. Many of them were left simply because their sites were too small to be reconstructed to apartments or office buildings. A mixture of prewar wooden houses, postwar quick-fix buildings, and newly rebuilt concrete buildings existed together in Osaka, inevitably creating indecent townscapes.

Ando did not desire to refurbish Osaka.

Pursuit of beauty is common in art and architecture, but pictorial art is created on a white canvas, while architecture is not. As an architect, Ando accepted Osaka as-is with an accumulation of buildings that were constructed over time since the prewar period. He put his efforts into materialization of natural human peace — being lost behind rapid modernization and comfortable life as a result — by substituting wooden houses with concrete boxes.

At this point, he looked back on ROW HOUSE, SUMIYOSHI from such perspective.

If the Japanese measuring system is used, the frontage of the former row house was 2 kens (about 3.6 meters), and the depth was 8 kens (about 14.6 meters), which were cut off and a concrete box was inserted. The external wall surface on the street side was completely closed, and the light garden was arranged inside. This made the already narrow house be an extreme space.

In the process of designing, he realized what the true richness of life was. The immovable condition of low-cost helps us develop an eye for seeing basic things. When one understands the mental and physical limits, a simple living space must turn into a rich space. Ando recognized a significant theme in house designs: a definite response from life, which was lost in exchange for comfort and convenience.

Three Dimensional
TOWN HOUSE IN KUJO

TOWN HOUSE IN KUJO located in Kujo in Osaka, not far from an everyday shopping street with a downtown atmosphere. There is a modest-sized green park nearby, and the area was not as densely built-up as ROW HOUSE, SUMIYOSHI. However, there were small factories and shops in addition to detached houses and housing complexes in the neighborhood. The design was for a typical townscape in Osaka, i.e., in the midst of a "not white canvas". The design process began from framing the mixed townscape, and ensuring a realm by using a concrete box, like ROW HOUSE, SUMIYOSHI.

In contrast to the evenly tri-sectioned ROW HOUSE, SUMIYOSHI (the light garden at the center, and the residential spaces divided into two), TOWN HOUSE IN KUJO was divided into two sections (internal spaces for residential spaces, and an outdoor space). The outdoor space is surrounded by walls as high as the building. A courtyard and outdoor stairs were made in the outdoor void space. The area of the outdoor section and that of the inside residential spaces were about the same. In this sense, the design was bi-sectioned. The building has three stories, while ROW HOUSE, SUMIYOSHI has two stories, and this promoted challenges to new spaces.

Ando came up with a design in which the indoor residential part for everyday life and the outdoor courtyard

九条の町屋——井筒邸　1982
town house in kujo — izutsu house

1. 西側外観
   Exterior appearance on the west side
2. 全体俯瞰
   Bird's-eye view
3. 2階から3階への階段部分
   Stairs from the second floor to the third floor

感じることで生活を彩ると考えた。

　光庭に玄昌石を敷きつめ、屋内の床、扉、家具はすべて木製にした。それらは自然素材であって、光、風、雨に呼応しながら、棲み手の記憶が刻み込まれ、住宅は身体の延長と化していくに違いない。

　光、風、雨といった自然を暮らしのなかに引き込むことが、生活者にとって厳しい状況をもたらすことは認識していた。だいいち、自らの住居内なのに、光庭という屋外を通らなければ移動できない不便はいかばかりか。その意味では「住吉の長屋」の暮らしは一般解とするには厳しすぎる。建築家がそんな住宅をつくったときに、彼は住みこなせるのか、暮らすことによって建物がさらに生きてくるのか、そこはもう棲み手の生活感の問題であり、ないがしろに出来ない課題だと認識した。

　建築家の立場では、こうした思考の重なりこそが、住居のありかたそのものを考えていく有意義な手だてと考えるようになった。一貫してコンクリートの住宅を設計していたこともあって、密集地の老朽化した木造住宅建替えの設計を依頼される機会が増えた。「九条の町屋」もそのような依頼のひとつだった。ここでは「住吉の長屋」から一歩踏み出す構成に挑戦した。

立体化した「九条の町屋」

　「九条の町屋」は、大阪・九条の下町風情豊かな生活商店街から少し外れたところに位置する。近くにそこそこの大きさの公園の緑があり、「住吉の長屋」ほどの密集地でもなかったが、周囲には、独立住宅、集合住宅だけでなく、町工場や商店が揃っていた。ここもまた大阪の典型的な街並み、つまり、まさに「白くはないキャンバス」の真っ只中での設計となった。その雑多な街並みを切り取り、そこに「住吉の長屋」と同じく、コンクリートボックスを持ち込んで、まず領域を確保するところから、設計作業は始まった。

　全体構成は、「住吉の長屋」が中央の光庭と二つに分かれた居室部分をそれぞれに均等にした三分割だったのに対して、「九条の町屋」は、居室となる内部空間と屋外空間の二分割にした。屋外といっても、建物の高さいっぱいの壁に囲われている。そのヴォイドの屋外空間に、中庭と外部階段を配した。屋外部分と、屋内の居室部分の広さはほぼ同じで、その意味でも二分割といえる仕立てである。階数は「住吉の長屋」の2階に対して、こちらは3階であり、そのことが新たな空間への挑戦を刺激した。

　屋内にあたる生活を営む居室部分と屋外に位置する中庭とが、屋外階段で交差する仕立てを考えた。ここでも、階段と広場の仕上げは黒い玄昌石を採用し、コンクリートとの対比を意識した。中庭の短辺は二間半、3階の屋外から、まるで井戸を覗くような

were intersected by the outdoor stairs. Black-colored Genshouseki (a type of slate) was used for stairs and the finish of the open space, in order to contrast with the concrete. The short side of the courtyard is about 4.5 m. The courtyard can be viewed from the outdoor space on the third floor, as if peeking into a well. At the bottom of the well, the courtyard appears to be a spot garden.

Whereas the light garden in Row House, Sumiyoshi is described as centripetal, Town House in Kujo is mobile, since travelling to other floors requires using the outdoor stairs. For this reason, the outdoor stairs were likened to a three-dimensional pathway with three layers.

The living space for the son and his wife is on the ground level (partially underground). The courtyard is facing their bedroom. The client couple live on the upper floors (2nd and 3rd). The lives of the two generations were vertically stacked. Since the common bathroom is on the first floor, multiple trips via the outdoor stairs are necessary in everyday scenarios, in addition to when leaving home.

Entering the entrance on the first floor, residents reach the courtyard at the back after going through a passage-garden-like path, as if in *machiya* in Kyoto. The courtyard is indeed a spot garden at the back, surrounded by concrete walls. The residents turn at the stair landing and ascend the outdoor stairs. The feeling of ascending can be considered similar to going through a three-dimensional pathway.

Above all, the residents come into contact with nature including light, wind, and rain, whenever they use the outdoor stairs. The urban nature was also brought into the living spaces in Town House in Kujo, via the dense, surrounding outdoor space.

Because of being made three-dimensional, it turned to be a complicated spatial composition. This was consequence of narrowness, and it relates to both life and nature in a different way from Row House, Sumiyoshi, creating a scenery of interaction with materials. Here again, he hoped that the building would question what the true nature of living is, and give human bodies a realization of being alive.

小篠邸　1981
koshino house

1. リビングルーム
   Living room
2. 寝室棟外観
   Exterior appearance of the bedroom building
3. コートヤード夜景
   Night view of the courtyard

趣で、底の位置に坪庭のような中庭を望むことができた。

「住吉の長屋」の光庭が求心的とするなら、「九条の長屋」では流動的となった。他の階への移動に屋外の階段を利用するためである。それもあって、屋外階段を三層に及ぶ立体的な路地に見立てた。

少し掘り下げた1階に息子夫婦の生活空間があり、中庭は彼らの寝室に面している。上階の2、3階を施主夫婦が暮らす場にあて、二世帯の暮らしを立体的に組み上げた。両世帯の共用の浴室とトイレは1階にある。このため外出時にとどまらず、日常的な場面で外部階段を日に何度も使わざるを得ない仕立てになった。

1階の玄関を入ると、京都の町屋にあるような通り庭風の通路を伝い、奥の中庭に至る。そこは、まさにコンクリートの壁で囲われた奥の坪庭である。この坪庭を見おろしながら、住み手は踊り場で方向転換して屋外階段を上階へと進む。それはまさに立体的な路地を巡る感覚に通じていると見なせるだろう。

なにより棲み手は外部階段を利用する度に、光や風、雨といった自然と接することになる。「九条の町屋」においても、囲われた稠密な屋外空間を介して、都市の自然が生活の場に持ち込まれたのである。

立体化したがゆえに、建物は複雑な空間構成になった。それは狭さがもたらした結果であり、「住吉の長屋」とは違ったかたちで、建築は生活とも自然とも関わり、素材と触れ合う光景を出現させる。ここでもまた、住まうことの本質を建物が問いかけ、生きていることの実感を人間の身体に喚起させることができればと願った。

「一枚の布の残像」を配する

兵庫県芦屋市。高級住宅地で知られるこの町には、奥座敷と呼べる高級住宅地がある。その名を奥池といい、住人は芦有ドライブウェイ（芦屋と有馬温泉を結ぶ）を利用して、日々の生活を送る、とても不思議な場所だ。その山の斜面を生かした住宅地の一角にファッションデザイナーのコシノヒロコの住宅として設計したのが「小篠邸」（1981年）である。道路から下っていく傾斜地を敷地とするこの住宅は2棟の直方体から成る。ずらした平行配置の住宅は、道路に近い側が2階建て、斜面の下の側が平屋で、両者は中庭を介して向き合い、斜面地に埋められた廊下で結ばれている。

安藤は足もとと両側をコンクリートで固めたこの中庭を、周囲の自然のなかに置かれた「一枚の布の残像」と見なし、住宅の象徴と位置づけた。昇降のための外部階段などの硬質なコンクリートは、周囲の自然との融和ではなく、もうひとつの人工の屋外を強く意識して設けられた。

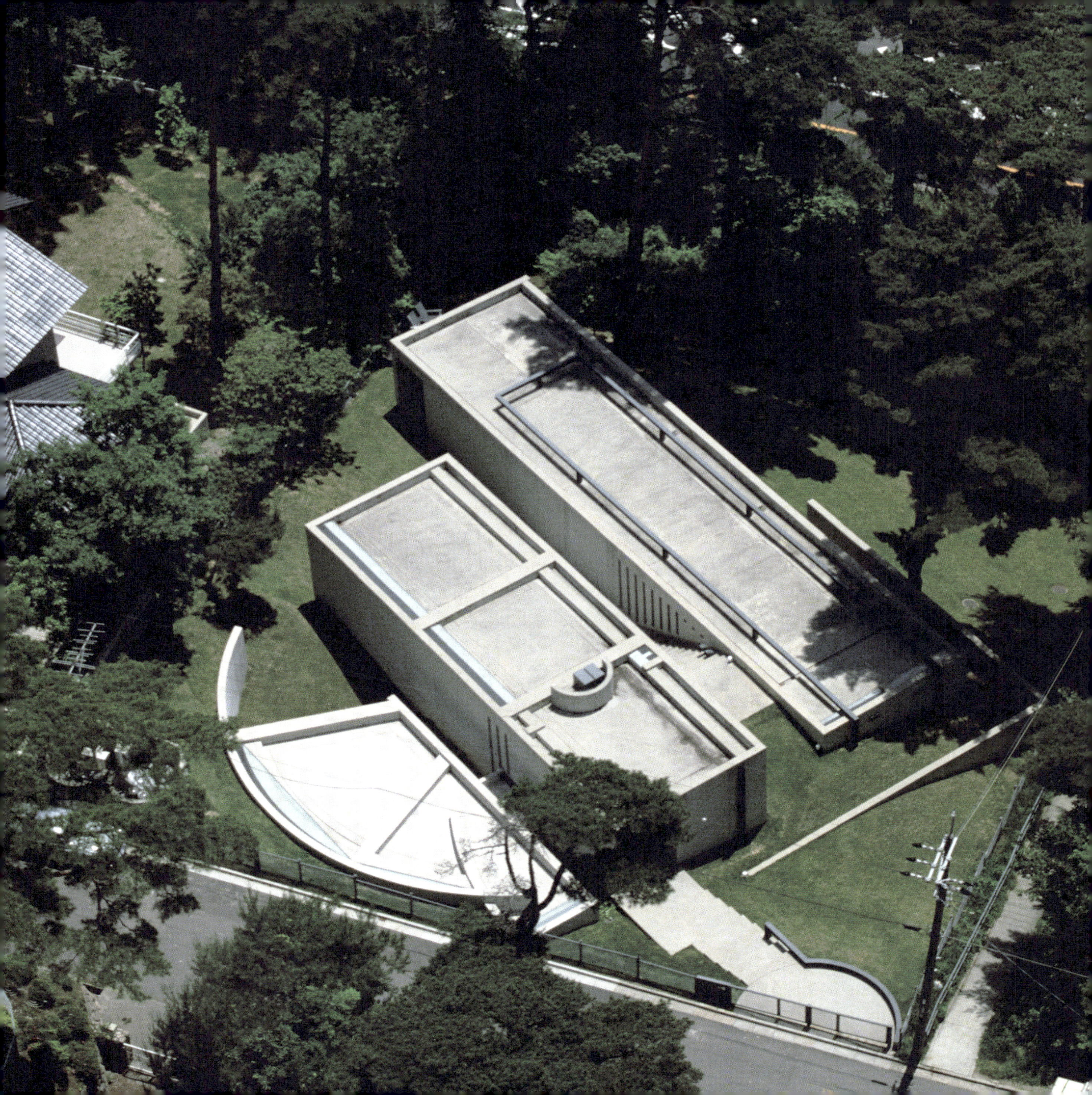

小篠邸　1981
koshino house

4. （前ページ）増築後の鳥瞰全景
    (previous page) Bird's-eye view after the extension
5. ゲストハウス廊下
    Corridor of the guest house
6. 増築棟内部
    Interior of the extension building
7. 断面図ドローイング
    Section drawing

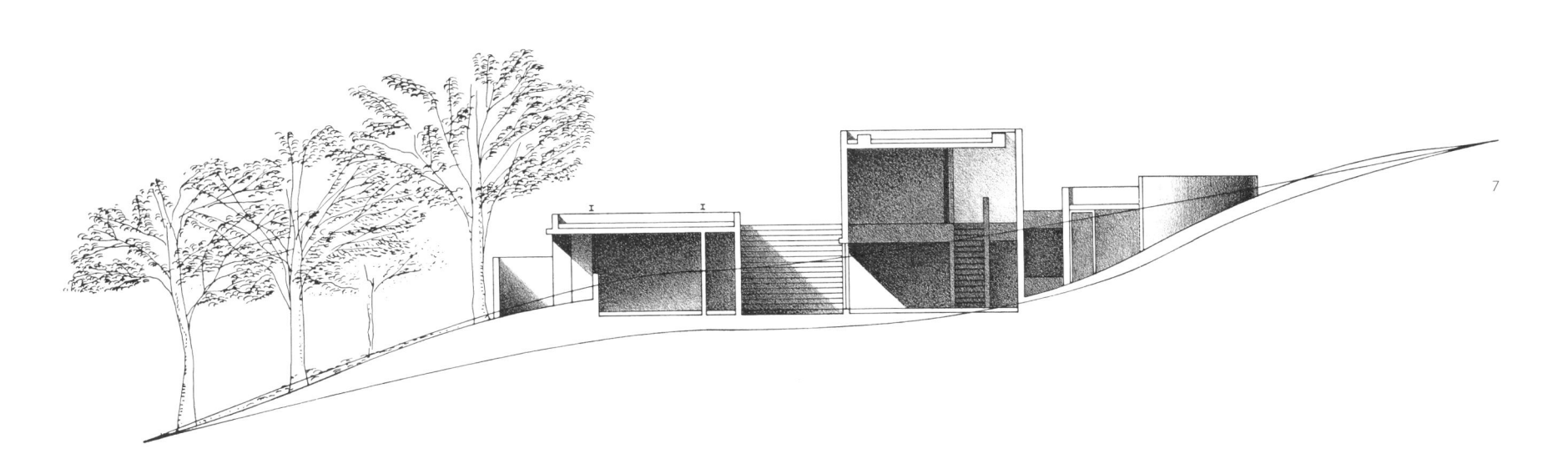

Arranging a
"Residual Image of a Piece of Cloth"

Ashiya City in Hyogo Prefecture is known as a fancy neighborhood. On its backside, there is a high-status residential area, called Okuike. It is a mysterious area, where residents use a toll road, Royu Driveway (connecting Ashiya and Arima Onsen) for everyday life. KOSHINO HOUSE (1981) was designed for fashion designer Hiroko Koshino at a corner of the residential area, and utilizing a mountain slope. The house consists of two cuboids and stands on a downhill site below a street. The misaligned parallel buildings face each other across a courtyard. The street side building has two stories, and the one at the bottom of the slope has one story. The two buildings are connected by an underground corridor in the slope.

Ando regarded the courtyard — surrounded by concrete on both sides and the ground — a "Residual Image of a Piece of Cloth" placed in the surrounding nature, and he positioned it as a symbol of the house. Hard concrete structures (such as outdoor stairs for going up and down) were added while being acutely conscious of artificial outdoors, rather than in harmony with surrounding nature.

Architectural critic Kenneth Frampton referred to this house as a typical example of "critical regionalism". "Critical regionalism" is a concept that connects the universal abstract language of modernism with unique regional expressive languages. It was different from both stateless modernism, and postmodernism that follows concrete historical forms. It is as if the light and wind are filtered and introduced into the concrete box, so that residents can feel the transitions of time and the seasons, and provoke thoughts about "places" as a concept. Frampton considered this idea of Ando as a part of "critical regionalism".

The referral of Ando's work to Western media by Frampton had an impact; attention to him was further increased after this KOSHINO HOUSE, raising more expectation as a savior of modernism.

Abstract and Physical Maze

A well-known larger house design by Ando in Japan is KIDOSAKI HOUSE. The client was an architect couple. The house was for three households: the couple and each of their parents. Ando described this as a condominium, in terms of prioritizing the privacy of each housing unit.

Overall, a concrete cube with 12m sides is located at the center, and concrete walls stand at the borders of the site. An arched slope to the house entrance is placed at a void between the cube and the walls. The outside scenery surrounded by the walls can be enjoyed from each housing unit. Two housing units for the parents are located on the first floor, and the client's residence is on the second and third floors. It can be said that Ando intentionally designed the complicated puzzle-like room arrangement.

It is said that Ando introduced a vibration of senses and an expansion of the senses, brought by abstract figures, as well as a coexisting physical maze in this house. An example of an abstract expression that affects the senses is "Homage to the Square" by Josef Albers (1888–1976). By painting the overlapping squares with different colors, Albers's figure was given a movement beyond an abstract frame, appealing to the senses of viewers. The cube in KIDOSAKI HOUSE is regarded as a three dimensional version of Albers's figure.

1

Chapter 1   Quest for "My Presence" and the "Fundamental Space of Pathos"

城戸崎邸　1986
kidosaki house

1. リビングルーム
   Living room
2. 鳥瞰全景
   Bird's-eye view

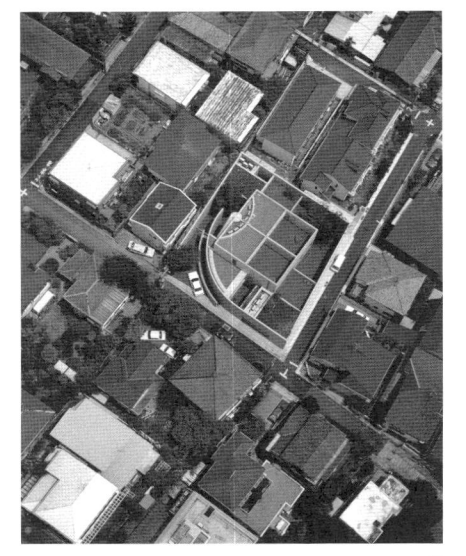

この住宅を「クリティカル・リージョナリズム」の典型例として言及したのは、建築評論家のケネス・フランプトンだった。「批評的地域主義」というのは、モダニズムの普遍的な抽象言語とその土地固有の表現言語を結びつける概念で、それは無国籍なモダニズムとも、具象的に歴史造形をなぞるポスト・モダニズムとも異なるものとした。コンクリートの箱のなかに、光と風をいわば濾過して引き込み、居住者に時間や季節の移ろいを実感させ、概念としての「場」への思いを抱かせる安藤の発想を、フランプトンは「クリティカル・リージョナリズム」の一翼を担うものと見なしたのである。

この概念は、当時のポスト・モダニズムによる批判のなかで、力を失ったモダニズムの抽象表現を延命させるための牽強付会な論法の色合いが濃かった。それでも、フランプトンによる欧米のメディアへの紹介は影響力を持ち、安藤への注目はこの「小篠邸」によっても高まり、モダニズムの救世主としての期待が自ずと拡大していった。

抽象と身体的迷路

安藤の設計による日本における邸宅の代表作として知られるのは「城戸崎邸」である。建築家夫妻を施主とするこの住宅は、夫妻とそれぞれの両親一家との三世帯住居であり、各住居のプライバシーを優先するという点では、コンドミニアムだったと安藤は述懐している。

全体形としては、中央に一辺が12メートルのコンクリートの立方体が置かれ、敷地境界にはコンクリートの塀が建てられた。この立方体と塀の余白の部分に住宅のエントランスへの円弧を描くスロープなどが配され、各戸も塀に囲われた屋外の風景を眺める仕立てをとっている。1階に両親の二世帯、2、3階に施主の住戸部分が配された。複雑なパズルのような間取りは、安藤の狙いだったといえるだろう。

安藤は抽象図形がもたらす感覚の振動と拡張、それと同居する身体的な迷路をこの住宅に配したという。感覚に影響を及ぼす抽象表現の例として現代画家ジョゼフ・アルバース（1888–1976年）の「正方形讃歌」をあげる。重ね合わせた正方形を塗り分けることによってアルバースの造形は、抽象の枠を超える動きをもち、それが鑑賞者の感情に訴える。「城戸崎邸」の立方体は、そのアルバースの造形が立体化したものだという見立てである。

そこに絡みつく円弧を描くスロープは、身体的な迷路なのだともいう。細く絞られたスロープは視線が遮られ、来訪者の視界は束縛される。この迷路的な空間イメージの原点として、18世紀後半のイタリアの版画家ジョバンニ・バチスタ・ピラネージの連作「牢獄」をあげる。脳を支配する観念的な感覚と、直接的な身体感覚。その二つは、安藤

城戸崎邸　1986
kidosaki house

3. アプローチ外観
   Exterior appearance of the approach way
4. コートヤード
   Courtyard
5. コートヤード
   Courtyard
6. 2階リビングルーム
   Living room on the second floor

4

5

6

第1章 「わたしの存在感」「情念の基本空間」を求めて 055

The arched slope entwined there can be called a physical maze. The narrowly made slope allows limited perspectives, containing the visitor's view. The origin of this maze-like spatial image could be the "Prison" series of work by Italian printmaker Giovanni Battista Piranesi of the latter half of 18th century. A conceptual sense that governs the brain, and a direct physical sense: needless to say, these two senses were Ando's architectural view, which he explored in a series of small concrete urban houses, including Row House, Sumiyoshi. He attempted to accomplish this in the mansion-like sized Kidosaki House. The word condominium has the same meaning and concept as "Row House" in this respect, suggesting that Ando's view of residence was unwavering.

*Never Ending Pursuit of
Nature and Urban Life*

4×4 House was completed in 2003 and gathered attention from society, partly because the client was publicly sought through general magazines. Since Ando put his efforts into rehabilitation from the Great Hanshin earthquake in 1995, the architect's creative urge as an origin was stimulated by the small site in Kobe City facing the Seto Inland Sea. Sandwiched between a busy motorway and seashore, the site only has a 6m depth, and therefore the house became a cuboid with 4m sides. Stair halls take up much space from the first to third floors of the four story house, significantly limiting the room arrangement. The living room is located on the fourth floor, where a relatively larger space was available. From a large window on the ocean side, the Akashi Kaikyo Bridge can be viewed. On the other hand, the façade was closed by a bare concrete wall with consideration for noise reduction.

While former regeneration of row houses was attempted in a densely built-up area, the spaciousness and natural environment are totally different in this case, albeit with an area constraint. In this house, Ando also chose a composition somewhat similar to his early houses. There exists a constant pursuit of the proposition: how much of a size restriction can be compensated for by opening a space towards nature?

In that sense, House in Utsubo Park (2010) also represents Ando's unalterable belief in houses. The back of the narrow and long concrete box, which reminds us of a row house, was opened to one of Osaka's best urban parks, "Utsubo Park" through a glass window. With this composition, he proved that living in this three story house with 5m width and 27m length can bring a benefit as if having the large park all to themselves. As Ando's architect activities expand, he has less opportunities to design small houses. However, by designing these concrete boxes once every few years, Ando is perhaps trying to return to his starting point.

1

4×4の住宅　2003
4×4 house

1. 鳥瞰全景
   Bird's-eye view
2. 海側からの夜景
   Night view from the seaside
3. 4階リビングから瀬戸内海を望む
   View of the Seto Inland Sea from the fourth floor living room

が「住吉の長屋」をはじめとする一連のコンクリートの狭小な都市住宅で突き詰めてきた建築観なのはいうまでもない。それを邸宅と呼べる規模の「城戸崎邸」でも貫徹することを目指した。コンドミニアムという言葉は、その点では「長屋」と同義語、同観念であり、安藤の住宅観が揺るぎないものであることを物語っている。

終わりなき自然と都市の暮らしの探求

　2003年に完成した「4×4の住宅」は一般雑誌で施主を公募したこともあり、社会的にも注目を集めた。1995年の阪神淡路大震災のあと、安藤は復興に取り組んできただけに、神戸市垂水区の瀬戸内海に面した狭小な敷地は創作意欲をかきたてた。交通の激しい自動車道路と海岸に挟まれた敷地の奥行きは6メートルしかなく、住宅は4メートル角の直方体となった。内部は四層構造で、3階までは階段室に多くの面積をとられ、間取りの制約は大きい。比較的広さが確保できる4階にリビングが配され、大きな窓が明石海峡大橋を望む海側にとられた。一方、自動車道路側の正面は騒音対策も考慮して全面がコンクリート打ち放しの壁で閉ざされた。

　かつての長屋の再生が、住宅の密集地で企てられたのに対して、面積の制約はあっても、周囲の開放感、自然環境は全く異なっている。ここでも安藤は、初期の住宅に通じる構成を選択した。寸法上の厳しさを、自然に向かって空間を開くことで、どれだけ補えるかという命題の変わりない追求がそこには存在しているのである。

　その意味では「靭公園の住宅」(2010年)もまた安藤の住宅に賭ける不変の信念を物語っている。それこそ長屋を思わせる間口が狭く奥深いコンクリートのボックスの背後を、大阪でも指折りの都市公園「靭公園」に向かってガラスの窓で開いた。その構成により、この間口5メートル弱、奥行き27メートル、3階建ての住宅に住み続ける行為が、広大な公園をあたかも独り占めするかのような恩恵をもたらすことを証明してみせた。建築家としての活動が拡大するなかで、小住宅を手がける機会は限られてきたが、それでも数年に一度、こうしたコンクリートボックスを手がけることで、安藤は原点に立ち返ろうとしているのかもしれない。

靭公園の住宅　2010
house in utsubo park

1. 靭公園側外観
   Exterior appearance of the Utsubo Park side
2. 2層吹き抜けのリビングルームよりコートを見る
   View of the south side court
   from the double-height living room

1

2

Chapter 1　Quest for "My Presence" and the "Fundamental Space of Pathos"　058

第2章　商業建築に都市の〈公性〉を託す
道、広場、都市の文脈

Chapter 2　Expect the City's 'Publicness' in Commercial Buildings
Streets, Open Spaces and Urban Context

アーバンスプロールから街を救う

　安藤忠雄はずっと大阪に住み、事務所も構えてきたので、かなりの数の作品が大阪にある。一方、神戸市でも多くの建築を設計してきた。安藤が初めて神戸に行ったのは小学校の遠足。そのとき、なんてきれいなところだと思ったという。阪神淡路大震災で大きな被害を受けた先代の神戸市役所は1957年の完成で、三宮の広い通りに面して花時計を足元に添えて建ち、子ども心にも、実にすがすがしい姿だと感心させられた。設計の仕事をするようになって、その目で眺めても、大阪と異なる美しい町の印象は変わることがなかった。

　今でこそ、神戸というと北野町の西洋館が思い浮かぶが、1977年にNHKが朝の連続テレビ小説「風見鶏」を放映するまでは、そこまでの観光スポットとは言いがたかった。北野町は明治に始まる西洋館が残る古い住宅地で、1960年代には安手のホテルが相次いで建設されるなど危機的な状態にあった。せっかく神戸ならではの歴史遺産を抱えた町なのに風前の灯火のように思えた。

　三宮駅につながる地下街「さんちかタウン」の商店主たちとの付き合いは、ショッピングタウン設計の先駆者だった西脇顕正の建築事務所のアルバイトとして6軒の店舗のインテリア設計を手がけたところから始まった。店主たちは、西洋館をハイカラな神戸の「原点」と位置づけ、打ち合わせをしているときに、その大切さを語ってくれた。そんな縁で、彼らと一緒に「うろこの家（旧ハリヤー邸、明治38年）」を見学に行くなど、北野町とのつきあいが始まった。

　市民に対して、西洋館の価値を訴えている坂本勝比古（のちに千葉大教授）と知り合ったのもそのころだった。神戸市役所に席を置きながら、学術的な価値を粘り強く理解し

Rescue the City from Urban Sprawl

As Tadao Ando has lived and had his office in Osaka, a considerable number of his works are in Osaka. In the meantime, he has also designed many buildings in Kobe city. It was on a school excursion at elementary school that he first went to Kobe. He thought it was such a beautiful place, as he recalled. The former Kobe City Hall that was heavily damaged by the Great Hanshin-Awaji Earthquake had been built in 1957. The building standing along a main street of Sannomiya with a flower clock arranged at its foot looked so dignified and imposing to the child's eyes that he got a strong positive impression from the figure. Even after he started to work as an architect, the impression of the beautiful town that is different from Osaka, never seemed to have changed to his eyes.

Although "Kobe" now reminds us of the Western-style houses in Kitano-cho, it was far from a popular sightseeing spot before 1977, when NHK broadcasted a morning TV drama series called "Kazamidori". Kitano-cho, an old residential district retaining Western-style houses built in Meiji-era, was once in a critical condition in 1960's when cheap hotels were constructed one after another. The town seemed to be on the verge of ruin although it had historical heritages unique and precious to Kobe.

He met Katsuhiko Sakamoto (later, a professor of Chiba University) who was insisting on the values of Western-style houses to the citizens. While working for the Kobe city office, he was persistently trying to make them understand their academic values. Ando, who wanted to support him, started to join the conservation action. Learning about the Western-style houses in this manner offered him numerous suggestions as to the designing of multiple commercial facilities that he worked on in Kitano-cho, including ROSE GARDEN, and these let him think about fusion of history and modern times.

When he was offered the job to design ROSE GARDEN, he had no choice but to think about the urban sprawl that was threatening the existence of Western-style houses. New architecture, especially construction of commercial facilities can be feasible when they are based on capital investment and its recovery. Under such conditions, he considered what should be inherited from the history in Kitano-cho.

For ROSE GARDEN, first, he conceived an idea of securing "a place characteristic of Kitano-cho" by creating two walls so that it would not get eroded by its surroundings. The two walls were to be arranged in parallel to one another from the mountain to the sea direction. This was in line with the history that Western-style houses have been located on the slope stretching to the sea to enjoy the panoramic view. Since Kitano-cho is a town created based on the sea-oriented culture, he made a choice to inherit it and maintain the characteristics of Kobe as a port town.

ローズガーデン 1977
rose garden

1. 北側外観
   Exterior appearance on the north side
2. 切妻屋根が見える
   View of the gabled roof

てもらおうとする坂本を支援したいと考え、保存活動にも参加するようになった。そうやって、西洋館のなんたるかを知ったことは、「ローズガーデン」をはじめ、北野町で手がけた複数の商業施設の設計にあたって、歴史と現代の融合を考える多くの示唆を与えてくれた。

「ローズガーデン」設計の依頼を受けたとき、西洋館の存在を危うくしているアーバンスプロール化について考えざるをえなかった。新しい建築、しかも商業施設は資本投下と回収を前提に成立している。そうした条件のもとで、北野町において歴史からなにを継承していくのかという考察である。

「ローズガーデン」ではまず2枚の壁によって、周囲から浸食を受けない「北野町らしい場」を確保しようと構想した。壁の配置は、山から海の方向に向かって2枚を平行にすることに決めた。それは西洋館が斜面地を生かして、海への眺望が開けるように立地してきた歴史を踏まえてのことである。北野町は海に向かう方向性に基づいて形成された街なのだから、それを継承し、神戸ならではの港町らしさを持続させようとする選択だった。

海へ向かう北野町の視線

壁の仕上げを煉瓦にしたのは、西洋館らしいテクスチュアを考えてのことだが、それ以上に組積造を意識した。日本人の大工がひとつひとつ煉瓦を積むところから、日本の近代は始まった。その組積造を北野町の街角で未来に向けて確認することによって、肌合いを超えて、ここで育まれてきた歴史を後世へと伝えうると考えたのである。

肌合いは西洋館を意識したものの、形としての類似性は求めなかった。意識したのはヴォリュームであり、建物の規模を既存の街並みに見合うように抑制した。そのうえで、2枚の平行な壁のうち、街路に面した1枚は、三つに分割して、高さも傾きも少しずつずらして配置した。そうすることによって、北野町ならではの坂道のロケーションを来訪者にはっきりと認識してもらうのを意図した。また、壁を三つに分割したことで生じる間隙、つまりスリットから海の側への視界が開かれる。これもロケーションへの気づきをもたらす仕掛けだった。

2枚の壁が挟む建築の躯体は、坂道の傾斜を強調するように床の高さを違えて、中庭にあたる広場をレベルの異なるデッキで囲むように仕立てた。この上階に進むにつれてセットバックするデッキは、広場に立ったとき、躯体の高さを和らげ、より人間的なスケールをそこに出現させた。

こう記すと、2枚の壁の設営をはじめ、全体を決定して部分を従属させていったよ

Vision from Kitano-cho to the Sea

Although brick was used for the wall finishing in consideration for a Western-like texture, he paid more attention to the masonry structure. The modern age of Japan started when Japanese carpenters laid bricks one by one. He thought it would be possible to hand down the history developed here to new generations, beyond the texture, by reconfirming the masonry structure on a street corner in Kitano-cho for the future.

Although the texture was decided by taking into account the Western-style houses, similarity in shape was not pursued. What he cared about was the volume, and the size of the building was restricted to fit into the existing streetscape. On that basis, one of the two parallel walls facing the street was divided into three parts, each of which was arranged with different height and angle from one another. By doing so, he intended to let visitors clearly recognize the location of the slope that is unique to Kitano-cho. The gaps created by dividing the wall into three parts, in another word, slits, also provide views of the sea side. This is also a device to provide awareness of the location.

The body of the building sandwiched by two walls was designed to have floors in different height to emphasize inclination of the slope, with open space surrounded by step decks as a patio. The decks were designed to set back as they go higher, and thereby, when visitors stand in the open space, the height of the building is reduced and more humanly scale is produced there.

The description so far may give an impression that the overall design including construction of two walls was determined first and details were added to it as subordinate elements. In fact, however, the image of detailed space produced by the patio and decks was exactly the starting point of ROSE GARDEN. The perspective of the sea, and the space experience provided by wind and light around the patio are what was meant to be designed. The way the decks cut off the sky over the patio, and intentional misalignment of the walls of stairs added some movement to the space. The space of ROSE GARDEN was produced precisely by accumulating images of partial spaces and weaving them into the whole design.

ローズガーデン　1977
rose garden

3. デッキから望む中庭の賑わい
   Crowded courtyard viewed from the deck
4. 中庭にひとびとが集う
   People gathering in the courtyard
5. 北東角からの透視図
   Perspective drawing from the northeast corner

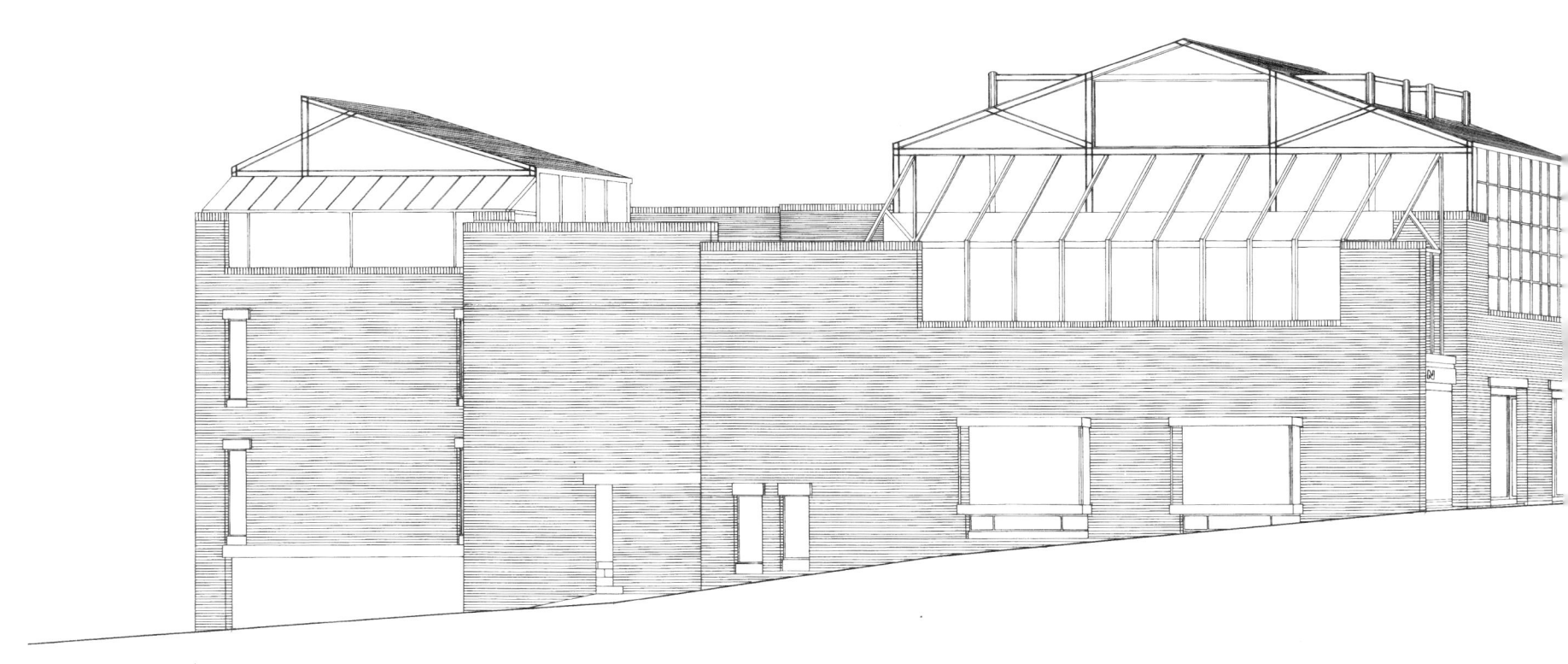

うに思えるかも知れないが、実際には、広場やデッキのもたらす細部空間のイメージこそが「ローズガーデン」の出発点となった。海へのパースペクティブ、広場を中心に風や光がもたらす空間体験がそれである。広場の頭上のデッキが空をどう切り取るか、階段の壁を意図的にずらせたことが空間に動きを与えた。まさに部分の空間のイメージが集積して、全体を織りなすことによって、「ローズガーデン」の空間が設えられたのであった。

西澤文隆の評価

　この「ローズガーデン」を専門誌で評したのは、坂倉建築研究所の西澤文隆だった（「新建築」1977年5月号、「近頃の安藤さん」）。関西の建築界にあって、指導的な立場にあり、数々の箴言を残した孤高の建築家である。
　煉瓦の組積造について西澤は、まず「囲い込むことはオーソドックスであるがいかにも古めかしい形態に堕しやすい」と危惧を語り、そのうえで、煉瓦壁を面に解体することが、そうした陥りやすい癖を脱する技法だと指摘する。そして、それはミース・ファン・デル・ローエに通じるものだと述べている。街路側の壁を3枚に分割して「海を垣間見させよう」とした意図を、そのように的確に解釈してくれた。さらに「本計画では外壁を透かしながらも囲い込み、南北の棟をスキップにして中庭で連絡する。囲われた中庭はまったく自由と見せながら外の通りとの連りも十分考えられているのである」と設計意図を理解してくれた。
　それまで励ましも込めて辛口の批評に終始していた西澤から、やっと合格点に近いものをもらえた。
　西澤は、安藤が「あらゆる場所のアイソメを描いて、各個所が納まっているかどうかをチェックすることにしている」ことを評価したうえで、「それは途方もなく手間のかかる仕事ではある」と努力を認めてくれた。さらに「住吉の長屋」以降、「細部にわたって細かく注意を行き届かせ、見事に納めているのである。文句をいうところがなくなってきたというのが今日このごろである」とまで褒めそやした。
　ちなみに、この「ローズガーデン」の街路側の1階に入居したテナントのひとつが「神戸コロッケ」だった。のちに全国のデパートの惣菜売り場に系列店舗を展開する「ロックフィールド」の創業者、岩田弘三との出会いはここから始まった。やがて、工場、本社を設計することになるとは、その時点では想像もつかなかった。
　西澤の寄稿は次のように結ばれている。

Lessons Learned from Western-style Houses

Almost eight years had passed since he worked on designing of ROSE GARDEN, the first work in the town of Western-style houses in Kitano-cho, Kobe. With this commercial complex building as a start, and having obtained some advocates among land owners in Kitano-cho, he was given opportunities to design some more commercial buildings. Within a radius of 200 meters or so, he designed ROSE GARDEN, KITANO ALLEY, followed by RIN'S GALLERY and KITANO IVY COURT, so he decided to summarize their architecture and how the town should be like.

At the beginning of an article he contributed to the magazine "Shinkenchiku", he wrote as quoted below. This can be interpreted as "one declaration". It was an architectural view, almost a conviction, that he gained as a result of coming face-to-face with the town of Kitano-cho and taking on the design so intently.

Architecture stands on its own with its logic following behind.
Architecture forms the town's context as well as its environment. Newly created architecture also becomes a part of the context from that moment.

In designing commercial buildings in Kitano-cho, he addressed this problem head-on in the first place — that is, which characteristics of the area should be inherited as an image, and how new values can be created. Attacked by the wave of development, with condominium buildings planned here and there, and pushed by sleazy commercial facilities, Western-style houses were demolished. What could he do as an architect? With commercialism as one principal axis, he thought of giving a new potential to Kitano-cho that will be inherited to the next generation of the town of Western-style houses.

Looking back now, the Western-style houses taught him many things.

He realized that in the case of Western-style houses, the spirit of the builder is infused in every hole and corner of the building, unlike the modern-day buildings that are quickly built with emphasis on economic efficiency. He thought that in Meiji Era, the builders could not have achieved the construction of Western-style houses without having conflicted feelings, since they were something they had never seen before. He felt the builder's heart was infused, say, in the windows or even in the outdoor fence.

Now, since he was going to design new commercial architecture, he knew that it would take a lot of time at any rate. The slope and the site, the open space within the building, how the shops relate to the whole architecture, how the light provides bright and dark within the space, and how the architect should see and solve the continuity of segments. He tried to hold his design plan in mind for a long time. By doing so, he could feel that distance between the building and himself was getting closer. Most of all, he could develop a deeper affection for the buildings.

北野アレイ　1977
kitano alley

1. 細い通路を介して2棟が交差する
   Two buildings cross each other via the narrow pathway
2. エントランスの通路見おろし
   Downward view of the entrance path
3. 通路から地下階への屋外階段
   Outdoor stairs from the pathway to the underground level

「1年に5つつくれば70歳までに200つくれる。3つとしても120つくれる。たとえ時間がかかってもこつこつとつくって行けばよい。あとは少しでも長生きしてたくさん作品を世に残すことだ。」トツトツとして安藤さんは語る。上気して本当に美しく見えた。

西澤が鬼籍に入った現在、感慨なくして読みえない心温まる励ましのメッセージである。

西洋館の教え

神戸北野町の西洋館街の最初の作品「ローズガーデン」の設計にとりかかってから8年の歳月が過ぎようとしていた。この複合商業ビルをきっかけに、北野町に土地を所有するオーナーから賛同者が現れて、複数の商業ビルを設計する機会を得た。半径200メートルそこそこのエリアに「ローズガーデン」「北野アレイ」に継いで、「リンズギャラリー」「北野アイビーコート」を手がけることになり、それらの建築と街のあり方を総括することにした。

「新建築」誌に寄稿した論文の冒頭に安藤は次のように記した。これは「ひとつの宣言」と読めるものだ。北野町の街に向き合い、夢中で設計に挑んだ結果として得られた確信に近い建築観だった。

建築は、自身(みずから)の論理を従え自立する。
建築は、その環境とともに、街のコンテクストを形成する。新たにつくられる建築もまた、その時点より、街のコンテクストの一部となる。

西洋館が残り、良好だったはずの北野町の住宅地が、あけすけな商業施設の浸食を受けて、無秩序な場に変わりつつあるのを、なんとかしなければとの思いだった。建築家として自ら商業建築を手がける立場にあり、営利と建築本来のあり方の突き合わせに向き合わざるを得なかった。

北野町での商業建築の設計にあたって、まず、地域のどの特性をイメージとして継承するか、そして新たな価値をどう生み出すかに正面から挑んだ。北野町がもはや高級住宅地でいられなくなっている状況は誰の目にも明らかだった。開発の波が押し寄せ、いわゆるマンションがそこここで計画され、低俗な商業施設に押されて、西洋館は取り壊されていった。建築家としてなにができるか、そこで商業をひとつの基本軸に、西洋

He believed that, by putting some thought into segments just as the carpenters who built the Western-style houses used to do, the segments with his thoughts would turn into a rich architecture, and by making a sequence of such architecture, he could produce a new environment in Kitano-cho.

It may still take a long time before new architecture will become a scenery of Kitano-cho. However, he thought that when they do, the architecture would evolve from private existence to public one as common properties that constitute the scenery.

*A Turning Point Brought by
the Great Hanshin-Awaji Earthquake*

In response to the emergence of such new commercial architectures by Ando, many people have come to enjoy strolling in Kitano-cho. There were also people visiting just to see the modern architecture such as ROSE GARDEN.

However, due to the serious damages caused by the Great Hanshin-Awaji Earthquake in 1995, the entire city of Kobe lost its dynamism as a city. The society was in a state of prolonged exhaustion after the collapse of bubble economy, and the economic position in Kansai was deteriorated. People's consumption behavior also changed drastically in the wave of collapse of prices. Although Kitano-cho has been providing fancy places for sightseeing that were established as a continuation of daily lives, it seems to be reaching a big turning point today.

With ROSE GARDEN as a starter, He has designed seven architectures in Kitano-cho. The scar left by the great earthquake appears to have been healed by the redevelopment, but how does the Kobe city itself overcome the disaster and create a new vision for urban development? The current state of Kitano-cho makes us think about many things. It was certain that the time had come to reconsider the figure of Kitano-cho for the next era, not just to be reminiscent of the glory of the past.

リンズギャラリー　1981
rin's gallery

1. 坂道に面した正面
　 Façade facing a slope
2. 階段からの眺望
　 View from the stairs

館の街の次代につながる新しいポテンシャルを北野町に持たせようと考えた。

　思えば西洋館はいろいろなことを教えてくれた。

　経済性重視で手早くつくられる今日の建築と違い、西洋館はつくり手の気持ちが隅々まで行き渡っていることに気づいた。明治になって、それまで見たこともなかった西洋建築を構築するのに、葛藤なくしてはそれらは実現せず、窓ひとつとっても、あるいは外構の塀でさえ、彼らの思いが塗り込められていることを感じた。

　そこで新たに商業建築を手がけるのであるから、とにかく設計に時間を要することは覚悟した。坂道と敷地、建築内の広場、店舗はどう全体に関わっていくのか、光は空間のなかで明暗をどうもたらすのか、部分の連続を建築家はどのように解決していくのか。設計案を長く頭のなかに滞留させることを心がけた。そうすることによって、建物と自分との距離が近づいていく手応えがあった。なにより、建物への愛着も深まった。

　西洋館を建設した大工たちがそうしたように、部分に思いを込め、その思いのこもった部分が密度の高い建築をもたらし、そのような建築を連続させることで、北野町に新たな環境を出現させられると考えた。

　それでも新たな建築が北野町の風景となるには長い時間を要するかもしれない。しかし、それがなったとき、建築は風景を構成する共有財産として、私的存在から公的なそれへと昇華しうると思ったのである。

自らを律する三つの原則

　そこで自分なりに北野町で商業建築を設計するにあたって心すべき「三つの原則」を考えた。

　第1の原則は、新たに設計する建物が、既存の街並みを壊さないようにヴォリュームを設定すること。そのためには、北野町ならではの坂道の多い傾斜地の地形がもたらす高低差の積極的な活用を常に意識した。

　第2の原則は、建物に都市のアルコーブとなるような空間を持たせ、それが界隈性を獲得して、北野町の街へと連続させることだった。そうすることによって、建築は私有地に位置していても、街のひとびとが、アルコーブとしての建築内の広場などを、みんなで共有する公有財産と認識できるようになるはずだと考えた。

　第3の原則は、煉瓦塀や、やはり煉瓦で出来ている側溝、西洋館を囲う背の高い擁壁、そこを這うアイビーなどの具体的な要素と起伏のある土地、背後の山の稜線と眼前に広がる青い海など、北野町の住人が記憶のなかに保持し続けてきた街のイメージの継承である。新たな建築の出現がそれらの記憶を断ち切ってしまわないための周到な配

"Site Work" and "Site Craft"

For commercial buildings, the focus was on the pursue of how the external environment can be drawn into the interior considering interrelationship between external environment and the building as a core of design. At that time, Ando was thinking about the concepts of "site work" and "site craft" in terms of commercial buildings.

"Site work" is an approach to think about how to constitute an architecture on the flat surface, that is, within the site. For example, in the case of KITANO ALLEY in Kitano-cho, Kobe, he pondered the meaning of mutual interference between "blanc space" created by arranging solid geometry on an atypical site in a misaligned manner and the architectural body itself. On the other hand, as ROSE GARDEN also in Kitano-cho is structured in a way that the decks surrounding the open space have different levels, "site craft" puts focus on how to construct a three-dimensional structure.

From such viewpoint of "site craft", in the case of STEP that he designed in Marugame-cho Shopping Street in Takamatsu city, he considered the whole concept of a commercial building that would face the existing shopping arcade, and tried to design an architecture that might change the mindset of the shopping street. Marugame-cho Shopping Street is one of the busiest shopping district in Shikoku, and STEP was planned as a commercial complex building that could hold many boutiques as tenants.

Before developing an idea for the architecture, Ando thought shopping arcades that could be seen around local cities in Japan were lacking individualities and did not represent their regionalities in the first place. Arcades cover the third floor and above of the shops, which makes the space in the shopping street seem closed and exclusive. Marugame-cho Shopping Street is no exception. And so, in designing STEP, from the standpoint of site craft-like mindset, three flights of stairs were inserted. By positioning the stairs as the core of the space, the commercial building from the ground floor to the top fourth floor was regarded as a three-dimensional structure.

STEP is located at a corner plot, with its front facing to Marugame-cho Shopping Street. On the left, as one faces, was a side street which leads to the shopping street. Although the frontage was not so wide, the first flight of stairs that go straight up to the third floor were introduced at the center. The idea was that, in this building, the most probable targets are the shoppers approaching from the shopping street, so they would be lead to these stairs and drawn into the top floor of the building.

北野アイビーコート　1980
kitano ivy court

1. 既存の壁も活用
　Utilizing the existing wall
2. 煉瓦の肌合いの入り口へのアプローチ
　Approach to the brick-textured entrance

慮の必要性を痛感した。

　それを「住吉の長屋」で目指したヴォキャブラリーを限定した建築でいかにして体現するのか。それには建築自らが厳密な論理を有していなければならないし、空間の操作は概念が明確であれば単純になり、建築は自ずと端正なものになっていくはずと考えた。現実には、北野町のなかの狭い一角で四つの建築を手がけたこともあり、これらの建築は自ずと共通する仕立てをとることになった。

　「ローズガーデン」で試みた自立した平行な2枚の壁による場の設定とそこに架かる鉄骨造の屋根については、他の建築でも援用した。建築はヴォリュームを分割し、それを階段でつなぐ。同時に平面の整合性と位相のずれを持たせて空間の多様性を演出した。

　地形の傾斜を生かし、ひとつの建築内のフロアは南北でスキップさせた。建築は外部空間としての広場を内に包み込む。道と広場と建物内部を結ぶ路地、光や風など建築によって切り取られた自然と来訪者が呼応する場を設定した。これらが、四つの建築の共通要素としてあげられる。

　北野町としっかり向き合うことで編み出された自分なりの解答だったといえるだろう。それらの基本的な骨格が部分のイメージの集積と呼応して、建物全体の物語が織りなされていくと考えたのである。

阪神淡路大震災がもたらす曲がり角

　こうした安藤の手になる新たな商業建築の出現に呼応して、多くのひとたちが北野町の散策を楽しむようになった。「ローズガーデン」をはじめ、現代建築を目当てに訪問するひとたちも現れた。それはこの土地固有の西洋館の歴史的な文脈と現代の創造が理想的な形で呼応した姿だった。北野町の新たな未来像を垣間みるかのような光景が出現した。

　しかし、1995年の阪神淡路大震災による致命的な被災により、神戸全体が都市としての活力を失ってしまった。バブル経済崩壊後の長引く社会の疲弊、関西経済圏の地盤沈下もあった。ひとびとの消費行動も価格破壊の波のなかで、大きく変化していった。日常の延長として地に足のついたしゃれた場所を提供してきた北野町の観光も、今日ひとつの大きな曲がり角にさしかかっているように思える。

　「ローズガーデン」を手始めに、北野町で手がけた建築は七つを数えた。大震災の傷は再開発で一見癒えたように思われているが、神戸そのものが震災を乗り超えて新たな都市像をどう結ぶか、北野町の現状はさまざまなことを考えさせる。あの時代は輝いて

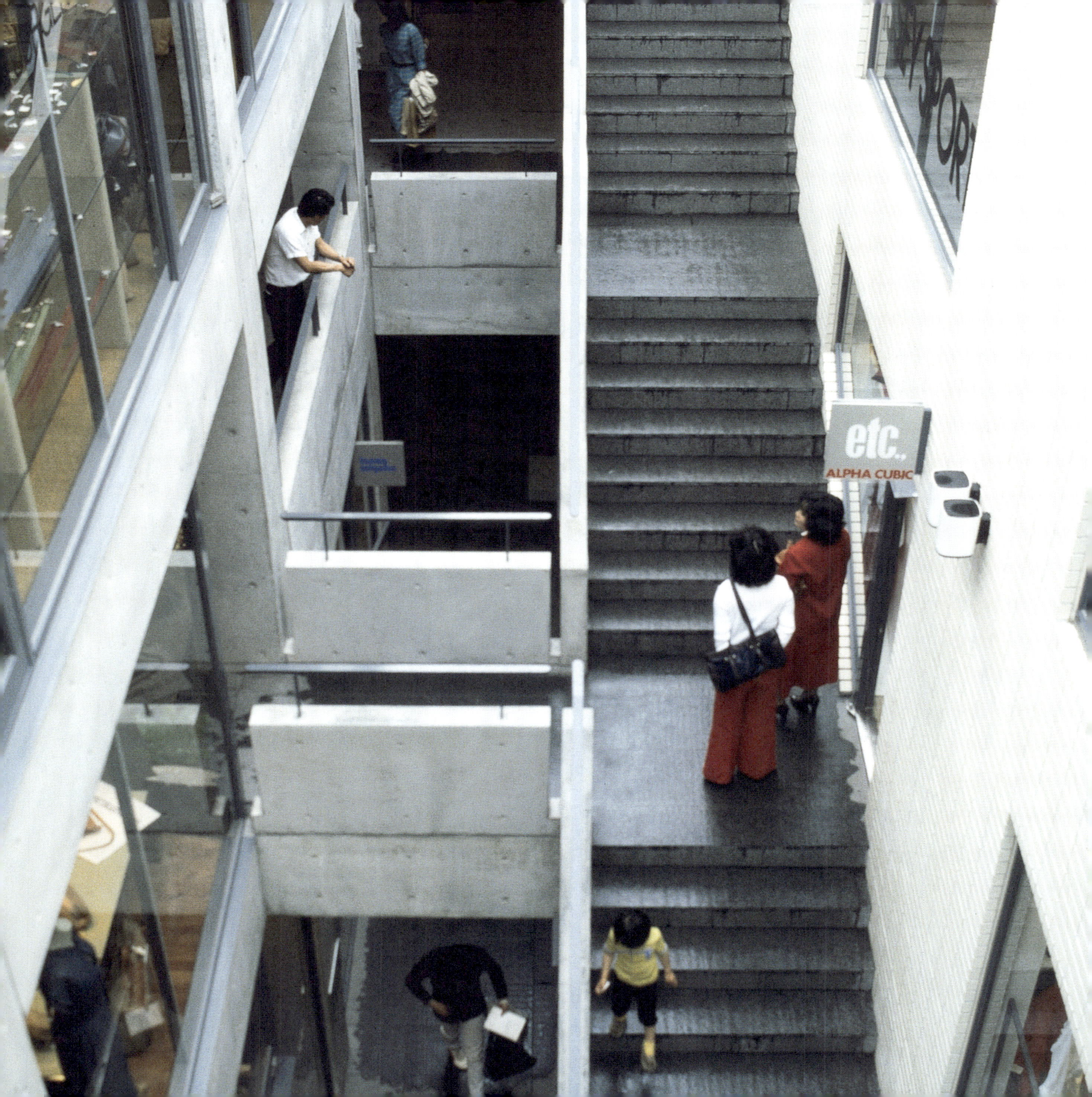
etc.
ALPHA CUBIC

STEP 1980
step

1. （前ページ）建物中央の屋外主階段
   (previous page) Main outdoor stairs at the center of the building

いたというだけではすまない、次の時代の北野町の姿を再考するときが来ているのは間違いあるまい。

サイトワークとサイトクラフト

　商業建築に関しては、外部環境と建物との相互の関係を設計のひとつの核として、外部環境をいかに内部に導入するかの探究に力点を置いた。その頃、商業建築に関して、安藤の考えていた概念に「サイトワーク」と「サイトクラフト」がある。

　「サイトワーク」とは平面、つまり敷地のなかでいかに建築を構成するかという考え方で、例えば、神戸・北野町の「北野アレイ」では、変則的な敷地に幾何立体をずらして配置することで生じる「余白」と建築の躯体との相互干渉の意味を考えた。一方、「サイトクラフト」とは、同じ北野町の「ローズガーデン」が広場を囲むデッキに高低差を持たせて構成したように、立体造形をどう構築するかが主眼点になった。

　そのような「サイトクラフト」の視点から、高松市の丸亀町商店街で手がけた「STEP」では、既存のアーケード商店街に面した商業建築のありかたを考察し、商店街に対する発想転換を促すような建築を試みた。丸亀町商店街は、四国でも指折りの繁華な商店街で、「STEP」はブティックなどの集まる複合商業ビルとして計画された。

　どのような建築にするかを構想する前に、そもそも日本の地方都市のあちこちに見られるアーケード商店街は、個性に欠けていて、地域性を象徴しているわけでもないと安藤は考えた。アーケードは商店の三層から上の部分を覆い隠していて、そのことが商店街の空間を閉鎖的にしている。丸亀町商店街も例外ではない。そこで「STEP」の設計にあたっては、「サイトクラフト」的な発想に立って、3本の階段を挿入することにした。階段を空間の中核に位置づけて、この商業建築の地上階から最上階の4階までを立体として捉えたのである。

　「STEP」は角地に位置していて、正面は丸亀町商店街に面し、向かって左側は商店街につながる脇道になっていた。さほどの間口ではなかったが、中央に3階まで一直線に登る1本目の階段を持ってきた。このビルにおいて、まず想定するのは商店街からアプローチする買い物客なのだが、彼らをこの階段に誘導し、ビルの上階まで引き込もうと考えたのである。

"STEP" Involved with the Street
as a Three-dimensional Structure

This was a proposition that he thought, if realized, would allow the architecture to be involved with the city in its three-dimensional cross-section. In general, commercial structures in shopping streets could get involved with the street only through the facade and plane surface. This was an attempt to break the status quo by introducing these stairs.

To offer an approach from the side street to the top floor, the second flight of stairs were arranged. Although these are turn-around stairs, they were not surrounded by walls so that people can feel open air and enjoy watching tenants' show windows while going up and down. The third flight of stairs were arranged on the back of curved wall behind the building. The intention here was that people, with adversely limited visibility, go up and down the moderate curved-incline using stairs.

As a result of featuring the stairs that way, the shared space occupied one third of the whole area. This shared space is a void, and it is literally an empty space. This space spreads from the ground floor through to the top floor of the building, where natural lights including direct light and reflected light are reaching out to the cross section of each layer of the building. For the shopping street, it was a space where people would linger around.

Since more shoppers were using the stairs on their feet than expected, and a scenery that nobody had ever seen before in Marugame-cho Shopping Street appeared, connoisseurs of architecture including Atsushi Ueda wrote articles for magazines and newspapers such as Asahi Shimbun. Involvement with nature, which had once been lost in return for the convenience of shoppers' being able to shop whatever the weather under the arcade, was regained in STEP in a visible manner by the intervention of light.

He deeply considered the design of three flights of stairs to make them induce the shoppers to go to upper floors. Not only the position of opening and arrangement of stair landing, but also the dimensions of stairs, including tread, height and width, were examined in detail. He aimed to make stairs that would allow visitors to reach the fourth floor while having the feeling that they are walking there on their own. For flooring of the stairs, he chose black granite stone with jet-induced rough finishing. He expected that the feeling they have through their feet would also inform them of the spatial composition.

STEP　1980
step

2. 商店街から上る主階段
   Main stairs ascending from the shopping street
3. 主階段の見おろし
   Downward view of the main stairs
4. 背後の曲面壁と屋上
   Curved backside wall and rooftop

立体として街路に関与する「STEP」

そうすることによって、建築が立体的な断面形状で街と関わることが可能になると考えての空間の提案だった。一般に、商店街の商業建築は、ファサードと平面の形状でしか街と関われなかった。それをこの階段で打破しようと企てたのである。

脇道から上階へのアプローチのために、2本目の階段を配した。こちらは折り返し階段だが、壁で囲うことはせず、外気に触れ、テナントのショーウインドーを見ながら昇降できるようにした。3本目は建物の背後の曲面壁の裏側に配した。ここは逆に視界を制約されながらカーブした緩やかな傾斜を階段で昇降する仕立てをとった。

そのように階段を主役にした結果、共有スペースが全体の3分の1の面積を占めることになった。この共有スペースは、ヴォイドであり、それはまさに空間であった。この空間は建物の地上階から上階まで貫き、そこでは直射光や反射光など自然の光が、いわば建築の断面の各層に働きかけてくる。それは商店街にとって、淀みの空間となった。

想定した以上に多くの買い物客が、自らの足で階段を昇降し、それまでの丸亀町商店街にはなかった光景が出現した。上田篤ら建築の目利きのひとたちが朝日新聞などに紹介の筆をとってくれた。アーケードによって天候に左右されない買い物の利便は確保されたが、その引き換えに失ってしまった自然との関わりが、「STEP」においては、光の介在によって目に見えるかたちで回復された。

安藤は、買い物客が自然に上階へと進めるように、三つの階段について、詳細な検討を重ねた。開口部の位置、踊り場の配置はもちろん、踏面、蹴上、幅など、階段の寸法について、事細かに研究を重ねた。来訪者自身が、そこを自らが歩いているという歩行感覚を自覚しながら、4階まであがっていける階段を目指した。階段の床材には、わずかに凹凸を持たせたジェット仕上げの黒御影石を選択した。それは靴を通してでも足触りの感覚が得られるもので、そうした触覚からも空間の構成が伝わることを期待した。

自然を感じさせる銀行支店

「住吉の長屋」がそうであったように、このころは単純化した平面と断面によって、どのようにすれば複雑な空間を創り出せるかが、設計のテーマとなっていた。単純化すれば建築の構成は明確になる。また、そうやって建築の内側に思考が向かえば、建築は自ずと自己完結型になる。それは街との関わりからいうと正反対になりそうだが、むしろ、そこを突き詰めることで逆説的に街と関われるのではと安藤は考えた。

Bank Branch with a Feeling of Nature

As with ROW HOUSE, SUMIYOSHI, theme of design at that time was how complicated spaces can be created by using simplified plane surfaces and cross-section surfaces. When they are simplified, the architectural composition will be clear. And if thinking goes inward to the design like this, architecture will be spontaneously self-contained. Although this might seem totally opposite in terms of relationship with the town, Ando thought architecture could rather get involved with the town paradoxically by pursuing it to the farthest extent.

When external factors in nature such as light and wind act on the architecture, and human beings intervene in between, an internal scenery is newly produced. The internal scenery is what confronts the external, and the mutual interference itself must be the relationship with the town. When he saw people walking up and down the stairs of STEP with no elevators and escalators under natural light, he knew that he got a definite answer. In fact, what he found there a shopping street that was expanded three-dimensionally by the people in town who acted in response to the concept of STEP.

Ando had an opportunity to design SUN PLACE in one corner of Minami-shinmachi Shopping Street that is connected to Marugame-cho Shopping Street by arcade. This project aimed to combine shops and a small culture hall centering around a bank.

Banks are closed quite early, and this brings a vacant area to the street. Since the site was also a corner lot fortunately, the bank was put away to the side of off-street, tenants were located on the main street of the shopping street, and the bank counter was arranged in such a manner that people approach through a small open space within a building adjacent to the bank, so that the effect of the vacancy would be minimized.

It would more appropriately be called an alley space rather than an open space, and by drawing in the street's stagnation into this space, he attempted to expand the street. This alley was also designed to enable people to go from the main street through to the off-street. It was expected that events like cultural activities to be held in the small hall on the third floor of this SUN PLACE and the preceding STEP would create a harmony, bringing breath and a new lively scene to the street.

The thought behind this idea was that Ando wanted to do something to the situation where the fundamental image of Japanese life had been lost. Although the life in Japanese society was simple and strict, there was a rich essence of life in the inner domain. Being convinced of the necessity to regain it, he worked on the designing of these commercial buildings.

What deprived commercial buildings of the inner nature of life was pursue of comfort and utilitarianism in modern times. They ended up turning to easiness. He was convinced that the key element needed to bring back the liveliness there one more time would be nature after all. He attempted to create a space with urban nature, where people involved there can be reminded of true selves they have forgotten.

About a quarter-century after the opening of STEP, Marugame-cho Shopping Street was transformed drastically by local people to construct a new shopping arcade. After part of the arcade was demolished, a street that gets a lot of sunshine came back. While STEP also changed itself to a new architecture, SUN PLACE has been exploring how it should be in such a big trend of the times and change in society.

サンプレイス　1982
sun place

1. 上階ラウンジのトップライト
   Skylight of upper floor lounge
2. 脇道側の外観
   Exterior appearance on the side street

建築に光や風といった自然に根ざした外部の因子が作用し、そこに人間が介在することで新たな内部風景が創出される。その内部風景は、外部と対峙するものであり、その相互干渉こそが街との関わりなのではないだろうか。自然光のもと、エレベーターもエスカレーターもない「STEP」の階段を昇降するひとたちの姿を見たとき、ひとつの確かな回答をもらった手応えがあった。商店街という街路が、「STEP」の構想に呼応したひとたちの行動によって、立体的に拡張された姿をそこに見出せたからである。

丸亀町商店街とつながるアーケードの南新町商店街の一角に「サンプレイス」を設計する機会も得られた。こちらのプロジェクトは銀行を中心に店舗、小さな文化ホールを複合するものだった。

銀行は閉店時刻がはやく街に空白地帯をもたらしてしまう。幸い、ここも角地だったので、その影響を最小限に抑制するために、銀行の店舗を脇道側に追いやり、商店街の表通り側はテナント店舗を配し、銀行の窓口へは店舗に隣接する建物内の小さな広場を介してアプローチするようにした。

いや広場というよりは、むしろ路地空間と呼ぶほうがふさわしい仕立てで、街の淀みを商店街からそこに引き込むことによって街路の拡張を企てた。この路地は表通りから脇道へと抜けられるようにもした。先行した「STEP」と、この「サンプレイス」の3階の小ホールでの文化活動などが共鳴して、街に生気を吹き込み、新たな賑わいがもたらされることを期待した。

こうした考えに立ち至ったのは、日本の生活の原像が失われてしまったことをなんとかしたいと安藤が考えたからである。日本社会は、素朴で厳しかったが、その内なる領域に濃密な生活の本質が存在していた。それを回復する必要を痛感して、これらの商業建築の設計に臨んだ。

商業建築において、生活の本質を奪い去ったのは、現代の快適さの追求と功利性だった。それらは互いを損ねないようにしながら、結果的には安易さへと流れてしまった。そこにもう一度生気を取り戻させる鍵は、やはり自然しかないと確信していた。なによりまず建築は自立し、ひとつひとつの建築が、街の特性を新たに開いていく。建築が、ひとびとの拠点となる場所を提供していけば、失われた界隈を回復していくきっかけになるのではと考えたのである。そのためにも、そこに関わるひとびとに、日々の暮らしに流されているうちに見失ってしまった自身の本来の姿に気づかせる、都市の自然を演出する空間の創出を試みた。

「STEP」の開場から、およそ四半世紀後、丸亀町商店街は、地元のひとたちの手で、新たなアーケード商店街を構築するべく、大きくその姿を変えた。アーケードの一部は撤去され、光の射し込む通りが復活した。「STEP」は新たな建築に衣替えし、「サンプレイス」も、そうした大きな時間の流れと社会の変化のなかで自分なりのあり方を模索している。商業建築と時代の変化について、考えさせられることは少なくない。

Milestone of 15th Anniversary,
Challenge in Naha, and General Overview

For Ando, the commercial complex building called Festival that opened on the International Street in Naha in 1984, Okinawa was a piece of his work in which he had a strong awareness of "milestone in his creative activities". Since Okinawa was a perfect stage for modern architecture to express natural features of the land, Ando tried a block architecture that is unique to Okinawa, and realized an open-ceiling stairwell that harnesses natural ventilation and an Indian laurel-planted terrace where people can enjoy the subtropical blue sky from upper floors and breeze blowing through the stairs. Highly expected by the locals, it was welcomed with so much enthusiasm that at the time of opening there was a long queue of people waiting to enter.

When this Festival was announced, what he could do as a budding architect was designing "residential houses and commercial buildings", noted Ando, looking back on his prior creation. As the starting point as an architect, he also pointed to Masuzawa Makoto's residence, a minimal house, and "Fugetsudo" in Ginza, Tokyo as well as a series of Antonin Raymond's works. The combination of Masuzawa who was like a genuine original form of modernism on one hand, and Raymond who was also a modernist and yet freely used diverse techniques on the other hand, seems interesting when we try to know Ando's disposition. In addition, reference to Masuzawa's residence and commercial buildings is associated with his early works, suggesting that his real motive was there.

Small houses and commercial buildings. Starting from the minimal house built in an era of 1950's when contribution to postwar construction was expected, small houses had always been a focus of the portfolio for ambitious architects' debut works until 1970's. A collection of all sorts of small houses that "play the eccentric artist" was a popular and essential item for both architecture magazines and their readers in 1970's. However, Ando suggested, by presenting a series of works including Row House, Sumiyoshi, a concept of legitimate ordinary house in city that would make us feel the city's nature by means of spatial instrument (specifically, "light garden"), and he shifted out of the trend.

"Extraordinary space becomes incarnated by living in the space." These words that Ando wrote in the announcement of Festival exactly suggest how houses should be, and they were true with commercial buildings as well. In terms of commercial buildings, Ando devoted himself to walking around the town of Western-style houses in Kitano-cho, Kobe to find out any signs for such "incarnation". He says he tried to deeply understand the history, memories of the land and lifestyle and to apply the images of those elements to his architectural context. Such efforts have led to the series of brilliant works, namely Rose Garden in Kitano-cho, Step in Takamatsu, and Festival in Naha.

His attempt to let local people feel the context of the city's indigenous lifestyle through commercial buildings achieved another success in Kyoto with Time's.

1

フェスティバル　1984
festival

1. 国際通り側の正面外観
   Façade facing the International Street
2. 南国の光に輝くブロックの建築
   Block building shining in the tropical sun

15年の節目、那覇での挑戦、そして総括

　1984年、沖縄・那覇の国際通りにオープンした複合商業ビル「フェスティバル」は、安藤にとって、自身の「創作活動の節目」を強く意識した作品だった。沖縄は現代建築にとって風土性を表現できる格好の舞台であり、安藤は沖縄固有のブロックの建築に挑戦し、自然換気を生かした中央吹き抜けの階段室、上階の南国の青空と吹き抜ける風を満喫できるガジュマルの木が植わったテラスなどを実現した。地元のひとびとの期待も高く、開場時には入場を待つ長蛇の列が出来るほど熱狂的に受け入れられた。

　この「フェスティバル」の発表時点で、安藤は、自身のそこまでの創作について、建築を始めたばかりの自分が仕事に出来たのは住宅と商業建築だったと振り返っている。また、建築家としての出発点に、増沢洵の最小限住居の自邸と東京・銀座の「凬月堂」を、アントニン・レーモンドの一連の作品とともに挙げている。モダニズムの純粋な原形のような増沢と、同じくモダニストでありながら屈託なく多彩な技法を駆使したレーモンドという取り合わせは、安藤の心性を考えるうえで興味深い。加えて、増沢の住宅と商業施設に言及しているのは、初期の仕事とオーバーラップし、彼の本質の一端がそこにあったのだと実感させる。

　小住宅と商業施設。1950年代の戦災復興への貢献が意識された時代の最小限住居の試みに始まり、1970年代に至っても、小住宅は意欲的な建築家のデビューにあたってのポートフォリオの中心を占めてきた。「奇を衒う」小住宅の百花繚乱は、1970年代の建築専門誌にとっても読者にとっても欠くことの出来ない人気アイテムだったが、安藤は「住吉の長屋」など一連の作品で、都市のなかの自然を空間の装置（具体的には「光庭」）で体感させる正当な都市における庶民住宅のありかたを提案し、そこから抜け出した。

　「非日常的空間は生活によって受肉する」。安藤が「フェスティバル」の発表時に記したこの言葉こそが、住宅のありかたを端的に物語り、そして、それは商業施設にも当てはまっていた。安藤は商業施設に関しては、神戸北野町の西洋館街を実際に歩き回って、そうした「受肉」のための萌芽を探りあてることに没頭した。歴史、土地の記憶、生活様式を感得し、イメージとして残るそれらを自身の建築の文脈のなかに生かすことを心がけたという。そうした成果が、北野町においては「ローズガーデン」、高松では「STEP」、そして那覇では「フェスティバル」という一連の秀逸な作品に結びついた。

　商業建築を介して、そこに住むひとびとに、その土地固有の都市生活の文脈を感知させる企てば、京都においては、「TIME'S」によって成功を収めるに至った。

フェスティバル　1984
festival

3. 屋上のコンクリートフレーム
   Concrete frame on the rooftop
4. 吹き抜けを囲むブロックの肌
   Block skin surrounding the open ceiling
5. 穴開きブロックがもたらす陰影
   Shadows created by hollow blocks

第2章　商業建築に都市の〈公性〉を託す

Awakening of "Water Garden"

For young fellows from Osaka aiming to be designers, Kyoto is a place for learning with a row of old temples. There are still many people who visit there frequently to learn through architecture and garden what the Japanese culture is all about.

When Ando stood at the side of Takase River which runs across Sanjo Street, a concept of "water garden" came up to his mind. It was of course associated with "Rock Garden" in Ryoanji Temple. As one takes steps there, the cluster of rocks silently arranged on white sand with no trees nor grass start to draw a beautiful scroll of painting so impressively. The inorganic rocks and sand gains a feeling of vitality and provides a scenery that is unique to Kyoto.

Takase River is a river that branches off from Kamo River, then called "Misogi River", and flows into the site under the above name. Although it used to play a role in shipping transportation between Kyoto and Fushimi, it is now maintained as a cultural heritage, contributing to improvement of the surrounding environment. With the water level and quality being controlled, it is so transparent and beautiful that people cannot help putting their hands into the flow when they see the surface up close. Through this river, people in Kyoto must have spent each year feeling the seasons, such as autumn leaves on the water, and snow scene along the shore. It shouldn't be forgotten that such history has been inspiring people after Meiji Era, as in the case of "Takasebune" written by Ogai Mori.

TIME's that he was requested to design is located at the foot of "Sanjo Kobashi" on its southwest side, a stone bridge over Takase River with *giboshi* (a kind of ornament which resembles the bulbous flower of onion) on its main poles. It is a busy place with a lot of passersby and there remain some wooden machiya (merchant houses) around. Now that he was going to create a new building there, Ando thought of bringing back the relationship between people and water by connecting it to Takase River. That was the idea of "Water Garden".

When designing a new building in a city where historical landscape remains, it should be approached in concert with the tradition of the land. Coordination with the existing scenery, such as to put on inclined roof, or to paint walls in *Juraku* color (ocher) is generally practiced. However, that alone is not enough to go deeper into the true meaning. So, efforts are needed to find out the true nature of the city's heritage that remains in the present, and to distill and inherit it. In other words, he had to feel the sense of space and materials, which cannot be found on the surface but is hidden in the deepness of the city, and furthermore to read the story enshrined therein, so that he could make use of them in his own creation. To that end, architects are required not only to stick to softness of the superficial finishing, but also to have an intent to achieve finely-tuned architectural beauty while giving care to the city.

1

Chapter 2 Expect the City's 'Publicness' in Commercial Buildings

TIME'S I 1984
time's I

1. 手前のカマボコ屋根がI、その奥のドーム屋根がII
Time's I (building with a semicircular roof in front) and Time's II (one with a dome roof at the back)

2. 1階は高瀬川の水面に接する
First floor facing the water surface of the Takase River

「水の庭」の気づき

　大阪出身で建築を志す若者にとって、京都は古刹のならぶ学習の場である。日本の文化はいかなるものなのか、建築、庭を介して学ぶために、足繁く通う姿は、今なお見られる。

　安藤が三条通りを貫いて流れる高瀬川のほとりに立ったとき、思い浮かべたのは「水の庭」という概念だった。もちろん、龍安寺の「石の庭」からの連想である。一木一草をも排した静寂の白砂に配された石の群れが、歩を進めるたびに動感を伴って、美の絵巻を描き始める。無機的な石と砂が生命感をもって、京都ならではの風景をもたらすのである。

　高瀬川は、鴨川から分かれて市街地を流れる「みそぎ川」がさらに名前を変えて現地に至る。京都と伏見を結ぶ舟運を担ったが、今では文化遺産として整備され、周辺の環境の向上に寄与している。水位と水質も管理されており、間近で川面を見ると、流れに手を入れたくなるほど透明度が高く美しい。京のひとびとは、この川を介して、水面に浮かぶ紅葉や岸辺の雪景色など、季節を感じながら一年を過ごしてきたに違いない。そうした歴史が森鷗外の「高瀬舟」のように、明治以降の表現者に刺激を与えてきたことも忘れてはなるまい。

　設計を依頼された商業施設「TIME'S」は、その高瀬川に架かる擬宝珠のついた親柱を持つ「三条小橋」の南西側のたもとに位置している。ひと通りが多く繁華な場所で周囲には木造の町屋も残る。そこに新たな建物を造るのであるから、高瀬川と結びつけ、ひとと水との触れ合いを取り戻すことを安藤は考えた。それが「水の庭」という発想だった。

　歴史的な景観の残る都市に新たな建物を設計するときは、いかにその地の伝統に呼応するかの取り組みが求められる。傾斜屋根を架ける、聚落色の壁に仕立てるなど既存の風景との協調が一般的だろう。しかし、それだけでは本質を究めることは難しい。現代に残された、その都市の遺産のなにが本質かを抽出し、継承していく努力が求められる。つまり、表層ではなく、都市の奥行きのなかに隠されている空間や素材の感覚、さらにはどんな物語がそこに秘められているかを読み取り、それを自らの創造に生かしていかねばならない。

　そのためには、上辺の仕上げのやわらかさにとどまることなく、街に配慮しながらも、研ぎすました建築の美に高める意識が建築家には求められる。

Distressed Condition of Takase River

When Ando was looking with his own eyes at the buildings along Takase River, he realized that many of them were so big as to disturb the quiet flow of the river, and that was solely weakening Takase River's "power of site". This is no good. If that should be the case, a newly designed building should play a role to remind contemporary people of the values of Takase River.

As a result, TIME's was designed to have a different style from those applied to the surrounding buildings.

The entire building was confined to be a low rise of three stories. However, it is not a regular three-storied structure above the ground; the first floor was arranged barely above the water surface of Takase River, the second floor was several steps above the road surface of Sanjo Street, and another floor was laid above it. The second and third layers were structured to be set back against the first layer. This was his decision not to let the building protrude toward the river nor the town.

The first floor facing the river on the Sanjo Kobashi's side was designed to have a small open space by arranging the wall deeper inside. The floor in contact with the water surface draws a gentle curve of sextant. Visitors can descend the steps from Sanjo Street to enter this open space. That alone should be exciting, because they can get close to the water that they could only see from some distance before, and can even put their hands into the river flow if they go to the curve's edge and crouch. Ando has a memory of his first impression that when he first came by the river, he almost touched the clear waterflow unconsciously, and this memory took shape as architecture.

As with this first floor, tenant shops were basically arranged in a way that they would be open towards Takase River. On the first floor, visitors come in and out through the open space arranged towards the waterflow, and on the second and third floors, through the aisle-type decks that also face the river side. On either floor, an aisle was arranged as a "path" to approach the shops from the open space or the decks, which allowed for practical realization of the device he tried with "path" and shops in Kitano-cho, Kobe. "Path" comes into the building on each floor, and when it wanders into the small open space ahead, there awaits another experience of being surprised at the blue sky above.

Before TIME's appeared, all the surrounding buildings were designed to have their back turned to Takase River. Because of being back sides, they were poorly cared for and not taking advantage of the location facing the water. It even seemed as a kind of rejection to Takase River. Probably because they saw the structure of TIME's facing to the river, many of the rebuilt or reconstructed commercial facilities that appeared later along Takase River followed the same style to utilize the river's historical environment, for instance, by arranging a café space on the riverside. This was a result of increased attention to the environment and history in the wake of TIME's. It is such a pleasure to be able to feel that the town is changing in a positive direction.

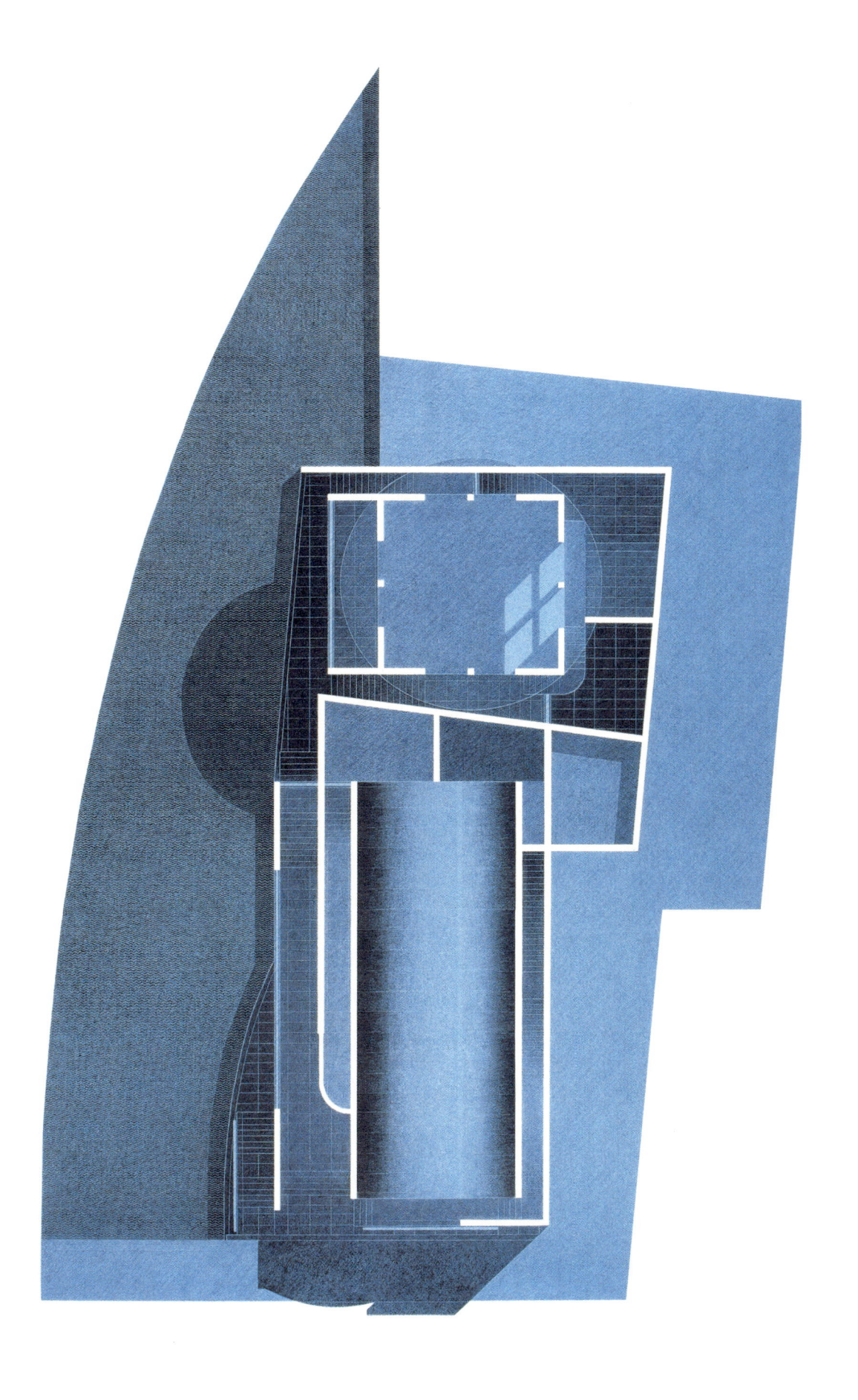

TIME'S I 1984
time's I

3. (前ページ) ドローイング
   (previous page) Drawing
4. 水辺に降りる階段
   Stairs leading to the water front

高瀬川の窮状

　安藤がその目で高瀬川に面した建物を見ていくと、高瀬川の静かな流れを乱すかのような規模のものが多く、それだけでせっかくの高瀬川ゆえの「場の力」が弱められてしまっていることに気づいた。これではいけない。そうだとするなら、新たに手がける建物は、高瀬川の価値を現代のひとびとに思い起こさせる役割を担わねばならない。

　その結果、「TIME'S」は、周囲に付加されてきた建物とは異なる仕立てをとることになった。

　建物の全体は三層の低層に抑えた。しかし、通常の地上3階ではなく、1階は高瀬川の水面すれすれに位置させ、2階が三条通りの路面から階段を数段あがったレベル、さらにそのうえに一層を重ねた構成となった。二、三層は、一層目に対して、後退するセットバックの構成とした。川に対しても、街に対しても、建物を突出させないための選択だった。

　川に面した1階の三条小橋側は、壁を奥まらせて小さな広場とした。水面に接する床は6分の1円の緩やかな曲線を描く。来訪者は三条通りから階段を降りて、この広場に進むことができる。それだけでわくわくするはずだ。かつては眺めていただけの高瀬川の川面に接近し、曲線の淵にたたずんでしゃがめば、高瀬川の流れに手を入れるのも可能だからである。最初にたたずんだとき、思わず透明な流れに触れそうになった安藤の第一印象の記憶が、ここに建築の形をとった。

　この1階もそうであるように、テナントの店舗は原則的に高瀬川に向かって開く配置とした。1階では流れに向かって開かれた広場、2階、3階ではやはり川の側に面した通路形式のデッキから、来訪者は店舗に出入りする。いずれの階も、広場やデッキから店舗にアプローチする「道」としての通路を設けて、神戸北野町で試みた「道」と店舗に関する実践がここに生きるかたちとなった。「道」は各階で建物のなかに入り込み、その先の小さな中庭などに迷い込むと、上空に広がる空の青さに驚かされる体験も待ち受けている。

　「TIME'S」が登場するまで、周囲の建物のすべてが高瀬川に背を向けて建っていた。背面ゆえに手入れも事欠き、水に面した立地を活かせずにいた。まるで高瀬川に対する拒否反応とさえ思えるほどだった。それが変った。「TIME'S」の川に対して開かれた構成を見てのことだろう、以後、改築などで出現した高瀬川沿いの商業施設の多くが、川に対してカフェのスペースを設けるなど、高瀬川の歴史的な環境を活かす形式をとることになった。「TIME'S」をきっかけに環境、歴史などへの注目が高まった成果である。街がよい方向に動いている手応えを感じるのは、とても喜ばしいことだ。

5

30th Anniversary of the Commercial Building

Time's purposely used concrete blocks for the exterior. It was an attempt to let the modern creation respond to the traditional landscape by carefully laying seemingly-coarse concrete blocks, as well as paying attention to the texture.

The size of each block being fixed, dimensions of architectural composition are quite limited. However, as it is designed in a manner that details are accumulated, the limitation is not necessarily a problem. Instead, there is a strong feeling that design image is being improved because of the limitation. Space construction using blocks requires consistency from parts to the entire structure because predefined building materials are placed in layers. Ando thought this greatly helped to establish logicality in drawing an answer to the site of the building.

The deck and footsteps of the stairs were roughly finished with black granite. This was because of an expectation that people can surely feel the walking sensation when they walk on the deck arranged in the setback space. That will also be an essential factor for developing a firm image of the new architecture in the historical city. Among other materials that are used, iron, which expresses heaviness and hardness, is also expected to enhance its definite image.

When he drops by the site while visiting Kyoto, there are always people who linger around on the decks of the second and third floors looking down the flow of the river quietly. In the open space of the first floor, outdoor seats are arranged for a restaurant, where again people are constantly seen. Visitors from overseas are often seen, too. It would undoubtedly be so honorable for the architect if they become aware of the historical environment in Kyoto, and Japan, by taking a cue from the spatial experience that this architecture provides.

After Time's underwent multiple enlargements during 30 years of establishment, the owner passed away and a different company took over its operation. Taking this as an opportunity, maintenance and renovation of the entire building was carried out. In 2016, it became as beautiful as it had been at the time of establishment.

It is often said that modern architecture is at its peak when completed, and will be on the decline afterwards. In spite of this accepted view, Time's will continue to live its life. It is expected that the relationship between water and people will last in a visible manner on the stage of riverside with eternal flow of Takase River.

TIME'S I　1984
time's I

5. 川面からの外観
   Exterior appearance viewed from the river
6. さくら越しのテラス
   Terrace behind cherry blossoms
7. 上階の通路
   Pathway on the upper floor

30年目の商業建築

　「TIME'S」は、敢えてコンクリートブロックを外装に採用した。一見、粗末に思われるコンクリートブロックを丁寧に組み上げ、肌合いにも配慮することで、伝統的な景観への現代の創造の呼応を試みた。

　ブロックはひとつひとつが決まったサイズなので、建築を構成するにあたっての寸法面での制約は大きい。しかし、細部を積み上げていく設計の方法をとっているので、制約の存在は必ずしも問題ではない。むしろ、その制約ゆえにイメージが鍛え直されていく感覚のほうが強い。ブロックによる空間構築は、定型の建材を重ねるがゆえに、部分から全体への整合性を求められる。それは、この建物の立地への回答を導き出すにあたって、論理性を確立するのに、大きな助けとして作用したと安藤は考えている。

　デッキや階段の足もとは、黒御影石の粗面仕上げとした。セットバックで生み出された空間に配したデッキをしっかりした歩行感覚で進めることを期待したためだ。それもまた、歴史都市における新しい建築の揺るぎない姿の確立のために不可欠な要素であろう。他の素材も、鉄は重さと硬さを伝え、やはり確たる印象を高めることを託されている。

　京都に出向いた際に立ち寄ると、いつも2、3階のデッキにひとがたたずみ、じっと川の流れを見おろしている。1階の広場にはレストランの屋外席が設けられ、そこにもひとの姿が絶えない。海外からの訪問客の姿もよく見かける。彼らがこの建築のもたらす空間体験をひとつの手がかりに、京都の、そして、日本の歴史的な環境に気づいてくれれば、それは設計者冥利につきることなのは間違いない。

　「TIME'S」は開設後30年の時間の経過のなか増築も重ねてきたが、オーナーが亡くなり、新たな企業が運営することになった。それを機に建物全体の保全改装が進められ、2016年には開設当時の美しさを取り戻した。

　近代建築はしばしば完成時が頂点で、その後は下降線をたどるとされる。そのなかで「TIME'S」は、これからも生き続けるだろう。高瀬川の悠久の流れに身を添わせて、そこを舞台とする水とひととの関わりが、これからも目に見えるかたちで続いていくことを期待したい。

表参道への思い

　商業施設に求める社会の要求は、情報環境の著しい進化、本来の利用者層である若

GALLERIA [akka] 1988
galleria [akka]

1. ヴォールト屋根
   Vault roof
2. 最上階のギャラリー
   Gallery on the topmost floor

1

2

Chapter 2 Expect the City's 'Publicness' in Commercial Buildings   086

者の経済状態の悪化などで、1990年代初めの土地バブル崩壊をきっかけに根本的なところでの変化を余儀なくされた。それは建築家の、都市における庶民の生活への思いを吹き飛ばすほどの勢いで浸透していった。ファストファッションと呼ばれるブランドの拡大により、消費は非日常の憧れではなくなり、郊外の米国流のショッピングモールなどが日常のハレの場となっていった。そうした流れのなか、安藤は地下空間の可能性を探究した1988年の「GALLERIA [akka]」、1989年の「COLLEZIONE」のあとは、2006年の「表参道ヒルズ」に至るまで商業施設の設計から遠ざかった。

その「表参道ヒルズ」には、若き日の安藤が、上京の際に訪れた「都市東京の記憶」が託されていた。関東大震災後の帝都復興事業の一環として建設された「同潤会青山アパート」の建て替え事業だった「表参道ヒルズ」において、安藤は、日本の都市集合住宅の原点の継承を実現するべく努めた。かつては複数の中層のコンクリート・アパートが囲っていた敷地内の中庭の三角形の形状が、「表参道ヒルズ」の吹き抜けに再現され、商業施設内のスロープは、屋外の表参道と同じ傾斜に仕立てられた。その意味では、「表参道ヒルズ」は、安藤にとって特別の存在であり、こうした安藤の都市への思いに応えてくれる施主、森ビルの総帥、故・森稔があってこその作品だったといえるだろう。

残念なことに、商業施設そのものに対する建築界の位置づけは、あいも変わらず低いままだ。建築家としてのデビューの時期に、安藤がそうした風潮に敢然と立ち向かい、成果を残したことを今さらながら評価したい。

COLLEZIONE 1989
collezione

1. 北側外観
   Exterior appearance on the north side
2. 屋外階段が内部にも続く
   Outdoor stairs extending inside

1

Feelings for Omotesando

Social requirement in commercial facilities was forced to change fundamentally in the aftermath of the collapse of land bubble economy in early 1990's, due to significant progress in information environment, or deterioration in economic conditions among the young who should be their primary users. The trend became widespread so swiftly as to blow off architects' feelings for ordinary people's life in cities. With the expansion of brands called fast fashion, consumption was no longer an extraordinary desire, and American-style shopping malls in the suburbs were stepping into the spotlight in everyday life. In this context, Ando stayed away from designing of commercial facilities after GALLERIA [AKKA] in 1988 and COLLEZIONE in 1989 in which Ando explored possibilities of underground space, until OMOTESANDO HILLS in 2006.

In OMOTESANDO HILLS, the young Ando's "memories of city Tokyo" during his visit was infused. In OMOTESANDO HILLS, a reconstruction project of "Dojunkai Aoyama Apartments" that had been constructed as a part of Teito (Tokyo) reconstruction project after the Great Kanto earthquake, Ando strived to realize inheritance of the origin of Japanese urban complex housing. The triangle shape of the patio once surrounded by several midrise concrete apartments was reconstructed as a wellhole of Omotesando Hills, and the slope within the commercial facility was arranged with the same inclination angle as the outside street, Omotesando. In that sense, OMOTESANDO HILLS is a very special piece to Ando, and it is not too much to say that this work can exist solely thanks to the client who would understand Ando's such feelings for cities, that is, the leader of Mori Building, late Minoru Mori.

Unfortunately, the position given to commercial facilities themselves in the architectural industry remains as low as ever. It should be belatedly recognized that at the time of his debut as an architect, Ando stood firmly against such trend and achieved results.

表参道ヒルズ　2006
omotesando hills

1. 商業棟のうえに住宅棟が載る
   Residential building on top of the commercial building
2. 表参道の並木道に面した配置
   Arrangement facing Omotesando boulevard
3. 三角形は同潤会アパートの中庭の形
   Triangular shape is the shape of the courtyard of Dojunkai apartments
4. 吹き抜けの大階段
   Grand stairs with open ceiling
5. （次ページ）ドローイング
   (next page) Drawing

明治神宮

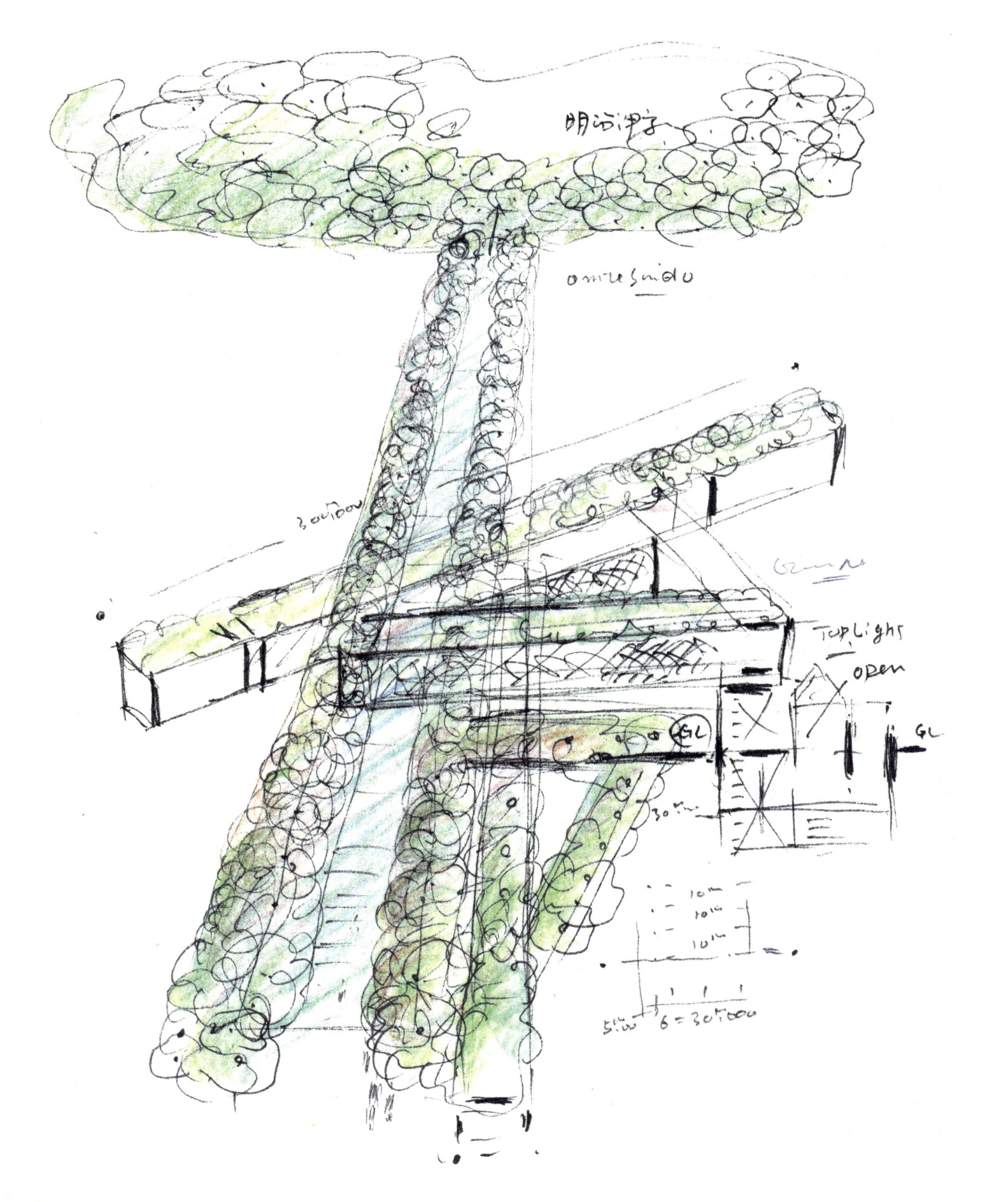

omotesnido

30,000

toplights
open

GL GL

30m

10m
10m
10m

5m × 6 = 30,000

第3章 〈美〉は〈自然〉と融合し、母なる大地に還る
国境を超える美術館の挑戦

Chapter 3 'Beauty' Collaborates with 'Nature' to Return to Mother Earth
Challenges with Museums Crossing National Borders

美術界が指名したモダニズムの継承者

　まさに建築家として疾風怒濤の最初の20年を駆け抜け、1990年代にさしかかろうとしたとき、安藤忠雄の前にはそれまでと異なる世界が待ち受けていた。美術、しかも、国内から発して海外へと広がる建築家冥利につきる舞台であった。1990年、わたしはパリの郊外にカイネティック・アートの主唱者マルタ・パンを訪ねたことがあった。ル・コルビュジエの後継者のひとりと目されるアンドレ・ボジャンスキーを夫に持つ彼女は、夫が設計したモダニズムの極致のような住宅に迎え入れてくれた。面談の主題はフランスにおける屋外アートの展開の話だったが、それを終えて雑談になったとき、マルタ・パンは、当時、世界を席巻していたポスト・モダンの批判を口にした。安易な歴史回帰に走るマイケル・グレイブスらの世代への嫌悪だった。「しかし、アンドウだけは違う」と彼女が確信に満ちた口調で語ったとき、わたしは少なからぬ驚きを感じた。

　確かに夫がボジャンスキーであり、自身、現代建築家との協同が多い彼女なのだから、現代建築の動向に関心を持っているのはなんらの不思議もない。しかし、その時点では、国際的な知名度は醸成過程にあり、まだ極東のひとりの個性的な建築家でしかなかった安藤の名が、フランスの指導的な立場にある芸術家から、しかも「唯一無二」の存在として聞かされようとは、思いもしなかった。マルタ・パンは厳格なひとであり、わたしが日本人だからリップサービスをするようなことはない。彼女の考えるル・コルビュジエに発するモダニズムが、当時の建築界において激しい否定の波に見舞われ、存在すら見失われようとしている状況において、すがるに値する救世主として、アンドウという名が飛び出してきたのだった。

　マルタ・パンを現代彫刻の巨匠のひとりと呼んで差し支えあるまい。その彼女が指名した意味を、1990年代以降、安藤が世界各地で美術館を手がけていった軌跡を踏まえて振り返るなら、「住吉の長屋」で世界にデビューした日本の建築家に、現代美術の世

*Successor of Modernism Designated by
the Art World*

After the first two decades of dramatic and stimulating years as an architect, a different world was waiting in front of Tadao Ando just before entering the 1990s. It was a stage that extends outside Japan to the world, a true blessing as an architect.

In 1990, I visited Marta Pan, an advocate of kinetic art in suburbs of Paris. She invited me into her home that perfectly reflected the modernism designed by her husband, André Wogenscky, who is known as the successor of Le Corbusier. Although the theme of the interview was about the development of outdoor art in France, while we were having a general conversation after the interview, Marta Pan criticized the postmodernism that was dominating the world at that time. It was her dislike toward the generation including Michael Graves who were advocating recurrence of history without much thought. I was surprised when she said this in a convinced manner, "However, Ando is different".

It is no wonder that she was interested in trends of modern architecture because her husband is Wogenscky and she was doing a lot of collaborative work with modern architects. However, I was not expecting to hear the name of Ando from an artist who has been in a leadership position in France since Ando at that time was merely a unique architect in the far-east and not fully known yet internationally. Furthermore, she viewed him as a unique architect.

Marta Pan may be regarded as a master of contemporary sculpture. Given the achievement of his work on museums around the world since 1990s, the meaning of her designation could be explained as a symbol that the world of contemporary art viewed the architect who made his international debut with ROW HOUSE, SUMIYOSHI as the person who would embody and inherit the "pure space" of modernism and was ready to entrust perpetual realization of beauty of modernism.

*Naoshima Becoming
the Fort of Art at Setouchi*

The first person in the art world who would notice the use of space of Ando in Japan would be Soichiro Fukutake. He is the first son of the founder of Fukutake Publishing Co, Ltd and developed Benesse Holdings, Inc. to a conglomerate. He planned to make Naoshima, an island of Kagawa Prefecture where his father accepted the assignment to promote tourism, to a resort area unprecedented in Japan where nature and art can be enjoyed fully. Although Naoshima is located in the Seto Inland Sea in Kagawa, it is just a little away from Okayama where Benesse has its headquarters. In 1987 he visited Ando to request the first work in Naoshima, to design and supervise the Seaside Park that mainly has a camp site for children. Following this job, his designing of art facilities in Naoshima started, and his works extending over two centuries continue to be completed today.

ベネッセハウス ミュージアム 1992
benesse house museum

1. 桟橋につながる階段
   Stairs to a pier
2. 上空からの眺望
   Bird's-eye view
3. 丘のうえに建物が続く
   Group of buildings on a hill
4. 遠景スケッチ
   Distant view sketch
5. (次ページ見開き) 石壁と青空、瀬戸内海
   (next two pages) Stone wall, blue sky and Seto Inland Sea

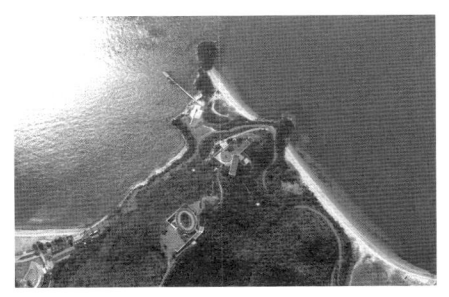

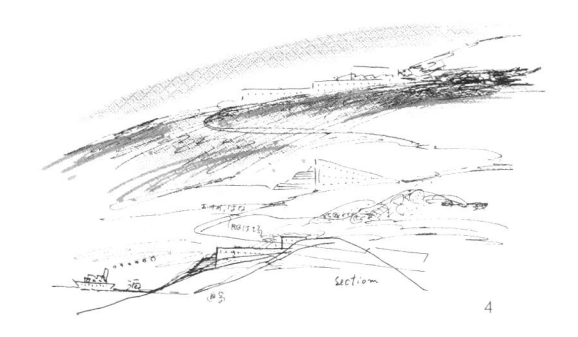

界がモダニズムの「純粋な空間」の具現者、継承者として着目し、モダニズムの美の永続的な実現を託そうとしていた、ひとつの象徴と捉えることができるだろう。

直島、瀬戸内の美術の砦へ

　美術に関わるひとで、日本において最初に安藤の空間に着目したのは、福武總一郎だろう。福武書店の創業者の長男であり、ベネッセ・コーポレーションを複合企業に育て上げた彼は、父の代に観光振興を引き受けた香川県の直島を、自然とアートを堪能できる、それまでの日本にはなかったリゾート地にする計画を立てていた。直島は、香川県の瀬戸内海上に位置するが、地理的にはベネッセが本拠を置く岡山と目と鼻の先にある。その彼が安藤のもとを訪ねて、直島における最初の仕事となる子どものためのキャンプ場を中心とする「シーサイドパーク」の設計監修を依頼したのは1987年のことだった。その仕事を皮切りに、直島でのアート関連施設の設計が始まり、世紀をまたぐかたちで作品の完成は今日なお続いている。福武の依頼からすでに30年、この直島での継続は、欧米からアジア各国における目覚ましい数の美術館の完成を下支えするものとなった。

　30年の歳月を経て、アートの島となり、国際的な現代芸術家の創作の場となった直島の中心となっているのは「ベネッセハウス ミュージアム」(1992年) である。当初、「直島コンテンポラリー・アート・ミュージアム」として登場したこの美術ギャラリーは、今や世界から島を訪れるひとびとの「聖地」になっている。いや、この建物の完成以前に安藤への期待を語ったマルタ・パンの慧眼に、わたしとしては改めて敬服の念を抱くのである。

　「ベネッセハウス ミュージアム」の見どころは、なんといっても瀬戸内の海へ広がる視界のなかで、福武が収集した現代美術作品が鑑賞できるところだろう。訪問者は島の斜面を山道を伝って登り、小高い丘のうえに位置する建物に至る。そこから館内への誘導路は自然石の独立壁で両側を囲われ、豊かな自然とは対比的な小さなエントランスから内部に進む。次に待ち受けるのは、三層分の吹き抜けとなったコンクリート打ち放しの円筒形のギャラリーで、ここには立体造形が展示される。この円筒に巻きついて昇るスロープを進むと、一気に瀬戸内海の海原と自然光があふれるギャラリーに至る。絵画作品は、その視界に負けない大きな寸法のものが壁に掲げられ、来訪者はここでしか味わえない美術鑑賞の場を得た幸福感に満たされるのである。

　安藤はこの立地を見たとき、建築をすべて地中に埋め込みたいと感じたという。建築の素材は屋外ではコンクリートと自然石。自然石は瀬戸内の砂を思わせる白い肌合いで表面は粗さをとどめた仕上げになっている。安藤は斜面地の傾斜を生かして、建築の

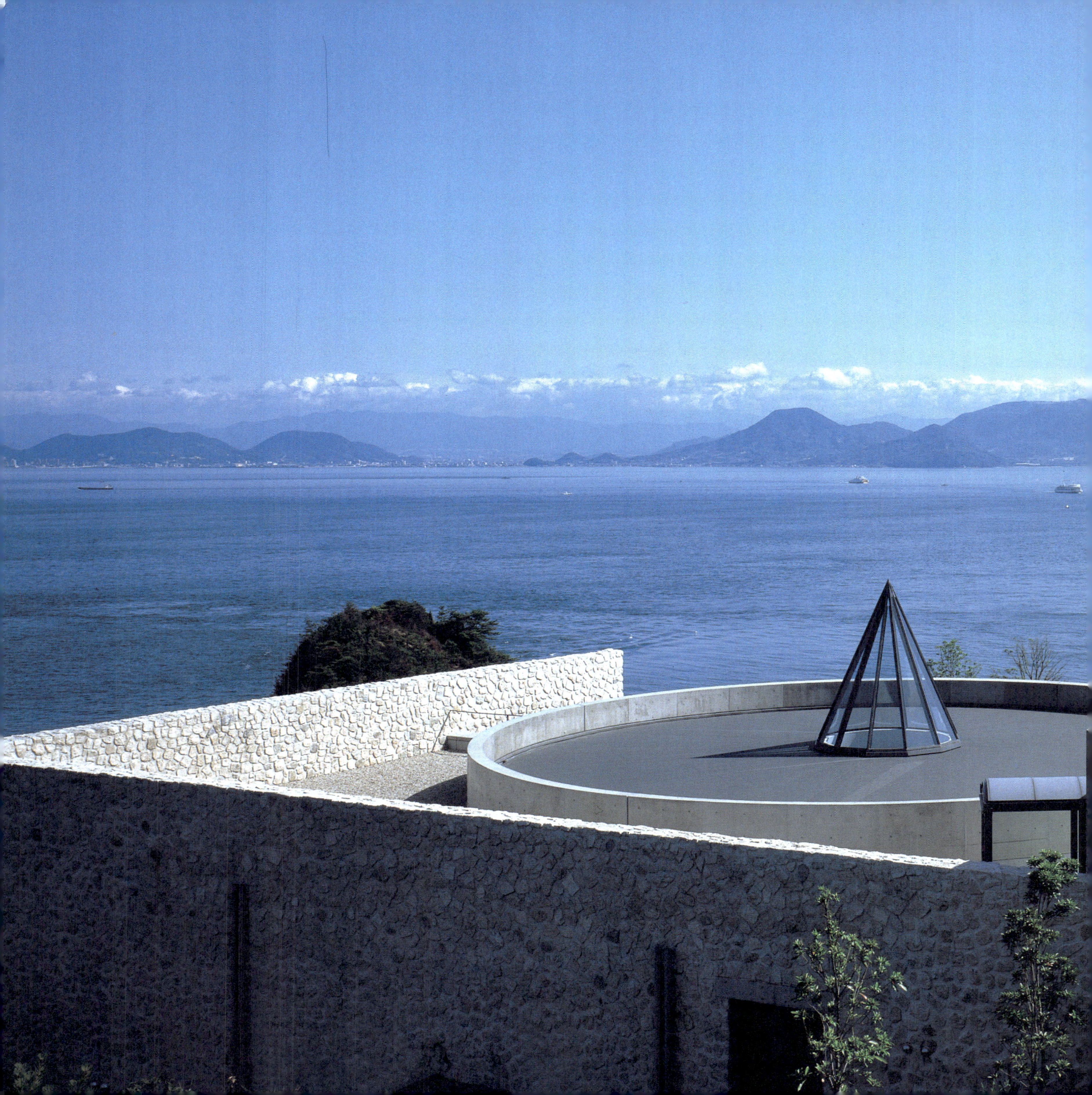

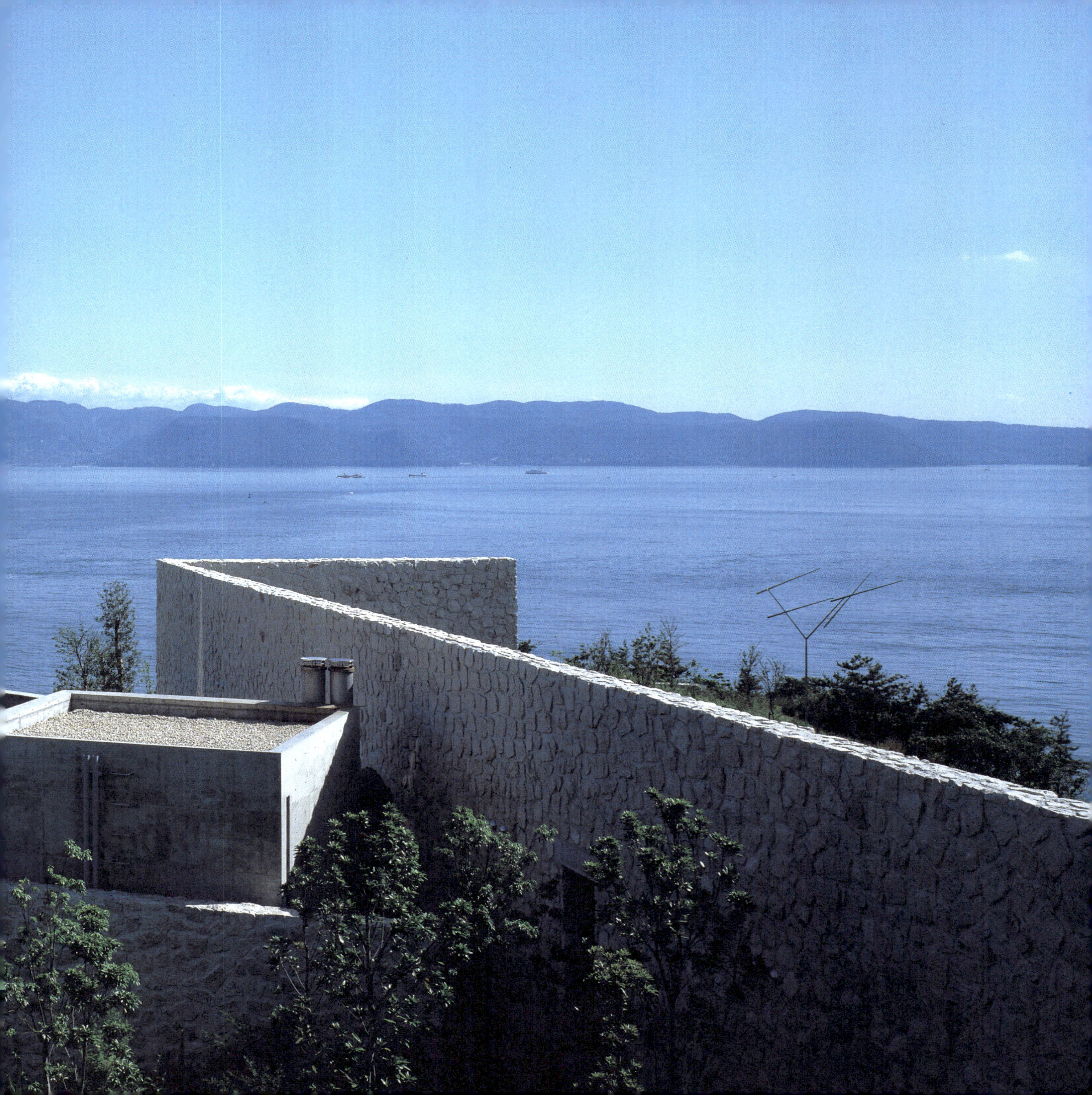

ベネッセハウス オーバル　1995
benesse house oval

1. 瀬戸内海を望むテラス
   Terrace with a view of the Seto Inland Sea
2. 水庭を配した楕円の中庭
   Oval courtyard with the water garden
3. 楕円の中庭の夜景
   Night view of the oval courtyard

   The main facility in Naoshima, which has become an island of art and a creation site for international modern artists after 30 years, is BENESSE HOUSE (1992). This art gallery, which first appeared as the "Naoshima Contemporary Art Museum", is treated as a "holy place" from people who visit the island from all over the world. Here again, I feel respect and admiration for Marta's perceptiveness.
   The highlight of BENESSE HOUSE is to view contemporary arts collected by Fukutake with the scenery of the Inland Sea. Visitors climb the pathway of the slope of the island to approach the building standing on top of a small hill. The pathway guiding to the entrance from there is surrounded by independent walls made of natural stones on both sides and they enter an entrance small in size compared to the vast nature. The next area is the cylinder-type gallery of exposed concrete where it has an open ceiling through three floors where three-dimensional molding will be exhibited. After climbing this slope that goes up along the cylinder, the gallery with a view of the Inland Sea with an abundance natural light suddenly appears. Paintings with large sizes that can show their existence against the outdoor view will be put on the wall, and visitors will be filled with happiness viewing the arts that are available only at this location.
   Ando mentioned that he thought of embedding the building completely underground when he saw this property. The materials for the exterior of this construction are concrete and natural stones. Natural stones have a white tone that resembles sand of Setouchi and there is roughness on the surface. Ando took advantage of the sloped ground and embedded half of the architecture underground. Furthermore, the layout in accordance with the slope creates a vector of the view to the ocean as the whole architecture, allowing us to see beautiful and precious artwork in the gallery with a sense of spaciousness.
   The BENESSE HOUSE ANNEX was added in 1995 as an accommodation facility closer to the peak than BENESSE HOUSE. A planform oval in shape to surround the courtyard was adopted. The curved wall of the courtyard is a stucco finish. Ando chose stucco to associate the Mediterranean Sea and the Inland Sea of Japan. Ando said he found the Seto Inland Sea "more beautiful than the Mediterranean". It is almost certain that Fukutake's intention to let visitors not only appreciate art but also stay there and enjoy the rich nature took a definite shape.

Collaboration with Other Artists

   For BENESSE, creation of work is requested to contemporary artists to fit the scene of traditional houses that remain in Naoshima. This is called the ART HOUSE PROJECT. Ando worked in one of them named MINAMIDERA in 1999 with James Turrell. Ando decided to design a wooden architecture on his own that would hold Turrell's work that is characterized by geometric forms placed in dark spaces where the shape could be acknowledged when eyes get used to the darkness. The wooden works of Ando using square timbers as the base of representation originates continuous vertical lines according

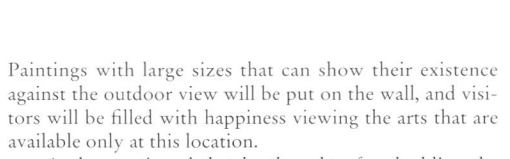

半分を地中に埋めてみせた。そして、その斜面に沿った配置が、建築全体として海への視界のベクトルをつくりだし、わたしたちは開放的なギャラリーで眼福にあずかることができるのである。

　この「ベネッセハウス　ミュージアム」のさらに山頂にあたる場所に宿泊施設として「ベネッセハウス　オーバル」が1995年に付加された。平面形は楕円で中庭を囲う形式が採用された。中庭の曲面壁は、スタッコの仕上げとなっている。当時、安藤がイタリア北部のトレヴィゾで「FABRICA（ベネトンアートスクール）」を手がけていたこともあり、地中海と瀬戸内海の連想でスタッコが選ばれた。安藤は、瀬戸内海を「地中海より美しい」と感じたといい、美術の鑑賞だけでなく、そこに宿泊する来訪者に、豊かな自然を満喫させたいとする福武の意図がひとつの確たる形をとったとみなしてよいだろう。

芸術家との協同

　ベネッセは、現代美術家に、直島に残る民家などを舞台にした創作を依頼している。「家プロジェクト」と呼ばれるもので、安藤はジェームズ・タレルとともに、そのなかのひとつ「南寺」を1999年に手がけている。暗黒空間のなかに幾何図形を配し、目がそこに慣れると形が認識できるタレルの作品を収める器として、安藤は木造建築を自身で設計する道を選んだ。角材を表現の基本とする安藤の木造は、身上とする厳格なプロポーション感覚に従って垂直線の連続が構築され、伝統木造とは異なるオリジナリティー豊かな現代の日本美を実現している。それは1992年の「セビリア万博日本館」に始まる安藤の木造への挑戦の延長線上にも位置づけられよう。

　そしてなにより「南寺」という名乗りが、この島への安藤の愛着を体現している。今は空き地となった敷地に、かつては寺院があり、寺が姿を消したあとも、地元のひとびとはそこを「南寺」と呼んできた。空き地の隅にあたる山裾には往時を偲ばせる石碑や石像、小さな木造の会所も残っている。安藤はその記憶が、未来へと語り継がれることを期待して、タレルの表現とは対比的な木造を敢えて選んだのである。

　そして、その効果は十分に持続している。2010年から3年に1回開催されている「瀬戸内国際芸術祭」の期間は、タレルと安藤のこのコラボレーションを目当てに多くの美術愛好家が「南寺」を訪れる。安藤が現代美術を島の現実の生活と遊離した存在ではないことを示す努力を重ねている点でも、好小品として評価したい。

　2004年の「地中美術館」は、「ベネッセハウス　ミュージアム」とならぶ世界の美術愛好家が目指す「場」となっている。現代美術家のウォルター・デ・マリア、ジェームズ・タレル、そして、印象派のクロード・モネの作品がそれぞれ独立した地下展示室に配され、

南寺（直島・家プロジェクト）　1999
minamidera (art house project in naoshima)

1. 和風を基調とする外観
   Japanese-style based exterior appearance
2. ジェームズ・タレルの造形
   Formative art of James Turrell

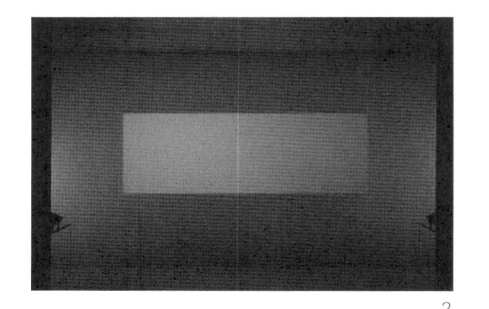

Chapter 3 'Beauty' Collaborates with 'Nature' to Return to Mother Earth

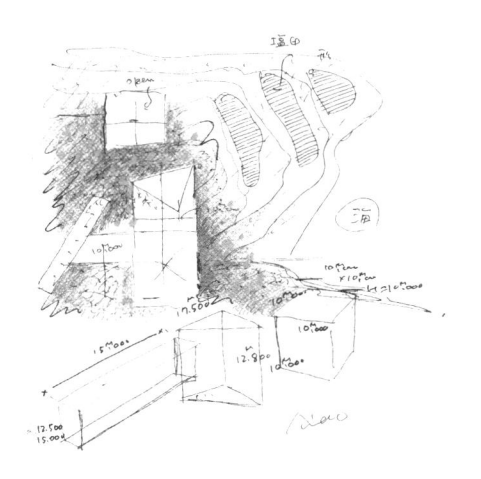

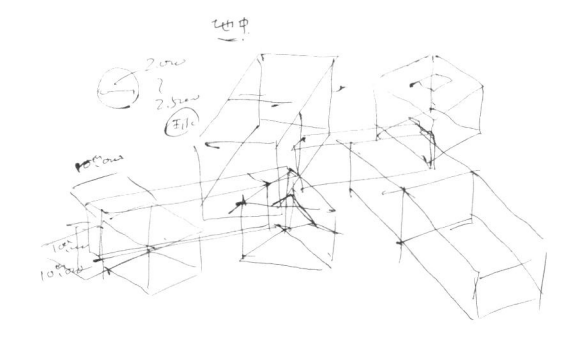

地中美術館　2004
chichu art museum

1. 展示室をつなぐ空間の幾何学が連なる
   Series of spatial geometries connecting the exhibition rooms
2. 空間スタディーのスケッチ
   Sketch for spatial study
3. ウォルター・デ・マリアの展示室
   Exhibition room of Walter De Maria
4. モネの展示室
   Exhibition room of Claude Monet

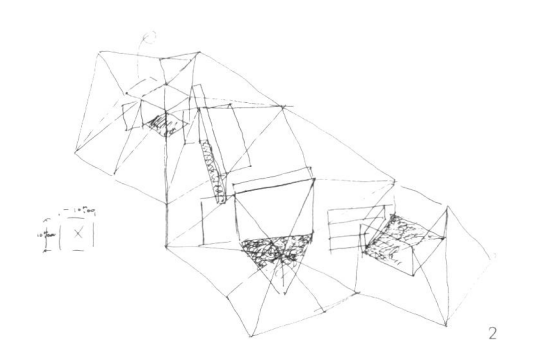

地中美術館　2004
chichu art museum

5. エントランスのコンクリートの通路
   Concrete entrance pathway
6. 通路を歩む来訪者
   Visitors on the pathway

to strict proportional sensitivity. The design is realizing the modern Japanese beauty with rich originality different from traditional wooden building. This is in the same orientation as the challenge Ando is taking to seek the possibility of wooden buildings that started with the JAPAN PAVILION, EXPO'92 / SEVILLA in 1992.

Furthermore, the naming MINAMIDERA demonstrates Ando's attachment to this island. Local people continued to call an open space where a temple was standing as Minamidera (south temple), even after the temple was gone. Ando deliberately selected a wooden architecture in contrast with Turrell's expression anticipating that the memory of the open space area would be passed on to future generations.

The effect is still sufficiently continuing. During the "Art Setouchi" festival, which is held every three years since 2010, a number of art lovers visit "Minamidera" to see the collaboration work by Turrell and Ando.

The CHICHU ART MUSEUM in 2004 is the "place" where art lovers around the world aim for similar to BENESSE HOUSE. Arts of contemporary artists Walter De Maria, James Turrell, and an impressionist, Claude Monet, are displayed in individual underground exhibition rooms respectively. Visitors move around using an outdoor passage that connects the three rooms.

The underground architecture was Ando's "unfulfilled dream". He found one of the starting points of his architecture when he was a newly-fledged architect in a space where there was intersection of light in an underground well in India. It is very interesting that the underground work was materialized while taking a side glance at the outside world with rich nature in Naoshima. As a matter of fact, he didn't turn his eyes away from nature, but he buried his works completely underground to preserve the nature.

The space that has a route to connect the three exhibition rooms is in a geometric shape of a regular triangle and square. The form that guides visitors who have lost their sense of orientation due to the underground space is the absolute geometric shape of modernism. The heated contrast between contemporary artists and Ando's space can be felt only because Ando himself has unmovable belief in his stance toward space.

Strength of Architecture, Strength of Art

Ando's works related to Naoshima are drifting to BENESSE HOUSE PARK (2006) that has a purpose of a welcoming center of the island and then to the LEE U-FAN MUSEUM in 2010. An exhibition room was embedded in the landscape of the mountain skirt that extends to the coast in continuous search for an architecture that merge in the natural landform and blends in the scenery. The strict rising exposed concrete walls and the symbolic rectangular column that emphasizes the verticality are arranged on the ground level to give connotation of the underground exhibition space. This is where Ando's unique approach is fully shown.

ANDO MUSEUM built in 2013 is, as the name indicates, a gallery exhibiting Ando's architectural work. A concrete box was inserted in a 100-year old wooden house with wooden board sidings with battens that still remains in the Honmura area in Naoshima where the ART HOUSE PROJECT was planned. Natural light shines in through the gap between the box and the existing wooden roof frame creating light and shadow unexpected to exist inside the building. Ando anticipated the overlay of confrontation between the past and present, wooden and concrete, and light and darkness. A meditation space (it resembles the meditation yard at the headquarters of UNESCO in Paris) covered by concrete with minimal space of 2.7 meters in diameter was created to offer an area where the true nature of Ando's architecture.

李禹煥美術館　2010
lee ufan museum

1. 角柱のそびえる広場
　Plaza with a towering square column
2. 「関係項―沈黙」の展示
　Exhibition of "Relatum-Silence"
3. 配置のスケッチ
　Layout sketch

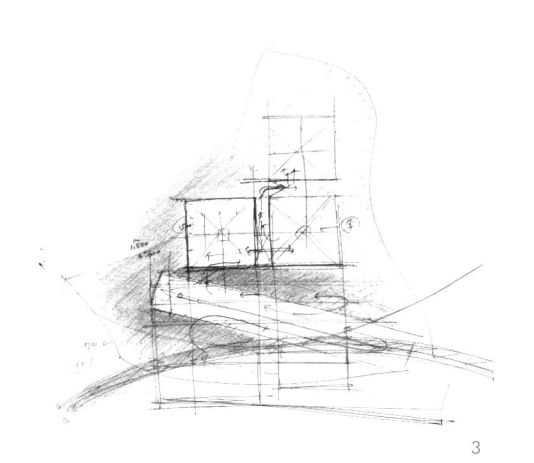

来訪者は三つの部屋を結ぶ屋外の通路を伝って移動する仕立てである。敷地は高台に位置していて、製塩のための段状塩田の跡も残る。「ベネッセハウス　ミュージアム」とは、600メートル離れた場所だ。

　地下建築は、安藤の「見果てぬ夢」だった。建築家として駆け出しのころ、インドで見た地下の井戸で光の交錯する空間に、彼は建築のひとつの原点を見出した。そして、その体験が、安藤の作品をいわば自閉的な洞窟の空間のイメージで染め上げてきたことに、建築家本人としても強い自覚を抱いている。それが初期の「渋谷プロジェクト」に始まる「地下空間の提案」に結びついた。もっとも、それらの計画は、実現することなく終わったが、この直島の外界の豊かな自然を横目に「地下に潜る」形で実現したのは実に興味深い。彼は自然に目を背けたのではなく、自然を保全するために、自作を完全に地下に埋没させたのである。

　三つの展示室の繋ぎとなる順路を配した空隙は、正三角形や正方形の幾何図形の形をとる。地下空間ゆえに方位感覚を失った来訪者を導くのは、それらのモダニズムの絶対的な幾何図形である。現代美術家と安藤の空間が見事な火花を散らすのを体感できるのは、そのような安藤自身の空間に対する揺るぎない信念があればこそなのだ。

建築の力、芸術の力

　安藤の直島における作品は、島のウエルカムセンター的な性格を持つ「ベネッセハウス　パーク／ビーチ」（2006年）を経て、2010年の「李禹煥美術館」へと至る。海岸に開けていく山裾の地形に展示室を埋め込み、「自然の地形と一体化し、風景に溶け込む建築」の探究がやむことなく続けられている。ここでも厳格に屹立するコンクリート打ち放しの壁、垂直性を強調した象徴的な角柱が、背後の展示空間を暗示する形で地表に配され、安藤らしさが発揮されている。

　2013年の「ANDO MUSEUM」は、その名の通り、安藤の建築資料を展示するギャラリーである。「家プロジェクト」が企画されている直島本村地区に残る築100年の下見板張りの木造民家に、コンクリートボックスを挿入した。ボックスと既存の木造の小屋組の隙間からは自然光が射し込み、室内に思わぬ光と影がもたらされる。そこに安藤は、過去と現代、木造とコンクリート、光と闇という対立の重層を期待したという。地下には、コンクリートで囲われた直径2.7メートルの極小の瞑想空間（パリのユネスコ本部の「瞑想空間」を連想させる）を設けて、安藤の建築の本質を体感できる場としている。

　直島に始まるベネッセの自然とアートを融合したリゾート空間つくりは、豊島、犬島など近隣の島々に広がりを見せる。銅の製錬所跡地や廃棄物の不法投棄で汚染が進

Prototype of Art Museum Architecture

Ando designed the JAPAN PAVILION at the international expo held in Seville, Spain in 1992. The large space created with wood became popular and Ando's architectures started to be acknowledged as the realizable space of beauty in Europe. First company that sent a request was Benetton, an apparel company in Italy. A design of an architecture of an art school named FABRICA, which Benetton had planned to establish, was requested to Ando around the time the expo was held, so in July of that year, he went to see the site in Treviso in North Italy where Benetton has its headquarters. This architecture with most of its function gathered underground required a long construction period, and completed in the year 2000.

In 1990 before the project for FABRICA, Ando was requested to create design for a seminar house of a furniture manufacturer, Vitra in Basel, Switzerland, which was completed in 1993. He became a prominent member of this development project that gathered aspirational contemporary architects from all over the world at a vast property where an art museum by Frank Gehry is also located.

It was in 1994 when designing of an art museum named LANGEN FOUNDATION / HOMBROICH was requested. It will be assumed that around this time, Ando's popularity started to rise and clients who wanted to specifically delegate the space of beauty to Ando appeared one after another. Karl-Heinrich Müller who opened an art museum in Hombroich Island in the suburb of Dusseldorf, Germany requested Ando to design a new art museum planned at a former NATO missile launching site near the island. Due to lack of budget, it took 10 years to materialize the plan. By funding of Marianne Langen who was a collector of oriental arts and contemporary arts, the LANGEN FOUNDATION / HOMBROICH was built.

Although the special exhibition building of this art museum is embedded underground, the permanent exhibition building seen on the ground has a "nest" structure where a concrete box is inserted in the coating of glass external walls. This nest structure with glass and concrete is one of the trademarks of Ando's design for art museums. Many of art museums in Japan use the same structure including the Hyogo Prefectural Museum of Art. The MODERN ART MUSEUM OF FORT WORTH has a nest structure that brings major effects with the spatial variation.

Although the completion was delayed, LANGEN FOUNDATION / HOMBROICH is one of the starting points of Ando's art museum architecture. This design of nest structure with double coating was actually based on the design Ando proposed in 1992 for an art museum requested by the Roi Baudouin Foundation in Brussel, Belgium, which did not materialize. Although the project was never realized in spite of three visits paid to the site, according to Ando, the design experience was embodied one after another, for instance as LANGEN FOUNDATION / HOMBROICH.

ANDO MUSEUM 2013
ando museum

1. 民家を再生した外観
   Exterior appearance of a restored private house
2. 入れ子で挿入されたコンクリートの壁
   Concrete wall inserted in a nesting manner

Chapter 3 'Beauty' Collaborates with 'Nature' to Return to Mother Earth

1992年セビリア万国博覧会 日本館　1992
japan pavilion, expo'92 / seville

木造の外観
Wooden exterior

FABRICA（ベネトンアートスクール）2000
fabrica (benetton communication research center)

地下に施設を埋めた
Facilities buried underground

ヴィトラ・セミナーハウス　1993
vitra seminar house

広大な緑に立地
Located in vast greeneries

んでいたところも、安藤の尽力もあり汚染物の除去が進み、本来の瀬戸内の穏やかな環境の復原が進んでいる。建築と美術の力が一帯を甦らせ、国際的にも注目される場となったことを祝福したい。

美術館建築の祖形

　1992年、安藤はスペイン・セビリアで開催された国際博覧会で日本館を設計した。木造による大空間は評判を呼び、先に述べたようにマルタ・パンをはじめとする芸術関係者の注目を集めていた「ANDO」の建築は、ヨーロッパにおいて「実現可能な美の空間」と認識されるようになった。まず声をかけてきたのは、イタリアのアパレル企業ベネトンだった。安藤は、ベネトンが設立をはかっていた「FABRICA」と呼ぶ施設の設計を、万博の会期と前後して依頼され、その年の7月にはベネトンが本拠地としている北イタリア・トレヴィゾの現地を確かめに出かけた。地下に機能の大半を収容するこの建築の工事は長きにおよび、完成は2000年となった。

　安藤は「FABRICA」に先立つ1990年には、家具メーカー、ヴィトラからスイス・バーゼルでセミナーハウスの設計を依頼され、1993年に完成を迎えている。広大な敷地にフランク・ゲーリーによる美術館も揃う、世界から意欲的な現代建築家を集めた開発プロジェクトの有力な一員とされた。こうした実績がヨーロッパにおいて多くの美術館の設計を手がける大きな原動力となった。

　のちに「ホンブロイッヒ／ランゲン」と命名される美術館の設計を依頼されたのは1994年だから、安藤の名声がこの時期に高まり、具体的に美の空間を委ねようという施主が相次いで現れたことになろう。ドイツ・デュッセルドルフ郊外のホンブロイッヒで美術館を開設していたカール・ハインリッヒ・ミューラーは、近くの旧NATOのミサイル発射基地の跡地に計画している新たな美術館の設計を打診してきた。資金難から実現には10年を要した。東洋美術と現代美術のコレクターであるマリアン・ランゲン夫人が資金援助を申し出て、「ホンブビロイッヒ／ランゲン美術館」は実現した。

　この美術館の企画展示棟は地中に収められているが、地上に顔を出している常設展示棟は、ガラスの外壁の被膜のなかに、コンクリートの箱が挿入される「入れ子」の構成をとっている。このガラスとコンクリートの入れ子構造こそ、安藤の美術館のひとつのトレードマークといってよい。兵庫県立美術館を筆頭に国内外の美術館の相当数が同じ構成をとり、安藤の美術館で最も優れた建築と目される「フォートワース現代美術館」では、入れ子のもたらす空間の変化が大きな効果をあげている。

　完成は遅れたが、その意味では「ホンブロイッヒ／ランゲン美術館」こそが、安藤の

ホンブロイッヒ／ランゲン美術館　2004
langen foundation / hombroich

1. ガラスのなかにコンクリートが入れ子に
   Nested concrete structure inside of the glass
2. ロビーから展示室を望む
   Exhibition room viewed from the lobby
3. 地下展示室にはスロープで降りる
   Slope leading to the underground exhibition rooms
4. 配置図のスケッチ
   Layout plan sketch

第3章 〈美〉は〈自然〉と融合し、母なる大地に還る

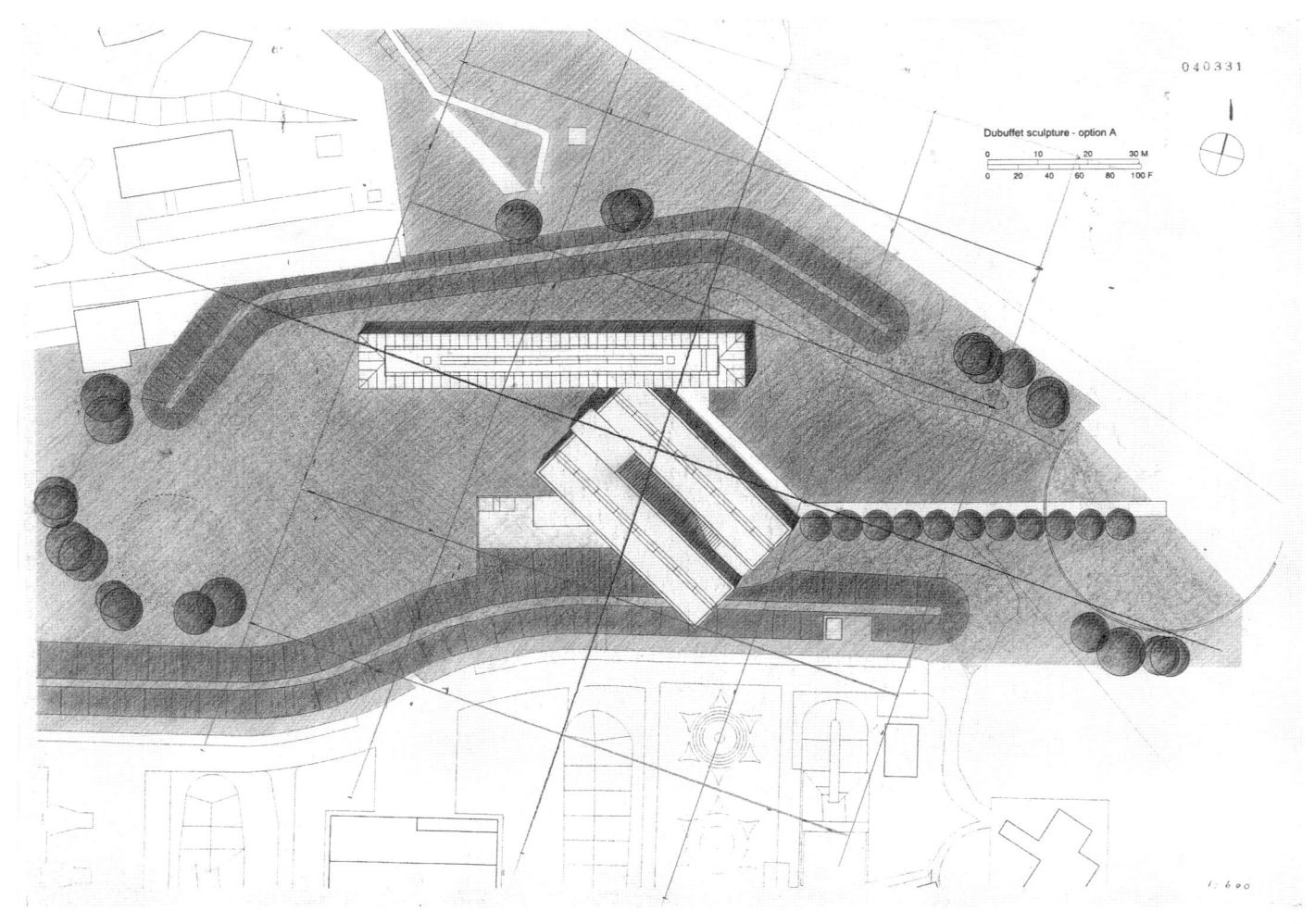

seguin   plaza   gallery

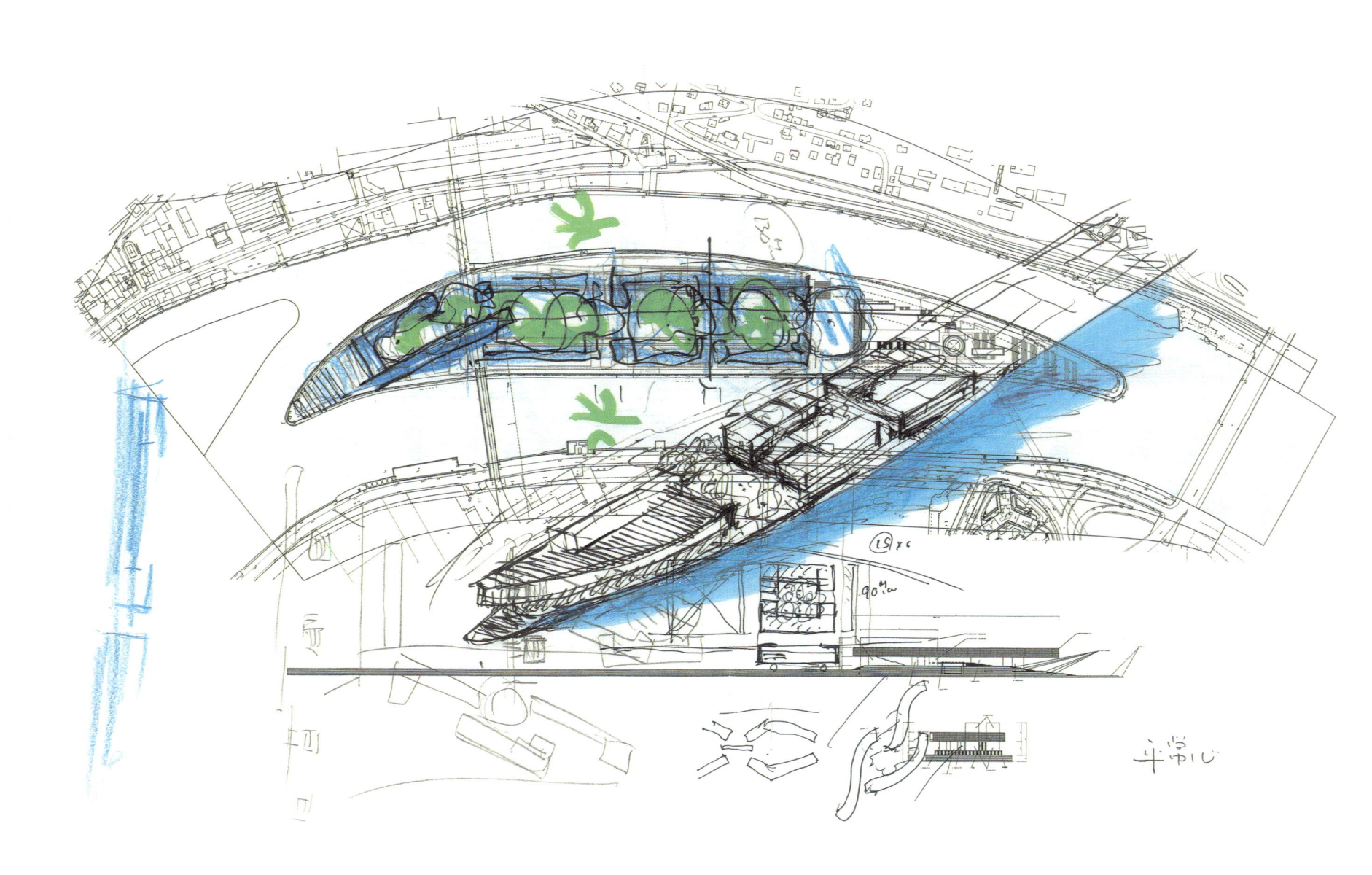

Seine

ピノー現代美術館　2001
françois pinault foundation for contemporary art

1. （前ページ）セーヌ川とのつながりを示すスケッチ
   (previous page) Sketch showing a connection to the Seine
2. 展示空間などの模型
   Model of the exhibition spaces
3. セガン島の模型
   Model of Seguin Island

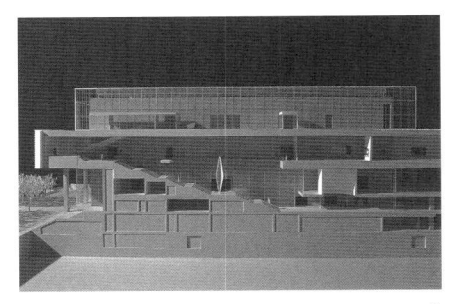

美術館建築のひとつの原点といえるものだ。実は、この二重被膜の入れ子構造は、1992年に提案されて実現しなかったベルギー・ブリュッセルのボードワン国王財団から依頼された美術館で、安藤が提案したものが下敷きになっている。安藤によると3度現地を訪ねたが実現にはいたらなかったプロジェクトだが、その設計の体験が「ホンブロイッヒ／ランゲン美術館」などで相次いで具現化していったわけだ。

美術館建築の最高の果実は、フォートワースという米テキサスの砂漠のなかに実を結んだにせよ、ヨーロッパが出発点となったことは、ひとまず記憶しておいてしかるべきだろう。

パリからヴェネチアへ、再びパリへ

1996年、安藤の建築家人生にとって、ひとつの節目となる人物との出会いがあった。安藤は、ファッションデザイナーのカール・ラガーフェルドの住宅の設計をしており、彼にひとりの実業家を紹介された。フランソワ・ピノーがそのひとで、一代で財閥を築き上げた立志伝中の人物だった。何事をも自身の信念で実現してきた実業家人生と、安藤の独学で世界を代表する建築家となった身上が重なりあい、ふたりは運命的な出会いを実感した。

現代美術のコレクターとしても知られるピノーは、パリ西郊のビヤンクールに自身のコレクションを展示する大規模な「ピノー現代美術館」を計画していた。立地はセーヌ川の中洲に浮かぶセガン島、そこはフランスを代表する自動車メーカーのルノーの工場があった場所で、美術館の計画段階ではまだ工場の建物が残っていた。

ピノーはこの美術館の設計者をコンペで選ぶことにし、安藤が当選者となった。しかし、諸般の事情で美術館は実現せず、安藤は大いに落胆した。

ピノーは、そこで諦めず、舞台をイタリアのヴェネチアに移して、新たな美術館計画を立案した。フィアット財団が展覧会場としてきた「パラッツォ・グラッシ」（1772年、ジョルジョ・マッサーリ設計、安藤による改装2006年）を引き継ぎ、安藤に新装の設計を依頼した。この邸宅の背後には、ビデオアートやパフォーマンスのための「テアトリーノ」（2013年）が設置され、これも安藤の手になる。また、大運河がアドリア海に流れ込む突端に位置する旧税関（15世紀）の現代美術ギャラリーへの改装（2009年）も安藤に委ねた。

「パラッツォ・グラッシ」と、旧税関の「プンタ・デラ・ドガーナ」の二つのプロジェクトにおいて、安藤は謙虚ともいえるほど、自分の表現を抑制して成功に結びつけた。ヴェネチアならではの文化財保全の規制を柔軟に受け入れ、まず「パラッツォ・グラッシ」では、後年の改装を18世紀後半のマッサーリの原形に戻す処置がとられた。そのう

Paris to Venice and Back to Paris

In 1996, Ando met a person that changed his course in the life as an architect. Ando was designing the residence of a fashion designer, Karl Lagerfeld, who introduced one business person to Ando. Francois Pinault is his name and he was a self-made person who built a financial conglomerate in one generation.

Pinault who is known as a collector of contemporary arts was planning to build a large art museum to display his own collection in Billancourt at the western suburb of Paris. The location is Seguin Island in the middle ground of Seine River where a plant of Renault, an automobile manufacturer representing France, use to stand. The building of the plant still remained when the art museum was planned.

Pinault decided to select the designer for the art museum through a contest, in which Ando was selected. However, Ando was very disappointed later since the art museum could not be built due to various reasons.

Pinault did not give up there and planned a new art museum in a different location, Venice in Italy. Inheriting the Palazzo Grassi (designed by Giorgio Massari in 1772 and renovated by Ando in 2006) where the Fiat Foundation was using as an exhibition site, he requested Ando to design the new interior. Teatrino (2013) also designed by Ando was established at the rear area of this residence for video arts and performances. Additionally, the renovation of a contemporary art gallery (2009) of the former customs house (15th century) located at the tip where Canal Grande flows in Adriatic Sea was entrusted to Ando as well.

パラッツォ・グラッシ　2006
palazzo grassi

1. 邸宅の内装を活かした展示室
   Exhibition room utilizing the interior of the mansion
2. 階段室の展示
   Exhibitions in the stair hall
3. 大運河に面する正面外観
   Façade facing the Grand Canal

テアトリーノ　2013
teatrino

1. エントランス
   Entrance
2. ホールのホワイエ
   Foyer of the hall

第3章 〈美〉は〈自然〉と融合し、母なる大地に還る

Ando had success by humbly controlling his own expression with the two projects of Palazzo Grassi and the former customs house Punta della Dogana. Flexibly accepting the regulations for preservation of cultural assets of Venice, he first restored the original shape of Palazzo Grassi by Massari in the latter 18th century. After that, he limited his own expression to setting the interior white exhibition walls in a nest structure and creating the area of collision of the modern and historical styles partially. His pride for his spatial interpretation has created this natural style exhibition space. It is also certain that there is a solid relationship of trust with Pinault as a great background. In addition, the Italian project team he worked with on Fabrica in Treviso joined the project, which was another great force. He recalled that the precise workmanship could only be achieved by them who conveyed Ando's intention to the site as an intermediate.

With Punta della Dogana as well, Ando removed walls that were set only for convenience in later years and first restored the original shape. As a result, wooden roof frame and brick walls appeared in a form to show the weight of the history there. A concrete box, which is the highlight of Ando's works, was inserted in that space and tactfully made the inside and outside areas as an exhibition space. The structure offers historical value with the pre-existed wooden frame with a space regulated by Ando underneath. It is not so rare in Europe to use historical architecture for an art exhibition. Even in that environment, the exhibition space of Punta della Dogana is in an outstanding level full of charm in intertwining of history and modern space. The reality feeling of the practical space, neither a palace nor a mansion house, conflicts with the contemporary sense of modern art in some times, and responds to it in other times, providing a real-size space of beauty. Both works exhibit his deep insight and tolerance as a modern architect.

However, the art world was astonished when Pinault's commitment to the project in Paris was shown in 2016 without being diminished after the success in the project in Venice. Pinault obtained the long-term right to use the building of the Commodity Exchange that remains in the Les Halles District in Paris and announced a plan to renovate the building into a gallery. Although it is not so close, the Centre Pompidou, which is the sanctuary of the world's contemporary art exists in the Les Halles District. Pinault requested Ando to design the renovation of the gallery of this Commodity Exchange. The journey of contemporary art started in Seguin Island took Ando to Venice and brought him back to Paris. The construction period was set unusually short for the locality to be completed at the end of 2018, and expectation for the space of beauty that Ando was involved in is rising. It is hoped that the dream of the two will come true.

Since the end of the 20th century, construction of facilities called art sites is increasing around the world; an art site is a place where multiple modern architects hold independent galleries on a vast ground. In those facilities, Ando became very much in demand from the world.

1

プンタ・デラ・ドガーナ　2009
punta della dogana contemporary art center

1. 大運河の先端に位置する
　Located at the tip of the Grand Canal
2. もとの建物の内部
　Interior of the original building
3. 煉瓦壁が残る
　Remaining brick walls

えで、内部に白い展示壁を入れ子に収め、現代と歴史が衝突する場を部分的につくりだすのにとどめた。自身の空間解釈への自負が、このような自然体の展示空間を生み出した。そして、それはピノーとの揺るぎない信頼関係を大きな背景としているのは間違いあるまい。加えて、トレヴィゾの「FABRICA」で一緒に仕事をしたイタリア人のプロジェクトチームが計画に参加したのも大きな力になった。精密な施工は建築家の意志を現場に仲介して伝える彼らの存在があってこそだったと安藤は振り返る。

　「プンタ・デラ・ドガーナ」でも、後年の改造で便宜的に設けられた壁などは撤去され、まずは原形への復原が優先された。その結果、木造の小屋組や煉瓦壁が、内部の空間に歴史の重みを実感させる形で姿を現した。そこに安藤の真骨頂であるコンクリートの箱が挿入され、内外を巧みに展示空間に仕立て上げた。既存の木造の架構が歴史を実感させ、その下に安藤の規定した空間が展開するという構成である。歴史的な建築を美術の展示に転用する試みは、ヨーロッパでは珍しいことではない。なかでも、この「プンタ・デラ・ドガーナ」の展示空間の歴史と現代が交錯する魅力は群を抜いた水準に達している。もともと王宮でも邸宅でもない実用的な空間のもっている実在感が、現代美術の今日的な感覚と時には衝突し、時には共鳴し、等身大の美の空間がもたらされている。両者とも、現代建築家としての懐の深さと器の大きさを感じさせる作品となっている。

　しかし、ピノーのパリに賭ける執念は、そうしたヴェネチアのプロジェクトの成功があったにせよ衰えていないことが2016年になって示され、美術界を驚かせた。パリのレ・アール地区に残る「商品取引所」（ブルス・ドゥ・コメルス）の建物の長期の利用権をピノーが獲得し、ギャラリーに改装する計画が発表された。レ・アール地区には、少しは離れているが、世界の現代美術の殿堂ポンピドーセンターが存在する。ピノーはこの「商品取引所」のギャラリーへの改装の設計を安藤に依頼し、パリ郊外のセガン島で始まった現代美術の旅は、ヴェネチアを経て、パリへと戻って来た。2018年末完成という現地では珍しい短い工期の設定がされており、安藤が関与した美の空間への期待は高まっている。二人の夢の結実を確かめたい。

　20世紀末以降、広大な敷地に複数の現代建築家が独立したギャラリーなどを手がけるアートサイトと呼べる施設の建設は、世界各国に広がりをみせつつある。そうした施設において、安藤はまさに世界から引く手あまたの存在となった。

Chapter 3 'Beauty' Collaborates with 'Nature' to Return to Mother Earth

プンタ・デラ・ドガーナ　2009
punta della dogana contemporary art center

4. 歴史的な空間に現代美術がならぶ
　 Contemporary artworks in a historic space
5. 木造の架構の下の展示
　 Exhibitions under wooden frameworks
6. コンクリートの壁からギャラリーを望む
　 Gallery viewed from a concrete wall side

第3章　〈美〉は〈自然〉と融合し、母なる大地に還る　113

Architect as a Priest of Beauty

CHÂTEAU LA COSTE is a contemporary art gallery and outdoor exhibition facility on a vast property of a winery at the Aix-en-Provence in Southern France. It is also the facility owned by a wine brewery from Ireland who is expanding investment business internationally. Ando designed the main ART CENTER, restoration of a church using remains of Roman Era, wooden gallery he will exhibit his own installation, and supervised the whole site of the project.

The ART CENTER is quietly positioned with smooth skin of exposed concrete at the property with spreading vine field which symbolizes Southern France. A vertical wall with stunning proportion protrudes the main building and regulates the area while rows of rectangular columns provide strength in the spatial setting. The wind blowing in the area draws wave pattern on the water surface of an artificial pond facing the building where the building reflected on the surface sways beautifully.

A small chapel rebuilt using rough stones of remains of the Roman Era, located at an upland apart from there, is Ando's homage to the European history. When pondering over the lives of people in the ancient times that took place at this location, one will come to realize that the creation of contemporary artists such as Ando and Richard Serra are forming a page of the history.

The wooden gallery looks as if MINAMIDERA of Naoshima was invited to that location. When entering the dark space inside from outside with bright sunlight, Ando's introspective space different from the spacious ART CENTER can be experienced.

It is refreshing to see that Ando displayed his ability to the full in this facility.

The STONE SCULPTURE MUSEUM, which is a private art museum that collects works of Wolfgang Kubach and his wife Wilmsen known for the piled literature shape stone sculptures, is located at Bad Münster am Stein-Ebernburg (Germany), which is the location where Kubach was born. Ando received a request to design an art museum from Kubach when he was still alive and completed it with his wife and the foundation who carried out his will. The appearance of the art museum created from a house with an inclined roof and impressive irregular-shaped wood frame transferred to the location and the foundation covered with exposed concrete walls demonstrates the resonance of the European history and modern creation. If people see the figure of the museum on a green hill containing concomitant multiple values, they would realize that Ando himself has been involved in activities in an effort to steadily grow into more tolerant person, like a priest who dedicates himself to the nature and beauty.

シャトー・ラ・コスト　2011
château la coste

1. アートセンター、水上のカルダーの彫刻
   Calder's sculpture on the water at the Art Center
2. 人工池を望む
   View of artificial pond

美の司祭としての建築家

　南仏エクス・アン・プロヴァンスのワイナリーの広大な敷地を生かした現代美術のギャラリーと屋外展示施設「シャトー・ラ・コスト」は、アイルランド出身で世界規模で投資事業も展開するワインの醸造元が施主となった施設である。安藤はその中心となるアートセンター、ローマ時代の遺跡を生かした教会の再建、自身のインスタレーションを展示する木造のギャラリーの設計、さらにこのサイト全体の監修役を担当した。

　南仏らしいぶどう畑の広がる敷地に、アートセンターはコンクリート打ち放しの平滑な肌を纏って、静かに身を横たえている。見事なプロポーションの垂直壁が建物本体から突出する形で場を規定し、林立する角柱がその空間設定に力を添える。吹き抜ける風が、建物に面した人工池の水面に波紋を描き、そこに映し出される建築の姿を美しくゆらめかせる。直島において自然との融合を意図した建築家の想念は、この南仏の豊かな緑のなかで、確かな形をとっている。人工の幾何学と自然が織りなす、交響詩を聞く思いがする。

　そこから離れた高台に位置する、ごつごつしたローマ時代の遺跡の石を使って再構築された小さな聖堂は、安藤のヨーロッパの歴史へのオマージュそのものだ。この場での古代のひとびとの営みに思いを馳せるとき、安藤、そして、リチャード・セラら現代美術家たちの創造が、歴史のひとこまをつくろうとしていることに気づくだろう。

　木造の独立棟のギャラリー「4グラス・キューブス・パビリオン」は、それこそ直島の「南寺」がそこに勧請されたかのようだ。陽光あふれる屋外から、内部の闇の空間に歩を進めるとき、アートセンターの開放的な表現とは異なる、内省的な安藤の空間に触れることができる。思う存分に腕を揮った爽快さがこの施設にはあふれている。

　ドイツに目を移そう。積み重ねた書籍を型取った石彫で知られるヴォルフガング・クーバッハと妻のヴィルムゼンの作品を収蔵する個人美術館「ストーン・スカルプチュア・ミュージアム」は、クーバッハの生地バート・ミュンスター・アム・シュタイン＝エーベンブルグに位置する。安藤は、生前のクーバッハから美術館設計の依頼を受け、遺志を継いだ未亡人と財団によって完成にこぎ着けた。傾斜屋根で、不整形な木組みが印象的な現地の民家を移築再生し、その足もとをコンクリート打ち放しの壁で囲った美術館の姿は、ヨーロッパの歴史と現代の創作の共鳴を感じさせる。その多義的な価値観を両立させる姿を緑の丘陵地に眺めるとき、安藤自身がかつての「住宅」と「商業施設」を主たる作品とする「都市の建築家」から、より器の大きな自然と美を奉じる司祭のような存在への弛まない成長を心がけて活動してきたことが実感できる。建築家の歩みとして実にすばらしいことだといえよう。

シャトー・ラ・コスト　2011
château la coste

3. チャペル
   Chapel
4. チャペルのインテリア
   Interior of the chapel
5. 4グラス・キューブス・パビリオン
   Four glass cubes pavilion
6. パビリオン内の展示
   Exhibitions of the pavilion

Chapter 3　'Beauty' Collaborates with 'Nature' to Return to Mother Earth

ストーン・スカルプチュア・ミュージアム　2010
stone sculpture museum

1. 内部の木造の架構
   Wooden interior framework
2. コンクリート壁で囲われた屋外展示
   Outdoor exhibitions enclosed by concrete walls
3. 民家を活用した仕立て
   Design utilizing a private house

第3章　〈美〉は〈自然〉と融合し、母なる大地に還る　117

Challenge in the U.S.

Also with a recommendation of the late James N. Wood who was the director of The Art Institute of Chicago, Ando received a letter of request to design a gallery to display the art collection of the owner, the head of the Pulitzer family, known with the Pulitzer Prize, in 1990. First it was a plan to restore an old automobile plant to a gallery to encourage recovery of Saint Louis where it was affected by the hollowing-out, however, a new art museum was considered to be built by Ando on a new property since the Joseph Pulitzer Jr., the family head, passed away.

At times heated discussion took place with the wife of Joseph Pulitzer Jr., who is an artist and curator, regarding the style of the exhibition space and it took 11 years for completion in 2001. Although the "space of nil" is the area to express the permanent universal value for Ando, sculpture artists such as Richard Serra naturally pursued to obtain space where their own exhibition works would be highlighted and heated discussion continued.

This circumstance was caused by having artists join as advisors who have right to express opinions regarding the architecture. However, Ando was able to pursue the "space of nil" and created buildings of rectangular solids by exposed concrete that are positioned in parallel with an artificial pond in between. The process of discussions Ando had in this project brought him major ideas of how to form space in an art museum. The results were firmly expressed in the MODERN ART MUSEUM OF FORT WORTH.

I remember Ando's nervous face, which was unusual, when he talked about his plan after winning the contest of the MODERN ART MUSEUM OF FORT WORTH. He explained to me several times while drawing a rough sketch of five parallel buildings on a sheet of paper napkin at a restaurant.

The largest cultural facility in Fort Worth in the south of the U.S., is the Kimbell Art Museum. The architecture of the art museum with high-quality collections form Michelangelo to impressionist is known in the architects' world as the masterpiece of Louis Isadore Kahn. The property of the MODERN ART MUSEUM OF FORT WORTH Ando was going to handle was right next to that location. The concrete vault ceiling of Kimbell Art Museum shines glamorously that looks silver in filtered natural light. Everyone agrees that it is the world's most beautiful concrete architecture.

As an architect who uses exposed concrete as his trademark, Ando had to achieve creation of a work that is equivalent to the Kimbell Art Museum. The exhibition rooms with vault ceiling are lined in parallel at the Kimbell Art Museum. On the other hand, Ando placed five rows of rectangular solid buildings in parallel as if he was challenging the layout of the Kimbell Art Museum.

ピューリッツァー美術館　2001
pulitzer foundation for the arts

1. 幾何立体の外観
   Geometric-shaped exterior
2. 展示空間から人工池を望む
   Artificial pond viewed from the exhibition spaces
3. スリットからの自然光
   Natural light through a slit

米国での試練

　シカゴ美術館の館長だった故・ジェームス・N・ウッドからの推薦もあって1990年、ピューリッツァー賞で知られるピューリッツァー家の当主から安藤に、美術コレクションを展示するギャラリーの設計依頼が封書で寄せられた。この時期、ヨーロッパのみならず米国の美術関係者の間でも、安藤のモダニズムへの期待が高まっていたことがうかがえる。当初は空洞化が進むセントルイスの街の復活を期して、旧自動車工場をギャラリーに再生する案だったが、当主であるジョセフ・ピューリッツァー・JRが亡くなったこともあり、新たに敷地を求めて安藤による新しい美術館が建てられることになった。

　完成まで11年、アーティストたちに、キュレーターでもあるピューリッツァー未亡人も交えて、展示空間のありかたを巡って時には激しい議論が交わされ、2001年ようやく完成をみた。安藤は「無の空間」こそが、永続する普遍的な価値を体現するとしたが、彫刻家のリチャード・セラらアーティストは、当然のように自身の展示作品を引き立たせる空間を求めて激論が続いた。

　建築に関して発言権を持つアドバイザーとしてアーティストたちが参加したことがこうした経緯の背景にあったが、安藤は「無の空間」を押し通し、コンクリート打ち放しの直方体の棟が人工池を挟んで平行する構成が実現した。この議論の過程が、美術館空間のありかたについて大きな示唆を与えることになったのは、安藤自身が認めるところである。その成果は「フォートワース現代美術館」においてしっかりと結実することになった。

　「フォートワース現代美術館」のコンペの勝利者となった安藤は、その案を語るとき、いつになく緊張した面持ちだったのが、わたしの記憶に残っている。平行する5本の棟のスケッチなどをレストランの紙ナプキンなどに走り書きのように描いて構想を説明してくれる機会が何度もあったが、美術館の建築を手がけるにあたって、他にはない立地が安藤の緊張状態を高めさせた。

　米南部の有力都市のひとつであるフォートワースの最大の文化施設は「キンベル美術館」である。ミケランジェロから印象派まで質の高いコレクションを誇る同美術館は、建築の世界では、ルイス・カーンの最高傑作として知られる。安藤が手がけることになった「フォートワース現代美術館」の敷地は、まさにその隣地に位置していた。カーンは1960–70年代の米国を代表する建築家であり、「キンベル美術館」のコンクリートのヴォールト天井は濾過された自然光で銀色と思わせるほど妖艶に輝き、すべてのひとが「世界一美しいコンクリート建築」と認めるものだ。

　コンクリート打ち放しをいわばトレードマークとする安藤にとって、「キンベル美術館」にひけをとらない作品の実現を、なんとしても達成しなければならなかった。「キン

Milestone at the Fort Worth and Continued Struggle

I was sitting at the café and looked up the ceiling of Kahn with Ando in the Kimbell Art Museum at the end of 2002 on the day of the completion ceremony. It is absolutely beautiful. However, the MODERN ART MUSEUM OF FORT WORTH we walked together before the ceremony was overwhelming the masterpiece of Kahn with the style of exhibition space.

Although it is only 10 minutes by car from the center of Fort Worth, this area in the suburbs gives somewhat a hazy impression. In that environment, Ando placed an artificial pond and placed three rectangular-solid exhibition buildings to float on the water. Each of exhibition buildings is surrounded by glass walls where an exposed concrete box is contained in a nest form. Visitors would view the reflection of dry light in Texas on the water surface through the glass walls. Then they follow the path route to inside the concrete box, come out of the glass wall space and again be led to the next concrete box.

The appreciation flow line of the space of glass walls and concrete boxes was effectively designed. The scale of the passage is comfortable and the features that differ between the buildings excite visitors, such as movement of space between the waterfront with rich sunshine and space surrounded by concrete as well as the open ceiling provided inside the box.

I wanted to congratulate Ando as I remembered him drawing rectangular solids in parallel as if he was teaching himself before I visited the site.

The creation of this art museum is showing to the whole world Ando Tadao is an architect who is not inferior compared to any architect of Europe and the U.S. and it was the moment in which a milestone was established.

CLARK ART INSTITUTE (2014) was completed in Williams Town in the eastern part of the U.S. Two facilities that are positioned in the vast green land were entrusted to Ando. Taking into consideration the context of soil of America that is different from the dry sand of south area, Ando's aesthetic value in concrete is gently developing in the nature. This shows Ando's level of maturity in creation as an art museum architect.

フォートワース現代美術館　2002
modern art museum of fort worth

1. 直方体の棟の連続
　Sequence of cuboid buildings
2. コンクリート箱内の展示室
　Exhibition room inside the concrete box
3. Y字のフレーム越しに人工池を望む
　View of the artificial pond through Y-shaped frame

ベル美術館」はヴォルト屋根の展示室が平行に並ぶ。一方、安藤はその構成に挑戦するかのように、直方体の棟を五列平行に並べたのである。

　安藤はこの自作の並列棟を繰り返して描いてわたしに示した。そして、紙の余白の「キンベル美術館」にあたる位置に、カーンの並列棟を正確な方向に基づいて描いた。それは、20世紀にコンクリートの美しさで頭角を現した2人の王座を巡る避けられない闘いを思わせた。

フォートワースのマイルストーン、そして闘いは続く

　2002年の終わり、竣工お披露目の日に、わたしは「キンベル美術館」のカフェに安藤と一緒に腰掛けて、カーンの天井を見上げていた。確かに、圧倒的に美しい。それでも、竣工を前にともに歩いた「フォートワース現代美術館」は、展示空間のありかたでカーンの名作を圧倒していた。

　フォートワースの都心から車で10分ほどとはいえ、郊外地は茫漠たる印象を与える。安藤はそこに人工池を設け、展示棟は3本の直方体を水に浮かべる構成をとった。個々の展示棟はガラス壁で囲われ、そのなかにコンクリート打ち放しのボックスが入れ子となって収容されている。来訪者はガラス壁を通して、テキサスの乾いた光を反射する水面を眺め、順路に従ってコンクリートの箱のなかに誘導され、そこからまた、ガラス壁の空間に出て、次のコンクリートボックスへと移動する。美術品はコンクリートの壁の内外に配されている。

　このガラス壁とコンクリートボックスの空間の鑑賞動線が実に巧みに設えられていた。通路のスケール感は心地よく、陽光あふれる水辺とコンクリートで囲われた空間との移動は、ボックス内に吹き抜けを設けるなどの、棟ごとに異なる仕掛けが来訪者の心を躍らせてくれる。

　建築家が美術館でなにが出来るかは難しい話だ。しばしば、建築家は展示空間には手を出さず、エントランスホールや外部との繋がりのあるカフェなどで、自身の主張を展開する傾向にある。しかし、「フォートワース現代美術館」は違った。展示空間そのものが、安藤の掌のうえにあった。数々の仕掛けを楽しませながら、鑑賞動線は流れるように設定されていた。

　わたしは、現地を訪れる前に、安藤が自身に教唆するかのように、直方体の並列を描いていたことを思い出して、祝福したい気持ちになった。「あなたは、カーンを凌ぐものを見事にやってのけたではないか」と声をかけたくなった。そして、これはピューリッツァー美術館でのアーティストたちとの時間をかけた議論の成果なのだと確信した。

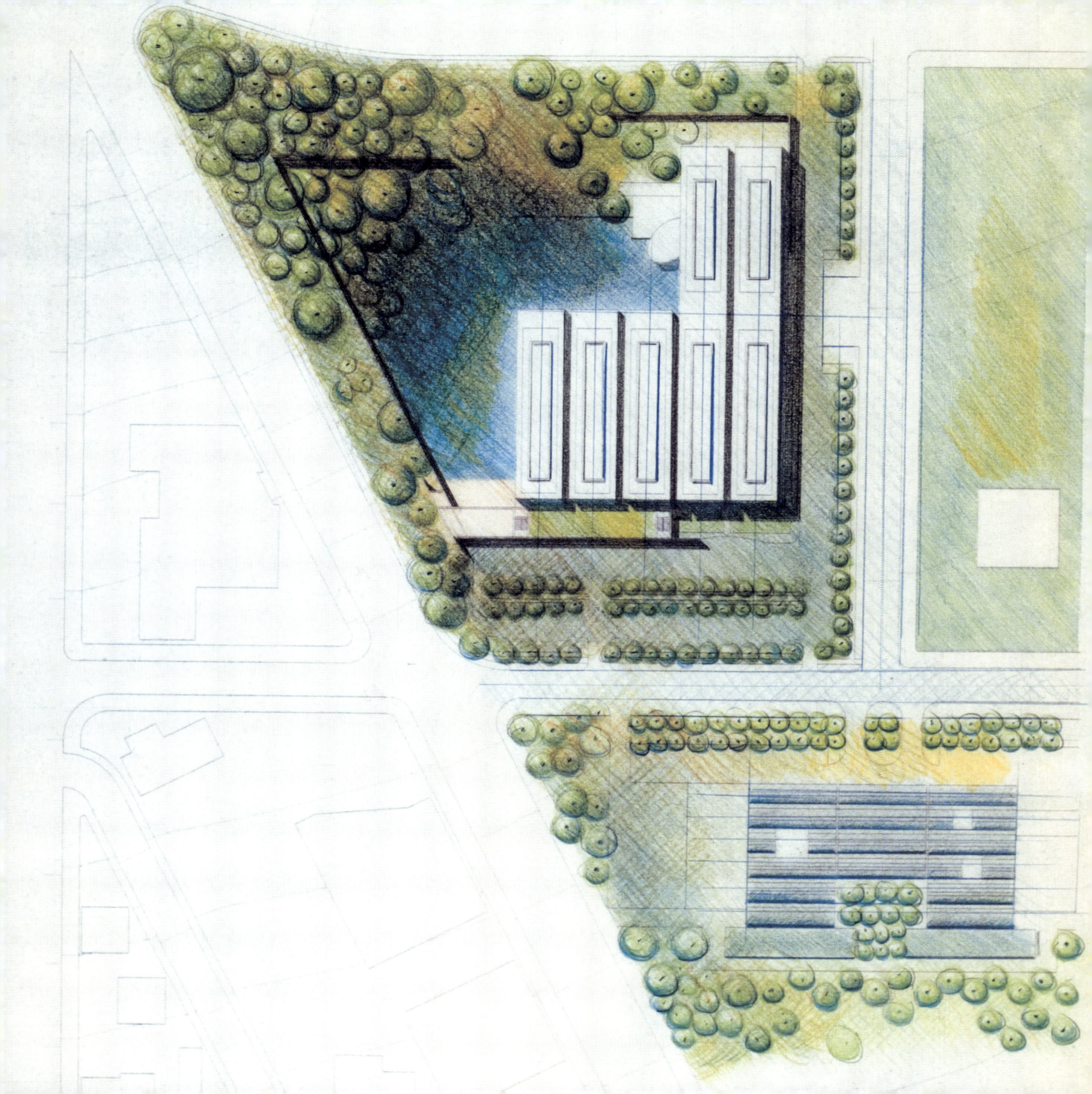

フォートワース現代美術館　2002
modern art museum of fort worth

4. (前ページ) 配置図のドローイング
   (previous page) Layout plan drawing
5. 屋内の展示空間
   Indoor exhibition space
6. リチャード・ロングの作品
   Artwork by Richard Long
7. ヴォールト屋根の階段室
   Stair hall with a vaulted roof
8. 棟の間からの眺望
   View from a gap between buildings

第3章　〈美〉は〈自然〉と融合し、母なる大地に還る　123

クラーク美術館／クラークセンター　2014
clark art institute / clark center

1. 水辺に浮かぶエントランス
   Entrance on the waterside
2. 新館とつながる既存の建物のロビー
   Lobby of the existing building connected to the new building
3. 人工池に臨む外観
   Exterior appearance facing the artificial pond

　この美術館の誕生は、安藤忠雄が欧米のどの建築家にもひけをとらない存在であることを国際舞台において示し、ひとつのマイルストーンが打ち立てられた瞬間だった。日本の建築家が海外で手がけた美術館建築は相応な数にのぼるが、これほど見事な展示空間を実現した例をわたしは知らない。

　安藤は米国でも、ヨーロッパと同じく美術界から手厚く迎えられ、このような大きな成果を打ち立てた。際立った作品を残すことこそが、厚遇へのなにより返礼であり、それが実現したことを評価したい。

　米東部マサチューセッツ州のウィリアムズタウンでは「クラーク美術館」の美術品修復施設「ランダーセンター」（2008年）と美術館新館にあたる「クラークセンター」（2014年）が相次いで竣工を迎えた。広大な緑地に点在する施設の二つが安藤の手に委ねられた。南部の乾いた砂地とは異なるアメリカの土地の文脈を踏まえて、安藤のコンクリートの美学が、自然のなかに静かに展開されている。そこに美術館建築家としての安藤の創造のひとつの熟成を見ることができよう。しかし、彼は、刺激があれば、またフォートワースのような挑戦に打って出るに違いない。そこにも闘う建築家の揺るぎない姿勢を確かめることができるだろう。

第4章 「生き続ける近代建築」を目指して
建物と建築家の「30年の物語」

Chapter 4　In Pursuit for "Modern Architecture That Will Continue to Exist"
"Story for 30 Years" of Buildings and the Architect

自然と葛藤する建築家の決意

　60度の急勾配の斜面地という、常識では住宅地になりえない厳しい立地条件が、「六甲の集合住宅」(1983年) の生みの親だった。完成する5年前、斜面地の開発を相談された安藤は、依頼者が宅地として想定していた緩やかな斜面より、背後の急勾配に心惹かれた。

　まるで建築することを拒むかのような急斜面。しかし、ひとたびそこに住宅を建てることがかなえば、斜面を覆う野生の樹木に建築は埋もれ、得られる眺望を独り占めできる。自然と眺望は集合住宅にとって、ここでしか獲得できない特性ではないかと、彼は考えたのである。

　安藤は斜面に立ってみた。緑に囲われた場所に風が吹き渡っていくのを感じた。大阪湾から神戸港まで期待通り、一望できる。しかし、集合住宅を設計するのなら、なにより緑を壊したくない。その思いが、自然のなかに、ひっそりと息づく建物の姿となって安藤の脳裏で形をとりはじめた。

　かつて安藤が神戸で斜面地の集合住宅「岡本ハウジング」(1976年) を構想したとき、法的規制や採算、技術的な課題を解いていくと、ごく普通のいわゆるマンションになってしまって、断念に追い込まれたことがあった。

　その轍は踏みたくない。社会の複雑なシステムをもちろん受け入れ、そのうえで頭のなかのイマジネーションを極限まで働かせなければ実現にこぎ着けられない。いや実現したとしても数々の制約との妥協が、建物の端々に見えてしまえば、せっかくのイメージも歪んでしまう。やはり、この集合住宅での生活像を踏まえた構想力こそが大切だと安藤は思った。あとはその実現を後押しする、なんとしてもやるのだという熱意。

岡本ハウジング　1976
okamoto housing project

1. 模型の俯瞰
　 Elevated view of the model
2. 斜面に配された住棟の模型
　 Model of the residential building on a slope

*Architect with Determination
to Struggle with Nature*

Rokko Housing (1983) was born in extremely strict environments for building a residence, that is, a very steep slope with an angle of 60 degrees. 5 years before the project was completed, Ando was offered to develop a low-angled slope for the residence, but he was rather interested in constructing the residence on much steeper slope behind the originally offered area.

A slope that seemed as if it resisted to have something built on. However, if it was possible to build a residence there, the architecture would be hidden by surrounding indigenous trees and residents would have the great view all for themselves. Ando thought that the natural environment with the view at this site was so unique that it could only be obtained here.

He stood on the slope for a while. He could feel a breeze through the area with full of greenery. You could have a panoramic view from Osaka Bay to Kobe Port if you live here. He wanted to design a collective housing here, but he didn't want to destroy its natural environment. The image of the architecture which was quietly nestled in the forest was gradually formed in his mind.

Okamoto Housing Project (1976), a collective housing project on a hillside in Kobe, which Ando once planned but couldn't realize because it turned out that the housing would become nothing more than just an ordinary apartment in order to meet various restrictions including legal regulations, profitability, and technical challenges.

He didn't want to make the same mistake again. He knew that it was necessary to use his imagination as fully as possible, not to mention he followed a complex social system at the same time, for making Rokko Housing come true. Even if he could manage to complete the project, it would surely spoil the image of the architecture once you could see through a series of restrictions and compromises behind every corner of the housing. The most important thing was, he believed, the imagination based on people's life in this collective housing from the very realistic point of view. In addition to that, strong ambition and determination pushing towards its realization must have been required. Without them, such imagination could never take shape.

According to the legal regulation, no architecture higher than 10 meters was allowed. The completed Rokko Housing, however, was built along the slope of which height difference was 40 meters. The architecture was built in a way that was half-buried underground along the slope, and thus it was possible to have such a scale while following the regulation. Besides, he was fully aware of the risk associated with constructing a collective housing on a slope so that extensive geological survey was conducted for checking the safety not only within the building site but also in its surrounding area.

The nature seemed to seek a chance to penetrate into the completed architecture. The architecture, on the other hand, claimed itself as an artificial concrete object in accordance with the geometry. I could see that the existence of this architecture enhanced the beauty of surrounding natural environment even further. A panoramic view appeared when an architecture was completed and independent.

六甲の集合住宅 I 1983
rokko housing I

1. 正面外観
Façade

それがあって初めてイマジネーションは形をとることができる。

　法的な規制に従うと建物の高さの制約は10メートル。現実に完成した「六甲の集合住宅」の斜面の高低差は40メートルに達している。建物を斜面に添う形で地中に埋め込むような形式にしたため、高さ10メートルの規制を守りながら、それだけの規模の建物が実現できた。斜面地のリスクを十分認識し、安全性を確かめるため、地質調査の網を敷地の周囲にまで広げ、丹念に確認を進めた。

　自然は完成した建物の内部への浸透をうかがっているように見えた。それに対して、建物は幾何学に則ったコンクリートの人為的なオブジェとしての存在を主張していた。その建築の存在によって、自然はさらに際立って見える効果が確かめられた。建築が自立して初めて可能になる風景がそこに出現した。

「余白」から回遊庭園へ

　安藤が集合住宅の計画にあたって、最も重視するのは「道」だ。そこには路上という共同空間のありかたを復権したいという、彼の思いが込められていた。

　西欧の都市にはひとの集う中心的な広場があるが、木造住宅が肩寄せ合って密集する日本の都市では、路上が生活と密接な関わりを持ってきた。そこは近隣のひとびとにとっての共同空間で日々立ち話もすれば、小さな集まりが持たれることもしばしばだった。道路の両側の連続する住宅を「壁」だと見なせば、道路は壁に囲われた「連続する屋外の部屋」と見なすことができるだろう。そして、そこは公共の空間でありながら、両側の住宅の暮らしと結びついている点で、私的な空間の延長線上に位置していた。

　「六甲の集合住宅」で、安藤は道から直接住戸に入る形式を採用した。近代建築がもたらした集合住宅は、敷地に入った瞬間に、外部の道との関係を遮断されてしまう。そうではなく斜面を昇降する階段を主要な道と位置づけ、それをひとつの軸に住宅の各戸はその道に向き合う玄関を持つ独立住宅と見なして、全体計画を押し進めた。

　つまり、建物としては一棟なのだが、独立住宅が道を媒介にして斜面に重なり合っている姿を構想したのである。集合住宅内の廊下は、どうしても閉ざされた通路になりがちだ。それを排するためにも、玄関は道に面する必要があった。

　このような「六甲の集合住宅」の構想を練る経緯は、安藤に「余白」という概念について考えを深めさせるきっかけになった。

　一般に、建物は敷地のなかで「余白」を支配しようとする。しかし、実際は「余白」も建物を支配しようとする。建築と「余白」がそのような関係にあるなら、建築はもちろんのこと、「余白」もまた自身の論理を持ち、しっかりした意図のもとに、敷地のなか

From "Vacancy" to Stroll Garden

When Ando designs a collective housing, what he emphasizes the most is "roads". Behind his design, he had a strong feeling for the road being restored as public space.

There are commonly central plazas and squares for people to gather in European cities, while cities in Japan are crowded with wooden houses so that the road has been closely related to life in the neighborhood. People often stood talking to neighbors, and even small gatherings were held on the road. If you consider a series of houses on both sides of the road as "walls", then the road between these walls can be considered as "a series of outdoor rooms". It was the public space which was at the same time closely connected to the residents living on both sides, thus was placed on the extension of their private space.

For ROKKO HOUSING, Ando designed the entrance of each unit facing directly to the road. For typical collective housings in modern architecture, the connection between external road and residence is cut off immediately at the entrance of the residential site. In general planning, Ando placed steps along the slope and considered them as the main road, and each unit was regarded as detached with individual entrance facing toward the road.

What he imagined was, therefore, that a single building with independent units being layered with each other on the slope, and that the road would mediate those units. Corridors of a collective housing tend to be closed passages, and in order to avoid that, the entrance needed to be placed facing toward the road.

As he developed the planning of ROKKO HOUSING, he started to think deeply about the concept of vacancy.

In general, an architecture tries to control the vacancy within the site. In fact, however, the vacancy also tries to control the architecture. If there is actually such kind of relationship between the architecture and vacancy existed, not only the architecture but also the vacancy should appear on site with their own logics and strong determination. It also takes a form of gap in the structure. When such vacancy becomes the core of the architectural scene, Ando thought that the vacancy would become the architecture itself. It means that the architecture and the vacancy would stimulate each other to create a place with great magnetic force.

Courtyards designed in ROW HOUSE, SUMIYOSHI and TOWN HOUSE IN KUJO — IZUTSU HOUSE are vacancies within buildings, but for a collective housing it is a challenge how to design vacancies not only inside but also outside of the building.

For ROKKO HOUSING, the architecture consisted of a group of units, each of which is $5.8m \times 4.8m$. The units were arranged along with the slope in a vertical direction, and the plane symmetrically in principle but leaving vacancies intentionally. That created gaps vertically, and a flat roof of a residence downstairs became a terrace for each unit upstairs. Setback landings of steps for each floor created changes in view. People spending their time at terrace would have eye contacts with people in the terraces at the same level as well as people walking up and down the steps. Ando hoped that such design would create positive interactions among residents.

2

3

六甲の集合住宅 I 1983
rokko housing I

2. 小広場と通路
   Small plaza and a pathway
3. 外部階段と空中通路
   Outdoor stairs and skyway

の「空き」として出現しなければなるまい。また、それは構造的にも位置づけられる間隙の形をとることがある。そうした「余白」が建築のもたらす場面の集合のひとつの軸となるとき、「余白」は建築化されるのだと、安藤は考えた。建築と「余白」は互いを触発し合い、大きな磁力を持った場をつくりあげることになるわけだ。

「住吉の長屋」や、その後の「九条の町屋（井筒邸）」に設けた中庭は、建物のなかの「余白」だが、集合住宅では内だけではなく、外の「余白」をどう設営するかが課題になってくる。

「六甲の集合住宅」では、建物は5.8メートル×4.8メートルをひとつのユニットとして、その集合体とした。これを垂直方向では斜面に沿わせて配置し、平面はシンメトリーを原則にしながらも意図的に「空き」をつくった。そうすることによって垂直方向にずれが生じ、下階の住宅の水平屋根が、上階の各戸ごとのテラスとなった。階段の踊り場は1階ごとにセットバックさせて昇降時の視界の変化をもたらした。テラスでくつろぐひとびとは、同じレベルのテラスの住民とも、階段を昇降するひととも視線を交わす。そこに住民同士の出会いが生まれることを期待した。

その点では、あとになって気づいたことだが、この「六甲の集合住宅」は、「住吉の長屋」などで突き詰めた、人間にとって根本的なリアリティとはなにかという設問への答を拡張したものだったといえよう。

都市のなかの閉ざされたローコストの空間のなかで、ひとは光庭を介して浸入してくる光や風、雨と直接触れ合い、そして、思いは光庭をさまよい続ける。そのとき、ひとは人間にとって根本的なものを、ローコストゆえの制約のなかで見つけ出すことができる。生活の仕方に始まり、自身の精神力や体力に至るまでの限界を思い知らされることになる。それは光庭による個人の内的な風景への訴求だと考えた。そして、そこから都市的な視点に基づいて視界は外部へと開いていく。

個人としての人間からスタートして全体へ。「六甲の集合住宅」では、それをひとつの「開放的な型」として実現できた手応えが安藤にはあった。住戸としては閉ざして守りながら、道や「余白」によって開き、個々の空間を組み立てていくと、全体に至る。単なる部分の結合にとどまらず、また、外部から部分が規定されるわけでもない。あくまでも個を基盤に、全体との関係を見定めながらの内から外、個から全体への展開が「六甲の集合住宅」において実現できた。

これに先立つ「九条の町屋」では、光庭は三層の吹き放ちの屋外空間を昇降する流動的な構成に展開していた。それを集合住宅という個の集合体にまで踏み出せたといえよう。そのとき「住吉の長屋」を原形とする「六甲の集合住宅」の光庭は、幾何学的な秩序を守りながら、重層的に連なることによってあたかも「回遊式庭園」のようになった。「回遊式庭園」は、三次元的な多様な視点を有しており、それはのちの開放的な回廊を持つ多くの作品の構想に結びついていった。

From that point of view, I later noticed that ROKKO HOUSING could be an extension of the answer for the question that Ando sought to find in the design of ROW HOUSE, SUMIYOSHI, asking what was the fundamental reality for humans.

Within an enclosed, low-cost space in the city, people directly feel the light, wind, and rain through the light court, and their minds keep wandering about there. That is when people can find what really fundamental is for them under a budget constraint. They will know their limits in their lifestyles, in addition to their mental as well as physical strengths. Ando thought this as an appeal for personal inner scenery by the light court. The sight will be open to the outer world, based on the urban point of view.

Human as an individual begins and then becomes the whole. ROKKO HOUSING was satisfying enough for Ando to actually realize a form of openness. It is enclosed and secured as a residence, but is open with the road and with the vacancies at the same time. Individual spaces were assembled together to create the whole. It is neither a mere connection of parts, nor the parts defined from outside. The development from individuals to the whole, and from inner space to outer space could be successfully achieved with ROKKO HOUSING while having the individual as a core and determining the relationship with the whole.

In his previous work, the TOWN HOUSE IN KUJO, the light court was developed a structure that flowed up and down the three-level open air space, and it was adopted into the collective housing, that is, an assembly of individuals.

The light court of ROKKO HOUSING that was originated from ROW HOUSE, SUMIYOSHI was constructed as if it was a circuit style garden, since its structure was multi-layered while it kept certain geometric order. The circuit style garden had a diversity of three-dimensional perspectives, and it influenced many of Ando's designs that had open corridors.

Expansion into the Second Phase

The construction of ROKKO HOUSING II was completed in 1993, which was after 15 years from Ando's first visit to the site, and 10 years after the completion of the first block. It was situated next to the first residence on the left, on the same slope with the gradient of 60 degrees. But the size was four times larger than the first one. It was because the demand for this type of collective housing was increased among people who found the life in Kobe attractive, after the completion of the first block. Although it was much desired by many people, it still took nine years for the second to be completed. Ando's ambition as an architect to challenge a new design of collective housing, rather than a mere extension of the first block, also made the project delayed.

The concept of "stroll garden", which was realized in the first phase, became deeper with the second phase. Front yard of each unit is a terrace where residents can enjoy the greenery, light, wind, and view in their daily life, which also means to the individual residents always being aware of their life in relation to the place they live, that is, the society.

There is a buffer zone between the first and second residential blocks, providing a square for residents from both blocks gather together. There is also an indoor swimming pool building in the buffer zone, and the residents from both blocks can use it. It was hoped that individual life of these residents would eventually form a community through the use of these facilities.

六甲の集合住宅 I 1983
rokko housing I

4.（前ページ）斜面のドローイング
(previous page) Slope drawing

第II期への拡大

　1993年、「六甲の集合住宅」の第II期が完成した。安藤が初めて敷地を訪ねてから15年、第I期が完成してからでも10年の歳月が過ぎようとしていた。敷地は第I期の右隣り、傾斜60度の急勾配は変わりなかった。規模はほぼ5倍にあたる。第I期によって神戸での暮らしの新たな魅力に気づいたひとびとが、同じような住宅を求める需要が高まったためだ。それでも第II期の実現には9年を要した。やるからには第I期の単なる拡張ではない新たな集合住宅像に挑戦したいという建築家としての熱意が、計画の実行を慎重にさせたこともあった。

　第I期で実現した「回遊式庭園」の構想は、第II期によって、さらに深みを増すことになった。住宅の各戸に設けられた前庭は、日々の暮らしのなかで、緑、光と風、そして眺望を満喫するテラスであり、それは、個人の暮らしがその立地する場、つまりは社会との関係を常に意識させる役割を果たす。

　ブロックとしての第I期と第II期の間は緩衝地帯と位置づけ、双方の住民の集う広場を設けた。そこには第I期、第II期の住民が共用する室内プール棟も設えた。プライベートな暮らしが、そこでひとつのコミュニティーのかたちをとることを期待してのことである。

　段状になった住棟の屋上を利用して、季節ごとに開花が続くように草花を配したテラスもまた庭園の喜びをもたらし、各戸の後庭は散策路となることを想定して植栽が施された。

　しかし、そこでも安藤の身上とする「幾何学」が貫徹された。住棟は一辺5.2メートルの正方形グリッドの連続が基本となり、それゆえ庭園のすべても幾何学に規定される「余白」となった。幾何学は不整形の崖地をよじ登り、自らをそこに埋没させ、放恣な感覚の自然と対峙して、安藤の美学を植えつけている。崖地に寄り添うことで住戸は垂直と水平の二つの方向でずれを生じ、その幾何学のずれがもたらす段差や空隙に自然が侵入し、視覚的にも多様さが実現している。無機質な幾何学と自然が邂逅することによって、両者は新たな関係性をつくりだし、それがここでの生活風景を一段と魅力的なものにしている。

　この第II期の完成により、崖地への挑戦に始まる「六甲の集合住宅」が、総合的な住環境の形成へと拡大していく確かな手応えを安藤は得るに至った。その建築家の確証が第III期、そして第IV期へとこの仕事を持続させていく大きな原動力となった。

The stepped rooftop of the residence was utilized as a garden with various seasonal flowers blossomed throughout the year. Besides, backyard of each unit was planted so that it was used as a walking path.

The geometry, Ando's philosophy, was also used in the design of these areas. The residential unit was basically a series of square grid with 5.2m on a side, and therefore all of these gardens became vacancies which were defined by the geometry. The geometry climbing up the irregularly-shaped hillside, buried itself, confronting the nature with no restriction, and planted Ando's aesthetics.

By the completion of the second block, Ando became confident that the ROKKO HOUSING project could expand to form a comprehensive living environment from his challenge to build a housing on the steep slope. Such confidence gave the architect great motivation to continue the project to the third and the fourth phases.

After the Earthquake

ROKKO HOUSING III (1999) was constructed mainly on a flat area on top of the hill, and the second block was situated on the left side of the slope of that hill. It used to be a company dormitory of Kobe Steel, Ltd. During the construction of the second block in 1991, Ando had already submitted a proposal in which he suggested to reconstruct the aging dormitory into ROKKO HOUSING III without first seeking the company's approval. He hadn't received a good response until the Great Hanshin-Awaji Earthquake occurred in January 1995 and facilities of Kobe Steel, including the factory in the coastal area as well as the dormitory on the hilltop, were seriously damaged and not be able to use anymore. The dormitory was decided to be rebuilt as a post-earthquake housing, and Ando was in charge of its design. It was nothing more than an odd coincidence that ROKKO HOUSING III became true due to the serious disaster.

There was a major budget constraint for construction, since it was a post-earthquake housing with subsidy. Having considered such difficulty, Ando designed the housing from a different point of view; finding a value of the collective housing in its public space.

Although the first block was advocated to be a collective housing, its design was planned to be a series of detached houses which were connected to each other at the courtyard of three dimensional structure. In fact, the structure of the first block was confirmed as a building of "two stories above the ground and one underground story" in the building certification, Similarly, the second block was planned to be a series of detached houses which were connected three dimensionally, although its building certification showed that it was a building of "four stories above the ground and six underground stories". For the third block, however, it was not possible to create a unique assembly of detached houses due to its construction costs. Instead, the three residential blocks, tall, medium, and low, were placed around a public space.

The low-rise block was constructed on the right side of the second block, creating a continuity from the slope, and a triangular site protruded from the rise toward the ocean. From this block, same as the first and the second, you can enjoy the panoramic view from the Kobe Port to the Osaka Bay. You can also enjoy the planting on the rooftop garden of the second block.

1

六甲の集合住宅 II　1993
rokko housing II

1. 斜面を上る屋外階段
   Outdoor stairs ascending the slope
2. ロビーから見る緑
   Greeneries viewed from the lobby
3. 中間階のロビー
   Lobby on the intermediate story

震災を経て

　「六甲の集合住宅」の第III期（1999年）は、第II期のさらに右側の斜面を登った高台の平坦地を主な敷地としていた。そこには神戸製鋼所の社員寮が建っていた。安藤はすでに第II期の建設中の1991年、老朽化した社員寮を第III期として建て替える、いわば「勝手に提案」をまとめて同社に賛同を呼びかけた。色好い返事をもらえないままかと思えたが、1995年1月に起きた「阪神淡路大震災」は臨海地にあった同社の工場施設に大被害を与えただけではなく、この山上の社員寮も設備関係が利用不能となった。そして、大震災からの復興住宅として建て替えることになり、安藤に設計が委ねられた。大災害によって第III期が実現にこぎ着けたのは奇遇としかいいようがなかった。

　公的な支援を受ける復興住宅ゆえに工費の面では大きな制約が生じた。それを受けて、安藤は、集合住宅の価値を「パブリックスペース」に見出すという発想転換で設計に臨んだ。

　集合住宅をうたうが、第I期は建築確認上の構造が「地上2階、地下1階」となっている事実が示すように、立体構成の中庭で結ばれた一戸建て住宅の連続体として計画され、「地上4階、地下6階」と表示されている第II期もまた同じく戸建て住宅の立体的な連結の想定だった。しかし、第III期は工費の関係で、変化を持たせた戸建て住宅の集合体とすることは無理だった。それもあって高層、中層、低層の三つに分かれた住棟が公共のスペースを囲う配置をとらせた。

　低層の住棟は、第II期の向かって右側、斜面地との連続を活かし、台地から海側に三角形の敷地が飛び出す構成にした。そこでは第I期、第II期と同じく神戸港から大阪湾にかけての広大な眺望と第II期の屋上テラスの植栽が目を楽しませる。

　高層の住棟は東西軸の配置で、低層棟の背後に聳え立つ。ここもまた海への眺望が堪能できるだけではなく、コンクリートの格子を埋めるように配した低層棟の屋上緑化の恩恵も受けられる。中層棟は高層棟の東端の背後の位置に90度で交差する南北軸上に配されている。ここでは住戸内からは左右に連なる六甲山の自然を視界のなかに収めることができる。制約がありながらも、立地の優位性を活かした住棟配置が、まず集合住宅としての質を高めている。

　それだけではない、高層棟と中層棟が背後で形成する「L字型」の外構を、安藤は見事な「パブリックスペース」に仕立て上げた。その外構の地上階を駐車場とし、2階レベルにあたるその屋上に植栽を施して屋外庭園としたのである。さらにこの屋外庭園の緑に臨む、大きなガラスの曲面壁を持つプールが配された。プールを利用する入居者は、第I期、第II期とは違って、背後の六甲山の緑を眺めながら健康維持に励むことができる。安藤自身が語る通り、ここでは「パブリックスペース」が、第I期、第II期に匹敵す

The high-rise block was situated through east to west, behind the low-rise block. From here, you can not only have a great ocean view, but also benefit from the rooftop greenery of the low-rise block which was arranged as if it fills the blanks of concrete grids. The medium-rise block was situated through south to north, intersecting at a right angle with the east end of the high-rise block from behind. From windows of this block, you can see the nature in the mountain range of Rokko. Despite of constraints, the arrangement of blocks which took advantage of the site enhanced the quality of buildings as collective housings.

Moreover, L-shaped exterior behind the high- and medium-rise blocks became a beautiful public space by Ando's design. The ground floor of the exterior was a parking space, and above it (equivalent level of the second floor) was a roof garden with greenery. Furthermore, indoor swimming pool building with a view of the roof garden from a large curved glass wall was constructed, too. Different from the swimming pool for the first and second blocks' residents, the users of this swimming pool can maintain their health while they enjoy the greenery of Mt. Rokko right at the back of the building. As Ando himself mentioned, this public space made the third block as attractive as the first and second blocks.

The fourth project of ROKKO HOUSING was the reconstruction of KOBE KAISEI HOSPITAL, on the slope a little far west side of the first, second, and third blocks. It consists of three buildings with the hospital and a nursing home for the elderly called "Comfort Hills Rokko", designed by Ando and completed in 2009. The rooftop greenery was also introduced in this project, securing the view full of greenery among buildings within the facility. A permanent home for the elderly was constructed as the fourth project of ROKKO HOUSING, which seems to represent the aging society and reflects changes in times and society.

六甲の集合住宅 III　1999
rokko housing III

1. 高層棟が面するルーフガーデン
   Rooftop garden facing the high-rise building
2. 低層棟を見おろす
   Downward view of the low-rise building
3. 住戸のテラス
   Terrace of a housing unit

る集合住宅の魅力をもたらしているのである。

　ちなみに第IV期に相当する施設は、第I期―III期の敷地から少し離れた西側の斜面にあった「神戸海星病院」の建て替えで、同病院と介護付き有料老人ホーム「コンフォートヒルズ六甲」が安藤の設計による3棟の建築で2009年に登場している。ここでも屋上緑化を進め、施設相互の緑の眺望の確保に努めている。高齢化社会を象徴する「終の棲み家」が、第IV期となったことは社会と時代の変遷を物語っていよう。

熱意がモダニズムの限界を突破する

　「六甲の集合住宅」の時間の流れを振り返ってみよう。第I期のために現地を訪ねたのが1978年、第I期の完成が1983年。安藤は1941年生まれだから、30代後半から40代前半の時期に相当する。「住吉の長屋」が1976年なので、まだ建築家として社会に知られるようになってそれほど時間は経っていなかった。その5年ほどの期間は、若き建築家にとって相応な長さに感じたに違いない。

　当時の安藤は、発表する作品のいずれもが注目され、次作を期待されていた。建築家としてまさに飛ぶ鳥を落とす勢いにあるとき、5年という時間をちょっと見には実現の危ぶまれる急斜面の計画案に投じたのは、ある意味、とても不可思議な選択といってよい。しかし、彼は、斜面地を訪れたときに「六甲の集合住宅」という「幸運の時の神」の前髪をしっかりつかんで放さなかった。いや、安藤は出現した神が幸運の神であり、そして、時間的な涵養を神が認めてくれて、やがては大きな果実を彼にもたらすことなど、露ほども期待しなかったに違いない。

　安藤にあったのは真剣に創作に向き合う熱意であり、傾斜60度の崖地は建築家たる彼の魂を揺さぶった。そこに阪神間ゆえの海に眺望の開く集合住宅を実現するためには、人生のかなりの時間を投じるのになんら臆さない建築家としての純粋な魂が彼には宿っていた。崖地との出合いから30年に及ぶ集合住宅群の設計にあたって、安藤はどの期においても自らに「新たな課題」を負わせてきた感がある。崖地の克服、すでに完成した前の期の作品との有機的な連携の模索、制約ある条件の克服による住空間の水準維持などである。

　崖地の克服は劇的だった。しかし、そのあとの闘志は煮えたぎるようなものとは違って、ともすれば「完成時がピーク」になりがちなモダニズムの建築、しかも自作のそれに静かに向き合い、その時点での課題を解決しながら、建築家として成熟の道をたどっていったと思えてならない。なかでも1995年の阪神淡路大震災後、復興住宅をその場で実現した熱意には大きな共感を抱く。まさに社会的に「建築家としてなにができ

Passion Overcomes the Limit of Modernism

Let me look back in time and the series of projects of ROKKO HOUSING. It was in 1978 when Ando first visited the site for the first project, and that was completed in 1983. He was born in 1941, and spent in his late thirties to early forties for this project. Back then, it was not a long time since he designed ROW HOUSE, SUMIYOSHI in 1977 and became widely recognized as an architect. That five years must have been felt such a long time for him, as a young architect.

At that time, the public paid a lot of attention to Ando's works, expecting what came next. It seems, in a way, a quite mysterious choice that Ando, as an up-and-coming architect, spent five years for the project which looked difficult to realize at first glance. He did, however, timely seize the Fortune by the forelock, that is, ROKKO HOUSING, when he first visited the slope.

It was very dramatic how he overcome the steep hill. There is a tendency for modernist architecture that it reaches a peak at the completion of the architecture. However, Ando kept his motivation and ambition constantly as he calmly confronted his own works and solved problems at that time, even after overcoming the initial challenge. That, I believe, made him grow and mature as an architect. I particularly feel great sympathy for his motivation when Ando timely constructed the post-earthquake housing after the Great Hanshin-Awaji Earthquake in 1995. It was indeed a practical example of what you really could do for the society as an architect.

It was also a great opportunity for Ando to decide how he and other architects in general would address challenges on modern architecture and its perpetuity and sustainability.

Ando designed ROKKO HOUSING to challenge the rigorous nature. He excavated the steep hill, replaced the design of nature with his own design which was basically made of a concrete grid, and from there expanded his "universe of modernism" through four consecutive ROKKO projects. Compare with the long history of the nature, nearly forty years was of little significance. However, considering the history of modernism which was established in the 1930s, what Ando had achieved could be seen as "an experimental work" for a modern architect.

He always kept his architect's eye on his own work, observing it from the beginning through the process of aging, and did whatever possible for the architecture to be continuously utilized as a historical property in the society. His attention never left ROKKO HOUSING as he was always planning its next project. It may be worth reviewing for the meaning of his ROKKO project for the first time in the 21st century when conditions are right to calmly judge advantages and disadvantages of the modernism.

六甲プロジェクト IV　2009
rokko project IV

1. 低層棟が病院、高層棟が老人ホーム
   Hospital in the low-rise building
   and a nursing home in the high-rise building
2. 老人ホーム内低層集合住宅棟の屋上緑化
   Roof planting on the low-rise housing complex building
   for the nursing home
3. （次ページ見開き）左からIV、I、II、上部にIIIが連なる
   (next two pages) IV, I, and II from left to right. III on top

るか」の実践だったといえるだろう。

　そして、それはまたモダニズムの建築の永続性、持続性への疑問に、建築家がどう応えていくかという「現代建築の課題」への安藤の姿勢を決めるひとつの大きなきっかけになった。

　建築は時間の経過とともに間違いなく朽ちていく。物体としても社会的な存在としてもである。コンクリートの寿命に関しても、社会の多くのひとびとは疑問なしとはしない。さらにいえば、モダニズムの建築が18世紀後半の産業革命以後の建材の工業生産を基盤に成立し、また、20世紀に顕著だった数々の化学的な素材の開発を取り込みながら自らの「様式」を決定してきたこともまた、古来からの伝統的な素材との比較で永続性に疑問の目を向けられる原因となっている。

　安藤が「六甲の集合住宅」をぶつけた相手は、思えば厳然たる存在としての自然だった。彼は峻厳な崖地を削って、コンクリートのグリッド（格子）を基本にした自らの造形を自然の造作に替えて挿入し、そこを起点に4期に及ぶ自らの「モダニズムの宇宙」の拡大をはかった。自然の生成から見れば40年近い歳月といえども、いかほどもない時間であろう。しかし、1930年代にモダニズムが成立してから80余年という時間の経過を踏まえれば、それは「ひとつの実験」と受けとめてよい、近代建築家の営みだったと見なせるだろう。

　彼は自作に常に寄り添い、その生成から経年変化の過程を建築家として眺め、建築が歴史的な資産として社会で機能し続けることに力をつくしてきた。「次の期のプロジェクト」を構想することで、建築家の関心は不断に「六甲の集合住宅」に向けられてきた。そのことの意味は、モダニズムの長所も短所も冷静に判断できる条件が整った21世紀において、初めて検証するに値するのかもしれない。

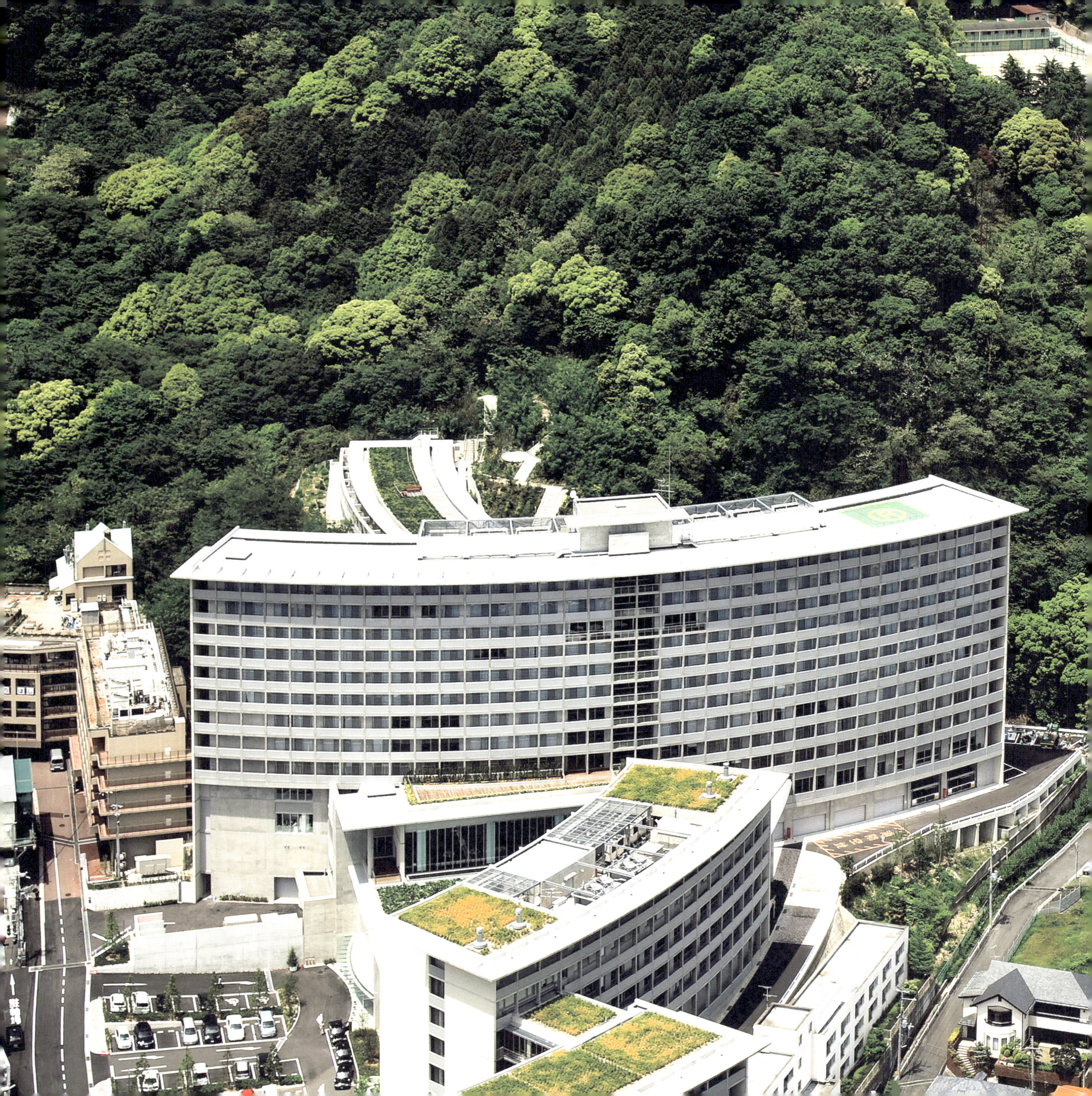

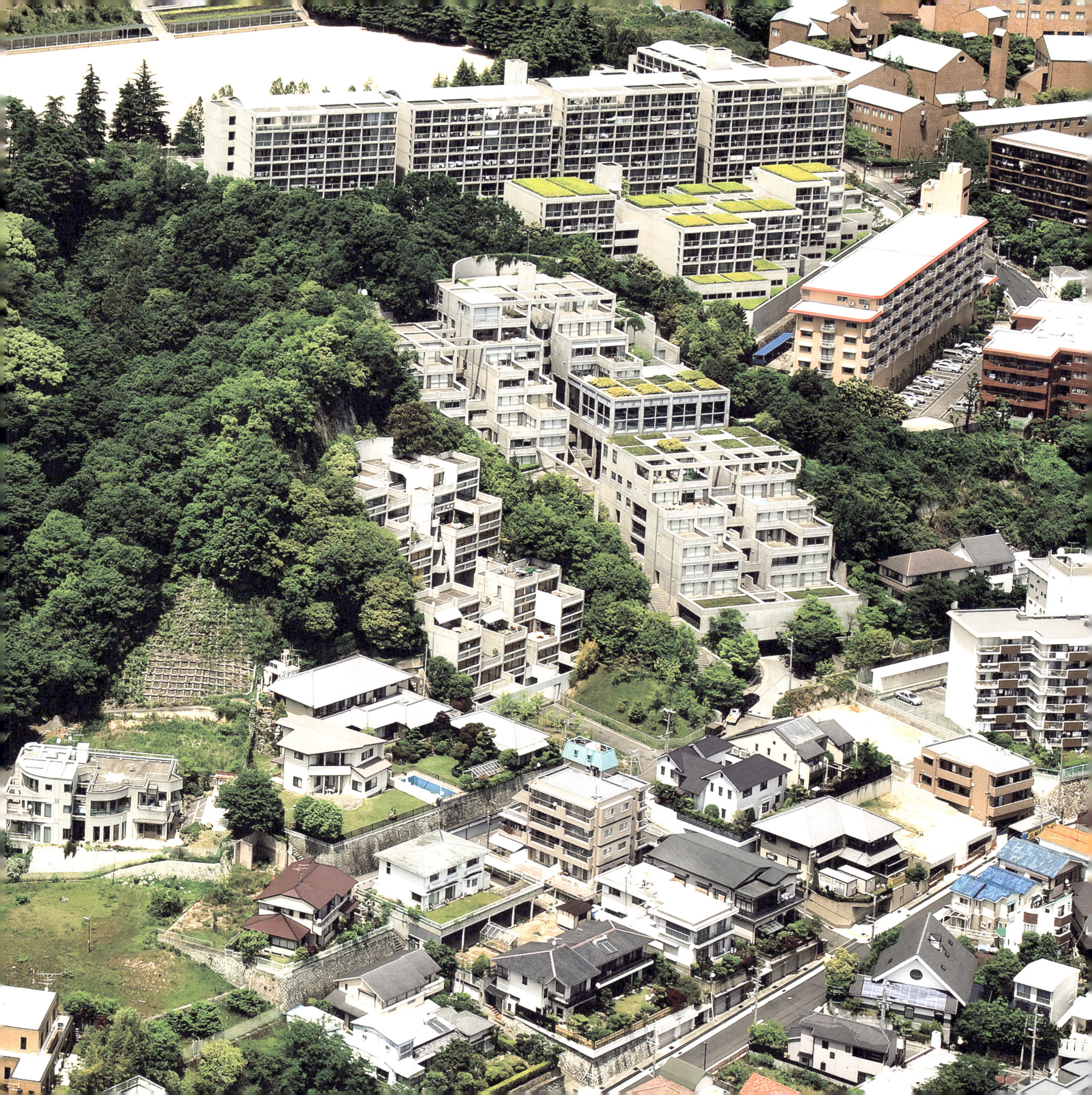

*Architecture That Transcends
History, Climate, Time and Space*

"While in this modern world, we can only construct architecture with full control over the nature, ancient people could whether utilize or aggressively oppose to the power of living nature in order to take such power into the architecture and created a magnificent space."

This is what Ando said when he designed KUMAMOTO PREFECTURAL ANCIENT BURIAL MOUND MUSEUM in Aso in 1992. The construction site was around Yamaga district, Kumamoto Prefecture where many decorated kofun (ancient Japanese tombs) were closely built. When Ando inserted the space made of his concrete grids, he paid respect to the ancestor as well as gave thoughts to the majesty of nature.

Having experienced interactions between the architecture and the nature in the series of ROKKO HOUSING project, Ando's words cited above made me realize that his view of architecture is rooted in the view of universe based on the time axis which goes beyond a life of a man.

His respect, or almost awe, for the history and nature, but he never hesitates to bring a space of what he believes into life. You don't see the social mission of modern architecture in which the space was created for labors in the 20th century anymore; what you see is a creator who confronts the architecture with nature and abstract beauty. The beauty of modernism is sublimed there, and the architecture looks as if an austere modernist knight who challenges a tough enemy. When the architect had to face the absolute value of history and nature, he departed to "a journey that never ends" for engraving his name on the ground.

Ando himself became aware of such thing stronger than ever when he designed CHIKATSU-ASUKA HISTORICAL MUSEUM in 1994.

In the history of the Yamato Dynasty which began in ancient Kofun Period, Asuka district in Nara Prefecture was called "Totsu Asuka", whereas Kanan area in Osaka Prefecture where the Museum is situated was called "Chikatsu-Asuka". These names were originated from distances from "Naniwa no Miya" or "the tomb of Emperor Nintoku" in Osaka before the Capital was relocated to Nara: "Chikatsu-Asuka" was closer to Osaka than "Totsu-Asuka". CHIKATSU-ASUKA HISTORICAL MUSEUM was planned to construct on Fudoki-No-Oka Historical Park where more than a hundred of small kofun called "Ichisuka Kofun Gun" were preserved and maintained.

On a rise of land of the mountainside where the Museum is situated, you have a clear view in the west. In that direction, you can see Osaka Bay which used to be called Naniwazu in ancient times. As you see the tomb of Emperor Nintoku in the northwest at the center of the vision, you can have a panoramic view from Sennan to Kobe. Ando was said to stand there, be moved somehow and to make a firm decision on the upcoming work when he was commissioned to design this facility. That was because almost all of his works existed within the area that he could see from that site. Initially, it was rather natural that Ando was strongly aware of himself as an architect from the downtown of Osaka City. That was not a regional concept that widely covered the Kansai area, but an extremely small universe that was represented by the downtown Osaka where houses and small shops were densely built. Since his initial works were the pursuit of "basic space for emotions", it was highly logically compatible with his creation at that time.

When Ando stood on the planning site of CHIKATSU-ASUKA HISTORICAL MUSEUM, he found what was in common among his works each of which had different requirement: architecture helped to visualize the history and climate that existed in the place, and to keep them in people's memories. While, for example, architects such as Togo Murano tried to glamorize "what modern is" by the architecture from the orthodox Kansai architects' point of view and to make it as a shared property for the public,

熊本県立装飾古墳館　1992
kumamoto prefectural
ancient burial mound museum

1. 古墳に接した敷地配置
   Site adjacent to an ancient tomb
2. 円形の中庭
   Circular courtyard
3. 配置のドローイング
   Layout drawing

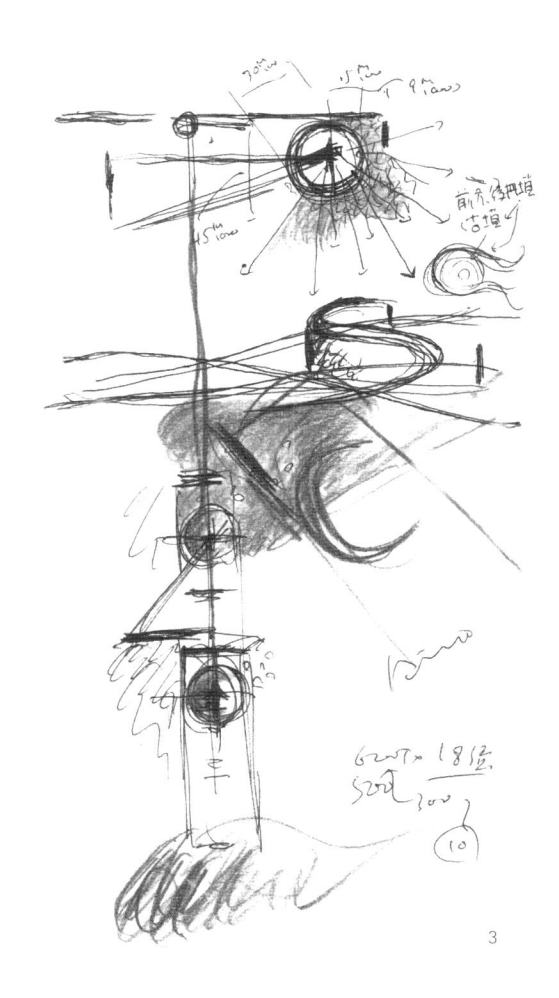

歴史と風土、時空を超越する建築

「自然を十分手なずけておいたうえでしか建築物を構築できない現代に対して、古代人は自然の生の力を利用し、あるいはそれと激しく拮抗しながらその力を建築に宿し、壮大な空間を創造してきた」

1992年、阿蘇の「熊本県立装飾古墳館」の設計に際して、安藤はこのように述べている。立地は、熊本県山鹿周辺に装飾古墳が密集する一帯。そこに自身の造作のコンクリートの空間を埋め込むとき、建築家は先人に敬意を払い、同時に自然の壮大さに思いを馳せている。

一連の「六甲の集合住宅」における建築と自然との応答の経験を踏まえて、安藤の言葉を読み返すとき、彼の建築観がひとりの人間の営みを超えた時間軸に基づく宇宙観に根ざしていることに気づかされる。

歴史と自然への畏怖にも近い敬意。しかし、決して臆することなく、そこに自らの信じる空間を出現させる。そのとき、モダニズムが背負ってきた20世紀における労働者のための空間造営という社会的な使命はもはや影もなく、抽象美で自然と対峙する創造者の姿がある。モダニズムの美の側面がそこに昇華され、建築はあたかも難敵に挑む禁欲的なモダニズムの騎士の趣きさえ漂う。歴史と自然という絶対価値と向き合わざるを得なくなったとき、建築家は大地への刻印を続ける「終生続く旅」に赴くことになったのである。

安藤にそのことをさらに強く自覚させたのは、間違いなく「大阪府立近つ飛鳥博物館」(1994年) だった。

古代の古墳時代に始まる大和朝廷の歴史のなかで、奈良の飛鳥を「遠つ飛鳥」と呼ぶのに対して、博物館が位置する大阪府河南町一帯は「近つ飛鳥」と称されてきた。奈良に遷都する以前の「難波の宮」や「仁徳天皇陵」など大阪の地を基準に「近い飛鳥」「遠い飛鳥」と命名されたのである。小さな古墳が100以上も残る「一須賀古墳群」を保存整備した「風土記の丘」に、「近つ飛鳥博物館」は計画された。

この博物館の立地する山腹の高台は、西の方角に大きく視界が開けている。視線の先にあるのは大阪湾、即ち古代の難波津である。ちょうど北西にあたる「仁徳天皇陵」を視界の中心に据えると、泉南から神戸までを一望することがかなう。安藤はこの施設の設計を委ねられたとき、そこに立って、ある種の感慨とこれからの創作に臨む決意を固めたという。なぜなら、まさに眼前に広がる風景のなかに、彼のそれまでのほとんどの仕事が存在していたからである。もちろん、初期の安藤は大阪の町場の建築家ということを強く意識していた。しかし、それは関西といった広範な地域概念ではなく、住宅と小さな商店が綾なす稠密な大阪下町に代表される極小な宇宙であった。初期の創作

Ando has developed his work by "ultimate abstraction of architectural view based on disregarding impurities in this world". By doing so, he achieved to go beyond not only this world but also the time and space.

The architecture of the Museum was buried into the mountainside adjacent to the Fudoki-No-Oka Historical Park. A water conduit goes along the mountainside, water flowing into a pond right below the site. Gigantic outdoor stairs that are placed to look down the water indicates visitors the existence of the Museum which was buried underground. At the top of the stairs, there is a thirty-meter tall square pillar standing straight.

Beginning of a Journey That Never Ends

Tower of Hades — this is what Ando named for the square pillar. It makes me imagine that the underground exhibition facility of the Museum acts in concert with Hades where the ancient lie underground. While pursuing ideological modernism as an ideal form, the space that Ando designed had reached an ultimate concept which cherished the vibrant memory of life in the ancient times. You may find the actual exhibition being rather miscellaneous, but as you ignore those and witness the architecture and imagine to extract the framework of Ando's design, you can recognize that everything including the circular outline and baroque stairs leading to the underground space were ideologically arranged underneath the Tower of Hades and the gigantic outdoor stairs.

Ichisuka Kofun Gun (Ichisuka tumulous clusters) was said to be constructed in the late 6th century, and thus it has approximately 1400 years of history. It will soon be 25 years since the Museum was opened. The time lapse between the two is so enormous beyond imagination. However, you may consider that the Kofun Gun and the Museum as a modern architecture go together on a journey that never ends. Crude and disrespectful view on the ancient civilization which the Japanese society used to believe will never come back again no matter how significantly the society will change in the future. The Museum has a responsibility to hand down the value of important historical heritage for the world, for Japan, and for the region to people of our time.

Every year on March 3rd, Ando gives a lecture at the Museum. When I attended the lecture, he spoke to the audience, "architecture will age over time. However, it is an architect's job to keep an eye on the architecture as time proceeds." He also asked the audience to cooperate with planting plum trees, which started at the opening of the Museum and still continues to do every year. At the opening, 150 plum trees were planted on the mountainside, facing right in front of the Museum. The number of trees has increased every year, and now there are nearly 400 plum trees planted and blossomed beautifully in spring. Many people visit here repeatedly during the time of bloom.

"Taking over to the future" by the modernist architecture and architect began at the completion of the facility, and there is no shortcut to the goal. Rather, it is a way that never ends.

As I listened to his lecture, I understood that planting plum trees every year is what Ando prepared for relaying a baton to the future. I also understood that in every spring, Ando makes a rule for himself to come here for reaffirming such trip that never ends. This hilly area has become one of the famous plum blossom viewing sights in neighboring region, which shows the architect's philosophy has gradually been shared by many people.

1

大阪府立近つ飛鳥博物館　1994
chikatsu-asuka historical museum, osaka

1. 大階段の下に施設が収まる
   Facilities packed under the grand stairs
2. 円形スロープで巡る展示
   Exhibitions along the curved slope
3. エントランスの地階アトリウム
   Underground atrium at the entrance

が「情念の基本空間」の追究にあったわけだから、その宇宙は創作との論理的な整合性が高かった。

その意味では、同じ大阪を拠点とした建築家村野藤吾の商都感覚とは、明らかに拠って立つところが異なっていた。村野が裕福な経済人たちを生み出した大阪の「実業の空間」をモダニズムに依拠しながら艶やかに仕立て上げたのに対して、安藤はまさに「貧困の美学」を地で行き、建築家として一家をなしたのであった。それは明治以来の武田五一、安井武雄、渡辺節、そして村野へと連なる関西の建築家の系譜からすれば異端ともいえる歩みだった。

しかし、「住吉の長屋」において、「貧困の美学」の珠玉の空間を達成したがゆえに、その美学はあたかもコペルニクス的な転回を遂げて、「桂離宮」の精神性に接近した。海外の評者たちは、そこに安藤の美学の極点を見出した。

だとするのなら、安藤が「近つ飛鳥博物館」の計画にあたって、自らが数多の作品によって刻印した土地を、古代の難波津に重ね合わせたのは、まさに的確に時空を跳んだことになるだろう。

「近つ飛鳥博物館」の計画地に立った安藤は、自身の建築作品について、個別の条件が異なる仕事の共通点として「建築によって場所に内在する歴史、風土といったものを顕在化し、その記憶を留めていくことにあった」という認識に至った。例えば、村野らがそれこそ関西人流の「現世的なもの」を建築によって美化して市民共有の資産としようとしたのに対して、安藤はあくまで「現世の夾雑物の捨象に基づく、建築観の究極の抽象化」によって自作を展開してきた。そして、そのことによって現世はおろか時空の超越をなしとげた。

「風土記の丘」に接する山腹に、博物館の建築は埋め込まれた。山腹を伝うように流れる水路が敷地のすぐ下では青々とした水をたたえた池になっている。その水面を見おろすように配された「巨大な屋外階段」が、地下に埋め込まれた博物館施設の存在を来訪者に示している。そして、階段の最上部には高さ30メートルの角柱がそびえ立つ。

終わりなき旅の始まり

黄泉の塔——安藤は、このコンクリートの角柱をそう名付けた。地下に古代人の眠る黄泉の国があり、地下に配した博物館の展示施設が呼応する姿を想像させる。理念的であるはずのモダニズムを理想の形態として追究しながら、安藤の空間は、地下に息づく古代への追慕と記憶に彩られ、まさに極限の思考に到達したのである。現実の展示は

4

Chapter 4 In Pursuit for "Modern Architecture That Will Continue to Exist" 144

大阪府立近つ飛鳥博物館　1994
chikatsu-asuka historical museum, osaka

4.「黄泉の塔」が階段にそびえる
　Tower of Hades soaring above the stairs
5. 階段にひとが集うドローイング
　Drawing of stairs with people gathering
6. 植樹された梅林
　Plantation of plum trees
7.（次ページ見開き）全体図のドローイング
　(next two pages) General drawing

雑多なものが多すぎるが、そこに居合わせたとき、それらをまさに捨象し、安藤の空間の骨格だけを抽出想起してみれば、円形の外郭も、その地下空間に降下するバロック風の階段も、すべてが「黄泉の塔」と大階段の地下に観念的に配されていることが理解できるだろう。

「一須賀古墳群」は6世紀後半とされるから、約1400年の歴史を持つ。この博物館が完成してほどなく25年を迎えようとしている。この時間差は気の遠くなるほどのものに違いない。しかし、古墳群とこの現代建築は、竣工の時点から、それこそ「終わりなき旅」をともにすることになったと見なせるだろう。かつてのような古代文明を顧みない粗雑な文明観は、どんなに社会が変わろうと、日本社会のなかに舞い戻ることはあるまい。博物館の役割は、世界にとって、日本にとって、さらには地域にとって大切な歴史遺産の価値を現代のひとびとに知らしめ、未来へと継承していく責任のまっとうである。

毎年3月3日、桃の節句に、安藤はこの博物館で講演の壇上に立っている。わたしがその講演に立ちあったとき、安藤は「建築は時間と共に古びていきます。しかし、その時間の経過をしっかりと傍らから見つめていくのが建築家の仕事なのです」と聴衆に語りかけた。そして、開設時から継続している梅の木の植樹への協力を呼びかけた。開館当初、この博物館が向き合う山腹に150本が植樹された。それを毎年少しずつ増やして、今では400本近くが春先の山に彩りを添える。開花時期にあわせて、何度も足を運ぶひとたちも少なくない。

現代建築と現代建築家による「未来への継承」のスタートは、施設が完成した時点で切られ、ゴールへの近道はない。いや終点のない営為なのだ。

講演を聞きながら、わたしは、梅の木は、1年さらに1年とそのことを確認していくために安藤が用意したバトンなのだと受け止めた。毎年、この季節、ここに来ることを自分に課している安藤もそうした「終わりなき旅」の再確認をしているのだろうと考えた。この丘陵地帯が、周辺地域でも指折りの観梅の名所に数えられるようになったと聞くと、着実に建築家の理念が共有されている手応えが確かめられる。

永遠は1年1年を積み上げることで現実のものとなる。建築は本来、完成すれば千年の命を求められる。だが、モダニズムはそのことを忘却して、不毛の空間を増殖してきた。その轍を踏むまいと安藤は考えている。外観は、安藤も認めるように多少なりとも経年の綻びを生じる。しかし、建築家が現代建築に持続的に関わり続け、その都度、的確な技術的対応を怠ることがなければ、来館者は綻びをある種の必然と受け止めてくれるのではないだろうか。古び、そしてほころびてはならないのは、まさに精神の矜恃なのだ。季節ごとに巡って来る梅の開花は、人間が陥りがちな怠惰への的確な叱咤激励と、これからも続く努力への餞(はなむけ)の役割を担ってくれるのである。

第4章「生き続ける近代建築」を目指して　145

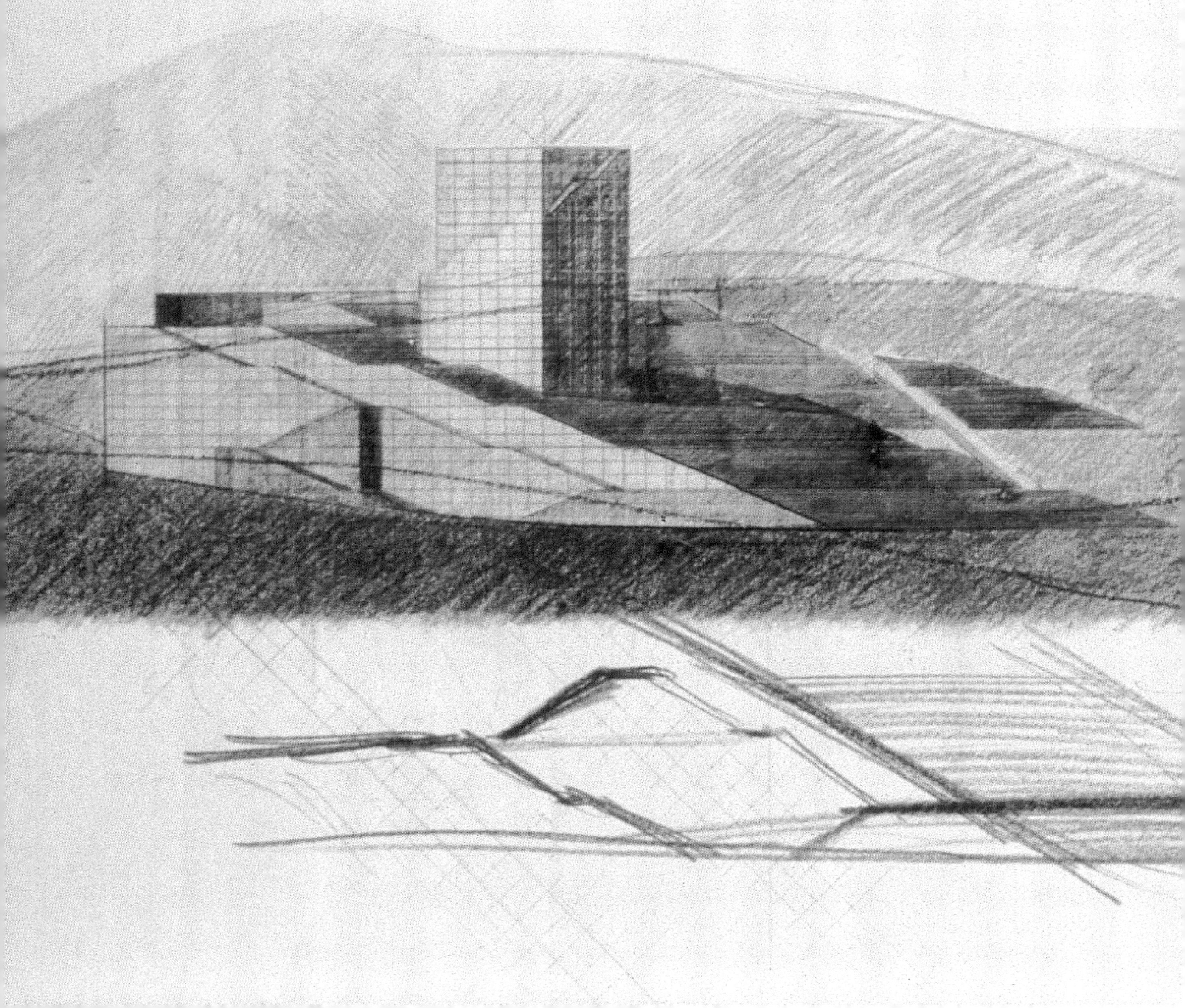

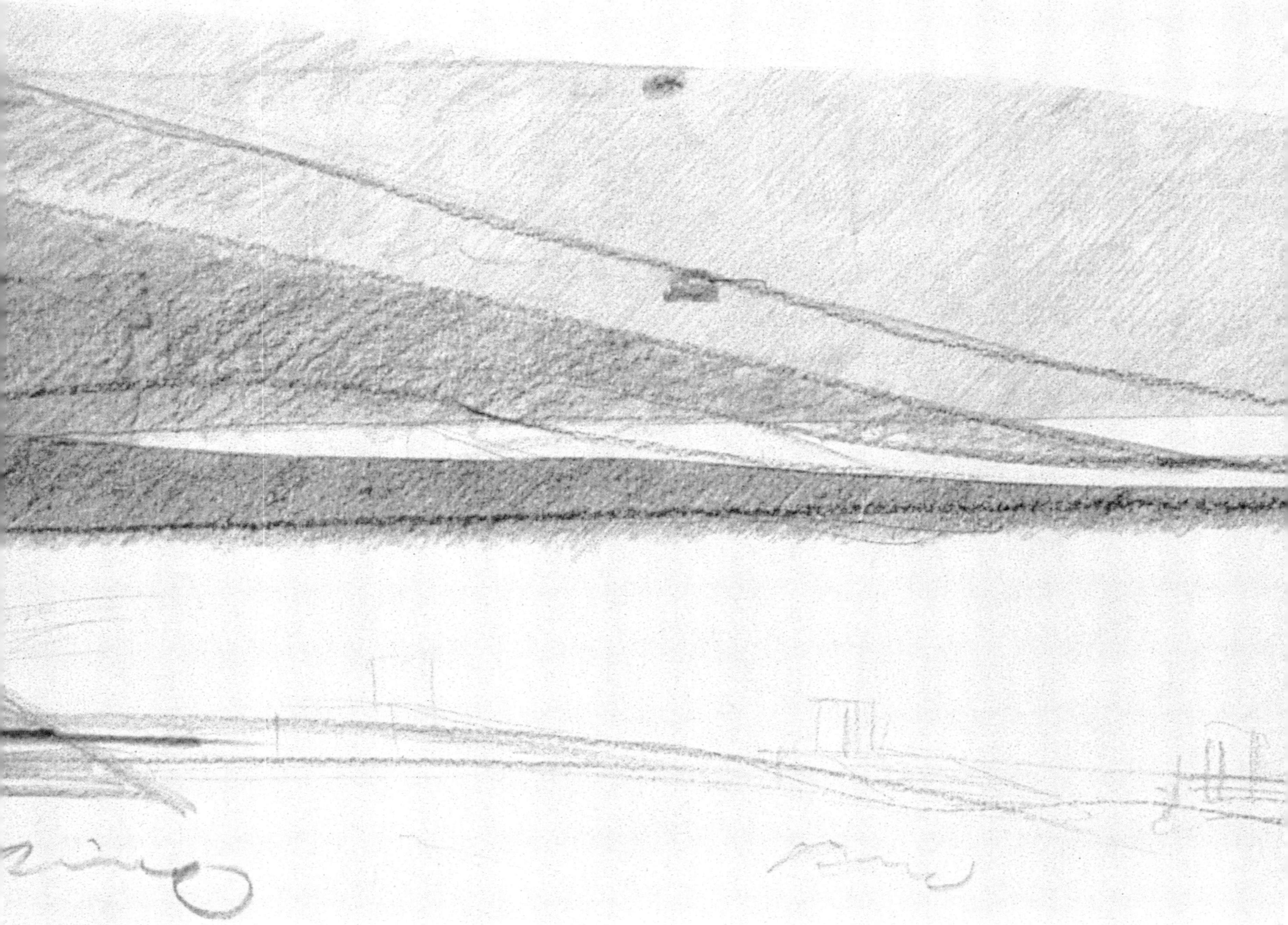

Succeeding a High Priest's Heritage

Ando's passion for the history and the land has further increased in the design of SAYAMAIKE HISTORICAL MUSEUM in 2001. Sayamaike is said to have been built here in Osakasayama for the purpose of irrigation in neighboring area in 616, a little after Ichisuka Kofun Gun was constructed. It has long brought good harvest in the area and thus become an important heritage that historical figures including Gyoki in Nara Period, Chogen in Kamakura Period, and Katsumoto Katagiri in Momoyama Period supervised the construction or reconstruction of the pond. Moreover, considering that Sayamaike is still used as an irrigation pond now, it is a valuable place where you can see the greatness of people's life in ancient times.

The biggest exhibition at this Museum is the "dam body" where the cross-section of the dam was cut out. Its cross-section, over 15 meters high and 60 meters wide, has geological layers that indicate the construction and reconstruction of the dam in different times. There are seven layers that you can closely examine the history from Asuka to Meiji, Taisho, and Showa Periods. With exhibitions not only the cut-out of dam body, but also findings during the excavation such as watershoots which prove maintenance works from time to time, this is a unique and interesting "civil engineering museum".

SAYAMAIKE HISTORICAL MUSEUM which collects and exhibits artifacts from such excavation work was designed by Ando with two concrete cuboids arranged at the angle of 70 degrees from outdoor colosseum. The biggest installation by Ando is the "water garden" which goes along the bigger concrete cuboid.

The water garden is situated below the level of the dam of Sayamaike and the water regularly flows down along the sidewalls of the garden, beautifully demonstrating a theme of the Museum, that is, the history of Sayamaike. The sound of water flowing down gets very loud, and walking along corridors on both sides of the water garden is a unique experience you can only get here at this Museum.

I was surprised to see the amount of water in the water garden, but I understood the reason as I walked along the Sayamaike until I reached to the actual floodgate at the opposite side of the dam.

The spillway, a structure used to release the water from a dam into a downstream conduit, is a small round concrete embankment, and the water flowing down from there makes loud sound. This is no secret at all, but I'm sure Ando felt vitality of Sayamaike from the sound that had been existed there for 1400 years. It is more understandable to see the shape of the bench placed at the center of the exterior of the Museum referred to the round shape of the spillway. This fact shows that Ando observed every detail of the dam in order to find the source of his design, rather than he designed the structure of the Museum based simply on his aesthetics.

Sayamaike dam stands higher than 18 meters above the ground level. You can only see the head of the structure that Ando designed behind the dam, since the Museum was constructed on a site that was one level lower, controlling the dominance of the architecture. I guess that Ando might want to design this Museum as another underground architecture. The idea is that the main feature is the dam itself and the exhibition facility is only for making such valuable resource widely known to the public.

大阪府立狭山池博物館　2001
sayamaike historical museum, osaka

1. 狭山池越しの外観
   Exterior appearance behind the Sayamaike
2. 水庭の落水
   Waterfall in the water garden
3. 堤体の展示
   Exhibition of a dam body

高僧の遺産を継ぐ

　安藤の歴史と風土への思いは「大阪府立狭山池博物館」（2001年）でさらに高まっていった。周囲の農地への灌漑を目的として「狭山池」が大阪狭山市の現地に築造されたのは616年ごろとされるから、「一須賀古墳群」より少しあとの時期ということになる。広域にわたり、実りをもたらした狭山池は、奈良時代には行基、鎌倉時代には重源が築造を指導し、桃山時代には片桐且元も改修に手を染めており、そうした歴史上の人物が関わってきた重要な遺産となっている。しかも、現在も灌漑池として機能している点では、上古のひとびとの営みの偉大さが確かめられる貴重な場でもある。

　この博物館の最大の展示物は、堤の断面をそのまま切り出した「堤体」だ。高さ15メートル、幅60メートルを超える断面は、各時代の築造、改修のあとを物語る地層となっている。地層は七層に及び、飛鳥時代から明治・大正・昭和の三代までの堤の履歴が眼前で確かめられる。切り出された「堤体」だけでなく、各時代の補修を裏付ける樋などの発掘品も展示され、類例をみない「土木博物館」として魅力的だ。

　それらの発掘成果を物語る遺物を収蔵展示するために安藤の設計した「狭山池博物館」は、二つのコンクリートの直方体の棟が、屋外の立体円形広場から70度の交差で配されている。ここで安藤が設営した最大の仕掛けは、大きなほうの直方体に沿って配した「水庭」だ。

　「水庭」は、狭山池の堤の高さからすれば掘り下げた位置にあり、定時になると両側の壁に沿って水が流れ落ち、池の歴史をテーマにした博物館ならではの光景が展開される。流れ落ちる水音はかなりの音量に達し、それを耳にしながら、「水庭」の両側の回廊を歩く体験はここでしか味わえないものとなっている。

　この「水庭」の水量には驚かされたが、狭山池の周囲を巡り、池の水面を挟んで向かい側にある実際の水門までたどりついたとき得心がいった。

　灌漑池として外部の水路に水を流す「洪水吐」は、円形の小さなコンクリートの堤になっていて、そこを池から下る水流は轟音を立てていた。種明かしというほどでもないが、安藤はその水音に1400年の歴史を超えて生き続ける狭山池の生命力を感じたに違いない。そのことは、この「洪水吐」の円形の堤の形が、博物館外構の中心に位置するベンチのシルエットに引用されているのを見れば、さらに納得がいくだろう。それは安藤が単に博物館の躯体を自らの美学で構築したのではなく、池の細部にまで目を光らせて造形の源を求めたことを物語る。

　ちなみに狭山池の堰堤の高さは18メートルを超えている。安藤による博物館の躯体は堰堤から頭を覗かせてはいるが、堤から一段下がったところにあり、建築としての自己主張を抑制している。安藤の気持ちを推し量るなら、ここも「地中の建築」にした

*Cherry Blossoms Bloom,
and Butterflies Fly along the Dam*

It is clear that Ando believed such idea by starting a civil movement to plant cherry trees along the dam since he designed the Museum. In fact, the area around the dam was simply barren with a few trees when Ando first visited. Therefore, he planted 1,000 cherry trees to begin with, and called the citizens to add planting 50 trees every year, which was successfully realized. It has been more than fifteen years since the completion of the Museum, and now nearly 2,000 cherry trees get in full bloom every spring and visitors enjoy the sight.

The question is how a modern architect contribute the succession of history. If you go classic, you can build a modern architecture which stands out enough to attract people to a forgotten historical site. However, there are always some constraints on location and budget. Besides, it is not favorable to have an architecture oddly stood out from the environment, especially in a historical site. The way Ando chose to go by the design of SAYAMAIKE HISTORICAL MUSEUM was not at all an easy way around as an architect. If you say the role of architect is to reach out to hearts of citizens, then he should be recognized well enough to fulfill his responsibility.

As you walk along the dam in anti-clockwise direction from the Museum, you will find a small forest, and a sign that reads "The Butterfly Garden". This is a place where children in the neighborhood raise Sasakia charonda, the national butterfly of Japan, and a variety of plants that bear flowers also grow here. 34 kinds of butterflies come to this garden spontaneously, and more than 16 kinds of butterflies has been born and raised here. It is the natural education using wonderful natural education materials, and this can only be done in the environment of Sayamaike with full of water and greenery. There will be nothing more brightening in the future of Sayamaike as the cultural heritage than having these children feel attached to this place.

I could see his face brightening up as he mentioned this. Not many architects in the world get so naturally involved in the architecture that they designed, and become a main force to create civil movements around their architectures. It may show that the modern architecture is being empowered to survive with the citizen for a thousand years, along with Ando being matured as an architect. CHIKATSU-ASUKA HISTORICAL MUSEUM and SAYAMAIKE HISTORICAL MUSEUM are both monumental for bringing another phase in Ando's work, that is, the phase of co-working with the citizen.

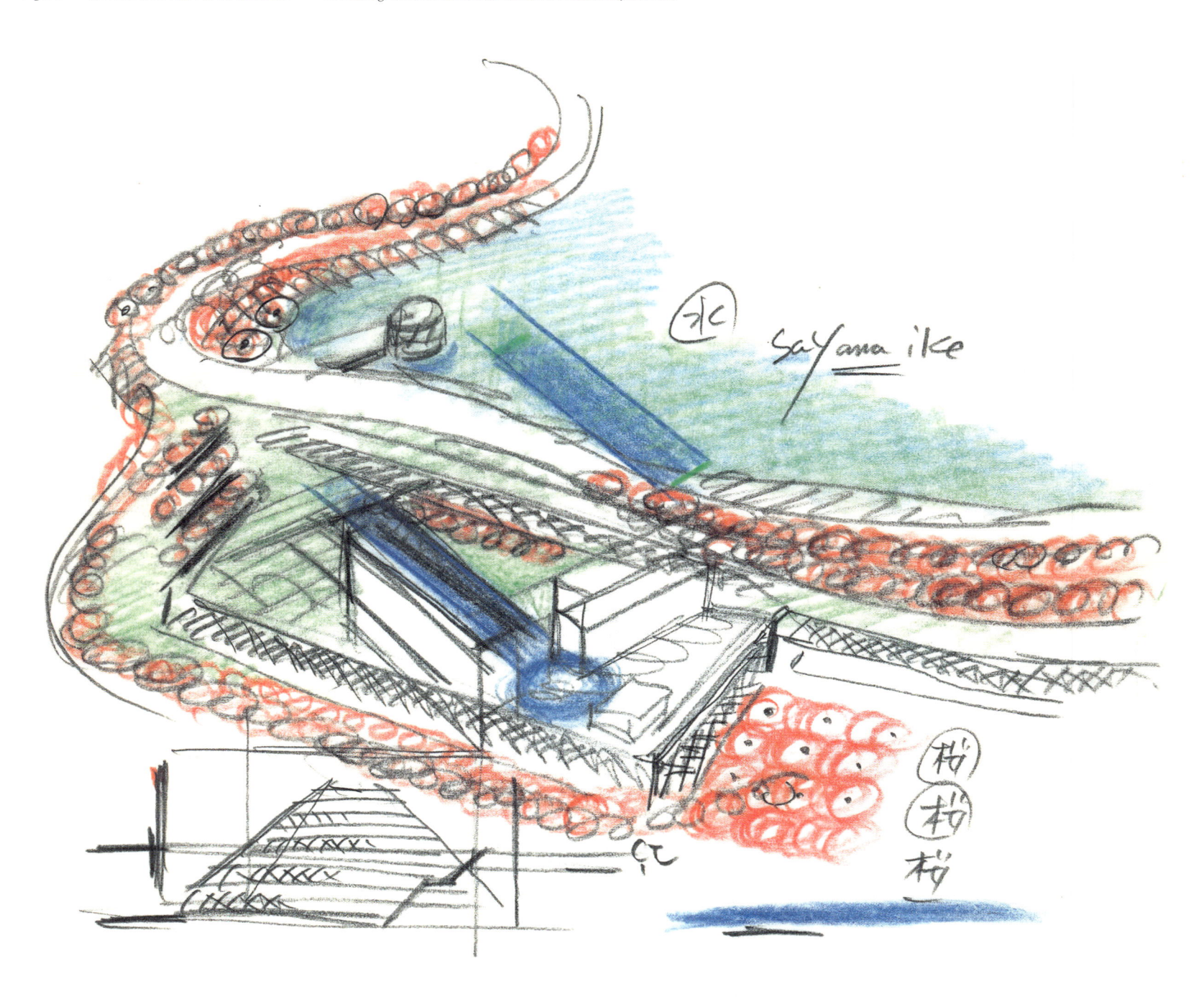

大阪府立狭山池博物館　2001
sayamaike historical museum, osaka

4.（前ページ）堤のサクラも描いたドローイング
(previous page) Drawing with cherry blossoms on the levee

かったのかもしれない。あくまでも主役は池そのものであって、展示施設は池という資産を広く知らしめるのが担うべき役割であるという考え方である。

堰堤に桜咲き、蝶が舞う

　その彼の考えは、博物館の設計を機に、堰堤に桜を植樹する市民運動をおこしたところに如実に示されているだろう。実は、安藤が初めて訪ねたとき、堰堤は樹木もまばらで殺風景きわまりない姿だったという。そこで安藤はひとまず1000本の桜を植樹し、以後、市民の手で毎年50本ずつ増やしていくことを呼びかけ、実現させた。完成から15年余り、今では2000本近い桜が春には満開になって来訪者の目を楽しませる。

　わたしは満開の桜の季節の賑わいを見たことがある。堤に数えきれないほどのひとびとが腰を下ろし、家族連れがにこやかに談笑する光景に接すると、身近にありながら、なかなか訪問の機会のなかった遺産が、安藤という建築家の営為によって、再び、関心の対象に復帰したことをとてもうれしく感じた。きっと行基さんも重源さんもこの姿を喜んでおられるに違いない。

　歴史の継承に現代建築家がどのように貢献できるか。もちろん、王道をいくなら、現代建築の施設が、忘れられた歴史の場にひとを呼ぶだけの突出したものになるにしくはない。しかし、立地にも、予算にも限りがあるし、歴史的な地であれば、建築だけが目立つのは望ましくない。安藤が「狭山池博物館」で選んだ道は、決して建築家として逃げを打ったわけではない。市民の心に働きかけるのが建築家の役割だとするのなら、安藤はその責任を十二分に全うしたと評価してよいだろう。

　博物館の位置から逆時計回りに堤のうえを歩いていくと、小さな森の存在に気づく。「蝶の森（バタフライガーデン）」という看板が掛かっている。ここは地元の子どもたちが国蝶オオムラサキを飼育している場所で、小さな森には花をつける植物が数多く植えられている。自然に集まる蝶も34種類を数え、この森で育って羽化した蝶も16種類に達している。見事な天然の素材を使った自然教育であり、水があり、緑のある狭山池だからこそできる試みだ。子どもたちにこの場への親しみを抱かせることほど、文化遺産としての狭山池の未来を開くものはない。

　そのことを語る安藤の表情は明るい。自身の設計した建築にこれほど自然体で関わり、その建築を起点にきっちりと市民を動かしている例は、世界広しといえどもそれほど多くはあるまい。それは建築家、安藤忠雄の成熟とともに、モダニズムの建築もまた市民とともに千年を生き抜く力をつけつつある姿なのかもしれない。「近つ飛鳥博物館」「狭山池博物館」の二つの作品は、安藤の作品に市民との協働という、「もうひとつ

The Brain of Ryotaro Shiba

While Ando's works became realized worldwide around 2000, he designed SHIBA RYOTARO MEMORIAL MUSEUM in 2001, about the same time he designed SAYAMAIKE HISTORICAL MUSEUM. By these works, he became conscious of the history and climate of Osaka stronger than ever before.

Ryotaro Shiba, a novelist who had his base for writing in Osaka, tried to express the nature of the Japanese after the modern times from history of world civilization point of view. One of his best-known works "Saka no Ue no Kumo" depicted how young people in Meiji Era such as Akiyama Yoshifuru and Saneyuki brothers, and Masaoka Shiki struggled to build the modern state rapidly after the Meiji Restoration. In the 21st century, the story won a great sympathy among the Japanese who struggle to establish their identities in the trend of globalization, and who want to know how the forerunners in Meiji Era challenged such issue.

What connected Shiba and Ando was their pride for Osaka. Ando favored urban density which was represented by Nagaya, residence for ordinary people. Shiba also liked hustle and bustle in Osaka, but he decided to own a house in order to store the collection of books and move to Tondabayashi, where he described "the east suburb that resembled Osaka in its vulgarity". When I visited the house, now the Memorial Museum, I saw yellow flowers of field mustards bloomed around the place, especially in front of the study room where Shiba used to write.

Shiba discovered that the area used to be a swamp, and turned into a cultivated field by the flood control work done in the Edo Period. It was also found out during the boring work that the construction site was a bottomless swamp several meters beneath the ground surface, so that, Shiba stated, the house was constructed on a concrete base that had sunk into the water. This episode of flood control work is interesting as it made me recall the Sayamaike and its irrigation facility, even though these two are far apart.

The residence was preserved and the Memorial Museum with concrete structure and curved glass wall was designed by Ando and constructed next to the residence. The most significant exhibition room in the Museum is the Library with huge bookshelves. It is a two-story open ceiling space with the basement and the first floor, and the both sides of walls are shelves with full of books by Shiba's collection. There are 20,000 books in total.

The shelves were precisely measured so that all books fit in perfectly, and spines of books consist of the curved wall. Meticulously finished bookshelves with books perfectly in order made me feel as if I peeked into Shiba's well-ordered brain. Tadao Ando is also a dedicated reader of books. He was an avid and enthusiastic reader in his youth, in order to satisfy the hunger for knowledge. Whenever someone recommended a good book, he usually followed the recommendation without doubt and read it to the end no matter how difficult it was. Knowledge obtained from those books has become his source of creation. Architecturizing the books was the ultimate way for Ando to express his respect to Shiba. This library with huge bookshelves is a tribute for the world of Shiba which was accumulated from tremendous amount of resources from all ages and cultures.

1

Chapter 4 In Pursuit for "Modern Architecture That Will Continue to Exist"

司馬遼太郎記念館　2001
shiba ryotaro memorial museum

1. 大書架の展示空間
   Exhibition space with huge bookshelves
2. 外観
   Exterior

の顔」をもたらした点において、記念碑的な意味をもっている。

司馬遼太郎の脳内

　2000年前後の安藤の作品の舞台は世界に広がるとともに、国内では「狭山池博物館」と同時期に「司馬遼太郎記念館」（2001年）も手がけ、大阪の歴史、風土をより強く自覚する方向にも向かっていった。世界を視野に入れながら、地に足のついた歴史文化的な文脈への意識の高まりは、建築家としてのスケールをより大きなものとした。それがまた世界を舞台とする創作にあたっての足元を、確かにしたのは間違いない。

　作家、司馬遼太郎は大阪に執筆の拠点を構え、近代以降の日本人の心性を世界文明史的な視点で見出そうとした。代表作『坂の上の雲』の秋山好古、秋山真之兄弟、正岡子規ら明治の若者が、明治維新後の急速な近代国家造営にどのように挑んだかは、21世紀のグローバル化のなかで、近代における日本人のたゆまぬ努力を再発見するという次元での共感を集めた。

　司馬と安藤を結びつけたものは大阪への自負だった。安藤は庶民が暮らす長屋に代表される都市的密集を好んだ。司馬もまた「大阪の雑鬧が好き」だったが、蔵書の収蔵のために「大阪の猥雑さに似た東郊」に居を求め、富田林の地に居宅を構えた。今は「記念館」となった居宅を訪ねると、司馬が執筆の場とした書斎の前などに菜の花の黄色が散りばめられていた。

　転居してきた司馬は、そこが「摂津の国」ではなく、「河内の国」であっことに多少の戸惑いを覚えたが、豪農の名残をとどめ、立派な日本家屋の集まる野趣あふれる農地の風景に惹かれるようになったという。

　一帯が江戸時代の治水によって出現した耕作地で、もとは沼だったことを司馬はつきとめている。このため居宅を新築するときにボーリングすると数メートル下が底なし沼になっていることがわかり、コンクリートの基礎を水中に沈めてそのうえに住宅が乗る構造とした経緯も司馬は明かしている。この治水工事の逸話は、距離は離れているが狭山池の灌漑機能との繋がりを連想させる点も興味深い。

　居宅部分はそのまま保存し、隣地にコンクリート打ち放しの躯体にガラスの曲面壁を持つ別棟の「記念館」が安藤の設計で建設された。記念館の最大の見せ場は大書架の「展示室」だ。1、2階と地下の三層になった吹き抜け空間の両側の壁が書架になっていて、司馬の蔵書がびっしりと収められている。その数は2万冊にのぼる。

　綿密に計算された奥行きに書物はきっちりと収まり、書物の背がそのまま曲面壁を構成している。精巧な仕上げの書架と相まって収蔵された書籍は、あたかも整理された

Modernism Surrounded by Field Mustards

It was February 12, 1996 when Shiba passed away. Since one of his novels was titled "Nano Hana no Oki", and he was also very fond of flowers of field mustards, the anniversary of his death is called "Nano Hana Ki (Anniversary of field mustard)". Every year on this day, the symposium is held, remembering his achievements and personality. Ando has appeared in this several times.

On March 3, 2012, after Ando's annual lecture was held at CHIKATSU-ASUKA HISTORICAL MUSEUM, Ando and I visited the SHIBA RYOTARO MEMORIAL MUSEUM and saw the library that Ando designed was covered with yellow flowers of field mustards. Along the pathway from the entrance to the library, as well as in the "New Garden" designed by Ando and built in 2010, there were a number of planters with beautiful yellow flowers placed orderly. In addition, there were a line of vases with yellow flowers inside the curved glass wall on the way to the library. Not only it originated from the anniversary of Shiba's death, but also it provided the celebrating atmosphere for coming spring.

There was more to that. The movement of Nano Hana Ki, in which people plant field mustards on the street, had expanded and firmly rooted among civil volunteers and schools, and the Museum played a central role for that. From the end of January to April, the street becomes full of yellow flowers grown by people in the city. I found it so favorable and even jealous while I enjoyed the view.

In the chapter of Kawachiji in Shiba's lifetime exertion "Travelling the old roads", there is a mention of Tondabayashi near CHIKATSU-ASUKA HISTORICAL MUSEUM. The author also referred to the theory of Masaaki Ueda, a historian, about the Kawachi Dynasty, which was ruled by Emperor Nintoku. This reminded me of the episode that Ando looked over the Naniwazu from the site of CHIKATSU-ASUKA HISTORICAL MUSEUM, as it got mixed up with the planting activity of plum trees that I just saw earlier at the Museum, and the field of yellow flowers in front of me. Standing next to me, Ando smiled and said, "isn't this wonderful?" as he look at people taking care of the flowers.

Design of architecture is not only the process of producing a structure, but Ando goes beyond that and always runs side by side with his own works while he keeps carefully considering the city, the nature, and the surrounding environment even after the completion of architecture. His sincere attitudes and his love of hometown will surely open the door of modernist architecture in the 21st century.

司馬遼太郎記念館　2001
shiba ryotaro memorial museum

3. ステンドグラスの壁
Stained glass wall
4. 庭の草花の見えるアプローチ
Approachway with garden views

司馬の脳内をのぞくかのような趣がある。安藤忠雄は読書家でもある。彼は青年時代に知識欲を満たすために書物を貪るように読んだ。知人に名書を奨められると必ずといってよいほど素直に従い、苦吟しながらも読み通した。書物から得た知識は、彼の創造の源泉となっている。書物そのものを「建築化」する選択は、司馬に対するなによりの敬愛の表現そのものだ。古今東西の資料を駆使して構築された司馬の世界への賛辞が、この大書架の展示室なのである。

竣工後、歳月を重ねて、書架の木製の棚も方立ても、経年変化による色付きが顕著で、そのことがますます司馬の蔵書の背の劣化と相まって一体化し、空間を引き締める役割を果たしている。

間違いなく、この大書架の空間は竣工当座よりも落ち着きを見せ、司馬と安藤の願った姿に近づいている。それを眺めながら、そこにも安藤が手がけるモダニズムの建築の熟成があると直感した。生前の司馬との強い結びつきがもたらす哀悼の気持ちが何年も生き続け、そのようなエージングとともに美の高まる空間を醸成したのだと確信した。

菜の花に包まれるモダニズム

司馬が亡くなったのは1996年2月12日。作品に『菜の花の沖』があり、また、当地の農地に咲く菜の花を好んだことから、命日を「菜の花忌」と呼び倣わしている。毎年、この日に司馬の業績、ひととなりを語るシンポジウムが開催され、安藤も何度か出演している。

2012年3月3日、桃の節句に安藤が「近つ飛鳥博物館」で講演した帰路、わたしは安藤とともに「司馬遼太郎記念館」を訪ねて、安藤の設計した資料館が黄色い菜の花に包まれている姿を見た。エントランスから資料館に続く足元のあちこちに鉢植えの菜の花が配され、安藤が2010年になって設営した「新庭」にも、植木鉢がずらりと置かれていた。展示室への誘導路となっているガラスの曲面壁の内側にも切り花の花瓶がびっしりと並び、命日に由来しながらも、近づく春を言祝ぐ祝祭の雰囲気にあふれていた。

いや、それだけではない。菜の花を一帯の街角に植える「菜の花忌運動」は、記念館という核になる施設の登場もあって、市民ボランティアや学校も参加して広がりを見せ、しっかりと根付いているのが確かめられた。1月末から4月の開花期に合わせて育てた菜の花が町を飾る風景は、とても好もしく、うらやましく思えた。

司馬遼太郎の生涯の労作『街道をゆく』の河内路の項には、「近つ飛鳥博物館」に近い富田林に言及がある。また、仁徳帝を頂点とする河内王朝のことを、歴史学者、上

司馬遼太郎記念館　2001
shiba ryotaro memorial museum

5. 記念館の前庭のイメージスケッチ
Image sketch of the greenery front yard of the memorial museum

田正昭の説を引くかたちで紹介している。安藤が「近つ飛鳥博物館」の敷地に立って難波津を遠望した話がそこに重なり、さっき見た「近つ飛鳥博物館」の梅林の植樹活動と、眼前の菜の花の群れが交錯した。一緒にたたずんでいた安藤が甲斐甲斐しく菜の花を整える市民の姿を見ながら「いいでしょ、これは」と目を細めていた。

　建築の設計を構造物を生み出す過程にとどめず、完成後も町や自然など周辺環境としっかり関わりながら、自作と併走を続けていく。安藤の地元への愛を忘れない真摯な姿勢が、モダニズムの建築の21世紀を拓いていく手応えを感じた。

第5章 〈無〉は魂の安らぎをもたらす
己の精神と向き合う宗教施設

Chapter 5　'Nil' Brings Repose of Soul
Religious Facilities to Face Own Spirit

シトー会の絶対空間

　南仏プロヴァンスのラベンダーの野で知られるセナンクに中世から生き続ける「ノートル・ダム・ドゥ・セナンク修道院」。その姿こそが、安藤の考える「聖なる空間」であり、彼の考える教会の原型がそこにあるのだという。12世紀半ばに建設されたロマネスクの建築は、回廊形式の中庭を囲うクロイスターと聖堂が接した配置をとる。若き日にここを訪れた安藤は、谷あいの立地、粗削りの石材のこの修道院に、近代建築家の手からこぼれ落ち、現代において忘れ去られた「聖なる空間」を見出した。

　原始修道制への回帰を目指したシトー会の修道院は、辺鄙な山里に立地を求め、宗教者たちは自ら進んで世俗からの隔離をはかった。そこに立ち合った安藤は「浄化」の強い意志を感じた。厳しい戒律を守る毎日を送ることで、肉体を浄化し、精神を高めることを目指したと見なすのである。

　空間がそれをどう体現したのか。安藤は粗削りの石材が積まれたぶ厚い壁に穿たれた小さな窓から聖堂内に射し込む光こそが、空間の聖性演出のなによりの主役だと考えた。そして、このセナンクの光を制御した空間こそが、彼の考える教会建築の原形となり、周囲の世俗と距離を置き高い密度を持つ「聖なる空間」と考えるようになった。

　この空間体験を、彼が最初に作品として実現したのは「六甲の教会」（1986年）だった。安藤は施主である神戸の老舗ホテル「六甲オリエンタルホテル」から、このウェディング・チャーチの設計依頼を受けたとき、セナンクでの体験を実現する好機ととらえ、絶対純粋の「浄化空間」の実現を試みた。

　港町神戸の背後にそびえる六甲山頂に位置するホテルの敷地内に独立して設計された建築の美しさは際立っていた。緑の絨毯のような芝生のうえに、安藤の完璧なプロ

The Cistercian and Absolute Space

Notre-Dame de Senanque was founded in the Middle Ages and is still used as a Cistercian abbey in Provence, southern France. The abbey is also well-known for its lavender fields. In Ando's opinion, the Senanque Abbey is his ideal "sacred space" as well as the genuine form of church. This Romanesque architecture was constructed in the mid-12th century, with the cloister around the inner courtyard and the church adjoined to it. Young Ando visited here, and discovered the "sacred space" as if it had fallen from a hand of a modern architect and left forgotten in the modern world, in this crude stone abbey in a valley.

The Cistercian advocated a return to the original monastic practices so that they built abbeys in remote villages and monks were willing to withdraw themselves from the world. Ando witnessed their way of living and felt their strong determination for purification. It is considered that living a life with strict rules will purify the body and enhance the spirit.

How did the space embody the purification? Ando thought that the light coming through small windows on crude and thick stone walls was the main feature for creating sacred atmosphere in the space. The Senanque Abbey where the amount of light was controlled was, Ando thought, the genuine form of church architecture and the truly "sacred space" that was highly dense and remote from the world.

The first project that he actually reflected his experience at the Senanque Abbey into the design was CHAPEL ON MT. ROKKO in 1986. When he had an offer to design a wedding chapel from Rokko Oriental Hotel, one of the oldest hotels in Kobe, he thought it was a good opportunity to put his experience at the Senanque into practice and tried to create a purifying space with absolute genuineness.

The hotel was situated on top of Mt. Rokko, looking down the port city of Kobe in front. The chapel was designed to be independent from other facilities in the hotel, and it was strikingly beautiful. On green velvety lawn, perfectly proportioned concrete structure was laid down beautifully by Ando. The main structure of the chapel was 6.5 meters wide by 13 meters deep by 6.5 meters high, and in Ando's drawing, a circle 6.5 meters in diameter (a sphere in three dimensions) inscribed in the main structure. You can see from the drawing that these are the basis of dimension in each part. The glassed colonnade leading to the chapel and concrete walls that enclose the architecture were determined where to be placed by drawing a 6.5 meters circular arc and expanding it to outdoor.

The tower is 13 meters above the ground, being integrated with the main structure of the chapel. It means that the tower is twice the size of the diameter of the chapel's inscribed circle. The idea of drawing circular arcs is similar to the idea of "Regulating Lines" espoused by Le Corbusier. He claimed that structures of facades in historical architectures, Notre-Dame Cathedral in Paris for example, could be understood as systematic layers of geometrical figures by drawing inscribed circles. According to the concept of Regulating Lines, the great Gothic Cathedral and Ando's little chapel can be described as architectures based on the same genealogy of aesthetics.

六甲の教会　1986
chapel on mt.rokko

1. 柱廊が聖堂に延びる
   Colonnade extending to the church building
2. 柱廊の内部
   Inside of the colonnade
3. 聖堂のインテリア
   Interior of the church

ポーションのコンクリートの躯体が美しい姿態を横たえていた。礼拝堂の本体は、間口6.5メートル、奥行き13メートル、高さ6.5メートルで、安藤の作図には、本体に内接する直径6.5メートルの円（三次元立体としては球体）が描かれ、それが各部の寸法の基になっていることがわかる。礼拝堂に参列者を導く回廊としてのガラス張りの「コロナード」、建物を囲うコンクリートの塀、それらの位置は、6.5メートル円弧を屋外にも拡張して描くことによって決定されていった。

　安藤は密集地にコンクリートボックスの小住宅を置くとき、「建築家のキャンバスは白くはない」と綴ったが、この「六甲の教会」では、芝生の緑に覆われた敷地は、求めようのなかった純白のそれだったといってよい。まさに「浄化」にふさわしいキャンバスがここでは用意されたのである。

　礼拝堂本体と一体となった塔の高さは地表面から13メートル。つまり、内接円の直径の2倍になっている。この図面に円弧を描くのは、ル・コルビュジエが歴史的な名建築、例えばパリのノートルダム大聖堂のファサードの構成が、内接円を描くと、幾何図形の体系的な積み重ねであることを解明しうるとした「規整線」の発想に通じている。ゴシックの大聖堂と安藤の小さな礼拝堂が、同じ美の系譜に則っていると考えることができる。

　ル・コルビュジエが代表作のひとつ「ラ・トゥーレット修道院」の設計にあたり、やはり南仏プロヴァンスに残る、シトー会の「ル・トロネ修道院」を参考にしたのは建築界では知られている。ル・トロネは、建設時期もセナンクと重なり、両者にシルヴァカンス修道院を加えて「プロヴァンスの三姉妹」と称される教会建築である。また安藤がル・コルビュジエに心酔して建築家を目指したこともよく知られている。セナンクの体験を「聖なる空間」の起点と語る安藤は、その意味では思慕するル・コルビュジエへのオマージュとして「六甲の教会」を設計したと見なせるだろう。

「水の教会」、抽象化された自然

　「聖なる空間」をいわば宗教とは一線を画して、絶対美の建築として追究する安藤の試みは、1988年完成の「水の教会」（北海道勇払郡占冠村）で次なる次元に進んだ。アルファリゾート・トマムのウェディング・チャーチとして登場した「水の教会」において、安藤は日本らしい「縁側」という発想を持ち出した。

　ここでは参列者は安藤の設えた人工池に面した屋外のテラスに腰掛けて、池のなかにそびえる鉄骨の十字架に向き合うことになる。このテラスは背後の礼拝堂から池に向かって延びる配置となっている。安藤は、これを日本の伝統的な住宅になぞらえて縁側

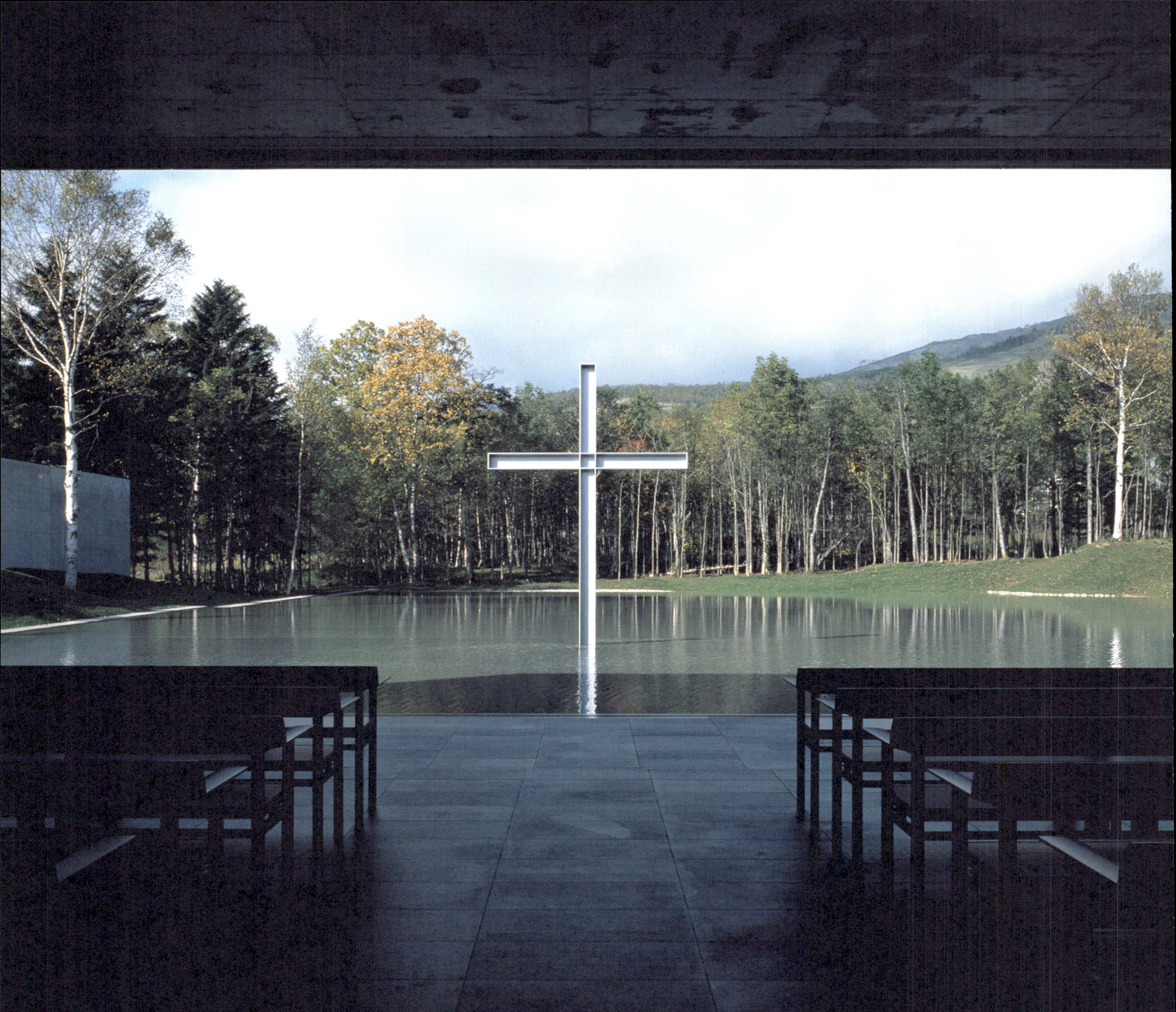

水の教会　1988
church on the water

1. （前ページ）水上に立つ十字架に向き合う
(previous page) View of the cross on the water

と表現する。内なる空間の延長線上にある半屋外の縁側から屋外の自然と向き合う姿を、縁側に準えたのである。

　この「水の教会」において「聖なる空間」への意識は、安藤の内面において、ますます極まっていった。礼拝堂本体は、一辺が10メートルと15メートルの二つの正方形を平面形とし、それは人工池とともに、敷地の周囲に巡らせたコンクリートの壁によって囲い込まれている。人工池の深さは、わずかな風でもさざ波が立ちやすいように決められた。自然はそこで安藤の手になる造営物で切り取られ、参列者はそれに正対する空間構成となっている。自然と一体化することで参列者は自身の内面と向き合うと安藤は述べている。その自然は、季節の変化、1日の時間の流れのなかで、さまざまな移ろいの表情を示し、ひとの感情に作用していく。

　ここでもまた北海道の広大な自然が空間の聖性を保証したのである。視界のなかに、他の人工物が入って来ない、日本では稀に見る立地。自然は、都市のなかのコンクリートボックスの住宅に引き入れられるような、ある意味、危うい存在ではなく、人工物を飲み込むかのような自由奔放な存在となって参列者の前にある。安藤は自分自身にとっての「聖なる空間」とはなにかをその環境で突き詰めていった。彼の言葉を借りるなら、西欧世界の「聖なる空間」は超越的であるが、自分にとってのそれは自然との関わりに見出されると記している。

　しかし、八百万の神が自然のなかに存在するといった日本古来の汎神論、アミニズム論ではなく、安藤は自らが切り取った「人工的な自然」、建築化された自然と向き合う場こそが、「聖なる空間」だという論を展開している。そして、それはあるがままの自然を「抽象化」することだと、ひとまず結論づける。自然を人為的に切り取り、抽象化したとき、「聖なる空間」の欠かさざる要件が成立するという発想である。

　これは「小篠邸」に関して、海外の評者から持ち出された「クリティカル・リージョナリズム」と呼応するものといってよい。普遍的な存在としての自然と、モダニズムの表現言語を、時空を超えて結びつける安藤の資質に対する賛辞として「クリティカル・リージョナリズム」があるとすれば、それはまさにこの「水の教会」において発展継承されていったと考えられるだろう。

　「六甲の教会」は六甲オリエンタルホテルの廃業により、残念ながら閉鎖されたままになったが、「水の教会」は星野リゾートが経営を継承し、ウェディング・チャーチとして現在も、この北限のリゾートのひとつのセールスポイントであり続けている。いや、安藤にとって、そうした世俗はもとより関心の対象ではなく、これらの施設は、まさに「聖なる空間」探究の場として、自身の建築観を深める舞台と考え、純粋な気持ちで創作に臨んだのである。その気概があってこそ、「水の教会」は時代の変化をものともせず、生き延びているのだろう。

Besides, it is known in the architecture community that Le Corbusier referred to "Le Thoronet Abbey", another Cistercian abbey in Provence, southern France, when he designed one of his major works "Sainte Marie de La Tourette". Le Thoronet Abbey was constructed about the same time as the Senanque Abbey, and together with Silvacane Abbey, these three church architectures are known as the "three sisters of Provence". It is also a well-known fact that Ando became an architect because he sincerely admired Le Corbusier. Ando said that his experience at the Senanque was the origin of what he considered as the "sacred space". In that sense, it is reasonable to say that he designed the Chapel on Mt. Rokko as an homage to his respected Le Corbusier.

Church on the Water:
Abstracted Nature

Ando pursued the "sacred space" as the architecture of absolute beauty, rather than a religious facility. In 1988, he took his pursuit a step further by the completion of the Chapel on the Water in Shimukappu, Yufutsu, Hokkaido. The Church on the Water was made as a wedding chapel at former Alpha Resort Tomamu, and Ando came up with the idea of engawa (Japanese style veranda) for its design.

In this chapel, guests may sit on benches at the terrace, facing an artificial pond and the iron cross standing in the water. This terrace is situated next to the chapel at the back and extends towards the pond. Ando called it engawa, as he used the analogy of a Japanese traditional house. The terrace of the church is a semi-outdoor space and extended from the inner space, which is similar to engawa. From there, you can interact with the nature outside.

By designing the Church on the Water, Ando had become even more conscious about the "sacred space". The main structure of the chapel consists of 2 squares with 10 meters and 15 meters on sides respectively to make a planar shape, and together with the artificial pond, is fully surrounded by concrete walls. The depth of artificial pond was determined to be at the level that the water ripples easily with a little breeze. The nature was cut out by structures designed by Ando, and the space composition of the chapel provides guests no choice but to face to it. Ando commented that guests would face to their inner selves when they felt united with the nature. And the nature shows various expressions depending on the change of seasons and the time of a day, which affects human emotions.

It was the vast nature of Hokkaido that assured the sacredness of this place. There are no other artificial objects in sight here. A very rare site in Japan. Borrowing his words, he wrote that the "sacred space" in Western Europe is transcendent while, for him, it could be discovered in relation to the nature.

However, it is not Japanese ancient pantheism or animism that Ando believed, in which yaoyorozu no kami (eight million deities) reside in nature. Instead, he argued that the place he could face to the "artificial nature" that he cut out himself, or architecturized nature was the "sacred space". He concluded that it was about the "abstraction" of nature as it was. The idea is that essential requirements of the "sacred space" will come into effect when a person artificially cuts out the nature and makes an abstract from it.

水の教会　1988
church on the water

2. 自然を囲いとる壁
    Walls enframing nature
3. 人工照明で十字架が浮かびあがる
    Cross lit up by artificial lighting
4. 水に面する聖堂
    Church facing water
5. コンクリートと緑の対比
    Contrast between concrete and green

第5章　〈無〉は魂の安らぎをもたらす

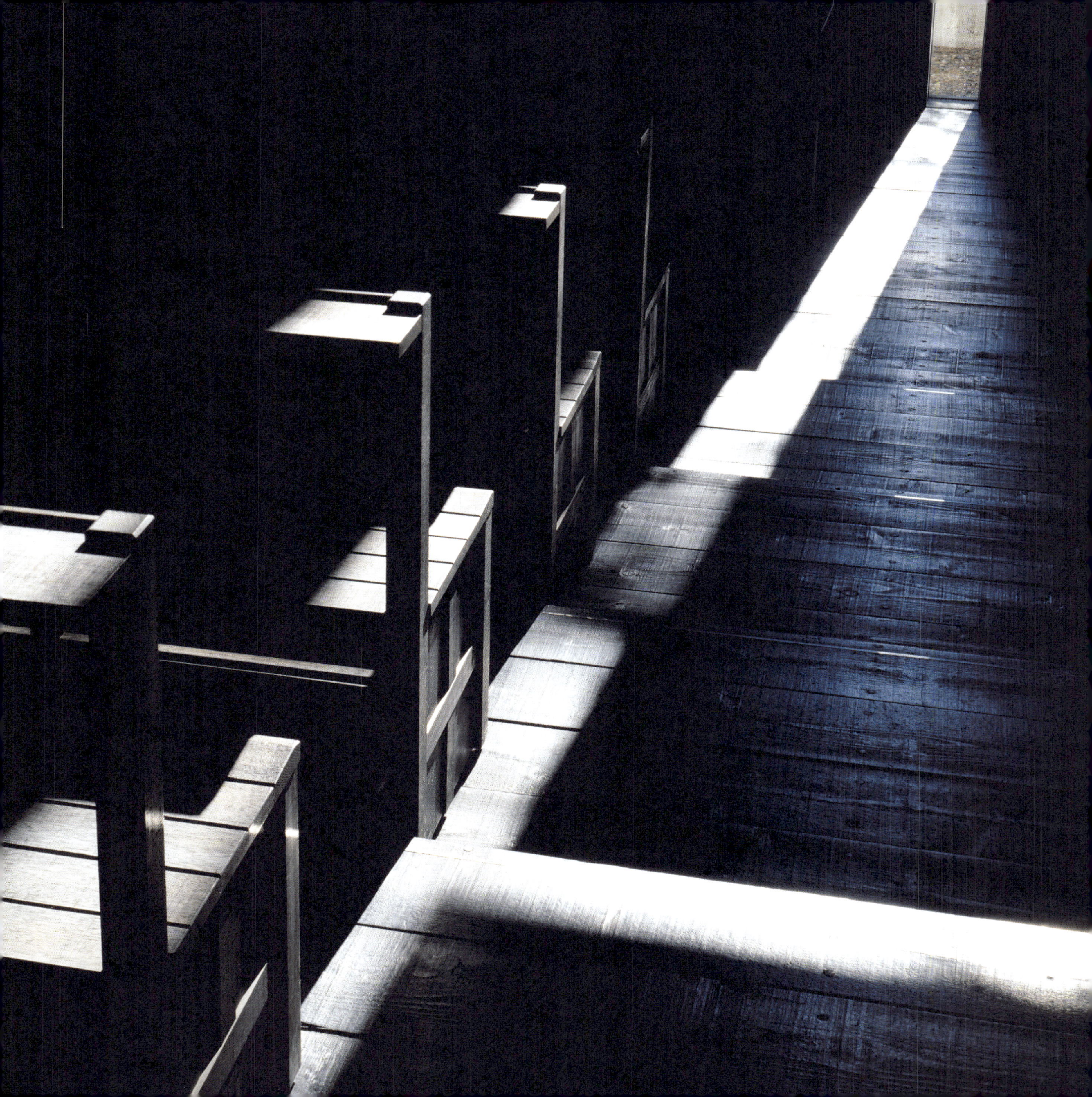

光の教会　1989
church of the light

1. (前ページ) 足場板の床に自然光が射す
   (previous page) Natural light on floor boards
2. 外壁に切られた十字のスリット
   Cross-shaped slit on an exterior wall

自然を「光」に凝縮する

　安藤は「六甲の教会」を「風の教会」とも呼んだ。六甲山上を吹きわたる風を踏まえてのことだ。「水の教会」はその名の通り、人工池に面した北海道の大自然のなかの建築のあり方の反映だった。ここまで見て来たように、彼の内面において「聖なる空間」を突き詰める創作意欲は作品を追って高まりを見せ、「三部作」と称されるなかでの最後の作品「光の教会」(1989年)において、自然の要素を「光」に限定することによって、セナンクの体験に始まる一連の創作の集大成がなった。

　大阪府茨木市の住宅街のなかに「光の教会」は立っている。日本基督教団茨木春日丘教会が正式の名称である。安藤がこの教会の依頼を受けたとき、信者からの寄進に頼る教会ゆえに2500万円しか予算がなく、安藤は「壁だけで屋根のない聖堂」を覚悟したともいう。それでも新しい聖堂を求める信者の努力と建設会社の熱意によって、安藤の代表作のひとつとなる教会建築が実現した。

　建物の本体は、図化すると、内側に直径5.9メートルの球体が3個連なって内接する寸法に収められた。この直方体に15度の急角度で屋外から切れ込む独立壁が設えられ、来訪者はその独立壁の切れ込みから礼拝堂の奥の部分にアプローチする動線になっている。正面には、十字のスリットを穿たれたコンクリートの壁が屹立し、そのスリットを通した「光の十字」が側壁にかすかな光を放ちながら出現する。

　それは自然の要素の建築化、抽象化に他ならない。六甲山上や北海道のような開放的な自然ではなく、閑静な住宅地のなかでやっと知覚できるほどの微かな自然が、十字の形で礼拝堂に立ち現れ、信者たちに働きかけるのである。コンクリートは空間を囲い込み、内部はほとんど闇に近い。そこに光が十字の形で射し込むとき、ひとびとは空間の聖性を実感しうるのではないかと安藤は考える。信仰の象徴であるところの十字架が、自然の極限の要素である光そのものであることの意味は大きい。そして、それは安藤のいう建築によって自然が抽象化、人工化された結果だということを忘れてはならないだろう。

　安藤は光が空間に緊張をもたらすことを期待する。それこそがセナンクで体感した「浄化の空間」に通じるという思考である。そして、この「浄化」は、予算の事情ゆえに、礼拝堂内部の床や家具に、足場板が活用されたことによっても強く印象づけられる。

　この教会の建設が進められたとき、日本は「土地バブル」の熱狂のなかにあった。当時、安藤は建築と経済合理性の関係について深い憂慮を抱いていた。建築が、ヴァルター・ベンヤミンのいうように「空間の総商品化」にさらされ、そのことに違和感を覚えないバブル期の社会のありかたと逆行するかのように、「光の教会」は出現したのである。コストに基づく経済効率ではなく、空間とその肌触りこそが建築を決めるという発

Condensation of Nature into the Light

The CHAPEL ON MT. ROKKO was also called by Ando the CHAPEL OF THE WIND. That was because the wind blowing over Mt. Rokko. The CHURCH ON THE WATER is, as the name suggests, the architecture with an artificial pond in the vast nature of Hokkaido. As shown earlier, Ando's creative urge for pursuing the "sacred space" had increased over his career, and the pursuit was completed by the design of the CHURCH OF THE LIGHT (1989), the last work of his trilogy in church architecture. Since his experience at the Senanque, he designed a series of church architectures, and in the CHURCH OF THE LIGHT, he chose to use the "light" as the only element of the nature.

The CHURCH OF THE LIGHT was constructed in a residential area in Ibaraki, Osaka. The official name of the Church is the Ibaraki Kasugaoka Church, United Church of Christ in Japan. When Ando was offered to design this church, he was prepared to build a church "with walls and no roof", since the budget was only 25 million yen, all from donations by followers. However, the followers' efforts and the constructor's enthusiasm to build a new church, the project successfully realized and this church also became one of Ando's major works.

In the drawing, the main structure was within the size that three spheres 5.9 meters in diameter would be successively inscribed. This cuboid has a freestanding wall which has been inserted from outside at the sharp angle of 15 degrees, and visitors will approach towards the back of the church from the slit of this freestanding wall. At front, a concrete wall with a crossed slit rises, and the light through the slit comes in and a cross shaped light appears on the sidewall.

It is indeed the architecturization and abstraction of the natural element. It is not the nature as open as the one in Mt. Rokko or Hokkaido, but the nature that can only be felt slightly in a quiet residential area, which appears in the form of the cross, a religious icon, in front of the followers. The space is enclosed by concrete walls and thus it is almost dark inside. When the cross shaped light comes through into the dark, Ando believes that people can feel the sacredness of the space. It means significantly that the cross as the symbol of religious belief is made from the light, that is, an ultimate element of the nature. We should not also forget, as Ando described, that it has been achieved as a result of abstraction and artificialization of the nature by means of architecture.

He expects the light to bring tension into the space. That is what he believes to create the "space of purification" which he experienced at the Senanque. In the case of the CHURCH OF THE LIGHT, the "purification" was further enhanced by using scaffold planks for its floor and furniture, due to the limited budget.

When this church was under construction, Japan was in the middle of the land bubble fever. Ando was having deep concern about the relationship between the architecture and the economic rationality. As Walter Benjamin stated, the architecture was exposed to "the commercialization of every space", and the CHURCH OF THE LIGHT appeared in such time as if it regressed the trend of the bubble society which didn't question such commercialization. Ando never conform such exhilarating trend, and held onto the idea that the architecture should not be evaluated by its economic efficiency based on the cost, but be evaluated by the space and its texture.

光の教会　1989
church of the light

3. 自然光の十字架
   Cross formed by natural light
4. 十字架の映り込み
   Reflection of the cross
5. 平面のドローイング
   Drawing of the plan

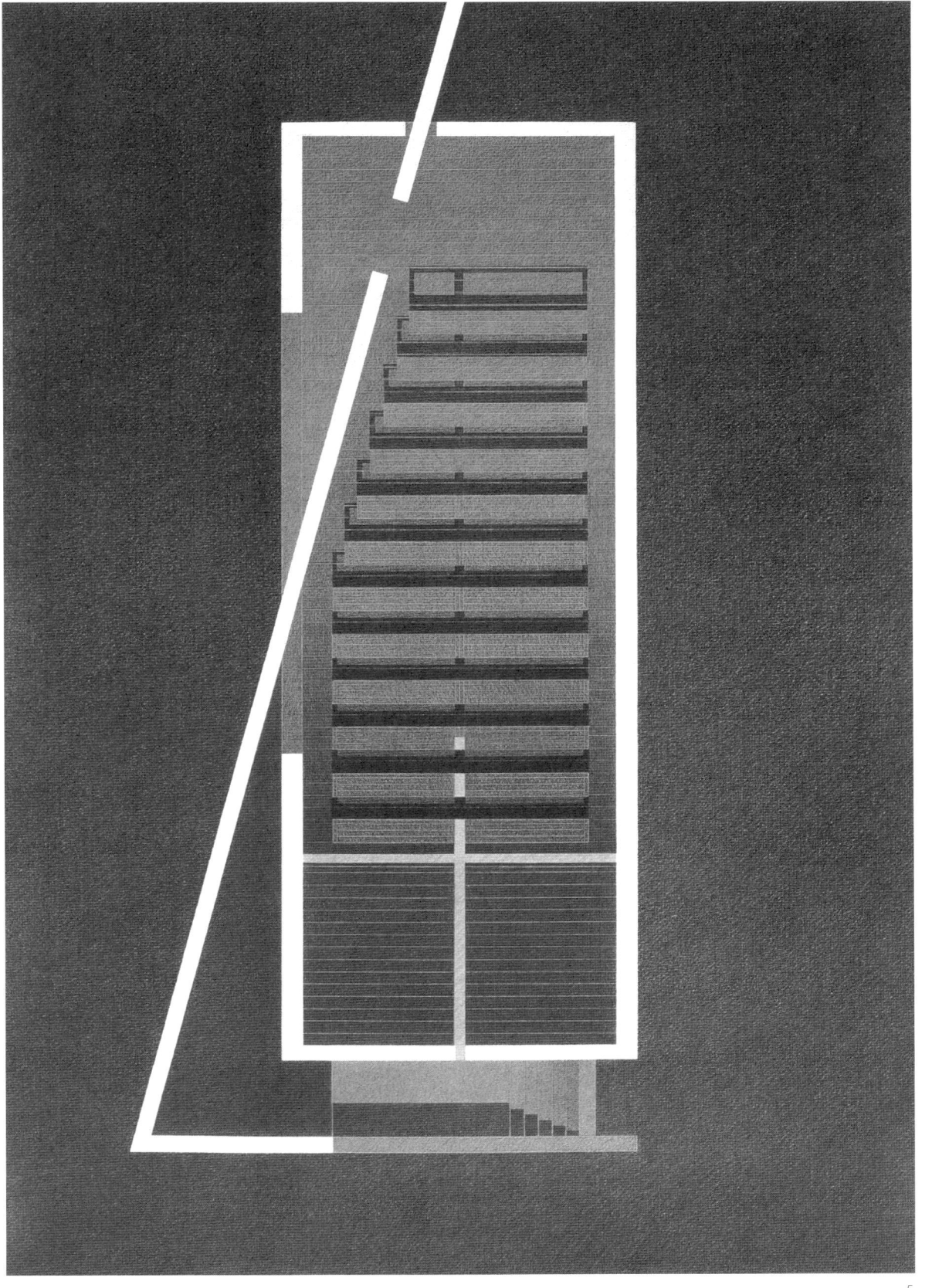

The reason why the CHURCH OF THE LIGHT could become one of his representative works seems to be the result of Ando's step-by-step pursuit in his "sacred space". It was getting matured through the previous two works. The Church represents a perfect unification of the "sacred space" and the principle of modernism. The modernism has been nothing else but "the aesthetic of poverty" in which the means of expression was limited, and it was originally the concept of creating an ultimate space for the socially vulnerable such as labors by eliminating every affectation. Undoubtedly, we witnessed that Ando's architecture had reached the far north of modernism beyond the limited concept of the "critical regionalism".

CHURCH IN HIROO (21st Century Christ Church), built in 2014, is located in a densely populated area within the JR Yamanote Line in Tokyo. From the main street, you can only see a concrete wall that is a side of isosceles triangle with a sharp angle, a distinctive shape of this church. On the walls, there are windows in the shape of right triangle being upside down, and a pure white cross appears by lighting-up at night. The light comes in effectively from a frosted window at the apex of triangle on the left end of the wall.

Going into the chapel, you see the walls on both sides, floor, and benches for followers to sit are all made by solid wood, and only the ceiling is made by concrete. Different from Ando's previous churches which were mostly made by concrete, it provides a feeling of comfort.

From the window at the apex of triangle, the natural light is filtered through a slit. The light is so bright that creates a band of light on the floor and the ceiling, and the followers get amazed by it. Two windows with the shape of upside-down right triangle are placed symmetrically on both sides of the walls, and the chapel is filled with light that is filtered through these frosted glasses. The floor at the tip of the triangle is made of glass, so that the band of light reaches to the baptistery in the basement directly underneath.

The major constraint on constructing this church was to have a limited space. According to Ando's architectural view, constraints are indeed the parents of aesthetic in his architecture. Taking advantage of the site limitation, he designed a layer of chapels on the ground floor and the basement and allowed the band of light from the slit to come in. The light is blight enough to directly appeal for people on the ground floor, while it is filtered by the glass floor and controlled to be thrown into the basin that is used for baptism at traditional churches. You can see the architect's true worth in his full control over the light in such a limited space.

広尾の教会　2014
church in hiroo

1. 鋭角の三角形の頂点に十字架
   Cross at a sharp triangular end
2. 外壁のガラス壁
   Exterior glass wall
3. ガラス床は地下空間のトップライト
   Glass floor serving as a skylight for the underground spaces

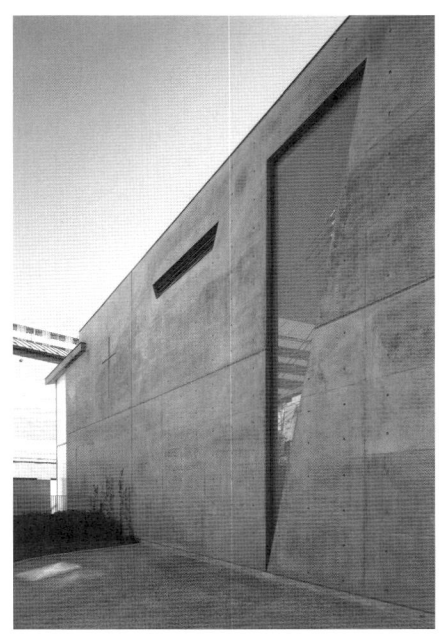

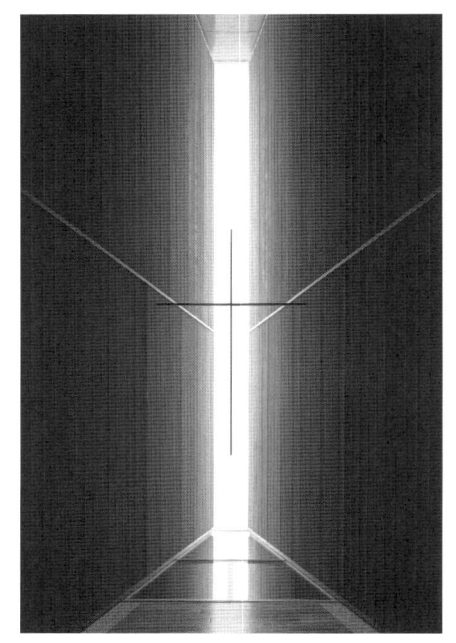

想を、安藤は浮かれがちな世相に流されず、堅持し続けた。それは彼が長屋の再生に始まる大阪の庶民の小住宅を数多く手がけ、その一方でコスト志向を超えた都市に貢献する商業施設の空間の案出に余念がなかったことと深く関係している。

「光の教会」を作品録のなかに刻印できたのは、安藤が前二作において、自身の考える「聖なる空間」の探究を、段階を追って熟成させていった成果といってよい。それは創作における安藤の緊張感のなせる業なのだと、わたしは受けとめている。多くのひとびとが、この「光の教会」の完成に祝福を送り、海外からやってきた芸術の関係者からも訪問の希望が重なった。「聖なる空間」とモダニズムの本義そのものが、ここで見事な合体を示した。モダニズムは、表現の手段を限定した「貧困の美学」であり、元来、虚飾を排して労働者ら社会のなかの弱者のための極限の空間を構築する発想に他ならなかった。「クリティカル・リージョナリズム」という限定的な概念を超越したモダニズムの極北に安藤の建築が到達した姿を、わたしたちは目の当たりにした。純文学という用語に倣うなら、それはまさに純化された建築の極限の姿だった。

「広尾の教会（21世紀キリスト教会）」（2014年）は、東京の山手線内の密集地に立地している。表通り側からは、この教会の特徴である鋭角の頂点を持つ二等辺三角形の一辺を占めるコンクリート打ち放しの壁しか見えない。壁には上下を逆さにした直角三角形の窓がうがたれ、夜には、純白の十字架が浮き上がるライトアップの仕掛けも凝らしてある。壁の左端で三角形の頂点の位置にはめ込まれたすりガラスの窓からは、堂内に印象的な光がもたらされる。

礼拝堂内に進むと、天井はコンクリート打ち放しだが、両側の壁も床も、信者の座るベンチも無垢の木材で構成される。それ以前のコンクリート打ち放しの安藤の教会とは異なる、温かな空間が心地よい。

三角形の頂点に位置するガラス窓からは、自然光がスリットによって絞り込まれて射し込む。その強い光は、床と天井にも光の帯を生み出し、信者の目を驚かせる。逆さ直角三角形の窓が両側の壁の対称の位置に配され、そのすりガラスで濾過された光が淡く堂内を潤していく。三角形の先端の足元はガラスの床になっていて、自然光の帯は、真下の地下階に配した小礼拝堂にももたらされ、地下の床にうがたれた洗礼槽まで届けられる。

この教会での一番の制約は土地の狭さであった。安藤の建築観に従うなら、彼の建築においては、制約こそが一番の美の生みの親である。敷地の制約を逆手にとり、礼拝堂を地上階と地下階で重ね合わせ、そこに強烈なスリットからの光を地上階では目に直接訴えかけるように印象的にあしらった。地下ではその光を1階床のガラスで濾過したあと、さらに伝統的な教会建築にみられる装置としての洗礼槽で受けるように制御した。限られた空間のなかで光を自在に操る建築家の真骨頂をそこに見ることができるだろう。

The Spirit of Buddhism

Having discussed the church architecture, I would like to move on to the story of Buddhist temples.

Concrete temples had been awkward in the post-war architect world in Japan. From the 1960s to 1970s, many temple buildings all over the country were constructed with reinforced concrete instead of traditional wooden materials. However, most of those concrete temples were far from the delicate and magnificent beauty of wooden temples. Comparing with highly abstractive shrines, temples are mainly constructed with indigenous wooden inclined roof, so that it has long been a difficult challenge for architects to succeed their tradition and beauty by using modern building materials. Ando successfully came up with a solution, showing his in-depth understanding of Japanese culture.

When Ando was offered to design the WATER TEMPLE by the Iue family who was the founder of Sanyo Electric Co., Ltd. and a representative of parishioners, he came up with an idea of "creating a space with the spirit of Buddhism without relying on its conventional style." The site is located on a hill with an ocean view in the northern part of Awaji-shima Island. Along the right hand side of the pathway to the top of the hill, there is a terraced graveyard with lines of graves looking down the calm sea of Osaka Bay. This is a safe refuge that lasts forever for people born and brought up in this part of the Island.

Ando visited there and walking around the site, and had a vision in which the main hall, also called Mido Hall, was embraced by a lotus, rather than a glorious Mido Hall was constructed. In his image, Buddha and mankind were also embraced by lotus flowers.

Then the bold design of "Mido Hall under the lotus pond" was brought into life. At the surface of the ground appears an oval shaped pond with concrete edge, as well as a curved wall surrounding the pond. The oval is 40 meters long-side by 30 meters short-side, and lotuses are floating on the surface of the pond with full of water. The curved concrete wall blocks the sight climbing up the slope, and reaches to the pond from the entrance on the wall. There is nothing in sight that associates with the Buddhism. Strictly abstract expressions are used for the walls and the pond, and only the lotuses floating on the glassy surface of water assert their existence in reality.

The Mido Hall is located underground, right underneath the pond. To the Mido Hall, you go down the stairs in the middle, placed as if they cut the pond in half. Below the lotus pond, there is a secret entrance to Gokuraku-Jodo (the Heaven). It is in fact a dramatic design that makes people feel that way.

Further inside, there is the Mido Hall waiting for you, and its structure is so bold that goes well beyond the expectation. The underground Mido Hall is outlined with a square with 17.4 meters on a side, located on the basement level. The outlined wall is made of concrete, and a wooden cylinder of 14 meters in diameter is placed inside the wall. This cylinder is vividly vermilion-lacquered, and visitors feel a kind of dizziness when they step into the world full of bright colors from the gray-colored concrete world which is familiar with Ando's architecture.

1

Chapter 5 'Nil' Brings Repose of Soul

真言宗本福寺水御堂　1991
water temple

1. 本堂は水盤の下に位置する
   Main hall is located below the water basin
2. 地下の本堂への入り口
   Entrance to the underground main hall
3. 蓮池の隙間を降りる
   Descending path in a gap in the lotus pond

その意味では、「広尾の教会」において、安藤が「光の教会」の空間の精神を継承しながら、「情念の基本空間」と呼ぶところの、一連の「長屋」に発するコンクリートの小住宅で試みた、都市のなかの自然を素材にした空間構成を援用した軌跡を認めることができよう。

仏教の精神

教会から仏教寺院に話を広げていこう。

コンクリート寺院は、日本の戦後の建築界において、厄介な存在だった。1960-70年代に、日本の伝統的な木造の伽藍をそのまま鉄筋コンクリートに置き換えた寺院が全国各地で建設された。しかし、その大半は木造の繊細かつ雄渾な美からはほど遠いものになった。元来、抽象性の高い神社に比べて、木造の傾斜屋根という土着の構成が中心の寺院建築は、建築家にとってモダニズムの建材でどのようにその伝統と美を継承するか、長く難題のままだった。安藤はそれに対する見事な解答を導き出し、彼の日本文化に対する理解力の高さをあらためて示した。

「真言宗本福寺水御堂」の設計を、檀家を代表する三洋電機創業者の井植家から依頼されたとき、安藤は「様式に頼らない仏教精神の空間化」を考えたという。淡路島北部の海を見おろす小高い丘の立地。そこまで登る道の右側には、大阪湾の穏やかな海面を見おろすように段状に区画された墓地に墓石がならんでいる。先祖代々、この地で生まれ育ったひとの永遠の安住の場である。

敷地を確かめて歩いた安藤は、伽藍、つまり、壮大な御堂を建てるのではなく、蓮のなかに御堂が抱かれる姿を夢想した。御仏、衆生も御堂とともに蓮の花に包まれるイメージが浮かんだという。

「蓮池の下の御堂」という大胆な構成はそうやって生まれた。導入路を過ぎると、地表にはコンクリートで縁取りされた楕円の池とそれを囲う形の曲面壁だけが存在する。楕円の長径は40メートル、短径は30メートル、いっぱいに張られた水面に蓮が浮かんでいる。コンクリートの曲面壁は斜面を登ってきた視界を無化するかのようにいったん遮り、壁に穿たれた入り口から池に至る。そこには仏教を連想させる一切の造形はない。壁も池も抽象表現を遵守し、鏡のような水面に浮かぶ蓮だけが現実のものとして存在を主張している。

御堂は地下、即ち池の真下にある。そこへは池を二分するように構成された直線階段を降りていくことになる。蓮池の下に極楽浄土への密やかな入り口がある。そのように思わせる実に劇的な仕立てだ。

第5章　〈無〉は魂の安らぎをもたらす　171

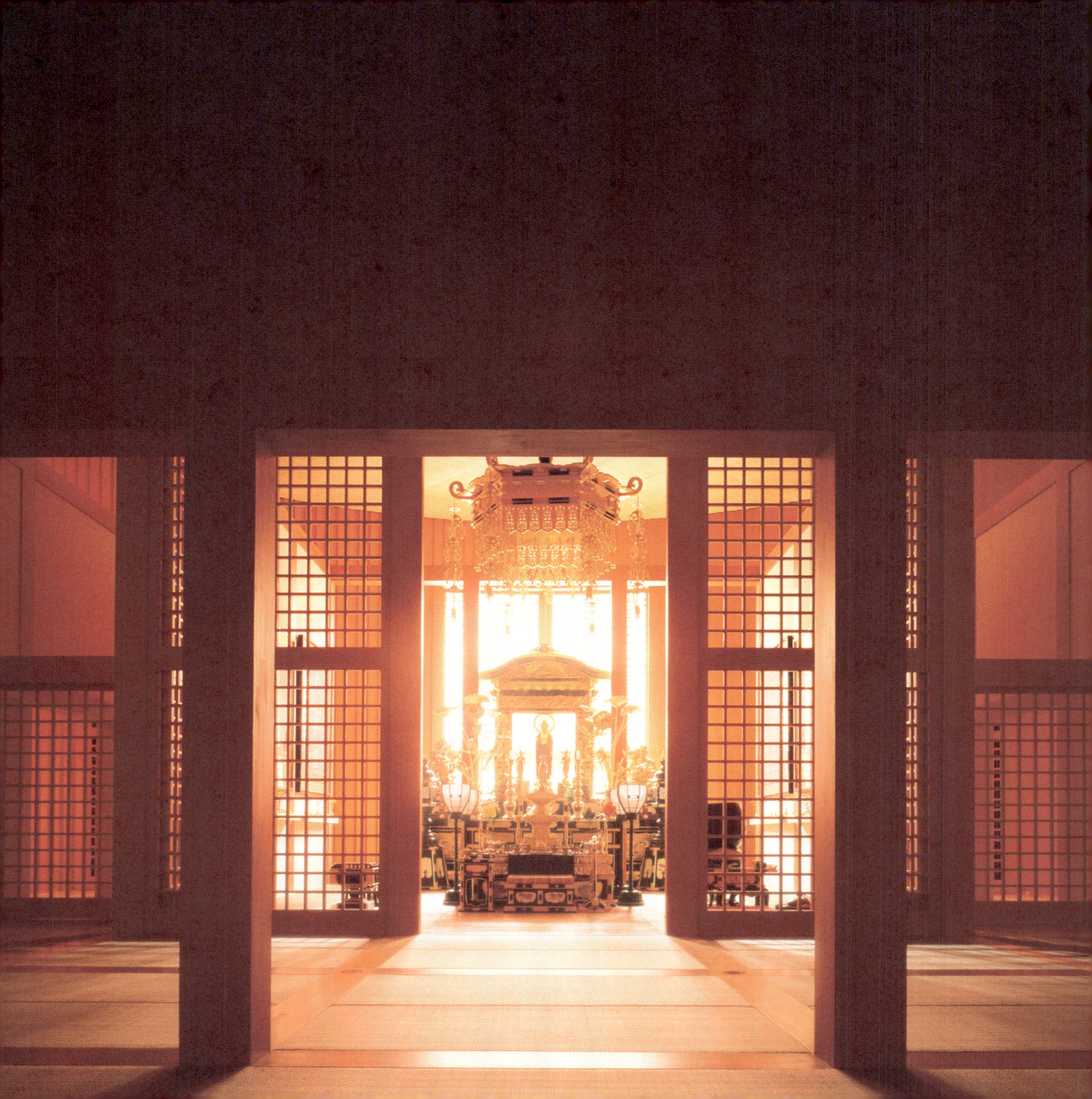

真言宗本福寺水御堂　1991
water temple

4. (前ページ) 西からの夕陽で輝く本尊
   (previous page) Principal image shining in the setting sun
5. 地下から階段を見上げる
   Stairs viewed from the underground level
6. 本堂を囲む格子
   Lattice enclosing the main hall

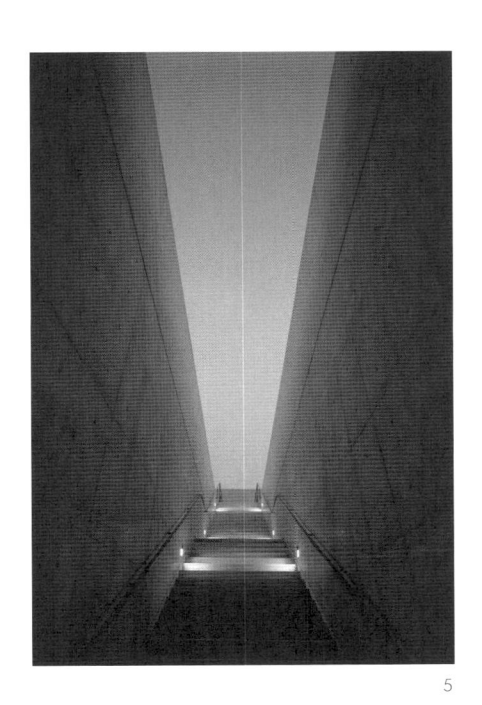

　内部に進むと、御堂が期待をさらに上回る大胆な構成で待ち受けている。地下の御堂の外周は一辺が17.4メートルの正方形で、それが地下1階のレベルに位置している。その外周壁はコンクリート打ち放しで、そのなかに直径14メートルの木造の円筒が配されている。この円筒は目にも彩やかな朱塗りになっており、来訪者は、安藤らしい彩度を消したコンクリートの宇宙から、突然、極彩色の世界に足を踏み入れ、目眩さえ覚えることになる。

現代に甦る重源の空間

　朱塗りの壁は、格子を組んだ部分が大半を占め、御堂の内部を透かして見通せる。木造寺院の本堂の内部に見え隠れする御本尊を、格子を通して覗き見るような感覚といってよいだろう。規則正しくならぶ角柱をはじめ、真言宗の寺院の配置を遵守したと安藤がいう通り、この格子の壁に至ると、地上とは異なる仏教の伝統的な空間に誘われたことに気づく。

　抽象から具象へ、現代から伝統へ、安藤の大胆な場面転換に誰しもが喝采を贈りたくなるに違いない。そして、本尊を見やると背後からの強い西日で光り輝いているお姿が目に入る。まさに西方浄土を連想させる演出である。自然光は内壁の朱を堂内のあちらこちらに浸潤させて、夢幻の空間をつくりだしている。朱は、光源となる本尊の背後の窓からの距離と角度によって、微妙なグラデーションをコンクリート壁や円形の天井にもたらし、幻想性は一段と高まりを見せて、鑑賞者を虜にする。

　わたしは1980年代の半ば、安藤とともに兵庫県小野市の浄土寺を訪ねたことがあった。夕暮れが迫り来るなか、東大寺などで独自の木造建築を開拓した重源による国宝「浄土堂」のなかに西日が低く射し込むと、堂内が朱に包まれ、本尊の阿弥陀三尊像を中心に極楽浄土を想起させる空間が広がるのを感動とともに眺めた。そのため「本福寺水御堂」に始めて足を踏み入れて、安藤の空間が朱に染まるのを体験したとき、「浄土堂」の空間が見事にそこに再現されていることに気づいた。

　建築はなにより空間体験の積み重ねの反映が重要であり、安藤がそれをもとに浄土堂の空間の真髄を的確に現代の素材で再現したことに驚きを覚えた　安藤忠雄ほど「住吉の長屋」をはじめ、コンクリートと自然のありようについて熟考を重ね、試行錯誤を重ねてきた建築家は存在しまい。キリスト教文化の集積としての教会の礼拝堂では、敢えて世俗や歴史から離れてモダニズムの「浄化された空間」を追究してきたのは、教会三部作を見れば得心がいくだろう。一方、自身の肉体にいわばDNAのように入り込んでいる日本の伝統精神の一翼を担う仏教の空間においては、御仏に託す衆生の気持ちを

The Space of Chogen back to the Present

The most part of the vermilion-lacquered walls were grid-like structure, and thus the inside of the Mido Hall can be seen through the grids. It is similar to wooden temples where visitors may try to peak the Buddha statue placed inside the main hall through the grid. As Ando mentioned, he followed the traditional style of a Shingon temple, such as orderly placed square columns, and visitors find themselves in traditional Buddhist space as they reached to the grid wall, and that this space was nothing similar to the space above the ground.

Anyone who experience such bold change of the scene, from abstract to embodiment and from modern to traditional, will surely give high credit to Ando. As you have a look at the Buddha statue, it shines golden bright with the afternoon sun coming in at its back. It conjures up the image of the Pure Land in the West. The natural light infiltrates the vermilion color into every part of the hall, creating a heavenly space. Depending on the distance and the angle of light source from the window, the vermilion creates delicate graduations on the concrete wall and the circular ceiling, and attracts visitors with its highly illusional sight.

In the mid-1980s, Ando and I visited Jodo-ji in Ono, Hyogo Prefecture. With dusk approaching and late afternoon sunlight slanted into the Jodo-do, a national treasure by Chogen who developed his original wooden architecture including Todai-ji, the hall was enveloped in vermillion. We were utterly moved to see the space around the Amida Sanzon (Amida triad) invoking Gokuraku-Jodo. Later, when I first visited the completed WATER TEMPLE and saw the space being enveloped in vermillion, I realized that Ando beautifully reproduced the space of Jodo-do.

Accumulating spatial experiences is ever so important for the architecture. It was surprising that he could grasp the essence of Jodo-do based on his spatial experience and precisely reproduce it with modern building materials. As you see three churches of Ando's design, it is understandable that he deliberately stayed away from the world and history when he pursued to create the "space of purification" in modernism in those chapels as accumulation of Christian culture. Buddhism, on the other hand, takes part in Japanese traditional spirit and is engraved in our bodies like DNA. Therefore, for the space of Buddhism, he designed the splendid Mido Hall to express the entrance of Gokuraku-Jodo which enhances the feeling of mankind to rely on Buddha. This is not a residence or commercial facility. This is another masterpiece that is completely different from his previous works, addressing the Japanese concept of life and death.

The wedding chapel of the hotel located at AWAJI-YUMEBUTAI which is known for its terraced flowerbeds, by the way, was also constructed below the stepped artificial pond. This artificial pond on the rooftop has a walking path, and as you walk along there you can see scallops that cover the bottom of the shallow water. Looking at the square bell tower that resembles the one at the CHAPEL ON MT. ROKKO standing in the water, I feel almost confused as if I look at the CHAPEL ON MT. ROKKO being framed into the water. Considering that the design of "underneath the water" was created based on the concept of space with the spirit of Buddhism, then the CHAPEL ON MT. ROKKO in the water also seems interesting.

淡路夢舞台／海の教会　1999
awaji-yumebutai / church of the sea

1. 聖堂は人工池の下に配置
   Church building under the artificial pond
2. 斜面側の外観
   Exterior appearance on the slope side
3. 聖堂内部
   Interior of the church

高ぶらせる極楽浄土への入り口を本福寺の華麗な御堂の姿で表現してみせた。それまでの住宅とも商業施設とも異なる、日本人の死生観までをも踏まえた名作の出現であった。

ちなみに、同じ淡路島の段状花壇などで知られる「淡路夢舞台」に併設されたホテルのウェディング・チャーチ「海の教会」は、段状の人工池の下に配された。この屋上の人工池には歩行できる通路が設けられ、浅い池の底に敷きつめられたホタテ貝の貝殻も確かめられる。「六甲の教会」を思わせる四角いコンクリートの鐘楼が水面にそびえる姿を眺めるとき、あたかも「六甲の教会」が眼前の水面下にはめ込まれているかのように思えてくる。「水の下」が、仏教精神の空間化という発想のもとに生まれたことを考えると、これはこれで興味深い構成になるだろう。

「組む」と「集まる」

仏寺では愛媛県西条市の「南岳山光明寺」（2000年）もまた寺院の今日のありかたを考えさせる空間で、自身が蓄積してきた木造建築の表現に磨きをかけた。旧建物を撤去して、新たに本堂などを建て替える工事に際して、若い住職から寄せられたのは「ひとの集まる場」にしてほしいとの要望だった。湧水池の豊かな水を生かして、そこに木造の本堂が浮かび、その周囲を客殿、礼拝堂、庫裏が取り囲む構成を採用した。

中心となる本堂は、百畳の広さの大空間で、すりガラスを木製の格子にはめ込んだ内壁で囲われる。畳敷きの屋内は、すりガラスの濾過した柔らかな光が隅々まで行き渡り、快適な集合空間となった。この大空間を、4本ひと組の柱の束が四隅で大空間を支えている。座敷に腰を下ろし、頭上の木造の架構と柱の構成を眺めると、そこには実に豪快な木組みの交差があり、空間の力強さも実感できよう。

この内壁の外側には回廊が回り、外壁の仕上げは透明ガラスを木の垂直材にはめ込んだ「入れ子」の構造となっている。緩い勾配のつけられた屋根は深い庇となって建物本体から飛び出し、その下には四層の垂木が深い陰影をもたらしている。

夜間、周囲を漆黒の闇が支配するなか、内部の照明がガラスを通して洩れ来て、本堂が水面に姿を移すとき、究極の美しさが出現する。安藤自身、伝統木造との接点はほとんどないと語る通り、この木造建築は集成材を多用した「安藤流の新木造」と呼ぶに値するものだ。そして、その新木造は現代の美を余すところなく、全身から発信していると思えてくる。

安藤が木造にこだわったのは、「組む」という木造建築の精神こそが、住職の期待する「ひとの集まる場」にふさわしいと考えたからである。また「組む」は、「浄土堂」な

Framing and Gathering

Another Buddhist temple that Ando designed is the KOMYO-JI TEMPLE in 2000 in Saijo, Ehime. He refined his experience in designing the wooden architecture to create a space which also addressed the way a temple should be like today. It was a complete reconstruction that the old structure was destroyed and replaced with the new one, and the young priest asked Ando to design the hall where people can gather together. There was a pond with rich spring water, and Ando decided to place the wooden main hall floating on the pond, and the reception hall, the chapel, and priest's quarter were arranged in a way that surrounded the pond and the main hall.

The main hall is a vast space with 100 tatami mats, and inner walls are made of wooden grids and frosted glasses. The natural light is filtered through the frosted glass and provides soft lighting over the vast hall with tatami, making the space comfortable for people to gather. A bundle of four pillars is placed at every corner of the hall, supporting this vast space. You can feel the strength of the space as you sit on tatami and look up the wooden frame crossing over pillars to enjoy dynamic timberwork.

The inner walls are enclosed by the cloister, and the exterior walls are finished in the embedded structure with transparent glasses and wooden vertical members. The low-angled roof protrudes from the structure to create wide eaves, and below that there are four-layered rafters to provide deep shade.

You can witness its ultimate beauty at night when the main hall is reflected on the surface of the water by the light from inside through the window in the jet-black darkness. Ando had little connection with the traditional wooden structure, as Ando himself admitted, therefore this wooden architecture which made great use of laminated lumber deserves to be called as "the new wooden structure in Ando's way".

Ando thought that it was the most appropriate approach to design this temple with wood, since the framing was the spirit of wooden architecture which went perfectly well with the place for gathering, as the priest desired. He also claimed that the timberwork is back to the source of Japanese traditional wooden architecture in which, as Chogen showed at Jodo-do for example, even the smallest members are kept tightened until they are framed together to contribute to the overall beauty. Such wooden architecture with framed members, he claimed further, reflects daily life in Japan where communities of parishioners are formed around temples.

As a modernist, Ando's pursuit for new wooden architecture began in 1992 with JAPANESE PAVILION AT THE UNIVERSAL EXPOSITION OF SEVILLE, and the MUSEUM OF WOOD (1994) which may be considered as the conversion of the pavilion into the context of Japan. He successfully took a step forward in his continuous efforts on wooden architecture by designing the KOMYO-JI TEMPLE, as an everyday Japanese Buddhist architecture. Ando's inquiring mind shows no sign of slowing down.

南岳山光明寺 2000
komyo-ji temple

1. 既存の建物と新本堂（左）の屋根
   Roofs of the existing building and the new main hall (on left)
2. 格子の木造建築が水に浮かぶ
   Wooden structure with lattices floating on the water
3. 本堂のガラス壁と格子
   Glass wall and lattice of the main hall
4. 格子がもたらす陰影
   Shadows cast by the grid
5. 本堂内の本尊
   Principal image in the main hall

Space of 'Nil' for Autocatharsis

Here, I would like to mention the UNESCO's MEDITATION SPACE, built in 1995. It was a space design that Ando worked on as "a place for praying for world peace" beyond races and religions. The site for the Meditation Space was next to the Japanese garden designed by Isamu Noguchi for the UNESCO headquarters (designed by Marcel Lajos Breuer) in Paris, and the construction funds were raised in Japan as a victim of nuclear bombing. Ando placed a concrete cylinder with 6.3 meters in diameter in a way that it is as if floating on an artificial pond, which became the Meditation Space.

As you walk inside the cylinder, it is indeed a space of 'nil' where there is nothing. The natural light slightly comes in through a circular slit at the top along the circumference of the cylinder. This is what Ando described "a building made of the light and the concrete only, with no fittings or finishing."

His idea of "a place for the repose of soul" is a place of 'nil' where the geometry dominates with only the filtered light coming through, and people can only face themselves in such place, which projects his architectural view. Ando wishes that people's calling for peace will be purified in the space of 'nil', and feeling for the repose of soul emerges spontaneously when the light from the ceiling is softly casted on the floor and on the stone exposed to nuclear bombing in Hiroshima. More stones exposed to nuclear bombing in Hiroshima were also placed at the bottom of the pond around the cylinder. The idea here is that the stones being washed by the flow of water will become the repose of the dead soul.

The foyer of NISHIDA KITARO MUSEUM OF PHILOSOPHY (2002) in Kahoku, Ishikawa was named as "the Meditation Space". The open ceiling space of three levels from the ground floor was designed by Ando as the place of 'nil', only with the sky to look up through the glass of top light, and the inverse conically shaped concrete.

I feel a kind of being intimidated when I sit on a clear acrylic chair at the center of the foyer. It is the inverse conically shaped structure that makes a person at the chair feel that way, and asks the person to purify themselves as they understand the philosophy of Nishida. I cannot help realizing that fierceness of the space identifies the meaning of existence for Ando's space of 'nil' and "sacred space" where people in modern age are forced to think who they really are. I'm sure it is not only me to feel how formidable this architect is.

ユネスコ瞑想空間　1995
meditation space, UNESCO

1. 円筒の空間と直線のアプローチ
   Cylindrical space and linear approach
2. 水が広島の石を洗う
   Stones from Hiroshima washed by water
3. 円筒の内部
   Inside of the cylinder
4. （次ページ見開き）天井の見上げ
   (next two pages) Ceiling viewed from below

どで重源が示した小さな部材に至るまでが緊張感を失わず、それらが組み合わさることで全体の美に貢献する、日本の伝統木造の原点への回帰に通じているとも思った。そして、その部材が組み上げられた木造の姿こそが、寺院を中心に多くの檀家が共同体を形成し、日々が送られていく日本の暮らしの写しなのだと論は展開する。

　安藤は、敷地との対話を重ねて、建築のあるべき姿を構築したこの寺院建築は、自身の建築手法の原点の確認作業だったとも述べている。安藤は、1992年の「セビリア万博日本館」に始まり、その日本移植版とでもいうべき「兵庫県木の殿堂」（1994年）などでモダニストとして新たな木造のありかたを追究してきた。「本福寺水御堂」では、身上とするコンクリートによって、伝統美を現代に表現する道を選んだが、この「南岳山光明寺」では、一連の木造への取り組みを、日常的なスケールの寺院建築で進化させることに成功した。衰えを知らない探究心のなせる業である。

自己浄化を迫る「無の空間」

　ここで「ユネスコ瞑想空間」（1995年）に言及しておきたい。安藤が宗教、民族を超越した「世界平和希求の祈りの場」と位置づけ、空間の設計に臨んだからである。敷地は、マルセル・ブロイヤー設計のパリの「ユネスコ本部」の敷地内にあるイサム・ノグチによる「日本庭園」の隣地、建設資金は被爆国として日本国内の募金によって集められた。安藤は直径6.3メートルのコンクリートの円筒を人工池に浮かぶ形で配して、そこを「瞑想空間」とした。

　その内部に歩を進めると、なにもない、まさに「無」の空間となっている。頭上からは円筒の外周に沿ったリング上のスリットを通した自然光が微かに降り注いでくる。安藤のいうところの「建具も仕上げも一切を排除した光とコンクリート打ち放しのみの建物」なのである。

　この幾何学が支配し、濾過された光だけが入り込む「無」の場こそ、人間が自身に向き合う「鎮魂の場」になりうるという安藤の発想は、彼の建築観を投影している。平和を希求する願いは、この「無」の空間のなかで純化し、天井からの光が、床に配された広島市が寄贈した「原爆の石」をほんのりと照らしだすとき、自ずと「鎮魂」の感情が生まれることを安藤は期待する。広島の被爆の石は、円筒を囲む池の底にも配された。池の水が流れてその原爆の石を洗えば、亡くなったひとびとの鎮魂につながるという発想である。

　石川県かほく市の「西田幾多郎哲学記念館」（2002年）のホワイエは「瞑想の空間」と名付けられている。地階から三層の吹き抜け空間には、トップライトのガラス越しに見

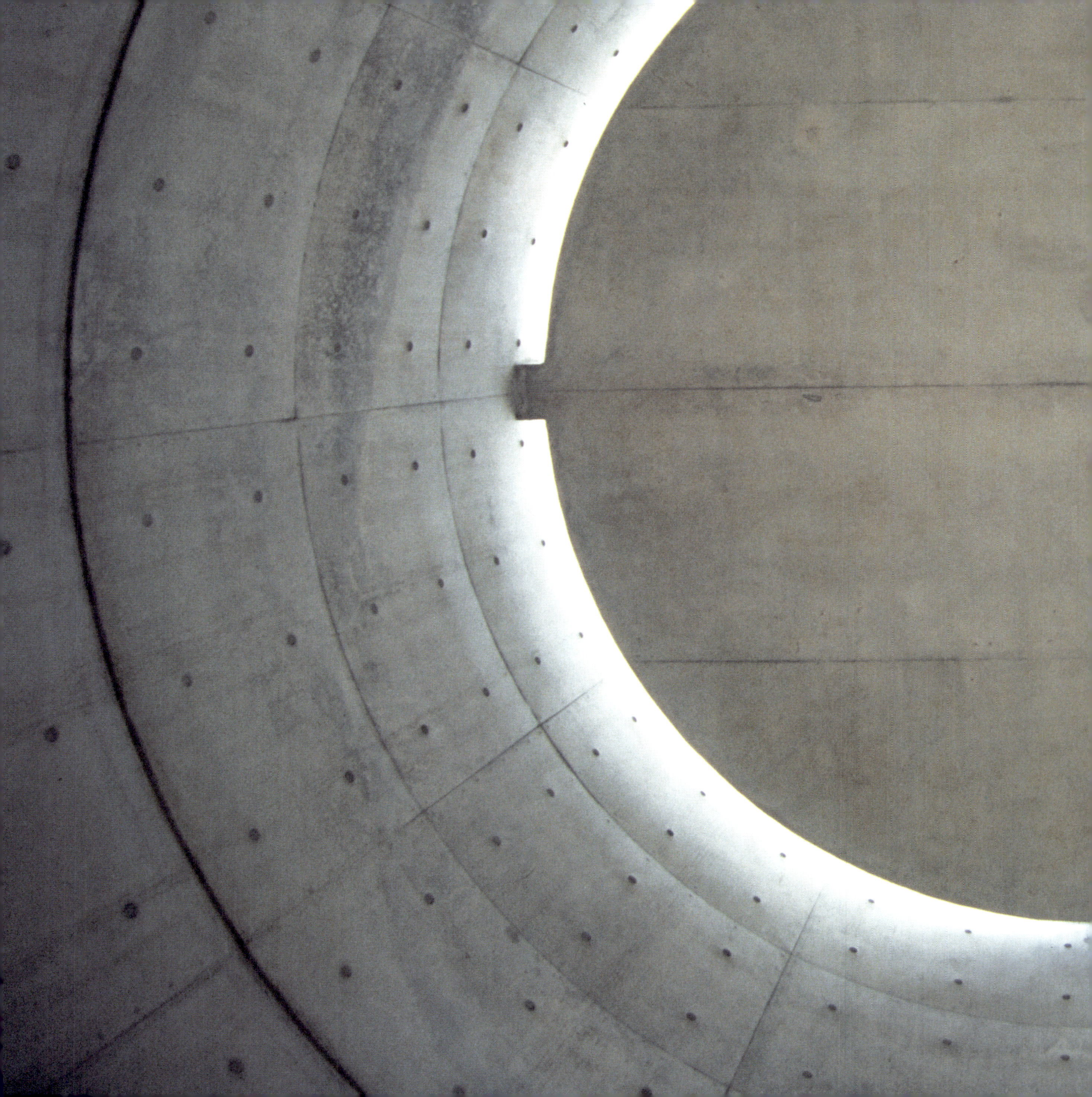

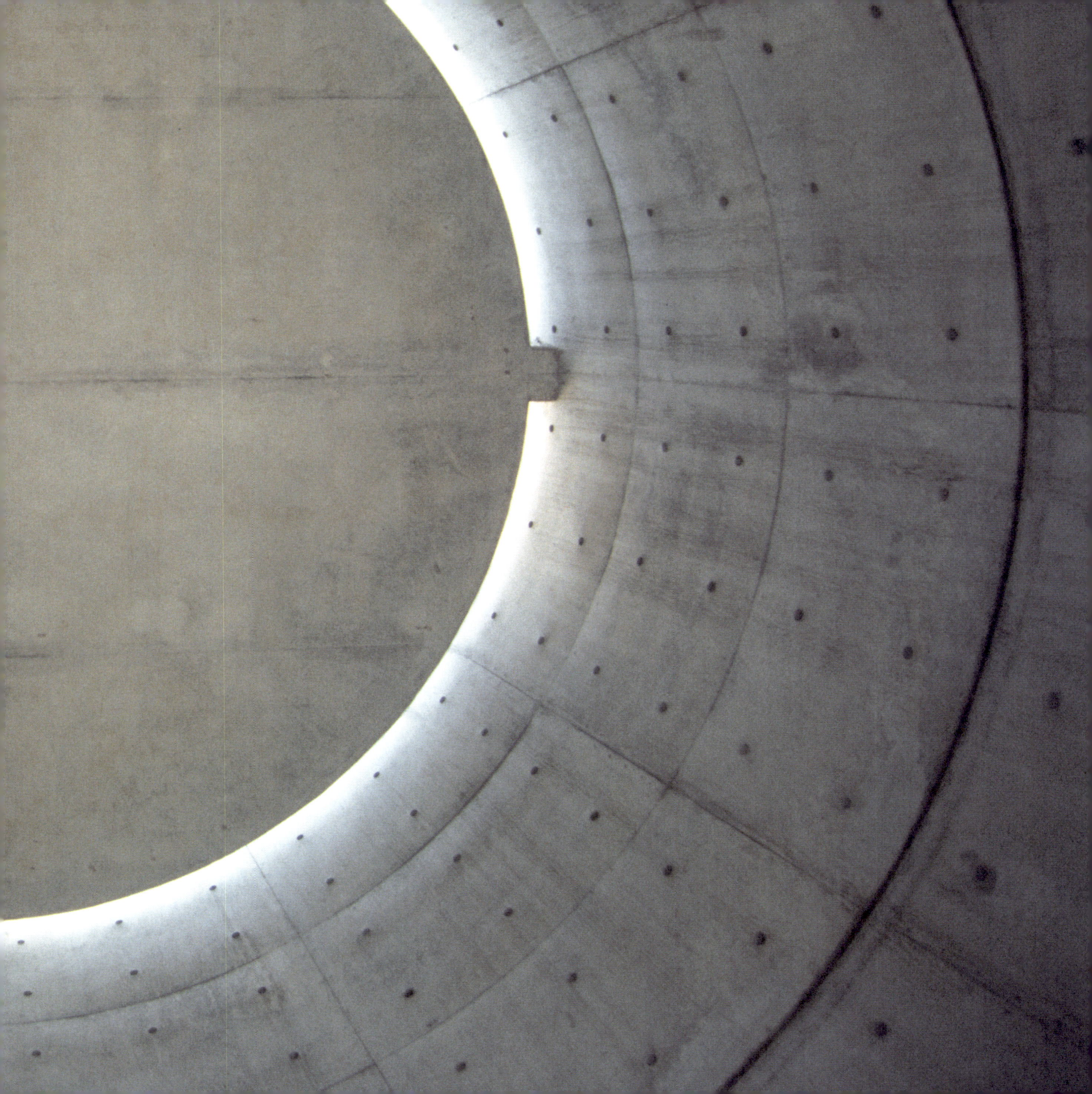

上げる空と、覆い被さるような逆円錐形のコンクリートだけが存在する、安藤の設えた「無」の場となっている。

　安藤は、西田と和辻哲郎を青年期に最も影響を受けた哲学者と語っている。『風土』の著作で知られる和辻が「現実の旅を思想の契機とした」のに対して、禅に根ざす純粋経験を西洋的思想と対比的に融合させた西田は「物理的な移動もなくひとつの場所にとどまっても内面を覗き、世界の無限へ旅した」と考える。その考えに基づき、館内の何か所に「自身と向き合う場」が設けられた。日本独自の思想体系の構築に挑んだ西田へのオマージュとしての「無」の空間である。

　ホワイエの中央に置かれた透明アクリルの椅子に座ると、ある種の圧迫感を覚える。逆円錐の造形のなせる業であり、安藤はそうやって、座する者に西田哲学の理解にあたって、自身の「浄化」を迫ってくる。その空間の凄味こそが、現代人に自分とはなにかを考えさせる安藤の「無の空間」「聖なる空間」の存在意義となっていることに気づかされる。恐ろしい建築家なのだとそのとき思いを新たにするのは、わたしだけではあるまい。

西田幾多郎記念哲学館　2002
nishida kitaro museum of philosophy

1. 丘の上に位置する
   Located at the top of a hill
2. 階段庭園からの見上げ
   Upward view from the tiered garden
3. ホワイエのトップライト
   Skylight of the foyer
4. 「空の庭」と呼ぶ吹き抜け空間
   Space with an open ceiling, called the "Garden of Sky"

Chapter 5　'Nil' Brings Repose of Soul　182

第6章　ランドスケープ、まちづくりへ
〈建築〉に始まり、〈建築〉を超える

Chapter 6　Towards Landscaping and Urban Development
Beginning with 'Architecture' and beyond 'Architecture'

人間の暴挙を回復する「淡路夢舞台」

　カナダのブリティッシュコロンビア州、英国風の街並みで知られるビクトリアの街から車で北に30分ほど走ったところに「ブッチャート・ガーデン」がある。セメント王ロバート・ピム・ブッチャートが石灰石を採掘した跡地を、夫人のジェニーが歳月をかけて美しい緑の庭園に整備した。建設が始まったのは1906年。初期の日本庭園は、当時、北米で活動していた庭師、岸田伊三郎の手で整備された。公園全体の広さは22ヘクタール、第2次世界大戦前でも年間50万人が訪れ、現在は毎年100万人の訪問者を数える世界でも指折りの観光庭園となっている。

　このブッチャート・ガーデンこそが、安藤忠雄と兵庫県知事貝原俊民にとって「淡路夢舞台」建設の手本だった。入り江に面したブッチャート・ガーデンが石灰石採石場跡地の再生だったのに対し、建築家と政治家の眼前には大阪湾岸埋め立てで土砂を削り取られ放置されたままの赤茶けた岩盤が広がっていた。瀬戸内海に浮かぶ淡路島に似つかわしくない広さ140ヘクタールの荒涼たる空き地。その一角を再生させるプロジェクトが始まったのは1990年。何事も徹すればかなうという信念を持つ安藤でさえ先行きは覚束なかった。

　1960年代以降、埋め立てで運び出された土砂は1億立方メートルに達したとされる。その土砂で大阪湾岸の臨海部が埋め立てられ、工場や港湾施設が建設された。1980年代には、大阪泉南沖の「関西国際空港」もここから運び出された土砂で建設された。

　安藤と貝原はこう考えた。関西の太平洋戦争後の経済復興のために損なわれた自然を、荒れ果てた姿のままで放置することは忍びない。おりから近畿、中国地方と四国を結ぶ本州四国連絡橋のひとつ、明石海峡大橋が建設途上であり、淡路島の観光振興の

Awaji-Yumebutai:
Recovering What Human Destroyed

About 30 minutes drive to north from Victoria, a city in British Columbia, Canada, that is well-known for its British style streetscape, there is the Butchart Gardens. This place used to be a limestone quarry owned by a cement tycoon Robert Pim Butchart, and his wife Jenny took a long time to make this place become beautiful gardens with full of greenery. The construction started in 1906. The initial Japanese garden was designed by a Japanese gardener Isaburo Kishida who was at that time working in North America. The size of the Gardens is about 22 hectares, and it has become one of the most famous gardens in the world with approximately 500,000 visitors a year before the World War II, and currently one million visitors a year.

On construction of Awaji-Yumebutai, Tadao Ando and Toshitami Kaihara, the governor of Hyogo Prefecture, chose the Butchart Gardens as its model. The Butchart Gardens is located nearby harbor and used to be an exhausted limestone quarry, while in the planned site for the Awaji-Yumebutai, what the architect and the governor saw was a reddish bedrock which was left abandoned after soil had been scraped down for the landfill of Osaka Bay area. It was a desolate site of 140 hectares, unlikely to be seen on the Awaji-shima Island in the Seto Inland Sea. The project which would recover a corner of the site started in 1990. However, there were clouds on the horizon for this project, and even Ando who had strong will to make the impossible possible found it hard to achieve.

The soil which had been moved out from here for the landfill is said to reach 100 million cubic meters since 1960s. The waterfront area along Osaka Bay was landfilled with such soil, and factories and harbor facilities were constructed there. In 1980s, Kansai International Airport off Sennan, Osaka was also constructed with the soil from here.

Ando and Kaihara thought: the nature was destroyed due to economic reconstruction in Kansai area after the Pacific War, and it shouldn't be left abandoned, and; from tourism development point of view, nature recovery in Awaji-shima Island would surely reflect the social trend as the Akashi Kaikyo Bridge, one of the Honshu Shikoku Bridges that would connect the Kinki, Chugoku and Shikoku areas had been under construction.

The Awaji-Yumebutai would become the main facility for the development and Ando was commissioned to design it. In January 1995 when the design was ready and construction work was about to start, however, the Great Hanshin-Awaji Earthquake occurred. Revegetation work had already started there but the design of the Awaji-Yumebutai was forced to change, since a fault was discovered at the site during the post-earthquake investigation.

Five years after the Earthquake, Japan Flora 2000 (Awaji Flower Expo) exhibition was held as a part of reconstruction support in Awaji-shima Island, and the once desolate site had been turned into the welcoming site with full of greenery. It was then the Awaji-Yumebutai first opened as the Yumebutai Zone of the Exhibition site.

Awaji-Yumebutai is a complex facility with garden, glasshouse, international conference center, hotel, and restaurant. Soon after the completion, Ando and I walked along together in this hilly site to visit facilities, I remember that Ando kept talking about how a lot of people took the revegetation work seriously here.

The slope at the back with exposed rocks was as steep as 30 degrees, due to the soil being scraped away. The revegetation work started with planting 250,000 seedling trees of 10 centimeters tall. These seedling trees were all planted manually on the very steep and uneven slope. Ando couldn't help appreciating gardeners as he saw them doing such hard work that seemed endless. The gardeners did their best for this work, learning the know-how for the maintenance of greenery in very dry area of Iran.

淡路夢舞台　1999
awaji-yumebutai

1. 緑を失っていた旧状
   Previous condition with poor greenery
2. 整備された姿
   After development
3. 施設中央部の見おろし
   Downward view of the center of the facilities
4. 水際に施設が広がる
   Facilities spread near the waterfront

第6章 ランドスケープ、まちづくりへ

It was almost the first time for Ando's atelier with 30 staff members to design a complex facility simultaneously. Whenever I heard Ando saying "well, it's hard", I imagined him and his staff members working doggedly towards its absolute deadline, Japan Flora 2000 exhibition, while they had a strong determination for the reconstruction of the disaster-affected area.

Green Garden: Water Creates Life

The must-see sight at AWAJI-YUMEBUTAI is the "Hyakudan En": a sloped garden with 100 concrete grids, 4.5 meters square each, in which flowers are planted beautifully. The bright Setouchi sunlight shines onto the south-facing flowerbeds, making flowers in full bloom look even more beautiful. As you look out, the blue water stretching in front. The design that can enjoy blessings of nature makes visitors feel fully satisfied with coming here.

The visitors need to walk up and down the concrete stairs to see the Hyakudan En. Although it is the stairs with 30 meters height difference, steps are perfectly designed by Ando, as they are of ROKKO HOUSING, in terms of the height of risers and the depth of threads so that you can go up and down smoothly without pain. I was so impressed to know that he was as meticulous about detailed dimensions for the 100 large-scale flowerbeds as he was for a house.

On the right side of the Hyakudan En, there is a courtyard walkway, Hillside Gallery, with a shallow artificial pond surrounded by lines of concrete pillars. You can feel its cold aesthetic through Ando's strict sense of proportion, similar to works of Mies van der Rohe. As you walk through the courtyard, there is a huge open ceiling glasshouse.

There are a series of facilities in the AWAJI-YUMEBUTAI where visitors can enjoy various concrete frames to the fullest which only Ando could design, including an oval park which utilize the height difference of the site. This is the best place to enjoy the world of Ando as thoroughly as possible, from the tower to the walkway. What makes such concrete space even more distinctive is the flow of water.

The water flows fast from up high near the stairs of the Hyakudan En, and vertically down to the ground level at the bottom. At the rooftop of the hotel, however, the water stops flowing and the calm surface stretches out. This is the rooftop of a wedding chapel called the Marine Chapel, with a concrete tower standing in the artificial pond beautifully. The surface of water at the rooftop was designed to look as if it stretches toward the larger surface of Osaka Bay.

The water flows along the slope into a vast artificial pond called "the Shell Beach" at the ground level. The shell here particularly means scallops and bottoms of artificial ponds and stepped conduits in AWAJI-YUMEBUTAI are all covered with orderly lined scallops. A bit yellowish color of the scallops matches perfectly with the color tone of natural granitoid soil from the coast of Seto Inland Sea. Ando visited a waste site of a canning company in order to obtain these scallops. His passion bore fruit and the artificial pond gives the place a warm and favorable touch.

The water flows with splash, and the sound becomes louder when it spouts like a fountain. The splashing sound gives energy to break the silence in the place, which makes visitors realize that the landscape designed by Ando is always alive and well. Besides, you may feel a sense of cleansing as you see the gushing water running down from the top near the stairs of the Hyakudan En. The Hyakudan En was added to the AWAJI-YUMEBUTAI after the Earthquake, showing Ando's remembrance of the victims. The water flowing down can be considered as ablution, and the water inside our bodies acts in concert to make us feel the soul. The constant splashing sound in the garden lingers exquisitely in the ear, like the proof of eternal life.

淡路夢舞台　1999
awaji-yumebutai

5. コンクリートの柱がならぶ山回廊
   Hillside Gallery with lines of concrete pillars
6. 楕円フォーラムの吹き抜け見下ろし
   Downward view of the Oval Forum
7. （次ページ見開き）斜面に広がる百段苑
   (next two pages) Hyakudan En on a slope

観点からも自然の回復は社会の趨勢に見合っている、と。

安藤は中核となる複合施設「夢舞台」の設計を任され、実施設計も終えたが、着工寸前の1995年1月、阪神淡路大震災が起きた。自然を回復する工事は一足先に始まっていたものの、震災後の調査で敷地内に新たに断層が見つかり、「夢舞台」は設計変更を余儀なくされた。

5年後、淡路島復興の一助として、緑が復活した土砂採取場跡地で「ジャパンフローラ2000（淡路花博）」が開催された。このとき「淡路夢舞台」は、博覧会場の一角を占める「夢舞台ゾーン」としてお披露目された。

「淡路夢舞台」は、庭園、温室、国際会議場、ホテル、飲食施設などを備える複合施設だ。完成直後に安藤と一緒に起伏に富んだ敷地に広がる施設群をくまなく歩いたとき、彼が、いかに多くのひとびとが緑の再生に真剣に取り組んだかを語り続けたのを思い出す。

土砂を切り出したため、背後の岩肌の露出した斜面は30度の急傾斜になっていた。そこに高さ10センチの樹木の苗、25万本を植樹する作業から跡地の再生は始まった。急勾配の足場が悪い斜面に、ひとが一本一本手作業で植樹していく。いつ終わるとも知れない気が遠くなりそうな職人たちの作業を目の当たりにし、建築家の胸には感謝の思いが込み上げてきた。造園技術者たちも、水の乏しい中東イランにおける緑の維持管理のノウハウを学ぶなど知恵をつくした。

30人規模の安藤のアトリエにとって、同時並行で複合施設の設計を進めるのも初めてといってよい経験だった。「いやあ大変ですよ」と彼が洩らすのを耳にする度に、被災地を必ず復興させなければならない強い決意を胸に、安藤や所員たちが、花博開催という絶対的期限を目標に、黙々と作業に勤しむ姿を想像した。

水が生命を演出する「緑の庭園」

完成した「淡路夢舞台」の最大の見どころは「百段苑」と名付けられた、急斜面に4.5メートル四方のコンクリートの格子で区切られた花壇（実際に100面が存在する）の広がる庭園だ。南向きにつくられた花壇は、瀬戸内ならではの明るい陽光を浴び、開花した花々がひときわ輝いて見える。視界の先には青海原が広がる。「ああ、ここまで来てよかった」と自然の恵みあふれる仕立てに納得させられる。

来訪者はそこをコンクリートの階段で昇降する。高低差は30メートルあるが、安藤の階段は「六甲の集合住宅」もそうだが、蹴上げ、踏面とも絶妙の寸法で、昇り降りとも足がごく自然に運び、苦痛を感じさせない。スケールの大きな100の花壇を造りながら、

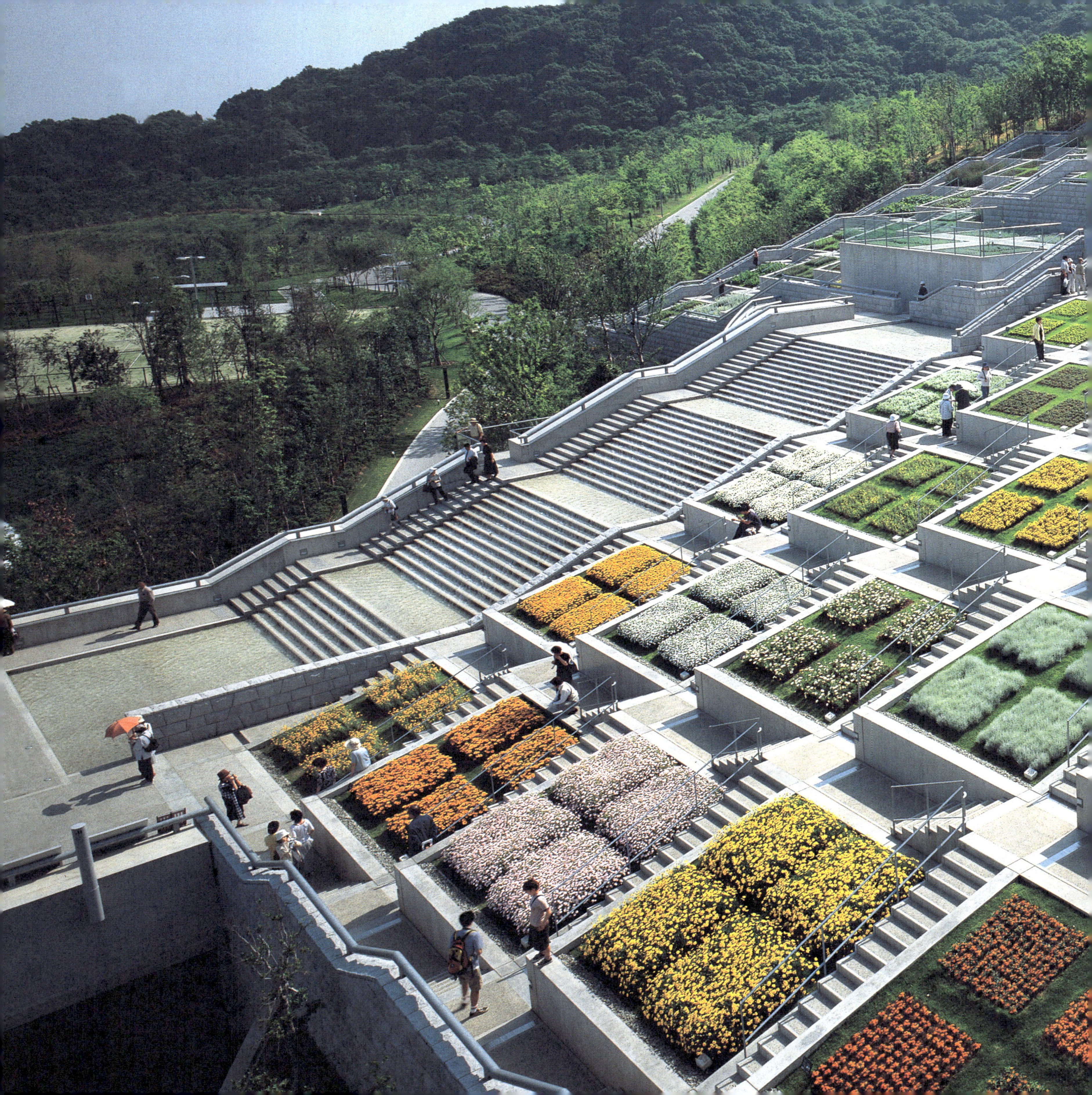

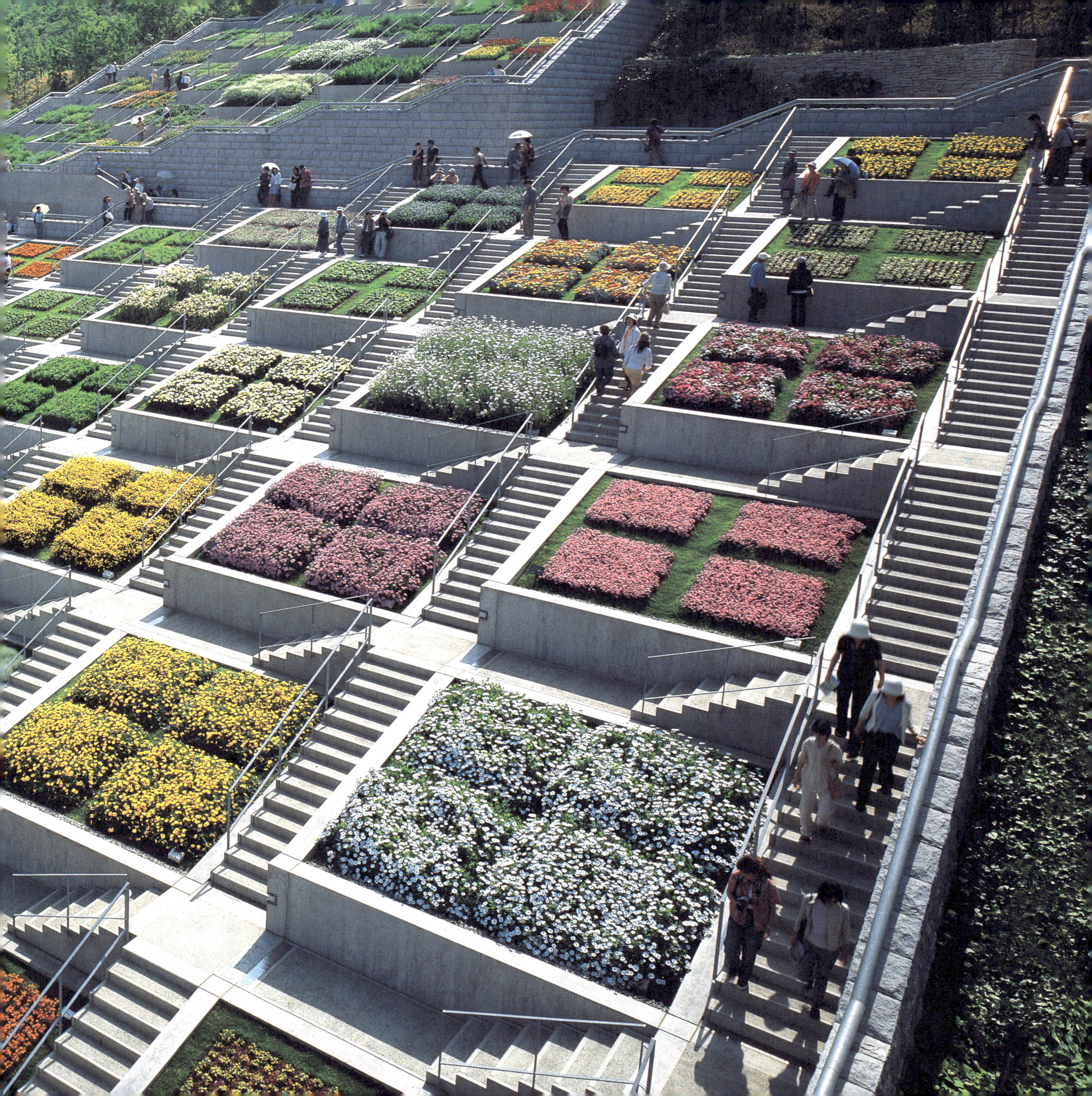

8

Chapter 6　Towards Landscaping and Urban Development

淡路夢舞台　1999
awaji-yumebutai

8. 山麓の段状の水の流れ
   Tiered water flowing at the bottom of the hill
9. 温室の外観
   Greenhouse exterior
10. 温室の内部
    Inside of the greenhouse

いわば住宅レベルの微細な寸法を疎かにしない姿勢に、わたしは感心させられた。

　この「百段苑」の右側に位置する「山回廊」は、浅い人工池をコンクリートの円柱の列が囲む中庭形式の通路になっている。安藤の厳格なプロポーション感覚が生かされ、ミース・ファン・デル・ローエに通じる冷徹な美学を体感できる。そこを抜けると吹き抜けの巨大なガラスの温室が待っている。

　敷地の高低差を活かした楕円の広場など、安藤ならではのコンクリートの躯体の醍醐味を感じさせる場が「夢舞台」にはびっしりと配されている。塔や回廊などを伝いながら、安藤の空間をここまで徹底的に堪能できる作品は他にない。そのようなコンクリートの空間を一段と特徴あるものに仕立てているのは、水の流れである。

　水の流れは「百段苑」の階段の傍らに始まり、高所から地上レベルまで勢いよく、敷地を縦断するように流れていく。ホテルの屋上には、その水の流れが小休止したかのような静寂の水面が広がる。そこはウェディング・チャーチ「海の教会」の屋上でもあり、コンクリートの塔が人工池にそびえる光景は美しい。屋上の水面は、視界のなかで大阪湾の海面へと連なる空間の広がりが演出されている。

　斜面を駆け下りた水は、地上レベルでは「貝の浜」と呼ばれる広大な人工池に至る。貝とは、ホタテ貝の貝殻であり、「淡路夢舞台」の人工池や水の流れ落ちる段状の水路の底には、帆立て貝の貝殻が規則正しく敷きつめられている。少し黄味がかった貝殻は、瀬戸内海沿岸の花崗岩質の自然土と同じ色調で違和感なく納まっている。安藤はこの貝殻の調達のため、缶詰会社の廃棄場を訪ねた。その熱意が実を結び、人工池の温かみを感じる肌合いが好もしい。

　水は音を立てて流れ、噴水状に吹き上げるときも威勢のいい音が響く。音は静寂を破る活力をこの場に与え、安藤の仕立てたランドスケープが常に息づいていると思わせる。「百段苑」の傍らの高所から地上までの水の勢いを目の当たりにすると、それはなにかを洗い落とし、清めていくように思えてくる。震災後に「淡路夢舞台」に追加された「百段苑」に安藤は、震災の犠牲者への追悼の気持ちを託した。流れ落ちる水は、慰霊の清めの水に思え、鑑賞者の体内の水と呼応して魂の存在を想起させる。庭園の絶えることがない水音は、永遠の生命の証のように耳のなかに響きわたり、えも言われぬ余韻を残していく。

第6章　ランドスケープ、まちづくりへ

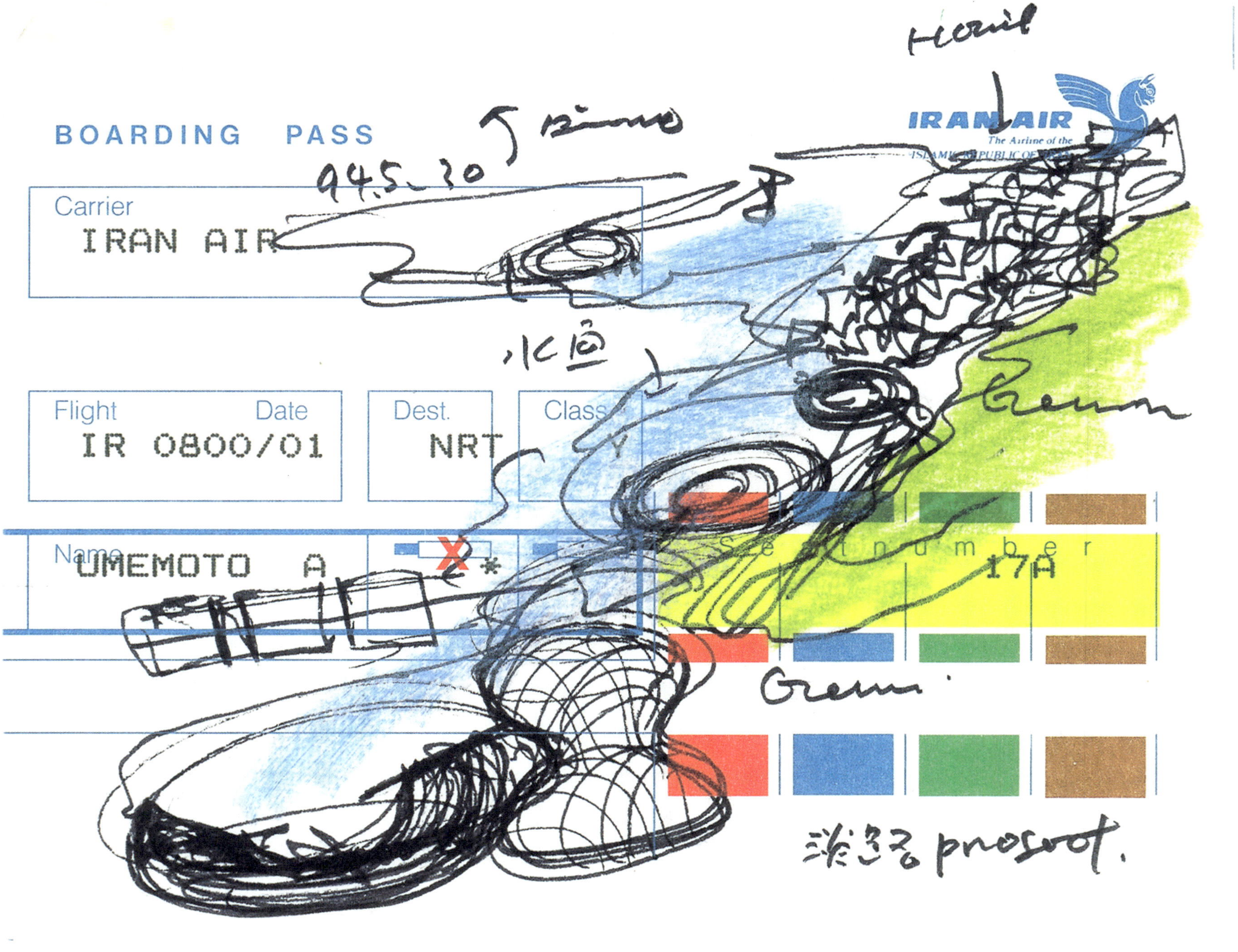
BOARDING PASS
IRAN AIR
Carrier
IRAN AIR
Flight
Date
IR 0800/01
Dest.
NRT
Class
Name
UMEMOTO A
Seat number
17A
94.5.30
Green
Green

淡路夢舞台　1999
awaji-yumebutai

11. （前ページ）搭乗券に描いたスケッチ
    (previous page) Sketch on a boarding pass
12. 海の教会の鐘楼
    Bell tower of the Marine Chapel
13. 水底に敷きつめたホタテの貝殻
    Scallop shells paved on the bottom of the water

The Turning Point as an Architect

When you look at the AWAJI-YUMEBUTAI from the architect's career point of view, it may be said that this project became a turning point for his architectural view. Ando said, "development typically destroys the nature, but in this project, development started with recovering the nature." The planning of AWAJI-YUMEBUTAI project started in about 1990 when Ando had been working on designing a series of projects in Naoshima, Kagawa Prefecture. In Naoshima, Ando was forced to face the fact that islands in the Seto Inland Sea were suffering from prioritizing industry and wastes, including copper refining in Naoshima and illegal dumping of wastes in Teshima, another island near Naoshima.

From that perspective, it surely became a great opportunity for Ando to shift his architectural view into a larger view that considered not only the architecture but also the environment, as he cooperated with Kaihara the governor who also faced to address the great earthquake, while multiple projects going on around Ando, including the one in Naoshima.

In the same period, SUNTORY MUSEUM TEMPOZAN and adjacent MERMAID PLAZA in the waterfront area of Osaka Nanko were Ando's another ambitious challenge to create the environment that went beyond the architecture. Ando had put so much effort on overcoming administrative constraints particularly for waterfront development, and the facility was finally opened in November 1994, two months before the occurrence of the great earthquake. He was motivated to make this waterfront area open for everyone by eliminating administrative barriers among the national government, local governments, and sections within the governments. He achieved to make it come true and constructed the PLAZA where a lot of people could sit on its steps, facing the water.

Since 1980s, the development of waterfront area had been the worldwide trend and industrial facilities such as factories were replaced with cultural and commercial facilities. Pollution and the citizen's attempts to avoid any adverse effect from it, as well as changes in industrial structure such as distribution accelerated such trend. The SUNTORY MUSEUM TEMPOZAN was also planned as a part of such development, and Ando claimed the necessity of space where people could use for free along with the "commercialized space (that is, payment required to use the space) and he created both.

1

サントリーミュージアム
＋マーメイド広場　1994
suntory museum + mermaid plaza

1. 幾何立体がならぶ外観。足元右端がマーメイド広場
   Appearance of geometric solids in a row.
   MERMAID PLAZA on the right at foot
2. 背後からの階段
   Stairs from behind
3. マーメイド広場の俯瞰
   Bird's-eye view of MERMAID PLAZA

建築家としての転機

　建築家としての歩みという観点から「淡路夢舞台」を見るとき、安藤の建築観にひとつの転機をもたらしたことに思いあたる。安藤曰く「開発は自然を破壊するものなのに、ここでは自然を再生するところからスタートが切られた」。1990年前後に「淡路夢舞台」の計画は実現に向けて動き出したが、ほぼ同じ時期に安藤は香川県直島の一連の作品の設計に取り組んでいた。直島の銅精錬、直島に近い豊島の廃棄物の不法投棄など、瀬戸内の島々が産業優先の排出物で悲鳴をあげている姿に目を背けるわけにはいかなかった。それはある意味、神戸北野町で西洋館が破壊されていく以上に深刻な島民の生活被害を伴っており、建築家としてそこでの創作の機会があるからには、本腰を入れて向き合わざるをえなかった。

　そうした観点に立つなら、貝原俊民という震災に正面から向き合う自治体首長と二人三脚の「淡路夢舞台」が、同時進行の直島などのプロジェクトを複眼的ににらみながら、安藤が建築を超えて環境へと建築観をより巨視的に転換していく、ひとつの大きなきっかけとなったのは間違いない。気候に恵まれ、歴史も積み重なる瀬戸内海への強い関西人の思いも、その転換を後押しした。大震災からの復興になんとしても建築家として力を尽くさねばという切迫した責任感もあった。「淡路夢舞台」はそのような観点から眺めるとき、安藤の真摯な瀬戸内への深い愛着の結実だったと受けとめられよう。

　同時期の、やはり建築の枠を超える環境の創造への意欲的な挑戦は、大阪南港のウオーターフロントに立地する「サントリーミュージアム」と連続する「マーメイド広場」だった。阪神淡路大震災発生の2カ月前の1994年11月にオープンしたこの施設の実現にあたって、安藤は湾岸エリア特有の行政の壁を乗り超える努力を重ねていた。国、自治体相互にも、また、それぞれの組織内のセクションごとの縄張りをいかに超えて、岸辺を市民に開くか、安藤は熱心にそのことに取り組み、海に向かって多くのひとが座ることのできる段状の広場を実現した。

　都市の岸辺は、近代産業国家建設の過程で工場施設に占拠され、市民を遠ざけた。大阪南港を市民に愛される場とするには、市民が自由に往来できて、海辺ならではの自然の移ろいを堪能できる広場が必要だと安藤は考えた。

　おりから1980年代以降、公害の悪影響の回避に加え、流通をはじめとする産業構造の変化が、工場などの産業施設を都市の水辺から追いやり、文化・商業施設によってそこを活性化するウオーターフロント開発が世界的に流行した。「サントリーミュージアム」もその流れの一環として計画され、安藤はその足元に「商品化された空間（対価を払わないとそこが使えない）」とは異なる無償の広場の必要性を訴え、実現にこぎ着けた。

　この「マーメイド広場」の実績が、震災後の神戸での実践につながった。震災で「兵

His experience with the MERMAID PLAZA helped him to deal with practical issues in Kobe after the great earthquake. Hyogo Prefectural Museum of Modern Art (designed by Togo Murano in 1970) was damaged by the earthquake, and Ando was chosen as the designer of the new Hyogo Prefectural Museum of Art (2002). The site for the new museum was situated at a corner of the waterfront area called "Tobu Shintoshin (HAT Kobe)", and there used to be a factory of Kobe Steel, Ltd. until it was destroyed by the earthquake.

Ando was commissioned to design the Museum and Kobe Waterfront Plaza (Nagisa Park) as a unit, since the sites of the two facilities were next to each other. The Plaza is located on the west side of the Museum, and is 500 meters long along the pier. You can see a forest of camphor trees stretching along the clear axis that goes through the elongated plaza. Ando requested government-designated cities in Japan for donating these trees to Kobe. Those camphor trees were orderly planted so that people expected to see a deep forest appeared in the shore. A folly with wide concrete eaves was constructed by the water, as well as an outdoor amphitheater at the center of the axis.

It was such a new experience for me who knew the old Hanshin Industrial Zone to appreciate the exhibition at the museum and to walk along the Waterfront Plaza.

White Flowers for the Remembrance

There is a freestanding wall which intersects with the axis of the Plaza. I found a stainless plate being placed on the wall. I got closer to the plate and it read "In Memory of Hyogo Green Network Planting Activity." Ando is a leader of the Hyogo Green Network, a volunteer group by citizens for greening activities, and I found out that its planting activity was carried out in this Plaza, too.

The objective of the Hyogo Green Network was to keep remembering the victims of the great earthquake by planting trees in cities of Hyogo. Its main activity was to distribute two seedlings to 125,000 households in the Reconstruction Housing, which were constructed in ten cities and ten towns in Hyogo. Residents look after these seedlings which grow and eventually bear white flowers such as magnolia denudata, magnolia kobus, and cornus florida. In response to Ando's call, a lot of people gathered for support and the donation of 380 million yen was generated.

It was Ando's words that moved people's heart,"every year when white flowers bloom, we all remember the victims of the great earthquake." 130,000 seedlings were procured by the donation, and 154,000 seedlings were purchased by volunteers and the group, and all of them were distributed. I could feel very well how passionate Ando was about people in the disaster-affected area when I heard him talking enthusiastically about this movement.

Eventually, more than 300,000 seedlings were distributed. So many people acted voluntarily in response to his call. Ando's message was widely understood.

兵庫県立美術館＋神戸市水際広場　2001
hyogo prefectural museum of art + kobe waterfront plaza

1. 神戸港の水辺に下りる階段
   Stairs down to the Kobe port
2. 神戸市水際広場の俯瞰
   Bird's-eye view of Kobe Waterfront Plaza
3. テラスに上る螺旋階段
   Spiral stairs up to the terrace

庫県立近代美術館」（1970年、設計・村野藤吾）が被災したことを受け、新たに計画された「兵庫県立美術館」（2002年）のプロポーザルで安藤が設計者に選ばれた。震災で被災した神戸製鋼所の跡地に計画された「東部新都心」と呼ばれる臨海地の一角が、新しい敷地となった。

美術館の設計は、敷地が連なる新都心の「神戸市水際広場（なぎさ公園）」と一体の形で安藤の手に委ねられた。広場は美術館の西側に位置し、岸壁に沿って500メートルの長さがある。細長い広場を貫く明確な軸線が意識され、それに沿い、安藤からの依頼を受けて全国の政令指定都市から神戸市に贈られたクスノキの森が延びている。クスノキは規則正しく植樹され、海辺に鬱蒼とした森が出現することが期待された。水辺にはコンクリートの深い庇を持つフォリー（あずまや）、軸線の中央には円形の屋外劇場が配された。

かつて工場施設がならび近寄ることも出来なかった水辺が、散策のひとびとの眼前に出現した。広場は摩耶埠頭との間の水路に沿って東西方向に伸び、視界の先には摩耶大橋の姿もある。美術館の展覧会を鑑賞したあと、この水辺の広場を歩く体験は、かつての阪神工業地帯を知るわたしにとって、とても新鮮だった。安藤が無償の広場を設営した功績は大きなものがあろう。

震災慰霊を「白い花」に託す

この広場の軸線と交差する形で一枚のコンクリートの独立壁が立っている。そこにステンレスのプレートが掲げられているのを見つけた。傍に寄って印字された文字を見ると「ひょうごグリーンネットワーク植樹記念」とある。この「ひょうごグリーンネットワーク」は、安藤を呼びかけ人代表とする市民の植樹運動で、この公園でも植樹が行われたことがわかった。

「ひょうごグリーンネットワーク」が目指したのは、震災で失われたひとびとへの鎮魂の気持ちを、植樹によって都市に刻印し、いつまでも記憶にとどめることだった。被災した10市10町に建設される復興住宅12万5千戸に、白い花をつけるモクレンやコブシ、ハナミズキなどの苗木を一軒あたり2本を配布し、住人に育ててもらうのを事業の中核とした。安藤の呼びかけに多くの賛同者が現れ、3億8千万円の寄付が集まった。

「白い花が咲くたびに震災で亡くなったひとを忘れないように思いをあらたにする」という安藤の呼びかけが、ひとびとの心を打った。寄付金で13万本が調達されたが、それを超える15万4千本がボランティアや団体の購入でまかなわれ、配布された。震災から間もない時期、この運動の目的について熱っぽく語る安藤の姿に接したとき、被災

第6章　ランドスケープ、まちづくりへ

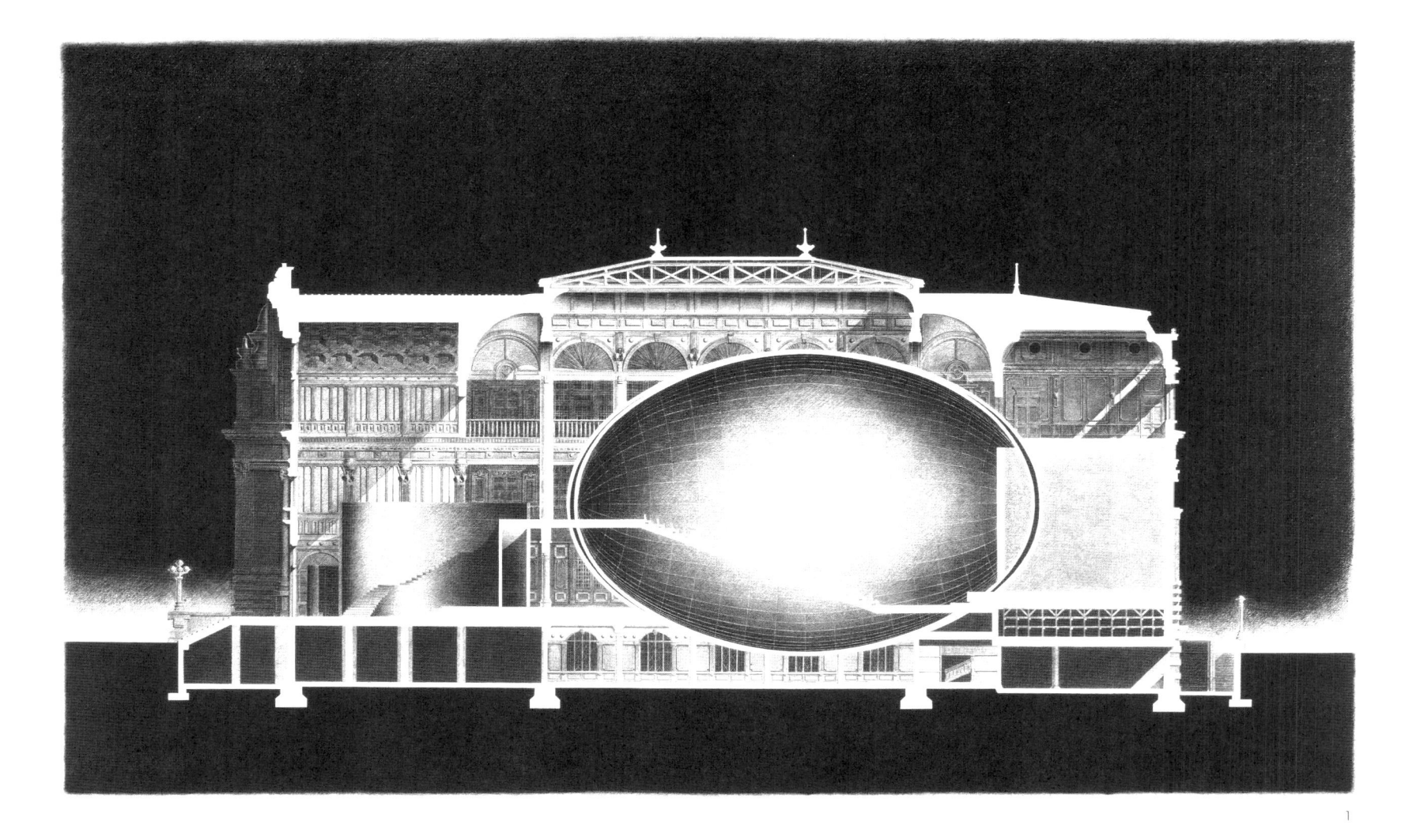

Ando's activities to improve the environment had further expanded and more and more citizens were encouraged to get involved. In 2000, Ando then established the Setouchi Olive Foundation, which objective was to plant one million olive trees on the islands of the Seto Inland Sea. The Seto Inland Sea was polluted and exhausted because the industry had been considered to be the first priority, and the activity to plant olive trees was expected to improve such situation.

A lawyer Kohei Nakabo was a leader of the movement for cleaning up 600,000 tons of illegally disposed industrial wastes which were left abandoned in Teshima Island of the Sato Inland Sea, and Ando got to know about such movement and agreed with the idea. Thus, Ando and Nakabo cooperated for the establishment of the foundation. The public survey at that time showed that Nakabo was considered to be the best person who would become the prime minister. Cooperation of Ando, an internationally recognized architect, and Nakabo made a great appeal and the number of supporters for the Setouchi Olive Foundation as well as the public concern about Teshima Island had both increased largely. In 2003, the Law on Special Measures concerning Removal of Environmental Problems Caused by Specified Industrial Wastes was enacted and Teshima Island was the first case to apply that law.

Flower Bloomed by
the Proposal for Nakanoshima,
Evolving into the Urban Construction

Nakanoshima, Osaka is situated in a sandbank on the Kyu-Yodogawa River. The current Yodogawa River runs through the northern part of the city, which was newly excavated after the great flood occurred in 1885. Therefore, the Kyu-Yodogawa River that runs through Nakanoshima was originally called the Yodogawa River. Currently, the Kyu-Yodogawa River is subdivided into sections and called in different names: the Okawa River from Kema Lock to Nakanoshima, the Dojima River from Nakanoshima (the left shore is called Tosabori River), and the Ajigawa River at the mouth into the Osaka Bay. Names of these rivers change chaotically even though the total length of the Kyu-Yodogawa River is as short as 15 kilometers. Nevertheless, people in Osaka are familiar with these names, showing that Nakanoshima and the Kyu-Yodogawa River are closely attached to the people's living.

The best seasonal attraction along the Okawa River of the Kyu-Yodogawa River is the Osaka Mint Bureau Cherry Blossom Tunnel in April. Every year, a large number of citizens come to enjoy watching 400 cherry trees in full bloom. It started in 1883 for not only the employees of the Bureau but also anyone to enjoy the arrival of spring, and it became a traditional event in this area that lasts over 130 years. Movement of planting cherry trees along the basin of Kyu-Yodogawa River had gradually expanded from this tunnel, and the Kemasakuranomiya Park near a point of river diversion has now over 4,000 cherry trees blooming in every spring.

Ando thought that the citizen's admiration for the cherry blossoms could help recovering the politics, economics and other situations of Osaka which had declined significantly. In December 2004, he established the executive committee of "Sakura no Kai: Cherry Blossom Tunnel in the Heisei Era", and called for support for expanding the cherry blossom tunnel to Nakanoshima by donations. Initially, it was at least 10,000 yen per donation to plant 1,000 cherry trees, but it received a great response since the Prime Minister Junichiro Koizumi visited the tree-planting ceremony on 8th January 2005 (a year after his visit to Teshima Island, and it was also his birthday). The project ended in 2015 as its objective had been achieved, with donations of 450 million yen generated in total, and the number of planted trees reached 3,000 which were distributed to areas other than the Kyu-Yodogawa River area. Plates with names of donators, 30 names per plate, are placed along with the cherry trees.

Chapter 6 Towards Landscaping and Urban Development

中之島プロジェクト II　1988
nakanoshima project II

1. 中央公会堂に卵を挿入
   Egg inserted into the Central Public Hall
2. 模型の内部
   Inside of the model

地への思いの強さが痛いほど伝わってきた。

　最終的には30万本を超える苗木が配布された。多くのひとが呼びかけに応じて自発的に動いた。思いは通じたのである。復興のまちは「白い花」という共有できるシンボルを手に出来た。神戸近辺の自治体のなかには、ウェブサイトでこの運動によって植樹された木がどこにあるかを案内しているところもある。

　安藤のこうした環境づくりに市民の参加を促す活動はさらに広がり、瀬戸内海の島々に100万本のオリーブの木を植える運動「瀬戸内オリーブ基金」を2000年に立ち上げるに至った。産業優先の思考が瀬戸内海を汚染し、疲弊させた状況を広く社会に訴え、その回復をオリーブの植樹に託した。

　運動のきっかけは、瀬戸内海に浮かぶ豊島に不法投棄され、放置されたままになっていた60万トンに達する産業廃棄物の除去運動を、弁護士の中坊公平が主導していることへの共感だった。基金設立の呼びかけは、安藤と中坊の連名だった。当時の世論調査では、中坊は首相にしたい人物の筆頭に擬せられていた。その中坊と世界的評価を集める安藤の連携は訴求力があった。「瀬戸内オリーブ基金」への賛同の声の広がりとともに、豊島問題への社会的な関心も高まり、2003年には「産廃特措法（特定産業廃棄物支障除去特別措置法）」が成立し、豊島はその適用第一号になった。

　それを受けて、小泉純一郎首相が、2004年1月8日に豊島を訪れ、産業廃棄物の掘削や下水の無害化処理の作業現場を、安藤らの案内で視察した。1月8日は、小泉の誕生日にあたる。「産廃特措法」は10年間の時限立法だったが、改正法によりさらに10年間延長され、現在に至っている。

「中之島」への提案から開花、そして都市造営の結実

　大阪・中之島はその名の通り、旧淀川の中洲に位置している。今の淀川は市域の北部を流れているが、これは明治18年（1885年）の大洪水を受けて新たに開削した流路で、それまで淀川といえば、中之島を流れる旧淀川のことを指した。現在では旧淀川は、分流の閘門にあたる毛馬から中之島までを「大川」、中之島からは「堂島川（左岸は土佐堀川）」、大阪湾に注ぐ河口は「安治川」と呼ぶ。せいぜい15キロほどの流れが、目まぐるしいほど呼称を変える。それらの河川名も大阪のひとびとの間には定着しており、中之島はもちろん、旧淀川が暮らしに密着していることをうかがわせる。

　この旧淀川の大川界隈の最大の風物詩は、毎年4月初旬に開催される造幣局の「桜の通り抜け」だ。その数400本、多くの市民が春の到来を楽しむ風景が定着している。この通り抜けが始まったのは明治16年。局員だけが楽しむのではなく、広く春の到来

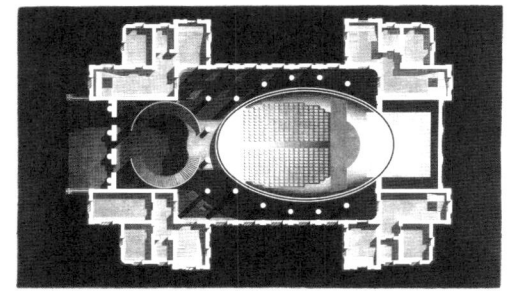

Ando first got involved with Nakanoshima when he started the NAKANOSHIMA PROJECT I in 1980. In this project, he proposed to renovate Osaka City Hall, originally constructed in 1921, in a way that the entrance part would leave as it was but enclose it by a large latticed frame so that the new City Hall could emphasize the relationship between the internal and external environment. In 1989, NAKANOSHIMA PROJECT II (URBAN EGG SPACE STRATA) was also proposed by Ando, in which a huge egg-shaped hall would be inserted into the Osaka City Central Public Hall, the symbol of Nakanoshima originally constructed in 1918. The egg-shaped hall was 32 meters long-side by 21 meters short-side with an oval flat surface and the capacity of 400 people, and expected to place a gallery outside the egg. The bottom part of the egg would be buried underground.

Ando's proposal was so unique for preservation of the historic building that some researchers disagreed with it. Nevertheless, Ando claimed that it was essential to have stimulus and conflict by catabolism between its historical context and modern creation in order to succeed the vitality of Nakanoshima to the future. His passion for the city was brought to fruition by "Sakura no Kai: Cherry Blossom Tunnel in the Heisei Era", and as he kept passionate about the city, a particular urban facility, as a bridge, eventually started to take shape.

The Sakuranomiya Bridge, commonly called "Gin-bashi (silver bridge)" by citizens of Osaka due to its steel-framed metallic exterior, is a bridge on the Kyu-Yodogawa River near the Osaka Mint Bureau. It was constructed in 1930 by the design of Takeda Goichi who was a leading figure of architect world in Kansai area from the Meiji Era to the pre-war Showa Era. Ando had also been familiar with the Gin-bashi since he was a child. Even when the renovation project of Gin-bashi for widening the road was brought up, it was decided that the bridge would stay as it was and a new bridge would be constructed next to the original one. Ando was commissioned to supervise the design the new bridge.

Ando showed his respect to the silhouette of original Gin-bashi and thus referred to the structure as much as possible to decide the external design of SHIN SAKURANOMIYA BRIDGE (completed in 2006). As I see the old and new Sakuranomiya Bridges with cherry blossoms in the Mint Bureau area being full in bloom in the background, I feel like celebrating Ando's contribution for the city and these bridges are the monument of his successful work. The citizen knew well about Ando's intention, and they started to call the new bridge "Shin Gin-bashi". A wonderful urban story in the 21st century had begun here.

Ando was also commissioned not only to design the entrance of a new railway station "Naniwabashi Station" on the Keihan Nakanoshima Line, located nearby the Osaka City Central Public Hall, but also to be in charge of improving the surrounding streetscape. In this area, there are many cultural facilities, including Osaka Prefectural Nakanoshima Library (1904) and the Museum of Oriental Ceramics, Osaka (1982). Ando further proposes construction of the Center for Children's Literature, Osaka, next to the Museum of Oriental Ceramics, Osaka, and still continues to work passionately for the future of Nakanoshima.

Chapter 6 Towards Landscaping and Urban Development

新桜宮橋
Shin Sakuranomiya Bridge

1. 手前が新しい橋
   New bridge in front
2. 中之島遠景
   Distant view of Nakanoshima
3. 中之島の模型の展示
   A model of Nakanoshima

を謳歌してもらう、130年以上続く「市民のための伝統行事」となっている。この通り抜けに始まり、旧淀川流域に桜を植樹する動きは年を追って拡大し、分流地点に近い「毛馬桜宮公園」には4000本を超える桜が植わり、満開時には市民の目を楽しませてきた。

安藤はこの桜を愛でる市民の心情を、政治、経済など各方面で地盤沈下著しい大阪の復興に役立てることを考え、2004年12月、「桜の会・平成の通り抜け」実行委員会を立ち上げ、市民から寄付を募り、中之島界隈まで「桜の回廊」を延伸させることを呼びかけた。当初1000本を目標にひと口1万円で寄付を求めたが、2005年の1月8日に小泉純一郎首相（豊島訪問の1年後のやはり誕生日だった）が記念植樹に足を運んだこともあり、大きな反響を呼んだ。結局、2015年に目的を達したとして事業が終了するまでに4億5千万円の寄付が集まり、植樹のエリアは旧淀川流域以外まで広がり、植樹は3000本に達した。寄付者の名前は30人ひと組でプレートに記載、桜の木の傍に掲げられている。

大阪のみならず、日本のひとびとが季節の設えを今なお尊重する心情を見抜いた見事なまでの市民運動家としての安藤の姿をそこに見出すことができる。確かに、わが国において、建築の話題を文化的な次元で広く語ることは、困難を極める。では諦めるのか。いや、安藤は市民感情を踏まえて、大阪や神戸、淡路島の被災地、瀬戸内の島々を少しでもよくしようと、敢えて建築の領域には踏み込まずに植樹などの運動を呼びかけ、大きな成果をあげた。

安藤自身の「中之島」との関わりは、1980年の「中之島プロジェクトI」に始まる。これは中之島に現存していた「大阪市役所」（1921年）の保存問題が持ち上がっていたなかで、市役所のエントランス回りを残し、大きな格子のフレームで囲うことによって、内部空間と外部環境の関わりを浮かび上がらせる新しい市役所の提案だった。そして、1989年には、この「I」に続いて、中之島のシンボルとされる「大阪市中央公会堂」（1918年）の内部に、巨大な卵形の新たなホールを入れ子として挿入する「中之島プロジェクトII、地層空間、アーバン・エッグ」を提案した。卵形のホールは、長径32メートル、短径21メートルの楕円の平面を持つ立体で、そこを400人収容のホールとし、卵の外側にギャラリーなどの配置を想定していた。卵形の下部は地中に埋め込む提案だった。

歴史的建造物の保存としては研究者から異論も出る独創的な提案だったが、安藤は中之島の活力を未来に継承するためには、歴史的な文脈と現代の創造の相互異化作用による刺激と対立が欠かせないものだと主張した。「桜の会・平成の通り抜け」はその思いの結実であり、信念の持続は、やがて橋梁という具体的な都市施設としても形をとることになった。

旧造幣局の傍らで旧淀川（大川）に架かるのは「桜宮橋」で、大阪のひとびとは、鉄骨を組み上げたこの橋を金属質の外装ゆえに「銀橋」と呼び倣わしてきた。昭和5年架橋の「銀橋」は、明治から昭和戦前期に関西建築界の重鎮として君臨した武田五一の設

Into the Development of
Sakura Hiroba and Sea Forest

Panasonic Corporation, an electronics manufacturer of the Osaka origin, supported the movement of "Sakura no Kai: Cherry Blossom Tunnel in the Heisei Era", and later Ando and the company agreed to construct Sakura Hirobas in four places in Kanto and Kansai areas. These four sites used to be the company's factories but now the idle lands. The largest Sakura Hiroba was constructed in Makuhari New City of Narashino, Chiba. An artificial pond, water conduit, and undulating circular path were designed by Ando, and many citizens visit here when the blossoms are in full bloom.

The site is located in the extended area of Makuhari New City, and the 3 hectares of Sakura Hiroba was designed to become what Ando called a cherry garden with "modern landscape". He created slopes for what originally was a flat land, and visitors could have panoramic view on top of the hill. From there, visitors could enjoy the cherry blossoms to the fullest. There are 505 trees of Prunus x yedoensis in total, orderly planted in accordance with square grids divided the site. The most attractive area in the Sakura Hiroba is a large oval pond, located close to the far end from the entrance, and visitors can walk along its gentle slope. The pond has a fountain and a disk with planted roses protrudes from the water surface. There are also a small circular pond, a conduit stretching from the entrance to the large pond, and an azumaya, all of which add beauty to the park.

When I visited here with full bloomed cherry blossoms, a lot of people also knew that it was the best time to see them bloom so that they came here and enjoyed walking around. These cherry trees are expected to become as tall as 6 meters.

The other three Sakura Hirobas are smaller than the one in Makuhari, but located in Chigasaki, Kanagawa, Kadoma (where the headquarters of Panasonic is) and Toyonaka in Osaka. All of them utilized the idle lands of Panasonic Corporation to construct Sakura Hirobas and Ando designed the landscape of these sites in order to create modernism gardens. He thanked Panasonic for making efforts to maintain Sakura Hiroba in waterfront area such as developing the windbreak.

さくら広場　2006
sakura hiroba

1. 幕張のさくら広場
   Cherry Plaza of Makuhari
2. 幕張のあずまや
   Azumaya of Makuhari

計による。安藤も子どものときから「銀橋」を近しい存在として認識してきた。そして、道路幅を広げるために「銀橋」改修の計画が持ち上がったとき、もとの「銀橋」はそのままに、すぐ傍に平行する新しい橋を架けることになり、安藤がその意匠監修を依頼された。

もとの「銀橋」のシルエットを尊重し、構造体の形式も可能な範囲で援用する形で「新桜宮橋」（2006年）の外観は決まった。新旧2本の橋が造幣局と一帯の満開の桜を背景にならぶ姿を眺めると、安藤がこの街に貢献した「記念碑」の誕生として祝福したい気持ちになる。市民もそのことをよく認識していて、今では、安藤の新しい橋を「新銀橋」と呼ぶようになった。すばらしい21世紀の都市の物語の誕生だ。

さらに安藤は「中央公会堂」に近い京阪電車中之島線の新駅「なにわ橋駅」の出入り口のデザインと周辺の景観整備の担い手ともなった。この一帯には「大阪府立中之島図書館」（1904年）、「東洋陶磁美術館」（1982年）など文化施設が集積している。安藤は「東洋陶磁美術館」の隣地に児童文学館の新設も提言しており、中之島の未来を見据えた活動にさらに本腰を入れている。

「さくら広場」「海の森」への展開

「桜の会・平成の通り抜け」への協賛を受けたのをきっかけに、安藤は、大阪由来の電機メーカー「パナソニック」と相談し、同社の関東、関西一円の工場跡の遊休地4か所に「さくら広場」を実現させた。なかでも大規模な千葉の幕張新都心に近接する「さくら広場」（習志野市）は、安藤の手で人工池、水路、起伏をもたせた回遊路が設計され、満開時には多くの市民がつめかけ、活況を呈している。

立地は幕張新都心の拡大地区と呼ばれるエリアで「さくら広場」の広さは3ヘクタール、安藤がいうところの「モダン・ランドスケープ」の桜の園に仕立て上げた。平坦だった敷地に緩やかな勾配を持たせ、高いところからは桜並木が俯瞰できるようにした。満開の桜を堪能してもらうための仕掛けだ。樹種はソメイヨシノで総数505本、正方形のグリッドに従って規則的に植樹した。一番の見どころはエントランスから最奥に近い場所に配した楕円形の大池で、緩やかなスロープの縁を歩くことができる。この池では噴水が水を吹き上げ、バラを植えた円盤が水面に突き出している。他に、小さな円形の小池、エントランスから大池に向かって伸びる水路やあずまやも散策に彩りを添えて目を楽しませる。

満開の日にわたしが訪れたとき、多くのひとびとが開花日を把握してつめかけ、そぞろ歩きに興じていた。桜は6メートルの高さに成長することを期待されている。1980

The Sea Forest in Tokyo Bay was Ando's another achievement. A development project was adopted in 2005 that would turn the 88 hectares of the east part of the landfill site inside the central breakwater, which had been built with 12.3 million tons of garbage from Tokyo in 14 years since 1973, into a green island by planting trees. That is the Sea Forest. This was another project to recover the environment which was destroyed by the economic activity of the human.

Ando gathered supporters all over the world, and started to plant trees in 2008. In the same year, Bono from an Irish rock band U2, and Wangari Maathai, a Kenyan environmental activist who made the word "Mottainai" popular worldwide, also joined the planting and appealed that Tokyo was proactively dealing with environmental issues. The amount of donation had reached its goal, 500 million yen, in four years.

Since the site is on the sea, trees that will tolerate salty winds such as Machilus thunbergii, and that will collect birds and insects around their flowers and fruits such as Japanese camellia and Morella rubra are chosen for planting. The project aims to plant 480,000 trees in total. The site has been under construction since it will be used as the venue for rowing matches in the 2020 Summer Olympics in Tokyo.

While Ando has been working on a series of projects that are not the architecture but the environment, he mentioned, in a way to criticize himself, as follows: Eco-friendly architecture is no excuse to be unattractive. I am an architect and not a social activist, and therefore I will be nothing if I cannot create good architecture. I want to keep the balance between the two. He said this before the Great East Japan Earthquake occurred on 11th of March, 2011. However, it may be a foreseen statement about his attitude toward the post-earthquake architecture, when the main focus of architecture in general tends to the disaster prevention and texture of wood, which might be an easier solution, is more likely to be favored.

海の森　2007
sea forest

1. （前ページ）ドローイング
(previous page) Drawing
2. 植樹するボランティア
Volunteers for planting trees

年代後半から開発の進んだ幕張新都心は、最寄り駅のJR京葉線海浜幕張駅の東側にあたる一帯が住宅や緑地公園など市民の憩いのゾーンになっている。この「さくら広場」は同駅西側の大規模商業施設などが多いエリアの一角に位置し、一帯の都市空間のイメージアップに寄与している。

　なにより、入場料を徴収するわけでもなく、無償の空間として新都市に貢献しているのがすばらしい。わが国において、パナソニックという大企業が植生を管理し、市民の季節の喜びに貢献している姿は、土地という私有物を公的な資産として活用する先例として好もしい。

　幕張以外の3か所は、幕張よりも小規模だが、神奈川県の茅ヶ崎、大阪の門真市と豊中市に位置する。いずれもパナソニック所有の遊休地を整備して「さくら広場」が実現した。この3か所も安藤の手で敷地内のランドスケープがデザインされ、モダニズムの庭園が出現した。

　安藤は、パナソニックが「さくら広場」を臨海地で維持するため、防風林を整備するなど努力を重ねたことに感謝を述べている。その意味でも、「さくら広場」は、市民が「桜の会・平成の通り抜け」を個人の寄付で支えた実績を踏まえ、企業がその成果を大阪以外の地域にも拡大する役割を果たしたことになる。寄付を個人が持ち寄る一方、企業体力の範囲内でどのように公的空間の質向上の道が見出せるか、日本社会の現実を踏まえた安藤の賢明な判断もそこからは読み取れるだろう。

　安藤のこうした活動のもうひとつの成果に、東京湾の「海の森」がある。1973年から14年間、都内のゴミ1230万トンを集めて造られた「中央防波堤内側埋立地」の東側部分にあたる広さ88ヘクタールを、植樹によって「緑の島」に再生する整備計画が2005年に決定された。それが「海の森」だ。ここもまた人間が経済活動によって破壊した環境を回復するプロジェクトとなった。

　安藤が世界から賛同者を募って2008年から植樹が始まった。同年にはアイルランドのロックバンド「U2」のボノ、ケニアの環境運動家で「MOTTAINAI」を世界的な流行語にしたワンガリ・マータイらも植樹に参加し、東京が環境問題に積極的に取り組んでいることをアピールした。募金額は4年間で目標額の5億円を達成した。

　海上に位置するため、潮風に強いタブノキをはじめ、鳥や昆虫が果実や花に集まるヤブツバキやヤマモモなどの樹種が選ばれ、最終的には48万本の植樹を目指している。2020年東京オリンピックのボート競技の会場に予定され、工事が続いている。

　1年のうち何日か公開される日を選んで訪れた。もともとゴミの累積が高さ30メートルに達していたこともあり、埋立地とは思えない築山のようになっていた。完成すれば、視覚的にも変化に富んだ緑の島に仕立てられそうだ。東京都は「海の森」の登場によって、東京湾から都心部への風の流れを変化させ、地球温暖化に伴うヒートアイランド現象の解消につなげたいとしている。

*Architecture That Is Productive
and Is Eco-friendly at the Same Time*

Ando and Kozo Iwata, a chairman, president and CEO of Rock Field Co., Ltd. which sells delicatessen at the shop called RF1 on the basement food floor in department stores nationwide, had a long-time friendship. In 1977, on the ground floor of Rose Garden which was Ando's masterpiece of commercial building in Kitano-cho, Kobe, a takeout shop called Kobe Croquette was tenanted. Iwata first opened a small restaurant in Kobe in 1965, and later started to sell delicatessen which went on track so that he tried to find a new market in Kitano-cho where many tourists come to visit Western style buildings.

Ando received acclaim for the Row House, Sumiyoshi and also this Rose Garden, and became a world famous architect. Iwata expanded the delicatessen business with unique menus and shops until it became an essential shop in the food floor of department stores. The name "Rock Field", which is an English translation of the two kanji characters of his surname, became a well-known food brand. The encounter of the two successful persons became a rare story in Japanese society at the time of experiencing stagnant economy.

Ando designed a series of Rock Field buildings, from the headquarters to factories. It started from the first project of the factory in Shizuoka (Iwata, Shizuoka) in 1991, the second project in 2000, the third project in 2009, and now the fourth project is planned. Tamagawa Factory in the Tokyo metropolitan area was also designed by Ando and completed in 2003.

In 2004, he also designed the Rock Field's new headquarters with a factory attached in a landfill site in Kobe. For this project, he utilized a warehouse that used to be a logistics center for Sogo Kobe but was destroyed by the Great Hanshin-Awaji Earthquake. In this project, Ando opened a new frontier as an architect by renovating the existing building. Having a strong relationship of mutual trust between Ando and Iwata and the continuing expansion of his business of Rock Field, 40 years of groundbreaking story of architecture is woven, and it will lead to the future.

The series of Rock Field architectures were designed with the essence of what Ando had achieved in the environmental movement in the Seto Inland Sea, Osaka, and Kobe. The Rock Field company calls its factory in Shizuoka "the Factory Park". This is because the company considers that the factory is not only a place for production, but also a comprehensive facility with surrounding natural environment. The history of this factory has been in parallel with Ando's increasing interest in the environment.

Iwata obtained the site for a production facility in an industrial complex in Toyooka (later Iwata by annexation). The site was located near an interchange of the Tomei Expressway and thus beneficial for the shipment of products to areas including the Tokyo metropolitan area, Kinki area, and Chukyo area. It was always the case, however, that the developed industrial complex had no particular urban infrastructures nor convenient facilities for living, except a reservoir. Iwata, who made the current business successful from his knowledge about delicatessen in Europe, had an image of his production facility located in a forest, and thus asked Ando to create the forest. The first factory construction project started when Ando gave advice for Iwata to plant trees.

ロックフィールド静岡ファクトリー　1991, 2000
rockfield shizuoka factory

1. 風力発電の風車もそびえる
   Towering wind turbines for power generation
2. 段差のある敷地をつなぐ空中廊下
   Skywalk connecting tiered sites
3. アプローチから中庭を望む
   Courtyard viewed from the approachway

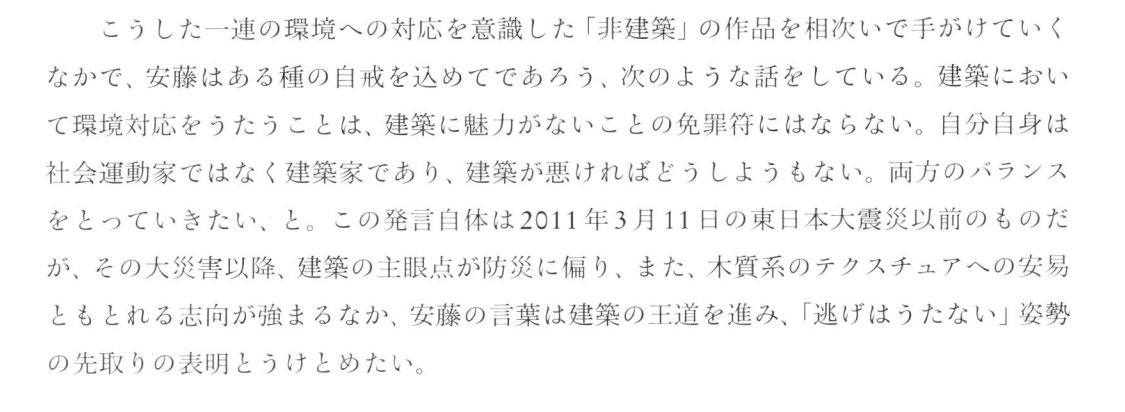

こうした一連の環境への対応を意識した「非建築」の作品を相次いで手がけていくなかで、安藤はある種の自戒を込めてであろう、次のような話をしている。建築において環境対応をうたうことは、建築に魅力がないことの免罪符にはならない。自分自身は社会運動家ではなく建築家であり、建築が悪ければどうしようもない。両方のバランスをとっていきたい、と。この発言自体は2011年3月11日の東日本大震災以前のものだが、その大災害以降、建築の主眼点が防災に偏り、また、木質系のテクスチュアへの安易ともとれる志向が強まるなか、安藤の言葉は建築の王道を進み、「逃げはうたない」姿勢の先取りの表明とうけとめたい。

生産の場でありながら、自然を尊重する建築

　全国の百貨店の地下惣菜売り場で「RF1」という店を構える「ロックフィールド」の経営者、岩田弘三は、安藤の古くからの知己である。1977年、安藤が神戸・北野町で手がけた商業建築の名作「ローズガーデン」の1階にはテイクアウトの店「神戸コロッケ」がテナントとして入っていた。岩田は1965年、神戸市内で小さなレストランを開業、その後始めた高級惣菜の販売が軌道に乗り、西洋館目当てに観光客の集まる北野町に新たな販路を求めた。

　安藤は「住吉の長屋」に続き、この「ローズガーデン」でも高い評価を受け、世界的な建築家に成長していった。岩田もまた惣菜のイメージを一新する店舗とメニューで、百貨店の食品売り場に欠かせない存在となるまで業務を拡大、姓を英語に写した「ロックフィールド」は、食の領域のブランドとして定着した。二人の出会いは、停滞著しい日本の社会にあって、希有な成功者の物語となった。

　その「ロックフィールド」の本社、工場など一連の施設は、一貫して安藤が設計を手がけてきた。1991年の静岡工場（静岡県磐田市）の第1期に始まり、2000年に第2期、2009年には第3期と関わり続け、第4期の計画も検討されている。2003年完成の首都圏の施設「玉川ファクトリー」も安藤の設計による。

　安藤はさらに2004年には神戸の埋立地に工場併設の新本社を設計した。阪神淡路大震災で被災した「そごう神戸店」の物流センターの倉庫建築を活用し、減築再生で、建築家としての新境地を開いた。「ロックフィールド」の業務拡大の勢いそのままに、創業者岩田との強固な信頼関係のうえに、40年の画期的な建築の物語が綴られ、それは未来へと繋がっていこうとしている。

　この「ロックフィールド」の一連の作品は、安藤が瀬戸内海や大阪や神戸で呼びかけてきた自然を取り戻す社会運動の成果が凝縮された仕立てになっている。同社は「静

ロックフィールド静岡ファクトリー 1991, 2000
rockfield shizuoka factory

4. 屋外彫刻と風車
Outdoor sculpture and a wind turbine

It was Iwata who decided to plant persimmon trees. 250 seedlings, same as the number of employees in the factory at that time, were planted. When persimmons are ripe, employees can help themselves to the fruits. Three years after planting those trees, Iwata sent Ando a box of persimmons as a gift at the end of the year, and ever since it continues every year. It took five years for the factory complex with soil being exposed to become "the factory in a forest" as Iwata first imaged.

The exterior of this factory seems to be the abstraction image of the Senanque Abbey in Southern France with which Ando was deeply impressed. The company describes this factory as "the factory like a museum", which is understandable given the Senanque Abbey as its origin.

The great proportion of the building was occupied mainly by the production department on the first and second floors. At both ends of the building, long and thin parts with vaults are the third floor where a cafeteria and a kitchen for food research are placed. Looking down from the third floor, you can see the green lawn extending on the roof of the second floor which provides pleasure and relaxation for the employees.

As the factory developed in the second and third projects, a biotope was placed for improving the ecology of surrounding nature. With this biotope, a conduit of 180 meters long was also constructed and they contribute to improve the quality of environment along with the forest of persimmons, zelkovas, and sweet viburnums. There are also three windmills for generating electricity at the site, which visually represents the company's practices for the circulating society. This factory procures ingredients from neighboring farmers, and employs workers in the area. The community-based approach of the factory perfectly corresponds to what Ando has proposed in a series of social movements.

Renovation of the Damaged Architecture

After the Great Hanshin-Awaji Earthquake occurred in 1995, Kobe was forced to change its way fundamentally. A department store Sogo Kobe is one of the major commercial facilities in Kobe, and its logistics center was located at a corner of the landfilled factory complex in Uozakihamamachi. The logistics center, however, was seriously damaged by the earthquake and the company was forced to sell it. The landfilled site caused ground liquefaction, and the unequal settling occurred by the earthquake and buildings on that site were shook and undulated. Since it owned its initial office nearby, Rock Field became a new owner of the facility, and Ando was commissioned to design the company's new headquarters with a factory attached.

Although the floor of the warehouse was heaved with up to 30 centimeters height difference, the architect chose to renovate the building as he utilized the structure as much as possible. Considering the damage by the earthquake, the top floor of the five-story building was torn down and the four-story structure was left for renovation. The idea was to reduce the load on the structure so that the existing building could be utilized. Surprisingly, he decided that the heaved floor with 30 centimeters height difference caused by the unequal settling would basically be left as it was. As a result, slopes and stairs were placed on each floor, creating expressions in a large space.

The third floor is mainly used for the employees to prepare themselves before work, and the production floor is on the ground level. Going up the stairs to the fourth floor, the administrative department and the cafeteria are placed around the light garden at the center of the building. The original building was so large that the frontage of the building was as long as 160 meters. By utilizing the original structure, the light garden became as long as 100 meters. The large-scale light garden provides a plenty of natural light and a view of the blue sky in corridors and the cafeteria, as well as the refreshing office environment in the waterfront. Although the ceilings of each floor were not high since it was originally a warehouse, the cafeteria on the top floor provides openness with the gently curved and elevated ceiling.

In the corridor of the fourth floor, there is a panel that explains how the original building was renovated into the current building, and a sample of the stainless exterior material unit used to cover the exterior of the original building is displayed, too. The company is proud of this architecture.

The architect Tadao Ando started expressing his philosophy in the design of a little concrete house, and as his work became acclaimed worldwide, he used his name and status to change the society. Then, he gets feedbacks from his social activities and reflects them into the architecture. He demonstrates what he believes. Ando always says, "If you are an architect, doing social activities is not enough. Creating superior architecture is what the architect is for." Indeed, he embodies his words. One of his ideals that he aimed to achieve is "architecture that transcends the architecture", and such architecture truly exists here. It is worth celebrating the fact that he achieved his ideal by the design of the production facility for people's everyday life, rather than the architecture of authoritarian character.

岡工場」を「ファクトリーパーク」と呼ぶ。単なる生産場所ではなく、食品メーカーらしい、自然環境を生かした総合空間との位置づけである。この工場の歩みは、安藤が環境への関心を高めていく過程と並走する形で進んでいった。

　岩田は、工場用地を静岡県の豊岡村（のちに合併で磐田市）の工場団地に求めた。東名高速のインターチェンジに近く、首都圏、近畿圏、中京圏への商品出荷に地の利があった。しかし、造成された工業団地の常で、調整池以外にはこれといった都市インフラも生活利便施設も存在しなかった。ヨーロッパでデリカテッセンを知って現在の業態を成功させた岩田は「森のなかの工場」を自社の生産施設として想定、安藤に「森をつくりたい」と持ちかけた。安藤は木を植えるのを勧め、そこから第1期の工場建設プロジェクトが立ち上がった。

　樹種を柿の木にするのを決めたのは岩田だった。苗木の本数は250本、当時の工場の従業員数にあわせた。柿の実がなれば遠慮なく従業員が食べられるようにと考えた。3年後、岩田から安藤のもとにお歳暮として柿が送られてくるようになり、毎年続いている。森がそれらしい姿になるのに5年を要したが、土が剥き出しだった工場団地は岩田の求めた「森のなかの工場」に姿を変えた。

　この工場の建築の外観は、安藤が感銘を受けた南仏セナンクの聖堂のイメージを抽象化したように思える。エレベーターシャフトのガラスの塔が建物の屋根を見おろすように中央に聳え、塔を中心にガラス壁の回廊が1階から3階までスロープとなって半円を描く。来訪者はこのガラスの回廊を登って3階のエントランスに至る。

　安藤の同時期の作品に南仏セナンクの修道院と聖堂を意識した「六甲の教会」がある。その「六甲の教会」で直線だった柱廊（コロナード）が、「ロックフィールド静岡ファクトリー」では立体的な曲線に置き換えられた。同社はこの工場を「美術館のような工場」と説明しているが、セナンクに原形をたどれるとなれば合点もいこう。このスロープからアプローチする工場本体の建築も安藤のトレードマークである幾何立体を組み合わせた造形で清楚な美しさを湛え、食品の生産現場として望ましいイメージを醸しだすことに成功している。

　建物の大部分は2階までに抑制され、そこに主として生産部門を配した。両端のヴォールト屋根の架かった細長いところだけが3階で、そこに従業員食堂、調理研究のためのキッチンなどが配されている。3階から見やると、床を延長した位置に広がる2階の水平屋根が芝生によって緑化され、勤務の合間の食事時間に従業員の目を楽しませ、心を和ませる役割を果たしている。

　第2期、第3期と、いわば工場そのものが成長する過程で、自然の生態を生かしたビオトープも設けられた。このビオトープは、長さ180メートルの水路が配され、柿の木やケヤキ、サンゴジュなどの林と一体になって、環境の質の向上に寄与している。敷地内には、電力を自力でまかなう風力発電の風車3基が立ち、循環社会の実践が目に見え

第6章　ランドスケープ、まちづくりへ

る形で表現されている。食材を周辺の農家から調達し、農家のひとびとを工場の従業員に採用する地域尊重型の工場のありかたは、安藤が提唱してきた数々の社会運動と見事に符合している。

再生された被災建築

　1995年に起きた阪神淡路大震災の発生により、神戸は好むと好まざるに関わらず、地域と社会の根底からの激変を余儀なくされた。百貨店「そごう神戸店」は、神戸の消費施設の一翼を担う存在で、魚崎浜町の埋立工場団地の一角に「流通センター」を所有していたが、震災によって建物は大きな被害を受け、手放さざるをえなくなった。埋立地ゆえに地盤は液状化し、建物は不同沈下に見舞われ、軒線が波うっているように見えたという。近隣に最初の事業所を持っていた縁で、「ロックフィールド」が施設の新たな所有者となり、工場を併設する本社の設計が安藤に委ねられた。

　床のうねりの高低差は最大30センチにも達していたが、既存の社会資産の活用という観点から、流通センターの建物を可能な限り活用して、本社と工場に再構成する道が選ばれた。震災によるダメージを考慮して、まず、既存の最上階を解体し、5階建てを4階に「減築」する道が選ばれた。構造面での負荷を小さくして、既存の建物を活用するための選択だった。そして、驚くべきことだが、不同沈下によって30センチもの高低差のついてしまった床も基本的にそのまま活用することにした。その結果、各階のいくつかの場所にスロープや階段がつくられ、長大な空間に多様な表情がもたらされた。

　岩田は「静岡工場」に倣って、この本社でも外来の受付を3階に配することにし、来訪者は安藤の設えたコンクリートの直線のスロープを3階まで歩いてあがることになった。このスロープは緩い傾斜で、途中で方向を代える踊り場もある。訪問者は安藤のコンクリート打ち放しの壁に沿って歩き、途中でやはり安藤が設計した低層の社内保育所と緑の庭を俯瞰して受付に進む。受付は、もとの建物に安藤が斜めに貫通させたガラスの直方体の位置にあり、このガラスの箱には、アーティストによる"銀のいちご"のオブジェも置かれている。

　3階は主として従業員が工場での作業のための身辺清掃などの準備空間にあてられ、生産部門は地上レベルに配されている。3階から階段で4階にあがると、建物の中央に配した長大な光庭を囲う形で事務部門と職員食堂が配されている。もとの流通センターは、間口が160メートルに達する大建築だった。それをそのまま生かしたこともあり、光庭は100メートルに達するほどの長さがある。そのスケールは、潤沢な自然光を廊下や食堂にあふれさせ、垣間見える青空が臨海地ならではの爽快感をオフィスに与えてい

ロックフィールド神戸ヘッドオフィス／
神戸ファクトリー　2005
rockfield kobe headquarters / kobe factory

1. 4階の水庭
   Water garden on the fourth floor
2. 被災建物を減築した社屋
   Office building downsized from disaster-stricken building

（次ページ見開き）幕張のさくら広場
(next two pages) Cherry Plaza of Makuhari

る。もともと流通倉庫だったために各階の天井は低く抑えられているが、職員食堂は最上階の配置を生かして、緩い曲面を描きながら競り上がる天井で開放感を演出している。

　流通倉庫にしては珍しく、各階とも途切れることなく窓が配されていたのも幸いし、転用建築ゆえの違和感を覚えない仕立ては、安藤と岩田が目指した社会資産の活用として高く評価されよう。4階の廊下には、もとの建築をどのように改築したかを示す説明のパネルと、旧外壁の外側に取り付けたステンレスの外装材のユニットの見本が展示されている。再生について社会に胸を張って強調できる作品になった。

　建築家安藤忠雄は、小さなコンクリートの住宅に自己の想念を込めて、世界で注目される存在になり、その立場を存分に生かして、社会を動かす運動家となった。さらに彼は、社会的な活動の結実を「ロックフィールド」という建築作品の形で世に送ったのである。範を自ら示すとはこのことだろう。安藤が常々口にする「建築家である限り、社会的な活動だけではだめだ。建築が優れていてこそ建築家の存在意義がある」という言葉は、見事に形をとっている。安藤の目指してきた理想形のひとつ「建築を超える建築」がここに確かに存在する。権威的な作品ではなく、等身大の生活のための生産施設でそれがかなったことは、なにより祝福されるべきだろう。

第6章　ランドスケープ、まちづくりへ

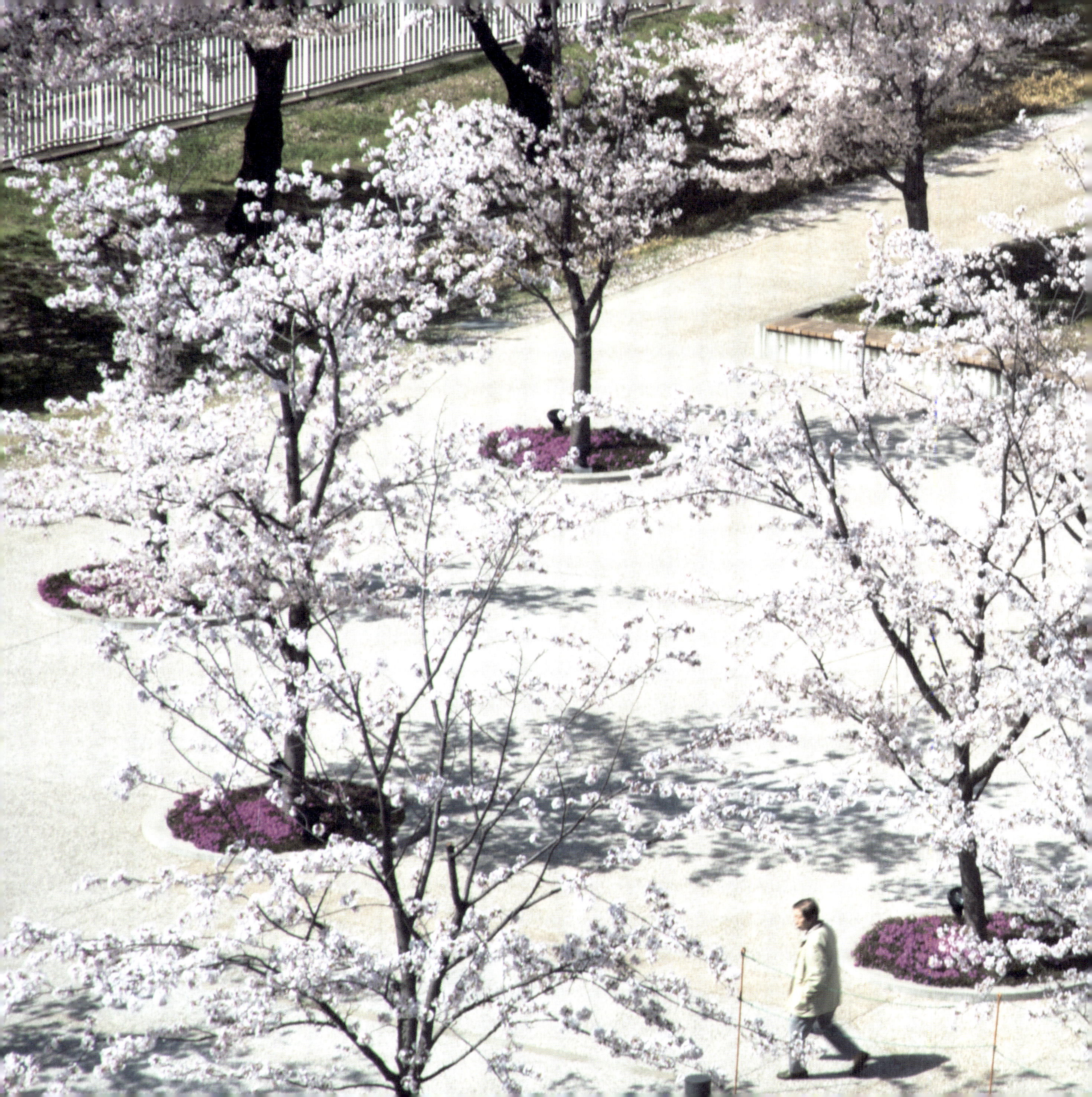

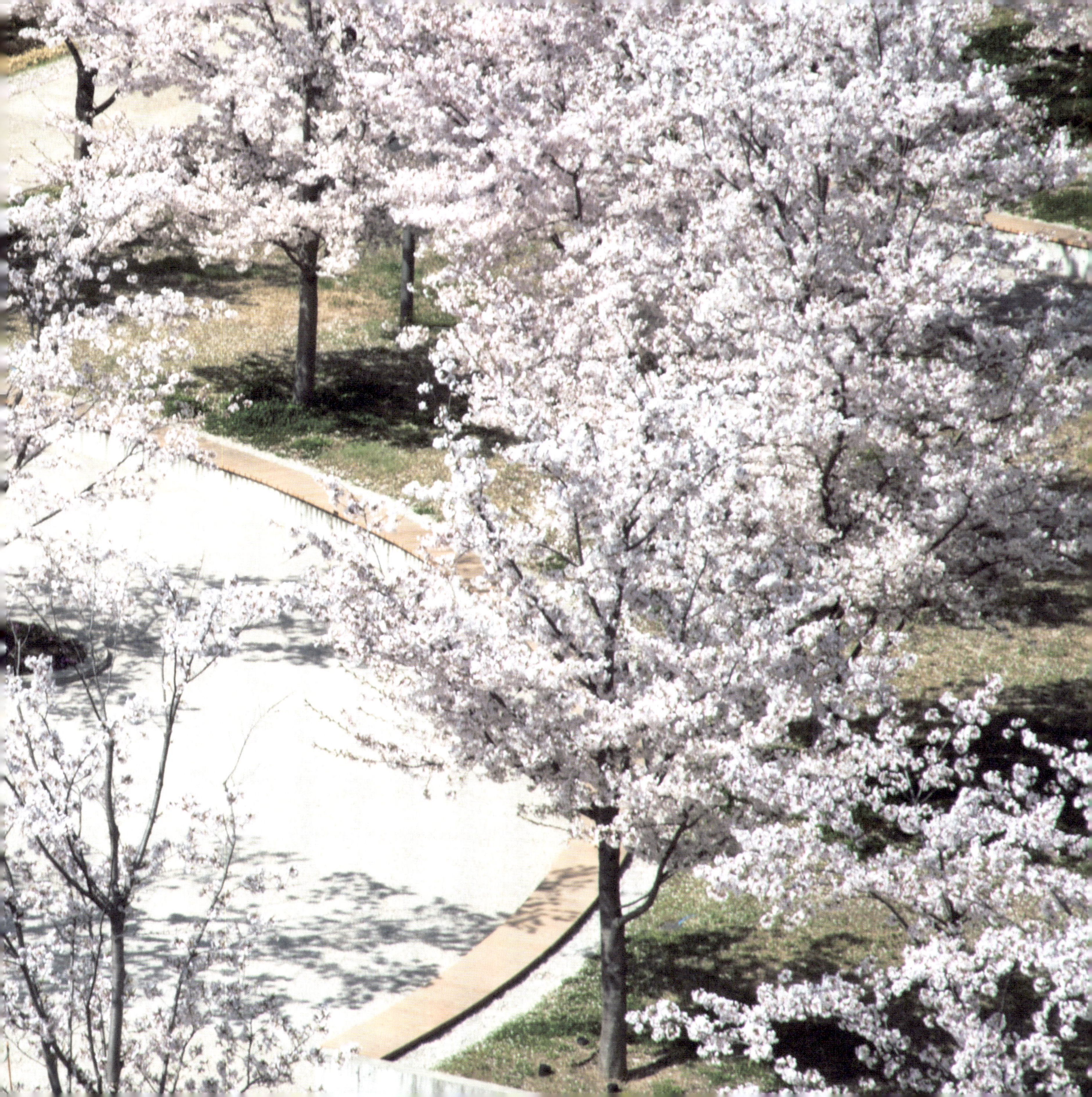

Aiello

エピローグ　アンドウは如何にして建築家となりし乎
Epilogue　How ANDO Became an Architect, out of His Memory

求道者へのオマージュ

　1969年に独立した建築家としてのスタートを切った安藤忠雄が、どれだけの作品を世に送ってきたのか。2017年の時点で、発表作品を網羅する作業を進め、全作品のリストアップを試みた。結果は、本書の「全作品録」に示す通りで、実現したものだけで300作品を超える。このほかにコンペ応募案、アンビルトに終わったもの、継続中が数十件は存在する。半世紀近くにわたる建築家としての活動の成果である。

　朧げには安藤が大変な数の仕事をしてきたことはわかっているつもりだったが、具体的な数字を目の当たりにして仰天した。まず、この数自体が、所員30人の規模の事務所として、想像の域を超えている。しかも、安藤は一作一作について細部まで妥協することなく所員を督励して設計に挑んできた。必ずといってよいほど、夕刻、自身の事務所に戻り、進行中の作品の進捗状況を確認し、あらためて所用に出向いた。

　建築家という職業に多くのひとが抱くような華やかな暮らしとは無縁だった。贅沢も飽食も遊興もせず、仕事を終えたあと、ジムで身体を動かすこと以外に趣味も持たず、ひたすら建築家であり続けた。いや、建築家の多くが、自身が建築家であることに陶酔しているのに対して、安藤は「設計する表現者」としての建築家にこだわり続け、それを自負していた。

　その結果、もたらされた「住宅」の数は100に達する。米国の東西両海岸、新興国にも、安藤の「美」とともに暮らしたいと考えるひとがひきもきらない。安藤の原点が「住宅」にあるのは確かだが、「美術館」「博物館」、文化関係の「上演・展示施設」の数も肩をならべる水準に到達している。国内の「美術館」「博物館」の数は優に30を超え、海外のそれらも二桁を数える。一方、「オフィス」は国内外で20件そこそこにとどまる。

Homage to a Seeker

How many works have been produced by Tadao Ando, since he began his career as an independent architect in 1969? A list of his entire works up until 2017 was made, based on published works. The result is shown in "Part II" of this book: there are almost 300 realized designs, and more than dozens of designs for competitions and unbuilt / ongoing projects — a result of his 48-year career as an architect.

I was vaguely aware of Ando's amazing number of works, yet the actual number still surprised me. The number itself — produced by a design office with 30 employees — was beyond imagination. Furthermore, Ando never compromised over any detail in each work, and encouraged his employees to challenge the designs. He would go back to his office almost every evening to see the progress of ongoing works, before going out for business again.

He was indifferent to a glamorous life, of which many people would imagine about architects. He was not interested in luxury, gourmet food, or pleasure. He had no hobby other than exercising at a gym after a day's work. He just continued to be an architect. Ando pursued being an architect as an "expressive person who designs" and felt proud of it, in contrast to most architects who are self-absorbed for being architects.

As a result, the number of "houses" produced by Ando approaches 100. On the west and east coasts of the U.S. and in emerging countries, there are always some people who desire to live with the "beauty" of Ando. It is obvious that Ando's starting point is "houses", yet the numbers of "art museums", "museums" and "performing arts and exhibition facilities" for cultural activities reach the same level. "Art museums" and "museums" in Japan total more than 30, and those overseas also reach two digits. However, less than ten "offices" were designed. This indicates how often Ando has been chosen to design temples of "art" and "history".

安藤がいかに、「美」や「歴史」の殿堂の設計者に選ばれてきたかがわかるだろう。

　文化の受容が、1989年の「ベルリンの壁」の崩壊によって国境を超え、さらに、より多くの社会層にも広がっていく。そのような地球規模での大きな流れが、安藤を「美の担い手」として奉じられる存在にした。安藤は東西冷戦が終結したあと、まさに「平和の時代の文化の寵児」となって、世界に羽ばたいて行った。それはあの丹下健三でさえかなわなかった「美術的建築家」としての輝かしい軌跡だったといえよう。

　安藤とともに、わたしが訪問した彼の作品は100を遥かに超える。ほとんどの場合、多数のメディアを現場に招くお披露目の場ではなく、彼はひとりで待ち合わせ場所に現れ、たったひとりの見学者のために、自作をどう考えて構成したかを熱心に説いてくれた。広報を期待しての打算など、どこにもなかった。安藤は、いわば造物主として、実に朗らかに誇らしく自作を語った。施主の思いを受け、全身全霊をもって作品を実現した達成感、昂揚感。その横顔を見ながら、こんなに建築が好きで、そこに打ち込める建築家が他にいるだろうか、とわたしはいつも思った。同行の機会を重ねるに連れ、表現者と評者の間に作品を自由に論じる信頼感は自ずと深まっていった。

　実現した作品数300超。そのなかに事務所維持のために受けた仕事は皆無だったと断言してよいだろう。つまり、所員を含めて生計をたてるための「身過ぎ世過ぎ」は、安藤事務所には存在しなかった。300を超える作品名を通覧すると、どの作品にも彼が投じた熱意が思い出される。もちろん、すべての作品が成功したわけではない。しかし、初めから、手を抜いた作品は断じて存在しない。肩の力を抜いたものさえない。海外を含め、多くの建築家の軌跡をたどるなら、20世紀以降、ル・コルビュジエやフランク・ロイド・ライト、ルイス・カーンらいわば一国の一世代にひとりぐらいしか、生涯の作品のすべてに施主の求めに対応して自身の表現者としての課題を設定して創作を続けた建築家はいない。

After the fall of the Berlin Wall in 1989, acceptance of cultures spread beyond countries and into wider social stratums. This huge global trend made Ando a person to be respected as a "bearer of beauty". Ando indeed became a "cultural hero in peaceful times" after the end of the Cold War, and his activities expanded worldwide.

I visited much more than 100 of Ando's works with him. On most of the occasions, they were not for gaining publicity such as inviting mass-media. He appeared at the meeting site by himself, and enthusiastically explained to one visitor how he thought about and composed his works. There was no calculation for publicity. Ando merrily and proudly talked about his own works, as if the Creator. Senses of accomplishment and uplift after accepting the clients' passions and realizing works with his heart and soul into them, Gazing at his face in profile, I was always wondering if any other architect could love architecture and be able to devote themselves into it. As we met many times, a feeling of trust between the expressive person and the critic naturally grew into free discussions of the pros and cons of Ando's works.

300 designs were actually built. I am certain that no project was done just to keep the design office running. In other words, Ando's design office has never worked for one's (including the employees') "livelihood" to earn bread. When reviewing the titles of more than 300 works, Ando's passion in every work can be remembered. Of course, not all works were successful. However, there was no work in which he did a careless job from the beginning, and no work was taken easily.

I have closely followed his attitude towards his works since he was in his 30s. He is a great architect, yet he also had setbacks and disappointments. However, he always stoically restrained himself, never gave up, gave another try as an architect to address the task head-on, and overcame numerous barriers to ascend to even higher levels. Tadao Ando is no doubt a "seeker of architecture". Uchimura Kanzo wrote an autobiography, "How I

わたしは彼が30代の時から、傍らで多くの作品を手がける姿を見てきた。これだけの建築家でありながら、やはり、挫折も、あてはずれもあった。しかし、その度に、彼は禁欲的に自己を律して、決して諦めることはせず、建築家として正面から課題に再挑戦して、いくつもの壁を打ち破り、さらなる高みへと移行していった。安藤忠雄は、紛いなき「建築の求道者」である。内村鑑三に多言語に翻訳された自伝「余は如何にして基督信徒となりし乎（How I became a Christian, out of my Diary）」がある。同じ求道の姿勢を安藤に見出す。以下、安藤と語り合った「如何にして建築家となりし乎」を綴り、本論の結びにしたい。

原点としての森小路、区画整理の町

物語は、大阪市旭区森小路の町から始まる。森小路の地名を聞いたことがある大阪人でさえ確かな場所を知るひとは少ないだろう。南北に長い大阪市の北の端、淀川の左岸に沿った一帯に広がる大阪市旭区の中心商店街が「森小路」である。一帯は、最寄りの鉄道駅はあっても、商店街には間口の狭い商家がならび繁華街の風情はない。商都大阪にあって、第2次世界大戦後の高度経済成長期にも、発展から取り残されたかのような町だった。

安藤は兵庫県西宮市鳴尾で生まれて、少年時代はその森小路一帯で育った。双子が生まれたら、祖父母のもとへという約束があり、双子の弟、さらにそのしたの弟、妹とは離れた暮らしとなった。両親一家とは年に一、二度、顔を合わせる程度だった。小学校1年の秋に祖父が他界、祖母の手で育てられた。貿易商だった父も、小学校3年のと

became a Christian, out of my Diary", which was translated into multiple languages. The same attitude of a seeker can be found in Ando. I would like to conclude this book by describing "How Ando became an Architect" based on a dialogue with Ando.

*Morishoji as an Origin,
a Town of Land Readjustment*

The story begins in the town of Morishoji, Asahi Ward in Osaka City. Not many people know the exact location of Morishoji, even residents in Osaka who have heard of the name. Morishoji is a central shopping district in Asahi-ku in Osaka City, spread along the left bank of the Yodo River at the north end of Osaka City (extending north and south). There is a railway station in the area, but the shopping district is just rows of stores with narrow fronts, unlike busy downtown streets. The area in the mercantile city Osaka was left behind from development even in the rapid economic growth after WWII.

Born in Naruo, Nishinomiya City in Hyogo Prefecture, Ando spent his youth in the area of Morishoji. Due to a promise to give one twin baby to the grandparents, Ando lived away from his twin brother, younger brother, and sister. He only met his parents' family once or twice a year. His grandfather died in the autumn of Ando's first year in elementary school, and he was raised by his grandmother. His father was a trading merchant and died when he was in the 3rd grade.

The grandparents' house was in the Morishoji area. They returned from the evacuation area during the wartime and started living there just after the war. Since the area is along the Yodo River, large military and private factories from the prewar period stood there, surrounded by groups of wooden houses. When returning from school after hearing the news of his grandfather's death, a determination arose in the child to "live by learning a trade by

きに亡くなった。

　その祖父母の家が、森小路の一帯にあった。暮らし始めたのは、戦時中の疎開地から戻った戦後間もない時期だった。淀川の川べりゆえに、戦前から軍関係、民間の大規模な工場があり、それを木造の民家の群れが取り巻いていた。祖父の訃報を聞いた下校時、「ああ、自分で手に職をつけて生活していかなければならない」という、子どもなりの決意が芽生えた。その思いが後年、建築家を目指すひとつの原動力となった。

　開発から取り残された下町一帯には、家業でさまざまな「ものつくり」をしている民家が散在していた。ちょっと見には、それぞれが勝手に営業しているようだが、実はそれらの「ものつくり」は見事に連携し合い、全体としては、ひとつのまとまりのある工場のようだった。

　碁盤をつくる職人がいる。碁盤には碁石が必要だ。碁盤のための木材を扱う材木屋が要るし、碁石には石屋も要る。家業を営むひとびとは互いの技術で助け合い、仕事も融通し合って生きていた。そのことを口には出さないが、下町のひとたちが自然発生的につくりあげた「無言のネットワーク」だった。それゆえに、ひとびとの関係は緊密であり、仲がよかった。そして、時には本気で喧嘩をする声が道路まで響きわたった。仲がいいから喧嘩になるのだと、安藤は子ども心に理解していた。そのような、ひとびとのつながりを目の当たりにしながら、少年時代を過ごした。

　大阪の下町というと、木造住宅の密集を連想するかも知れないが、祖母の家の周囲はそうした先入観念とは少し違う成り立ちだった。

　2ブロック分、ほんの2分ほど歩いたところに、住宅地らしい近隣公園がある。広さは、小学校の運動場にひけをとらないから、かなりゆったりしていて近所のひとたちの憩いの空間でもある。公園の一角に、見上げるほどの高さの真っ黒な粘板岩の碑が、2段になった基壇のうえに聳え立っている。

himself". This thought later became a driving force in him becoming an architect.

There were houses "manufacturing" various products for family businesses across the downtown area, which was left out from the development. At a glance, they appeared to be individually run businesses. However, the "manufacturing" in fact beautifully cooperated with each other, as if forming a coherent factory together.

There were artisans of Go boards. The Go boards required Go stones. Lumber businesses were necessary for making the Go boards, and so were stone businesses for making the Go stones. People with family businesses helped each other, using their own skills, and accommodated each other with their works. Though it was not openly discussed, it was a spontaneously built "silent network" among the downtown citizens. Hence, people had intimate and friendly relationships. Sometimes, serious fighting voices could be heard around the streets. Ando understood in a child's own way that people fought because they were good friends. Ando spent his childhood witnessing such relationships between people.

One might imagine densely built wooden houses in downtown Osaka, but the neighborhood around his grandmother's house was developed a bit differently from such preconceptions.

In 1940, the year before Ando was born, a large scale land readjustment was conducted in the Morishoji area, involving road improvements and replotting.

Due to the Bombing of Osaka in June 1945 by the American army, a considerable part of the area was burned down. The story continues to be passed down that people escaping from the fire reached the Yodo River bank and were killed by machine-gun fire from battle planes. Large holes in the ground from the bombing, called "bomb ponds", remained on the grounds of an elementary school for a length of time after the war.

Several land readjustments were conducted within Asahi-ku around the same time, and large-scale land

　正面から眺めると、碑文には「竣功記念碑」とある。背後に回ると、「皇紀二千六百年」「昭和十五年十一月建之」「大阪市榎並ノ荘土地区画整理組合」と三列の文字がならび、寄進者であろう「大阪　新川橋　太田傳」と個人名が刻まれている。「榎並ノ荘」という荘園に由来する気品のある名前を区画整理組合は名乗った。

　昭和15年、安藤の生まれる前の年に、森小路一帯で大規模な区画整理があり、換地を伴う道路整備がされたことがわかる。

　昭和20年6月の大阪大空襲の際、米軍の爆撃で周辺は相当程度、焼け落ちた。火災を逃れ淀川べりまで逃げ落ちたひとびとが、戦闘機の機銃掃射で命を落としたことが今なお語り継がれる。小学校のグラウンドには、爆撃で地面に大穴が開いた「爆弾池」が戦後しばらく残っていた。

　同時期の区画整理は、旭区内で数カ所あり、大阪市のあちこちでも昭和10年代に大規模な区画整理事業が施行された。いずれも関東大震災による東京の密集地火災の怖さを知った当局が音頭をとったものだ。当時の大阪には、日本一の商都としての気概と財力があり、大都市への自負は、庶民の居住する地域にまで広く及んでいた。

　その後、戦災で焼け落ちたにせよ、道路は残った。長屋の多くは、密集地とは異なる碁盤の目のように規則正しく区切られた道路に面して建てられている。道路幅も6メートルはある。都市部の住宅地の生活道路としては余裕さえ感じさせる。

　長屋のイメージと整然とした計画道路のイメージはそぐわないかも知れない。しかし、下町のひとびとが屈託なく日常を送り、相互の繋がりが良好に保たれていたことと、この庶民の町らしからぬ「計画都市」は無関係ではない。大阪は昭和2年、関一（せきはじめ）市長の強い指導力のもとに、幅44メートルの「御堂筋」を完成させる。そこから市内の区画整理の完成まで10年余り。その時期に、大阪の誇りが広く庶民にまで浸透していった。

　下町の日常を楽しくするのは、大阪人ならではの豊かなコミュニケーション力と町

readjustment projects were performed from 1935 to 1945 throughout Osaka City. The municipality led all projects, after recognizing the threat of fire in densely built-up areas, which was experienced in Tokyo at the time of the Great Kanto Earthquake. Osaka had enough fighting spirit and financial ability as the largest commercial city at that time. Its self-pride as a large city broadly covered general residential areas.

The area was burnt down due to the war damage later, but the streets remained. Most row houses were built along regularly divided streets following a grid pattern, rather than in a densely built-up area. The street widths are at least six meters, which is plenty for community roads in an urban residential area.

An image of row houses and that of well-organized planned roads may not go together. However, the "planned city" that is unlike a common people's town and the fact that the downtown residents lived cheerfully and maintained good relationships among themselves are not unrelated. The pride of Osaka widely spread to the general population.

Modernism in the Downtown: His Early Days

His grandparents' house was in a row house with three housing units. The room arrangement of the house was generally of common people's houses: the front of the three units was on the main street side, and residential spaces stretched towards the back side. When Ando was in the 9th grade (age 15), a plan was made to add a second floor to his one-story house, which was part of a three-unit row house. This extension work crystalized into a significant motivating factor in him becoming an architect.

There was a woodworking shop, "N Wood Pattern Factory", across from Ando's house. He visited the workshop and observed the works of three artisans beginning when he was in elementary school, and he was impressed in

衆としての自負だ。それを「お上＝公共体」が「道路＝インフラストラクチュア」で支える、市民と公共の好もしい関係は、先人の賢明さがもたらしたものだ。その点でも、森小路の暮らしには、教えられるところが多かった。

下町のモダニズム ── 事始めの日々

祖母の家は三軒続きの長屋で、表通りに面して三戸が間口をならべ、奥に向かって生活空間の延びる庶民住宅の間取りだった。15歳、中学生3年生のとき、平屋の一軒だったわが家に2階を増築する話が持ち上がった。この増築が建築家を志望する大きな動機付けになった。

向かいに「N木型製作所」と屋号のあがる木工所があった。小学生のころから作業場に出入りし、3人の職人さんたちの仕事ぶりを眺めて、子ども心に感心したものだった。2階を増築することになったとき、見よう見まねで覚えていた木工の手作業を生かせるのではと考え、自分で増築部分をつくってみようと思い立った。木造建築なら木工の手作業の延長で出来るのではと考えたのである。建築の勉強などしたことはなく、建築家になりたいと思っていたわけでもなかった。

どんな2階にするかは「こんなんでどうやろ」という調子で施工する大工さんと話し合った。向いの木工所の職人さんには折に触れて、大工さんとの相談結果に対する意見を求め、自ずと形態は決まっていった。

屋根は「切妻」だが、棟木の位置をぐっと奥に寄せて、緩い傾斜の「片流れ」の雰囲気を持たせた黒い瓦葺きに、増築部分の正面と両脇の壁は、杉の焼き板の外装とした。

a child's own way. When the extension was planned, he had the idea of building the extension by himself, by utilizing woodworking skills that he had learned by watching the woodworkers. He thought that a wooden structure could be constructed by applying manual woodworking skills. He had never learned architecture and never dreamed of being an architect.

He casually discussed the design of the second floor with the working carpenters. He occasionally solicited opinions from the workers of the carpentry shop across the street about the result of the discussions with the carpenters, and the design was naturally formed.

The roof was "gabled" but the ridge beam was placed further back, providing an atmosphere of a gently-sloped "shed roof" with black tiles. Burnt cedar boards were used for the exterior walls of the front and both sides of the extension. A wide window was made under the front eaves on the exterior wall. Glass was put on two horizontally-long wooden window frames, and arranged side by side. Glass windows were also placed on the side walls near the ridge beam. The burnt boards were used in a longitudinal direction, and the front and both sides were finished with regularly arranged boards.

The interior was indeed an "empty" open space, and no room arrangement was necessary. A drying space for drying laundry and beddings, commonly seen in similar row houses, was constructed at the back of the second floor.

Ando was interested in the carpenters' work and observed them almost every day. The carpenters enthusiastically worked as if devoting all of their time. They did not stop working even at lunchtime, and ate bread they kept in a pocket to relieve hunger. Ando was very impressed by their attitude.

Ando wondered if people can dedicate themselves as much, in order to achieve something. He thought an architect might be an interesting job. It is interesting that whenever Ando sees this extension that still exists, he is

正面の庇のかかる部分の外壁は、窓をいっぱいに開けて、二連の横長の木製建具にガラスを嵌めた。側壁も棟木に近い位置にガラス窓を配した。焼き板は垂直方向を長手にして、正面も両脇も規則正しくならぶ仕上げとした。

内部はワンルームのそれこそ「がらん洞」の空間で、間取りもなにもなかった。2階の奥には、これもこの手の長屋でよくするように、洗濯物や布団を干せる物干し台を設けた。

興味があったので、大工さんの仕事ぶりを毎日のように眺めた。寝食を忘れてというのはこのことかというほど大工さんは熱心に働いていた。昼時でも作業の手は休めず、ポケットにねじ込んだパンを口に運んで空腹を紛らわしていた。その姿に大いに心を打たれた。

ひとはひとつのことをなし遂げるのに、ここまで熱心にやるものか、ひょっとして建築というのは面白い仕事なのかも知れないと考えた。今も残るこの増築を眺めるたびに、造形としてそうおかしくはない、モダニズムとして様になっている、と安藤は自分で納得してしまうというから面白い。

木工所の親方Nさんには、モダニズムの造形原理に近いことを教えてもらった。

発注が来ると、Nさんは、数時間、ずっと図面を眺めている。どの種類の材木でそれを作るかを徹底的に突き詰めて考えるのだという。そのプロセスを経ないと、彼の手は1ミリたりとも動かない。しかし、いったん動き出すと一気呵成に大工さんのための図面が出来上がる。

感心したのは、注文がどんな形状であれ、削りだすもとの材木は「立方体」などの幾何立体に近いものが選ばれるところだった。どんなに長かろうか、薄かろうが、である。例えば薄くて長い形のものを求められたら、通常は板材を使いそうなものである。しかし、彼は、必ず、立方体の材木から削りだすのである。不思議に思ったので「なぜ、

convinced that the design was not too silly, and that it is in good shape as modernist architecture.

He learned something like modernist design principles from the master N. at the woodworking shop.

When he received an order, N. stared at the drawing for a few hours while he thoroughly examined which types of lumber would be used for it. Without completing this process, his hands never moved an inch. Yet once they started moving, a drawing for the carpenters was completed all at once.

What impressed Ando was that wood material was always something like geometric solids such as "cubic", regardless of the shapes of the orders — no matter how long or thin the final products were. When a thin- and long-shaped product was required, for example, a board might be commonly used. However, he always carved the product from cubic material. Ando wondered and asked why.

N. answered that he was "returning everything to its origin". He believed that woodworking would be quicker when returning to its origin and beginning from there, regardless of the final product shape. The origin was "geometric shapes". N. attentively taught woodworking skills to the artisans, always based on his principle that challenged "the truth of the universe".

Grownups in Morishoji strived to do their jobs. Ando was very much impressed by their attitude of dedication to one thing. Closely feeling the seriousness of adults gave him lifetime lessons. In that sense, Morishoji was a live school where Ando learned the truth of life and the essence of designs. He lived in Morishoji town until 1984 and still keeps in touch with the neighbors. An old neighborhood lady occasionally calls and visits his office. The news of the woodworking master's death was also brought by the lady.

However, Ando had not yet aimed to become an architect. Since an architecture major was not available at the technical high school he attended, Ando majored in mechanical engineering. His aimless journey began.

そうするのか」と訊ねた。

戻ってきた答えは「なんでも原点に戻す」というものだった。つまり、形がどうであれ、一度、原点に立ち返ってスタートした方がはやいというのが彼の信念だった。その原点が「幾何立体」だったわけだ。Nさんは職人に手取り足取り技術を教えていたが、彼の方法は「宇宙の真理」に肉薄する原理的な思考に貫かれていた。

多くの建築にまつわることを学んだあとで思うに、20世紀の造形表現の本義を下町の木工の親方が体得していたわけだ。驚くべきだろう。モダニズムの黎明期において新造形の原点を原初的な幾何立体に求めた芸術家に通じる思考がそこにはあった。熱意をもって仕事を突き詰めていった結果？ 20世紀はなべて抽象志向の時代だったから？ いずれにせよ、不思議で有意義な体験が、下町の子どもゆえに出来たことに、安藤は感謝している。

森小路で見た大人は自分の仕事に必死だった。彼らのひとつことに打ち込む姿に感じるところは多かった。間近でおとなの本気を感じられたことは、人生の大きな収穫だった。その意味では、森小路は生きた学校だった。人生の真理も、造形の奥義もそこで学んだ。結局、森小路の町に1984年まで住み続けた。そのつきあいはまだ続く。近所住まいだったおばあさんが突然、電話をくれて事務所までやって来るし、先日は木工所の親方の訃報も伝えてくれた。

だが、まだ建築家という目標は、皆目見えていなかった。中学から進学先に選んだ工業高校に建築のコースはなく機械工作を選んだ。あてのない道を歩き始めた。

Aiming to become an Architect:
Fellows in the Same Generation

In the 1960s, Osaka was full of vibrancy. Soon after completing the war damage reconstruction, the framework of society was not yet established, and the young generations felt hopeful about their future.

The city gave a somewhat dull impression, due to damages from the war. The sky was dirty with soot and smoke from factories. At subway stations, women earned daily cash incomes by breaking up books of tickets and individually selling the tickets. There was no internet or cell phones. Young people hung out in the downtown areas without purpose, excitedly waiting for something to happen. They might talk overnight at a café in north or south Osaka, whenever they felt like it.

Ando's desire to become an architect was encouraged by the heat and energy of the time, and understanding from young people who were heading towards the future together.

In 1956, Ando graduated from middle school and proceeded to a technical high school and majored in mechanical engineering. In fact, when he was in the 8th grade, he began to think it might be difficult for him to go to college due to both financial and academic limitations. He majored in mechanical engineering since there were only mechanical engineering and electrical engineering courses in his technical high school. His choice was made for a merely casual reason, which was that the one-year older neighbor boy was also in the school.

There was one hour each of mathematics and English classes, and three hours of social studies classes per week. The rest was practical training and there was no cultural atmosphere. Students concentrated on turning a lathe from 8am to 5pm. For this extremely precise process, the students continued cutting metal without talking, occasionally looking through a microscope. The school was somewhat unusual, with at least one graduate entering

建築家を志して――乗り合わせた同世代

1960年代の大阪は、活気にあふれていた。戦災復興をやり遂げて間のない時期、社会の枠組みは確定しておらず、若者は自分たちの未来に希望を持っていた。

町には戦争の爪痕が残り、どこかくすんだ印象があった。工場の煤煙で空は曇り、地下鉄の駅には、回数券をばら売りして日銭を稼ぐおばちゃんたちの姿があった。インターネットも携帯電話もなく、若者は用もないのに繁華街にたむろし、なにかが起こることをワクワクしながら待っていた。気が向けばキタやミナミの喫茶店で夜を徹して話し込んだ。

その時代の熱気と活力、そして、一緒に未来へ向おうとする若者たちの共感が、建築家になりたい願望を後押ししてくれた。

1956年に中学校を卒業、工業高校の機械科に進んだ。実は、中学2年生のとき、これでは財力、学力とも、大学に行くのは難しいと思うようになった。進学した工業高校には、機械と電気の学科しかなく機械科を選んだ。近所の1歳年上のおにいさんがそこに通っていたから程度の動機だった。

カリキュラムは1週間に数学、英語が1時間、社会が3時間で、あとはすべて実習だった。文化的な雰囲気はなかった。朝の8時から夕方の5時までひたすら旋盤を回し続ける。作業は精密を究め、顕微鏡ものぞきながら無言で金属を削り続けた。1学年にひとりは東大に合格していたから不思議な学校だった。堅実な校風ゆえに、大阪発祥の「椿本チエイン」など優良企業からの求人は引く手数多で、中堅技術者として会社員人生を送る卒業生が多かった。

いざ、社会人になろうとしたとき、森小路のわが家を増築したときの建築の面白さ

the University of Tokyo every year. Due to the reliable school reputation, graduates were popular among quality companies including Tsubakimoto Chain Co., founded in Osaka, and many worked for such companies as mid-level engineers.

When Ando was about to start working, he remembered the appeal of architecture when he built the extension to his house in Morishoji, and his passion increased for seeking a career as an architect. Partially due to the economic context, he could not go to college. He began a part time job in interior design, in order to learn architectural works. While he needed to earn his bread, he could not be occupied too much with immediate tasks and fell behind competitors learning in colleges. After careful thought, he concluded that he would learn from literature.

Ando was supported by friends of his generation attending Kyoto University and Osaka University. Ando asked them to get him textbooks used in the universities and avidly read them every day. Naturally, understanding everything in the books was impossible, but he struggled to read through them. The friends in the universities had a piano at home, and had grown up while listening to Mozart and Bach music. In Morishoji, there was no classic music, literature, and philosophy, let alone architecture books. It was hard to catch up.

In fact, he did not even know the term "modern architecture". He was given a recommendation to read Sigfried Giedion, who established the theoretical pillars of modern architecture, and he struggled to read the two volumes of "Space, Time and Architecture". Although Ando could not fully understand the contents, it was vaguely understood that modern architecture overtook decorative eclecticism in Beaux-Arts architecture. He also learned that modern architecture pursued a functionalist c and consistent morality. However, he did not yet feel sympathy towards modern architecture.

When he heard how interesting Bruno Taut was, he began reading Taut's books. His interest in Taut deepened

がよみがえり、どうしても建築を生涯の仕事にしたいとの思いがつのった。経済的な事情もあり、大学への道は閉ざされていた。なにより仕事を覚えようとインテリア設計のアルバイトを始めた。食べていかなければならないし、眼前の仕事にかまけて、大学に進んだ競争相手に負けるわけにはいかないと思った。どうしようかと悩み、書籍で学ぶしかないと考えるに至った。

　助け船を出してくれたのは、京大や阪大に進んだ同年代の仲間たちだった。彼らに依頼して大学の教科書を買ってきてもらった。それを読みふける毎日が続いた。すべてを理解するのは、当然、無理な話だったが、それでもなんとか読破しようと苦闘した。大学に進んだ彼らの家にはピアノがあり、モーツアルトやバッハを聞くなどして育った。森小路には、クラシック音楽も文学も哲学もなかった。建築論の書籍などあろうはずがなかった。追いつくのは大変だった。

　実のところ「近代建築」という言葉さえ知らなかった。近代建築の理論的支柱を確立したジークフリート・ギーディオンを読めというから、『時間、空間、建築』の上下巻を四苦八苦しながら読み通した。内容はよく理解できなかったが、近代建築がボザール流の装飾的な折衷主義を克服したことは漠然とわかった。機能主義的で首尾一貫した倫理観を近代建築が目指していることもわかった。しかし、だからといって近代建築に共感を覚えるところまではいかなかった。

　ブルーノ・タウトが面白いと聞くとタウトの本を読みはじめる。大丸の当主、下村正太郎が、ナチスの難を恐れてドイツを離れ、敦賀から日本に入国したタウトを、ウィリアム・メリル・ヴォーリズ設計の京都の自邸に招き、翌日に「桂離宮」に案内したという話を知って、タウトへの興味が深まった。

　タウトを媒介に、日本の古建築を新たな目で見るようになった。また、タウトが抱いていた近代建築との距離感に共感を覚えた。本を読むまでタウトの存在さえ知らな

after discovering the fact that Taut had come to Tsuruga, escaping from Germany to avoid the persecution of the Nazis. Taut was invited to the house of Shotaro Shimomura (the owner of the Daimaru department stores at that time) in Kyoto, designed by William Merrell Vories. Shimomura brought Taut to the Katsura Imperial Villa on the following day.

Ando began seeing old Japanese architecture from a new perspective through Taut. He also felt a sympathy for Taut's sense of distance from the modern architecture. He never knew the existence of Taut before reading his books. Ando was led to the architectural world by literature.

He held discussions with friends of his generation through editing the architectural magazine "Hiroba", published in Osaka. He appreciated having plenty of opportunities to straightforwardly discuss architecture, while acquiring actual work in architectural design through part time jobs.

Encounter with the Gutai: Jazz and Art

The "Hankyu East Shopping Street" is in Umeda, the largest downtown area of Osaka, and casual restaurants stand under the arcade. Unexpectedly, the street mysteriously anticipated the waves of advanced cultures in the Kansai region. The jazz café "Check" was located near the entrance of the Hankyu East Shopping Street.

Ando began hanging out at "Check" after first going there with workers from the sake brewery "Tamon". First, he woke up to modern jazz music. Musicians from the U.S. provided live music there as well. Ando had precious experiences of hearing live drum performances of Elvin Jones and Max Roach.

Above all, Ando met people from the avant-garde artist group "Gutai" at this café.

The café was designed by architect Takamitsu Azuma, who later became famous for designing the "Tower House" at a 20m² site in central Tokyo. Azuma was working at

かったのは確かで、書籍の力で建築の世界に導かれていった。

同年代の友人たちとは、大阪で発行されていた建築専門誌「ひろば」の編集で議論を戦わせた。建築設計の実務をアルバイトで習得する一方、建築を真正面から論じる機会に恵まれていたことにも感謝している。

具体との出会い──ジャズ、そして美術

大阪きっての繁華街、梅田の一角を占めながら、アーケードの下に、気の張らない飲食店のならぶ「阪急東商店街」は、一方で先端的な文化の波を、関西で先取りしている不思議なところだった。大映画館「OS劇場」もあれば、裏通りに入るとジャズやロックの輸入レコードの店が並んでいた。今では高層ビルも建ち、かつての風情は乏しくなったが、その阪急東商店街を入ってすぐのところに、ジャズ喫茶「チェック」があった。

「チェック」には清酒メーカー「多聞」のひとたちに案内されたのをきっかけに入り浸るようになった。まず、モダン・ジャズに目覚めた。それまでは、ジャズといえば、江利チエミの「カモナ・マイ・ハウス（家へおいでよ）」にとどまっていたが、「チェック」で聴いたモダン・ジャズは新鮮だった。店はアメリカから来日するプレーヤーの演奏の場でもあった。エルビン・ジョーンズやマックス・ローチのドラム演奏に生で接する貴重な体験もした。

そしてなにより前衛美術家集団「具体美術協会」のひとたちとここで出会った。

店舗の設計者は建築家の東孝光だった。東京都心の6坪住宅「塔の家」で後に名を馳せる東は、当時、坂倉建築研究所（坂倉準三主宰）の大阪事務所に所属していた。そし

the Osaka office of SAKAKURA ASSOCIATES Architects and Engineers (directed by Junzo Sakakura) at that time. Together with architect Yasutaka Yamazaki (who also worked for SAKAKURA ASSOCIATES, and designed the unique Ashiya City Center Luna Hall), Azuma established the "Check club". The members of the "Gutai" had an interaction with the "Check club".

The interior of "Check" was filled with "symbols" endlessly drawn by Shuji Mukai, a member of the Gutai. Ando was working on shop interiors around that time. He was surprised that something like that was possible, and someone like Mukai existed. Ando was personally acquainted with Mukai.

A diversity of artists gathered in the "Gutai", established in 1954. There was Mukai who continued drawing symbols, and there was Takesada Matsutani who just continued coloring screens with pencils. Matsutani won the grand prize in the first Mainichi Art Awards in 1966 and studied abroad in Paris in his 20s after receiving the French Government Scholarships. This served as a great stimulus to Ando.

He was also surprised when Norio Imai also went to Paris after being awarded first prize in the 10th Shell Art Award. Imai was still around 20 years old. Ando saw close examples of which a road to the world can be opened if one's ability is recognized, even at a young age. When traveling to Europe for the first time, Ando was reunited with Matsutani, who moved to Paris. His friendship with Matsutani still continues to this day.

Everyone had eccentric personalities, including the founding members Jiro Yoshihara and Shozo Shimamoto, and others like Atsuko Tanaka and Sadamasa Motonaga. They teased Ando and said "workers of Sakakura are excellent, and you are eccentric". Ando felt encouraged by knowing these eccentric people, and understanding that there were many people who lived with self-respect.

They did not behave like artists. They did not care about their livelihood, and were in a pursuit of their

て、建築家で同じく坂倉事務所の山崎泰孝（独創的な芦屋市民会館ルナ・ホールの設計者）らと「チェックの会」を結成していた。その「チェックの会」と交遊があったのが「具体美術協会」の面々だった。

「チェック」の内装は、具体のメンバーのひとり、向井修二が延々と描き続けた「記号」で埋めつくされていた。そのころ、店舗のインテリアの仕事をしていたので、「ほう、こんなことが出来るのだ。こんなひとがいるのだ」と驚き、向井とも面識が出来た。

1954年結成の「具体」には多様な芸術家が集まっていた。記号を描き続ける向井がいれば、ただ、鉛筆で画面を塗り続ける松谷武判もいた。松谷が1966年に第1回毎日美術コンクールでグランプリを獲得、フランス政府給費留学生となって20代でパリに渡ったのは大きな刺激になった。

今井祝雄が第10回シェル美術賞1等賞を受けたのを機に、やはりパリに行ったのにも驚いた。今井はまだ20歳そこそこだった。彼らのように認められれば、若くても世界への道が開けることを身近で知った。パリに移住した松谷とは、初めてヨーロッパに行ったときに再会し、現在も親交は続いている。

結成メンバーの吉原治良、嶋本昭三もそうだし、田中敦子、元永定正ら、みんな一風変わったひとびとだった。その彼らに「坂倉のひとたちは優秀、あなたは変わったひと」とからかわれたが、変わり者の彼らの存在を知って、自分を大切にして生きている人間が、この世にはいっぱいいるのだと心強かった。

彼らは芸術家然とはしていなかった。生活のこともかまわずに、自分の表現を追い求めていた。2013年にニューヨークのグッゲンハイム美術館で「具体：素晴らしい遊び場」展が開かれた。当時のあの熱気があればこそ、海外での再評価が、今日起きているのだと思う。

この具体のひとびと、なかでも元永、嶋本、白髪一雄らが、横尾忠則、田中一光、倉

expressions. In 2013, the exhibition "Gutai: Splendid Playground" was held at the Solomon R. Guggenheim Museum in New York City. I believe that today's re-evaluation overseas is a result of the heat at that time.

Ando should appreciate that these people in the Gutai, in particular, Motonaga, Shimamoto and Kazuo Shiraga, gave him opportunities for interactions with Tadanori Yokoo, Ikko Tanaka, Shiro Kuramata, and Juro Kara. Ando worked in collaboration with these people after the 1980s, but it started from "Check".

Due to the influence of "Check", Ando developed a taste for American culture, in particular, American arts. It was new for Ando to experience Jackson Pollock and others, whom he had never heard of. Ando was learning European modern architecture, and previously had no particular interest in American culture. However, Ando also followed trends in art as well as jazz, and realized that the U.S. was indeed moving. It motivated him to travel to the U.S. in 1968 to see the "Seagram Building" and "Lake Shore Drive Apartments" by Mies van der Rohe.

Ando then experienced the fertile architectural ground of Osaka. It began from designing TEZUKAYAMA TOWER PLAZA in his early days, and KITANO ALLEY in Kitano-cho in Kobe for Chishima Real Estate Co., Ltd., established by Osaka merchant Shibakawa Mataemon.

Mataemon Shibakawa (1853–1938) asked for Goichi Takeda to design his own house in Kotoen (Nishinomiya City) in the Hanshin area. Takeda was a major player in the architectural world of the Kansai region before the war and established the department of architecture at Kyoto University. The SHIBAKAWA HOUSE (1911) was transferred to the Museum Meiji-mura. Shibakawa was well-versed in architecture, and actively made an effort to patronize architects. He can be called a benefactor of the architectural world in the Kansai region. He was also a practitioner of prewar modern life in the Kansai region, by establishing the Takarazuka Golf Club and managing an orchard near his house (Kotoen).

俣史朗、唐十郎らとの交流の道を開いてくれたことにも感謝せねばなるまい。それらのひとびとと協同での仕事は1980年代以降となるが、その萌芽は「チェック」から生まれた。

安藤が「チェック」から受けた影響のひとつに、アメリカ文化、ことにアメリカ美術について目を開かせてくれたことがある。それまで名前も知らなかったジャクソン・ポロックらの存在を知ったのは新鮮だった。ヨーロッパの近代建築について学習していたこともあり、それまで特段、アメリカの文化についての認識はなかった。しかし、ジャズと同時に美術の動向も耳に入り、「ああアメリカは動いているんだ」と認識した。それは1968年に米国を旅行し、ミース・ファン・デル・ローエの「シーグラムビル」や「レイク・ショア・ドライブ・アパートメント」を見る動機にもなった。

やがて大阪の建築の土壌の豊かさにも触れることになった。きっかけは、大阪の財界人芝川又右衛門が設立した「千島土地」が、初期の作品「帝塚山タワープラザ」と神戸・北野町の「北野アレイ」を発注してくれたことに始まる。

芝川又右衛門（1853–1938年）は、阪神間の甲東園（西宮市）の自邸を、戦前の関西建築界の重鎮で京都大学建築学科を創設した武田五一に設計させた。この「芝川邸」（1911年）は現在は明治村に移築された。芝川は建築に明るく、積極的に建築家のパトロンとなることを志した。関西建築界の恩人といってよいだろう。また宝塚ゴルフクラブを開設し、自邸近傍で果樹園（これが甲東園だった）を経営するなど、関西の戦前のモダンライフの実践者でもあった。

芝川邸を設計した武田五一による「銀橋」（1930年）は、「御堂筋」、「中央公会堂」、「ライオン橋」とならぶ戦前からの大阪市民の誇りだった。正式の名前は「桜宮橋」というのだが、金属のアーチ橋で銀色に光っていることから、その呼称が広まった。

「御堂筋」建設の話は、小学校で教えられた。中之島の「中央公会堂」の建設の経緯

Osaka citizens had been proud of "Silver Bridge" (1930) by Goichi Takeda, the designer of Shibakawa House, since the prewar period, along with "Midosuji", "Osaka City Central Public Hall", and "Lion Bridge". The official name of the bridge is "Sakuranomiya Bridge", but the nickname was spread since the metal arch bridge has a shiny silver color.

He was taught about the construction of "Midosuji" in elementary school. The background of constructing the "Osaka City Central Public Hall" in Nakanoshima is also well known. The hall construction was funded by donations to Osaka City from stockbroker Einosuke Iwamoto. Iwamoto later went bankrupt but refused to accept the donation refund, and committed suicide by handgun. There is no such anecdote for "Silver Bridge", but Osaka people — who love new things and are looking for things that exceed Tokyo — are attracted by the shiny appearance, and spontaneously began using its nickname.

"Naniwa Bridge" in front of the stock exchange is commonly called "Lion Bridge", since the newel posts are decorated with lion statues. But the common name "Silver Bridge", representing the texture of the modern city, was spontaneously born and shared among Osaka citizens even now. In Osaka, episodes on architecture and the city were well-known to that extent, making us realize the existence of the rich architectural climate.

When Ando walked "Tenroku Shopping Street" with former Prime Minister Keizo Obuchi, he was asked by Obuchi if there was something to invigorate Osaka. With Taichi Sakaiya, Ando proposed construction of "New Silver Bridge" and got an opportunity to supervise its design. Coincidentally, the Ministry of Land, Infrastructure, Transport and Tourism was also planning a new bridge construction next to "Silver Bridge", while preserving the old bridge. Ando determined the shape of "New Silver Bridge" with respect to the architectural climate of Osaka and Takeda Goichi. Today, the combination of the old and new bridges creates an urban scene, suitable for the water city Osaka.

も、広く知られている。相場師岩本栄之助が私財100万円を市に寄贈して建設された。前後して破産した岩本は寄付金の返却を断り、短銃自殺した。「銀橋」にそんな逸話はないが、新しもの好き、東京を凌げるものはないかと心に期している大阪人が、きらきら光る姿に心惹かれ、誰いうともなく「銀橋」と呼ぶようになった。

　　証券取引所前の「難波橋」は、ライオンの彫像が親柱を飾っているのでまさに「ライオン橋」そのものだが、「銀橋」は、モダン都市の肌触りを表現する呼び名が自然発生的に生まれ、今なお大阪市民に共有されている。大阪において建築や都市の話題が人口に膾炙していたわけで、豊かな建築風土の存在を実感させる。

　　安藤は、小渕恵三首相と「天六商店街」を歩いたとき、「なにか大阪を元気に出来るものはないか」と聞かれたので、「新銀橋」の架橋を堺屋太一とともに提案して意匠監修の機会を得た。おりから国土交通省も「銀橋」をそのまま保存し、傍らにもう一本架橋する工事を検討中だった。そうやって、大阪の建築風土と武田五一に敬意を込めた「新銀橋」の姿を決めることになった。新旧二つの銀橋が並んで、水の都大阪にふさわしい都市風景がもたらされた。

裏切りのル・コルビュジエ

　　1965年、初めてヨーロッパに行った。同世代の仲間から「建築を志すならパルテノンを見なければ」といわれたが、それよりもル・コルビュジエの建築を見たかった。

　　「天牛書店」のウェブサイトに逸話として紹介されているが、道頓堀のこの大阪一の古書店で、5巻本のル・コルビュジエの作品集に出合い、欲しくてたまらなかった。アルバ

Treachery Le Corbusier

In 1965, Ando visited Europe for the first time. He was told by friends of his age to see the Parthenon if he wanted to become an architect, but he was more eager to see the works of Le Corbusier.

A story about Ando is introduced on the website of Tengyu Bookstore — the largest old bookstore in Osaka, located in Dotonbori. Ando saw a five volume portfolio of Le Corbusier at the bookstore. He desperately wanted the books but they were too expensive for someone with a part time job. In order to prevent other people from buying them, Ando buried the books under a stack of books before leaving the bookstore. When he went back the next time, the books were in the most visible place, on top of the stack, so he buried the books again. After repeating this process, Ando bought a volume with "Notre Dame du Haut, Ronchamp", and then he truly desired to visit Europe to see the architect Le Corbusier with his own eyes.

A ban on foreign travels had just ended in the previous year, 1964. Prior to that, travels without clear purposes, such as for businesses and studying abroad, were prohibited. In order to afford the high expense, he saved money and used the 100,000 yen he received for designing a café as seed money.

He took a ship to Nakhodka, USSR from Yokohama, and a train to Khabarovsk. From there, he took the Trans-Siberian Railway. Only 500 USD in foreign currency was allowed to be taken abroad. It was equal to 180,000 yen at a fixed rate of 360 yen per dollar at that time.

It took nine days to reach Moscow. After arriving in a European city for the first time, Ando was shocked at seeing Red Square and Moscow State University.

Ando arrived in Paris in September, and Le Corbusier had passed away the month before. Ando visited there without much preparation, hoping something would turn up. He wandered in Paris without any concrete plan for visiting the atelier of Le Corbusier.

イトの身で購入するには高価すぎた。他の客に買ってしまわれないようにと、平積みの書籍の下の方に移動させて店を去る。次に立ち寄ると、一番上の目につくところに戻してある。また本の山に潜らせる。そんなことを繰り返して、5巻のなかの「ロンシャン教会堂」の掲載されている巻を入手した。そして、ル・コルビュジエとはどんな建築家なのか、それを確かめにヨーロッパに行ってみたいと思うようになった。

海外旅行は前年の1964年にやっと解禁になったばかりだった。それ以前は、業務や留学などの明確な目的がなければ渡航できなかった。とにかく費用がかかる。喫茶店の設計料10万円を元手に暮らしを切り詰めて貯金した。

横浜からソビエト連邦のナホトカに船で渡り、ナホトカからハバロフスクに汽車で移動して、ハバロフスクでシベリア鉄道に乗車した。持ち出せる外貨は500ドルまで。1ドル360円固定レート時代だから18万円しか持参できなかった。

9日間かけてモスクワまで移動した。初めて降り立ったヨーロッパの都市はモスクワで、赤の広場、モスクワ大学を見た衝撃は大きかった。

パリに着いたのは9月で、前の月にル・コルビュジエは亡くなっていた。ろくな準備もせず行けばなんとかなるという認識だったので、アトリエを訪ねたいとあてどなくパリの町を彷徨った。

パリ郊外の「サヴォア邸」は作品集で見ており、「近代建築の五原則」がどう実現されているかも知っていた。その意味での感激は薄かった。パリを離れて見に行った「ラ・トゥーレット修道院」でル・コルビュジエの真髄に触れた思いがした。そこでは近代建築の原則が見事に棄却されており、さらに見るひとをも裏切る空間が眼前に展開されていたからである。「サヴァワ邸」の前後の時期、つまり1920-30年代に提唱していた近代建築の論理性、倫理観とは異なる芸術的な感情のほとばしりに仰天した。

それまで近代建築は、機能主義にせよ、構造尊重であれ、一貫性のある思考だと受

He had seen "Villa Savoye" in the portfolio, and already knew how the "5 Points of Modern Architecture" were materialized. In that sense, he was not overly impressed. He thought he found the essence of Le Corbusier in "Sainte Marie de La Tourette", away from Paris. The building was completely contrary to modern architecture, and even the space developed there was also contrary to visitors' expectations. Ando was amazed by the flowing artistic passion, which was different from the logicality and ethics of modern architecture that were proposed around the time when Le Corbusier designed "Villa Savoye" (the 1920s to 1930s).

Ando had recognized modern architecture as a consistent concept, regardless of functionalism or structural respect. Furthermore, he thought that it was based on economy, i.e., the logic of industrial production, and the continuity would be maintained even in a construction member. However, "Sainte Marie de La Tourette" was completely contrary to all of them.

The discontinuity of "Notre Dame du Haut" also attracted Ando. A commonality between these buildings is a robust relationship between the client and the architect. Ando thought that the building in front of him — based on the secure relationship with the client — was a materialization of the client's explicit desire to build this type of structure on this site.

The site in Ronchamp was believed to be a spiritual spot since the time of the Celts. With that in mind, the client asked Le Corbusier for a design. Indeed the results of cohesion of three elements: the clients, the architect, and the site location. Ando concluded that such discontinuity could be intentionally designed only by Le Corbusier.

In the two Christian buildings, the industrial production logic and the 5 Points of Modern Architecture were both excluded. The structures were incoherent, and the spaces were disconnected and segmented everywhere. An object and another object were not connected, yet the spatial experience itself formed an expression. This largely

け止めていた。それには経済、つまり工業生産の論理が下敷きになっていて、建築の部材ひとつをとっても連続性を保つものだと考えていた。しかし、「ラ・トゥーレット修道院」は、そのすべてを裏切っていた。

「ロンシャン教会堂」も、同じように不連続に魅せられた。両者に共通しているのは、施主と建築家の強固な関係だ。この土地にこんな建築が欲しいという施主側の明快な意志。それを施主との確かな信頼感のもとに実現した結果が、眼前にあるのだと感じた。

ロンシャンの立地は、ケルト文化時代からの、霊力を感じる場所であり、それを施主が意識して、ル・コルビュジエに設計を依頼した。まさに施主、建築家、そして、その土地、この三つが密着してこそ生まれた空間だった。そこまでの不連続を意図的に手がけられるのは、ル・コルビュジエしかいないと自分なりに結論づけた。

二つのキリスト教建築では、近代建築の掲げた工業生産の論理も、いわゆる五原則も退けられていた。構造もちぐはぐ、空間もほうぼうで断ち切られて不連続になっていた。モノとモノが繋がっていない。しかし、空間体験そのものが表現となっていて、それがすごく魅力的に映った。そして、ああこれは人生なのだと思えてきた。ル・コルビュジエ本人が自身の掲げたスローガンを裏切る人生を選んだとも受けとめた。第2次世界大戦前に彼の提起したスローガンがにべもなく捨て去られている。彼は裏切ることに良心の呵責を感じない。すべてを空間の芸術的表現に供するためにそうしているのだと気づいた。

attracted Ando, and he thought of it as representing life itself. It was perceived that Le Corbusier chose a life that was contrary to the slogans, which he had proposed himself. The slogans, proposed by Le Corbusier before WWII, were bluntly discarded. He did not feel guilty to renege. Ando realized that Le Corbusier was doing so in order to devote everything to artistic spatial expressions.

Kenzo Tange: Spiritual Architecture

In 1964 (according to Ando's memory), Ando audited a lecture by Masami Naka, which was the pen name of architectural researcher Hiroshi Sasaki. The lecture was about modern architecture in Northern Europe, mainly on Finnish architect Alvar Aalto. Ando was very much interested. A desire to see modern architecture in Northern Europe was one of the triggers for travelling to Europe, before encountering the works of Le Corbusier.

When Ando visited the atelier of Aalto in Helsinki and hovered around outside on the street, Aalto asked him from inside if he was Japanese. Aalto invited Ando to tour the atelier. Aalto was still alive and it was a great pleasure to see him.

Ando visited the experimental Tapiola Apartment Buildings, partly designed by Aalto. It was far from interesting, since only a group of mid-rise housing complexes with pure white walls was visible, and he was unable to see inside. Nonetheless, Ando visited many works by Aalto and was fascinated by Northern European modern architecture.

He traveled to Europe twice by using the Trans-Siberian Railway, and visited various buildings old and new. A conviction grew as Ando taught himself: lack of architectural education in college can be substituted by learning through reading, and visiting the actual buildings. It was a confidence that literature and actual buildings can provide a learning experience that is comparable to a school

丹下健三——魂の建築

1964年だったと記憶するが、建築研究者の佐々木宏が、ペンネームの中真己の名前で開いた講演会に聴衆として出かけた。内容はフィンランドの建築家アルヴァ・アアルトを中心とする北欧の近代建築の話で、これが面白かった。ル・コルビュジエの作品との出合い以前に、北欧の近代建築を見たいというのが、ヨーロッパに出かけるひとつの動機になった。

ヘルシンキのアアルトのアトリエまで行って、道路をうろうろしていると、なかから声をかけてくれて、「日本人か？」と言ってアトリエを見学させてくれた。アアルトはまだ存命で謦咳に接することが出来たのは、なによりの喜びだった。

アアルトも参加した実験集合住宅タピオラを訪ねた。純白の壁の中層の集合住宅の建ち並ぶ姿を見ただけで、住宅内部には入ることはかなわず、面白さにはほど遠かった。それでもアアルトの多くの作品を訪ね、北欧の近代建築に魅了された。

結局、シベリア鉄道を使ってのヨーロッパ行は2回に及び、新旧さまざまの建築に出合った。大学の建築教育を受けなかったことに代わるものは、ひとつは読書による学習であり、もうひとつは現物を訪ねるということだという確信が、自分なりの経験を重ねるうちに生まれた。書籍と現物があれば、学校に匹敵する学習が可能だという自信である。それがあったからこそ、北欧では、暮れない白夜に、目的の建築を求めて歩き通せた。

歴史的な名作ばかりではない。ウィーンの中心市街地で、ハンス・ホラインが設計した「レッティ蝋燭店」（1965年）の完成から間もない姿を見たときには感動を覚えた。ステンレスの肌の冷たい美しさに、これは建築でありながら、「ひとつの宝石」だと感じ

education. This enabled Ando to walk under the midnight sun in Northern Europe to visit buildings, i.e., actual architectural works.

He was impressed not only by historical masterpieces, but also by seeing the brand-new "Retti Candle Shop" (1965), designed by Hans Hollein, in central Vienna. The cool beauty of stainless steel surfaces formed the building but it was perceived as "a jewel". Ando realized that a newly built building could also create happy feelings for viewers at the moment they saw the building. He re-recognized the importance of seeing the actual buildings on site.

When looking back, Ando had no interest in the architectural world at that time. He was desperate for learning, and had no room to see other things. He was focused on learning through seeing actual works on site, rather than the trends of architects.

In 1963, two years before his international travels, Ando traveled through Japan at age 22. He went around Japan in two months, with the exception of Okinawa.

By seeing sceneries of traditional Japanese farming communities with houses and terraced rice fields while traveling, Ando came to know that a variety of beauty — different from the beauty of downtown Osaka — existed throughout Japan. His traveling experiences gave Ando an epiphany about the Japanese beauty sought by Isamu Noguchi, whom Ando only knew by name.

Ando traveled to Tokyo for the first time. He visited the former "Tokyo Metropolitan Government Building" in Marunouchi, a work of Kenzo Tange that Ando saw for the first time. At that time, Ando could not understand what pilotis were, since he knew almost nothing about Le Corbusier. He deepened his understanding of Tange's works as he traveled further and visited more of his works, including "Kagawa Prefectural Government Hall" and "Hiroshima Peace Memorial Museum".

When Ando saw the concrete cross sections arranged in an orderly fashion, like rafters of Japanese architecture, under the deep eaves of "Kagawa Prefectural Government

た。生まれて間もない建築でも、見た瞬間に幸福な感覚に包まれることを知った。現物に現地で接することの大切さを、そのときも実感した。

思い返すに、そのころは建築界というものには関心がなかった。自分が学ぶことに必死で、脇目をふるような余裕はなかった。建築家の動向よりも、自分の目で現地で作品を見て、学習することだけを心がけていた。

日本国内を旅したのは、海外行より遡ること2年、1963年、22歳の時だった。2カ月かけて沖縄を除く日本を一周した。

旅をするうちに民家と棚田が織りなす日本の伝統的な農村集落の風景を眺めて、大阪下町とは異なる美が、日本のあちこちにあることを知った。名前だけしか知らなかったイサム・ノグチが目指していた日本美とはなにかを、そうした旅の体験が直感させた。

この旅で初めて東京に行った。現在は失われた丸ノ内の「東京都庁舎」を訪ね、丹下健三の作品に初めて接した。ル・コルビュジエについてほとんど何も知らなかったので、ピロティといわれてもよくわからなかった。丹下の作品は、旅が進むに連れて「香川県庁舎」、広島の「原爆資料館」と実見を重ねて、理解を深めた。

「香川県庁舎」の深い庇の下に、日本建築の垂木のようにコンクリートの断面が規則正しくならぶ姿を見たとき、「日本美」の表現として間違いなく最高傑作だと確信した。そして、広島で、ピロティの向こうに平和記念公園と原爆ドームの姿を確かめたとき、建築がひとの思いも歴史も、その土地の文脈来歴も、すべてを巻き込んで成立しているのだということを実感した。

丹下は、敗戦間際に、病気と空襲で、日を置かずに相次いで両親を失った。

それもあって丹下の魂が「原爆資料館」には込められていた。その静かな激情が1964年の東京オリンピック、さらに1970年の日本万博まで持続し、世界から注目される大作を生み出した。自分の心を揺り動かす動機があってこそ、初めて見るひとを感動

Hall", he was certain that the building was a masterwork as an expression of "Japanese beauty". In Hiroshima, he saw the Hiroshima Peace Memorial Park and the Atomic Bomb Dome behind pilotis. Then he realized that buildings were established by including everything from people's thoughts, histories, and the contexts of the site.

Tange lost his parents in a short period of time due to an airborne attack and illness, right before Japan's losing war.

Therefore, Tange put his soul into the "Hiroshima Peace Memorial Museum". His quiet passion was sustained up until the Tokyo Olympics in 1964, and even through the Japan World Exposition, Osaka 1970, by creating globally-noticed masterpieces. Ando learned from visiting works of Tange from his golden age that an architectural work that would move viewers was only created by a motivation that moved the architect himself. This became Ando's attitude for designing, which still endures in his mind.

After listening to Ando's words, I re-recognized the strong willpower of Ando as an architect, who perseveres after overcoming two major illnesses. His goalless journey was morphed into an endless pilgrimage of a seeker of the truth of architecture. By seeing the great works of the SHANGHAI POLY THEATER (2014) and ROBERTO GARZA SADA CENTER FOR ARTS, ARCHITECTURE AND DESIGN (2012), which exceeded the scales of his earlier creations, I can imagine that Ando will keep going without rest after age 80, and on toward ages 90 and 100.

させる建築が出来るのだということを、丹下の絶頂期の作品に接して学んだ。それはそのまま安藤自身の設計にあたっての心がけとなり、今なお心のなかに生き続けているという。

わたしは、こうした安藤の言葉に耳を傾け、二度の大病を超えて持続する建築家としての彼の強固な意志の力を改めて実感した。あてどのなかった旅は、建築の真理を求める求道者の終わりなき巡礼の道行きへと昇華されていく。「上海保利大劇場」(2014年)と「モンテレイ大学RGSセンター」(2012年)のこれまでの創作のスケールを打破する大作の揃い踏みに接すると、齢80を超え、90、さらに100歳を目指して、なお休むことなく歩み続ける安藤の姿が目に浮かんだ。

第II部　全346作品録

解説：松葉一清

Part II　346 Complete Works

synopsis by Kazukiyo Matsuba

凡例（Legends）：

［作品番号　number］
作品名　完成年
name of works　completion year

1. 住所 | location
2. 設計 | design
3. 施工 | construction
4. 構造 | structure
5. 用途 | use
6. 敷地面積 | site area
7. 建築面積 | building area
8. 延床面積 | total floor area

掲載順は原則として完成年による。
未完の作品については、完成年に替えて設計年を表示。
Works are basically in the order of completion year.
For the unfinished works, design year is noted instead of completion year.

作品総覧
List of Works

1960s:

001 JR大阪駅前プロジェクト'69 1969
JR osaka station area reconstruction project

1970s:

002 スワン商会ビル──小林邸 1971
swan — kobayashi house

003 ゲリラ──加藤邸 1972
guerrilla — kato house

004 高橋邸 1973
takahashi house

005 冨島邸 1973
tomishima house

006 平岡邸 1974
hiraoka house

007 立見邸 1974
tatsumi house

008 芝田邸 1974
shibata house

009 内田邸 1974
uchida house

010 宇野邸 1974
uno house

011 松村邸 1975
matsumura house

012 双生観──山口邸 1975
soseikan — yamaguchi house

013 ツインウォール 1975
twin wall

014 四軒長屋 1975
tenement house with four flats

015 住吉の長屋──東邸 1976
row house, sumiyoshi — azuma house

016 貫入──平林邸 1976
interpenetration — hirabayashi house

017 番匠邸 1976
bansho house

018 帝塚山タワープラザ 1976
tezukayama tower plaza

019 岡本ハウジング 1976
okamoto housing project

020 ローズガーデン 1977
rose garden

021 帝塚山の家──真鍋邸 1977
tezukayama house — manabe house

022 領壁の家──松本邸 1977
wall house — matsumoto house

023 北野アレイ 1977
kitano alley

024 アートギャラリー・コンプレックス 1977
art gallery complex

025 甲東アレイ 1978
koto alley

026 ガラスブロックの家──石原邸 1978
glass block house — ishihara house

027 大楠邸 1978
okusu house

028 ガラスブロックウォール──堀内邸 1979
glass block wall — horiuchi house

029 片山ハウス 1979
katayama building

030 大西邸 1979
onishi house

031 松谷邸 1979
matsutani house

032 上田邸 1979
ueda house

1980s:

033 STEP 1980
step

034 松本邸 1980
matsumoto house

035 北野アイビーコート 1980
kitano ivy court

036 福邸 1980
fuku house

037 中之島プロジェクト I（大阪市役所） 1980
nakanoshima project I

038 小篠邸 1981
koshino house
小篠邸増築 1984
koshino house addition

039 リンズギャラリー 1981
rin's gallery

040 大淀のアトリエ 1981, 1982, 1986
atelier in oyodo

041 児島の共同住宅──佐藤邸 1981
kojima housing — sato house

042 番匠邸増築 1981
bansho house addition

043 ファッション・ライブ・シアター 1981
fashion live theater

044 サンプレイス 1982
sun place

045 石井邸 1982
ishii house

046 双生観の茶室──山口邸増築 1982
tea house for soseikan — yamaguchi house addition

047 九条の町屋──井筒邸 1982
town house in kujo — izutsu house

048 赤羽邸 1982
akabane house

049 ドールズハウス 1982
doll's house

050 六甲の集合住宅 I 1983
rokko housing I

051 BIGIアトリエ 1983
bigi atelier

052 梅宮邸 1983
umemiya house

053 茂木邸 1983
motegi house

054 金子邸 1983
kaneko house

055 フェスティバル 1984
festival

056 植条邸 1984
uejo house

057 太田邸 1984
ota house

058 MELROSE 1984
melrose

059 岩佐邸 1984
iwasa house

060 南林邸 1984
minamibayashi house

061 TIME'S I, II 1984, 1991
time's I, II

062 畑邸 1984
hata house

063 ジュン・ポートアイランドビル 1985
jun port island building

064 中山邸 1985
nakayama house

065 アトリエ・ヨシエ・イナバ 1985
atelier yoshie inaba

066 モン・プティ・シュ 1985
mon-petit-chou

067 青葉台アトリエ 1985
aobadai atelier

068 吉本邸 1985
yoshimoto house

069 大淀の茶室（ベニヤ、ブロック、テント） 1985, 1986, 1988
tea house in oyodo (veneer, block, tent)

070 服部邸ゲストハウス 1985
guest house for hattori house

071 渋谷プロジェクト 1985
shibuya project

072 城戸崎邸 1986
kidosaki house

073 福原病院 1986
fukuhara clinic

074 リランズゲート 1986
riran's gate

075 沖辺邸 1986
okibe house

076 孫邸 1986
son house

077 佐々木邸 1986
sasaki house

078 太陽セメント本社ビル 1986
taiyo-cement headquarters building

079 六甲の教会 1986 chapel on mt. rokko	105 夏川記念会館 1989 natsukawa memorial hall	127 熊本県立装飾古墳館 1992 kumamoto prefectural ancient burial mound museum	149 大山崎山荘美術館 1995 oyamazaki villa museum
080 TSビル 1986 ts building	106 城尾邸 1989 shiroo house	128 宮下邸 1992 miyashita house	150 市立五條文化博物館 1995 museum of gojo culture
081 ゲストハウスOLD／NEW六甲 1986 guest house old / new rokko	107 矢尾クリニック 1989 yao clinic	129 姫路市立星の子館 1992 children's seminar house, himeji	151 ベネッセハウス オーバル 1995 benesse house oval
082 細工谷の家──野口邸 1986 town house in saikudani ─ noguchi house	**1990s:** 108 B-LOCK北山 1990 b-lock kitayama	130 奈良市民ホール国際設計競技案 1992 nara convention hall, international design competition	152 綾部工業団地交流プラザ 1995 ayabe community center
083 渋谷神社総合開発計画 1986 shibuya shrine redevelopment project	109 伊東邸 1990 ito house	131 六甲アイランドプロジェクト 1993 rokko island project	153 かほく市立金津小学校 1995 kanadu primary school, kahoku
084 BIGI 3rd 1986 bigi 3rd	110 国際花と緑の博覧会「名画の庭」 1990 garden of fine art, expo'90 / osaka	132 兵庫県立大学 看護学部・看護研究科 1993 college of nursing art and science, university of hyogo	154 ユネスコ瞑想空間 1995 meditation space, UNESCO
085 田中山荘 1987 tanaka atelier	111 Sビル 1990 s building	133 六甲の集合住宅 II 1993 rokko housing II	155 テートギャラリー現代美術館 国際設計競技案 1995 tate gallery of modern art, international design competition
086 唐座 1987 kara-za	112 ストックホルム現代美術館・建築美術館 国際設計競技案 1990 the modern art museum and architecture museum, stockholm, international design competition	134 ヴィトラ・セミナーハウス 1993 vitra seminar house	156 大淀のアトリエ・アネックス 1995 atelier in oyodo annex
087 天王寺公園植物温室 （天王寺博覧会テーマ館） 1987 tennoji park, greenhouse (main pavilion for tennoji fair)	113 十文字美信仮設劇場 1990 temporary theater for bishin jumonji, photographer	135 YKK津田沼寮 1993 YKK seminar house	157 海の集合住宅 1995 seaside housing
088 水の劇場 1987 theater on the water	114 姫路文学館 1991 museum of literature, himeji	136 垂水の教会 1993 church in tarumi	158 大谷地下劇場計画 1995 the theater in the rock, oya
089 六甲山バンケットホール 1987 banquet hall on mt. rokko	115 石河邸 1991 ishiko house	137 李邸 1993 lee house	159 丘の集合住宅 1995 hilltop housing
090 伊豆プロジェクト 1987 izu project	116 佐用ハウジング 1991 sayo housing	138 ギャラリー野田 1993 gallery noda	160 姫路文学館 南館 1996 museum of literature south annex, himeji
091 Iプロジェクト 1987 i project	117 ロックフィールド静岡ファクトリー 1991, 2000 rockfield shizuoka factory	139 サントリーミュージアム ＋マーメイド広場 1994 suntory museum + mermaid plaza	161 平野区の町屋──能見邸 1996 town house in hirano ─ nomi house
092 Iハウス 1988 i house	118 ミノルタセミナーハウス 1991 minolta seminar house	140 大阪府立近つ飛鳥博物館 1994 chikatsu-asuka historical museum, osaka	162 白井邸 1996 shirai house
093 水の教会 1988 church on the water	119 大淀のアトリエ II 1991 atelier in oyodo II	141 京都府立陶板名画の庭 1994 garden of fine art, kyoto	163 ギャラリー小さい芽（澤田邸） 1996 gallery chiisaime ─ sawada house
094 GALLERIA [akka] 1988 galleria [akka]	120 真言宗本福寺水御堂 1991 water temple	142 マックスレイ本社ビル 1994 maxray headquarters building	164 ローマ司教区教会国際設計競技案 1996 vicariato di roma ─ international design competition for the church of the year 2000
095 小倉邸 1988 ogura house	121 JR京都駅改築設計競技案 1991 the reconstruction of JR kyoto station, international design competition	143 鹿児島大学稲盛会館 1994 inamori auditorium	165 スタジオ・カール・ラガーフェルド 1996 studio karl lagerfeld
096 B-LOCK神楽岡 1988 b-lock kaguraoka	122 甲南大学スチューデントサークル プロジェクト 1991 konan university student circle project	144 兵庫県木の殿堂 1994 museum of wood	166 マンハッタンのペントハウス 1996 penthouse in manhattan
097 吉田邸 1988 yoshida house	123 大手前大学アートセンター 1992 otemae art center	145 高梁市成羽美術館 1994 nariwa museum	167 シカゴの住宅 1997 house in chicago
098 Iギャラリー 1988 i gallery	124 1992年セビリア万国博覧会 日本館 1992 japan pavilion, expo'92 / seville	146 日本橋の家──金森邸 1994 house in nipponbashi ─ kanamori house	168 越知町立横倉山自然の森博物館 ──横倉山・牧野富太郎展示室 1997 the yokogurayama natural forest museum, ochi
099 中之島プロジェクト II （アーバン・エッグ＋地層空間） 1988 nakanoshima project II (urban egg space strata)	125 ベネッセハウス ミュージアム 1992 benesse house museum	147 安藤忠雄建築展 ／Palladian Basilica 1994 tadao ando exhibition in palladian basilica	169 TOTOセミナーハウス 1997 TOTO seminar house
100 COLLEZIONE 1989 collezione	126 シカゴ美術館屏風ギャラリー 1992 gallery for japanese screen, the art institute of chicago	148 播磨高原東小学校 1995 harima kogen higashi primary school 播磨高原東中学校 1997 harima kogen higashi junior high school	170 八木邸 1997 yagi house
101 モロゾフP&Pスタジオ 1989 morozoff p&p studio			171 青木の集合住宅 1997 ogi housing
102 光の教会 1989 church of the light			172 小海高原美術館 1997 koumi kogen museum
103 兵庫県立こどもの館 1989 children's museum, hyogo			
104 ライカ本社ビル 1989 raika headquarters building			

173	ライン世界文化博物館 1997 the museum of world cultures on the river rhine	193	セント・ポール寺院聖台 デザインコンペティション 2000 a new font for st. paul's cathedral, international design competiton	216	砂漠の家・乗馬施設 2002 house & stable for tom ford and richard buckley	237	滋賀の住宅 2006 house in shiga
174	ダイコク電機本部ビル 1998 daikoku denki headquarters building			217	野間自由幼稚園 2003 noma kindergarten	238	モリモト ニューヨーク （モリモト・ニューヨーク） 2006 morimoto nyc
175	渡辺淳一記念館 1998 junichi watanabe memorial hall	194	カルダー美術館 2000 calder museum	218	4×4の住宅 2003 4×4 house	239	ベネッセハウス パーク／ビーチ 2006 benesse house park, beach / naoshima
176	エリエール松山ゲストハウス 1998 elleair matsuyama guesthouse	195	大阪府立狭山池博物館 2001 sayamaike historical museum, osaka	219	マリブの住宅 2003 house in malibu	240	小篠邸ゲストハウス 2006 guest house for koshino house
177	ネパール子供病院 1998 shiddhartha children and women hospital	196	ピューリッツァー美術館 2001 pulitzer foundation for the arts	220	県立ぐんま昆虫の森　昆虫観察館 2004 gunma insect world / insect observation hall	241	さくら広場 幕張 2006 sakura hiroba makuhari 同 門真 2006 sakura hiroba kadoma 同 茅ヶ崎 2007 sakura hiroba chigasaki 同 豊中 2009 sakura hiroba toyonaka
178	織田廣喜ミュージアム 1998 daylight museum	197	兵庫県立美術館＋神戸市水際広場 2001 hyogo prefectural museum of art + kobe waterfront plaza				
179	セーヌ川橋国際設計競技案 1998 passerelle de bercy-tolbiac, international design competition	198	司馬遼太郎記念館 2001 shiba ryotaro memorial museum	221	ホンブロイッヒ／ランゲン 美術館 2004 langen foundation / hombroich		
180	六甲の集合住宅 III 1999 rokko housing III	199	四国村ギャラリー 2001 shikokumura gallery	222	見えない家 2004 invisible house	242	パラッツォ・グラッシ 2006 palazzo grassi
181	淡路夢舞台 1999 awaji-yumebutai	200	神宮前の集合住宅 2001 jingumae housing	223	地中美術館 2004 chichu art museum	243	游庵 2006 yu-un (obayashi collection)
182	光の教会／日曜学校 1999 church of the light, sunday school	201	国際芸術センター青森 2001 aomori contemporary art center	224	仙川・安藤ストリート 2004–2012 sengawa, ando street	244	2016年東京オリンピック構想 2006 tokyo oliympic games 2016 project
183	西宮市貝類館 1999 shell museum of nishinomiya city	202	アルマーニ・テアトロ 2001 armani teatro	225	絵本美術館 2004 iwaki museum of picture books for children	245	アブダビ海洋博物館 2006 abu dhabi maritime museum
184	南寺（直島・家プロジェクト） 1999 minamidera (art house project in naoshima)	203	ピノー現代美術館 2001 françois pinault foundation for contemporary art	226	加子母ふれあいコミュニティセンター 2004 kashimo community center	246	谷間の家 2006 crevice house in manhattan
185	レイナ・ソフィア美術館国際設計競技案 1999 museo nacional centro de arte reina sofia, international design competition	204	グラウンド・ゼロ・プロジェクト 2001 ground zero project	227	2004 サイトウ・キネン・ フェスティバル松本・オペラ 「ヴォツェック」舞台構成 2004 set design for 2004 saito kinen festival matsumoto / opera "wozzeck"	247	デミアン・ハースト・スタジオ 2006 damien hirst studio
		205	4×4の住宅（東京） 2001 4×4 house (tokyo)			248	21_21 デザインサイト 2007 21_21 design sight
186	ネルソン・アトキンス美術館 国際設計競技案 1999 nelson atkins museum, international design competition	206	西田幾多郎記念哲学館 2002 nishida kitaro museum of philosophy			249	曹洞宗太岳院 2007 taigakuin temple
		207	国立国会図書館国際子ども図書館 （レンガ棟） 2002 the international library of children's literature	228	ICED TIME TUNNEL ／THE SNOW SHOW 2004 2004 iced time tunnel / the snow show 2004	250	バーレーン考古学博物館 2007 bahrain archeological museum
187	ケ・ブランリー美術館国際設計競技案 1999 musée du quai branly, international design competiton			229	ゴールデン・ゲート・ブリッジの住宅 2004 golden gate bridge house	251	東京大学 建築資料館 2007 architecture reference library, the university of tokyo
		208	フォートワース現代美術館 2002 modern art museum of fort worth	230	森の教会 2004 chapel in the woods	252	ポズナニ美術館 2007 art stations poznan
2000s:		209	マンチェスター市ピカデリー公園 2002 piccadilly gardens regeneration, manchester	231	ロックフィールド神戸ヘッドオフィス ／神戸ファクトリー 2005 rockfield kobe headquarters / kobe factory	253	海の森 2007 sea forest
188	FABRICA（ベネトンアートスクール） 2000 fabrica (benetton communication research center)					254	マンハッタンのペントハウス II 2008 penthouse in manhattan II
		210	アサヒビール神奈川工場ゲストハウス 2002 guesthouse, asahi kanagawa brewery	232	高槻の住宅 2005 house in takatsuki	255	クラーク美術館／ランダーセンター 2008 clark art institute / lunder center at stone hill
189	南岳山光明寺 2000 komyo-ji temple	211	アウディジャパン本社ビル 2002 audi japan headquarters	233	hhstyle.com/casa 2005 hhstyle.com/casa		
190	新潟市立豊栄図書館 2000 niigata city toyosaka library	212	加賀市立錦城中学校 2002 kinjo junior high school, kaga	234	回遊式住宅 2005 walk around house	256	スリランカの住宅 2008 house in sri lanka
191	ミュゼふくおかカメラ館 2000 fukuoka camera museum	213	灘浜ガーデンバーデン 2002 nadahama garden baden	235	坂の上の雲ミュージアム 2006 saka no ue no kumo museum	257	聖心女子学院 創立100周年記念ホール 2008 sacred heart school, 100th anniversary hall
192	アントワープ市立博物館国際設計競技案 2000 museum aan de stroom, antwerp, international design competition	214	コキュ・オフィスビル 2002 cocue office building	236	表参道ヒルズ 2006 omotesando hills		
		215	尾道市立美術館 2002 onomichi city museum of art			258	東急東横線渋谷駅 2008 tokyu toyoko-line shibuya station

259	東京大学情報学環・福武ホール 2008 interfaculty initiative in information studies, fukutake hall, the university of tokyo		
260	ハンファHRDセンター 2008 hanwha hrd center		
261	済州島〈石の門〉〈風の門〉 2008 gate of stone and gate of wind in jeju island		
262	北京国子監ホテル+美術館 2008 beijing guozijian hotel		
263	カペラ・ニセコ・リゾートホテル 2008 capella niseko resort & residence		
264	ヴィラ・ブダペスト（旧首相公邸改造計画） 2008 villa budapest		
265	六甲プロジェクト IV 2009 rokko project IV		
266	プンタ・デラ・ドガーナ 2009 punta della dogana contemporary art center		
267	IPU環太平洋大学 2009, 2013 international pacific university		
268	横浜地方気象台 2009 yokohama local meteorological observatory		
269	俄本社ビル 2009 niwaka headquarters building		
270	ムンク美術館国際設計競技 2009 munch museum and stenersen museum collections		
271	北ヨーロッパの住宅 2009 house in northern europe		
272	上海建築文化センター 2009 architecture and culture center, shanghai		
273	北京紅楼夢ホテル 2009 hong lou meng hotel		
274	半山半島美術館+劇場センター 2009 serenity coast art museum + performing arts center		

2010s

275	ノバルティス研究施設棟 2010 novartis wsj-352
276	ストーン・スカルプチュア・ミュージアム 2010 stone sculpture museum
277	上海デザインセンター 2010 shanghai design center
278	竜王駅+南北駅前広場 2010 ryuo station + station square
279	靱公園の住宅 2010 house in utsubo park
280	李禹煥美術館 2010 lee ufan museum
281	チャスカ茶屋町 2010 chaska chayamachi
282	あてま森と水辺の教室〈森のホール〉〈水辺のホール〉 2010 atema project ‹forest hall› ‹waterside hall›
283	名古屋の住宅 2010 house in nagoya
284	石原邸 2010 ishihara house
285	光の美術館 2010 museum of light
286	中国太湖博物館 2010 china taihu museum, suzhou
287	シャトー・ラ・コスト/アートセンター 2011 château la coste / art center 同 チャペル 2011 château la coste / chapel 同 4グラス・キューブス・パビリオン 2011 château la coste / four glass cubes pavilion
288	モンテレイの住宅 2011 house in monterrey
289	東急大井町線上野毛駅 2011 tokyu oimachi-line kaminoge station
290	カルロス・プレイス「サイレンス」 2011 carlos place "silence"
291	韓屋のゲストハウス 2011 house with "hanok"
292	ミュージアム SAN 2012 museum san
293	マリブの住宅 III 2012 house in malibu III
294	モンテレイ大学RGSセンター 2012 roberto garza sada center for arts, architecture and design
295	秋田県立美術館 2012 akita museum of art
296	ボンテ・ミュージアム 2012 bonte museum
297	震旦美術館 2012 aurora museum
298	老木レディスクリニック 2012 oiki ladies clinic
299	高松の住宅 2012 house in takamatsu
300	上方落語協会会館 2012 kamigata rakugo house
301	マンガロールの住宅 2012 house in mangalore
302	亜洲大学 亜洲現代美術館 2013 asia museum of modern art, asia university
303	うめきた広場 2013 umekita plaza
304	芦屋の住宅 2013 house in ashiya
305	佐渡邸 2013 sado house
306	おかやま信用金庫 内山下スクエア 2013 okayama shinkin bank uchisange square
307	JCCクリエイティブセンター 2013 jcc creative center JCCアートセンター 2014 jcc art center
308	テアトリーノ 2013 teatrino
309	ANDO MUSEUM 2013 ando museum
310	希望の壁 2013 wall of hope
311	都市の大樹 2013 the tall green project
312	クラーク美術館/クラークセンター 2014 clark art institute / clark center
313	上海保利大劇場 2014 shanghai poly theater
314	広尾の教会 2014 church in hiroo
315	デュベティカ ミラノ ショップ 2014 duvetica milano shop 同 ショールーム 2014 duvetica milano showroom
316	ボスコ・スタジオ&ハウス 2014 bosco studio & house
317	マリブの住宅 I 2015 house in malibu I
318	良渚村文化芸術センター 2015 liangzhu village cultural ar center
319	森の教会 2015 church in the forest
320	十和田市教育プラザ 2015 towada education plaza
321	三河田原駅 2015 mikawatahara station
322	真駒内滝野霊園 頭大仏 2015 hill of the buddha
323	みやこ町立伊良原小学校 みやこ町立伊良原中学校 2016 miyako town irahara elementary and junior high school
324	国立国会図書館 国際子ども図書館アーチ棟 2016 the international library of children's literature / arch building
325	北菓楼札幌本館 2016 kitakaro sapporo honkan
326	元麻布の住宅 2016 house in motoazabu
327	森の中の家 安野光雅館 2017 anno mitsumasa museum
328	大阪商工信用金庫 新本社ビル 2017 osaka shoko shinkin bank

進行中 | in progress:

329	森の霊園・水の納骨堂 water charnel, cemetery in the woods
330	ボローニャ ISA bologna isa
331	GENESIS MUSEUM genesis museum
332	元祖夢世界 ganso dream world
333	ライトウッド ギャラリー wrightwood gallery
334	ヴァルスの広場 valser path
335	マンハッタンのペントハウス III penthouse in manhattan III
336	マンハッタンの集合住宅 condominium in manhattan
337	和美術館 he art museum
338	寿長生の郷 点心庵 sunainosato tenshinan
339	臥龍山安養院増築計画 garyozan anyoin temple
340	浅草の住宅 house in asakusa
341	新華紅星国際広場 xinhua redstar landmark
342	ブルス・ドゥ・コメルス bourse de commerce
343	フォートワース現代美術館増築計画 modern art museum of fort worth expansion project
344	BIGI青葉台 bigi aobadai
345	兵庫県立美術館増築計画 hyogo prefectural museum of art expansion project
346	中之島児童文学館プロジェクト nakanoshima children's library project

[001]
JR大阪駅前プロジェクト '69
1969
JR osaka station area
reconstruction project

1. 大阪市北区 | kita-ku, osaka
2. 設計 | design 1969
3. 構想案 | concept
5. 都市計画 | urban planning

活動の初期、大阪市の求めでまとめた大阪駅前の再開発案。ビル群の屋上に空中庭園を設けて、それを高低差を踏まえてエスカレーターで連結させる構想で、庭園の周囲に図書館、美術館、劇場などの都市の文化機能を配置することを提案した。駅前を、私的な経済活動を超えた公共の場とする構想だった。後年の「JR京都駅改築設計」コンペで示したJR線路をまたぐ広大な人工地盤案の萌芽を見ることもできる。

Redevelopment plan in front of Osaka station Ando proposed under the request of Osaka City during his initial phase of activity. The proposed concept was to create a hanging garden on the rooftop of buildings and connect them with escalators considering the height difference and provide urban cultural functions including a library, art gallery, and theater located around the garden. Also, the area in front of the station was designed to be a public area outside of private commercial activities. The sprouting of the vast artificial ground plan that pcsses across the JR railways proposed at THE RECONSTRUCTION OF JR KYOTO STATION contest that held later can be seen in this plan.

[002]
スワン商会ビル ── 小林邸
1971
swan — kobayashi house

1. 大阪市旭区 | asahi-ku, osaka
2. 設計 | design 1971
3. 構想案 | concept
5. 住宅、店舗 | house, shop
6. 敷地 | site 198 m²
7. 建築 | building 101 m²
8. 延床 | total floor 218 m²

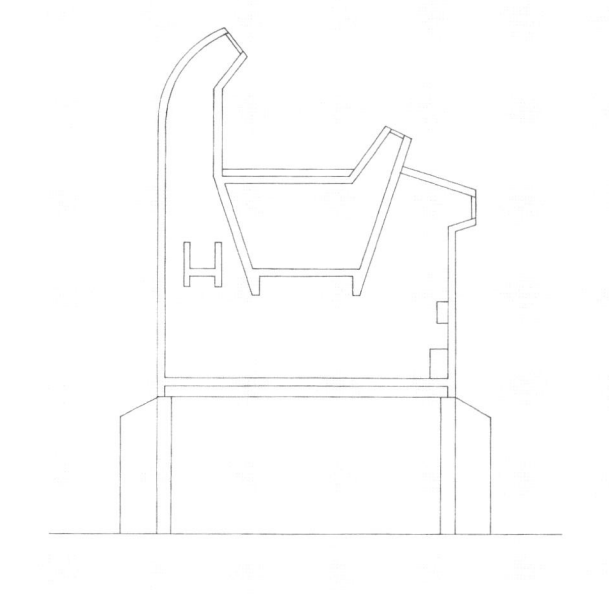

安藤が設計活動の初期に提案した「都市ゲリラ住居」のコンセプト案のひとつ。クリーニング店の2、3階に居室を配し、狭さを克服するため、吹き抜けが活用されている。光を室内に浸潤させるトップライトの特異な形、さらに、黒く仕上げられた模型そのものが、都市ゲリラという過激な概念を体現して、多くのひとの関心を集めた。なんとしても都市に凄み続けたいという大阪下町の庶民の意志を、建築家が実現していく決意が読み取れる。

One of the conceptual ideas of the urban guerrilla housing Ando proposec in his initial designing activity. Living rooms are situated on the 2nd and 3rd floors of a dry-cleaning store with effective use of open ceiling to solve the narrow space. A top light with an unusual shape that makes light to soak into the interior and the model finished in black attracted much attention as an object that materialized the extreme concept of urban guerrilla. It demonstrates the architect's determination to realize the will of common people in the old area of Osaka to by any means continue living in the city.

[003]

ゲリラ —— 加藤邸　1972
guerrilla — kato house
.
1. 大阪市旭区 | asahi-ku, osaka
2. 設計 | design　1972
3. 構想案 | concept
4. 鉄骨 | steel
5. 住宅 | detached house
6. 敷地 | site　126.0 m²
7. 建築 | building　80.1 m²
8. 延床 | total floor　109.6 m²

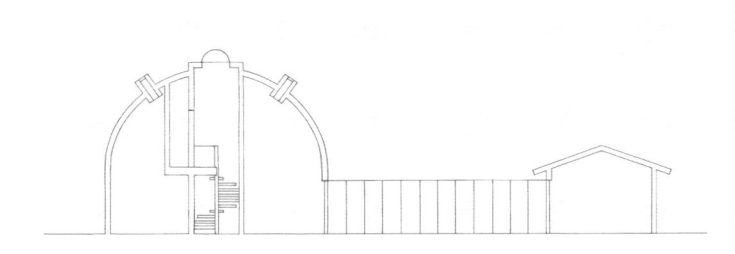

安藤が大阪下町を舞台に想定して提唱した「都市ゲリラ住居」のひとつ、実現を前提にせず、都市に対する思考を凝縮した。壁で敷地を囲い両端に住棟を置いた。大きな住棟はヴォールト屋根が架かり、小さな方は平屋で畳敷き、切妻屋根の和風の仕立てになっている。ヴォールト屋根の下には大きな空洞がとられ、絞られた採光窓から自然光が射し込む。二つの住棟の間はコートとして整備され、親子二組の家族がそこを挟んで向き合って暮らす姿が考えられた。
.
One of the urban guerrilla housings Ando advocated based on the environment of an old town of Osaka. The plan was for condensing thoughts on urban areas, not for actual implementation. The property is surrounded by walls and residential buildings are placed on both ends. A vault roof is set on the large residential architecture meanwhile the small architecture is a one-story Japanese-style house with tatami mats inside and a gable roof on top. A large hollow area is provided under the vault roof where natural light narrowed by lighting window shines inside. A courtyard is arranged in between the two housings for families of two generations could live facing each other on both sides of the courtyard.

---

[004]

高橋邸　1973
takahashi house
.
1. 兵庫県芦屋市 | ashiya, hyogo
3. 施工 | construction　1973.1–1973.6, 1975.4–1975.5 [addition]
4. 鉄筋コンクリート（壁式）、上部木造 | RC (wall), wood
5. 住宅 | detached house
6. 敷地 | site　158.5 m²
7. 建築 | building　70.6 m²
8. 延床 | total floor　154.6 m²

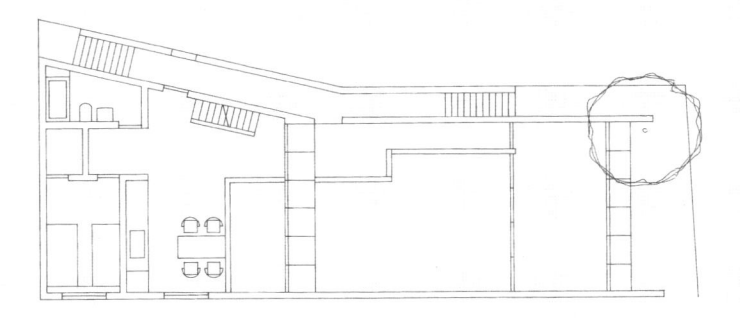

芦屋に立地する個人住宅。外部環境との繋がりを演出する目的で、街路に面した位置に高さ4メートルに達する2枚の塀を立てて、その1.5メートルほどの隙間に2階のエントランスに至る階段を設けた。2枚の壁の内側にはアーチが切られ、そこから「コート」と呼ばれる庭に出入りできる。安藤は、この庭を住宅内外の空間が相互貫入する場と位置づけ、外部に閉じた建築において、そこに「よどみ」が生まれることを期待した。

This is a private residence located in Ashiya City. Two walls in 4m high are built at the position facing to the town street, and a staircase leading to the entrance on the 2nd floor is provided in a space with 1.5m width between those two walls. One of these walls built on the inner side is cut out in arch shape, to allow entry to a garden space named "court". Ando looks at this garden as a place where both exterior and interior spaces interpenetrates into the space, expecting some "sedimentation" would occur within an architecture closed to the outside.

[005]
冨島邸　1973
tomishima house

1. 大阪市北区 | kita-ku, osaka
2. 設計 | design 1972.1–1972.11
3. 施工 | construction 1972.12–1973.2
4. 鉄筋コンクリート（壁式）| RC (wall)
5. 住宅 | detached house
6. 敷地 | site 55.2 m²
7. 建築 | building 36.2 m²
8. 延床 | total floor 72.4 m²

安藤自身、この建物がコンクリート打ち放しの第一作と述べている。大阪駅からもさほど距離を置かない木造住宅の密集地で近隣に木造の寺院もあった。角地を占める木造長屋をコンクリートボックスに置き換える発想は「住吉の長屋」の先取りだった。間口11メートル、奥行き4メートルしかない狭小の住宅で、壁には開口部はなし。屋根に配したガラスのトップライトから、間取りの中央に位置する階段室の空洞を通して届く自然光が、季節の移ろいを暮らしにもたらした。のちに安藤の事務所がここに置かれた点でも記念すべき一歩だった。

Ando himself said this is the first building he made in exposed concrete finish. There was also a wooden temple in the clustered area of wooden houses, which is not too far from Osaka station. The Idea of replacing a wooden building occupying the corner lot with a concrete box was taken prior to ROW HOUSE, SUMIYOSHI project. This is a tiny house in 11m wide and 4m deep, without any opening on the exterior walls. Natural light is brought in from the glass top light on the roof, and it comes down through the void space of the staircase room positioned in the center of this house, allowing residents to feel the change of seasons in daily life. This building shall be the memorable first step in Ando's career, considering his office was later placed here.

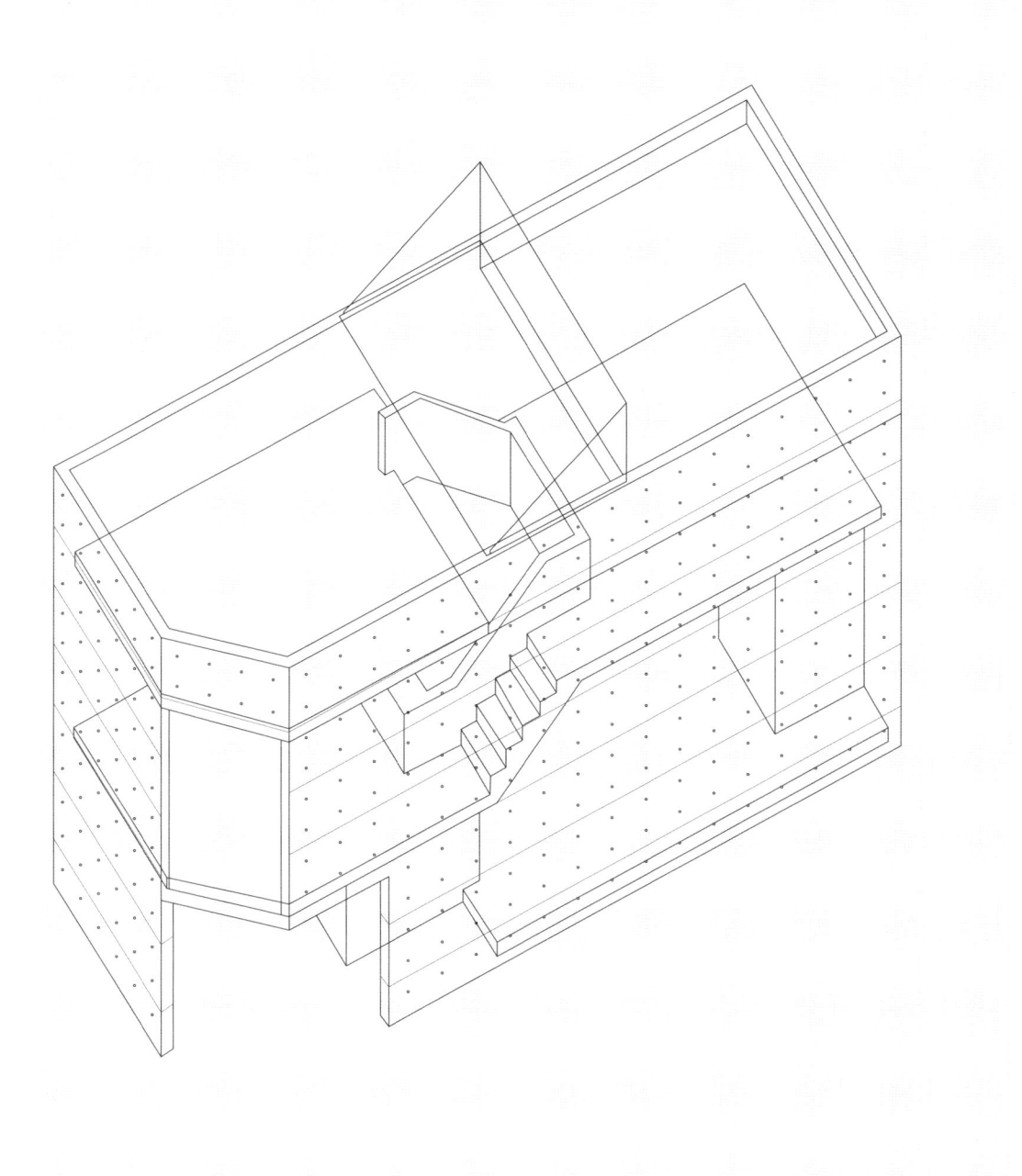

[006]

平岡邸　1974
hiraoka house

1. 兵庫県宝塚市 | takarazuka, hyogo
2. 設計 | design　1972.1–1973.5
3. 施工 | construction　1973.8–1974.2
4. 鉄筋コンクリート（壁式）、上部木造 |
   RC (wall), wood
5. 住宅 | detached house
6. 敷地 | site　238.0 m²
7. 建築 | building　58.0 m²
8. 延床 | total floor　87.9 m²

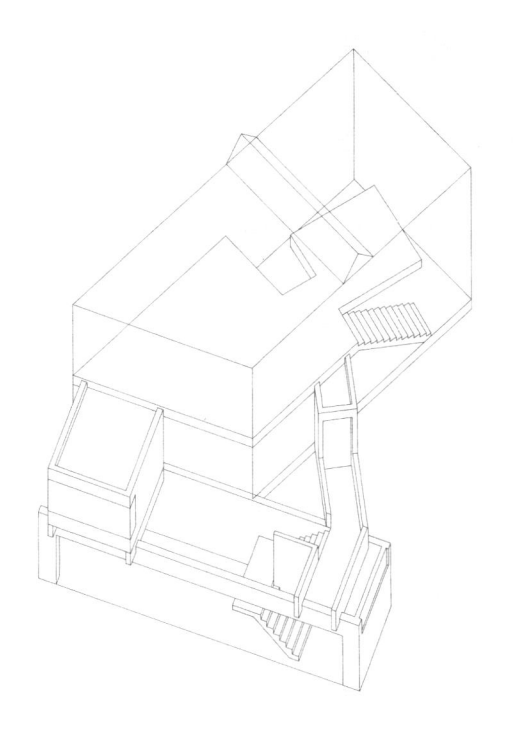

兵庫県宝塚市の傾斜地の戸建て住宅。表通り側から見ると3階だが、庭側からは2、3階の二層分だけが見える。表通り側の1階には主フロアである2階への階段とガレージだけがあり、そのうえに表通りに対して60度振った配置の2、3階が載る。2、3階には50度で振った和室と子ども部屋が配される。平面の配置は入り組み、さまざまな軸線の衝突が暮らしの空間をトリッキーなものにしている。安藤によると、その仕立てそのものが、プレハブ住宅のならぶ単調な住宅地への批評なのだという。

A residential house built on a slope in Takarazuka City, Hyogo Prefecture. Although it is a three-story building when observed from the front street, only the 2nd and 3rd floors can be seen from the garden side. Only a garage and a stairway to the 2nd floor, which is the main floor, are on the 1st floor. The 2nd and 3rd floors are turned in a 60-degree angle against the front street. A Japanese-style room and children's room are arranged on the 2nd and 3rd floors turned in a 50-dgree angle. The plan is complicated with collision of various axis lines making tricky spaces in residents' lives. Ando described that the idea of the design is to criticize the monotone atmosphere brought by numerous pre-fabricated houses in the residential area.

[007]

立見邸　1974
tatsumi house

1. 大阪市大正区 | taisho-ku, osaka
2. 設計 | design　1972.5–1973.7
3. 施工 | construction　1973.9–1974.1
4. 鉄筋コンクリート（壁式） | RC (wall)
5. 住宅、店舗 | house, shop
6. 敷地 | site　61.8 m²
7. 建築 | building　56.1 m²
8. 延床 | total floor　135.5 m²

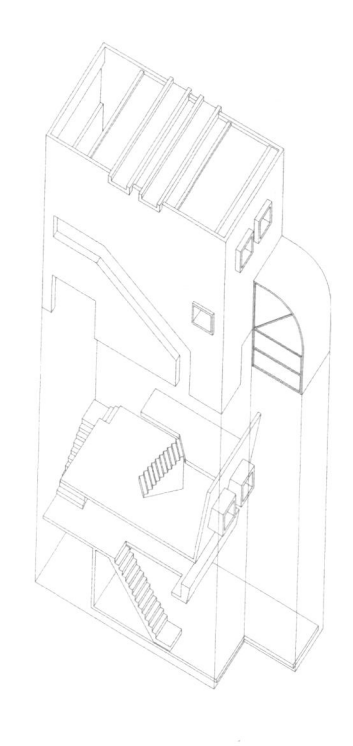

大阪の生活商店街に面する間口6メートル、奥行きが13メートル弱の狭小地に立つコンクリートボックスの店舗兼住宅。1階に家業の喫茶店を配し、主な生活空間は3階に置いた。3階は吹き抜けのスプリットフロアになっていて、リビングから階段をあがったところが寝室にあてられた。住居部分は、傾いた壁が外壁の内側に挿入され、そのために壁は下すぼまりになっている。スリットなどから侵入する自然光が、空間の仕立てに呼応して、思わぬ表情をつくりだす。都市に棲み続ける強固な意志の凝縮した印象的な空間だ。

A concrete box building for a shop and house in a narrow property of 6m in width and 13m in length facing a street with commodity shops in Osaka. The owner's coffee shop is on the 1st floor and the main living space is on the 3rd. A split floor design is used on the 3rd floor in a wellhole structure where the bedroom is arranged by going up the stairs from the living room. In the residential area, walls are tapered in downward direction since inclined walls are inserted in the inner part of exterior walls. Natural light coming through slits and other openings create unexpected expression in the rooms. The space that condensed the determination to keep living in the city is impressive.

[008]
芝田邸　1974
shibata house

1. 兵庫県芦屋市｜ashiya, hyogo
2. 設計｜design　1972.10–1973.6
3. 施工｜construction　1973.9–1974.4
4. 鉄筋コンクリート（壁式）｜RC (wall)
5. 住宅｜detached house
6. 敷地｜site　186.9 m²
7. 建築｜building　73.8 m²
8. 延床｜total floor　144.6 m²

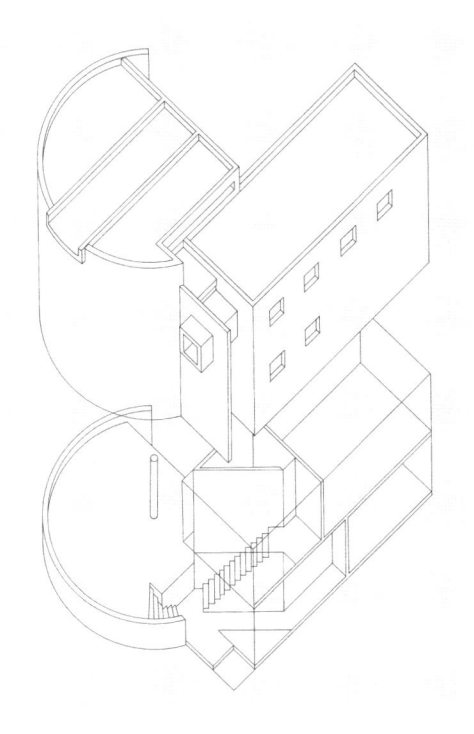

芦屋市の住宅地に位置する。直方体とシリンダーが付き合わされた形式をとる。1階はガレージで、2階は、シリンダー内部がホール、直方体には和室、3階は後者に寝室のみというシンプルな間取りになっている。円筒を切断したシリンダーは、面した街路を庭に引き込む視覚的な動感をつくりだす。シリンダーが回り込んだ内側に位置する庭に起伏を持たせ、躯体が地面に埋め込まれているかのように見せている。郊外住宅地にありがちな単調さの打破が託されている。

This is a detached house built within a residential area of Ashiya City. It is brought into a form in which a cuboid and a cylindrical volumes are associated. Floor plan is simple; 1st floor is for a garage space; 2nd floor is for a hall in the cylinder and a traditional Japanese room in the cuboid; 3rd floor is for a bedroom in the cuboid. The partial cylinder provides a dynamic visual appearance, pulling the faced street into the garden space. Having unculations in the garden inside the cylinder which wraps around, it shows the building as if it were embedded in the ground. It is expected to break down the monotonous tendency in suburban residential area.

[009]
内田邸　1974
uchida house

1. 京都市左京区｜sakyo-ku, kyoto
2. 設計｜design　1972.10–1973.9
3. 施工｜construction　1973.10–1974.6
4. 鉄筋コンクリート、一部木造｜RC, wood
5. 住宅｜detached house
6. 敷地｜site　3,641.3 m²
7. 建築｜building　84.6 m²
8. 延床｜total floor　106.7 m²

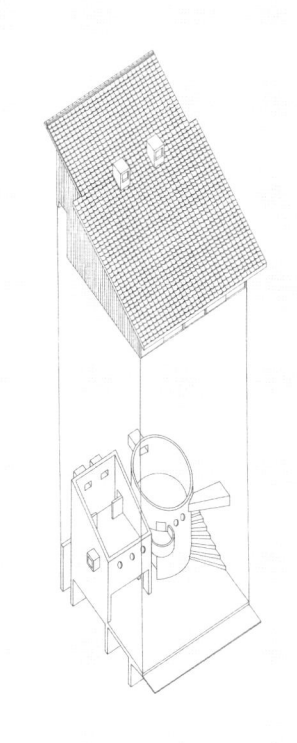

京都市北部、八瀬の美観地区の歴史的な環境を考慮して、コンクリートのシリンダーと切断した直方体を並立させ、その外側に片流れの傾斜した瓦屋根の木造建築が皮膜として被る構成をとる。そのような木造とコンクリートの二重の仕立てを踏まえて、発表時には「皮膜の激突」を作品名称とした。基本的な生活の場を確保するコンクリートと木造の隙間の空間は、ホール、和室に充てて、皮膜の衝突がもたらす非日常性を演出している。

In consideration of the historic environment of the aesthetic area of Yase in the north part of Kyoto City, a concrete cylinder and a cut cuboid are arranged side by side, and a wooden construction of a single pitch tied roof is covered as a membrane on the outside thereof. Based on the double construction in wood and concrete, the "crash of different membranes" was used as the title of the work at the time of release. The space of the gap between concrete construction as basic living place and wooden construction as a membrane is used as a hall and a Japanese traditional room, and it produces extraordinary character derived from the crash of those membranes.

[010]
宇野邸　1974
uno house

1. 京都市右京区 | ukyo-ku, kyoto
2. 設計 | design　1973.9–1974.8
3. 施工 | construction　1974.9–1974.12
4. 木造 | wood
5. 住宅 | detached house
6. 敷地 | site　84.5 m²
7. 建築 | building　42.0 m²
8. 延床 | total floor　63.7 m²

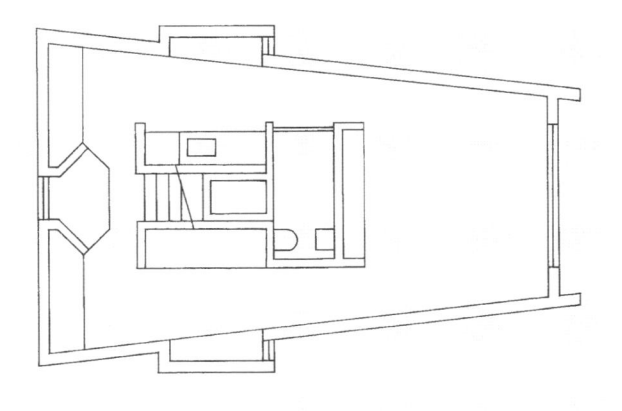

平面が台形なら、断面もまた台形で、室内の壁は傾斜し、加えて屋根も傾斜している特異な姿の木造の小住宅。安藤の幾何学のなかでの暮らしの姿が想像できる。2階の床は長方形に区画され、両側から迫る壁とその床の間に意図的にスリットが設けられた。大きな窓とトップライトからの光が2階を明るく照らしだすとともに、スリットによって絞られた微妙な自然光が1階まで届くことで、都市生活における季節の移ろいを実感させる。

A small residential house with an unusual appearance that has plane surface in a trapezoid shape and cross section in a trapezoid shape with slanted interior walls and a slanted roof. A life in the geometry of Ando can be imagined in this house. The floor of the 2nd floor is sectioned in rectangular shape where slits are intentionally provided at the area between the floor and walls on both sides. Light from the large window and top light brightly shines throughout the 2nd floor with subtle natural light narrowed by the slit reaching the 1st floor provides an area where transition of seasons can be felt in the urban life.

[011]
松村邸　1975
matsumura house

1. 神戸市東灘区 | higashinada-ku, kobe
2. 設計 | design　1974.6–1975.10
3. 施工 | construction　1975.6–1975.10
4. 鉄筋コンクリート（壁式）、上部木造 | RC (wall), wood
5. 住宅 | detached house
6. 敷地 | site　491.1 m²
7. 建築 | building　81.0 m²
8. 延床 | total floor　145.6 m²

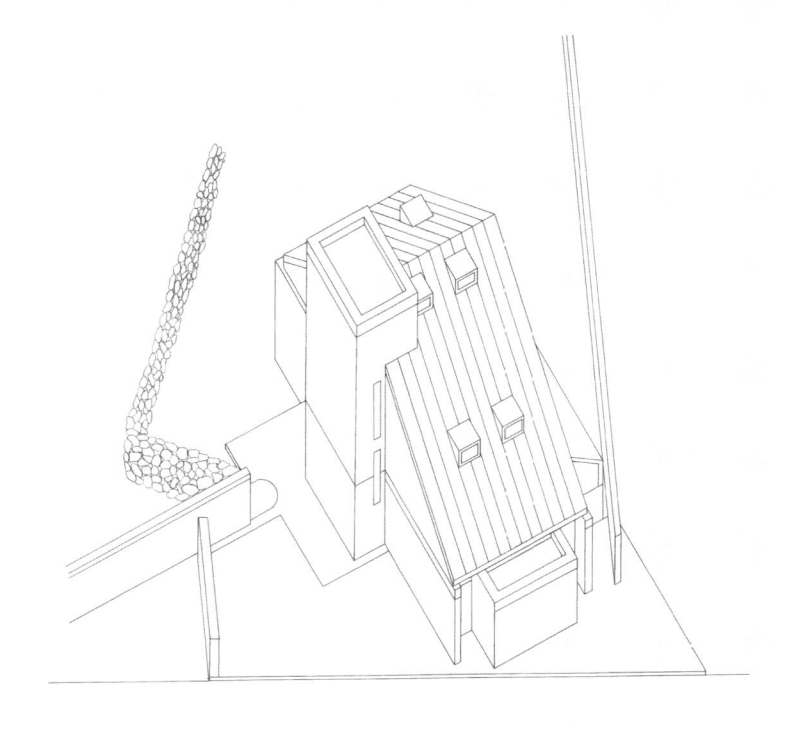

神戸市の住宅地に位置する煉瓦壁と傾斜屋根の戸建て住宅。敷地は道路に向かって開かれ、足元にも煉瓦が敷きつめられている。屋根は木造で白壁に柱と梁が露出する真壁造りの仕立てとなっている。道路側と側壁、そして塔状の階段室のいずれも煉瓦タイルの仕上げで、そのなかに住空間が入れ子となって展開する。大きくかぶさった屋根裏が大胆な空間を造り出し、2、3階に配したスリット状の吹き抜けなどから入り込んだ光が劇的な暮らしを演出する。

A residential house with brick walls and an inclined roof in a residential area of Kobe City. The property is opened toward the road and the ground is covered with bricks as well. The wooden roof is made with the half-timber style, which exposes columns and beams on white walls. Brick tiles are used on the walls on the street side, side areas, and the tower-shape stairways with living spaces expanding in a nest form. The attic that largely covers the building creates a bold atmosphere with light entering from areas such as slits of the open ceiling created on the 2nd and 3rd floors produces dramatic life.

[012]
双生観——山口邸　1975
soseikan — yamaguchi house

1. 兵庫県宝塚市 | takarazuka, hyogo
2. 設計 | design　1974.1–1975.2
3. 施工 | construction　1975.3–1975.7
4. 鉄筋コンクリート（壁式） | RC (wall)
5. 住宅 | detached house
6. 敷地 | site　523.6 (255.4+268.2) m²
7. 建築 | building　97.5 m²
8. 延床 | total floor　161.9 (81.0+81.0) m²

二つの同形態の鉄筋コンクリートの住棟がひと組となった戸建て住宅。屋上に配されたヴォールト状のガラスのトップライトも目をひく。丘陵を立地として同形態の住宅を並列に置く選択は、極限の原初的な形を目指す宣言だと安藤はいう。二つの棟を少しずらした配置にすることにより、原初的なイメージはさらに強まるとも。両棟を結ぶ空中のデッキについて、安藤が「双生」の住居を大地に結びつける〈へその緒〉と述べたことが、一卵性双生児である安藤とこの作品を結びつけて語る背景になった。→参照［046］

This is a detached house with a pair of houses in a same shape, both built in reinforced concrete structure. The glass top light on the rooftop in vault shape draws attention from the outside. Ando says, the choice to place houses in a same shape in parallel with the hill as its location means his declaration to aim at an extreme original form. He says also, the original image will become even stronger by arranging the two building slightly misaligned. He described the sky deck connecting two wings as an "umbilical cable" linking up those "twin" houses to the ground — this became a background story to relate this project with Ando's background as an identical twin. → see also [046]

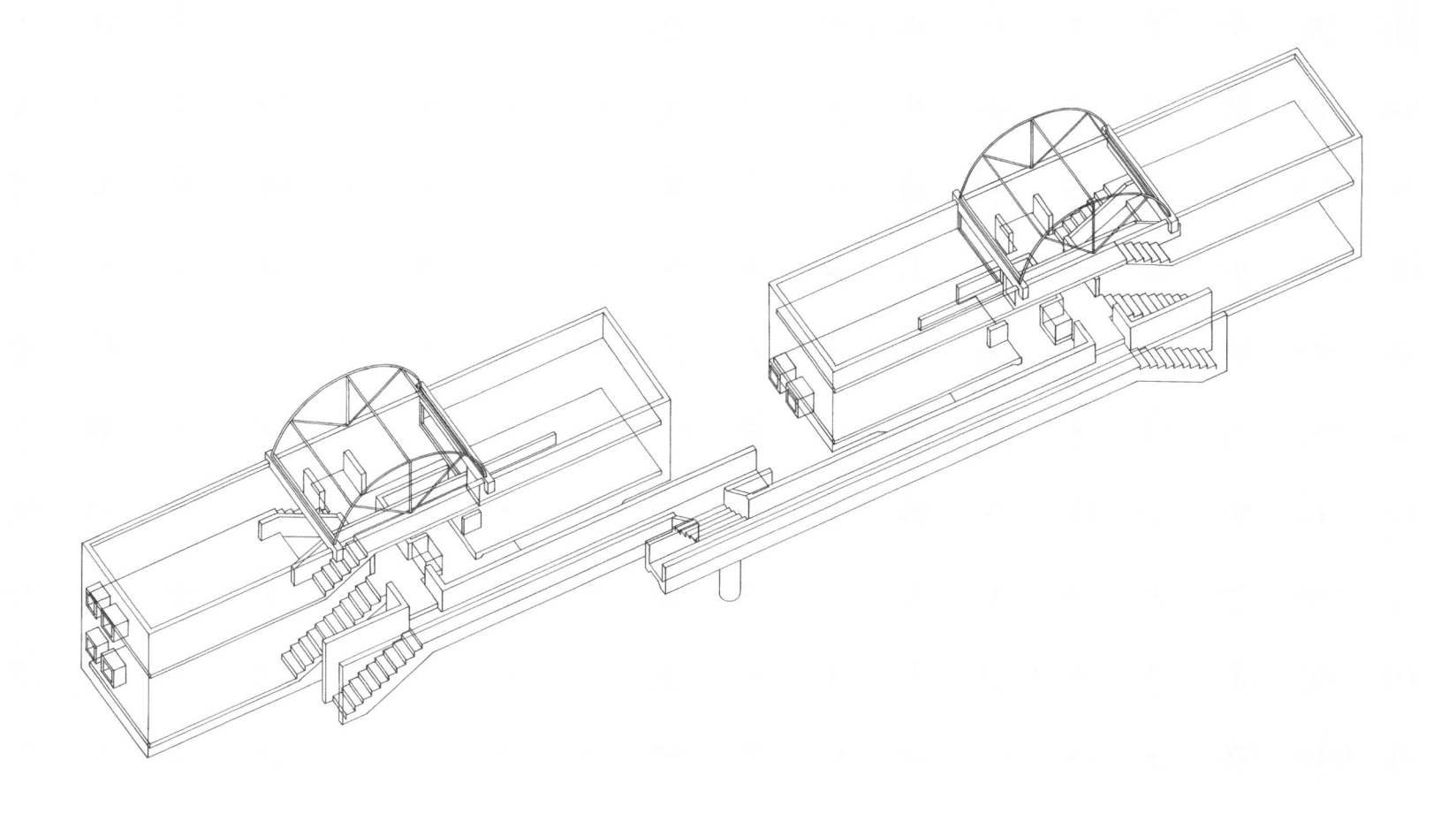

[013]
ツインウォール　1975
twin wall

2. 設計 | design　1975
3. 構想案 | concept
4. 鉄筋コンクリート | RC
5. 住宅 | detached house
6. 敷地 | site　85.1 m²
7. 建築 | building　70.6 m²
8. 延床 | total floor　107.2 m²

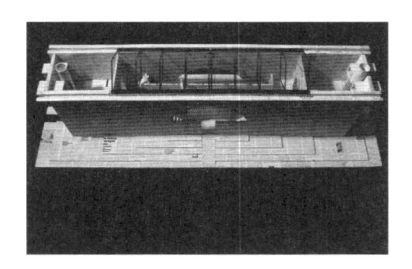

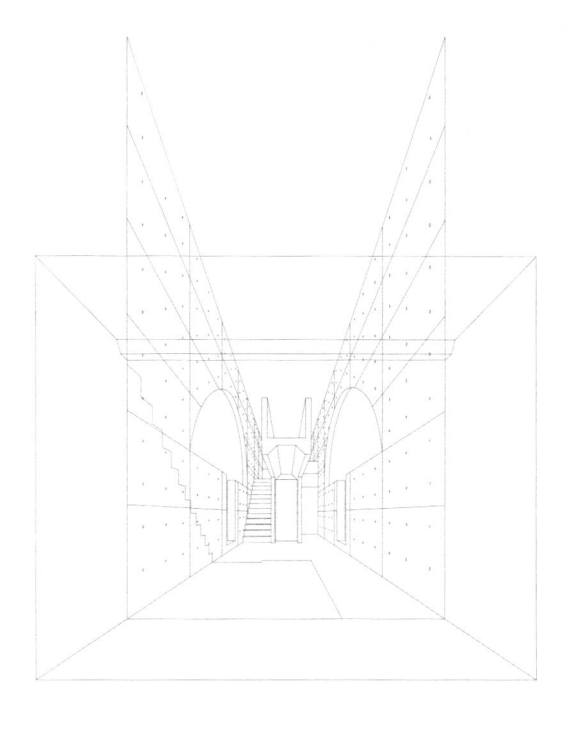

想定した狭い敷地そのものを安藤は壁になぞらえ、この住宅プロジェクトは、その壁をうがって内部に居住空間を求めるものと説明する。1階の空間のほとんどがホールに充てられ、そこに斜めの配置で立方体の寝室が挿入されている。平面は二分されて対称を構成し、中心から二方向にわかれて2階の個室にあがる階段もまた対称が遵守されている。壁をうがつ半円など初期の安藤の住宅作品のヴォキャブラリーが随所に見受けられる。

Ando explains that he viewed the expected narrow property as a wall and obtained a living space by penetrating inside the wall. The space of the 1st floor is occupied almost completely by a hall and a cube bedroom is inserted on a diagonal composition. The planform is divided in two to have a symmetric form. The stairs divided in two directions from the center that go up in the private room on the 2nd floor is also keeping in symmetric form. Architectural vocabularies of early residential house works of Ando such as a semicircle engraved in the wall are observed at various areas.

[014]
四軒長屋　1975
tenement house with four flats

1. 大阪市住吉区 | sumiyoshi-ku, osaka
2. 設計 | design　1975.3–1975.10
3. 構想案 | concept
4. 鉄筋コンクリート（壁式）| RC (wall)
5. 集合住宅 | apartment house
6. 敷地 | site　171 m²
7. 建築 | building　84 m²
8. 延床 | total floor　226.8 m²

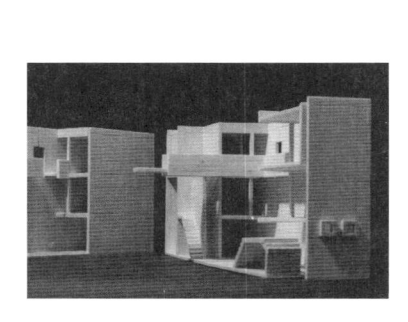

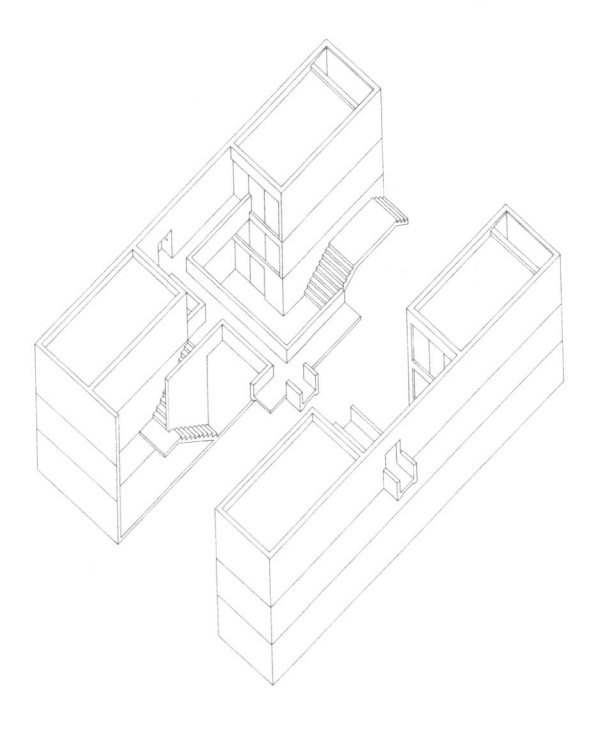

住宅内でありながら一度屋外空間に出なければ居室を移動できない「住吉の長屋」を4戸、立体的に積み上げたような集合住宅の計画。3階建てで4戸を構成するため、1階と3階に各戸のリビングとダイニングを配し、メゾネット形式の各戸の寝室を2階に集めた。H字型の住棟配置をとり、空隙の空間に各戸の中庭を設け、家族内のコミュニケーションをはかるとともに、他の家族の存在する気配も感じられる空間構成が企てられた。

A plan to build a condominium that has a design of four housings of ROW HOUSE, SUMIYOSHI piled up on top of each other where the residents have to go outside to move to a different room although it is in the same residence. Since four units are composed in a three-story building, a living room and a dining room of each maisonette type unit is provided on the 1st and 3rd floors and a bedroom is located on the 2nd floor. The H-shape layout of the residential building allows each unit to have a courtyard between the gaps to provide a spatial structure that contributes to having a good communication within the family and feel the presence of other families.

[015]
住吉の長屋 —— 東邸　1976
row house, sumiyoshi — azuma house

1. 大阪市住吉区 | sumiyoshi-ku, osaka
2. 設計 | design　1975.1–1975.8
3. 施工 | construction　1975.10–1976.2
4. 鉄筋コンクリート（壁式）| RC (wall)
5. 住宅 | detached house
6. 敷地 | site　57.3 m²
7. 建築 | building　33.7 m²
8. 延床 | total floor　64.7 m²

安藤忠雄を世界的な建築家として知らしめるに至った文字通りの代表作。住吉大社の南側に広がる木造住宅密集地に位置する三軒長屋の真ん中の一軒を、コンクリートボックスに置き換えた。中央に設けた屋外空間の光庭を介して自然の光、風、雨が都市の暮らしに季節感をもたらした。安藤自身が長屋で育ち、暮らしの真理を探究する揺るぎない姿勢が具体化された。広告代理店勤務の若い施主と建築家の意気投合が名作をもたらした。棲みこなした施主にも称賛を贈りたい。

This is literally the most prominent work of Ando Tadao to be known as a global architect. This building is designed to replace one building in the middle of three row houses with to a concrete box, and this area is located in a condensed wooden residential area spreading on the south side of Sumiyoshi Taisha shrine . The natural light, wind and rain brought a sense of the season to the life of city through the light court in the outdoor space that was set in the center of this building. Ando himself grew up in such row house, and his determined attitude to seek for the sincerity of living enabled to realize this building. This is a masterpiece produced by getting along with a young client working in an advertising agency and an architect — I would also like to praise the client who digested the concept and the quality of this building to live.

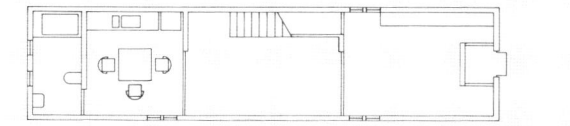

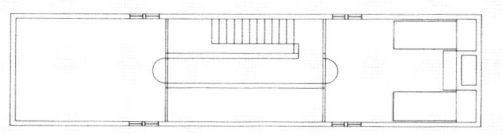

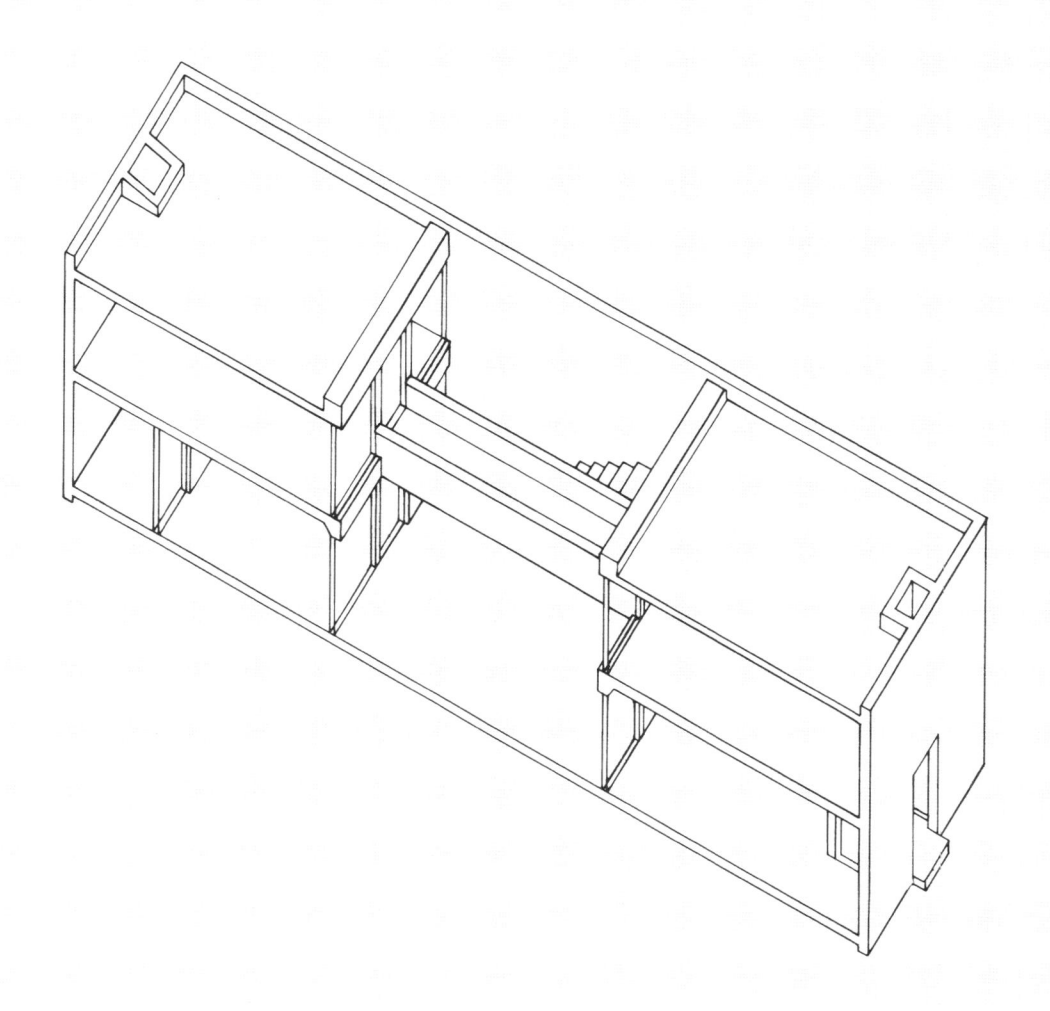

346 Complete Works

[016]
貫入──平林邸　1976
interpenetration — hirabayashi house
.
1. 大阪府吹田市 | suita, osaka
2. 設計 | design　1975.1–1975.9
3. 施工 | construction　1975.10–1976.7
4. 鉄筋コンクリート（ラーメン、壁式）| RC (frame, wall)
5. 住宅 | detached house
6. 敷地 | site　394.4 m²
7. 建築 | building　143.3 m²
8. 延床 | total floor　211.7 m²

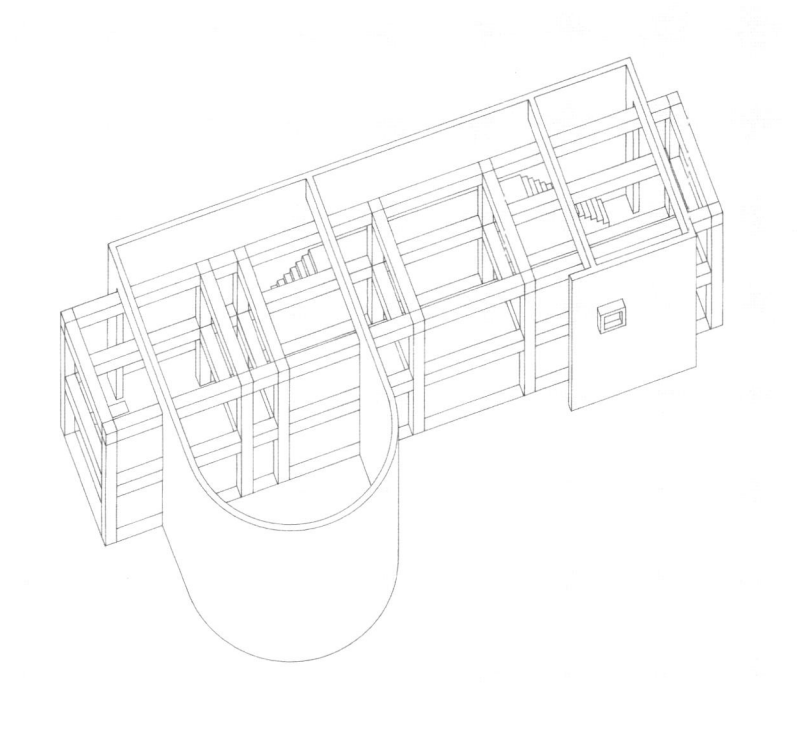

コンクリートの立体的な格子のフレームと、壁構造の膨張した曲面。違いの明確な二つの構造体を、個人住宅のなかに持ち込むことにより、その対峙がもたらす空隙に期待したと安藤は語っている。住宅の間取りは、格子の直方体の躯体のなかに客間、和室、台所を一直線に連ねて単純化し、それをアルコーブを形作るコンクリートの曲面壁のホールと突き合わせた。その相互貫入が生み出す間隙こそが、棲まい手自らが暮らしの実像を構築していくきっかけになるとの想定である。
.
A 3 dimensional grid frame built in concrete structure and an expanded curved surface of wall structure — Ando said, he hoped that the two structure of distinct differences is brought into private houses, and then "gaps and voids" are produced by the confrontation. The layout of this house is simplified by linearly distributing guest room, traditional Japanese room, and kitchen within a grid cuboid building volume; then, this volume was placed against a hall space with a curved concrete wall forming an alcove — so that gaps and voids are created by reciprocal penetration to the other spaces would become the trigger for the residents to establish his / her own reality of living.

[017]
番匠邸　1976
bansho house
.
1. 愛知県三好町 | miyoshi, aichi
2. 設計 | design　1975.2–1976.1
3. 施工 | construction　1976.4–1976.7
4. 鉄筋コンクリート（壁式）| RC (wall)
5. 住宅 | detached house
6. 敷地 | site　168.3 m²
7. 建築 | building　62.5 m²
8. 延床 | total floor　85.7 m²

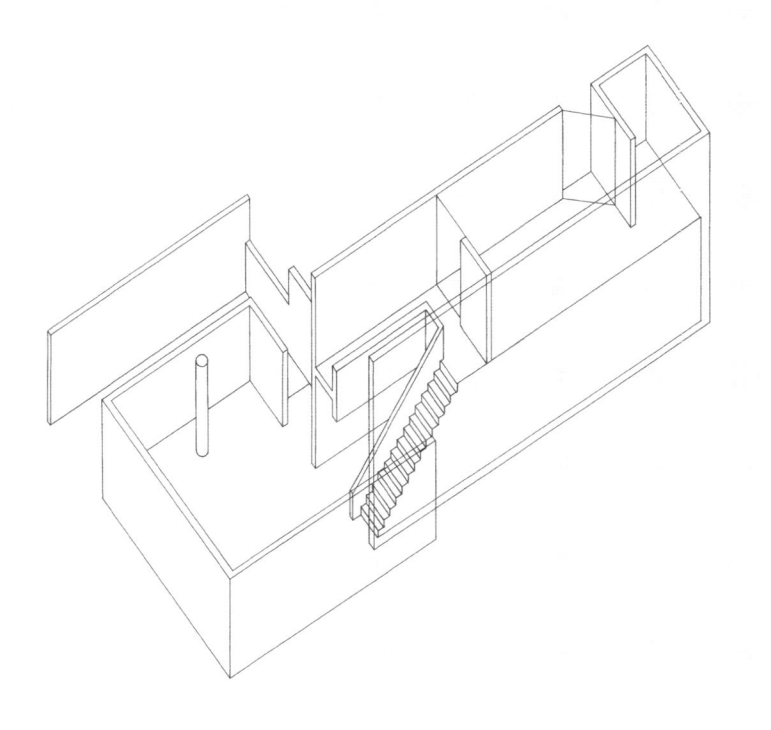

表通り側はコンクリートの立方体の平屋。その背後からコンクリートの直方体の2階屋が直交する形で突き刺さる。特異な形態の住宅において、2階の開口部からの光を階段室を介して絞り込み、1階の居間などへ侵入させる構成がとられている。もたらされた光はあたかも暖をとるための炎のようで、そこに家族が集まる姿を想定した。極限まで要素を限定することで、暮らしの原像を棲まい手に体感させる、初期住宅に共通の思考が読み取れる。→参照 [042]
.
A flat cube in concrete is placed on the main street. From the back, a cuboid in two-floor stuck in orthogonal form. In a unique type of housing, a structure is adopted that natural light from the opening on the 2nd floor narrows down through the staircase room and comes in the living room and other spaces on the 1st floor. Such natural light brought in was like a flame of warming up, supposing the family gathered there. You can read common thoughts of the initial housing, which allows residents to feel and experience the original image of living by selecting elements to extremes. → see also [042]

[018]
帝塚山タワープラザ　1976
tezukayama tower plaza
.
1. 大阪市住吉区 | sumiyoshi-ku, osaka
2. 設計 | design　1975.2–1976.1
3. 施工 | construction　1976.2–1976.9
4. 鉄筋コンクリート（ラーメン）| RC (frame)
5. 集合住宅、店舗 | apartment house, shop
6. 敷地 | site　376.2 m²
7. 建築 | building　161.4 m²
8. 延床 | total floor　754.4 m²

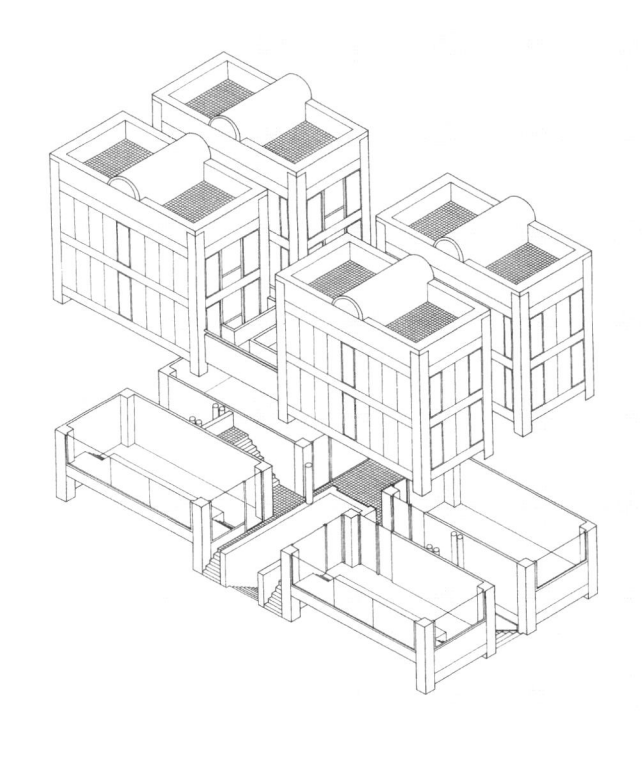

大阪の繁華街、阿倍野から南に3キロ弱、帝塚山は良好な住宅地として知られる。そこに位置する「帝塚山タワープラザ」は、敷地の四方にタワーが立つ複合商業ビル。4本のタワーが囲む「余白」に1階では「プラザ」と呼ぶ小広場が、2階では各棟を結ぶデッキが設けられている。商業テナントへの来訪者は、そのオープンエアを介して空間性を堪能できる。すべての床を商品化せず、空白の活用による新たな商業建築像を目指す意欲が読み取れる。3、4階はメゾネット形式の住戸に充てられている。
.
Tezukayama is about 3km south of the busy street of Abeno area, known as a good residential area. As its name suggest, this TEZUKAYAMA TOWER PLAZA building is located in this residential area as a complex commercial building where 4 tower buildings stand on the 4 corners of the site. The "blank space" enclosed by those 4 towers houses a small square named "Plaza" on the 1st floor, and a deck element connecting each tower at the 2nd floor. Visitors to the commercial tenants of this facility can fully enjoy the spatial quality of this building through those open-air spaces. This project reveals the eagerness of Ando to seek for a new image of a commercial building, by actively utilizing void spaces without entirely using floor spaces for commercial reasons. The 3rd and 4th floor are used for apartment units in maisonette style.

[019]
岡本ハウジング　1976
okamoto housing project
.
1. 神戸市東灘区 | higashinada-ku, kobe
2. 設計 | design　1976.6–1976.12
3. 構想案 | concept
4. 鉄筋コンクリート（ラーメン）| RC (frame)
5. 集合住宅 | apartment house
6. 敷地 | site　1,774.9 m²
7. 建築 | building　556.4 m²
8. 延床 | total floor　1,404.7 m²

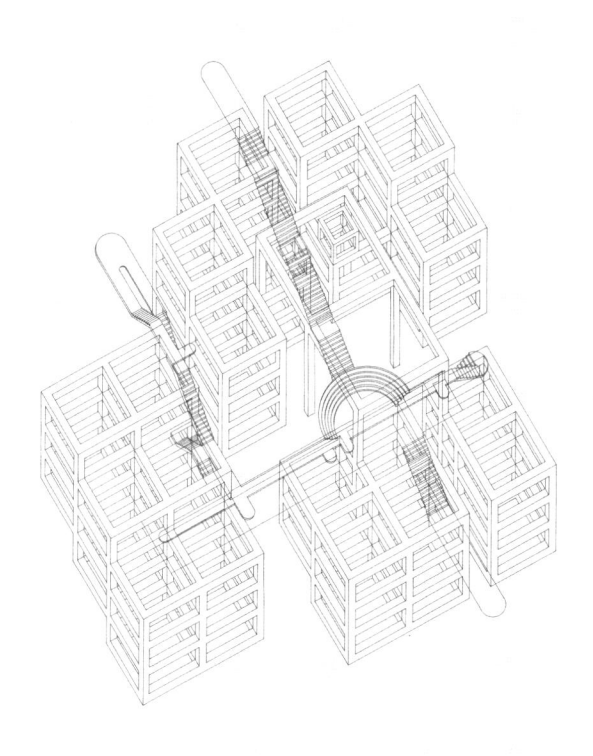

のちに安藤の代表作となる「六甲の集合住宅」の構成理念の先駆けがここに読み取れる。神戸市東部の六甲山麓の斜面地に計画した17戸の小規模な集合住宅で、連続するコンクリートの立体格子の均等なフレームを基本に住戸が割り振られた。それぞれの住戸には配置によって生まれたずれを生かして吹き抜けやルーフガーデンが配された。このずれの部分に階段状の広場を設けるなど「六甲の集合住宅」の外部空間が先取りされている。
.
The initial stage of the structural principle of Ando's masterpiece ROKKO HOUSING that was built later can be seen in this complex. A small-scale housing complex with 17 housings planned on a slope area at the base of Mt. Rokko on the east area of Kobe City, which has housings with a continuous cubic lattice frame made of concrete. Gaps between housings made by the arrangement are used to place an open ceiling and a roof garden. A terraced open space is provided at these gaps, which is later used for the outer space of ROKKO HOUSING.

[020]
ローズガーデン 1977
rose garden

1. 神戸市中央区 | chuo-ku, kobe
2. 設計 | design   1975.8–1976.3
3. 施工 | construction   1976.4–1977.3
4. 鉄筋コンクリート、鉄骨 | RC, steel
5. 複合商業施設 | commercial complex
6. 敷地 | site   410.2 m²
7. 建築 | building   270.9 m²
8. 延床 | total floor   933.1 m²

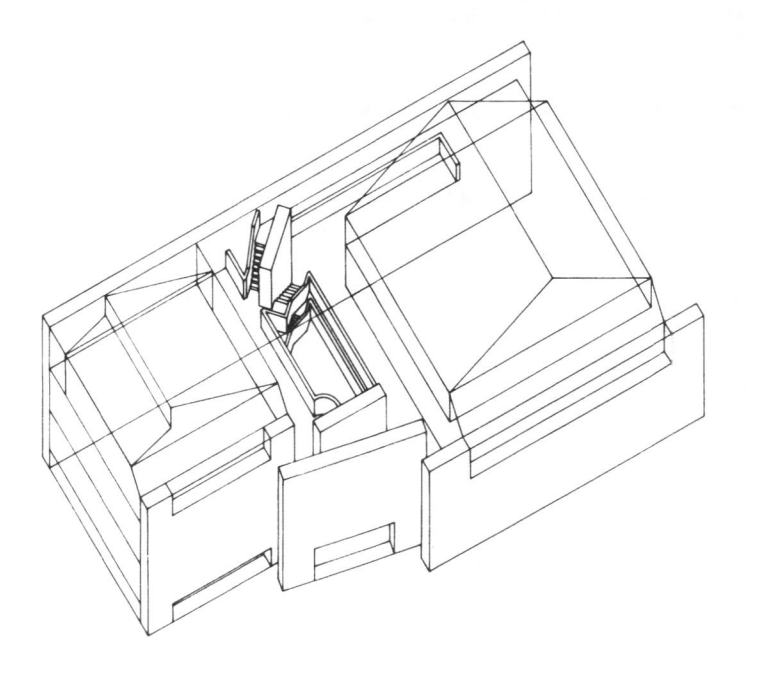

西洋館群で知られる神戸・北野町で安藤忠雄が手がけた一連の商業施設の最初の作品。正面の外壁の煉瓦の肌が、この街らしい急な傾斜の坂道に面し、歴史の文脈を連想させる。街路側から望む二つの傾斜屋根も、西洋館へのオマージュだ。内部に進むと、周囲にコンクリート打ち放しの通路の巡る中庭が待ち受けている。通路の位置が上階に進むにつれセットバックする仕立てで、来訪者は豊かな自然光の恩恵にあずかりつつ、店舗での買い物を楽しめる。商業施設を都市に貢献させる建築観を示した点でも、大きな存在意義を有している。

This is the first work designed by Ando Tadao for a series of commercial facilities in Kitanocho in Kobe City, known for classic western style residences. The brick exterior of the front façade is facing to the steep sloped street, which remind us of the historical context of this area. Two pitched roofs visible from the town street appear to be the hommage to those western style residences. When visitors going into the site, a courtyard space enclosed by a corridor in exposed concrete finish appears. The position of this corridor is applied with a setback as the corridor rises up, for visitors to enjoy shopping in stores while receiving the rich natural light. This building has a significance in that a commercial architecture can contribute to urban conditions.

[021]
帝塚山の家──真鍋邸 1977
tezukayama house—manabe house

1. 大阪市阿倍野区 | abeno-ku, osaka
2. 設計 | design   1976.3–1977.3
3. 施工 | construction   1977.4–1977.9
4. 鉄筋コンクリート（ラーメン、壁式） | RC (frame, wall)
5. 住宅 | detached house
6. 敷地 | site   273.3 m²
7. 建築 | building   108.8 m²
8. 延床 | total floor   147.3 m²

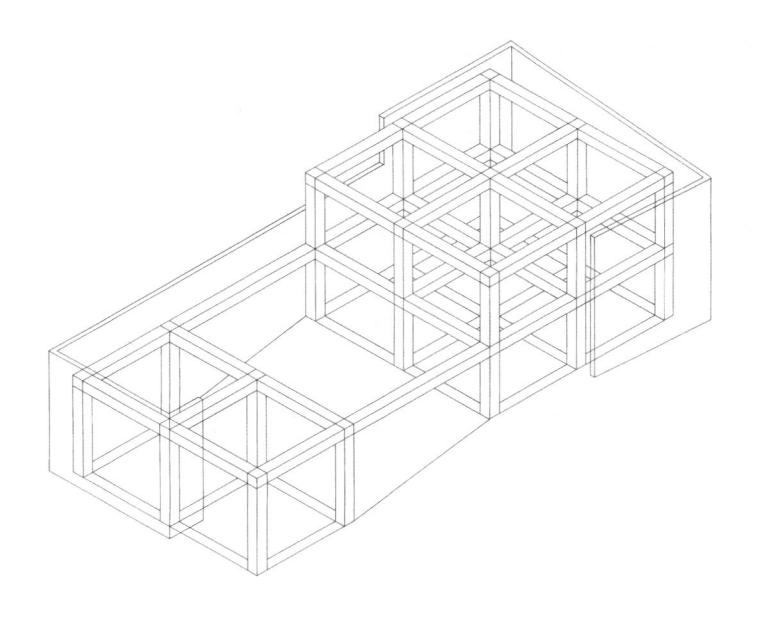

格子状に組んだコンクリートのフレームが住宅全体の空間を規定している。六つのグリッドのうち四つが居室にあてられ、残りの二つがテラスとエントランスにあてられている。居室部分では、フレームを媒介に光と風が戯れ、日常の暮らしの場としての空間に多様性をもたらす。それを安藤は陰陽でいうなら「陰画」だと考える。一方、屋外の幾何学的なコンクリートのグリッドは、良好な住宅街が劣化していく都市の状況に抗する棲み手の意思表示であり、「陽画」としての役割を担うと述べている。

The spaces of the entire house are defined by concrete frames assembled in grid pattern. 4 of the 6 grid patterns are defined as rooms, while 2 grid patterns are used as terrace and entrance. Rooms are provided with diverse conditions for a place to spend daily lives, with the play of light and wind mediated by the frame. Ando thinks the quality of the spaces as "negative image" if considering the principle of duality as positive and negative in photographic film. On the other hand, the exterior concrete grid pattern in geometric shape states that it is an expression of the resident's will to resist the situation of the city where the former good residential area is deteriorating, and to play a role as a "positive image" of such context.

[022]
領壁の家 ── 松本邸　1977
wall house ─ matsumoto house

1. 兵庫県芦屋市 | ashiya, hyogo
2. 設計 | design　1976.6–1977.2
3. 施工 | construction　1977.2–1977.7
4. 鉄筋コンクリート（ラーメン、壁式）| RC (frame, wall)
5. 住宅 | detached house
6. 敷地 | site　1,082.1 m²
7. 建築 | building　128.4 m²
8. 延床 | total floor　237.7 m²

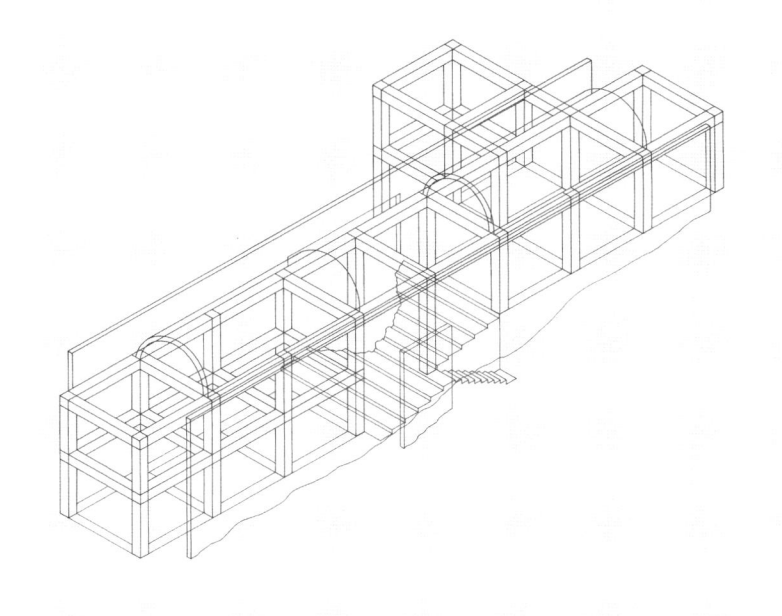

兵庫県芦屋市の奥座敷のような山間地の奥池。その傾斜した街路に沿って荒々しいコンクリートの壁が屹立している。内部はヴォールト屋根を持つ住宅で、傾斜した土地の形状に従って、居室は屋根のない中庭を挟んで二つの部分に分かれている。その分かれた空間を統御するのが、街路側の住宅全体を外界から遮断する一枚の壁であり、安藤はその壁こそが現代にあって「個人の領域」をつくりだす「領壁」であると述べる。そこにインドの地下の井戸で体験した、光のグラデーションの投影を試みたという。

The site is situated in an up-country location within a mountainous region as a back room of Ashiya City, Hyougo Prefecture. Along a sloped town street, rough concrete wall stands. The inside is a house with a vault roof, and the rooms are separately distributed in two volumes divided by a courtyard without a roof. Those separate spaces are integrated by a wall, which isolates the entire house from the outside world of the town street. Ando describe this wall is the "territory wall" of modern days to establish "a territory of a person". He also tried to project gradation of light, which was experienced in an underground well in India.

[023]
北野アレイ　1977
kitano alley

1. 神戸市中央区 | chuo-ku, kobe
2. 設計 | design　1976.8–1977.2
3. 施工 | construction　1977.3–1977.10
4. 鉄筋コンクリート、鉄骨 | RC, steel
5. 複合商業施設 | commercial complex
6. 敷地 | site　345.4 m²
7. 建築 | building　190.4 m²
8. 延床 | total floor　427.4 m²

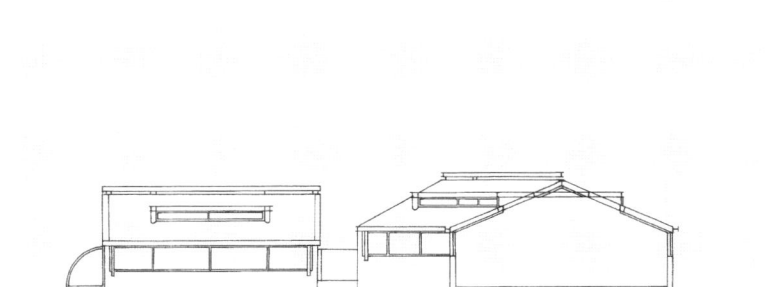

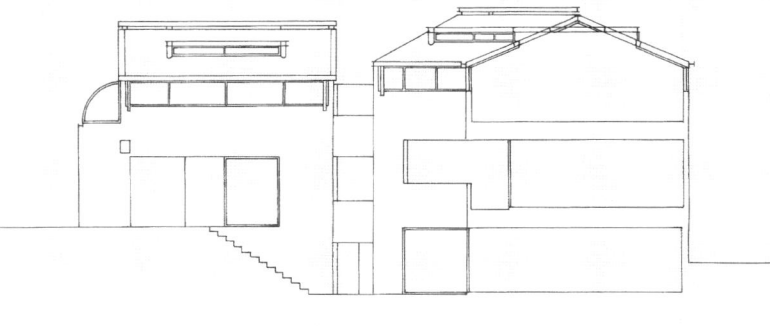

「ローズガーデン」に近い立地の神戸・北野町の商業施設。狭い間口の奥に広がる敷地を考慮して、表通りから階段を介して繋がる通路を「道＝路地」に見立てて、建物内に来訪者を引き込む構成をとる。この通路の右側は煉瓦の仕上げで、西洋館の街のイメージを継承しているが、建物全体はコンクリート打ち放しとなっている。二つのブロックに分かれた建物は、周囲に配慮して高さを抑制しながら、地下にも店舗を配置し、「道」は立体的な街路の様相を帯びる。

This is another commercial facility located near ROSE GARDEN building in Kitano-cho in Kobe City. Considering the site condition with narrow entry and deep lot, this building was configured to bring in visitors to the interior space through the passage with a staircase connecting to the main street—which is considered as a "street=alley" to the building. The right side of this alley is finished with brick, reflecting the context of this town with western style residences, while the building itself is entirely finished in exposed concrete. This building, separated into 2 blocks, is controlled in height to fit in the surrounding neighborhood, and store spaces are also placed on the underground level; then the "street=alley" takes on the appearance of a "3-dimensional urban street".

[024]
アートギャラリー・コンプレックス
1977
art gallery complex

1. 東京都港区 | minato-ku, tokyo
2. 設計 | design 1977
3. 構想案 | concept
4. 鉄筋コンクリート | RC
5. 劇場＋事務所

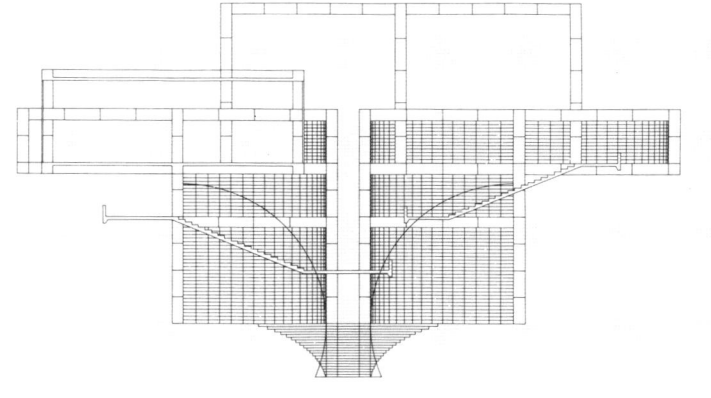

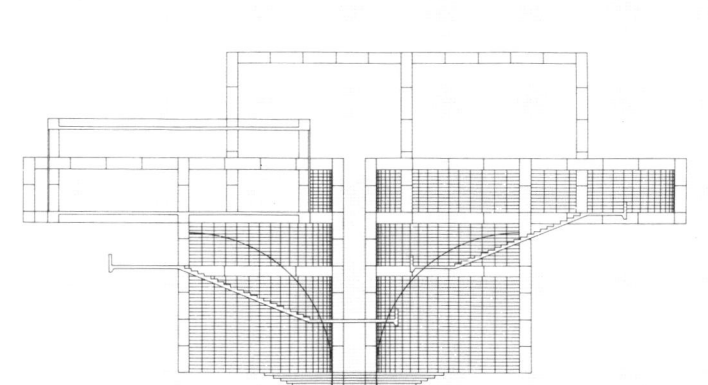

台形に近い敷地の外周に沿って置いた直方体の躯体、挿入された円筒形の二つのガラスブロック、さらにそこにコンクリートの立体格子を配することで、さまざまなズレが生じる。安藤はそのズレにテラスを配して、全体形の統御を意図した。内部から発せられる美術、演劇などの現代芸術の活気が、そうしたズレによって交錯することが期待された。若き日々から「具体美術」など、現代の表現芸術の傍らで創作を続けてきた安藤の現代表現への解釈がそこに込められている。

Various gaps are created with a cubic concrete lattice placed with two cylindrical glass blocks inserted in a body of a rectangular solid placed along the circumference of the trapezoidal property. Ando built a terrace to fill the gaps to control the whole shape. There is an anticipation of energy of modern art emitted from inside by fine arts and theatrical performances to intertwine in these gaps. This architecture demonstrates an interpretation of the contemporary expression of Ando who has been creating works from his youth next to modern expressionist art including the "Gutai".

[025]
甲東アレイ　1978
koto alley

1. 兵庫県西宮市 | nishinomiya, hyogo
2. 設計 | design 1976.6–1977.8
3. 施工 | construction 1977.10–1978.7
4. 鉄筋コンクリート | RC
5. 複合商業施設 | commercial complex
6. 敷地 | site 362.8 m²
7. 建築 | building 297.7 m²
8. 延床 | total floor 804.1 m²

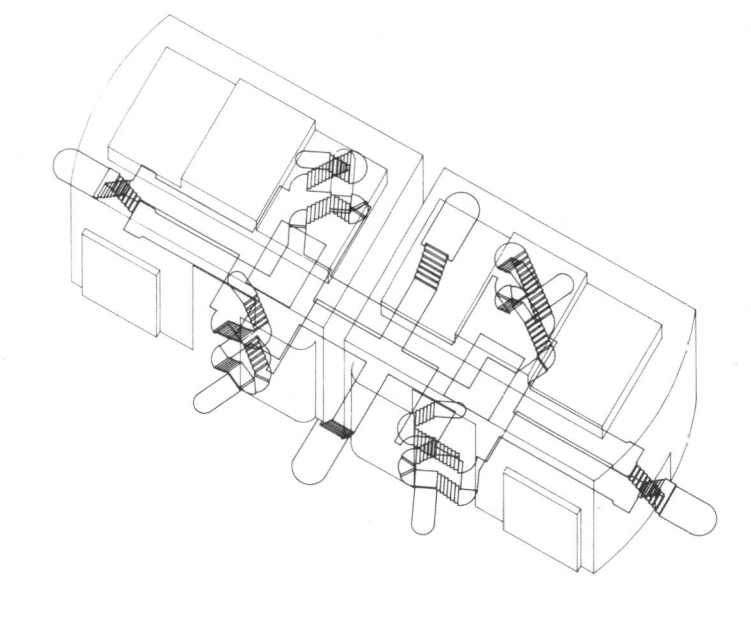

関西の私鉄阪急沿線には成熟した住宅地が広がるが、駅前は必ずしも安定した環境というわけでもない。そうした駅前の再開発として計画された。区画整理は当初の予定通りに進まず、そのため、4面の外壁を見ることができる。駅に向き合う西側の外壁は、屋外階段の開口部のところでシリンダー状の造形をとり、また、北側では壁面全体が曲面を描く。内部は半階分高い位置の1階に広場が設けられ、中央の床の切欠きから地下の光庭に自然光がもたらされる構成だ。隣接地に同形態の「2」も計画されたが、実現しなかった。

Even though a mature residential neighborhood spreads along with the railway lines of Hankyu Corporation in Kansai region, station front spaces of this private railway are not always well managed and established then this project was planned to redevelop those station front spaces. This building has various expressions; the west side exterior wall facing toward the station shows a cylindrical shape at the opening of the exterior staircase; the entire wall of the north side has a curved surface. The interior space consists of a courtyard on the 1st floor level elevated to the half-height of the floor height. Light court is placed on underground level, while daylight is taken into this space from the cut opening at the center of the floor slab of the 1st floor.

全346作品録

[026]
ガラスブロックの家――石原邸
1978
glass block house — ishihara house

1. 大阪市生野区 | ikuno-ku, osaka
2. 設計 | design　1977.7–1978.4
3. 施工 | construction　1978.6–1978.12
4. 鉄筋コンクリート | RC
5. 住宅、事務所 | house, office
6. 敷地 | site　157.4 m²
7. 建築 | building　92.0 m²
8. 延床 | total floor　221.5 m²

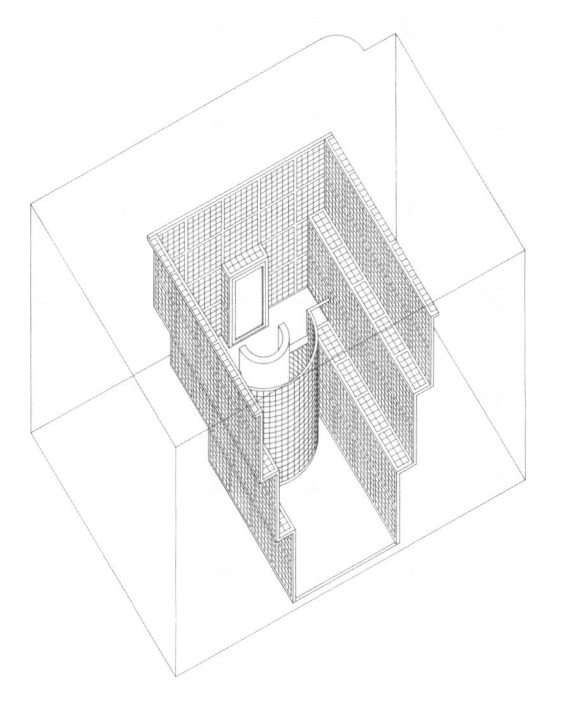

大阪市生野区の工場と住宅が混在するなかに、三層のコンクリートの箱を置いた。重量感のある箱は生活の場を周囲から保護する壁で囲い、内部は中庭に向き合うように各室が配された。なによりの特徴は、中庭に面する壁がすべてガラスブロックによって構成されたことだ。ガラスブロックは生活の場で間近に眺めると、コンクリートに匹敵するような重量感がある。しかし、光を濾過し、その先にある視界を溶解させるという点において、安藤の住宅作品に新境地をもたらすものであった。

A concrete box with three levels is placed amid factories and houses in Ikuno Ward, Osaka City. The massive looking box is enclosed by walls to protect the living space from the surroundings. Rooms inside are allocated to face the courtyard placed in the center of the house. The main feature is that all walls facing the courtyard are made of glass blocks. Glass blocks also provide a massive look similar to concrete when looking at them closely in a daily environment. This point of the project brought a new scope in Ando's work of residential houses to filter light and dilute the view on the other side.

[027]
大楠邸　1978
okusu house

1. 東京都世田谷区　setagaya-ku, tokyo
2. 設計 | design　1977.9–1977.12
3. 施工 | construction　1978.1–1978.8
4. 鉄筋コンクリート（壁式）| RC (wall)
5. 住宅 | detached house
6. 敷地 | site　531.1 m²
7. 建築 | building　194.2 m²
8. 延床 | total floor　288.4 m²

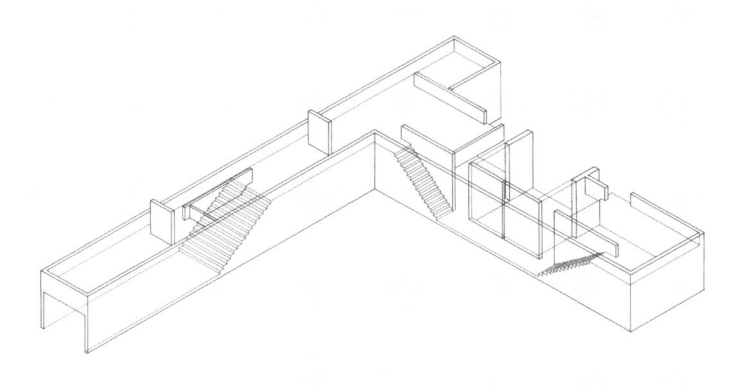

L字型の不整形な敷地そのままに住宅が計画された。ファッションメーカーのオーナーが施主であったため、表通りに近い部分には接客空間が配され、住棟の右に折れたところからが、私的な生活スペースとなっている。細長い形状ゆえに動線は一方向に制約され、視線の先に隠れるように配された階段を上がるところから建築空間が始まる。階段や吹き抜けなどが設定され、意外性のある体験が用意されている。

A house was planned to be built to fit the irregular land with an L shape. Since the client was an owner of a company in the fashion industry, a space for visitors was made at the area close to the main street and a private living space was located in the section from where it bends to the right. The flow line was limited to one direction due to the narrow plan form, where it starts after climbing the steps of the stairway hidden from the visual line. Stairs and an open ceiling are provided along the space to offer an unpredictable spatial experience.

[028]
ガラスブロックウォール
── 堀内邸　1979
glass block wall — horiuchi house

1. 大阪市住吉区 | sumiyoshi-ku, osaka
2. 設計 | design　1977.10–1978.6
3. 施工 | construction　1978.7–1979.2
4. 鉄筋コンクリート（壁式）| RC (wall)
5. 住宅 | detached house
6. 敷地 | site　237.9 m²
7. 建築 | building　95.0 m²
8. 延床 | total floor　243.7 m²

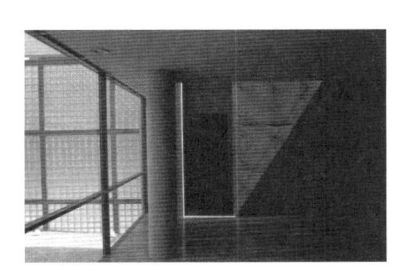

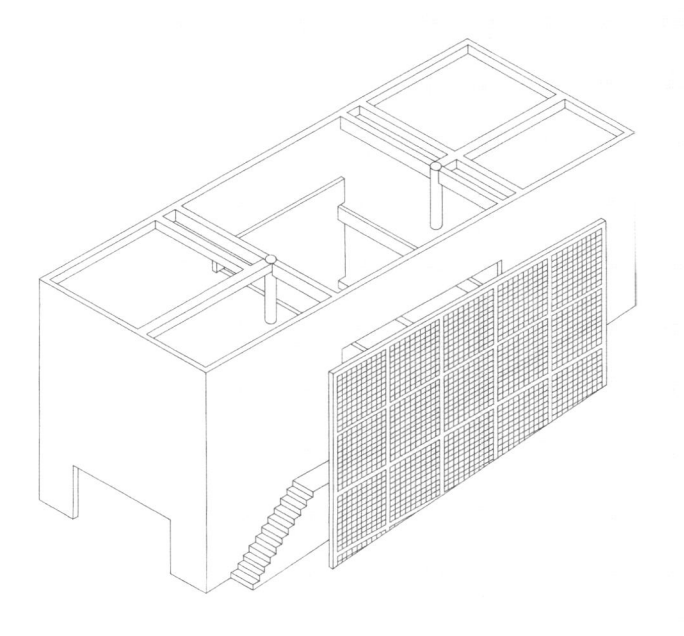

大阪市住吉区の住宅地の一角を占める、地下階を持つ2階建てのコンクリートボックスの住宅。中央に中庭をとり居住部分は各階がこの中庭に面する形で大きく二分されている。それは「住吉の長屋」に通じる形式だが、異なるのは、この住宅では中庭がコンクリートの壁で囲われるのではなく、大きく東に開いた開口部からガラスブロックを濾過した自然光が入ってくるところだ。しかも、ガラスブロックの壁は、建物本体から街路側に踏み出したところに配され、それが自然の浸潤をさらに印象的なものとしている。

A box-shaped concrete residential house with a basement and two stories located on the corner of a residential area in Sumiyoshi Ward, Osaka City. A courtyard is placed in the center, which largely divides each floor of the living space facing the courtyard. The style is similar to ROW HOUSE, SUMIYOSHI; the difference is that the courtyard of this house is not surrounded by concrete walls but has a glass block wall that penetrate natural light entering from the large opening on the east side. The glass block wall is placed only a step away beyond the main structure to the road, which emphasizes an impression of the infiltration of nature.

[029]
片山ハウス　1979
katayama building

1. 兵庫県西宮市 | nishinomiya, hyogo
2. 設計 | design　1978.1–1978.9
3. 施工 | construction　1978.10–1979.4
4. 鉄筋コンクリート（壁式）| RC (wall)
5. 住宅、店舗、事務所 | house, shop, office
6. 敷地 | site　78.3 m²
7. 建築 | building　62.9 m²
8. 延床 | total floor　232.2 m²

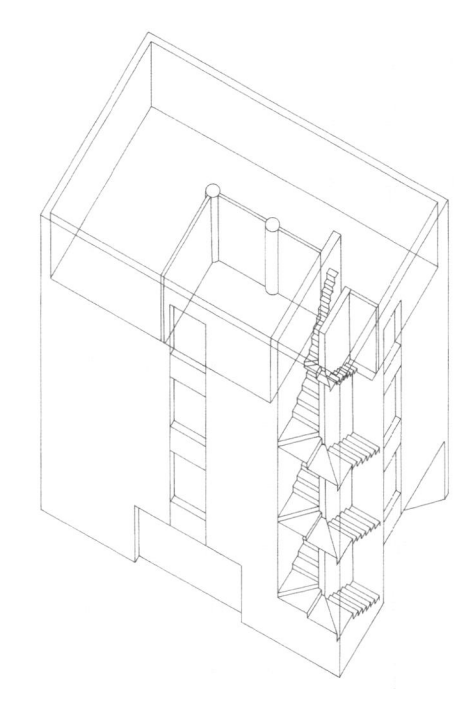

兵庫県西宮市の生活商店街の入り口に位置していた店舗兼集合住宅。強固な守りをイメージさせるコンクリートの躯体が、小規模な建築ながら力強さを体現していた。道路側の2–4階には垂直につながる縦長の三つの窓を設け、1階には店舗の入り口を斜めに突き刺さるように配した。2、3階は事務所、4階に住居を配し、住居部分には中庭を置いて上階の光庭とした。都市部の狭小な敷地を踏まえて、コートハウスを上階に配する可能性の模索だった。

A condominium with a shop located at the entrance of a street with commodity shops in Nishinomiya City, Hyogo Prefecture. The concrete structure that gives an impression of solid protection demonstrates the strength even with its small-scale architecture. Three vertically long windows are provided that connect vertically from the 2nd to the 4th floors on the road side and the shop entrance on the 1st floor was arranged to stick in diagonally. The 2nd and 3rd floors have office rooms and the 4th floor has a residential area with a courtyard and a light court on the top floor. The aim was to search the possibility to provide a courthouse on the top floor in a small property located in an urban area.

全346作品録

[030]

大西邸　1979
onishi house

1. 大阪市住吉区 | sumiyoshi-ku, osaka
2. 設計 | design　1978.7–1979.1
3. 施工 | construction　1979.2–1979.8
4. 鉄筋コンクリート（ラーメン）| RC (frame)
5. 住宅 | detached house
6. 敷地 | site　165.2 m²
7. 建築 | building　60.5 m²
8. 延床 | total floor　144.3 m²

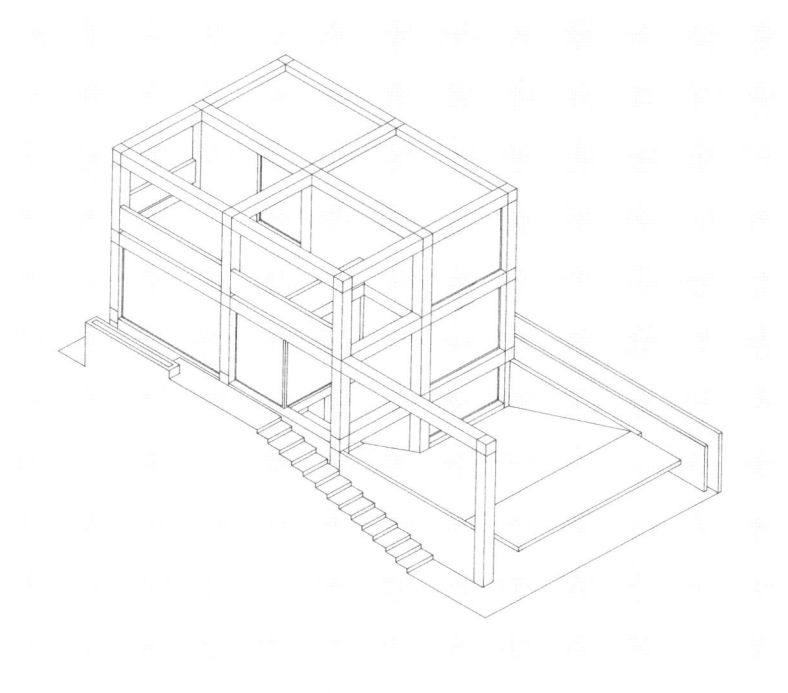

大阪市住吉区の成熟した住宅地の個人住宅。骨太なコンクリートの格子が力感あふれる外観をもたらすとともに、間取りもこのフレームに従って区画されている。法的な壁面後退を逆手にとり、そこに庇を配して駐車場に充て、玄関へのアプローチ、時には子どもたちの遊び場として活用される場をつくった。地下のテラスと寝室に至る道路側からの空隙を斜面緑化し、この規模の住宅としては多様な空間構成で生活の豊かさに寄与させている。

A private residential house located in Tezukayama, which is a matured residential area of Sumiyoshi Ward, Osaka City. Thick concrete lattice brings the appearance an outflow of strength and the house's layout is also arranged according to this lattice frame. Turning the legal regulation requiring retraction of the wall to its advantage, hoods are provided to create a parking lot, also an area for the entrance approach and an area at times to be used as a children's playground. Greenery was provided on the slope of the open space from the road to the underground terrace and bedroom contributing to having a high level of various spatial structure and rich life for this size of housing.

[031]

松谷邸　1979
matsutani house

1. 京都市伏見区 | fushimi-ku, kyoto
2. 設計 | design　1978.7–1979.3
3. 施工 | construction　1979.8–1979.11
4. 鉄筋コンクリート（壁式）| RC (wall)
5. 住宅 | detached house
6. 敷地 | site　143.1 m²
7. 建築 | building　56.6 m²
8. 延床 | total floor　91.9 m²

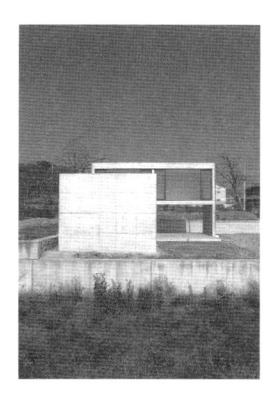

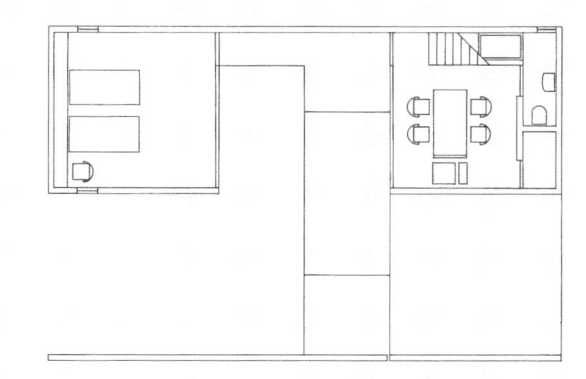

京都市郊外のローコストのコンクリート住宅。美術教師の一家からの依頼で設計した。間取りは、正方形グリッドに従って、中庭を挟んで二つのブロックにダイニングと子ども部屋、寝室を配した。床を土間と見なしてコンクリートのタタキにして、屋外の庭まで広げることで、自然が室内に侵入する仕掛けとした。完成から11年後の増築では、寝室だった棟を居間に変え、Y字の鉄骨のフレームが支えるヴォールト屋根のアトリエを付加した。この屋根はもとの2階の軒線より高く、庭の側にも既存の壁を超えて張り出す。自身の作品が完成した形ゆえに、増築では、もうひとつの完結形を付加したと安藤は述べている。

The design was requested by a family of an art teacher. The layout of rooms is in a square grid form with a dining room, children's room and bedroom located in two blocks sandwiching the courtyard. The exposed concrete floor that resembles a dirt floor is extended to the outside yard to provide an atmosphere where nature is intruding inside the house. Since an extension was requested 11 years after a bedroom was changed to a living room and added an atelier with vault roof supported by a Y-shape steel frame. Ando mentioned that since this was a completed form, he added another completed form in handling the extension.

[032]
上田邸　1979
ueda house

1. 岡山県総社市 | soja, okayama
2. 設計 | design   1978.8–1979.6
3. 施工 | construction   1979.8–1979.11
4. 鉄筋コンクリート（壁式）| RC (wall)
5. 住宅 | detached house
6. 敷地 | site   180.4 m²
7. 建築 | building   70.1 m²
8. 延床 | total floor   94.4 m²

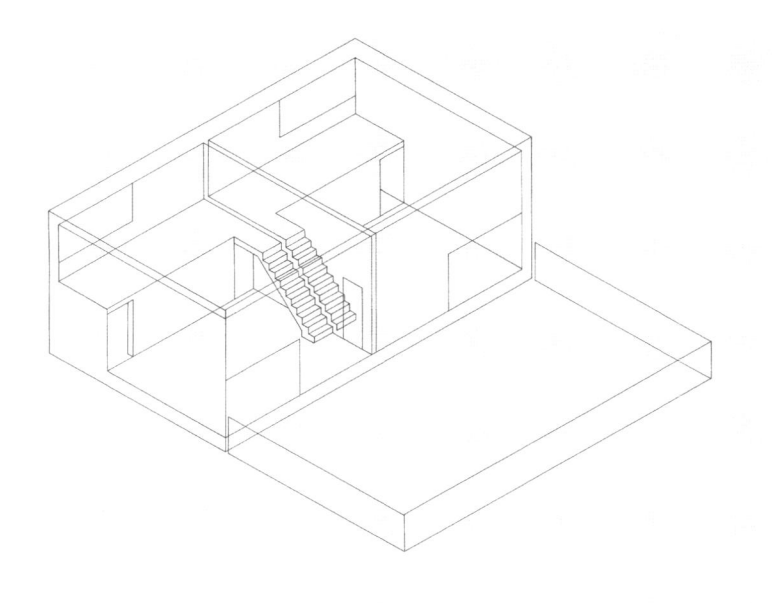

岡山県総社市の音楽教育者を施主とする個人住宅。1979年の第1段階の完成時の平面は、コンクリートボックスのなかで、完全に二分され、1階では音楽家の施主のためのピアノの置かれたホール＋納戸、寝室＋食堂＋台所が、各ひと組となっていた。2階も二分された中2階を持ち、書斎にあてられた。8年後、庭の南側に、中庭を挟む配置で平屋が増築され、今度はそこがピアノのホールとなり、もとのホールはリビングに転用された。増築部分と元の建物は、新たに設けられた細長い廊下によって結ばれ、劇的に構成が変わった。

According to the plan of the first stage was completed in 1979 with areas completely divided in two within a concrete box. The first floor had a hall for a piano and a storeroom for the owner who is a musician, being located against the bedroom, dining room and kitchen. The second floor has a separate mezzanine floor where the study room is located. Eight years later, a one-story house was added on the south side where a yard existed creating the courtyard between the buildings. The extended area is now the piano hall and the former hall was changed to the living room. The extended area and the original house are connected with a new narrow corridor, which drastically changed the layout of this small residential house.

[033]
STEP　1980
step

1. 香川県高松市 | takamatsu, kagawa
2. 設計 | design   1977.4–1978.10
3. 施工 | construction   1979.2–1980.3
4. 鉄筋コンクリート | RC
5. 複合商業施設 | commercial complex
6. 敷地 | site   466.4 m²
7. 建築 | building   365.1 m²
8. 延床 | total floor   1,142,0 m²

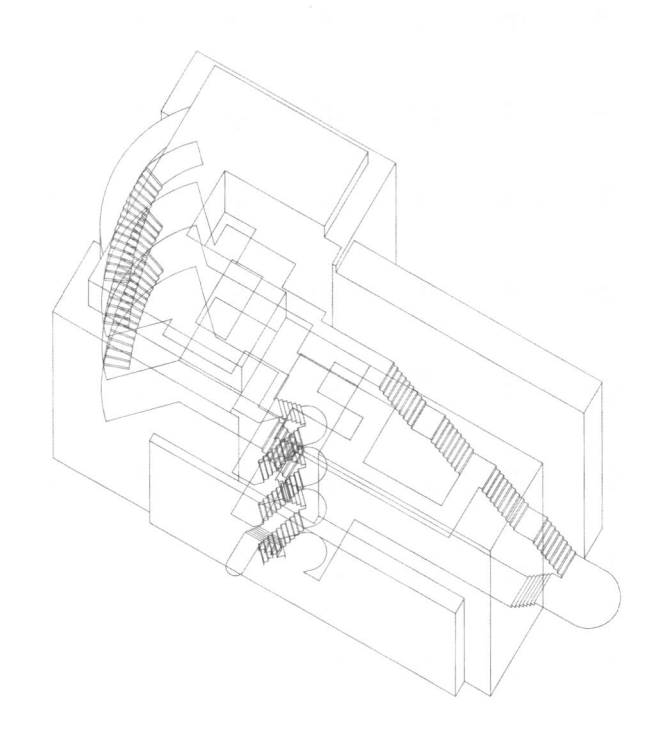

地方都市の商店街再生のモデルとされる香川県高松市の丸亀町の商業施設。アーケード商店街の一直線の動線に対して、建物の正面中心にそれと直交する屋外階段を設けた。来訪者が四層分に及ぶ階段を昇降し、買い物を楽しむ姿が見られた。間口が狭く奥深い敷地の形状を活かし、階段を主役にして、新たな賑わいをもたらすことに成功した。アーケードの下の薄暗さを払拭した開放的な階段が支持された。現在は安藤の設計による新たな施設に建て替えられたが、「STEP」の提案した空間のありかたは不朽の価値を持つ。

This commercial facility in Marugame-cho, Takamatsu in Kagawa has become a role model for regenerating shopping streets in local cities. For the straight line of the arcade shopping street, an exterior staircase on the front center of the building is set up, positioned orthogonal. It was seen that visitors are going up and down the stairs extending to the 4 levels and enjoy shopping. Taking advantage of the shape with narrow frontage and the depth of the site and the stairs as the main character, this building succeeded to bring a new bustle. The open staircase dispelling the gloominess of the space under the arcade was generally supported. As this shopping street succeeded to regenerate, this building was rebuilt as a new facility by Ando's design.

[034]
松本邸　1980
matsumoto house

1. 和歌山県和歌山市 | wakayama, wakayama
2. 設計 | design　1978.2–1979.2
3. 施工 | construction　1979.4–1980.2
4. 鉄筋コンクリート（ラーメン）| RC (frame)
5. 住宅 | detached house
6. 敷地 | site　952.1 m²
7. 建築 | building　317.4 m²
8. 延床 | total floor　484.1 m²

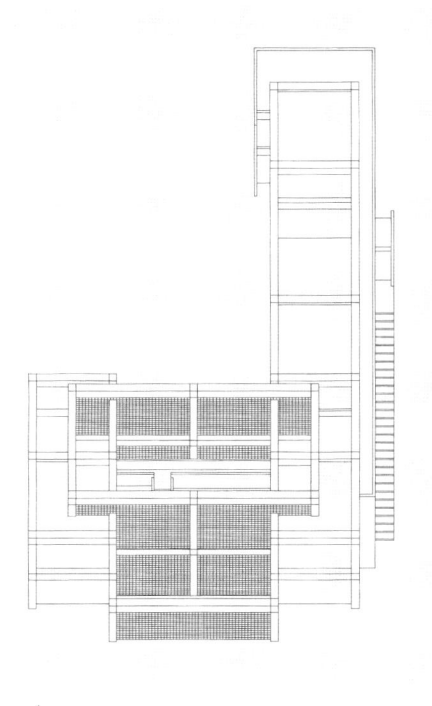

スリットからの光の強烈さとは対照的に、ガラスブロックの光は、トップライトからの天空光の方向性まで溶かしてしまい、空間をよい意味で曖昧にする。二つに分かれた住居部分を5.2メートル角のグリッドで構成し、連結には7.8メートル×7.1メートルの同じくコンクリートの格子を採用した。その骨格をどれだけ融解しうるか、外観でガラスブロックの重量感とコンクリートの格子の力感を示し、内部においては柔らかさを求める住宅建築となっている。

In contrast with strong light through slits made by splitting certain areas of a concrete wall, light through glass blocks disambiguate even the orientation of the natural light through a top light and it makes the space obscure in a positive means. Layout with grids of 5.2 meters on each side was arranged to the residential area divided in two and concrete lattices of 7.8 meters by 7.1 meters were used for the connection area. It is a residential architecture that shows the weightiness of glass blocks and strength of concrete lattices by appearance where softness is pursued inside through fusion of the two types of framework.

[035]
北野アイビーコート　1980
kitano ivy court

1. 神戸市中央区 | chuo-ku, kobe
2. 設計 | design　1978.7–1979.9
3. 施工 | construction　1979.12–1980.12
4. 鉄筋コンクリート | RC
5. 集合住宅、診療所 | apartment house, clinic
6. 敷地 | site　575.7 m²
7. 建築 | building　344.8 m²
8. 延床 | total floor　1,211.9 m²

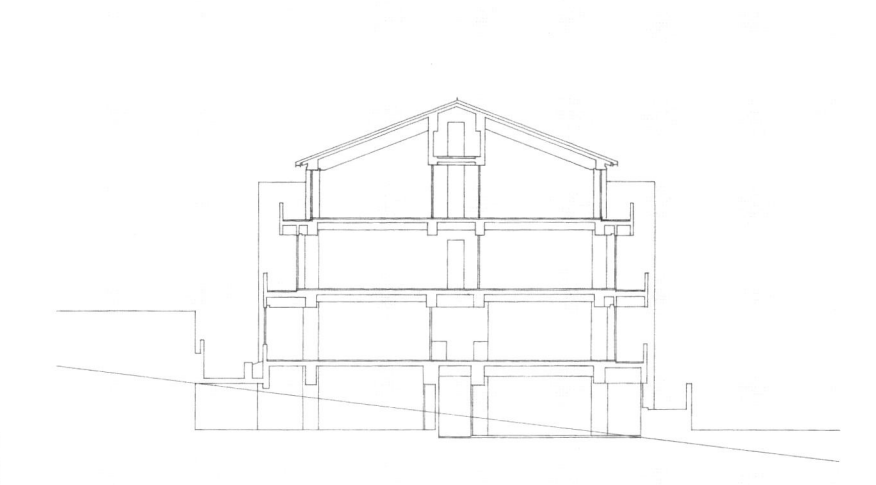

神戸・北野町の5戸の集合住宅。地階のクリニックは急傾斜の坂道に面する立地を活かした入りやすいエントランスを持ち、1–2階には4戸の住宅が配されている。建物全体は二つのブロックに分割され、住戸の独立性を確保すると同時に、表通りから「道」を引き込む構成をとる。煉瓦壁の肌合いは西洋館の街に似つかわしい落ち着きをもたらしている。坂道に残っていた塀の一部を活用したのは、住環境継承への安藤の思いを感じさせる。

This is an apartment building with 5 units in Kitano-cho Town, Kobe City. The medical clinic on the basement has an easily accessible entrance which made use of the location facing a steep slope; 4 apartment units are arranged on the 1st and 2nd floor. The whole building is divided into 2 blocks, in order to maintain privacy of each apartment while bringing in the "street" into the building from the main street. The texture of the brick wall brings quite calm to the atmosphere of this town with western style residences. This building reused parts of Oya Stone (volcanic rock) masonry wall remaining in the site — this reflects the consideration of Ando trying to succeed the living environment from the past to the future.

[036]
福邸　1980
fuku house

1. 和歌山県和歌山市 | wakayama, wakayama
2. 設計 | design　1978.10–1979.4
3. 施工 | construction　1979.8–1980.6
4. 鉄筋コンクリート（ラーメン）| RC (frame)
5. 住宅 | detached house
6. 敷地 | site　800.0 m²
7. 建築 | building　345.4 m²
8. 延床 | total floor　483.6 m²

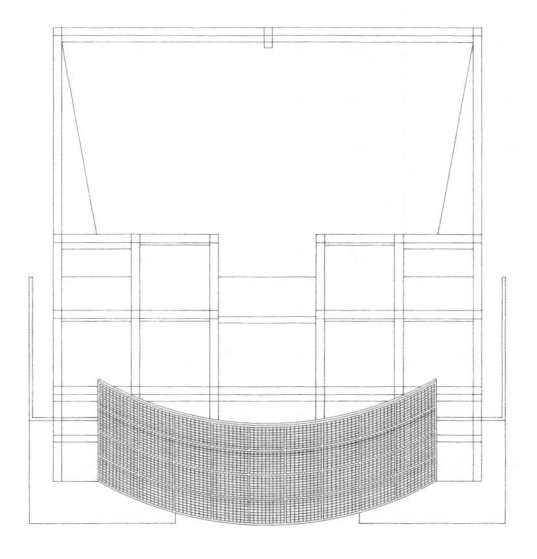

和歌山市の個人住宅。二重に設営されたガラスブロックの壁が室内に、明るく、かつ非日常的な感覚をもたらす空間構成が目をひく。建物の外周を受け持つガラスブロックの壁は大きな円弧を描き、その内側に垂直の内壁がある。住宅内部にコンクリートの格子が出現しているのも、明快な構想を感じさせる。住居部分は2階から1階に下りる傾斜した人工盤上の中庭に面し、緑の庭の下に駐車スペースなどがとられた。

A private residential house in Wakayama City. The spatial structure with double-layered glass block walls, provides a bright and an extraordinary sensation and attracts attention. The glass block walls that surround the periphery of the building have a large circular shape with vertical inner walls. The appearance of concrete lattice inside the house also gives an impression of perspicuous concept. The residential area is facing the courtyard on the artificial ground that is inclined from the 2nd floor to the 1st floor and a parking space was provided under the yard with greenery.

[037]
中之島プロジェクト I
（大阪市役所）　1980
nakanoshima project I

1. 大阪市北区 | kita-ku, osaka
2. 設計 | design　1980
3. 構想案 | concept
4. 鉄筋コンクリート | RC
5. 都市計画 | urban planning

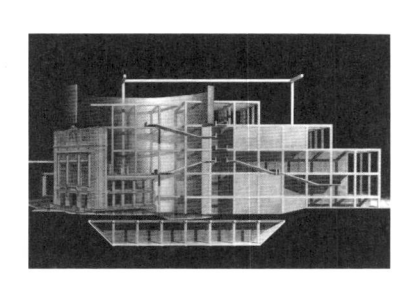

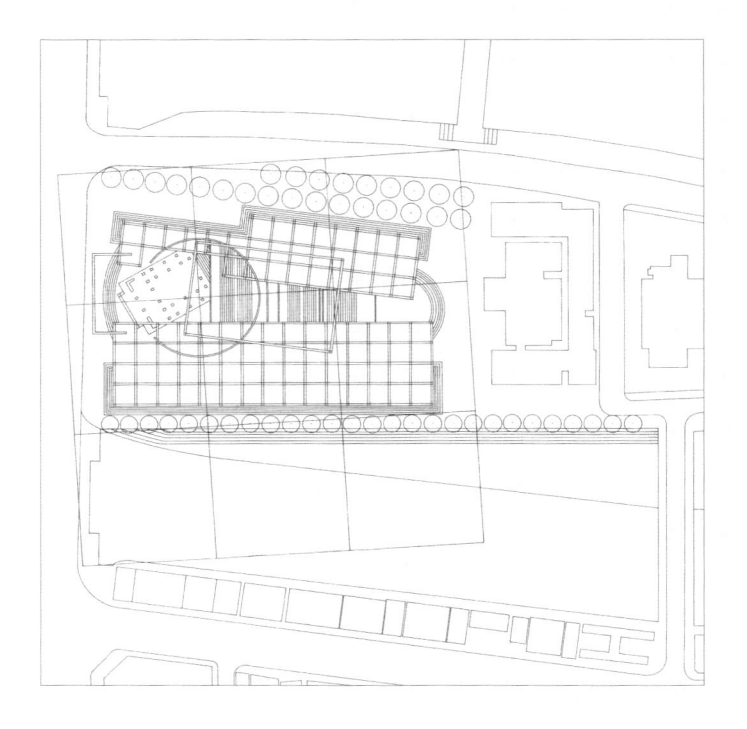

旧大阪市役所の建て替え話が持ち上がったとき、中之島における歴史的な資産と現代における創造を問いかけるため、旧庁舎（1921年）を部分保存し、周囲をコンクリートの格子を基本とする新たな庁舎建築で包み込む案を提起した。御堂筋に面して立つ市役所の正面性を踏まえて、中洲である中之島の東西方向の軸線に揃えた回廊を設定し、一帯の環境に対するこの場所の重要性を訴求した。安藤が中之島に関わる第一歩となるプロジェクトの提案だった。→参照 [099]

When the renovation of the former Osaka City Office was announced, it was proposed a plan to partially save the former government office (built in 1921) and surround it with a new government office architecture that has a concrete lattice as the basic design, in order to draw attentions to the historical assets and modern creativities in Nakanoshima. Keeping in mind that the façade of the city office is facing Midosuji, a corridor was placed along the line toward east and west of Nakanoshima, which is a middle ground between rivers, to appeal to the importance of this location amid the environment of the area. The project was the first step for Ando to be involved with Nakanoshima. → see also [099]

[038]

小篠邸　1981
koshino house

1. 兵庫県芦屋市 | ashiya, hyogo
2. 設計 | design　1979.9–1980.4
3. 施工 | construction　1980.7–1981.3
4. 鉄筋コンクリート（壁式）| RC (wall)
5. 住宅 | detached house
6. 敷地 | site　1,141.0 m²
7. 建築 | building　224.0 m²
8. 延床 | total floor　241.6 m²

芦屋・奥池は、大規模な現代住宅が点在する阪神間の奥座敷の邸宅街。「小篠邸」は、そこの緑地に見目麗しいコンクリートの肌で身を横たえる。傾斜した敷地に、並列配置されたコンクリートの細長い箱。二つの建物の間は屋外の中庭とし、そこをコンクリートの外壁が囲う「居間」に見立てた。下段の棟には細分化された個室がならび、新しい家族の形を連想させた。完成から3年後、道路側の一角に、施主であるファッションデザイナーのためのアトリエが4分の1円を描く外壁で付加され、安藤の幾何学がひとまず完結した。→参照 [240]

Okuike area of Asyiya City is the inner room of Hanshin area with modern and large-scale residential buildings. KOSHINO HOUSE is sitting on the green area with a beautiful concrete skin. Two slender concrete boxes are placed in parallel on a sloped site. Their in-between space was an outdoor courtyard, while this space is designated as a "living room" enclosed by the concrete exterior walls. The lower wing has a series of subdivided rooms, and it reminds of the shape of a new family. 3 years after its completion, an atelier space for the client as a fashion designer was added to the road side corner of the site, with an exterior wall in a shape of a quarter circle. The geometry of Ando is completed for now. → see also [240]

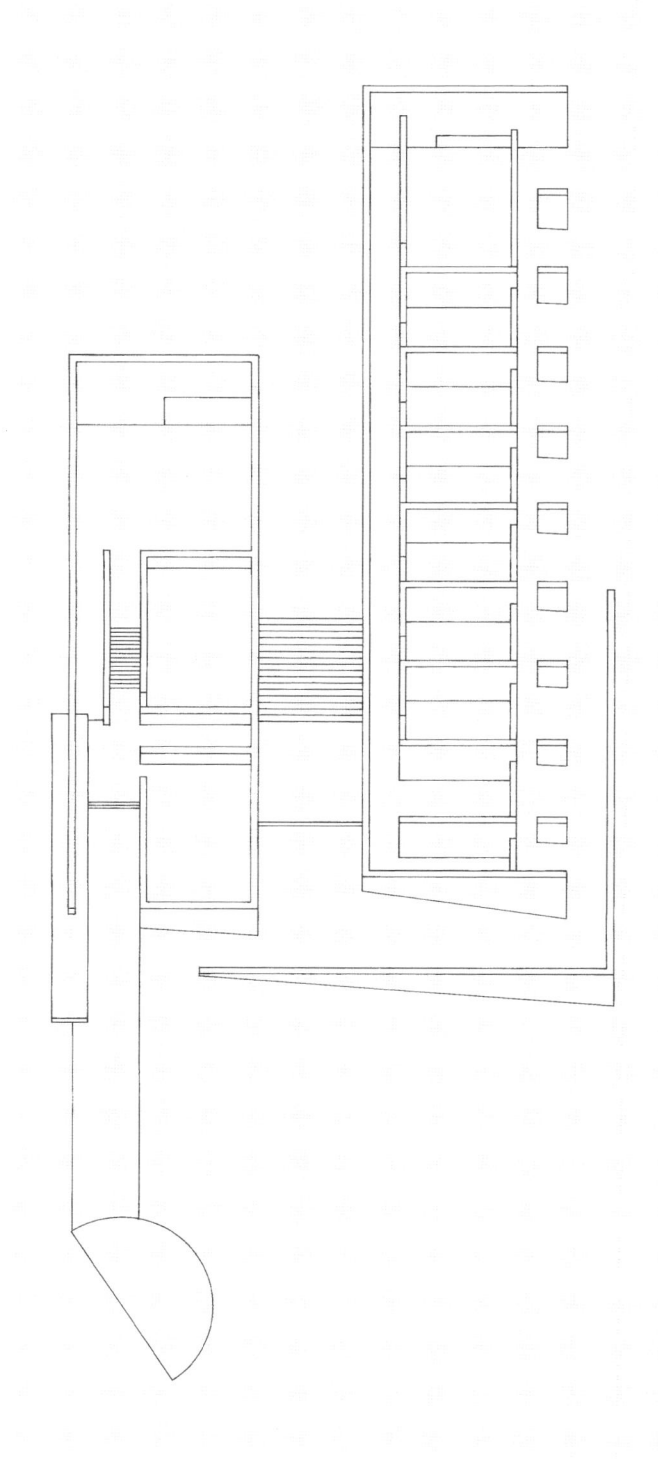

[038]

小篠邸増築　1984
koshino house addition

1. 兵庫県芦屋市 | ashiya, hyogo
2. 設計 | design　1983.1–1983.6
3. 施工 | construction　1983.11–1984.3
4. 鉄筋コンクリート | RC
5. 住宅 | detached house
6. 敷地 | site　1,141.0 m²
7. 建築 | building　52.7 m²
8. 延床 | total floor　52.7 m²

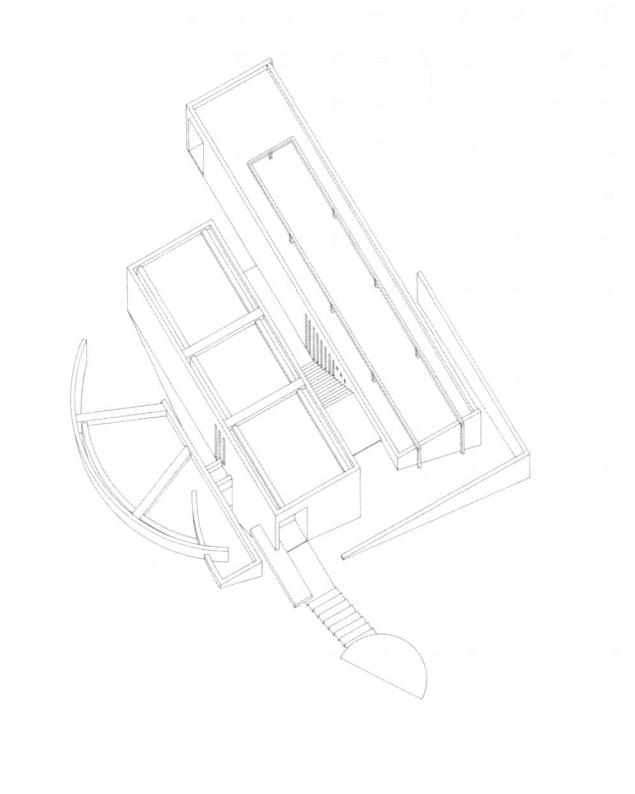

←解説は前ページ参照

← see previous page

[039]

リンズギャラリー　1981
rin's gallery

1. 神戸市中央区 | chuo-ku, kobe
2. 設計 | design　1979.6–1979.12
3. 施工 | construction　1980.3–1981.5
4. 鉄筋コンクリート | RC
5. 店舗、住宅 | shop, house
6. 敷地 | site　703.7 m²
7. 建築 | building　361.6 m²
8. 延床 | total floor　1,594.9 m²

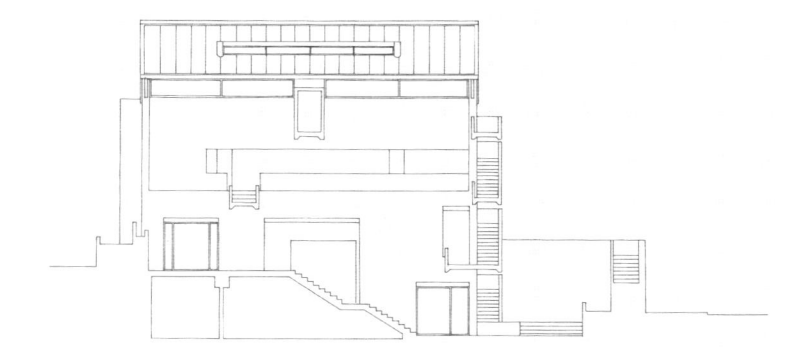

広場、「道」としての通路、細長い吹き抜け、下階の屋根を活用した屋外テラス、「ローズガーデン」から4年、北野町における商業施設の表現言語が存分に活用されている。それらの要素は、建物の屋内、屋外を意識し、煉瓦とコンクリートの肌の対比を踏まえながら、立体的に構成され、多彩な表情をもたらしている。また、坂道に面した煉瓦の塀は、独立しているがゆえに、安藤が多くの北野町の作品で示唆しようとした海への視線の方向性を認識させる。この地での安藤の商業施設のひとまずの完成形が読み取れる。

After 4 years from the completion of ROSE GARDEN — the architectural language of a commercial facility in Kitano-cho Town context is fully reflected in this building, with those elements of plaza, a passage as "alley", an elongated void space, and an exterior terrace utilizing the roof of the lower floor. Those elements are paid attention to the interior and exterior of the building, are structured in 3 dimensions based on comparison of brick and concrete skin, and are bringing a variety of facial expressions. As the brick wall facing to the sloped street is independent in its presence, its directionality makes us recognize the direction of the visual line toward the ocean, also indicated by Ando in various works of Kitano-cho Town.

[040]
大淀のアトリエ
1981, 1982, 1986
atelier in oyodo

1. 大阪市北区 | kita-ku, osaka
4. 鉄筋コンクリート（壁式）| RC (wall)
5. アトリエ | atlier
6. 敷地 | site   114.8 m² [phase 3]
7. 建築 | building   76.1 m² [phase 3]
8. 延床 | total floor   225.3 m² [phase 3]

安藤が建築家として第一歩を印したと自認する「冨島邸」を取得し、自らの設計事務所に転用して使ってきた。10年ほどの間に3期の増築を重ね、創造の拠点を整えていった。第1期ではガラス窓の連なりに載る屋根を架けた。第2期は隣地に曲面壁を持つ新棟を増築、3期では二つの棟を結ぶヴォールト屋根のペントハウスを付加した。この過程は即興的な実験の連続で、その結果、内部は思わぬ迷宮の仕立てとなったと安藤は振り返っている。→参照［119］、［156］

TOMISHIMA HOUSE that Ando recognizes the first step as an architect was later acquired by Ando himself to be converted and used as his own design office. This building received repeatedly three phases of extension in 10 years to be organized as a base of their creation; a roof was added over the series of glass window in the 1st phase; a new wing with curved wall was added to the adjacent lot in the 2nd phase; a penthouse with a vault roof connecting two wings was added in the 3rd phase. According to Ando, the process of these extension was a series of improvised experiments — as a result, the interior space became an unexpected labyrinth. → see also [119], [156]

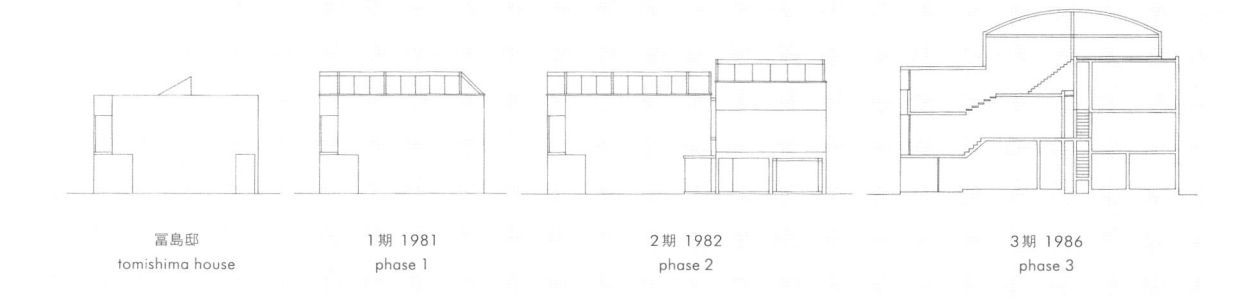

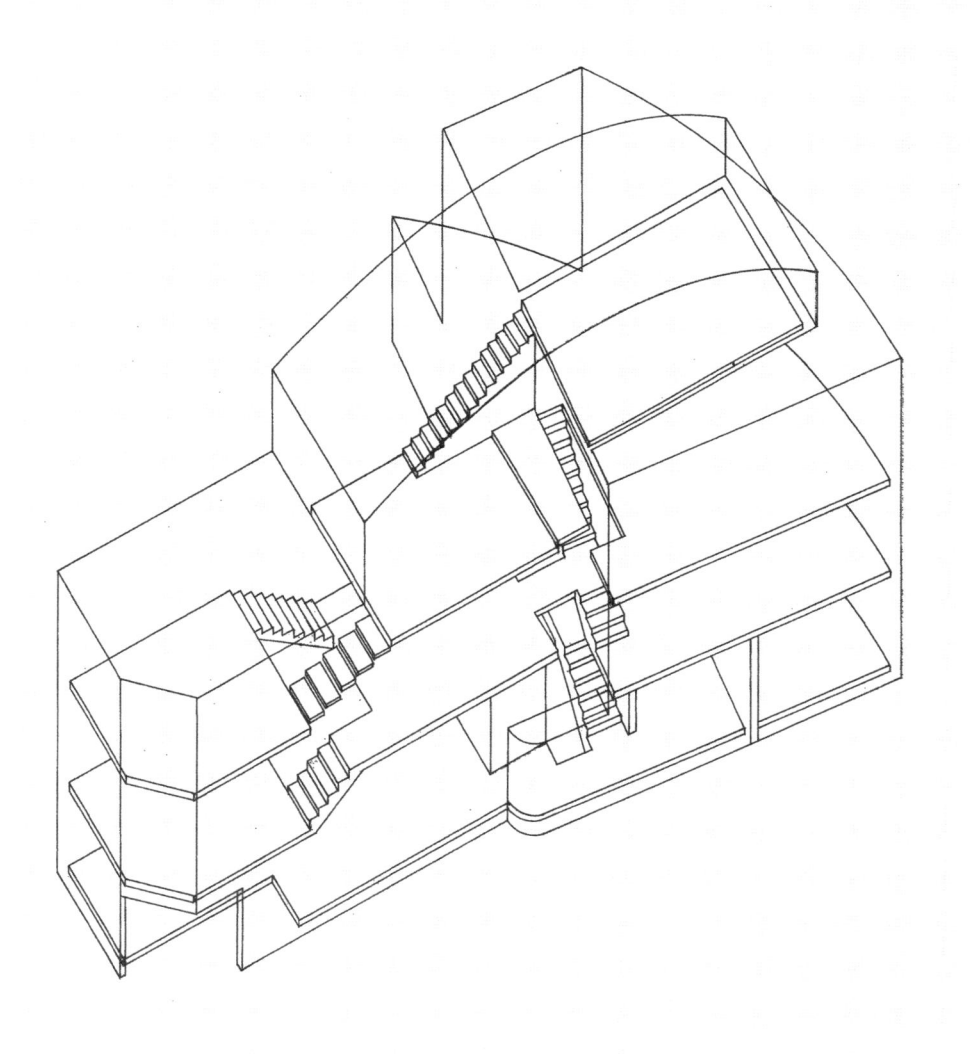

冨島邸 | tomishima house

1期 1981 | phase 1

2期 1982 | phase 2

3期 1986 | phase 3

3期 | phase 3

346 Complete Works   262

[041]
児島の共同住宅 ── 佐藤邸
1981
kojima housing — sato house

1. 岡山県倉敷市 | kurashiki, okayama
2. 設計 | design　1980.1–1980.10
3. 施工 | construction　1981.1–1981.8
4. 鉄筋コンクリート（壁式）| RC (wall)
5. 住宅、集合住宅 | house, apartment house
6. 敷地 | site　655.3 m²
7. 建築 | building　145.6 m²
8. 延床 | total floor　238.3 m²

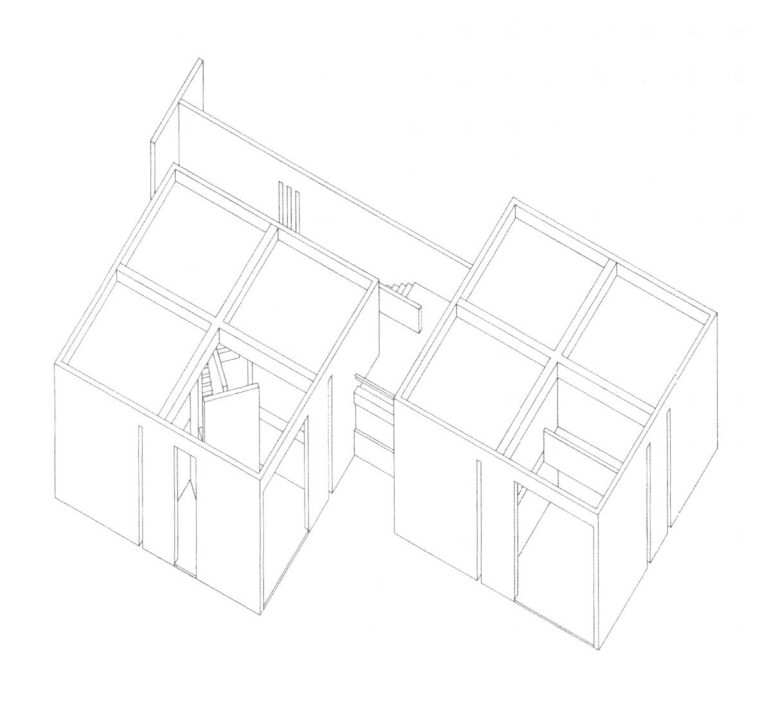

3戸で構成する小規模集合住宅。1戸にオーナーが暮らし、2戸が賃貸居住者用。二つのコンクリートの箱をずらして平行配置した。いずれも高さは2階で、エントランスに近い側の箱は1、2階ともオーナー一家が住み、奥の箱は2組の入居者が1、2階に分かれて入居する。内装にもコンクリート打ち放しの仕上げを徹底し、簡素な素材のなかで、自然の変化を味わえる暮らしを想定している。オーナー宅の間取りは対角線の位置に階段を配して45度振った配置にして、小規模ながら変化のある空間構成を達成している。

A small housing complex consisting of three apartments. The owner is living in one apartment and the other two apartments are for tenants. Two concrete boxes are placed offset in parallel. Both of them are two-stories high where the 1st and the 2nd floor of the box close to the entrance is for the owner and his family and the 1st and the 2nd floor of the other box is for two pairs of tenants. The whole interior is finished with an exposed concrete to offer a taste of natural transition in the simple material. The layout on the owner's side is based on the stairway that is placed on the diagonal line of the house at a 45-degree angle to achieve variation in spatial structure in the small scale architecture.

[042]
番匠邸増築　1981
bansho house addition

1. 愛知県三好町 | miyoshi, aichi
2. 設計 | design　1980.7–1980.10
3. 施工 | construction　1980.12–1981.2
4. 鉄筋コンクリート（壁式）| RC (wall)
5. 住宅 | detached house
6. 敷地 | site　168.3 m²
7. 建築 | building　35.4 m²
8. 延床 | total floor　28.2 m²

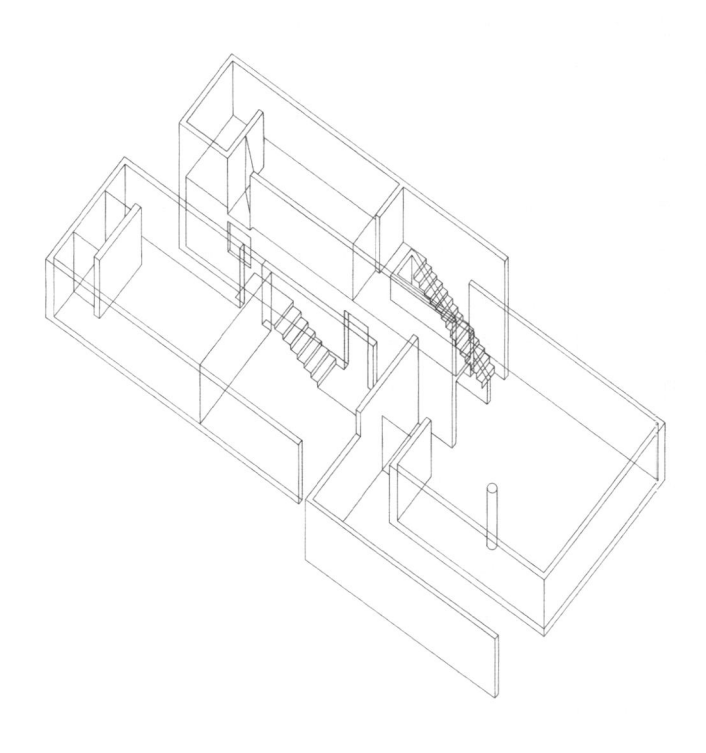

初期の住宅作品の増築。既存の居住部分に加えて、アトリエが増築された。アトリエといっても1室にすぎないが、深い庇の下に秘匿するかのような空間として付加された。背後の隣地と高低差があることを生かし、アトリエは既存住宅の2階のレベルに設営された。そのことによって、狭小な敷地のなかに、空中庭園のようなテラスを獲得することになった。完結した自身の造形に対する増築について、安藤は「空間のスケールやリズムの連続性を重視した」と述べており、その発想が新たな迷路的魅力をもたらした。→参照 [017]

An extension of one of Ando's early residential house works. An atelier was added to the existing living area. The atelier consists of only one room but it was added as a space that has an atmosphere of a hiding area under a deep hood. Using the height difference with the adjacent property at the back, an atelier was added on the level same as the second-floor in the existing house. By doing so, a terrace that resembles a hanging garden was obtained in the narrow property. Regarding the shape of the completed extension, Ando mentioned that he "placed importance on the scale of the space and sequence of rhythm", which provides the attractiveness of a maze that did not exist before the extension. → see also [017]

[043]
ファッション・ライブ・シアター
1981
fashion live theater

1. 神戸市中央区 | chuo-ku, kobe
2. 設計 | design   1979.11–1980.6
3. 施工 | construction   1980.7–1981.3
4. 鉄骨 | steel
5. 展示場、店舗 | exhibition hall, shop
6. 敷地 | site   2748.1 m²
7. 建築 | building   1092.7 m²
8. 延床 | total floor   1732.2 m²

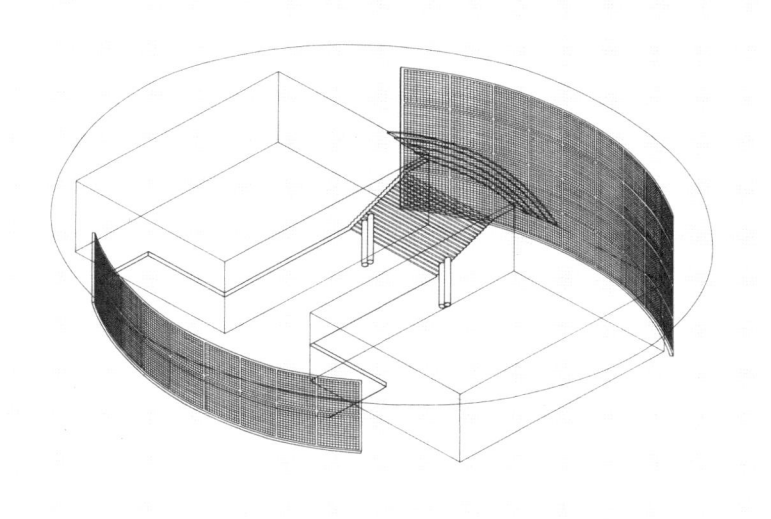

神戸港を埋め立てた造成地ポートピアのお披露目として開催された地方博覧会のパビリオン。ファッションの原点としてバリ島の民族衣装を展示するために設営された。安藤は敷地を円形として片側に高さ12メートル、もう片側に6メートルのガラスブロックの壁を配し、段差を付けたテラスと広場を階段で昇降する仕立てを選択した。ローマのスペイン階段のように入場者が集う場となってほしいとの想定で造られた。6カ月間の仮設建築だった。

A pavilion of a regional expo held as an opening event of Portopia, a developed area of reclaimed land in Kobe Port. It was situated to exhibit native costumes of Bali as the origin of fashion. Ando arranged glass block walls with a height of 12 meters on one side and 6 meters on the other side with a plaza that can approach a terrace on a different level using stairs in a circle property. It was created with the intention to make an area where visitors gather similar to the Spanish Steps of Rome. It was placed temporarily for six months.

[044]
サンプレイス   1982
sun place

1. 香川県高松市 | takamatsu, kagawa
2. 設計 | design   1979.10–1980.12
3. 施工 | construction   1981.3–1982.2
4. 鉄骨鉄筋コンクリート | SRC
5. 銀行、店舗、多目的ホール | bank, shop, auditorium
6. 敷地 | site   663.7 m²
7. 建築 | building   551.2 m²
8. 延床 | total floor   1,793.2 m²

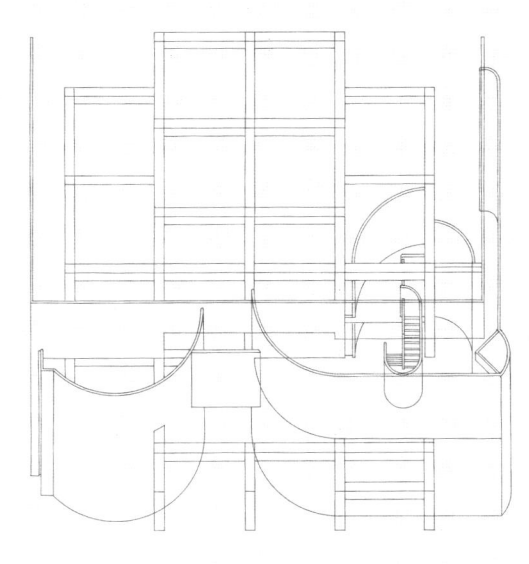

「STEP」から続くアーケード商店街に位置する複合商業ビル。地元の銀行の支店の建て替えに際して、営業時間の短い銀行窓口を脇道側に後退させ、アーケード商店街から路地を設けて、町の賑わいを引き込む仕掛けを凝らした。脇道側のエントランスはコンクリートのフレームで構成し、明確な骨格が読み取れる仕立てになっている。3階に設けられたコミュニティーホールは、ライブハウス系音楽のコンサートなどに活用され、現在も活動を続けている。

This is a commercial complex located in the arcade shopping street leading from the STEP building. When a branch building of a local bank was planned to be reconstructed, the bank teller area with short business hours was moved back to the side street. Then an al eyway leading from the arcade shopping street to the bank teller area was provided, in order to bring in the bustle of the town to the building. The entrance on the side street is composed of a concrete frame, and its clear framework of the building can be read. The community hall provided on the third floor is used as a live house for concerts, and it works still today.

[045]
石井邸　1982
ishii house

1. 静岡県浜松市 | hamamatsu, shizuoka
2. 設計 | design　1980.5–1981.6
3. 施工 | construction　1981.8–1982.4
4. 鉄筋コンクリート（壁式）| RC (wall)
5. 住宅 | detached house
6. 敷地 | site　371.2 m²
7. 建築 | building　154.1 m²
8. 延床 | total floor　235.3 m²

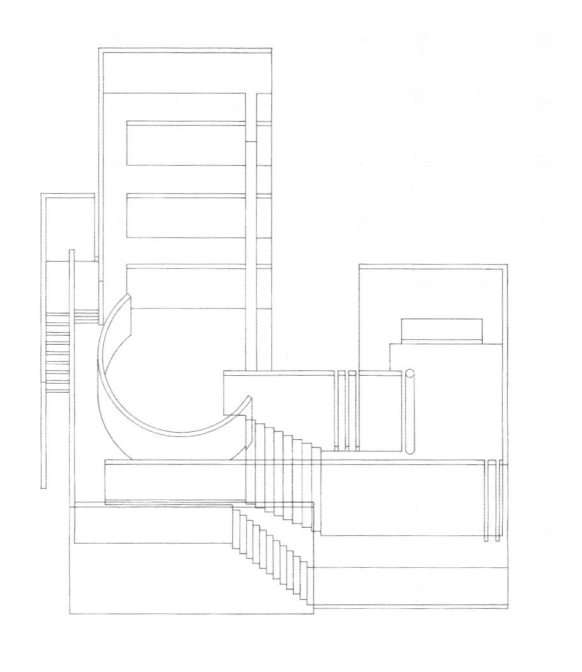

L字型の間取りの転換点の部分に円筒を配して食堂に充てている。玄関を入ると円筒の縁にあたるトップライトからの光がふり注ぐホールが待ち受けている。この住宅の空間の出発点であるとともに、L字型に垂直交差する二つの棟の結節点となっている。安藤はトップライトに加えて、コンクリートの壁で囲われた空間の、節目となる位置に縦長のスリットを切って自然光を導き入れ、人工と自然の劇的な衝突を演出している。

A dining room is allocated with a cylinder space at the turning point of an L shape layout. Light emitting from the top light along the edge of the cylinder welcomes visitors at the hall after entering the entrance. It is the starting point of the space of this house and the nodal point of the two sections where they meet perpendicularly in an L shape. In addition to top lights, Ando added vertical long slits at suitable points to guide in natural light in the space surrounded by concrete walls to present dramatic collision of human work and nature.

[046]
双生観の茶室――山口邸増築
1982
tea house for soseikan
――yamaguchi house addition

1. 兵庫県宝塚市 | takarazuka, hyogo
2. 設計 | design　1981.5–1982.2
3. 施工 | construction　1982.3–1982.7
4. 鉄筋コンクリート（壁式）| RC (wall)
5. 茶室 | tea-ceremony room
6. 敷地 | site　255.4 m²
7. 建築 | building　15.5 m²
8. 延床 | total floor　12.8 m²

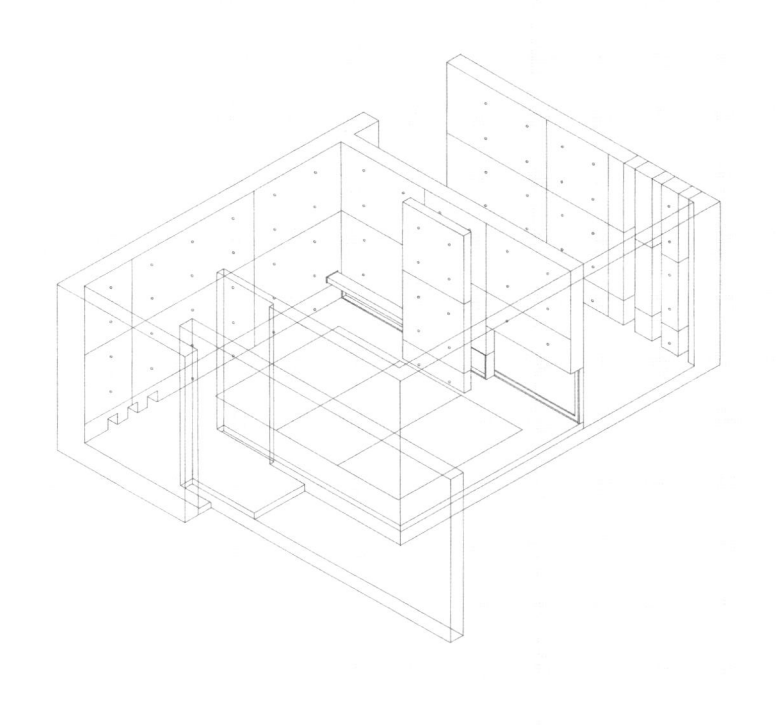

初期の代表的な住宅作品「双生観」に増築されたコンクリート打ち放しの茶室。全体を平滑なコンクリートの壁で構築した。にじり口にあたる切欠きからは、コンクリートの外壁にうがったスリットの列が顔をのぞかせ、茶室内には「鉄扉」を開けて入るなど「無」の空間の仕立てのなかに、安藤の考える「作意」が込められた。近代建築の素材に徹することで、むしろ自然にアプローチできるとする建築家の信念が凝縮している。→参照 [012]

A tea-ceremony house made of exposed concrete added to SOSEIKAN, which is one of Ando's representative works during his initial phase. The overall structure is made of smooth concrete walls. Ando's thoughts are demonstrated through the space of "nil" by rows of penetrating slits on concrete exterior walls that can be seen from the notch that forms the small entrance to the tea ceremony room as well as the iron door placed to enter inside. An architect's belief of thoroughly using materials for modern architecture allows more natural approach in the design is condensed in this work. → see also [012]

[047]
九条の町屋――井筒邸　1982
town house in kujo — izutsu house

1. 大阪市西区 | nishi-ku, osaka
2. 設計 | design　1981.11–1982.4
3. 施工 | construction　1982.5–1982.10
4. 鉄筋コンクリート（壁式）| RC (wall)
5. 住宅 | detached house
6. 敷地 | site　71.2 m²
7. 建築 | building　46.0 m²
8. 延床 | total floor　114.5 m²

大阪下町、九条の雑多な環境に位置している。自宅内を移動するのに、壁で囲われた庭に面しているとはいえ、屋外階段を利用する構成が選ばれた。「住吉の長屋」が囲われた屋外の光庭を通らざるを得なかったように、棲まい手は屋外に出る度に都市の自然を感得するというわけだ。実際、この住宅の上階からは、玄昌石を敷きつめた地面が「坪庭」のように見え、日本の都市居住の文脈が生かされたことを実感する。「住吉の長屋」を中層化した変奏曲の趣がある。

This building is situated in a mixed environment of an old downtown district of Kujo area in Osaka City. Although it faces a garden surrounded by walls, a structure to use this "exterior" staircase is selected to move in the house; therefore, residents feel nature in the city every time he/she goes outside, as the resident in the ROW HOUSE, SUMIYOSHI had no choice but to pass through the enclosed outdoor light court. Actually, the ground surface finished in a slate material appears to be a "tsubo-niwa" inner garden as seen from the upper floor level of this house, making us realize the context of "urban residence and living" in traditional Japanese culture. This work sounds like a variation piece of the ROW HOUSE, SUMIYCSHI in a medium rise housing.

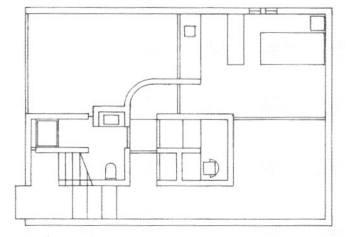

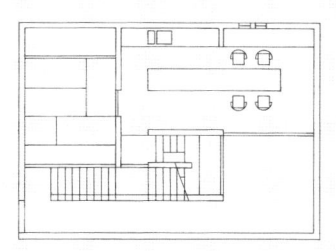

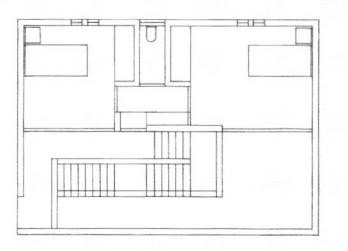

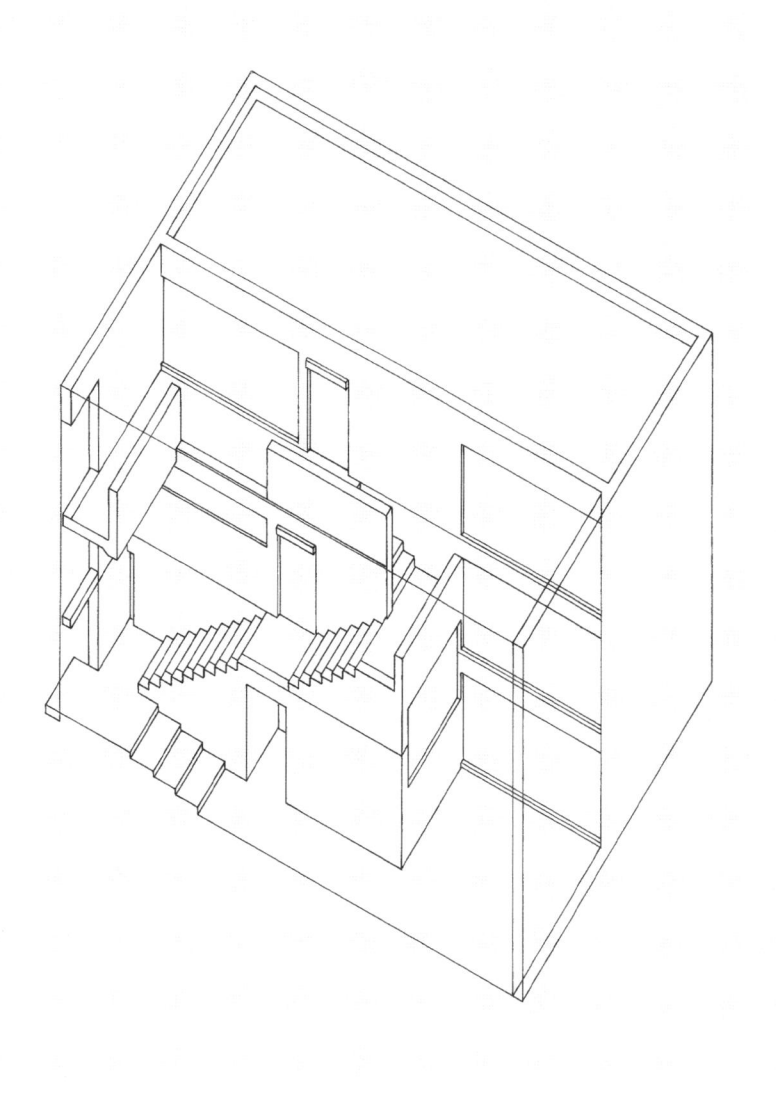

346 Complete Works

[048]
赤羽邸　1982
akabane house

1. 東京都世田谷区 | setagaya-ku, tokyo
2. 設計 | design　1981.6–1982.4
3. 施工 | construction　1982.5–1982.10
4. 鉄筋コンクリート（壁式）| RC (wall)
5. 住宅 | detached house
6. 敷地 | site　240.8 m²
7. 建築 | building　61.1 m²
8. 延床 | total floor　119.0 m²

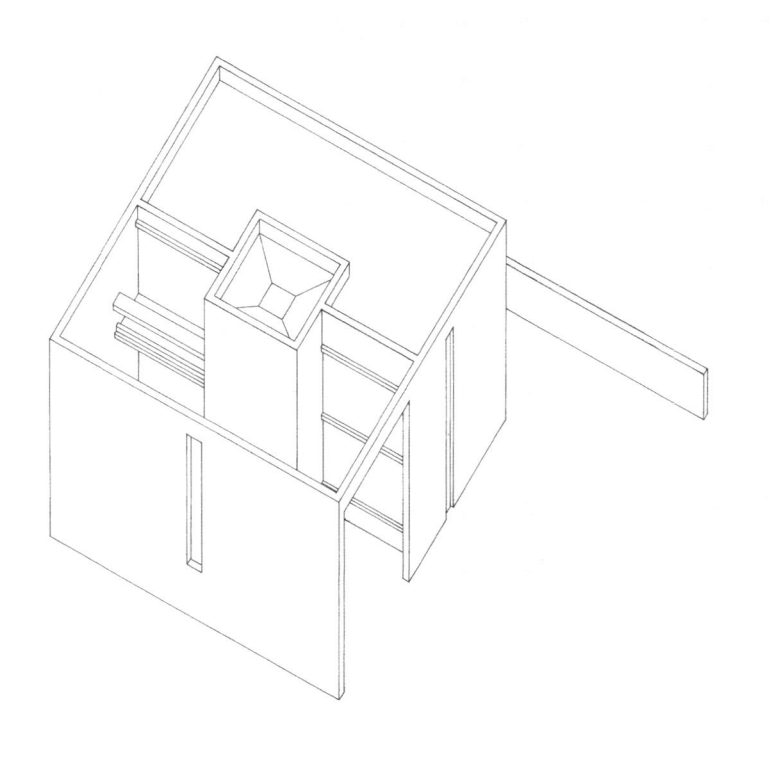

「文学界」新人賞受賞の小説「住宅」の作家が施主。四周をコンクリートの壁で囲った正方形の平面の中央に階段がコアとして配され、民家を思わせる「田の字型」で部屋を区切った。スリットは各所にあるが、開口部はダイニングキッチンなど必要最小限としたため、各部屋へ浸潤する光源は階段室上部のトップライトからの天空光だ。壁が生活を守り、自然を感知させる光が支配する空間のありようは初期の住宅の共通項で、原初的な形が確認できる。

The client of this residence is the author of the novel "Jutaku (A House)" that received the rooky of the year award by Bungakukai ("Literary World") magazine. The staircase was arranged as a core in the center of a square plan surrounded by concrete walls for periphery of the square lot, and the room was divided into 4 spaces as often seen in traditional private houses in Japan. Minimum number of openings are provided in dining kitchen and other places, while there are slits in various places — therefore the light source coming into each room is the sky light from the top light in the upper part of the staircase room. The spatial conditions of this house — walls protect the living and the light controls the space to allow residents feel the nature — are common language found in the early residential projects of Ando. This house also reveals the original form of his architecture.

[049]
ドールズハウス　1982
doll's house

2. 設計 | design　1982
3. 構想案 | concept
4. 鉄筋コンクリート | RC
5. 住宅 | detached house
7. 建築 | building　75.4 m²
8. 延床 | total floor　128.4 m²

大阪下町の長屋を思わせる家並みの模型のなかに、正方形に4区分され、そのなかのひとつがさらに四つの正方形に区切られた立体が配されている。「ドールズハウス」は、ヨーロッパでは貴族の趣味に始まり、子弟の生活教育のツールとして発達した。安藤のそれは、地上に一層、地下に二層が収められた。4区画のうち三つが三層の吹き抜けを持ち、光を介して自然と戯れる。安藤によると区画は無限拡大もできるし、逆に無限に区分していくこともできる。それは人間の身体から解放された人形なればこそ可能なのだという。

A solid formed by dividing a square in four from one section that is also from a square divided in four is placed in a model of housed similar to terrace houses in the old area of Osaka City. Doll houses were developed as a tool for educational purpose for children that started as a hobby among the aristocratic class in Europe. Ando's work has one layer aboveground and two layers underground with an open ceiling of three layers for three sections among four sections to allow interaction with nature through light. Ando described that sections could be increased indefinitely and also they can be sectioned indefinitely. That was possible with dolls that are liberated from limitations of human body, he mentioned.

[050]
六甲の集合住宅 I 1983
rokko housing I

1. 神戸市灘区 | nada-ku, kobe
2. 設計 | design 1978.10–1981.10
3. 施工 | construction 1981.10–1983.5
4. 鉄筋コンクリート（ラーメン）| RC (frame)
5. 集合住宅 | apartment house
6. 敷地 | site 1,852.0 m²
7. 建築 | building 668.0 m²
8. 延床 | total floor 1,779.0 m²

「六甲の集合住宅」は、大阪から神戸にかけての海の風景を独り占めできる立地にある。しかし、急斜面の崖地での住宅建設は不可能に思えた。綿密に地質を調べ、崖地にコンクリートの箱がへばりつく形で実現した。住棟は、中央の階段を軸にした配置で、階段から両側の住戸へは、各戸に設けられた屋外の展望テラスを眺めながら、路地に見立てた通路を通る。そこでの住民同士のアイコンタクトがコミュニティーを育むことが期待された。それらを支えるディテールへのこだわりが、昇降が苦にならない階段の寸法などに反映され、秀作が実現した。
→参照 [133]、[180]、[265]

ROKKO HOUSING is in a location that can take over view of the ocean spreading from Osaka to Kobe areas. Although it seemed impossible to build a house on steep sloping cliff areas, this design can be realized by careful geological survey in a form that the concrete boxes stick to the cliff ground. The residence building is arranged with the staircase placed in the center as a main axis; the access from the staircase to the dwelling on both side passes via alley-like passage, while seeing an exterior observation terrace provided to each unit. It was expected such design to form the sense of community through eye contacts among residents. This masterpiece was realized with Ando's keen attention to details for supporting the concept, as seen in the dimensions of the stairs allowing to go up and down without harshness. → see also [133], [180], [265]

[051]
BIGIアトリエ　1983
bigi atelier

1. 東京都渋谷区 | shibuya-ku, tokyo
2. 設計 | design　1980.10–1982.3
3. 施工 | construction　1982.5–1983.3
4. 鉄筋コンクリート | RC
5. アトリエ | atlier
6. 敷地 | site　742.7㎡
7. 建築 | building　286.3㎡
8. 延床 | total floor　998.5㎡

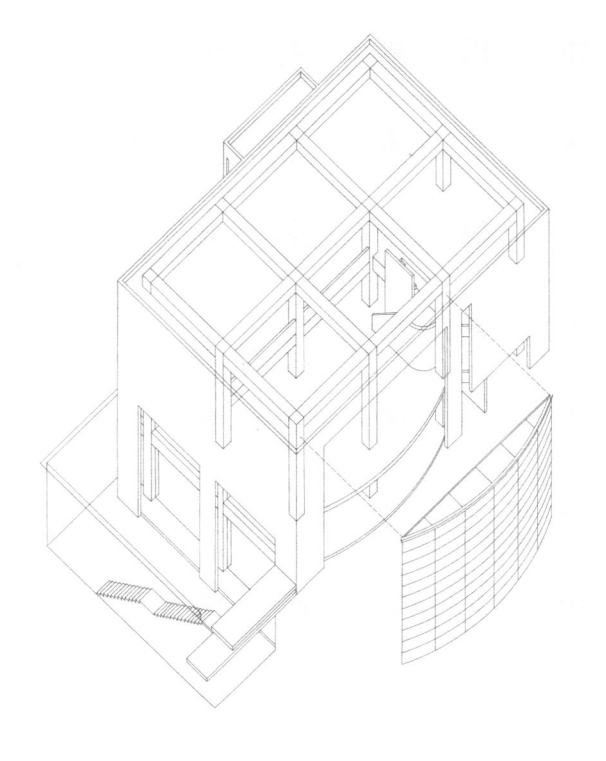

1980年代、デザイナーズ・キャラクターと呼ばれる国内のファッションブランドが人気を集めた。安藤のコンクリート打ち放しの空間は、その担い手であるデザイナーから支持され、多くのファッション関係の施設を手がけた。そのひとつ東京・代官山のBIGIのためのアトリエは、コンクリート打ち放しのボックスに曲面のガラス壁を備え、半透過のガラス壁で濾過した光が建物内へと及び、柔らかな空間を実現した。曲面壁の左側には階段で下りるサンクンガーデンも設け、自然との融合が試みられた。

In the 1980's, domestic fashion brands called "designer's and character's" gained popularity and attention. Ando's concrete space is supported by designers as a leader, and he designed many buildings for fashion-related facilities — The atelier for one of them, BIGI in Daikanyama in Tokyo is set up with a curved glass wall in an exposed concrete box, and light filtered through the semi-translucent glass wall is brought into the interior space to create a gentle atmosphere. A sunken garden accessed by a staircase was provided on the left side of the curved wall, in order to unify with the nature.

[052]
梅宮邸　1983
umemiya house

1. 神戸市垂水区 | tarumi-ku, kobe
2. 設計 | design　1981.6–1982.9
3. 施工 | construction　1982.10–1983.3
4. 補強コンクリートブロック | RC block
5. 住宅 | detached house
6. 敷地 | site　681.7㎡
7. 建築 | building　68.0㎡
8. 延床 | totcl floor　119.9㎡

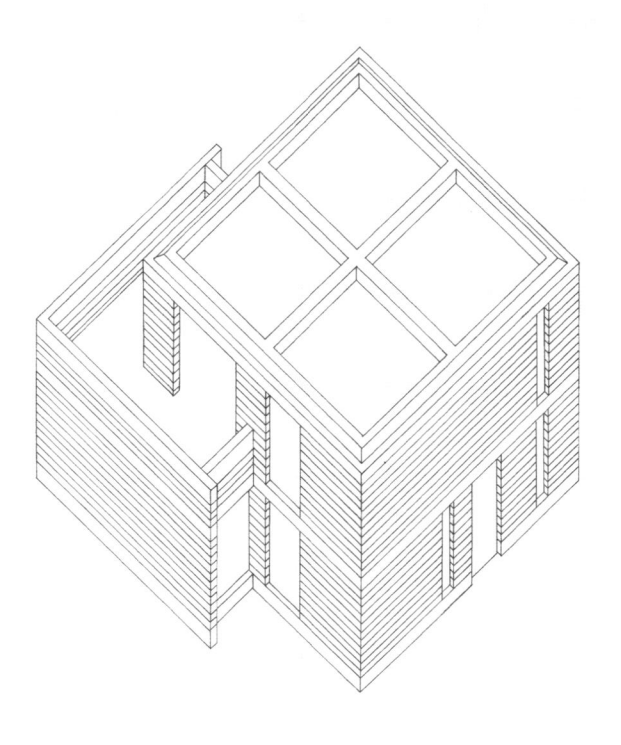

神戸市舞子の瀬戸内海を見おろす丘陵地に立地する。コンクリートブロックのざらざらした感触と、自然豊かな環境がもたらす陽光、風との出合いが、コンクリート打ち放しとは異なる空間のイメージをもたらしている。間取りは二つの正方形を重ね合わせた形をとる。この規則的な幾何図形の配置と、ブロックならではの定型サイズの制約されたイメージが、住宅全体に規律をもたらし、安藤らしい結晶化された空間が実現している。

Located at a hilly area that views the Seto Inland Sea in Maiko in Kobe City. The combination of the concrete block texture, sunlight and wind from the rich natural environment brings the different impression of a space from an exposed concrete structure. The rooms are crranged in a form of two squares with one on top of the other. This regular geometric layout and the controlled image from the standard size of blocks bring order to the whole house expressing a crystallized space that characterizes Ando's work.

[053]

茂木邸　1983
motegi house

1. 神戸市長田区 | nagata-ku, kobe
2. 設計 | design　1982.5–1983.6
3. 施工 | construction　1983.7–1983.12
4. 鉄筋コンクリート（壁式）| RC (wall)
5. 住宅 | detached house
6. 敷地 | site　32.1㎡
7. 建築 | building　25.0㎡
8. 延床 | total floor　94.7㎡

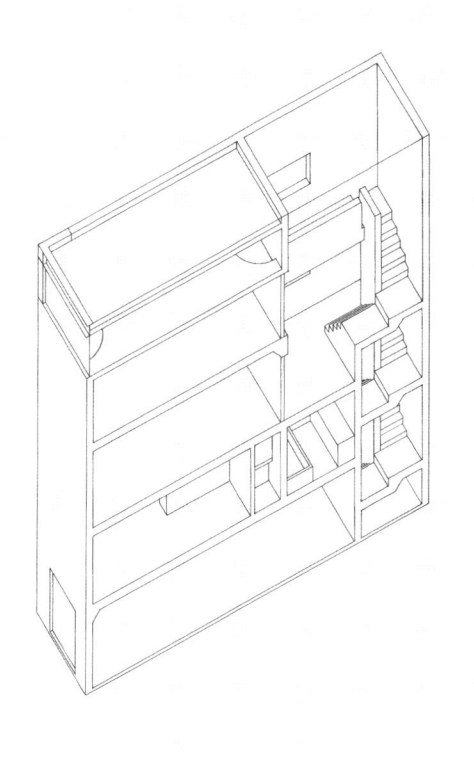

神戸市の商店街の一角に立つ店舗付き住宅。間口は2.5メートルしかなく、奥行きは10メートルの細長い平面に、表通りから眺めると高さ12メートル近いコンクリートの塔がそびえる風情だ。内部は1階が店舗、2、3階にリビングルームと寝室、3、4階に子ども部屋を配した。各階の行き来は、最奥の中庭に面した階段を利用する。安藤は細い間口を、ヨーロッパの歴史的な建築の「壁厚」だと受けとめ、壁のなかに住空間をうがつ発想で、生活の器を設定した。

A residential house with a shop located in a shopping street of Kobe City. The house expresses the atmosphere of a concrete tower when seen from the front street with its narrow structure of 2.5 meters wide, 10 meters long and 12 meters high. The shop is on the 1st floor, a living room and bedroom on the 2nd and 3rd floors, and children's rooms on the 3rd and 4th floors. A stairway is placed facing the courtyard at the very end of the house. Ando viewed the narrow width as "wall thickness" of European historical architectures and set a place of living with an idea of drilling a living space inside a wall.

[054]

金子邸　1983
kaneko house

1. 東京都渋谷区 | shibuya-ku, tokyo
2. 設計 | design　1982.11–1983.4
3. 施工 | construction　1983.5–1983.11
4. 鉄筋コンクリート（壁式）| RC (wall)
5. 住宅 | detached house
6. 敷地 | site　172.9㎡
7. 建築 | building　93.6㎡
8. 延床 | total floor　169.0㎡

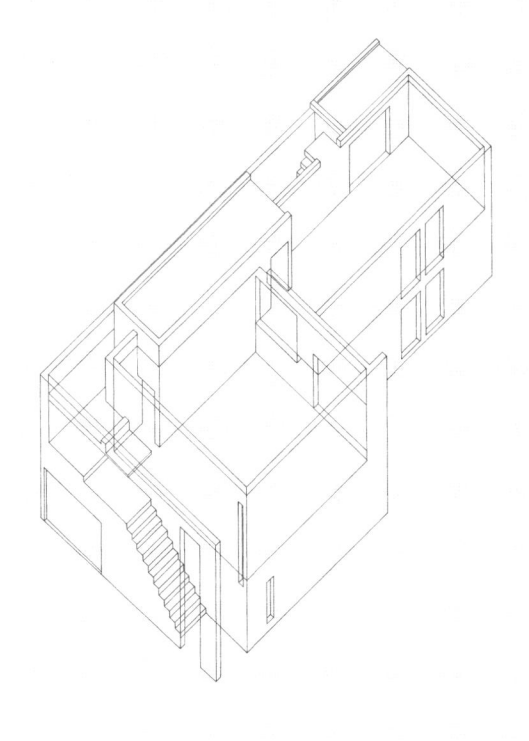

東京・渋谷の松涛美術館に近い立地の小住宅。面積の制約から、廊下を排して階段による各室の移動を前提に計画された。この階段中心の発想が四つの異なるレベルの床という構成をもたらした。また二つの中庭が配され、南側の大きな中庭が開放感を、北側の小さな中庭はそこに面する居室の一体感を、自然の変化とともに感じられる仕立てとなっている。居住者はこの二つの中庭とレベルの異なる床がもたらす空間体験を堪能することになる。

A small residential house at a location close to the Shoto Museum of Art in Shibuya, Tokyo. Due to limitation of the property space, it was designed to use stairs instead of corridors to move to each room. The idea centered on the stairway resulted in bringing four different levels of floors. Additionally, two courtyards were provided in which the larger courtyard on the south side offers a sense of spaciousness, while the smaller courtyard on the north side provides unity with the room facing the courtyard to feel the transition of nature. The residents would fully enjoy the spctial experience from these two courtyards and floors with different levels.

346 Complete Works

[055]

フェスティバル 1984
festival

1. 沖縄県那覇市 | naha, okinawa
2. 設計 | design   1980.1–1983.2
3. 施工 | construction   1983.3–1984.9
4. 鉄骨鉄筋コンクリート | SRC
5. 複合商業施設 | commercial complex
6. 敷地 | site   1,658.1 m²
7. 建築 | building   1,510.7 m²
8. 延床 | total floor   7,936.4 m²

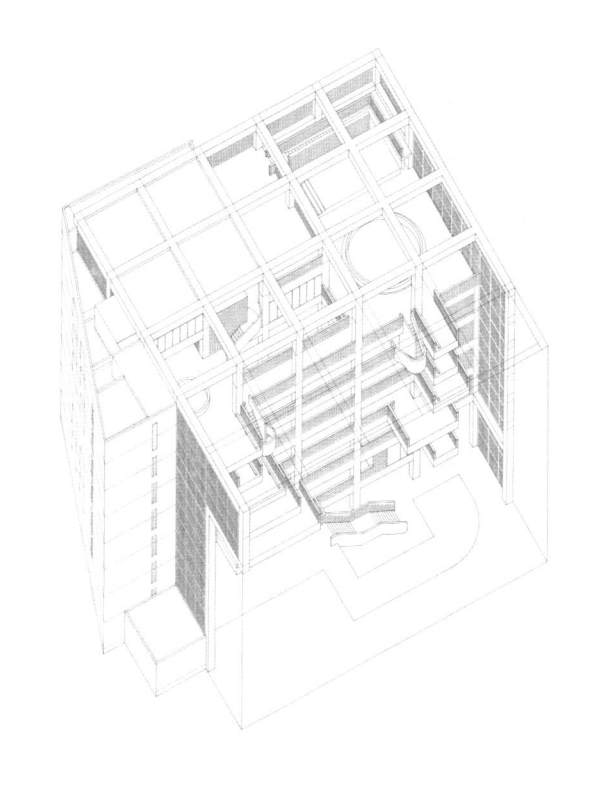

沖縄・那覇の国際通りに面して立つ。第二次世界大戦後の沖縄の主建材ブロックを多用して、当地らしい商業建築のありかたを提案した。7階までを貫く吹き抜け空間には、穴開きブロックが濾過した南国ならではの鮮烈な光線が射し込み、強い陰影がもたらされた。そのスケール感を伴った美しさは沖縄の建築にはなかったもので、的確な地脈の読解力の成果だった。屋上の広場にはガジュマルの木が緑陰をつくりだし、そこで寛ぐ若者たちの姿が見られた。

This building stands facing toward Kokusai-dori Street in Naha City, Okinawa Prefecture. The building proposed the possibility of a commercial architecture suitable to this area, by fully utilizing concrete blocks, the main buiding material in Okinawa after the World War II. In the open void space going up to the 7th floor, a brilliant daylight unique to southern regions through perforated blocks come in and a strong shadow was brought. Such aesthetics derived from a sense of scale, had not been seen in the architecture of Okinawa, while it was the result of Ando's precise comprehension of the site context. In the plaza on the rooftop, the banyan tree created a shade of green, and the young people who relax there were seen.

[056]

植条邸 1984
uejo house

1. 大阪府吹田市 | suita, osaka
2. 設計 | design   1982.1–1983.5
3. 施工 | construction   1983.7–1984.3
4. 鉄筋コンクリート（壁式） | RC (wall)
5. 住宅 | detached house
6. 敷地 | site   330.6 m²
7. 建築 | building   105.6 m²
8. 延床 | total floor   272.1 m²

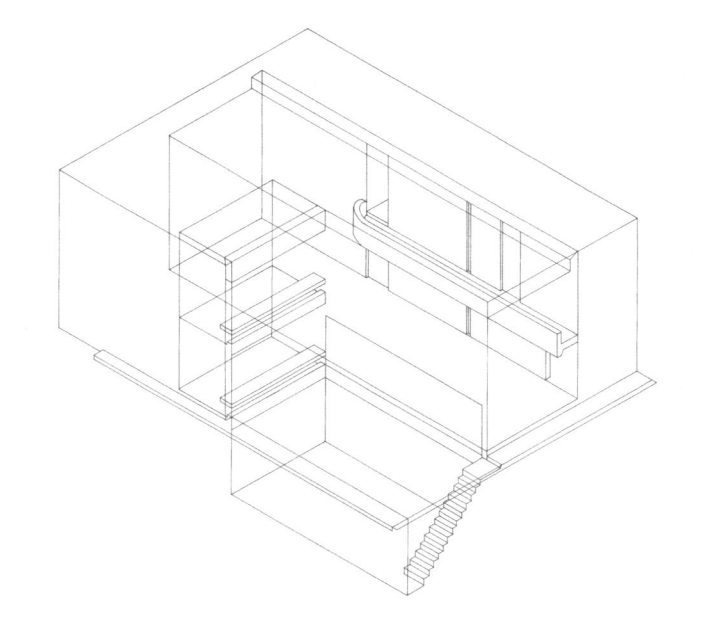

平面図を一見すると、直方体のコンクリートボックスの地階から2階までの三層を規則正しく区分して、リビングや書斎、寝室などが配置されているように見える。しかし、実際は三層すべてに部屋が配されたのは西側の部分だけで、残りは吹き抜けとテラスを大胆に各階に置いて、居室からの中庭の眺めを自然の変化によって多彩に仕立てた。明快な構成が大阪郊外の落ち着いた住宅地にふさわしい制御された美をもたらしている。

The floor plan gives an impression that a rectangular solid concrete box are systematically sectioned in three layers from the ground floor to the 2nd floor with living rooms, studies, and bed rooms. However, the rooms are actually located only on the west side in all three layers with open ceiling and terrace boldly positioned on each floor in the remaining space. The view from the courtyard has the wide variation with the seasonal transition. The distinct design provides reduced beauty adequate to the tranquil residential area in a suburb of Osaka.

[057]
太田邸　1984
ota house

1. 岡山県高梁市 | takahashi, okayama
2. 設計　design　1982.2–1983.1
3. 施工　construction　1984
4. 鉄筋コンクリート（壁式）| RC (wall)
5. 住宅 | detached house
6. 敷地 | site　137.7 m²
7. 建築 | building　71.4 m²
8. 延床 | total floor　145.9 m²

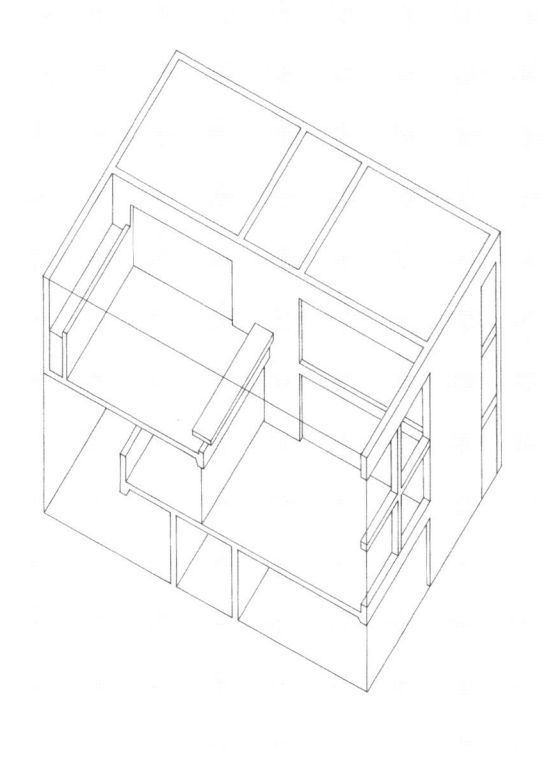

歴史の街並みで知られる岡山県の備中高梁に位置するが、周囲は密集住宅地のため、南側の表通りに壁を立て、背後に生活空間を展開する構成がとられた。正面右側の縦長の開口部は、1階では玄関、2階は和室、3階は寝室に外光をもたらす。左側の十字の格子が4分する大きな開口部は、2階の広いテラスと3階奥側の小さなテラスに光と風を運び入れる。その開放的な仕立てが、ダイニングと書斎の1階、リビングの2階、寝室の3階の暮らしに季節ごとの変化を演出している。

Although it is located in Bitchu-Takahashi where it is well-known for its historical street in Okayama Prefecture, a wall was placed on the south side by the front street and the living space was developed behind the wall since the property is in a dense residential area. The vertically long opening on the right side of the front wall provides outside light on the 1st floor entrance, 2nd floor Japanese-style room, and 3rd floor bedroom. The large opening on the left divided in four sections by a cross-shaped lattice delivers light and wind to the wide terrace on the 2nd floor and small terrace in the rear part of the 3rd floor. The design that gives spacious feeling provides variation in life according to the seasonal changes on the 1st floor with a dining room and study, 2nd floor with a living room, and 3rd floor with a bed room.

[058]
MELROSE　1984
melrose

1. 東京都目黒区 | meguro-ku, tokyo
2. 設計 | design　1982.8–1983.9
3. 施工 | construction　1983.10–1984.12
4. 鉄骨鉄筋コンクリート | SRC
5. アトリエ、事務所 | atlier, office
6. 敷地 | site　1,659.9 m²
7. 建築 | building　839.1 m²
8. 延床 | total floor　3,531.8 m²

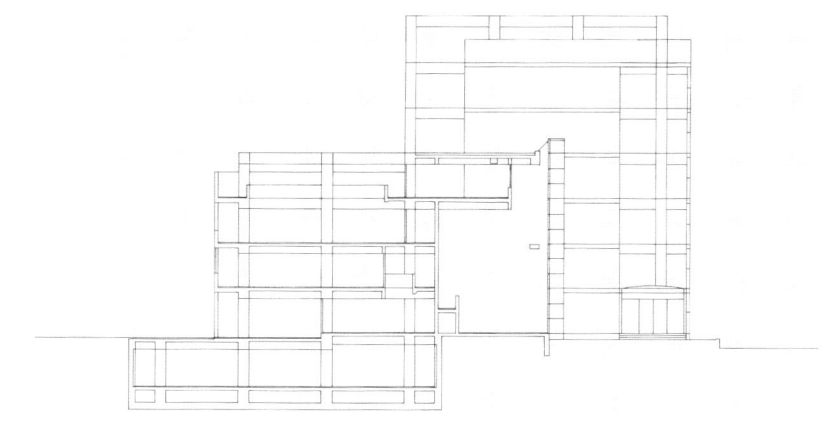

ファッションブランドのためのオフィスビルでアトリエも備える。L字型を構成する棟はそれぞれ7階と4階で高さが異なる。7階のほうに事務所機能を、4階のほうにアトリエを割り振った。両者を結びつけるのは、4分の1円の平面を持つすりガラス張りの円筒で、そこが働くひとたちが共有するアトリウムとなっている。濾過された光が内部に入ってくるため、柔らかで心地よい空間が広がっている。アトリエの2階部分はルーフガーデンに面している。

An office building for a fashion brand company with an atelier. The building is an L shape with a 7-story part and a 4-story part. The office function was arranged on the 7-story side where an atelier is on the 4-story side. The area that connects the two is a cylinder area with a quarter-circle planform that is covered by frosted glass. This area forms an atrium where people who work here share the space. Soft and comfortable space is extended here since filtered light shines inside. The 2nd floor area of the atelier is facing the roof garden.

[059]
岩佐邸　1984
iwasa house

1. 兵庫県芦屋市 | ashiya, hyogo
2. 設計 | design　1982.11–1983.10
3. 施工 | construction　1983.11–1984.6
4. 鉄筋コンクリート（壁式）| RC (wall)
5. 住宅 | detached house
6. 敷地 | site　821.4 m²
7. 建築 | building　188.0 m²
8. 延床 | total floor　235.6 m²

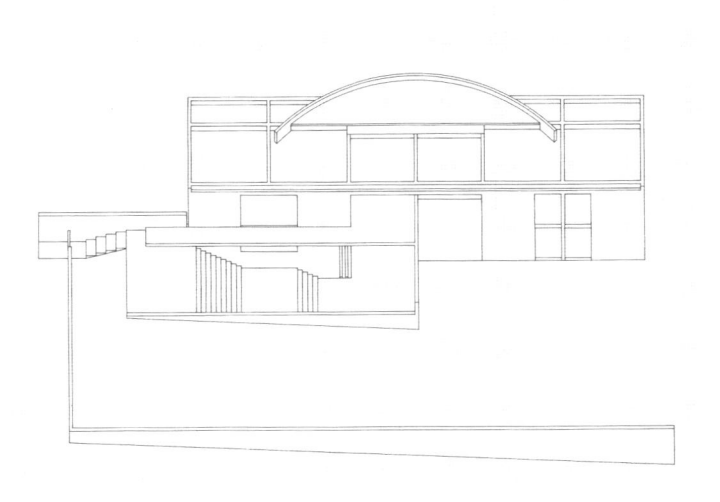

兵庫県芦屋市の国立公園の自然環境のなかに安藤のコンクリートの美学が身を横たえている。建築制限を受けて、住宅の躯体の半分は地中に埋もれているが、その抑制も手伝い、曲面壁と直方体のコンクリート打ち放しの住宅は見事な幾何学となって好もしい形で姿をのぞかせている。この曲面壁の部分は最初に完成した住宅に、6年後、ゲストルームを増築することで出現した。安藤の住宅の多くはこうした増築によって既存部分との間に魅力的な空隙の場がもたらされる。この住宅でも新旧の棟がハーモニーを奏でている。

Ando's aesthetics is expressed in the concrete placed in the natural environment of a national park in Ashiya City, Hyogo Prefecture. Although half of the building is buried in the ground due to the building restrictions, the restraint is adding to the pleasant style of outstanding geometry with curved walls and the rectangular-solid house being made of exposed concrete. These curved walls appeared when a guestroom was added to the residential house that was completed first. Many of the residential house expansion designed by Ando have attractive areas of void between the existing and new architecture, while this house has a harmonious flow between the new and old sections.

[060]
南林邸　1984
minamibayashi house

1. 奈良県生駒市 | ikoma, nara
2. 設計 | design　1983.3–1984.2
3. 施工 | construction　1984.3–1984.9
4. 鉄筋コンクリート（壁式）| RC (wall)
5. 住宅 | detached house
6. 敷地 | site　237.5 m²
7. 建築 | building　74.5 m²
8. 延床 | total floor　165.4 m²

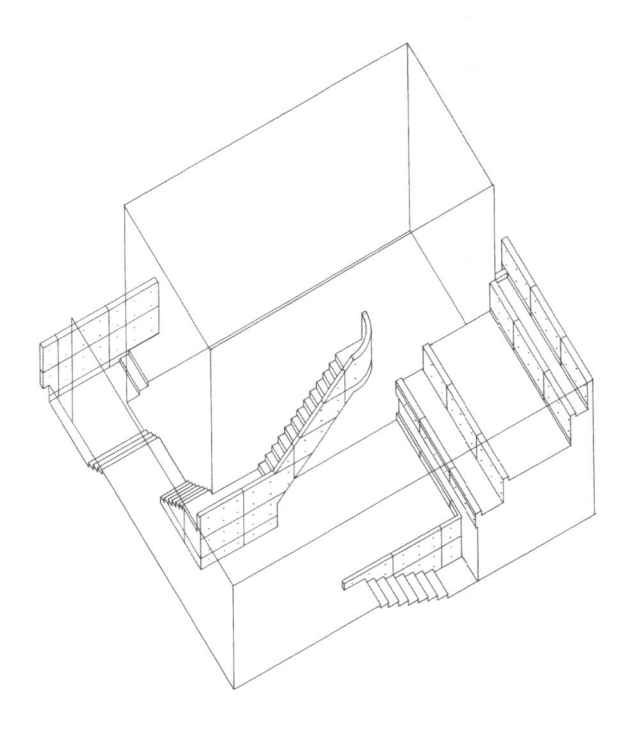

奈良県生駒市の地階を持つ三層の集合住宅。三世帯居住のため、各階でそれぞれ家族が生活する間取りが選ばれた。下層部分をコンクリート壁で囲っており、道路からは階段をあがった位置に設定された中庭に至る。そこを起点に地下に降りるエントランス、上階へ階段を昇る2戸のアプローチが設定されている。各階にリビングダイニングが配され、それぞれが中庭のオープンな空間に向き合った配置になっており、自然の恩恵を感じながら生活できる。

A three-story condominium with a basement floor in Ikoma City, Nara Prefecture. Since the house is for three families, a family layout was designed on each floor. The lower area is surrounded by concrete walls with a courtyard that can be approached by going up the stairs from the street. An entrance to go downstairs to the basement and an approach to two units by going up the stairs are provided starting from the courtyard. A living & dining room is positioned on each floor to face the open space of the courtyard to feel the gifts from nature in their daily lives.

[061]
TIME'S I, II 1984, 1991
time's I, II

1. 京都市中京区 | nakagyo-ku, kyoto
2. 設計 | design 1983.4–1983.10 (1期 phase 1)
3. 施工 | construction 1983.11–1984.9 (1期 phase 1)
4. 補強コンクリートブロック、一部鉄筋コンクリート | RC block, RC
5. 複合商業施設 | commercial complex
6. 敷地 | site 351.3 m² [phase 1], 485.8 m² [phase 2]
7. 建築 | building 289.9 m², 107.9 m²
8. 延床 | total floor 641.2 m², 274.2 m²

京都の都心を流れる高瀬川が三条通りと交差する橋のたもとに位置する。歴史ある高瀬川に背を向ける多くの商業施設と異なり、川に面した側を「表の顔」とするべく、堰堤を削って水面から四層の商業施設を立ち上げた。水が間近の地階にはオープンなテラスが設けられた。コンクリートブロックの外壁は、抽象の幾何学で構成され、控え目な清楚さをたたえて水面に向き合う。多くの来訪者が三条通りから屋外階段を通って地階のテラスまで下る姿に、地脈のひとつを「都市河川」に見出した慧眼を感じる。川に平行にヴォールト屋根が架かるところが1期、奥の一段高いドーム屋根の棟は2期の増築（1991）で付加された。

Located at the foot of a bridge where Sanjo-dori Street is crossing over Takase River going through the center of Kyoto City. On the contrary to the other commercial facilities facing its backside to the river, this building is facing toward the river to make that side as the "front façade". A dike was dismantled to build this commercial facility in 4 layers, standing from the surface of the river water. The ground floor near the water level is provided with an open terrace. The exterior wall in concrete blocks is composed in abstract geometry, facing the surface of the water with subtle cleanness This is the result of Ando's keen insight to focus on the "urban river" as one of the context of this building — reflected in the fact that many visitors are going down to the terrace on the ground floor via the exterior staircase leading from Sanjo-dori. 1st phase is the part where the vault roof is built in parallel to the river, and 2nd phase (1991) is the extension where the dome roof building is added, which is one step higher farther from the bridge.

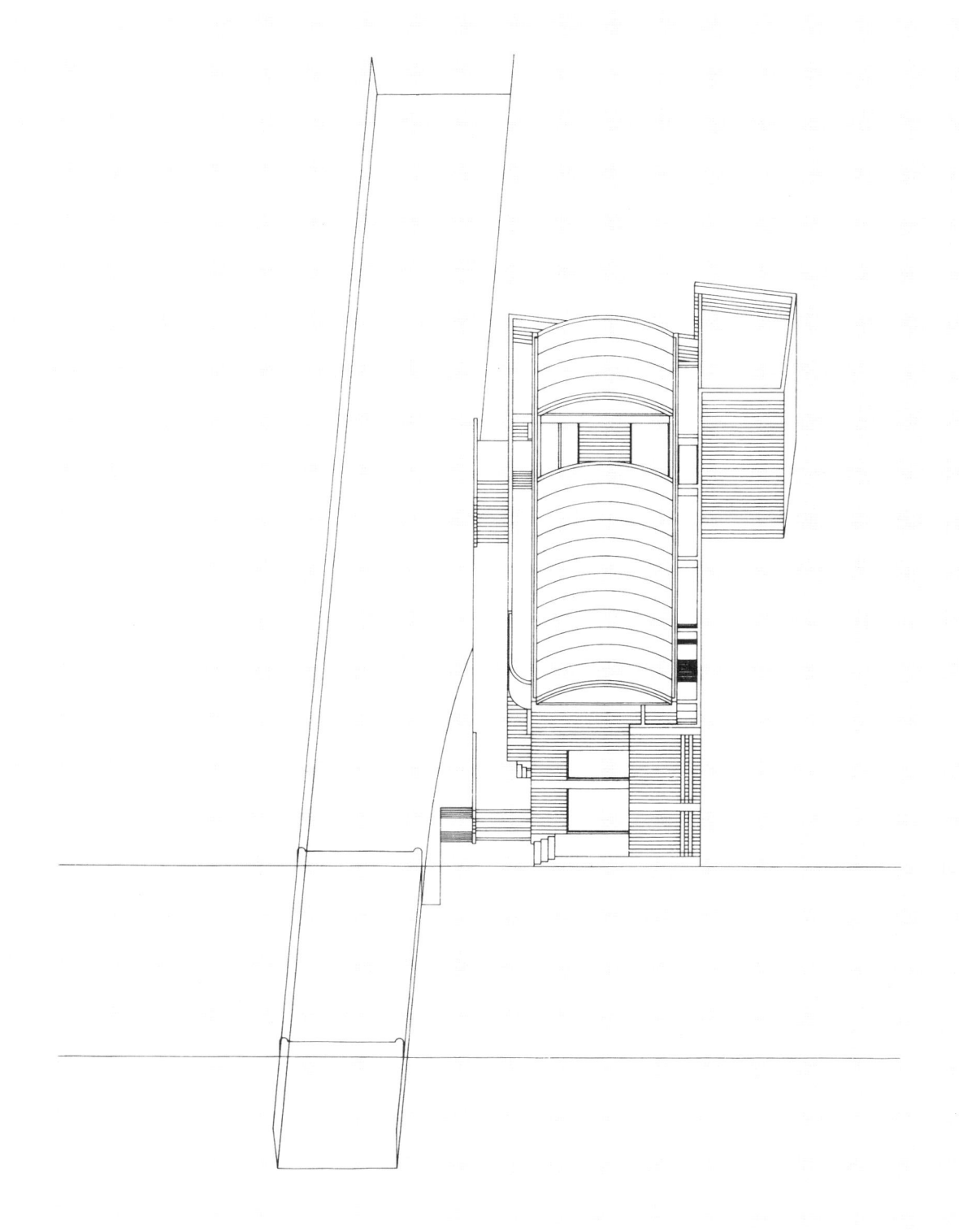

[062]
畑邸　1984
hata house

1. 兵庫県西宮市 | nishinomiya, hyogo
2. 設計 | design　1983.7–1984.2
3. 施工 | construction　1984.3–1984.9
4. 鉄筋コンクリート（壁式） | RC (wall)
5. 住宅 | detached house
6. 敷地 | site　441.5 m²
7. 建築 | building　118.7 m²
8. 延床 | total floor　207.2 m²

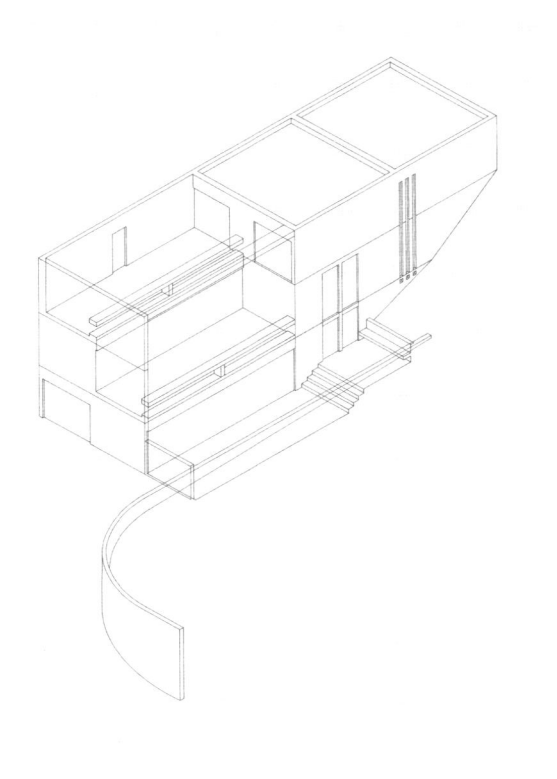

西宮市の山間部に立地する住宅。建物の後の4分の1ほどは傾斜地に埋め込まれた配置をとる。敷地は、交差する表通りに接する位置にあり、来訪者は安藤がしつらえたコンクリート打ち放しの曲面壁によってこの住宅の正面に導かれる。道路側に建てたコンクリートの壁の背後には、段状のテラスが設けられており、そこを介して豊かな自然が室内へと侵入してくる。完成から30年以上を経て、新たなオーナーの手で完成当時の姿を取り戻した。

A house located in the mountainous area of Nishinomiya City. About a 1/4 of the rear area of the building is embedded on sloping ground. The property is by an intersection of a main road. Visitors approach the entrance of the house guided by the curved wall of exposed concrete designed by Ando. Graduated terraces are provided behind the concrete wall standing by the road, from which rich nature trespasses inside the room. 30 years after completion, the original shape was recovered by the new owner.

[063]
ジュン・ポートアイランドビル
1985
jun port island building

1. 神戸市中央区 | chuo-ku, kobe
2. 設計 | design　1983.4–1984.9
3. 施工 | construction　1984.10–1985.11
4. 鉄骨鉄筋コンクリート | SRC
5. 事務所、ホール | office, auditorium
6. 敷地 | site　6,238.7 m²
7. 建築 | building　2,114.3 m²
8. 延床 | total floor　5,361.2 m²

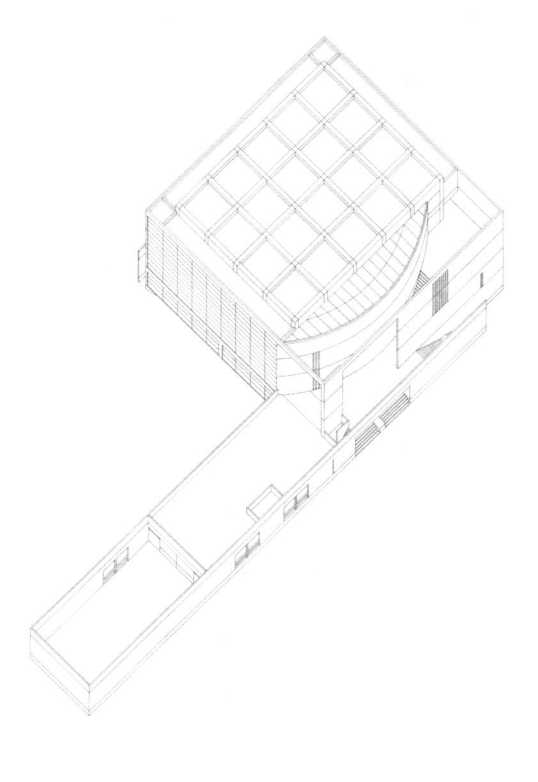

ポートアイランドは神戸市の人工埋立地。そこにファッションメーカーのオフィスビルを設計するにあたって、安藤は敷地の半分を緑地とし、築山を配して起伏を持たせた。とりつくしまのない茫漠たる埋立地に、建築の拠って立つところを、背後の六甲山の緑に呼応する形でつくりだすことが重要と判断したからである。密集した市街地で闘う姿勢を表明するコンクリートボックスとは異なる開放感のなか、幾何学の美がのびやかだ。吹き抜けを活かした開放的なオフィスも立地に似つかわしい。

Port Island is a reclaimed land in Kobe City. To design an office building for a fashion manufacturer, Ando created a greenery area on half of the property and placed an artificial hill to have undulating areas. He considered important to form an area that resonates the greenery of Mt. Rokko rising behind the building on a reclaimed land that is left utterly obscure. Geometric beauty is presented in a spacious atmosphere that differs from concrete boxes that express an aggressive attitude in concentrated urban areas. Offices with openness using the wellhole style gives an atmosphere suitable for the surrounding sites.

[064]

中山邸　1985
nakayama house

1. 奈良県奈良市 | nara, nara
2. 設計 | design　1983.6–1984.7
3. 施工 | construction　1984.10–1985.4
4. 鉄筋コンクリート（壁式）| RC (wall)
5. 住宅 | detached house
6. 敷地 | site　263.3㎡
7. 建築 | building　69.1㎡
8. 延床 | total floor　103.7㎡

京都と奈良の境に位置する住宅地の一角を立地とする。ごく日常的な,周辺の風景を安藤は「散漫」と受けとめ、それとは一線を画す発想で、コンクリートの直方体で周囲との遮断を選択した。この直方体の外側にコンクリートの独立壁を配して、居住者が自らの敷地に足を踏み入れると、直ちに純化された住空間に入り込むように仕立てた。内部には直方体の棟のコンクリート壁によって視界を切り取ったテラスが配され、郊外生活における暮らしの場の提案とした。

Located in a residential area on the border of Kyoto and Nara. Ando takes normal surrounding scenery as "loose" and he selected to use a rectangular solid made of concrete to draw a line from the surroundings. An independent concrete wall is placed outside this rectangular solid where once the residents step inside their property, they will enter their refined living space. A terrace that cuts the view with a concrete wall of the rectangular solid building is provided to propose the living space in a suburban area.

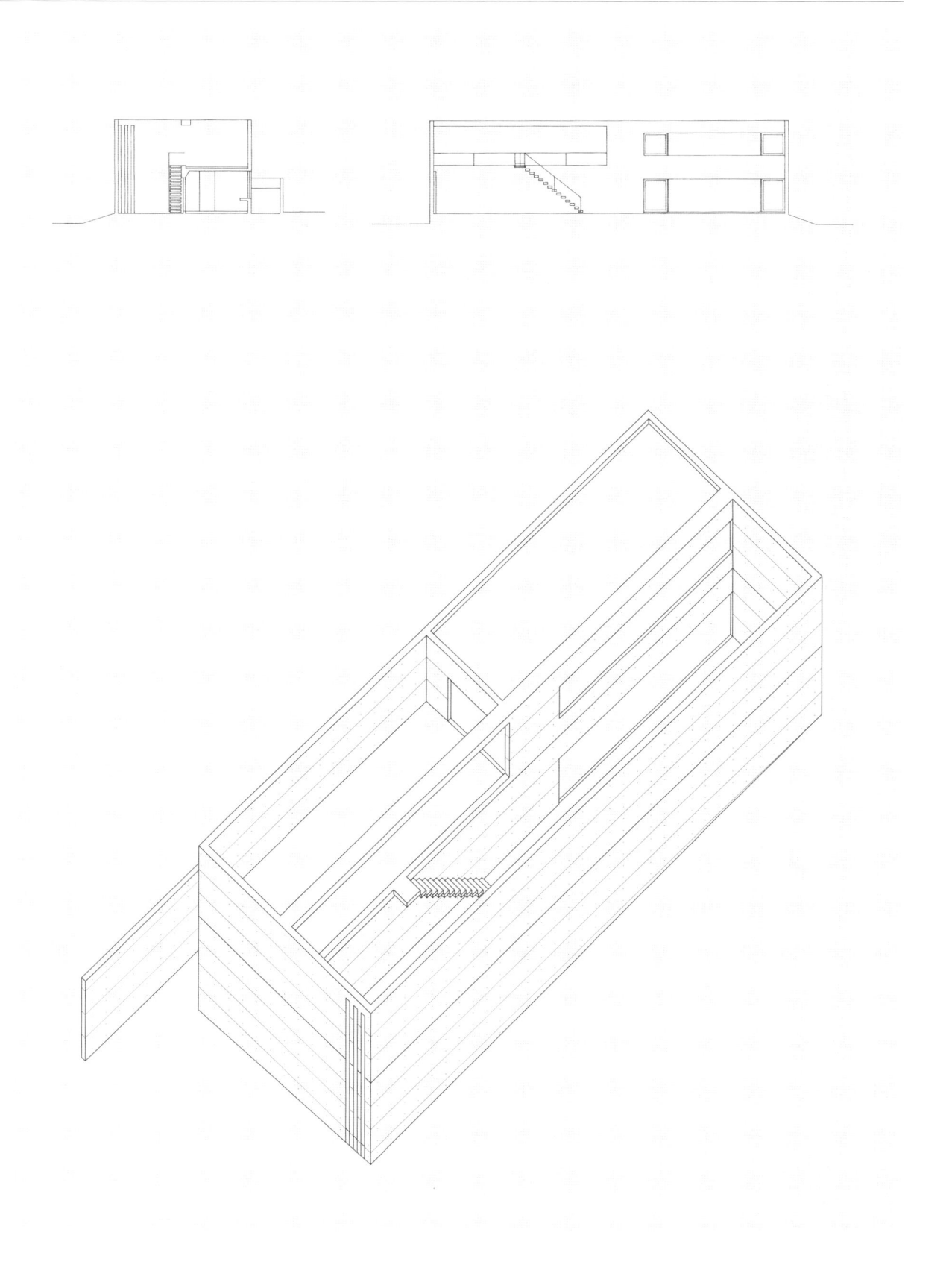

346 Complete Works

[065]

アトリエ・ヨシエ・イナバ　1985
atelier yoshie inaba

1. 東京都渋谷区 | shibuya-ku, tokyo
2. 設計 | design　1983.5–1984.4
3. 施工 | construction　1984.5–1985.4
4. 鉄筋コンクリート | RC
5. 事務所 | office
6. 敷地 | site　374.0 m²
7. 建築 | building　181.9 m²
8. 延床 | total floor　756.2 m²

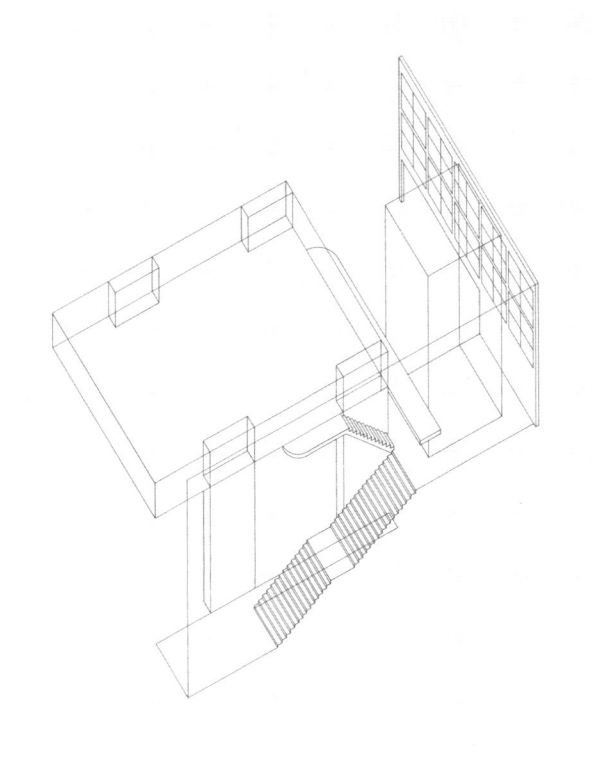

ファッションデザイナーのアトリエの建築。渋谷の住宅街の環境を考慮して、コンクリート打ち放しの全体の形態を単純化したうえで、ヴォリュームの半分を地下に配した。通りに面した壁はコンクリートの美しいグリッドに厳密なプロポーションに基づいて、規則正しくならぶすりガラスの大きな窓が設えられ、アトリエの「顔」となった。この壁の背後は街路と繋がる開放的な中庭であり、それを視覚的に確認させる吹き放ちの仕立ても上出来だった。

This is an atelier building for a fashion designer. In the consideration of the residential neighborhood of this Shibuya area, the entire volume of exposed concrete finish was simplified and half of the volume was placed underground. Frosted glass windows were set up in a beautiful grid of concrete on the wall facing the street, based on strict proportions, which became the "face" of this atelier building. Behind this wall is an open courtyard connected to the street, and it is well articulated to enable visual recognition of the courtyard space through its column-free design.

[066]

モン・プティ・シュ　1985
mon-petit-chou

1. 京都市左京区 | sakyo-ku, kyoto
2. 設計 | design　1983.6–1984.11
3. 施工 | construction　1984.12–1985.4
4. 鉄筋コンクリート | RC
5. 店舗 | shop
6. 敷地 | site　516.8 m²
7. 建築 | building　180.4 m²
8. 延床 | total floor　322.9 m²

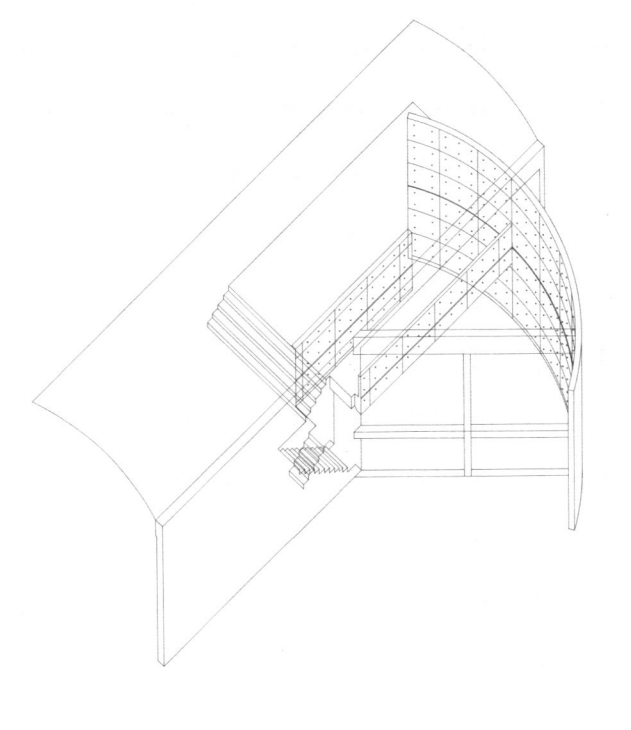

京都市北部の住宅地に位置するケーキハウス。コリドーを思わせる6分の1円のヴォールト屋根の架かる細長い棟がメインで、その背後の脇に4分の1円の円筒の棟が交錯する。来訪者はエントランスに近いショップを抜けて、背後の地下への吹き抜けになった客席ホールに至る。隠されたかのようなホールは大きな窓から地下レベルの植栽を堪能することができる。都市のなかの憩いの空間がきめ細かな配慮で設定されている。

A cake house located in a residential area in the north part of Kyoto City. The long narrow building with a one-sixth-circle vault roof that resembles a corridor is the main section where a building of a quarter circle is intersecting on the side at the at the back. Visitors pass through the shop near the entrance and arrive at the hall where it has a wellhole to the basement level at the back. Plants on the basement level can be enjoyed from a large window of the hall that seems to be hidden in the building. A refreshing space in the city is arranged with careful consideration.

[067]
青葉台アトリエ　1985
aobadai atelier

1. 東京都目黒区 | meguro-ku, tokyo
2. 設計 | design　1983.11–1984.4
3. 施工 | construction　1984.4–1985.2
4. 鉄筋コンクリート | RC
5. アトリエ | atelier
6. 敷地 | site　191.4 m²
7. 建築 | building　138.3 m²
8. 延床 | total floor　520.3 m²

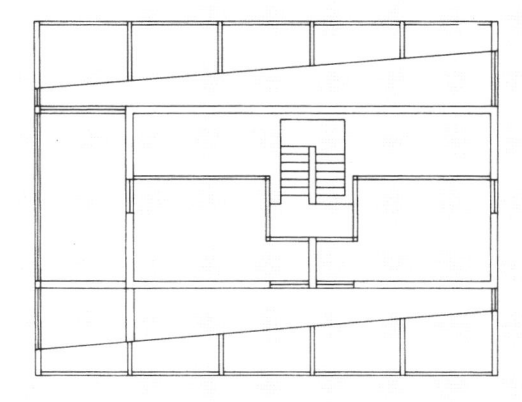

ファッションブランド、BIGIのアトリエ。東京・目黒の住宅地に位置した。角地の立地に、コンクリートのフレームが区切るガラスブロックの外壁が質感を伴って屹立、軒から最頂部までは傾斜したガラスのトップライトの壁が続く。モダニズムの極致としてのグラスハウスが創造的なイメージを漂わせる。最上階と直下の階は吹き抜けで、最上階の壁際は光あふれる開放的な廊下になっている。地階にもガラスブロックを透過した自然光が入り込む。

This is an atelier of fashion brand BIGI, located in a residential area in Meguro, Tokyo. Glass block exterior walls, partitioned by concrete frames, stand with texture feelings at the corner site. A sloped glass wall with skylights continues from the eaves to the tip. The glass house — the pinnacle of modernism — has a creative image. The topmost level and the level underneath have open ceilings. An open and well-lit corridor is located by a wall on the topmost level. Natural light through the glass block reaches to the underground level as well.

[068]
吉本邸　1985
yoshimoto house

1. 大阪市西区 | nishi-ku, osaka
2. 設計　design　1984.3–1984.12
3. 施工 | construction　1984.12–1985.12
4. 鉄筋コンクリート（壁式）| RC (wall)
5. 住宅　detached house
6. 敷地 | site　41.3 m²
7. 建築 | building　28.7 m²
8. 延床 | total floor　62.1 m²

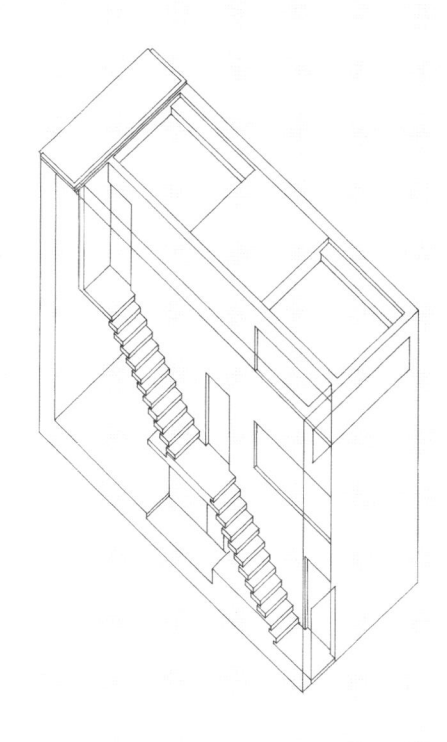

立地は大阪下町。間口も狭く、奥行きも短い。その限界のある条件のなかで実現したコンクリートボックスの戸建て住宅。1階にリビングダイニング、2階は床を切って面積を半分程度にした寝室、3階も最奥の床を切り欠いた寝室とした。この吹き抜けを介して、屋上のトップライトからの自然光が各階に届けられ、狭さのもたらす息苦しさから生活を解放している。各階の移動はすべて屋外階段によるもので、最小限住宅の厳しさが見てとれる。

The property is in the old area of Osaka with a narrow width and short length. A concrete box residential house created within the limit of the dimensional condition. A living & dining room is placed on the 1st floor, a bed room by cutting the floor area in about half is placed on the 2nd floor, and another bedroom with the rear-end floor cut off is positioned in the 3rd floor. Through this wellhole structure, natural light is distributed throughout each floor from an open ceiling, which is liberating from the suppressing atmosphere from the narrow space. An outdoor stairway is used to move to the next floor showing the severity of a minimum housing.

[069]
大淀の茶室（ベニヤ、ブロック、テント）
1985, 1986, 1988
tea house in oyodo (veneer, block, tent)

1. 大阪市北区 | kita-ku, osaka
5. 茶室 | tea-ceremony room

事務所に近い木造民家の屋上に、ペントハウス状に飛び出す「ベニヤの茶室」と「テントの茶室」が、そして、屋内の1階には入れ子の形で「ブロックの茶室」がつくられた。数寄の精神とは建築における自由と安藤は述べている。「テントの和室」は、切妻屋根の棟木に載り、強い風が吹けば飛んで行ってしまいそうな危うさだ。重量感のない仮の素材なればこそ茶室の数寄の感覚は強まる。「ベニヤの茶室」も屋根勾配のうえに飛び出している。形は「妙喜庵待庵」に由来する五尺八寸の円弧を描いて決定された。危うい素材なればこそ、日本的な寸法は身体化された空間のモジュールとして認識されうると安藤は語る。

A wooden house with TEA HOUSE IN OYODO (TENT TEA HOUSE) and TEA HOUSE IN OYODO (VENEER TEA HOUSE) that protrude out like a penthouse on a rooftop and a nested shape TEA HOUSE IN OYODO (BLOCK TEA HOUSE) on the 1st floor was built close to the office. Ando described that the freedom in architecture is the spirit of refined taste. The TENT TEA HOUSE looks unstable since it is placed on top of the ridge beam on an inclined roof and it may be blown away by strong wind. Temporary light materials emphasize the refined taste of a tea house. The VENEER TEA HOUSE is protruding from the slant of the roof. The shape was determined by drawing a circular arc of about 176cm; the dimension derived from Myokian Taian. Ando said that Japanese dimensions can be recognized as the module for physicalized space only when using unstable materials.

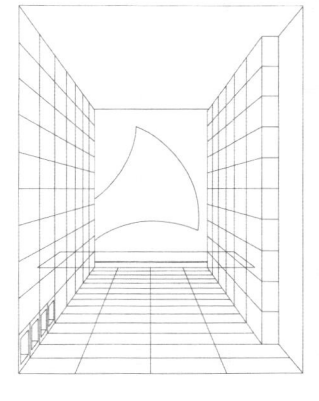

ブロックの茶室 1986 | block tea house

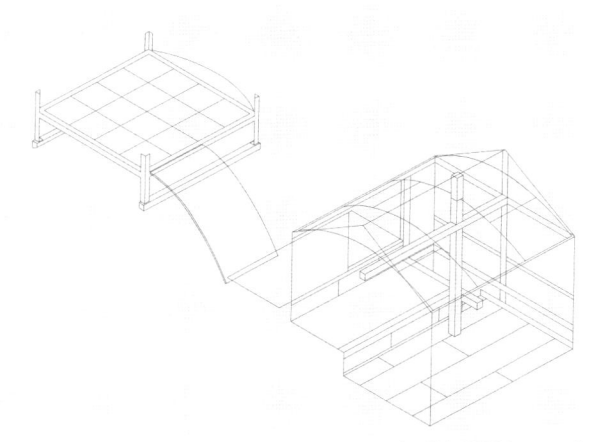

テントの茶室 1988 | tent tea house

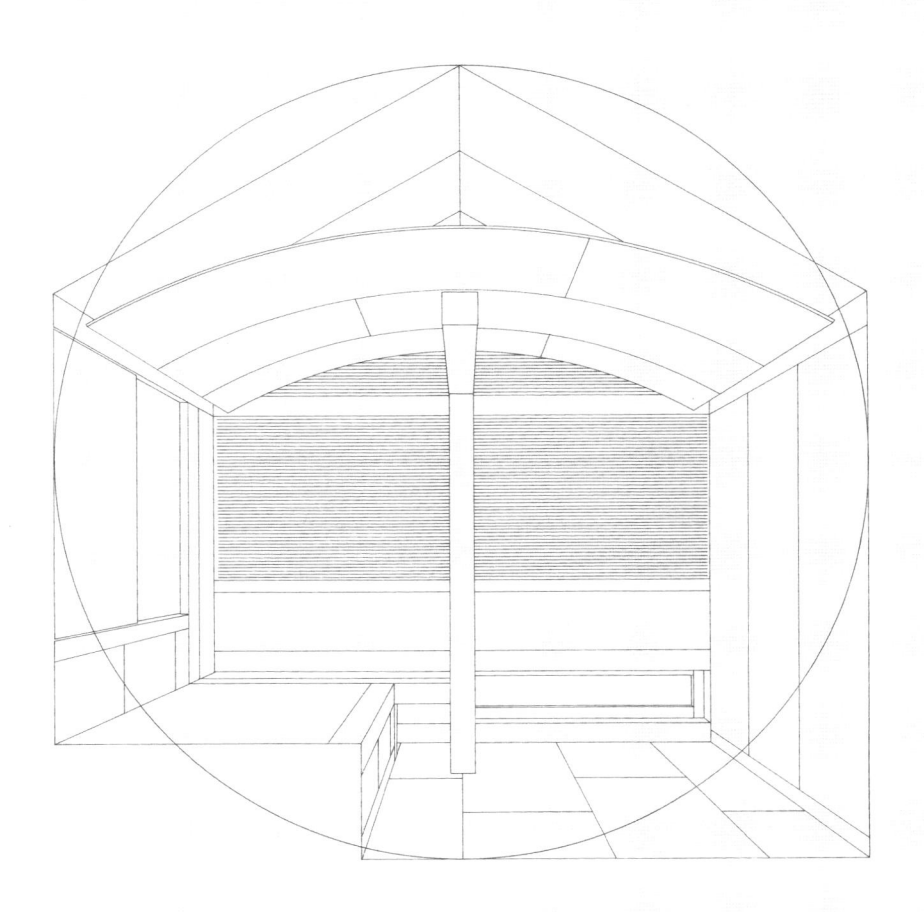

ベニヤの茶室 1985 | veneer tea house

[070]
服部邸ゲストハウス　1985
guest house for hattori house

1. 大阪市阿倍野区 | abeno-ku, osaka
2. 設計 | design　1984.10–1985.3
3. 施工 | construction　1985.6–1985.12
4. 鉄筋コンクリート〈壁式ラーメン構造〉
   RC (wall-type frame structure)
5. ゲストハウス | guest house
7. 建築 | building　32.3 m²
8. 延床 | total floor　68.3 m²

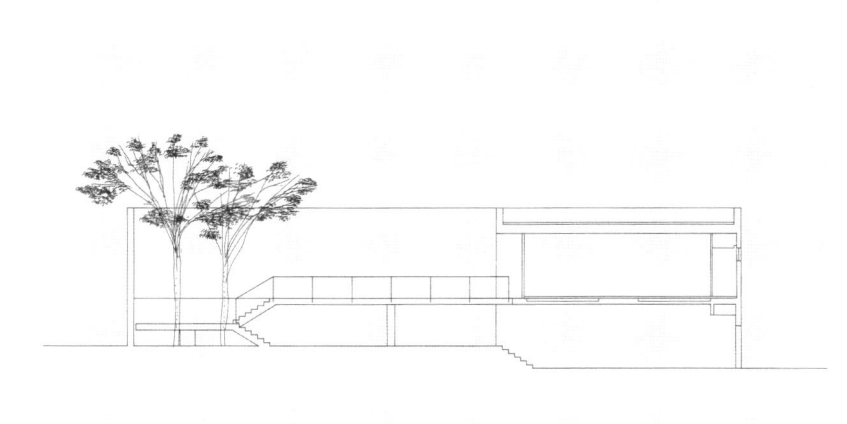

既存の木造住宅をコンクリートの壁で囲い、その壁の一角にゲストハウスを増築した。ゲストハウスは近隣のひとびとが集まるお茶やお花の会のためのスペース。訪問者は既存の住宅の脇を飛び石伝いで抜けて敷地の背後まで行き、そこから塀沿いに進んで階段を上がり、ブリッジ上をさらに歩いて、ゲストハウスにたどりつく。安藤はゲストハウスの床の高さを既存の住宅の中二階に合わせ、付加される新しい建築の量塊感の緩和に努めた。

Concrete walls were built to surround the existing wooden house and a guesthouse was added to one corner of the wall. The guesthouse is a space where neighbors visit to enjoy tea parties and flower arrangement gatherings. To approach the guesthouse, visitors need to follow the stepping stones along the side of the preexisting house to the back of the property, walk along the fence, go up the stairs, walk farther on the bridge and enter the guesthouse. Ando made the floor height of the guesthouse to match the mezzanine floor of the preexisting house to mitigate the massive impression of the added new architecture.

[071]
渋谷プロジェクト　1985
shibuya project

1. 東京都渋谷区 | shibuya-ku, tokyo
2. 設計 | design　1985.4–1987.3
3. 構想案 | concept
4. 鉄筋コンクリート | RC
5. 複合商業施設 | commercial complex
6. 敷地　site　1,130.7 m²
7. 建築　building　867.1 m²
8. 延床　total floor　6,210.1 m²

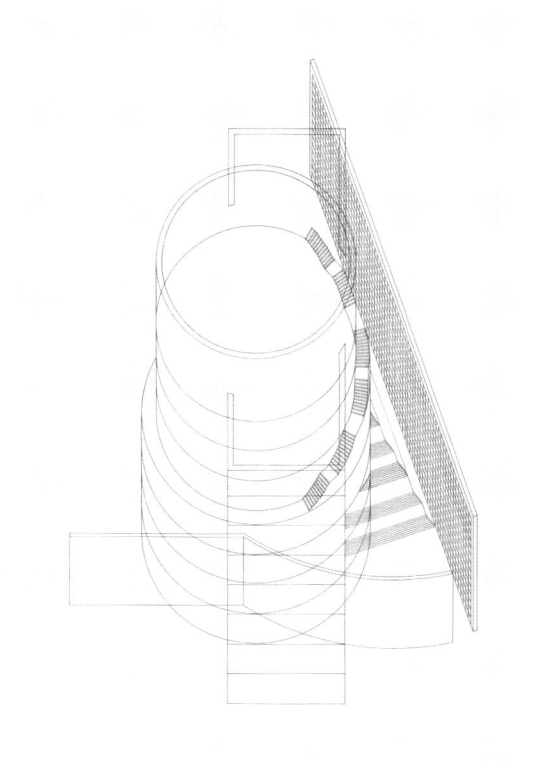

地上四層、地下十層の複合商業ビルの提案。地下に比重を置く建築の構成は、高さ制限で地上階の上限が四層なのを受け、地下に空間の自由度を求める発想で構想された。道路境界に建てるガラスブロックのスクリーンと建物本体の間は地下三層までの屋外階段とし、それを主動線に設定した。安藤は活動の初期に訪れたインドで体験した地下の井戸の空間的な醍醐味に感動して、光が地表から深く射し込む地下建築の実現を期していた。その後の地下空間を主題とする建築のプロトタイプがここに認められる。

A proposal of a complex commercial building with four levels aboveground and ten levels underground. The building has a structure with more levels underground, which comes from an idea to obtain spatial freedom underground since the height regulation allows for only four levels above the ground. The area between the glass block screen on the border by the road and the main building will have an exterior stairway up and down to the third underground level and set as the main flow line. Ando was touched by the spatial attractiveness of an underground well in India when he visited during his initial period of his activity and he was waiting for an occasion to materialize the underground space where light shines down deep from the ground surface.

[072]

城戸崎邸　1986
kidosaki house

1. 東京都世田谷区 | setagaya-ku, tokyo
2. 設計 | design　1982.10–1985.10
3. 施工 | construction　1985.10–1986.10
4. 鉄筋コンクリート（壁式）| RC (wall)
5. 住宅 | detached house
6. 敷地 | site　610.9 m²
7. 建築 | building　351.5 m²
8. 延床 | total floor　556.1 m²

戸建て住宅を代表する作品のひとつ。東京・世田谷の住宅地の一角を占めるこの邸宅は、3家族が独立しながら、お互いの存在を感じられるコンドミニアムでの暮らしを想定して設計された。正方形に近い敷地を囲う塀としてのコンクリート壁の内側に、躯体の本体となる曲面壁を挿入することで生まれる余白が、住宅内に自然の移ろいを導き入れ、同時に、家族間の気配を感じさせる装置となっている。安藤は、住人が幾何立体を身体化する仕掛けとして迷路性をあげており、余白がその役割を担う。現代生活における家族相互のありかたを問いかける意欲的な住宅作品となった。

One of Ando's works that represents his detached residence architecture. This house that is located in a residential area of Setagaya, Tokyo was designed imagining life in a condominium that allows three families to live independently while feeling the existence of one another. Curved walls of the main building placed inside the concrete walls surrounding the nearly square property creates a space, where it brings changes of nature in the house and also becomes a device to let families feel the existence of each other. Ando described that a labyrinth structure is the trigger to make the residents to physicalize a geometric body. In this case, the space plays that role. It is an aspirational residential house work that questions the mutual relationship of families of modern life.

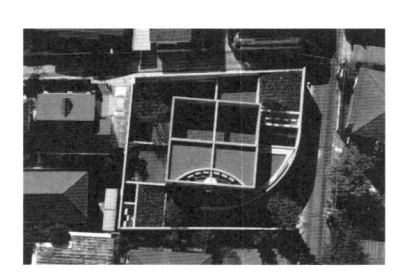

[073]
福原病院　1986
fukuhara clinic

1. 東京都世田谷区 | setagaya-ku, tokyo
2. 設計 | design　1981.9–1985.8
3. 施工 | construction　1985.9–1986.12
4. 鉄骨鉄筋コンクリート | SRC
5. 病院 | hospital
6. 敷地 | site　627.0 m²
7. 建築 | building　424.2 m²
8. 延床 | total floor　2,638.7 m²

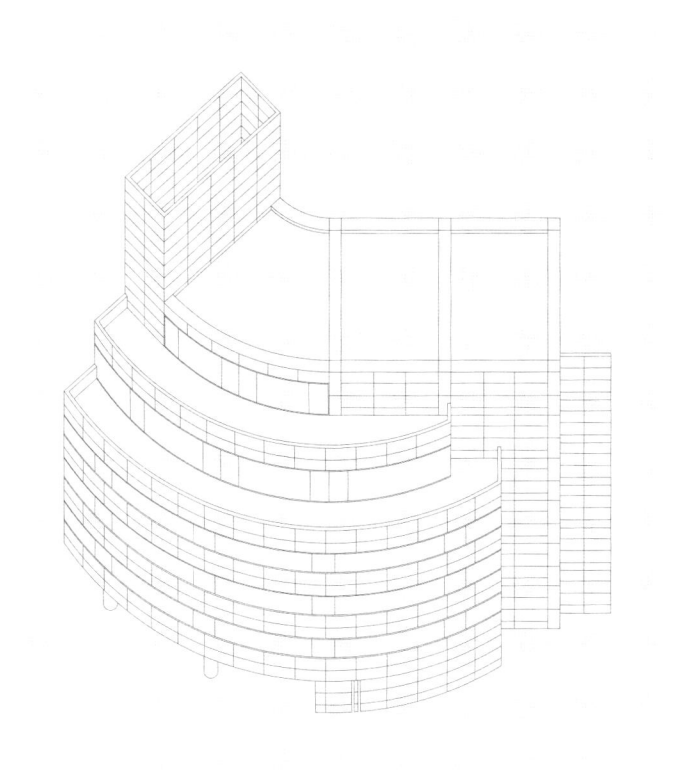

東京・下北沢近傍のリハビリテーションのための病院。カーブを描く道路の角地に位置していることを受けて外壁は曲面としている。この曲面壁の背後の診察、運動療法室、病室の入る部分は、グリッドを基本とした空間で、上下の空間を一体化させ、地階の緑化空間につながる吹き抜けが背後に配されている。曲面壁の内部には、3階に横長窓からの光が射し込む吹き抜けのカフェテリア、地階には機能回復のためのプールが配され、開放感あふれる空間となっている。

A rehabilitation hospital located close to Shimokitazawa, Tokyo. The exterior wall is curved since the property is on a corner of a curved road. The consultation room, therapeutic exercise room, and entrance to patient's rooms behind the curved wall are arranged in a grid form and an open ceiling where the upper and lower space is unified, connecting to the greenery area on the ground floor is provided at the back. Inside the curved wall has a liberating space with an open ceiling cafeteria on the 3rd floor with light shining in from wide windows and a pool for functional recovery on the ground floor.

[074]
リランズゲート　1986
riran's gate

1. 神戸市中央区 | chuo-ku, kobe
2. 設計 | design　1984.1–1984.11
3. 施工 | construction　1985.1–1986.3
4. 鉄筋コンクリート | RC
5. 複合商業施設 | commercial complex
6. 敷地 | site　620.3 m²
7. 建築 | building　367.6 m²
8. 延床 | total floor　2,079.7 m²

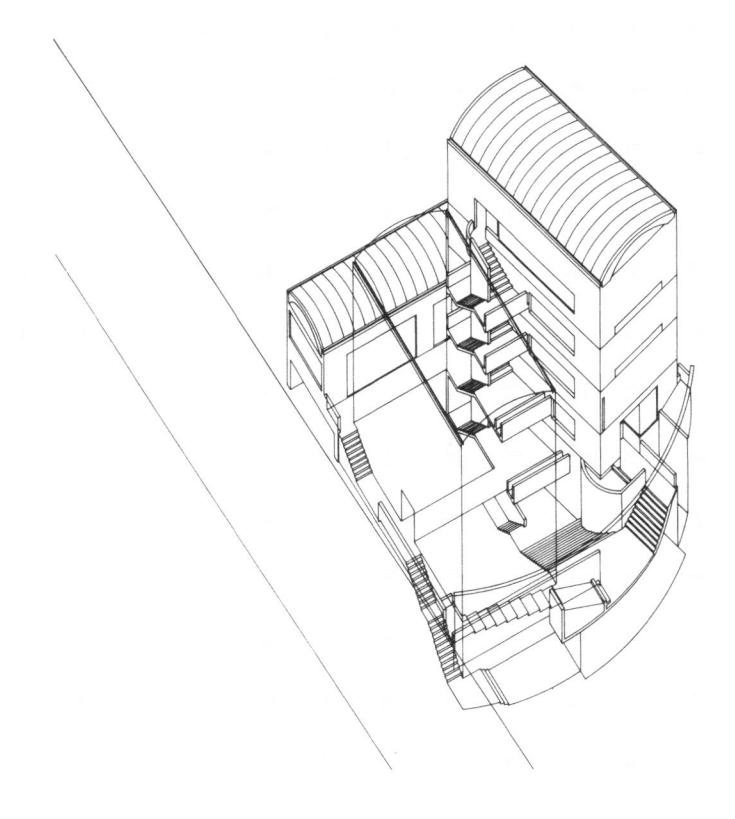

神戸北野町には、一連の商業建築のスタートとなった「ローズガーデン」から「リランズゲート」まで7件の安藤の作品が勢ぞろいする。「リランズゲート」は、コンクリート打ち放しの躯体に、三つのヴォールト屋根が架かる。うち二つは建物の前の坂道に沿う方向に配した棟の屋根として設えられ、もうひとつは二つの棟の南側の低層部分に載る。1階にギャラリー、2階より上には店舗・オフィスなどがあるが、二つの棟の空隙の広場、上階に進むに連れてセットバックする棟に合わせた通路などが、小さな建築に迷路の感覚を実現している。

Seven of Ando's works exist in Kitano-cho, Kobe from ROSE GARDEN that iritiated series of commercial buildings to RIRAN'S GATE. Three vault roofs are set on exposed concrete structures of the RIRAN'S GATE. Two of those roofs are placed on the building positioned perpendicularly to the hill road in front of the building and the other roof is on the lower area on the south side of the building. A gallery is arranged on the 1st floor and stores and offices are on the floors from the 2nd floor up. The plaza in the gap between the two buildings and passages according to the buildings that have been set backward as they go upstairs brings a feeling of being inside a maze to enjoy various passageways.

[075]

沖辺邸　1986
okibe house

1. 大阪市北区 | kita-ku, osaka
2. 設計 | design　1984.1–1985.9
3. 施工 | construction　1985.10–1986.9
4. 鉄筋コンクリート（壁式）| RC (wall)
5. 住宅 | detached house
6. 敷地 | site　89.6 m²
7. 建築 | building　64.0 m²
8. 延床 | total floor　245.7 m²

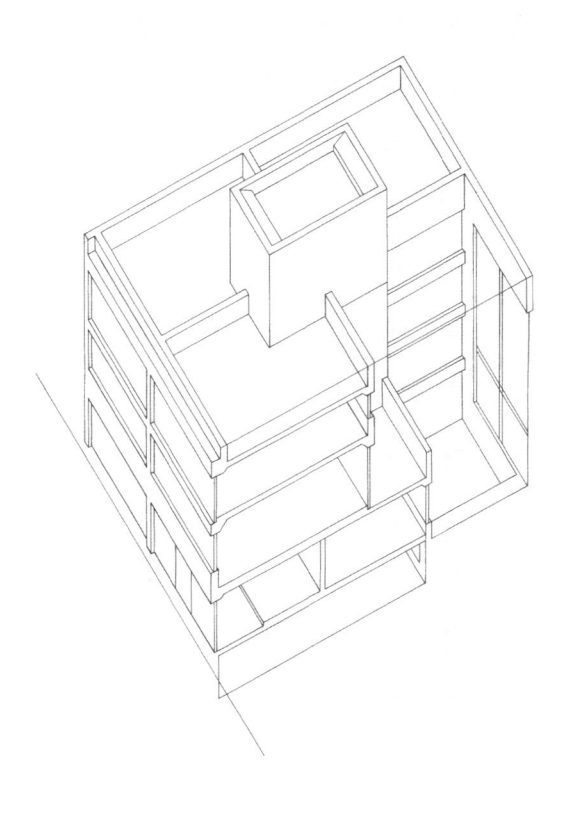

大阪市北区の市街地に位置する戸建て住宅。家並みのなかにコンクリートボックスがはめ込まれ、道路からは正面だけを望むことができる。玄関を入り内部に進むと階段は中央に配され、各階の間取りは階段を中心に「田の字」に4等分された。特筆すべきは各階の床を2分する間取りで、二つに分けた床の落差は80センチ近くに設定されている。階高が2メートル20センチ前後なので大胆な仕立てだが、それによって小住宅を超えた空間構成が実現した。

A residential house located in an urban area of Kita Ward, Osaka City. A concrete box is inserted in rows of houses where only the front face can be seen from the road. The stairway is positioned at the center after entering the entrance and the layout of each room is equally sectioned in four squares with the stairway at the center. The highlight is the structure of each floor, separated in half where the height difference is about 80cm between the two separated floors. A bold spatial structure is provided in the floor height of 2.2 meters creating a spatial structure that exceeds the scale of a small residence.

[076]

孫邸　1986
son house

1. 大阪市天王寺区 | tennoji-ku, osaka
2. 設計 | design　1984.9–1985.4
3. 施工 | construction　1985.5–1986.3
4. 鉄筋コンクリート（壁式）| RC (wall)
5. 住宅 | detached house
6. 敷地 | site　103.3 m²
7. 建築 | building　85.2 m²
8. 延床 | total floor　206.5 m²

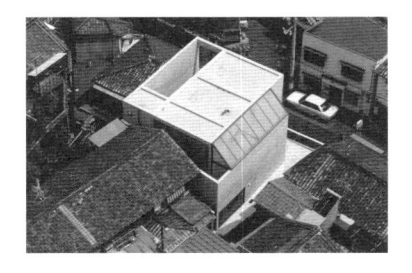

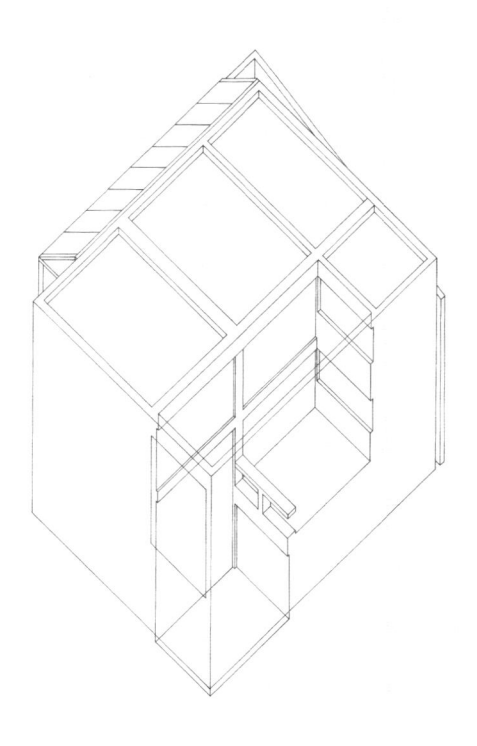

大阪市天王寺区の市街地の角地に位置する戸建て住宅。3階建てのコンクリートボックスの中心の位置に、1階は和室と付属の水回り、2階に食堂、3階には寝室という生活機能を配して、それぞれが光の射し込むテラスに面する間取りとした。守りの固さを思わせる外観のなかに、季節の変化が投影する仕立てになっている。軒回りに大きくとったガラスのトップライトが昇降のための階段を開放的な装置とするとともに道路側の表情を柔和にする役割も果たす。

A residential house located in an urban corner of Tennoji Ward, Osaka City. Necessary functions for daily life are arranged at the center of the three-story concrete box such as a Japanese-style room and plumbing on the 1st floor, dining room on the 2nd floor, and bed room on the 3rd floor. Each room is facing the terrace to have the light shine inside. Changes of the seasons are projected in the appearance that gives an impression of solid protection. Top light by large windows around the eaves transforms the stairway for going upstairs and downstairs to a device that adds spaciousness inside the house and softens the impression from the road side.

[077]
佐々木邸　1986
sasaki house

1. 東京都港区 | minato-ku, tokyo
2. 設計 | design　1984.9–1985.8
3. 施工 | construction　1985.10–1986.7
4. 補強コンクリートブロック | RC block
5. 住宅 | detached house
6. 敷地 | site　382.1 m²
7. 建築 | building　227.1 m²
8. 延床 | total floor　373.1 m²

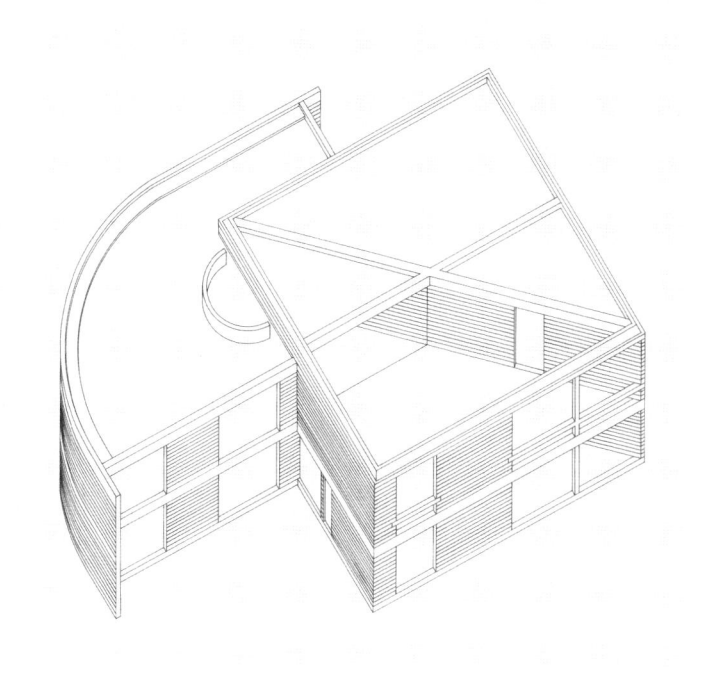

東京・南麻布の住宅街に位置しているが、敷地が三叉路に面して交通量が多く、暮らしの防御を担うコンクリートブロックの曲面壁が、この住宅の性格を端的に物語っている。曲面壁の円筒の棟は内部に平面が4分の1円のリビングを抱え、そこには正方形平面の生活空間を配したもう一つの棟がズレを持たせて配置されている。この二つの棟は、正方形の対角線方向の動線で結ばれており、それが住空間に変化をもたらしている。

Although the house is located in a residential area in Minamiazabu, Tokyo, the property is facing a three-way junction with heavy traffic. The curved concrete block wall that protects the life of residents straightforwardly depicts the characteristics of this house. Inside the cylindrical building of this curved wall has a living room in which the planform is a quarter-circle and another building with a square living space is attached in an offset position. These two buildings are connected with a flow line in diagonal direction of the square providing another variation in the living space.

[078]
太陽セメント本社ビル　1986
taiyo-cement headquarters building

1. 大阪市福島区 | fukushima-ku, osaka
2. 設計 | design　1984.10–1985.10
3. 施工 | construction　1985.10–1986.9
4. 枠型コンクリートブロック、鉄筋コンクリート | fill-up concrete-block, RC
5. 事務所 | office
6. 敷地 | site　1,059.3 m²
7. 建築 | building　300.6 m²
8. 延床 | total floor　742.6 m²

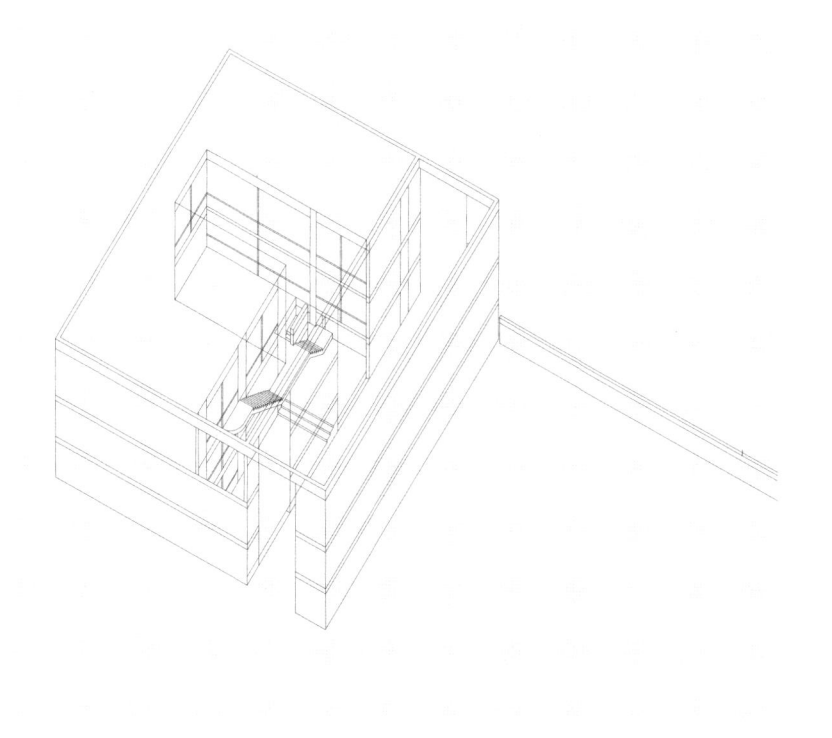

自社製品のブロックを用いた建材メーカーの本社ビル。表通りから見通せる中庭にコンクリートの立体的なグリッドを配して建築の骨格を暗示し、外装材にブロックを採用した。重厚な仕立ては風格さえ漂わせ、ブロックの表現の可能性を最大限に引き出している。オフィス空間の構成は、外部空間の扱いとなっている中庭（ガラス屋根が張られている）に主階段を配して、働くひとびとは一度そこに出て、オフィス内を行き来する。

This is the headquarters building of a building material manufacture, using blocks of their own products. 3 dimensional concrete grid structure is placed in the courtyard visible from the street, the framework of this building is implied, and the block for the exterior material is adopted. The building in dignified style represents a distinguished atmosphere even for its small scale, and brings out the possibilities of expression of block to the maximum. The composition of the office space is to arrange the main staircase placed in this courtyard which works as the external space (the ceiling of the courtyard is covered by a glass roof), and working people go out into the external space once and go around inside the office.

[079]

六甲の教会　1986
chapel on mt. rokko

1. 神戸市灘区 | nada-ku, kobe
2. 設計 | design　1985.1–1985.7
3. 施工 | construction　1985.8–1986.3
4. 鉄筋コンクリート | RC
5. 教会 | church
6. 敷地 | site　7,933.9 m²
7. 建築 | building　220.3 m²
8. 延床 | total floor　220.3 m²

設計の原点に、安藤は南仏プロヴァンスの「ノートルダム・ド・セナンク修道院」をあげる。12-13世紀に建設されたこのロマネスクの修道院の礼拝堂に感銘を受け、六甲ではセナンクの中庭を囲う列柱廊を、直線の形に展開したという。礼拝空間は、コンクリート打ち放しの躯体に直方体の塔が載る。そこへの柱廊は、壁、天井とも、すりガラスの半透過の空間とした。周囲も見事な緑地に整備され、山上の爽快な環境も踏まえて「風の教会」と呼んだ。→参照 [089]

Ando points out "Notre-Dame de Sénanque" in Provence of Southern France as the origin of his design. Impressed by this chapel of Romanesque monastery built in 12th to 13th century, he says that the concept of cloister in Sénanque (a corridor around a courtyard with a series) is developed as a linear colonnade. In the chapel space, a cuboid tower is built on the skeleton in exposed concrete. In the colonnade to the chapel, both walls and ceiling is made as a semitransparent space with frosted glasses. The surrounding area was also well developed with rich greenery, and it was called "Chapel of a wind" based on the refreshing environment of a hillside. → see also [089]

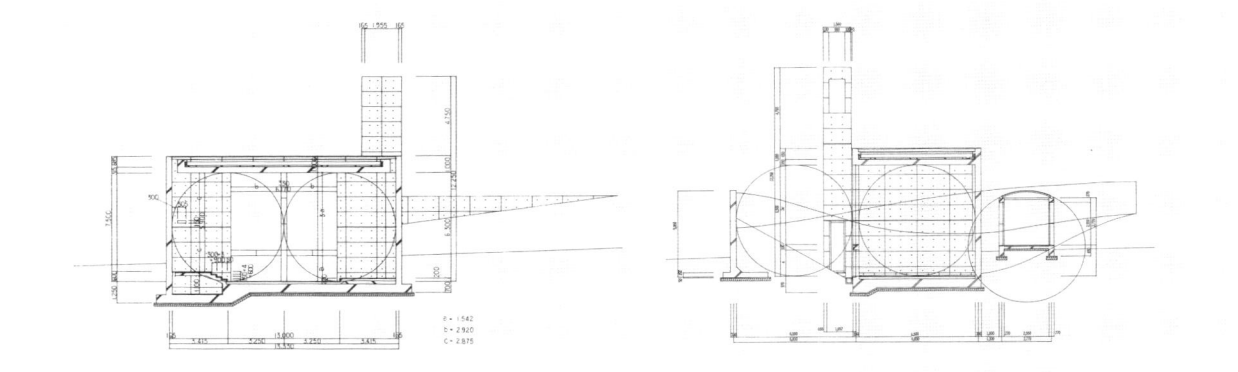

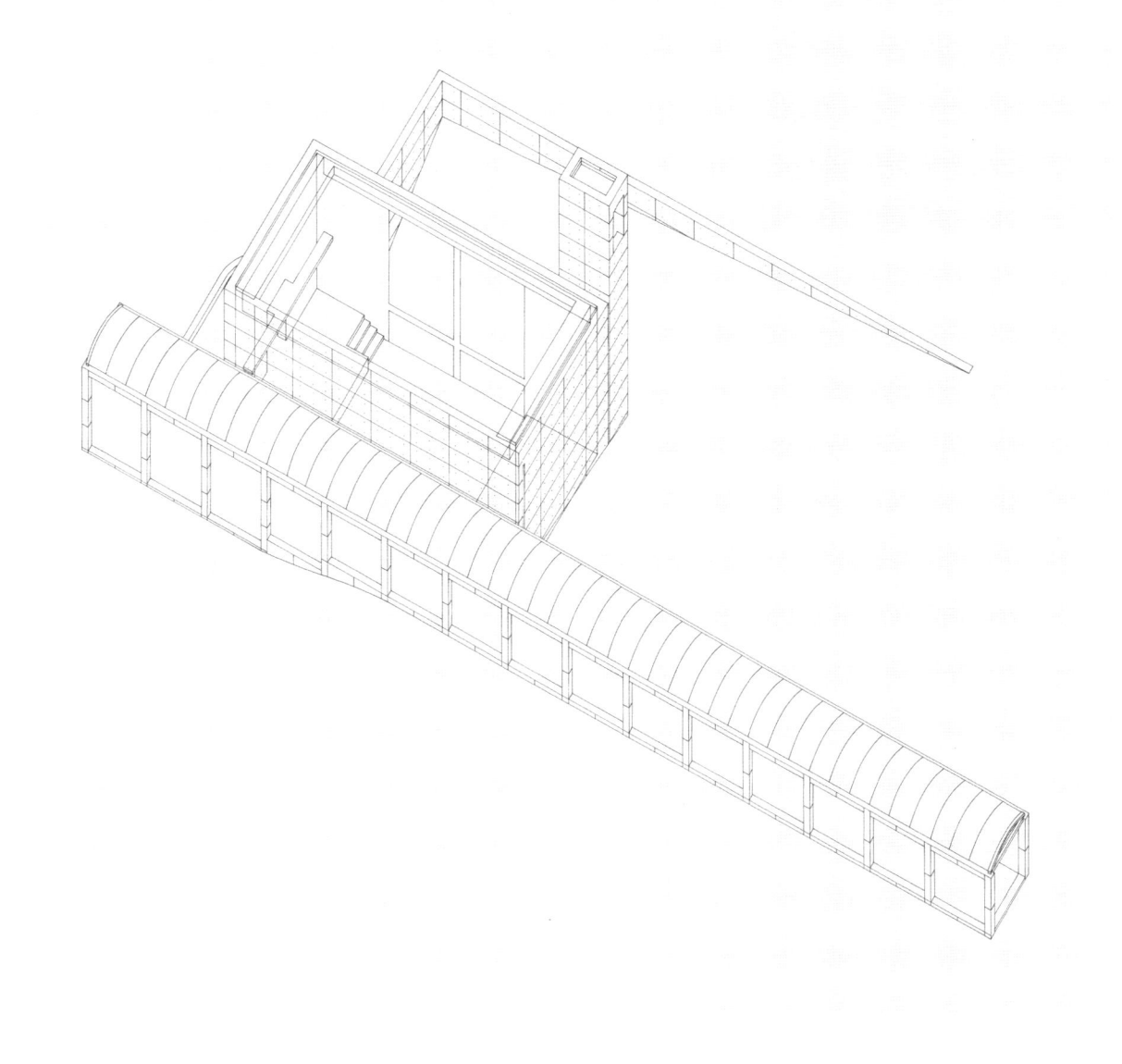

[080]
TS ビル 1986
ts building

1. 大阪市北区 | kita-ku, osaka
2. 設計 | design　1984.11–1985.8
3. 施工 | construction　1985.9–1986.8
4. 鉄筋コンクリート（壁式）| RC (wall)
5. 住宅、事務所、店舗 | house, office, shop
6. 敷地 | site　160.7 m²
7. 建築 | building　118.1 m²
8. 延床 | total floor　665.0 m²

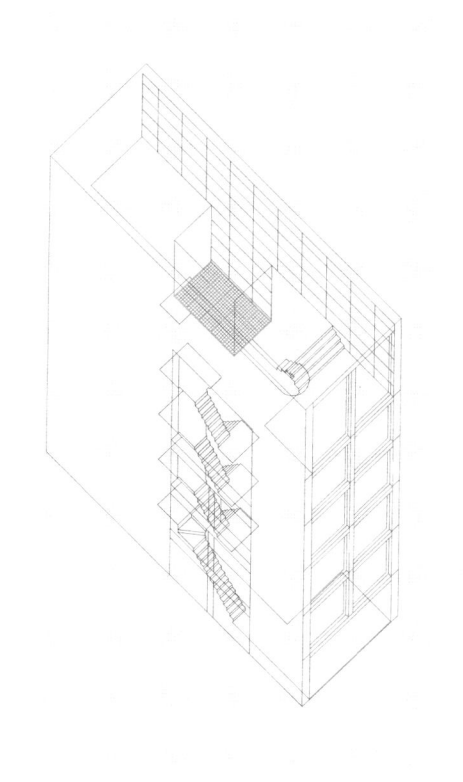

大阪都心の堂島川に面したオフィスビル。間口は狭く、奥行きのほうがずっと長い。堂島川に開く眺望は、年に一度の天神祭りの日に川面を賑わす舟の灯を見るという喜びを味わえる。上階の二層はそのお祭りのためのゲストルームに設えられた。この細長い建築の中央に光庭を配し、上階を吹き抜けにし、5階の床にガラスブロックをはめ込んで、下階のトップライトとした。季節の移ろいに応じて、変化する自然光が射し込み、多彩な表情を各階に生み出す。

This is an office building located in the center of Osaka City facing to Dojima River. The width is narrow, yet the depth is much longer. For people in Osaka, the open view to Dojima River means that they can enjoy the pleasure of seeing the river to be full of the boat's lights in the day of Tenjin Festival, an annual event. The top two floors are designated as guest rooms to enjoy the event. A light court is placed in the center of this building in elongated shape, the top floor is open to below, and the glass blocks is fixed on the 5th floor to function as a top light for the lower levels. Depending on the seasons, the changing natural light is reflected, and various conditions are generated in each floor.

[081]
ゲストハウス OLD／NEW 六甲
1986
guest house old / new rokko

1. 神戸市灘区 | nada-ku, kobe
2. 設計 | design　1985.1–1985.11
3. 施工 | construction　1985.12–1986.12
4. 鉄筋コンクリート | RC
5. 複合商業施設 | commercial complex
6. 敷地 | site　1,233.0 m²
7. 建築 | building　481.1 m²
8. 延床 | total floor　806.5 m²

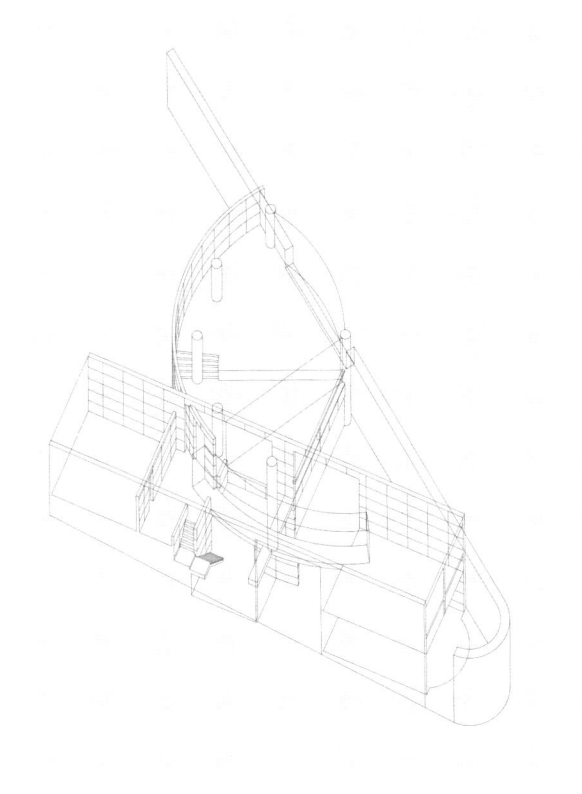

神戸に愛着を持つ安藤は、この飲食施設の設計にあたって、敷地に残る樹齢200年とされるクスノキの大木を残し、一帯の住宅地に多い御影石の石垣を敷地の外周に巡らせた。日常風景の欠かせない要素を読み解くところから設計を立ち上げた。三角の角地の地形を生かし、ヴォールト屋根の細長い棟をその一辺に添わせて配置し、そこに4分の1円より少し大きな分円の棟を交錯させた。レストランは開放的なガラス窓を持ち、神戸ならではの港への眺望を楽しむこともできた。

Ando feels attachment to Kobe area. For designing this restaurant, he provided granite masonry wall to the periphery of the site as often found in this residential area, and he kept a large camphor tree with age of 200 years on the site — he started to design from the point of fully reading and understanding the essential elements of ordinary landscape. Making use of the topography of the triangle corner, a slender shaped wing with vault roof was placed along the side, and then another wing with the circle slightly larger than the quarter circle was crossed there. This restaurant had an open glass window to be able to enjoy the view to the harbor specific to Kobe.

［082］

細工谷の家──野口邸　1986
town house in saikudani
—noguchi house
.

1. 大阪市天王寺区｜tennoji-ku, osaka
2. 設計｜design　1985.5–1985.9
3. 施工｜construction　1985.10–1986.5
4. 鉄筋コンクリート（壁式）｜RC (wall)
5. 住宅｜detached house
6. 敷地｜site　68.5 m²
7. 建築｜building　40.0 m²
8. 延床｜total floor　106.3 m²

下町商店街の木造長屋の一角にコンクリートのボックスを突っ込んだ。「住吉の長屋」が2階建てだったのに対し、こちらは3階建て。奥行きは15メートル、間口3.5メートル。住吉と同じく中央に光庭を配して、各階のどの部屋もこの吹き抜けに面する構成をとった。高さがあるため細長い吹き抜けは「光の井戸」となって、季節によって変化する自然光を住宅の隅々まで届ける役割を演じる。3階には小さなオープンスペースが生まれ、コンクリート壁で囲った屋上とともに都市生活を楽しめる場になっている。
.

A concrete box is integrated in a wooden terrace house located in an old shopping area. The ROW HOUSE, SUMIYOSHI was a two-story house but this house has three stories. The length is 15 meters and the width is 3.5 meters. Similar to ROW HOUSE, SUMIYOSHI's composition, a light garden with an open ceiling is placed where all rooms in each floor are facing. Since this building is taller, it forms like a light well that delivers natural light which changes each season throughout the house. With a rooftop surrounded by concrete, a small open space is provided on the 3rd floor to enjoy urban life.

---

［083］

渋谷神社総合開発計画　1986
shibuya shrine redevelopment project
.

1. 東京都渋谷区｜shibuya-ku, tokyo
2. 設計｜design　1986
3. 構想案｜concept
5. 劇場、ギャラリー、店舗｜theater, gallery, shop

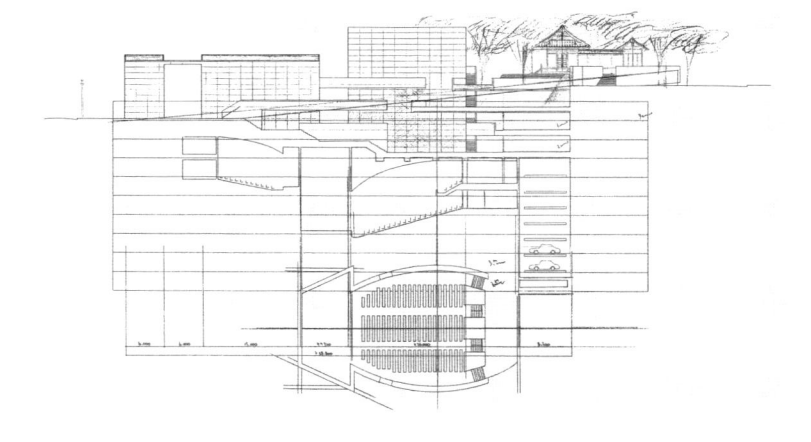

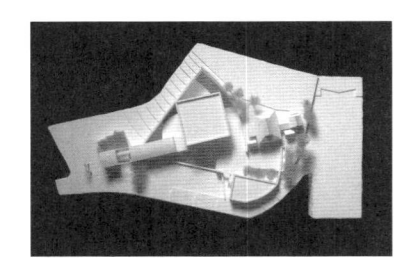

東京・渋谷の繁華街に近い神社の再開発計画。傾斜した敷地の最奥の高台に社殿を置き、そこに至るまでの参道に立方体と直方体の施設を配置、地下の劇場、ギャラリー、ブティック、レストランなども入居させることが想定された。そうした機能の過半は地中に埋めて、神社の境内の雰囲気を壊さないことに配慮した。宗教施設がもう一度、ひとびとの日常生活の核となることを、都市施設の複合に託した。

A redevelopment plan of a shrine close to a busy area of Shibuya, Tokyo. The main shrine is placed on an elevated area of the most inner part of the inclined property. A cube and rectangular solid facilities are situated on the approach to the main shrine. It was also planned to have tenants including an underground theater, gallery, boutique, and restaurant. Consideration was paid not to destroy the atmosphere of the precincts of the shrine by embedding more than half of the space for those facilities underground. An idea to once again make a religious facility into a center for people's daily lives was reflected in this composite urban facility plan.

[084]
BIGI 3rd　1986
bigi 3rd

1. 大阪市中央区 | chuo-ku, osaka
2. 設計 | design　1986.3–1986.8
3. 施工 | construction　1986.9–1986.11
5. 店舗 | shop
6. 敷地 | site　55.2 m²
7. 建築 | building　43.5 m²
8. 延床 | total floor　43.5 m²

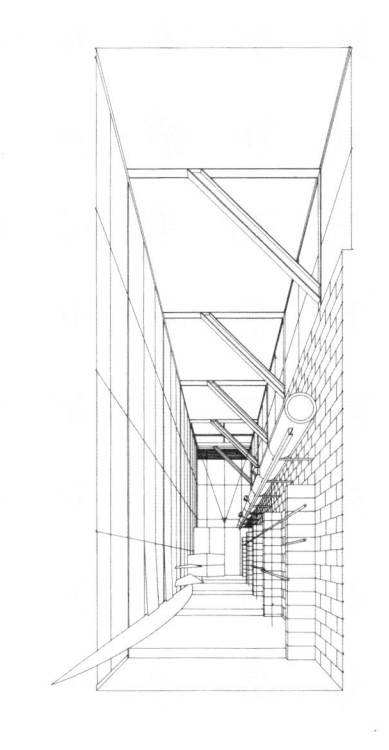

建物の実寸は間口3メートルに対して奥行きは15メートルに満たず、高さは7.5メートルに収められている。安藤は大阪都心に出現した建物と建物の隙間のような敷地に、構造的な工夫を凝らし、このファッション・ブティックを「建築的な遊戯」の精神で構築した。構造柱を片側に集め、そこから伸ばした梁によって対面の壁を構造耐力を担わないカーテンウォールに仕立てた。屋根は構造柱から斜め材を伸ばして支えた。狭小な空間にコンクリートボックスを挿入するのとは異なる空間構成が興味深い。

The actual dimension of the building is only 3 meters wide, while being 15 meters long and 7.5 meters high. Ando elaborated the structural design and built a fashion boutique with a spirit of architectural play in a property that seems to be a gap between buildings in the center of Osaka. Structural columns are gathered on one side and beams extended from those columns support the wall on the other side that form a curtain wall that does not bear structural resistance. The roof is supported by the material diagonally extended from the structural columns. It is interesting the spatial structure different from inserting a concrete box in a narrow space.

[085]
田中山荘　1987
tanaka atelier

1. 山梨県南都留郡 | minamitsuru, yamanashi
2. 設計 | design　1985.4–1986.4
3. 施工 | construction　1986.5–1987.5
4. 鉄筋コンクリート（壁式）、上部木造 | RC (wall), wood
5. 住宅（別荘）| resort villa
6. 敷地 | site　693.6 m²
7. 建築 | building　71.9 m²
8. 延床 | total floor　100.5 m²

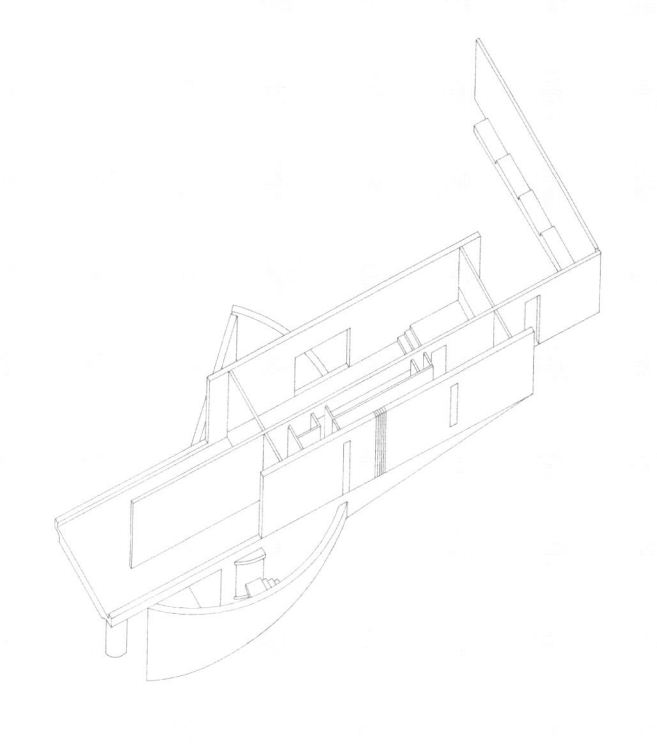

著名なグラフィックデザイナーの別荘。山間地の別荘らしく外観は傾斜屋根が架かっているが、内部の天井はヴォールトの形に仕立てられている。傾斜面を生かして、二層の建物の下半分は地中に埋められた。上階では、L字型の独立壁が建物全体を二分するように配された。玄関への誘導とともに、室内ではリビングと台所を分け、斜面から空中に飛び出したテラスを二分している。下層階は、半円形の壁が建物本体に食い込み、豊かな自然を別荘に囲い込む役割を演じている。

A vacation house for a famous graphic designer. The house has an inclined roof, which is a common appearance for a vacation house in a mountainous region. However, the ceiling inside is a vault shape. The lower half of the building is embedded underground taking advantage of the sloped surface. An L-shaped independent wall is placed on the upper floor to divide the building in two. It approaches to the entrance and also divides living room and kitchen inside the building and the terrace protruding in the air from the sloped surface in two. The lower floor has a semicircle wall that cuts into the building to satisfy its function to enclose the rich nature inside the vacation house area.

[086]
唐座　1987
kara-za

1. 宮城県仙台市｜東京都台東区｜
   sendai, miyagi / taito-ku, tokyo
2. 設計｜design　1985.7–1987.4
3. 施工｜construction　1987.5–1987.6 [sendai],
   1988.2–1988.3 [taito-ku]
4. 単管パイプ造｜single pipe structure
5. 仮設劇場｜temporary theater
7. 建築｜building　1,145.0 m²
8. 延床｜total floor　601.4 m²

唐十郎主宰の赤テント「状況劇場」の仮設劇場。構造体として足場に使うパイプを組み上げ、外装は木材を使った十二角形の漆黒の建築が出現した。多角形の屋根には赤テントをイメージしたビニールが張られ、劇場への入場には太鼓橋が設えられた。劇空間という異界への橋渡しだった。最初は宮城県で開催された「未来の東北博」のセゾングループのパビリオンとして建設され、一度、解体のあと、台東区の協力で、隅田川の河岸に奇想の建築は出現した。

This is a temporal theatrical space for a red tent theater called "Situation Theater" directed by Kara Juro. A completely black colored architecture in a dodecagonal shape appeared after building up pipes that are used for the scaffold as a structure, covered with wooden materials for its exterior finish. Its polygonal shaped roof is set up with a plastic sheet representing the image of a red tent theater, while an arched bridge was provided to enter the theater space. It was a bridge to the parallel world of the theater space. This building was first built as a pavilion of Saison Group in "EXPO '87 TOHOKU" held in Miyagi prefecture, and after the demolition, unique architecture appeared on the banks of Sumida River, with the aid from Taito Ward in Tokyo Prefecture.

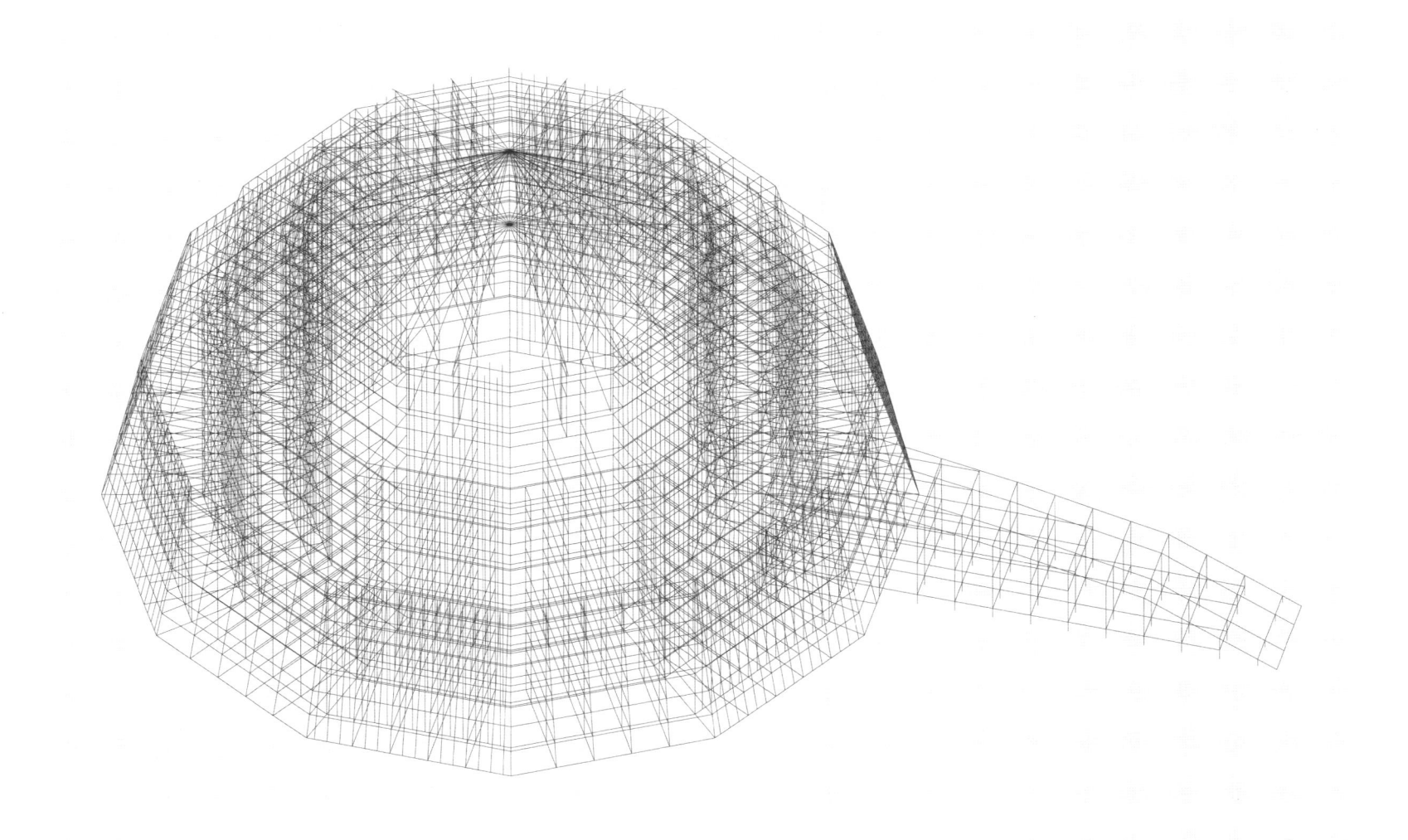

[087]
天王寺公園植物温室
(天王寺博覧会テーマ館) 1987
tennoji park, greenhouse
(main pavilion for tennoji fair)

1. 大阪市天王寺区 | tennoji-ku, osaka
2. 設計 | design 1986.4–1986.10
3. 施工 | construction 1986.12–1987.7
4. 鉄筋コンクリート、鉄骨 | RC, steel
5. 展示場 | exhibition hall
6. 敷地 | site 251,725.0 m²
7. 建築 | building 1,101.5 m²
8. 延床 | total floor 1,853.2 m²

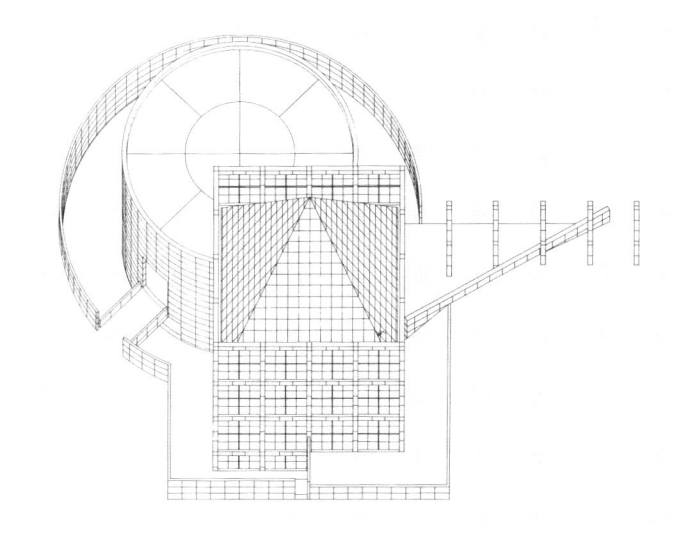

大阪の天王寺公園を舞台に、いきものをテーマとして開催された博覧会のメインパビリオン。厳格な仕立ての立方体、正四角錐、円柱を組み合わせて、幾何学の結晶を思わせる完結した外観が目をひく。コンクリートのフレームとガラス壁の取り合わせは、安藤の美学を透明感によって強調し、魅力的な光景を緑豊かな広大な公園の一角に添えることになった。博覧会ではさまざまな映像展示の舞台ともなったが、植物の温室に転用されて現在に至る。

The main pavilion of an exposition opened focusing on living creatures as the theme at Tennoji Park in Osaka. The completed appearance that resembles geometric crystal attracts attention combining with rigorous looking cubes, square pyramid and cylinder. The combination of the concrete frame and glass walls emphasizes the aesthetic value of Ando with its transparency adding attractive scenery in part of this extensive park. Although it was used to show various videos during the exhibition, currently it is being used as a greenhouse for plants.

[088]
水の劇場 1987
theater on the water

1. 北海道占冠村 | shimukappu, hokkaido
2. 設計 | design 1987
3. 構想案 | concept
4. 鉄筋コンクリート | RC
5. 野外劇場 | open-air theater

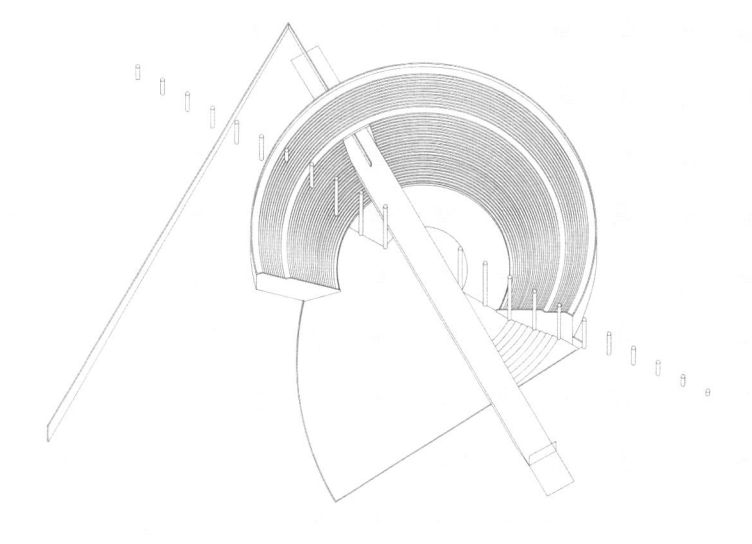

「水の教会」の傍らで構想した屋外シアターの建築。劇場は6千人収容の規模で半円形のアンフィシアター形式。舞台は幅13メートル、長さ200メートルに達し、客席と60度で交差する。ファッションショーやコンサートの利用を想定した。コンクリートの列柱がもうひとつの軸線も形成し、それらが相まって安藤による大地の造形が展開する計画だった。極寒の冬季には傍らの池をスケート場とすることにもなっていた。→ 参照 [093]

An architecture of outdoor theater planned to be created beside the plan of CHURCH ON THE WATER. The theater was designed in a semicircle amphitheater style that can hold about 6,000 people. The stage was 13 meters in width, 200 meters in length, and it intersects with the audience in 60-degree angle. It was designed to be used for fashion shows and concerts. A row of concrete columns form another axis line where Ando was going to develop styling of the earth. The pond on the side was going to be an ice skate rink during the harsh cold winter. → see also [093]

[089]

六甲山バンケットホール 1987
banquet hall on mt. rokko

1. 神戸市灘区 | nada-ku, kobe
2. 設計 | design　1987
3. 構想案 | concept
5. 宴会場 | banquet hall

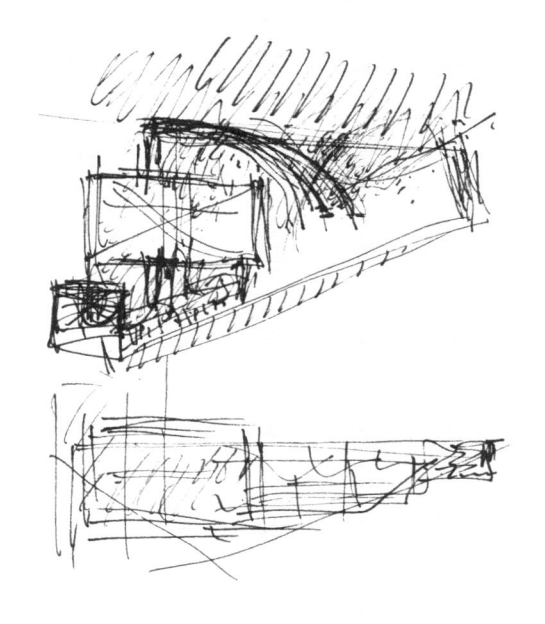

港町・神戸の背後にそびえる六甲山頂に近い「六甲の教会」と同じホテルの敷地内に計画された宴会棟。パーティーや宴会での利用を想定した。ホテルと教会の軸線を意識した配置で、もうひとつの幾何立体を既存ホテル棟と教会の場に追加し、三つの建築が一体となることで自然を際立たせる効果を意図した。建物の半分を地中に沈め、環境と建築が共振しあう効果も考えた。のちに直島で複数の施設が連携する一体化した配置を構想するとき、この試行が役立ったという。→参照 [079]

A banquet building planned inside the property of the same hotel as a CHAPEL ON MT. ROKKO close to the peak of Mt. Rokko standing behind the port town of Kobe. It was designed to be used for parties and banquets. The layout was planned taking the axis line with the hotel and church into consideration where another geometric solid was added in the area of the existing hotel building and church to unite the three architecture and give an effect to highlight the nature. Half of the building was embedded underground to have a resonance effect between the environment and the architecture. Trials in this project was useful when an integrated layout that allow cooperation between various facilities was planned for Naoshima. → see also [079]

[090]

伊豆プロジェクト 1987
izu project

1. 静岡県賀茂郡 | kamo, shizuoka
2. 設計 | design　1987.6–1989.12
3. 構想案 | concept
4. 鉄骨鉄筋コンクリート | SRC
5. 集合住宅、ホテル、展望台 | apartment house, hotel, observation deck
6. 敷地 | site　1,775.0 m²
8. 延床 | total floor　1,405.0 m²

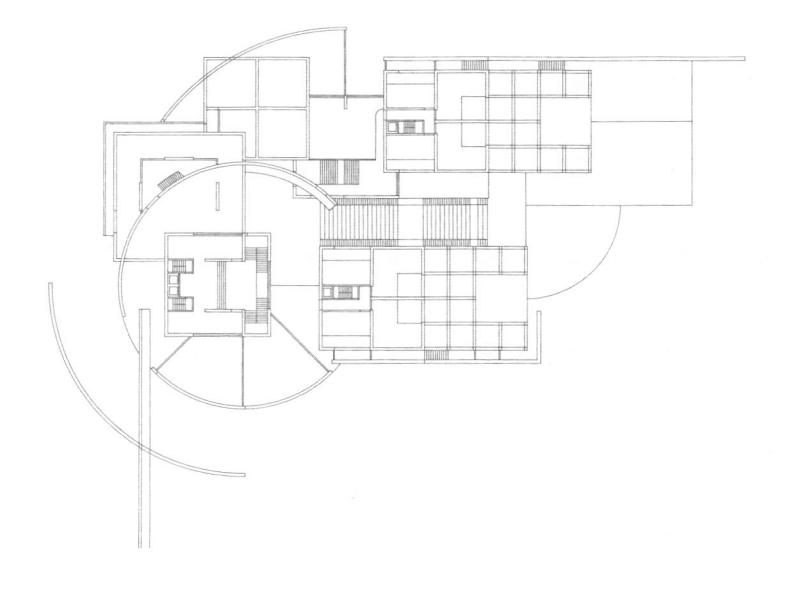

伊豆半島南部の岬を想定したリゾート施設の開発計画。岬全体の建築化が目標だったといい、安藤は、最頂部の展望台から海に向って水が流れる人工池まで、斜面のあらゆる場所に造作を施そうとした。宿泊施設を中心にギャラリー、レストランなどを分散的に配し、壁や宿泊棟で区切られた散策路を伝い歩きしながら、海に面した空間を堪能する配置が企てられた。のちに「淡路夢舞台」で実現するランドスケープの前触れといえるだろう。

A development project of a resort facility supposing the cape of southern Izu Peninsula. The target was to make the whole cape filled with architecture. Ando designed to create architecture at various locations of the inclined plane including an artificial pond that flows water toward the ocean from the observation deck on the highest point. Galleries and restaurants were arranged sporadically with the accommodation facility at the center to allow visitors to enjoy the space facing the ocean while walking along the promenade sectioned by walls and lodgings. This was the prelude of the landscape materialized by the AWAJI-YUMEBUTAI (Awaji Island Project).

[091]
I プロジェクト　1987
i project

1. 静岡県伊東市 | ito, shizuoka
2. 設計　design　1987.3–1990.10
3. 構想案 | concept
4. 鉄骨鉄筋コンクリート | SRC
5. 集合住宅 | apartment house
6. 敷地 | site　10933.6 m²
7. 建築 | building　4922.5 m²
8. 延床 | total floor　21068.9 m²

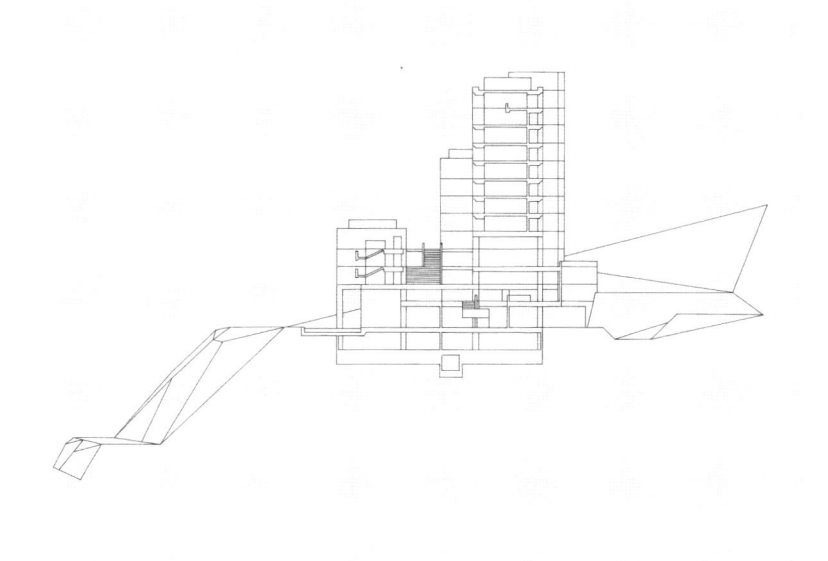

伊豆半島東部の相模湾に面した崖地の開発計画。高層から低層まで18の建築が集合し、住宅、レストラン、温泉が配置された。個々の棟はそれぞれ11.25メートルの正方形平面を規格にして収められ、それが全体の街区にリズムをもたらすことが期待された。住棟へは4階レベルに設定されたロビーからアプローチし、各戸からは相模湾の海の風景が堪能できる仕立てだった。展望テラス、読書ラウンジなど公的な空間を確保して他のリゾート開発とは一線を画する提案だった。
.
Development plan of a cliff facing Sagami Bay at the east area of Izu Peninsula. 18 of low-rise to high-rise buildings are located with housing, restaurant, and hot spring. Each building is in a square planform of 11.25 meters each side to provide rhythm in the city block as a whole. A lobby situated on the 4th-floor level is used to approach inside the residential area where scenery of the ocean of Sagami Bay could be enjoyed from each residence. It was a proposal different from other resort developments because that had public spaces such as an observatory terrace and reading lounge.

[092]
I ハウス　1988
i house

1. 兵庫県芦屋市 | ashiya, hyogo
2. 設計 | design　1985.8–1986.11
3. 施工 | construction　1986.11–1988.6
4. 鉄筋コンクリート（壁式）、一部鉄骨造 | RC (wall), steel
5. 住宅 | detached house
6. 敷地 | site　987.0 m²
7. 建築 | building　263.0 m²
8. 延床 | total floor　907.9 m²

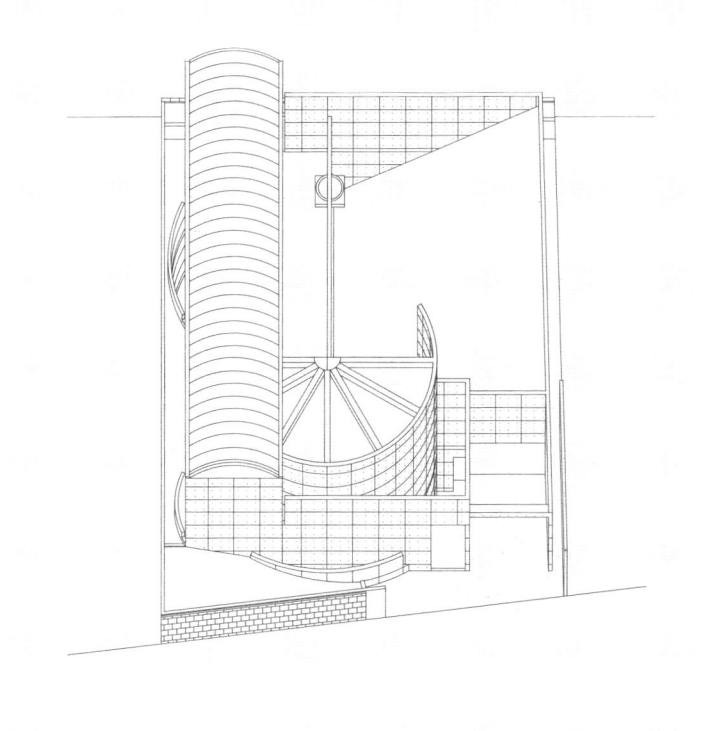

兵庫県芦屋市の芦屋川沿い、高級住宅地の一角を占めるゲストハウス。敷地の中心に置いた半円筒を中心に空間が展開している。目をひくのはヴォールト屋根で、この屋根の下に寝室、ゲストルームなどが配されている。円筒の外周を巻く形で配された屋内階段をのぼるとき、ヴォールト屋根を介して射し込む自然光が、住宅内部のコンクリートの壁につくりだす陰影に目を見張らされる。円筒内にはリビング、ホールなど共有空間が配されている。敷地内の余白には傾斜した庭があり、各室から季節の花々が咲き誇る風景を楽しむこともできる。
.
A guesthouse in an exclusive residential area along Ashiya River of Ashiya City, Hyogo Prefecture. The space is expanding around the half cylinder place at the center of the property. The vault roof attracts attention under which the bedroom and guestroom are provided. By climbing up the indoor stairs built in spiral along the circumference of the cylinder, the shade that appears on the concrete wall inside the house by the natural light shining in through the vault roof offers a spectacular sight. A shared space including a living room and a hall is arranged in the cylinder space. An inclined garden is situated in the open area of the property and the scenery of seasonal flowers can be enjoyed from each room.

[093]
水の教会　1988
church on the water

1. 北海道占冠村 | shimukappu, hokkaido
2. 設計 | design　1985.9–1988.4
3. 施工 | construction　1988.4–1988.9
4. 鉄筋コンクリート | RC
5. 教会 | church
6. 敷地 | site　6,730.0 m²
7. 建築 | building　344.9 m²
8. 延床 | total floor　520.0 m²

縁側に面した教会が日本にあってもよい。安藤はこの建築をそう説明している。十字架は室内ではなく、新たに設けられた人工池のなかに、鉄骨を組んだ形でそびえ立つ。その十字架に向き合うには、礼拝空間の大きく開け放った開口部に向かって座ることになる。縁側たる所以だ。人工池はコンクリートの壁で囲われ、屋外でありながら、確たる領域を確保する。礼拝空間にアプローチするエントランスには、十字架を思わせるコンクリートのグリッドが配されている。安藤の作品がランドスケープを意識したものに変化していく転換点となった。
→参照［088］

Ando explained that a church facing to En'gawa (a strip of flooring before windows) may be in Japan, and this architecture as such. The Cross is not inside of the building, but stands in a newly constructed artificial pond in the form of a steel frame. In order to face with The Cross in the pond, prayers sit down to the wide open window of the chapel space — it is a reason to be built on En'gawa. The artificial pond is enclosed by concrete walls, keeping the definite area even in outdoor. The entrance to access the chapel space is placed with a concrete grid as an image of The Cross. This work became the turning point for Ando to think more consciously about the landscape. → see also [088]

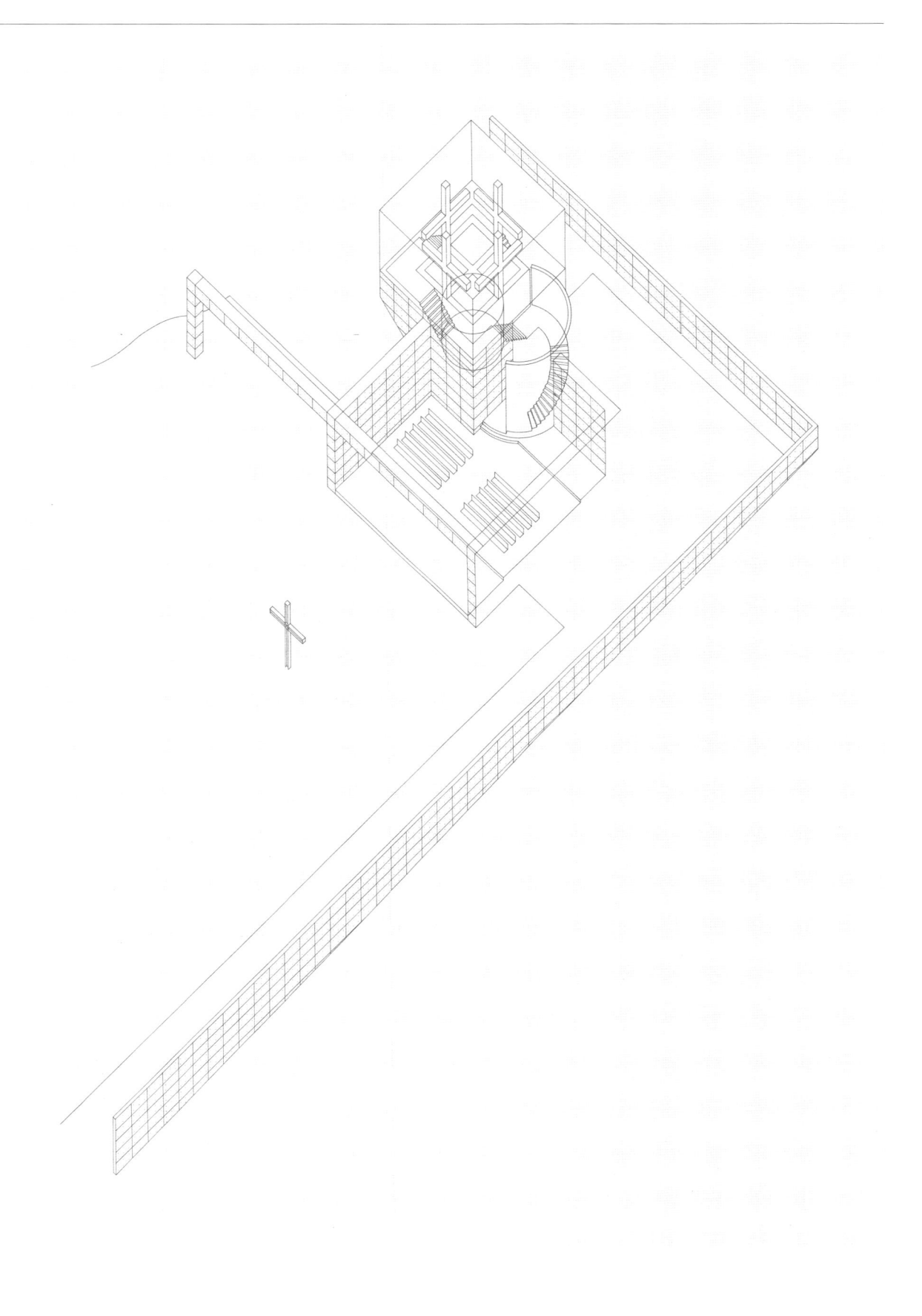

[094]
GALLERIA [akka]　1988
galleria [akka]

1. 大阪市中央区 | chuo-ku, osaka
2. 設計 | design　1985.10–1987.3
3. 施工 | construction　1987.3–1988.4
4. 鉄筋コンクリート | RC
5. 複合商業施設 | commercial complex
6. 敷地 | site　324.2 m²
7. 建築 | building　226.0 m²
8. 延床 | total floor　1,027.1 m²

敷地は、大阪きっての繁華街に位置し、間口8メートル、奥行き40メートル。そこで飲食中心の商業ビルを手がけた。細長い平面の中途を緩やかな円弧で区切り、円弧の外側を空洞として残し、立体的な迷路のイメージを実現した。屋上にはすりガラスのヴォールト屋根が架かり、自然光はそこから地階まで続く狭く深い空隙を下りてゆく。この光がもたらす陰影の変化こそが、迷路たる所以であり、安藤はこれを都市に対する「異化作用」と位置づけている。

This commercial building mainly for food and drink services is realized in the prime center of Osaka, on a site in 8m wide and 40m deep. The elongated plot was divided by a gentle arc shape in the middle part, while the outside part of the circular arc was left as a void to realize the image of a 3 dimensional labyrinth. The rooftop has a frosted glass vault roof, and the natural light goes down the narrow and deep void space from the roof to the basement. This shadow change caused by lights is the reason for being a labyrinth, and Ando positions it as the "dissimilation effect" against cities.

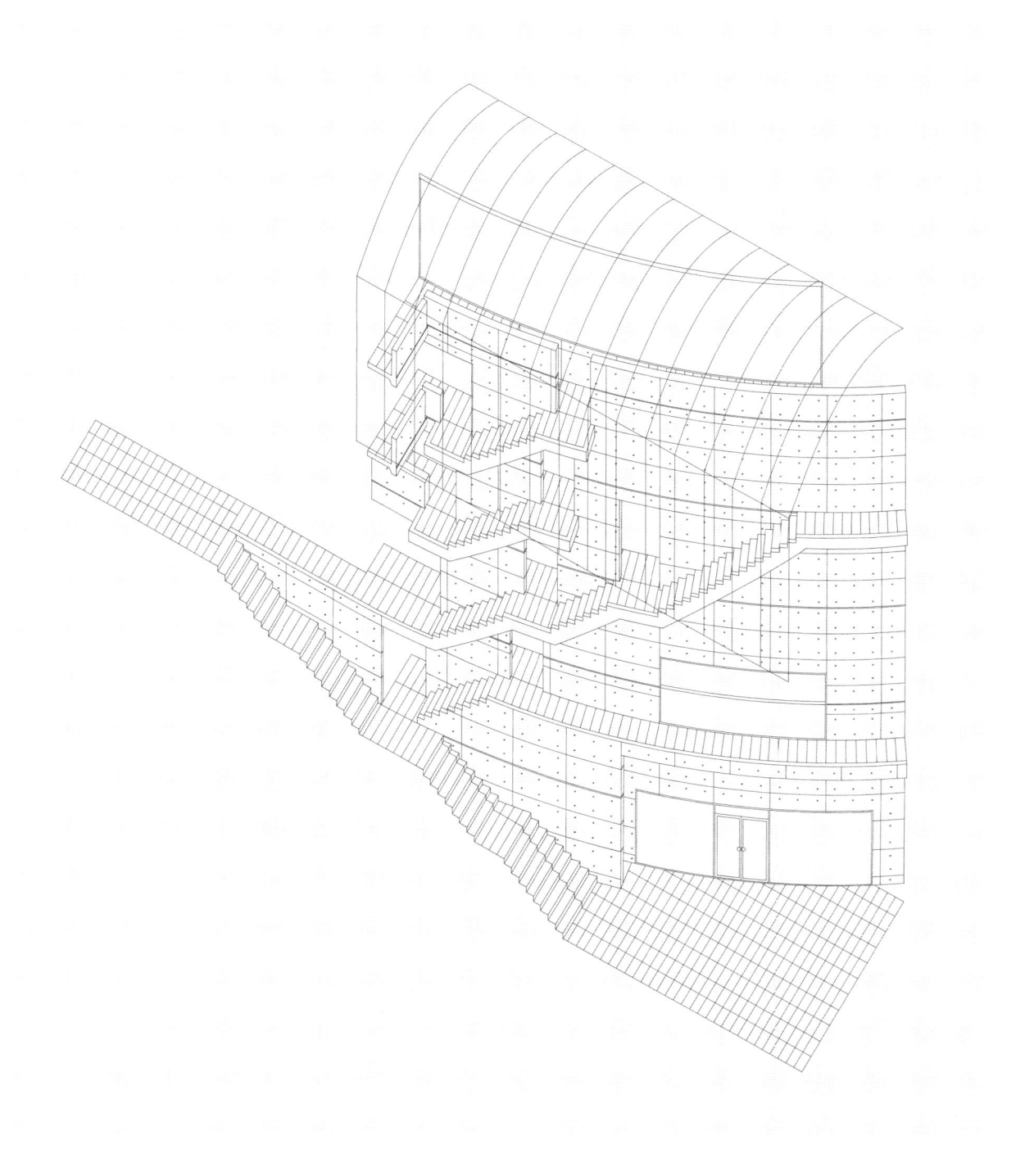

[095]
小倉邸　1988
ogura house

1. 愛知県名古屋市｜nagoya, aichi
2. 設計｜design　1986.2–1987.2
3. 施工｜construction　1987.4–1988.2
4. 型枠コンクリートブロック｜fill-up concrete-block
5. 住宅｜detached house
6. 敷地｜site　214.9 m²
7. 建築｜building　106.6 m²
8. 延床｜total floor　189.4 m²

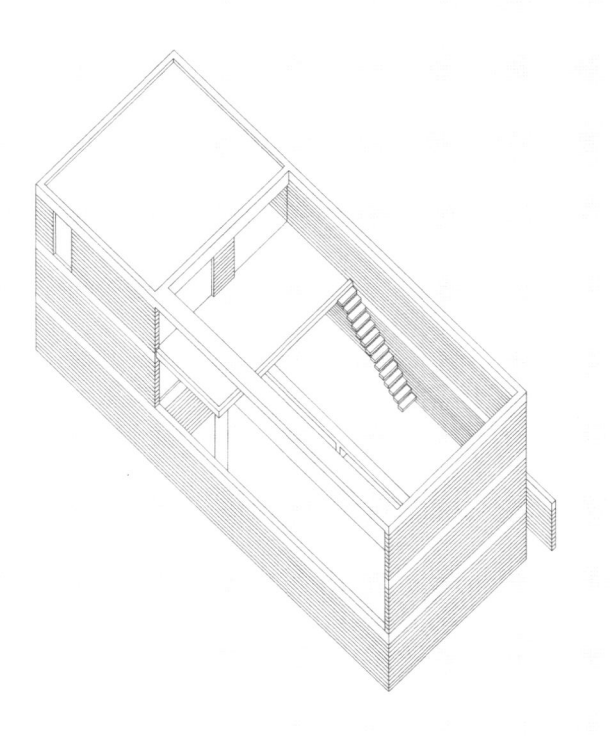

長方形の住宅の3分の2が、安藤にいわせると外部の扱いになっている。敷地を囲うコンクリートブロックの壁は、表通りに向って大きく開かれ、わずかに1階の一角だけに玄関や客間などが配され、2、3階は開放的なテラスとなっている。高級住宅地に位置し、傍らに緑豊かな斜面地が保持されていることを受け、住宅内部にそうした立地環境の利点を取り込もうとしたためだ。玉砂利を敷きつめた1階のコートなど細部に外部環境への配慮を示し、そのことが厳格なコンクリートブロックで守られた室内からの眺望を多様なものにしている。

Ando described that 2/3 of the rectangle house is viewed as the outside. Concrete block walls that surround the property are widely open toward the street in front. Only one corner of the 1st floor is for the entrance and the drawing room while the 2nd and 3rd floors are an expansive terrace structure. This design was adopted to bring the advantage of the location environment inside the house since it is located in an exclusive residential area and slope ground full of greenery is preserved on the side of the property. Consideration to the external environment is shown in detail by, for example, laying pea gravel on the court of the 1st floor, which provides diverse and rich view from inside the house that is protected by rigorous concrete blocks.

[096]
B-LOCK神楽岡　1988
b-lock kaguraoka

1. 京都市左京区｜sakyo-ku, kyoto
2. 設計｜design　1986.3–1987.9
3. 施工｜construction　1987.9–1988.3
4. 型枠コンクリートブロック｜fill-up concrete-block
5. 集合住宅｜apartment house
6. 敷地｜site　244.0 m²
7. 建築｜building　118.0 m²
8. 延床｜total floor　211.0 m²

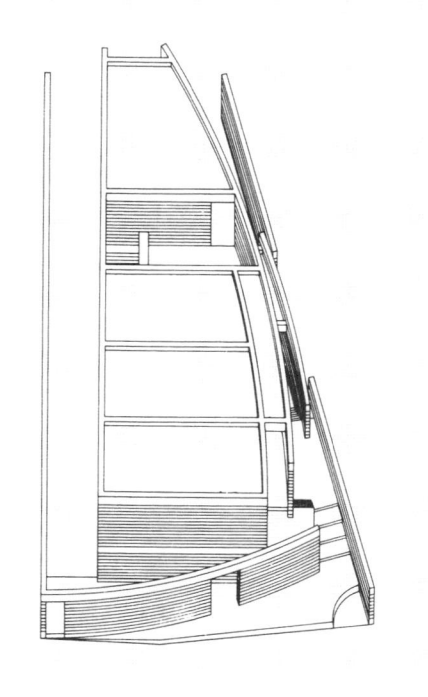

京都市東部、緑豊かな吉田山の北端に広がる住宅地に位置する集合住宅。ワンルーム7戸、メゾネット1戸の小規模なもので、表通り側からはエントランスのゲート以外は開口部のない囲われた仕立てをとり、コンクリートブロックの厳格さが強固な守りを実感させる。小さな敷地だが、コンクリートブロックの壁を曲面とすることによって、背後の吉田山の自然を敷地内に呼び込み、視線と光線の予期せぬ交錯による空間の多様化を狙った。

A condominium located in a residential area that spreads on the north end of Mt. Yoshida that is full of greenery at the east area of Kyoto City. It is a small scale condominium; seven studios and one maisonette where except the entrance gate, it is completely covered by concrete blocks from the front street, which their rigorous look gives sense of strong protection. Although the property is small, the nature of Mt. Yoshida standing at the back of the property is brought in by making the concrete block walls in curved shape to obtain diversity of space by an unexpected crossing of line of sight and light ray.

[097]
吉田邸　1988
yoshida house

1. 大阪府富田林市 | tondabayashi, osaka
2. 設計 | design　1986.5–1987.5
3. 施工 | construction　1987.7–1988.2
4. 鉄筋コンクリート（壁式）| RC (wall)
5. 住宅 | detached house
6. 敷地 | site　252.0 m²
7. 建築 | building　124.0 m²
8. 延床 | total floor　211.0 m²

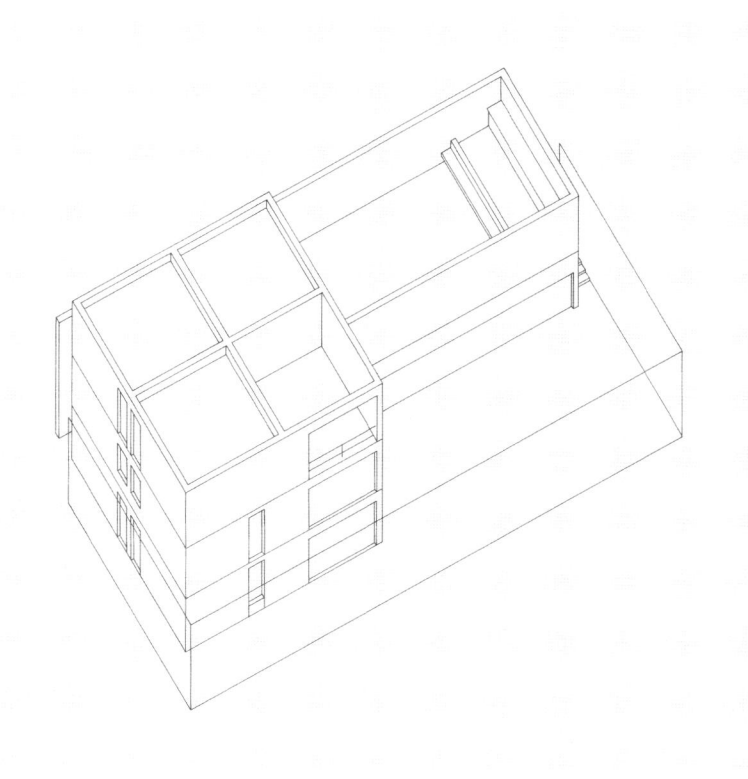

大阪・富田林市のアトリエ兼住宅。コンクリートの壁構造の仕立てで、安藤は敷地を一段掘り下げて、1階ではアトリエと食堂が面する位置に壁で囲われた庭を配した。2階では、1階アトリエの屋上、3階では2階リビングの屋上に、それぞれ位置をずらしたプライベートなテラスを設け、各階で異なる空間体験が楽しめるようにした。1階がアトリエで作業するひとのための、樹木の緑陰が涼しげな半ば開かれた場なのに対して、2、3階は家族の私的な空間であることを考慮し、上階のテラスは壁で囲われている。

An atelier and residential house in Tondabayashi City, Osaka. The structure is of concrete walls. Ando lowered the ground level of the property and placed a garden surrounded by walls on the 1st floor where it faces the atelier and dining room. Private terraces were built in each offset position on the roof top of the 1st floor atelier in the 2nd floor and on the roof top of the 2nd floor living room in the 3rd floor to offer enjoyable spatial experience that varies on each floor. The 1st floor atelier is a semi-open area for work under the shade of trees and the terrace on the 2nd and 3rd floors are surrounded by walls considering that are private spaces.

[098]
I ギャラリー　1988
i gallery

1. 東京都世田谷区 | setagaya-ku, tokyo
2. 設計 | design　1988
3. 構想案 | concept
4. 鉄筋コンクリート（ラーメン）| RC (frame)
5. 住宅、ギャラリー | house, gallery
6. 敷地 | site　520 m²
7. 建築 | building　208 m²
8. 延床 | total floor　445 m²

東京・世田谷の住宅街に計画された住居とギャラリーの複合施設。二世帯居住、そして近隣にも開放するギャラリーの機能を違和感なく充足するためのスタディーが重ねられた。敷地にもとからあった樹木を尊重して建物の外形を定め、3階にオーナーの住居、2階に母親の住居、そして、1階と地階にギャラリー機能を振り分けることを前提に配置が決定された。ギャラリーへは建物中央のサンクンガーデンに渡されたブリッジを通る。二つの住戸はこの1、2階を通す吹き抜けやテラスに面して自然との関わりを持つ。

A composite facility of a residence and gallery planned in the residential section of Setagaya, Tokyo. A design was examined to satisfy function as the housing for two generations of mother and child as well as a gallery opened for neighbors. The external shape of the building was decided by paying high regard to the trees that exist on the property. The layout was determined by arranging the owner's residence in the 3rd floor, the mother's residence in the 2nd floor, and the gallery function on the 1st floor and the basement. A bridge is provided over the sunken garden placed at the center of the building to approach the gallery, and the two housings make a connection with nature through the terrace and open ceiling that go through the 1st and 2nd floors.

[099]

中之島プロジェクト II
(アーバン・エッグ＋地層空間)　1988
nakanoshima project II
(urban egg space strata)

1. 大阪市北区 | kita-ku, osaka
2. 設計 | design 1988.1
3. 構想案 | concept
5. 都市計画 | urban planning

1980年の「中之島プロジェクト」は建替えが議論された旧大阪市役所を対象としていた。それから9年後発表の「中之島プロジェクト II」と銘打つ提案は、大阪市中央公会堂のなかに、安藤の造形による新たな卵形の劇場空間を挿入する大胆な内容だった。相場師、岩本栄之助が寄付した文化遺産をどう継承するか、この提案はやがて「平成・桜の通り抜け」など、大阪に残る貴重な都市資産としての中之島全体に、安藤が積極的に関わっていく大きなきっかけとなった。美術館などの施設は地下に収容する構成をとり、「地層空間」をうたった。卵形の造形は、「鹿児島大学稲盛ホール」や「東急東横線渋谷駅改築」などの複数の作品で具体化した。→参照 [037]

The NAKANOSHIMA PROJECT in 1980 was for the former Osaka City office that was discussed to be renovated. Nine years later, the NAKANOSHIMA PROJECT II was proposed. This had a bold design of Ando's new form with an egg-shaped theater space inserted in the Osaka City Central Public Hall. This project was the beginning of Ando to be actively involved with determining how to inherit the cultural heritage contributed by the stockjobber Iwamoto Einosuke as well as preserving Osaka's precious heritage in Nakanoshima such as Sakura No Kai Heisei Cherry Blossom Viewing. The facilities such as museum are located underground to be called "stratum space". The egg-shaped form was realized in various works such as INAMORI AUDITORIUM of Kagoshima University and renovation of TOKYU TOYOKO-LINE SHIBUYA STATION. → see also [037]

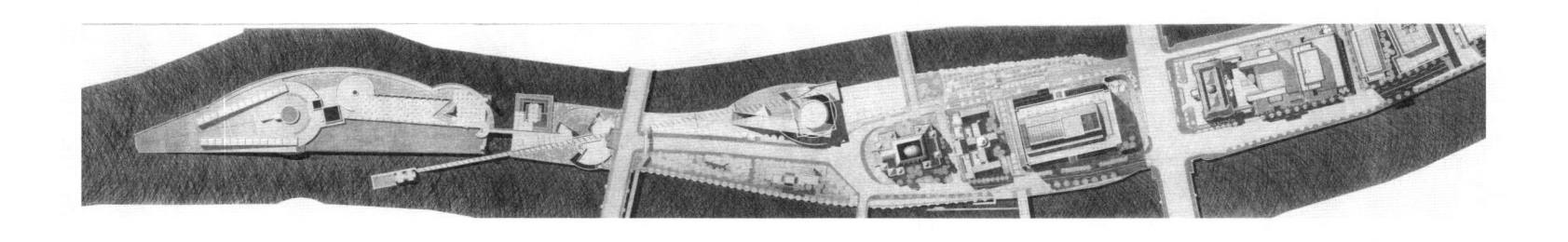

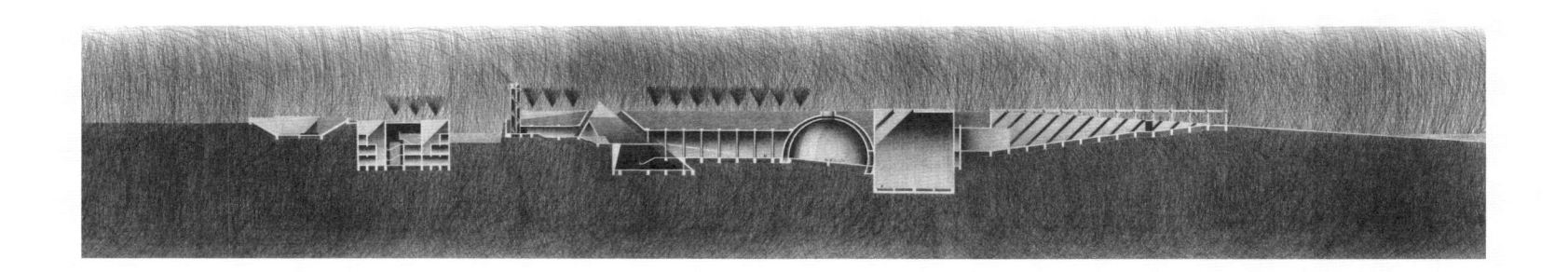

[100]
COLLEZIONE 1989
collezione

1. 東京都港区 | minato-ku, tokyo
2. 設計 | design 1986.3–1987.8
3. 施工 | construction 1987.9–1989.9
4. 鉄骨鉄筋コンクリート | SRC
5. 店舗、事務所 | shop, office
6. 敷地 | site 1,683.5 m²
7. 建築 | building 1,175.3 m²
8. 延床 | total floor 5,709.7 m²

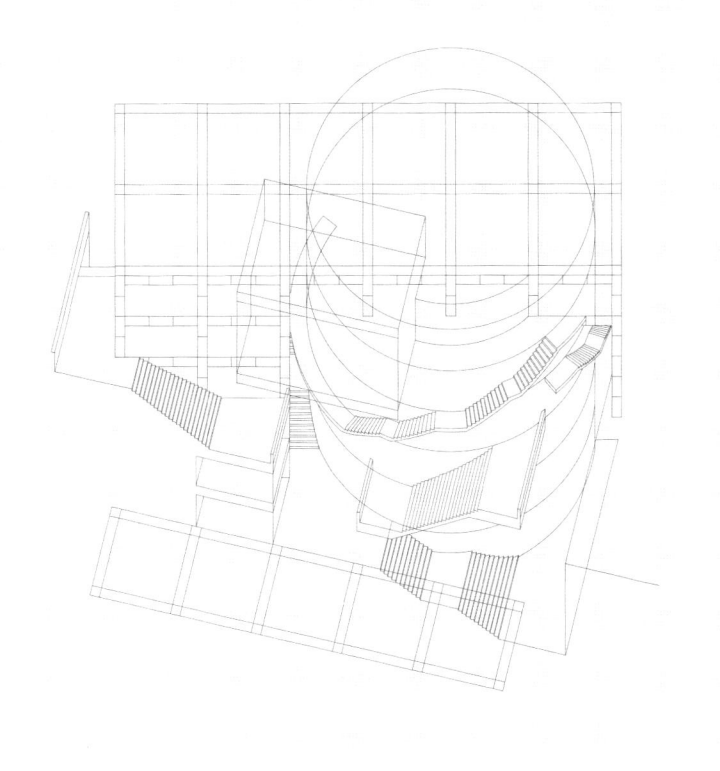

「地層建築」をテーマとした複合商業ビル。道路を挟んだ向かいに「根津美術館」の緑豊かな庭園があり、それら周囲の環境への影響を最小にするためにも、建築のヴォリュームの半分を地中に埋設する必然性があった。相応な部分を円筒形にして、この円筒形と敷地境界などの余地を活用し、井戸の底を覗くような立体空間を生成した。円筒形の外側に巻きつく階段は、そうした空間のダイナミズムを来訪者が堪能するための装置となっている。

This is a commercial complex building based on a concept as "stratum architecture". There is a lush garden of "Nezu Museum" across the road, and it was necessary to embed half of the building volume in the ground in order to minimize the influence to such surrounding environment. The corresponding part was designed in cylindrical shape, and the space of this cylindrical form and the boundary of the site is utilized to generate a 3 dimensional space, as if looking into the bottom of a well. The staircase circulating around the outside of this cylindrical form becomes a device for visitors to enjoy the dynamism of such space.

[101]
モロゾフ P&P スタジオ 1989
morozoff p&p studio

1. 神戸市中央区 | chuo-ku, kobe
2. 設計 | design 1986.4–1988.5
3. 施工 | construction 1988.5–1989.5
4. 型枠コンクリートブロック | fill-up concrete-block
5. 事務所 | office
6. 敷地 | site 985.5 m²
7. 建築 | building 530.2 m²
8. 延床 | total floor 1,620.6 m²

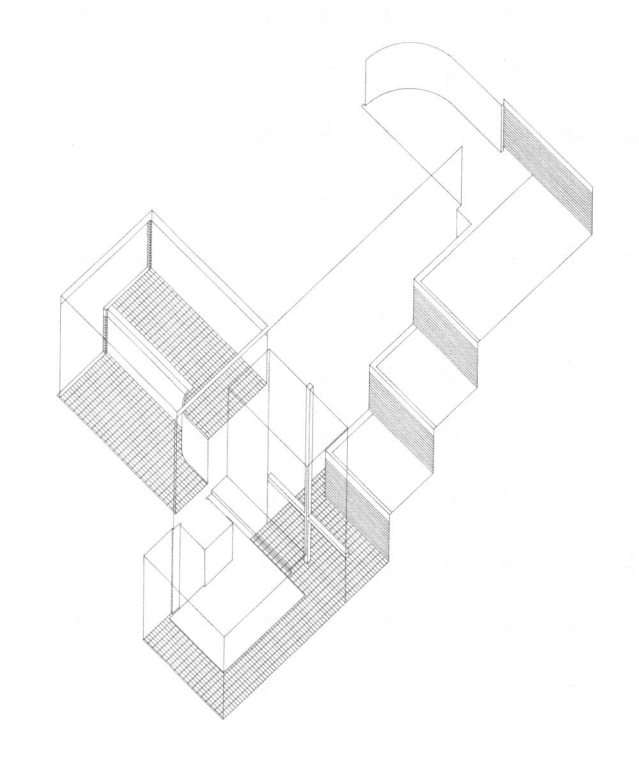

神戸港の埋立地ポートアイランドに位置した菓子メーカーの研究開発スタジオ。ここで開発されたチョコレートは「P&Pスタジオ」というブランド名で販売されていた。安藤がこの時期にいくつかのオフィスビルや商業施設で使っていたブロックの壁が、コンクリート打ち放しとは異なる落ち着きを建物に与えた。埋立地の四角く区切られた道路の四つ角に位置し、角向いは、やはり安藤が設計した「ジュン・ポートアイランドビル」の広大な敷地となっている。

A studio for research and development of a confectionery manufacturer located at the Port Island, which is reclaimed land in Kobe Port. The chocolate products developed at this studio was sold with the brand name P&P Studio. Block walls Ando was using around this time for various office buildings and commercial facilities provide a calm atmosphere to the buildings that is different from that of exposed concrete. The studio is located at a crossroad of the reclaimed land sectioned in squares where the vast property on the other side of the corner is the JUN PORT ISLAND BUILDING, which also was designed by Ando.

[102]

光の教会　1989
church of the light

1. 大阪府茨木市｜ibaraki, osaka
2. 設計｜design　1987.1–1988.5
3. 施工｜construction　1988.5–1989.4
4. 鉄筋コンクリート｜RC
5. 教会｜church
6. 敷地｜site　838.6 m²
7. 建築｜building　113.0 m²
8. 延床｜total floor　113.0 m²

日本基督教団の教会の敷地内の増築として計画されたこの建築は、十分な予算がなく、安藤は壁だけで屋根の架からない礼拝の場を想定した。関係者の熱意は低予算の限界を打破し、代表作のひとつとなる教会建築が実現した。四角い箱型の本体の躯体と、15度で交差する壁が奥行きのなかほどで交錯する。この貫入する壁を切り欠いてエントランスが設けられ、来訪者は斜めの壁によって一度転換させられた視線を四角い箱の奥に転じると、壁を切り欠いた「十字」が視界に飛び込んでくる。劇的な演出が、宗教空間としての神秘性や荘厳さを高める効果をあげている。→参照［182］

This is an extension of a church building within its territory of the United Church of Christ in Japan, although the project was in short of budget. Then, Ando came up with an idea of a chapel space built only with walls without any roof structure. The eagerness of the stakeholders broke the limit of the low budget, and realized the church building which is one of the masterpieces of Ando. The main volume of the building in square box shape and a wall intersect in the middle part of the box at 15°angle. This piercing wall is cut out to provide an entrance. When visitors turn the view, which was changed by the diagonal wall, to the back of the square box, and then "The Cross" cut out of the wall jumps into their sight. This dramatic setting raises the mystique and majesty in a religious space. → see also [182]

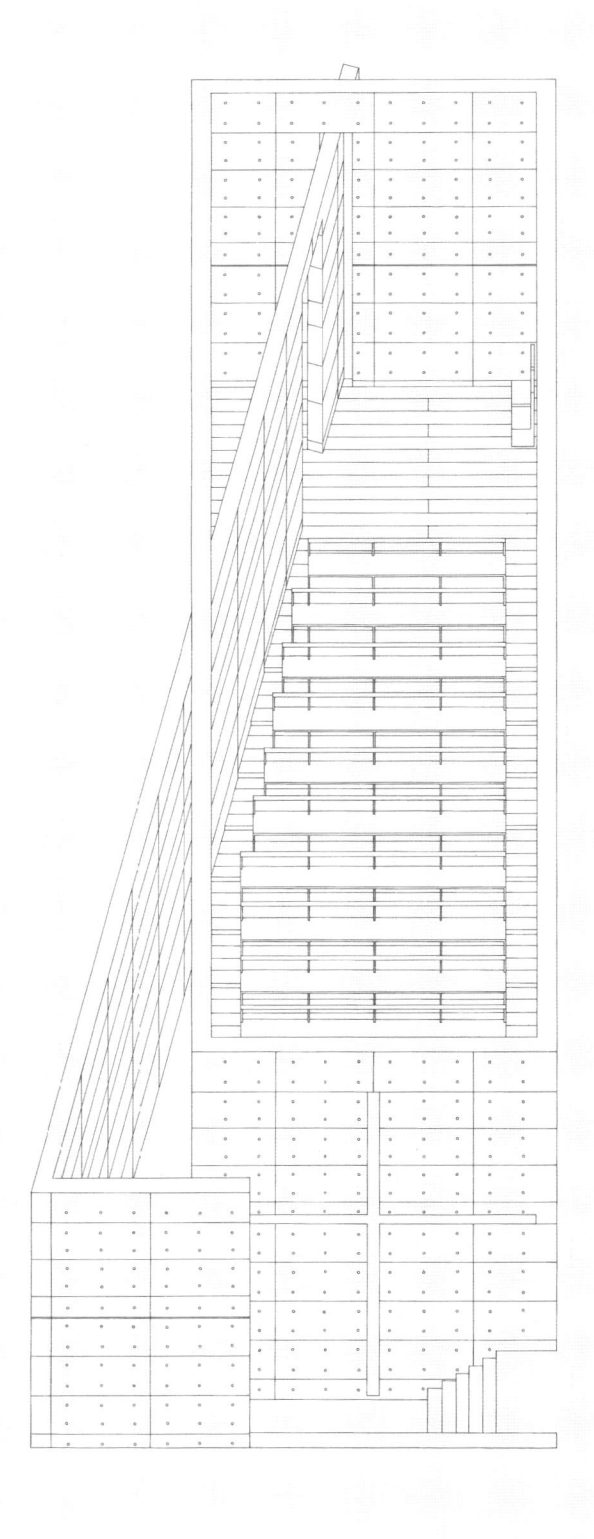

全346作品録

[103]
兵庫県立こどもの館　1989
children's museum, hyogo

1. 兵庫県姫路市 | himeji, hyogo
2. 設計 | design　1987.3–1988.3
3. 施工 | construction　1988.3–1989.7
4. 鉄骨鉄筋コンクリート、一部鉄筋コンクリート、鉄骨 | RC, SRC, steel
5. 多目的ホール、野外劇場、美術館、図書館、工作室 | auditrium, open-air theater, library
6. 敷地 | site　87,222.0㎡
7. 建築 | building　3,575.6㎡
8. 延床 | total floor　7,488.4㎡

兵庫県姫路市の山間地に位置する広大な貯水池を見おろす丘陵に、二か所に分かれて施設が設けられている。複合的な機能を持つ本館と200メートルほど離れた位置に配された工房である。両者は山林のなかの長大な通路で結ばれる。通路のコンクリートの壁が延々と続く光景は、建築家の環境への参画の意志をうかがわせる。本館は図書館、ギャラリー、ホールなどを併せ持ち、屋上には円形の野外劇場もある。人工池が本館を取り巻き、建物から池を見おろすデッキを張り出させるなど、貯水池の傍らに位置する環境との整合性が意識されている。
→参照 [129]

This facility stands in two places on a hill looking down on the vast reservoir in mountainous location of Himeji City, Hyogo Prefecture. It is a workshop located at a distance of 200 meters from the main wing with multiple functionalities. Both are connected by a long pathway in the mountainous forest. The sight that the concrete walls of the pathway continues indefinitely shows the intention of the architect to get involved with the surrounding environment. The main wing has a library, galleries and a hall space, with an open-air amphitheater on the rooftop. The main wing is surrounded by an artificial pond, and a deck structure is extended out to look down at the pond from the building. It is the design to make the building consistent with the environment next to the reservoir. → see also [129]

[104]
ライカ本社ビル　1989
raika headquarters building

1. 大阪市住之江区 | suminoe-ku, osaka
2. 設計 | design　1986.6–1987.12
3. 施工 | construction　1987.12–1989.12
4. 鉄筋コンクリート、鉄骨 | RC, steel
5. 事務所 | office
6. 敷地 | site　23,487.8 m²
7. 建築 | building　9,771.4 m²
8. 延床 | total floor　42,791.8 m²

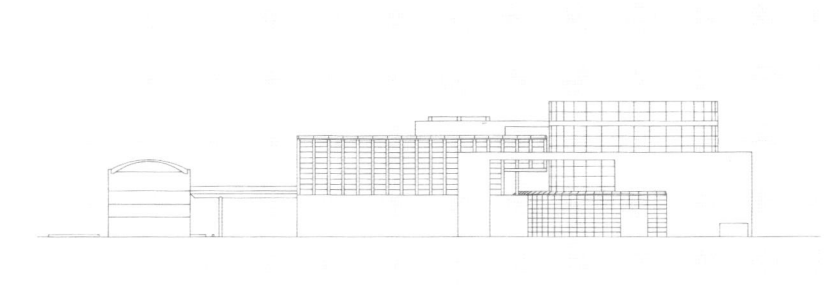

大阪・南港に位置したアパレルメーカーのオフィスビル。直径40メートルのガラスブロックの円筒を中心に矩形がオーバーラップする配置をとる。湾岸の立地らしい開放的な自然の恩恵を仕事の場でも受けられるように、屋上庭園や内側に昇降の螺旋のスロープを備えた吹き抜けホールなど、従来のオフィスビルにはない数々の装置を配した。また、敷地の一角にパブリックスペースとしての広場を配し、他企業で働くひとたちにもウォーターフロントを楽しんでもらおうとした。

An office building for an apparel manufacturer in Nanko, Osaka. The layout is arranged with a cylinder of 40 meters in diameter made of glass blocks placed at the center that is overlapped by a rectangle shape. Various apparatus that do not exist in normal office buildings were added to benefit from gifts of nature even in a work environment that provide a sense of spaciousness unique to the bay area such as a rooftop garden and a hall with an open ceiling that has a spiral slope inside to go upstairs or downstairs. Furthermore, a plaza is placed as a public space in the property to allow workers of other companies to enjoy the water front atmosphere.

[105]
夏川記念会館　1989
natsukawa memorial hall

1. 滋賀県彦根市 | hikone, shiga
2. 設計 | design　1987.4–1988.10
3. 施工 | construction　1988.10–1989.11
4. 鉄筋コンクリート、鉄骨 | RC, steel
5. 資料館 | resource center
6. 敷地 | site　768.2 m²
7. 建築 | building　521.1 m²
8. 延床 | total floor　1,205.0 m²

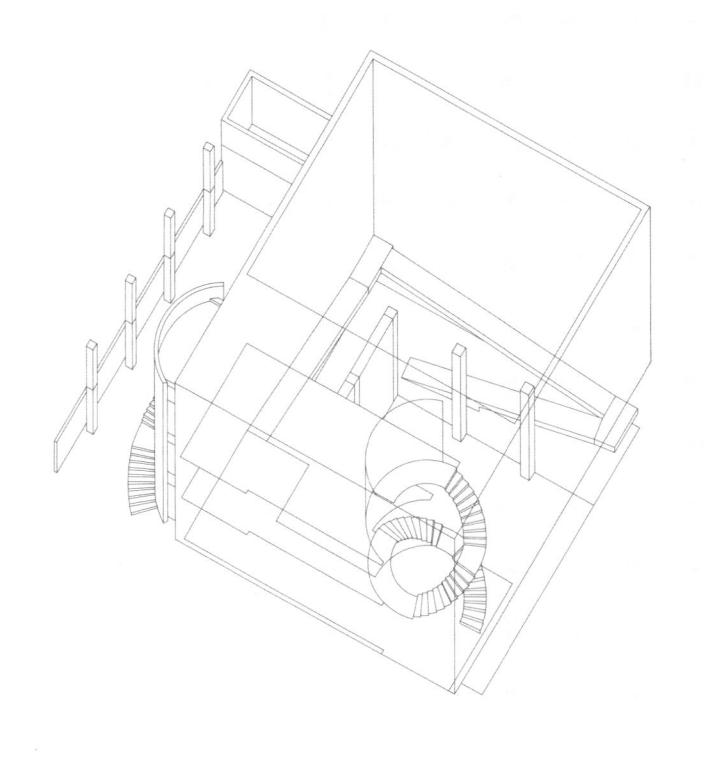

滋賀県彦根市の私立高校の会議場、多目的ホールなどを備えた施設。全体を直方体の単純なコンクリートの箱とし、外壁のひとつの面はコンクリートの格子から内部のヴォイドがうかがえる構成とした。屋上までの吹き抜けとなっているエントランスホールをはじめ、スロープ、階段などで屋外と繋がる開放的な内部空間を味わえる。屋上には樹木を配した庭園を設け、そこにたたずむ人影を路上から確かめることによる外部環境との交信も期待した。

This facility consists of a conference room and a multi-purpose hall for a private high school in Hikone City, Shiga Prefecture. Entire program is housed in a simple concrete cuboid box, and one of the faces of the exterior walls in concrete grid allows to look into the void space inside of the box. Through a space such as the entrance hall with an open ceiling extending up to the roof level, the building allows users to experience openness of the interior space that is also linked to the exterior conditions by slopes and a staircase. A tree lined garden space is provided on the rooftop, and people in this garden can be visible from the street level so that visual communication with the outside environment is promoted.

[106]
城尾邸　1989
shiroo house

1. 東京都渋谷区 | shibuya-ku, tokyo
2. 設計 | design　1987.6–1988.6
3. 施工 | construction　1988.7–1989.7
4. 鉄筋コンクリート | RC
5. 住宅 | detached house
6. 敷地 | site　111㎡
7. 建築 | building　57㎡
8. 延床 | total floor　201㎡

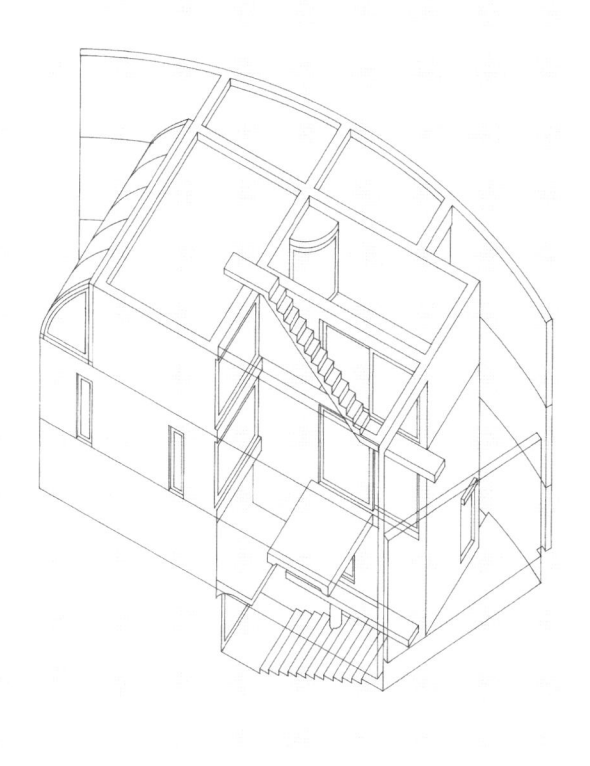

東京・渋谷の住宅街のアトリエ付属の住宅。限られた敷地に置いた直方体に三層のフロアを重ね、曲面壁と直方体の空隙の吹き抜けに昇降のための階段を配し、生活空間としての一体化をはかった。3階の寝室にはテラスを設けて、自然の変化を日々の暮らしのなかで実感できる仕立てをとった。3階の道路側は垂直方向の曲面のトップライトとするとともに妻壁の側に窓をとり、囲われたコンクリートボックスへの自然光の導入にも留意している。

A residential house with an atelier in a residential area of Shibuya, Tokyo. Three floors are put on top of each other in a rectangular solid placed on a limited amount of property and stairways were built in wellhole area made in the gap between the curved wall placed on the side and the rectangular solid to pursue integrated atmosphere as a living space. A terrace is set to the 3rd floor bedroom to create an area where seasonal changes can be felt in daily activities. A curved top light was provided on the 3rd floor in a vertical direction on the road side and a window was placed on the gable wall side in order to bring natural light inside the surrounded concrete box.

[107]
矢尾クリニック　1989
yao clinic

1. 大阪府寝屋川市 | neyagawa, osaka
2. 設計 | design　1988.1–1989.5
3. 施工 | construction　1989.5–1989.12
4. 鉄筋コンクリート | RC
5. 診療所 | clinic
6. 敷地 | site　137.9㎡
8. 延床 | total floor　174.2㎡

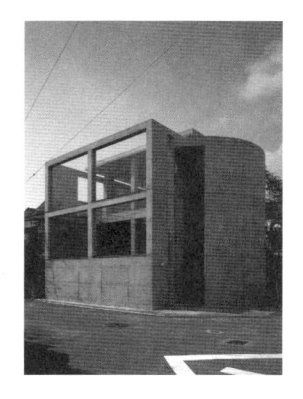

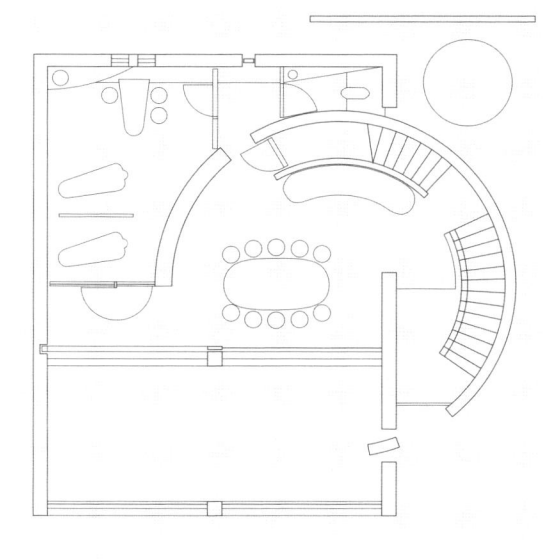

大阪・寝屋川の歯科医院。建物の躯体は円筒と直方体を組み合わせた。さらに、表道路の境界線から垂直の壁を立ち上げ、建物本体にも食い込ませた。道路に面した壁にはガラスの嵌まった大きな開口部があり、地階の中庭や各階の待合室などに自然光が届く。円筒の内壁に沿って上階の診察室などにあがる螺旋階段が配され、そこにはガラス屋根のトップライトから自然光が降り注ぐ。幾何立体とトップライト、開口部のダイナミックな組み合わせで、規模を超えた多様な空間が展開する。

A dental clinic in Neyagawa City, Osaka Prefecture. The structure is a combination of a cylinder and a cuboid. A vertical wall rises from the border of the front street and cuts into the building. Large fixed glass windows on the wall facing the street provide natural light to the underground courtyard and waiting rooms on each floor. Spiral stairs along the interior wall of the cylinder continue to the upper floors with a dentist's office. Natural light pours through a skylight on the glass roof. A dynamic combination of the geometric shapes, skylight, and openings develops a diversity of spaces beyond scale.

[108]
B-LOCK北山　1990
b-lock kitayama

1. 京都市左京区 | sakyo-ku, kyoto
2. 設計 | design　1985.5–1988.10
3. 施工 | construction　1988.12–1990.2
4. 型枠コンクリートブロック | fill-up concrete-block
5. 集合住宅 | apartment house
6. 敷地 | site　564.2㎡
7. 建築 | building　377.7㎡
8. 延床 | total floor　1,117.6㎡

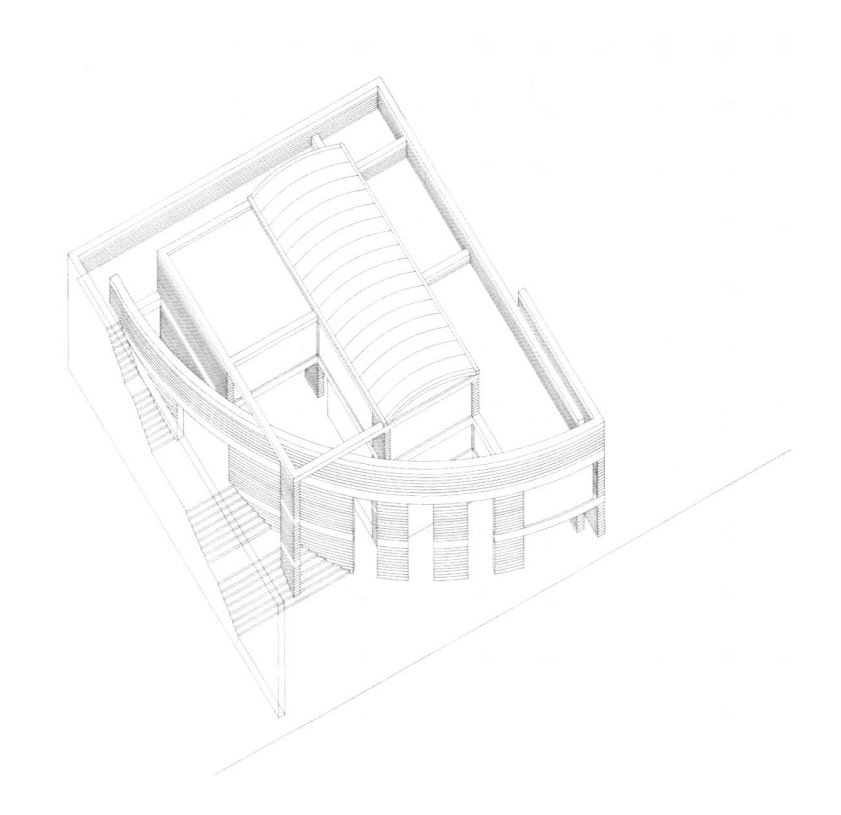

表通り側から見たとき、コンクリートブロックの大きな曲面壁と、そこに交差する太い骨格のコンクリートブロックのフレームに目がいく。この曲面壁の背後にヴォールト屋根の架かる住棟が配置され、居住者は曲面壁に沿う階段を上って住戸に向う。フレームは住棟のグリッドの一部を示し、円弧を描く曲面と格子の二つの幾何学の交差が、この小規模な集合住宅に重厚さを伴った存在感を持たせる効果をあげている。

A large curved wall made of concrete blocks and a thick frame made of concrete blocks that intersect with the curved wall gather attention when viewed from the front street. The residential building with a vault roof stands behind the curved wall where residents go up the stairs along the curved wall to their housing units. The frame is a section of the grid of the residential building in which the intersection of two types of geometry; the curved surface and the lattice contributes to have the profound presence of this small-scale condominium.

[109]
伊東邸　1990
ito house

1. 東京都世田谷区 | setagaya-ku, tokyo
2. 設計 | design　1988.4–1989.6
3. 施工 | construction　1989.7–1990.11
4. 鉄筋コンクリート（ラーメン、壁式）| RC (frame, wall)
5. 住宅 | detached house
6. 敷地 | site　567.7㎡
7. 建築 | building　279.7㎡
8. 延床 | total floor　504.8㎡

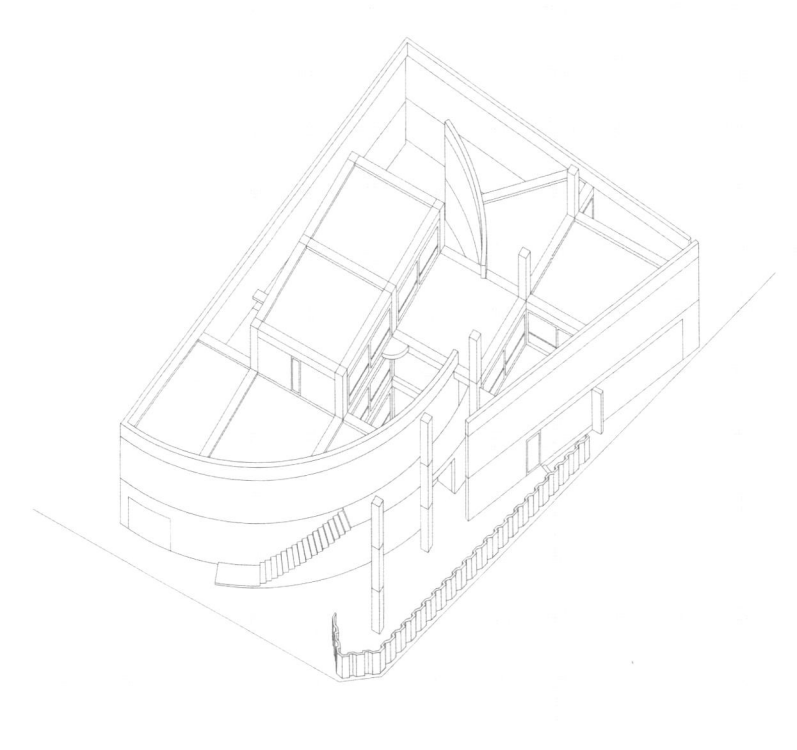

両親と息子、娘、各夫婦の三世帯住宅、息子の経営するブティックとアトリエ、それらの要素を満たすことが、この住宅では求められた。住宅の基本は5.6メートル角の格子で、それに従って1階から3階に三世帯の住宅が配置された。それぞれが中庭、テラス、吹き抜けで外部空間に面することにより独立性を確保し、自然を暮らしのなかに引き込む構成を実現した。格子の躯体に敷地に沿った円弧が交差し、コンクリートの独立柱をグリッドが連想できるように配した。ブティックとアトリエは円弧の外側に置いた。

A residential house for three families; parents, their son and daughter with a boutique and atelier managed by the son. Satisfying all those factors was required in designing this residence in Setagaya, Tokyo. The basic form of the residence is a lattice form of 5.6 meters on each side and housings for three families were arranged based on it from the 1st floor to the 3rd floor. Independency was secured by positioning each floor to face the outdoor space from the courtyard, terrace, and open ceiling and create a layout that draws nature into their daily lives. Isolated columns were placed where circular arcs along the property intersect with the lattice structure to remind of the 5.6-meter grid. The boutique and atelier were placed outside the circular arc.

[110]
国際花と緑の博覧会「名画の庭」 1990
garden of fine art, expo'90 / osaka

1. 大阪市鶴見区 | tsurumi-ku, osaka
2. 設計 | design   1988.6–1989.5
3. 施工 | construction   1989.7–1990.3
4. 鉄筋コンクリート | RC
5. パビリオン | exhibition hall
6. 敷地 | site   3,003.0 m²
7. 建築 | building   441.5 m²
8. 延床 | total floor   692.3 m²

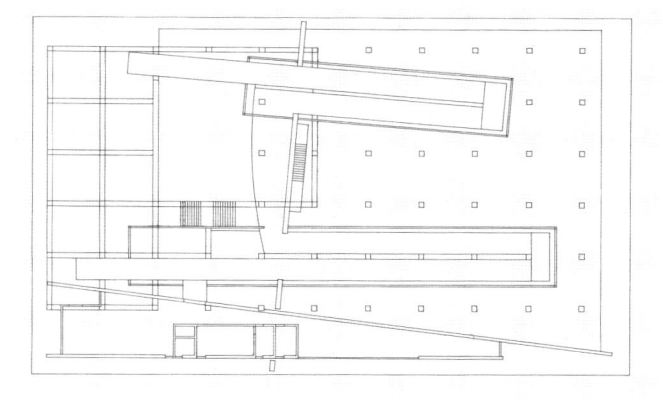

1990年、大阪の鶴見緑地での「花と緑の国際博覧会」に企業出展されたパビリオン。「水の庭」をテーマに、水の張られた敷地内に高さ12.6メートルの角柱45本を規則正しい間隔で林立させる屋外庭園を手がけた。展示としては、レオナルド・ダ・ヴィンチの「最後の晩餐」など名画をセラミックスで原寸大に再現した屋外展示を回遊しながら観賞するものであった。回遊路は2階レベルから地階までを周遊するように設えられた。安藤の手になるこの庭園は、光と風があふれ、博覧会のテーマと合致し、多くの来訪者を集めた。→参照 [141]

This is the pavilion for the exhibition of a company at "The International Garden and Greenery Exposition" in Tsurumi Park in Osaka. The theme of this project was to create a "Garden of Water", which is lined up with 45 square columns in 12.6m high in the outdoor territory space covered with water basin. This exhibition space was for presenting famous paintings reproduced on ceramic materials in actual size, including the painting by Leonardo da Vinci, "The Last Supper". Visitors move freely around the outdoor exhibition space to enjoy those paintings through a circulation passage installed to travel around from the 2nd floor level to the underground level. This garden space was consistent with the theme of the exposition, and gathered many visitors. → see also [141]

[111]
S ビル   1990
s building

1. 大阪市北区 | kita-ku, osaka
2. 設計 | design   1989.3–1989.11
3. 施工 | construction   1989.12–1990.12
4. 鉄骨鉄筋コンクリート 一部鉄骨 | SRC, steel
5. 事務所 | office
6. 敷地 | site   271.6 m²
7. 建築 | building   213.4 m²
8. 延床 | total floor   1,242.6 m²

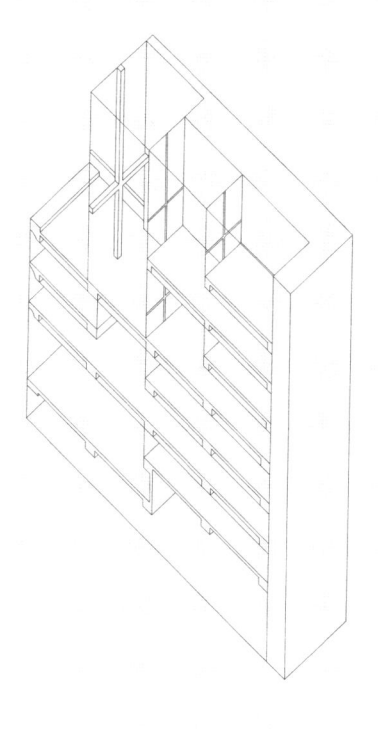

大阪都心の広告代理店のオフィスビル。敷地は、間口が狭く奥行きが深い。正面外観が示すように中層階で上下二つのブロックに分けて、6階から上をセットバックさせる明快な構成をとった。二つのブロックはそれぞれコンクリートの格子を十字型に外壁側に組むざっくりした構成。上部のブロックは十字の奥に屋外扱いのテラスを設け、深い陰影をもたせた。その外部のテラスに昇降のためのコンクリートの階段を配し、都市で働くひとびとが自然を感じられる仕立てとした。

This is the office building for an advertisement agency located in the center of Osaka. The site has a narrow entry with a deep elongated shape. As the front exterior presents, the building is clearly configured with two separate blocks in upper and lower layers divided at the middle floor level, with a setback applied to the upper volume above 6th floor. The façades of those two blocks are composed of concrete grids assembled in cross shapes on the exterior wall. The upper block houses an exterior terrace behind the cross shape to receive opaque shades from the cross structure. In addition, a concrete staircase was provided to go up and down from this exterior terrace, allowing people working in this urban environment to feel the nature through this element.

[112]
ストックホルム現代美術館・
建築美術館国際設計競技案
1990
the modern art museum and
architecture museum, stockholm,
international design competition
.
1. スウェーデン ストックホルム | stockholm, sweden
2. 設計 | design   1990
3. 設計競技 | design competition
4. 鉄骨鉄筋コンクリート | SRC
5. 現代美術館、建築美術館
   museum of contemporary art and architecture
6. 敷地 | site   153,000 m²
7. 建築 | building   10070 m²
8. 延床 | total floor   17,350 m²

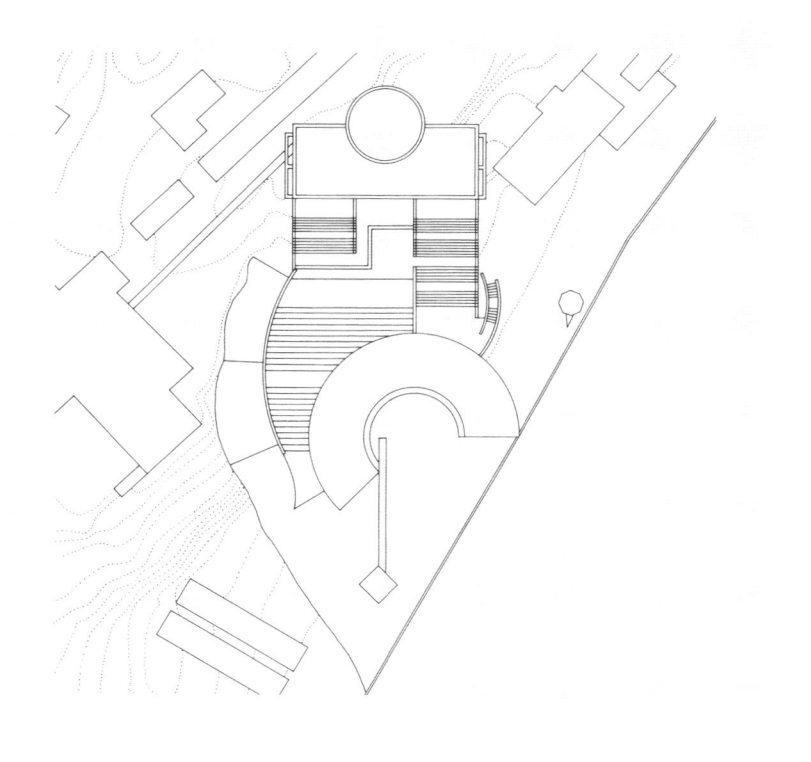

入り江に面したスウェーデン・ストックホルムのシェップスホルメン島は、美術館、博物館が集まる「美術館島」と呼ばれる。この島の現代美術館コンペに、安藤は、モネオ、ゲーリーらとともに指名されて参加した。安藤が提案したのは、水辺の環境を踏まえて屋外にも現代美術の展示を実現する階段をセールスポイントとする計画で、陸側に現代美術館を、海側に建築博物館を配した。ストックホルムは北のヴェネチアと呼ばれる都市のひとつだが、水辺を想定したコンペは後年の安藤のヴェネチアでの仕事に継承されている。
.
Skeppsholmen Island of Stockholm, which is a town facing the bay of Stockholm in Sweden, is known as the "Art Gallery Island" since there are several art galleries and museums. For the competition for modern museums of this island, Ando was designated to participate with Moneo and Gehry. Ando proposed a plan to have stairs as the strong point to materialize exhibition of modern arts outdoors as well as considering the waterfront environment. He placed the modern art gallery on the land side and the architecture museum on the ocean side. Stockholm is one of the cities called the northern Venice. For Ando, however, this contest in Stockholm with waterfront in view was succeeded by his work later in Venice.

[113]
十文字美信仮設劇場   1990
temporary theater for bishin jumonji,
photographer
.
1. 東京都新宿区 | shinjyuku-ku, tokyo
2. 設計 | design   1990.2–1990.3
3. 施工 | construction   1990.4
4. 木造 | wood
5. 仮設劇場 | temporary theater
6. total: 80.0 m²

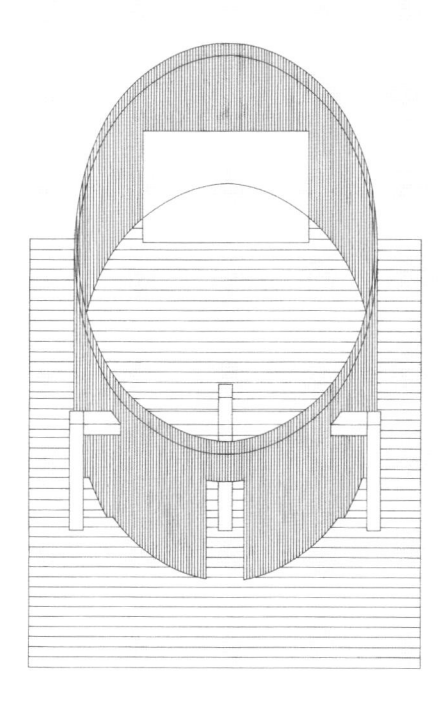

テレビの3Dハイビジョンシステムのプレゼンテーションのために4日間の限定で開設された木造の小劇場。東京・四ツ谷のギャラリーの地下空間が会場に充てられた。杉の足場板を張りつめた木造の四角い箱が造られ、その内部に床と同じ杉材の高さ4メートルの楕円の筒が置かれた。定員30人の鑑賞者はそこで、写真家十文字美信の撮影した仏像を立体映像で見る仕掛けだった。黒くステイン塗装された木材が縦に張られた空間は強い垂直性によって厳粛な雰囲気をもたらした。
.
This is a temporal theater space only for 4 days in small wooden structure, for making a presentation of 3D high definition TV system. The venue was held in the underground space of a gallery in Yotsuya, Tokyo. A wooden square box with a cedar wood scaffolding board was built, and an oval shaped cylinder form in 4m high with the same cedar wood material as the flooring was placed within the space. A viewer with a capacity of 30 people was there to watch the 3D video image presentation of a Buddha statue filmed by a photographer, Bishin Jumonji. The space is covered by vertical wooden strips stained in black color, providing a sense of solemnity through its strong verticality.

[114]
姫路文学館　1991
museum of literature, himeji

1. 兵庫県姫路市｜himeji, hyogo
2. 設計｜design　1988.7–1989.11
3. 施工｜construction　1989.7–1991.3
4. 鉄骨鉄筋コンクリート｜SRC
5. 文学資料館｜literature museum
6. 敷地｜site　15,600.9 m²
7. 建築｜building　1,324.1 m²
8. 延床｜total floor　3,814.5 m²

国宝姫路城から北西に500メートル離れた男山の山麓に立地している。建物の本体は、一辺22.5メートルの二つの立方体を30度ずらして重合させた。ずれは内部の展示空間などにトリッキーな動線を生み出す効果をあげている。立方体を取り巻くように設けられた人工池の水は、一般道へと下るスロープに沿う水路を流れ、姫路城に視線を誘導する役割を与えられている。姫路ゆかりの和辻哲郎の木造の書斎が文学館に隣接する竹林に保存され、安藤のコンクリートボックスと新旧の対比を示す。→参照 [160]

This building is located at the foot of Otoko-yama Mountain. The main building volume is composed of two cubes in 22.5m, and layered them on top of each other by rotating 30° against each other. The gap created by this rotation affects the interior exhibition space by promoting unique, unpredictable circulations. The water of an artificial pond set around the cubes runs through a water channel along with a slope going up from a public road to the facility, and also given a role to guide the visual line of visitors to Himeji-jo Castle. A wooden study room of Tetsuro Watsuji, a closely related figure of Himeji, is preserved within a bamboo forest located next to this literature museum, showing a contrast between this old building with the new structures of Ando's concrete box. → see also [160]

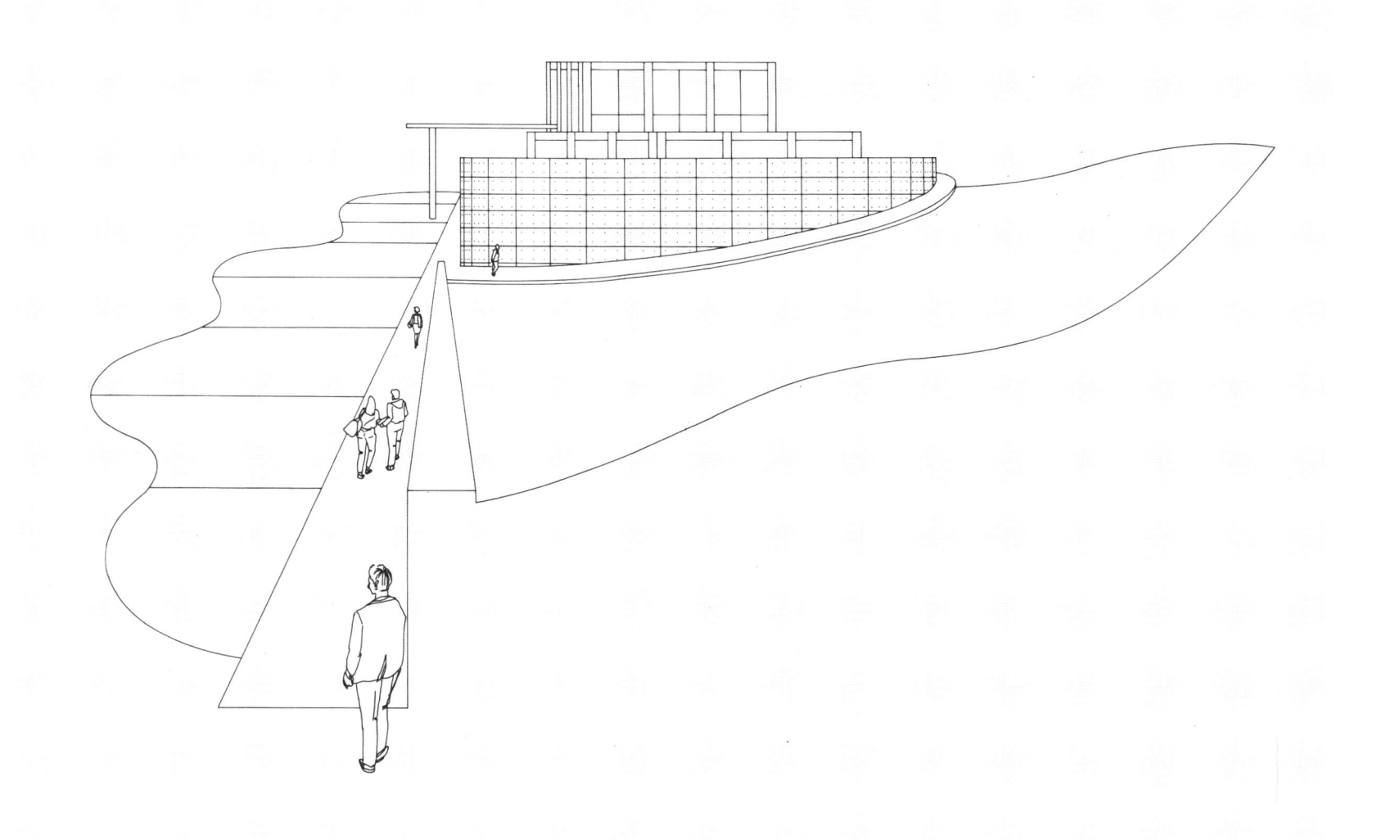

[115]
石河邸　1991
ishiko house

1. 大阪府高槻市 | takatsuki, osaka
2. 設計 | design　1989.1–1990.4
3. 施工 | construction　1990.5–1991.5
4. 鉄筋コンクリート（壁式）| RC (wall)
5. 住宅、診療所 | clinic
6. 敷地 | site　179.3 m²
7. 建築 | building　107.0 m²
8. 延床 | total floor　239.8 m²

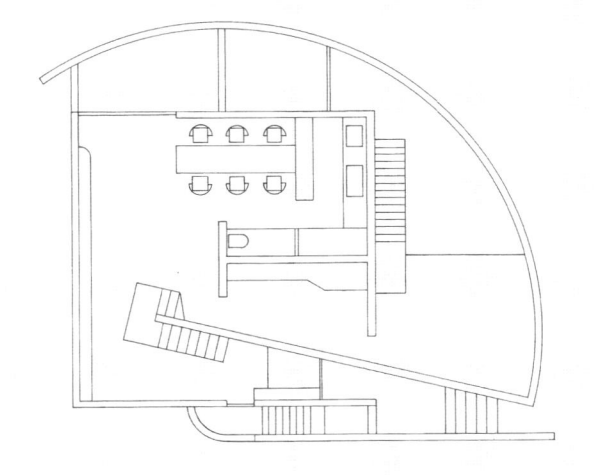

角地の立地にコンクリート打ち放しの円筒を立てて、外部と生活空間を切り離す構成を選択した。居室は円筒の内部に立方体で配され、そこには上部のスリットから絞られた自然光が浸潤してくる。内部の階段は正方形に設定され、屋内の各階の床も矩形に収められているため、吹き抜け空間は曲線と直線の隙間に展開してダイナミックな様相を呈する。傾斜した道路に合わせて、建物と歩道との間に生じた小さな空間に植栽を施し、住宅が大地にしっかり根を下ろす風景を演出している。

An exposed concrete cylinder was situated on the corner property and separated the living space from outside. Cubes were placed inside the cylinder to form living rooms and narrowed natural light plugs into through its slits above. Since the inner stairway is a square shape and the floor of each story is a rectangle shape, the open ceiling area has a dynamic appearance developed in a gap between a curved line and straight lines. Plants were set on a small space between the building and a sidewalk on a sloped road giving the scenery as if the house was deeply rooted in the ground.

[116]
佐用ハウジング　1991
sayo housing

1. 兵庫県佐用郡 | sayoh, hyogo
2. 設計 | design　1989.3–1990.3
3. 施工 | construction　1990.5–1991.8
4. 鉄筋コンクリート（ラーメン）| RC (frame)
5. 集合住宅 | apartment house
6. 敷地 | site　6,989.0 m²
7. 建築 | building　1,270.0 m²
8. 延床 | total floor　3,854.2 m²

岡山県境に近い兵庫県のリゾート集合住宅。近隣の温泉地やスキー場の利用を目的としている。山頂に3本のコンクリートの塔が立つ。この塔は高層棟と呼ばれ、足元の斜面に直方体の低層棟が控えている。合わせて四つの棟は屋外のスロープや回廊で結ばれ、利用者は山頂ならではの眺めを楽しみながら歩き、リゾートの非日常的な感覚を堪能できる。「六甲の集合住宅」などで試みてきた斜面の集合住宅の外部空間構成の成果が反映されている。

A resort condominium in Hyogo Prefecture close to the border with Okayama Prefecture. It was built for visitors who come for hot springs in the area and to enjoy skiing. Three concrete towers are situated on the mountain peak. These towers are called the high-rise buildings and a rectangular solid low-rise building is situated on an inclined plane. These four buildings are connected with a slope and corridor for visitors to enjoy the walk while viewing the scenery from the mountain peak and fully experiencing the extraordinary feeling of the resort area. The outcome of the external space structure of an inclined plane used at works such as ROKKO HOUSING is reflected in this project.

[117]
ロックフィールド
静岡ファクトリー　1991, 2000
rockfield shizuoka factory
.
1. 静岡県磐田市｜iwata, shizuoka
2. 設計｜design　1989.7–1990.4 (phase 1),
1998.3–1998.8 (phase 2)
3. 施工｜construction　1990.5–1991.5 (phase 1),
1998.9–2000.5 (phase 2)
4. 鉄骨鉄筋コンクリート造、鉄骨｜SRC, steel
5. 工場｜factory
6. 敷地｜site　76,277.4 m²
7. 建築｜building　9,318.1 m²
8. 延床｜total floor　14,783.9 m²

デパートの地下売り場で惣菜を販売しているロックフィールドの工場。1990年代初めと2000年前後の2期に施工された。第1期の時点で円形のコロネードに囲われた緑の屋外広場、広大なルーフテラスなど、働くひとびとにとって快適な工場建築を実現した。続く2期の工場施設の増築に際しては、風力発電のための3基の風車が立てられた。その電力で排水を浄化してビオトープの維持に活用した。環境との共生があってこそ、地元のひとたちが進んで働く食品産業の工場になりうると考える旧知の経営者と安藤の信念が形をとった。→参照 [231]

This is a factory building of ROCK FIELD CO., LTD., a company producing and selling take-out dishes at food courts in department stores. The building was constructed in two phases, 1st phase in early 1990s and the 2nd phase in around 2000. The 1st phase building realized a factory building pleasant and comfortable for workers, by providing a green outdoor plaza space surrounded by colonnade in circle, and a vast rooftop terrace space. For the 2nd phase to expand the factory facility, 3 wind turbines for wind power generation were built, and the electricity generated by the turbines is utilized for purifying waste water of the factory to be used for maintaining a biotope. With the harmonious coexistence with the environment, the beliefs of Ando and the president of the company, an old acquaintance of Ando, took a shape as a factory building, thinking that a factory in the food industry may become the place where local people can work efficiently. → see also [231]

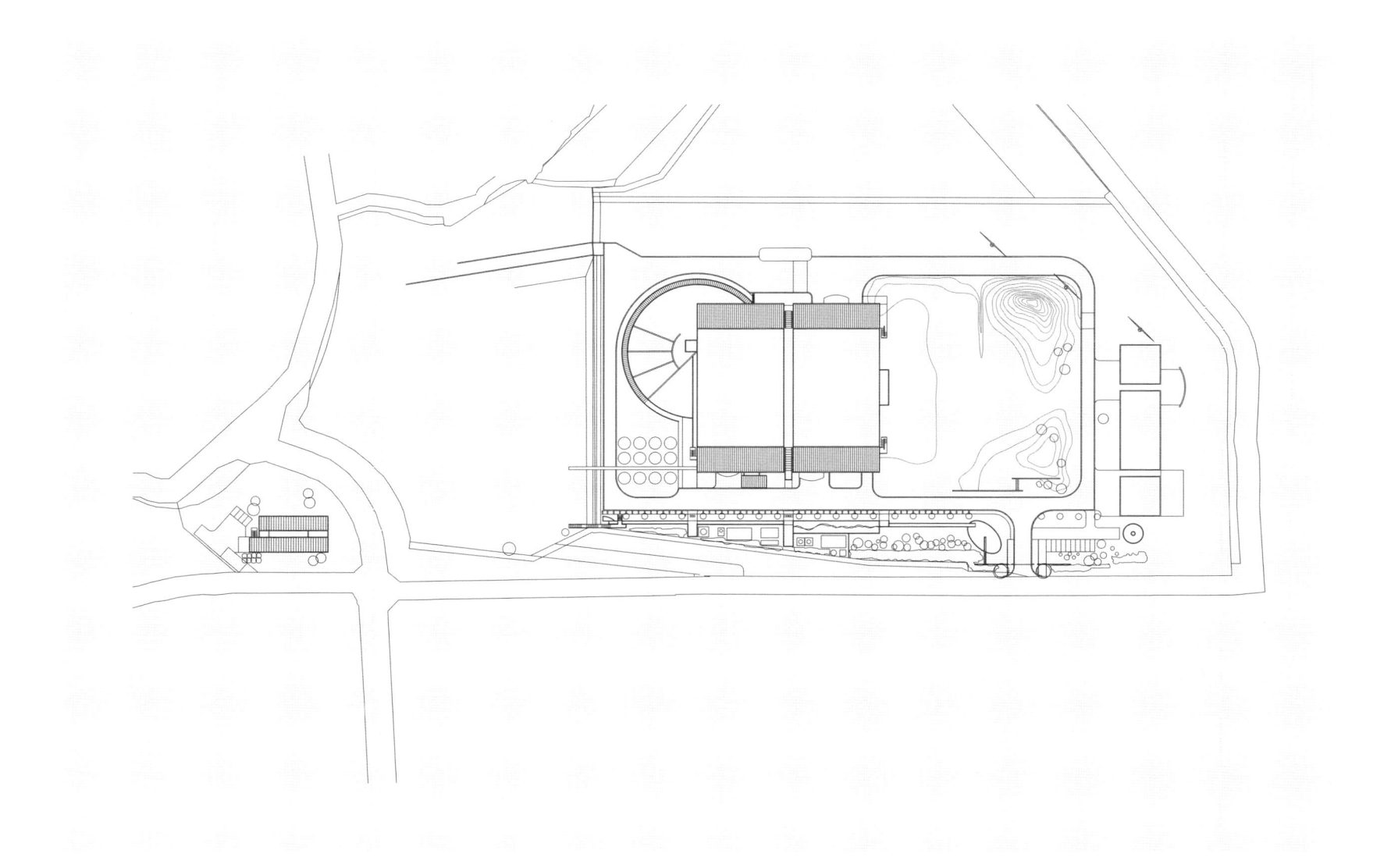

[118]
ミノルタセミナーハウス 1991
minolta seminar house

1. 神戸市西区 | nishi-ku, kobe
2. 設計 | design　1989.4–1990.6
3. 施工 | construction　1990.6–1991.9
4. 鉄筋コンクリート | RC
5. 社員寮 | company dormitory
6. 敷地 | site　4,132.9 m²
7. 建築 | building　1,859.3 m²
8. 延床 | total floor　4,556.4 m²

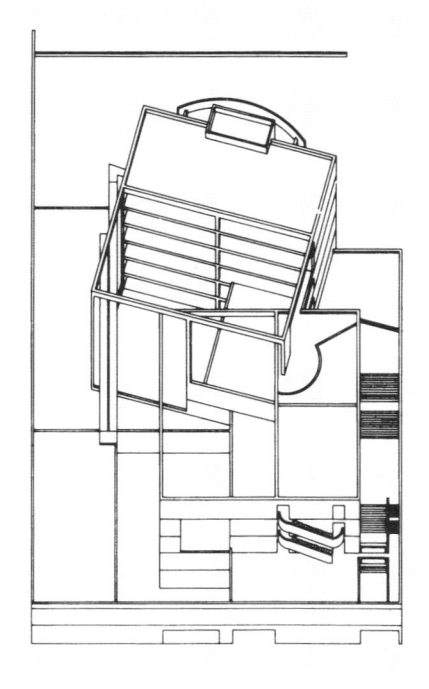

立地は神戸市の郊外。道路側の背面から眺めると開口部の少ない曲面壁が周囲から内部を守るかのようにそびえ立つ。一方、反対の中庭に面した側に回ると、居室、宿泊室のガラス窓が低層部の屋上緑化で自然を感じさせる場に向かって開かれている。低層から中層へは、途中で180度切り返す直線の屋外スロープが設けられ、利用者に外部空間の存在を意識させる。また、屋外の中層と低層の施設をひとまとめにするように、板状のコンクリートのフレームが敷地を囲い込み、建物の一体感を演出した。

The property is located in a suburb of Kobe City. A curved wall with small openings is standing as if it protected inside when seen from the road behind. However, when seen from the side facing the courtyard, the area is open to feel the nature on the rooftop greening from glass windows of living rooms and guest rooms. A straight outdoor slope that bends in 180-degree angle is provided for the passage between the lower level and middle level floors to make the users aware of the existence of the outdoor space. Plate concrete frames are surrounding the property to unite the outdoor facilities on the lower level and middle level floors to produce sense of integration of the building.

[119]
大淀のアトリエ II 1991
atelier in oyodo II

1. 大阪市北区 | kita-ku, osaka
2. 設計 | design　1989.6–1990.5
3. 施工 | construction　1990.6–1991.4
4. 鉄筋コンクリート（壁式ラーメン構造） | RC (wall-type frame structure)
5. アトリエ | atlier
6. 敷地 | site　115.6 m²
7. 建築 | building　91.7 m²
8. 延床 | total floor　451.7 m²

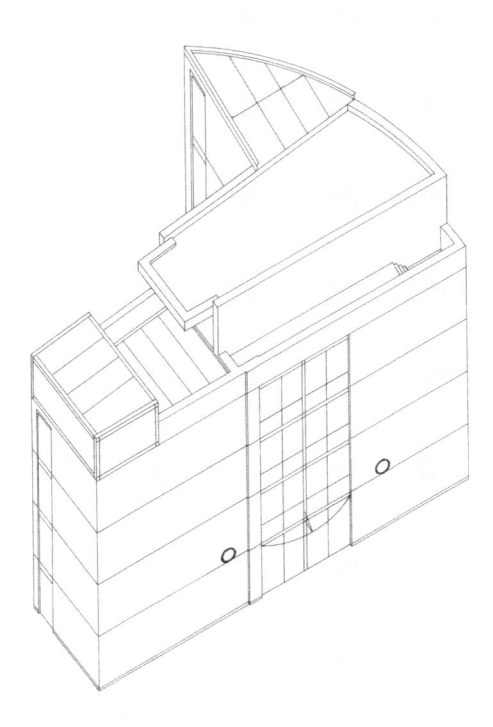

安藤は初期の作品「冨島邸」を3期にわたって改装した事務所を拠点としてきたが、それを解体して跡地に新たなアトリエを新築した。敷地の広さは120平方メートルほどで事務所建築としては広くないが、地上5階、地下2階の建築は、安藤の考える事務所としてのあるべき姿がそのまま形をとっている。中央に位置する五層分の吹き抜けは、この空間を介して所員たちの活気が各階相互に感じられ、ひと声かければ意志の伝わるコミュニケーションのツールとしても機能している。安藤は、この吹き抜けを「光の井戸」と呼んでいる。→参照 [040]、[156]

Ando had been using his early work, the TOMISHIMA HOUSE, as his office by renovating it three times. He demolished it and built a new atelier on the same property. Although the size of the property is about 120m², which is not spacious as an office building, the architecture with five floors and two underground floors is demonstrating the ideal form of office for Ando. The open ceiling in the center that exposes five levels of the building allows the staff working in this office to mutually be affected by the energy they emit in each floor and it is also used as a communication tool since voices from any floor can be heard at this area. Ando named this open ceiling the 'light well'. → see also [040], [156]

[120]
真言宗本福寺水御堂　1991
water temple

1. 兵庫県淡路市 | awaji, hyogo
2. 設計 | design　1989.11–1990.12
3. 施工 | construction　1990.12–1991.9
4. 鉄筋コンクリート | RC
5. 仏教寺院 | buddhist temple
6. 敷地 | site　2,990.8 m²
7. 建築 | building　859.5 m²
8. 延床 | total floor　417.2 m²

淡路島の大阪湾に面した緩い傾斜の丘陵地の地下に建築の本体は埋め込まれている。地上にあるのは誘導のためのコンクリート壁と、楕円の人工池。来訪者はこの楕円池を二つに割る位置の階段を降りて本堂に至る。池には蓮が浮かび、地下の聖なる場の存在を暗示する。地下に降り立つとそこは朱に彩られた強烈な空間で、本尊の背後、西方からドライエリアを介して侵入する自然光に目を奪われる。仏教の西方浄土の教えに全身が包まれるとき、日本の、そして東アジアの秀逸な現代の宗教空間が実現していることに称賛の念を抱く。

The main part of the architecture is embedded under the ground on a gentle slope on a hilly area facing Osaka Bay of Awaji Island. Structures situated on the ground are only the concrete curved wall placed as a guide and an artificial oval pond. Visitors go down the stairs that extend from the middle of this oval to enter the main temple. Lotuses floating on the pond suggest the existence of a holy site located underground. When entering the underground area, the visitors will face an intensive space colored with vermilion and be captivated by the natural light entering from the west through the dry area behind the principal image of Buddha. When covered with the teaching of the Western Pure Land of Buddhism, people are filled with admiration that the superb and modern religious space of Japan and East Asia is materialized in this architecture.

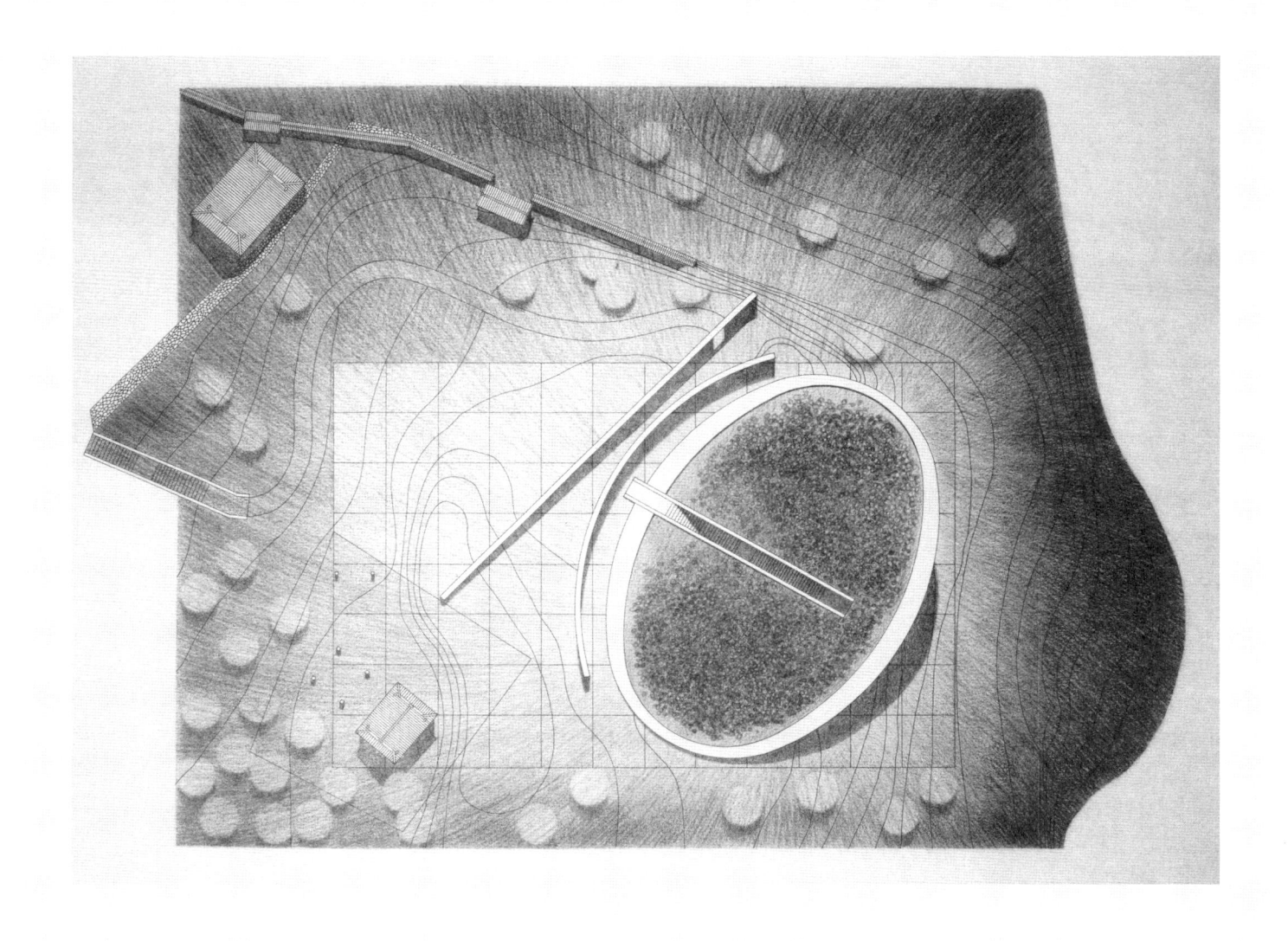

[121]
JR京都駅改築設計競技案 1991
the reconstruction of JR kyoto station, international design competition

1. 京都市下京区 | shimogyo-ku, kyoto
2. 設計 | design　1991
3. 設計競技 | design competition
4. 鉄骨 | steel
5. 駅舎、店舗、ホテルなど | station, commercial complex, hotel
6. 敷地 | site　38,000 m²
7. 建築 | building　34340 m²
8. 延床 | total floor　201,000 m²

景観問題など社会的に大きな反響を呼んだ京都駅の改築コンペ案。設定された大きなテーマは、国際観光都市京都の玄関口にどのような建築を配するかだった。安藤は「ツインゲート」と命名したゲート状の建物が二列にならぶ案を提示した。このゲートは広大な人工地盤（中央にはサーカスと呼ぶ巨大な光の井戸を配する）の上に位置し、ひとびとは人工地盤から明治の鉄道開通によって分断された京の町を一望することで歴史都市の今昔を考えるという設定であった。審査員のなかに支持者も多かったが、建設コストなどを理由に当選案にはならなかった。提案の正当性は高く評価され、ひとびとの記憶にとどまる。

A contest project for renovation of Kyoto station that gathered social attention due to issues including landscape problem. The main theme was an architecture suitable for the entrance of Kyoto, a city of international tourism. Ando submitted a design that has two rows of gate-type buildings named as the Twin Gate. This gate was to be located on an extensive artificial ground (a huge light well was to be placed on the center, which was named Circus) where people will stand and think about the past and present of this historical city by seeing the whole Kyoto that is separated by opening a railway during the Meiji Era. Many judges supported this design but did not accept it due to the construction cost. However, the rightfulness of the proposal received high reputation and it still remains in the memory of many people.

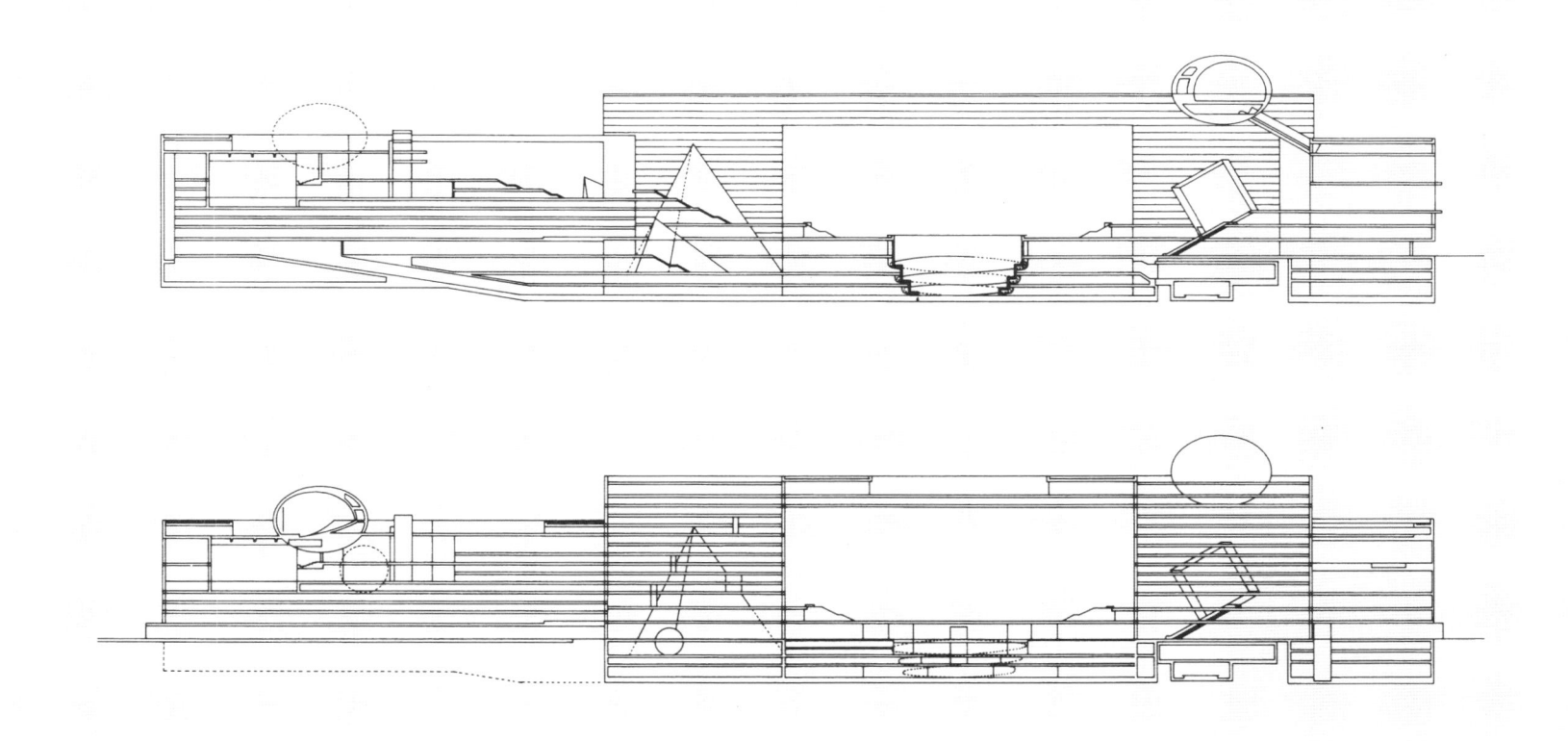

[122]
甲南大学スチューデント
サークルプロジェクト　1991
konan university student circle project

1. 神戸市東灘区 | higashinada-ku, kobe
2. 設計 | design　1991.4
3. 構想案 | concept
5. 学生会館 | student union building
6. 敷地 | site　7,885 m²
7. 建築 | building　3,031 m²
8. 延床 | total floor　7,314 m²

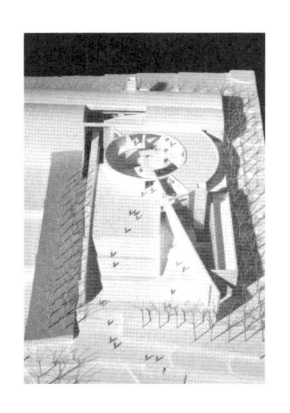

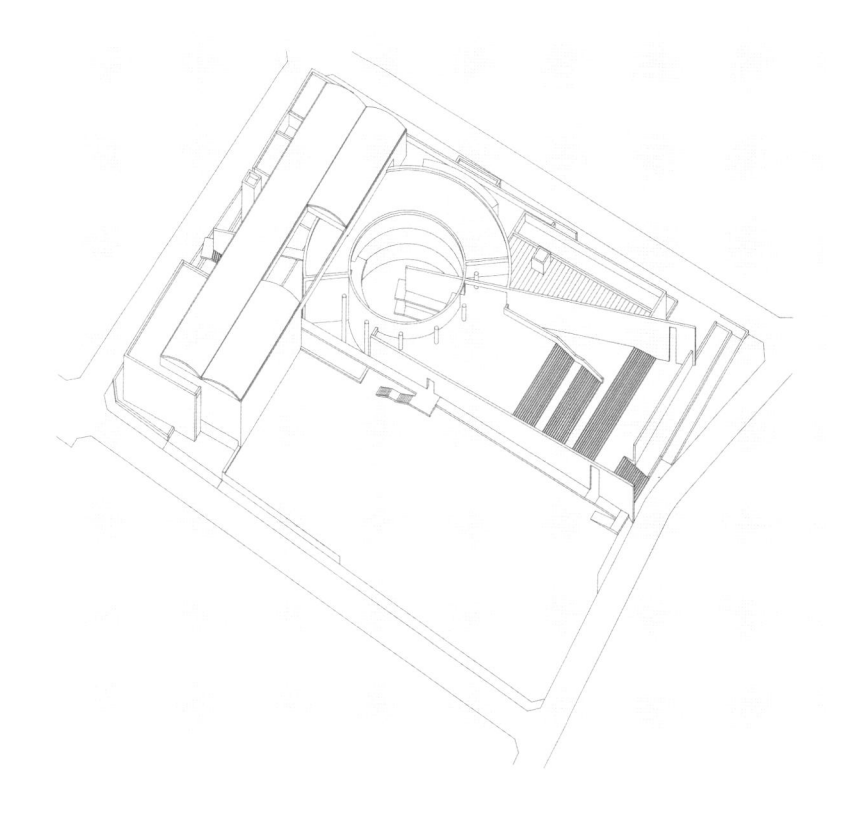

阪神間の六甲山を背景にする私立大学の学生のための利便施設の計画。二つのシリンダーが、施設の動線を流動的にする目的で置かれた。ひとつは内部が三層の円筒で、そこにはカフェを設け、円筒の端部に二列のヴォールト屋根を架け、物販施設を配する計画だった。また、このひとつめのシリンダーへのアプローチとして屋外の大階段を設営、地下には三層吹き抜けの二つ目のシリンダーを設けて、多目的ホールに充てることになっていた。幾何立体が既存のキャンパスにもたらす空間的刺激が学生時代の記憶に残ることを想定した。

A plan for a facility to be used by students of a private university where it has Mt. Rokko between Osaka and Kobe as the background. Two cylinders were to be placed to mobilize the flow line of the facility. Inside one of them is a three-layer cylinder where a café was to be provided and two rows of vault roofs were to be attached for placing retail facilities. In addition, a large outdoor stairway approaching the first cylinder and an underground multi-purpose hall with a second cylinder that has a three-layer open ceiling were planned. It was designed to let spatial stimulation from the geometric objects in the preexisting campus remain the memories of the campus life.

[123]
大手前大学アートセンター
1992
otemae art center

1. 兵庫県西宮市 | nishinomiya, hyogo
2. 設計 | design　1989.4–1990.11
3. 施工 | construction　1990.12–1992.3
4. 鉄筋コンクリート | RC
5. 大学施設 | university facilities
6. 敷地 | site　2,267.9 m²
7. 建築 | building　1,122.5 m²
8. 延床 | total floor　1,999.6 m²

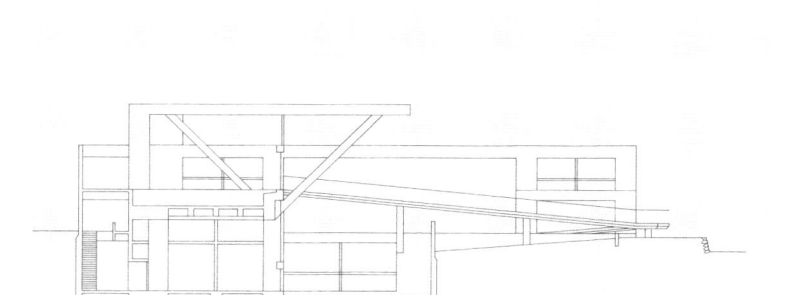

建設場所に関西の相場師、岩本栄之助の住宅があったと聞き、安藤は創作意欲を刺激された。私財を大阪の中央公会堂建設に拠出した財界人の気風が関西の文化を築き上げたとの思いがあるからだ。残っていた茶室や門、石垣の保存を前提に設計が進められた。多目的ホール、教室、ギャラリーなど主な機能の過半を地下に配し、上階の多くの空隙により周囲の自然や環境と継ぎ目なく繋がることを意図した。屋外から建物内部を貫通するスロープを昇降するとき、周囲の閑静な雰囲気が内部に引き込まれ、安寧の場をもたらしていることを実感する。

Ando said his creative urge was stimulated when he was told there had been a residence of Einosuke Iwamoto on the construction site of this project. The design was developed with a precondition to preserve the remaining elements such as a tea room, entrance gate and masonry walls. Most of the main functionalities including multi-purpose hall, classrooms and galleries are placed at underground level, while many void spaces are provided on upper floor levels to link with the surrounding nature and environment seamlessly. When visitors go up and down the slope piercing through the building from the outside to the inside, they will feel a quiet air of the surrounding environment is brought in to the interior space, in order to provide a calm atmosphere to the place.

[124]
1992年セビリア万国博覧会 日本館　1992
japan pavilion, expo'92 / seville

1. スペイン セビリア | seville, spain
2. 設計 | design　1989.9–1990.12
3. 施工 | construction　1990.9–1992.2
4. 木造 | wood
5. パビリオン | exhibition hall
6. 敷地 | site　5,660.6 m²
7. 建築 | building　2,629.8 m²
8. 延床 | total floor　5,660.3 m²

スペインのセビリアで開催された万国博覧会に日本が出展したパビリオン。安藤は、木造をコンクリートで直写することは避け、オリジナルの現代木造を造り上げた。間口60メートル、奥行き40メートル、高さは25メートル、世界最大級の木造建築をうたうこのパビリオンはこだわりにあふれている。反りを持たせた外壁は無垢材で構成、館内へはその木の外壁を二分する位置に架けられた太鼓橋でアクセスする。それを登り切ったところで見上げると東大寺南大門を思わせる豪快な組物に出くわす。イベリア半島が、ヨーロッパとイスラムの異種配合による独自文化を保持していることを意識し、異文化としての木造を実現したかったという。

This is a pavilion building presented by Japan, constructed for the international exposition held in Seville, Spain. Ando represented an original modern wooden structure without directly copying and replacing a wooden structure by a concrete one. This pavilion, said to be one of the largest wooden architecture in the world, is in 60m wide, 40m deep, and 25m high — and it is filled with Ando's original ideas. A curved exterior wall is finished with solid wood materials, and the access to the inside of this pavilion is provided by an arched bridge positioned in the middle point of the wooden exterior wall. When visitors go up to the top of this bridge and look up, a magnificent wooden structure — as if like the ones on the Great South Gate of Todai-ji Temple — becomes visible. Ando sought for realizing a wooden structure building of a different culture for the site — because he was aware of the context of the Iberian Peninsula, where unique culture was produced by the mingling of European and Muslim cultures, and today such culture still remains there.

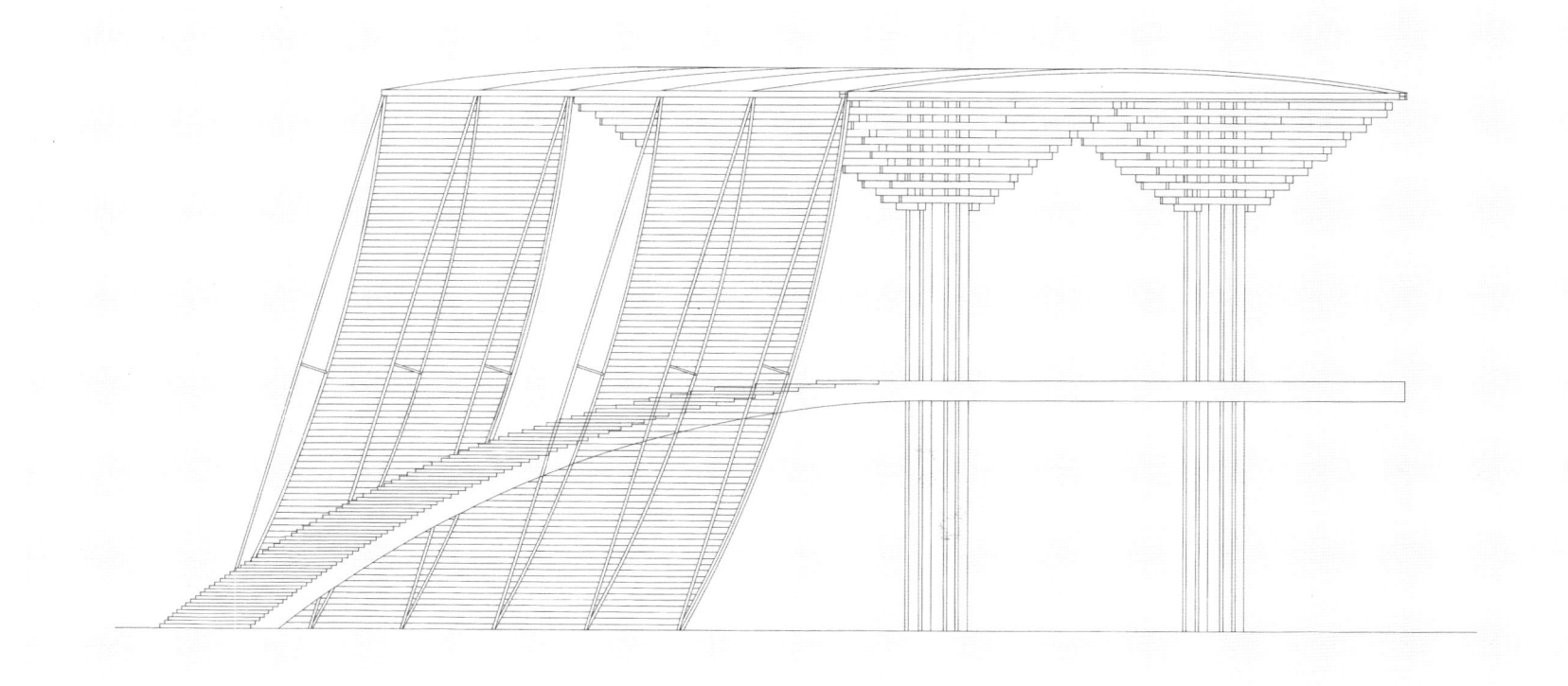

[125]
ベネッセハウス ミュージアム
1992
benesse house museum

.

1. 香川県直島町 | naoshima, kagawa
2. 設計 | design　1988.5–1990.10
3. 施工 | construction　1990.10–1992.3
4. 鉄筋コンクリート造 | RC
5. 美術館 | museum of art
6. 敷地 | site　44,700.0 m²
7. 建築 | building　1,775.5 m²
8. 延床 | total floor　3,643.4 m²

直島における安藤の最初のギャラリー。フェリー乗り場からのバスを降りると自然石を張った壁が待ち受け、その向うにコンクリート打ち放しの円筒形のギャラリーが目に入る。隣には箱型の石張りのギャラリー棟が並列する。人工物としての建築と直島の自然を対比させる強固な意志を物語る風景だ。円筒形のギャラリーから海の方向へ延びる重層の展示室に至る。自然と現代美術が邂逅し、展示室から屋外テラスに出られる仕掛けがここならではの鑑賞の雰囲気を高める。→参照［151］、［184］、［223］、［239］、［280］、［309］

The first gallery space designed by Ando for Naoshima. As the visitors get off the bus from the ferryboat landing area, they face with a wall finished in natural stone, with the sight to the gallery space in a cylindrical shape behind. A box shaped gallery wing finished in natural stone is situated adjacent to the cylindrical gallery in parallel. This is a view to represent the strong will to juxtapose architecture as an artificial element with the nature of Naoshima. Visitors access from the cylindrical gallery in exposed concrete to the multi-layered exhibition rooms extending toward the ocean—the nature and modern art come across at this building. The program allowing visitors to go directly to the exterior terrace from the exhibition room. → see also [151], [184], [223], [239], [280], [309]

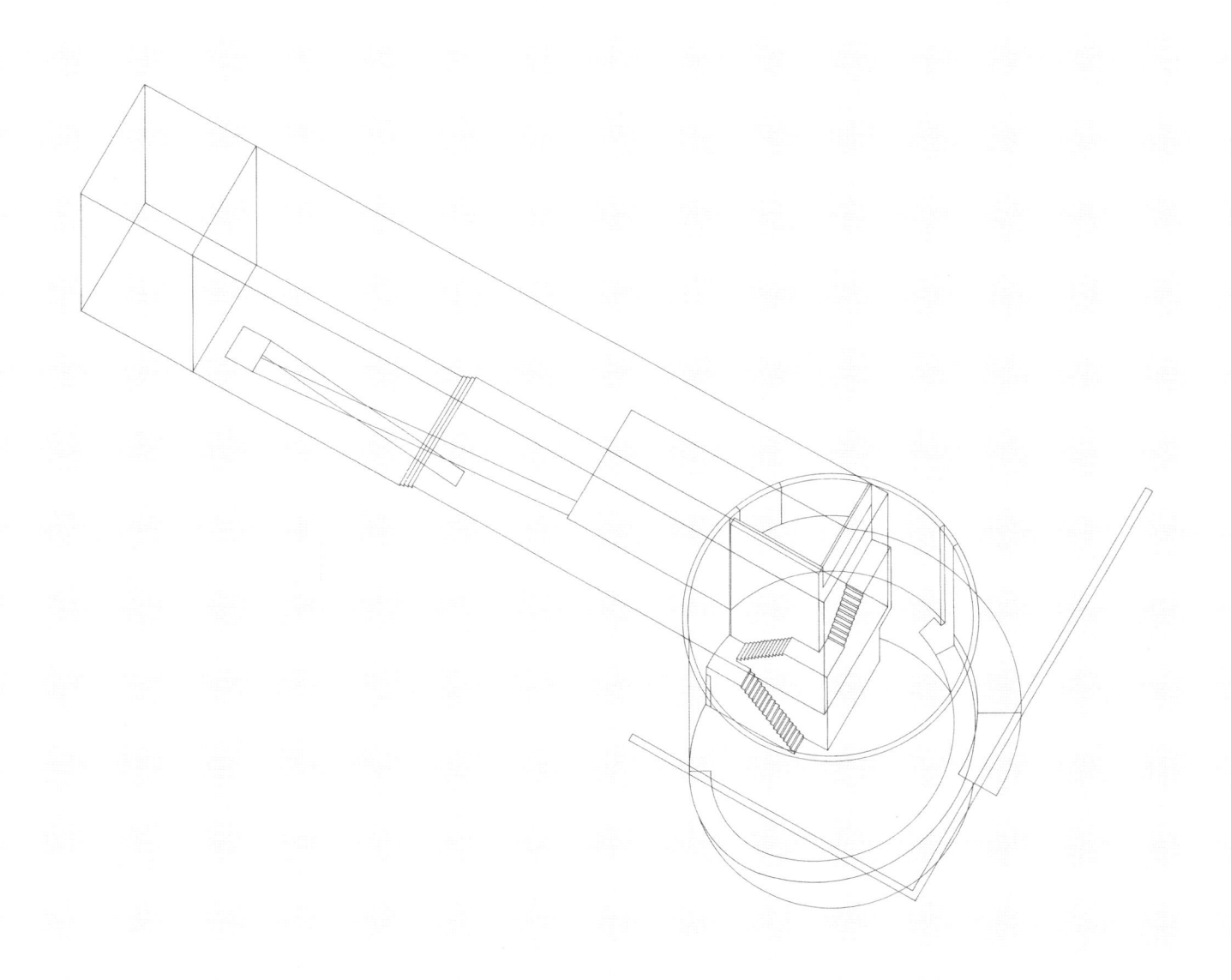

[126]
シカゴ美術館屏風ギャラリー
1992
gallery for japanese screen,
the art institute of chicago

1. アメリカ シカゴ | chicago, USA
2. 設計 | design　1989.2–1991.4
3. 施工 | construction　1991.5–1992.5
5. 展示室 | exhibition room
8. 延床 | total floor　160.0㎡

シカゴ美術館の東洋部門増築を機に屏風の展示室が新設された。広さは160平方メートル。そこを二分して一方には一辺が30センチ、高さ3メートルの16本の角柱を並べた。柱の素材はオーク（樫の木）で、床も同じくオークの仕上げ。柱が展示を遮ることにより、かえって空間に奥行きが生まれ、鑑賞者の歴史への敬意をかき立てるとの発想だ。木柱の向うに屏風の見える光景が、日本の屏風に親しむ暮らしの姿を彷彿とさせるとも考えた。

A new exhibition room for Japanese byobu folding screens was added when The Art Institute of Chicago went through an expansion for Eastern art. The total area of the room is 160sqm, and the space was divided into two zones. One of them is lined up with 16 columns made from Oak wood in 30cm wide and 3m high, and the flooring of the space is also finished in Oak wood material. As the columns interrupt the direct view toward those exhibited art pieces, the space appears to have more depth in the field. Audience would feel more respect toward the history — and the scenery of the space behind those wooden columns also reminds audience of the life in Japan with byobu screens used in daily lives.

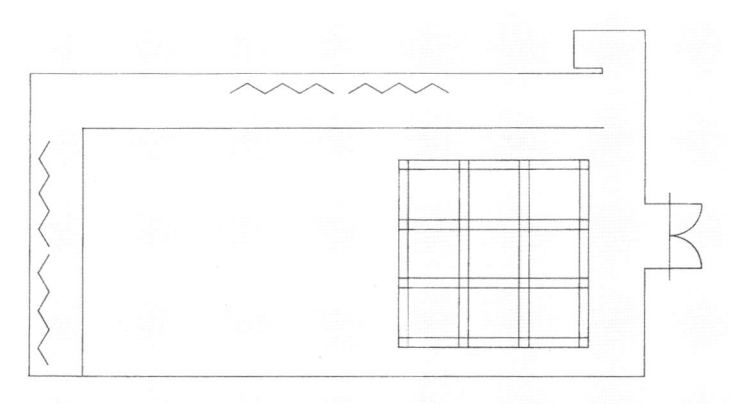

[127]
熊本県立装飾古墳館　1992
kumamoto prefectural
ancient burial mound museum

1. 熊本県山鹿市 | yamaga, kumamoto
2. 設計 | design　1989.12–1990.6
3. 施工 | construction　1990.10–1992.3
4. 鉄骨鉄筋コンクリート | SRC
5. 博物館 | museum
6. 敷地 | site　6,338.0 m²
7. 建築 | building　1,448.8 m²
8. 延床 | total floor　2,099.0 m²

熊本県山鹿市鹿央町一帯に残る岩原古墳群を体験するための博物館施設。立地の傍にも、前方後円墳の「双子塚古墳」を中心に8基が集中する。平面形のシルエットは、この双子塚古墳の形を借りて歴史への賛辞とした。建築はL字型の壁が、円形の建物本体に突き刺さる形をとる。入館者はまず古墳群を展望する上階のテラスに登り、そこから円形の建物の内側のスロープをくだって展示室に向かう。展望テラスで「目の前の遺物」を確かめるところから歴史への旅は始まる。

This is a museum to feel and experience Iwabaru Barrow group remained in the whole region of Kao-machi, Yamaga in Kumamoto. 8 bases are concentrated in the vicinity of the location, centering on "Futagozuka" of the mound which the trapezoid jutted out of the circle type, called ZENPOKOENFUN. The silhouette of the plan is borrowed from the shape of this Futagozuka Barrow to pay homage to the past history. This building is composed of a L-shaped wall piercing into the main volume in a circular shape. Visitors first go up to the terrace on the upper floor overlooking the group of barrows; then go down to the exhibition rooms through the slope on the inner side of the circular volume. Visitors' experience begins by the presence of the "past remains in front of themselves" on the viewing terrace.

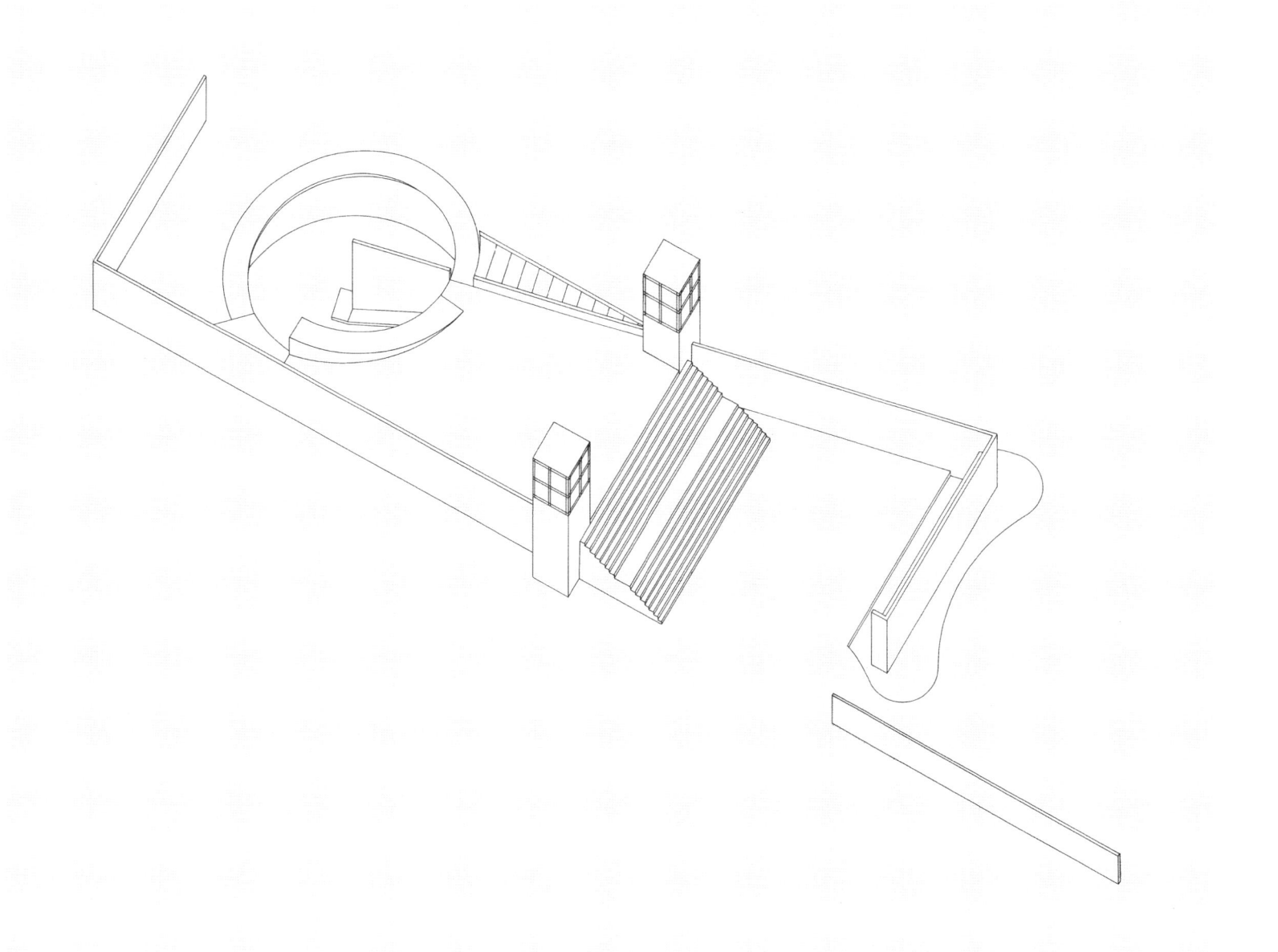

[128]
宮下邸　1992
miyashita house

1. 神戸市垂水区 | tarumi-ku, kobe
2. 設計 | design　1989.12–1990.12
3. 施工 | construction　1991.1–1992.4
4. 型枠コンクリートブロック | fill-up concrete-block
5. 住宅 | detached house
6. 敷地 | site　332.0 m²
7. 建築 | building　148.7 m²
8. 延床 | total floor　250.9 m²

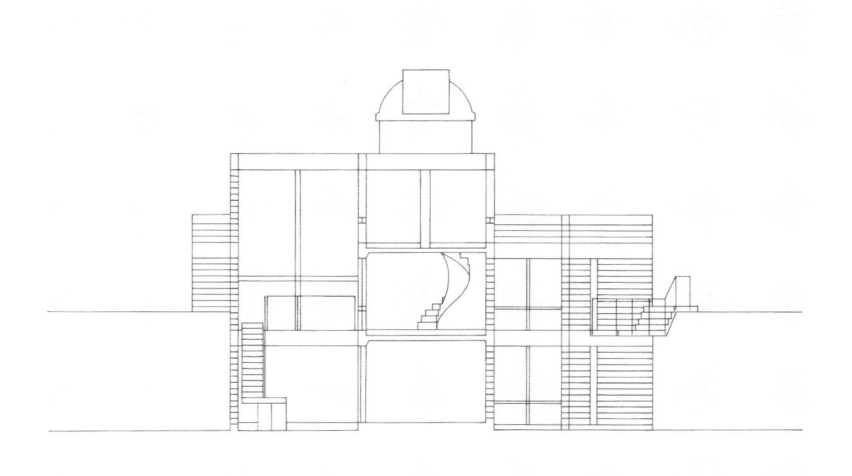

神戸市西部の瀬戸内海を見おろす小高い丘陵地に位置するアトリエ付属のコンクリートブロックによる小住宅。目につくのは屋上に飛び出した「天文台」の観測施設。安藤が天文台に登るために設営した螺旋階段は片側のみ手すりのあるもので、きりりとした曲線は魅力的に映る。対照的にコンクリートブロックの躯体は強固な空間イメージをつくりだし、建物内のテラスや中庭にさまざまなかたちで各室が接する配置が、内なる自然を小住宅に充満させている。

Small residential house made of concrete blocks with an atelier located in west part of Kobe City on a hilly area that has a view of Seto Inland Sea. What attracts attention is the astronomical observatory facility protruding from the rooftop. The spiral stairway Ando designed to climb up to the observatory has a handrail only on one side and is creating an attractive sharp curve line. On the other hand, the structure made of concrete blocks create a rigid spatial image and the scenery of each room connected in various forms to the internal terrace and courtyard makes residents to fully enjoy the nature inside the small house.

[129]
姫路市立星の子館　1992
children's seminar house, himeji

1. 兵庫県姫路市 | himeji, hyogo
2. 設計 | design　1990.4–1990.12
3. 施工 | construction　1991.1–1992.3
4. 鉄筋コンクリート | RC
5. 宿泊施設、展望台
   lodging facilities, observatory
6. 敷地 | site　26,078.0 m²
7. 建築 | building　817.9 m²
8. 延床 | total floor　2,810.5 m²

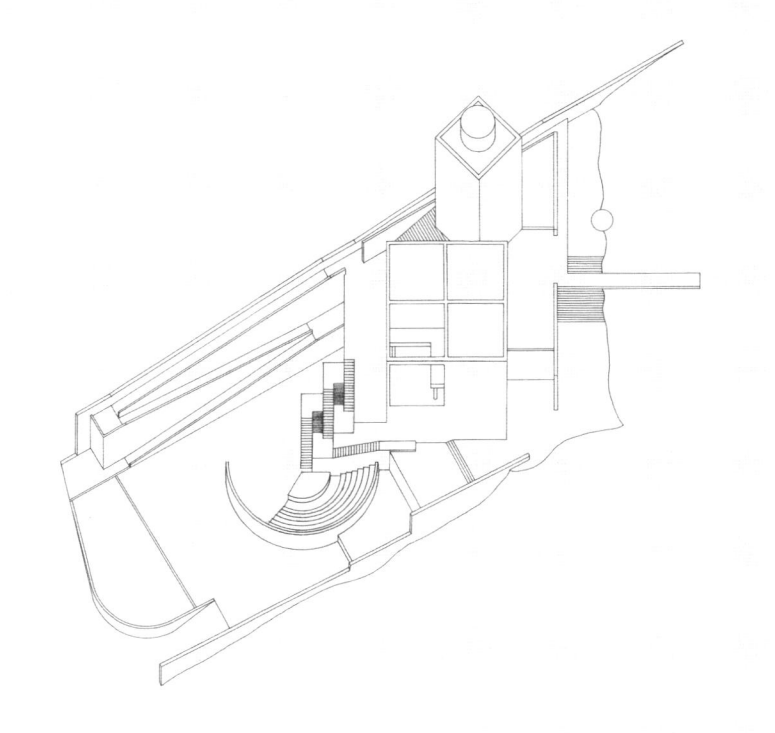

兵庫県立こどもの館と連携する児童の宿泊研修施設。塔状の天文観測棟、足元の宿泊棟、そしてさらにその基壇部に位置する屋外円形劇場などからなる。天文観測棟と宿泊棟は、前者が一辺が10.8メートルの正方形の平面を持ち、後者は二倍に相当する21.6メールを一辺とする正方形を平面としている。二つの棟は45度振られており、下段の直径30メートルの野外円形劇場へは、その余白から屋外階段で降りていく。安藤のコンクリートの幾何学が小規模ながら豊かな自然を背景に確かな存在感を示している。→参照［103］

The facility consists of a tower astronomical observation building, an accommodation building at the base, and the outdoor amphitheater situated at the platform area of the building. The astronomical observation building has a square planform of 10.8 meters each side and the accommodation building has a square planform of 21.6 meters, which is double of the former. These two buildings are positioned on a 45-degree angle to each other and the space between the buildings connects to an outdoor stairway that goes down to the outdoor amphitheater with a diameter of 30 meters. Although it is on a small scale, Ando's concrete geometry has a strong presence with the rich nature in the background. → see also [103]

[130]
奈良市民ホール国際設計競技案
1992
nara convention hall,
international design competition

1. 奈良県奈良市 | nara
2. 設計 | design 1992
3. 設計競技 | design competition
4. 鉄骨、鉄筋コンクリート | steel, RC
5. コンベンションホール | convention hall
6. 敷地 | site 16,390 m²
7. 建築 | building 5,282.0 m²
8. 延床 | total floor 16,037 m²

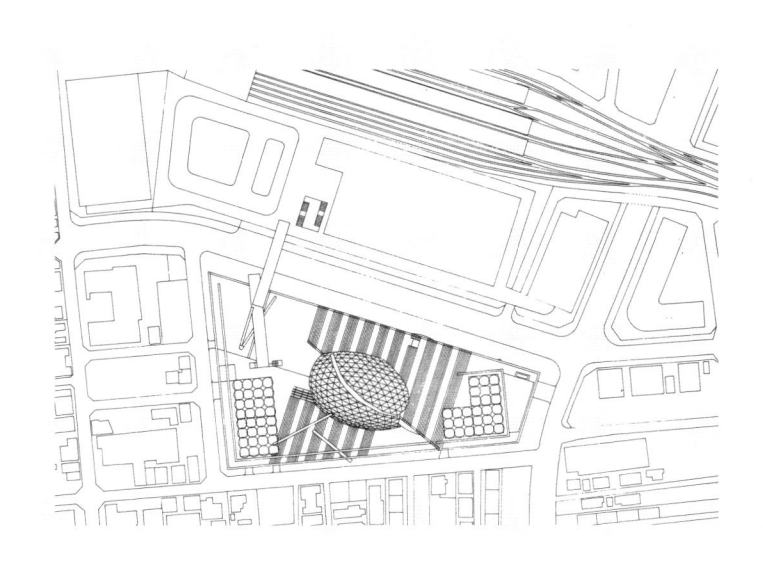

1990年代初め、奈良市はJR奈良駅周辺の再開発を計画し、その中心となる市民ホールの国際設計競技を実施した。安藤は指名された5人のひとりとして参加した。建物全体をツインフォーラムと呼ぶ二つの屋外階段を中心に構成し、その階段に覆い被さるかのようなジオメトリック・サイクロイド曲面のシェルターを配置した。シェルターの内部は、屋外でも屋内でもない空間とする計画で、その新奇な形態こそが、景観が破壊され、活力を失いつつあった一帯を大胆に再生するシンボルと位置づけた。

Nara City was planning for redevelopment of the area around JR Nara station in the early 1990s and held an international design competition of their community hall, which was the main structure of the project. Ando participated as one of the five designated contestants. The whole building was arranged to have the two outdoor stairways, which are called the Twin Forum, at the center and a shelter with geometric cycloid curve was placed to cover those stairways. Inside the shelter was designed to be a space that is neither outdoor nor indoor in which the unprecedented form was positioned as a symbol to boldly revitalize the area where the scenery was destroyed and was losing its vitality.

[131]
六甲アイランドプロジェクト
1993
rokko island project

1. 神戸市東灘区 | higashinada-ku, kobe
2. 設計 | design 1989.2–1991.9
3. 施工 | construction 1991.10–1993.3
4. 鉄筋コンクリート、鉄骨 | RC, steel
5. 店舗 | shop
6. 敷地 | site 3,740.0 m²
7. 建築 | building 1,798.6 m²
8. 延床 | total floor 2,570.2 m²

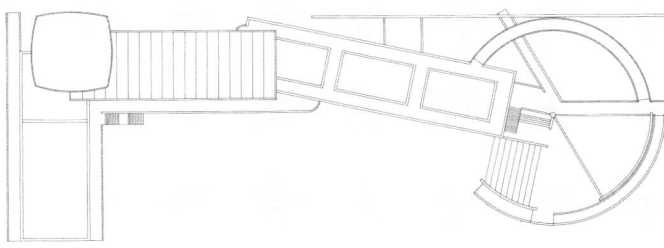

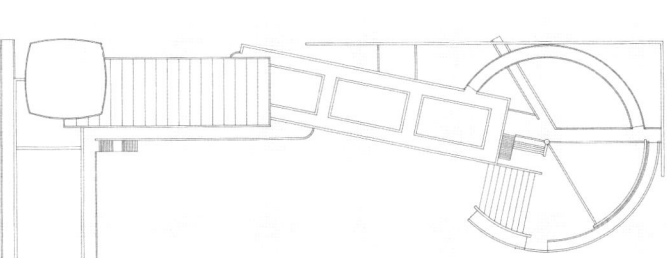

リバーモールは、神戸港東部の埋立地六甲アイランドの親水公園。新交通システムの六甲ライナーの高架に沿って広がっている。公園の東西両側に商業施設があり、安藤は「イースト」のほうを設計した。京都の「TIME'S」の2期でも採用されたドーム屋根が架かる。埋立地の常で大きなタウンブロックを前提にした巨大建築が多いが、安藤の低層の建築はヒューマンスケールの公共空間を実現した。2階の通り抜けの屋外テラスで、新交通システムの駅と結ばれている。

River Mall is a water park in Rokko Island, a reclaimed land in the east part of Kobe Port. It is located along the overhead railway of a new transportation system, Rokko Liner. Ando designed the East side of the commercial facilities situated on east and west sides of the park. A dome roof adopted at the second term of TIME'S in Kyoto was used here as well. Although there are huge architectures for large town blocks located in reclaimed lands, a human scale public space was created with Ando's low-rising architecture. The outdoor terrace that passes through the 2nd floor is connected to a station of the new transportation system.

346 Complete Works

[132]
兵庫県立大学
看護学部・看護研究科　1993
college of nursing art and science,
university of hyogo

1. 兵庫県明石市 | akashi, hyogo
2. 設計 | design   1990.3–1991.9
3. 施工 | construction   1991.10–1993.3
4. 鉄骨鉄筋コンクリート | SRC
5. 大学 | university
6. 敷地 | site   36,000.0 m²
7. 建築 | building   5,128.0 m²
8. 延床 | total floor   13,872.8 m²

大学としては小規模なキャンパスながら、安藤ならではの徹底した幾何学の完結が達成されている。三つの棟の平面形は、高層棟が正方形、低層棟とアネックスが長方形であり、それらは貫入する形で連続する。アネックスには6分の1円のヴォールト屋根が架かり、低層棟とともにサークル広場と呼ばれる円形の造園のなかに位置している。多様な表現を恣意的にならべることを排除した配置という。低層棟の内部は吹き抜けで、そこに入れ子になった講義室が面する姿は学校建築の新たな空間のありかたを印象づける。

Although this college has a small scale campus as a university, completion of the thorough geometric forms unique to Ando has been achieved. The shapes of three buildings on a plan layout are in square shape for a high-rise wing, and rectangle shapes for a low-rise wing and annex wing—and they are continuous in penetrating form. The annex building has a vault roof in a shape derived from the one-sixth of a circle. This building is positioned within a circular garden space called "circle plaza" along with the low-rise wing, as a result that Ando eliminated to arbitrarily place various expressions within a space. The interior space of the low-rise wing is open to below and lecture rooms are nested within the space—this configuration and atmosphere gives impression for a new space of an educational facility.

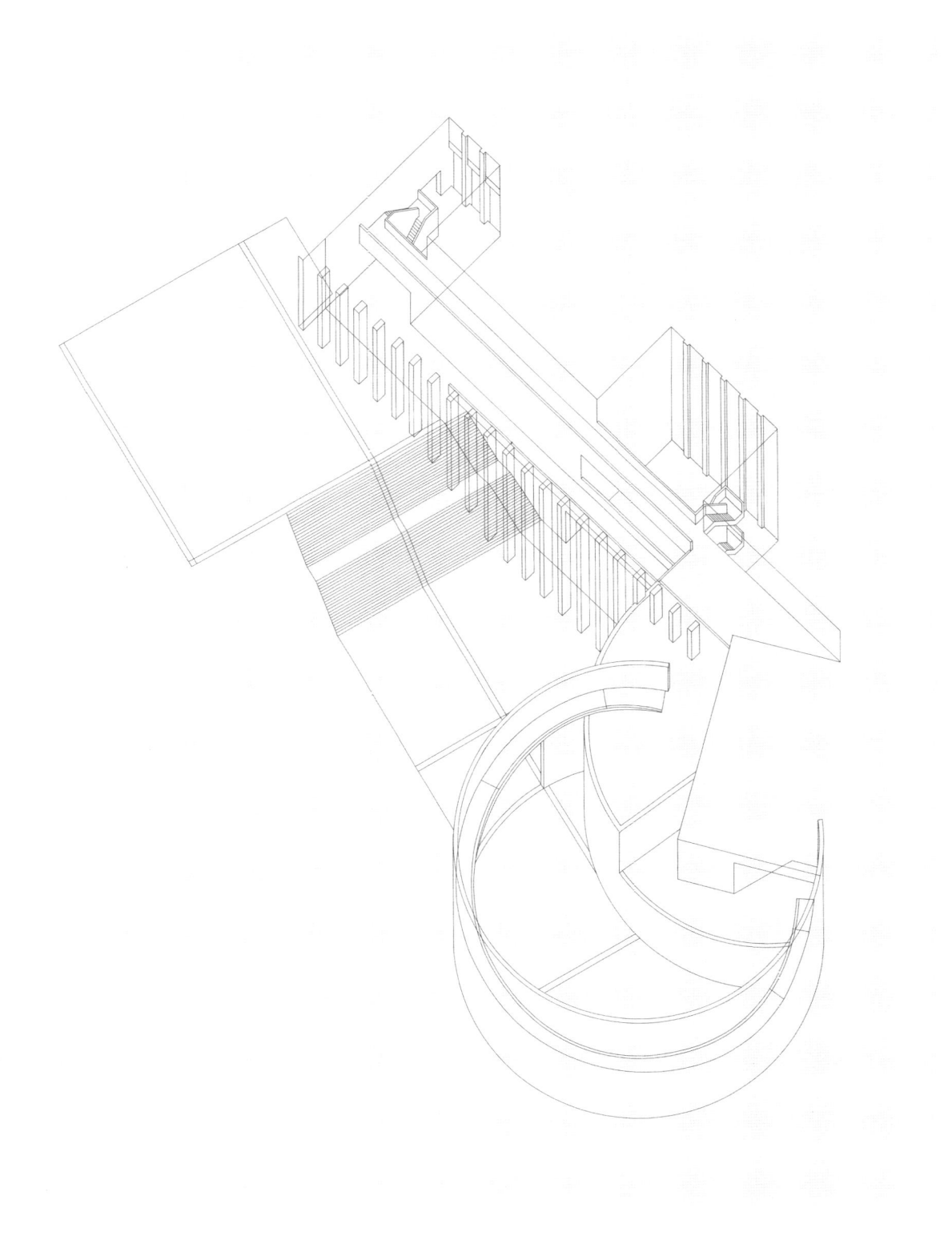

[133]
六甲の集合住宅 II　1993
rokko housing II

1. 神戸市灘区 | nada-ku, kobe
2. 設計 | design　1985.8–1987.4
3. 施工 | construction　1989.10–1993.5
4. 鉄筋コンクリート | RC
5. 集合住宅 | apartment house
6. 敷地 | site　5,998.1 m²
7. 建築 | building　2,964.7 m²
8. 延床 | total floor　9,043.6 m²

第1期に隣り合う崖地にさらに大規模な集合住宅が建設された。第1期が1978年の構想から5年かかったのに対し、第2期はさらに長い9年間を要した。第2期では「庭」がテーマとなった。前庭は社会との繋がり、中庭は1期との緩衝地帯、後庭は散策路の役割を託された。順にパブリック、セミパブリック、プライベートとの位置づけだ。50戸の集合住宅は、5.2メートルの正方形のグリッドを重ね、視覚的には箱を積み上げた形態で第1期とともに景観を形成する。新たな「庭」を介して、住民同士の積極的なコミュニティーの形成が期待された。
→参照 [050]、[180]、[265]

Larger scale collective housing building was constructed on the cliff-like site adjacent to the "Rokko Housing" 1st phase. Compare to the 1st phase project that took 5 years to realize since the proposal in 1978, this 2nd phase project took even longer for 9 years to complete from the proposal in 1985. The theme of the 2nd phase project was a "garden" space. Each garden space was given particular role; front garden was meant to promote communication with society; middle garden became the buffer zone with the 1st phase programs; the back garden function as stroll paths; thus, each garden is designated as a public, a semi-public and a private garden, accordingly. This 50 unit's collective housing is configured by the composition of a square grid in 5.2m scale; visually, the building appears to be composed of piled up boxes, forming a landscape along with the 1st phase building. → see also [050], [180], [265]

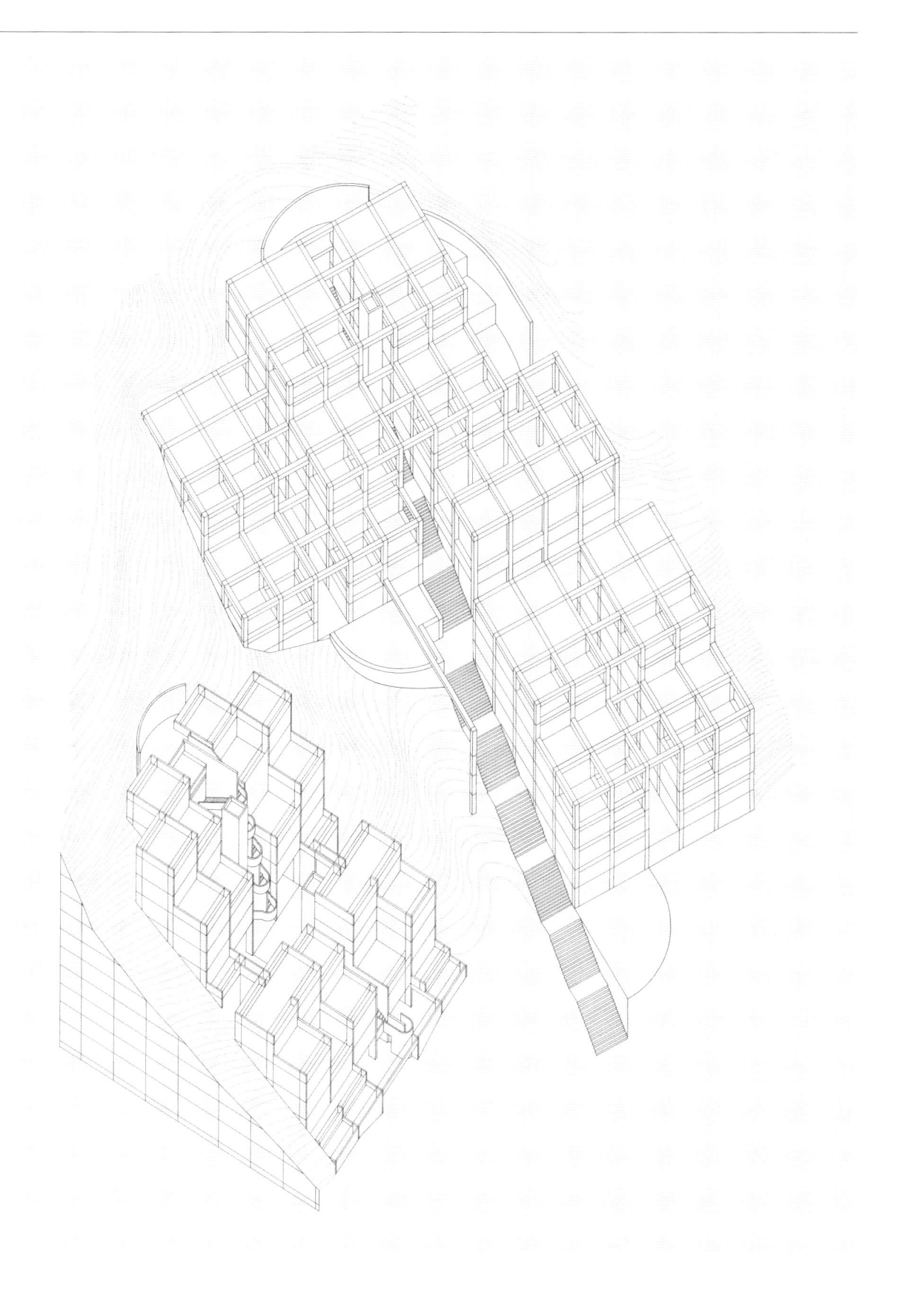

[134]

ヴィトラ・セミナーハウス　1993
vitra seminar house

1. ドイツ　ヴァイル・アム・ライン｜ weil-am-rhein, germany
2. 設計｜design　1987.4–1992.5
3. 施工｜construction　1992.6–1993.7
4. 鉄筋コンクリート（ラーメン）｜RC (frame)
5. 会議・研修施設｜training facilities
6. 敷地｜site　19,408.0 m²
7. 建築｜building　360.9 m²
8. 延床｜total floor　508.3 m²

スイス・バーゼル近郊の家具メーカー、ヴィトラが工場の一角で運営する広大なアートサイトのなかのセミナーハウス。すぐ傍らでフランク・ゲーリーが脱構築派らしい動的な造形の家具博物館を手がけていたことが、広大な緑地のなかに埋没する建築を安藤に考えさせた。ゲーリーの動きをせき止めるかのような長いコンクリートの壁を建てて、自らの作品を沈黙させることに専念している。ザハ・ハディドの消防署など他の建築家の激しい戦いをよそに、信念に基づく沈黙が、安藤の建築の美を高めていく。

This is a seminar building located within a vast site for art-oriented programs operated by a furniture manufacture, Vitra, at the corner lot of its factory near Basel, Switzerland. There was another on-going project for furniture museum next to this seminar building designed by Frank Gehry, with a dynamic form in "Deconstructivist" language — that made Ando to consider this seminar building to be buried under the vast green ground. A long concrete wall was built as if it is to keep back the flow of the dynamic movement of Gehry's building, and Ando focused to silent down the building he was designing. Compare to the other projects by other architects, strongly confronting and contrasting each other — including such project as the "Fire Department" designed by Zaha Hadid — Ando's own pursuit of a silent architecture within those buildings further elevates the beauty of his architecture.

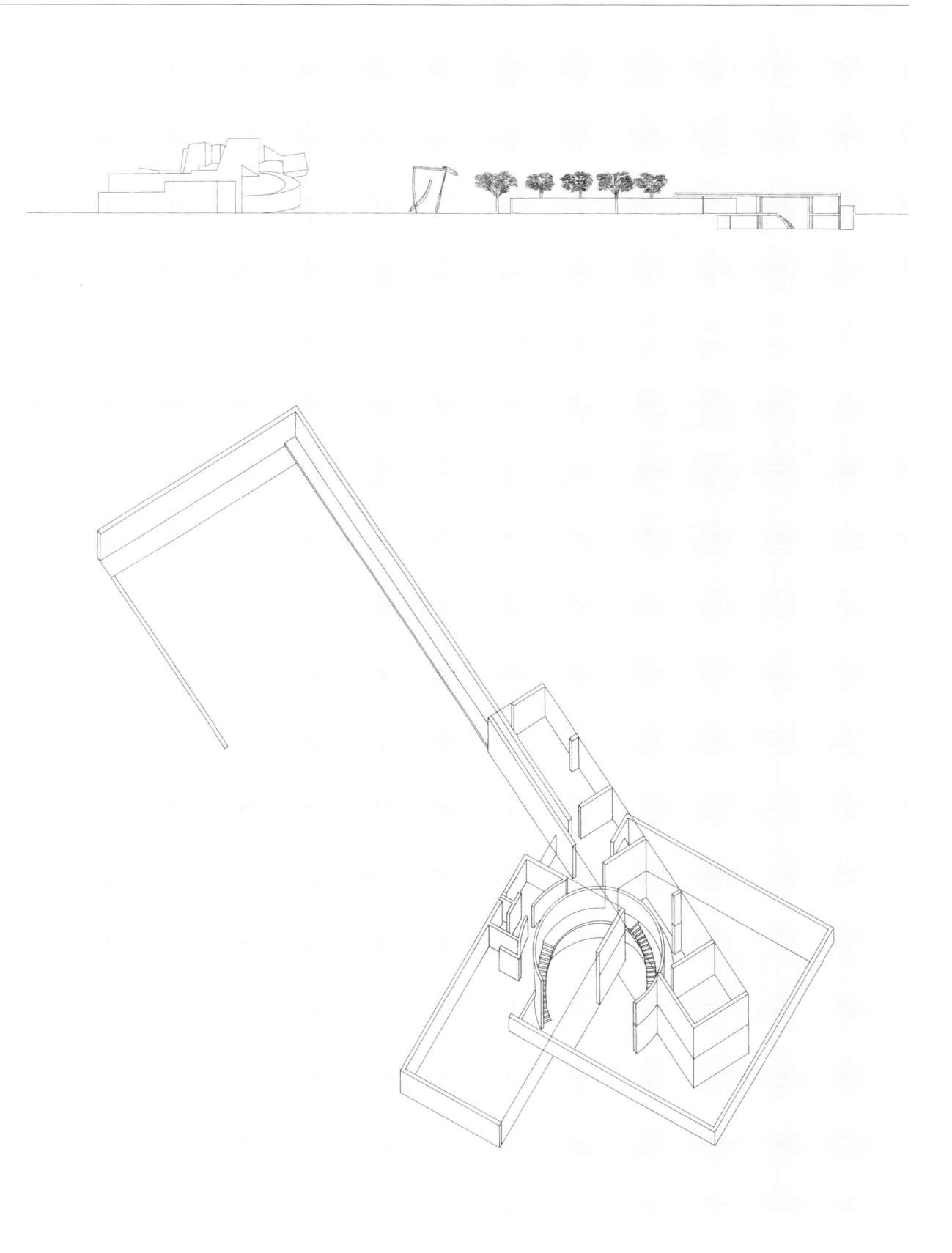

全346作品録

[135]
YKK 津田沼寮　1993
YKK seminar house

1. 千葉県習志野市 | narashino, chiba
2. 設計 | design   1990.5–1991.6
3. 施工 | construction   1991.7–1993.2
4. 鉄筋コンクリート（壁式ラーメン構造）|
   RC (wall-type frame structure)
5. 社員寮 | company dormitory
6. 敷地 | site   2,067.8 m²
7. 建築 | building   870.5 m²
8. 延床 | total floor   4,199.8 m²

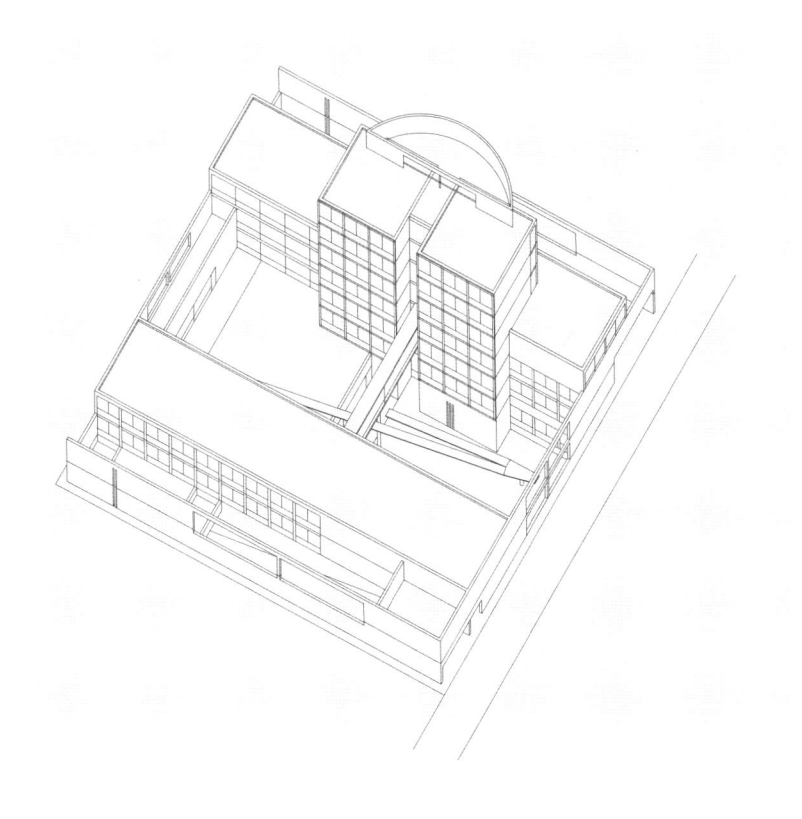

千葉県習志野市に位置する、若い社員を対象とした企業のセミナーハウス。中、低層の二つの棟が敷地の両端に配され、壁が残りの二辺を囲うことで中庭が確保された。壁にうがった大きな開口部を通して、歩行者は内部の緑の空間を見ることができる。中層と低層の居室の窓は、この中庭に向けて設けられており、窓の外に目をやると自然の変化が確かめられる。さらに中庭を2分する位置に180度で切り返す屋外のスロープを歩くと、緑の空間を実感できる。

A seminar house for young employees of a company located in Narashino City, Chiba Prefecture. A middle-rise building and a low-rise building are positioned on both sides of the property where a courtyard is secured by covering the two remaining sides by walls. A big opening is made in the walls for pedestrians to observe the green area inside the property. Windows of living rooms of middle level and lower level floors are facing the courtyard to observe the transition of nature outside. An outdoor slope that bends in 180 degrees at the center of the courtyard is situated to be able to feel the green atmosphere.

[136]
垂水の教会　1993
church in tarumi

1. 神戸市垂水区 | tarumi-ku, kobe
2. 設計 | design   1991.4–1992.5
3. 施工 | construction   1992.6–1993.5
4. 鉄筋コンクリート | RC
5. 教会 | church
6. 敷地 | site   622.1 m²
7. 建築 | building   187.5 m²
8. 延床 | total floor   304.5 m²

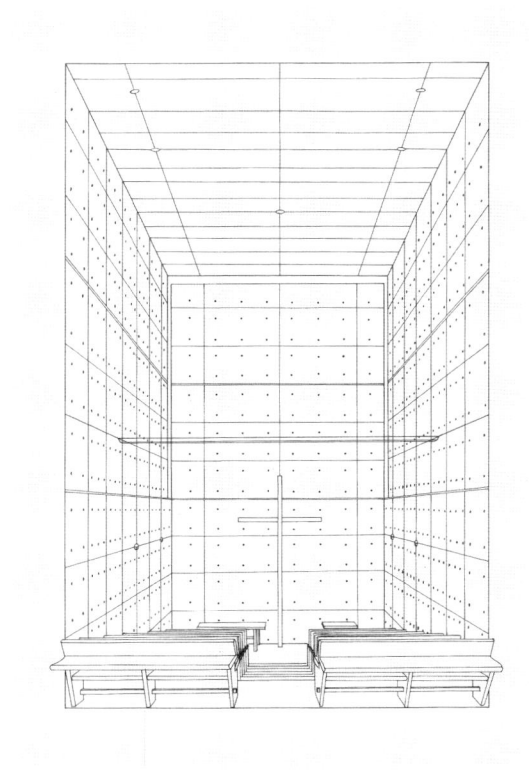

神戸市の西部、垂水の小さな丘に立つ教会。アプローチはコンクリート壁の谷間からで、そこには元からあったケヤキが青々とした葉を繁らせている。右側の独立壁は敷地に沿って曲線を描き、建物本体との間に静かな庭の空間をもたらしている。礼拝堂内部には、スリットから自然光が入り込み、独立した十字架がコンクリート打ち放しを背に屹立する姿は、聖なるものの存在の気配を感じさせる。外観はコンクリートの幾何立体を積み上げるモダニズムの教会の典型的な姿を示している。

A church standing on a small hill in Tarumi, which is in the west area of Kobe City. The approach is provided between concrete walls where rich green leaves of Japanese zelkova trees that existed from the past are flourishing. An independent wall on the right side is in a curved form along the property providing calm atmosphere in the garden between the wall and the main building. With natural light entering from slits inside the chapel, the appearance of the independent cross on the exposed concrete gives sense of presence of a holy identity. The appearance demonstrates the typical Modernism form of church constructed with layers of geometric concrete solids.

[137]
李邸　1993
lee house

1. 千葉県船橋市 | funabashi, chiba
2. 設計 | design　1991.7–1992.6
3. 施工 | construction　1992.7–1953.7
4. 鉄筋コンクリート（壁式）| RC (wall)
5. 住宅 | detached house
6. 敷地 | site　484.1㎡
7. 建築 | building　174.8㎡
8. 延床 | total floor　264.8㎡

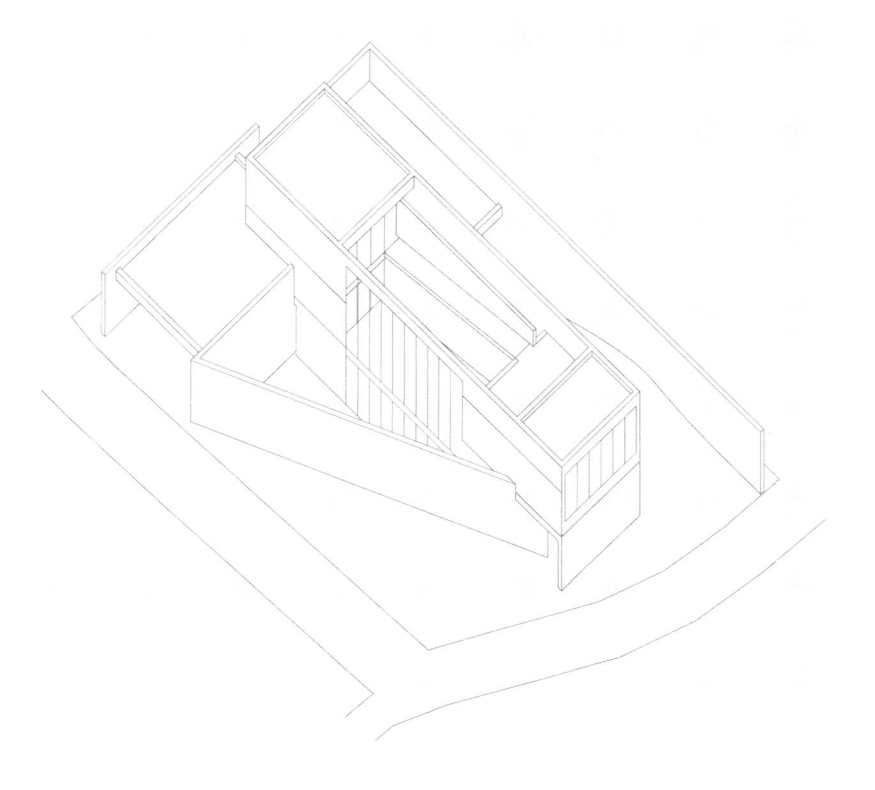

立体的な回遊性をもたせた、ギャラリーを思わせる住宅建築。長方形平面の下階には、L字型の壁面と3角形に区画した庭を配し、三層にオープンエアの空中の通路、独立したガラス壁のテラス、スロープを置くことで、レベルの変化を伴う豊かな自然光を楽しめる構成となっている。また、室内の各所に配した李朝の家具が、安藤のコンクリート打ち放しと調和し、アジアを超えたグローバルな空間の普遍解になりうる可能性を示唆している。

A residential building that resembles a gallery with three-dimensional excursion. An L-shape wall and a yard sectioned in a triangle are placed on the lower floor with a rectangular planform. By placing an open air pathway and a slope in three layers, independent glass wall terrace, rich natural light that changes at each level can be enjoyed. In addition, pieces of furniture of Joseon Dynasty placed in various locations inside the rooms match the exposed concrete of Ando indicating the potential of providing a universal solution for the space that extends globally beyond the range of Asia.

[138]
ギャラリー野田　1993
gallery noda

1. 神戸市灘区 | nada-ku, kobe
2. 設計 | design　1991.12–1992.5
3. 施工 | construction　1992.6–1993.1
4. 鉄筋コンクリート | RC
5. 住宅、ギャラリー | house, gallery
6. 敷地 | site　39.8㎡
7. 建築 | building　27.0㎡
8. 延床 | total floor　79.0㎡

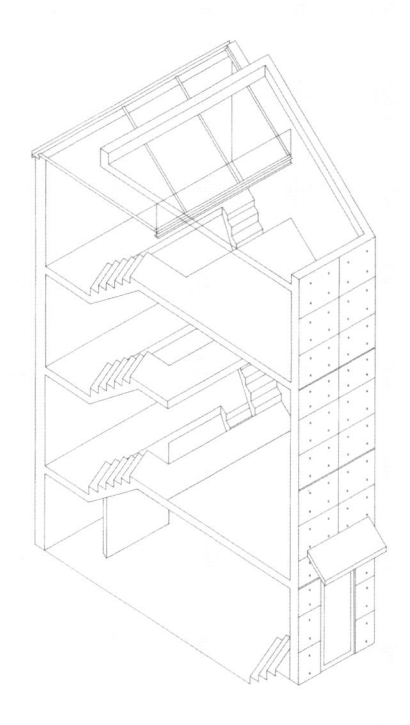

敷地は10坪、そこにギャラリー、アトリエ、住居の機能が求められた。工費にも限界があり設計作業は難航、最終的に、中央に四層の空間を貫く光庭を持つ、敷地いっぱいのコンクリートのボックスが実現した。トップライトからの自然光が各階に光をもたらし、来訪者は階段を昇降しながら、オーナーのアートへの思いを共有していく。最上階の居室は窓を大きく開き、そこからJRの駅に近い都市の喧騒を内部に引き込む仕立てになっている。

For this project, it was requested to house functionalities including a gallery space, atelier and residence within a small site in 33sqm. The budget was also limited, therefore its design process did not go smoothly. Finally, a building in a concrete box occupying the entire site space was constructed, with a light court in the middle of the building along with an open ceiling void space going up to the 4th floor level. Natural light coming down from the top light illuminate each floor level. As visitors to this building go up and down a staircase, they would share the same feeling with the owner toward art works. The top floor living room has a large window opening to bring in the bustle and noise of urban environment near a JR station.

[139]
サントリーミュージアム
＋マーメイド広場　1994
suntory museum + mermaid plaza

1. 大阪市港区 | minato-ku, osaka
2. 設計 | design　1989.8–1992.8
3. 施工 | construction　1992.9–1994.8
4. 鉄筋コンクリート、鉄骨鉄筋コンクリート、鉄骨、大屋根：立体トラス架構RC |
   RC, SRC, steel, space truss frame
5. 美術館 | museum of art, plaza
6. 敷地 | site　13,429.4 m²
7. 建築 | building　3983.3 m² [museum], 1362.2 m² [plaza]
8. 延床 | total floor　13804.1 m² [museum], 2696.6 m² [plaza]

大阪南港のウォーターフロント開発の一環として建設された。開放的な立地を踏まえ、巨大な幾何立体を相互に衝突させることで生まれるダイナミズムを建築のコンセプトとした。目を引くのは最大直径が48メートルにも達する逆円錐のドラムで、それに2本の直方体が突き刺さる。ドラムの内部には直径32メートルの球体の劇場が設けられ、直方体の内部にギャラリーが配された。安藤が力を入れたのは、美術館の足もとから岸壁に広がる広場。行政に働きかけ、来訪者が座れるよう岸壁を段状に造り替えた。海岸線を市民の憩いの場として取り戻す提案だった。

A part of the water front development for the South Port of the Port of Osaka. The concept was to create a dynamic gesture in the building, considering the openness of this site; enormous geometric volumes are juxtaposed to confront or crash with other volumes. The element gathering major attention is a reversed-cone shaped, drum-like volume with maximum diameter in 48 m, and two cuboid are penetrating into this drum. A theater of 32 m in diameter was installed inside the drum, and a gallery inside the cuboids. Ando paid strong attention to the plaza space spreading from the foot of the building to quaywall, so that the coast line area will be brought back to the hands of citizens as the place for relaxing and enjoying.

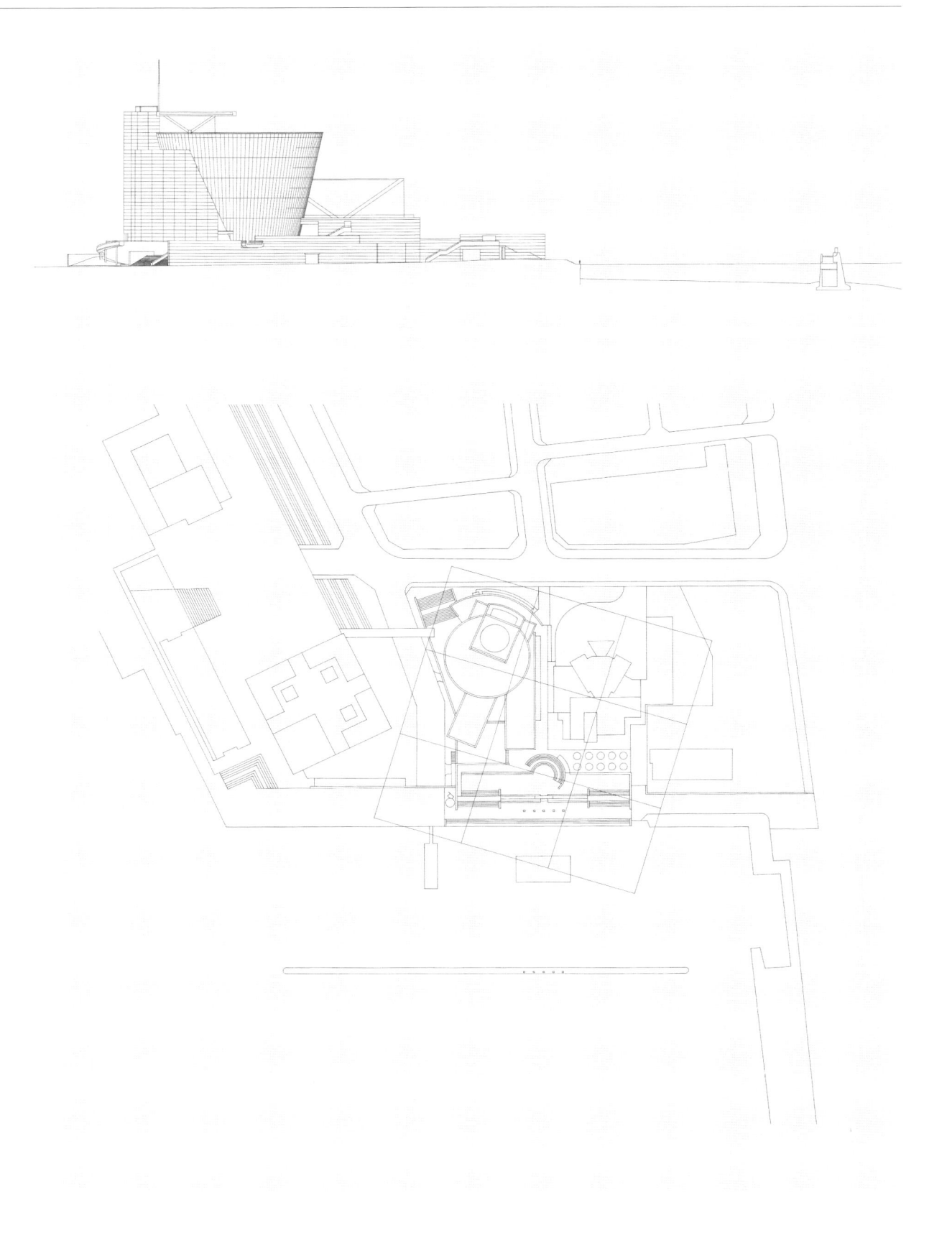

[140]

大阪府立近つ飛鳥博物館　1994
chikatsu-asuka
historical museum, osaka

1. 大阪府河南町 | kanan, osaka
2. 設計 | design　1990.4–1991.11
3. 施工 | construction　1991.12–1994.3
4. 鉄骨鉄筋コンクリート | SRC
5. 博物館 | museum
6. 敷地 | site　14,318.3 m²
7. 建築 | building　3,407.8 m²
8. 延床 | total floor　5,925.2 m²

古事記にある「近つ飛鳥」は、後の反正天皇が大和に赴く途上この地に泊まった際に命名したとされる。奈良の明日香が「遠つ飛鳥」、対して、難波津に近いこちらを「近いほうの飛鳥」と呼んだ。一帯は古墳群で知られ、博物館の近傍にも小さな古墳が集合する「風土記の丘」がある。安藤は、山腹に位置する博物館の来訪者に、この地を見てほしいと考え、外観らしい外観は持たせず、「黄泉の塔」と名付けたコンクリートのタワーだけがそびえる「大階段」の建築を構想した。大階段を昇降して歴史的な環境を身体で感じ取れば古代への思いをかきたてられると考えたのである。

Chikatsu Asuka, a place described in the book of Kojiki (Records of Ancient Matters), is said to be named by Emperor Hanzei when he stayed at this place on the way to the city of Yamato. Compare to Totsu-Asuka in Nara Prefecture, this place, located nearer to Naniwazu, was then called "Chikatsu-Asuka", meaning "The city of Asuka nearer". This area is known for the series of ancient Barrows, and there is also a park called "Fudoki-no-oka Historical Park" with groups of small barrows gathering near this museum building. Intention of Ando was to make visitors of this museum located on a hillside to see this area with historical background, then he proposed a building with a "large staircase" without any distinctive exterior appearance, except a concrete tower named "The Tower of Yomi" ("the land of the dead").

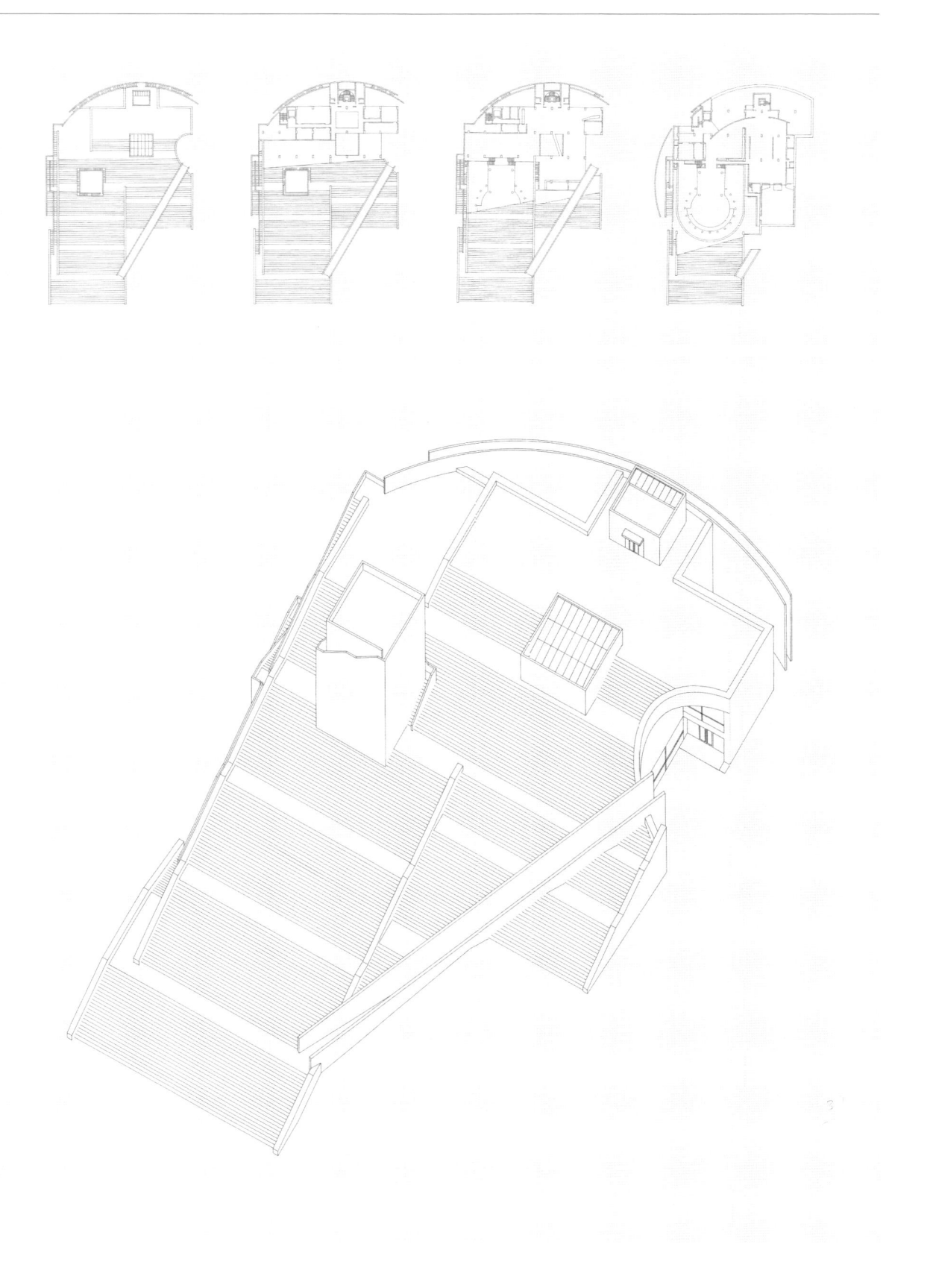

[141]
京都府立陶板名画の庭　1994
garden of fine art, kyoto

1. 京都市左京区 | sakyo-ku, kyoto
2. 設計 | design 1990.9–1992.2
3. 施工 | construction 1993.3–1994.3
4. 鉄筋コンクリート | RC
5. 野外美術館 | open-air museum
6. 敷地 | site 2,824.4 m²
7. 建築 | building 28.0 m²
8. 延床 | total floor 212.2 m²

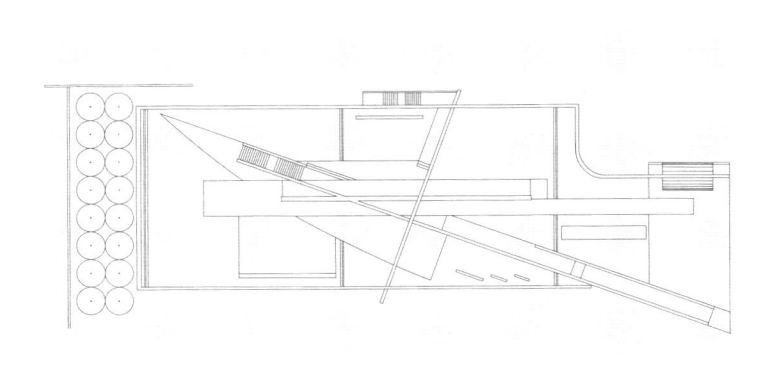

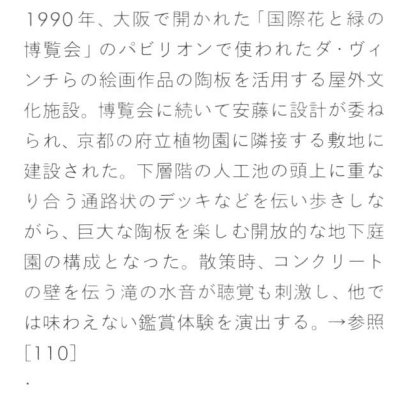

1990年、大阪で開かれた「国際花と緑の博覧会」のパビリオンで使われたダ・ヴィンチらの絵画作品の陶板を活用する屋外文化施設。博覧会に続いて安藤に設計が委ねられ、京都の府立植物園に隣接する敷地に建設された。下層階の人工池の頭上に重なり合う通路状のデッキなどを伝い歩きしながら、巨大な陶板を楽しむ開放的な地下庭園の構成となった。散策時、コンクリートの壁を伝う滝の水音が聴覚も刺激し、他では味わえない鑑賞体験を演出する。→参照 [110]

This is an outdoor cultural facility to present the works of painters including Leonard da Vinci on ceramic boards used in the pavilion of the International Garden and Greenery Exposition held in Osaka in 1990. As with the case of the pavilion design, this project was again commissioned to Ando, and the building was constructed on the site adjacent to Kyoto Prefectural Botanical Garden. The building as an "underground garden space" has an open atmosphere to enjoy paintings on ceramic boards in enormous scale, with a set up for visitors to walk around the passage deck bridging over the artificial pond situated on a lower floor level. The sound of a waterfall over the concrete wall also stimulates the hearing sense of visitors, providing a stage setting to appreciate paintings unlike any other places. → see also [110]

[142]
マックスレイ本社ビル　1994
maxray headquarters building

1. 大阪市城東区 | joto-ku, osaka
2. 設計 | design 1991.7–1993.1
3. 施工 | construction 1993.1–1994.9
4. 鉄筋コンクリート | RC
5. 事務所、ショールーム | office, showroom
6. 敷地 | site 345.7 m²
7. 建築 | building 204.3 m²
8. 延床 | total floor 972.5 m²

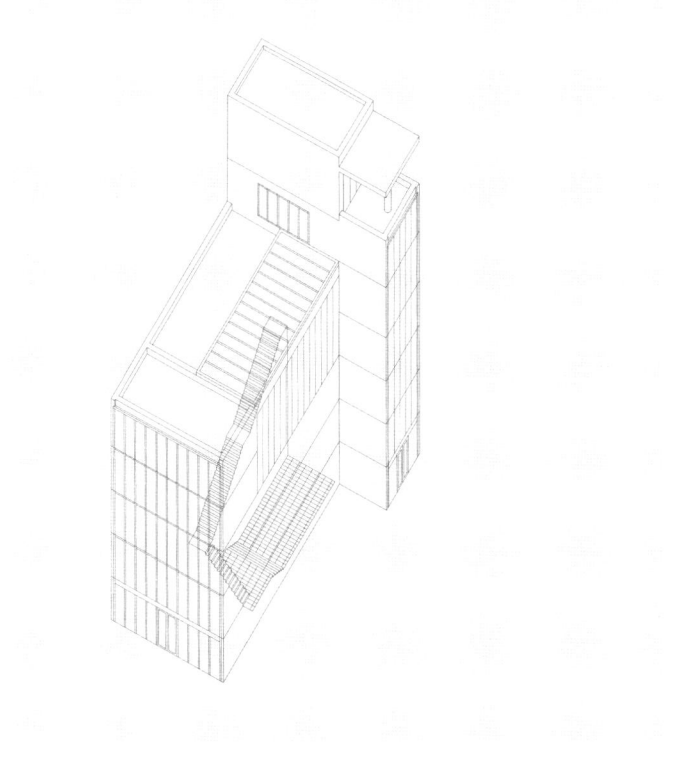

照明メーカーの本社ビル。旧知のオーナーの依頼に応じ、L字型の不整形な敷地に、当初、中庭を囲う形の構成を想定した。結果的にこの中庭はガラスの屋根で覆われた六層のアトリウムの形で実現した。ガラス壁のアトリウムを介して、周囲の下町らしい活気あふれる雰囲気がビル内に流入し、ものつくりの企業にふさわしい場が醸成された。また、アトリウムからの自然光により、事務空間を自社製品のショールーム的に使える利点もある。

A headquarters building of an illumination manufacturer. To answer the request from the owner Ando has known for a long time, the building was first designed to surround the courtyard on an irregular L-shape property. This courtyard was completed as a six-layer atrium covered with a glass roof as a result. The energetic atmosphere from the traditional working-class neighborhoods flows in through glass walls of the atrium, which builds a place suitable for a company who creates products. Additionally, there is an advantage that the natural light from the atrium allows the office space to be used as a showroom of their products.

[143]
鹿児島大学稲盛会館　1994
inamori auditorium

1. 鹿児島県鹿児島市｜kagoshima, kagoshima
2. 設計｜design　1991.7–1993.9
3. 施工｜construction　1993.10–1994.10
4. 鉄筋コンクリート造（シェル構造）、その他混構造｜RC shell, mixed structure
5. 大学施設｜university facilities
6. 敷地｜site　1,845.9 m²
7. 建築｜building　810.1 m²
8. 延床｜total floor　1,613.4 m²

京セラの創業者、稲盛和夫が出身大学の鹿児島大学に寄付したホール。「中之島計画II」で提案した卵形ドームを、稲盛自身が目にとめ、実現にこぎつけた。卵形のコンクリートの三次元曲面は、形状の決定をコンピューター、現場での打設を職人の手仕事が担って進められた。数々の技術革新で京セラを最先端企業に育て上げた稲盛にふさわしい作品になった。天井に散りばめた光ファイバーがもたらす点光源も手伝い、卵形の空間らしい広がりも感じさせる仕立てとなっている。

A hall donated by the founder of Kyocera, Inamori Kazuo to Kagoshima University where he graduated from. Inamori noticed the egg-shape dome designed for the NAKANOSHIMA PROJECT II and it was materialized by this hall. The shape of the three-dimensional curved surface of the egg-shape concrete was determined by use of a computer and the concrete installation was performed through the manual work of experienced workers. The completed work is very fitting for Inamori who developed Kyocera to a leading technology company by numerous technological innovations. With the expanse of point light source by optical fibers scattered on the ceiling, the special shape expresses movement suitable for an egg form.

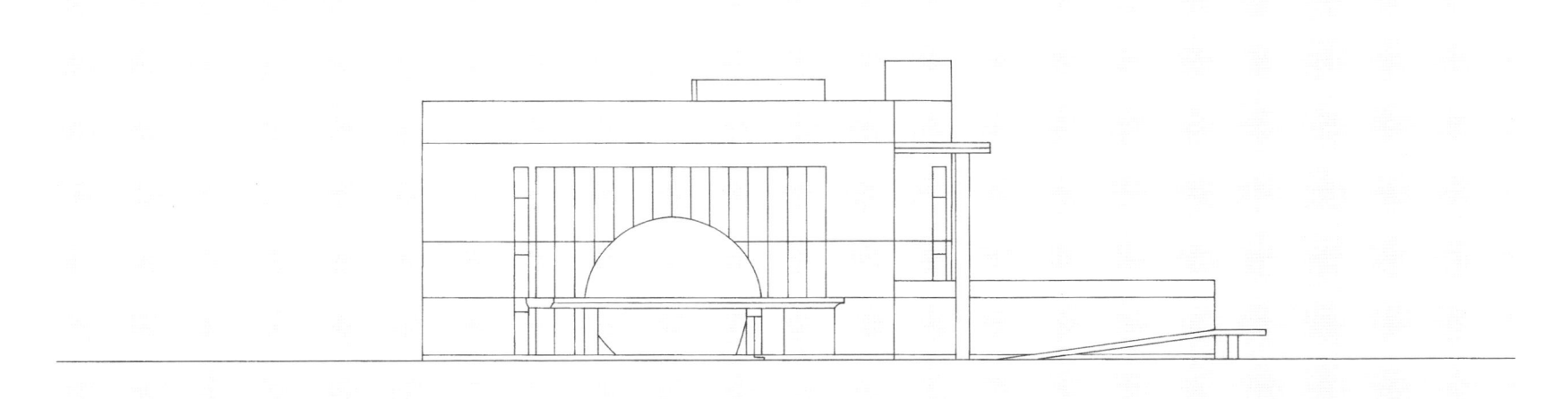

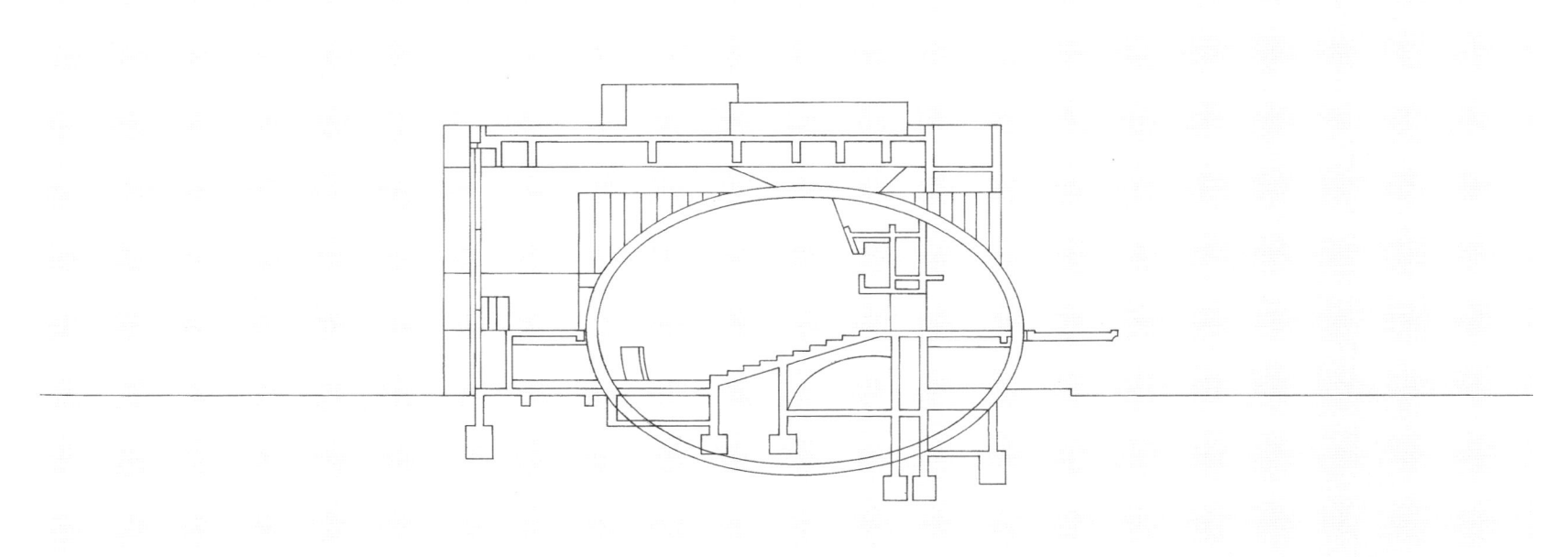

[144]

兵庫県木の殿堂　1994
museum of wood

1. 兵庫県香美町 | kami, hyogo
2. 設計 | design　1991.10–1993.4
3. 施工 | construction　1993.5–1994.4
4. 木造・鉄骨・鉄筋コンクリートによる混構造 | mixed structure (wood, steel, RC)
5. 博物館 | museum
6. 敷地 | site　168,310.0 m²
7. 建築 | building　1,951.3 m²
8. 延床 | total floor　2,694.6 m²

1992年、スペイン・セビリア万国博覧会に出展された木造建築の日本館を、日本で再建する試みは実現しなかった。代わって、1994年に兵庫県で開催された全国植樹祭に合わせて、安藤の手で博物館施設として「木の殿堂」が建設された。緑の森林のなかに、円錐状の台座の形をとった巨大な木造建築がそびえる。地元産の杉の集成材が活用され、展示室内部に入ると柱が林立している。屋内の展示空間はスロープで鑑賞する仕立てだ。円錐の中央は吹き抜けの広場になっていて、下層部に配された噴水が作動するとき、静寂の空間に動感が加わる。

It was not realized the proposal of reconstructing the Japanese pavilion in wooden structure presented for the 1992 International Exposition in Seville, Spain. Instead of this proposal, a museum facility named MUSEUM OF WOOD was built by the design of Ando for National Tree Planting Ceremony held in Hyogo Prefecture in 1994. A monumental large-scale wooden structure building with cone-shaped pedestal sits within a dense green forest. Laminated cedar wood material produced in local industry was used for this project, and series of columns is standing inside of exhibition rooms as if like a forest. Visitors are guided through a slope within the interior exhibition space to appreciate presentations. The center of the cone shape is a plaza space with open ceiling, and when fountains provided to the lower level is operated, this space is stirred up in dynamic movement within a calm, quiet space.

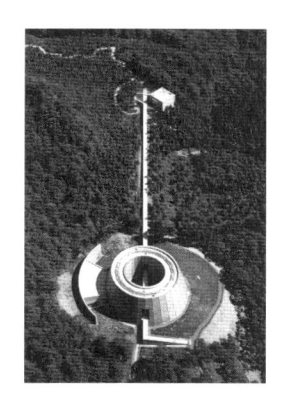

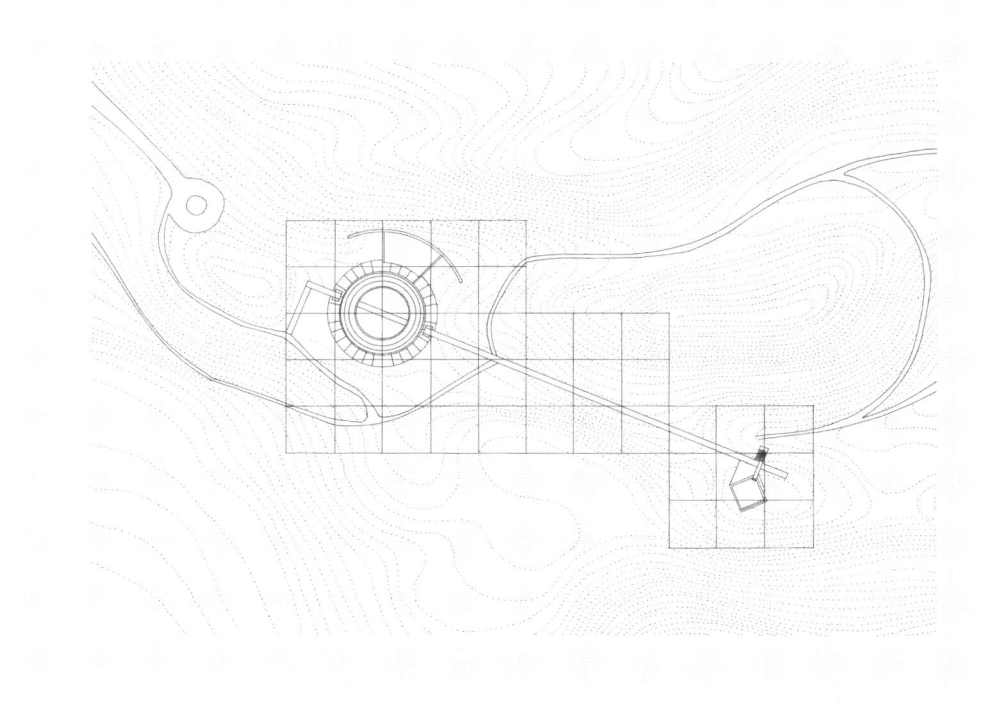

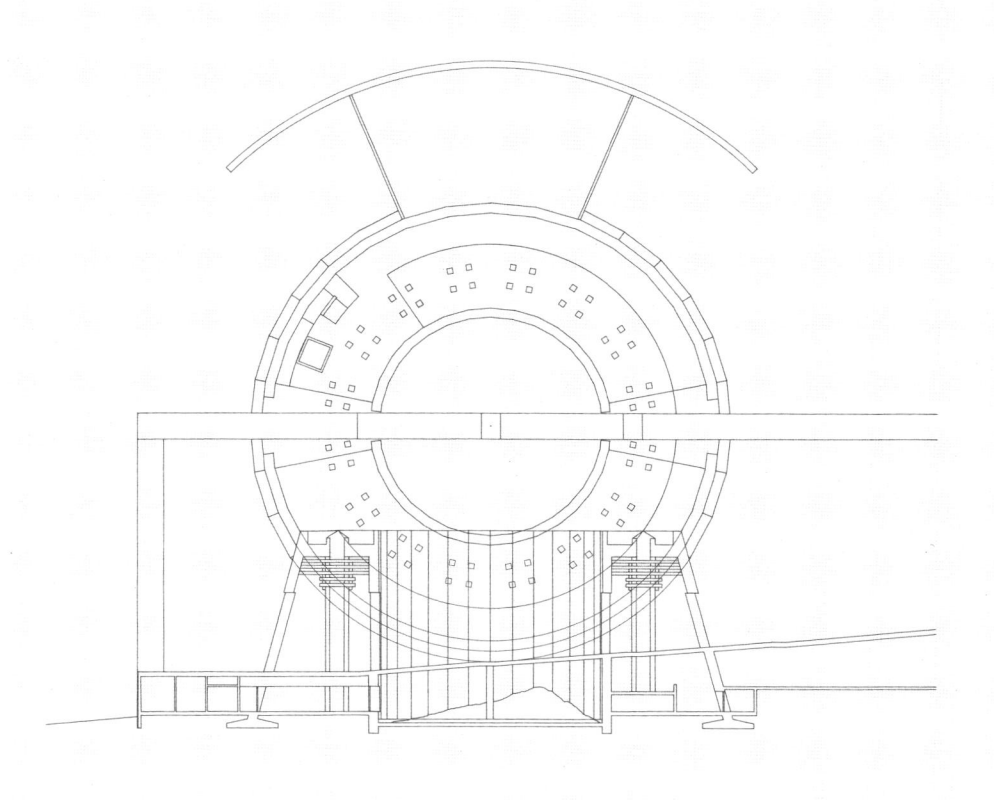

[145]
高梁市成羽美術館　1994
nariwa museum

1. 岡山県高梁市｜takahashi, okayama
2. 設計｜design　1991.12–1993.3
3. 施工｜construction　1993.4–1994.10
4. 鉄筋コンクリート、一部鉄骨鉄筋コンクリート｜RC, SRC
5. 美術館｜museum of art
6. 敷地｜site　7,607.9 m²
7. 建築｜building　1,490.0 m²
8. 延床｜total floor　2,691.1 m²

天領・成羽陣屋の跡地に今も残る屋敷の石垣の切れ目をくぐると、コンクリート打ち放しの建物が待っている。人工の浅い池がつくられ、美術館は水辺に幾何学の結晶となってたたずむ。小さな美術館だが、水面に灰色の幾何立体が映り込む姿は国際級の水準に達している。コレクションの中核は、成羽出身の画家児島虎次郎の作品。児島はパリに滞在して、大原美術館のコレクションを収集したことで知られる。美術館は、展示ギャラリーの周縁に外部の風景を堪能させる仕掛けを設え、来館者は水と緑にやすらぎを覚えながら館内を巡回する。

A building in an exposed concrete finish appears by passing through a gap of remaining stone walls of an estate on the site of the Nariwa Domain under shogunate control. An artificial shallow pond is created, and the museum stands as a crystalized geometric form on its waterside. Although this is a small museum building, the silhouette of this gray-colored building reflected on the water surface represents an international grade architecture. The main art pieces of the collection are the works of a painter, Torajiro Kojima. He is also known as a collector of the art works for Ohara Museum during his stay in Paris. The museum building has a feature to exterior scenery around the exhibition gallery, so that visitors can go around the hall, memorizing relaxation in water and green.

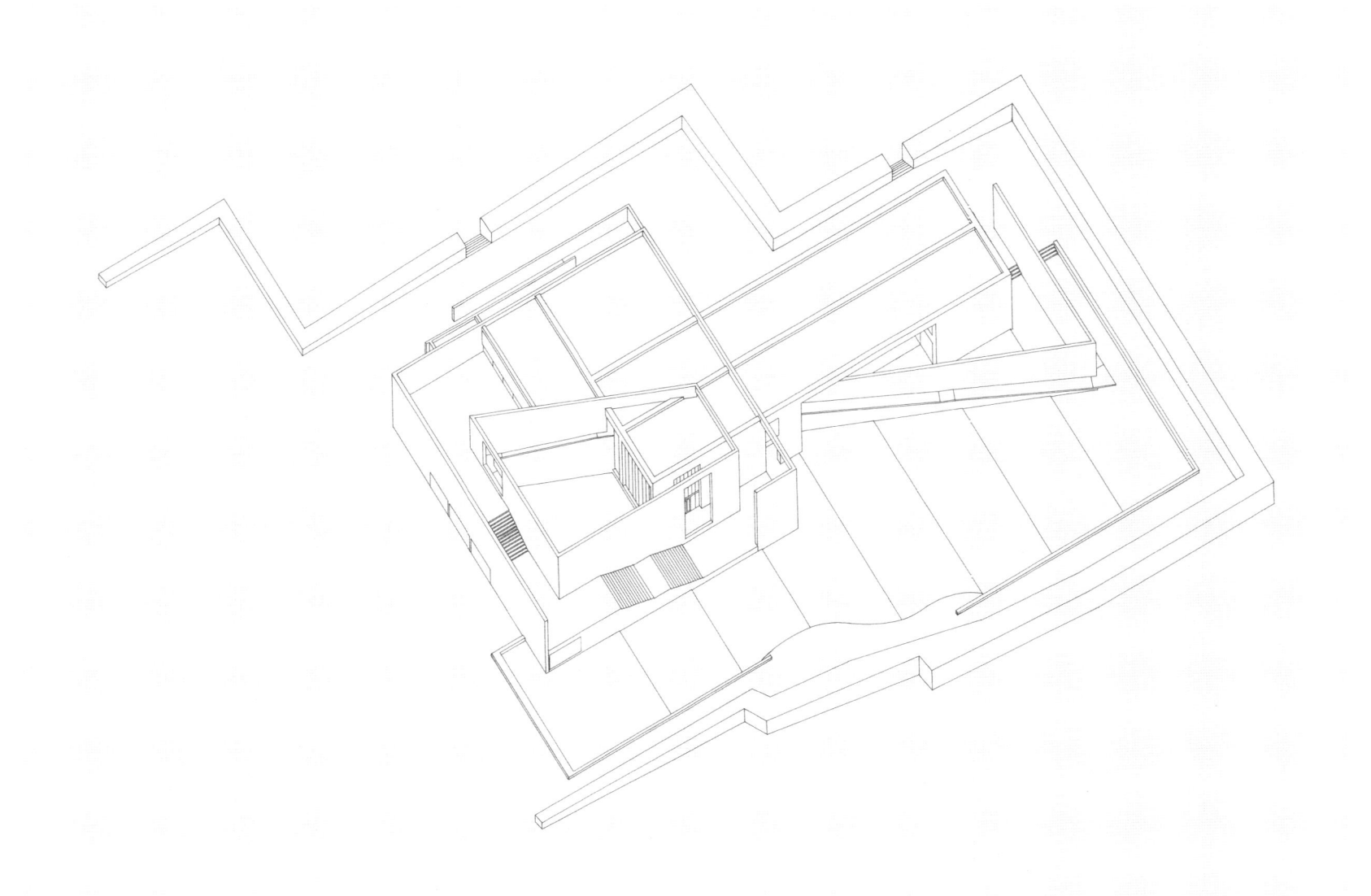

[146]

日本橋の家──金森邸　1994
house in nipponbashi
—kanamori house

1. 大阪市中央区 | chuo-ku, osaka
2. 設計 | design　1993.3–1994.1
3. 施工 | construction　1994.2–1994.9
4. 鉄筋コンクリート（壁式ラーメン構造） | RC (wall-type frame structure)
5. 住宅、店舗 | house, shop
6. 敷地 | site　57.8 m²
7. 建築 | building　43.5 m²
8. 延床 | total floor　139.1 m²

大阪にあって雑踏を実感させる日本橋に立地する小住宅。間口は3メートルに満たず、奥行きが15メートルの狭小な4階建てが実現した。安藤はただでさえ狭い敷地の3、4階に屋外の吹き抜け空間を設けた。自然光、風、自然の移ろいを感じさせる選択である。また、2–4階の内部の吹き抜けは昼夜で異なる役割を果たす。昼間は、正面のすりガラスの大きな窓を介して濾過された外部の活気がもたらされ、夜間は内部照明による発光体となって、街頭で存在感を示す。

A small residential house located at Nipponbashi in Osaka where the bustle of the city can be felt. A four-story building has a width of less than 3 meters and length of 15 meters. Although the property was narrow, Ando provided an outdoor wellhole structure on the 3rd and 4th floor. The natural light, wind, and transition of nature can be felt inside. Furthermore, the indoor open ceiling from the 2nd floor to the 4th floor plays different roles during the daytime and nighttime. During the day, energy from the outside is brought in through the frosted glass of the large window at the front. During the night, it becomes an illuminant by the interior lighting, which has a presence outside on the street.

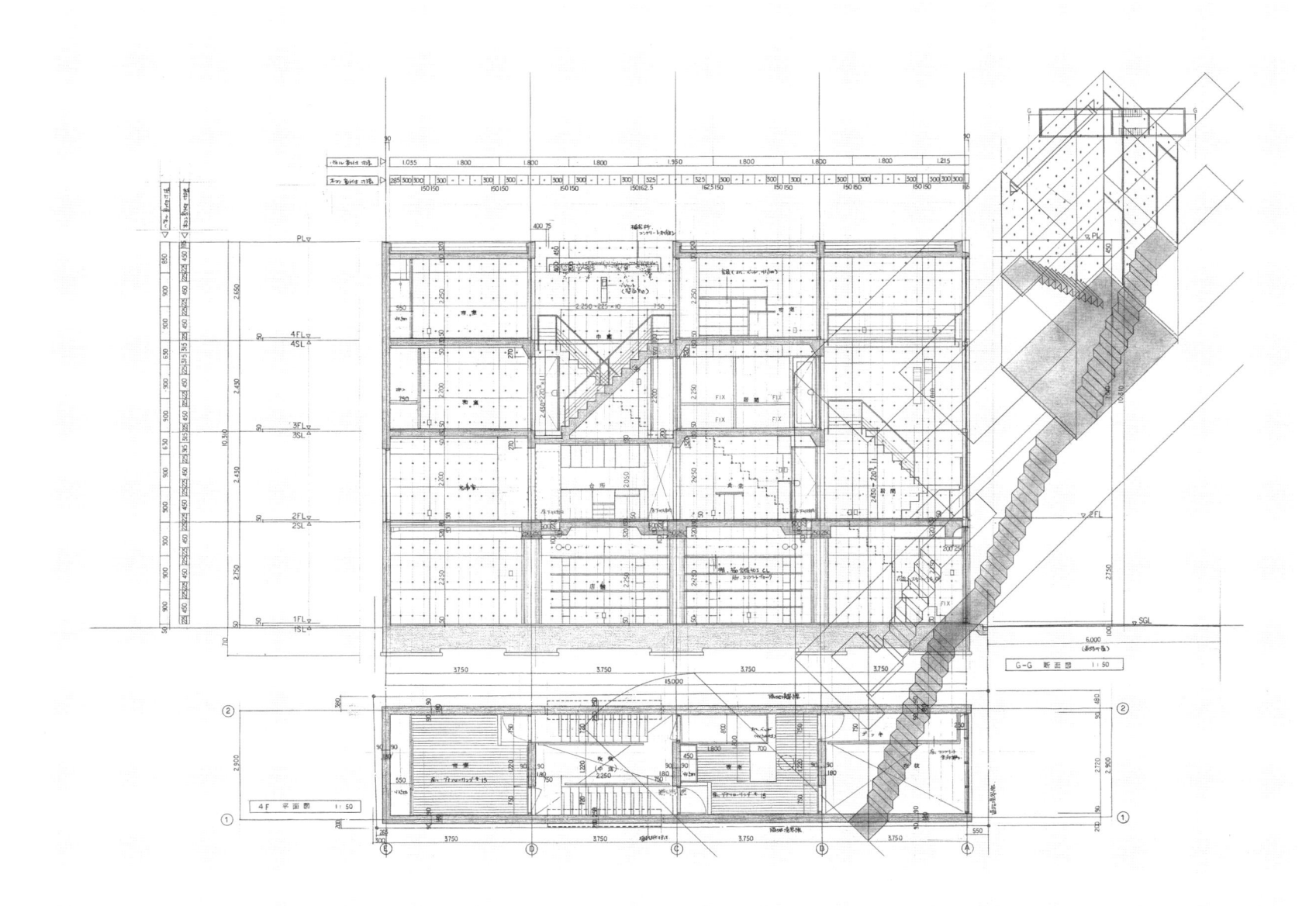

346 Complete Works

[147]
安藤忠雄建築展
／Palladian Basilica 1994
tadao ando exhibition
in palladian basilica

1. イタリア ヴィチェンツァ | vicenza, italy
2. 設計 | design 1994
3. 施工 | construction 1994
5. 展覧会展示 | exhibition

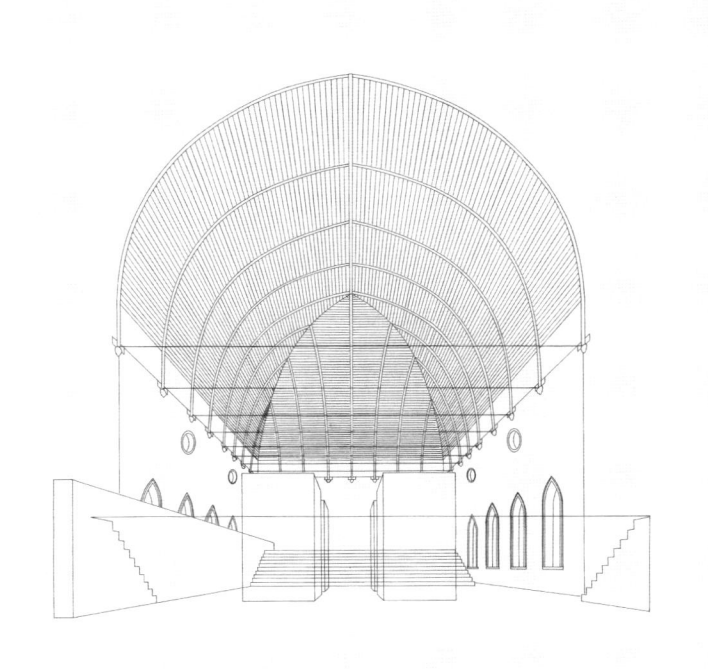

ルネサンスを代表するイタリアの建築家パラーディオの街として知られるヴィチェンツァのバシリカを会場にした展覧会のデザイン。パラーディオの手になる空間の内部の両端に一対の階段を配し、階段を包み込む壁を立て、囲われた空間を造りだした。そこには軸線上に四つの立方体が配された。鑑賞者は階段に腰掛けて立方体の厳格な配置を確かめ、立方体の内部に足を踏み入れると安藤の幾何学に支配される。原建築のルネサンスの均衡の美と安藤の現代の幾何学が交錯することによって、パラーディオの空間を際立たせることを意図した。

A design for an exhibition at Basilica in Vicenza known as the town of Palladio, an Italian architect who represents the Renaissance style. A pair of stairways are arranged on the both ends inside the big building which were by the design of Palladio, and walls that cover the stairways are placed to create a surrounded space. Four cubes were placed there on the axis line. Beholders can sit on the stairs to confirm the strict arrangement of the cubes and when stepping inside the cubes they will be dominated by the geometry of Ando. It is intended to highlight Palladio's space by mixture of the balanced beauty between former Renaissance architecture and the Modern geometry by Ando.

[148]
播磨高原東小学校* 1995
harima kogen higashi primary school
播磨高原東中学校** 1997
harima kogen higashi junior high school

1. 兵庫県たつの市 | tatsuno, hyogo
2. 設計 | design *1992.8–1993.11,
   **1992.8–1996.1
3. 施工 | construction *1994.2–1995.3,
   **1996.2–1997.3
4. 鉄筋コンクリート、鉄骨 | RC, steel
5. 小学校 | elementary school
   中学校 | junior high school
6. 敷地 | site *165,040.0 m², **30,000.0 m²
7. 建築 | building *5,157.8 m², **4,695.2 m²
8. 延床 | total floor *7,025.5 m², **7,707.7 m²

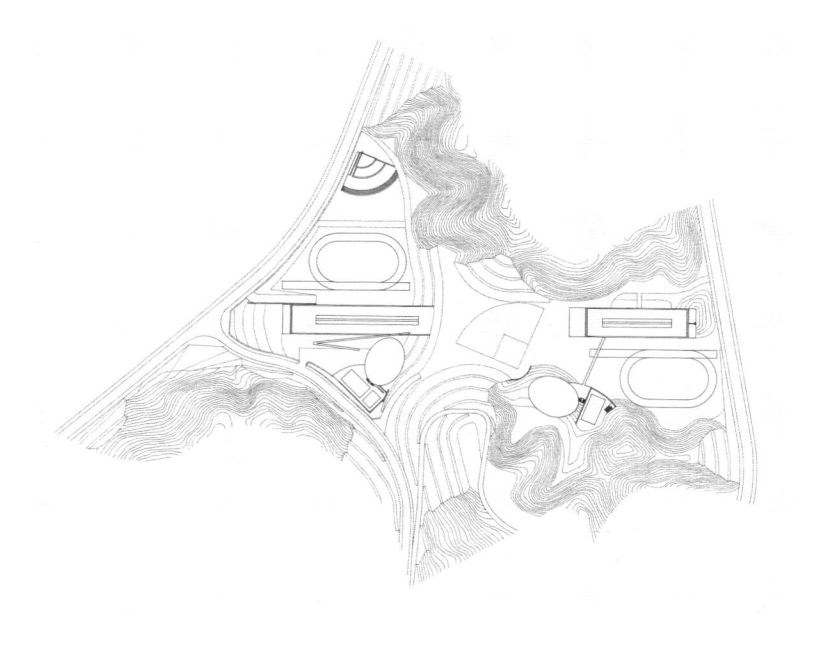

兵庫県が播磨科学公園都市に開設した小中学校を同じ敷地にひと組とする実験的教育施設。小学校と中学校は、教室棟、運動場、アリーナをそれぞれ持つ双子のような似通った構成で、新都市ならではの広大な敷地の東西両端に配された。各校舎の外回りは45度のコンクリートの斜材を連続させ、力強さと簡素さを表現している。アリーナの屋根は、安藤の幾何学の美が凝縮したスカイラインを形成し、新都市のなかで存在感を示している。

An experimental education facility opened by Hyogo Prefecture in the Harima Science Garden City that combines an elementary school and junior high school in one location. The arrangement of classroom buildings, playgrounds and arenas of the elementary school and junior high school are very similar in which they are located on both east and west ends of the vast property, which is distinctive of the new city. Concrete objects inclined at 45 degrees are positioned around both school buildings and express the strength and simplicity. Roof of the arena forms the skyline where Ando's geometric beauty is compressed into and is demonstrating the sense of existence in the new city.

[149]
大山崎山荘美術館　1995
oyamazaki villa museum

1. 京都府大山崎町 | oyamazaki, kyoto
2. 設計 | design　1991.4–1994.7
3. 施工 | construction　1994.8–1995.7
4. 鉄筋コンクリート | RC
5. 美術館 | museum of art
6. 敷地 | site　5,481.9 m²
7. 建築 | building　438.8 m² [改修／renovated part], 262.0 m² [新築／new part]
8. 延床 | total floor　730.7 m² [改修／renovated part], 271.5 m² [新築／new part]

大阪の実業家加賀正太郎の別荘として1920–30年代に建設された「大山崎山荘」を、1996年、美術館に保存再生して開館した。その際、本館にあたる元の別荘建築と45度で交差するコンクリートの回廊から地下の展示室に下りる「地中館」が安藤によって設計された。モネの「睡蓮」などの作品を展示し、「地中の宝石箱」と呼ぶ。加賀が指導したテューダー式の豪快な木造の本館とコンクリートが衝突するところに現代の創造が生まれた。2012年、本館を挟んでこの「地中館」と反対側に安藤設計のコンクリートの「山手館」が増築された。

In 1996, the "Oyamazaki Villa", built around 1920s–30s as the villa of an industrialist in Osaka, Shotaro Kaga, was renovated as an art museum to be opened. Along with this renovation, an "Underground Annex" was designed by Ando. This building has a structure descending from the concrete corridor crossing at 45°angle to the original villa building, now the main building, to the underground exhibition room. In this space, "Water Lilies", the paintings of Claude Monet, are exhibited—and it is named as "Underground Jewelry Box annex". Contemporary creation was produced where the tudor style wooden architecture of the main building produced under the instruction of Kaga, collided with the concrete structure of this new building.

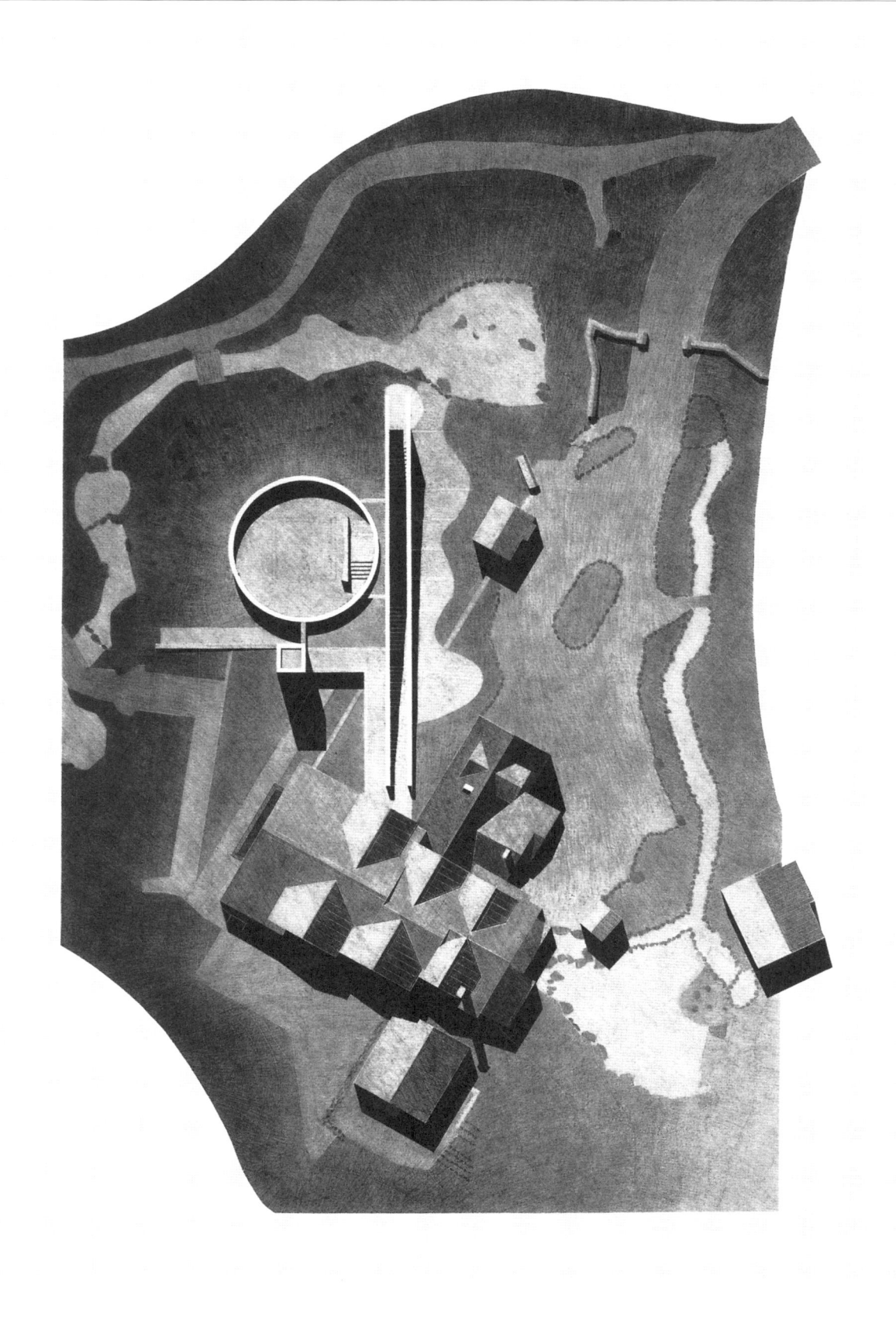

[150]

市立五條文化博物館　1995
museum of gojo culture

1. 奈良県五條市｜gojo, nara
2. 設計｜design　1991.12–1993.1
3. 施工｜construction　1993.2–1995.4
4. 鉄筋コンクリート、一部鉄骨鉄筋コンクリート｜RC, SRC
5. 博物館、茶室｜museum, tea-ceremony room
6. 敷地｜site　10,450.0 m²
7. 建築｜building　715.1 m²
8. 延床｜total floor　2,021.4 m²

古い歴史を持つ奈良県五條市の小高い丘に位置する博物館と地域文化活動の中核施設。ランドマークとなる立地を意識して、印象的なヴォールト屋根が円形の躯体に載る形態が選択された。屋根は、耐候性を意識して亜鉛引きの鉄板で葺かれ、出目地の仕上げも相まって、オリジナルの日本美を体現している。低層の建築が大地に根を下ろす仕立ては、基壇部階段のトラバーチンの乱尺積みでも強調されている。本館完成の3年後に茶室を中心とする別館が増築された。そちらも屋根材をはじめ、インテリアの造作にも亜鉛引きの鉄板を使っている。

A museum and a main facility for cultural activity of the community located on a slightly elevated hill of historical Gojo City of Nara Prefecture. Design with an impressive vault roof placed on top of the circle building was selected considering the purpose to be a land mark. Iron plates with zinc coating were used for its weather resistance and the beaded joint finish adds to the expression of unique Japanese beauty. The form of lower architecture taking root in the ground is emphasized by the random masonry of travertine at the stairway of the platform area. An annex for a tea-ceremony room was added three years after the completion of the main building. Iron plates with zinc coating were used as the roof material and for interior fixtures.

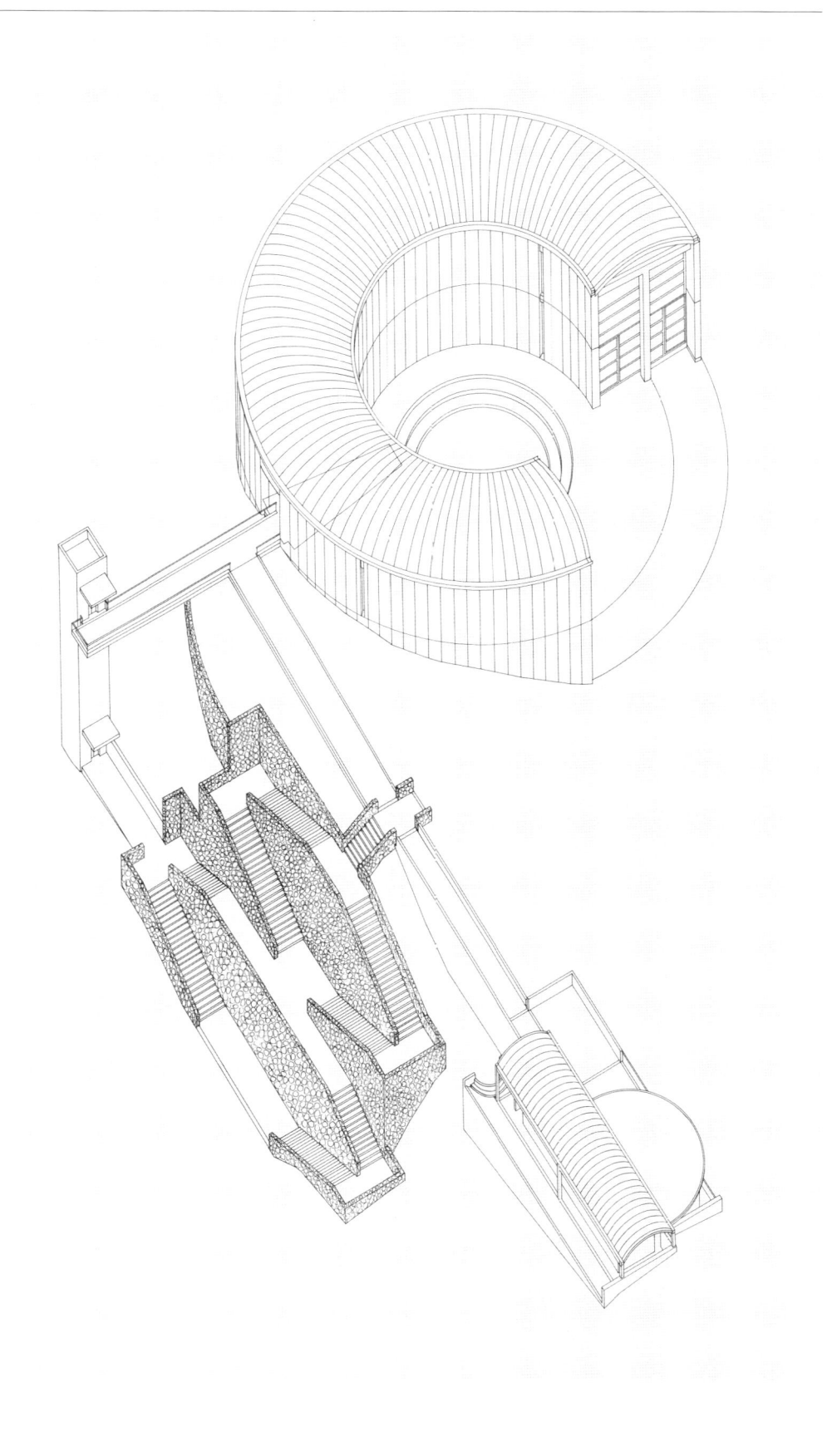

[151]

ベネッセハウス オーバル 1995
benesse house oval

1. 香川県直島町 | naoshima, kagawa
2. 設計 | design 1993.5–1994.9
3. 施工 | construction 1994.10–1995.6
4. 鉄筋コンクリート | RC
5. ホテル、美術館 | hotel, museum
6. 敷地 | site 53,369.0 m² [including the main museum]
7. 建築 | building 693.1 m²
8. 延床 | total floor 597.8 m²

山腹に位置する美術館「ベネッセハウス」の敷地から一段高い山頂にホテルを中心とした「アネックス」が設けられた。平屋の建物の全体形は楕円形で、内側に一回り小さな中庭が採られ、6室の客室とカフェテリアがそこに配されている。中庭の内壁はイタリアのスタッコの仕上げになっている。ここからの瀬戸内海の眺めはすばらしく、美術愛好家に対応する宿泊施設の登場により、直島の現代美術の島としてのイメージは確かなものとなった。→参照 [125]、[184]、[223]、[239]、[280]、[309]

"ANNEX" as a hotel wing was constructed on a mountain summit which is one step higher than the site of the museum BENESSE HOUSE located on the hillside. The form of a one-story building is in an oval shape, and another oval-shaped courtyard in a smaller dimension is provided within the building volume. 6 guest rooms and a cafeteria are distributed around it, and the inner wall of the courtyard space is finished in Italian stucco. The view to Seto Inland Sea from here is magnificent, thus the introduction of this hotel facility for art lovers has further strengthened the image of Naoshima as the island of contemporary art museum. → see also [125], [184], [223], [239], [280], [309]

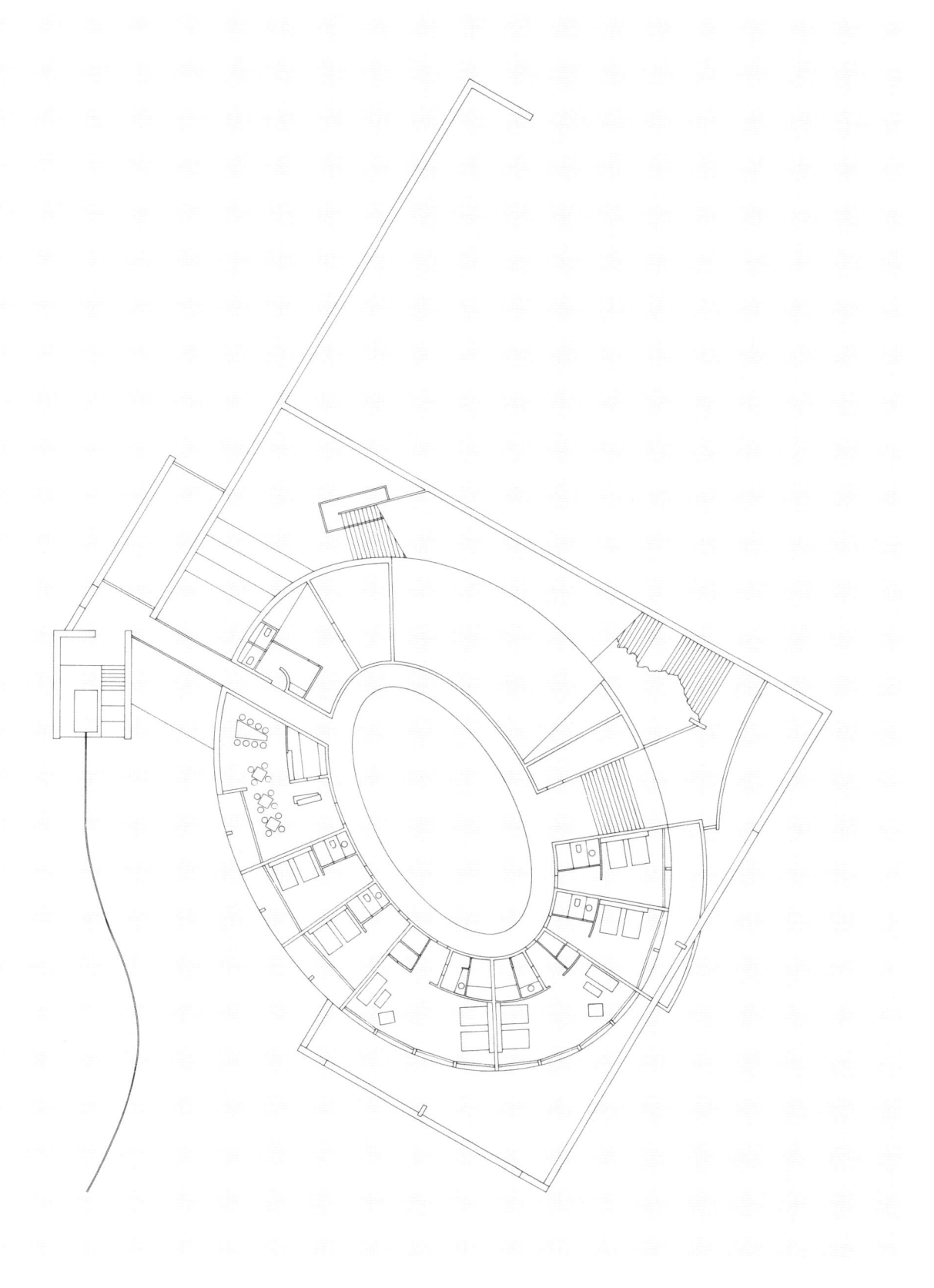

[152]
綾部工業団地交流プラザ　1995
ayabe community center

.

1. 京都府綾部市 | ayabe, kyoto
2. 設計 | design　1993.6–1994.6
3. 施工 | construction　1994.7–1995.4
4. 鉄筋コンクリート | RC
5. コミュニティーセンター | community center
6. 敷地 | site　19,774.8 m²
7. 建築 | building　525.7 m²
8. 延床 | total floor　595.6 m²

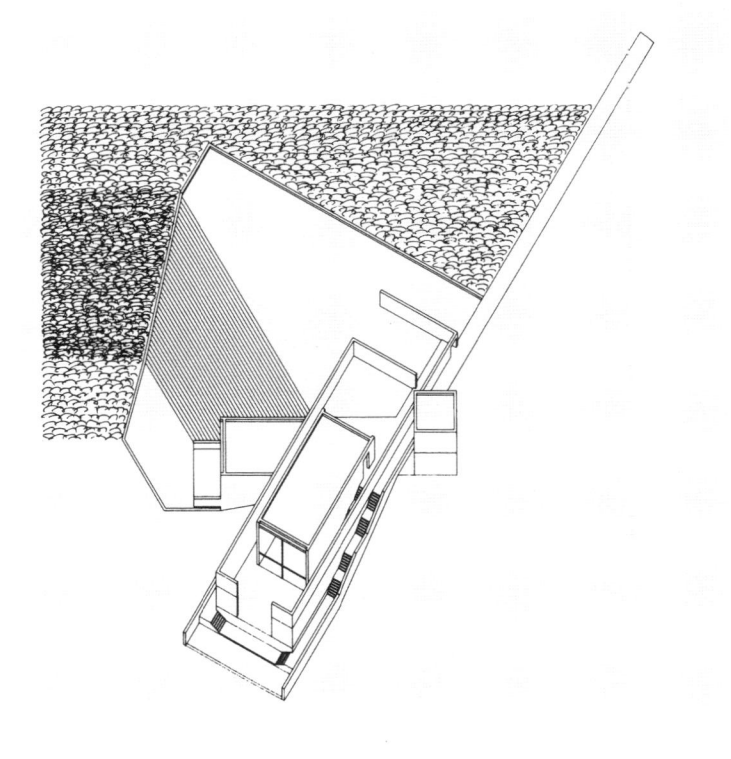

京都府北部の綾部に設けられた工業団地の交流施設。余裕のある敷地条件を活かし、建築は回遊路を意識した配置となっている。敷地の最後部では幾何立体のコンクリートボックスと自立壁が、豊かな水をたたえた人工池の傍らにそびえて、静寂の空間を演出する。一方、その人工池から絶え間なく水の流れ落ちる「水の階段」が、周囲の豊かな自然と呼応して存在感を示している。内部の交流、研修施設からは、安藤が壁で切り取った額縁のなかの自然が堪能できる。

.

A community facility of an industrial estate in Ayabe in the north part of Kyoto Prefecture. Using the property condition with less limitation, the architecture was designed considering the excursion route. A geometric concrete box and a self-sustaining wall are situated by an artificial pond full of water at the rear end of the property to produce a tranquil space. On the other hand, the Water Stairs where water keeps flowing down from the artificial pond is showing its presence among the surrounding rich nature. The nature shown in the frame Ando made by cutting out the wall can be enjoyed from the community and training facilities inside.

[153]
かほく市立金津小学校　1995
kanadu primary school, kahoku

.

1. 石川県かほく市 | kahoku, ishikawa
2. 設計 | design　1993.6–1994.10
3. 施工 | construction　1994.1–1995.10
4. 鉄筋コンクリート、木造 | RC, wood
5. 小学校 | elementary school
6. 敷地 | site　41,381.0 m²
7. 建築 | building　1,287.0 m²
8. 延床 | total floor　3,857.6 m²

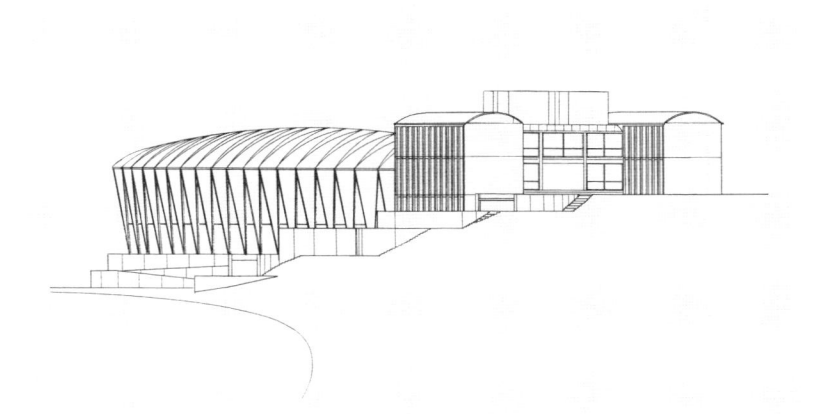

ステンレスで葺かれたヴォールト屋根が架かる2棟の同形の校舎、円形の広場に接した理科室などの半地下の教室棟、そして外壁が円弧の緩い膨らみを持つ独創的な木造の体育館が、校舎とは二層分低い敷地に配されている。設計前に訪れた安藤は「光と風と音のある学校」をつくろうと決意したという。高台ゆえに吹き抜ける風が創作者の心を刺激した。敷地を平坦に造成せず、高低差を積極的に生かし、三つの棟がゆったりとつながる配置がとられている。

.

Two schoolhouses that have the same shape with stainless steel vault roofs, a classroom building with a semi-basement that has a science room located to face the round school ground, and a unique wooden gymnasium with exterior walls shaped a circular arc on a property two floors lower than the classroom building. Ando was determined to create a school that has light, wind and music when he visited the property before designing. The wind blowing at the site due the elevated property stimulated the heart of the designer. The layout is arranged with a relaxed connection between the three buildings on different ground levels without flattening the whole property.

[154]

ユネスコ瞑想空間　1995
meditation space, UNESCO

1. フランス パリ ｜ paris, france
2. 設計 ｜ design　1994.1–1995.5
3. 施工 ｜ construction　1995.4–1995.10
4. 鉄筋コンクリート ｜ RC
5. 瞑想空間 ｜ meditation space
6. 敷地 ｜ site　350 m²
7. 建築 ｜ building　33 m²
8. 延床 ｜ total floor　33 m²

パリのユネスコ本部は、バウハウスの教員もつとめたマルセル・ブロイヤーの代表作として知られる。その背後の一角を占めるイサム・ノグチによる日本庭園の傍らに、コンクリートのシリンダーと2枚の壁で構成した「瞑想空間」が安藤の手で実現した。シリンダーは平和を祈念する瞑想空間で、直径と天井の高さはいずれも6.3メートルで仕立てられた。天井の隙間から射し込む自然光が幻想的で荘厳な雰囲気を醸成する。壁はそこに導く動線を担う。工費は日本国内の寄付でまかなわれ、日本庭園の維持管理も進められることになった。

The headquarters building of UNESCO in Paris is known as one of the major works of Marcel Breuer, who was the faculty stuff of Bauhaus. Next to the Japanese garden by Isamu Noguchi which is built on a corner behind it, "The Space of Meditation" which is composed of a concrete cylinder and two walls was realized with Ando's hand. This cylinder is designated as a meditation space to pray for peace, both diameter and height were in 6.3m. The space is filled with fantastic and majestic atmosphere by the natural light shining through the gap on the ceiling. Those two walls work as circulations to guide visitors into the space. The construction cost was covered by the donation from Japan, and the maintenance of the Japanese garden will be also conducted.

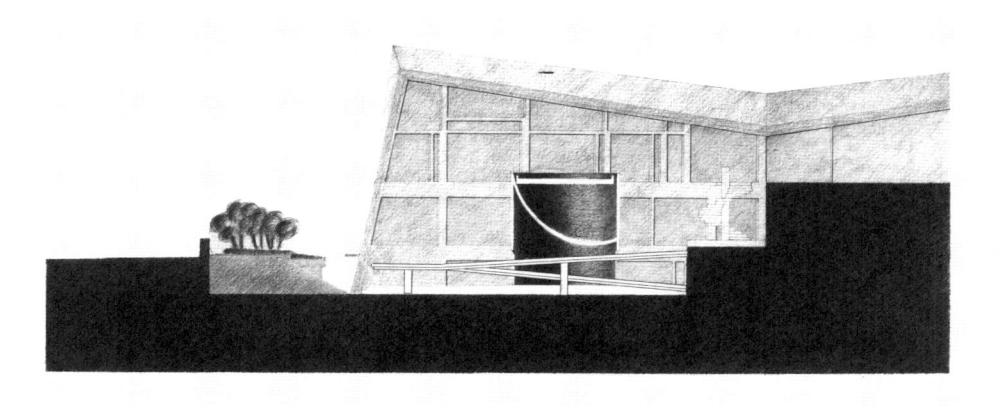

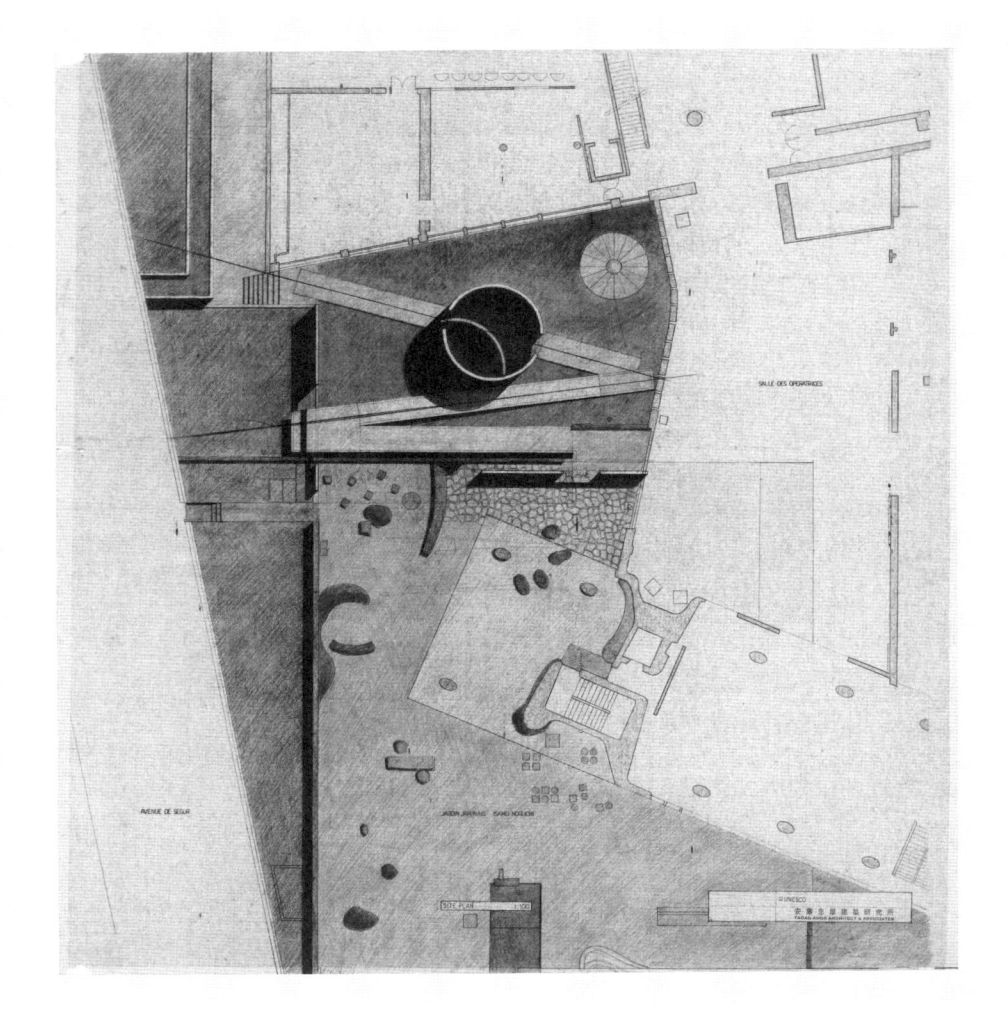

346 Complete Works

[155]
テートギャラリー現代美術館
国際設計競技案　1995
tate gallery of modern art,
international design competition

1. イギリス ロンドン ｜ london, UK
2. 設計 ｜ design　1995
3. 設計競技　design competition
4. 鉄骨鉄筋コンクリート ｜ SRC
5. 美術館 ｜ museum of art
6. 敷地 ｜ site　35,610 m²
7. 建築 ｜ building　13,660.0 m²
8. 延床 ｜ total floor　25,200 m²

ロンドンのテムズ川南岸に残る高塔を持つ火力発電所を現代美術館に改装するコンペの応募案。安藤は、対岸に位置するセント・ポール寺院に向って伸びるガラスの箱を、発電所の煉瓦の建物に突き刺す案を提案した。また、もうひとつのガラスの箱をテムズの川面に浮かべ、河岸は幅の広い階段として整備し、水面に浮かぶ細い橋を伝ってアプローチするようにした。ガラスと煉瓦という新旧の素材の衝突がもたらす緊張感が現代美術鑑賞の場にふさわしいと考えた。

A design submitted for the contest to renovate a thermal power station with a high tower located at the south bank of the Thames in London into a modern art gallery. Ando designed to make a glass box extend toward St. Paul's Cathedral located on the opposite bank to penetrate the brick building of the power plant. A narrow bridge for the pathway to approach the gallery was designed by floating another glass box on the Thames to provide a wider stairway on the bank. The tense atmosphere by collision of new and old materials, namely, glass and brick was considered suitable for the place to enjoy the modern arts.

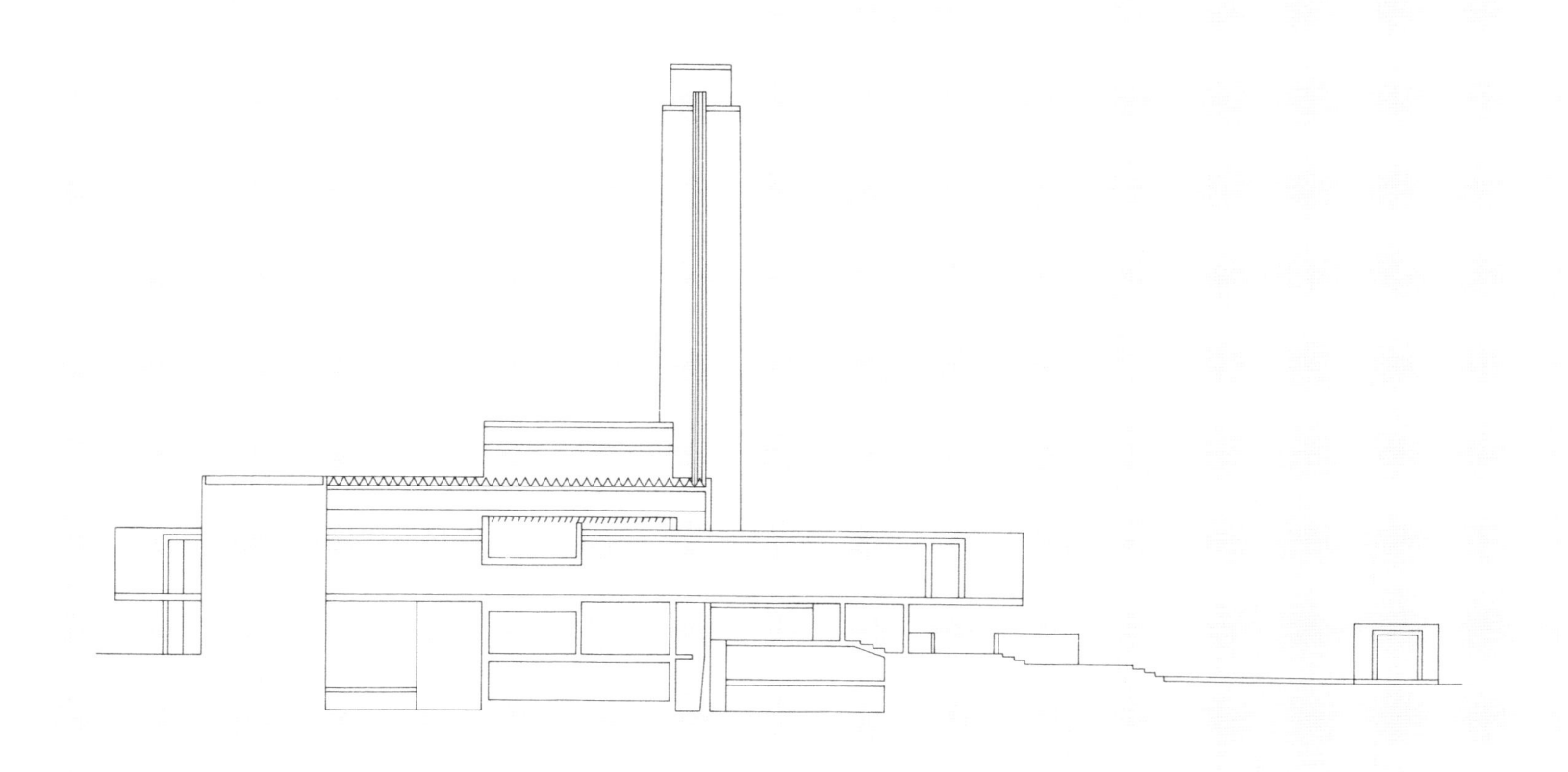

[156]
大淀のアトリエ・アネックス
1995
atelier in oyodo annex

1. 大阪市北区 | kita-ku, osaka
2. 設計 | design   1994.1–1994.4
3. 施工 | construction   1994.4–1995.3
4. 鉄筋コンクリート（壁式）| RC (wall)
5. アトリエ | atlier
6. 敷地 | site   182.8 m²
7. 建築 | building   104.3 m²
8. 延床 | total floor   247.4 m²

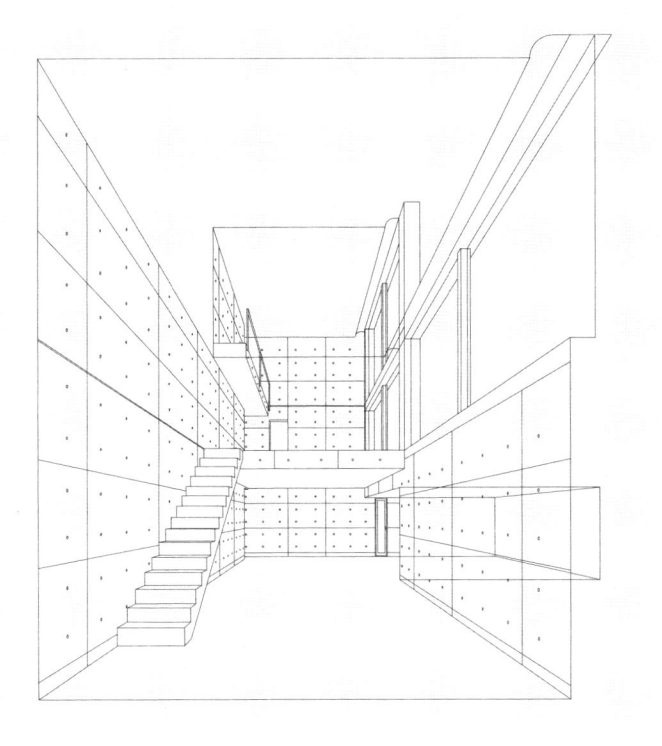

その名の通り、安藤の活動の拠点である設計事務所の通りを挟んだ場所に建設された別館。周囲は長屋のならぶ密集住宅地だったが、大阪駅に近い立地のため、オフィス街化が一気に進んだ。そこに3階建てのアトリエを付加するにあたって、安藤はコンクリートの壁で街路と区切った庭を設営、大きなクスノキを中心にハナミズキなどを植え、各階から都市のなかの自然を味わえる構成をとった。内部は吹き抜け空間のラウンジなどが設営された。→参照 [040]、[119]

As the name indicates, it is an annex built at a location on the other side of the street of a design office that is the center of Ando's activity. The surrounding area used to be a dense residential area with many rows of houses. However, since the location is close to Osaka station, the area rapidly changed to a business district. To add a three-story atelier in that location, Ando placed a yard separated from the street with a concrete wall and planted a large camphor tree in the center and other plants such as dogwood in the yard in order to provide an architectural structure where nature in the city can be enjoyed from each floor. An open ceiling lounge and other rooms were built inside the annex. → see also [040], [119]

[157]
海の集合住宅   1995
seaside housing

1. 兵庫県神戸市 | kobe, hyogo
2. 設計 | design   1995.2
3. 構想案 | concept
4. 鉄筋コンクリート | RC
5. 集合住宅 | apartment house

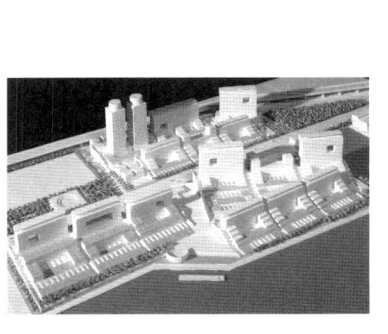

阪神淡路大震災後の神戸の臨海地を住宅街区として復興する提案。想定した場所は、現在の兵庫県立美術館と水際広場（いずれも安藤設計）の両側にあたる広大な工場跡地の埋立地。安藤はそこに海側から徐々に高くなる集合住宅群を提案した。想定戸数は7千戸、低層部は中庭を持つコートハウスで高齢者の住居に充て、その背後の中層棟は家族向けの屋上庭園を持つ。敷地の陸地側の奥には高層棟を配する計画だった。大阪、そして神戸に育てられた建築家として、明確な構想のもとでの速度感のある復興を促す気持ちが込められていた。

A proposal to restore the coastal area of Kobe to a residential district after the Great Hanshin Earthquake. The planned area is the vast reclaimed land where a plant used to stand on both sides of where HYOGO PREFECTURAL MUSEUM OF ART and KOBE WATERFRONT PLAZA (both designed by Ando) currently are located. Ando proposed a group of condominiums that gradually becomes higher from the ocean side. The total number of units is 7,000 units including court houses with courtyards at the low-rise area for elderly residents and middle-rise buildings at the back with rooftop gardens for families. High-rise buildings were to be built on the rear area of the property on the land side.

[158]
大谷地下劇場計画　1995
the theater in the rock, oya

1. 栃木県宇都宮市｜utsunomiya, tochigi
2. 設計｜design　1995.2–1996.9
3. 構想案｜concept
4. 石造（大谷石）｜stone
5. 劇場、美術館｜theater, museum
6. 敷地｜site　16,245.0 m²
8. 延床｜total floor　4,750.0 m²

栃木県宇都宮市は大谷石の産出地であり、地下には長年の採掘でできた坑道が網の目のように走っている。そこを活用した山海塾などのパフォーマンスの上演は文化的にも注目されてきた。安藤は坑道を世界に類をみないものと位置づけ、自身が追求してきた地下建築の可能性を見出した。彫刻美術館の設営、坑道を生かしたイベントスペースを順次整備し、イタリアの石材の産地ピエトラサンタから募った彫刻を配する広場の建設も提案した。

Utsunomiya City, Tochigi Prefecture is the place where Oya tuff stones are produced and mining galleries are made underground like a mesh due to mining for many years. Playing artistic performances such as Sankai Juku using that location gathered attention culturally. Ando viewed these mining galleries as unique space to this location and recognized the possibility of underground architecture he was searching for. Ando proposed for setting a sculpture art gallery, event spaces using the mining galleries, and situating a sculpture park installed with the works created by stone materials from Pietrasanta in Italy.

[159]
丘の集合住宅　1995
hilltop housing
.
1. 兵庫県宝塚市 | takarazuka, hyogo
2. 設計 | design　1995.2
3. 構想案 | concept
4. 鉄筋コンクリート | RC
5. 集合住宅、小学校 |
   apartment house, elementary school

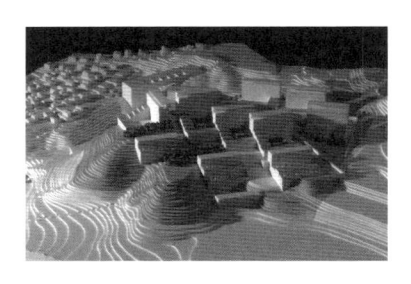

「海の集合住宅」と同時期に発表した宝塚市の丘陵地帯を想定した集合住宅の提案。立地は市街地から車で20分の場所で、丘全体を集合住宅群の敷地にあて、6棟800戸の規模とした。4棟を北斜面、2棟を南斜面に配して、それぞれの住戸はセットバックしながら丘をのぼる配置をとる。それによって生まれる屋上庭園が周囲の自然と一体になった緑の住空間の形成に貢献する。小学校の設置も提案、完結した住宅街区とすることを構想した。
.
A proposal of condominiums for a hilly area in Takarazuka City announced at the same time as the SEASIDE HOUSING. The property is at a location 20 minutes away from the urban area by car where 800 units in six buildings of condominiums were to be built on the whole hill. Four buildings were designed on the north slope and two buildings on the south slope where each unit would set back as it goes up the hill. Rooftop gardens created by the set back design contribute to the formation of a living space with green plants harmonizing the surrounding nature. An elementary school was to be built as well to create a complete residential district.

[160]
姫路文学館 南館　1996
museum of litercture south annex, himeji
.
1. 兵庫県姫路市 | himeji, hyogo
2. 設計 | design　1993.9–1994.9
3. 施工 | construction　1994.10–1996.5
4. 鉄筋コンクリート | RC
5. 文学資料館 | literature museum
6. 敷地 | site　13,918.8 m²
7. 建築 | building　1,360.0 m²
8. 延床 | total floor　2,532.6 m²

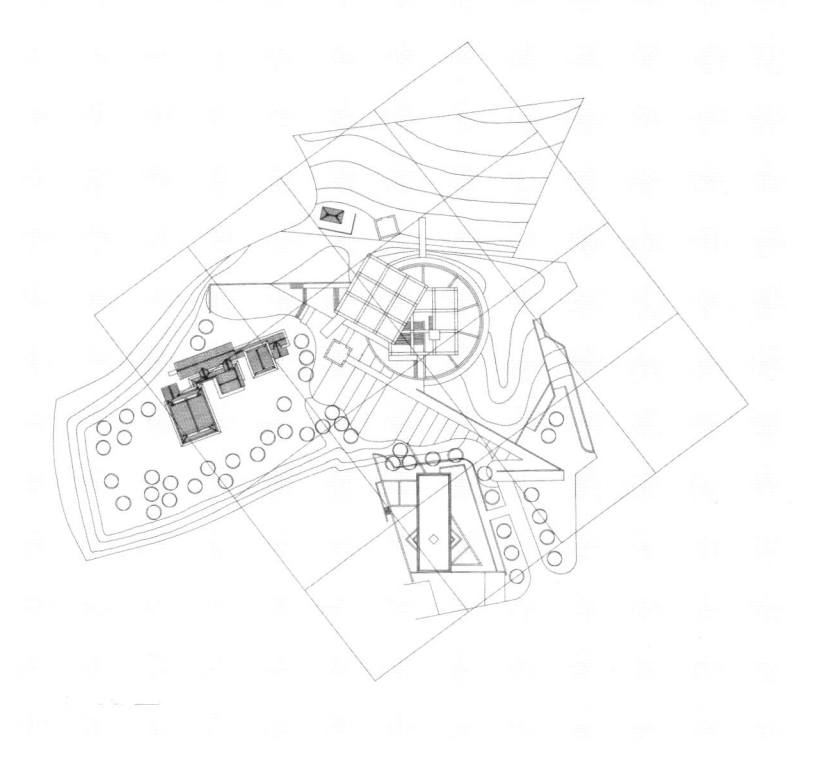

本館の山裾に新たな土地が取得できたのを機に、図書室棟にあたる南館が建設され、施設が拡張された。本館前から山裾に下る段状の水の庭と交差する形で、コンクリートの壁が新たに建てられた。その壁の一方の端が水の庭であり、逆側の末端を南館の建物に楔のように食い込ませることによって、本館と南館を結びつけている。展示を担う本館に対し、南館は図書室を設けるとともに、祖父の代まで姫路住いの作家、司馬遼太郎の記念室も併設された。→参照 [114]
.
As soon as the new lot was acquired at the foot of the main building, this south annex building as a library was built and the facility was expanded. In the form of crossing the stepped water garden going down the mountain from the front side of the main building, the new concrete wall was built. There is a water garden at one end of the wall, while the end on the opposite side is penetrating into the building volume of the south annex in a wedge like to link the main building with the south annex. Compared to the main building with exhibition functionality, this south annex is provided with a library and a memorial room for Ryotaro Shiba, whose family has lived in Himeji until his grandfather's generation. → see also [114]

346 Complete Works　340

[161]
平野区の町屋── 能見邸　1996
town house in hirano — nomi house

1. 大阪市平野区 | hirano-ku, osaka
2. 設計 | design　1995.2–1995.12
3. 施工 | construction　1996.1–1996.8
4. 鉄筋コンクリート（壁式） | RC (wall)
5. 住宅 | detached house
6. 敷地 | site　120.5 m²
7. 建築 | building　72.1 m²
8. 延床 | total floor　92.1 m²

大阪下町の一角に立地する。高さ5メートルほどのコンクリート打ち放しの壁が、家族の暮らしを周囲から保護するかのように敷地を囲っている。その内側の住空間は、伝統的な木造農家の「田の字」の間取りを踏襲した各室の配置になっている。ただ、安藤の「田の字」は、2階のテラスと1階の寝室をのぞいてはコートとして空隙の扱いになっており、この空隙に二つの寝室を個別に向き合わせることで独立性の維持に供している。

Located in an old town of Osaka. Exposed concrete walls with a height of about five meters surrounds the property as though they are protecting the life of the family from outside. As for the living space inside the house, each room is arranged following the four-square layout of traditional wooden farmhouses. However, the four-square layout by Ando has a gap, which is viewed as a court except the 2nd floor terrace and the 1st floor bedroom, and between this gap there are two bedrooms facing each other to provide independence.

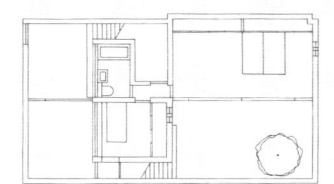

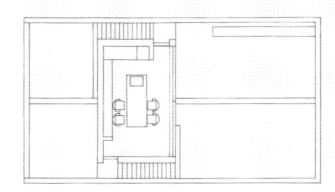

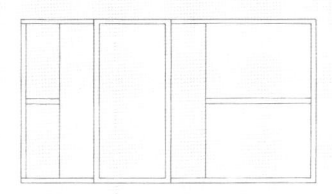

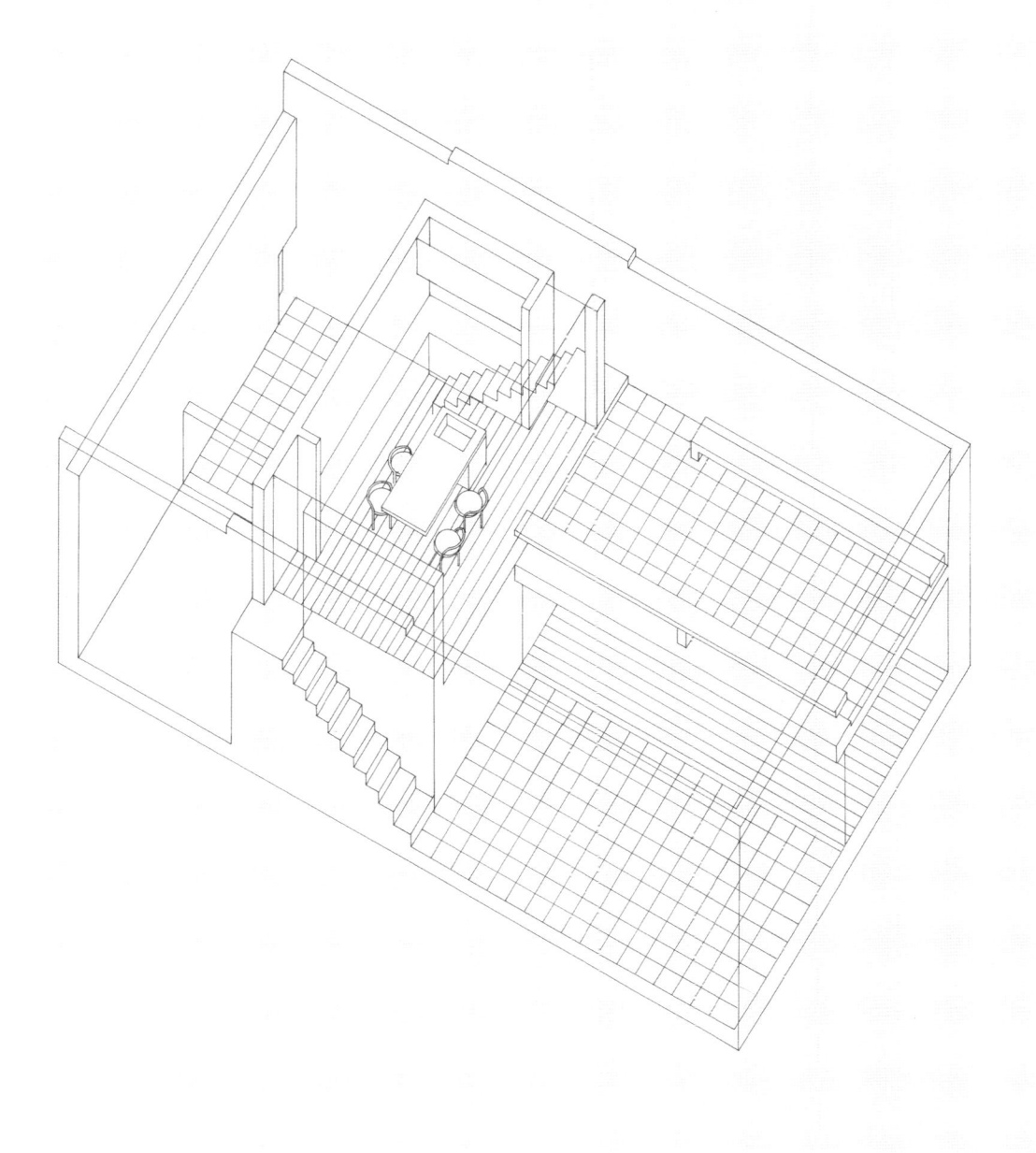

[162]
白井邸　1996
shirai house

1. 京都府八幡市 | yawata, kyoto
2. 設計 | design　1994.10–1995.6
3. 施工 | construction　1995.7–1996.2
4. 鉄筋コンクリート（壁式）| RC (wall)
5. 住宅 | detached house
6. 敷地 | site　247.3 m²
7. 建築 | building　84.1 m²
8. 延床 | total floor　94.1 m²

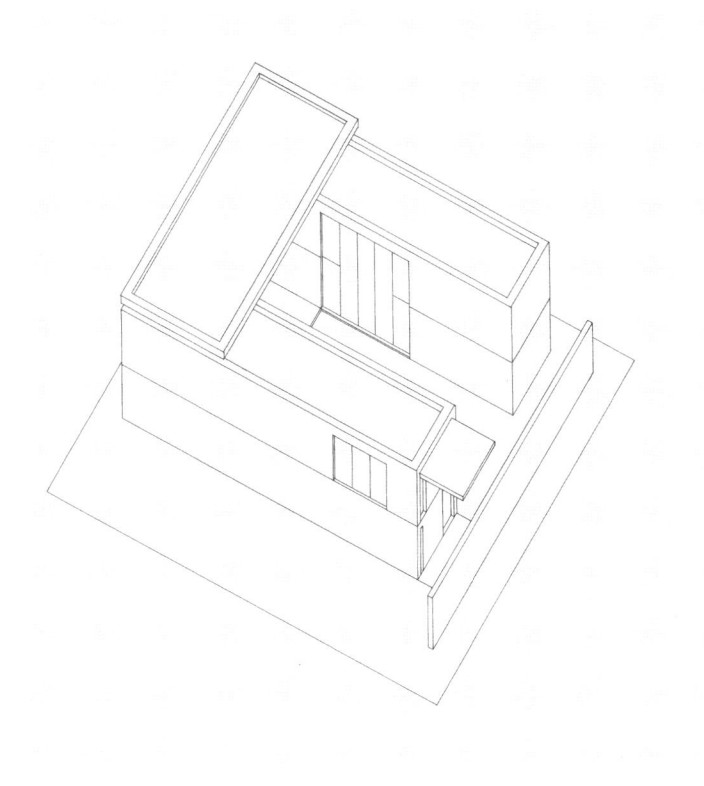

京都・八幡市の戸建て住宅。二つの直方体を距離を置いて並立させ、道路側には外からの視界を制御する低い独立塀を立てた。反対の敷地奥側は棟を結ぶ屋根を架け、その下の空隙は住宅内を行き来する屋外通路とした。そこには奥の壁を切り欠いた逆アーチと足元のスリットから光が射してくる。棟の間の庭にはケヤキの木がそびえ、両側の棟から大きく開いた窓を通して、囲い込んだ緑の庭の光景、降り注ぐ陽光、吹き抜ける風の変化が楽しめる。

A residential house in Yawata City, Kyoto. Two rectangular solids are in a parallel position placed apart where a low independent fence was placed on the road side to control views from outside. A roof is set to connect the buildings on the opposite rear area of the property and an outdoor passage to approach inside the residence was provided in the space underneath. Light shines through the openings made in an inverted arc shape and slits at the foot level. Transition of the enclosed green garden, shining sunshine, and blowing wind can be enjoyed through large windows of both buildings with Japanese zelkova planted in the garden between the buildings.

[163]
ギャラリー小さい芽（澤田邸）
1996
gallery chiisaime — sawada house

1. 兵庫県西宮市 | nishinomiya, hyogo
2. 設計 | design　1995.3–1995.12
3. 施工 | construction　1996.1–1996.8
4. 鉄筋コンクリート（ラーメン）| RC (frame)
5. ギャラリー、ゲストルーム | gallery, guest room
6. 敷地 | site　87.2 m²
7. 建築 | building　49.0 m²
8. 延床 | total floor　92.2 m²

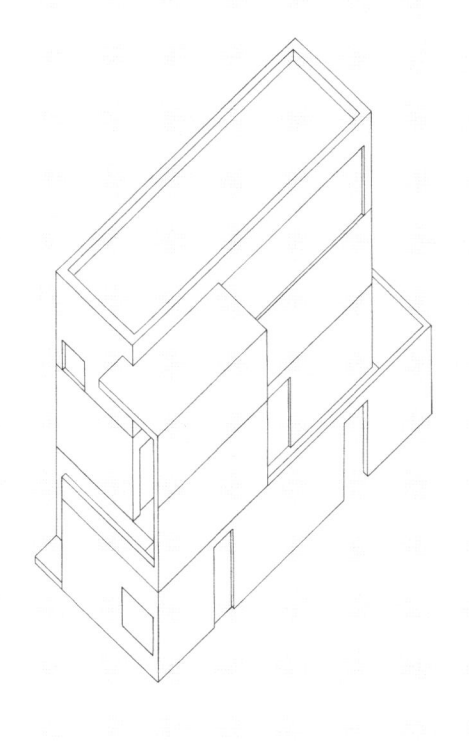

角地に位置する30坪に満たない細長い敷地に、阪神大震災後、建設された小さな美術のギャラリー。上階に進むに連れてセットバックする形式で3階建てのギャラリーが建設された。コンクリートの箱は、上階では板状の壁を組み合わせる開放的な仕立てをとる。震災前の街の記憶の継承を願い、敷地内のコートには高さ10メートルに成長するクスノキを植えて、地域再生のシンボルになることを願った。被災児童の絵画展などが定期的に企画されている。

A small art gallery built on a narrow corner property less than 100m² after the Great Hanshin Earthquake. A three-story gallery was built with a form that is set back as it goes up one floor. The concrete box has an open finish by combining plate walls on the top floor. To keep the memory of the town before the earthquake, a 10-meter tall camphor tree was planted in the court inside the property hoping that it will be a symbol of revitalization of the area. Painting exhibitions of children affected by the earthquake are planned regularly.

[164]
ローマ司教区教会国際設計競技案
1996
vicariato di roma
— international design competition
for the church of the year 2000
.
1. イタリア ローマ｜roma, italy
2. 設計｜design 1996
3. 設計競技｜design competition
4. 鉄筋コンクリート｜RC
5. 教会、教区センター｜church, parish center
6. 敷地｜site 5,717 m²
7. 建築｜building 1,334.4 m²
8. 延床｜total floor 1,554 m²

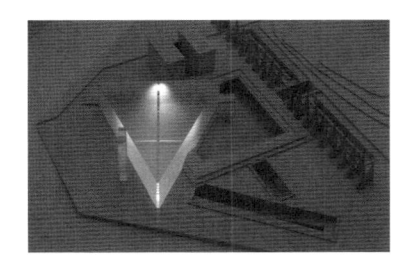

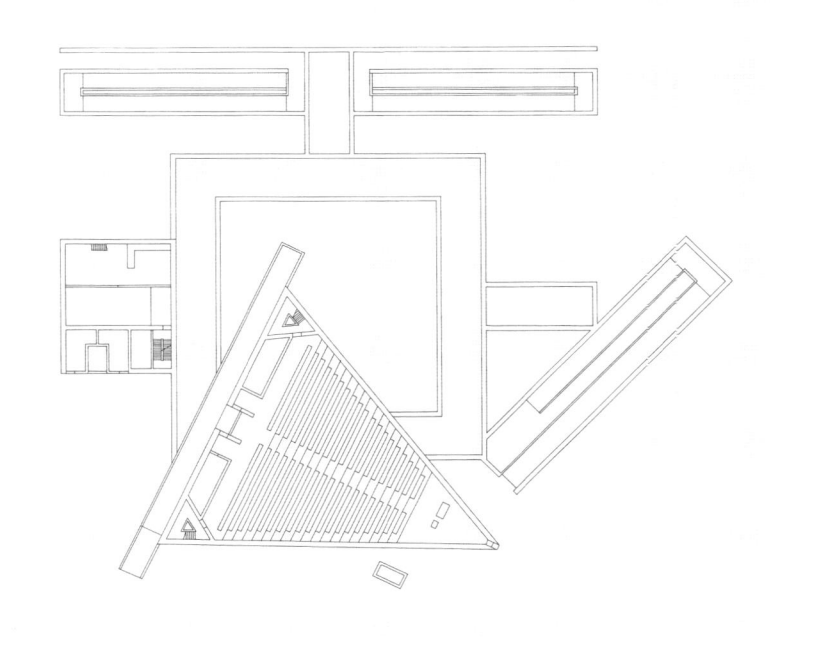

ミレニアムを機にローマ郊外に計画された教会と教区センターのコンペ応募案。聖堂は三角形の平面形で、一段掘り下げた位置の人工池を囲む回廊を持つ教区センターがそれに一部重なり合う形で配された。安藤は青春時代にヨーロッパ各地のロマネスクの聖堂を訪ねて、回廊と聖堂の原建築的な空間の成立ちに感動を覚えた記憶を大切にしている。ここではその聖なる非日常の空間を現代のコンクリートによって再生させようという意志が示された。
.
A design submitted for a contest of a church and a parish center to be constructed in the suburb of Rome with the new era of the Millennium. The cathedral is a triangle on the platform, which is partially overlapping the parish center that has a galleria surrounding an artificial pond located at the lower level. The impressive scene of spatial arrangement of fundamental architectures in galleries and cathedrals Ando had seen when he visited Romanesque cathedrals at various locations in Europe during his younger days is still an important memory for him. This project has shown Ando's will to recreate extraordinary holy space with the modern concrete material.

[165]
スタジオ・カール・ラガーフェルド
1996
studio karl lagerfeld
.
1. フランス ビアリッツ｜biarritz, france
2. 設計｜design 1996
3. 構想案｜concept
4. 鉄筋コンクリート｜RC
5. 住宅、スタジオ｜house, studio
6. 敷地｜site 約100 ha
7. 建築｜building 1,900 m²
8. 延床｜total floor 2,300 m²

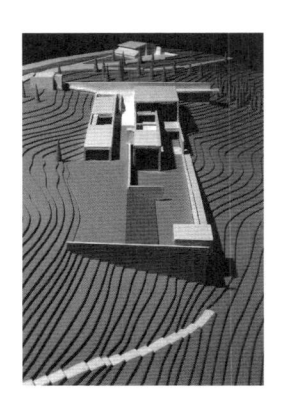

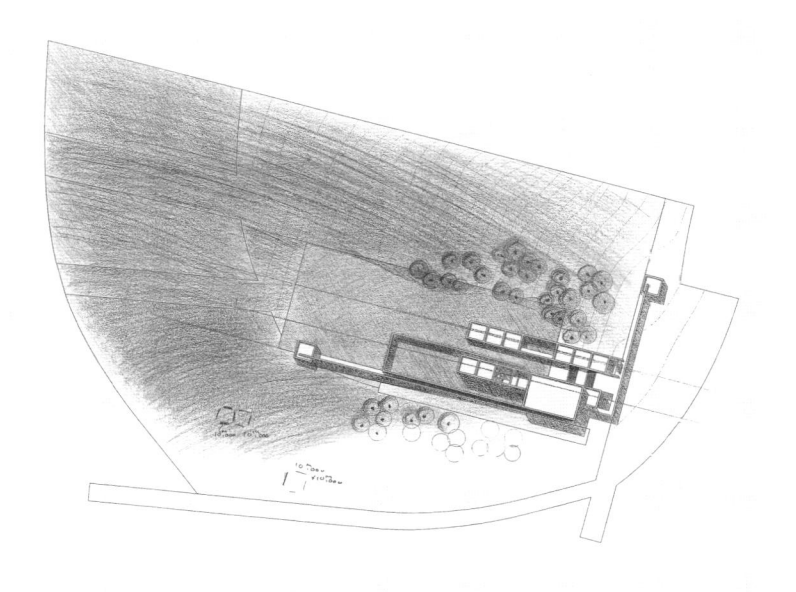

刺激的な造形で知られるファッションデザイナーのための住宅兼創作アトリエの計画。カール・ラガーフェルドは安藤の作品に共感を抱き、設計を依頼した。立地はスペイン国境に近いフランスの避暑地ビアリッツ。森林の豊かな自然を背景に、人工池の取り巻く並列の住棟とゲストハウス、そこから水上のブリッジで結ばれるプライベート・チャーチを配した。コンクリート打ち放しの幾何立体の徹底により、施主のファッションの表現とは異なるユニバーサルな空間を目指した。
.
A plan for a residential house and creation atelier for a fashion designer who is known for his sensational styling. Karl Lagerfeld sympathized with Ando's works and requested the design. The location is in Biarritz, a summer resort in France close to the border of Spain. A residential building and guesthouse were placed in parallel surrounded by an artificial pond and a private church that is approached by a bridge crossing the water was built in front of rich nature of the forest. Universal space different from the client's expression in fashion was aimed by thoroughly using geometric exposed concrete.

[166]
マンハッタンのペントハウス
1996
penthouse in manhattan

1. アメリカ ニューヨーク | new york, USA
2. 設計 | design 1996
3. 構想案 | concept
4. 鉄筋コンクリート、鉄骨 | RC, steel
5. 住宅 | detached house
8. 延床 | total floor 712㎡

マンハッタンに立つ1920年代の30階を超える高層ビルに、ガラスの箱が異物挿入されるかのように配された。ひとつは屋上からキャンティレバー状に飛び出し、もうひとつは上階から五層ほど下に突き刺さる。もとの建築の折衷主義風のざらざらした感触のヴォリュームに、20世紀の素材としてのガラス、鉄、コンクリートからなる箱を直截的に衝突させた。刺激的な都市活動がやまないニューヨークのありかたの投影を狙った。

Glass boxes were arranged as though foreign matter was inserted in a high-rise building with over 30 floors constructed in the 1920s in Manhattan. One is protruding from the rooftop in a cantilever form while another one is piercing about five layers from the top floor. The intent is to bluntly collide the volume with rough surface of American Beaux-Arts of the original architecture with boxes of the 20th century material such as glass, iron and concrete to project the style of New York where stimulating city activities never end.

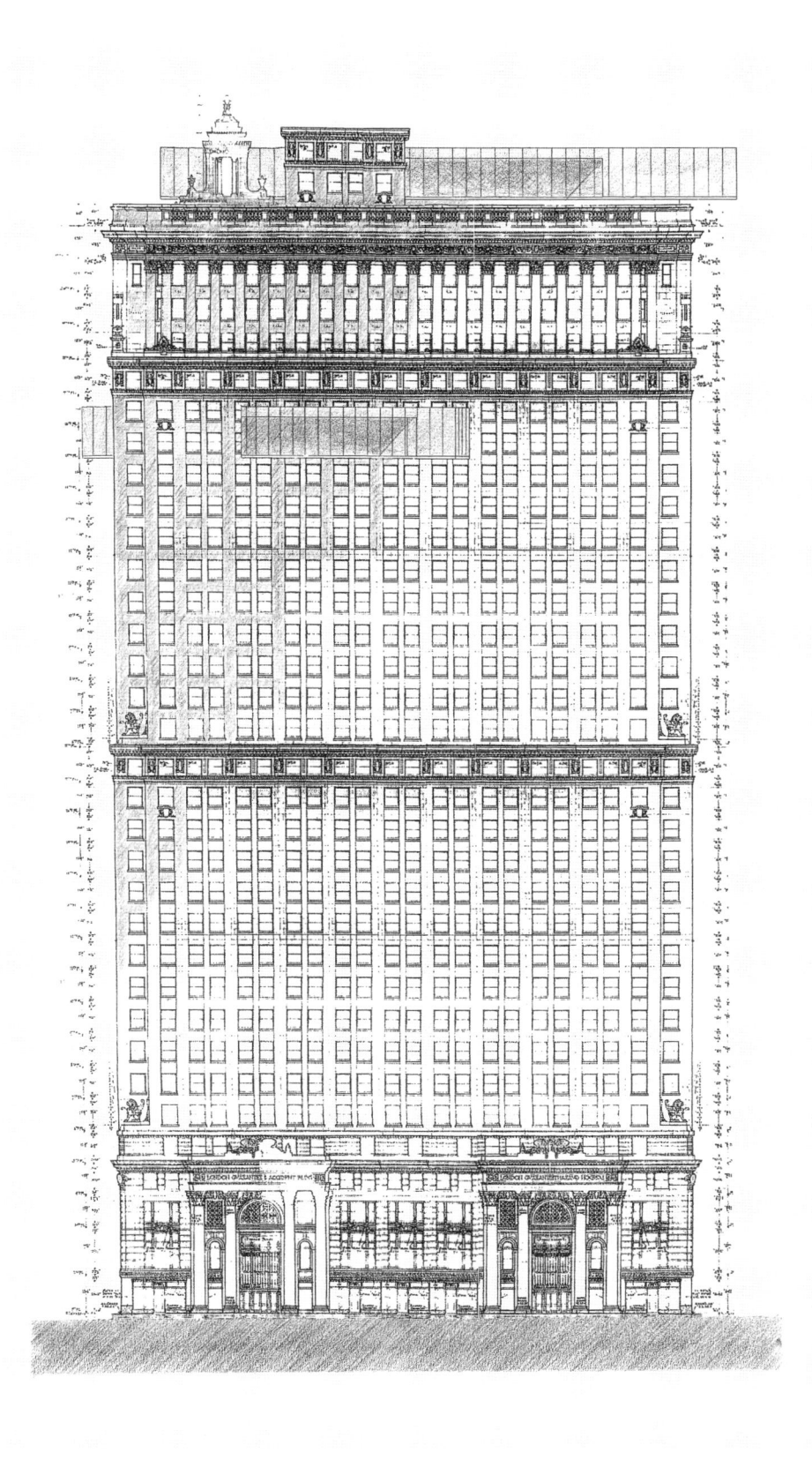

[167]

シカゴの住宅　1997
house in chicago

1. アメリカ　シカゴ ｜ chicago, USA
2. 設計 ｜ design　1992.5 –1994.12
3. 施工 ｜ construction　1993.12 –1997.12
4. 鉄筋コンクリート（壁式）｜ RC (wall)
5. 住宅 ｜ detached house
6. 敷地 ｜ site　1,935 m²
7. 建築 ｜ building　403.0 m²
8. 延床 ｜ total floor　835 m²

米国で最初に実現したシカゴの住宅建築。細長い敷地形状を踏まえ、地階から3階まで中央に配した屋外テラスの空間的な醍醐味を生かす構成がとられた。3階のアトリエ、2階のスタジオなど創造的な作業のための場では、スロープによって昇降するテラス、地表レベルの人工池を堪能できる仕立てをとる。もとの敷地にあったポプラの大木など土地の記憶を伝える植生も目を楽しませる有力な装置として継承され、豊かな住空間を実現している。→参照［333］

A residential architecture in Chicago that was materialized for the first time in the U.S. Considering the long and narrow shape of the property, it was designed to use the spatial taste of the outdoor terrace placed in the middle from the ground floor to the 3rd floor. A terrace that can be approached on a slope and areas to enjoy the artificial pond on the ground floor were provided on the 3rd floor atelier and the 2nd floor studio where creative tasks are handled. A large poplar tree that was originally growing in the property was kept as a means to inherit the memory of the land and for enjoyment contributing to the rich living space. → see also [333]

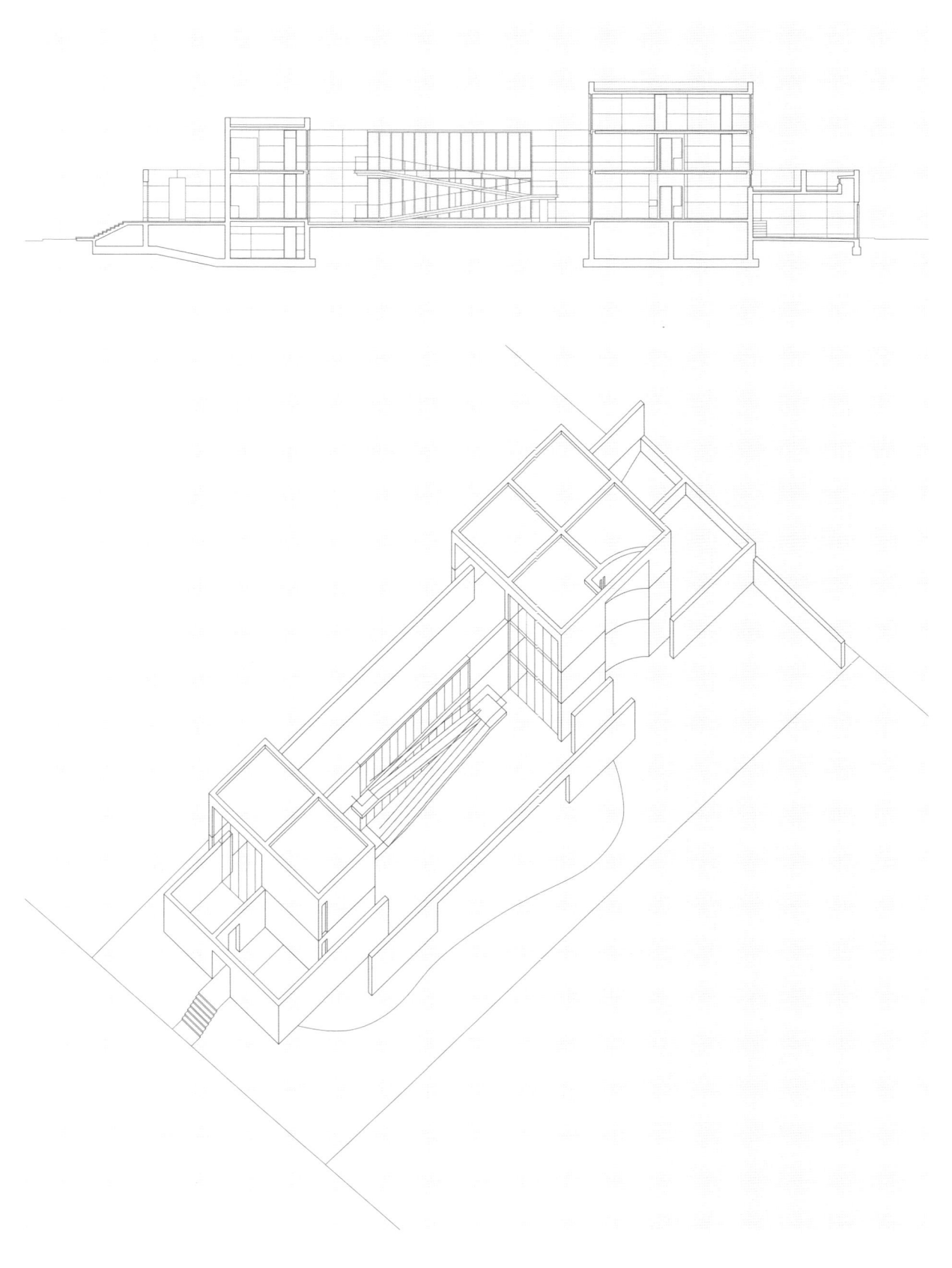

[168]
越知町立横倉山自然の森博物館
——横倉山・牧野富太郎展示室
1997
the yokogurayama
natural forest museum, ochi

1. 高知県越知町 | ochi, kochi
2. 設計 | design   1994.10–1996.1
3. 施工 | construction   1996.3–1997.9
4. 鉄筋コンクリート | RC
5. 博物館 | museum
6. 敷地 | site   7,284.2 m²
7. 建築 | building   1,163.2 m²
8. 延床 | total floor   2,093.7 m²

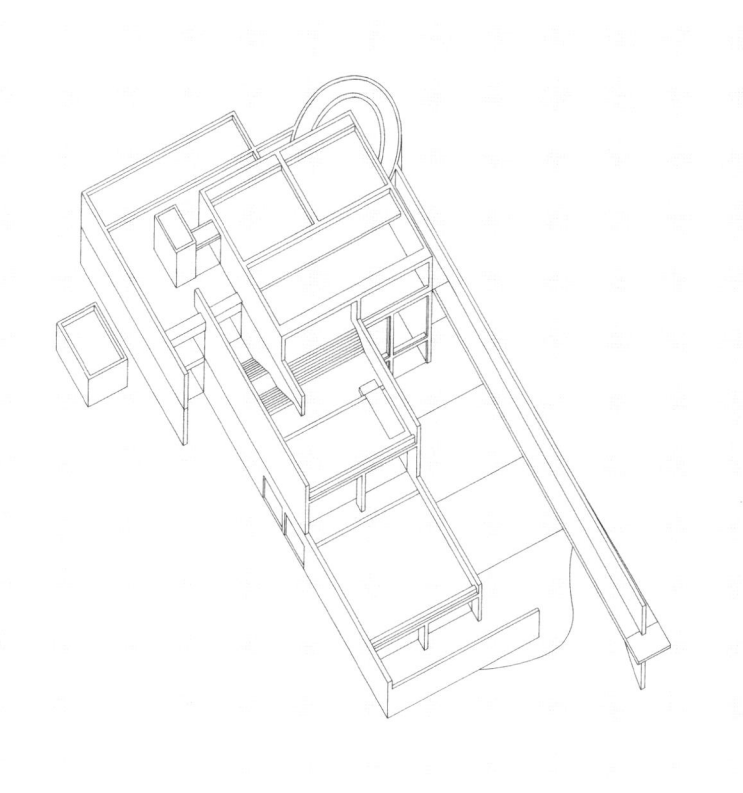

化石で知られる横倉山の中腹に位置する自然史博物館。アプローチに立つと長大なコンクリートの壁に直面する。この壁に沿って登りのスロープを上がり、反転して壁の裏側の上りのスロープに至ると、ようやく人工池に面した建物が目に入る。スロープの昇降が豊かな自然を感得させる仕掛けで、館内も大きなガラスを通して一帯の環境が満喫できる。展望テラスからは、コスモスで知られる仁淀川も見通せ、建築と環境の一体化を図る安藤の建築観が実現している。

This is a natural history museum building located on a halfway up the Mount Yokogura, which is known for the discovery of various fossils. Visitors face to an extensive concrete wall on the approach path. They go up the upward slope along this wall. When they turn around and reach the upward slope on the back side of the wall, they see a building facing to an artificial pond finally. This up and down of the sloping pathway allows visitors to feel the nature, while the surrounding environment can be fully experienced from the interior space of the building through the large glass. From the observation terrace, Niyodo River, known for cosmos flower, can be overlooked — it is realized here that Ando's architectural vision of integrating architecture with the surrounding environment.

[169]
TOTOセミナーハウス   1997
TOTO seminar house

1. 兵庫県淡路市 | awaji, hyogo
2. 設計 | design   1994.10–1996.2
3. 施工 | construction   1996.2–1997.12
4. 鉄筋コンクリート | RC
5. 研修所、保養所 | training facility, resort house
6. 敷地 | site   5,822.3 m²
7. 建築 | building   1,733.75 m²
8. 延床 | total floor   3,191.6 m²

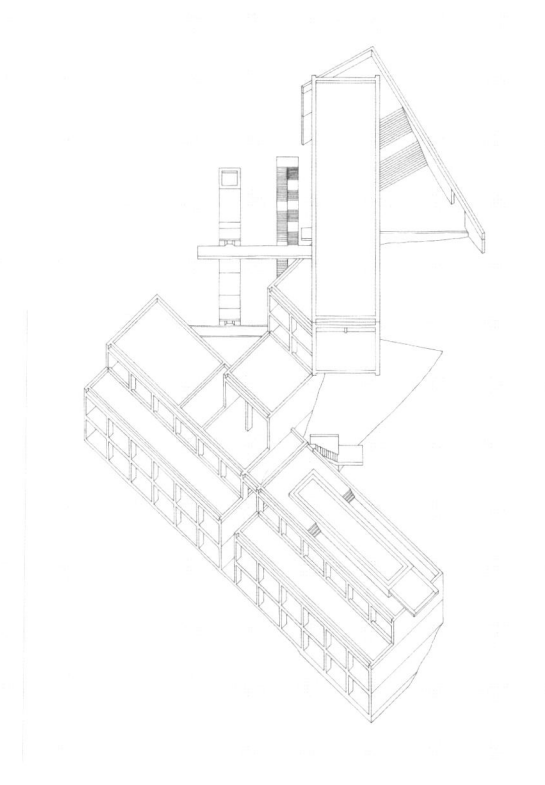

淡路島東岸、大阪湾に面した山腹に位置する。急斜面に沿って上下二つのブロックに分かれ、上段のエントランス棟は、ほぼ正方形の断面を持つ筒状、4階分下段にあるのが宿泊棟で、こちらは最上階がセットバックする直方体におさめられている。二つの立体は40度で交差し、エレベーター塔で結ばれている。来訪者はエントランス棟に入ると、コンクリートの筒の向うに広がる海の光景に迎えられ、そこから海上を歩くかのような屋外のブリッジを経てエレベーターのタワーに進み、下階の自室へ向かう。

This building is located on the hillside facing to Osaka Bay, on the east coast of Awaji Island. This facility is divided into two blocks in upper and lower volumes along the steep slope; the upper entrance wing has a tubular shape with nearly square plan section, and the other is placed 4 floor levels lower, which is set in a cuboid shape with a setback applied to the top floor level. Those two volumes are crossed at 40°angle and joined by an elevator tower. When they go into the entrance wing, visitor will be greeted by the ocean view spreading beyond the concrete tube. They go through the exterior bridge as if walking on the ocean, proceed to the elevator tower, and then go down to the guestroom on the lower floor level.

346 Complete Works   346

[170]
八木邸　1997
yagi house

1. 兵庫県西宮市 | nishinomiya, hyogo
2. 設計 | design　1995.3–1996.3
3. 施工 | construction　1996.5–1997.5
4. 鉄筋コンクリート | RC
5. 住宅 | detached house
6. 敷地 | site　1,757.1 m²
7. 建築 | building　362.2 m²
8. 延床 | total floor　500.9 m²

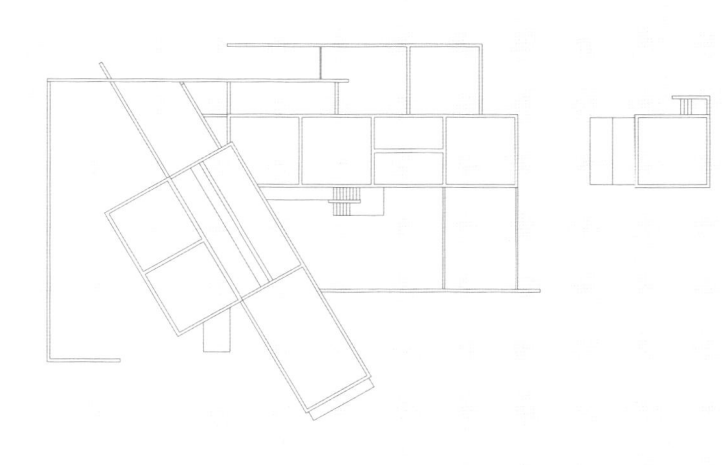

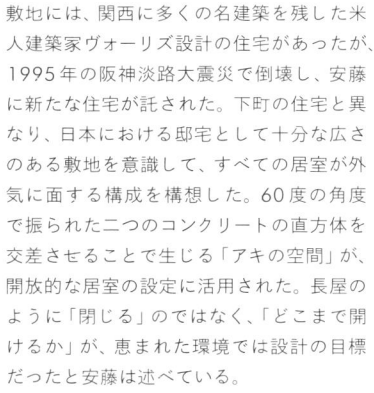

敷地には、関西に多くの名建築を残した米人建築家ヴォーリズ設計の住宅があったが、1995年の阪神淡路大震災で倒壊し、安藤に新たな住宅が託された。下町の住宅と異なり、日本における邸宅として十分な広さのある敷地を意識して、すべての居室が外気に面する構成を構想した。60度の角度で振られた二つのコンクリートの直方体を交差させることで生じる「アキの空間」が、開放的な居室の設定に活用された。長屋のように「閉じる」のではなく、「どこまで開けるか」が、恵まれた環境では設計の目標だったと安藤は述べている。

A residential house designed by Vories, an architect from the U.S., was on the property. However, it collapsed in 1995 due to the Great Hanshin Earthquake and a new house was requested to be built by Ando. Considering the property with sufficient space as a house in Japan, which is different from houses in the old town, it was designed that all living rooms would face outside. The gap created by locating two concrete rectangular solids to intersect each other on a 60-degree angle was used to arrange living rooms with a sense of spaciousness. Ando mentioned that the target of the design in the advantageous environment was to maximize the degree of openness instead of closing the space as seen at a terrace house.

[171]
青木の集合住宅　1997
ogi housing

1. 神戸市東灘区 | higashinada-ku, kobe
2. 設計 | design　1995.6–1996.4
3. 施工 | construction　1996.5–1997.3
4. 鉄筋コンクリート（ラーメン）| RC (frame)
5. 集合住宅 | apartment house
6. 敷地 | site　622.4 m²
7. 建築 | building　373.3 m²
8. 延床 | total floor　923.6 m²

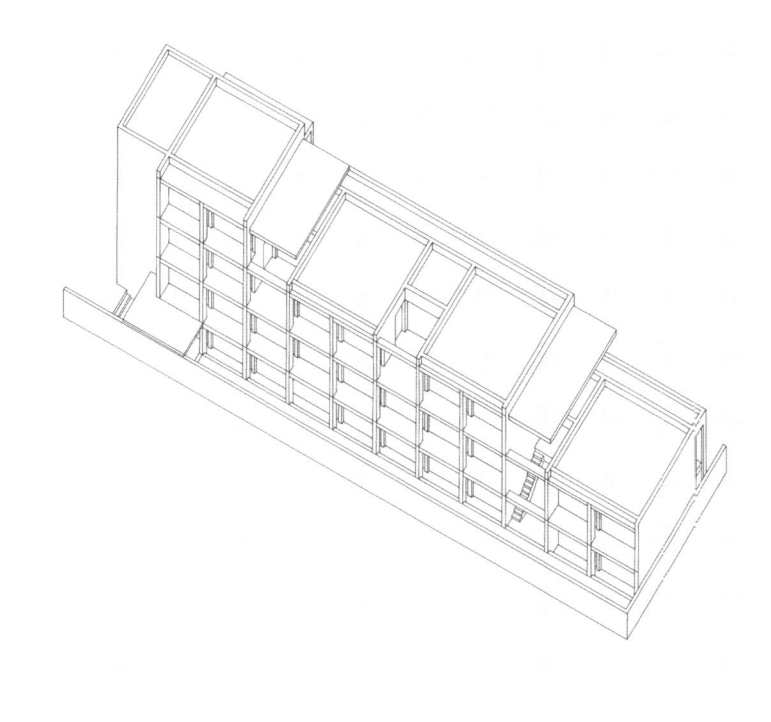

神戸市東部、阪神電車沿線の住宅密集地に計画されたローコストの集合住宅。阪神大震災後の住宅事情の逼迫に応える目的もあり、1、2階に学生などを入居者に想定した単身用の住戸、3、4階に家族用の居室を配した。細長い建物の1、2階には共用のテラスが置かれた。上階に進むに連れてセットバックする形式を活かし、2、3階の屋根にもテラスが設けられた。屋上緑化は隣地の都市公園との連続も意識した。

A low-cost condominium planed in a dense residential area along the railway of Hanshin Electric Railway located at the east area of Kobe City. Residences for single people such as students are provided on the 1st and 2nd floors where rooms for families are on the 3rd and 4th floors since it was necessary to respond to the lack of housing after the Great Hanshin Earthquake Disaster. Terraces to be shared by residents are designed on the 1st and 2nd floors of the narrow building. A terrace was to be built on the rooftop of 2nd and 3rd floors as well using the shape of the building that sets back toward the upper floor. The rooftop greening is provided to maintain continuity with the green of adjacent city park.

[172]
小海高原美術館　1997
koumi kogen museum

1. 長野県小海町 | koumi, nagano
2. 設計 | design   1995.6–1996.4
3. 施工 | construction   1996.8–1997.5
4. 鉄筋コンクリート | RC
5. 美術館 | museum of art
6. 敷地 | site   8,007.3 m²
7. 建築 | building   1,192.8 m²
8. 延床 | total floor   1,554.8 m²

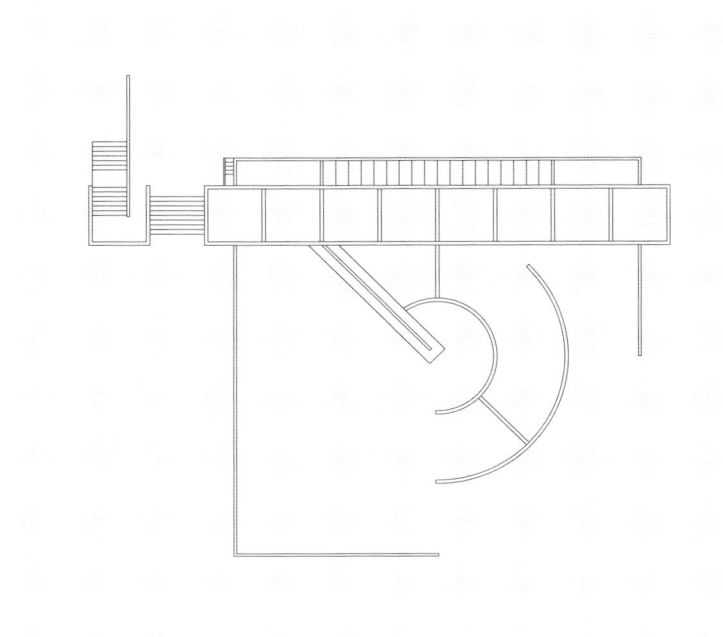

八ヶ岳の山麓、安藤の建築は広々とした緑豊かな風景のなかに、沈黙を保って身を沈めている。マウンドの敷地の1階から館内に進み、ガラスの箱のなかのくだりのスロープをたどって地下の主展示室に向う。主展示室は2枚の曲面のコンクリートの板に挟まれた空間で、そこからは屋外の植栽を楽しむこともできる。大自然のなか、美術という人間の営みをコンクリートで区画された場にしっかり根付かせている姿は、安藤の建築が美の極致を目指していることを認識させる。

Ando's building is silently sunken in an expansive scenery with rich greens at the foot of the Yatsugatake Mountains. Entering from the first level of the mound site, visitors follow a downhill slope inside a glass box and head towards the main exhibition room on the underground level. Plantings outside can be enjoyed from the main exhibition room, sandwiched by two curved concrete walls. Ando steadily rooted art, which is a human activity, at the site amongst Mother Nature, divided by concrete. The appearance of the building renews our awareness that Ando pursued the pinnacle of beauty in his architectural works.

[173]
ライン世界文化博物館　1997
the museum of world cultures
on the river rhine

1. ドイツ カールスルーエ、フランス ストラスブール | karlsruhe, germany / strasbourg, france
2. 設計 | design   1997.10
3. 構想案 | concept
4. 鉄骨鉄筋コンクリート | SRC
5. 博物館 | museum
8. 延床 | total floor   15,739.2 m²

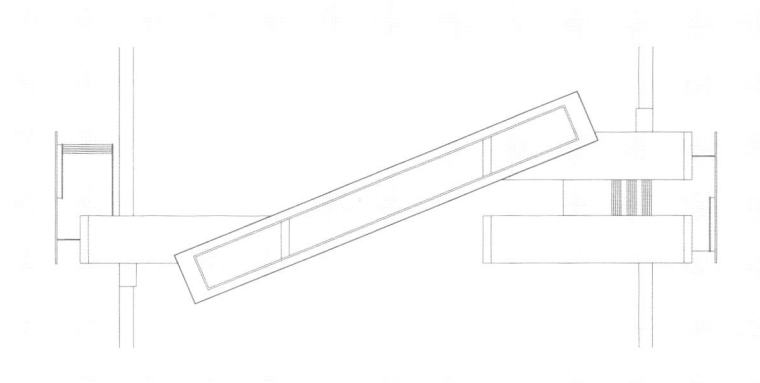

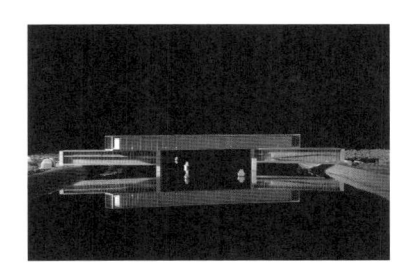

ドイツ・カールスルーエを流れるライン川をまたぐ橋のような形で計画された博物館。対岸はフランス領で、この博物館の配置そのものが「異文化を結ぶ」形態で構想された。それぞれの両岸から展示棟に渡るコンクリートの橋がはねだし、斜めになった二層の展示棟がそこに載る形態が提案された。展示棟の内部はコンクリートの箱が入れ子で設えられ、世界文化の多様性がテーマの展示を緩やかなスロープによる上下階の移動で鑑賞する動線が想定された。ガラス窓を通して両岸を眺めるとき、文化交流の意味が実感できると考えた。

A museum planned to form a bridge-like structure crossing the Rhine River that flows through Karlsruhe in Germany. The museum's location itself has a vision to connect different cultures since the other side of the river is a French territory. The proposed design had concrete bridges from both river banks extending across the river to the exhibition building where the slanted two-layered exhibition building is standing. Concrete boxes nested in form were created inside the exhibition building. For visitors to observe the exhibition focusing on the diversity of world's culture, a flow line was set to allow visitors to move between floors with a gradual slope. It was anticipated that the meaning of cultural interchange could be clearly felt by viewing both banks from the window.

[174]
ダイコク電機本部ビル 1998
daikoku denki headquarters building

1. 愛知県春井市 | kasugai, aichi
2. 設計 | design 1995.2–1995.11
3. 施工 | construction 1995.12–1998.3
4. 鉄骨鉄筋コンクリート | SRC
5. 事務所、ショールーム | office, showroom
6. 敷地 | site 4,051.1 m²
7. 建築 | building 2,360.1 m²
8. 延床 | total floor 9,543.0 m²

愛知県春日井市の郊外に位置する遊技機電子機器メーカーの本部事業所。事務所機能とショールームとしての利用を想定した本館に、外向きに15度の傾斜を持たせた楕円の曲面壁を全体形としている。この計画では駐車場も求められたため、道路を挟んだ向かいの敷地にツインタワーとして実現した。いずれもコンクリートが開放的な敷地環境のなかで存在感を示し、自動車交通を前提とした新たなランドマークの構築に成功している。

The headquarters of an electronic game equipment manufacturer located in the suburb of Kasugai City, Aichi Prefecture. The main building designed to be used for office work and a showroom has an overall shape of an oval curved wall with an inclination of 15 degrees toward the outside. A twin tower was placed in the property on the other side of the road since a parking lot was required. The concrete of both buildings are showing presence in the open environment of the property and successfully showed a new landmark where the automobile transportation is the norm.

[175]
渡辺淳一記念館 1998
junichi watanabe memorial hall

1. 札幌市中央区 | chuo-ku, sapporo
2. 設計 | design 1995.11–1996.11
3. 施工 | construction 1996.12–1998.1
4. 鉄筋コンクリート、一部鉄骨鉄筋コンクリート | RC, SRC
5. 文学資料館 | literature museum
6. 敷地 | site 622.2 m²
7. 建築 | building 344.1 m²
8. 延床 | total floor 1,120.6 m²

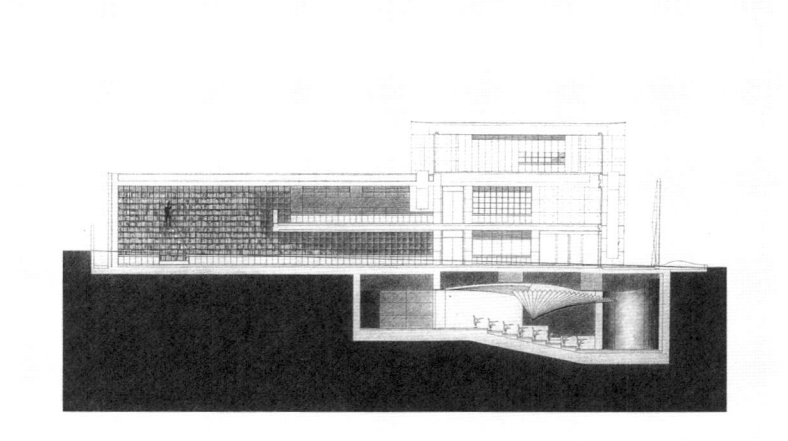

医師出身で大衆小説の人気作家だった渡辺淳一の文学館。彼が活動の拠点としていた札幌市の中島公園の傍らに位置している。建物の全体はコンクリートの直方体。エントランスの斜め材が目をひく。これは「白鳥の足」になぞらえられる。木質系で文学館らしい落ち着いたインテリアが心地よい。内部の見どころは吹き抜けになった二層の高さの書架。「司馬遼太郎記念館」の空間に通じる「本の建築」が、旺盛だった渡辺の作家活動を偲ばせる。

A literature museum of Junichi Watanabe who was a doctor and later became a famous writer in popular novels. It is situated next to Nakajima Park in Sapporo where his activity base was. The whole building is of a concrete rectangular solid. What attracts attention is the slanted material at the entrance. This design reminds the legs of swans. The interior is made of wood materials to give relaxing and calm atmosphere that fits for a literature museum. The highlight of inside the building is the two-story high bookshelf in the open ceiling. The architecture of books reminds visitors of Watanabe's vigorous writing activities and it is similar to the space at the SHIBA RYOTARO MEMORIAL MUSEUM.

[176]
エリエール松山ゲストハウス
1998
elleair matsuyama guesthouse

1. 愛媛県松山市 | matsuyama, ehime
2. 設計 | design　1996.1–1997.6
3. 施工 | construction　1997.7–1998.10
4. 鉄筋コンクリート、一部鉄骨鉄筋コンクリート | RC, SRC
5. 宿泊施設、ギャラリー | lodging facilities, gallery
6. 敷地 | site　8,095.5 m²
7. 建築 | building　1,629.8 m²
8. 延床 | total floor　3,772.1 m²

瀬戸内海を見晴らす製紙会社のゲストハウス。本館、別館の二つの飛び出した棟が目をひく。高さは異なっているが、いずれも側壁は亜鉛メッキを施された鉄板で覆われている。鉄板は目地の部分を敢えて隆起させ、陽光を受けると強い縦線が刻印となって現れる。壁面から4メートルほど飛び出した庇が、あたかも二つの棟が海を向いて立つかのような擬人的な印象を与える。足もとの人工池は、瀬戸内海の水面との視覚的な連なりを演出している。

This is a guest house to look over the Seto Inland Sea, designed for a paper manufacturing company. Two protruding buildings in the main building and the annex are attractive. While their height is different, the side walls of both buildings are covered with galvanized steel plates. The joint pats of the steel plates are intentionally protruded so that strong vertical lines appear as the marking of the buildings under the sunlight. The eaves protruding about 4m from the wall surface make those two buildings appear to be personified, and standing by facing to the ocean. The artificial pond on their footholds is directing a visual linkage to the water surface of the Seto Inland Sea.

[177]

ネパール子供病院　1998
shiddhartha
children and women hospital

1. ネパール　ブトワル | butwal, nepal
2. 設計 | design　1997.1–1997.10
3. 施工 | construction　1997.11–1998.11
4. 鉄骨鉄筋コンクリート | SRC
5. 子供病院 | children's hospital
8. 延床 | total floor　1,073 m²

阪神大震災救援の返礼として、子どもの死亡率の高いネパールに児童専門の病院が建設された。工法、予算などの制約が大きく、安藤は外壁に赤煉瓦を用い、内装にはモルタルにペンキ仕上げを採用し、清潔感を表現した。完成した姿は、あたかも北欧のモダニストが手がけたかと思えるような出で立ちで、安藤の厳格な幾何立体の造形が、赤煉瓦をまとって強い存在感を発揮している。南側の病室の窓の外にコロネードを設け日射対策とした。

In return for helping the relief work for Great Hanshin Earthquake, a hospital specialized for children was built in Nepal where children's mortality rate is high. Since it had strict restrictions on factors such as construction methods and budget, Ando used red bricks for exterior walls and mortar with paint finish for the interior walls to give a clean look. The completed style gives the impression of being designed by a Scandinavian modernist and Ando's strict geometric figures show a strong presence covered with red bricks. Colonnades are provided outside the windows of the south side to block the sunlight.

[178]
織田廣喜ミュージアム　1998
daylight museum

1. 滋賀県蒲生郡日野町 | gamo, shiga
2. 設計 | design　1997.2–1997.8
3. 施工 | construction　1997.10–1998.5
4. 鉄筋コンクリート（ラーメン）| RC (frame)
5. 美術館 | museum of art
6. 敷地 | site　178,225.1 m²
7. 建築 | building　210.1 m²
8. 延床 | total floor　196.2 m²

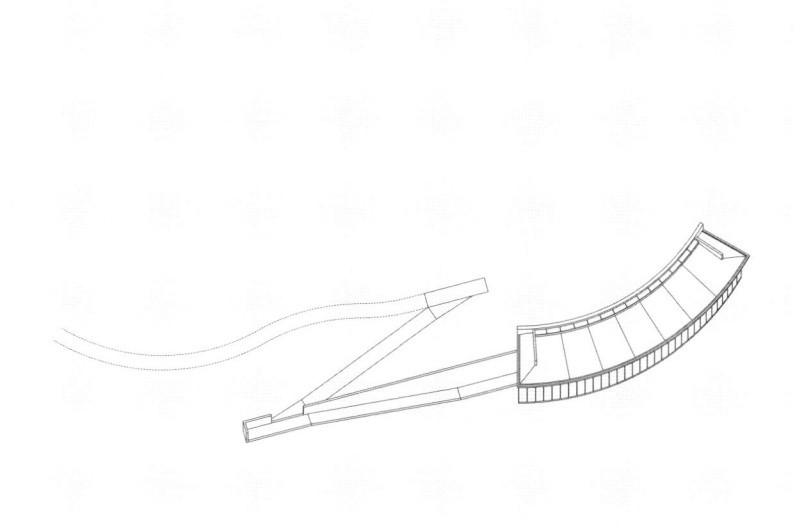

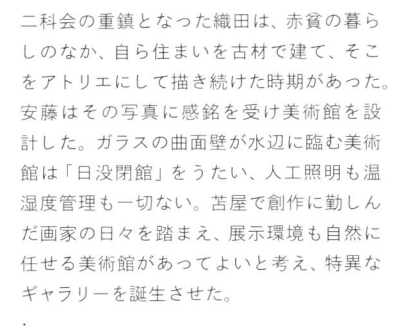

二科会の重鎮となった織田は、赤貧の暮らしのなか、自ら住まいを古材で建て、そこをアトリエにして描き続けた時期があった。安藤はその写真に感銘を受け美術館を設計した。ガラスの曲面壁が水辺に臨む美術館は「日没閉館」をうたい、人工照明も温湿度管理も一切ない。苫屋で創作に勤しんだ画家の日々を踏まえ、展示環境も自然に任せる美術館があってよいと考え、特異なギャラリーを誕生させた。

Hiroki Oda was a painter and the main member of Nika Association. He built his own house by using old and used material under the living in extreme poverty. He continued to paint by using this house as his atelier space, and Ando was impressed by the photograph of him painting in the house. Ando then designed an art museum for Oda's painting. This art museum, with curved glass wall facing to water surface, has a closing time at the sunset, and there is even no artificial lighting nor temperature / humidity control system at all. Based on the everyday life of this painter who worked at thatched cottage for the creation, he thought that there might be some art museum leaving the environment of its exhibition space to the surrounding natural conditions, and he create this unique gallery.

[179]
セーヌ川橋国際設計競技案
1998
passerelle de bercy-tolbiac,
international design competition

1. フランス パリ | paris, france
2. 設計 | design　1998.8–1998.10
3. 設計競技 | design competition
5. 橋梁デザイン | bridge design

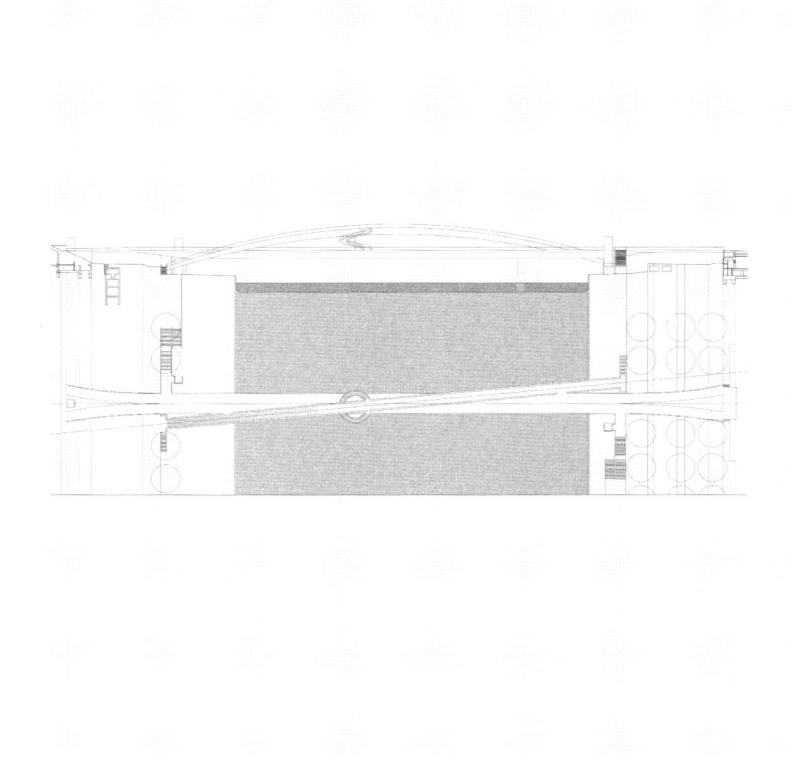

パリ東部、開発の進むベルシー地区と対岸の新国立図書館の一帯を結ぶ「シモーヌ・ドゥ・ボーボワール橋」のコンペ案。セーヌ川の流れを垂直に横断する幅8メートルの橋を国立図書館の人工地盤の高さで架け、その頭上を斜めに横切る幅4メートルのアーチ橋を交差させることを提案した。歩行者は河岸のレベルからアーチ橋を昇り、高所からセーヌ河岸の景観を楽しめる。直線の橋の真ん中に螺旋のスロープを配して交差橋に上がることも想定した。すべてシンメトリーが貫徹されているパリに、非対称の破調で刺激を与えたかったという。

A plan for a contest of the Passerelle Simone de Beauvoir bridge that connects the Bercy District where development is advancing and the new national library on the other bank of the river in the east area of Paris. The proposed design was to have an 8-meter width bridge to cross straight over the Seine River perpendicularly to the flow at the height of the artificial ground of the national library and have another 4-meter arched bridge to cross over in diagonal. Pedestrians climb up to the arched bridge from the river bank, which is at a lower level, and enjoy the scenery of the river bank of Seine from an elevated position. Additionally, an approach to the cross bridge was designed using a spiral slope from the center of the straight bridge.

[180]
六甲の集合住宅 III　1999
rokko housing III

1. 神戸市灘区 | nada-ku, kobe
2. 設計 | design　1992.9–1997.10
3. 施工 | construction　1997.11–1999.2
4. 鉄筋コンクリート | RC
5. 集合住宅 | apartment house
6. 敷地 | site　11,717.2 m²
7. 建築 | building　6,544.5 m²
8. 延床 | total floor　24,221.5 m²

第3期は、提案当初、建設の見通しがつかなかったが、阪神淡路大震災のあと実現にこぎつけた。敷地は2期までと異なり、山腹の平坦地。もとあった神戸製鋼所の社宅が被災し、その建替えプロジェクトとして実現した。復興住宅の一環のため、工事の坪単価は2期の3分の1。高層、中層、低層が連続する形で置かれ、中低層には屋上庭園が配された。2期に続いて入居者用のプールも設けられた。共用部分の充実こそ集合住宅の価値を決めるとする安藤の信念が託されている。→参照 [50]、[133]、[265]

In the 3rd phase of ROKKO HOUSING, the prospect of construction could not be obtained at the beginning of the proposal, but the project was finally realized after The Great Hanshin Earthquake. Unlike the earlier phases, the site is located on a flat land of a hillside. Existing company housing of Kobe Steel, Ltd. was damaged by the earthquake, and then it started construction as its rebuilding project. Because of part of the reconstruction housing program after the disaster, the prices per floor area of the construction was fixed at 1/3 of the 2nd phase. Upper floor levels, mid-floor levels, and lower floor levels are continuously distributed to the site, along with a rooftop garden for each unit of the mid to lower level housings. A swimming pool was also established for residents following the 2nd phase project — it is the reflection of Ando' belief that the enhancement of common spaces is the key aspect to define the value of a collective housing. → see also [50], [133], [265]

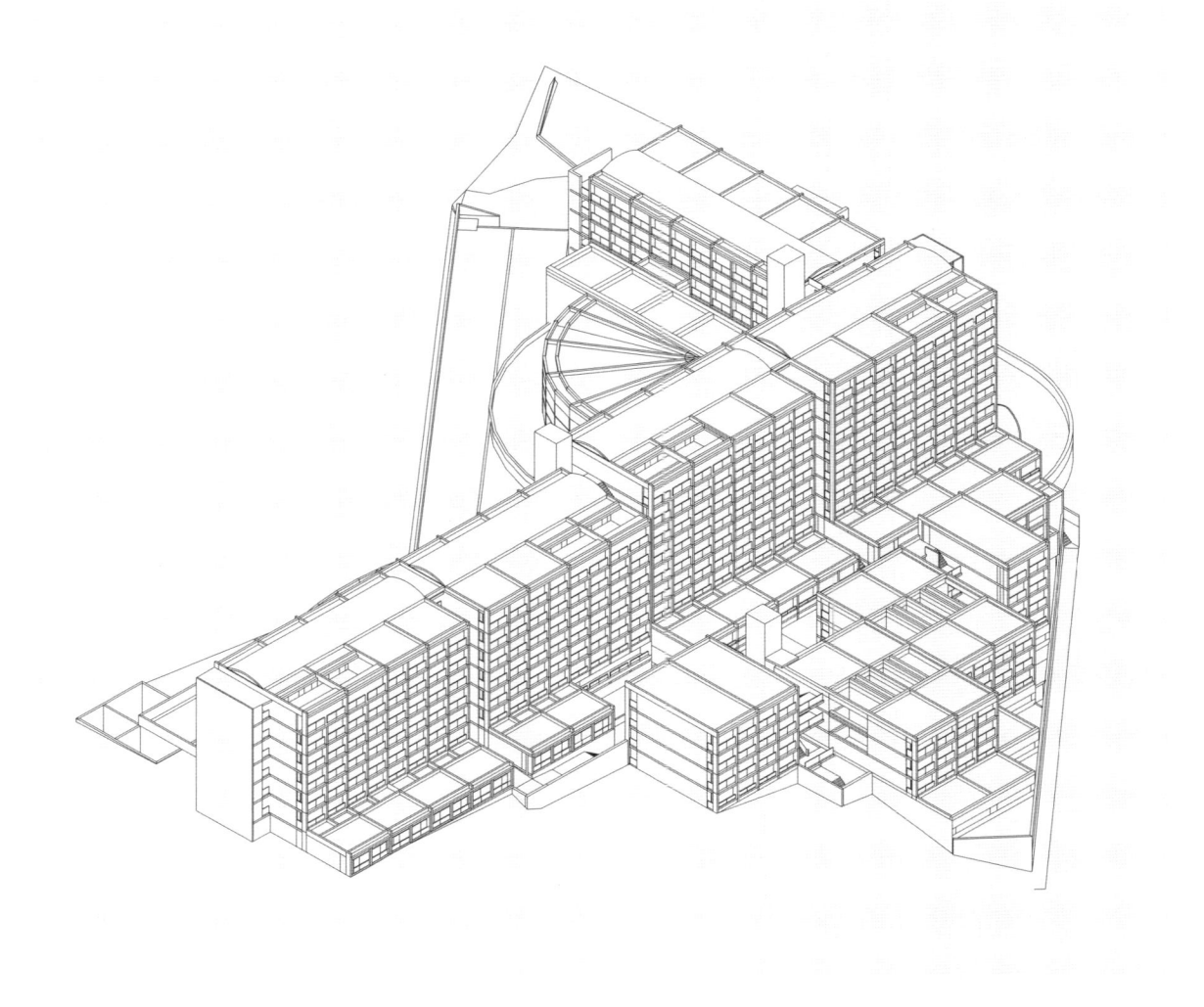

[181]
淡路夢舞台　1999
awaji-yumebutai

1. 兵庫県淡路市｜awaji, hyogo
2. 設計｜design　1993.4–1994.12, 1995.10–1996.12
3. 施工｜construction　1997.7–1999.12
4. 鉄筋コンクリート、一部鉄骨｜RC, steel
5. 国際会議場、ホテル、店舗、温室、野外劇場｜international conference center, hotel, shops, conservatory, open-air theater
6. 敷地｜site　213,930 m²
7. 建築｜building　38,429.1 m²
8. 延床｜total floor　95,078 m²

高度経済成長期に大阪一帯の経済発展を下支えした土砂採取の跡地には岩盤と急斜面が残されていた。そこを緑化して海と緑に囲まれた庭園にしたいというのが構想の出発点だった。だが、着工直前、阪神淡路大震災が起き、断層も見つかり、工期は延期、設計も変更を余儀なくされた。国際会議場などを備えたリゾートホテルを中心に、庭園、温室、野外劇場などが広大な敷地に広がる。目を引くのは、急斜面の敷地に格子状の花壇を集めた「百段苑」。「貝の浜」と呼ばれる広大な水底にはホタテの貝殻を敷きつめた。環境を踏まえた創造の手応えを感じさせる大規模プロジェクトの実現である。

An earth and sand excavation site, which had supported the economic growth of the entire Osaka area during the high economic growth period, was left with exposed bedrock and steep slopes. The starting point of this project was to turn such site into a garden space surrounded by the ocean and greenery by applying vegetation. Around a resort style hotel with international convention capability, garden space, glass house, and exterior theater space spread on a vast site territory. Eye-catching feature is "Hyakudan-en" ("Hundred step garden") with gridded flower beds on a steeply sloped site. The bottom of the basins on a wide open terrace space named Shell beach is covered all over with scallop shells.

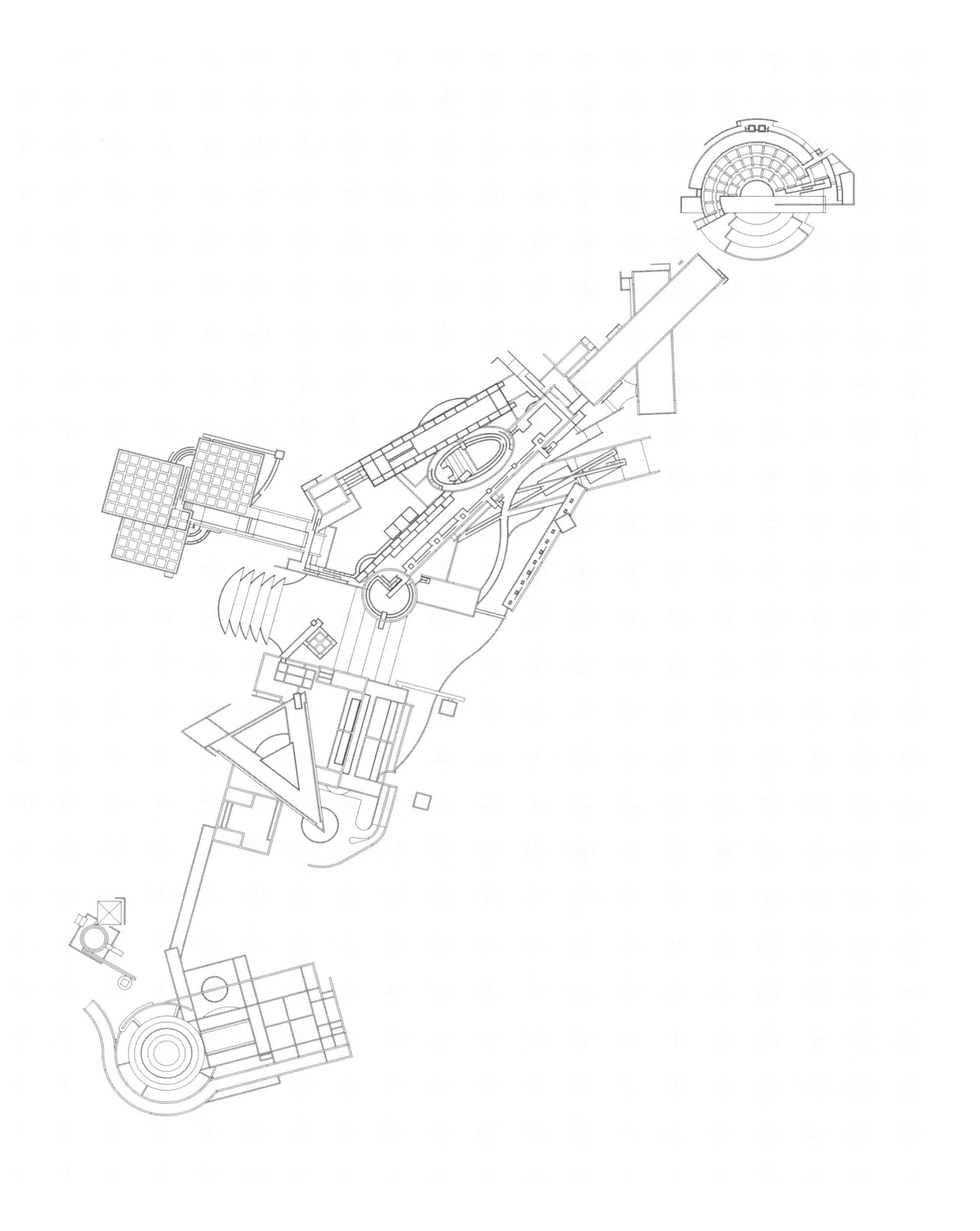

[182]
光の教会／日曜学校　1999
church of the light, sunday school

1. 大阪府茨木市 | ibaraki, osaka
2. 設計　1997.3–1998.5
3. 施工　1998.5–1999.2
4. 鉄筋コンクリート（ラーメン）| RC (frame)
5. 日曜学校 | sunday school
6. 敷地 | site　838.6 m²
7. 建築 | building　116.8 m²
8. 延床 | total floor　148.8 m²

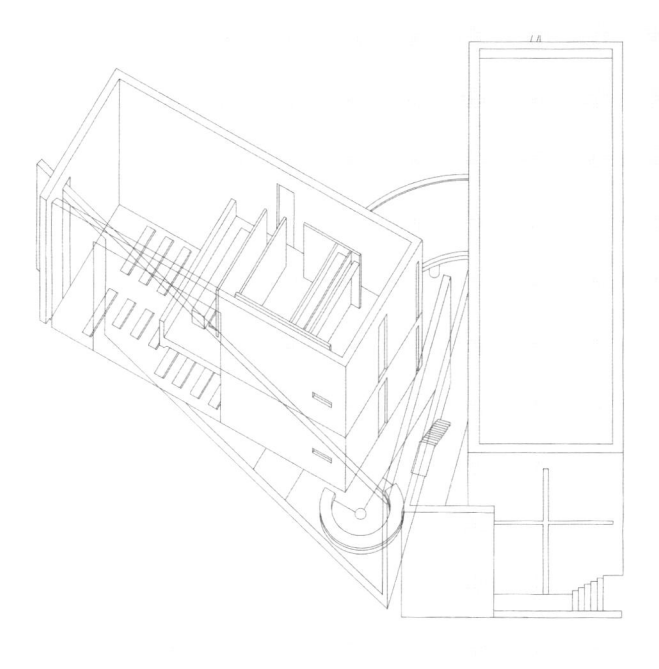

代表作のひとつ「光の教会」の増築。教会本体と50度斜めに振った建物の配置になっている。コンクリートのボックスは教会と同じだが、内装は外壁の一部と家具のすべてをシナベニヤ材で仕立て、「木の空間」が入れ子になる構成をとった。木を選択したのは、日曜学校に集う子どもたちの心に響く空間を目指したためという。そうすれば、永遠に「光の教会」が、成人したひとびとの心に生き続けるのではとの思いが素材選択に結びついた。→参照 [102]

This is the extension of CHURCH OF THE LIGHT, one of the masterpieces. This extension building is positioned 50°diagonally against the main church building. The concrete box is the same as the church, while the interior was constructed with a part of its exterior wall and the entire furniture in basswood plywood, and it had a structure that "space of wood" nests. According to Ando, the choice of wood material is to seek for a space to get to the hearts of children who come to the Sunday school. That way, the thought that "Church of the Light" would live forever in the hearts of those who grow up has led to the selection of such materials. → see also [102]

[183]
西宮市貝類館　1999
shell museum of nishinomiya city

1. 兵庫県西宮市 | nishinomiya, hyogo
2. 設計　1997.8–1998.6
3. 施工　1998.7–1999.5
4. 鉄筋コンクリート、一部鉄骨 | RC, steel
5. 博物館 | museum
6. 敷地 | site　2,605 m²
7. 建築 | building　432.0 m²
8. 延床 | total floor　591.0 m²

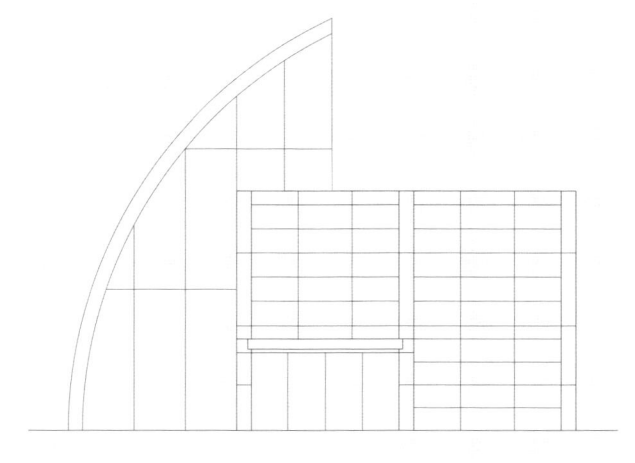

兵庫県西宮市の臨海部埋立地に位置する集合住宅団地の一角に建設された。個人のコレクションをもとに貝類標本を展示している。船の帆をイメージしたという曲面のドームで海に近い立地に呼応した。敷地の奥に位置する西宮浜公民館とを結ぶコンクリートのフレームとすりガラスの壁からなる回廊の存在が、空間に規律を与えている。貝類館と公民館の間の中庭に、太平洋横断で知られる堀江謙一の「マーメイド4世号」が置かれている。

This museum was built in an area with a collective housing complex located on reclaimed land of a waterfront area in Nishinomiya City, Hyogo Prefecture. Shellfish samples mainly from private collections are displayed. Ando applied a half-circle dome with the image of a sail of a boat in accord with the location close to the ocean. The corridor with a concrete frame and frosted glass walls that connect the community center of Nishinomiyahama provides a sense of order in the space. Mermaid IV of Horie Kenichi who is known for crossing the Pacific Ocean is placed in the courtyard between the SHELL MUSEUM and the community center.

[184]
南寺（直島・家プロジェクト）　1999
minamidera
(art house project in naoshima)

1. 香川県直島町 | naoshima, kagawa
2. 設計 | design　1998.8–1998.12
3. 施工 | construction　1999.1–1999.3
4. 木造 | wood
5. アートギャラリー | art gallery
6. 敷地 | site　395.5 m²
7. 建築 | building　202.6 m²
8. 延床 | total floor　163.0 m²

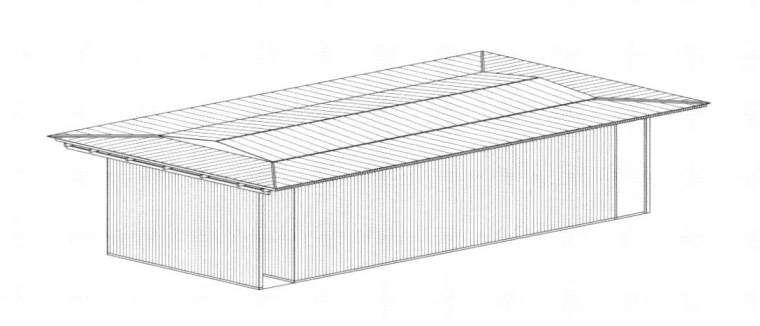

直島の「家プロジェクト」と呼ばれる島内民家などを活用したアート・コミッションワークのひとつ。空き地に地名だけが残り、寺の建物はすでに失われていたため、新たな木造の建築を安藤が設計した。焼き杉の板材を外壁に張りつめ、構造は集成材でまかなった。周囲には砂利を敷いて、コンクリートの舗石をならべ、アプローチの誘導とした。内部は暗黒の空間にジェームズ・タレルが仕込んだ光のインスタレーション「ザ・バックサイド・オブ・ザ・ムーン」が浮かび上がる。→参照 [125]、[151]、[223]、[239]、[280]、[309]

This is one of art related commissioned works called "ART HOUSE PROJECT", to utilize private houses in the island of Naoshima. The site was already empty after a temple building was lost, while the name was still valid to identify the site. Ando designed a new wooden building for the site; exterior walls are clad with burnt cedar wood boards; building structure was built in laminated wood material; the ground around the building is covered with gravel, and lined with some concrete pave stones for indicating the approach. Inside of the building is finished in black to create a dark space, while the light installation of James Turrell, "The Backside of the Moon" begins to appear to the eyes of visitors. → see also [125], [151], [223], [239], [280], [309]

[185]
レイナ・ソフィア美術館
国際設計競技案　1999
museo nacional centro de arte reina sofia, international design competition

1. スペイン マドリッド | madrid, spain
2. 設計 | design　1999
3. 設計競技 | design competition
4. 鉄筋コンクリート | RC
5. 美術館 | museum of art
6. 敷地 | site　26,000 m²
7. 建築 | building　16,000 m²
8. 延床 | total floor　16,000 m²

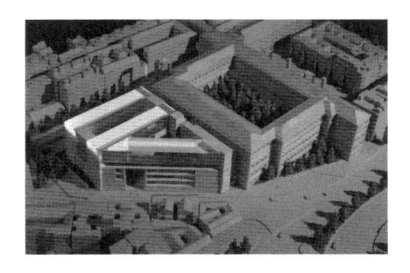

スペインの首都マドリードの国際的評価の高い歴史的な美術館の拡張コンペ案。都市の記憶をどう継承していくかを設計のテーマとした。18世紀に建設された本館の中庭を囲む形式を、増築する新たな棟にも採り入れて、空間体系の尊重と拡張を意図した。新館のヴォリュームも旧館と揃え、上階にガラスの箱を配することで、中庭の新たな連鎖とともに、新旧の対比がもたらす緊張感が都市の刺激になることを期待した。

A design for a contest for expansion of a historical art gallery that has been highly regarded internationally in Madrid, the capital of Spain. The theme of the design was focused on how to inherit the memory of the city. Respect and expansion of the spatial system were intended by adopting the style of surrounding the courtyard of the main hall built in the 18th century for the new building to be added. By designing the new building to have the same volume as the old building and by placing a glass box on the upper floor, it was anticipated to bring new sequence for the courtyard and give stimulation to the city through tense atmosphere by comparison of new and old.

[186]
ネルソン・アトキンス美術館
国際設計競技案　1999
nelson atkins museum,
international design competition

1. アメリカ カンザスシティー | kansas city, USA
2. 設計 | design　1999
3. 設計競技 | design competition
4. 鉄筋コンクリート | RC
5. 美術館 | museum of art
6. 敷地 | site　18,000 m²

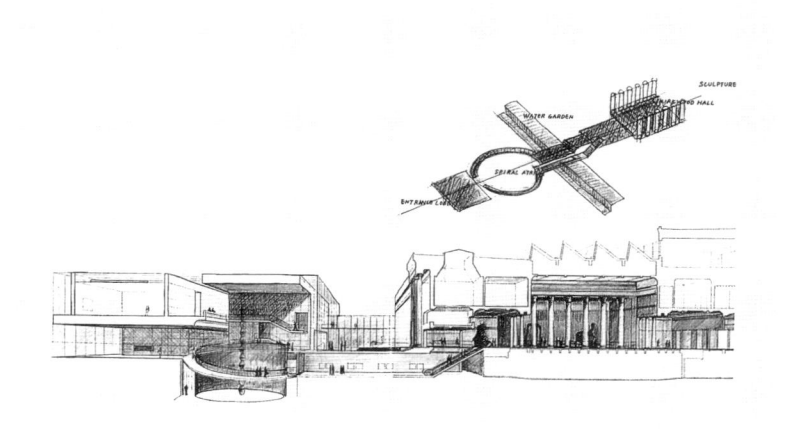

米カンザスシティーのネルソン・アトキンス美術館は、全米でも指折りのコレクションで知られる。1933年にワイト・アンド・ワイトの設計で完成した本館に向き合う形で2本の直方体が存在感を示す計画を提案した。新棟案のセールスポイントは、スパイラル・アトリウムと名付けた空間。本館の新古典主義の列柱に向き合う位置に吹き抜けを配し、上階にはアトリウム両端の階段、下階には螺旋のスロープを設けて、来館者が昇降時に本館を意識する仕立てとした。

The Nelson-Atkins Museum of Art located in Kansas City, U.S. is known for having one of the largest collections in the U.S. A plan was proposed to express the presence of two rectangular solids facing the main hall constructed under the design of White and White in 1933. The strong point of the new building plan is the space named Spiral Atrium. An open ceiling is provided at the position facing the Neoclassical style pillars in the main hall. Stairways on both sides of the atrium for the upper floor and a spiral slope for the lower floor are provided for visitors to always be conscious of the main hall when going up or down.

[187]
ケ・ブランリー美術館
国際設計競技案　1999
musée du quai branly,
international design competiton

1. フランス パリ | paris, france
2. 設計 | design　1999
3. 設計競技 | design competition
5. 美術館 | museum of art
6. 敷地 | site　40,000 m²

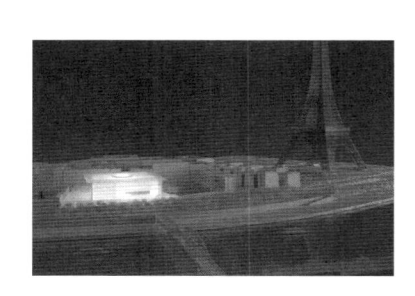

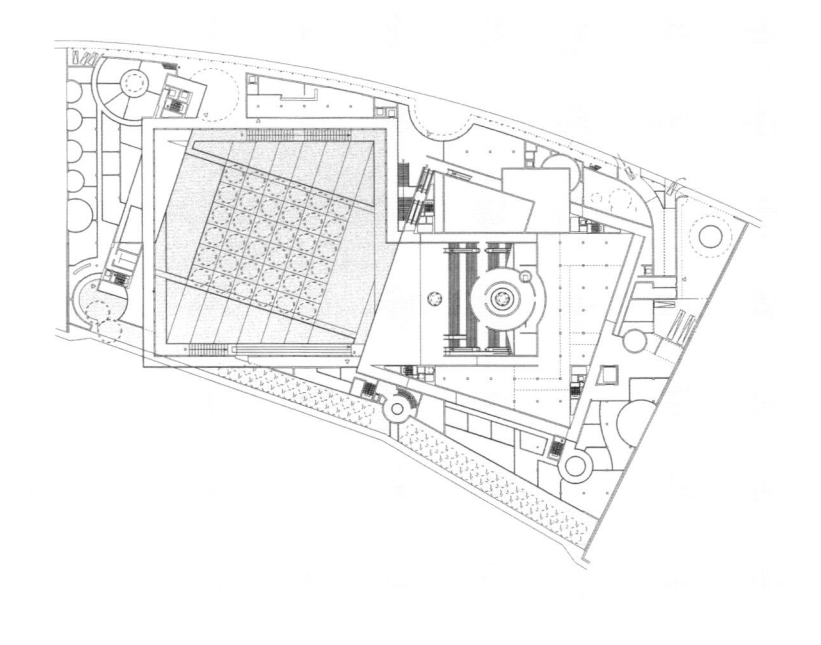

前面にはセーヌ川、背後にエッフェル塔の控える立地を踏まえて、二つの立方体が並列する構成を提案した。「知恵のキューブ」に美術館機能を収め、もう片方の「創造のキューブ」は中庭を囲う空隙の空間とした。前者をセーヌ川の流れに合わせた軸線に、後者をエッフェル塔に向う軸線に載せる配置とし、両軸線の生じるズレが、ミッテラン政権の「グランプロジェ」を継承発展させる新しい国立美術館に求められる「変化と奥行き」を体現できると考えた。

A composition with two cubes placed in parallel was proposed considering the location of the Seine River at the front and the Eiffel Tower at the back. The museum area consists of the Cube of Knowledge and the other Cube of Creation consists of an empty space that surrounds the courtyard. The former cube is placed on the axis along the Seine River and latter cube is located on the axis facing toward the Eiffel Tower. The offset of these axes is to demonstrate symbolize "change and depth" required of the new national museum for inheriting and developing the Grand Project of Mitterrand administration.

[188]
FABRICA（ベネトンアートスクール）
2000
fabrica (benetton communication research center)

1. イタリア トレヴィゾ | treviso, italy
2. 設計 | design　1992.4–1994.12
3. 施工 | construction　1992.10–2000.6
4. 鉄筋コンクリート造 [新築]、木造、煉瓦造 [修復] | RC, wood, brick
5. 教育、研究施設 | education, research center
6. 敷地 | site　48,834 m²
7. 建築 | building　1,250 m²
8. 延床 | total floor　5,172 m²

若者の創造性を育むための教育研究施設。イタリアのカジュアルブランドのベネトンが創設した。北イタリアのトレヴィゾに残る古い邸宅と納屋などの付属の建物を保全し、背後に地下の吹き抜け広場を中心とする建築を安藤は設計した。邸宅のエリアに人工池とコンクリートの列柱を新たに加え、歴史的風景の継承と更新に挑んだ。楕円の地下広場にスロープを下りて進む空間体験は、ここに集う若者に刺激を与えるに違いない。このプロジェクトの保存作業でイタリアの職人の技術の真髄に触れたことが、あとに続くヴェネチアのプロジェクトの大きな支えになった。

This is an educational research facility to foster creativity of the young generations produced by an Italian casual brand, UNITED COLORS OF BENETTON. Ando preserved the attached buildings, such as the old estate and the barn remaining in the North Italian city of Treviso, and he designed a new building with a double-height open plaza in the underground as the core space of this building behind the estate. An artificial pond and concrete colonnade were added into the estate area in order to challenge to inherit and update the historical landscape. Those young people coming to this place will be inspired by the spatial experience of going down to the oval-shaped underground plaza via a slope. Having touched the essence of Italian craftsmen' technical skill in conservation work of this project became the great help for the following projects in Venice.

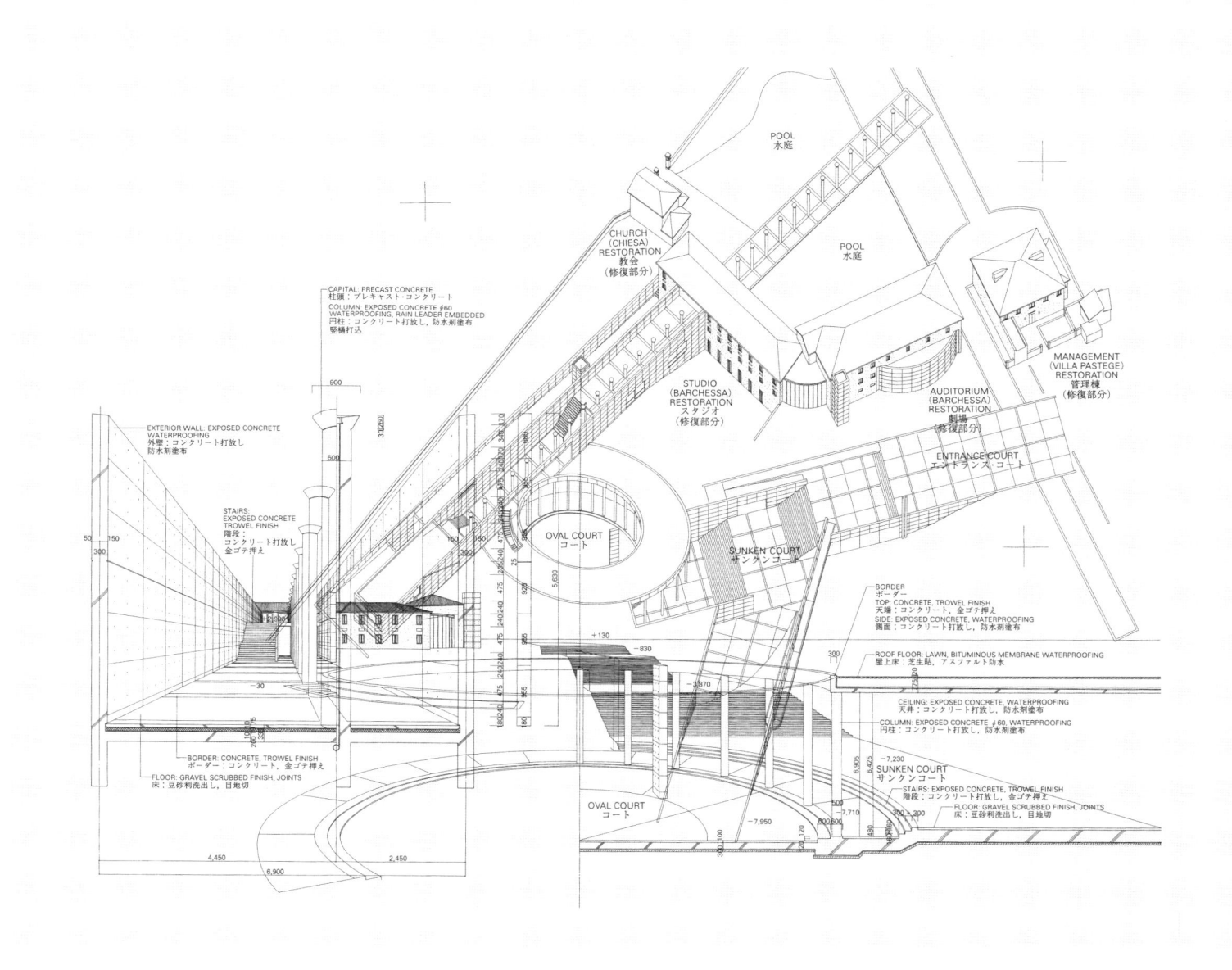

346 Complete Works

[189]

南岳山光明寺　2000
komyo-ji temple

1. 愛媛県西条市 | saijo, ehime
2. 設計 | design　1998.1–1999.3
3. 施工 | construction　1999.4–2000.6
4. 木造、鉄筋コンクリート | wood, RC
5. 仏教寺院 | buddhist temple
6. 敷地 | site　3,221.8 m²
7. 建築 | building　1,224.1 m²
8. 延床 | total floor　1,284.1 m²

若い住職と安藤の新たな寺院建築を求める熱意が、四国・西条の地に現代の木造建築を実現した。水に浮かぶ本堂は周囲を二層の壁で囲まれている。一番外側は、米松の角柱が15センチ間隔で垂直にならぶ。その内側ではすりガラスの壁が本堂の大空間を包み込む。複層で組まれた梁材が、深い庇の下に力強くせりだす。安藤は木造建築の本質は「組む」ことにあるとし、それは信仰を核にひとびとが集まり、手を組んで共同体を構成し、維持する姿に重なり合うと述べている。

This modern-day wooden building was realized in the place of Saijo City in Shikoku region, by the eagerness of Ando and a young chief priest of a temple to seek for a new kind of architecture in the form of a temple. The main hall of the temple is floating above a water basin and surrounded by walls in two layers. The outermost part of the building is lined up with a series of vertical square columns made in Douglas Pine in 15cm interval. Frosted glass walls are placed in the area surrounded by these columns to enclose the large space of the main hall. Under the deep eaves of the building, beam elements assembled in multiple layers boldly stick out. Ando says that the essence of wooden architecture is in the "wood joinery and framework", and that it overlaps with the image of people gathering and organizing a community, joining hands together under religious belief.

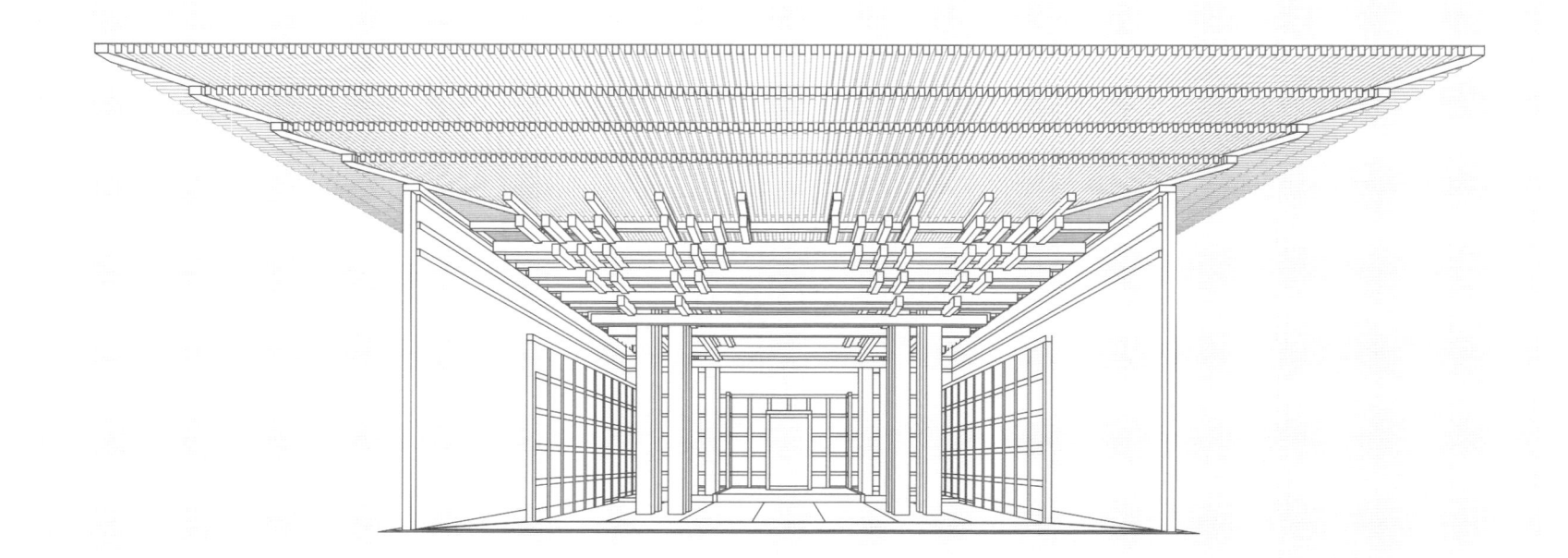

[190]
新潟市立豊栄図書館　2000
niigata city toyosaka library
.
1. 新潟県新潟市 | niigata, niigata
2. 設計 | design   1997.9–1999.3
3. 施工 | construction   1999.5–2000.9
4. 鉄筋コンクリート | RC
5. 図書館 | library
6. 敷地 | site   4,323.4 m²
7. 建築 | building   1,386.7 m²
8. 延床 | total floor   2,144.7 m²

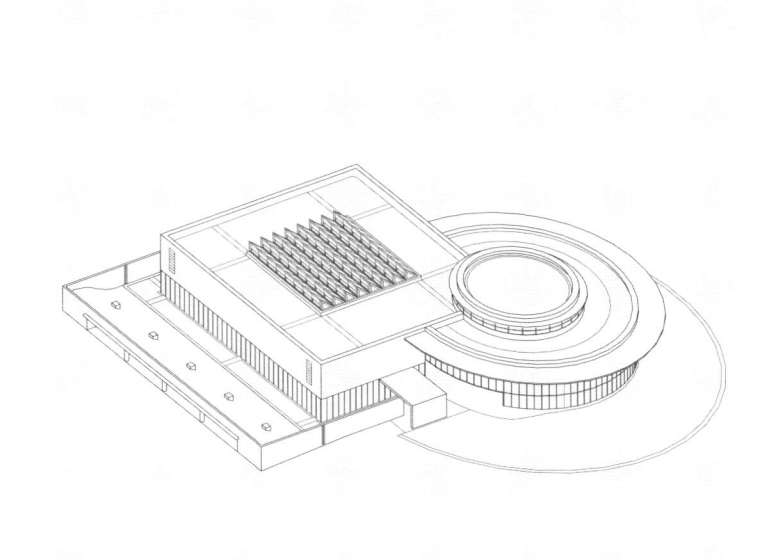

図書館の建築内に、二つの吹き抜けが配されている。ひとつは円形のトップライトを持ち、もうひとつは正方形のそれである。しかし、その下の閲覧机は、いずれも円テーブルとなっている。これは、天空からの柔らかな光線のもと、市民が車座になって集う姿を想定したためだ。敷地は小学校の跡地。地元で最初の独立した図書館であり、そこを核にひとびとの集うことが期待され、新築にあたっては既存の樹木を残す配置が選ばれた。
.
In this library building, two double-height spaces are arranged; one has a top light in circular shape, and the other has a square one. Even so, all the reading desks under those spaces are round tables, since the concept of the space is based on an image of citizens gathering in circle under the gentle light from the sky. The site is the remained land space of an elementary school. This is the first independent library of the area, expecting people will gather to this library as a core of the community. This new building is allocated in position so that existing trees can be preserved.

[191]
ミュゼふくおかカメラ館　2000
fukuoka camera museum
.
1. 富山県高岡市 | takaoka, toyama
2. 設計 | design   1999.1–1999.5
3. 施工 | construction   1999.7–2000.7
4. 鉄筋コンクリート | RC
5. 博物館 | museum
6. 敷地 | site   2,707.8 m²
7. 建築 | building   790.8 m²
8. 延床 | total floor   1,034.7 m²

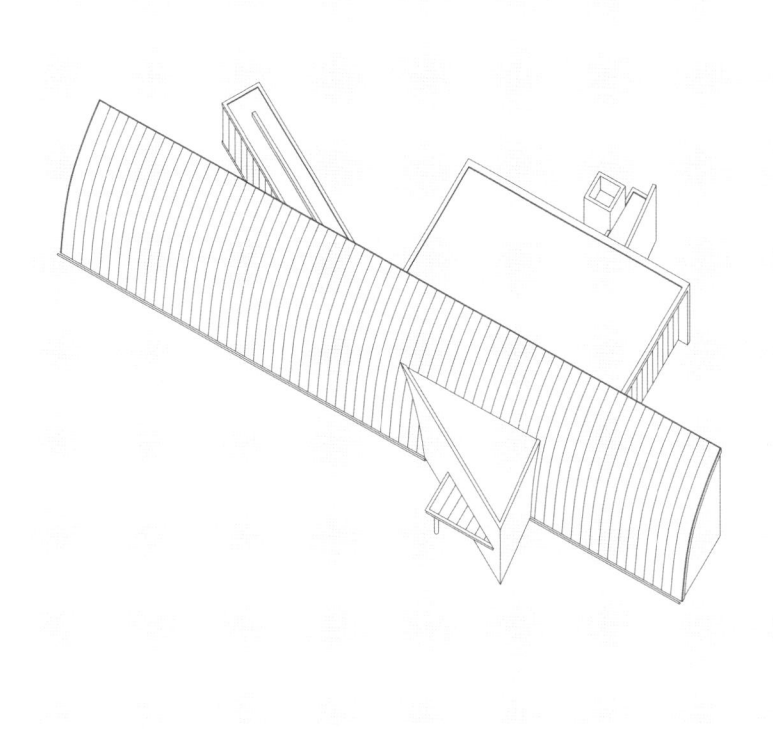

地表から曲面壁が立ち上がる展示棟。その外壁に、30度振った角度で三角柱が突き刺さる。エントランスを入ると1、2階に配された展示室を行き来するためのスロープが三角柱の壁の延長線上に鋭角で延びていく。アンティーク・カメラの小博物館だが、空間のすべてが抽象幾何学に従い、威厳をたたえている。カメラという工業製品を展示するからにはと、安藤はガラスの展示ケースの精密な仕上げにもこだわった。細部にまで緊張感が行き渡っている。

This is a building for exhibitions with a curved wall rising up from the ground surface. A triangular-shaped tower sticks into the wall by 30°shifted from orthogonal angle against the wall. When going through the entrance, there is a slope to access the gallery spaces on the 1st and 2nd floor extending at an acute angle on the extension of the wall of the triangular prism. Although it is a small museum for exhibiting antique cameras, everything in space follows abstract geometry and represents dignity. Ando also paid attention to the minute details of the glass exhibition cases for presenting cameras as industrial products. Tense atmosphere is spread all the way to details.

[192]
アントワープ市立博物館
国際設計競技案　2000
museum aan de stroom, antwerp,
international design competition

1. ベルギー アントワープ | antwerp, belgium
2. 設計 | design 2000
3. 設計競技 | design competition
5. 博物館 | museum
6. 敷地 | site 12,000 m²
8. 延床 | total floor 15,000 m²

ベルギーのアントワープのウォーターフロント開発の一環として水辺に新たな博物館が計画された。博物館の新設により、都市的活動の水辺までの拡大が期待されたため、逆円錐形の太い柱で建物全体を持ち上げ、足元の岸壁を広大な広場「都市の森」として、湾岸地区の活性化に寄与させることを提案した。このコンセプトはパリで計画した「ピノー現代美術館」の案に発展したが実現に至らず、安藤は次なる機会を待っている。

Construction of a new museum was planned as part of waterfront development in Antwerp, Belgium. Since expansion of city activities from the city center to the waterfront was required in addition to the exhibition function, a design that thick inverted cone-shaped pillars supporting the whole building to demonstrate the wharf of the base area as a vast open space of "City's Forest" was proposed to contribute to the revitalization of the bay area. Although this concept was developed as the design of Pinault Contemporary Art Museum, it did not materialize and Ando is waiting for the next opportunity.

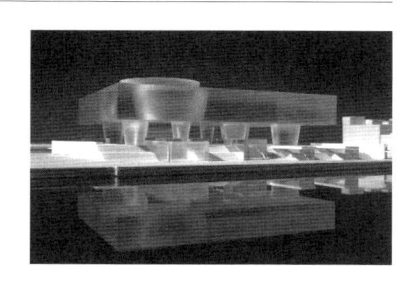

[193]
セント・ポール寺院聖台
デザインコンペティション　2000
a new font for st. paul's cathedral,
international design competiton
.
1. イギリス ロンドン | london, UK
2. 設計 | design　2000
3. 設計競技 | design competition
4. ガラス | glass
5. 洗礼盤 | baptismal font

ロンドンのセント・ポール寺院に置く新しい洗礼盤のコンペ。対岸のテート・モダンのコンペにおいて、旧発電所の煉瓦の肌にガラスの直方体を突き刺す新旧の衝突を企てたことを受け、ガラスによる洗礼盤を提案した。1メートル四方の厚さ5ミリのガラスの板を偏芯させて重ねた。ガラスの中央から少しずらした位置に穴を開け、聖水の受けとする仕立てだった。
.
A contest of a new baptismal font to be placed in the St Paul's Cathedral in London. A glass baptismal font was proposed in line with the glass rectangular solid piercing the brick wall of the former power generation plant on the other bank proposed for the contest of Tate Modern to demonstrate the collision of new and old. Square glass sheets of 1 meter on each side and 5 millimeters in thickness were laid on top of each other in eccentric positions. A hole is provided at a position slightly off center of the glass, which became a font for holding water.

[194]
カルダー美術館　2000
calder museum
.
1. アメリカ フィラデルフィア | philadelphia, USA
2. 設計 | design　2000.10
3. 設計競技 | design competition
5. 美術館 | museum of art
6. 敷地 | site　6,400.0 m²
8. 延床 | total floor　4,800 m²

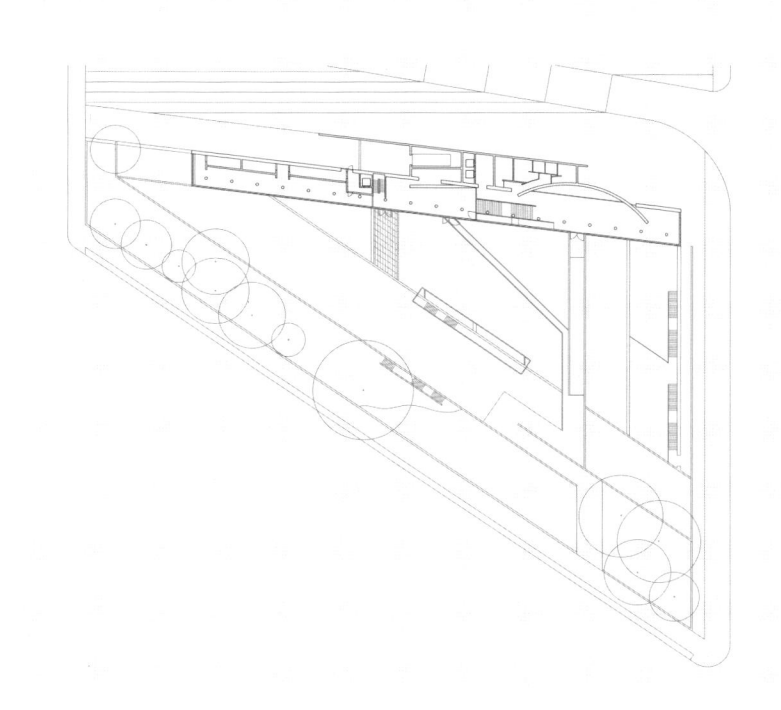

米フィラデルフィアゆかりの、屋外彫刻などで知られるアレクサンダー・カルダーの作品を集める美術館。国際コンペの結果、安藤が当選した。都市公園と隣り合う環境を尊重して、美術館は1階と地下の二層に抑え込まれた。来訪者は地下の広場の頭上に渡された地上レベルのブリッジなどから作品を鑑賞できる。地下の広場は人工池の仕立てで、立体作品がそこにも配される。フィラデルフィアの都市軸線に沿った敷地を踏まえて、建物は地下に埋没していく。カルダーこそが見えない「風」を感知して造形した最初の芸術家と考える安藤の思いが、「見えない建築」となった。
.
An art gallery that has a collection of works of the contemporary artist Alexander Calder who is known for his open-air sculptures and has connection with Philadelphia in the U.S. Ando's design for the art gallery was selected through an international contest. The art gallery was limited to a one-story building with two basement floors honoring the environment next to a city park. Visitors are able to view Calder's art works from areas including the bridge on the ground floor situated above the open area on the basement level. The basement open area has an artificial pond where Calder's three-dimensional works are placed.

[195]
大阪府立狭山池博物館　2001
sayamaike historical museum, osaka

1. 大阪府大阪狭山市 | osakasayama, osaka
2. 設計 | design　1994.6–1997.3
3. 施工 | construction　1997.7–2001.3
4. 鉄筋コンクリート、一部鉄骨鉄筋コンクリート | RC, SRC
5. 博物館 | museum
6. 敷地 | site　15,412.0 m²
7. 建築 | building　3,773.5 m²
8. 延床 | total floor　4,948.5 m²

起源を7世紀にさかのぼる狭山池は、日本最古のダム式貯水池。奈良時代に行基、鎌倉時代に重源ら高僧も開発、改修に携わり、一帯の灌漑に寄与してきた。鎌倉時代の樋の遺構に加え、改修の軌跡が確かめられる堤の地層の発見もあり、土木の歴史をたどる博物館が誕生した。主展示は堤の地層を切り出したユニークなもので、大空間が求められた。堤から一段下の敷地を踏まえ、地上のヴォリュームを抑え、地下に空間を展開している。水庭の両側に配した回廊を歩くとき、滝のような激しい流水のカーテンに包まれる。その力強い水音は感動的だ。

The history of Sayamaike Pond can go back to 7th century for its origin, and it is said to be the oldest dammed up reservoir in Japan. This pond was developed and improved under the leadership of Buddhist monk, Gyoki in Nara period, and Chogen in Kamakura period. The excavation investigations led to the discovery of the remains such as gutters from Kamakura period, and a stratum of embankment revealing the process of improvement works of those days. This newly established museum traces back the history of civil engineering in Japan unlike any other places. The main piece of exhibition in this museum is a unique cut-out stratum of the embankment requiring a large space for presentation. Considering the actual site with a ground surface one step lower from the embankment itself, this museum represents this particular condition by reducing the volume above the ground level and providing exhibition space in underground level.

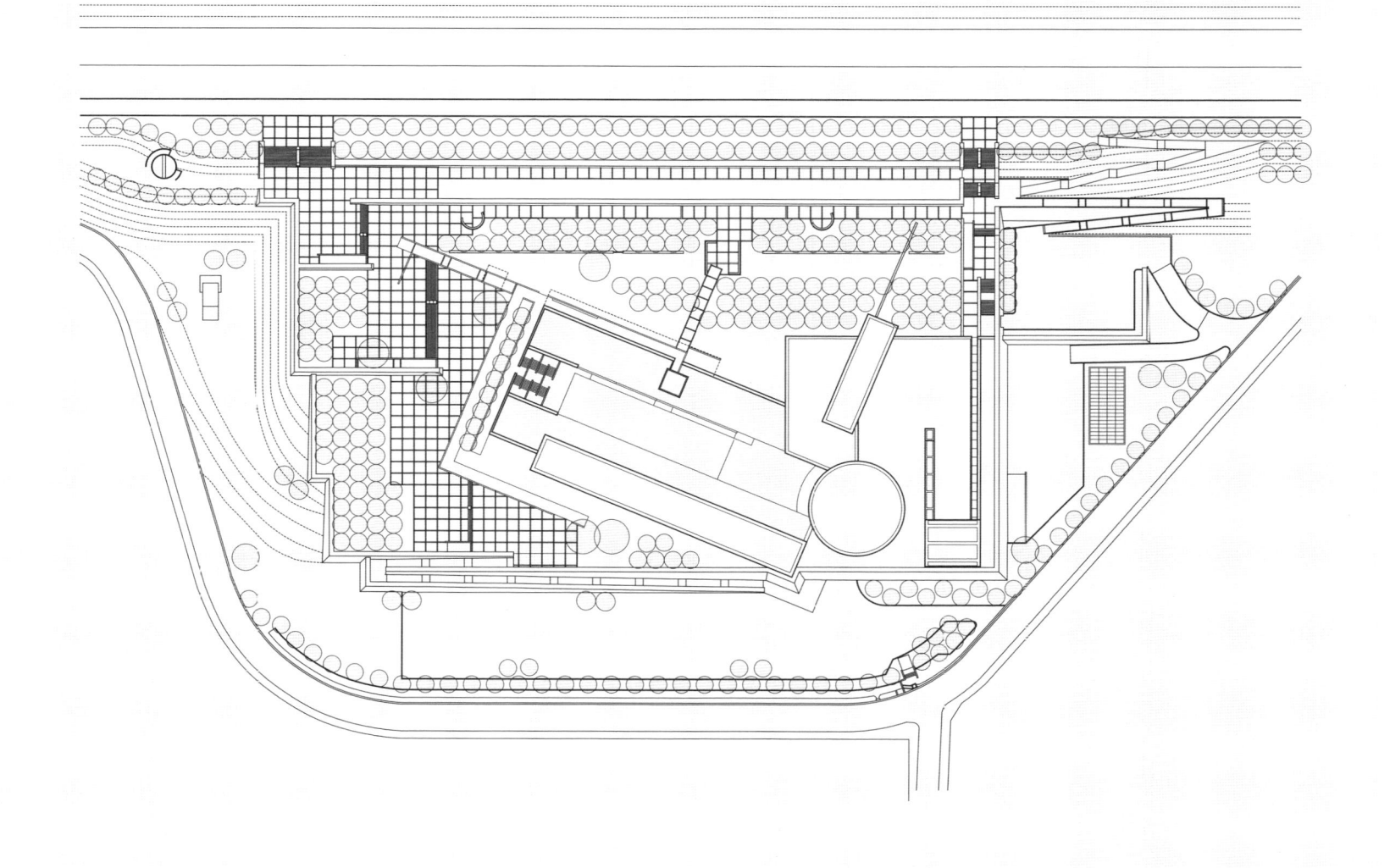

[196]
ピューリッツァー美術館　2001
pulitzer foundation for the arts

1. アメリカ セントルイス | st. louis, USA
2. 設計 | design　1991.5–1994.12 [旧案／phase 1], 1995.7–1997.10 [実現案／phase 2 for the new site]
3. 施工 | construction　1997.11–2001.7
4. 鉄筋コンクリート | RC
5. 美術館 | museum of art
6. 敷地 | site　3,920 m²
7. 建築 | building　1,040 m²
8. 延床 | total floor　2,380 m²

ピューリッツァー賞で知られる一族からの依頼で設計を初めてから実現まで10年を超す歳月を要した。敷地の変更、アドバイザー役の彫刻家、リチャード・セラらとの対立、キュレーターでもあるピューリッツァー夫人との合意形成の手順が求められた。自作の映える空間を求める芸術家と、どんな作品にも応えうる「無の豊穣」を求める建築家との立場の違いが議論を長引かせた。結局、「無の空間」が実現した。板状の壁が規定する抽象美のエントランス、並列する二つの直方体の展示棟の間には水が張られた。無であるがゆえの強靭さが、中西部の茫漠たる都市のなか、確たる存在感を発揮している。

It took more than 10 years from the start of design to the completion of the building at the request of a family known for "Pulitzer Prize". This process involved building site change, conflicts with artist including a sculptor, Richard Serra as an advisor to the project, and consensus building with Mrs. Pulitzer who also is a curator. Argument between artists who look for spaces where their own works shine, and an architect who seek for "richness of an untitled space" adapting and responding to any piece of work revealed differences in their viewpoints and prolonged the discussion. As a result, a "space of nil" was produced and realized. The entrance space is defined by a sheet of wall in abstract beauty; the in-between space of two exhibition wings in cuboid form is occupied by a water basin. This building exhibits positive presence with the boldness of being uncolored and untitled in a vast stretch of a city in Midwest part of the United States.

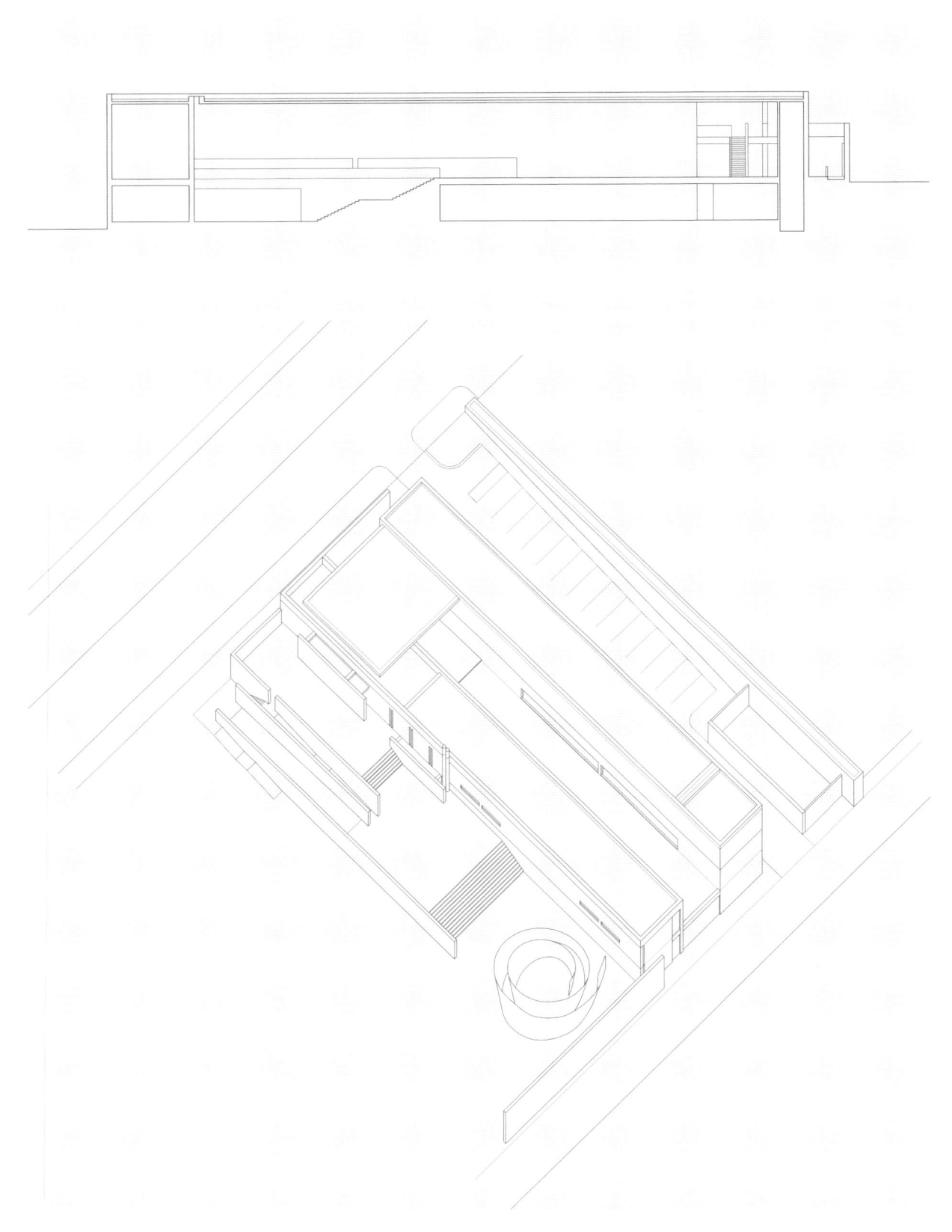

[197]
兵庫県立美術館＋神戸市水際広場
2001
hyogo prefectural museum of art
+ kobe waterfront plaza

1. 神戸市中央区｜chuo-ku, kobe
2. 設計｜design　1997.3–1998.3 [museum],
   1996.4–1998.3 [plaza]
3. 施工｜construction　1999.3–2001.9 [museum],
   1998.9–2001.9 [plaza]
4. 鉄骨鉄筋コンクリート｜SRC
5. 美術館｜museum of art
6. 敷地｜site　19000 m² [museum], 43107 m² [plaza]
7. 建築｜building　13807.7 m² [museum],
   1149 m² [plaza]
8. 延床｜total floor　27461.4 m² [museum],
   694 m² [plaza]

1995年1月の阪神淡路大震災で、元の美術館が被害を受けたため、神戸の臨海地、東部新都心に新たな立地を求め、安藤の設計による美術館が登場した。基壇の上に、三つの細長いガラスの箱を海に向かって平行に配置し、内部にコンクリートのボックスを入れ子で配して展示空間とした。美術館に繋がる「水際広場」は、震災前から計画されていたもので、円形の野外劇場、斜めに挿入されたコンクリートの自立壁、クスノキの樹木列などからなる。美術館の新設により存在意義が高まった。→参照 [345]

The original art museum building was damaged by The Great Hanshin Earthquake occurred in January, 1995, therefore a new museum building was designed by Ando on a new seaside location situated within HAT Kobe. On a podium, three slender boxes extending toward the ocean are arranged in parallel orientation, each with a concrete box nested inside to provide exhibition spaces. WATERFRONT PLAZA linked to the museum, which had been planned before the earthquake occurred, consists of an outside amphitheater, independent concrete wall inserted diagonally to the main building, and a series of camphor trees. The significance and value of this plaza space has increased by establishing a museum. → see also [345]

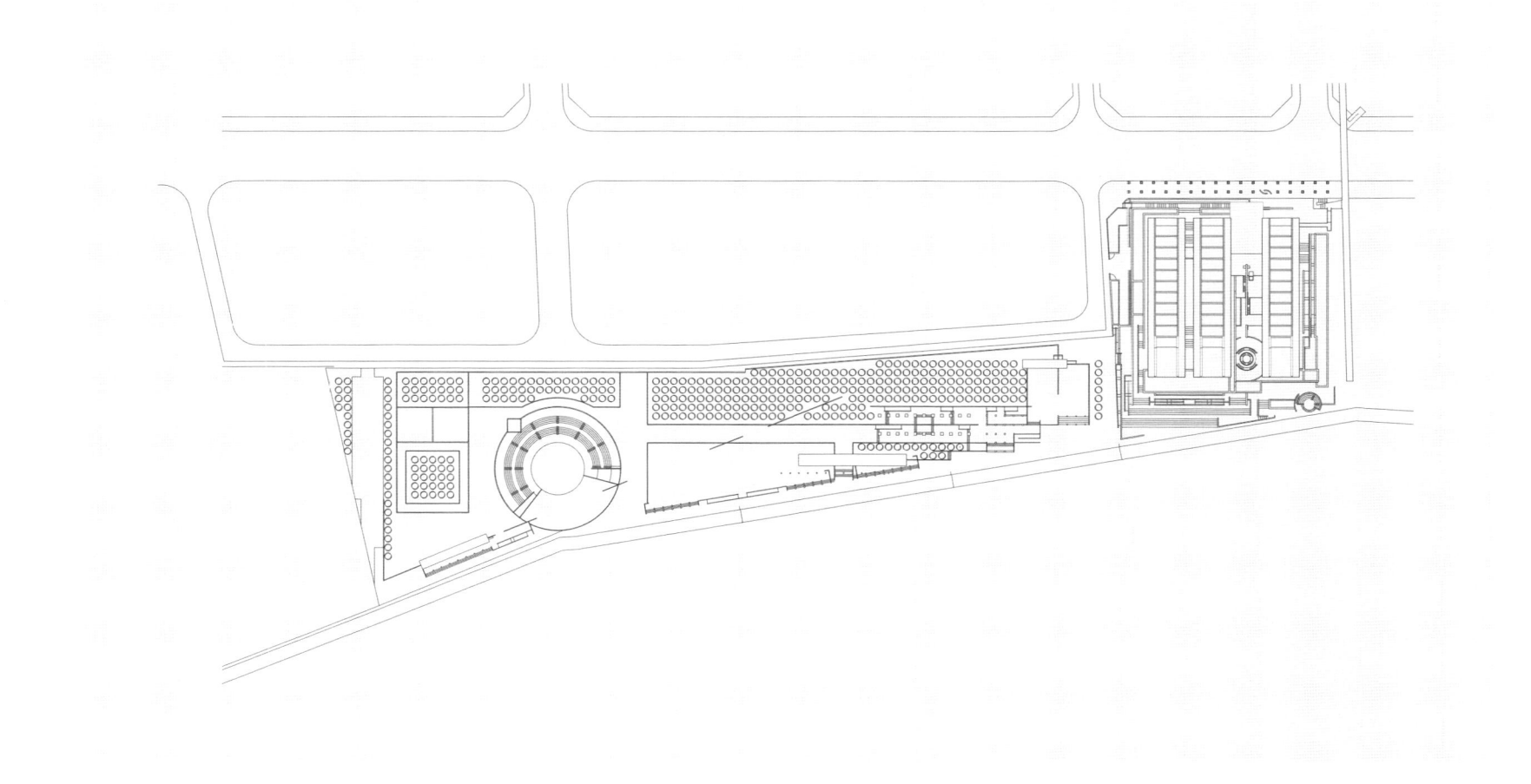

[198]
司馬遼太郎記念館　2001
shiba ryotaro memorial museum

1. 大阪府東大阪市 | higashiosaka, osaka
2. 設計 | design　1998.9–2000.6
3. 施工 | construction　2000.7–2001.10
4. 鉄筋コンクリート | RC
5. 文学資料館 | literature museum
6. 敷地 | site　1,010.0 m²
7. 建築 | building　455.9 m²
8. 延床 | total floor　997.1 m²

関西に縁の深い作家の司馬遼太郎は大阪府下の東大阪市に居宅を構えた。その自宅を資料館に整備する役割を、生前親交のあった安藤が担った。居宅は残して資料館を新築した。司馬がうずたかく資料を積み上げて執筆に勤しんでいた書斎の風景から、「司馬遼太郎・もうひとつの書斎」と呼ばれる吹き抜けの展示室を構想した。地階の床から2階の天井まで三層分の両側の壁を木製の書架で覆い、司馬の蔵書をならべた。資料館の周囲には、司馬の愛した豪農の民家が残り、心象風景に触れられる。

Ryotaro Shiba, well-known for his travel sketch essays, was deeply affiliated with Kansai region and established his house in Higashiosaka City, Osaka Prefecture. Ando played a role to renovate his house into an archive museum, since Ando used to be in close relationship with Shiba during his lifetime. For this project, the residence of Shiba was preserved, and an archive wing was added as a new building. From reminiscence of the scenery of Shiba's study room, where he devoted himself to write under a huge pile of the materials and books, Ando came up with a concept of an exhibition room in the double-height space, named as "Ryotaro Shiba and his another study room"—the walls on both sides of the room are built with wooden bookshelves extending in three floor levels from the floor of the basement to the ceiling of the 2nd floor, and those shelves are stuffed with the books Shiba had collected. In the vicinity of the museum, residences of neighboring wealthy farmers loved by Shiba remain, and it illustrates the scenery in Shiba's mind.

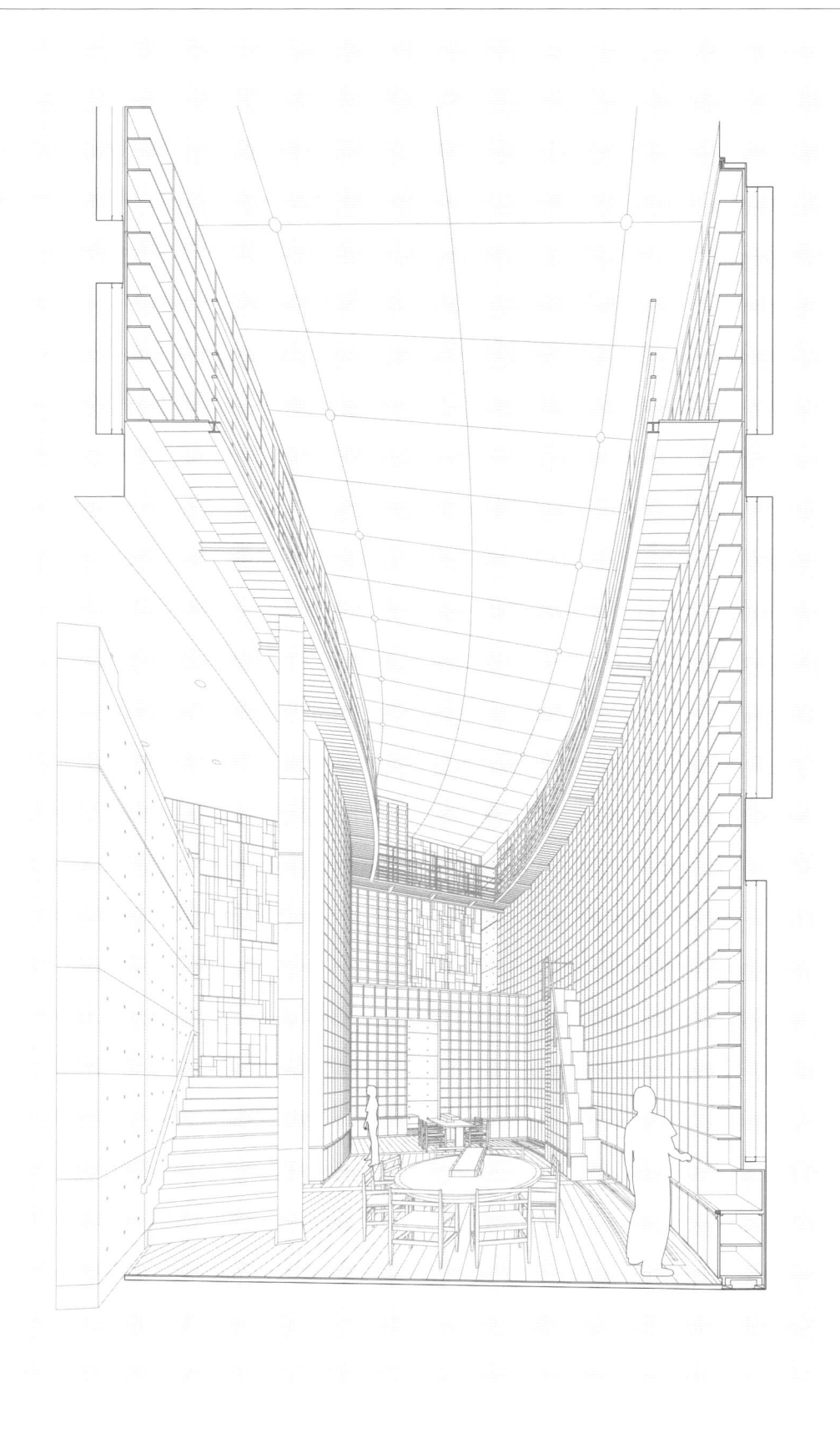

[199]
四国村ギャラリー 2001
shikokumura gallery

1. 香川県高松市 | takamatsu, kagawa
2. 設計 | design 1997.4 – 2000.6
3. 施工 | construction 2000.7 – 2001.12
4. 鉄筋コンクリート | RC
5. 美術館 | museum of art
6. 敷地 | site 4,960 m²
7. 建築 | building 473.3 m²
8. 延床 | total floor 698.4 m²

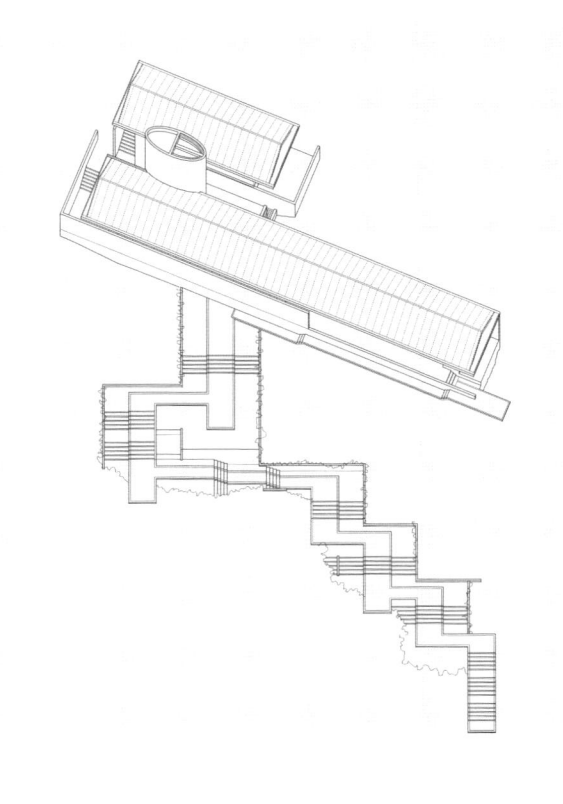

香川県高松市の屋島の山頂にある民家村の美術ギャラリー。古民家を移築した野外博物館の創設者加藤達雄の収集したコレクションを展示する。切妻屋根の平屋の棟が2棟、傾斜を生かして一層分の段差で並列する。入口は小さい方の棟に設けられ、一層分下がって大きな棟のギャラリーに至る。コンクリート打ち放しの館内でルノアールの絵画などを鑑賞したあと、ギャラリー棟から斜面に段差をつけて配置された水庭を散策できる。民家博物館に安藤の美学が新鮮さをもたらしている。

An art gallery in a village with traditional houses located on the mountain peak of Yashima, a historical battle field of Genji and Heike clans in Takamatsu City, Kagawa Prefecture. It displays a collection of Tatsuo Kato, the founder of an open-air museum built by transferring old Japanese-style houses. Two one-story houses with gabled roofs are placed in parallel with one house lower than the other by one floor using the gap of sloped ground. The entrance is at the smaller house to approach the gallery in the larger house located on the level one floor lower. After appreciating paintings of Renoir in the exposed concrete hall, visitors can enjoy the walk in the water garden situated on a gap of slope from the gallery. Ando's aesthetics provide a refreshing atmosphere to the village house museum.

[200]
神宮前の集合住宅 2001
jingumae housing

1. 東京都渋谷区 | shibuya, tokyo
2. 設計 | design 1998.8 – 2000.8
3. 施工 | construction 2000.9 – 2001.11
4. 鉄筋コンクリート | RC
5. 店舗、集合住宅 | shop, apartment house
6. 敷地 | site 901.2 m²
7. 建築 | building 537.6 m²
8. 延床 | total floor 2,211.1 m²

「表参道ヒルズ」の裏通りに位置する賃貸集合住宅。街路に面した側は低層におさめて屋上緑化し、背後の中層の居室から間近で緑を楽しめる仕立てをとった。全体の構成はグリッドを基本に、安藤らしい厳格な比例感覚で貫かれ、清新な印象を漂わせる。のちに竣工した「表参道ヒルズ」の上階には、もとそこにあった「同潤会青山アパート」の住人の集合住宅が配されている。その住宅部分も格子状の外観を採用、両者は呼応しあい新たな景観をもたらした。

Rental apartments located along the back street of Omotesando Hills. On the street side, the building is low-rise with the green roof, which can be enjoyed at the residences of the middle-rise behind. Total composition based on grids with a strict proportion of Ando gives a fresh impression. The upper floor of Omotesando Hills, which was completed later, has the residential zone for the residents of the former Dojunkai Aoyama Apartment. This residential zone has a grid appearance in harmony to create a new landscape.

全346作品録 367

[201]
国際芸術センター青森　2001
aomori contemporary art center

1. 青森県青森市 | aomori, aomori
2. 設計 | design　2000.1–2000.7
3. 施工 | construction　2000.10–2001.10
4. 鉄筋コンクリート、一部鉄骨、鉄骨鉄筋コンクリート | RC, steel, SRC
5. 創作・宿泊施設 | artist-in-residence program center
6. 敷地 | site　262,500.0 m²
7. 建築 | building　4,277.5 m²
8. 延床 | total floor　4,015.1 m²

アーティスト・イン・レジデンスを前提とする山間の立地。アトリエ棟は、起伏ある地形を踏まえて小さな谷間に架かる橋をイメージし、間口120メートル超、奥行き20メートルほどの極端に細長い平屋とした。近接する宿泊棟も低層の細長い形態で、安藤は二つの棟を2本の橋に見立てた。展示やパフォーマンス上演を想定した中央棟は低い円筒を切り欠いた形態で円形の屋外劇場を抱える。三つの棟は幾何学的な造形を貫徹し、それらと自然との衝突が表現者への刺激になることを、安藤は期待している。

This facility is located in a mountainous condition expected to provide features for "artist-in-residence" program. Considering the undulating topography of the site, atelier wing has 120m wide, 20m deep dimensions as a very long, single-floor building derived from an image of a bridge extending over a small valley. The accommodation building, which is close to one another, is also an elongated slender shape with low height based on the concept of Ando to look at those two buildings as two bridges. A central wing for exhibitions and performances holds an outside amphitheater in a form with a low, cut-out cylinder. Ando expects that those three wings realize the geometric forms, and that the collision between them and nature will be a stimulus to the artists.

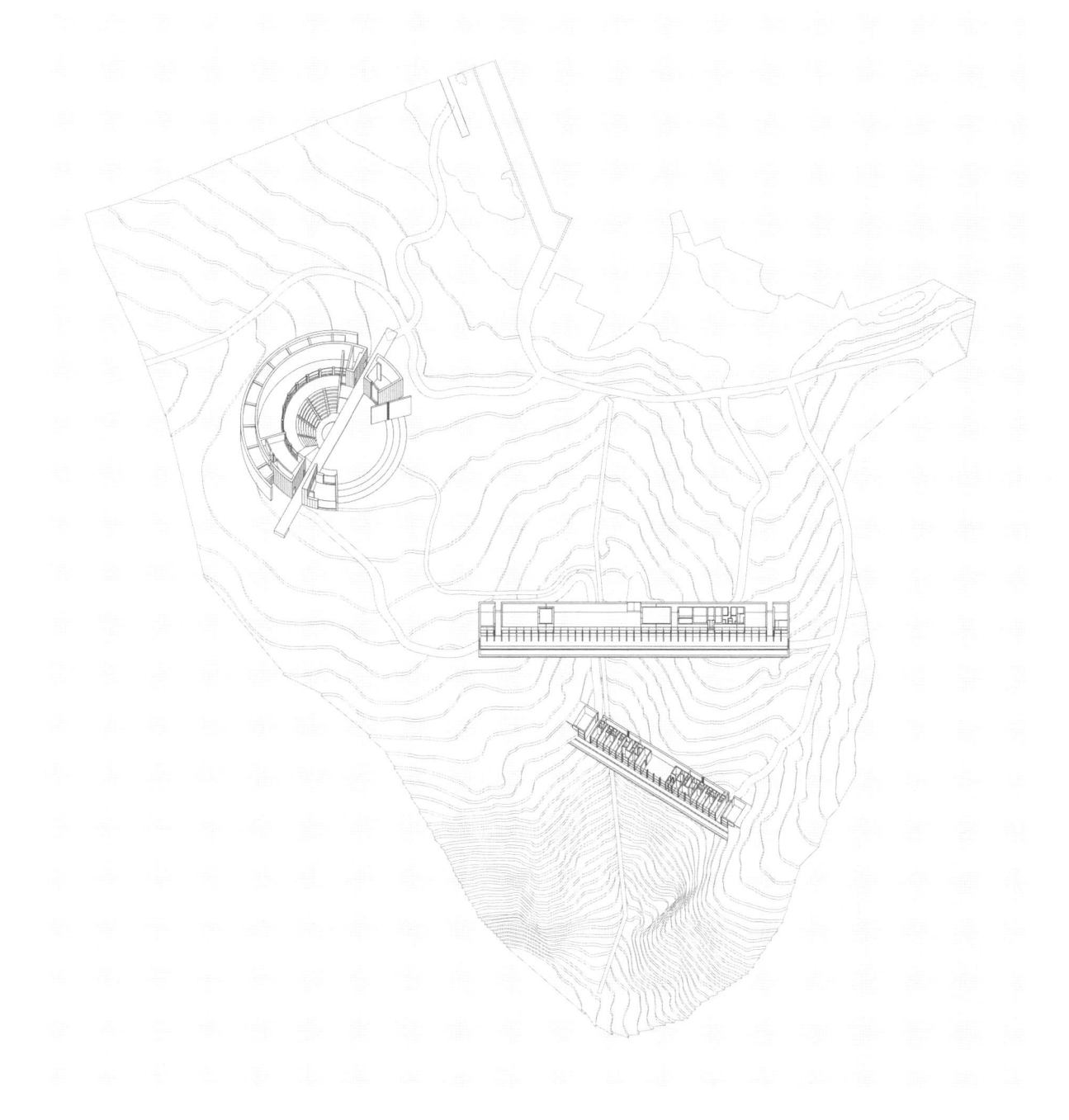

[202]

アルマーニ・テアトロ　2001
armani teatro

1. イタリア ミラノ | milan, italy
2. 設計 | design　2000.3 – 2000.9
3. 施工 | construction　2000.9 – 2001.7
4. 鉄筋コンクリート造［新築］、鉄骨［屋根部分］|
   RC, steel
5. 劇場、ギャラリー
6. 敷地 | site　9,700 m²
8. 延床 | total floor　12,300 m² [headquarters + teatro],
   3,400 m² [theater part]

世界的なファッションデザイナー、ジョルジオ・アルマーニの依頼により、ミラノ郊外の繊維工場を劇場に再生した。旧建物をひとつの敷地と見なし、そこに自立する新しい空間を誕生させた。エントランスから劇場まではパサージュと呼ぶ相応な長さの通路で、その中央には柱を一列でならべた。千席規模の劇場はファッションショーなど多様な用途を想定して可動式の客席を配した。入れ子になった新しい空間と元の建築との余白の部分に演出の余地があり、そこの活用を期待したいと安藤は述べている。

In response to a request from Giorgio Armani, the world-renowned fashion designer, a textile mill in the suburb of Milan was converted and regenerated as a theater. By looking at the old building as a "site", a new independent space was created on the site. A "passage" is a pathway in certain length to lead visitors from the entrance to the theater space, and a colonnade is positioned in the center of the passage. The theatrical space with a capacity of 1,000 spectators is expected to be used in various purposes, thus the seats of the theater are in movable type. Ando says that there is room for production in the void space between the original building and the new nested space, and that it is expected for the active usage there.

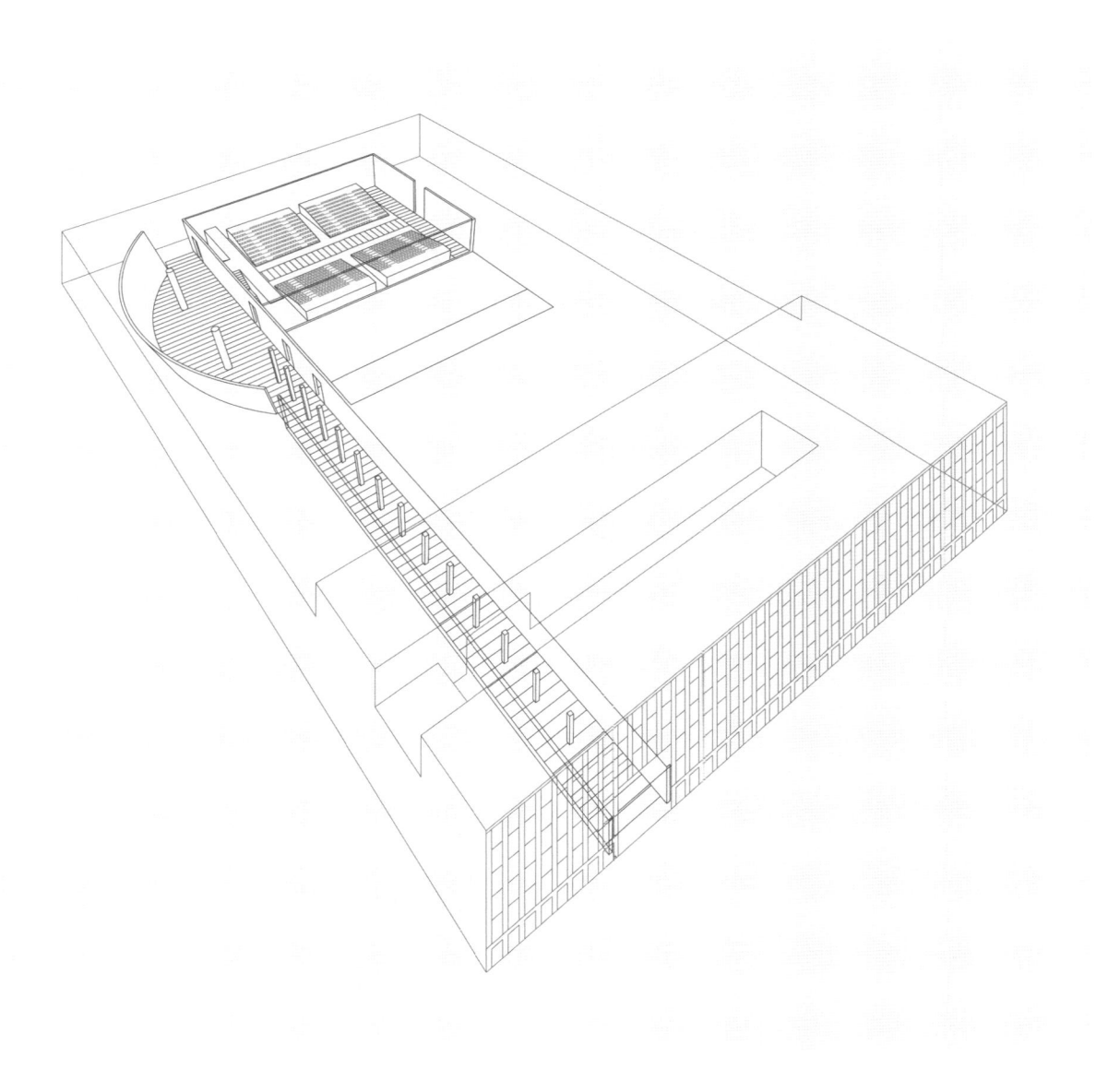

[203]

ピノー現代美術館　2001
françois pinault foundation
for contemporary art

1. フランス セガン島｜ile seguin, france
2. 設計｜design　2001.1 – 2005.4
3. 設計競技｜design competition
4. 鉄骨鉄筋コンクリート、一部鉄筋コンクリート、鉄骨｜RC, SRC, steel
5. 美術館｜museum of art
6. 敷地｜site　32,000 m²
7. 建築｜building　11,000.0 m²
8. 延床｜total floor　32,700 m²

パリの西郊外、ビヤンクールのセガン島に計画された美術館建築。セガン島は、フランスを代表する自動車メーカー、ルノーの工場があった場所としても知られる。ファッション関係の起業家として成功をおさめたフランソワ・ピノーは、この地に世界級の現代美術館の新設を計画し、国際コンペの結果、安藤が設計者に選ばれた。セーヌ川に浮かぶ立地を生かし、来訪者が川面に親しめる案だったが、諸般の事情で実現しなかった。ピノーは諦めず、安藤とともにイタリア・ヴェネチアの旧税関の現代美術のギャラリーへの改装などを実現、さらに2018年末には安藤とともにパリに帰還し、商品取引所を現代美術館に仕立て直す計画が実現する。

An art gallery planned in Seguin Island in Billancourt, a western suburb of Paris where Renault, an automobile manufacturer that represents France, used to have a factory. Francois Pinault, a successful entrepreneur in the fashion industry announced a plan to build world's largest contemporary art gallery where Ando was selected as the designer after an international contest. Although the architecture was designed fully using the location with rich nature of Seine River where visitors could feel close to the river surface, it was not materialized due to various factors. However, Pinault did not quit his endeavor. With Ando, he renovated the former customs office in Venice in Italy to a contemporary art gallery. In addition, Pinault will be back in Paris with Ando at the end of 2018 to transform the commodity exchange to a contemporary art gallery.

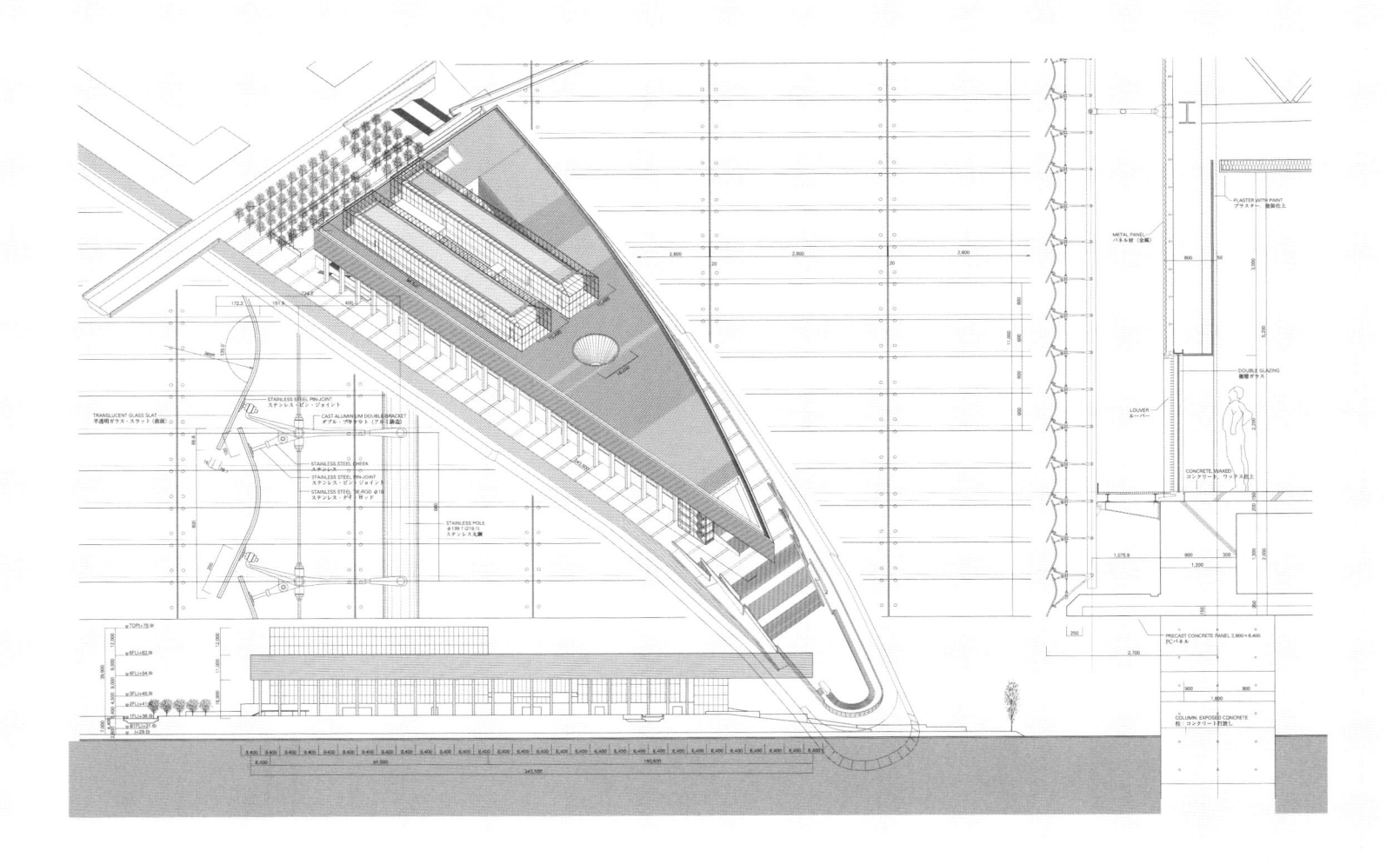

346 Complete Works

[204]
グラウンド・ゼロ・プロジェクト
2001
ground zero project

1. アメリカ ニューヨーク | new york, USA
2. 設計 | design　2001.12 – 2002.1
3. 設計競技 | design competition
5. 都市計画 | urban planning

2001年9月11日にニューヨークで起きた同時多発テロで倒壊した「ワールド・トレード・センター」の跡地の再開発プロジェクトとして、安藤は業務施設などをすべて排して、鎮魂のための「墳墓」を提案した。隆起した曲面は、地球の赤道半径を踏まえ、高さ20メートルに設定された。異文化の対立が悲劇を招いたと安藤は考え、資本主義と宗教的信念の衝突を克服する、モニュメントの前での新たな対話を期待した。

As the redevelopment project of the World Trade Center that collapsed due to terrorist attacks in New York on September 11, 2001, Ando proposed the Tomb that has no business facility but only for the repose of souls. The bulging round surface expresses the earth's equator and situated at the height of 20 meters. Ando considered that conflicts between different cultures resulted in this tragedy and anticipated that collision of capitalism and religious beliefs can be prevented by new dialogue exchanging thoughts in front of this monument.

[205]

4×4の住宅（東京）　2001
4 x 4 house (tokyo)

1. 東京都千代田区 | chiyoda-ku, tokyo
2. 設計 | design　2001.6
3. 構想案 | concept
4. 鉄筋コンクリート | RC
5. 住宅 | detached house
6. 敷地 | site　23.0 m²
7. 建築 | building　18.1 m²
8. 延床 | total floor　63.2 m²

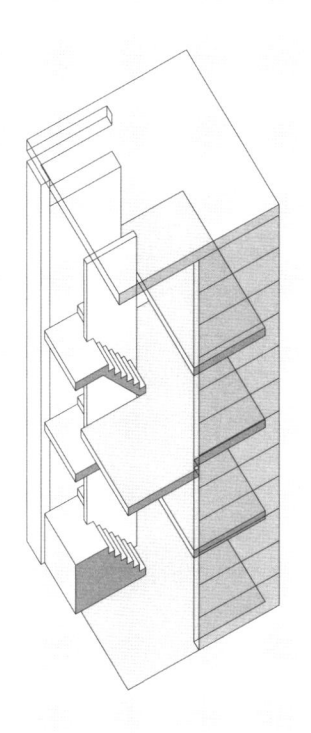

同様の作品名の神戸市の住宅が瀬戸内海の海岸際ゆえに制約があったのに対し、東京のこの住宅はビルの谷間の4.8メートル角の狭小地に計画された。そこに、その名の通り4メートル角の正方形を底面とする直方体の住宅が設計された。各階の面積の4分の1は昇降のための階段に充てた。2階の床の4分の1をエントラスにつながる吹き抜けとし、3階はテラスを設け、頭上の4階の床を4分の1の吹き抜けにした。残った面積に、1階はバスルーム、2階は子ども部屋、3階は食堂、4階は夫婦の寝室を配した。二つの吹き抜けを確保することで、容積以上の開放感を期待した。→参照 [218]

The residence with the same name in Kobe City had restriction due to being on a coast of the Seto Inland Sea, the residence in Tokyo was planned in a narrow space of 4.8m square located between buildings. A rectangular solid housing was designed with a 4m square floor area. A quarter of the area of each floor was used for a stairway, a quarter of the 2nd floor for open ceiling connected to the entrance, a terrace on the 3rd floor, and a quarter of the 4th floor for open ceiling. The remaining areas were used for a bathroom on the 1st floor, children's room on the 2nd floor, dining room on the 3rd floor, and the couple's bedroom on the 4th floor. → see also [218]

[206]

西田幾多郎記念哲学館　2002
nishida kitaro museum of philosophy

1. 石川県かほく市 | kahoku, ishikawa
2. 設計 | design　1997.4–1999.3
3. 施工 | construction　2000.1–2002.3
4. 鉄筋コンクリート造、一部鉄骨（壁式ラーメン構造）| RC, steel (wall-type frame structure)
5. 博物館 | museum
6. 敷地 | site　12,314.8 m²
7. 建築 | building　1,656.9 m²
8. 延床 | total floor　2,951.7 m²

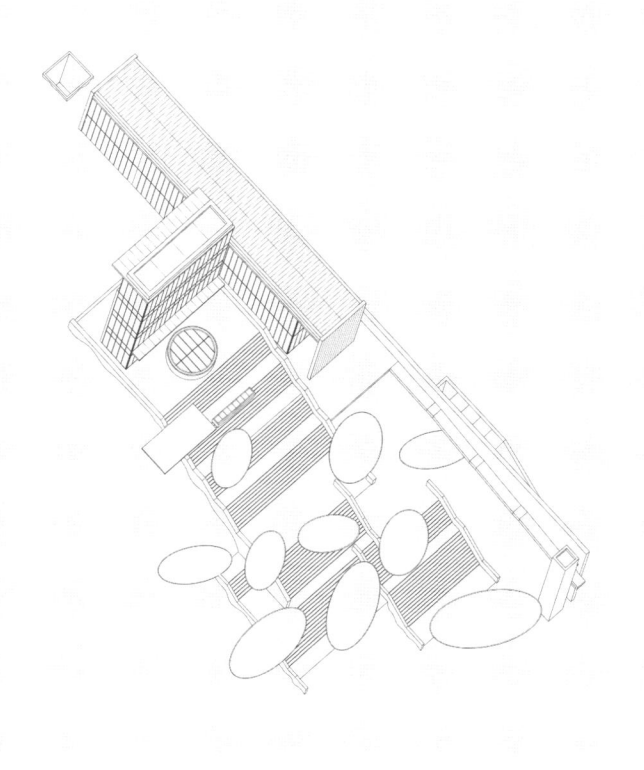

小高い丘のうえに建物は位置している。造園された斜面の階段を登るのは、西田哲学への旅だと安藤はいう。記念館にそびえるガラスの塔の最上階は四周を見渡せる展望ラウンジとなっており、登ってきた斜面に不規則に配されていた楕円形の花壇の位置が確かめられる。また、そこに座すことで自身の内面と向き合い、世界の広がりを体感できるとした。地下にはホールへのホワイエと展示室の端部の二か所に自然光の降り注ぐ空間が配され、「空（くう）」の心境に誘う場が設えられている。

This building is located on top of a small hill. Ando described that it is the journey to the field of Kitaro Nishida's philosophy to go up the staircase placed on the landscaped slope. The top floor of the glass tower rising up over the memorial hall building is a viewing lounge with 360°views, so that visitors can identify the location of the oval-shaped flowerbeds distributed irregularly over the slope they climbed up. By sitting there, visitors can face their own inner side, and feel the expanse of the surrounding world. There are two spaces shed by natural light, both located at the edge parts of a hall's foyer and a gallery room on underground level — those are the places to invite visitors to step into the state of "nil".

346 Complete Works

[207]
国立国会図書館
国際子ども図書館（レンガ棟）
2002
the international library of children's literature

1. 東京都台東区｜taito-ku, tokyo
2. 設計｜design　1996.8 – 2000.3
3. 施工｜construction　1998.4 – 2002.1
4. 鉄骨、鉄筋コンクリート［明治期建物］、鉄骨補強煉瓦造［昭和期建物］、鉄筋コンクリート｜steel, RC
5. 図書館｜library
6. 敷地｜site　5,433.8㎡
7. 建築｜building　2,018.2㎡
8. 延床｜total floor　6,671.6㎡

1906年開設の帝国図書館は、正面右側の部分のみが完成しただけで、日露戦争の戦費増大による財政逼迫で、車寄せのある正面玄関などはつくられないままに終わった。開場100周年を機に、子ども図書館に改装する計画を安藤が担当した。正面外観では、既存の建物と15度で交差するガラスのエントランスボックスを挿入して新旧の対比を試みた。また背後では、1階から3階までの外壁にガラスのカーテンウォールのボックスをかぶせて、もとの外壁の位置に設けた廊下から後庭が見通せるようにした。館内の機能配置も一新され、旧建物は新たな命を得た。→参照［324］

The Imperial Library of Japan, established in 1906, was built under the tight financial condition of expanding war expenditure for Russo-Japanese War. Therefore, the building was completed only for the front right side, and the main entrance with porte cochere was not constructed. Ando was in charge of planning to transform this library building into a children's library for the 100th anniversary of its establishment. In the front exterior, contrast between old and new was tried by inserting a glass entrance box intersecting with the existing building at 15°angle. Backside of the building is covered by a box with glass curtain wall extending from the 1st floor to the 3rd floor, and new corridors provided at the original exterior wall allow visitors to look over the backyard garden space. The functional arrangement inside the library was renewed, and the old building got a new life.
→ see also [324]

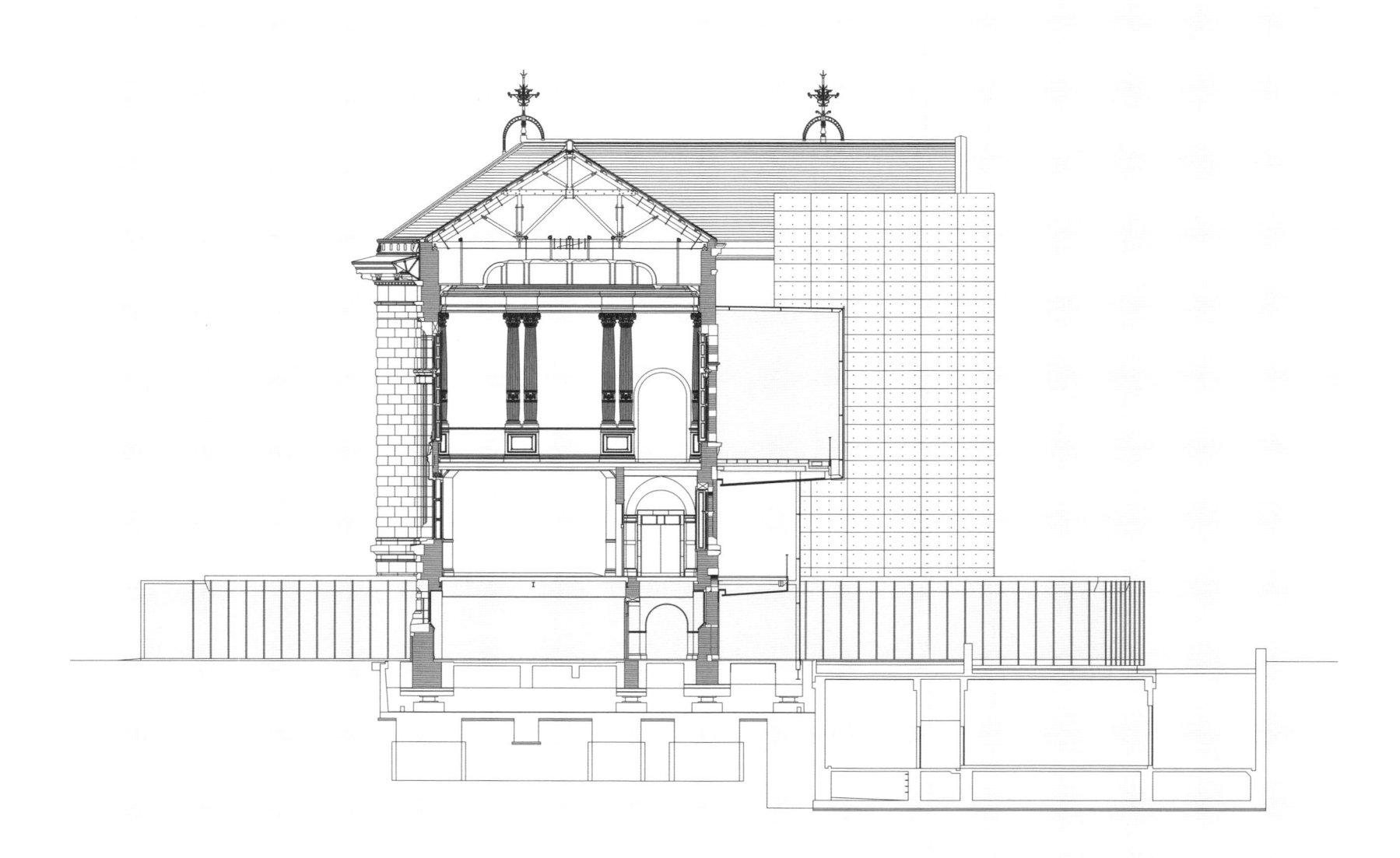

[208]
フォートワース現代美術館
2002
modern art museum of fort worth

1. アメリカ フォートワース | fort worth, USA
2. 設計 | design　1997.6–1999.9
3. 施工 | construction　1999.9–2002.9
4. 鉄筋コンクリート | RC
5. 美術館 | museum of art
6. 敷地 | site　44,370 m²
7. 建築 | building　9,240.0 m²
8. 延床 | total floor　14,820 m²

立地は、ルイス・カーンの名作「キンベル美術館」と隣り合わせ。安藤は臆することなくこの難題に挑んだ。カーンのヴォールトのシリンダーの並ぶ構成を意識して、5本のガラスの箱を並列させる展示空間を実現した。ガラスの箱の内部に、コンクリートの箱が入れ子となる展示室が挿入された。鑑賞者はコンクリートの箱のなかでは集中して作品に向き合い、そこを出て次の箱に移るときにはガラスを通して見る人工池のさざ波に心を和ませる。この緩急を持たせた鑑賞路の設定は、「キンベル美術館」のヴォールト天井がもたらす静かな豊穣と対比的な躍動感を実現している。→参照 [343]

The location is next to "Kimbell Art Museum", the masterpiece by Louis I. Kahn. Ando challenged this difficult project without hesitation. Considering the structure of Kahn's original museum building with vault cylinders placed in parallel, exhibition spaces of the new museum are composed of five glass boxes placed in parallel, with concrete boxes inserted and nested in the glass boxes for providing exhibition rooms. Visitors concentrate and face the art works inside of those concrete boxes. When leaving a box and moving to the next one, they feel at ease by the ripples on the artificial water basin viewed through a glass wall. This setting of the viewing path with the tempo has realized the feeling of spiritual dynamism in contrast with the quiet fertility produced by the vault ceiling of "Kimbell Art Museum". → see also [343]

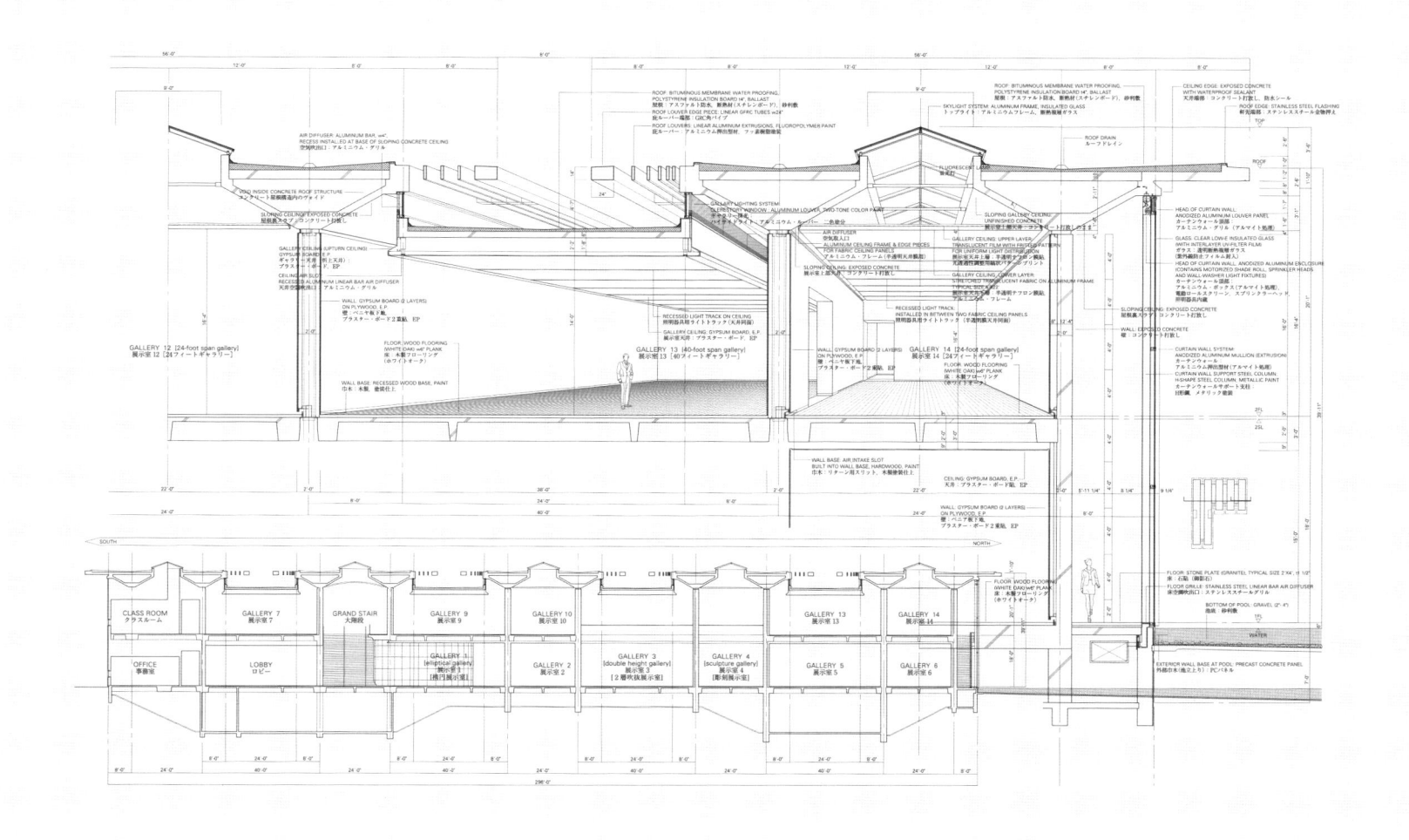

[209]

マンチェスター市
ピカデリー公園　2002
piccadilly gardens regeneration,
manchester

1. イギリス マンチェスター｜manchester, UK
2. 設計｜design　1999.5 – 2000.4
3. 施工｜construction　2000.4 – 2002.6
5. 公園｜park
6. 敷地｜site　80,000 m²
8. 延床｜total floor　500 m²

産業革命発祥の地のひとつ英マンチェスターの中心に位置する「ピカデリー公園」の再生コンペに当選し、実現にこぎつけた。公園は荒れ果てていたが、そこをヒューマンスケールの実感できる場とし、一帯の交通量の多い環境と遮断するために、大きな曲面壁を設けた。街路側から曲面壁の切れ目を通って公園に進むと、眼前に新設された楕円の池が目に入る。大阪とマンチェスターは姉妹都市でもあり、この公園をきっかけに工業都市の新たな表情が生まれることを安藤は期待した。

After winning the competition to regenerate "Piccadilly Gardens" located in the center of Manchester as one of the birthplaces of Industrial Revolution, this project has been realized. Although the park was desolated—in order to transform this place into a park in humane scale, and separate this place from the surrounding area with heavy traffic. a large, curved wall was built. When going into the park space from the town street through the boundary on this curved wall, a newly built oval shaped pond appears to the eyes of visitors. Osaka and Manchester are sister cities and Ando expected a new expression of this industrial city would be created through this park as a core.

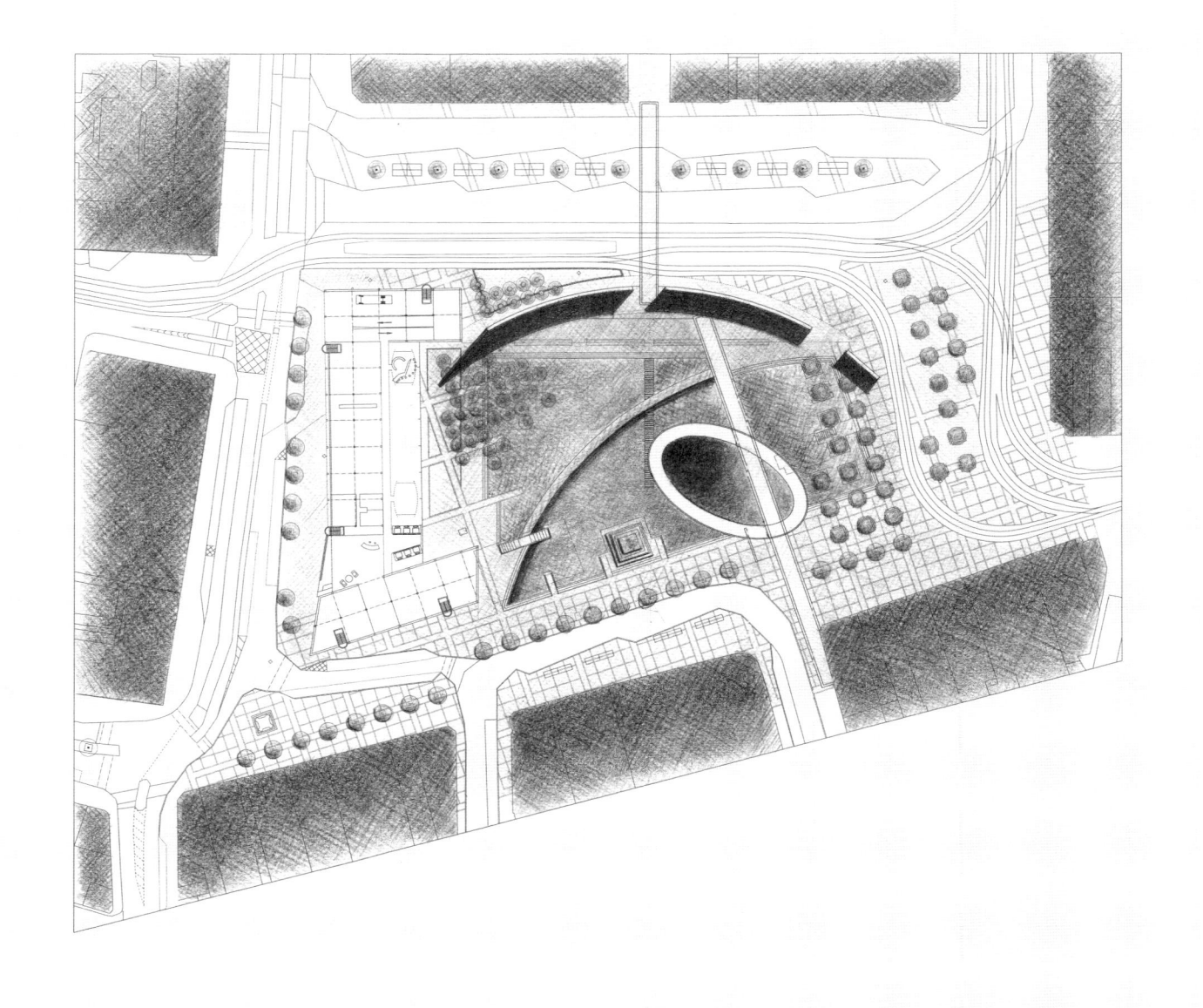

[210]
アサヒビール神奈川工場
ゲストハウス　2002
guesthouse, asahi kanagawa brewery
.
1. 神奈川県南足柄市 | minamiashigara, kanagawa
2. 設計 | design　1998.9 – 2001.9
3. 施工 | construction　2000.8 – 2002.4
4. 鉄骨 [ゲストハウス]、木造 [ビール園]、
   鉄筋コンクリート [物産館] | steel, wood, RC
5. 工場、店舗 | factory, shop
6. 敷地 | site　349,320.7 m²
7. 建築 | building　2,310.7 m²
8. 延床 | total floor　5,203.6 m²

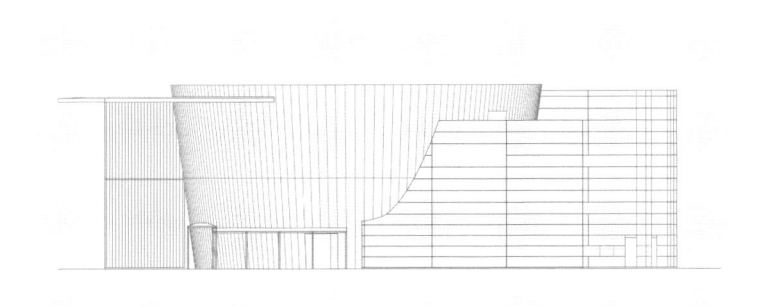

神奈川県南足柄市の広大な敷地に広がるビール工場見学者のためのウエルカムホール、レストラン、物産館から成る複合施設。傾斜したガラス壁のウエルカムホールと他の2棟は施設内道路を挟んだ離れた位置にあるが、段差を水が下るなど水路を配したランドスケープが一体感を演出している。敷地のマウンドで物産館の施設が隠れるようにするなど建築は控え目な存在とした。水庭に面したレストランの屋外席などで緑の環境を尊重した成果が確かめられる。
.
A composite facility for visitors who come for a beer plant tour and that includes the welcome hall, restaurant, and product exhibition area on a vast property in Minamiashigara City, Kanagawa Prefecture. Although the welcome hall with a slanted glass wall and another two buildings are separated by a road in the facility, the landscape arranged with flow of water in water channels provide integrated atmosphere to the facility. The product exhibition facility is hidden by earth mound to show the modest presence of architecture. A design that takes importance on green environment can be observed from the outdoor seats of the restaurant facing a water garden.

[211]
アウディジャパン本社ビル　2002
audi japan headquarters
.
1. 東京都世田谷区 | setagaya-ku, tokyo
2. 設計 | design　1999.11 – 2001.1
3. 施工 | construction　2001.2 – 2002.2
4. 鉄筋コンクリート（地下）、鉄骨鉄筋コンクリート、
   鉄骨 | RC, SRC, steel
5. ショールーム、本社 | showroom, head office
6. 敷地 | site　1,168 m²
7. 建築 | building　700.7 m²
8. 延床 | total floor　2,911 m²

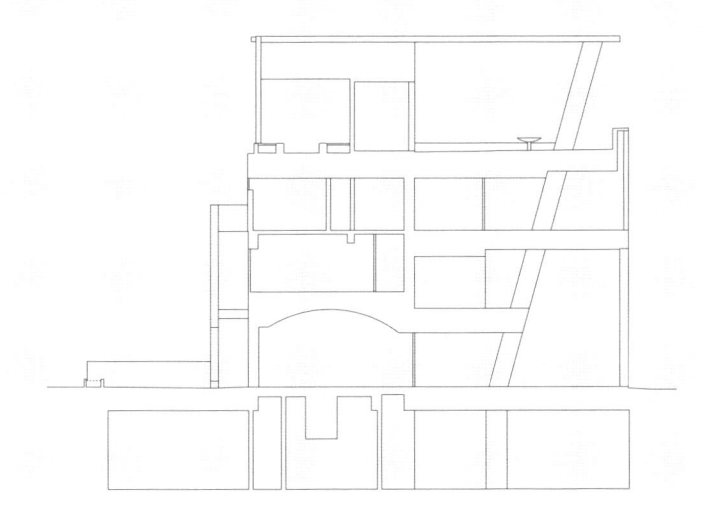

ドイツの自動車メーカー、アウディの製品を扱うショールームとオフィス。自動車交通が頻繁な世田谷・中原街道に面した立地。建物の上階をすりガラスで覆い、内部は傾斜したコンクリート柱のならぶショールームとした。この傾いた柱は屋上のペントハウスの部分にも顔をのぞかせ、建築にひとつのリズムを与えている。昼間は明るい自然光に彩られているが、日が落ちると内部照明が大きな行灯のようになって一帯を照らしだす。

A showroom of products and an office of Audi, a German automobile manufacturer. A property facing Nakahara-kaido Road in Setagaya, a location with heavy traffic. The top floor of the building is covered with frosted glass and the inside the building has a showroom with slanted concrete columns. These columns appear at the penthouse area on the rooftop to add a harmonic rhythm to the architecture. Bright natural light shines on the building during the day and the interior lighting shines the surrounding as a large street light at night.

346 Complete Works

[212]
加賀市立錦城中学校　2002
kinjo junior high school, kaga

1. 石川県加賀市 | koga, ishikawa
2. 設計 | design   2000.9 – 2001.8
3. 施工 | construction   2001.9 – 2002.12
4. 鉄骨 | steel
5. 中学校 | junior high school
6. 敷地 | site   51,102.0 m²
7. 建築 | building   5,615.3 m²
8. 延床 | total floor   7,514.9 m²

老朽化した中学校の建て替え。主たる教室棟を楕円とすることを基本に構成した。中央に楕円の吹き抜けの空間を設け、教室はそこに向き合うように配置した。吹き抜けの空間を学年を超えて子どもたちが一体化する場ととらえ、そこをまた自分たちで自由に発想して使う「もうひとつの教室」と位置づけた。吹き抜けのトップライトからの自然光が優しく、木質仕上げの教室にまで及ぶ。学校建築のあり方への積極的な提案がそこに読み取れる。

This is a rebuilding project of a deteriorated school building of a middle school. The building was configured with a basic concept of producing the main classroom building in oval shape. The double-height space in oval shape was provided in the core of the main building, while classrooms are arranged around the space to face with it. This open ceiling space is designated as the place for children to get mingled beyond grades, which is also freely defined by themselves to use as "another classroom". The natural light from the top light of the double-height space is gentle, and it extends to the classrooms finished in wood. This project reflects positive suggestions of Ando to propose a concept of an architecture for education purpose.

[213]
灘浜ガーデンバーデン　2002
nadahama garden baden
.
1. 神戸市灘区 | nada-ku, kobe
2. 設計 | design　1999.11–2000.10
3. 施工 | construction　2000.11–2002.3
4. 鉄筋コンクリート | RC
5. 健康運動施設 | wellness facilities
6. 敷地 | site　10,359 m²
7. 建築 | building　1,075.2 m²
8. 延床 | total floor　2,263 m²

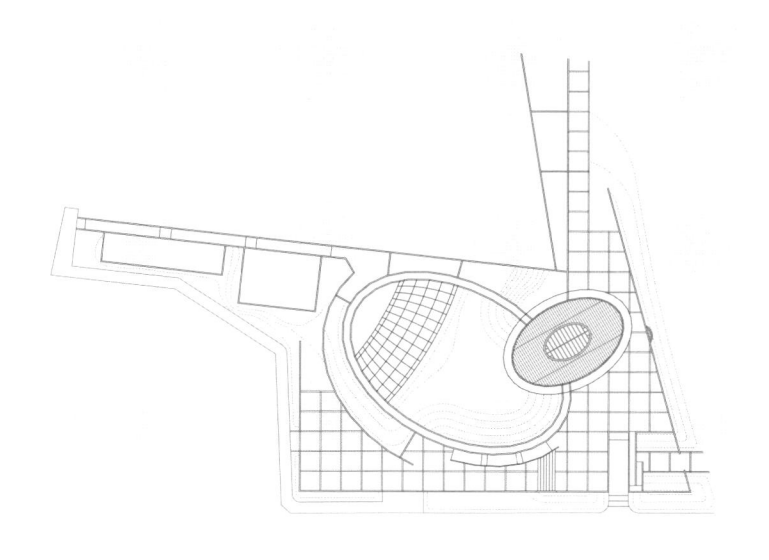

神戸の臨海部、神戸製鋼所などの工場施設と激しい自動車交通のために存在感の薄い運河沿いの都市公園が、温浴施設などで再生された。公園内の少し奥まった位置に楕円の区画を設定し、緑で覆われたサンクンガーデンを設けた。楕円の3分の1ほどを覆うシェル構造の屋根が北端に架けられ、その下に温水プールなどを備えた「バーデゾーン」を設けた。一方、地上レベルの南端に、大きな楕円の一部と重なる配置で小さめの楕円壁の棟が造られ、温泉の集まる「スパゾーン」となった。起伏ある緑の庭園を楽しみながら、健康維持に勤しめる。
.
An urban park at a seaside area of Kobe along a canal that had a weak presence due to heavy automobile traffic and plant facilities including Kobe Steel was restored to a new warm-bathing facility. An oval section was placed at a slightly deep position in the park where a large sunken garden covered by greenery is created. A shell structure roof was built to cover 1/3 of the oval on the north end and a Bade Zone with a heated swimming pool and other facilities were placed under the roof. On the other hand, a building with a relatively small oval wall was built on the south end on the ground level at a position to partially overlap the large oval to form a Spa Zone where hot spring facilities are gathered.

[214]
コキュ・オフィスビル　2002
cocue office building
.
1. 東京都渋谷区 | shibuya-ku, tokyo
2. 設計 | design　2000.4–2001.4
3. 施工 | construction　2001.5–2002.3
4. 鉄筋コンクリート | RC
5. 事務所 | office
6. 敷地 | site　249.3 m²
7. 建築 | building　143.2 m²
8. 延床 | total floor　382.5 m²

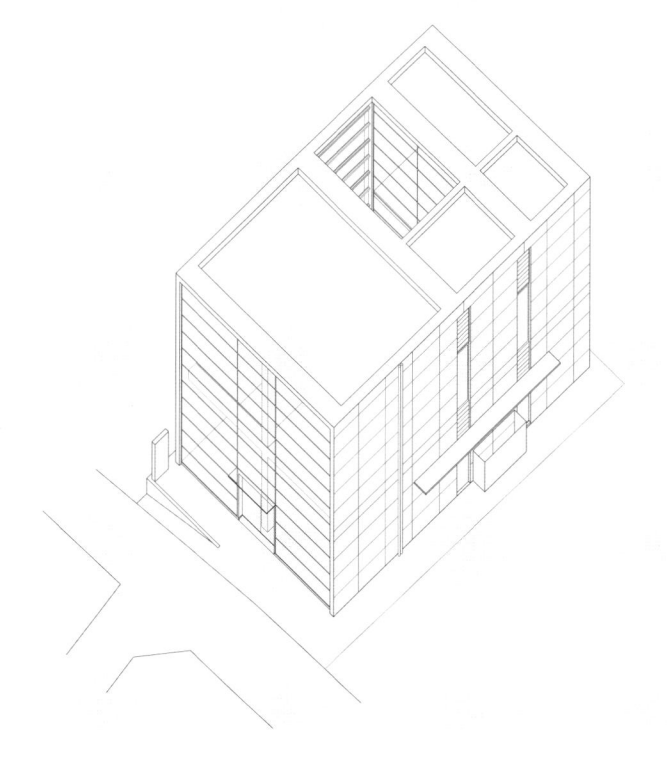

ファッションブランドのブティックとオフィスのために設計された東京・代官山の建築。表通りから眺めると両端の薄いコンクリート壁の間に大きなガラス窓が上階まで広がる。建設当初、1階はすりガラスになっていて、店舗内を敢えて通りからは見えにくい仕立てをとった。反対に2階から上の吹き抜けのオフィス部分は通常の透過ガラスで、開放的な空間が路上からでも確かめられた。背後に屋外のテラスがあり、前後から自然光が内部に流れ込む。現在は国内ブランドのショップとなっている。

An architecture designed for a boutique and office of a fashion brand company in Daikanyama, Tokyo. When observed from the front street, a large glass window extends to the upper floor on a concrete wall that is thin on both ends. The 1st floor had frosted glass when the building was constructed to intentionally block the view of inside the shop from the street. On the other hand, the office area with an open ceiling from the 2nd floor up had normal clear glass, which gave a sense of spaciousness that could be observed even from the street. A rooftop terrace is situated at the rear area allowing natural light to enter inside from the front and rear areas. This building is currently used as a shop of a Japanese brand.

[215]
尾道市立美術館　2002
onomichi city museum of art

1. 広島県尾道市 | onomichi, hiroshima
2. 設計 | design   2000.7 – 2001.3
3. 施工 | construction   2001.10 – 2002.9
4. 鉄筋コンクリート，一部鉄骨 | RC, steel
5. 美術館 | museum of art
6. 敷地 | site   3,088 m²
7. 建築 | building   1,118.5 m²
8. 延床 | total floor   1,498 m²

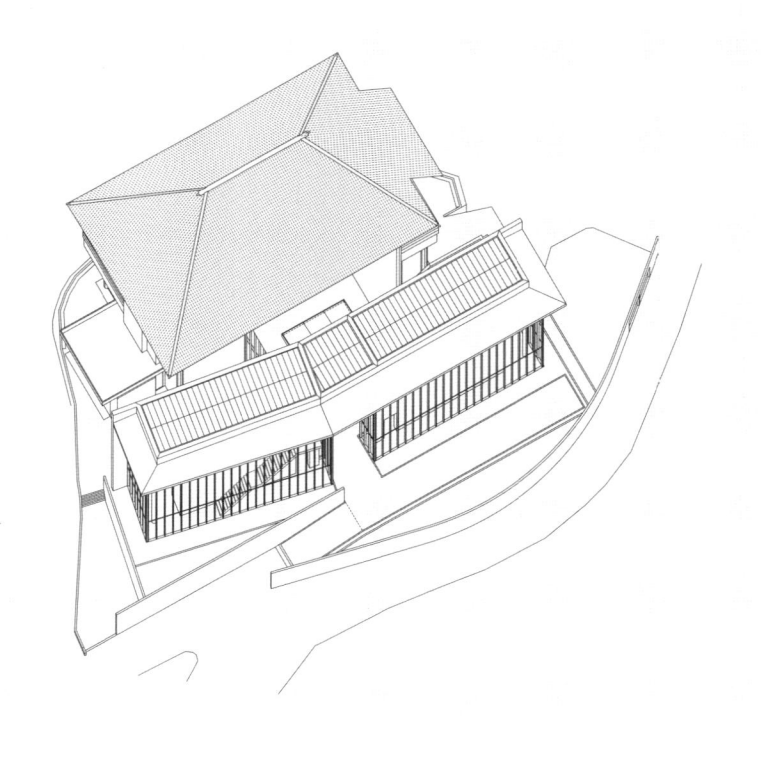

地元の文化遺産、西郷寺を模して1980年に造られた日本風傾斜屋根の旧美術館本館を保存し、背後に安藤のコンクリートの箱が置かれた。瀬戸内の海の眺望が楽しめる旧建物に対して、安藤は明確に区画するかのようなコンクリート打ち放しの壁を建て、自らの全面ガラスの窓からは山腹に広がる陸地側の公園の風景を堪能できるように仕立てた。人気の観光地、千光寺公園に新たな魅力が付加された。

Ando's concrete box was placed behind the conserved former main hall of the art gallery with a Japanese-style slanted roof built in 1980 imitating Saigoji, which is a cultural heritage standing in the local area. In contrast with the former building that offers an enjoyable view of the Seto Inland Sea, Ando built a wall of exposed concrete as it was blocking the view of the sea to fully enjoy the scenery of the park on the land side that expands on the mountain slope through the full-glass window. This architecture added another appealing piece to the well-known sightseeing area that was rearranged at Senkoji Park.

[216]
砂漠の家・乗馬施設　2002
house & stable
for tom ford and richard buckley

1. アメリカ ノース・ガリステオ | north galisteo, USA
2. 設計 | design   2002.7 – 2006.3
3. 構想案 | concept
4. 鉄筋コンクリート | RC
5. 住宅 | detached house
6. 敷地 | site   2,280 m²
8. 延床 | total floor   2,000 m²

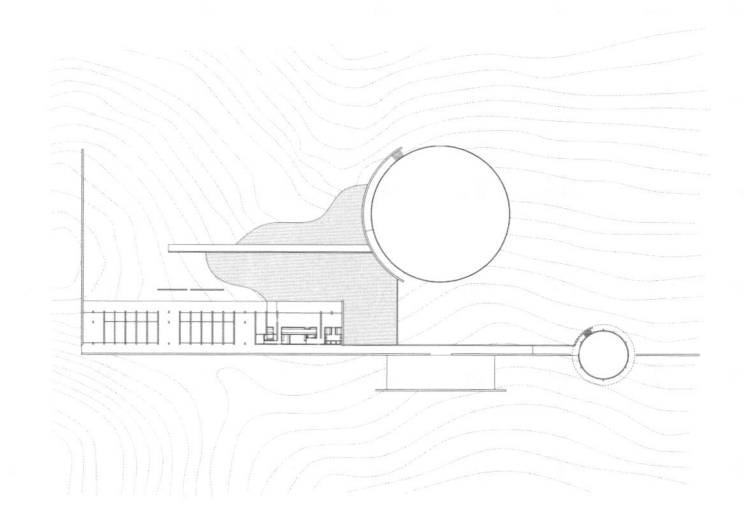

米ニューメキシコの乾燥地帯に、ファッションデザイナーのための別荘と乗馬施設が計画され、後者だけが2008年に実現した。乗馬施設は矩形平面の棟と、水を介して配された巨大な円形のグラウンドからなる。水を渡る直線的な橋も幾何学に貢献している。安藤は敷地のすべてが見渡せる小高い場所を立地に選び、広大なキャンバスに自身の美学を展開した。馬は10頭が飼われ、米国の多くの成功者に倣って、無限のフロンティアの国ならではの施設が実現した。

A vacation house and a horse riding facility for a fashion designer were planned in the dry region of New Mexico in the U.S., only the latter of which was realized in 2008. The facility has a rectangular solid building and a huge ground for horse riding with a pool situated in between. A straight line of the bridge is contributing to the geometry form as well. Ando chose the elevated area that can observe the whole property as a large canvas to develop his aesthetics. The facility in a country of infinite frontiers was materialized with 10 horses following many who have achieved success in the U.S.

[217]
野間自由幼稚園　2003
noma kindergarten

1. 静岡県伊東市 | ito, shizuoka
2. 設計 | design　2001.4 – 2002.2
3. 施工 | construction　2002.3 – 2003.1
4. 鉄骨 | steel
5. 幼稚園 | kindergarten
6. 敷地 | site　16,514.9 m²
7. 建築 | building　1,478.8 m²
8. 延床 | total floor　1,097.4 m²

北里柴三郎の別荘跡地で半世紀の歴史を持つ幼稚園の建て替え。大きなひとつの屋根の下に子どもたちが集うことを前提に木造を構想したが、防火面での法規制のため骨格を鉄骨にする一方、内部空間は可能な限り木で仕上げた。軒が緩やかな曲線を描く大屋根の下に、長大な縁側の空間がつくられた。その床も木製として園児が素足で遊べるようにした。手で触れる木の部分は不燃処理を施したスギ材を用い、壁などは木造で均質な平面になるように仕立てた。

This is a project to replace a kindergarten with a history of 50 years, which is built on a former site of a cottage owned by Shibasaburo Kitasato. In earlier stage of the design, the building was going to have wooden structure on the premise that children would gather under one large roof. However, the framework was made into steel frame due to the regulation on the fire prevention side, while its interior space was finished in wood material as much as possible. Under a large roof with eaves in gentle curve, a very long veranda space was provided, and the floor finish of this space in wood material allows children to play around in bare foot. The part of the wood touched with hands are made of Japanese cedar wood materials applied with incombustible treatment, while the walls are finished in uniformly smooth surface even though the use of wood material.

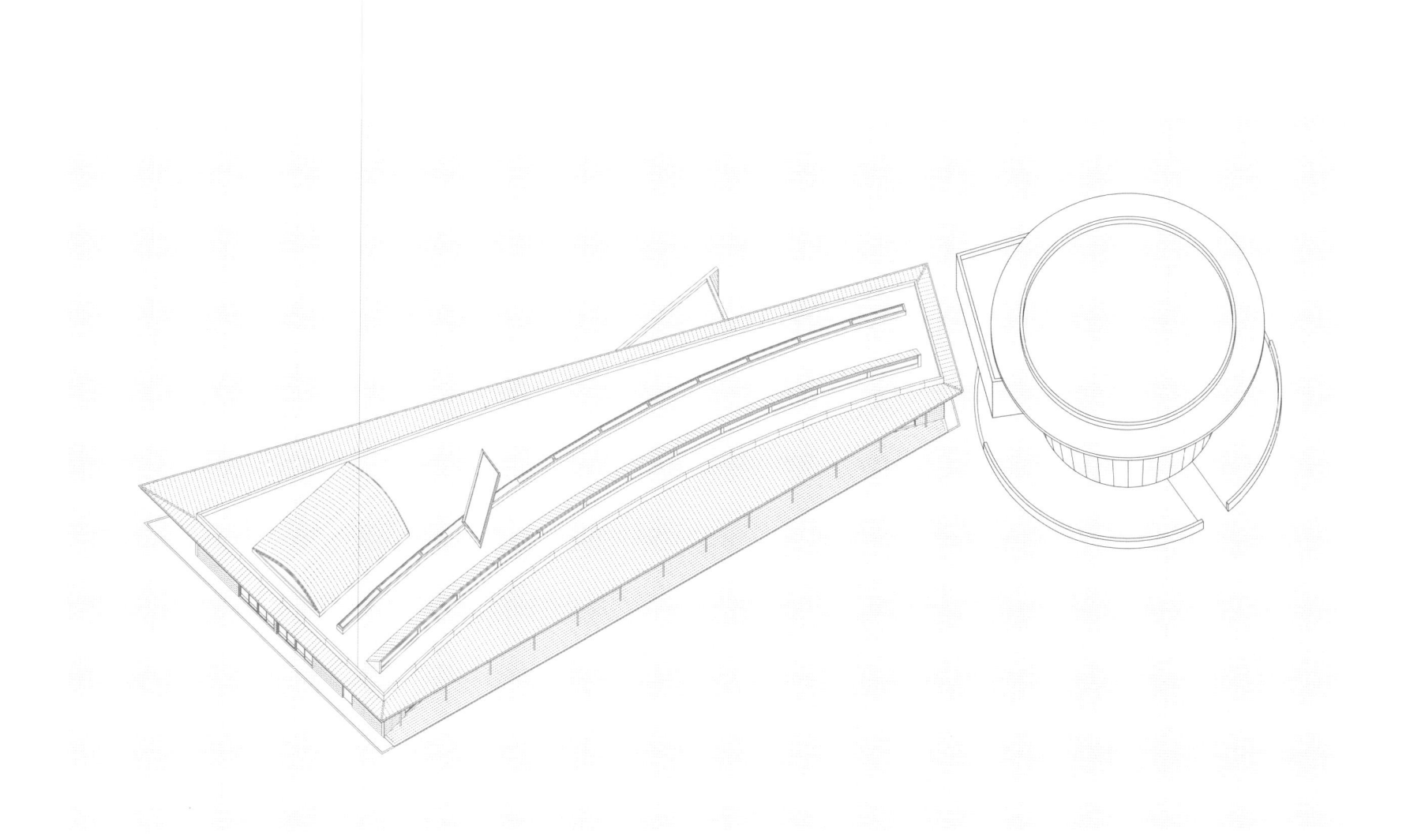

[218]

4×4の住宅　2003
4 x 4 house

1. 神戸市垂水区 | tarumi-ku, kobe
2. 設計 | design　2001.4–2002.4
3. 施工 | construction　2002.8–2003.2
4. 鉄筋コンクリート | RC
5. 住宅 | detached house
6. 敷地 | site　65.4 m²
7. 建築 | building　22.6 m²
8. 延床 | total floor　117.8 m²

神戸市垂水区の明石海峡、そこに架かる明石大橋を展望する砂浜に接した場所に立地している。雑誌が安藤の設計を希望するオーナーを募集する企画で、立地も勘案して、この住宅が実現した。4階建ての建物の平面はその名の通り4メートル角の正方形。階段の制約が小さい最上階は、1メートル左右にずらした配置になっている。海に向けて立方体の飛び出す印象的なシルエットが大きな風景と対峙しうると安藤は自負している。→参照 [205]

Located in Tarumi Ward, Kobe City next to a beach where Akashi Channel and the Akashi-Kaikyo Ohashi Bridge can be observed. It was a project of a magazine that invited an owner who would like Ando to design the house. Ando examined the location as well and the house was built. The planform for the four-story building is a square four meters on each side as indicated by the name. The top floor is offset by one meter on the right and on the left since the restriction of the stairway is limited. Ando is proud that the impressive silhouette of a cube projecting outward to the ocean is standing well against the wide scenery. → see also [205]

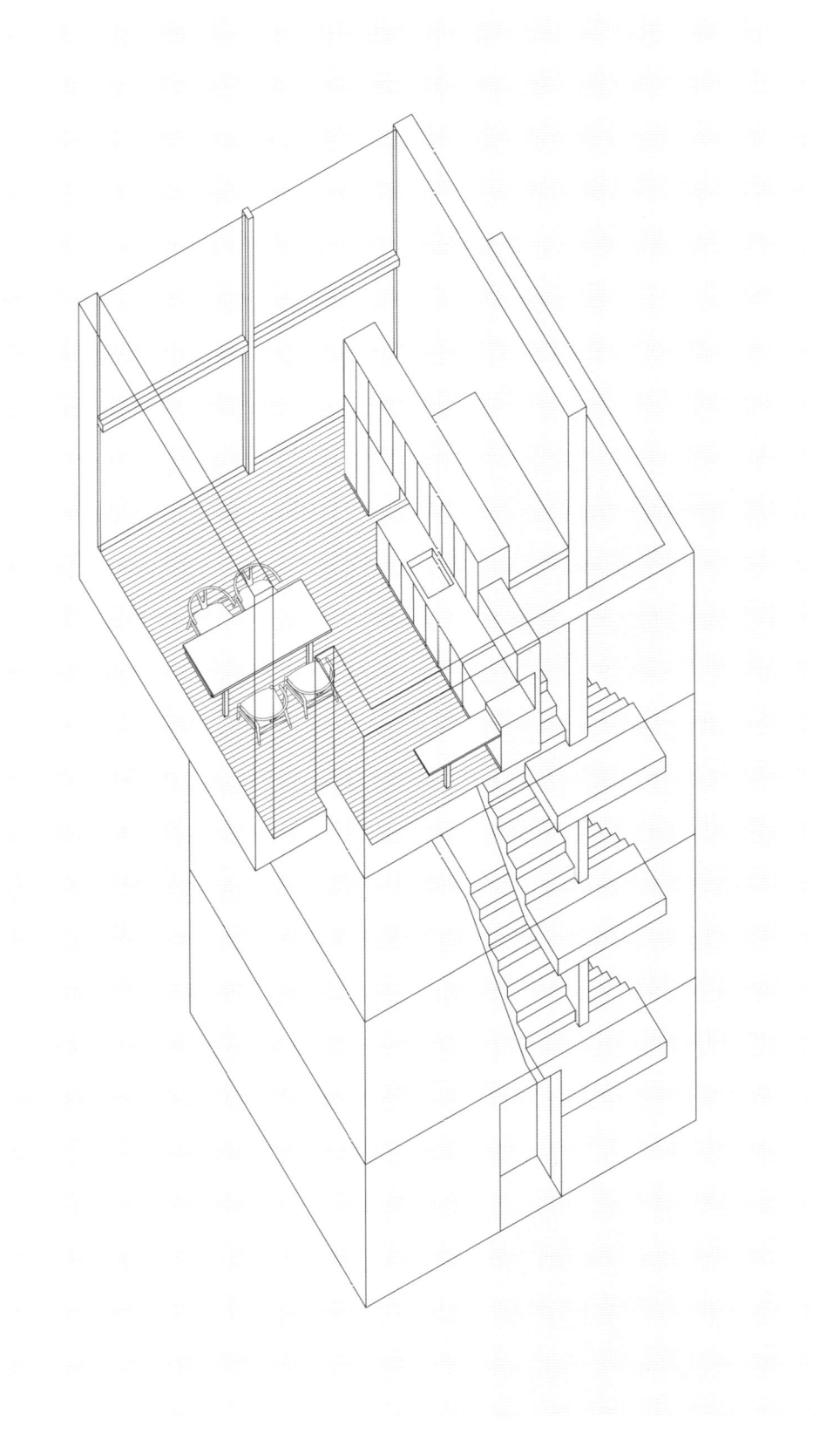

[219]
マリブの住宅　2003
house in malibu

1. アメリカ マリブ ｜ malibu, USA
2. 設計 ｜ design　2003.12
3. 構想案 ｜ concept
4. 鉄筋コンクリート　RC
5. 住宅 ｜ detached house
7. 建築 ｜ building　20.5 m²
8. 延床 ｜ total floor　411.9 m²

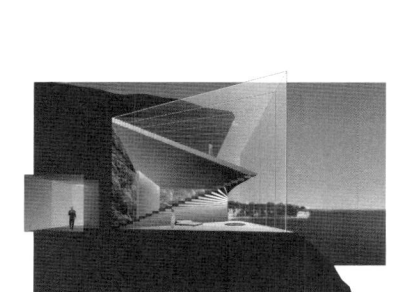

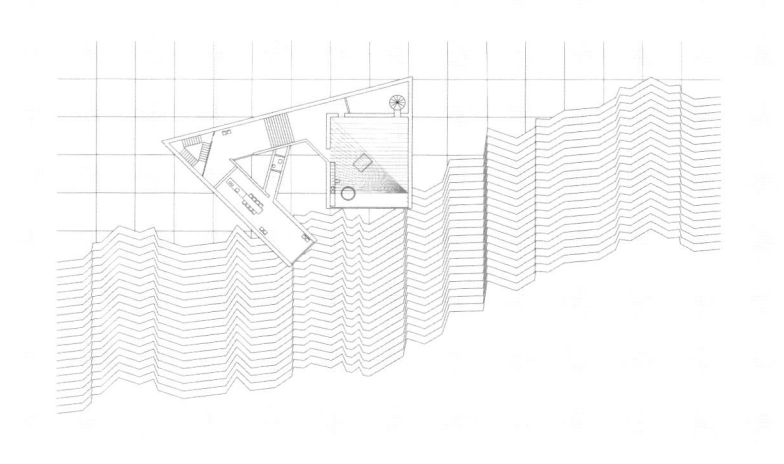

米西海岸ロサンゼルス郊外のマリブの海辺の崖地に幾何立体を挿入する形で、「光と、音と共に暮らす家」が計画された。直方体、三角柱、そして立方体が、住み手を包む住空間を構成し、内部では放物双曲線で壁を段状に仕立て、理想的な音響空間が出現するとした。また、マリブの明るい自然光、海の音も堪能することができる。1958年のブリュッセル万博で、クセナキスとル・コルビュジエが手がけたフィリップスのパビリオン「電子詩曲」へのオマージュを意識した提案となっている。

A house living with light and sound was planned in a form inserting geometric solids to the cliff by the coast of Malibu in the suburbs of Los Angeles on the west coast of the U.S. The living space is created by rectangular solids, triangle poles and cubes. Ideal acoustical space was provided by forming interior wall surfaces to have parabola and hyperbola lines in stages. In addition, bright natural light and the ocean sounds of Malibu can be enjoyed inside the rooms. It is designed as homage to "Le poeme electronique", which was the Philips pavilion created by Xenakis and Le Corbusier at the Brussels Expo in 1958.

[220]
県立ぐんま昆虫の森　昆虫観察館 2004
gunma insect world / insect observation hall

1. 群馬県桐生市 ｜ kiryu, gunma
2. 設計 ｜ design　1997.5 – 2001.8
3. 施工 ｜ construction　2002.6 – 2004.10
4. 鉄筋コンクリート、鉄骨鉄筋コンクリート、鉄骨 ｜ RC, SRC, steel
5. 博物館 ｜ museum
6. 敷地 ｜ site　483,000 m²
7. 建築 ｜ building　4,309.0 m²
8. 延床 ｜ total floor　5,084.3 m²

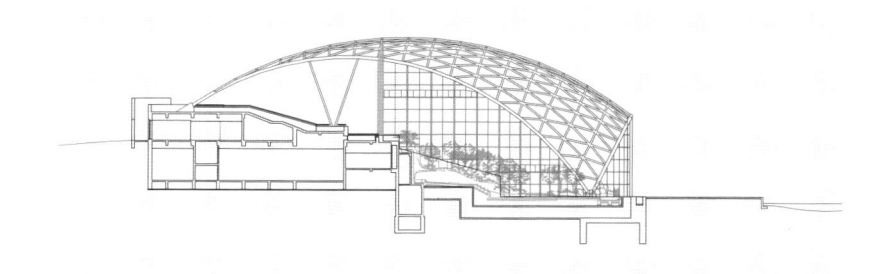

広さ48ヘクタールの「ぐんま昆虫の森」は、里山の自然を子どもたちをはじめ多くのひとに体験してもらう学習施設。一帯の自然の生態を理解し、里山を歩くための入り口が昆虫観察館とされる。一辺が70メートルのスペースフレームのガラスの大屋根が目をひく。その下の水辺の大階段に腰掛けると水面の向うに里山が望める。展示室、事務室は、この大階段を上った位置に配して隠れるように仕立てた。ガラスの大屋根の右半分は生態温室となっており、周囲の植生を移植したそこにはチョウも舞う。

GUNMA INSECT WORLD is a learning place in 48 hectares of vast territory, for many people especially for children to experience and feel the nature of country side forest. INSECT OBSERVATION HALL is the entry point to walk through the surrounding country side forest and understand the ecology of the nature of the areas. Eye-catching feature of this facility is the large glass roof in space frame structure, with a length of a side in 70m. When visitors sit on a waterside large-scale staircase under this roof, they can overlook the surrounding scenery of countryside forest beyond the water surface. The right half of the large glass roof is an ecological greenhouse enveloped by vertical glass walls, and the butterflies also dance there after transplanting the surrounding vegetation.

[221]
ホンブロイッヒ／ランゲン美術館
2004
langen foundation / hombroich

1. ドイツ ノイス | neuss, germany
2. 設計 | design　1994.7 – 2002.7
3. 施工 | construction　2002.8 – 2004.7
4. 鉄筋コンクリート | RC
5. 美術館 | museum of art
6. 敷地 | site　120,220 m²
7. 建築 | building　1,860 m²
8. 延床 | total floor　3,050 m²

安藤の美術館空間のトレードマーク「ガラスとコンクリートの二重皮膜」が、ここで実現した。ドイツ・デュッセルドルフ近郊のNATOのミサイル基地の跡地が敷地。発案者のカール・ハインリッヒ・ミュラーの構想に、東洋美術のコレクターとして知られるマリアン・ランゲンが賛同し、10年がかりで美術館は形をとった。入れ子のコンクリートの箱に加えて、地下にも企画展示室がある。二重皮膜の構成を構想した記念碑的作品と位置づけられよう。

This building is also realized by the application of trademark art museum design of Ando to utilize "double-skin layer structure of glass and concrete". This site is in a former NATO missile base near Düsseldorf, Germany. The concept of a museum proposed by Karl-Heinrich Müller was supported by Marianne Langen, who is known for the collection of Eastern art, then this museum was realized after 10 years of process. In addition to the nested concrete box exhibition room, there is a room in underground level for special exhibitions. This is a monumental work making the concept of the double-skin structure.

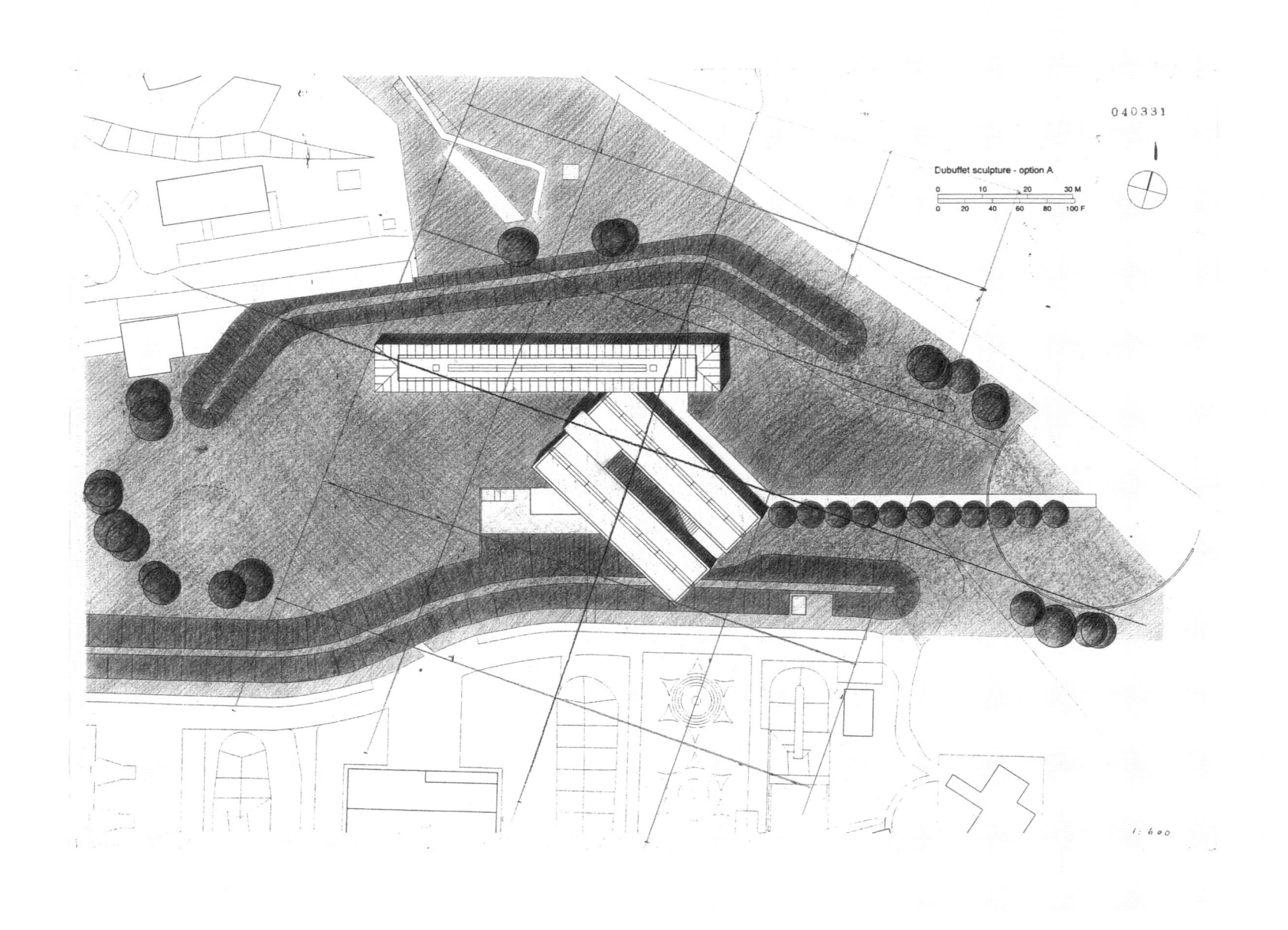

[222]
見えない家 2004
invisible house

1. イタリア トレヴィゾ | treviso, italy
2. 設計 | design　1999.6 – 2001.12
3. 施工 | construction　2002.2 – 2004.5
4. 鉄筋コンクリート | RC
5. 住宅 | detached house
6. 敷地 | site　30,600 ㎡
8. 延床 | total floor　1,450 ㎡

立地は、イタリア北部トレヴィゾの緑の平原。作品名通り、外部からの視界を遮断することがこの住宅の発注者からの最大の注文だった。広大な敷地は3ヘクタール、安藤が設計の自由度が高かったという通り、建物の本体を地下に沈め、床のレベルを何通りにも変化させ、中庭も多様に設定するなど、建築家として思う存分に腕がふるえた。地上に見えるのは直方体の開口部を持つ玄関アプローチと半地下の書斎だけで、文字通りの「見えない家」が実現した。

The site of this building is located in a green plain field of Treviso in Northern Italy. As the name of the project suggest, the most important request from the client of this house was to block visual lines from the outside into the building. According to Ando, the vast site territory in 3 hectares allowed freedom of design — the main volume of the building was buried underground, while floor levels are set in various height levels and series of courtyards in variation are provided — he could exercise his skill as an architect in full. Building elements visible above ground surface are only an entrance approach with an opening on a cuboid and a half-buried study room — as a result, literally "INVISIBLE HOUSE" was realized.

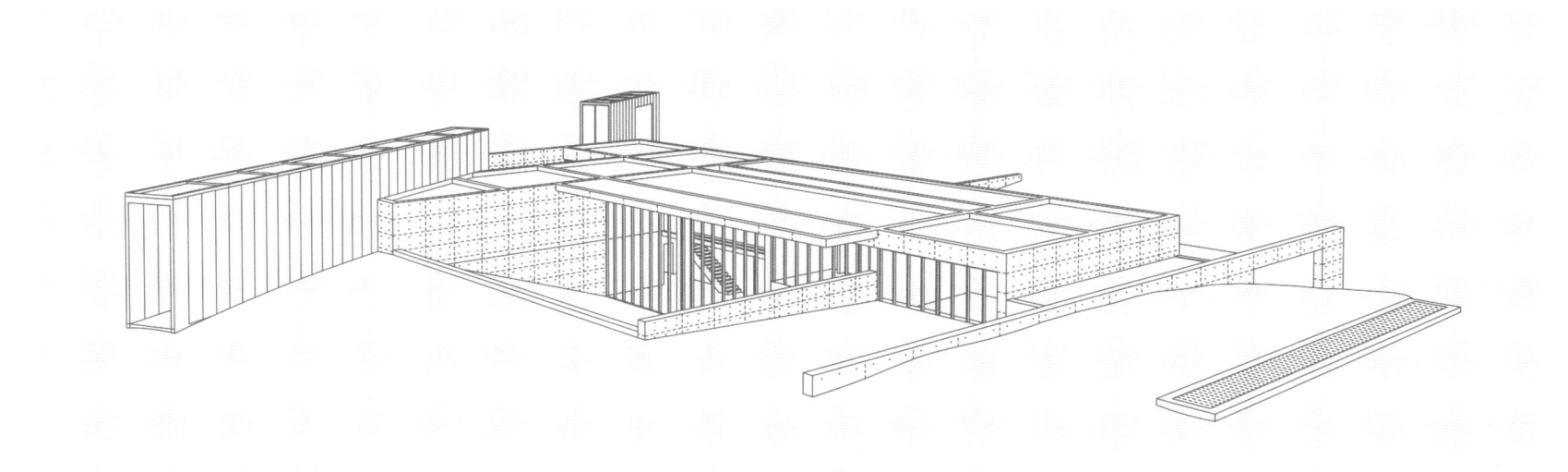

[223]

地中美術館　2004
chichu art museum

1. 香川県直島町 | naoshima, kagawa
2. 設計 | design　2000.8 – 2002.3
3. 施工 | construction　2002.4 – 2004.6
4. 鉄筋コンクリート | RC
5. 美術館 | museum of art
6. 敷地 | site　9,990.0 m²
7. 建築 | building　35.0 m²
8. 延床 | total floor　2,573.5 m²

上空からの眺めは、三角形と正方形のサンクンガーデンなどの空隙が、瀬戸内海を見おろす丘の突端に散りばめられている。安藤が追究してきた地下建築が直島の地で実現した。ウォルター・デ・マリア、ジェームズ・タレル、クロード・モネの3人の作品が固定展示されている。展示空間はそれぞれアーティスト、ディレクターとの議論を重ねて、仕上げなど最終形が決められていった。鑑賞者はまず地表のエントランスから通路を歩いて四角いサンクンコートに至り、地下の展示室のレベルに下りて、スロープや階段を昇降して3人の展示室を巡回する。→参照 [125]、[151]、[184]、[239]、[280] [309]

When viewed from the sky, this building appears as the scattered voids spaces of sunken gardens and other elements in triangle and square shapes, on the edge of a cliff looking down the Seto Inland Sea. The underground architecture concept that Ando had been pursuing was realized in the land of Naoshima. The art works of three artists, Walter De Maria, James Turrell and Claude Monet are in permanent exhibition. Those exhibition spaces were repeatedly discussed with the artists and the director, and final forms such as finishing were decided. Visitors start from the entrance on a ground level and walk through a pathway to access a sunken court in square shape; then they go down to the floor level with exhibition rooms; they go up and down slopes and staircases to move around the exhibition rooms of three artists. → see also [125], [151], [184], [239], [280], [309]

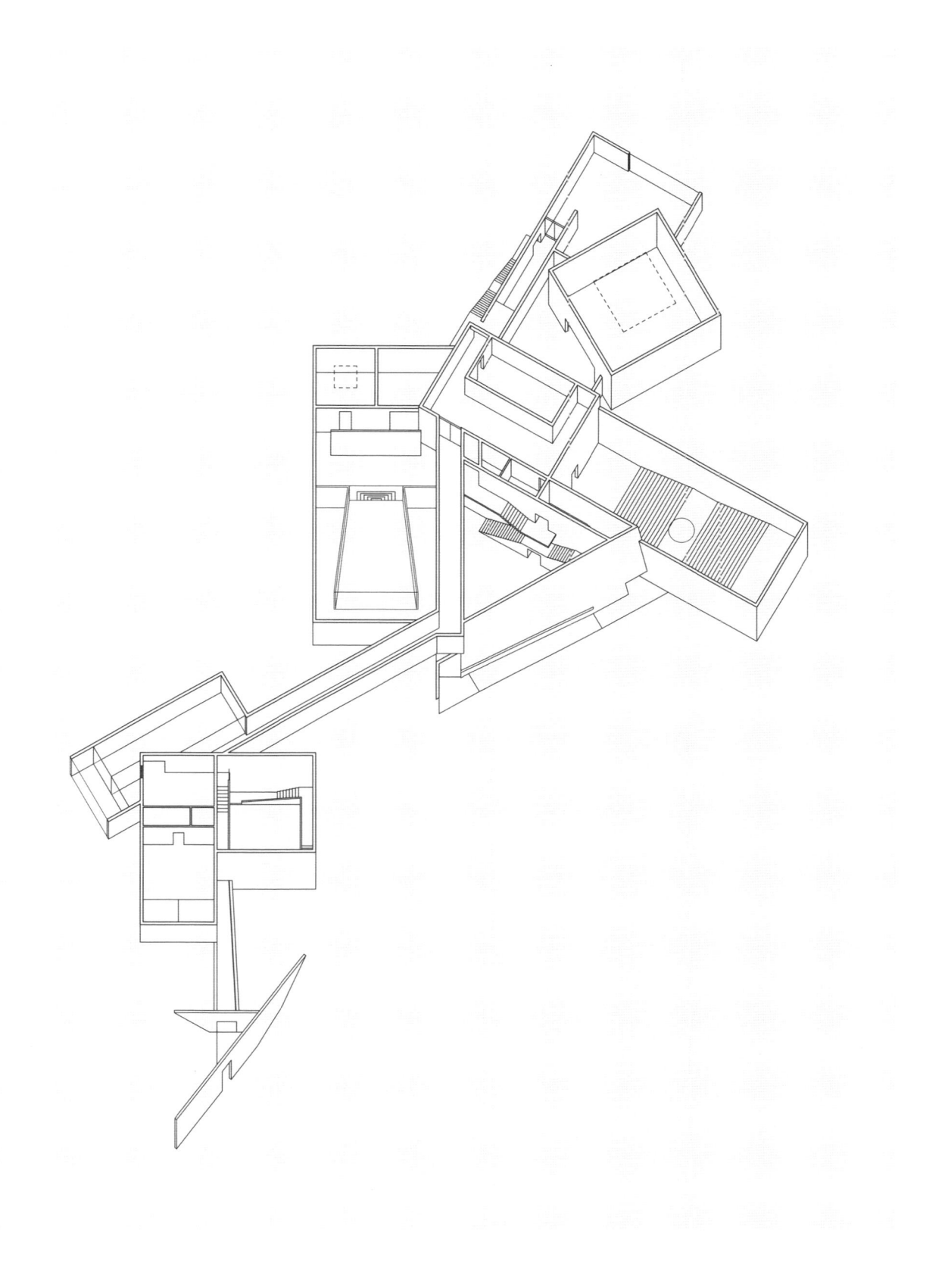

[224]
仙川・安藤ストリート
2004–2012
sengawa, ando street

東京郊外調布市の京王線仙川駅近くの住宅地を南北に貫通する都道114号線沿いの500メートルほどに安藤設計の六つの建物がならぶ。個人ギャラリーの「東京アートミュージアム」、2件の住友不動産の分譲集合住宅、小規模な賃貸オフィス、写真スタジオの入った住宅・店舗ビル、それと調布市の劇場、福祉センター、保育園が一体になった公共建築である。ハナミズキが街路樹として植えられ、安藤の考える街路の美が体感できる。

Six buildings designed by Ando stands next to each other within the range of 500 meters along the prefectural road No. 114 that passes through the residential area from north to south close to Sengawa Station of Keio Line in the suburb region of Chofu City. Those buildings consist of the private gallery the Tokyo Art Museum, two condominium buildings by Sumitomo Realty & Development, small leased offices, a building for residences, a photo studio shop, and an integrated public architecture of Chofu City with a theater, welfare center, and nursery school. Dogwood trees are planted as street trees and the beauty of an urban street of Ando's point of view can be experienced.

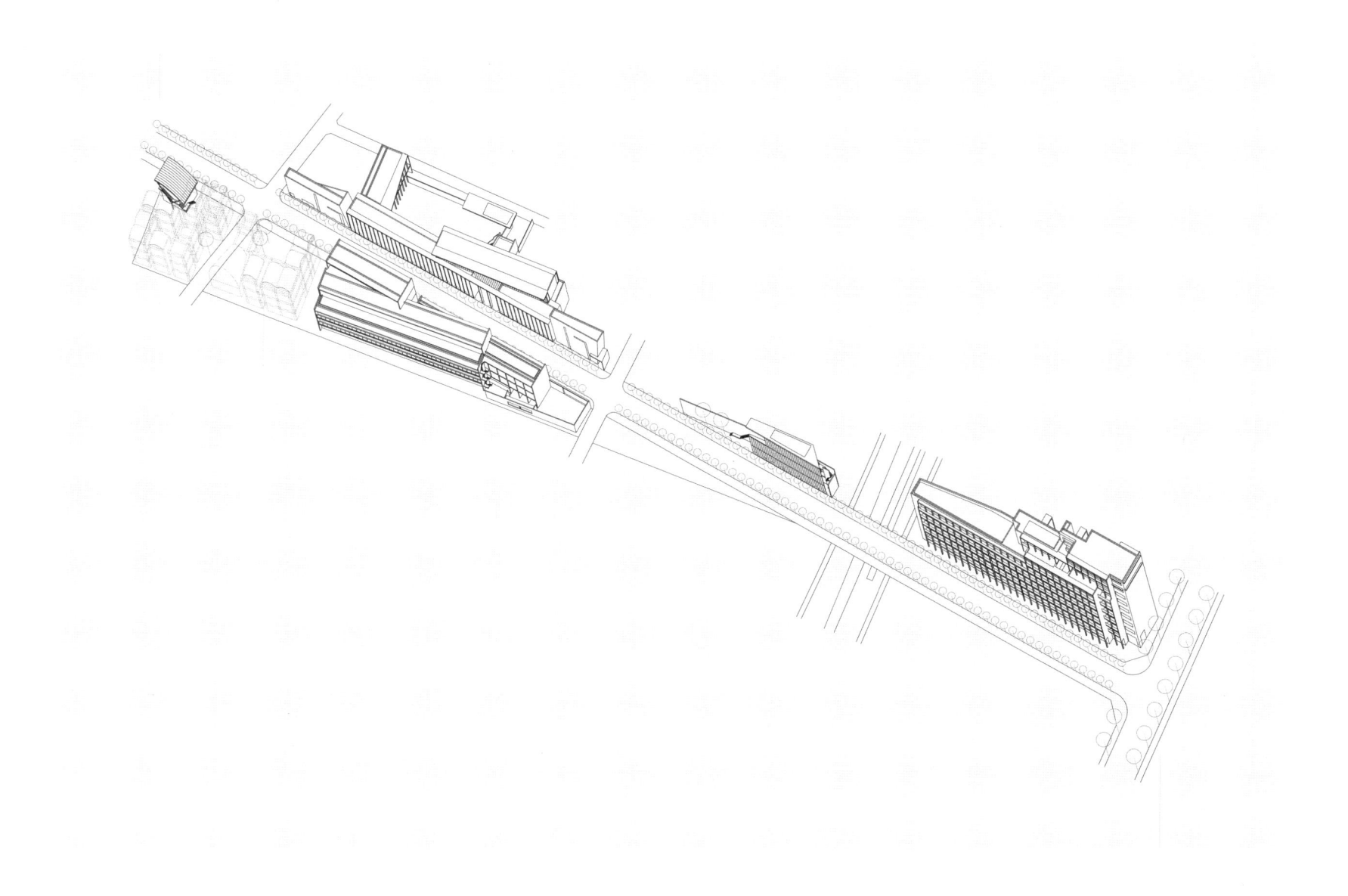

[225]
絵本美術館　2004
iwaki museum of picture books
for children

1. 福島県いわき市 | iwaki, fukushima
2. 設計 | design　2002.8 – 2003.10
3. 施工 | construction　2003.11 – 2004.12
4. 鉄筋コンクリート | RC
5. 美術館 | museum of art
6. 敷地 | site　3,237.9 m²
7. 建築 | building　492.1 m²
8. 延床 | total floor　634.1 m²

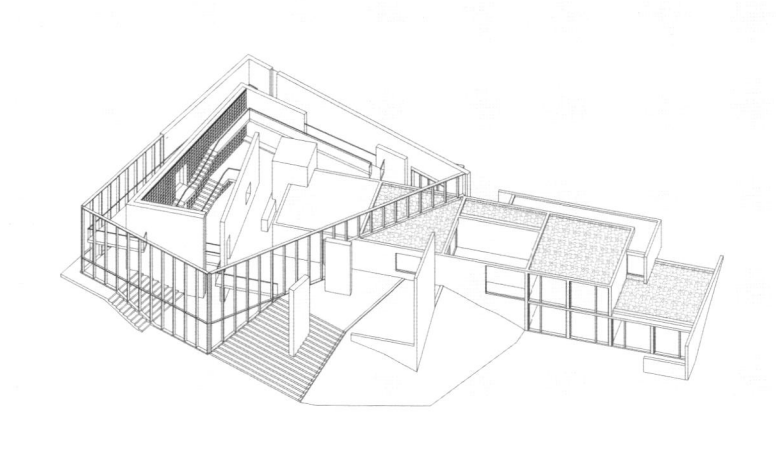

ガラスのカーテンウォールのボックスに、コンクリートの細長い箱を交差させた全体形は抽象の美学そのものだ。二つの箱が交差した部分のコンクリート壁の内側一面を書棚として展示空間にあて、クライアントの幼稚園経営者が30年の歳月をかけて集めた絵本をならべている。コンクリートとガラスの間に生じる空隙を安藤は縁側と位置づけ、子どもたちが自由に時間を過ごし、動き回れる場としている。

The whole silhouette which crossed a concrete slender box with the glass curtain box is the abstract aesthetic itself. An interior surface of a concrete wall, at the section where two boxes meet and intersect, is built as a bookshelf for exhibiting a collection of picture books gathered in 30 years, by the client of this building who runs a kindergarten. According to Ando, voids produced between the concrete box and the glass surface are viewed as veranda spaces, where children can freely move around and spend their own times.

[226]
加子母ふれあい
コミュニティセンター　2004
kashimo community center

1. 岐阜県中津川市 | nakatsugawa, gifu
2. 設計 | design　2003.3 – 2003.7
3. 施工 | construction　2003.7 – 2004.3
4. 木造 | wood
5. 研修施設 | training facilities
6. 敷地 | site　6,320.6 m²
7. 建築 | building　2,142.5 m²
8. 延床 | total floor　1,655.7 m²

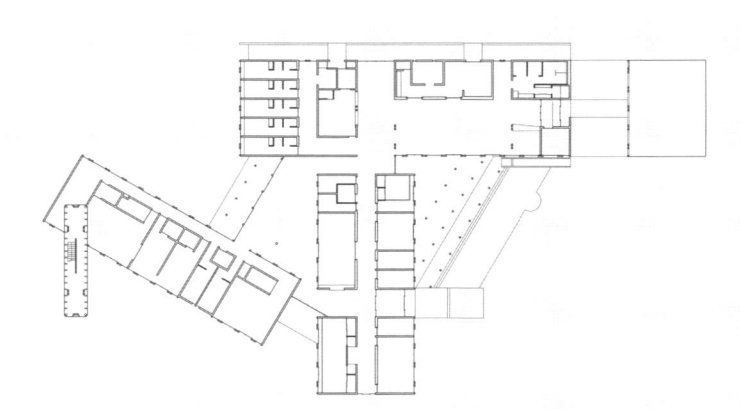

岐阜県の旧・加子母村は、伊勢神宮造営の材木を育ててきた歴史を持つ。林業を主産業とする村ということもあり、木造は設計の前提条件だった。地元産の木材の集成材を「V字」に組んだ外観は、木造建築の新たな表現への挑戦だ。山並みとの調和を考慮したゆるい傾斜の屋根の下はジグザグの特異な平面配置になっている。可能な限り、壁を排した柱による空間構成を目指し、林立する柱の空間にひとびとが集う集落の「居間」の実現を目指した。

Kashimo village in Gifu Prefecture has the history of growing trees for producing wood material used to construct Ise Jingu. The main industry of this village has been forestry, therefore the wooden structure was the prerequisite for designing this building. The exterior appearance of locally wood engineered wood in "V-shaped" is a challenge to a new expression in wooden structure building. The building has a unique floor plan in zigzag configuration under a gently sloped roof harmonized with the surrounding mountain range. The space is configured by eliminating wall structure as much as possible, in order to realize a "living room" of the village where people gather around in the space with a forest of columns.

[227]
2004 サイトウ・キネン・
フェスティバル松本・オペラ
「ヴォツェック」舞台構成　2004
set design for 2004
saito kinen festival matsumoto
/ opera "wozzeck"

1. 長野県松本市｜matsumoto, nagano
2. 設計｜design　2004
5. 舞台美術｜stage design

松本市民芸術館のこけら落とし公演、アルバン・ベルクのオペラ「ヴォツェック」の舞台デザイン。ステージ上にペットボトルを使った、内部に可動壁のある立方体空間をつくり、1920年代の孤立と絶望のオペラの舞台とした。指揮者は小澤征爾、ベルリン国立歌劇場のムスバッハが演出した。ベルクの重く沈痛な旋律が流れ、現代演目ならではの抽象的で、光が劇的な効果をもたらす舞台が実現した。前年に安藤が、やはりペットボトルで仕立てた田中一光展（東京都現代美術館）の展示の発展形だった。

A design for the stage of Alban Berg's opera Wozzeck for the opening performance of Matsumoto Performing Arts Center. Created a cubic space on the stage with a movable wall inside using plastic bottles and built the stage for an opera of isolation and despair of the 1920s. The conductor is Seiji Ozawa and the producer is Mussbach of Deutsche Staatsoper Berlin. Ando created a stage that is abstract and has dynamic light effect characteristics to the contemporary drama together with the profound and melancholy melody of Berg. It was a developed form of the Ikko Tanaka: A Retrospective (Museum of Contemporary Art, Tokyo) where Ando also created exhibition structure using plastic bottles.

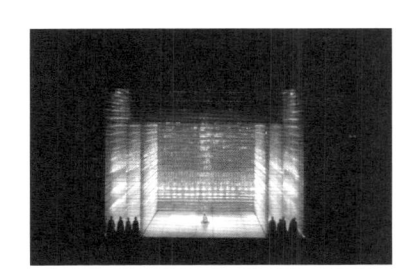

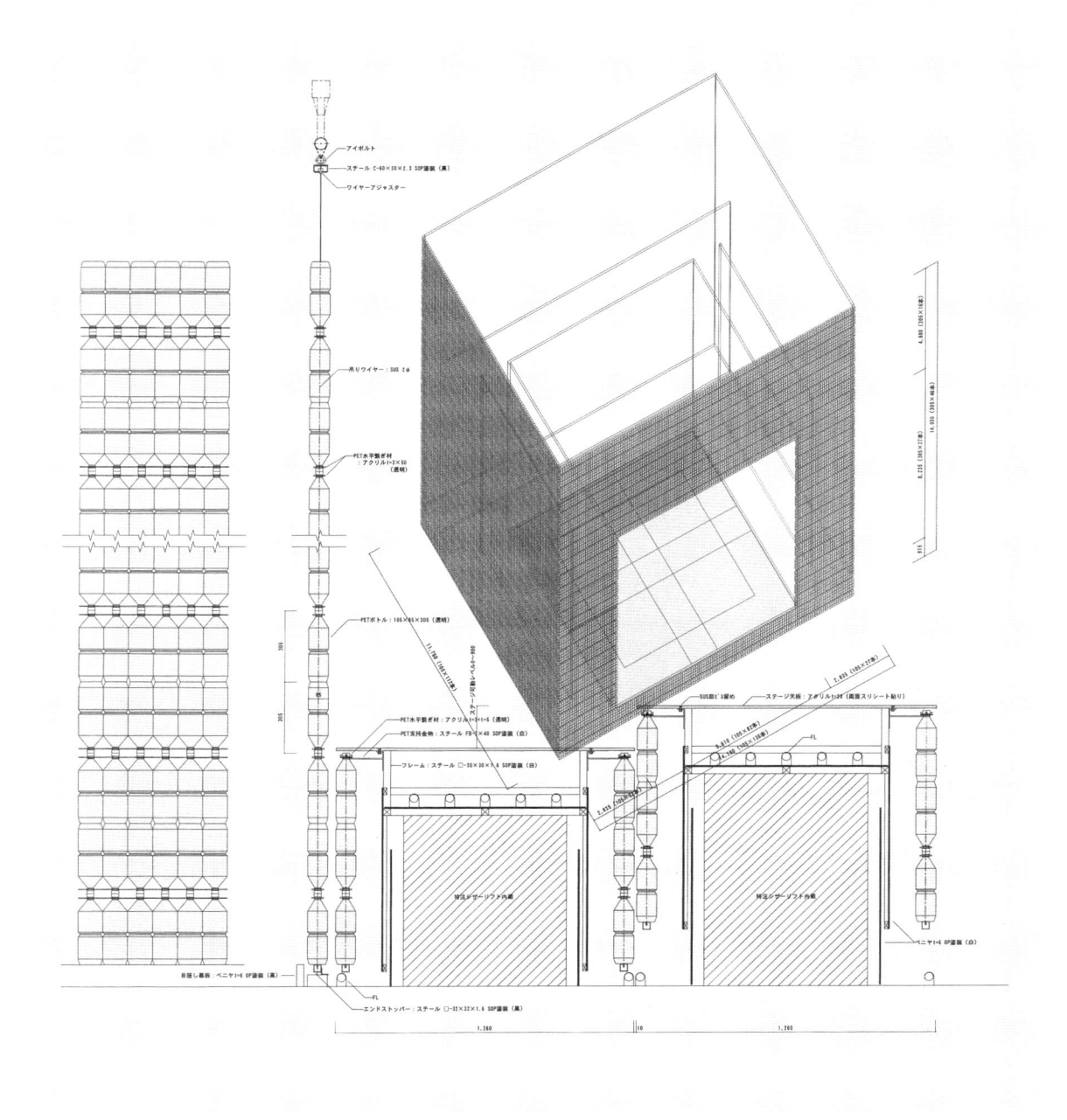

[228]
ICED TIME TUNNEL / THE SNOW SHOW 2004
2004
iced time tunnel / the snow show 2004

1. フィンランド ロヴァニエミ | rovaniemi, finland
2. 設計 | design   2003.6 – 2003.10
3. 施工 | construction   2003.12 – 2004.2
5. 野外展作品 | open-air sculpture
7. 建築 | building   244.9 m²
8. 延床 | total floor   188.4 m²

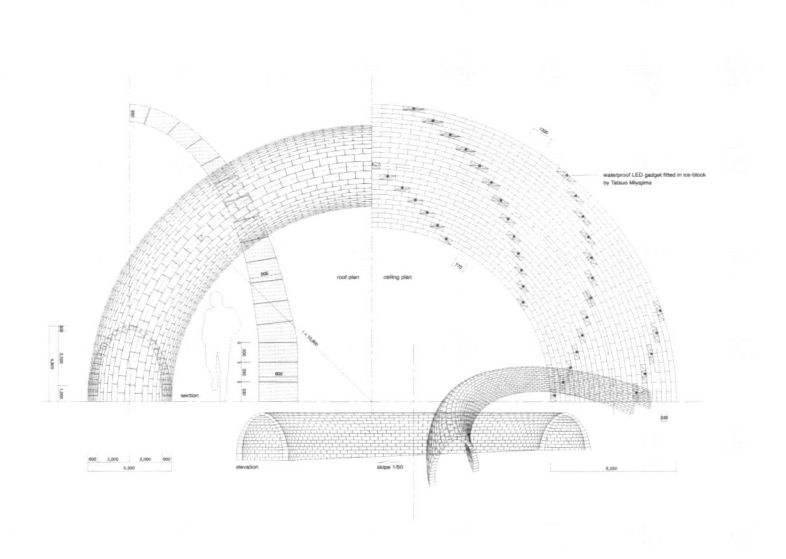

フィンランドで開催されたアーティストと建築家のコラボレーションによる「スノーショー2004」の安藤と宮島達男による出展作品。第2会場にあたるロヴァニエミのケミ川沿いの雪原に設置された。安藤が構築したのは「カテナリーアーチ（懸垂曲線）」のトンネル状の氷のチューブで、直径30メートルの半円を描く。宮島は氷の内壁に一桁の数字を継続的に赤く表示する「カウンター・ガジェット」と呼ぶ装置を70個埋め込んだ。

A work of Ando and Miyajima Tatsuo for the exhibition of The Snow Show 2004 held in Finland under the collaboration of artists and architects. It was placed in a snow field where the second venue was located along the Kemi River in Rovaniemi. Ando built an ice tube with a catenary arch in which it forms a half-circle of 30 meters in diameter when laid down. Miyajima embedded 70 units of devices called Counter Gadgets that continuously display a one digit number in red on the wall inside the ice tube.

[229]
ゴールデン・ゲート・ブリッジの住宅   2004
golden gate bridge house

1. アメリカ サンフランシスコ | san francisco, USA
2. 設計 | design   2004
3. 構想案 | concept
4. 鉄筋コンクリート | RC
5. 住宅 | detached house
7. 建築 | building   1,200 m²
8. 延床 | total floor   1,050 m²

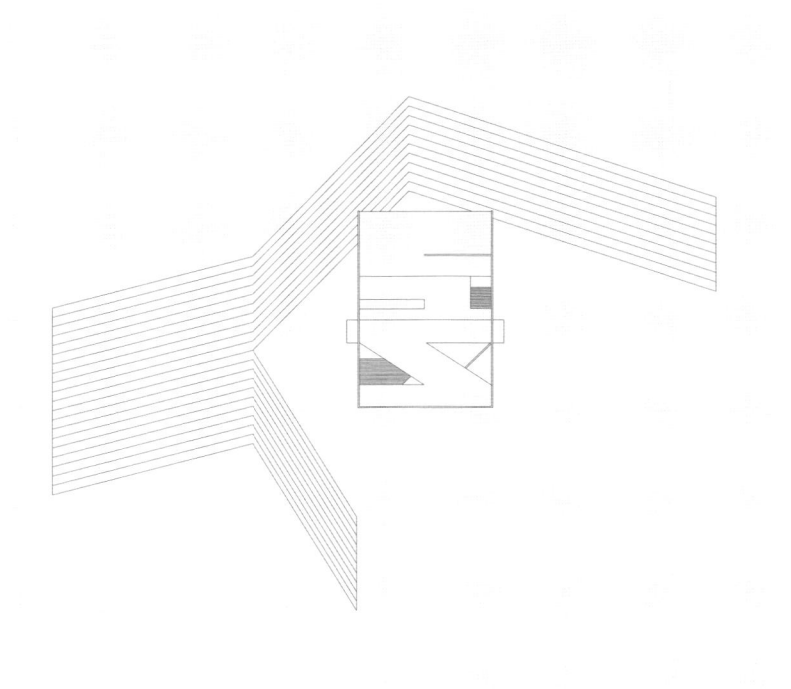

平面形は二つの平行する棟と、その2棟を斜めにもうひとつの棟が結ぶ「Z」型の配置をとる。米西海岸サンフランシスコの急な海辺の崖地に、水平屋根の低層な住宅を配する計画で、上階にあたる1階部分は水平屋根と床、垂直な壁、柱がいずれも板状で構成されて開放的な空間をつくりだし、自然豊かな環境と景観が堪能できる。この上階にリビングルームと視聴覚室を配し、他の生活空間は下階に配する構成で、環境の利点を堪能することも提案している。

The planform is in a Z shape with two building in parallel and one building connecting the two in a diagonal. A low-rising house with a horizontal roof was planned to be built on a steep cliff on the coastline of San Francisco on the west coast of the U.S. The first floor area, which is the upper floor, is designed with horizontal roof, floors, vertical walls and pillars all structured in a plate form to create openness in space composed and to fully enjoy the environment and scenery of the rich nature. A living room and an audiovisual room are arranged on this upper floor where other living space are located on the lower floor to take full advantage of the environment.

[230]
森の教会 2004
chapel in the woods
.
1. アメリカ シアトル | seattle, USA
2. 設計 | design   2004.1 – 2007.12
3. 構想案 | concept
4. 鉄筋コンクリート | RC
5. 教会 | church
6. 敷地 | site   27,600.0 m²
7. 建築 | building   3,900.0 m²
8. 延床 | total floor   4,840.0 m²

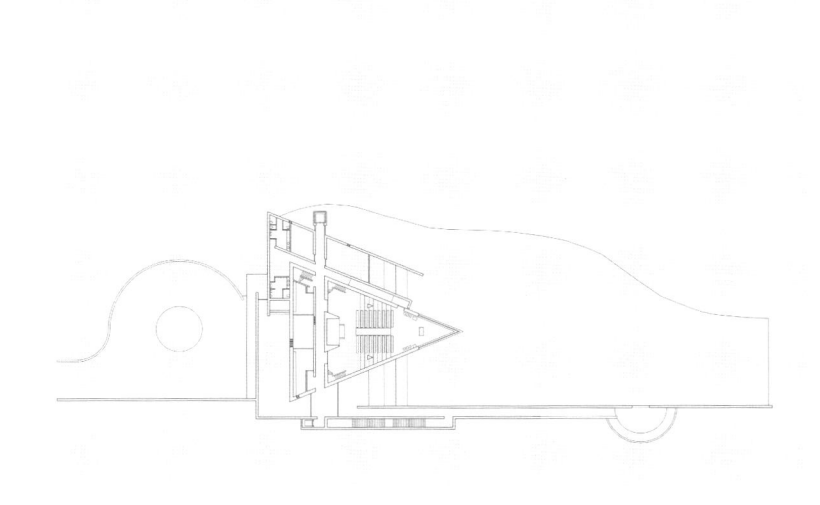

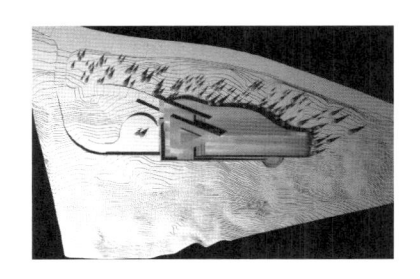

米シアトルに近いヴェルビュー郊外の森林のなかに計画された。敷地は緩やかな斜面を想定し、中核となる聖堂は二等辺三角形の平面を持ち、東端にあたる三角形の頂点の側に祭壇が配される。頂点に向かう視線の先はガラス壁となっており、祭壇の先に、教会から森に向って広がる人工池の水面が見える。トップライトからの自然光が聖なる空間に密やかに射し込み、礼拝者の心を和ませる。のちに実現した「広尾の教会」の原形を確かめることもできる。
.
This was planned to be built in a forest located in the suburbs of Bellevue close to Seattle, the U.S. On a property with a gentle slope, the chapel, which is the central object, has a planform of anisosceles triangle and an altar is placed on the apex of the triangle on the east end. A glass wall is placed in the direction of the line of sight where water surface of an artificial pond that extends from the church to the forest can be viewed behind the altar. The natural light from the roof quietly shines in to the holy space and calms the hearts of visitors. The original prototype of the CHURCH IN HIROO can be observed at this church.

[231]
ロックフィールド神戸
ヘッドオフィス
／神戸ファクトリー 2005
rockfield kobe headquarters
／ kobe factory
.
1. 神戸市東灘区 | higashinada-ku, kobe
2. 設計 | design   2003.2 – 2003.8
3. 施工 | construction   2003.7 – 2005.1
4. 鉄骨 | steel
5. 工場・事務所 | factory, headquarters
6. 敷地 | site   24,306.8 m²
7. 建築 | building   9,640.1 m²
8. 延床 | total floor   30,770.1 m²

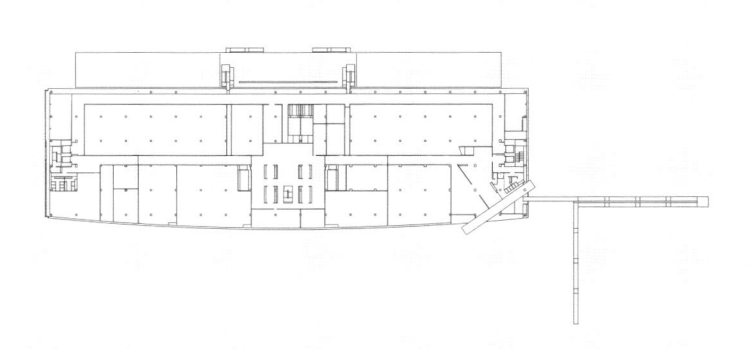

百貨店の倉庫だった神戸湾岸の建物がオフィスと工場に生まれ変わった。1995年の阪神淡路大震災で弱体になっていた構造を基礎杭の補強で強化、あわせて最上階の5階部分を撤去して上屋の荷重負荷を減じた。下層階に生産関係の機能を集め、最上階にオフィスと職員の休憩スペースを配した。長さ100mを超える光庭を設けることで、社員食堂を憩いの場とした。長大な外壁の圧迫感を軽減するため、鋼製床材「ファインフロア」で外壁を覆い、同じ部品の連続するリズム感を建物に添えた。建築のリサイクルへの挑戦と安藤は位置づけている。→参照 [117]
.
A warehouse of a department store in the coast of Kobe was transformed into an office and factory. The building, whose structure weakened by The Great Hanshin Earthquake in 1995, was reinforced by strengthening foundation pillars, while topmost 5th floor was removed in order to reduce the load of the building. Manufacturing related functions were gathered in lower levels, and the office and resting space of workers were allocated on the topmost floor. A light court in 160 m long was provided to a relaxing space accompanied to a staff cafeteria. A long exterior wall was covered with a series of metal flooring called "fine floor", to add a rhythmic appearance created by a sequence of a same part. → see also [117]

346 Complete Works

[232]
高槻の住宅　2005
house in takatsuki

1. 大阪府高槻市｜takatsuki, osaka
2. 設計｜design　2003.4 – 2004.6
3. 施工｜construction　2004.6 – 2005.3
4. 鉄筋コンクリート｜RC
5. 住宅｜detached house
6. 敷地｜site　273.9 m²
7. 建築｜building　125.4 m²
8. 延床｜total floor　218.3 m²

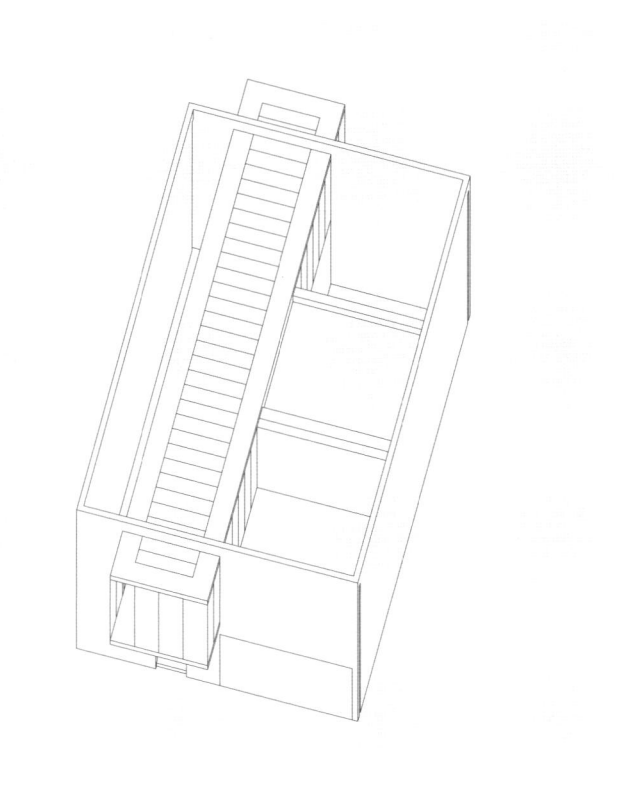

大阪府高槻市の住宅地に立地する戸建て住宅。270平方メートルの敷地をコンクリート打ち放しの壁でまず囲い、周囲に対して内部の暮らしの場を確保した。そこにコンクリートの住居部分を入れ子で挿入した。内部の吹き抜け、壁との空隙や1階部分の屋根をテラスに活用するなどして空間の多様化を実現、さらに2階部分に囲いの壁も貫通するガラスの直方体を挿入し、そこを生活の中心となるリビングとすることで、壁による保護の安心感と同時に開放感も獲得している。

A residential house located in a residential area of Takatsuki City, Osaka. The 270m² property was surrounded by exposed concrete walls and secured the living space inside. Then a concrete residential part was inserted in a nest form. Variation in space was provided by an interior open ceiling and placing terraces in the gap between the walls as well as on the 1st floor roof. Furthermore, a glass rectangular solid that penetrates the surrounding wall was inserted on the 2nd floor area to create a living room where daily activities are centered on, allowing acquisition of both peaceful sense of protection of closed walls and sense of spaciousness.

[233]
hhstyle.com/casa　2005
hhstyle.com/casa

1. 東京都渋谷区｜shibuya, tokyo
2. 設計｜design　2004.4 – 2004.8
3. 施工｜construction　2004.9 – 2005.2
4. 鉄筋コンクリート、鉄骨｜RC, steel
5. 店舗｜shop
6. 敷地｜site　352.7 m²
7. 建築｜building　210.5 m²
8. 延床｜total floor　469.8 m²

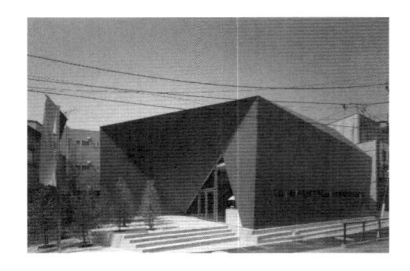

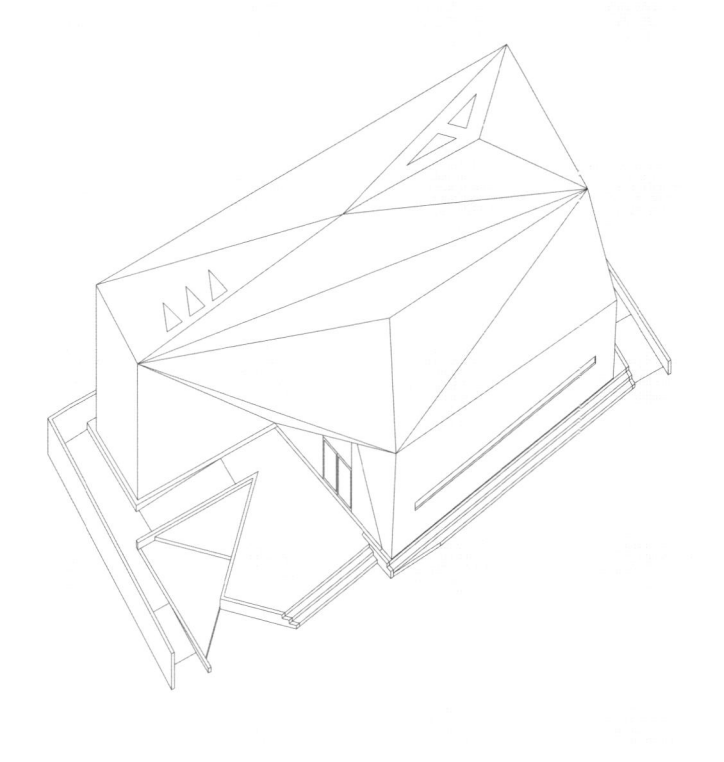

若者に人気の「裏原宿」「キャットストリート」と呼ばれる路地空間にある商業建築。計画道路が予定されている敷地ゆえの構造制限、借地の年限などを逆手にとり、鉄骨造の「軽い建築」を念頭に設計が進められた。屋根から外壁までのほとんどを、折り紙のように曲げた鉄板が覆う構成はそのような経緯から生まれた。内部も一部を吹き抜けにして空間の一体感を損ねないようにした。商業建築のための制約を自由な空間を実現する原動力にしたという。

This is a commercial building standing on a passage space called "Cat Street" in a "Ura-Harajuku" area, a popular destination among young people. There are various restrictions with the site for a construction plan of a road, such as the structural restriction and limited term tenancy. However, Ando took advantage of such restriction to promote a design process to create a "light architecture" in steel frame construction. Almost all parts of the roof and the exterior walls were built in folded steel panels for covering, as a result of the concept. The interior space was also produced without losing the sense of unity by applying a double height space in some part. Ando explained those restrictions of a commercial building were turned into a motivation of producing a space with a sense of freedom.

[234]
回遊式住宅　2005
walk around house

1. 大阪市 | osaka
2. 設計 | design　2005
3. 構想案 | concept
4. 鉄筋コンクリート | RC
5. 住宅 | detached house
6. 敷地 | site　154.3 m²
7. 建築 | building　81.0 m²
8. 延床 | total floor　133.5 m²

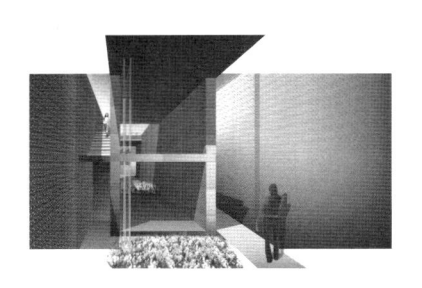

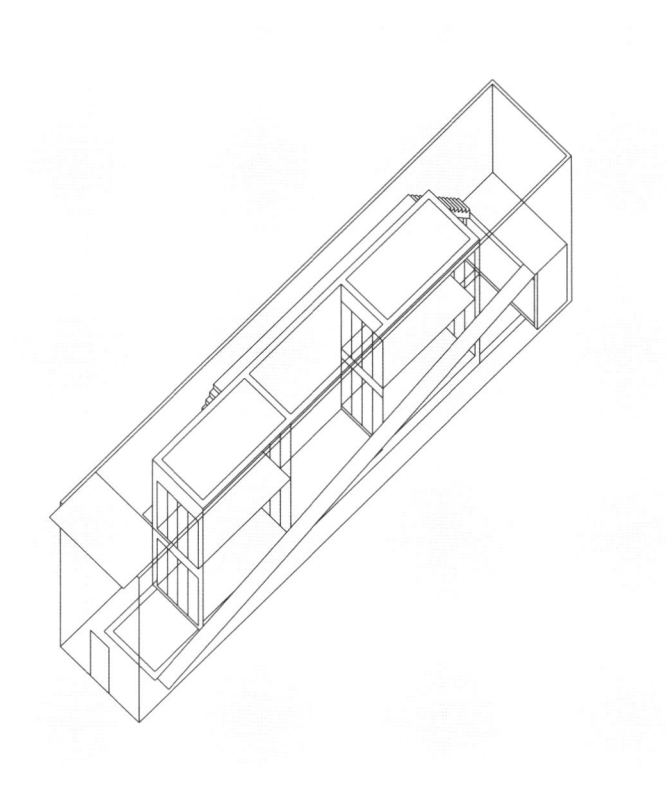

間口が5メートルに対して奥行き30メートル、大阪下町の短冊状の敷地に、夫婦2人のための住宅を設計した。敷地をパンチングメタルのアルミニウムの壁で囲い、そのなかに間口3メートル、奥行き18メートルの二層のコンクリートボックスを置き、住空間を確保した。ボックスの屋上庭園に加え、アルミニウムの塀と躯体との「空き」をテラスとし、都市のなかの囲いとられた自然を楽しめる仕立てをとった。2階の一室は、敢えてエントランスから建物を半周して屋上にあがったところで階段を降りる「回遊式」の配置とした。

A residential house was designed for a couple in a 5-meter wide and 30-meter long strip form property in the old area of Osaka. The property is surrounded by perforated aluminum walls where a two-layered concrete box of 3 meters in width and 18 meters in length was placed to secure a living space. A rooftop garden is situated on the box and a terrace is arranged in the gap between the aluminum wall and the building to enjoy the enclosed nature in the urban area. One room of the 2nd floor is intentionally arranged in a circuit style that requires residents to walk half around the building from the entrance to go up to the rooftop and then walk down to enter the room.

[235]
坂の上の雲ミュージアム　2006
saka no ue no kumo museum

1. 愛媛県松山市 | matsuyama, ehime
2. 設計 | design　2003.6 – 2004.9
3. 施工 | construction　2004.12 – 2006.11
4. 鉄骨鉄筋コンクリート、一部鉄骨 | SRC, steel
5. 博物館 | museum
6. 敷地 | site　3,384.6 m²
7. 建築 | building　936.8 m²
8. 延床 | total floor　3,122.8 m²

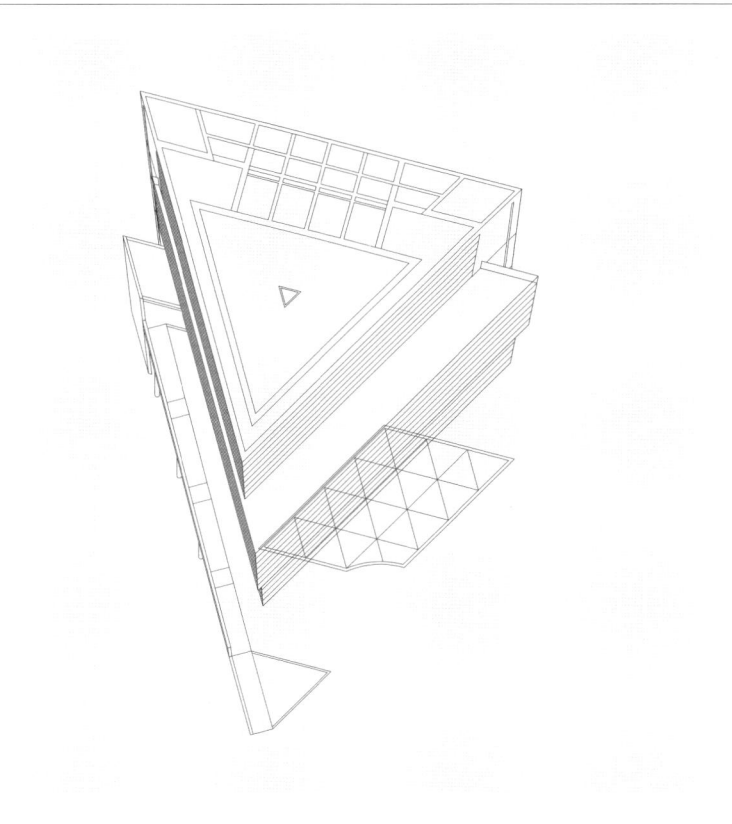

司馬遼太郎の小説『坂の上の雲』は、松山出身の正岡子規、秋山好古、真之兄弟が日本の近代化に貢献した物語。この小説にまつわる展示施設。司馬の記念館を東大阪市で設計した経緯があり、安藤がこの施設も手がけることになった。松山城のそびえる城山と市街地の境目に位置する立地を踏まえ、樹木の緑のなか、三角形の平面配置を採用した。3、4階の展示室にはガラスの外壁に沿って昇降するスロープが設えられ、城山の豊かな緑、傍らの大正建築「萬翠荘」など館外の歴史遺産を眺め、子規らの足跡に思いを馳せる仕立てをとった。

A novel written by Ryotaro Shiba, "Saka no ue no kumo" ("Clouds Above the Hill"), is a story of three characters from Matsuyama City, Ehime Prefecture, Shiki Masaoka, Saneyuki Akiyama and his brother, Yoshifuru, who had contributed the modernization of Japan in modern era. This is a museum building to exhibit related references and materials of this novel, and Ando was also involved in the design for this facility since he had previously designed the memorial building of Shiba in Higashiosaka City, Osaka Prefecture. Considering the site situated on in-between conditions of Shiro-yama Mountain where Matsuyama Castle is located and city area, the plan of this building adopted triangular configuration within the dense forest of trees.

[236]

表参道ヒルズ　2006
omotesando hills

1. 東京都渋谷区 | shibuya, tokyo
2. 設計 | design　1996.4 – 2003.3
3. 施工 | construction　2003.8 – 2006.1
4. 鉄骨鉄筋コンクリート、一部鉄筋コンクリート、鉄骨 | RC, SRC, steel
5. 商業施設、集合住宅 | commercial complex, apartment house
6. 敷地 | site　6,051.4 m²
7. 建築 | building　5,030.8 m²
8. 延床 | total floor　34,061.7 m²

表参道に面していた同潤会青山アパートは、関東大震災後の帝都復興期に建設され、東京におけるコンクリート集合住宅による都市居住のモデルとされてきた。その同潤会アパートを撤去して商業施設が建設された。もとのアパートが囲っていた中庭の平面のシルエットが、新しいビルの中央を占めるアトリウムの形に援用された。アトリウムを取り巻いて買い物客が昇降するスロープの傾斜は、建物が面している表参道の坂道にあわせた設定になっている。かつての同潤会アパートの住人たちは、最上階の住居部分に移住、表参道に面した一角に「同潤館」と命名した往時の姿を再現する棟が併設されている。

Aoyama Apartment of Dojunkai was standing along with Omotesando avenue. It was built during the reconstruction period of Tokyo after The Great Kanto Earthquake, and it became a model of a collective housing built in concrete structure, embodying an urban lifestyle of Tokyo. This commercial facility was built by demolishing this Aoyama Apartment. The apartment silhouette of the courtyard enclosed by the original apartment was adopted as the shape of atrium space occupying the core of this new building. The angle of inclination of a slope where shoppers go up and down around the atrium was adjusted to the same angle of the slope of Omotesando avenue that the new building faces. Residents of the former Aoyama Apartment moved to the top floor of the residential zone of this new building. There is a building that reproduces the appearance of the past which named "Dojunkan" in a corner facing Omotesando avenue.

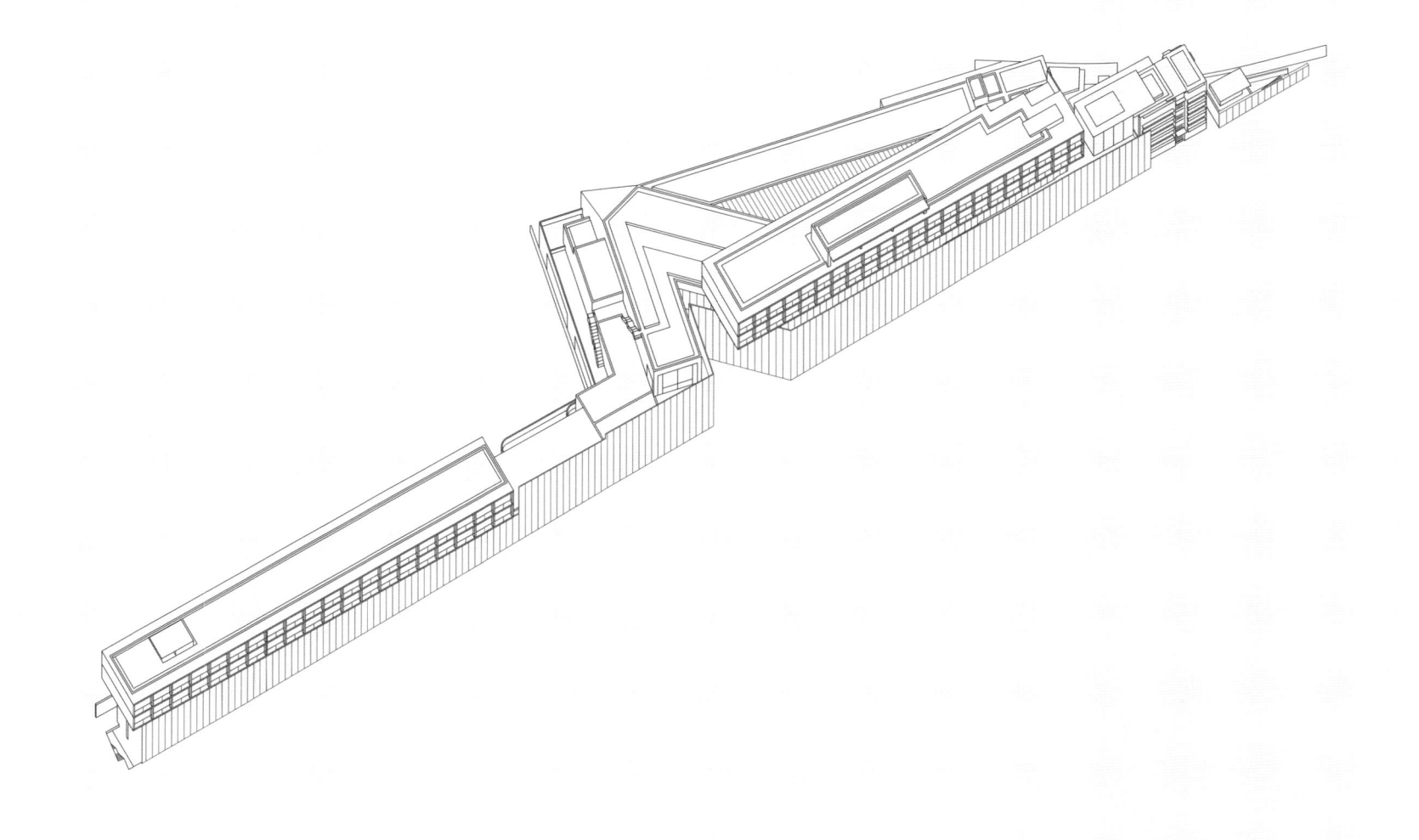

[237]

滋賀の住宅　2006
house in shiga

1. 滋賀県大津市 | otsu, shiga
2. 設計 | design　2004.1–2005.5
3. 施工 | construction　2005.8–2006.5
4. 鉄筋コンクリート | RC
5. 住宅 | detached house
6. 敷地 | site　598.5 m²
7. 建築 | building　225.5 m²
8. 延床 | total floor　312.5 m²

施主の家族と母親が同居する2世帯住宅。琵琶湖を見渡す眺望をどう生かすかが課題となった。コンクリートの塀で変則的な敷地の周囲を囲い、2階部分を空中に浮かせ、そこから眺望を堪能する構成を選んだ。1階に母親の居室と和室、2階にリビングルーム、寝室などを配した。2階はこの地ならではの明るい光を堪能し、一回り小さな1階では、2階床が太陽の直射を制御する庇の役割を果たし、自然光が静かに浸潤する落ち着いた空間となった。

A residential house for two families of the client's family and mother. The challenge was how to use the scenery of Biwa Lake viewed from the rooms. Concrete fences were used to surround the irregular-shaped property and the 2nd floor was designed to be in midair to enjoy the scenery fully. The client's mother's living room and Japanese room were arranged on the 1st floor and another living room and bed rooms were placed on the 2nd floor. Bright sunlight available in this area can be enjoyed on the 2nd floor and since the 1st floor is slightly smaller than the 2nd floor, the floor functions as a hood that controls the direct sunlight, thus, a tranquil space where natural light gently soaks is provided on the 1st floor.

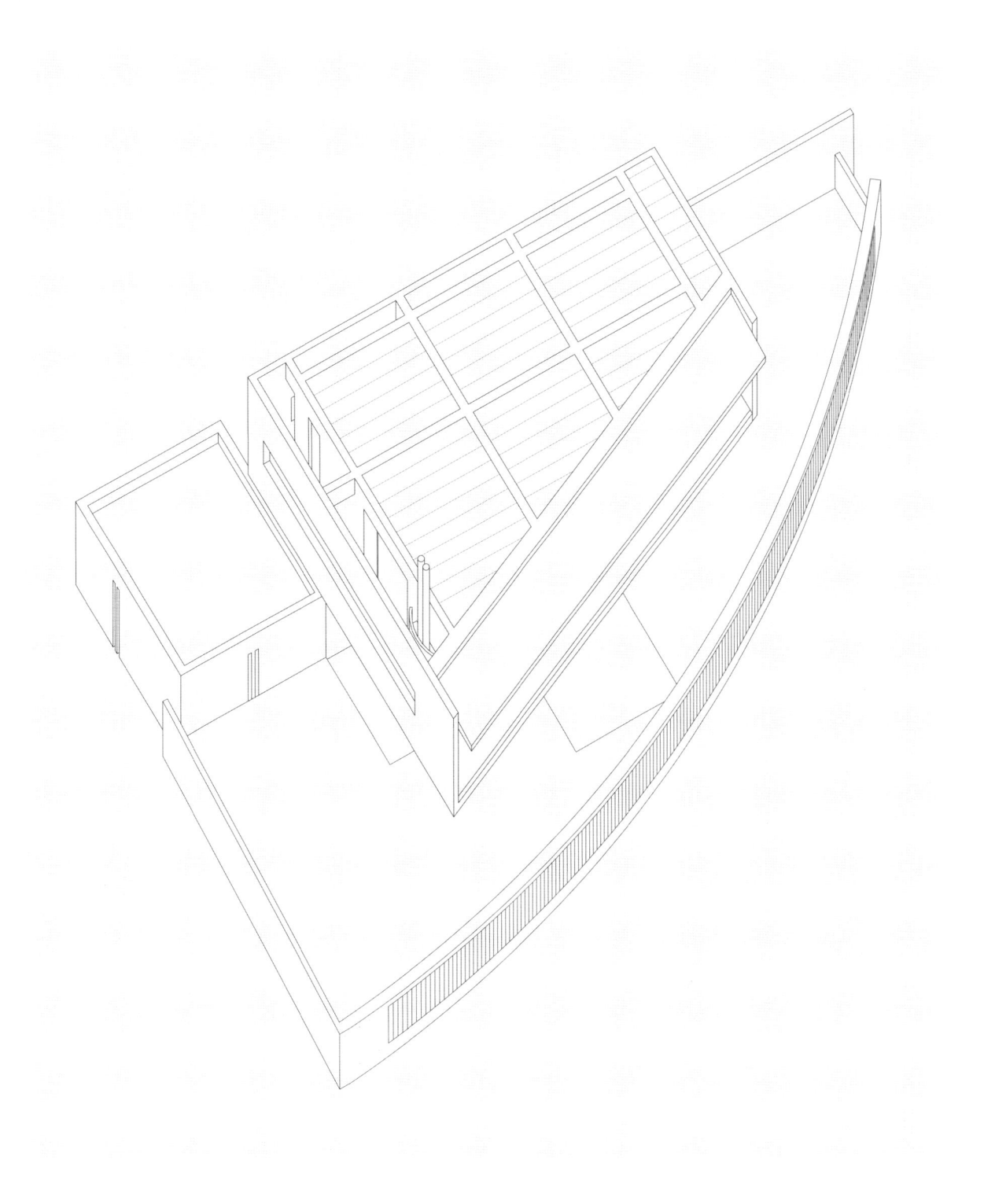

[238]

morimoto nyc
(モリモト・ニューヨーク) 2006
morimoto nyc

1. アメリカ ニューヨーク | new york, USA
2. 設計 | design   2003.11–2005.4
3. 施工 | construction   2005.5–2006.1
4. 鉄骨鉄筋コンクリート | SRC
5. レストラン | restaurant
8. 延床 | total floor   1,230 m²

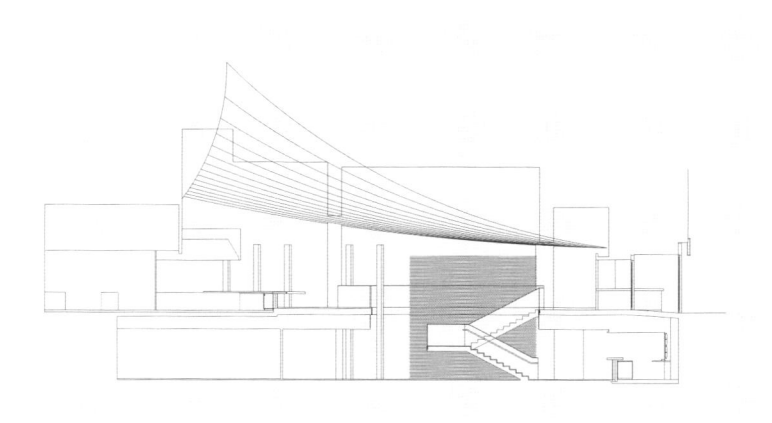

ニューヨークのハドソン川岸に近いミート・パッキング・ポイントはおしゃれな街として知られる。日本料理のシェフ森本正治のレストランをユニークなインテリアで仕立てた。チェルシーマーケットだった巨大建物の1階の一角を占める店の正面は水平目地の鉄材を張りつめ、緩やかなアーチのエントランスを設けた。地上階から一層下がったところにメインフロアの広がる店内で目をひくのは、水の入った500ミリリットルのペットボトルを埋め込んだ壁。店内で使ったペットボトルの総数は1万7千4百本。発光ダイオードの点光源のきらめきによって、滝のように水が流れているかのような光景がつくりだされる。

The Meatpacking point close to the Hudson River in New York is known as a fashionable town. A restaurant of Masaharu Morimoto, a Japanese food chef, was built with unique interior. The front of the store on the 1st floor of a large building of former Chelsea Market is covered by metal materials with horizontal joints and a gradual arch at the entrance. The area that captures attention in the main floor located one level lower is the wall embedded with 500ml plastic bottles that have water inside. 17,400 plastic bottles were used in total for the store, which creates the scenery as though water is flowing like a waterfall by the light of LED.

[239]

ベネッセハウス パーク／ビーチ
2006
benesse house park, beach

1. 香川県直島町 | naoshima, kagawa
2. 設計 | design   2004.4–2005.5
3. 施工 | construction   2005.5–2006.4
4. 木造、地下鉄筋コンクリート | wood, RC
5. ホテル、リゾート施設 | hotel, resort facilities
6. 敷地 | site   29,788.9 m²
7. 建築 | building   3,388.2 m²
8. 延床 | total floor   4,760.4 m²

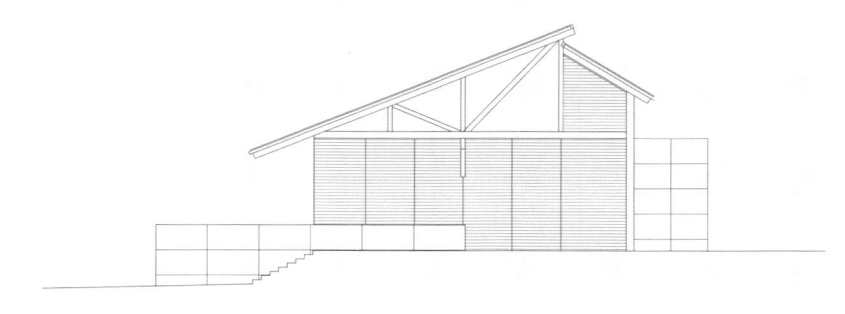

現代美術の島、直島のベネッセハウスの新館。国際キャンプ場の施設の一部を改修するとともに、集成材による木造のホテル棟などが新築された。ホテル棟の基壇部はコンクリートだが、インテリアはシナベニヤ材の簡素な仕立てで木造空間のイメージを徹底している。既存部分がエントランスにあてられ、島を周回する道路に近い位置には、ビーチ棟が木造で新たに建てられた。海に面した立地が、間近で瀬戸内の海を堪能できる場を提供している。→参照 [125]、[151]、[184]、[223]、[280]、[309]

The new building of BENESSE HOUSE of Naoshima, which became an island of contemporary arts. The preexisting facility of an international camping site was partially renovated and wooden hotel architectures were newly built using laminated wood. Although the foundation of the hotel building is concrete, the atmosphere of the space in a wooden house is thoroughly reflected inside the building using the simple finish of basswood veneer. The facility's general entrance was arranged to be located at the preexisting area and a wooden beach building was newly built close to the road that encircles the island. The location of one of the few facilities facing the ocean in Naoshima offers a place where visitors can fully enjoy the ocean of Setouchi. → see also [125], [151], [184], [223], [280], [309]

[240]
小篠邸ゲストハウス 2006
guest house for koshino house

1. 兵庫県芦屋市｜ashiya, hyogo
2. 設計｜design　2004.10–2005.5
3. 施工｜construction　2005.6–2006.5
4. 鉄筋コンクリート｜RC
5. ゲストハウス｜guest house
6. 敷地｜site　1,144.7㎡
7. 建築｜building　125.4㎡
8. 延床｜total floor　250.8㎡

最初の住宅が完成して4年後にアトリエが増築付加され、それからさらに20年後、家族構成の変化で、子ども部屋のあった南棟を撤去し、代わってホールを持つゲストハウスを新築した。当初の2棟は敷地の傾斜に従って高さに差をつける構成だったが、この増築にあたっては両方の棟の高さを揃えた。そのことによって中庭はより囲まれたイメージが強まった。新棟の中庭に向いた壁には連続スリットを刻み、中庭の自然光が内部に陰影をもたらす空間のダイナミズムを実現した。→参照 [038]

After 4 years of completion of the first house, an atelier space was added, and then another 20 years later, a new guest house with hall was built by replacing of the removal of the south wing for children's rooms due to the change of family structure. The existing two wing buildings were structured to make difference in height according to the slope of the site, but this extension was kept in the same height with the other wing. It strengthened the image of the courtyard more enveloped. On the wall facing to the courtyard of the new wing, a series of slits is carved to bring in daylight from the courtyard, and give contrast with various lights and shades to realize dynamic quality in the space. → see also [038]

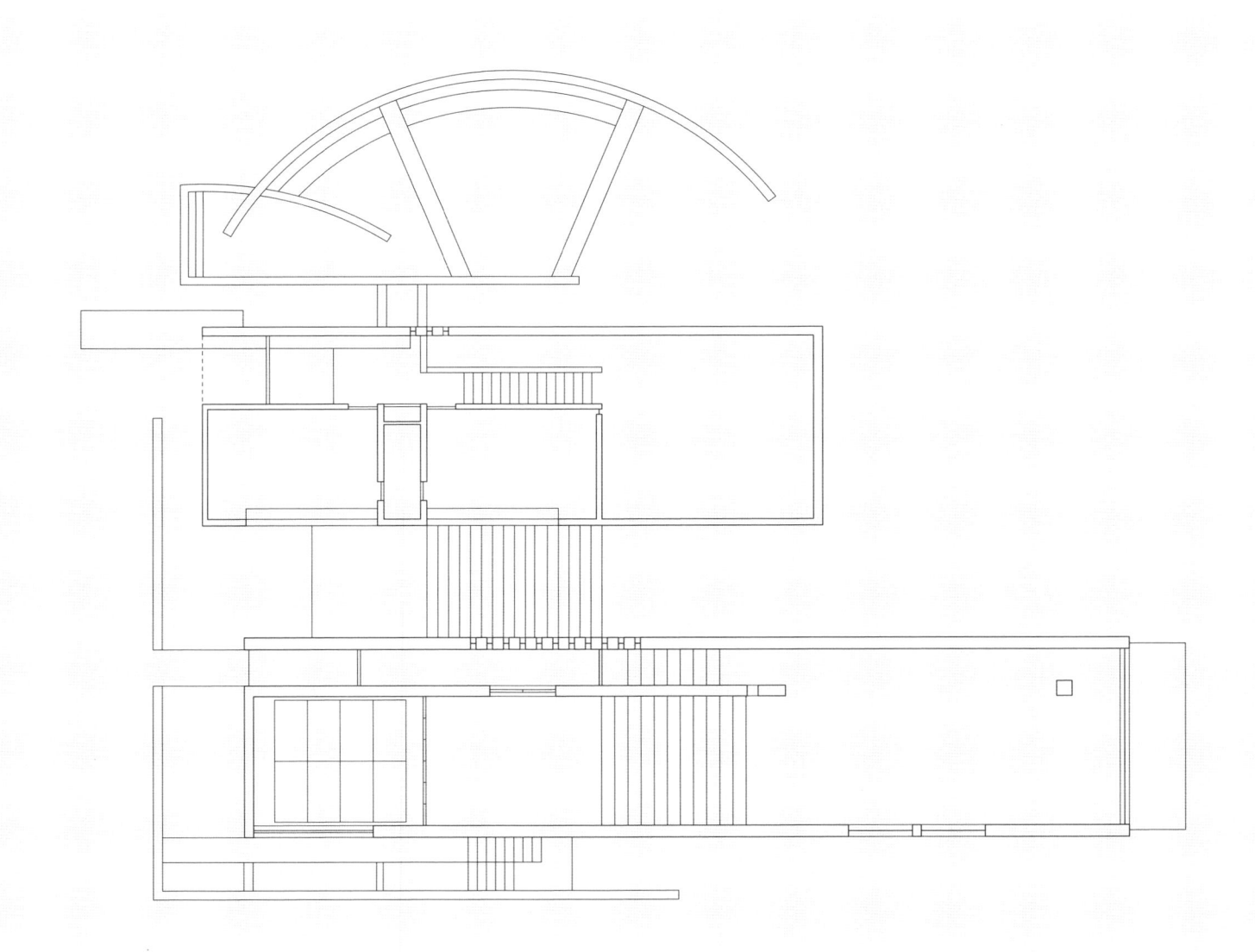

[241]

さくら広場 幕張　2006
sakura hiroba makuhari

1. 千葉県習志野市 | narashino, chiba
2. 設計 | design　2005.2 – 2005.10
3. 施工 | construction　2005.11 – 2006.3
5. 公園 | park
6. 敷地 | site　31,525 m²

同 門真　2006
sakura hiroba kadoma

1. 大阪府門真市 | kadoma, osaka
2. 設計 | design　2005.2 – 2005.10
3. 施工 | construction　2005.11 – 2006.3
5. 公園 | park
6. 敷地 | site　16,198 m²

同 茅ヶ崎　2007
sakura hiroba chigasaki

1. 神奈川県茅ケ崎市 | chigasaki, kanagawa
2. 設計 | design　2005.10 – 2006.8
3. 施工 | construction　2006.9 – 2007.3
5. 公園 | park
6. 敷地 | site　6,441 m²

同 豊中　2009
sakura hiroba toyonaka

1. 大阪府豊中市 | toyonaka, osaka
2. 設計 | design　2007.2 – 2007.9
3. 施工 | construction　2007.10 – 2008.3, 2008.7 – 2009.3
5. 公園 | park
6. 敷地 | site　9,970 m²

大手電機メーカー、パナソニックが保有していた遊休地を、さくらの広場とすることを提案、2006年に千葉の幕張新都心に近い臨海地と同社の本拠地、大阪・門真の二か所、次いで神奈川県茅ヶ崎と大阪・豊中で実現した。幕張では敷地の一角に楕円の大きな人工池を設け、その周囲を起伏をもたせた緑地で取り巻き、核となる場をつくりあげた。池から水路も設けてうるおいを演出した。さくらの木はグリッド状に規則正しく配置、季節感の希薄な臨海地に彩りを添えている。

It was a series of projects to transform unused land spaces of the major household electric appliance manufacturer, Panasonic, into parks with cherry trees. Proposals for seaside location near Makuhari New City of Chiba Prefecture, and two locations in Kadoma City in Osaka Prefecture were realized in 2006, and proposals for Chigasaki City in Kanagawa Prefecture and Toyonaka City in Osaka Prefecture were realized in 2007 and 2009. In the project of Makuhari, a central space was created by providing a large oval-shaped artificial pond on a corner of the site, and its surrounding is enclosed by a green space with undulation. A water channel is provided to render an image of refinement and purity. Cherry trees are regularly planted in a grid pattern, and add colors to the seaside locations with sparse seasonal changes.

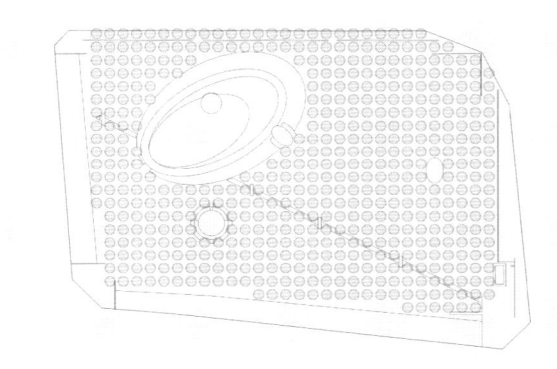

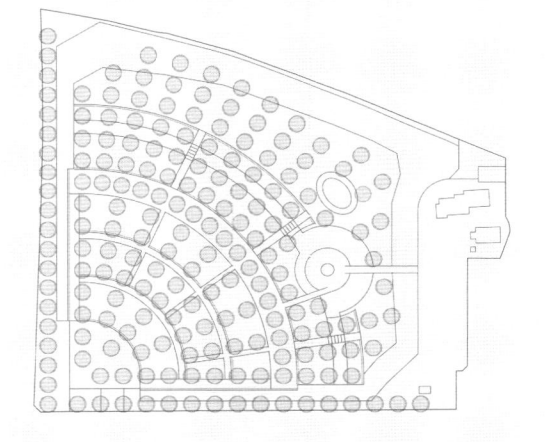

幕張 | makuhari

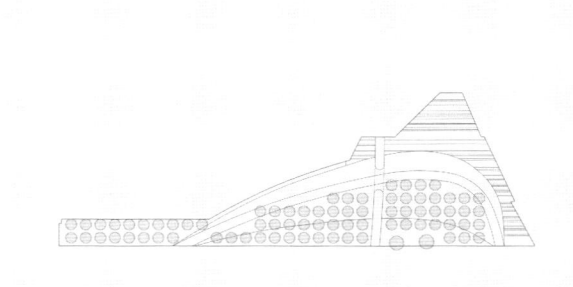

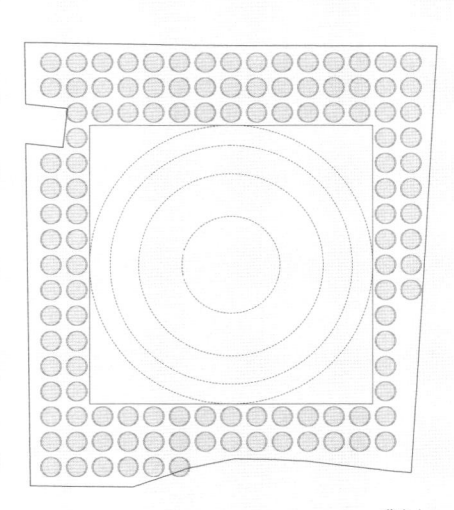

門真 | kadoma

茅ヶ崎 | chigasaki

豊中 | toyonaka

[242]
パラッツォ・グラッシ　2006
palazzo grassi

1. イタリア ヴェネチア｜venice, italy
2. 設計｜design　2005.6–2006.2
3. 施工｜construction　2005.9–2006.4
4. レンガ、木造｜brick, wood
5. 美術館（改修）｜museum of art (renovation)
6. 敷地｜site　1,450 m²
7. 建築｜building　1,400 m²
8. 延床｜total floor　6,320 m², 2,900 m² [renovated part]

パリ郊外で計画されていたピノー現代美術館の計画は日の目を見なかった。その実現に賭けたエネルギーはイタリア・ヴェネチアに向けられ、「パラッツォ・グラッシ」が現代美術のギャラリーとして新装開場した。大運河に面した1772年完成のこの居館はジョルジョ・マッサーリの設計によるが、1983年以降はフィアット財団が展覧会場として使ってきた。ピノー財団はそれを受け継ぎ、安藤はヴェネチアの厳しい規制のもと、装飾豊かな天井はもとのまま保全し、その下で白い壁の展示空間を展開、現代美術にふさわしい場に再生した。意欲的な展覧会が企画され、ヴェネチアの創作活動に不可欠な存在として認知されつつある。→参照［266］、［308］

The proposal of Pinault Modern Art Museum, to be constructed in a suburb of Paris, was unfortunately not realized. The energy to realize and establish new museum was then devoted to realize "PALAZZO GRASSI" in Venice, Italy, by renovating a space as a gallery for modern art. This former residential building facing to the Grand Canal was completed in 1772 by the design of Giorgio Massari. The building has been utilized as an exhibition space by Fiat since 1983, and François Pinault Foundation succeeded the concept. In spite of strict regulations of Venice, Ando regenerated the building into a space suitable for exhibiting modern art — while richly decorated ceiling was preserved as it is, new exhibition spaces enclosed by white walls were provided. A number of ambitious exhibitions have been planned, and this gallery has been recognized as an essential place for creative scene in Venice. → see also [266], [308]

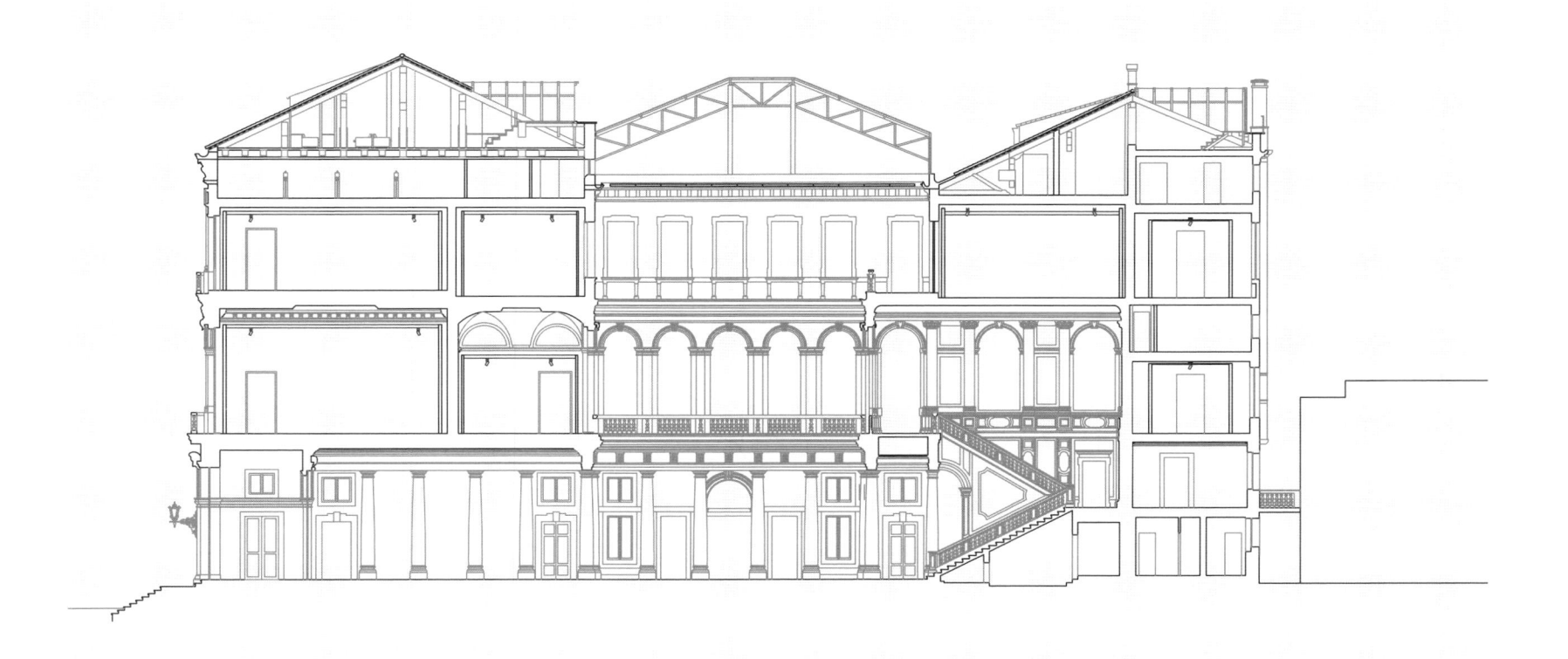

[243]
游庵 2006
yu-un (obayashi collection)

1. 東京都港区 | minato-ku, tokyo
2. 設計 | design 2004.9 – 2005.8
3. 施工 | construction 2005.8 – 2006.9
4. 鉄筋コンクリート | RC
5. ギャラリー、ゲストルーム | gallery, guest room
6. 敷地 | site 467.6 m²
7. 建築 | building 272.1 m²
8. 延床 | total floor 750.5 m²

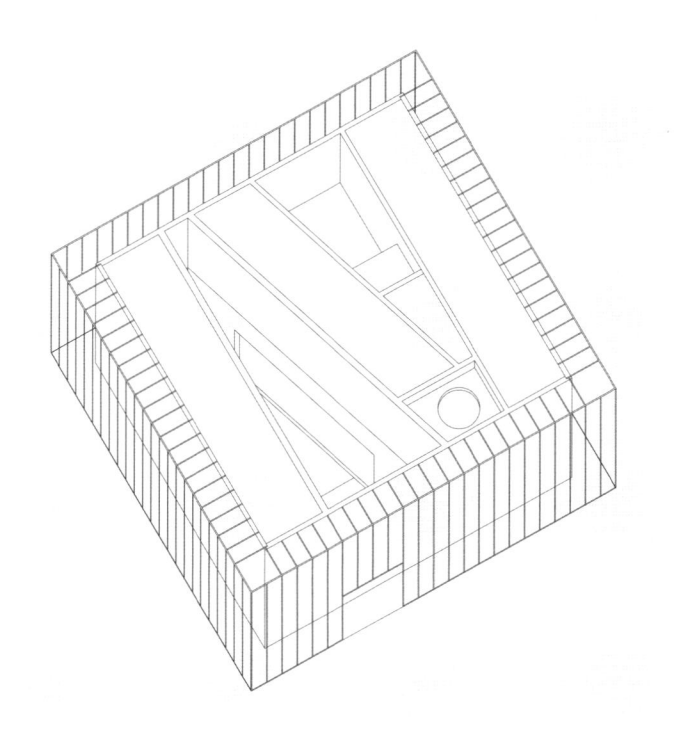

東京都内の住宅地のプライベートなゲストハウス。茶室と私的な美術収集品のギャラリーを併せ持つ。全体の構成は外装をガラスの壁とし、そのなかにコンクリートのボックスを入れ子で配した。中央の吹き抜けにオラファー・エリアソンによる立体形状を形成するタイルを張りつめたのをはじめ、吉岡徳仁によるガラスのカウンターが印象的なホームバーを配するなど他の領域の表現者も加わり、現代における「数寄」を体現した建築を目指した。

A private guesthouse of a residential area in Tokyo. It offers a tea ceremony room and a gallery of private art collection. The overall structure is using glass exterior walls where concrete boxes are nested inside. Creating an architecture that materializes the refined taste of modern times was aimed through a space covered with tiles that form solid geometry by Olafur Eliasson at the central open ceiling area and with participation of artists from a different field including Tokujin Yoshioka who designed a home bar with an impressive glass counter.

[244]
2016年東京オリンピック構想
2006
tokyo oliympic games 2016 project

1. 東京都 | tokyo
2. 設計 | design 2006.5 – 2009.10
3. 構想案 | concept
5. 五輪施設計画 | olympic facilities plan

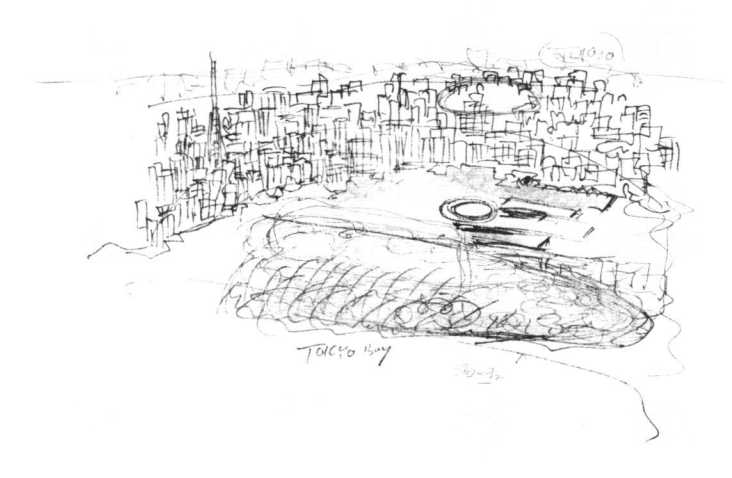

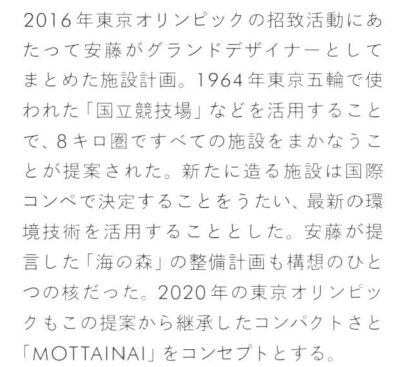

2016年東京オリンピックの招致活動にあたって安藤がグランドデザイナーとしてまとめた施設計画。1964年東京五輪で使われた「国立競技場」などを活用することで、8キロ圏ですべての施設をまかなうことが提案された。新たに造る施設は国際コンペで決定することをうたい、最新の環境技術を活用することとした。安藤が提言した「海の森」の整備計画も構想のひとつの核だった。2020年の東京オリンピックもこの提案から継承したコンパクトさと「MOTTAINAI」をコンセプトとする。

A facility plan organized by Ando for the campaign in 2016 to host the Tokyo Olympics. It was proposed to have all Olympic events held in facilities within eight kilometers by using the National Stadium where the 1964 Tokyo Olympics was held. Facilities to be built will be decided through international contests and the latest environment technologies will be applied. The SEA FOREST suggested by Ando was one of the core concepts for the preparation plan. Concepts for the plan of 2020 were the compactness succeeded from this plan and the idea of MOTTAINAI.

全346作品録　399

[245]
アブダビ海洋博物館　2006
abu dhabi maritime museum
.
1. アラブ首長国連邦 アブダビ｜abu dhabi, UAE
2. 設計｜design　2006.6
3. 構想案｜concept
4. 鉄筋コンクリート、一部鉄骨、鉄骨鉄筋コンクリート｜RC, steel, SRC
5. 博物館｜museum
6. 敷地｜site　61,000 m²
7. 建築｜building　25,400 m²
8. 延床｜total floor　33,300 m²

巨大な直方体の内側を三次元曲面で滑らかに削り取った建築が、アラビア海の水上に浮かぶ。アラブ首長国連邦のアブダビが沖合のサーディヤット島の開発の一環として実現をはかるプロジェクト。三次元曲面はアラビア海を航行する船舶の帆のイメージだ。来訪者は海上のブリッジを渡って、海に浮かぶ展示室内へアプローチする。同島の開発には、ジャン・ヌーヴェル、ザハ・ハディドらも起用されており、実現すれば中東における現代文化の拠点として注目を集めるだろう。

Architecture with a huge rectangular solid that is smoothly shaved inside in three-dimensional curve appears on the water in front of the Arabian Sea. It is part of the project of Abu Dhabi of United Arab Emirates to develop the offshore Saadiyat Island. The three-dimensional curve expresses the sails of vessels that pass through the Arabian Sea. Visitors cross the bridge above the ocean and enter in the exhibition room floating on the ocean. Jean Nouvel and Zaha Hadid are participating in the development of the island, which will gather attention as a base of modern culture in the Middle East after the completion.

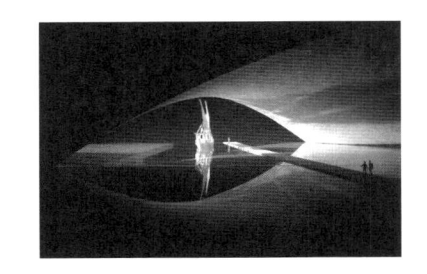

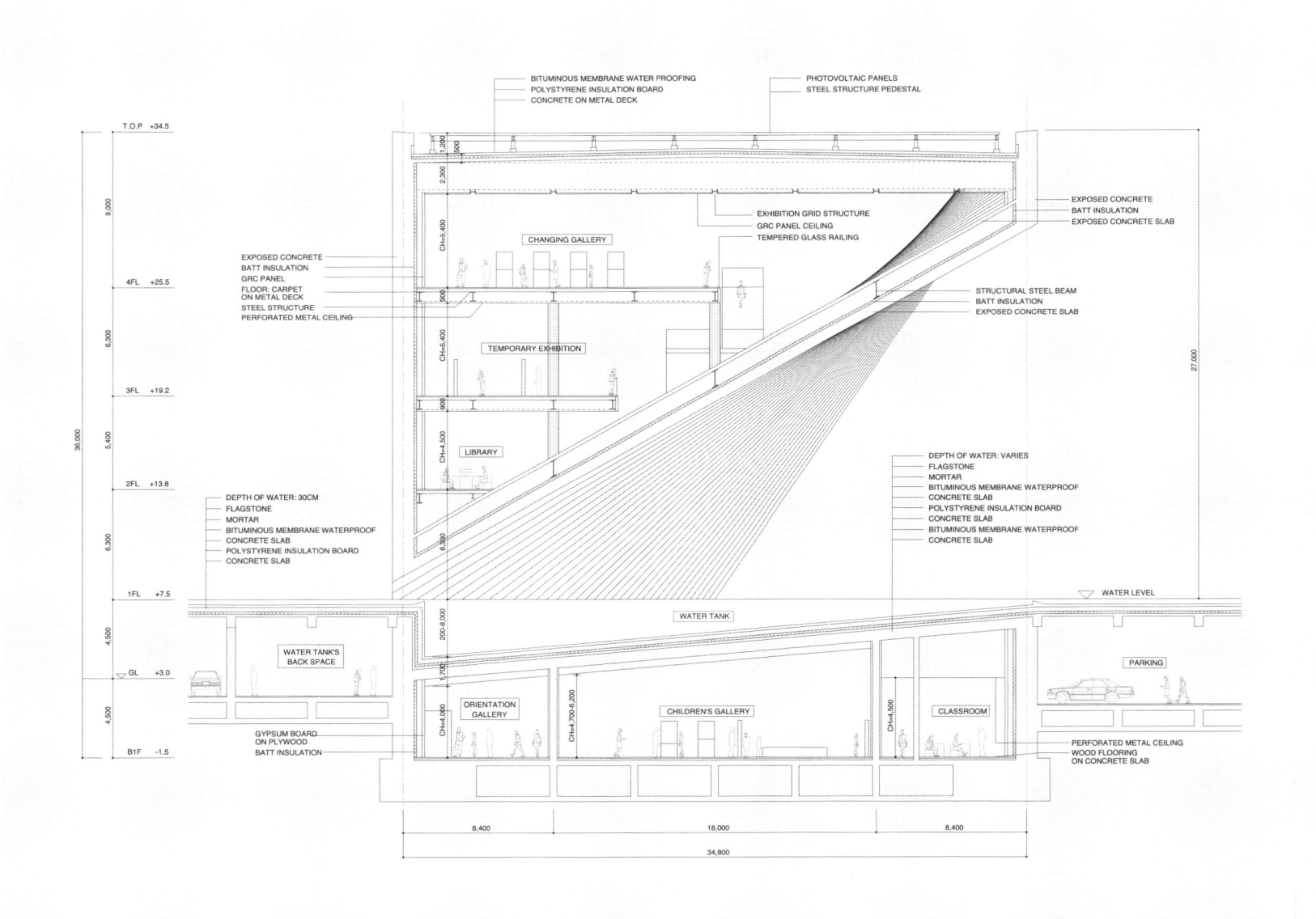

[246]
谷間の家 2006
crevice house in manhattan

.

1. アメリカ ニューヨーク | new york, USA
2. 設計 | design   2006.9
3. 構想案 | concept
4. 鉄筋コンクリート | RC
5. 住宅、ギャラリー | house, gallery
8. 延床 | total floor   317㎡

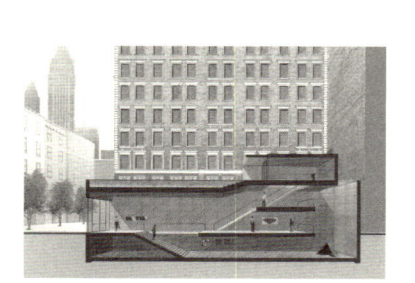

立地はメトロポリタン美術館の近く、ニューヨークの高層の建物のまさに谷間に位置する。そこの間口4メートル、奥行き30メートルの敷地に住宅を計画した。隣地との関係で高さ制限があり、2階までしか認められないことを逆手にとって、ニューヨークでは見られない住宅像を模索した。三層の直方体の建物の半分近くを地下に沈め、屋上にはプールとペントハウスを配することを提案した。内部は奥に進むに連れて上階に登っていく階段を主動線とする。谷間から都市を生け捕りにする提案という。

.

The location is close to the Metropolitan Museum of Art between high-rise buildings in New York. A residential house was planned on a property of 4 meters in width and 30 meters in length. Since a building of only up to two floors is allowed, a house that cannot be seen in New York was considered by turning the height regulation into an advantage. Almost half of a rectangular solid building with three layers is buried in ground and a pool and a penthouse are to be situated on the roof top. The stairs going up toward the inner part of the house is considered as the main floor line for the interior. The proposal is to capture the city from the valley.

[247]
デミアン・ハースト・スタジオ
2006
damien hirst studio

.

1. メキシコ ゲレーロ州 | guerrero, mexico
2. 設計 | design   2006.11
3. 構想案 | concept
5. ギャラリー、ゲストルーム | gallery, guest room
6. 敷地 | site   46,300 ㎡

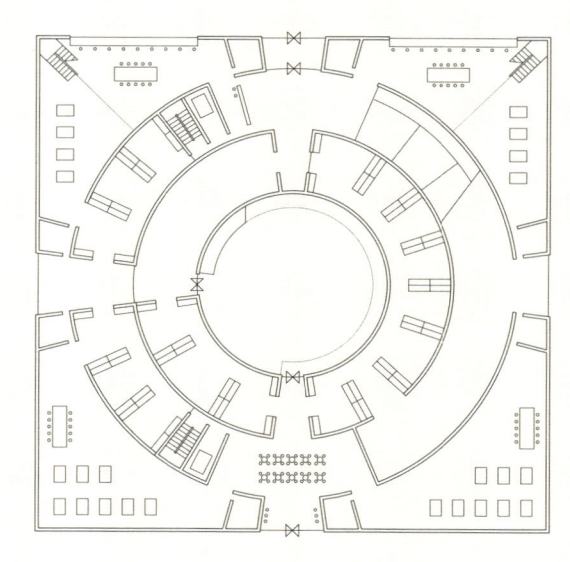

メキシコの太平洋に面した湾岸に位置する敷地は5万平方メートルにも達し、マングローブが密生している。陸地側の「スタジオ」の建物の外形は正方形の平面で、内部に同心円状の円筒の空間が入れ子となる。一方、海辺の「ビーチハウス」は、平行四辺形が斜めに交差する配置で、上階に家族のための空間、下階は外周に壁を持たない開放的なテラスに充てられ、彫刻作品もならぶ。上下階のいずれもが海に広がる視界を意識して計画された。マングローブの圧倒的な存在感と自作との対比に、安藤は幾何学に徹することで真正面から挑んでいる。

.

The vast 50,000m² property with a dense mangrove forest is located on the coast facing the Pacific Ocean in Mexico. The planform of external shape of the Studio building on the land side is a square with spaces of concentric circular cylinder are nested inside. On the other hand, the Beach House by the ocean is arranged in parallelograms intersecting diagonally and the space for the family is provided on the upper floor and an open terrace without any peripheral wall and several works of sculpture are arranged on the lower floor. Both upper and lower floors were designed to have a full view of the ocean in front. Ando straightforwardly talked to be compared with the overwhelming presence of the mangrove forest by thoroughly applying geometric forms.

全346作品録   401

[248]
21_21 デザインサイト　2007
21_21 design sight

1. 東京都港区｜minato-ku, tokyo
2. 設計｜design　2004.3 – 2005.9
3. 施工｜construction　2005.10 – 2007.2
4. 鉄筋コンクリート、一部鉄骨｜RC, steel
5. デザインミュージアム、レストラン｜
   design museum, restaurant
6. 敷地｜site　2,653.3 m²
7. 建築｜building　597.3 m²
8. 延床｜total floor　1,932.4 m²

東京・六本木の「東京ミッドタウン」の緑地の一角を占めるデザインミュージアム。デザインを展示する施設の必要性を訴え、実現の中心を担ったのはファッションデザイナーの三宅一生。三宅が自作を語る「一枚の布」という言葉を受けて、安藤は端部が地面に接する二枚の屋根がガラスの躯体を覆い、ギャラリーを地下に配する建築を構想した。地下の展示空間にはサンクンコートを介して自然光が入る。大規模開発をきっかけに複数の美術館が登場してアートの街となった六本木にあって、空間そのものが異彩を放っている。

This is a museum for designs, situated in a corner lot of a green area in "Tokyo Midtown" located in Roppongi, Tokyo. It was the fashion designer, Issey Miyake, who had appealed the necessity of a facility to exhibit works of design fields, and became the driving force to realize this facility. Inspired by the words of Miyake describing his design concept of "one piece of cloth", Ando thought of a building with a main volume in glass walls enveloped by two surfaces of roofs touching to the ground on their edges, and a gallery space buried underground. The underground exhibition space is illuminated by natural light through the sunken court. In the Roppongi area, art museums appeared after the large-scale development, and became a town of art. The space where this museum stands itself has the uniqueness.

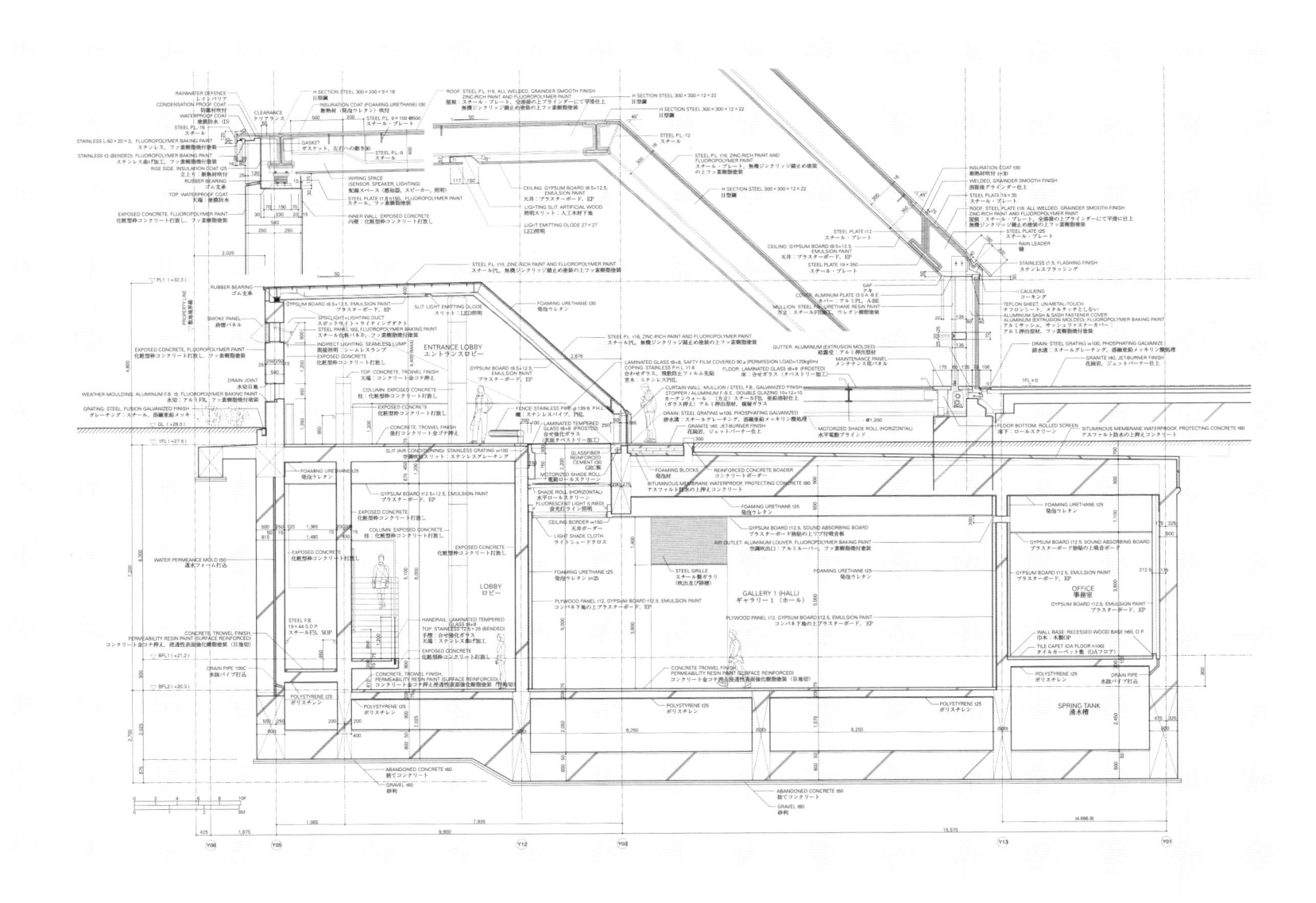

[249]
曹洞宗太岳院　2007
taigakuin temple

1. 神奈川県秦野市 | hadano, kanagawa
2. 設計 | design　2002.10 – 2006.7
3. 施工 | construction　2006.8 – 2007.10
4. 鉄骨 | steel
5. 仏教寺院 | buddhist temple
6. 敷地 | site　2,277.8 m²
7. 建築 | building　846.8 m²
8. 延床 | total floor　681.2 m²

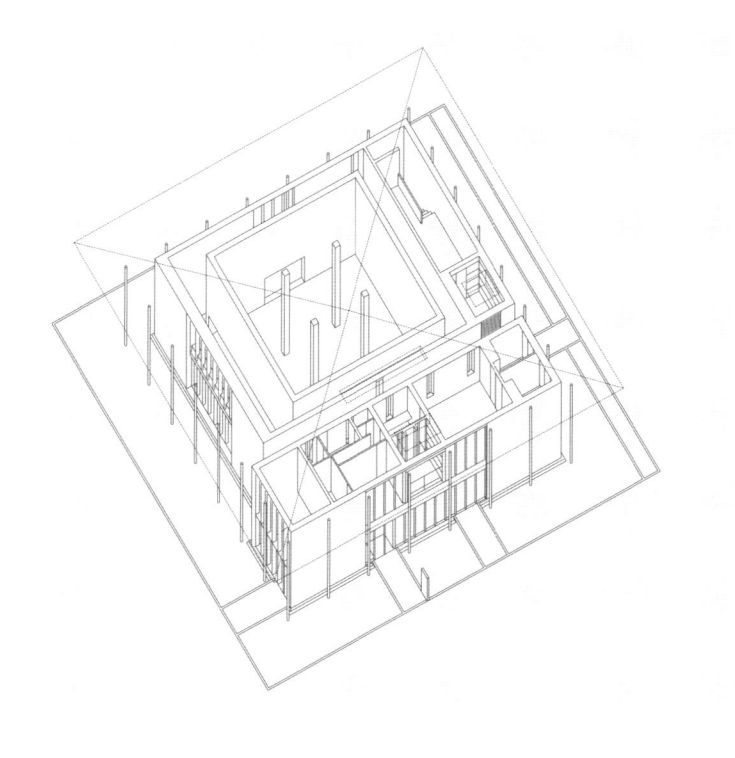

神奈川県秦野市の禅宗の古刹。関東大震災後に建設された旧本堂に代えて、安藤の和風への挑戦が形をとった。躯体は鉄骨造、深い庇の裏側の三段で列をつくる垂木や堂内の柱、格天井などは木を使い、大空間の豪快さと繊細さを両立させた。お堂全体は池に浮かぶ仕立てで、庇を支える細長い鋼管の列柱は水面で支えられているかのような仕立てをとる。傍らのさくらを楽しめる散策路を備えた「今泉名水桜公園」も安藤の構想に基づいて整備され、境内の水庭と連携して豊かな環境を形成している。

An old Zen temple in Hadano City, Kanagawa Prefecture. In replacing the former main hall (built after the Great Kanto earthquake in 1923), Ando's challenge to Japanese style materialized. In combination with the steel construction, Ando used wood for the triple rows of rafters behind the deep eaves, pillars in the hall, and the coffered ceiling, in order to balance the dynamism of the large space and daintiness. The hall itself was designed to float on an artificial pond. A narrow steel-tube colonnade — supporting the eaves — appears as if supported by the water's surface. The neighboring Imaizumi Meisui Sakura Park, which has trails for admiring cherry blossoms, was also developed based on Ando's vision. In cooperation with the water garden of the temple, a rich environment is created.

[250]
バーレーン考古学博物館　2007
bahrain archeological museum

1. バーレーン マナーマ | manama, kingdom of bahrain
2. 設計 | design　2007.6 – 2008.4
3. 構想案 | concept
4. 鉄筋コンクリート | RC
5. 美術館、研究施設 | museum, research facilities
6. 敷地 | site　28,500 m²
7. 建築 | building　2,450 m²
8. 延床 | total floor　5,950 m²

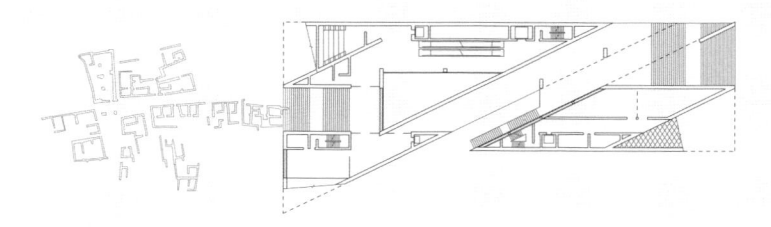

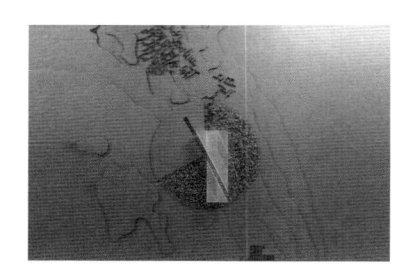

中東の砂漠の地でオアシスの跡地に計画した博物館。バーレーン全土に8500もの古墳が残ることを知り、その一角を望む場に計画した博物館を、安藤は墓標と対峙しうる強い幾何立体にすることを考えた。直方体を斜めに切断した全体形の採用はそのような意志に基づくものであり、また幾何学を基本とするモレスクの美学にも通じている。周囲に円形の人工池を配することで、水系に恵まれているバーレーンの風土やオアシスの記憶の継承も試みている。

A museum planned to be built at a site where it used to be an oasis in a desert in the Middle East. Acknowledging that there are about 8,500 ancient tombs in the whole land of Bahrain, Ando designed the museum, which was to be located where ancient tombs can be viewed, to have a strong geometric form that can stands out against the tombs. The adoption of a form of a rectangular solid that is cut on the diagonal as the overall shape of the architecture reflects Ando's will to take that challenge and also it connects to the aesthetic value of Moresque, which considers geometry as the principle of beauty. By placing artificial ponds around the building, succession of the natural features of Bahrain with a rich water system and memory of oasis is also attempted.

[251]
東京大学 建築資料館　2007
architecture reference library,
the university of tokyo

1. 東京都文京区 | bunkyo, tokyo
2. 設計 | design　2007.7
3. 構想案 | concept
4. 鉄筋コンクリート | RC
5. 大学施設 | university facilities
7. 建築 | building　829.2 m²
8. 延床 | total floor　1,367.1 m²

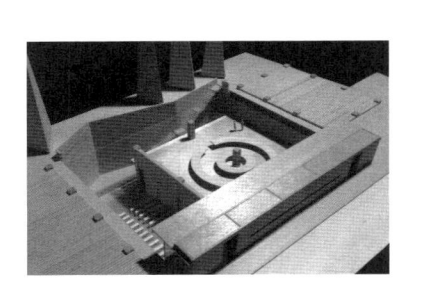

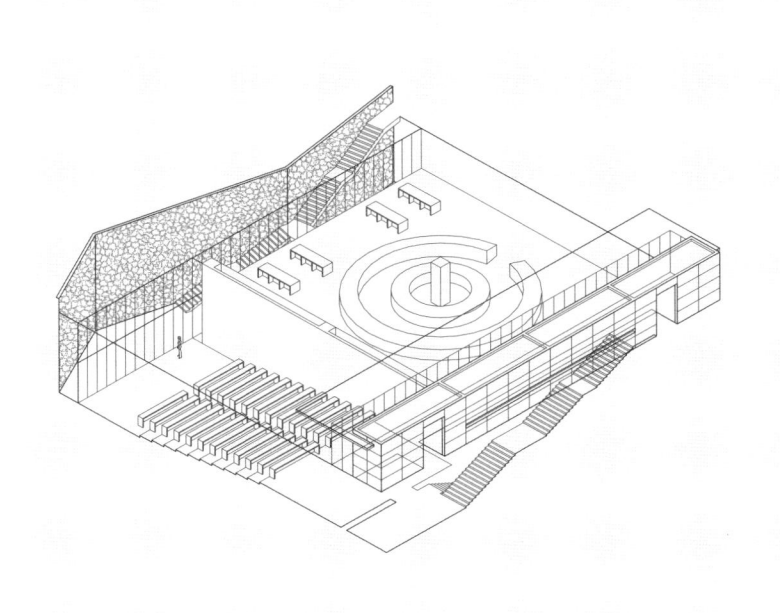

東大建築学科の先人の偉業を伝えるための展示室と講演ホールで構成する施設の計画。安藤が手がけた「福武ホール」と、赤門を挟んだ反対側の本郷通り沿いの敷地を想定した。東大本郷キャンパスの既存の景観を尊重するため、二層の建物の機能は地下に収め、地下1階に配した展示室にはサンクンガーデンから自然光が入るようにした。地下2階に講演のためのホールと資料閲覧室が配された。既存の樹木の列を尊重したことにより、サンクンガーデンの光庭は不整形な輪郭を持つ。

A plan for facilities including a lecture hall and exhibition room to pass on the achievement of predecessors of Department of Architecture, The University of Tokyo. The property is along Hongo Street on the other side of the Red Gate from FUKUTAKE HALL that Ando had worked on. Functions of the building with two floors are built underground to preserve the current scenery of the Hongo Campus of The University of Tokyo with a design to let natural light from the sunken garden enter the exhibition room located in the first basement. A lecture hall and a room to browse materials are provided in the second basement. The light garden of the sunken garden is formed in an irregular shape to preserve the row of existing trees.

[252]
ポズナニ美術館　2007
art stations poznan

1. ポーランド ポズナニ | poznan, poland
2. 設計 | design　2007.7
3. 構想案 | concept
5. 美術館 | museum of art
6. 敷地 | site　42,500 m²
7. 建築 | building　72 m²
8. 延床 | total floor　8,773 m²

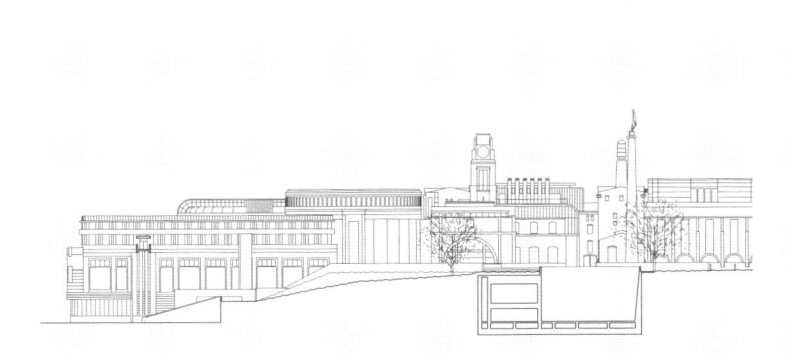

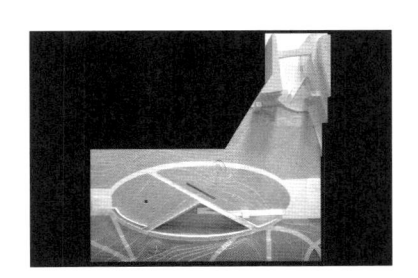

ポズナニはポーランド西部の古都として知られる。そこにある「オールド・ブリュワリー」傍らの公園に計画された美術館。既存の環境、景観に配慮して施設は地下に収めた。美術館のシルエットは地表では細長い楕円形。そのシルエットの一部に合わせてサンクンガーデンをうがつ。そこは深さ10メートル、幅55メートルに及ぶ絶え間なく水の流れ落ちる滝を想定した。水と風、滝の瀑布に反射する自然光が地下の空間に引き込まれる。来館者はこの滝を眺めながら半屋外の階段を降りて展示室へと至る。

Poznan is known as an ancient city in the west part of Poland. An art gallery was planned in a park located next to the Old Brewery in that city. The whole facility was to be built underground considering the existing environment and scenery. The silhouette of the art gallery is an oval shape on the ground surface. A sunken garden is formed along a part of the silhouette. A waterfall of 10 meters in height and 55 meters in width was planned there. Water, wind, and natural light reflected on the falling water sink down into the underground space. Visitors approach the exhibition room by going down the half-outdoor stairway while viewing this waterfall.

[253]
海の森 2007
sea forest

1. 東京都江東区 | koto-ku, tokyo
2. 設計 | design　2007.7
3. 施工 | construction　2008.5 –
5. 公園 | park

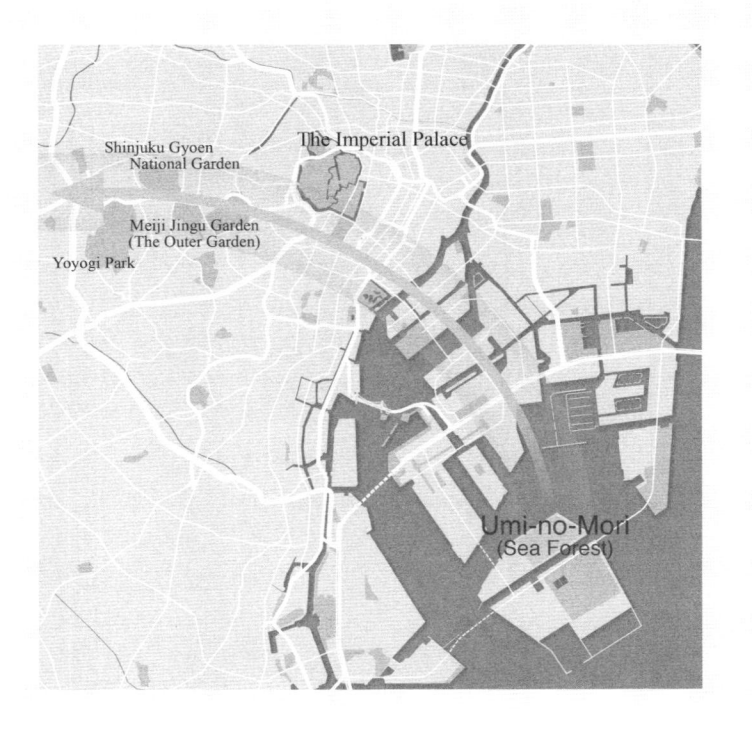

東京湾の「ごみの山」と呼ばれる埋め立て地を起伏のある88ヘクタールの広大な緑地に変身させる提案。ごみの山は、建設残土とごみが交互に重なり合う。そこに新たな地形を形成するにあたり、街路樹の剪定などで生じた葉からつくった堆肥を地表に用い、地質を一新する措置がとられた。安藤の呼びかけで募金が集まったこともあり、工事は年を追って進み、東京湾上に「緑の山」が形をとってきた。安藤の建築家としての社会的な使命感の成果のひとつ。

A proposal to change the reclaimed land called as the rubbish heap in Tokyo Bay to a large 88-hectare greenery area with hills. The rubbish heap is formed by layers of construction waste soil and rubbish. To form a new landscape to that area, an approach to change the nature of soil was taken by laying compost including leaves collected when street trees were trimmed. The construction continued year by year supported by donations gathered through the appeal made by Ando and a green mountain started to form its shape in Tokyo Bay. The project is one of the achievements of Ando led by his sense of social responsibility as being an architect.

[254]
マンハッタンのペントハウス II
2008
penthouse in manhattan II

1. アメリカ ニューヨーク | new york, USA
2. 設計 | design　2004.6 – 2006.4
3. 施工 | construction　2006.5 – 2008.7
4. 煉瓦、鉄骨、木造 | brick, steel, wood
5. 住宅、ギャラリー | house, gallery
6. 敷地 | site　230 m²
7. 建築 | building　210 m²
8. 延床 | total floor　1,050 m²

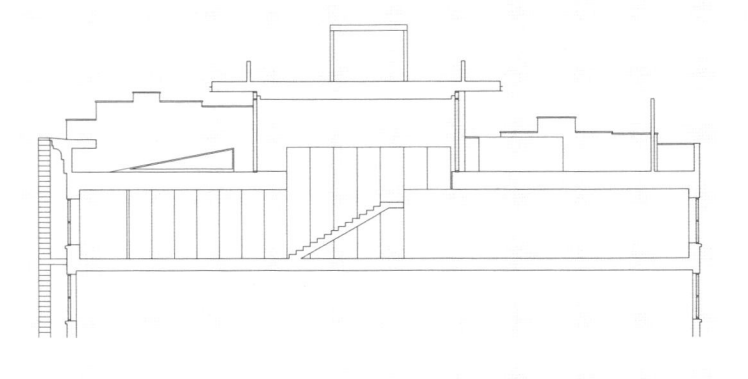

安藤は、ニューヨークでいくつか既存の住宅の増築やリノベーションの依頼を受けたなかで、ソーホーに位置する小ビルの最上階を改装するこの計画がまず日の目を見た。築100年の、間口7メートル、奥行き30メートルの小ぶりのオフィスビルが舞台だ。5階の居住スペースに屋根をうがって吹き抜けをつくり、屋上に水平屋根を架けて、既存のリビングと階段で行き来可能なペントハウスをつくった。ガラス張りの壁から下階の生活空間に自然光が入り、室内の表情が時間の移ろいとともに変化していく。ペントハウスの書斎に座るとニューヨークならではの都市の風景が一望できる。

This is the first realized project to renovate the top floor of a small building in SOHO, among requests Ando received to renovate or expand existing houses in New York. It was a small-scale office building in 100 years old, in 7m wide and 30m deep. The roof above the 5th floor living space was bored through to make a double-height space with a flat deck roof on the rooftop level. A penthouse space was provided by connecting the existing living space by a staircase. Natural light comes down from the glass wall of the penthouse to the living space of the lower floor. Sitting in the study room inside of the penthouse, whole views of the lively cityscape of New York City, unlike any other places, can be seen.

[255]
クラーク美術館
／ランダーセンター　2008
clark art institute
/ lunder center at stone hill
.

1. アメリカ ウィリアムズタウン | williamstown, USA
2. 設計 | design   2002.11–2006.3
3. 施工 | construction   2006.3–2008.6
4. 鉄骨、一部鉄筋コンクリート | Steel, RC
5. 芸術修復センター、展示室 |
    art conservation center, gallery
6. 敷地 | site   570,000 ㎡
8. 延床 | total floor   3,014 ㎡

米ウィリアムズタウンの緑の大地に施設を構える「クラーク美術館」は、印象派のコレクションに加えて、絵画修復技術など学術面でも知られる。安藤は施設全体の新たな計画を依頼され、まず芸術修復に取り組むランダーセンターを実現した。60度で交差するコンクリートの壁が直方体の建物を貫く。その壁には周囲の自然を堪能するための額縁としての大きな切り欠きがあり、そこから望む緑は、人工的な壁の質感ゆえに際立って見える。壁によって１階部分は「展示」と「修復」の二つのゾーンに分けられる。「展示」ゾーンはウッドデッキのテラスに面しており、鑑賞者はそこからも自然を味わうことができる。→参照［312］

"STERLING AND FRANCINE CLARK ART INSTITUTE" building standing on a green field of Williamstown, Massachusetts, is known for its collection of Impressionism paintings, as well as the position established in academic field for its restoration technologies of art works. Ando was asked for a new plan for the entire facility as new buildings, and the Lunder Center, where art restoration works take place, was realized first. The main volume of the building in cuboid shape is penetrated by a concrete wall intersecting at 60˚angle. This wall has a large cut out as a picture frame to fully appreciate the surrounding nature, and the view of the greenery through this wall stands out clearly because of the artificial quality and texture of the wall. The first floor part can be divided into two zones as "exhibition" and "restoration" by the wall. The "exhibition" zone faces the terrace of the wood deck, and visitors can enjoy the surrounding nature from there. → see also [312]

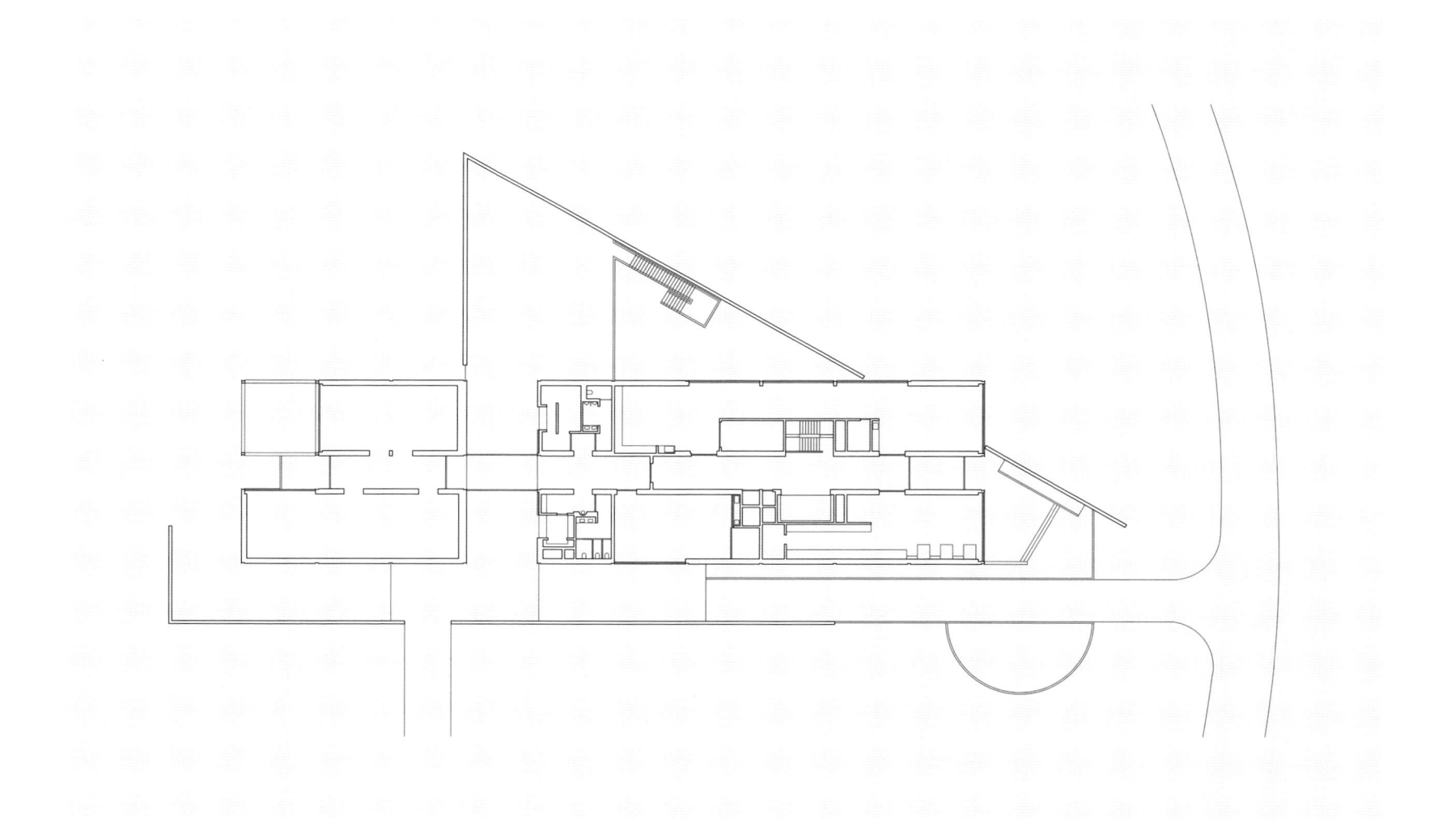

[256]

スリランカの住宅 2008
house in sri lanka

1. スリランカ ミリッサ | mirissa, srilanka
2. 設計 | design　2004.2 – 2006.2
3. 施工 | construction　2006.5 – 2008.12
4. 鉄筋コンクリート | RC
5. 住宅、アトリエ | house, atlier
6. 敷地 | site　131,621㎡
7. 建築 | building　955㎡
8. 延床 | total floor　2,577㎡

安藤自身、「住宅としての機能をジグザグに蛇行するヴォリュームに配した」と記している通り、海に面した小高い敷地に「N」の字を左右反転させ、その右から足を伸ばしたような不思議な屋根伏せが印象的だ。実業家と画家の夫婦のための住宅で、内部は生活空間をゆったりと配し、併せて、画家である妻の制作のために、天井のスリットから自然光が入るアトリエも設けた。コンクリートの精密な施工が難しかったため、日本の老練な技術者が、不安定な政治情勢をおして、現地に出向いて指導にあたった。スリランカで参照対象となりうる作品が出来たと安藤は自負している。

Ando described about this house as "functionalities of a house were distributed in a volume running in zigzag pattern". Roof plan of the house illustrates his words and attracts notice that a volume in horizontally flipped "N" character shape is located on a hilltop facing to the ocean, with an extension from its right side as if like a leg is stretched out. This is a house for a couple, a businessman and his wife as a painter. Interior spaces of the house for daily living are spaciously distributed, and an atelier space to paint for the wife of the client is also provided, which is illuminated by natural light coming down from slits on the ceiling. Because precise casting work of concrete was difficult, Japanese skilled engineers went to the field and instructed them in an unstable political situation of Sri Lanka. Ando is confident that a piece of architecture was realized to become a reference for local construction industry of Sri Lanka.

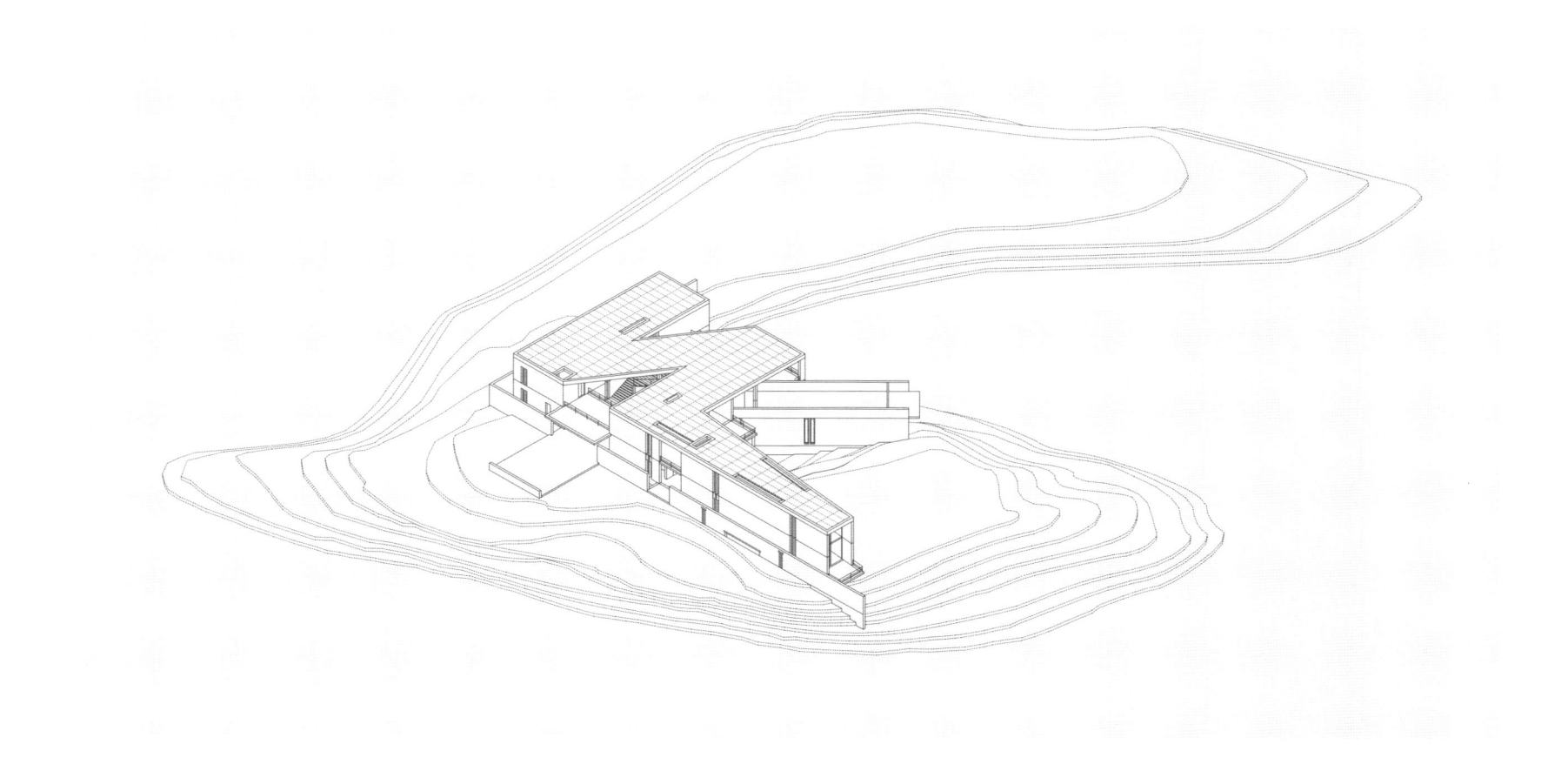

[257]
聖心女子学院
創立100周年記念ホール　2008
sacred heart school,
100th anniversary hall

1. 東京都港区 | minato-ku, tokyo
2. 設計 | design   2004.8 – 2007.6
3. 施工 | construction   2007.6 – 2008.7
4. 鉄筋コンクリート、鉄骨鉄筋コンクリート、鉄骨 | RC, SRC, steel
5. 大学施設 | university facilities
6. 敷地 | site   58,640.5 m²
7. 建築 | building   642.1 m²
8. 延床 | total floor   986.8 m²

もとのキャンパスは、日本のモダニズムを牽引したアントニン・レーモンドが手がけたもの。記念ホールは、1960年代に建設された屋内プール棟に覆い被さる形で計画された。プール棟の屋根から上は、傾斜した屋根とガラス壁で構成する多面体で、その内部がホールの空間となった。そこからは斜めのガラス壁を通して、キャンパスの緑が見通せる。またホールからプール棟の屋上を生かして新設された屋外デッキに進むことも可能で、そこでもキャンパスを見渡すことができる。幾何学と自然というテーマが、安藤のレーモンドへのオマージュとして追求されている。

The original campus was designed by Antonin Raymond, who became the guiding light of Modern Architecture in Japan. Proposal for this anniversary hall was made to provide a new structure to hang over the interior pool wing built in 1960s. The part above the roof of the pool wing was composed of a polyhedron derived from inclined roofs and glass walls, while its interior space became a hall. Sitting inside of this space, visitors can overlook the greenery of the campus through the glass walls. They can also proceed to the newly constructed exterior deck utilizing the space from the hall to the rooftop of the pool wing, and they can also see the views of campus area. This building illustrates the homage of Ando to Raymond, through the theme of geometric forms and nature.

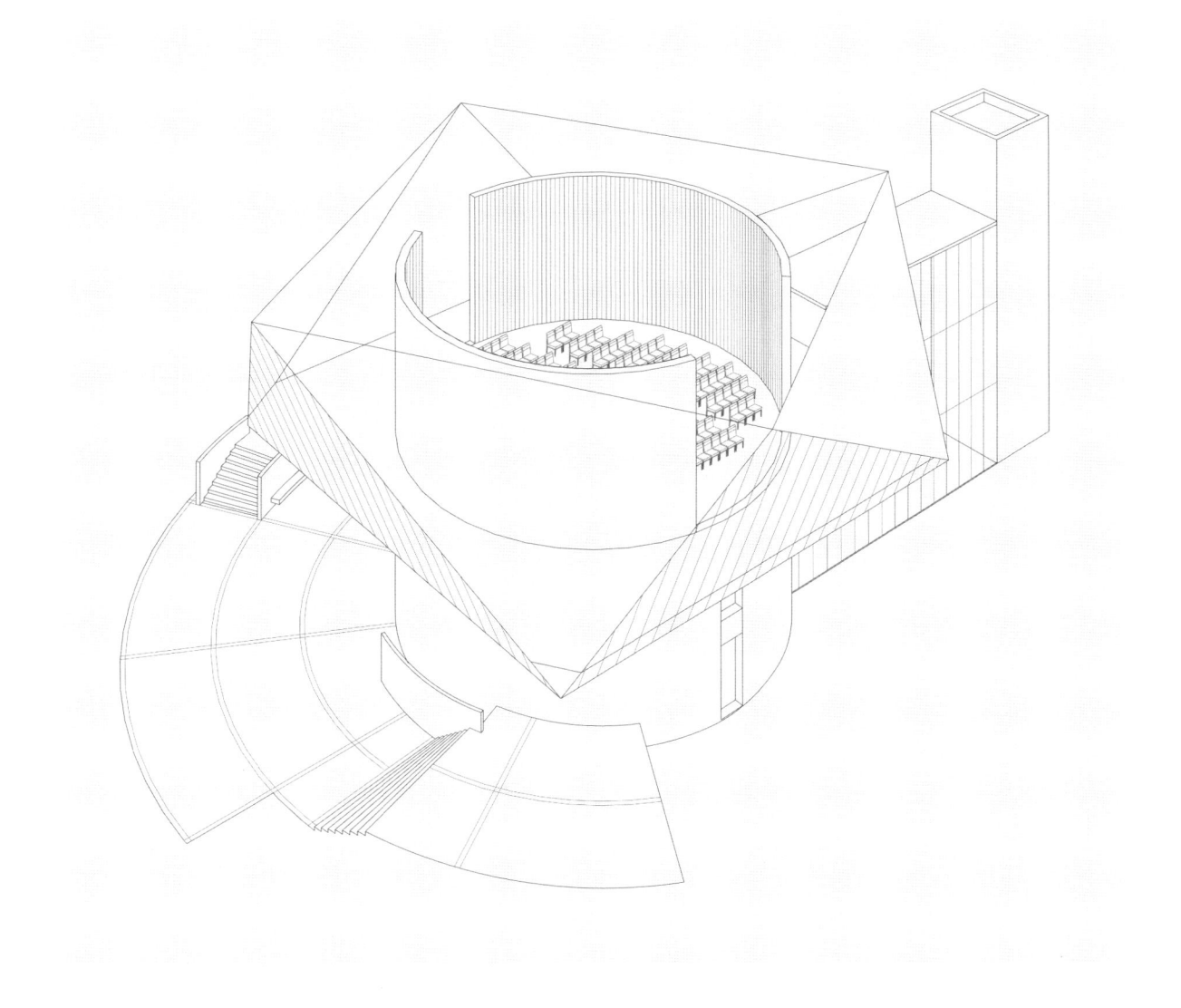

346 Complete Works

[258]

東急東横線渋谷駅　2008
tokyu toyoko-line shibuya station

1. 東京都渋谷区｜shibuya-ku, tokyo
2. 設計｜design　2005.1–2006.10
3. 施工｜construction　2006.12–2008.6
4. 鉄筋コンクリート、一部鉄骨｜RC, steel
5. 駅舎・鉄道施設｜railway station
6. 敷地｜site　15,278.6 m²
7. 建築｜building　109.5 m²
8. 延床｜total floor　27,725.1 m²

計画されながら長く実現できなかった渋谷駅周辺の開発が、この地下駅の実現で動き始めた。安藤は土木的な地下工事の大スケールの空間のなかに、自身が「中之島プロジェクトII」で提案した卵形ドームを地下のコンコースから電車の発着するホームまでのエスカレーターを覆う形で実現した。当初は、コンクリートによる構造を考えていたが、耐アルカリ性ガラス繊維補強セメントが採用された。卵型ドームの中央には楕円形の吹き抜けも設けられ、下層階を見通すことができる。

Development around Shibuya station that was planned but could not be initiated started to advance by the implementation of this station. Ando placed an egg-shape dome he proposed in NAKANOSHIMA PROJECT II over the area from the underground concourse to the escalator of the platform where trains arrive and leave inside the large-scale space of civil engineering underground construction. A structure with concrete was considered first but it was changed to use alkali resistant glass fiber reinforced cement. The center of the egg-shape dome has an oval wellhole structure to the lower floor.

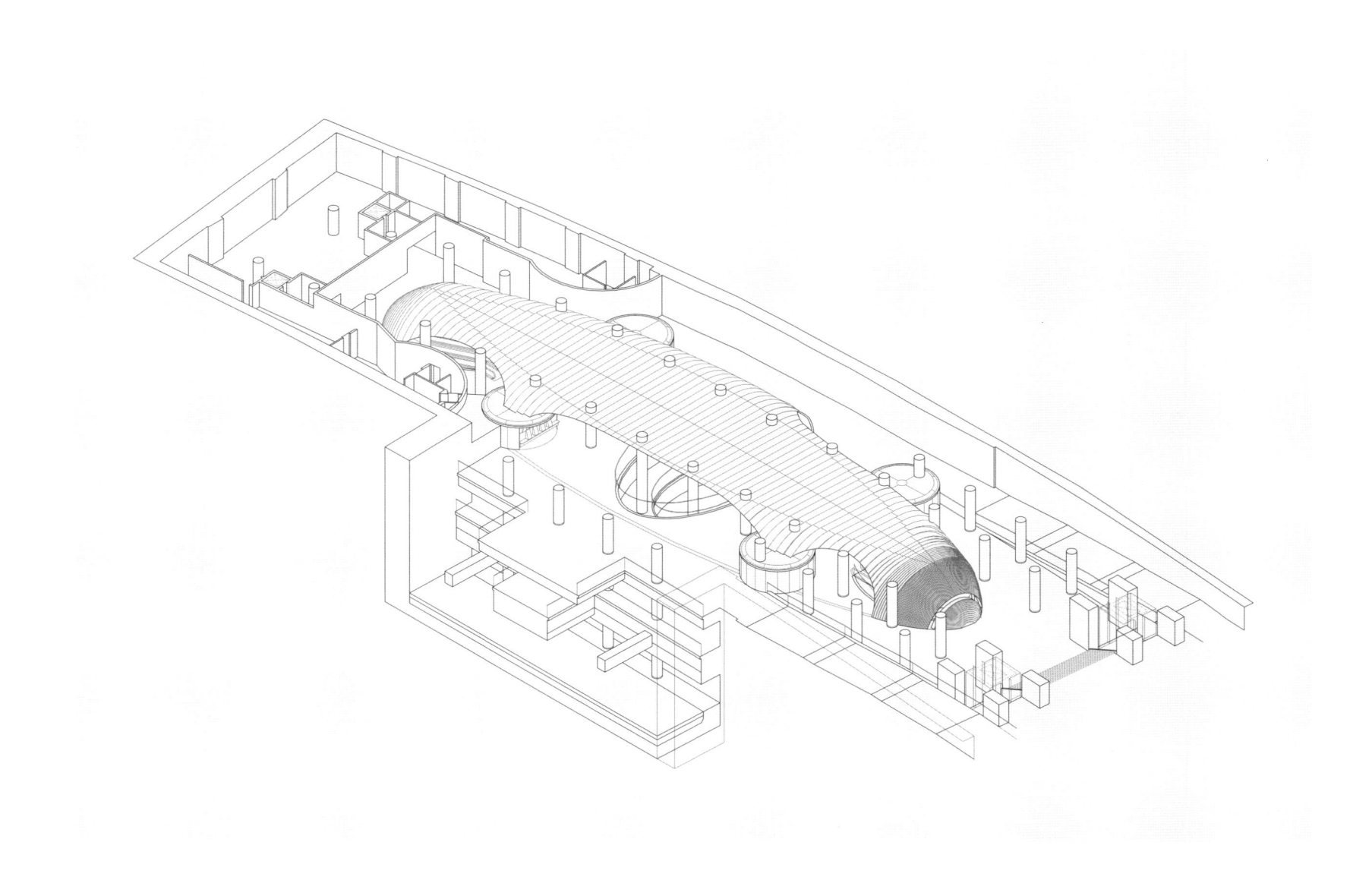

[259]
東京大学情報学環・福武ホール
2008
interfaculty initiative
in information studies, fukutake hall,
the university of tokyo

1. 東京都文京区 | bunkyo-ku, tokyo
2. 設計 | design   2005.9 – 2006.9
3. 施工 | construction   2006.12 – 2008.3
4. 鉄筋コンクリート | RC
5. 大学施設 | university facilities
6. 敷地 | site   402,682.2 m²
7. 建築 | building   1,454.2 m²
8. 延床 | total floor   4,045.7 m²

東大本郷キャンパスの赤門を入って左手の細長い敷地にコンクリートの壁が続く。敷地は奥行き10メートル、間口100メートルで極端に細長い緑地だった。施設の半分を地下に配し、構内通路側に高さ3.6メートルの独立したコンクリート壁が立てられた。その壁と建物本体との間には細長い地下のオープンスペースが設けられた。コンクリートの長大な壁のテクスチュアは、関東大震災後に整備された内田祥三設計のゴシックのキャンパスと衝突する。この建築の出現を刺激剤に新たなキャンパスへの挑戦が始まることを安藤は期待している。

When entering Aka mon ("The Red Gate") of Hongo Campus of the University of Tokyo, concrete walls continue on the slender site on the left. The site was an extremely elongated green area with a depth of 10m and an entrance of 100m. Half of the facility was placed underground, and an independent concrete wall with a height of 4m, the same length as the main volume of the building, was set up on the campus passage side. An elongated underground open space was provided between the wall and the main volume of the building. The texture of this extremely long concrete wall collides with the Gothic style campus design of Uchida Yoshikazu, which was developed after The Great Kanto Earthquake. Ando is expecting this new architecture will drive a challenge to become a new campus of modern days.

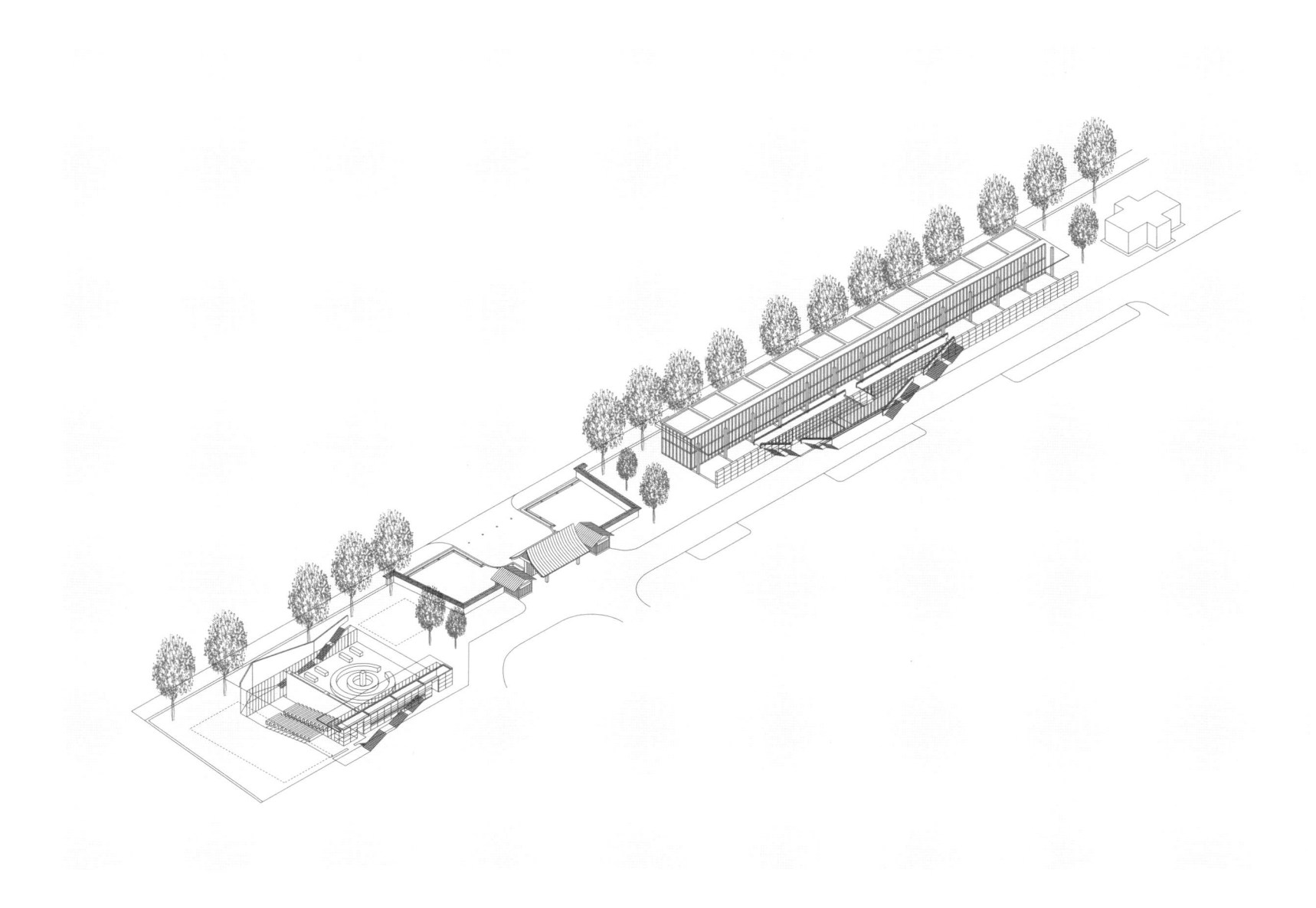

[260]
ハンファHRDセンター 2008
hanwha hrd center

1. 大韓民国 京畿道 加平郡 |
   gapyeong-gun, gyeonggi-do, south korea
2. 設計 | design 2005.10 – 2007.6
3. 施工 | construction 2007.6 – 2008.10
4. 鉄筋コンクリート | RC
5. 会議・研修施設 | training facilities
6. 敷地 | site 164,766 m²
7. 建築 | building 10,823 m²
8. 延床 | total floor 22,811 m²

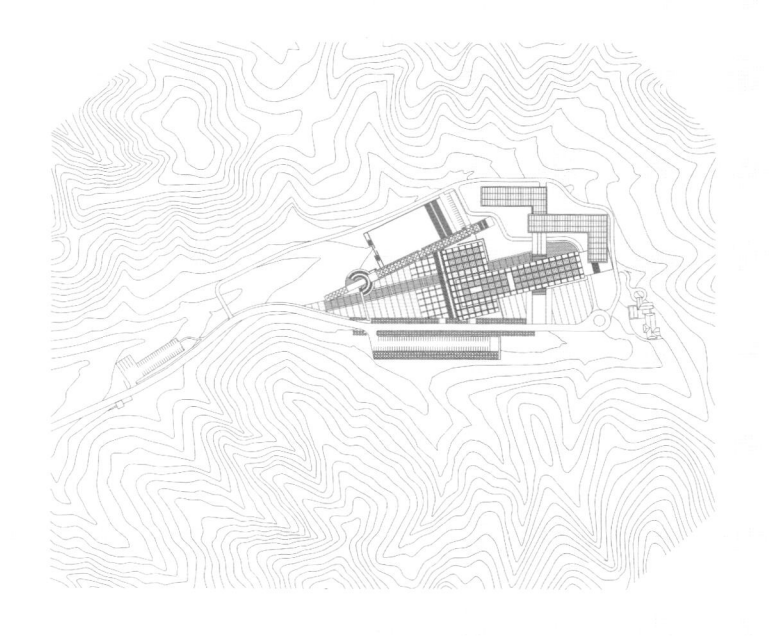

ハンファは火薬の製造会社から金融などに進出し、グローバルな存在になった韓国企業。ソウルから車で2時間ほど離れた自然豊かな立地に研修施設の設計を安藤に依頼した。ゆったりしたレイアウトの低層の研修棟、宿泊棟などの施設は自然を活かしたランドスケープデザインによって結ばれる。エントランスホールの繊細な柱列は、安藤ならではの造形の水準を示す。水庭とその傍らを緩やかに下る幅の広い屋外階段を歩みながら、自然に触れられる仕立てをとっている。

Hanwha is a Korean company that started as a gunpowder manufacturer and became a global enterprise by entering in the financial field. A training facilities design was requested for a property full of nature located in Gyeonggi-do, which is about a two-hour drive from Seoul. Facilities including a training building and accommodation building is designed with a spacious layout and harmonized with the landscape design effectively using the nature. The detailed column row of the entrance hall is demonstrating the standard of Ando's styling where nature can be felt while walking on the wide outdoors stairs that gradually descends to the water garden.

[261]
済州島〈石の門〉〈風の門〉 2008
gate of stone and gate of wind in jeju island

1. 大韓民国 済州島 | jeju-do, south korea
2. 設計 | design 2005.11 – 2007.4
3. 施工 | construction 2007.5 – 2008.6
4. 鉄筋コンクリート | RC
5. 美術館 | museum of art
6. 敷地 | site 16677 m² [stone], 9057 m² [wind]
7. 建築 | building 817 m² [stone], 1697 m² [wind]
8. 延床 | total floor 1302 m² [stone], 2039 m² [wind]

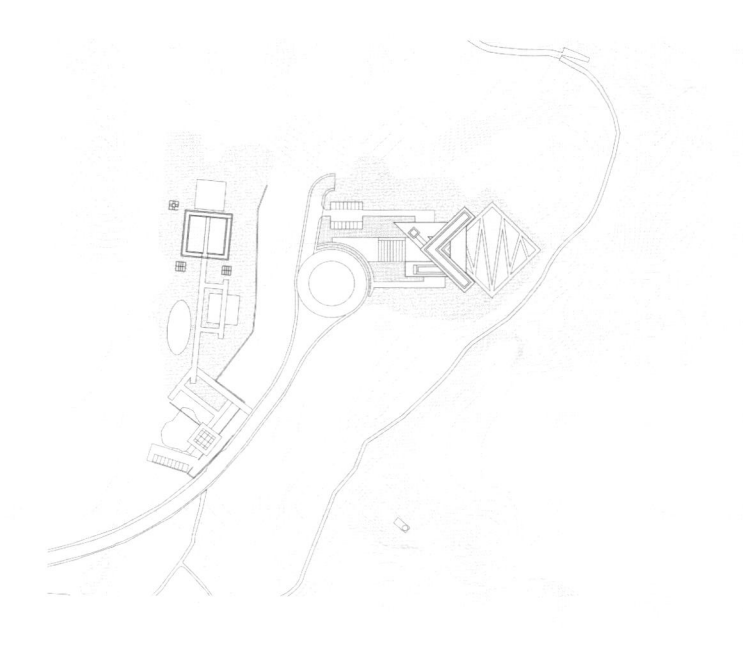

韓国・済州島東部のリゾート「ソプジコジ・フェニックス・リゾート」の施設。「石の門」と「風の門」はひと組で、前者は、荒々しい自然石の庭園をコンクリートのプロムナードで巡り、自然石を積んだ壁をくぐる仕立てになっている。ここを通ることで来訪者は、日常の暮らしから切り離された場にいることを認識する。一方、後者はコンクリート打ち放しの低い壁と足元を吹き放ちにしたレストラン、ギャラリーの取り合わせで、一段高いガラス張りの2階のレストランから海への視界を満喫できる。

Facilities for Seopjikoji Phoenix Resort located at the east area of Jeju Island, Korea. The GATE OF STONE and GATE OF WIND are formed as a pair and the former has a concrete promenade make a circle through the garden with rough natural stones and goes through a wall made by natural stones piled up. Visitors would acknowledge that they are separated from daily lives by going through this gate. On the other hand, the latter is a combination of a restaurant and a gallery with low exposed concrete walls that is open at the lower area. The glass-sided restaurant on the 2nd floor on a higher level offers an ocean view that visitors can fully enjoy.

[262]
北京国子監ホテル＋美術館
2008
beijing guozijian hotel

1. 中華人民共和国 北京 | beijing, china
2. 設計 | design   2008.4
3. 構想案 | concept
5. ホテル、美術館 | hotel, museum
6. 敷地 | site   16,496 m²
8. 延床 | total floor   42,760 m²

北京・故宮の北東部に位置する歴史的街区の一角を占める工場施設の改修計画。既存の建物のホテルへの改修とともに、油彩画を展示する美術館が新設される。改修は傾斜屋根を保持して、新たに設けた人工池と水路に見合うように外壁を再構成した。水が歴史ある場所に新たな空間イメージをもたらす効果を期待した。新築の美術館も屋上に配したクラブハウスの屋根を伝統的な四合院風の傾斜屋根とすることで周囲のスカイラインとの調和をはかっている。全体のレイアウトは中庭を囲う四合院を意識し、伝統と創造の融合を意図している。

A renovation plan of plant facilities of a historical area located at the northeast of the Forbidden City, Beijing. An art gallery that displays oil paintings was newly built by the renovation of the existing building. The sloped roof typical in Beijing was maintained while exterior walls were restructured to suit the artificial pond and water channel newly created. It was anticipated that water would provide a new spatial image to the historical location. A traditional Siheyuan-type sloped roof was arranged on the clubhouse where the new art gallery is located in harmony with the surrounding skyline. Harmony of tradition and creation is intended for the overall layout followed the design of Siheyuan that surrounds the courtyard.

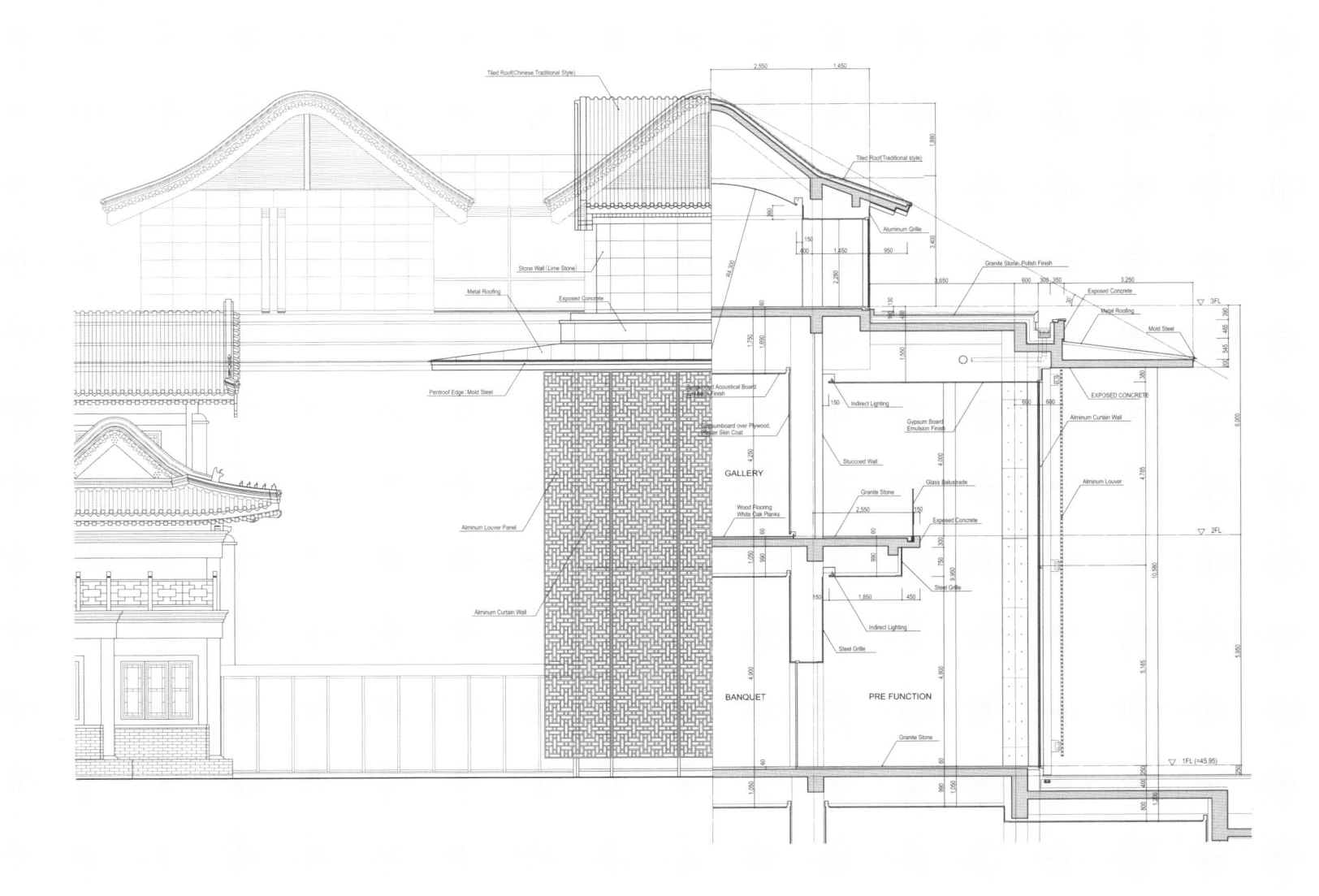

[263]

カペラ・ニセコ・リゾートホテル 2008
capella niseko resort & residence

1. 北海道ニセコ町 | niseko, hokkaido
2. 設計 | design 2008.2 – 2010.5
3. 構想案 | concept
4. 鉄筋コンクリート | RC
5. リゾートホテル | resort hotel
6. 敷地 | site 128,800 m²
7. 建築 | building 29,000 m²
8. 延床 | total floor 60,500 m²

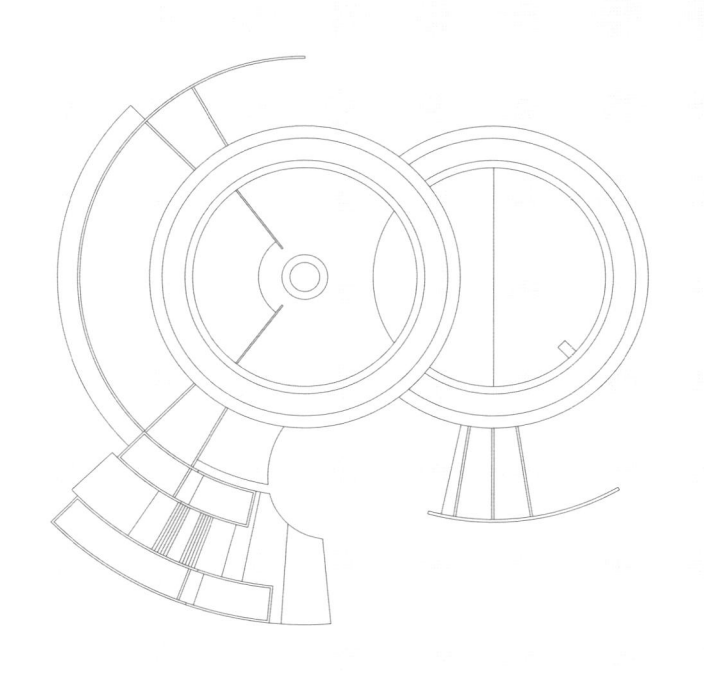

北海道のニセコに海外資本が立案したホテルと住居の複合開発。安藤は眺望を優先して、二つの円が鎖を繋ぐように重なり合う計画を提案した。低層棟の1階と、三層の棟の最上階に客室が配され、滞在中の窓から常に雄大な自然を眺める仕立てがとられた。円の内部はそれぞれ水庭と植栽された庭にする計画だ。「世界のどこにもない非日常が体験できるホテル」をという施主の求めに、自然の景観で応える配置が決定された。

A composite development project for a hotel and residential area planned by a foreign capital in Niseko, Hokkaido. Ando proposed a design to have two circles overlap each other in a chain form prioritizing the scenery. Guest rooms are provided on the 1st floor of the low-rising building and the top floor of the three-story building to offer a gorgeous view of nature from room windows during the stay. A water garden and plant garden are to be created inside each circle. The layout was decided to offer the scenery of nature as the response to the client's request to create a hotel that offers an extraordinary experience that cannot be found anywhere in the world.

[264]

ヴィラ・ブダペスト
（旧首相公邸改造計画） 2008
villa budapest

1. ハンガリー ブダペスト | budapest, hungary
2. 設計 | design 2008.10 – 2009.12
3. 構想案 | concept
5. 美術館 | museum of art
6. 敷地 | site 3,200 m²
7. 建築 | building 1,400 m²
8. 延床 | total floor 3,400 m²

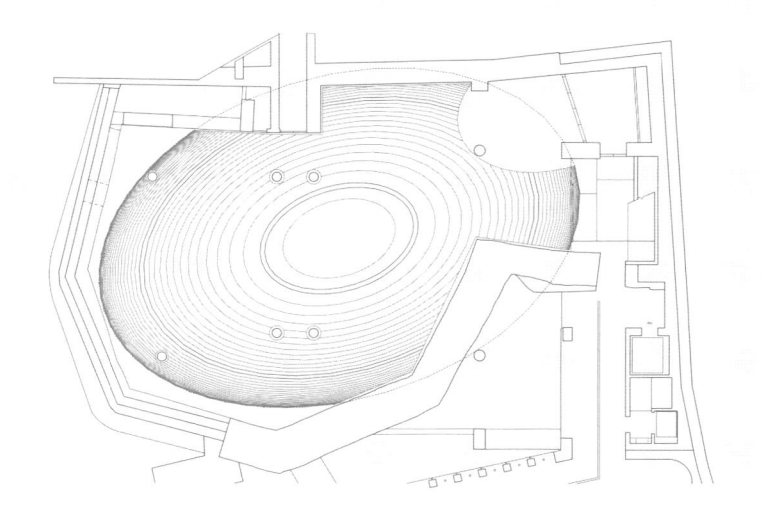

世界遺産のブダペストの歴史街区に旧首相官邸を復元、内部にホール、ギャラリー、レストランなどを収める計画。安藤はネオ・ルネサンスの復元建築の前庭を掘り下げ、楕円形の天蓋のあるホールを挿入することを提案した。ホールの周囲からは自然光が地下のフロアに入り込み、ホワイエは純白の空間となって旧建築の復元と対比的なイメージを醸しだす。復元した建築の1階には立方体のホールやシャンパンバーの巨大な三角形のカウンターを設え、そこでも新旧の衝突がもたらす活気を期待した。

A plan to restore the former prime minister's official residence in the historical section of Budapest registered as the world's heritage. Facilities such as a hall, gallery, and restaurant are to be located inside the building. Ando proposed to dig the front yard of the restored Neo-Renaissance architecture and insert a hall with an oval canopy. Natural light enters from periphery of the hall into the underground floor where the foyer creates a space of pure white that is opposite to the impression of restoring an ancient architecture. A huge triangle counter for the cubic hall and champagne bar is installed on the 1st floor of the restored architecture to create vigor from collision of the new and old.

[265]
六甲プロジェクト IV　2009
rokko project IV

1. 神戸市灘区 | nada-ku, kobe
2. 設計 | design　2002.1-2004.11
3. 施工 | construction　2004.12-2009.6
4. 鉄筋コンクリート、鉄骨鉄筋コンクリート | RC, SRC
5. 病院、有料老人ホーム | hospital, retirement home
6. 敷地 | site　26,691.7 m²
7. 建築 | building　5,412.6 m²
8. 延床 | total floor　32,080.5 m²

神戸の六甲山の傾斜を活用したプロジェクトの第4期。神戸海星病院2棟とセコム系の介護付き有料老人ホーム「コンフォートヒルズ六甲」1棟の計3棟が、1期から3期の集まるエリアの約100メートル西の斜面地に建設された。背後に位置する老人ホームから見おろす病院の屋根は屋上緑化が施され、3期までと同じく空と海、木々の緑を楽しめる仕立てとなっている。高齢化社会を踏まえて、こうした福祉施設が集合住宅群の一角に整備されたことは喜ばしい。
→参照 [50]、[133]、[180]

The fourth term of a condominium built using the sloped ground of Mt. Rokko in Kobe. Two buildings of Kobe Kaisei Hospital and one building of Comfort Hills Rokko, a private nursing home by an affiliate company of Secom were built on a sloped ground about 100 meters west from the area where the first term to the third term are located. A rooftop planted is provided on the roof top of the hospital, which is visible from the nursing home placed behind to offer the same enjoyable view of sky, ocean and green of trees as the view from the first to third term of the project. It is desirable that such welfare facilities were built in a group of condominiums in perspective of the aging society. → see also [50], [133], [180]

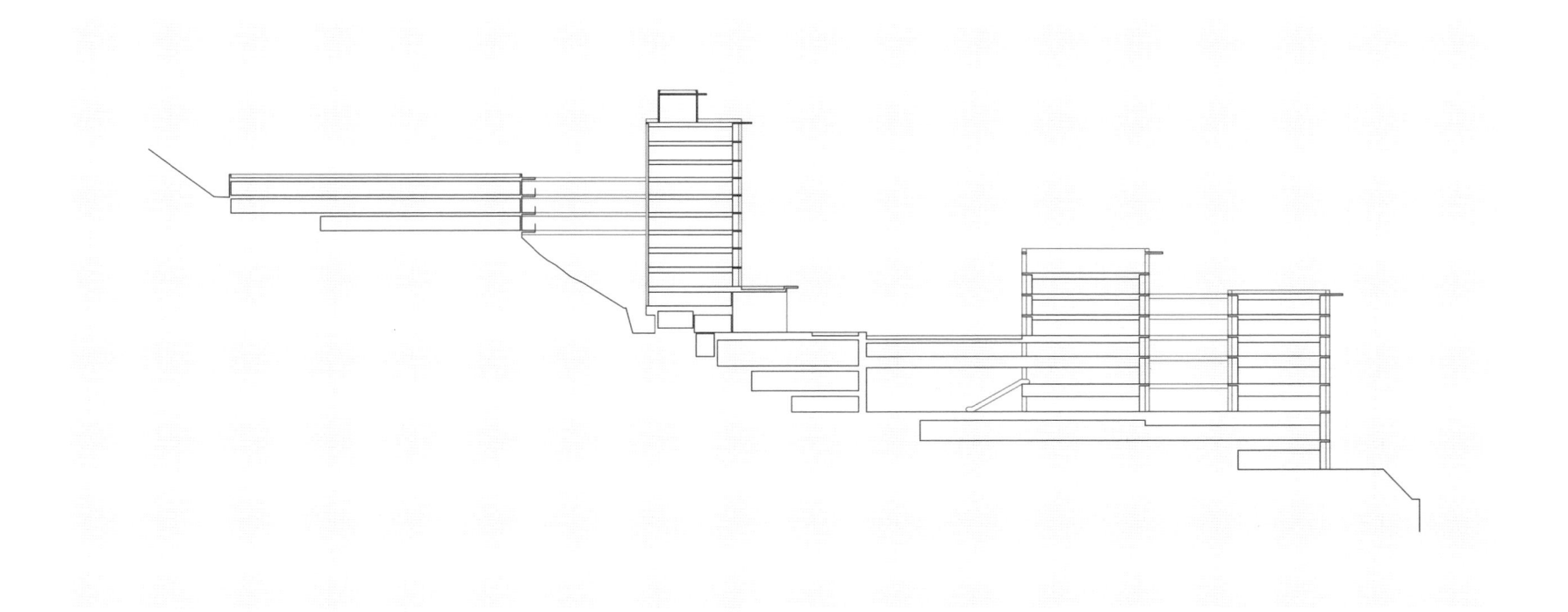

[266]

プンタ・デラ・ドガーナ　2009
punta della dogana
contemporary art center

1. イタリア ヴェネチア｜venice, italy
2. 設計｜design　2006.1–2007.9
3. 施工｜construction　2007.10–2009.5
4. レンガ、木造｜brick, wood
5. 美術館（改修）｜museum of art (renovation)
6. 敷地｜site　4,250 m²
7. 建築｜building　2,910 m²
8. 延床｜total floor　4,585 m²

イタリア・ヴェネチアの大運河の海への出口に位置する旧・税関の建物が、安藤の手で美術館に再生された。15世紀の躯体はそのままに、内側にコンクリートの箱が挿入された。入れ子のコンクリートは中央に配したセントラルコートと呼ばれる空間を囲う控え目なもので、館内に広がるギャラリーの区切りは、三角形の底辺と平行にならぶ、もとからあった煉瓦壁が活用された。そのことが木造と煉瓦の構造体を際立たせ、来訪者は、現代美術の展示、安藤のコンクリート、さらに歴史のテクスチュアの三つの要素が絡み合う静かなダイナミズムに魅了される。→参照［242］、［308］

By the hands of Ando, a building previously used as a custom house located at the gate of the Grand Canal to the ocean in Venice, Italy, was transformed into a museum. The skeleton of 15th century was kept as it is, and a concrete box was placed inside. This nested concrete box is a modest element to envelope a space allocated in the center of the space called the "central court". Existing brick walls placed in parallel at the bottom lines of triangle shapes are utilized as partition walls of the galleries extending inside of the building. This design highlights the structural elements in wood and brick. Visitors will be fascinated by combination of three elements to show quiet dynamism — exhibition presentation of modern art, the concrete element of Ando's design, and texture of historic context. → see also [242], [308]

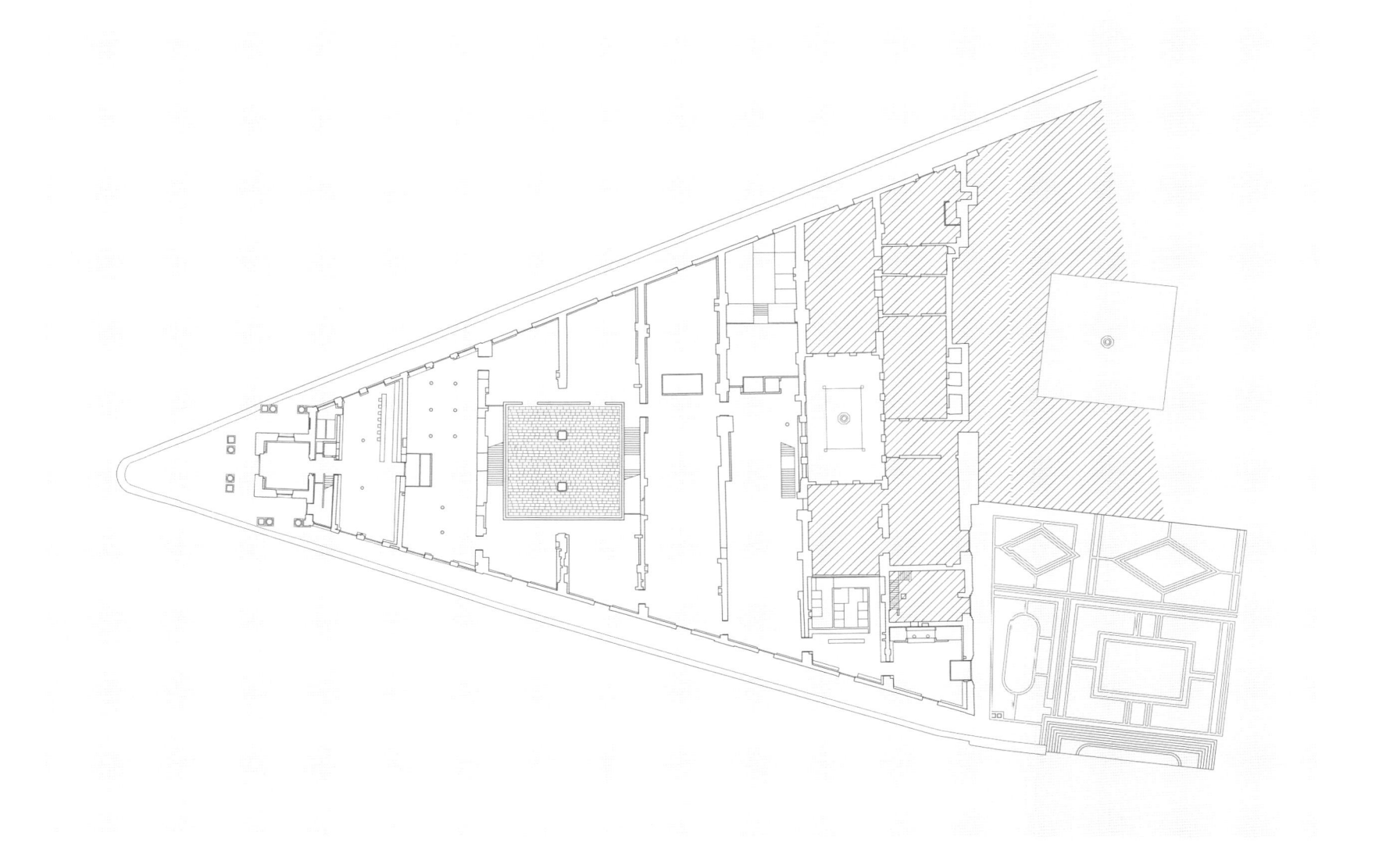

[267]

IPU環太平洋大学　2009, 2013
international pacific university

1. 岡山県岡山市 | okayama
2. 設計 | design　2006.8 – 2008.7 [TOP GUN]
3. 施工 | construction　2008.7 – 2009.8 [TOP GUN]
4. 鉄筋コンクリート、一部鉄骨、鉄筋鉄骨コンクリート | RC, steel, SRC [TOP GUN]
5. 大学施設 | university facilities
6. 敷地 | site　61,856.4 m²
7. 建築 | building　3,442.8 m² [TOP GUN]
8. 延床 | total floor　4,745.1 m² [TOP GUN]

2007年創立の大学の施設群。「TOP GUN」（アスリートホール）はキャンパスのエントランスに位置し、敷地の幅の相当部分を占める低層のガラス壁が立ちはだかる。この棟は屋上まで階段であがることの出来る構成で、建築がランドスケープの一翼を担うことが意識されている。「PHILOSOPHIA」（講義室棟、2013年完成）は、コンクリート打ち放しの空間で並列配置の教室、六角形平面のレクチャーホールで構成されている。緑豊かな周囲の環境と抑制した表現の建築が共存する。安藤設計のキャンパスの整備はアスリートホール近接の「Harmony」（カフェテラス）が実現し、「Discovery」と呼ばれる新しい講義室棟（実習棟）も建設されることになっている。

A complex of university facilities founded in 2007. TOP GUN (athlete hall) is located at the entrance of the campus with low glass walls placed along much of the width of the property. The rooftop of this building can be approached by stairs; it is anticipated that the architecture will be a part of the landscape of the area. On the other hand, the PHILOSOPHIA (building for lecture rooms, 2013) consists of classrooms in parallel layout and a hexagon shaped lecture hall. The architecture in reduced expression coexists with the ambient environment of rich greenery. Improvements of the campus designed by Ando have been realized by "HARMONY" (café terrace) built in the neighbour of the athlete hall and a new lecture building (building for training) called "DISCOVERY" is also planned to be built.

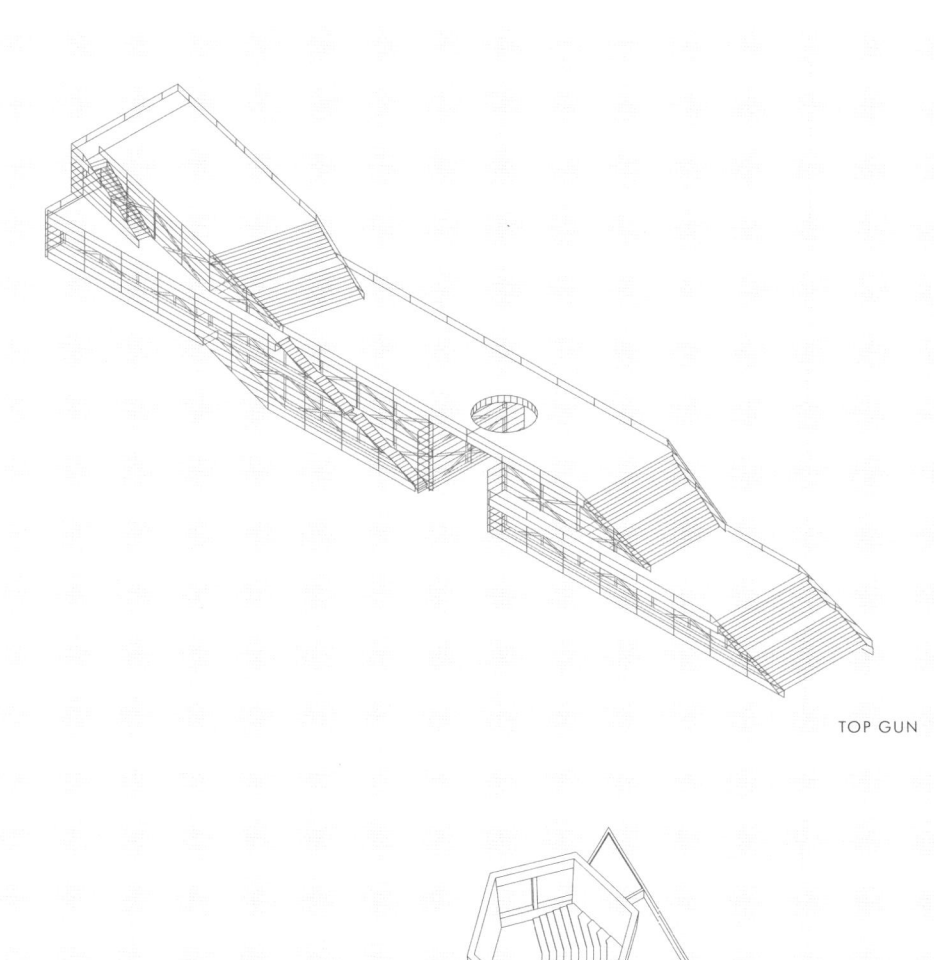

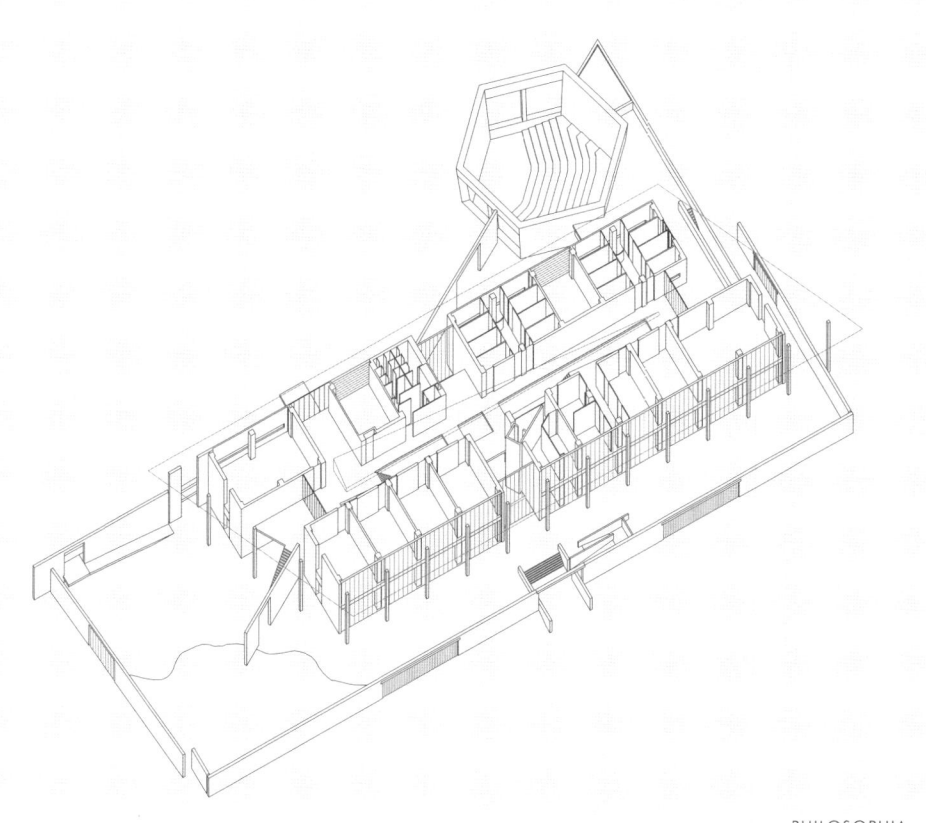

TOP GUN

PHILOSOPHIA

[268]

横浜地方気象台　2009
yokohama local
meteorological observatory

1. 横浜市中区 | naka-ku, yokohama
2. 設計 | design　2004.9 – 2006.03
3. 施工 | construction　2006.1 – 2009.3
4. 鉄筋コンクリート（既存棟）、
   鉄筋コンクリート（増築棟）、一部鉄骨 | RC, steel
5. 観測施設 | observatory
6. 敷地 | site　2,485.5 m²
7. 建築 | building　713.4 m²
8. 延床 | total floor　1,580.5 m²

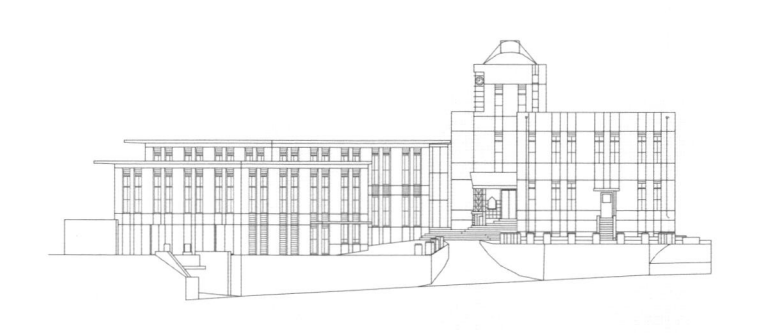

横浜山手の西洋館街の高台に位置する「横浜地方気象台」は1927年の建築。小振りながら塔を持ち、玄関回りを中心に当時流行のアール・デコの装飾が配されている。この建築に耐震補強を施し、隣接して増築棟が建てられた。もとの建物の意匠に合わせて安藤は珍しく縦長の窓を配し、歴史と現代の連続を企てた。来訪者は旧棟の石積みの階段が美しい玄関から入り、1920年代の造形に触れたあと、ガラスの回廊を通って増築棟を見学できる。常時公開で二つの建築を味わえる。

YOKOHAMA LOCAL METEOROLOGICAL OBSERVATORY is a building completed in 1927, located on the hillside of Yokohama city among the neighborhood of Western style residences. While the building itself is in a small scale, it has a tower volume and the building is decorated in Art Déco style, especially around the entrance area — a popular style in those days. This building was applied with seismic reinforcement, and annex building was built adjacent to the existing observatory building. Unusual for Ando, he provided vertically long windows by following the design of original building to create continuity between the past and the present. After seeing the design details of 1920s, visitors will see the annex building through the glass corridor.

[269]

俄本社ビル　2009
niwaka headquarters building

1. 京都市中京区 | nakagyo-ku, kyoto
2. 設計 | design　2007.1 – 2007.12
3. 施工 | construction　2008.3 – 2009.3
4. 鉄筋コンクリート　RC
5. 物販店、事務所 | shop, office
6. 敷地 | site　689.2 m²
7. 建築 | building　545.7 m²
8. 延床 | total floor　2,317.4 m²

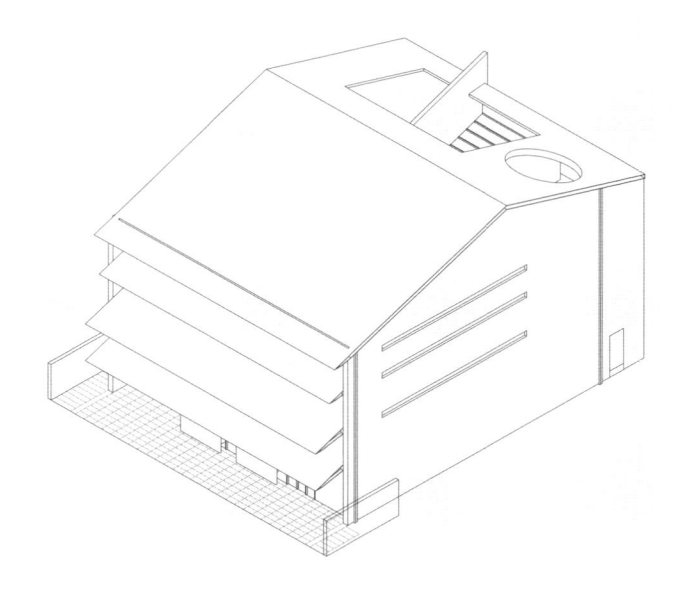

ジュエリーブランドがオーナーの複合商業ビル。京都の景観規制のために傾斜屋根を架けることが求められた。4階建ての躯体に、切妻の大屋根が架かり、この大屋根と同じ傾きの深いひさしが1–3階に設けられた。ひさしは歴史の街並みの商家にみられる下屋を思わせるもので、過去を参照したオリジナルの作品が実現した。街路から眺めると、ひさしもガラス窓も洗練された表現になっており、発想の豊かさを感じさせる。

A composite commercial building owned by a jewelry company. It was required by the landscape restriction of Kyoto to have an inclined roof. A large gable roof is set on the four-story building with deep eaves with the same inclination as the large roof provided on 1st to 3rd floors. With these eaves that resemble the penthouses of merchants in the historical town, an original work was created referring to the history. Creative richness is demonstrated by the sophisticated expression of the eaves and windows when viewed from the main street.

全346作品録

[270]
ムンク美術館国際設計競技
2009
munch museum and
stenersen museum collections

1. ノルウェー オスロ｜oslo, norway
2. 設計｜design   2009
3. 設計競技｜design competition
5. 美術館｜museum of art
8. 延床｜total floor   16,000.00 m²

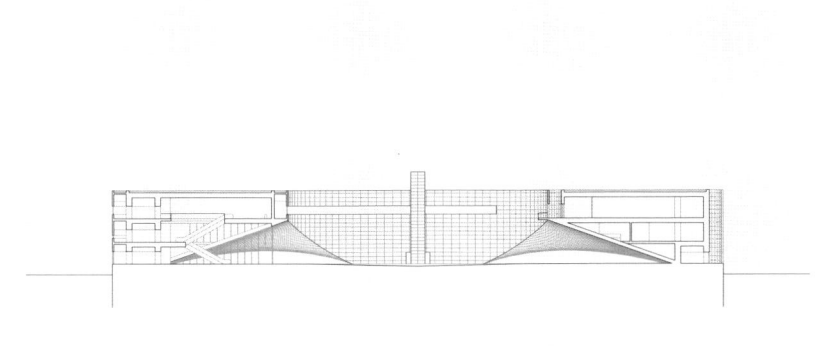

ノルウェー・オスロの水辺に計画されたエドワルド・ムンクのための美術館コンペ案。オスロの新しい顔になるようにというコンペの趣旨を踏まえて、強い正面性を意識した。カーブするアトリウムの稜線が建物の裏表で反対の凹凸を描く外観が想定された。来訪者はフィヨルドを超えて、このアトリウムに配された公共広場にアプローチし、ムンクの作品だけでなく豊かな自然も堪能できる仕立てとした。展示室は潮位の変化を考慮して上階に配した。

Design for a contest of an art gallery for Edvard Munch planned by the waterfront in Oslo, Norway. Attention was paid to give a strong frontality considering the purpose of the contest, which is to be the new symbol of Oslo. It is assumed that appearance of the curved ridge of atrium is formed in the opposite direction between the front and rear areas of the building. The property is designed to let visitors enjoy not only the works of Munch but the rich nature as well by allowing them to approach the public plaza located in the atrium across the fiord. The exhibition room is located on the upper floor considering the change in tide level.

[271]
北ヨーロッパの住宅   2009
house in northern europe

1. アイルランド ダブリン｜dublin, ireland
2. 設計｜design   2009
3. 構想案｜concept
5. 住宅｜detached house
6. 敷地｜site   8400 m²
7. 建築｜building   931 m²
8. 延床｜total floor   462 m²

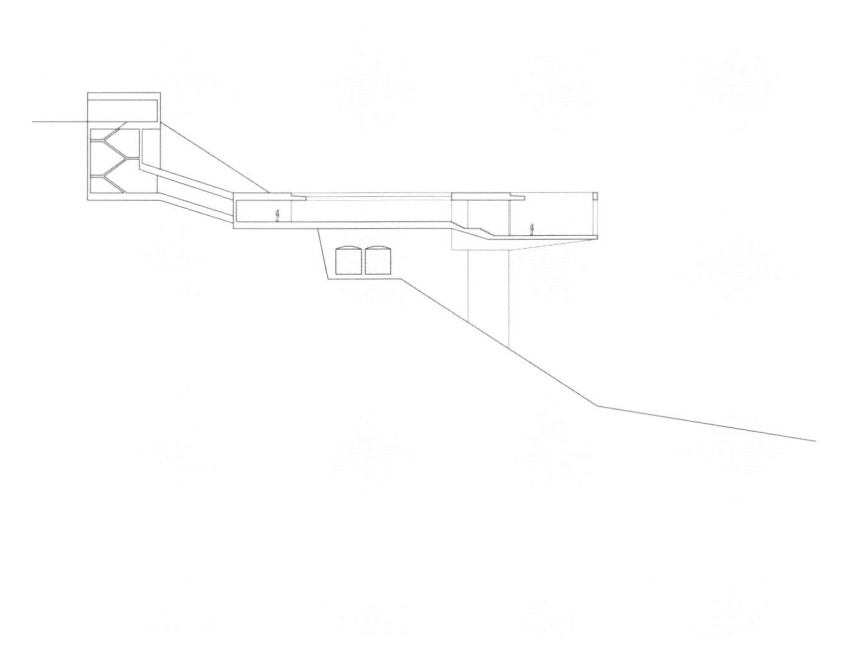

アイルランドの首都ダブリン郊外の住宅計画。安藤は、アイリッシュ海に面した敷地を実見して、海沿いに走る鉄道をまたぐ配置を決定した。線路を超えた陸地の側の崖地に埋もれる形で寝室棟を配し、そこから線路上を横断するブリッジでリビング、ダイニングを配した棟へと渡る。海側の棟は崖地からキャンティレバーで空中に飛び出した構成となっており、眺望を独り占めすることができる。法的な制約をクリアすることを含めて実現が検討された。

A housing program in the suburbs of Dublin, the capital of Ireland. A layout that crosses over a railway that runs alongside the ocean was designed by Ando when he actually observed the property facing the Irish Sea. Bedrooms are arranged in a style being buried under the cliff on the land side over the railway and a bridge is provided across the railway to approach the building with living room and dining room. The building has a structure hung over the ocean from the cliff in a cantilever shape and that offers an exclusive view from the room. Realization of the plan including satisfying regulatory requirements was examined.

[272]

上海建築文化センター 2009
architecture and culture center, shanghai

1. 中華人民共和国 上海 | shanghai, china
2. 設計 | design 2009.3 – 2009.11
3. 構想案 | concept
4. 鉄筋コンクリート | RC
5. 美術館、研究施設 | museum, research facilities
6. 敷地 | site 3,936 m²
7. 建築 | building 2,333 m²
8. 延床 | total floor 4,300 m²

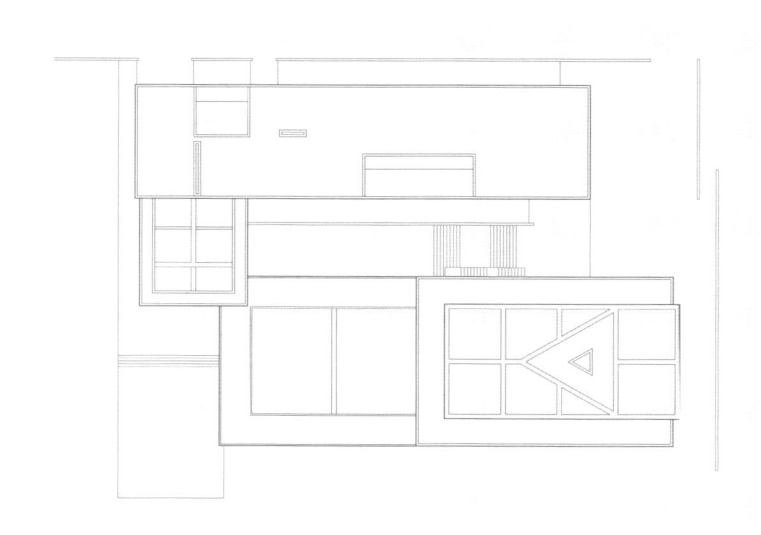

上海の郊外、嘉定区に計画された複合文化施設。創造のためのアトリエと資料を閲覧できるライブラリーが二つの棟を構成し、両者はずれを持った配置で、ともに深いひさしを特徴としている。一帯は水に恵まれた郊外地で、安藤は水路を生かすとともに新都市の空疎さを挽回するための植栽にも配慮して建築を計画した。ライブラリーの内部は三角形の平面を持つ三層吹き抜けで、壁は書籍で埋めつくされる。安藤の手になる「保利大劇場」一帯のオフィス街区との連携も期待されている。

A composite cultural facility planned at Jiading District in the suburbs of Shanghai. Two buildings consist of an atelier for creation and a library to browse reference materials and these buildings are arranged to be in an offset position to each other with characteristic deep hoods. Ando was taking advantage of water channels since this suburban area has a rich water source and planned the architecture considering the planting design to avoid hollow scenery in the new city. The interior of the library has a triangle planform with an open ceiling of three floors that has walls covered with books. Coordination with the office block of SHANGHAI POLY THEATER by Ando is anticipated as well.

[273]

北京紅楼夢ホテル 2009
hong lou meng hotel

1. 中華人民共和国 北京 | beijing, china
2. 設計 | design 2009.10
3. 構想案 | concept
4. 鉄筋コンクリート | RC
5. ホテル | hotel
6. 敷地 | site 193,591.26 m²
8. 延床 | total floor 78,703.29 m²

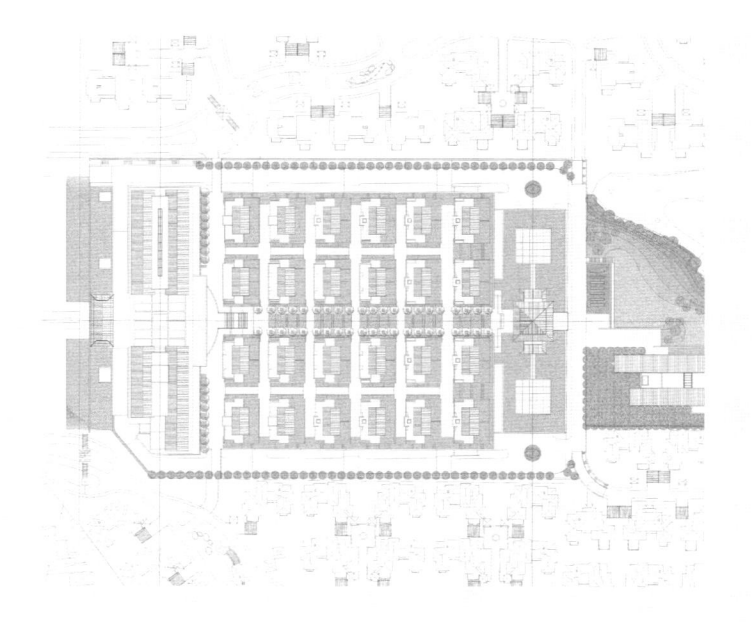

北京の北東60キロに位置する雁栖湖岸のリゾートホテル。傾斜した地形を生かし、段状の水路を湖に向って水が流れ落ちる「水のランドスケープ」を創造、宿泊の中心となるヴィラが水面に浮かぶかのような構成をとる。エントランスは低く抑えた石壁の中央にうがったアーチ状のゲートで、そこをくぐると伝統の瓦屋根の集落に見立てたコッテージが待ち受け、非日常の世界に足を踏み入れたと思わせる。全体の配置はシンメトリーを遵守し、中国らしい風景に仕立てた。

A resort hotel on the shore of Yanqi Lake, located 60km northeast of Beijing. Taking advantage of the sloped site, Ando created an "aquatic landscape" with flowing water from a tiered water route to the lcke. The cottages for guests appear as if they are floating on water. The entrance is an arched gate, bored at the center of a low stone wall. Entering the gate, cottages imitating a village of traditional houses with tiled roofs await the guests, providing an extraordinary feeling. The overall arrangement is symmetric, creating a Chinese-like scenery.

[274]
半山半島美術館＋劇場センター
2009
serenity coast art museum
+ performing arts center

1. 中華人民共和国 三亜 | sanya, china
2. 設計 | design   2009.12
3. 構想案 | concept
4. 鉄筋コンクリート、鉄骨鉄筋コンクリート | RC, SRC
5. 美術館、劇場 | museum, theater
6. 敷地 | site   63,270 m²
7. 建築 | building   26,566 m²
8. 延床 | total floor   36,060 m²

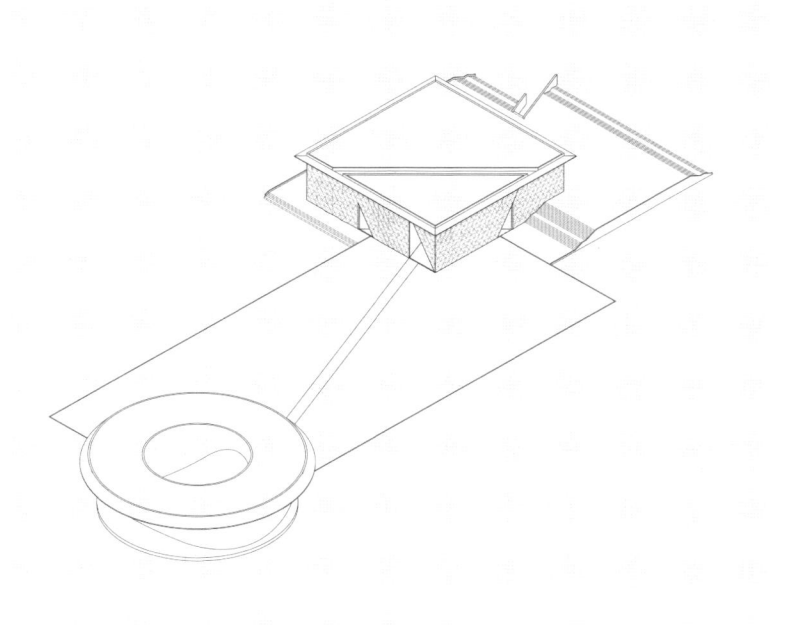

リゾート地として人気の高い中国南部の熱帯の島、海南島の芸術センターの計画。海岸の陸地側に劇場翼が配され、そこは高さ30メートル、平面は一辺が90メートルの正方形の仕立てになっている。壁のスリット部分は外部空間の扱いで、傾斜した壁が通路に覆い被さり、緊張感を与えている。一方、美術館棟は、劇場の足元から海岸を超えて海上に張り出した人工地盤のうえに三次元曲面の壁を配した円形の平面で建設される。海南島の雄大な自然と対峙しうる豪快な幾何学の展開だ。

A construction plan of an art center in Hainan Island, a popular tropical island as a resort area located in the south part of China. A theater wing is to be built on the land side of the coast with a structure of 30 meters in height and 90 meters each side in square planform. Slits on the walls are treated as external space where inclined walls are covering the passage in order to give tense atmosphere. On the other hand, the art gallery wing is to be built on a round planform with three-dimensional curved wall on an artificial ground extending out from the base of the theater on the coast over the ocean. Dynamic geometry is developed to be against the magnificent nature of Hainan Island.

[275]
ノバルティス研究施設棟   2010
novartis wsj-352

1. スイス バーゼル | basel, switzerland
2. 設計 | design   2004.4 – 2006.7
3. 施工 | construction   2006.8 – 2010.5
4. 鉄筋コンクリート | RC
5. 研究施設 | research facilities
6. 敷地 | site   1,995 m²
7. 建築 | building   1,766 m²
8. 延床 | total floor   22,385 m²

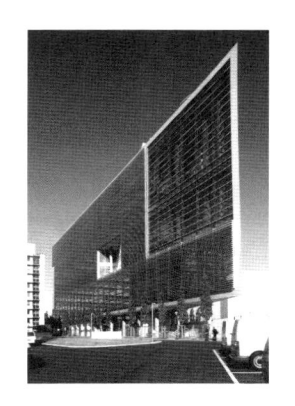

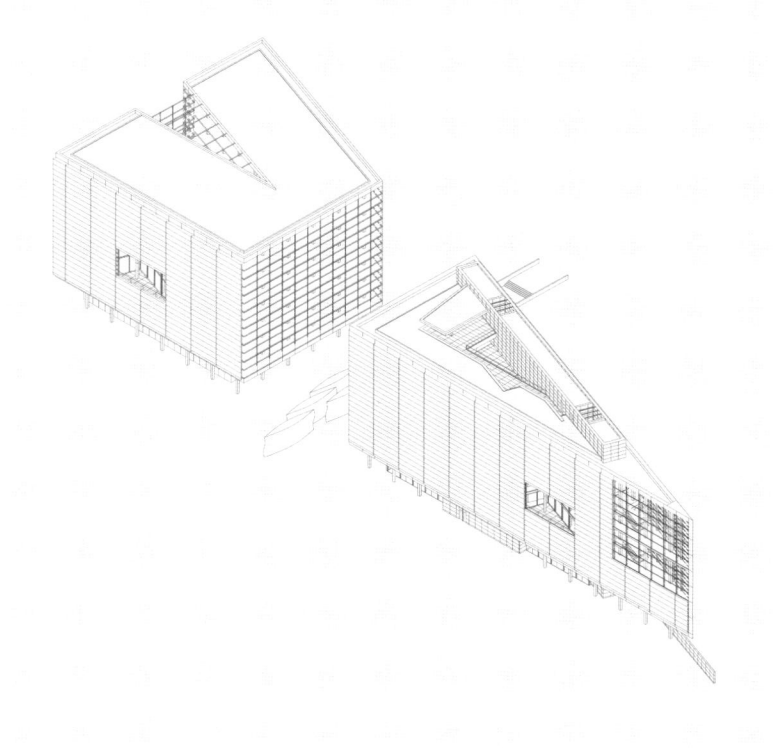

スイス・バーゼルの製薬メーカー、ノバルティスの研究施設。同社は広大な敷地に、世界から建築家を招聘して各種施設の設計を依頼しており、安藤もそのひとりに選ばれた。安藤は、スイスの清潔、完璧指向を、日本の繊細かつ器用さで実現することを目指した。スイスの厳しい環境基準に基づいて、ルーバーやダブルスキンの外壁構成を決定し、厳格なモダニズムを体現する建築が誕生した。三角形の敷地そのままの鋭角のヴォリュームが、安藤の美学を際立たせている。

A research facility of Novartis, a pharmaceutical company of Basle in Switzerland. The company selected architects from all over the world including Ando and requested them to design various facilities in the vast property of the company. Ando aimed to realize the Switzerland's tendency of cleanliness and perfection by the way of delicacy and dexterity of Japan. In accord with Switzerland's strict environment standard, louver and double skin exterior wall structures were adopted and created an architecture that materializes Modernism rigorously. The sharp-angled volume following the triangle property emphasizes Ando's aesthetic value.

[276]

ストーン・スカルプチュア・ミュージアム 2010
stone sculpture museum

1. ドイツ バート・ミュンスター・アム・シュタイン＝エーベルンブルク │ bad münster am stein-ebernburg, germany
2. 設計 │ design 1996.9 – 2009.4
3. 施工 │ construction 2008.1 – 2010.8
4. 鉄筋コンクリート、木造 │ RC, wood
5. 美術館 │ museum of art
6. 敷地 │ site 5,700 m²
7. 建築 │ building 158 m²
8. 延床 │ total floor 215 m²

彫刻家ウォルフガング・クーバッハの作品を収蔵する個人美術館。計画中に彫刻家は亡くなったが、妻がその遺志を継いで実現にこぎ着けた。ドイツ西部のバート・ミュンスター・アム・シュタイン＝エーベルンブルクの自然のなかに、18世紀に建設された木造民家の架構を移築、安藤が設営したコンクリートの基壇に載せる形で空間が構成された。敷地の周囲をコンクリートの壁で囲い、中庭に人工池が設けられ、クーバッハの宇宙を際立たせている。土着的な木造の骨組みとコンクリート打ち放しの取り合わせによって、彫刻家の精神世界に迫ろうとしている。

A private art gallery that collects works of a sculptor Wolfgang Kubach. Although the sculptor passed away during the plan, his wife succeeded the will and materialized the plan. The space is structured with the framework of an 18th century wooden house transferred and placed on the concrete base that Ando created among the nature field of Bad Münster am Stein-Ebernburg in the west part of Germany. The property is surrounded by concrete walls and an artificial pond is created to emphasize the Kubach's artistic universe. The sculptor's inner psychological world is implied through the combination of indigenous wooden frames and exposed concrete.

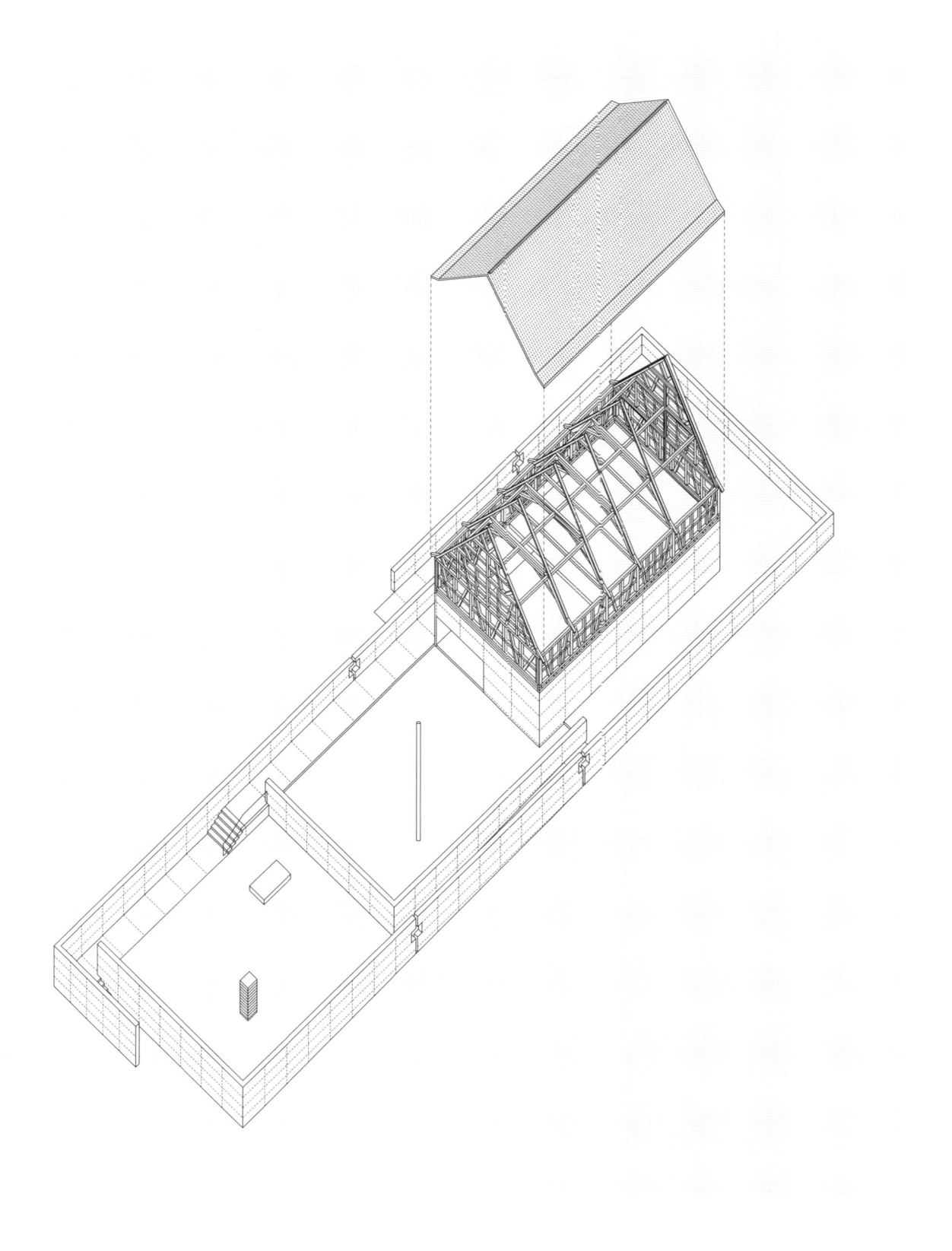

全346作品録

[277]
上海デザインセンター 2010
shanghai design center

1. 中華人民共和国 上海 | shanghai, china
2. 設計 | design 2004.7–2006.12
3. 施工 | construction 2008.12–2010.6
4. 鉄骨鉄筋コンクリート、鉄骨 | SRC, steel
5. 美術館、研究施設 | museum, research facilities
6. 敷地 | site 9,127m²
7. 建築 | building 3,867m²
8. 延床 | total floor 46,591m²

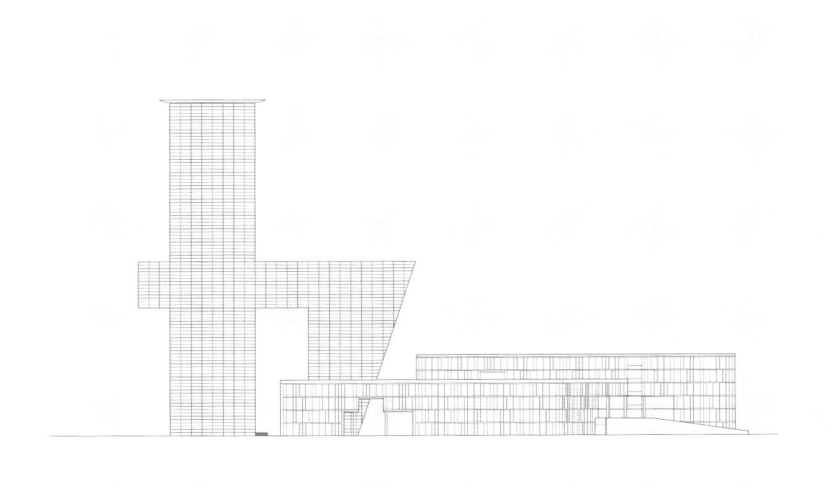

上海の同済大学を中心に進められている「同済科学技術地区開発プロジェクト」の中心施設。高さ100メートル近いガラスの高層棟に、壁を傾斜させた低層棟を組み合わせたスケールの大きな構成だ。新開発に求められるランドマークとしての役割を満たすために、ざっくりした外観が選択された。積極的なデザイン振興策を国家として進める中国は、安藤の造形力をプロジェクトの象徴として活用した。透過性の高い幾何立体の交錯が、現代建築ならではの新鮮な風景をもたらしている。

The central facility of the Tongji Science Technology Section Development Project being conducted around Tongji University in Shanghai. The large-scale facility is composed of a glass high-rise building with the height of about 100 meters and low-rise building with slanted walls. Such appearance was selected to satisfy the role as the landmark required for new development of the district. China used Ando's modeling ability as the characteristic of their national project to advance their proactive design promotion. A blend of highly transparent geometric solids demonstrates fresh scenery of modern architecture.

[278]
竜王駅＋南北駅前広場 2010
ryuo station + station square

1. 山梨県甲斐市 | kai, yamanashi
2. 設計 | design 2005.1–2006.2, 2007.11–2009.2
3. 施工 | construction 2006.3–2008.3, 2009.3–2010.3
4. 鉄骨 | steel
5. 駅舎、広場 | railway station, plaza
6. 敷地 | site 15,689.9 m²
7. 建築 | building 6,917.6 m²
8. 延床 | total floor 5,590.6 m²

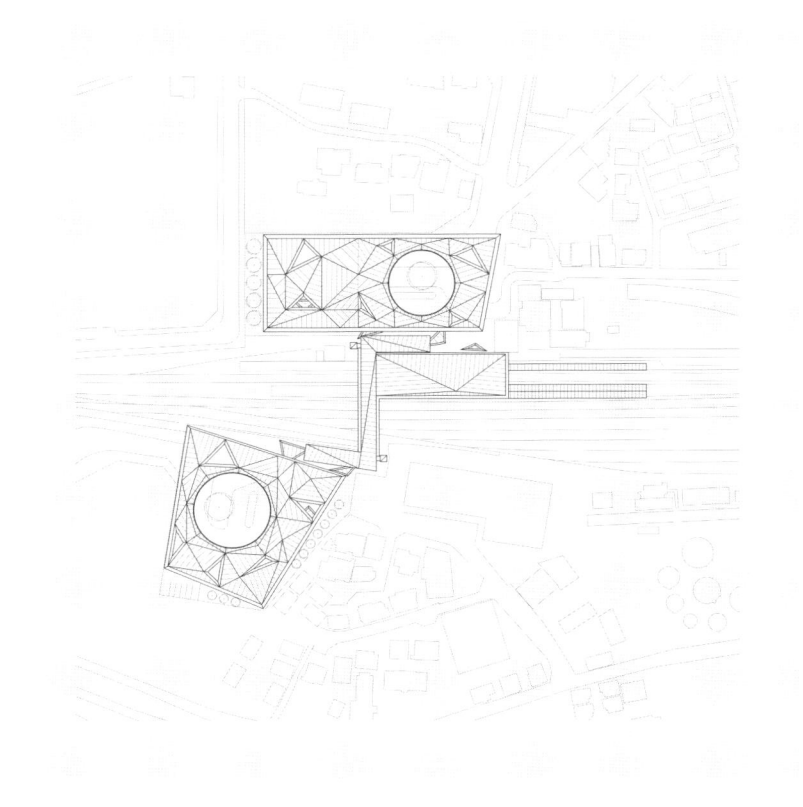

合併によって生まれた山梨県甲斐市の表玄関となるJRの駅舎と駅前広場。新駅では片側だけの広場が整備されがちだが、南北の両口にほぼ同じ規模の広場が新設された。安藤は武田信玄ゆかりの「信玄堤」に残る三角錐の構造物「聖牛」を見て、広場の屋根を三角形の集合体とすることを決めた。駅舎の屋根も三角形を組み合わせた大胆な幾何立体となっている。駅舎と広場は、合併した自治体住民を結ぶ「心の森」と位置づけられている。

This is a project to design a station building for JR line and its station front plaza space as the entrance gate to Kai City, a city newly established by municipal merger. For a development of a new station, it is common that only one side of the station front plaza space is developed, but two station front plaza spaces are newly provided in similar scale on the South and the North sides of the station for this project. By looking at "crib spur" structure in triangular pyramid shape remaining at the nearby "Shingen zutsumi" embankment built during the period of Shingen Takeda, the war load of the region, Ando decided to produce the roof of the plaza space by the assembly of scalene triangles. The roof of the station building is also produced in a bold geometric solid by combining triangle shapes. Ando described this station building and its plaza spaces as the "forest of souls" to unify the citizens of those merged municipalities.

[279]
靱公園の住宅 2010
house in utsubo park

1. 大阪市西区 | nishi-ku, osaka
2. 設計 | design 2007.9 – 2009.5
3. 施工 | construction 2009.6 – 2010.3
4. 鉄筋コンクリート | RC
5. 住宅 | detached house
6. 敷地 | site 142,6 m²
7. 建築 | building 89,4 m²
8. 延床 | total floor 186,1 m²

靱公園は大阪の都心で貴重な緑の空間を保持している。住宅の敷地は、間口5メートル弱に対して奥行きが27メートルある細長いもので、背後で靱公園に接している。その敷地いっぱいに三層のコンクリートボックスがしつらえられた。かつての町屋が奥に坪庭を持っていたように、公園に向き合う最奥の位置に、両側からコンクリートの壁で囲った光庭が配されている。1階では、この光庭に食堂と続きの居間が、2階では居間上部の屋内の吹き抜けに寝室が面する。3階の屋外テラスに主寝室から出ると、靱公園の開放感が味わえる。

Utsubo Park has a valuable green space preserved in the center of Osaka City. The site of this residence is a slender shaped lot with 5m or less in width, yet 27m in depth, and it is in contact with Utsubo Park on the backside. A concrete box on the 3rd floor was fully set up on this site. As the traditional town house had "tsuboniwa" in the back, a light court enclosed by concrete walls on both sides of the space is arranged at the innermost position of the lot facing to the park. Dining room and living room are linked together on the 1st floor and facing to the light court. Bedroom situated above the living room is facing to a double-height space on the 2nd floor. Going out from a main bedroom to the outside terrace space on the 3rd floor, openness of Utsubo Park can be experienced.

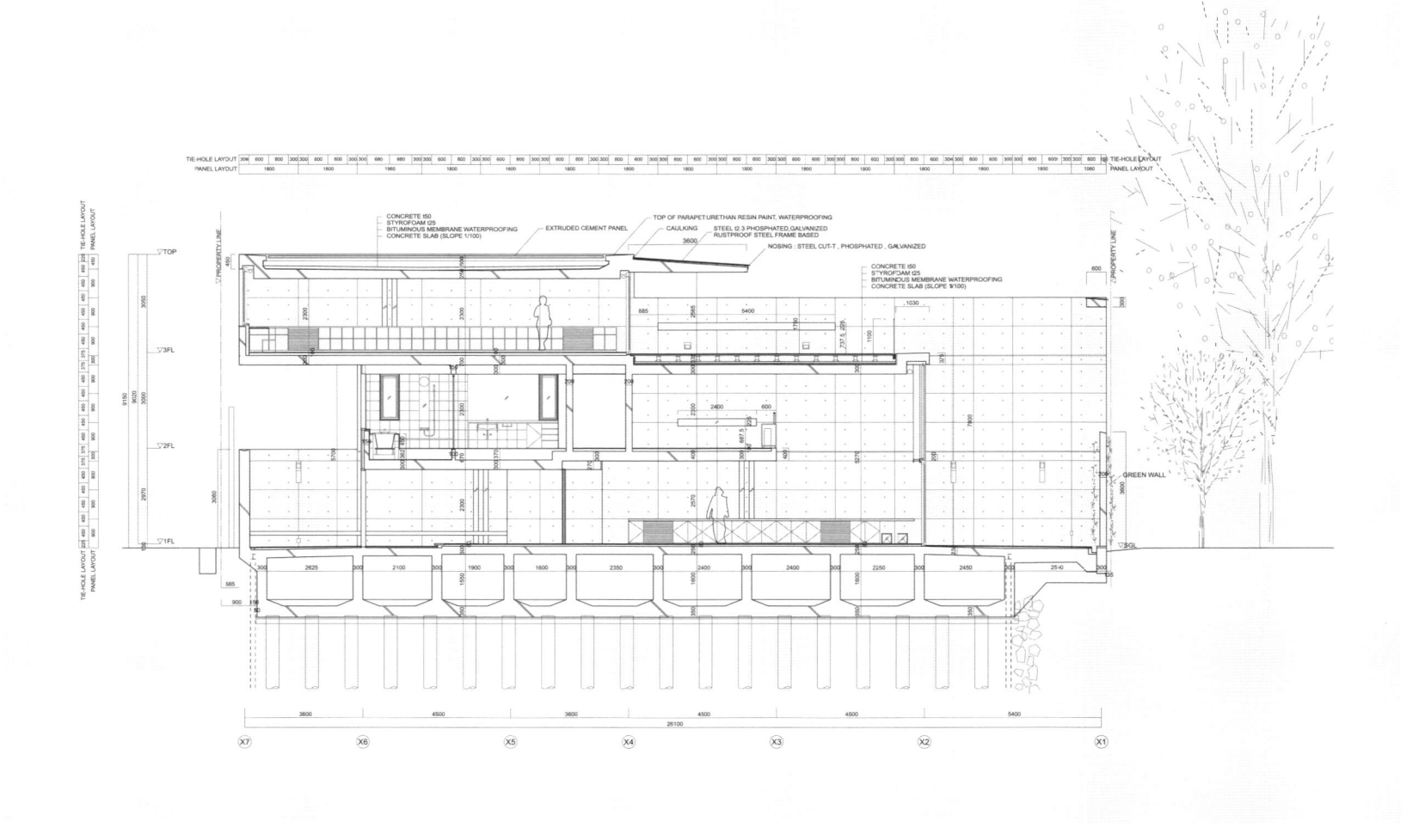

[280]
李禹煥美術館　2010
lee ufan museum

1. 香川県直島町 | naoshima, kagawa
2. 設計 | design　2007.12 – 2009.1
3. 施工 | construction　2009.2 – 2010.6
4. 鉄筋コンクリート | RC
5. 美術館 | museum of art
6. 敷地 | site　9,859.8 m²
7. 建築 | building　443.0 m²
8. 延床 | total floor　443.0 m²

香川県直島のベネッセ・アートサイトの美術館のひとつ。背後に傾斜地を抱えた海沿いの敷地に、安藤のコンクリートのボックスと、李による細長い角柱のそびえる広場が展開している。建物は背後の斜面にはめ込まれたかのような配置で、「地中美術館」と同じく、安藤の「地下建築」の一例となっている。建物の躯体に30度で接する直角三角形のコンクリート壁が立てられ、来訪者はその壁を伝ってギャラリーへと導かれる。トップライトからの自然光を重視した展示空間も「地下建築」のありかたの追求だ。→参照 [125]、[151]、[184]、[223]、[239]、[309]

This is one of the museum buildings of Benesse Art Site in Naoshima, Kagawa Prefecture. On the seaside location with a sloping land behind the site, a concrete box produced by Ando and the plaza space with a rising slender square column designed by Lee U-Fan are arranged. The building appears to be embedded to the sloping ground behind, making this building as one of the "underground architectures" of Ando as seen in the project such as the CHICHU ART MUSEUM. A concrete wall in right angled triangle shape is attached to the main volume of the building in 30°angle, and visitors are guided into a gallery space through this wall. The exhibition space illuminated by natural light from the top light is the result of Ando's pursuit for an "underground architecture". → see also [125], [151], [184], [223], [239], [309]

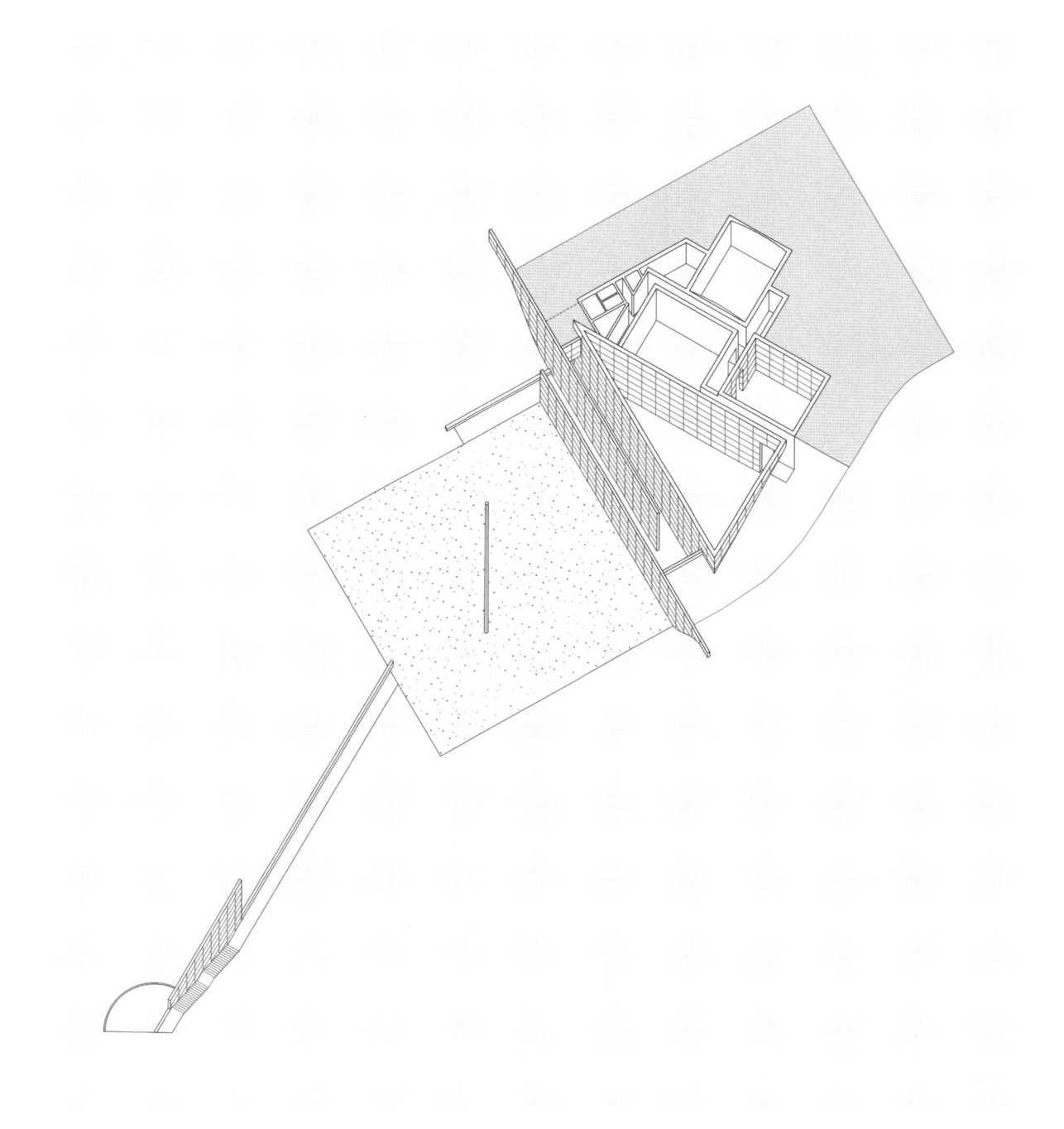

[281]

チャスカ茶屋町　2010
chaska chayamachi

1. 大阪市北区 | kita-ku, osaka
2. 設計 | design　2006.1–2007.02
3. 施工 | construction　2007.3–2010.4
4. 下層階・鉄骨鉄筋コンクリート、上層階・鉄骨 | SRC, RC
5. 商業施設、ホテル、集合住宅 | commercial complex, hotel, residence
6. 敷地 | site　2,670 m²
7. 建築 | building　1,877.2 m²
8. 延床 | total floor　24,308.5 m²

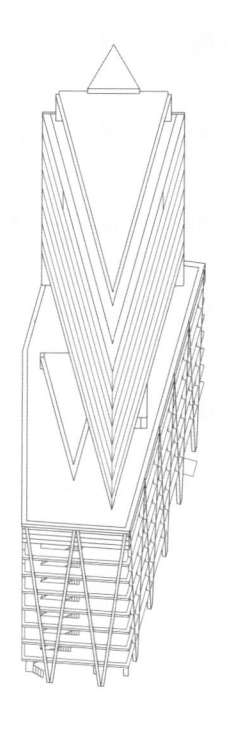

安藤には珍しい高層建築。大阪駅に近い繁華街の一角に位置し、低層部に商業施設、高層に集合住宅、ホテルが配されている。足元に「都市の広場」の創出を意識し、高層部は「ランドマーク」となりうる外観を目指した。Y字型のコンクリートのフレームが囲う低層部に、ガラスの三角柱の高層部が載る。最上階の高さ90メートルに位置するホテル付属のウェディング・チャーチは、宝石を建築化したイメージのガラス壁のきらめきが、都市施設ならではの興奮を覚えさせる場となっている。

A high-rising architecture, which is a rare case for Ando. It is located in downtown near Osaka station and has commercial facilities in lower floors as well as a housing complex and a hotel in the upper floors. Ando considered creating the city's plaza at ground level and aimed so that the upper area can achieve a landmark appearance. The glass triangular column of the higher floors is placed on the rectangular solid of lower floors surrounded by Y-shape concrete frames. The sparkle of glass walls that resemble jewelry of the hotel's wedding church on the top floor, which is 90 meters above ground, gives unique excitement to an urban facility.

[282]

あてま森と水辺の教室
〈森のホール〉〈水辺のホール〉
2010
atema project
‹forest hall› ‹waterside hall›

1. 新潟県十日町市 | tokamachi, niigata
2. 設計 | design　2008.5–2009.6
3. 施工 | construction　2009.7–2010.7
4. 鉄筋コンクリート | RC
5. ホテル、研修施設 | hotel, training facilities
6. 敷地 | site　13000 m² [forest], 7913.7 m² [waterside]
7. 建築 | building　1447.6 m² [forest], 1786.9 m² [waterside]
8. 延床 | total floor　1132.3 m² [forest], 1040.6 m² [waterside]

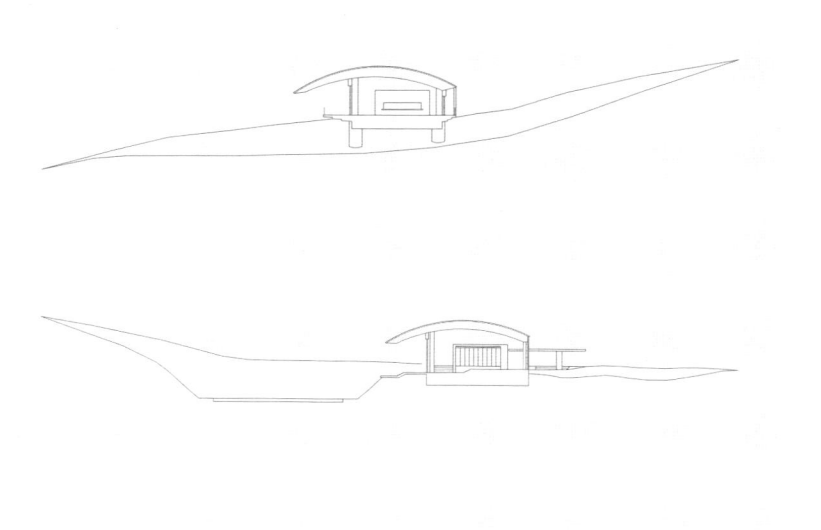

新潟県十日町に東京電力が開設している環境教育を目的とする自然学校。いずれも一枚の布のような大きな屋根が架かり、深いひさしの下に機能が配されている。「森のホール」は自然教育のための施設で、一帯のゲートの役割を持つ。「水辺のホール」は課外学習の一環で訪れる子どもたちのフィールドワークの基地として機能する。自然を残した池に面し、床は水辺の方向へ下る段状の配置をとり、水辺には来訪者が腰かけて豊かな自然を堪能するための屋外階段を設けている。

Resort facilities for environmental education held by TEPCO in Tokamachi City, Niigata Prefecture. A large roof with an appearance of a cloth is on each facility and functions are provided under the deep hood. The FOREST HALL is a facility for education of nature and also functions as the gate to the area. The WATERSIDE HALL has a function as a base for field work of children who visit as a part of school education. The facilities are located facing a pond that conserves the natural environment and their floors are arranged to descend in stages toward the waterfront. An outdoor facility is built by the waterfront allowing visitors to sit down and enjoy the rich nature.

[283]
名古屋の住宅　2010
house in nagoya

1. 名古屋市瑞穂区 | mizuho-ku, nagoya
2. 設計 | design　2008.5 – 2009.8
3. 施工 | construction　2009.9 – 2010.4
4. 鉄筋コンクリート組積造 | reinforced masonry
5. 住宅 | detached house
6. 敷地 | site　262.0 m²
7. 建築 | building　180.4 m²
8. 延床 | total floor　212.7 m²

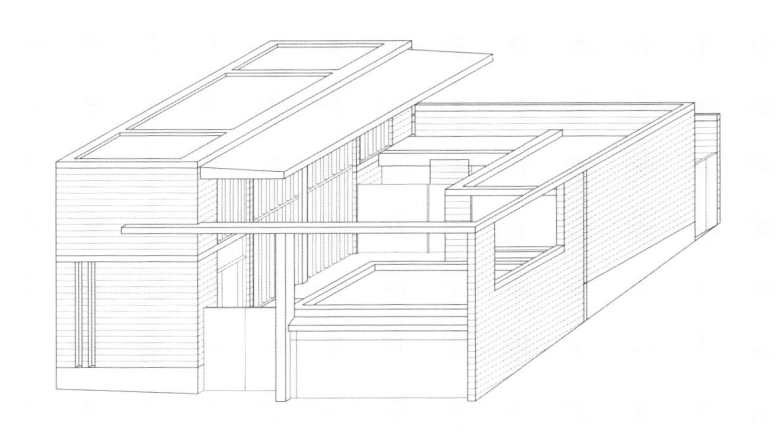

文教地区に位置する２階建ての個人住宅。コンクリートブロックの直方体に、やはりコンクリートブロックで構成したフレームが交差し、外部環境と敷地内の空間を仕切っている。角地の２面の外壁に大きな開口部を設け、そこからの光と風が、直方体の居住棟本棟とテラスを挟んで向き合う平屋のあずまやに届けられる仕組みだ。駐車スペースとなっているあずまやの屋根は緑化され、２階の居室での自然との触れ合いを豊かなものとする。

A two-story private residential house in an educational district where there is an accumulation of history. The external environment and the space inside the property are separated by rectangular solid of concrete blocks crossed by the frame that is also composed of concrete blocks. Large openings were provided on the two surfaces of exterior walls on the corner. This structure provides light and breeze to a one-story gazebo placed on the other side of the terrace in between the residence building. The roof greenery is provided on the gazebo, which is a parking space, to have rich contact with nature being in the living room on the 2nd floor.

[284]
石原邸　2010
ishihara house

1. 滋賀県大津市 | otsu, shiga
2. 設計 | design　2009.3 – 2009.8
3. 施工 | construction　2009.9 – 2010.2
4. 鉄筋コンクリート | RC
5. 住宅 | detached house
6. 敷地 | site　214.0 m²
7. 建築 | building　54.0 m²
8. 延床 | total floor　92.2 m²

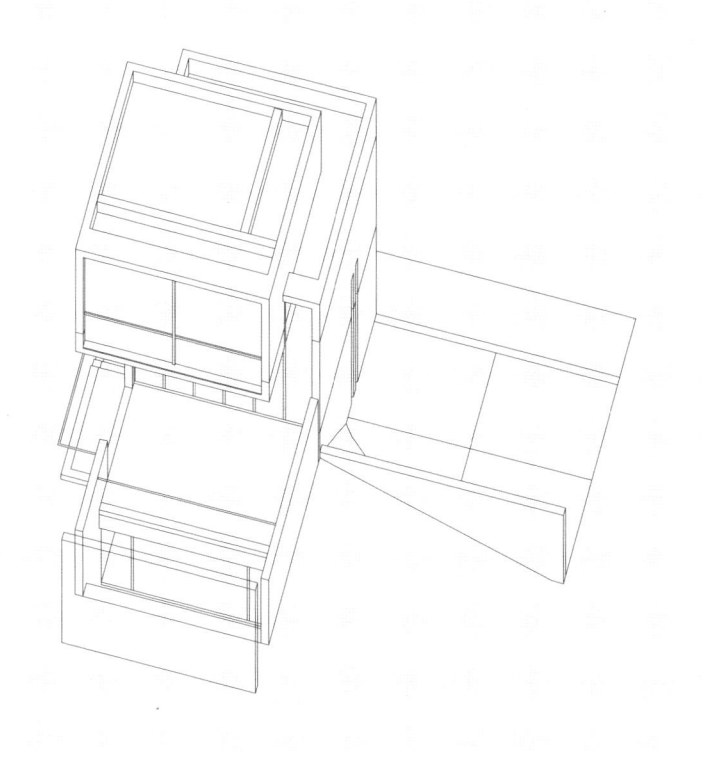

表通り側から眺めると４枚のコンクリートの壁と植栽された土盛りが、周囲の環境と切り離された、内なる住環境の存在を直感させる。壁の２枚は、二つの直方体をずらして重ねた住棟本体の壁で表通りに向って屹立する。もう２枚は道路と垂直方向の独立壁で、こちらは住宅の領域内にテラスなどの屋外空間を囲い込む。１階にテラスに面したダイニングキッチンを置き、２階と地階に吹き抜けやドライエリアを望む二つの寝室を配した。コンクリートの無化した住空間に光と風を誘い入れることで、現代の暮らしを体感させる。

The four concrete walls and land elevation with trees and plants give an intuition of presence of a residential environment inside the property separated from the peripheral environment when seen from the front street. Two walls are soaring facing the front street same as the walls of the house that are structured by overlapping two rectangular solids in an offset position. The other two walls are freestanding walls that extend perpendicular to the road surrounding the outdoor space such as the terrace within the area of the residence. A dining kitchen is placed on the 1st floor facing the terrace and two bedrooms facing the open ceiling area and dry area are placed on the 2nd floor and basement.

346 Complete Works

[285]
光の美術館　2010
museum of light

1. 山梨県北杜市 | hokuto, yamanashi
2. 設計 | design　2009.9 – 2010.4
3. 施工 | construction　2010.5 – 2010.10
4. 鉄筋コンクリート | RC
5. 美術館 | museum of art
6. 敷地 | site　18,345.8 m²
7. 建築 | building　78.0 m²
8. 延床 | total floor　120.9 m²

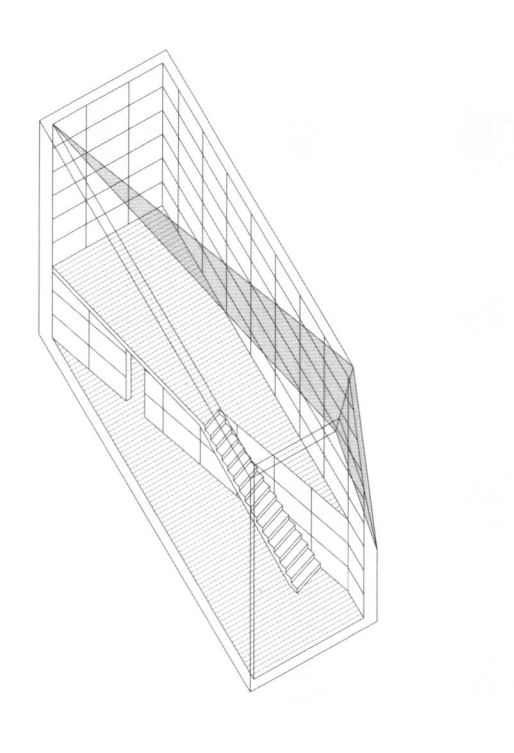

山梨県北杜市の清春芸術村のギャラリー。直方体の上部の一角を切欠き、館内に自然光を導き入れるシンプルな構成。人工照明に頼らずに、パリのモンパルナスにアトリエを構えて創作にいそしんだ画家アントニ・クラーベの絵画鑑賞を想定した。安藤の極小の幾何立体は、コンクリート打ち放しの美しい肌と相まって、複数の現代建築家の設計によるギャラリーやエッフェルのアトリエのレプリカなどが揃う施設内で、確固たる存在感を発揮している。

A gallery in Kiyoharu Art Colony located in Hokuto City, Yamanashi Prefecture. The structure is a simple form that guides natural light inside the gallery by creating a notch on the upper area of the rectangular solid. It was designed imagining art appreciation of Antoni Clavé, an artist who created his works at his atelier in Montparnasse, Paris without relying on any artificial lighting. Ando's minimum geometric solid demonstrates its solid presence in the facility with galleries of various contemporary architects and a replica of Eiffel's atelier.

[286]
中国太湖博物館　2010
china taihu museum, suzhou

1. 中華人民共和国 蘇州 | suzhou, china
2. 設計 | design　2010.3
3. 構想案 | concept
4. 鉄筋コンクリート | RC
5. 博物館 | museum
6. 敷地 | site　33,300 m²
7. 建築 | building　11,730 m²
8. 延床 | total floor　17,570 m²

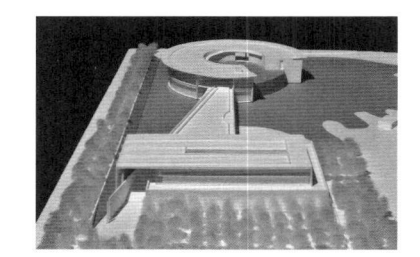

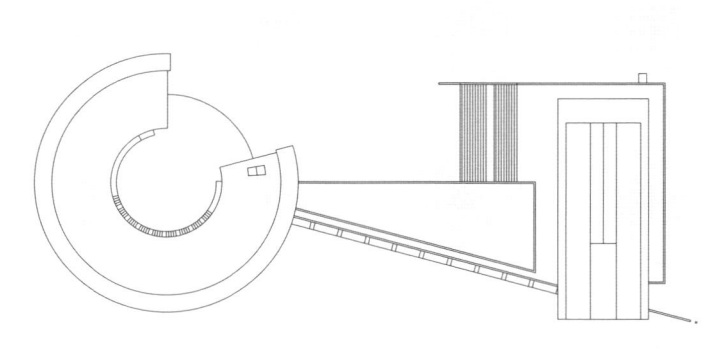

中国の蘇州は、昔ながらの水路の巡る観光地として人気が高い。その西方に広がる広大な太湖の岸辺の公園の一角に博物館が計画された。陸地側の直方体の企画展棟から、太湖の水を引き込んで造った池のなかの逆円錐形の常設展棟へは、水上のブリッジが伸びていく。そこを歩むとき、蘇州の市街地の密度の高い歴史的な環境とは対照的な、現代の雄大な幾何学が太湖を前に展開しているのを目のあたりにする。

Suzhou in China is a popular tourism spot to visit water canals from the past. Construction of an art gallery was planned in a park on the shore of vast Lake Tai that spreads toward the west. A bridge is extended over the water between the rectangular-solid-shaped special exhibition building on the land side and the inverse-cone-shaped permanent exhibition building in an artificial lake with water from Lake Tai. When walking on the bridge, the dynamic modern geometry expands in front of Lake Tai in contrast to the dense historical environment of the urban area of Suzhou.

[287]
シャトー・ラ・コスト
／アートセンター　2011
château la coste / art center
.
1. フランス エクス・アン・プロヴァンス｜
   aix en provance, france
2. 設計｜design　2006.6 – 2008.10
3. 施工｜construction　2008.11 – 2011.05
4. 鉄筋コンクリート｜RC
5. 美術館｜museum of art
6. 敷地｜site　1,910,000 m²
7. 建築｜building　4,562 m²
8. 延床｜total floor　5,020 m²

同　チャペル　2011
château la coste / chapel
.
1. フランス エクス・アン・プロヴァンス｜
   aix en provance, france
2. 設計｜design　2006.6 – 2009.10
3. 施工｜construction　2010.3 – 2011.5
4. 鉄骨、一部石造｜steel, stone
5. 教会｜church
7. 建築｜building　77.8 m²
8. 延床｜total floor　77.8 m²

同　4 グラス・キューブス・
パビリオン　2011
château la coste
/ four glass cubes pavilion
.
1. フランス エクス・アン・プロヴァンス｜
   aix en provance, france
2. 設計｜design　2008.10 – 2009.10
3. 施工｜construction　2010.3 – 2011.5
4. 木造｜wood
5. 美術館｜museum of art
7. 建築｜building　400 m²
8. 延床｜total floor　205 m²

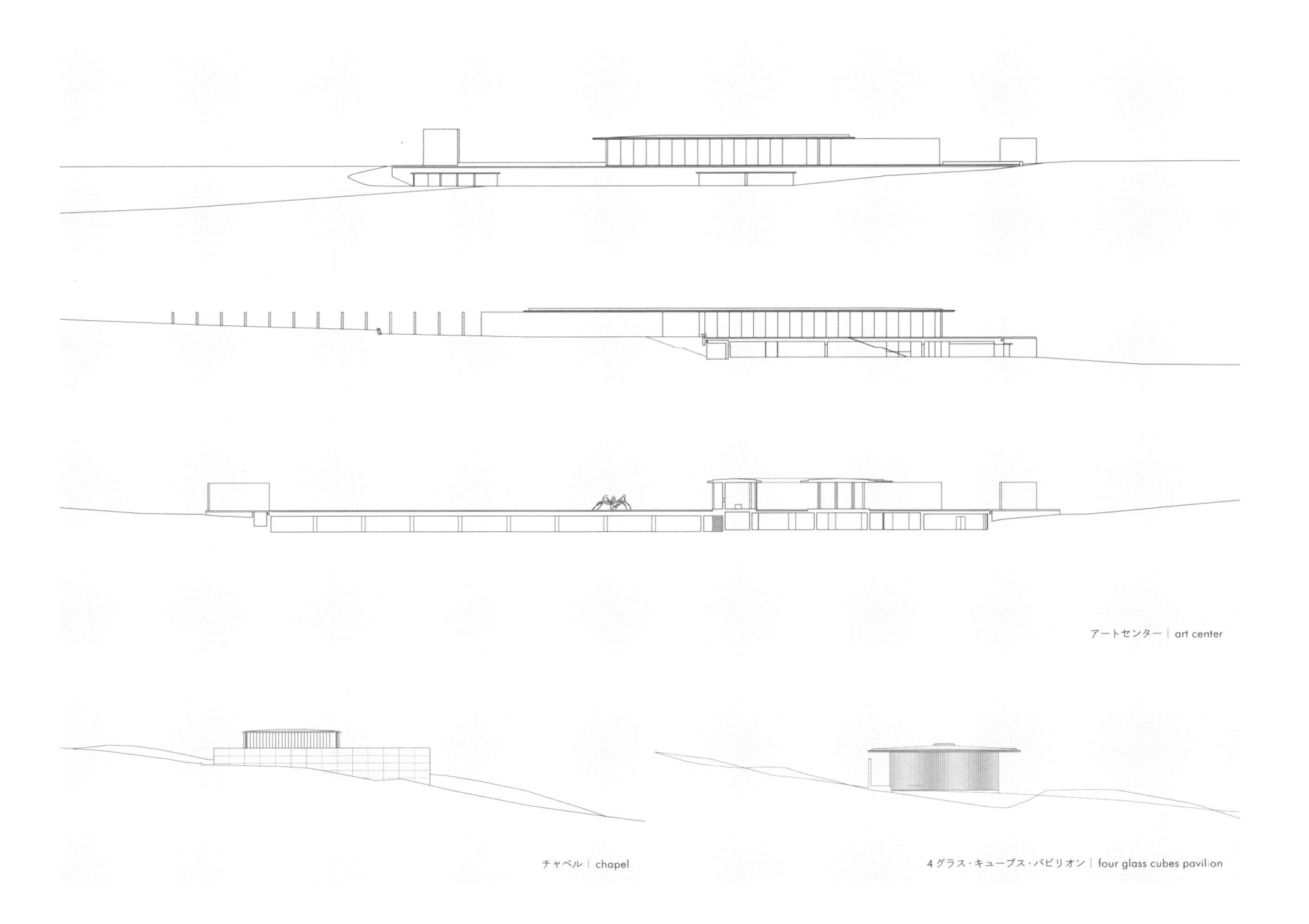

アートセンター｜art center

チャペル｜chapel

4 グラス・キューブス・パビリオン｜four glass cubes pavilion

346 Complete Works　428

セザンヌの出身地であり、大学都市としても知られるエクス・アン・プロヴァンス郊外に位置するワイナリー併設のアート・サイト。広大な緑のなかに現代美術家、国際的な建築家の手がけた作品や施設が点在する。安藤はその中心となるアートセンターと当地に残るローマ時代の聖堂の保存再生、自身のイメージを展示する木造のパビリオンを手がけた。アート・センターは人工池に低層のコンクリート打ち放しの建築が浮かぶように立つ。ゆったりしたレイアウトを生かして、鋭角に壁が交差する端部など抽象の美学が際立つ。聖堂の再生は残された遺構をガラスの壁で包み込み、歴史への敬意を表現した。木造のパビリオンは、セビリア万博以来手がけてきた現代木造を深いひさしとともに実現している。恵まれた環境のなかで存分に腕をふるった建築家の幸福な満足感に触れられる。

An art site built with a winery located in the suburbs of Aix-en-Provence, which is located in the place where Cezanne was born and known as a university town. Works and facilities created by contemporary artists and internationally known architects are scattered in the vast greenery area. Ando designed the art center, which is the main figure of the site, restored and recovered a chapel of Roman era that remains in the site, and a wooden pavilion that exhibits Ando's vision. The art center is standing as though the low-rising exposed concrete architecture was floating on an artificial pond. Abstraction aesthetics are highlighted such as the end of the walls intersecting at an acute angle using a wide layout. The chapel was renovated by wrapping the remaining wall with glass walls to express respect to the history. The wooden pavilion was created with a deep hood applying the modern wood work handled consistently since the Universal Exposition of Seville. Satisfaction with joy of an architect who was able to fully use his skill in a favorable environment can be felt at this site.

[288]
モンテレイの住宅　2011
house in monterrey

1. メキシコ モンテレイ ｜ monterrey, mexico
2. 設計 ｜ design　2006.8–2008.3
3. 施工 ｜ construction　2008.1–2011.4
4. 鉄筋コンクリート ｜ RC
5. 住宅 ｜ detached house
6. 敷地 ｜ site　10,824 m²
7. 建築 ｜ building　1,096 m²
8. 延床 ｜ total floor　1,519 m²

メキシコの山岳地に位置する中心都市モンテレイの国立公園内の個人住宅。傾斜地を活かし、低層部に配したロの字型の住棟と、それに重なり合うZの字型の翼棟が山腹をせり上がる構成をとる。ロの字の中庭を対角線の位置で横断するZ字の翼棟に図書室を置き、住宅の核としている。頂部に配されたプールと周囲の山々が重なり合う光景は感動的な次元に到達している。メキシコを舞台にモダニズムを確立したルイス・バラガンへのオマージュとして抽象表現に徹したと、安藤は述べている。

A private residential house in the national park of a central city of Monterrey located in the mountainous region of Mexico. Using sloped ground, the square shaped residential building on the lower floor and the Z-shape wing buildings that overlap the residential building are in a form that appears to climb up along mountainside. A library is shown as the center of this house as it is placed in the Z-shape wing buildings crossing the square courtyard diagonally. The scenery of the surrounding mountains behind the swimming pool on top of the building is very inspiring. Ando mentioned that he focused on describing the abstract expression as a homage to Luis Barragan who established Modernism in Mexico.

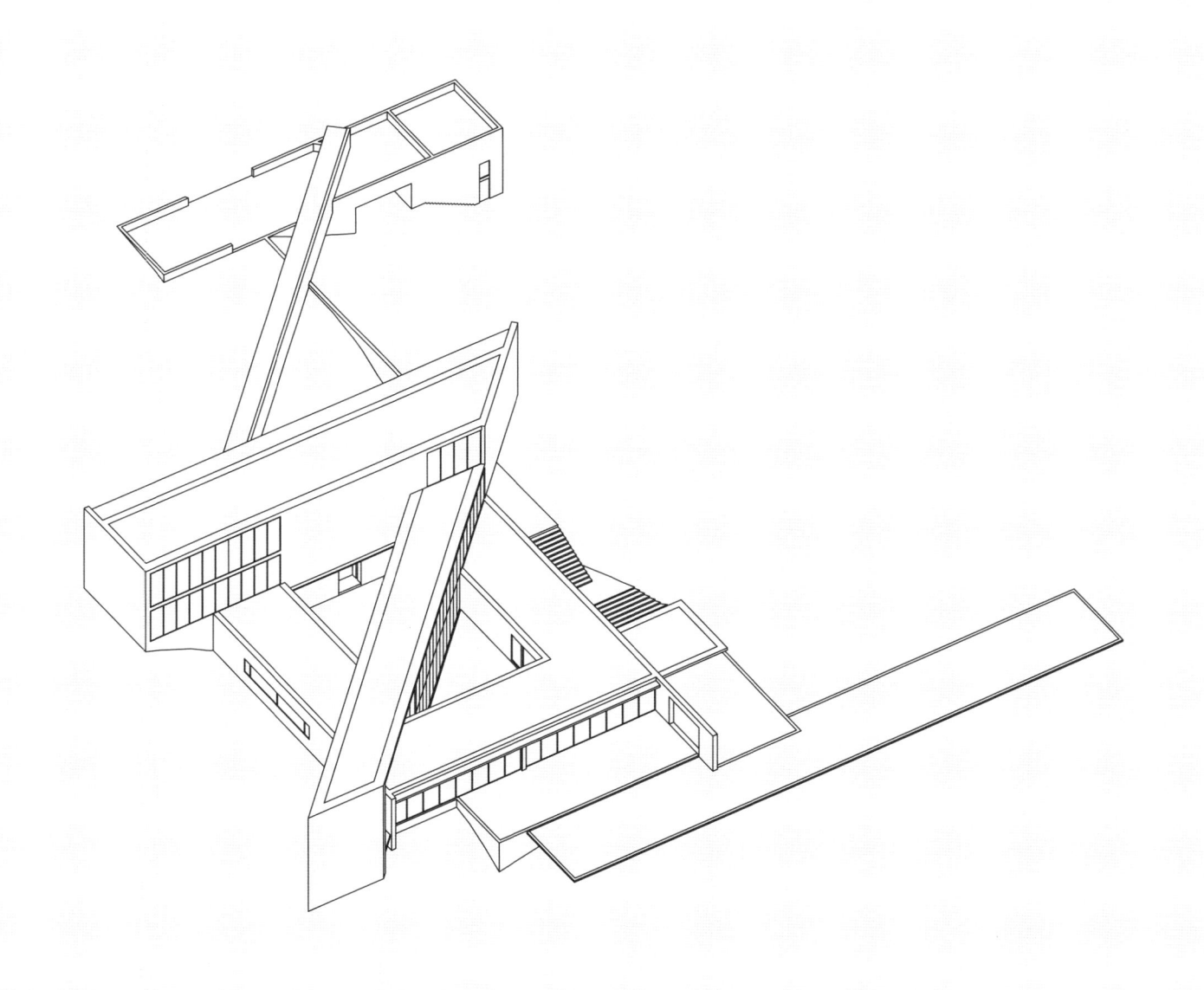

[289]

東急大井町線上野毛駅　2011
tokyu oimachi-line kaminoge station

1. 東京都世田谷区 | setagaya-ku, tokyo
2. 設計 | design　2006.10–2009.3
3. 施工 | construction　2007.6–2011.3
4. 鉄骨 | steel
5. 駅舎、バス停 | railway station, bus stop
6. 敷地 | site　2,175.1 m²
7. 建築 | building　1,217.7 m²
8. 延床 | total floor　2,587.8 m²

東急電車の大井町線は掘切に線路が位置し、上野毛通りを地下のレベルでくぐる。線路の複々線化を機に駅が新装された。長さ120メートルの緩い曲線を描く大屋根を、2階の軒の高さで上野毛通りをまたがせた。駅の出入口は通りの両側にあるが、大屋根の設置により一対のものと認識されるようになった。屋根にうがたれた直径8メートルの円形の穴は、上野毛通りのトップライトとなり、太陽が動くと光と影は異なる表情を路上につくりだし、時刻によって辺りの風景を一変させる。

Tokyu Oimachi Line is located in a trench, and it passes under Kaminoge street at the basement level. Kaminoge Station was remodeled along with the conversion of the line into quadruple tracks. A large, gently curved roof in 120m of length is crossing over Kaminoge street at the height of the eaves on the 2nd floor. The entrance gates to the station are located on both sides of the street, while those gates are now recognized as a pair after the large roof was provided over them. A circular hole in 8m diameter drilled on the roof became the top light of Kaminoge street. Light and shadow create different expressions on the street as the sun moves. It sometimes transforms the surrounding landscape.

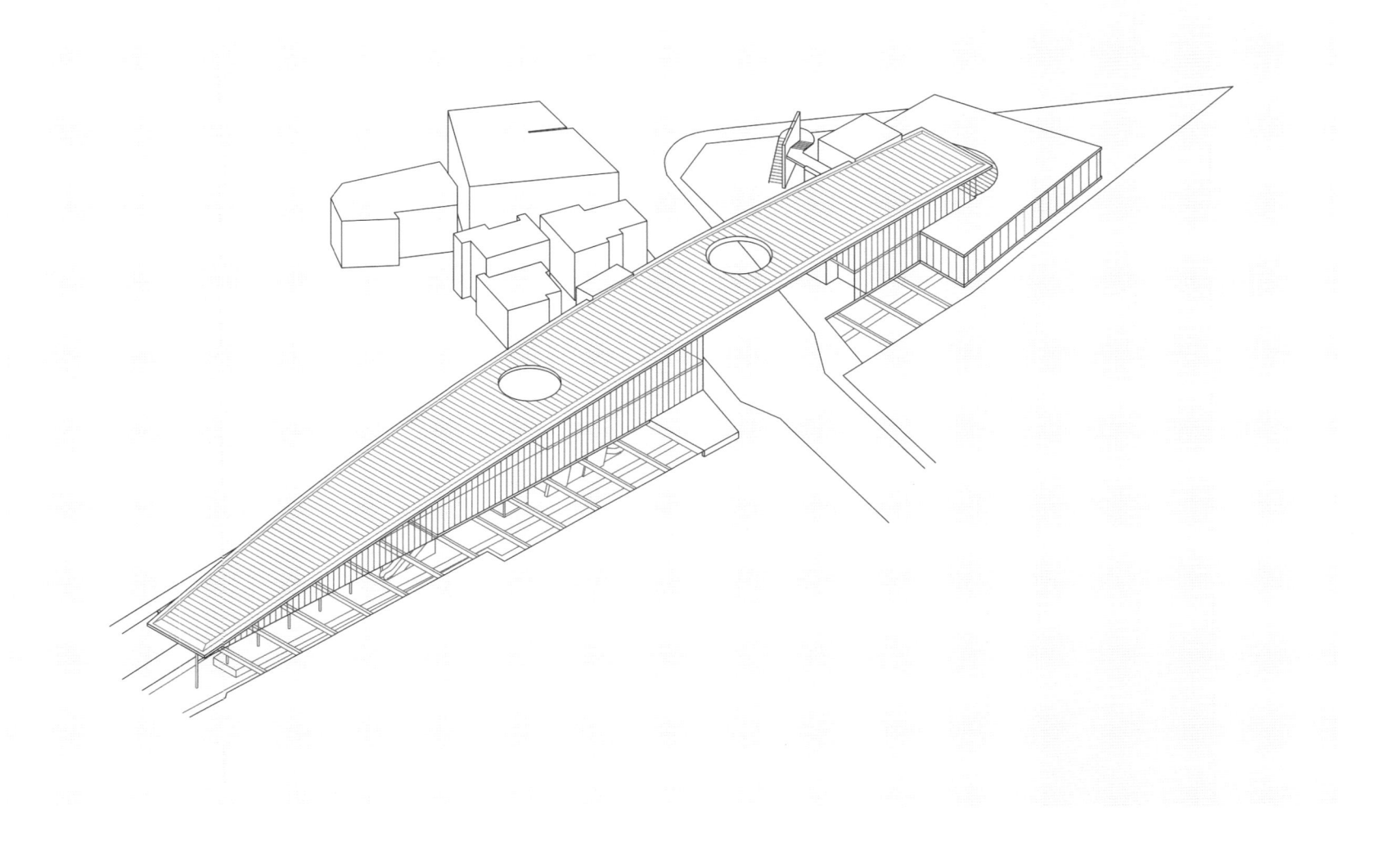

[290]
カルロス・プレイス「サイレンス」
2011
carlos place "silence"

.
1. イギリス ロンドン | london, UK
2. 設計 | design   2009.3 – 2010.12
3. 施工 | construction   2011.3 – 2011.6
4. 鉄筋コンクリート、鉄骨 | RC, steel
5. 噴水 | fountain
6. 敷地 | site   486 m²
7. 建築 | building   157 m² [fountain]

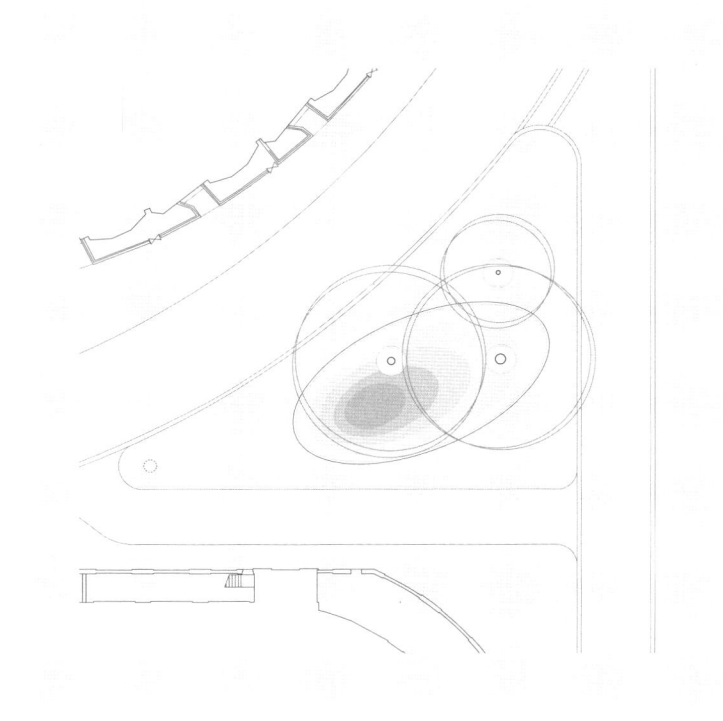

ロンドンの高級住宅街の一角、コンノート・ホテル前の広場に楕円形の水盤を置いた。楕円は長径が20メートル、短径が10メートルで、水中に円形のガラスブロックを敷き、時間が来ると噴水が霧を発生させる。自動車道路が交差するラウンドアバウトの中央に位置し、既存のメイプルの大木を水盤のなかに残すなど「場」の歴史にも配慮した。多くのひとが足をとめ、広場で日常の会話に興じる光景は、新しい施設が定着しつつあることを物語る。
.
An oval basin was placed at a plaza in front of The Connaught located in a high-end residential area of London. The oval's length and breadth are 20 meters and 10 meters respectively where round glass blocks are laid under water and mist is generated by the fountain at regular intervals. The location is in the center of a roundabout where motorways intersect. The history of the space was considered by leaving an existing large maple tree in the basin. The scenery where many people stop and enjoy conversations with each other shows that the new plaza is well rooted in this city.

---

[291]
韓屋のゲストハウス   2011
house with "hanok"

.
1. 大韓民国 京畿道 驪州郡 |
   yeoju-gun, gyeonggi-do, south korea
2. 設計 | design   2011.11
3. 構想案 | concept
4. 鉄筋コンクリート、木造 | RC, wood
5. ゲストハウス | guest house
6. 敷地 | site   6,317 m²
7. 建築 | building   1,054.2 m²
8. 延床 | total floor   1,344.92 m²

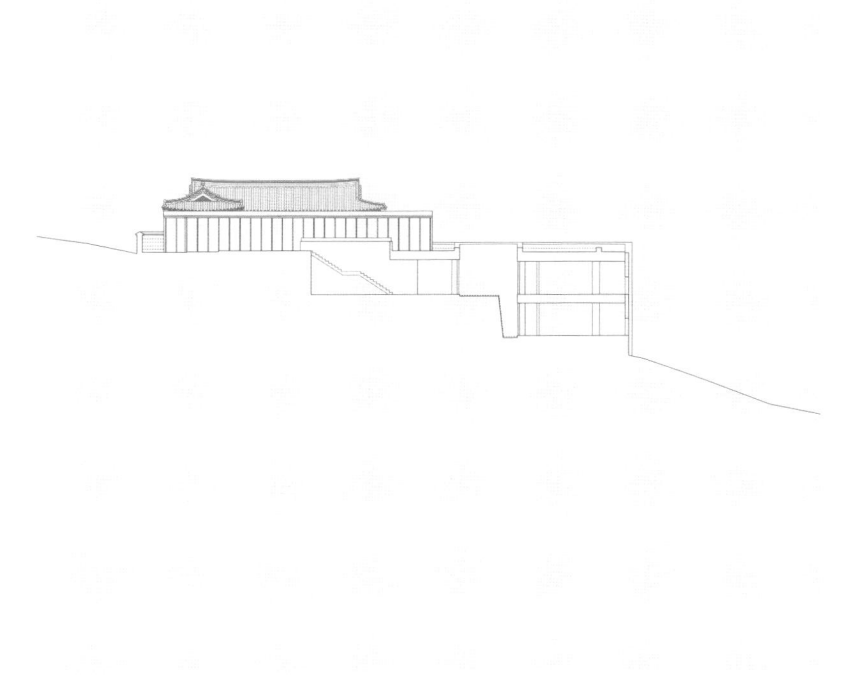

ソウル近郊の丘陵地に計画した企業グループオーナーのゲストハウス計画。「韓屋（ハノク）」と呼ばれる民家を移築したうえで、L字型の幾何立体の新たな住棟は、敷地の傾斜を活かし、屋上を緑化して「韓屋」のグラウンドレベルと揃えた。新旧の建物は、かつての「韓屋」がそうであったように中庭を囲う配置をとり、ヴォールト屋根の架かるガラス壁のエントランス棟で結ばれる。主棟の南面の開口部は、韓国の伝統的な格子のパターンを援用、そこでも新旧の融合を試みる。
.
A guesthouse plan for a hill site near Seoul for a corporate group owner. After relocating a house called "Hanok", a new L-shaped residential building was built to match the level of its green roof with the ground level of Hanok, taking advantage of the sloped site. The old and new buildings are arranged to surround the courtyard, like "Hanok" used to be. The entrance building with glass walls and a vaulted roof connects the two buildings. A traditional Korean lattice pattern is used for the openings on the south side of the main building, in pursuit of a fusion of old and new.

[292]

ミュージアム SAN 2012
museum san

1. 大韓民国 原州市　wonju, south korea
2. 設計｜design　2005.10 – 2008.7
3. 施工｜construction　2008.8 – 2012.5
4. 鉄筋コンクリート｜RC
5. 美術館｜museum of art
6. 敷地｜site　71,172 ㎡
7. 建築｜building　4,927 ㎡
8. 延床｜total floor　10,577 ㎡

韓国原州の現代美術館。韓国を代表する企業の文化財団がリゾート地の一角に美術館を建設、収蔵品を展示している。現地産の石材を張りつめた外観は、コンクリート打ち放しとは対比的な荒々しさで安藤の配した抽象立体を包み込む。人工池にその外観が映り込む姿は、韓国の文化的文脈を直感させる。安藤は四つの棟のうち三つを平行に配置、その二つを斜めに振った棟で結び、それぞれの棟の間に生じる空隙を、コンクリート打ち放しの幾何図形で構成し、現代美術館らしい空間を表現している。

A contemporary art gallery of Wonju, Korea. A cultural foundation of a representative company in Korea built an art gallery and exhibts the collection in a resort area. The external appearance covered with locally excavated stone material has a roughness opposite to exposed concrete and it enwraps the abstract solid arranged by Ando. Korea's cultural context can be grasped intuitively when one views the external appearance reflected on the artificial pond. Ando placed three out of four buildings in parallel, connected two of them with a building placed in diagonal, the gap made between the buildings are combined in geometric shape of exposed concrete to express a contemporary impression of art gallery.

[293]

マリブの住宅 III　2012
house in malibu III

1. アメリカ マリブ | malibu, USA
2. 設計 | design　2006.11–2009.10
3. 施工 | construction　2009.10–2012.6
4. 鉄筋コンクリート | RC
5. 住宅 | detached house
6. 敷地 | site　414 m²
7. 建築 | building　176 m²
8. 延床 | total floor　374 m²

米西海岸マリブの太平洋に面する個人住宅。施主はニューヨーク在住の美術収集家で、この住宅は別荘と個人ギャラリーとして設計された。太いコンクリートの柱列のピロティに、コンクリートの板材で構成された居室部分が載る。そこは海に向って窓を開き、当地ならではの開放感を演出している。最上階には外気に触れられるバルコニーも備える。各階の昇降には幅の広いコンクリートの階段を利用することで、レベルの変化も味わえる仕立てになっている。

A private residential house facing the Pacific Ocean of Malibu on the west coast of the U.S. The client is an art collector living in New York and this house was designed as a villa and a private gallery. The living room area composed of concrete plate material is placed on the pilotis with thick concrete column row. Windows open toward the ocean to make a sense of spaciousness unique to this location. The top floor has a balcony to feel the outside air. An impression of changing floor levels can be felt by using a wide concrete stairway for going up or down the stairs.

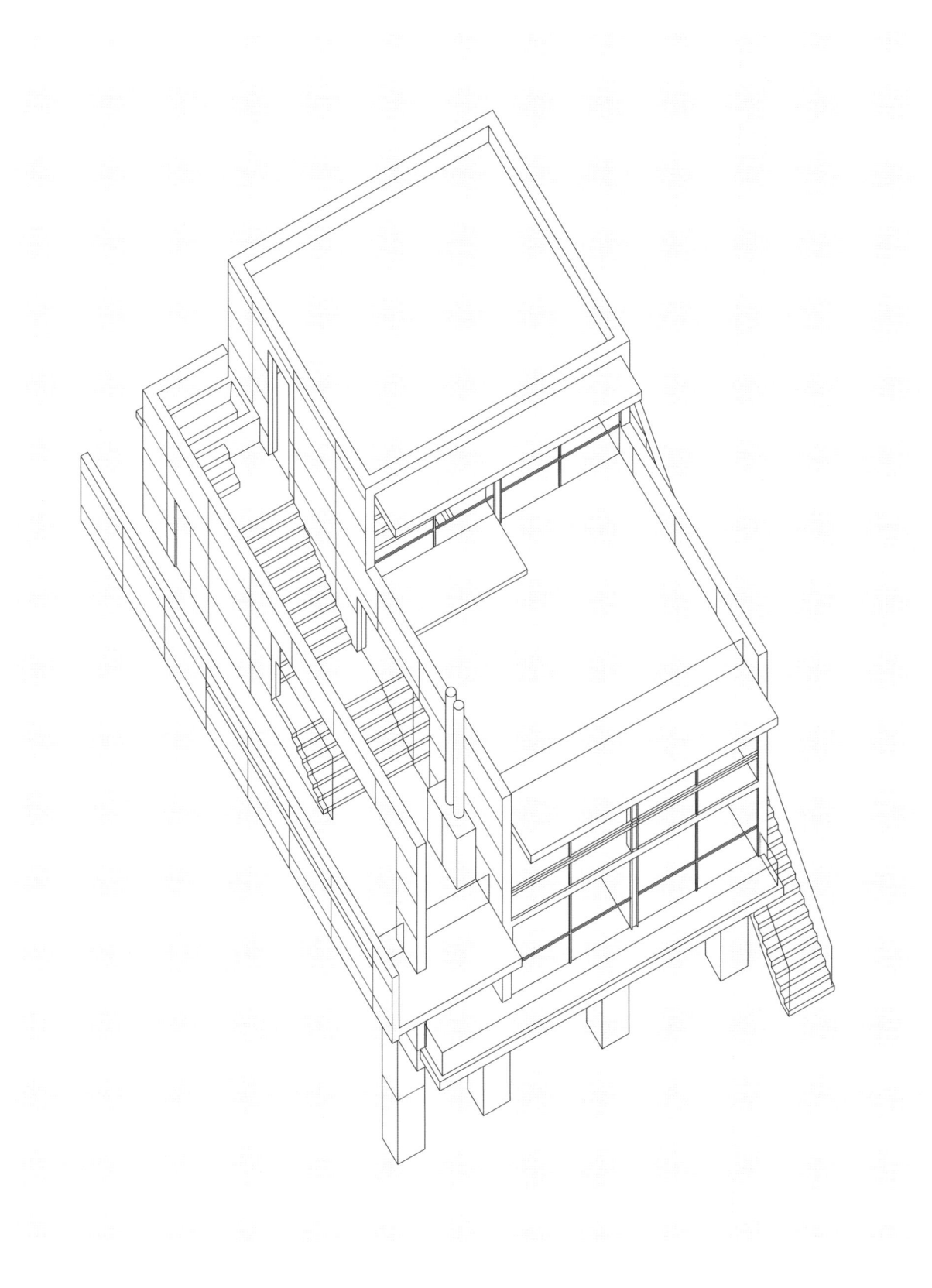

[294]

モンテレイ大学 RGSセンター
2012
roberto garza sada center for arts,
architecture and design

1. メキシコ モンテレイ | monterrey, mexico
2. 設計 | design 2007.4 – 2009.7
3. 施工 | construction 2009.7 – 2012.12
4. 鉄骨鉄筋コンクリート | SRC
5. 大学施設 | university facilities
6. 敷地 | site 20,700 m²
7. 建築 | building 2673 m²
8. 延床 | total floor 12,694 m²

メキシコの工業都市モンテレイの大学デザイン系学科の新校舎。ハイパーシェルと呼ぶ三次元曲面のゲートが目をひく。躯体は単純な直方体を基本とし、上階では長軸方向に3分割され、両側が教育施設、中央がパブリックスペースに充てられている。地上階レベルでは、両側から広がってきた三次元曲面がねじりの形で交差し、力感あふれる表現を見せている。安藤は、このデジタルエイジの申し子のような曲面を、周囲の国立公園の山並みと対比的に配して、新たな表現の一歩を踏み出した。

A new school building of a faculty of designing for Institute of Technology, Monterrey, an industrial city of Mexico. The three-dimensionally curved gate named "hyper shell" draws attention. The building frame is a simple rectangular solid. The upper floor is divided into three in the long axial direction where both sides are for educational facilities and the center is a public space. At ground level, the three-dimensionally curved surfaces extended from both sides intersect with each other showing their powerful expression. The curved surfaces that characterize this digital age were placed by Ando to make a contrast with the mountains of surrounding national parks that was a new step made by Ando from his former works.

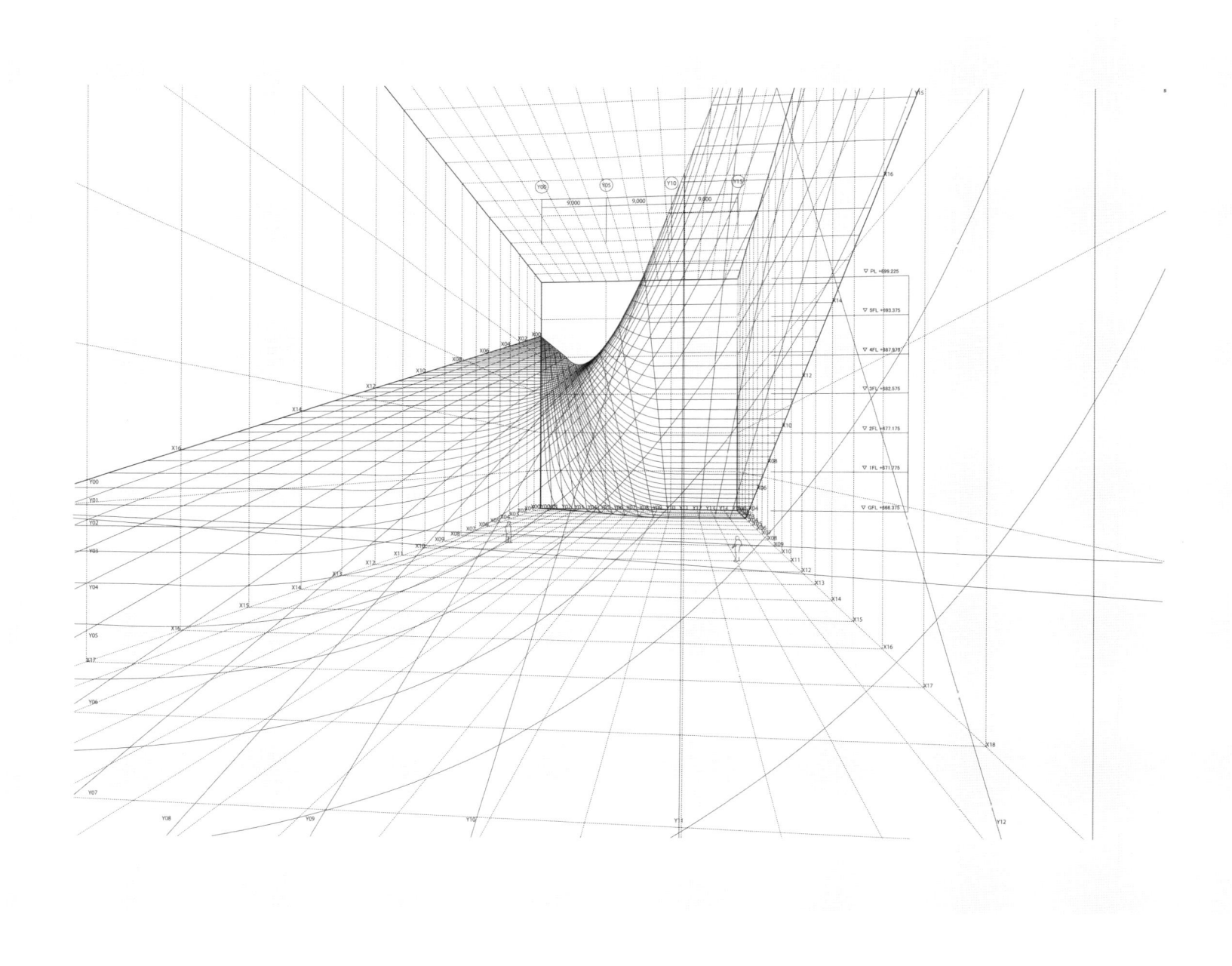

[295]
秋田県立美術館　2012
akita museum of art

1. 秋田県秋田市 | akita, akita
2. 設計 | design　2009.6–2010.3
3. 施工 | construction　2011.1–2012.6
4. 鉄筋コンクリート | RC
5. 美術館 | museum of art
6. 敷地 | site　17,365 m²
7. 建築 | building　1,977 m²
8. 延床 | total floor　3,746 m²

1937年に地元の素封家平野政吉の求めで藤田嗣治の描いた「秋田の行事」は、縦横が3.65メートル×20.5メートルの大作。パリで活躍しながら故国を忘れなかった画家の思いがこもる。恵まれない展示環境に置かれた時期もあったが、市街地の再開発を機に、美術館が新しい街の一角に場を求め、安藤の設計で新築された。主展示室は吹き抜けで、藤田の大作が大空間を飾っている。そこにつながるラウンジは1階の屋根上に設けた水庭に向かって開く構成をとり、水庭と道路をはさんだ秋田城址の「千秋公園」の堀の水が継ぎ目なしに連なるのが目に入る。

The painting of Tsuguharu Fujita, "Akita no Gyoji" ("Events in Akita"), was completed in 1937 by the request of Masakichi Hirano from a wealthy family—it is a very large painting work in 3.65m high, 20.5m wide, reflecting the thoughts of Fujita who had longed for Japan even after his success in Paris. Although it was in a disadvantageous exhibition environment for a long time, the organization of the museum sought a place in a new corner of the city with the development of the city, and it was newly built with Ando's design. The main exhibition room has a large-scale open ceiling space to present this large art piece of Fujita. A lounge space linked to this exhibition room has a configuration to open up toward the water garden provided on the rooftop of the 1st floor. When sitting down in this space, the water of the moat in "Senshu Park" of Akita Castle beyond the road and the water garden are seen like a continuous connection without seams.

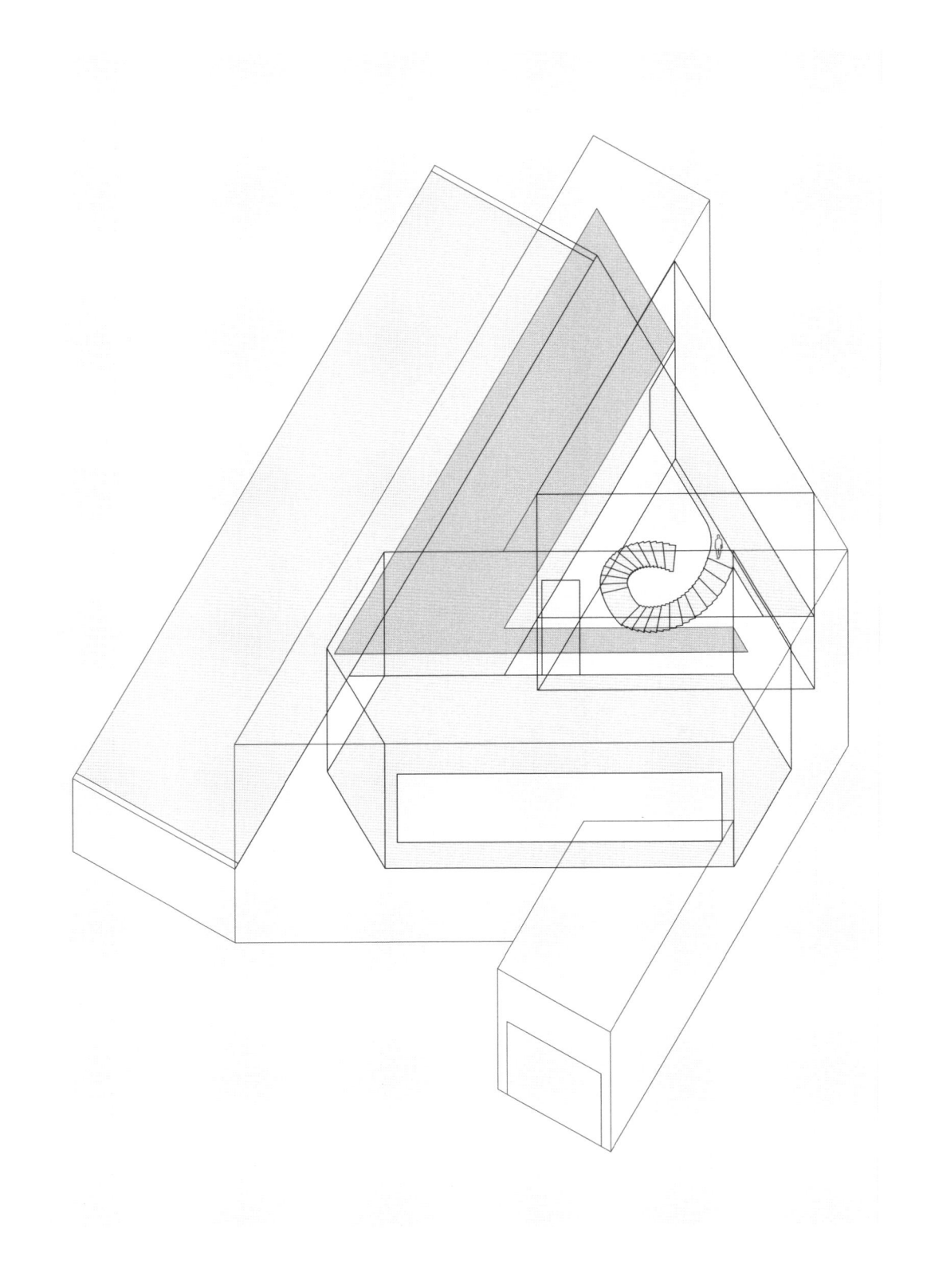

[296]

ボンテ・ミュージアム 2012

bonte museum

1. 大韓民国 済州島 | jeju island, south korea
2. 設計 | design 2009.9 – 2011.3
3. 施工 | construction 2011.4 – 2012.11
4. 鉄筋コンクリート | RC
5. 美術館 | museum of art
6. 敷地 | site 7,603 m²
7. 建築 | building 1,614 m²
8. 延床 | total floor 2,031 m²

韓国・済州島のリゾート施設の一角を占める美術館。海抜400メートルの立地だ。それぞれ同形のL字型の平面を持つ北館、南館の二つの棟から成る。南館は韓国の伝統美術を展示する場で、展示品の大きさ、性質を踏まえて小さな展示室が配されている。一方、北館は現代美術の展示空間のため、吹き抜けを配した開放的な空間が設営された。二つの建物をつなぐ位置に水庭を配し、南館から伸びる伝統的な塀の続く回廊によって両者の一体感を演出している。

An art gallery in a resort facility located at a property 400 meters above sea level in Jeju Island, Korea. The facility consists of a North building and South building, which both have the same L-shaped planform. The South building is for Korean traditional artworks where small exhibition rooms are provided suiting the size and characteristics of the exhibits. On the other hand, the North building has spacious areas with open ceilings for displaying contemporary arts. A water garden is arranged at the area connecting the two buildings and a cloister along traditional walls extending from the South building creates a sense of unity in these two buildings.

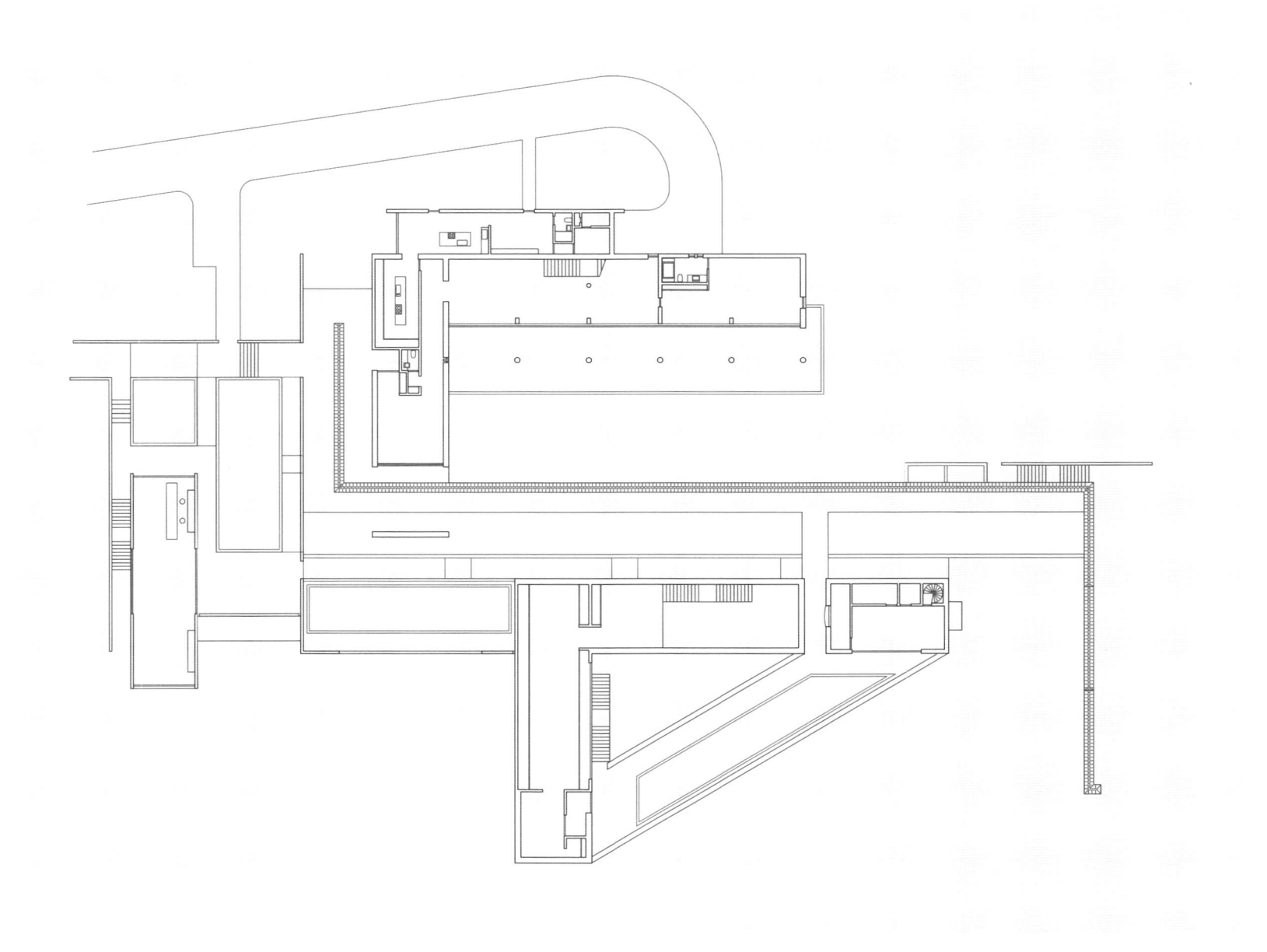

[297]
震旦美術館　2012
aurora museum

1. 中華人民共和国　上海 | shanghai, china
2. 設計 | design　2009.9 – 2010.11
3. 施工 | construction　2010.11 – 2012.2
4. 鉄筋コンクリート | RC
5. 美術館 | museum of art
6. 敷地 | site　9,720 m²
8. 延床 | total floor　5,282 m²

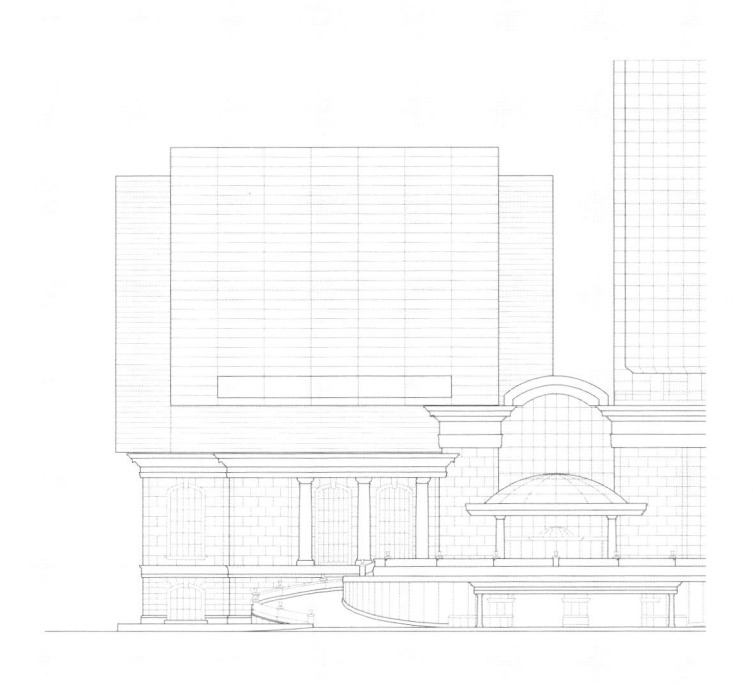

台湾系企業が中国・上海の本拠とする高層ビルの低層階に開設した美術館。五層の吹き抜け空間を持ち、階段で昇降して展示を鑑賞する。建物を取り巻くドライエリアからの自然光を生かしたフロアもあり、展示の多様性を追求している。中国古代からの磁器などコレクションは圧倒的で、安藤の展示空間は歴史遺物に敬意を払い、禁欲的な仕立てをとる。ガラスケースなど細部にまで造形の意志が貫徹されている。

An art gallery opened at the lower floors of the high-rise building of a Taiwanese company based in Shanghai, China. An open ceiling of six floors is provided to view the exhibition while going up or down the stairs. Certain floors take advantage of natural light from the dry area surrounding the building to pursue variation of exhibition. Ando used an ascetic approach to show respect to the exhibition space of historical relics for the overwhelming collection of artifacts including Chinese ancient porcelains. The styling concept is reflected thoroughly in details even such as glass cases.

[298]
老木レディスクリニック　2012
oiki ladies clinic

1. 大阪府和泉市 | izumi, osaka
2. 設計 | design　2009.12 – 2010.12
3. 施工 | construction　2011.4 – 2012.2
4. 鉄筋コンクリート | RC
5. 病院 | hospital
6. 敷地 | site　4,632.15 m²
7. 建築 | building　892.7 m²
8. 延床 | total floor　1,153.07 m²

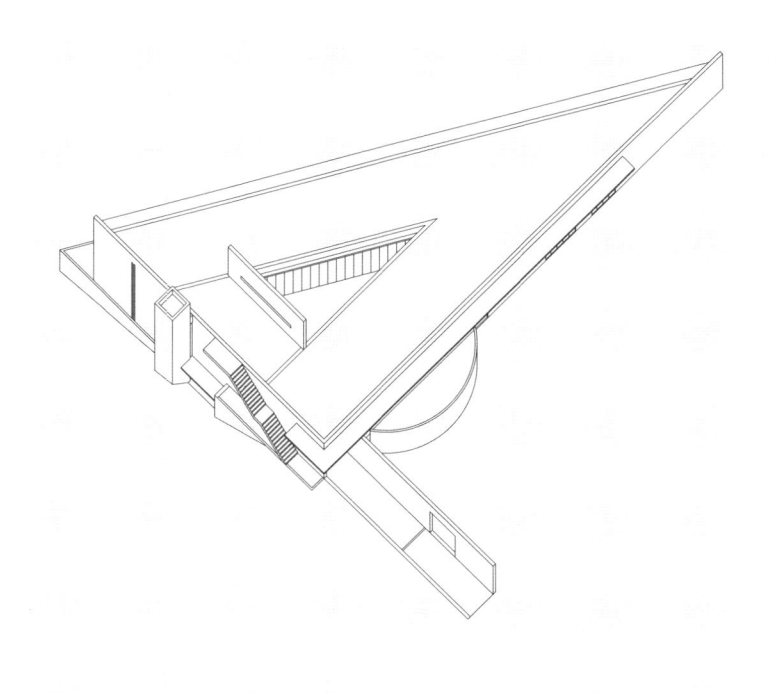

大阪府和泉市で地域医療に貢献している産婦人科医院の建築。造成地の高台にあるコンクリート打ち放しの建物の屋根は屋上緑化が施され、造成地斜面の緑との連続がはかられている。三角形の平面形で、中庭には浅い人工池が配された。入院病室はこの人工池を囲む廊下に面している。ここで生まれた子どもたちが、出生の場所として再訪したくなるような親しみの持てる空間構成を意識し、インテリアは柔らかなイメージに仕立てられている。

An architecture of a gynecology clinic that is contributing to the local medical care in Izumi City, Osaka. The roof of the exposed concrete building located on a hill of a developed land area that has a green rooftop to maintain the greenery on the slope of the developed land. The planform is a triangle and a triangle shallow artificial pond is situated in the courtyard. In patients' rooms that face these corridors that surround the artificial pond, rooms are finished with soft-looking interiors to create a friendly spatial structure where children who were born here would like to come back and visit their birthplace.

[299]
高松の住宅　2012
house in takamatsu

1. 香川県高松市 | takamatsu, kagawa
2. 設計 | design　2010.4 – 2011.11
3. 施工 | construction　2011.11 – 2012.8
4. 鉄筋コンクリート | RC
5. 住宅 | detached house
6. 敷地 | site　271.1 m²
7. 建築 | building　206.2 m²
8. 延床 | total floor　378.0 m²

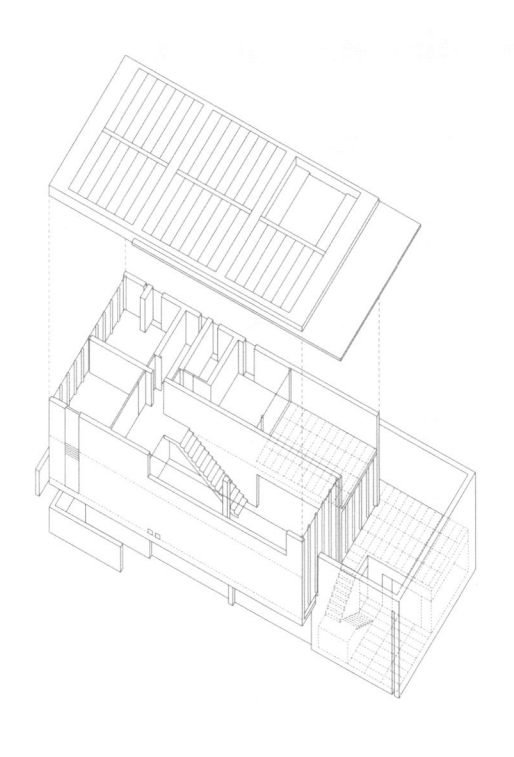

周辺環境に対して閉じつつ、〈自然〉に対して開かれた住空間。安藤はこの住宅の構成原理をそう説明している。オフィスビルもならぶ繁華な市街地の一角でいかに安寧の住環境を保持するか、規模は十分なこの住宅でも、「長屋」に通じる対応が求められた。角地の立地で、正面にあたる側の外観は、低層に抑制したコンクリートの壁が強固な保護の意志を表現し、一方の短辺のほうは、すりガラスの巨大な窓が外壁面のほとんどを占める。この窓を通して、5.6メートルの階高のリビングから外界を眺めることで、都市のなかの自然の移ろいが確かめられる。

A living space that shuts out the surrounding environment by letting the nature come in. That is Ando's exploration of the structural principle of this house. The challenge was how to maintain a tranquil living environment in a busy urban area where many office buildings are standing. Although the house had sufficient size, it had to be arranged similar to a terrace house. Since the house is on a corner plot, the front external view was made to express determination to securely protect using a concrete wall restricted to low height and the narrow side has a huge window with frosted glass that occupies almost the whole exterior wall. Transition of nature in the city can be observed by looking outside through this window from the living room that is situated at 5.6 meters in height.

[300]
上方落語協会会館　2012
kamigata rakugo house

1. 大阪市北区 | kita-ku, osaka
2. 設計 | design　2011.4 – 2011.8
3. 施工 | construction　2011.9 – 2012.4
4. 鉄筋コンクリート | RC
5. 事務所 | office
6. 敷地 | site　129.1 m²
7. 建築 | building　103.2 m²
8. 延床 | total floor　263.0 m²

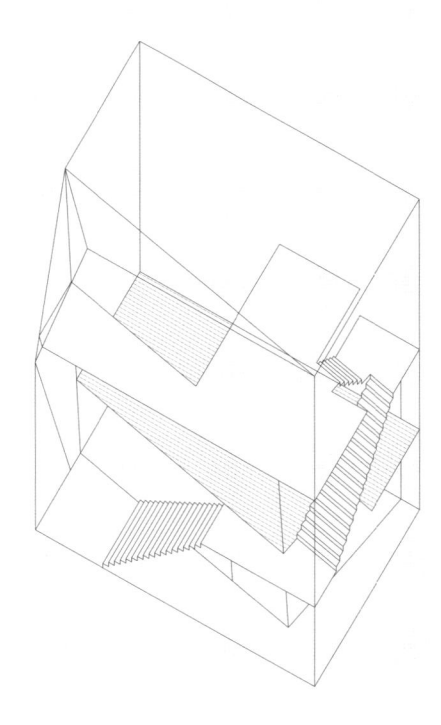

上方落語は大阪人の活力と屈託のない生き生きとした姿を今日に伝える。その本拠となる会館の建築は、間口が8メートル、奥行きと高さが12.5メートルの直方体を基本とし、そこに平面で9度、立面で9度斜めに振ったコンクリートの壁を挿入することで空間のダイナミズムが生まれた。階段は上段に進むに連れて幅が狭まり、事務室、会議室、資料室の廊下・階段側の壁は、向うに倒れるように傾いている。その傾斜した壁にガラス窓を設け、直方体の頂部を切り欠いたトップライトから自然光が室内に入り込むように仕立てた。

Kamigata rakugo shows the vitality and carefree attitude of Osaka people in the past. The architecture of the hall for Kamigata rakugo as its home has an 8-meter wide, 12.5-meter long and high rectangular solid as the basic form where a concrete wall is inserted in 9-degree angle on a horizontal surface and 9-degree angle on vertical surface to create dynamism in the atmosphere. The stairway gets narrower as it goes up and walls on the corridor and stairway sides of the office room, meeting room, and material room are inclined as if they were falling rearward. Glass windows provided on those inclined walls and the top light by creating a notch on the top part of the rectangular solid allow natural light to enter the building.

[301]
マンガロールの住宅　2012
house in mangalore

1. インド マンガロール | mangalore, india
2. 設計 | design　2012.2
3. 構想案 | concept
4. 鉄筋コンクリート | RC
5. 住宅 | detached house

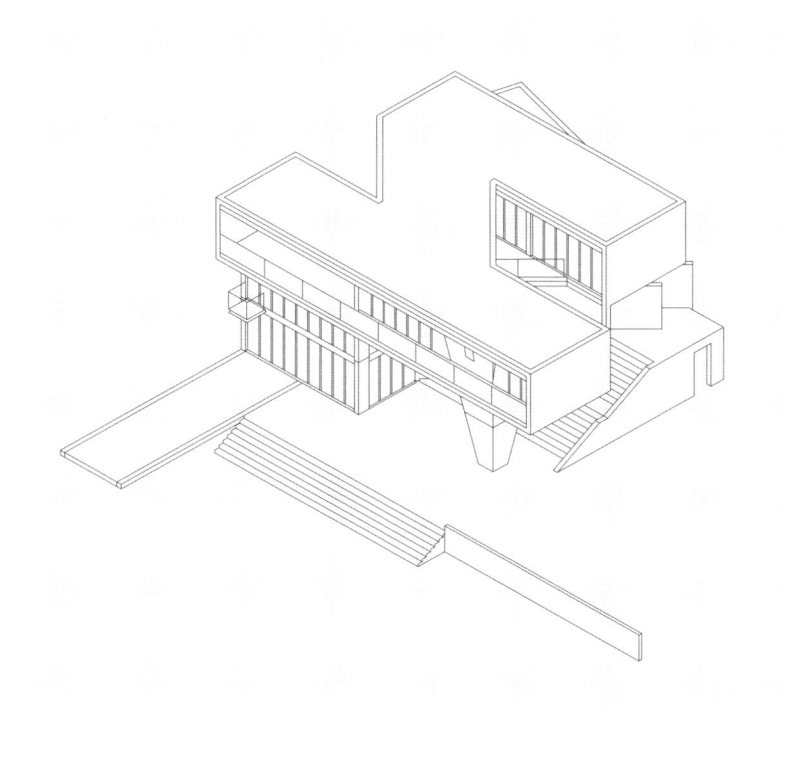

アラビア海に面したインド西部の港湾都市マンガロールの企業家の依頼に基づき、既存住宅にパーティースペース、ギャラリーなどを収める新棟の増築計画が立案された。海辺の開放的な敷地に、平面形が「Z」型の新棟を建設する。水平なコンクリートの板材が「Z」を描き、それを支える逆四角錐の柱、2階に配する屋根と床だけの空洞のテラスなど、豊かな自然のなかで安藤の幾何学が存在感を発揮する。地下にパーティースペース、1階にギャラリー、2階にゲストハウスなどの機能を置く。

An extension plan of a new building with a party space and gallery for an existing house, for an entrepreneur in Mangalore, a coastal city in western India facing the Arabian Sea. A new building having a Z-shaped plan is built on the open coastal site. Ando's geometry — horizontal concrete boards forming the Z shape, inverted quadrangular pyramid pillars that support the boards, and a hollow terrace on the second floor consisting of a roof and floor — has a massive presence in the abundant nature. Functions include a party space in the basement, a gallery on the first floor, and a guesthouse on the second floor.

[302]
亜洲大学 亜洲現代美術館
2013
asia museum of modern art,
asia university

1. 台湾 台中 | taichung, taiwan
2. 設計 | design　2007.6 – 2009.12
3. 施工 | construction　2011.1 – 2013.5
4. 鉄筋コンクリート、一部鉄骨鉄筋コンクリート | RC, SRC
5. 美術館 | museum of art
6. 敷地 | site　23,005.0 m²
7. 建築 | building　1,794.4 m²
8. 延床 | total floor　4,105.4 m²

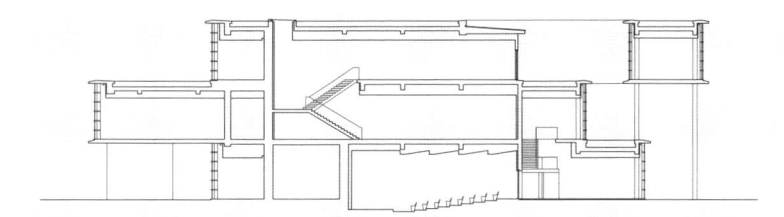

平面の基本形を正三角形とすることで、安藤は大学が保持しなければならない基本原理への回帰という教育機能を満たそうと考えた。価値観が変転、輻輳する現代社会における大学のありかたを踏まえた選択だ。空間としては三層の三角形の平面をずらすことで、ギャラリーを移動しながら、屋外彫刻の点在するキャンパスを鑑賞者に俯瞰させる効用を意識した。ガラスの外観を板状のコンクリートの柱が支える姿は、台湾中部大地震からの復興のために設立された同大学の起源を意識している。

By making regular triangles as the basic planform, Ando considered to satisfy the educational function of regression to fundamental principle that universities have to maintain. He chose the design to demonstrate how universities should function in modern society where the sense of values always keep changing and congesting. From spatial point of view, three layers of triangles are offset in planform to allow viewers to observe the greenery of the campus while moving through the gallery. The style of plate concrete columns supporting the mirror glasses is taken from the origin of this university established to revitalize after the Chi-Chi Taiwan Earthquake.

[303]

うめきた広場 2013
umekita plaza

1. 大阪市北区 | kita-ku, osaka
2. 設計 | design   2007.8 – 2010.3
3. 施工 | construction   2010.8 – 2013.3
4. 鉄筋コンクリート、一部鉄骨鉄筋コンクリート、一部鉄骨 | RC, SRC, steel
5. 広場の計画 | plaza plan
6. 敷地 | site   47,917.9 m²
7. 建築 | building   2,253.6 m²
8. 延床 | total floor   10,541.59 m²

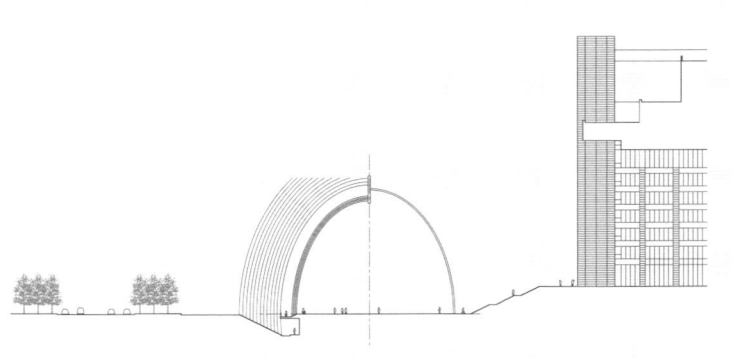

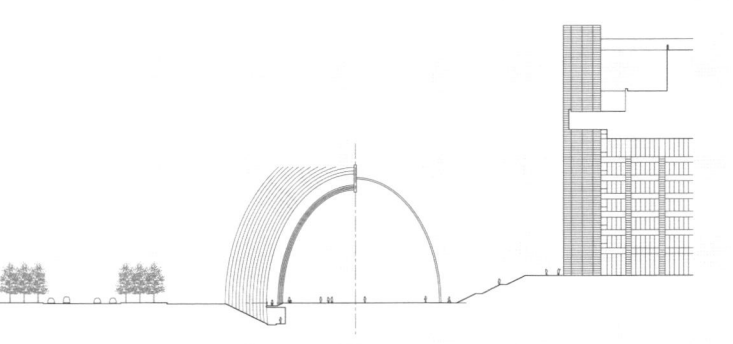

大阪駅北口の大規模再開発「北ヤード」の一角を占める都市広場。大阪駅に面した一角の地上レベルの高さに楕円形の立体広場が実現した。広さは1万平方メートルの大規模なもので、背後にある歩行者のためのブリッジを備えた人工池から、大量の水が楕円盤の脇に段状で構築された壁を轟音を伴って滝のように流れ落ちる。夜間は楕円の表面に規則的に散りばめられた発光ダイオードの点光源が、美しく造形を彩る。

An urban plaza in the North Yard of a large-scale redevelopment project at the north exit of Osaka station. An oval three dimensional plaza was created at the same level as the ground floor in an area facing Osaka station. The scale is wide as 10,000m² where a large amount of water runs down with loud noise like a waterfall on the wall built in stages by oval basin from an artificial pond with a bridge on the rear area for pedestrians. The LED lights scattered systematically on the oval surface make Ando's work shine beautifully during the night.

[304]

芦屋の住宅 2013
house in ashiya

1. 兵庫県芦屋市 | ashiya, hyogo
2. 設計 | design   2010.11 – 2012.1
3. 施工 | construction   2012.2 – 2013.1
4. 鉄筋コンクリート | RC
5. 住宅 | detached house
6. 敷地 | site   196.0 m²
7. 建築 | building   78.1 m²
8. 延床 | total floor   134.3 m²

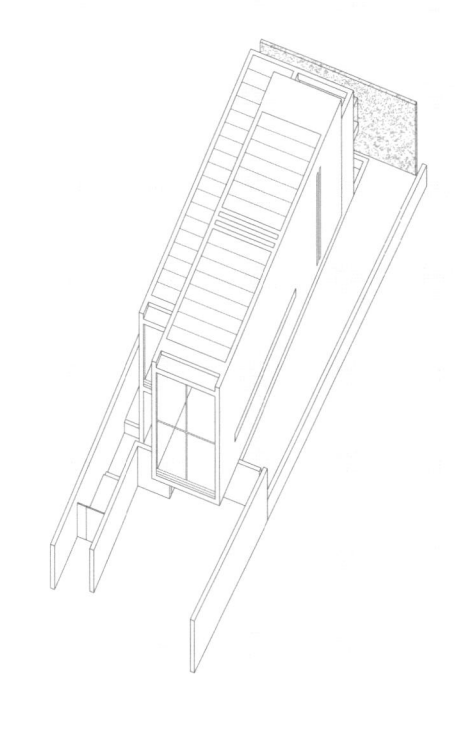

敷地は街区を突き抜けて、前後の道路を結ぶ位置取り。現地を見て、安藤は両側の風景をつなぐようなチューブ状の住空間を想定した。その発想は、間口7メートル、奥行25メートルの細長い敷地を、あたかも空中に浮遊して縦断するかのような2階リビングとなって実現した。空間ののびやかさを家族が実感できる仕立てを意図した。この細長い直方体のチューブには2か所スリットが切ってあり、そこからの光が住まいの中心となるリビングに、自然の変化をもたらしている。

The property passes through the city block and joins roads at the front and the back. Looking at the site, Ando imagined a tube-shape living space that joins the scenery of both sides. That imagination was materialized by the 2nd floor living room that appears to be floating across the long and narrow property with a width of 7 meters and a length of 25 meters. This arrangement allows the family to feel the freedom of space. There are two slits on this long and narrow rectangular tube where light shines in on the living room, which is the center of the home and brings in the transition of nature.

[305]
佐渡邸　2013
sado house

1. 兵庫県芦屋市 | ashiya, hyogo
2. 設計 | design　2010.4 – 2012.2
3. 施工 | construction　2012.2 – 2013.5
4. 鉄筋コンクリート | RC
5. 住宅 | detached house
6. 敷地 | site　331.2 m²
7. 建築 | building　129.6 m²
8. 延床 | total floor　263.9 m²

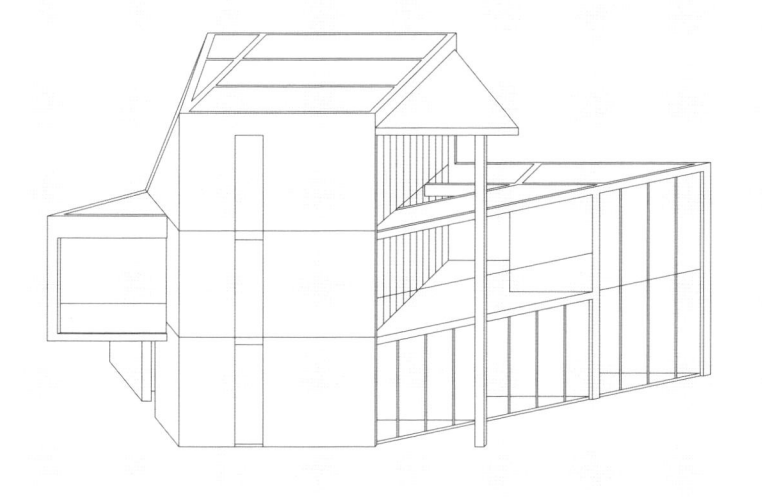

兵庫県芦屋市の斜面地に位置する音楽家の二世帯住居。海が望める立地の各部屋から眺望を優先して、大胆な幾何立体の重ね合わせが試みられた。中心を占めるのは、三層の台形平面の住棟。それに2層の三角形平面の棟を組み合わせ、1–3階の屋外に多様な庭やテラスを設けた。立体的に連続する半屋外空間を通じて、二世帯の生活が緩やかにつながる。各階の大きなガラス窓の壁面が方向を変えて重なる姿は、阪神間ならではの海を眺める暮らしの恩恵をうかがわせる。

This two-household house for a musician is located on a sloped site with ocean views in Ashiya City, Hyogo Prefecture. Prioritizing views from each room, venturesome combinations of geometric shapes were attempted. A solid at the center of the residential building is a square pillar with a trapezoid bottom. Combined with triangular prisms and other members, various gardens and terraces were made outside the 1st – 3rd floors. The roof is an irregular pentagonal shape - a trapezoid overlapped with a parallelogram with protruded eaves, and is supported by concrete through-pillar extending from the first floor. The appearance with large glass walls on each floor, overlapping in different directions, indicates the blessings of living with ocean views, which is special to the Hanshin area.

[306]
おかやま信用金庫
内山下スクエア　2013
okayama shinkin bank
uchisange square

1. 岡山県岡山市 | okayama, okayama
2. 設計 | design　2010.9 – 2012.5
3. 施工 | construction　2012.5 – 2013.2
4. 鉄筋コンクリート | RC
5. 銀行 | bank
6. 敷地 | site　694.0 m²
7. 建築 | building　507.7 m²
8. 延床 | total floor　997.0 m²

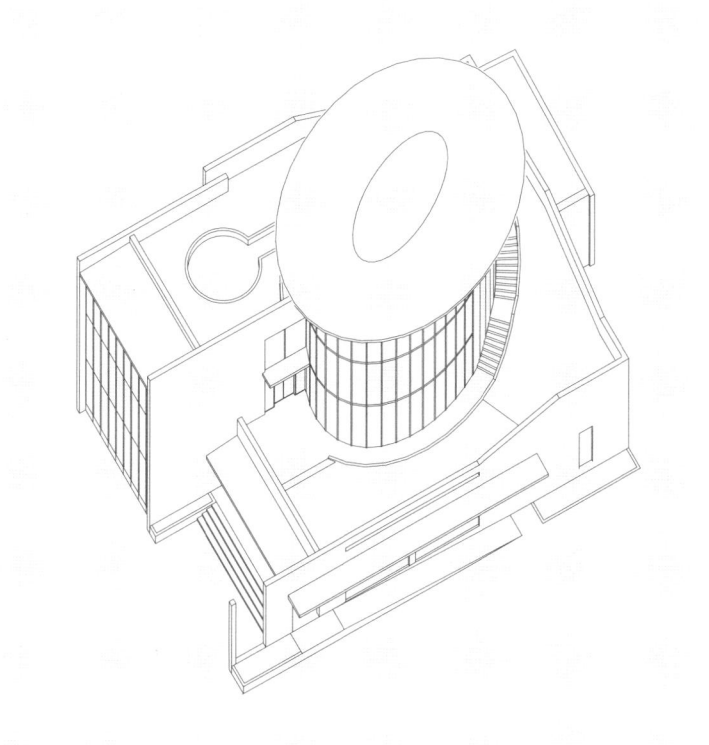

地方都市の信用金庫発祥の地に新たな店舗をつくるにあたって、開かれた支店をというのが施主の希望だった。支店の窓口機能などは低層階に収め、敷地の中心に楕円のシリンダーを置き、一帯でのシンボルとなる構成を目指した。シリンダーの外装はガラスで、内部にコンクリートの筒が入れ子になっている。ガラスとコンクリートの隙間に螺旋階段を配して、誰でも利用可能な4階屋上の野外庭園への順路とした。そこからは、すぐ傍らの旧・日銀岡山支店などの歴史遺産や都心に残る緑も堪能できる。

The client desired an "open" branch office, for a new office at the very place where the Shinkin Bank originated in the local city. The bank teller section and other sections were located on the lower levels. An oval cylinder was placed at the center of the site, in order to create a symbolic structure in the neighborhood. The exterior of the cylinder is glass, enclosing a concrete cylindrical structure. Spiral stairs were made between the glass and concrete, creating an access to the open-to-public rooftop garden on the fourth floor. The nearby Historic Heritage site (former Okayama Branch of Bank of Japan) and remaining greens in the urban area can also be enjoyed from the garden.

[307]

JCCクリエイティブセンター 2013
jcc creative center

1. 韓国 ソウル | seoul, south korea
2. 設計 | design 2010.1–2010.12
3. 施工 | construction 2011.5–2013.7
4. 鉄骨鉄筋コンクリート | SRC
5. 事務所 | office
6. 敷地 | site 2,135.9 m²
7. 建築 | building 1,204.1 m²
8. 延床 | total floor 5,424.2 m²

JCCアートセンター 2014
jcc art center

1. 韓国 ソウル | seoul, south korea
2. 設計 | design 2010.1–2010.12
3. 施工 | construction 2011.5–2014.2
4. 鉄骨鉄筋コンクリート | SRC
5. 劇場、ギャラリー | theater, gallery
6. 敷地 | site 1,120.7 m²
7. 建築 | building 672.3 m²
8. 延床 | total floor 4,098.1 m²

韓国の大手企業がソウルに開場した文化施設。近接する二つの敷地に2棟が建設された。アートセンターは、逆L字型断面の上階がV字型の脚部に載り、下層棟に覆い被さる大胆な造形。四つのギャラリーが1階から4階まで配され、最上階の4階では三角形の窓から自然光のもたらす光と影が時間につれて変化していく。地階にはコンサートホールがある。クリエイティブセンター（写真）は床面が傾斜した外観で、オフィスと多目的スペースがある。ともに屋上庭園を備えるとともに、各所に半屋外のテラスがあり、空間の多様性が実現している。

A cultural facility in Seoul, developed by a major Korean company. Two buildings were built on two neighboring sites. The art hall has a dynamic shape: the volume with an inverted L-shaped section are placed on V-shaped legs on top of the lower level building. Four galleries were made from the first floor to the fourth floor. On the topmost fourth floor, natural light through a triangular window provides illumination and casts shadows that change over time. A concert hall is on the underground level. The creative center — with offices and multipurpose spaces — appears to have sloped floors from the exterior. For both buildings, a diversity of spaces is materialized by rooftop gardens and semi-outdoor terraces in many locations.

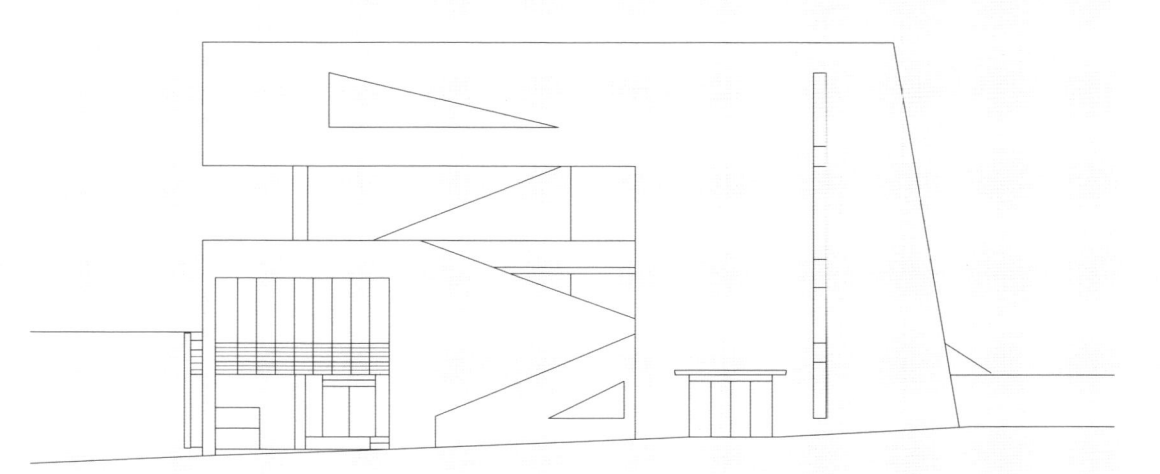

JCCアートセンター | jcc art center

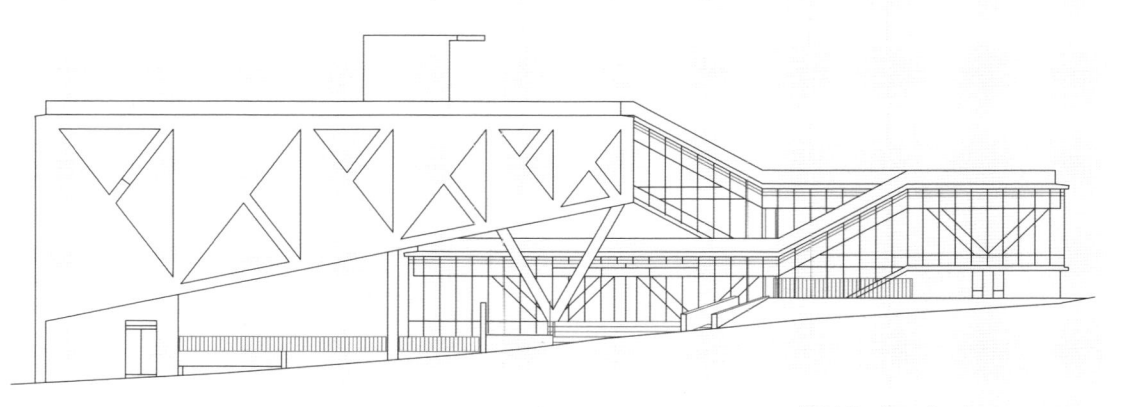

JCCクリエイティブセンター | jcc creative center

[308]
テアトリーノ　2013
teatrino

1. イタリア ヴェネチア | venice, italy
2. 設計 | design   2011.10–2012.5
3. 施工 | construction   2012.5–2013.5
4. 鉄筋コンクリート | RC
5. オーディトリアム、ギャラリー | auditrium, gallery
6. 敷地 | site   833.0 m²
7. 建築 | building   770.8 m²
8. 延床 | total floor   843.7 m²

安藤の手で、邸宅が美術館に改装された「パラッツォ・グラッシ」の背後に位置するパフォーミング・アーツのための小劇場。敷地は、もとは庭園だったが、1960年代から1980年代までは衣装関係のシアターとして使用された。美術館創設と合わせて、このスペースの新装開場が安藤に委ねられ、安藤は内部を大胆なうねる曲面壁で区画して、225席の小劇場をはめ込んだ。小さいながらも現代表現の躍動感あふれる場が、ヴェネチアの新たな文化発信拠点にふさわしい形で実現した。→参照 [242]、[266]

A small theater for performing arts located behind PALAZZO GRASSI where a residential house was renovated as an art gallery by Ando. This former garden was used as a theater for costumes from 1960s to 1980s. With the foundation of an art gallery, a new hall in this space was requested to Ando where he boldly used inclined walls to segment the interior and placed 225 seats in the small theater. The small area with lively expression of the modern age was materialized to appropriately fit the new cultural transmission point of Venice. → see also [242], [266]

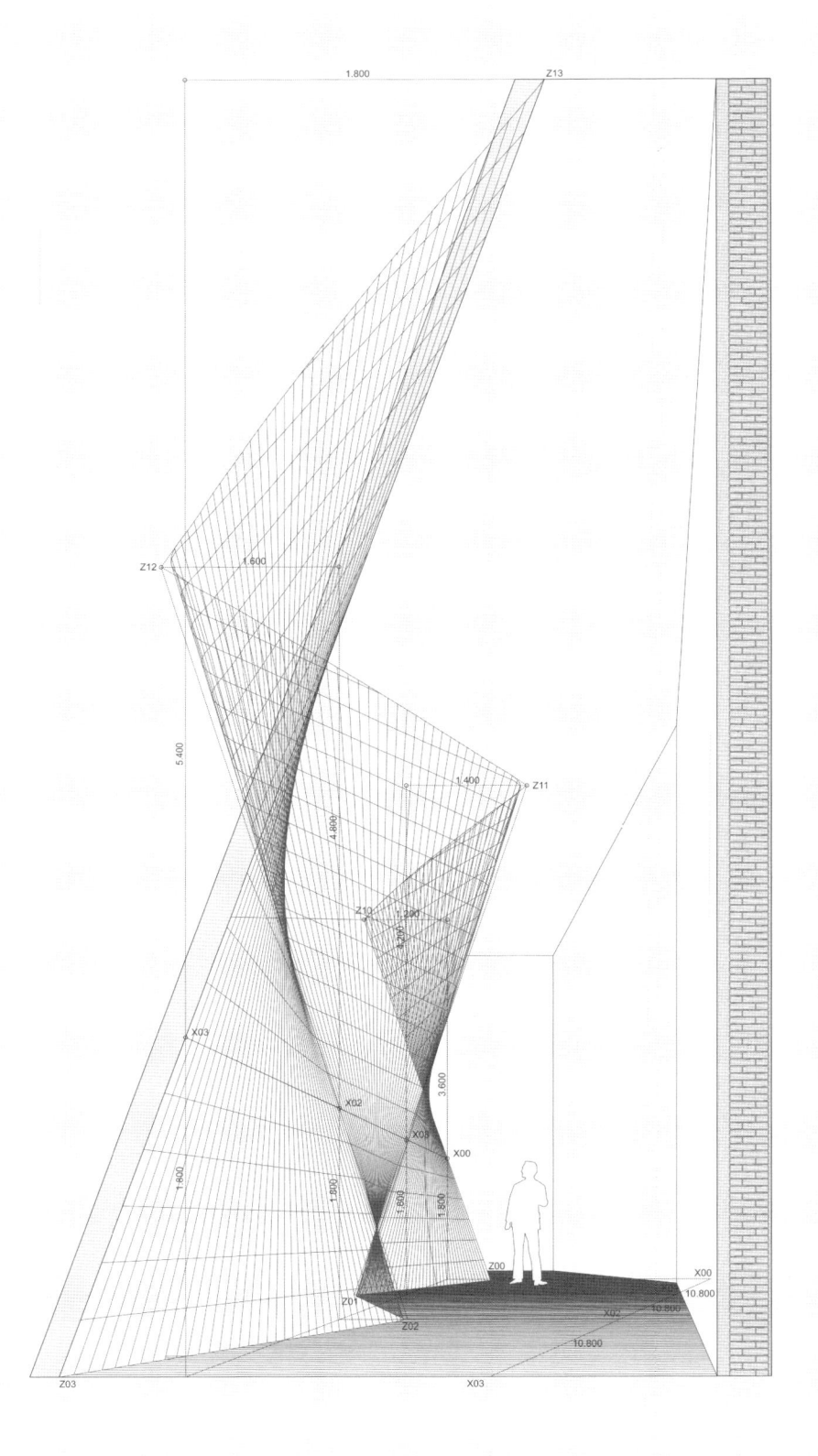

[309]
ANDO MUSEUM 2013
ando museum

1. 香川県直島町 | naoshima, kagawa
2. 設計 | design 2012.2–2012.6
3. 施工 | construction 2012.7–2013.2
4. 鉄筋コンクリート、木造 | RC, wood
5. 美術館 | museum of art
6. 敷地 | site 190.6 m²
7. 建築 | building 114.5 m²
8. 延床 | total floor 125.9 m²

直島の本村地区の民家を舞台に、現代美術家が創造を続ける「家プロジェクト」の一環として、安藤の建築美術館が設置された。100年を超える歳月を生きてきた民家のなかに、コンクリートのボックスを挿入し、展示空間にあてた。このボックスの天井は中央が緩やかに盛り上がり、そこに民家の屋根にガラス窓をはめたトップライトから自然光が入り込み、空間のふくらみを演出している。また、地下にはスリットから自然光が侵入する円筒状の瞑想の場が設けられ、凝縮された安藤の空間と出合うことができる。→参照 [125]、[151]、[184]、[223]、[239]、[280]

As a part of Art House Project underway in private residences of Honmura district in Naoshima for creative activities by contemporary artists, an architectural museum for Ando was constructed. An exhibition space was provided by inserting a concrete box into a traditional Japanese house with more than 100 years of history. The ceiling of this box gently swells in the center, and natural light enters from the glass window on the roof of the private house, to illuminate the bulge of the space. There is a place in the underground level to meditate in a cylindrical space, with natural light coming down from slits to face with the crystallized space of Ando. → see also [125], [151], [184], [223], [239], [280]

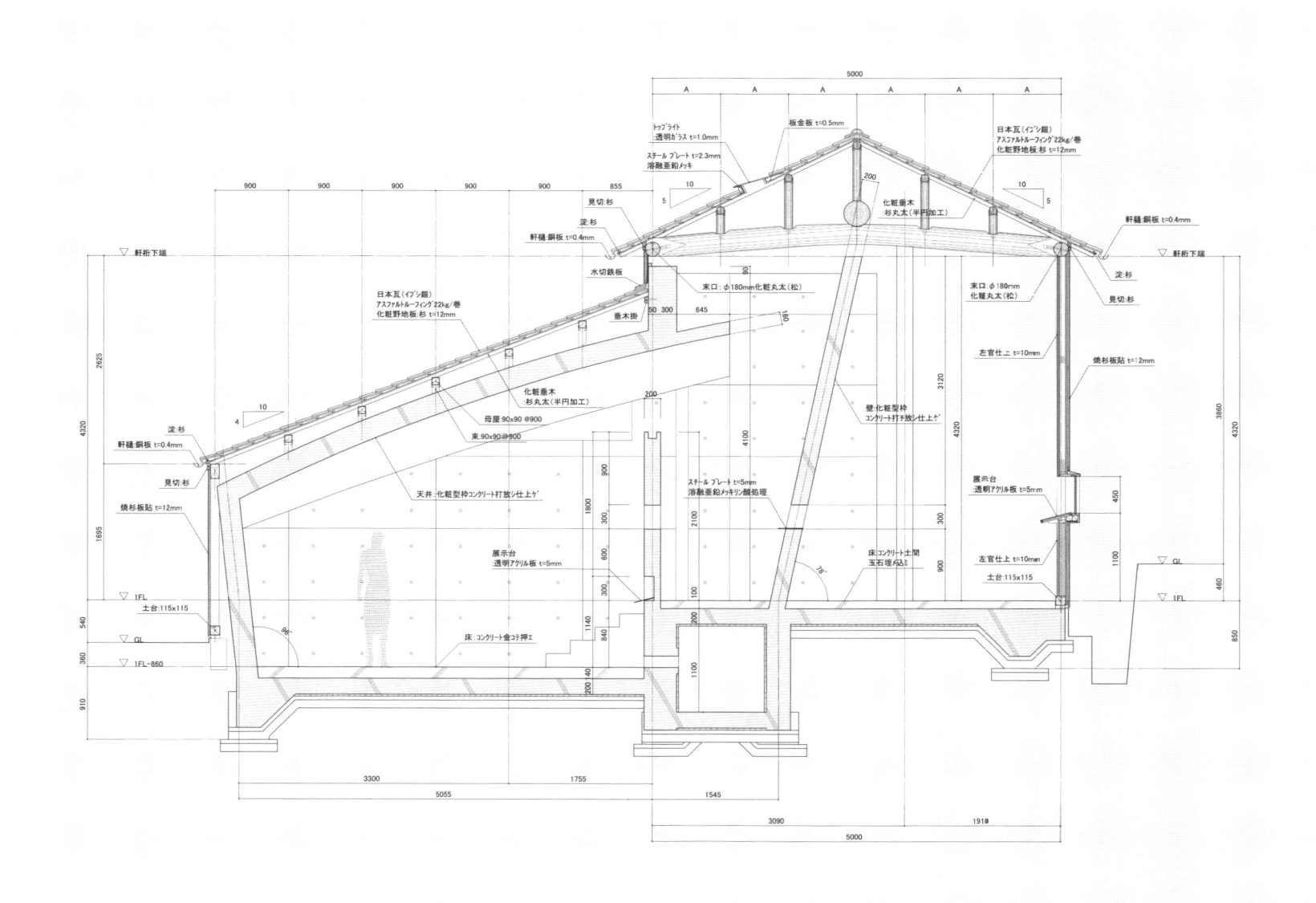

[310]
希望の壁　2013
wall of hope

1. 大阪市北区 | kita-ku, osaka
2. 設計 | design   2012.11–2013.4
3. 施工 | construction   2013.5–2013.9
5. 緑化壁 | greening wall
-. 全長 | length   78 m
-. 幅 | width   3 m
-. 高さ | height   9.45 m

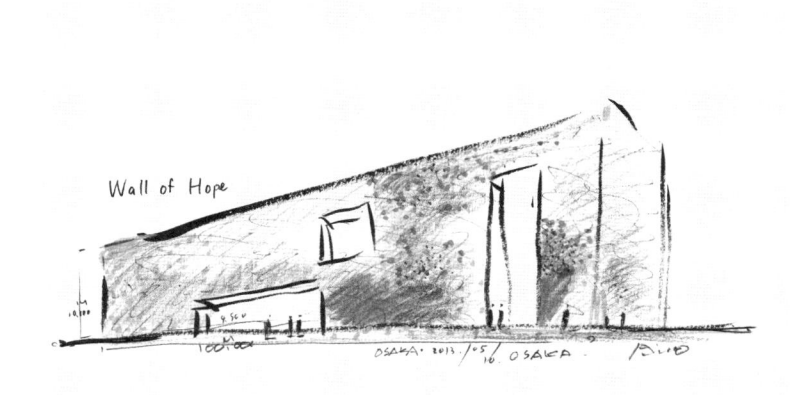

高層ビル「梅田スカイビル」の足元に立つ高さ9メートル、長さ78メートルの都市の緑化壁。安藤は大阪活性化の一環として、既存の庭園「新・里山」と連なる「希望の壁」を提案し、デザインを監修した。壁を覆う緑の背後には、植物が根を降ろすプランターと、植物を垂直に成長させるためのワイヤーメッシュがある。こうした工夫によって、ツツジやヤマブキなど100種、2万本の植物が壁を覆うことが可能になり、高層ビルの足元に新たな「緑の装置」が加わった。

An urban greening wall with height of 9 meters and length of 78 meters standing at the base of the high-rising Umeda Sky Building. Ando proposed and supervised the designing of the WALL OF HOPE in connection with the existing garden Shin Satoyama as part of Osaka's revitalization project. Planters the plants take roots in and wire mesh for plants to grow vertically are placed underneath the greenery covering the wall. This structure allowed the growth of about 20,000 plants of 100 varieties including azalea and kerria to cover the wall in order to add a new green device on the base of a high-rising building.

[311]
都市の大樹
2013
the tall green project

1. 大阪市北区 | kita-ku, osaka
2. 設計 | design   2012
3. 施工 | construction   2013
5. 外壁緑化 | outer wall greening

「大阪マルビル」は、大阪駅南口の高さ124メートル、直径30メートルの円筒形の高層ビル。その外壁面を10年計画で緑化して、植物で覆うプロジェクト。完成後の姿を巨木になぞらえたネーミングとなっている。安藤の提案に基づき、1階の公開空地の緑化と、1–3階の柱と4–6階の壁面緑化の工事が先行して進められた。官民協働で実現した「桜の会・平成の通り抜け」運動が実を結んだ中之島にも近く、大阪での都市緑化の広がりを示している。

The Osaka Marubiru is a cylinder-shaped high-rising building on the south exit of Osaka station with 124 meters in height and 30 meters in diameter. The project is to cover the exterior wall with plants in 10 years. The project is named imagining that the building would resemble a giant tree after its completion. Based on Ando's proposal, construction for greening of the public open space on the 1st floor, greening of the columns of 1st to 3rd floors, and greening of the walls of the 4th to 6th floors were initiated in advance. The location is close to Nakanoshima, where the activities of "Sakura no Kai: Cherry Blossom Tunnel in the Heisei Era" blossomed by public-private partnership, and this project demonstrates the active expansion of urban tree-planting in Osaka.

346 Complete Works

[312]

クラーク美術館
／クラークセンター　2014
clark art institute / clark center

1. アメリカ ウィリアムズタウン | williamstown, USA
2. 設計 | design　2001.2 – 2010.3
3. 施工 | construction　2010.4 – 2014.6
4. 鉄筋コンクリート、一部鉄骨 | RC, steel
5. 美術館 | museum of art
6. 敷地 | site　570,000 m²
8. 延床 | total floor　6,110 m²

印象派などの質の高いコレクションで知られる美術館の新古典主義風の本館は残し、新たに美術館の中心となる建物を設計した。低層の平屋にヴォリュームを抑制し、57ヘクタールの広大な敷地の風景の尊重と調和を重視した。ギャラリーはカフェとともに地下に収め、1階にはレセプション、ロビーなどを配し、訪問者を受け入れる機能を満たした。もとの本館との間は「水盤」に仕立て、そこが人工と自然、そして過去と現在を統合する新旧本館にふさわしい場となることを期待した。→参照 [255]

The main building of the museum in neoclassicism style, which is known for the valuable collection of art works including Impressionism and others, was decided to be preserved, while Ando designed a new building to become the center of this museum. The volume of the building was kept low as a single-story building, in order to pay respect to the scenery of the vast territory in 57 hectares and the building to harmonize with the surrounding environment. Gallery spaces and a cafeteria are arranged on the underground level, while 1st floor level has a reception and a lobby to welcome visitors. Ando expects the "water basin" provided between the original main building and this new building becomes the appropriate place for the old and new buildings, where artificial elements and natural elements, and the past and the present get unified. → see also [255]

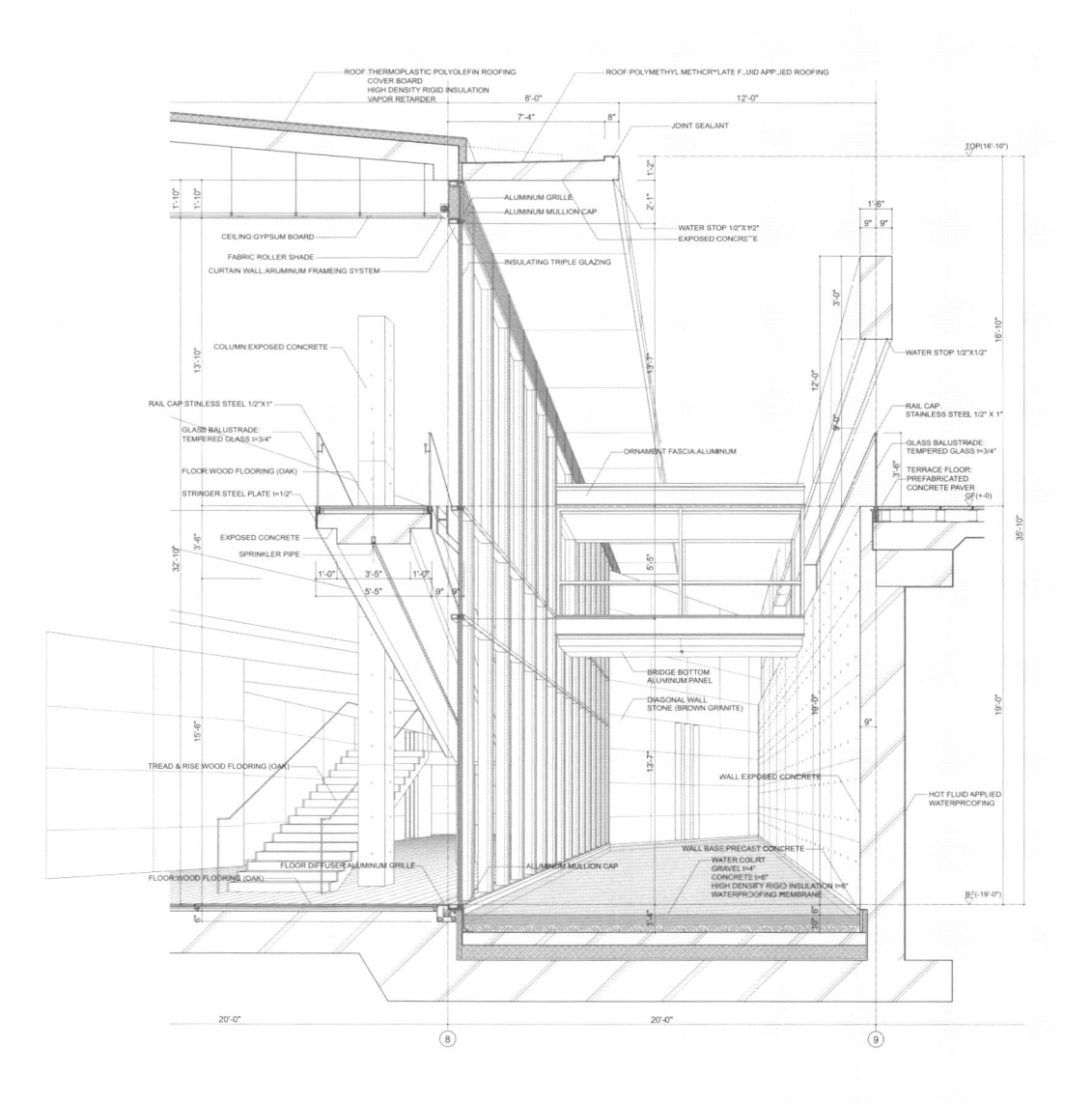

[313]
上海保利大劇場 2014
shanghai poly theater

1. 中華人民共和国 上海 | shanghai, china
2. 設計 | design 2009.3 – 2010.3
3. 施工 | construction 2010.8 – 2014.7
4. 鉄骨鉄筋コンクリート、一部鉄骨 | SRC, steel
5. 劇場 | theater
6. 敷地 | site 30,235 m²
7. 建築 | building 12,450 m²
8. 延床 | total floor 54,934 m²

上海の北西に位置する嘉定地区は、近傍にF1のサーキットが設けられるなど、中国自動車産業の成長を追い風に新都市の建設が進む。そこに新設するオペラ座の設計が安藤に委ねられた。全体形は底面が100メートル四方の直方体でガラスの壁で覆われる。内部に目を転じると5本の円筒のシリンダーが自由奔放に配され、その衝突が大胆な立体曲面の壁をそこここに生み出すことでもたらされた空間のダイナミズムに圧倒される。1600席のホールの内壁は集成材で仕上げられ、温かみのある空間が実現した。現地の丹念で精密な施工によって大胆な構成が実現したと安藤は語っている。

Jiading District, located in the northwest side of Shanghai, is under development as a new city with the following wind of growing automobile industry in China, as symbolized by the Formula One racing circuit built nearby. Ando was commissioned to design a new opera theater in the district. The silhouette of the building is in a cuboid, 100m each side on the bottom part, and the volume is covered by glass walls. Inside of this volume, 5 cylindrical volumes are freely positioned, and the collisions of those cylinders create bold, 3D curved surface walls here and there in overwhelmingly dynamic gestures. The interior wall of the theatrical hall with 1,600 seats capacity is finished in engineered wood to produce a space with warm atmosphere. Ando emphasized that such bold gestures of the building configuration were realized with the care of the local craftsmanship and precise construction.

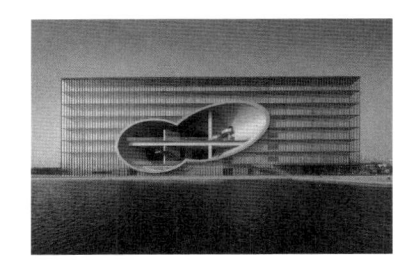

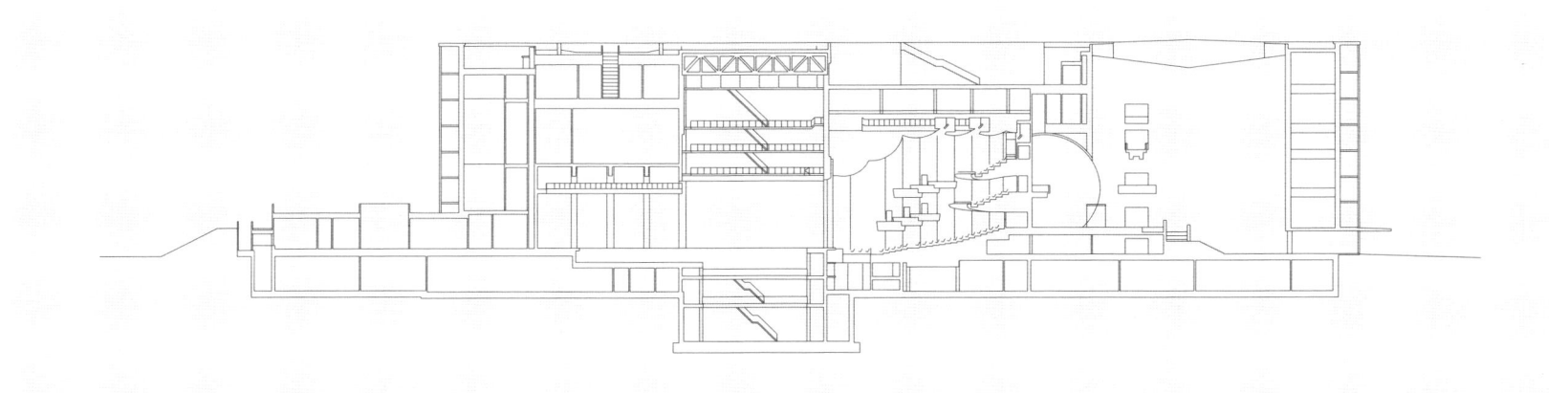

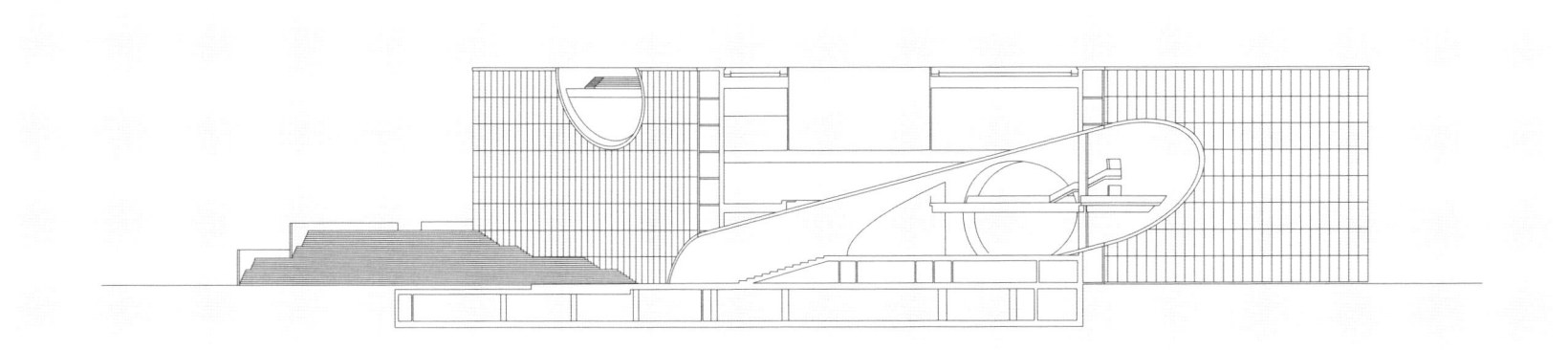

[314]
広尾の教会　2014
church in hiroo

1. 東京都渋谷区 | shibuya-ku, tokyo
2. 設計 | design　2012.11 – 2013.6
3. 施工 | construction　2013.6 – 2014.8
4. 鉄筋コンクリート | RC
5. 教会 | church
6. 敷地 | site　636.6 m²
7. 建築 | building　303.8 m²
8. 延床 | total floor　860.3 m²

東京・広尾の矩形の敷地に、とがった頂角30度の二等辺三角形のコンクリートの躯体が配されている。隣地との境にはコンクリートの壁が建てられ、三角形の躯体との隙間に余白の空間が設営されている。主礼拝堂は二層の吹き抜け空間で、内部の壁がツガ材、床はナラで木質の仕上げをとる。三角形の頂点に向かって座る配置で、床は10センチずつ段階を追って下降していく。その三角形の頂点に切られた縦長のスリットから堂内に光が射し込むと、劇的な光景が出現する。地下にも三角形の頂点の方向に従う小礼拝堂が設けられている。

A concrete skeleton in an isosceles triangle shape with 30°vertex angle is placed in a rectangular lot in Hiroo, Tokyo. A concrete wall is built at the boundary with the adjacent lot, creating a void space with the triangular-shaped main volume. The main chapel has a double-height space, finished in hemlock spruce wood for the wall surface and oak wood for flooring. Seats are arranged to the apex of the triangular space, while the floor height goes down by 10cm in 5 steps. Natural light comes in from the vertical slit on the apex of the triangular space — then a dramatic yet gentle atmosphere appears within the space. There is also another small chapel in underground level, following the same orientation to point at the apex of the triangle shape.

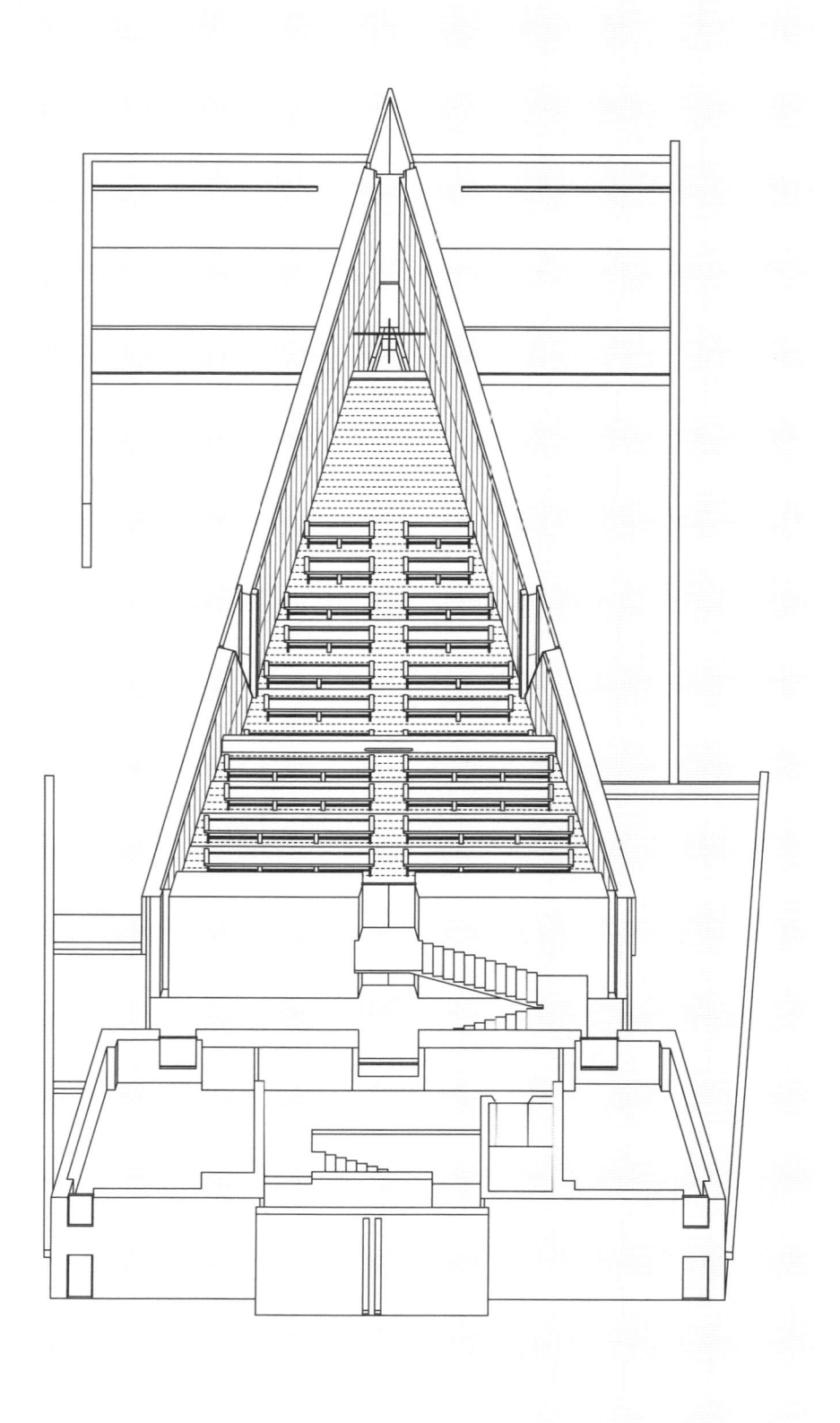

[315]
デュベティカ ミラノ
ショップ　2014
duvetica milano shop

1. イタリア ミラノ｜milan, italy
2. 設計｜design　2010.10 – 2011.4, 2013.9 – 2014.1
3. 施工｜construction　2011.5 – 2011.9, 2014.4 – 2014.6
4. 鉄筋コンクリート｜RC
5. 店舗｜shop
6. 敷地｜site　268.2 m²
7. 建築｜building　180.0 m²
8. 延床｜total floor　350.0 m²

同 ショールーム　2014
duvetica milano showroom

2. 設計｜design　2013.8 – 2013.11
3. 施工｜construction　2013.11 – 2014.4
4. 鉄筋コンクリート｜RC
5. ショールーム｜showroom
6. 敷地｜site　761.3 m²
7. 建築｜building　153.7 m²
8. 延床｜total floor　240.0 m²

ダウン衣料のファッションブランドのショップとショールーム。ショップはミラノのファッションストリートとして知られるモンテ・ナポリオーネ通り、ショールームは近傍のセナト通りに位置する。いずれも既存の歴史的な建造物内部の1階と地階にコンクリートの壁を建てることで、安藤の宇宙を実現した。ショップは吹き抜け空間を階段で昇降する開放的な仕立てをとる。歴史的な環境のなかでの一連の創作例のひとつと位置づけられる。

A shop and a showroom for a fashion brand of down products. The shop is located on Via Montenapoleone known as the fashion street in Milan and the showroom is located on the nearby Via Senato. Ando's architectural universe was materialized by creating concrete walls on the 1st floor and basement inside the existing historical architecture. The shop is structured to have a sense of openness by use of a stairway in the open ceiling area.

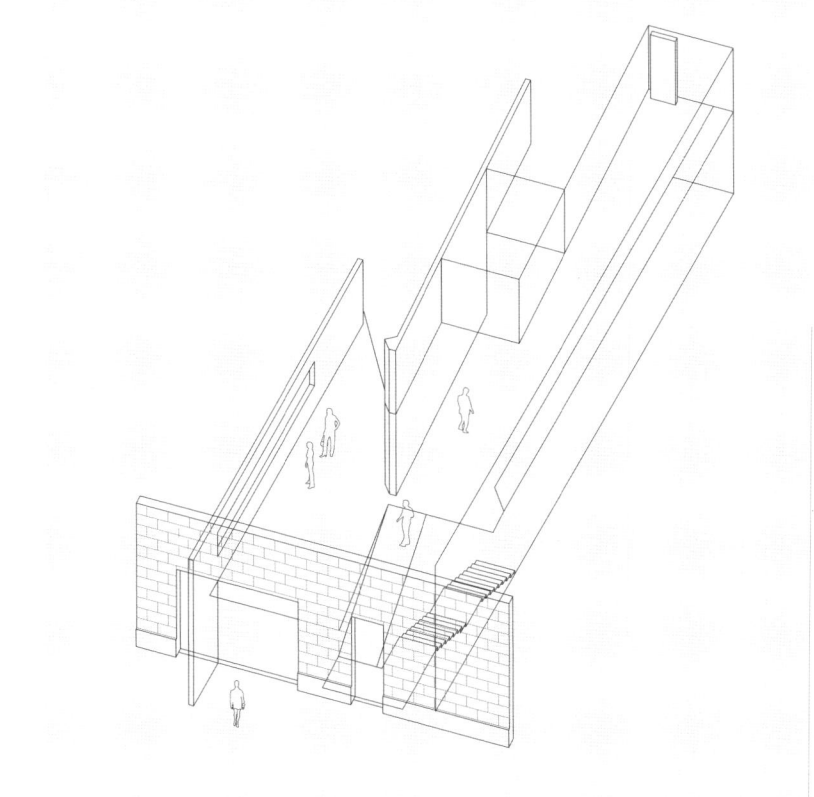

ショップ｜shop

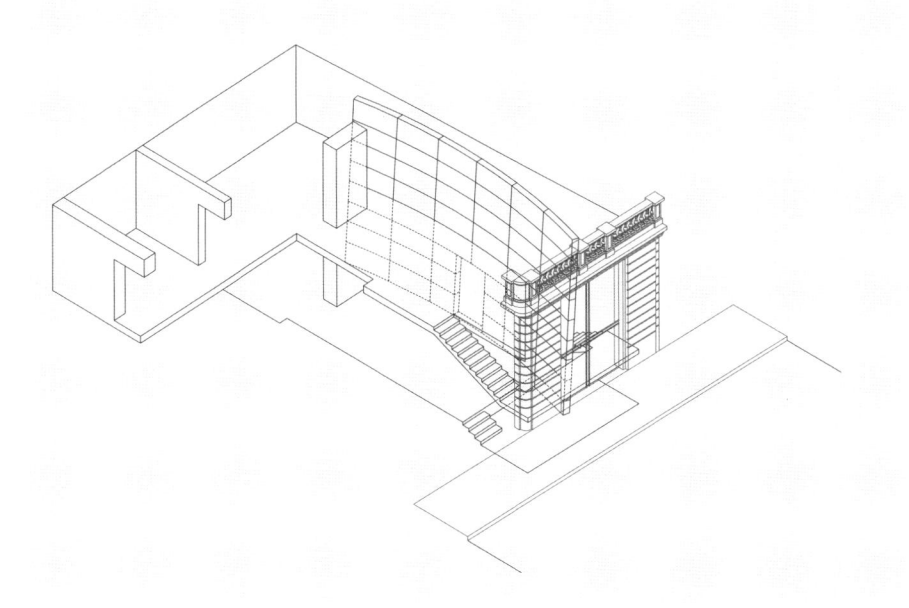

ショールーム｜showroom

[316]
ボスコ・スタジオ & ハウス
2014
bosco studio & house

1. メキシコ プエルト・エスコンディード | puerto escondido, mexico
2. 設計 | design 2011.11 – 2012.12
3. 施工 | construction 2013.1 – 2014.10
4. 鉄筋コンクリート、木造屋根 | RC, wood roof
5. アトリエ、住宅 | atlier, house
6. 敷地 | site 269,500 m²
7. 建築 | building 3,685 m²
8. 延床 | total floor 3,780 m²

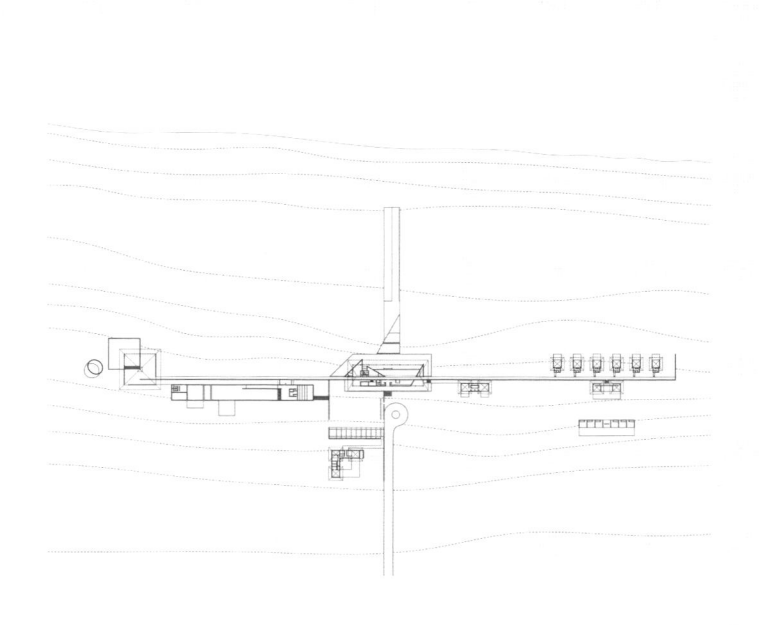

現代美術家ボスコ・ソーディのスタジオと住宅。メキシコの太平洋に面する港町プエルト・エスコンディードに位置する。施設の背景となる位置に長さ300メートルを超えるコンクリート打ち放しの壁が建てられた。その壁に寄りかかるように配した作家のためのメインヴィラを中心に、東側にスタジオ、西側にゲストヴィラが置かれた。それらの建物は、椰子の葉で葺いた伝統的な「パラパ」の傾斜屋根が架かる。ギャラリー以外は、半屋外で風が通り抜ける開放的な構成をとり、伝統的な空間の効用を現代に活かすことを心がけた。

The studio and residential house of a contemporary artist, Bosco Sodi. The architecture is located in Puerto Escondido, a port town facing the Pacific Ocean in Mexico. An exposed concrete wall that exceeds 300 meters in length was built at the background of the facility. With the main villa placed at the center along the wall, a studio and a guest villa were placed on the east side and west side respectively. A traditional sloped roof called Palapa, thatched with coconut leaves was used for the roofs of these buildings. Other buildings except the gallery have a structure of a half-outdoor open area allowing the breeze to pass through with an intent to apply the traditional spatial effect in modern architecture.

[317]
マリブの住宅 I 2015
house in malibu I

1. アメリカ マリブ | malibu, USA
2. 設計 | design 2003.11 – 2007.10
3. 施工 | construction 2007.10 – 2015.16
4. 鉄筋コンクリート | RC
5. 住宅 | detached house

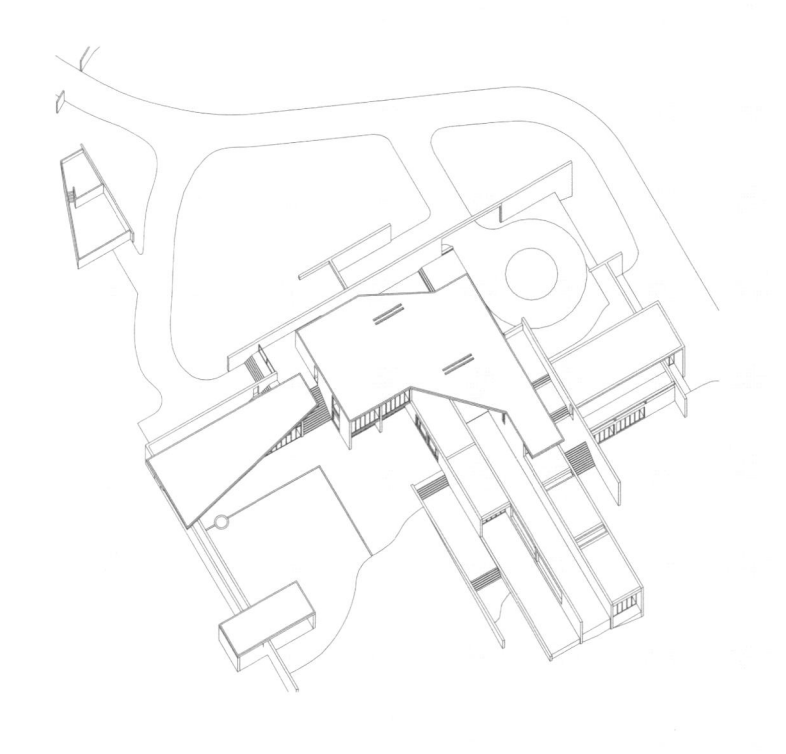

米カリフォルニア州マリブの太平洋に面した3ヘクタールの敷地に展開する現代美術コレクターのギャラリーを兼ねた住宅。中央に生活のための二列のファミリー棟、その両側にゲストルーム棟とスタディー棟が配された。建物は海に向って下る斜面に地階部分を埋めて三層で構成、ギャラリーはファミリー棟の1階から半階分降りたフロアに設けられた。ファミリー棟の中央には太平洋と視覚的につながる水庭を配した。水庭に屹立する厳格な比例感覚の壁が、水面しか見えないよう視覚を限定し、「無」の空間を出現させている。

A residential house with a gallery for a contemporary art collector in a three-hectare property facing the Pacific Ocean in Malibu, California in the U.S. Two family buildings as the living space were set at the center and a guestroom building and study building were built on both ends. Buildings have three floors including the basement floor that is embedded in the sloped ground descending toward the ocean and the gallery was placed on the semi-basement floor in the family building. A water garden was arranged in the center of the family buildings at a location where it is visually connected with the Pacific Ocean. Walls with a strict proportional concept facing the water garden limits the vision to be seen the water surface, which creates a space of nothingness.

[318]
良渚村文化芸術センター　2015
liangzhu village cultural art center

1. 中華人民共和国 杭州 | hangzhou, china
2. 設計 | design　2010.7–2013.4
3. 施工 | construction　2013.5–2015.7
4. 鉄筋コンクリート、鉄骨 | RC, steel
5. 多目的文化センター | multipurpose culture center
6. 敷地 | site　23,558 m²
7. 建築 | building　4,946 m²
8. 延床 | total floor　13,107 m²

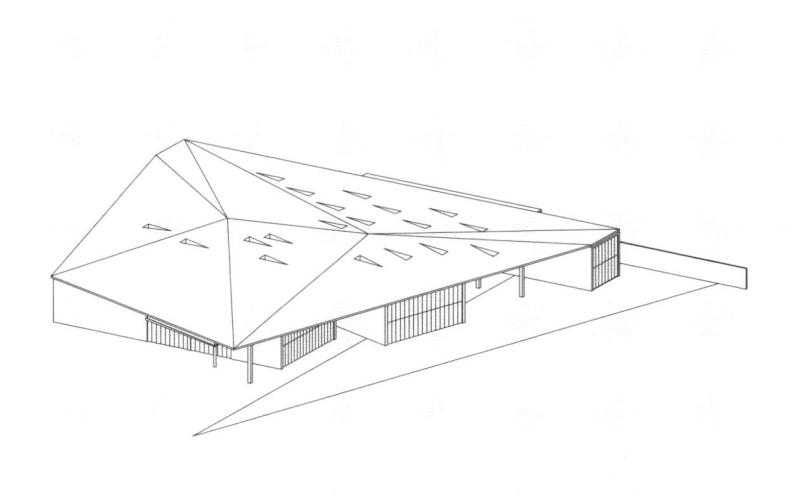

中国・杭州市の北方、新石器文化で知られる良渚村の複合文化施設。長江下流域の水の豊かな地域性を踏まえ、建物からはみ出した大きな傾斜屋根が新たに設けた水盤上にものびる。大屋根には三角形を切り欠いたトップライトがちりばめられ、屋根が館内と水上につくる陰に陽光のきらめきがもたらされる。大屋根は多面体の形態で、その下には吹き放ちの集いの場も広がる。良渚が育んできたコミュニケーションの継承を意図した。

A complex cultural facility in Liangzhu, a village known for its Neolithic culture at the north of Hangzhou, China. Taking into account the regional characteristics of abundant water in the downstream basin of the Yangtze River, the large sloped roof — oversized more than the building — extends above the newly-made water basin. Cutout triangular skylights are scattered across the large roof, providing shimmering sunlight indoors and on water surfaces where the roof cast its shadow. The roof is polyhedral shaped, under which an open plaza is located. Ando intended to support a succession of communications that have been fostered in Liangzhu.

[319]
森の教会　2015
church in the forest

1. 大韓民国 驪州 | gyeonggi-do, south korea
2. 設計 | design　2011.8–2012.8
3. 施工 | construction　2013.1–2015.3
4. 鉄筋コンクリート、鉄骨 | RC, steel
5. 教会 | church
6. 敷地 | site　94,482.0 m²
7. 建築 | building　798.2 m²
8. 延床 | total floor　936.2 m²

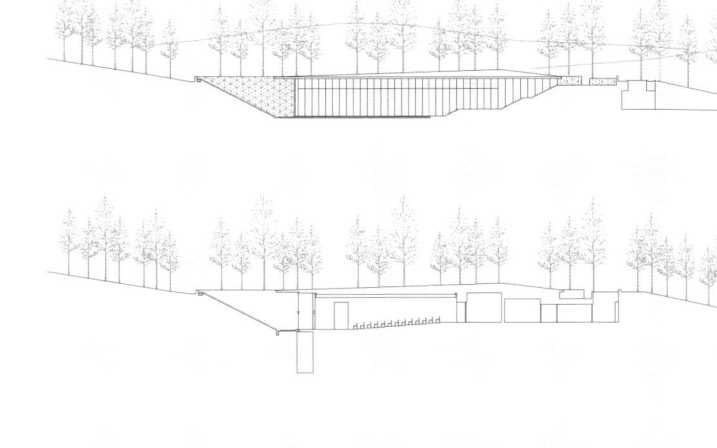

韓国の化粧品メーカーの研修施設。教会、ギャラリー、図書室の三つの建物から成る。安藤は、それらを純粋幾何学の結晶とすることで一体化を試みた。窪地を選んだ教会は、敷地を一段掘り下げ、荒々しい自然石の囲う人工池をつくり、周囲の石壁の高さに合わせた陸屋根の下に聖堂を配した。礼拝者は構造フレームがつくる十字に向き合い、その先の水と光の戯れを視界に入れる。ライブラリーとギャラリーは、継ぎ目のない鋼板をファサードに採用し、幾何立体の印象を高めている。ギャラリー内部のスペースフレームの架構の現代性も目をひく。

Training facilities for a cosmetics company in Korea. The facility consists of three buildings of a church, gallery, and a library respectively. Ando provided unification of these facilities by designing them as crystals of pure geometry. A depressed area was selected for the church where the land was dug a level deeper, an artificial pond with rough natural stones was created, and the chapel was placed under a flat roof arranged to be at the height of a surrounding stone wall. Worshipers face the cross made by the window frame and see the encounter of water and light beyond the window. The modernity of the structure of the space frame inside the gallery attracts attention as well.

[320]
十和田市教育プラザ　2015
towada education plaza

1. 青森県十和田市 | towada, aomori
2. 設計 | design　2011.12 – 2013.3
3. 施工 | construction　2013.6 – 2015.9
4. 鉄筋コンクリート | RC
5. 図書館、教育会館 | library, education center
6. 敷地 | site　9,159.5 m²
7. 建築 | building　3,407.9 m²
8. 延床 | total floor　3,199.04 m²

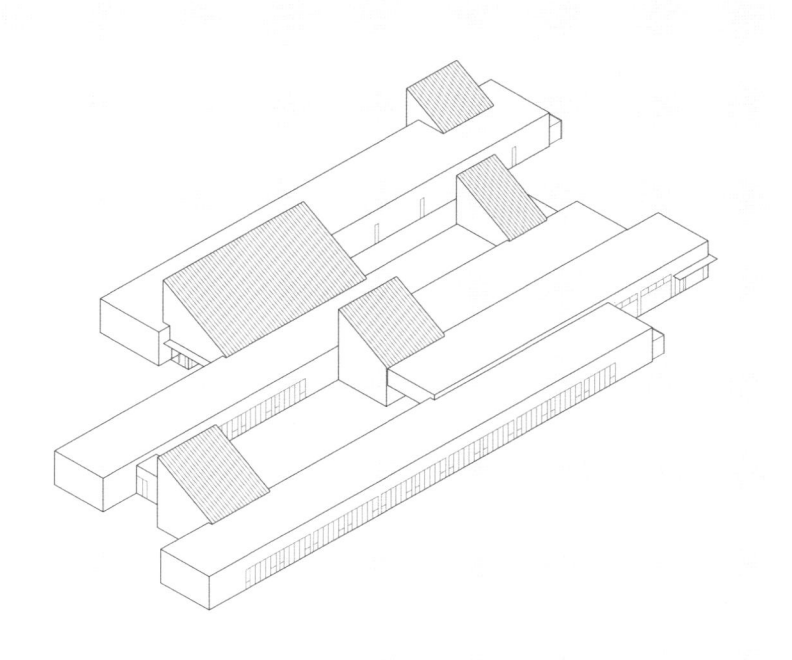

建物の側面にあたる東側から眺めると直方体の建物本体から五つの流れ屋根が同方向の傾きで連続しているのが目に入る。流れ屋根の下は教育センター、図書館などのロビーとエントランスの空間で、安藤が「本でない本」と呼ぶところの、人と人とが顔を合わせて情報交換する場との位置づけだ。そこには自然光が入り、ゆったりとした雰囲気が実現している。施設全体は3棟が平行に配置され、棟と棟との間の余白の空間が、既存の古木を保存した「中庭」として整備され、それがまた豊かな空間をもたらしている。

Continuous five single-flow roofs on rectangular solid buildings inclined in the same direction gathers attention when viewed from the east side, which is the side surface of the building. Under the single-flow roofs is the space of the lobby and entrance for facilities including an education center and library where it is positioned as the area for exchanging information face-to-face between people whom Ando describes as "books that are not books". Natural light enters in that area to provide a relaxing atmosphere. Three buildings are positioned to be in parallel making gaps between them where the existing old trees are preserved and it provide rich space in the facility as a whole.

[321]
三河田原駅　2015
mikawatahara station

1. 愛知県田原市 | tahara, aichi
2. 設計 | design　2011.5 – 2012.9
3. 施工 | construction　2013.3 – 2013.10
4. 鉄骨 | steel
5. 駅舎・鉄道施設 | railway station
6. 敷地 | site　5,501.7 m²
7. 建築 | building　504.3 m²
8. 延床 | total floor　440.1 m²

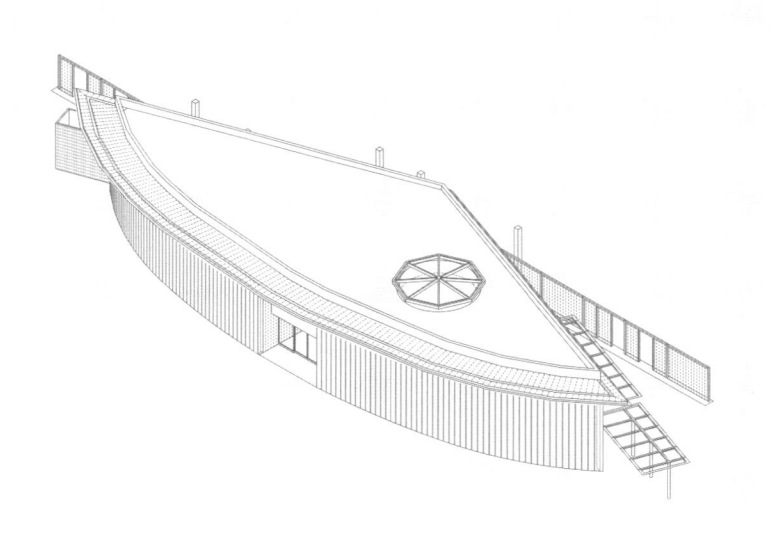

遠州灘に面した愛知県渥美半島。田原市の中心に位置する三河田原駅は、豊橋鉄道渥美線の終着駅にあたる。都市の顔の役割を期待されるターミナルの駅舎を、安藤は外観に「ふくらみ」と「広がり」をもたせ、町が未来に向う「始まり」になることを期待した。平面形は扇形。扇の要の位置で豊橋方面からの鉄道の線路を受けとめ、扇面の開きを市街地に向けた。外壁は縦のアルミ材の連続、外構には緑化壁が設けられている。白木の柱がならぶ二層吹き抜けは待合室と交流の場を兼ね、2階レベルに設けたテラスにはトップライトからの自然光がもたらされる。

For the exterior of the terminal station building — expected to be the face of the city — Ando gave a "swelling" and "expanding" feeling with an expectation of being the city's "starting point" for the future. The plan had a folding-fan-like shape. The railway lines from the Toyohashi direction end at the head of the fan, and the leaf of the fan spreads towards the urban area. The exterior walls are sequences of vertical aluminum materials, forming a curved green surface when covered with plants. A space under a two-level open ceiling with rows of plain wood pillars serves as both a waiting room and communication area. Natural light through a skylight illuminates the terrace on the second level.

全346作品録

[322]

真駒内滝野霊園 頭大仏　2015
hill of the buddha

1. 札幌市南区 | minami-ku, sapporo
2. 設計 | design　2012.5 – 2014.5
3. 施工 | construction　2014.5 – 2015.12
4. 鉄筋コンクリート | RC
5. 宗教施設 | religious space
6. 敷地 | site　401,587.9 ㎡
7. 建築 | building　402,12 ㎡
8. 延床 | total floor　1,105.39 ㎡

民間霊園にあった石像の大仏を、ランドスケープの中心に置いた。大仏は4000トンの原石から切り出された無垢の石像で、来訪者が大仏像と精神的に深い次元で邂逅する場の構築を目指した。周囲に築かれたコンクリートのマウンドから頭だけを出し、首から下は覆い隠されている。マウンドはラヴェンダーの花で覆われ、北海道らしい風景が展開する。アプローチから6分の1円のヴォールトの屋根を持つトンネル状の回廊が続き、来訪者はその闇を抜け出たところで、大仏の姿を仰ぎ見る。

The stone Buddha statue that used to be in a private graveyard was placed in the center of the landscape. The Buddha statue is made out of pure stone that weighs 4000 tons and was placed to form an area where visitors can encounter in a deep spiritual level. The Buddha statue has his head out of the concrete mound built around and the body under the neck is hidden. The mound is covered with lavender flowers displaying scenery that features Hokkaido. After going through the dark space in a tunnel corridor with a one-sixth circle vault roof extended from the approach, visitors are able to look up at the appearance of the Buddha.

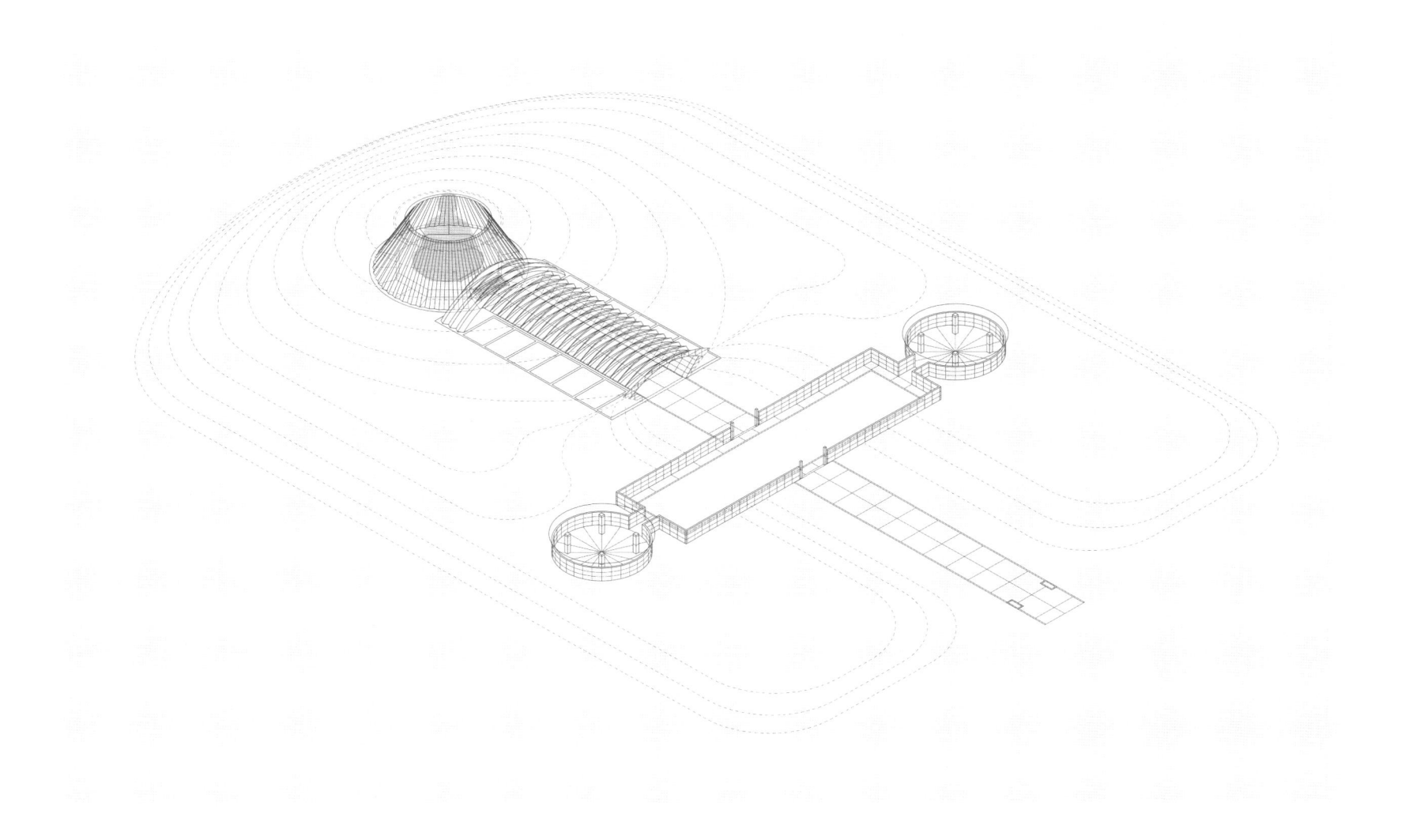

[323]
みやこ町立伊良原小学校
みやこ町立伊良原中学校　2016
miyako town irahara elementary
and junior high school

1. 福岡県みやこ町｜miyako, fukuoka
2. 設計｜design　2012.4 – 2013.3
3. 施工｜construction　2014.12 – 2016.1
4. 鉄骨、木造｜steel, wood
5. 小中学校｜elementary and junior high school
6. 敷地｜site　9,295.2 m²
7. 建築｜building　1,752.2 m²
8. 延床｜total floor　2,479.0 m²

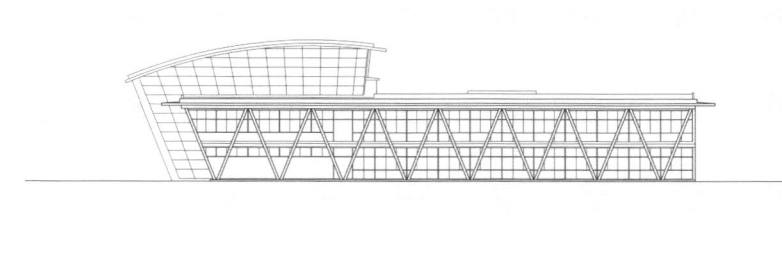

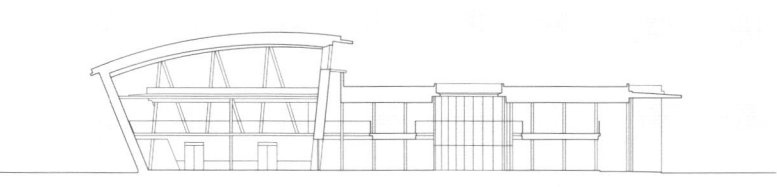

福岡県の大分との県境に近い山間部の小中学校。ダム建設で水没する旧校の移転新築が安藤に委ねられた。校舎と体育館をひとつの建築に収める構成で、二層になった教室を建物の両端に置き、木の肌が美しい吹き抜け空間を囲むようにした。その中央には楕円のガラスの筒が置かれ、屋内には豊かな自然光が射し込む。外観はW字型の木柱の連なる構成で、その柱の傾きが一段高い曲面屋根の体育館の構造体にも連なり、建築にリズムを持たせている。

An elementary school and junior high school in the mountainous area close to the prefectural boundary of Oita in Fukuoka Prefecture. The transfer and new construction of the former school that would be underwater by dam construction was entrusted to Ando. It was designed to put the schoolhouse and gymnasium in one building with two floors of classrooms on both ends of the building to surround an open ceiling area that shows beautiful wood grain. A glass cylinder is placed in the center to let rich natural light shine in the building. The external appearance is of connected wooden columns in a W shape where the inclination of the columns is reflected on the structure of the three-layered curved roof of the gymnasium situated on a higher level to provide rhythm to the architecture.

[324]
国立国会図書館国際子ども図書館
アーチ棟
2016
the international library of
children's literature / arch building

1. 東京都台東区｜taito-ku, tokyo
2. 設計｜design　2009.11 – 2011.10
3. 施工｜construction　2012.3 – 2016.2
4. 鉄骨鉄筋コンクリート｜SRC
5. 図書館｜library
6. 敷地｜site　7,735.31 m²
7. 建築｜building　1,105.0 m²
8. 延床｜total floor　6,185.67 m²

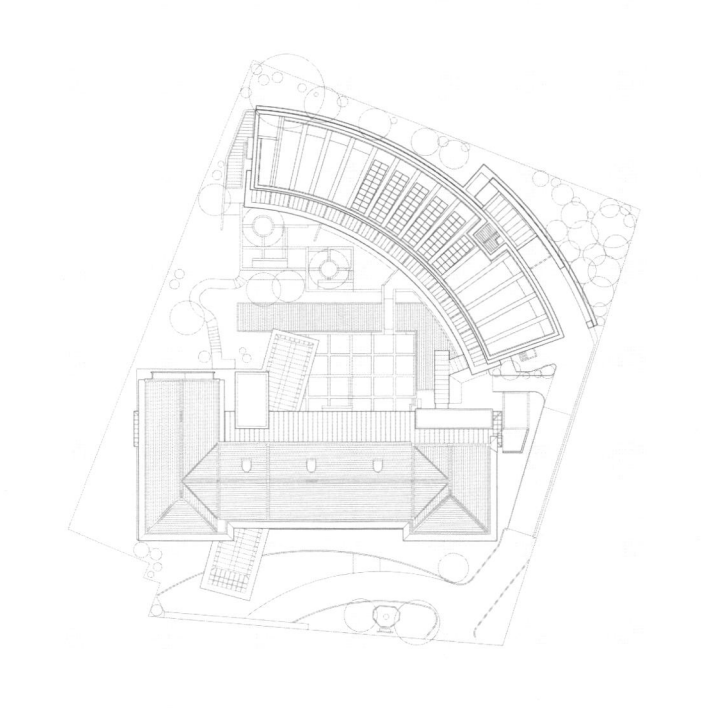

「国際子ども図書館」の増築。「れんが館」と呼ぶ旧館の背後に、4分の1円の平面形の「アーチ棟」が新築された。上野公園の景観に配慮して3階の高さに抑え、内部に児童書研究室や研修スペースなどを配した。外壁はガラスで仕立て、そのなかにコンクリートの躯体を入れ子で収めた。旧館背後の屋外庭園は保存再生時から利用可能だったが、「アーチ棟」の新設により、安藤の建築に囲まれたヒューマンスケールが実感できる中庭となった。「アーチ棟」の施工の美しさと相まって、快適に過ごせる場が上野にひとつ加わった。→参照 [207]

The "Arch Building" with a quarter circle-shaped plan was newly constructed behind the old building called the "(Old) Brick Building". With consideration of the scenery of Ueno Park, the building height was suppressed to three stories. Researchers' reading room and seminar rooms were made in the building. The outdoor garden behind the old building had been available since the time of preservation and renovation: however, due to the construction of the "Arch Building", it became a courtyard for experiencing the human scale, surrounded by Ando's buildings. Combined with the beauty of the workmanship of the "Arch Building", it appeared that another place of comfort was newly added in Ueno. → see also [207]

[325]
北菓楼札幌本館 2016
kitakaro sapporo honkan

1. 札幌市中央区 | chuo-ku, sapporo
2. 設計 | design   2014.8 – 2015.07
3. 施工 | construction   2014.12 – 2016.3
4. 鉄骨鉄筋コンクリート、一部鉄骨 | SRC, steel
5. 店舗、カフェ | shop, cafe
6. 敷地 | site   858.8 m²
7. 建築 | building   537.3 m²
8. 延床 | total floor   1,351.38 m²

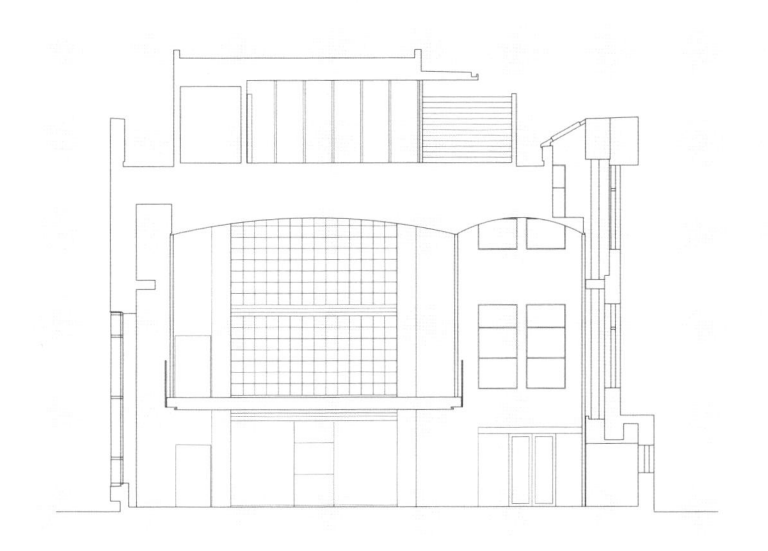

1926年建設の「旧北海道立図書館」の外観とインテリアの骨格を保存し、もとは三層の吹き抜け空間の2階部分にカフェテリアのフロアを挿入、道内砂川市に本拠を置く菓子店の札幌の店舗として再生した。カフェの天井は純白のFGボード（繊維混入石膏ボード）を交差ヴォールトの曲面仕立てにして、もとからある赤煉瓦の直立する壁と対比的な存在感を漂わせる。カフェの家具は白で統一、歴史的な空間に安藤の美学が浮遊している。

The appearance and the interior framework of the former Hokkaido Prefectural Library built in 1926 were preserved while a cafeteria floor was inserted in the 2nd floor area that used to be the space for open ceiling through three stories to restore the building as a Sapporo store for a confectionery based in Sunagawa City, Hokkaido. The ceiling of the café is of FG board (fiber-mixed gypsum board) finished to form a cross-vault curved surface to express presence in contrast to the vertical red brick wall that existed from the original building. The furniture of the café is harmonized in white where Ando's aesthetics is shown everywhere in the historical space.

[326]
元麻布の住宅 2016
house in motoazabu

1. 東京都港区 | minato-ku, tokyo
2. 設計 | design   2013.7 – 2014.11
3. 施工 | construction   2014.12 – 2016.7
4. 鉄筋コンクリート | RC
5. 住宅 | detached house
6. 敷地 | site   226.18 m²
7. 建築 | building   129.98 m²
8. 延床 | total floor   495.71 m²

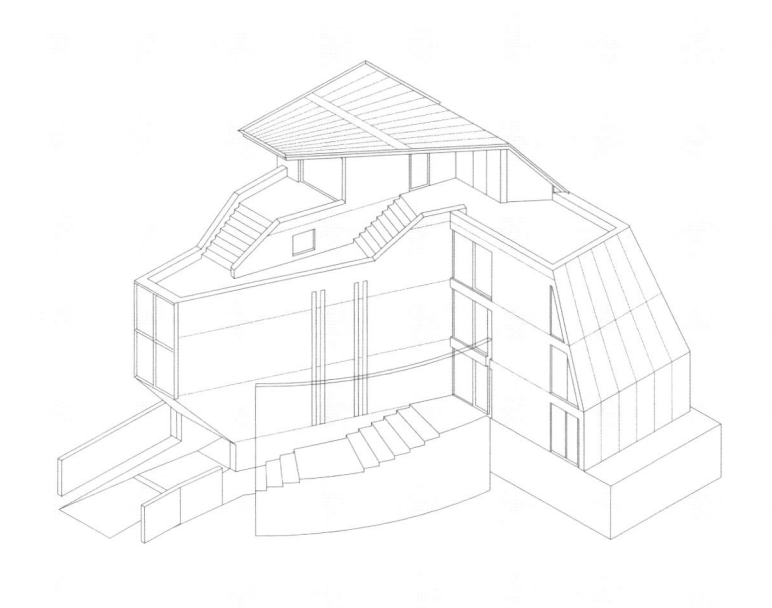

奥に進むに連れて面積の広くなる変則的な敷地に建つ4階建て住宅。地形に合わせ、Lの字を反転したような平面形が採用された。アプローチ右側の階段をあがると玄関があり、さらに一層上がって、メインのリビングに続く。3、4階に書斎、寝室などが配された。西側の壁は大きなガラス窓で構成、美術コレクションを自然光で楽しめる。隣地との斜線制限ゆえの傾斜した壁が不思議な形態をもたらし、屋上からの屋外階段は、都市的眺望を楽しむ装置となっている。

A four-story house built on an irregularly shaped site, of which area widens as you walk to the back. A plan similar to "L" shape upside-down was adopted to fit the configuration. Going up to the second floor through the stairs located at the right of the approach, you will find entrance leading to the main living room. Study and bedrooms were arranged on the third and fourth floors. The walls of the west side of each floor, consist of large glass windows and the owner's collection of art works can be enjoyed with natural light. Sloping wall designed by the set-back regulation creates a mysterious space in the house and the outdoor stairs from the roof penthouse are an observatory space to enjoy the urban city view.

[327]
森の中の家 安野光雅館 2017
anno mitsumasa museum

1. 京都府京丹後市 | kyotango, kyoto
2. 設計 | design   2015.7 – 2016.10
3. 施工 | construction   2016.10 – 2017.04
4. 鉄骨 | steel
5. 美術館 | museum of art
6. 敷地 | site   4254.25 ㎡
7. 建築 | building   323.96 ㎡
8. 延床 | total floor   444.49 ㎡

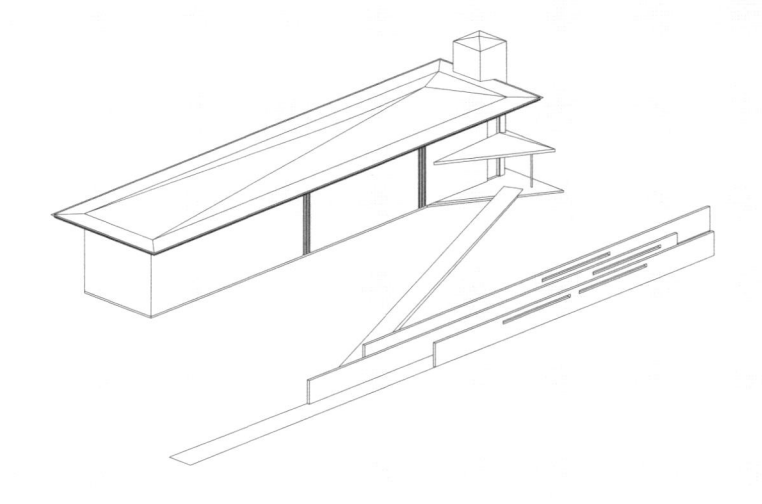

丹後ちりめんで栄えた京丹後市で旅館を営み、現在は弁当や和菓子を東京などで販売する「紫野和久傳」の女性経営者が運営する画家安野光雅の作品を展示するギャラリー。周囲に森を造成した環境のなか、低層の建築が身を横たえる。細長い長方形の平面に、方形を片側に低く引き延ばした形状の屋根が載る。外壁は真っ黒な杉板で、内部には吹き抜けがあり、2階に展示室を配した。来訪者はエントランスのコンクリート打ち放しの壁の隙間を抜けて、石を敷いた誘導路で前庭を横切り、建物に近づき、和と安藤のモダニズムの美の融合を味わう。

A gallery that displays works of the artist Mitsumasa Anno owned by a woman manager of Wakuden who was operating a Japanese inn in Kyotango City that prospered with Tango-chirimen (silk crepes). A low-rise building is laying in an environment where was prepared inside a forest. A roof with a low stretched rectangle shape is placed on a long rectangle architecture. Exterior walls are formed with black cedar boards and inside the building has an open ceiling and an exhibition room on the 2nd floor. Visitors approach the building by going through the gaps of exposed concrete walls at the entrance and passing the front yard on a stone-paved guide path while enjoy the fusion of beauty of Japanese style and Ando's Modernism.

[328]
大阪商工信用金庫
新本社ビル 2017
osaka shoko shinkin bank

1. 大阪市中央区 | chuo-ku, osaka
2. 設計 | design   2013.4 – 2015.12
3. 施工 | construction   2015.12 – 2017.9
4. 鉄骨、鉄筋コンクリート | Steel, RC
5. 銀行本店 | bank headquarters
6. 敷地 | site   1,795.4 ㎡
7. 建築 | building   1,229.1 ㎡
8. 延床 | total floor   9,621.8 ㎡

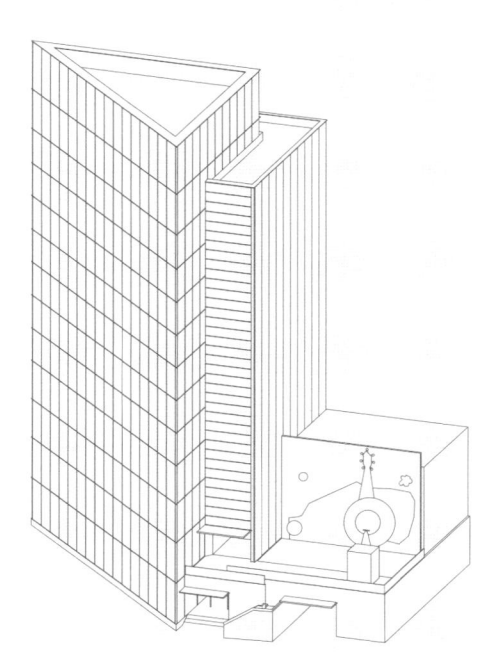

大阪船場の1960年代のオフィスビルを解体して、地元の金融機関の新本拠が建設された。三角形の平面を角地の立地に置き、それぞれの道路からガラスの鋭角の建築を見ることができる。内部には営業窓口、ホール、事務施設が配される。元のビルの屋上にあった今井兼次の巨大なタイルのレリーフ「フェニックス」が保存され、新しいビルの敷地内の2階レベルに設ける水庭に面する位置に再建される。ガウディに心酔した今井の工芸的な造形が、さらに多くのひとの目を楽しませることになる。

A new headquarters for a local financial institution were built after demolishing an office building from the 1960s in Semba, Osaka. Glassed sharp architecture with a triangle plan located on a corner property can be seen from each road. A sales counter, hall, and office facilities are placed inside. The Phoenix, which is a large sculptural relief created with tiles made by Kenji Imai, that was placed on the roof top of the former building would be conserved and restored on the 2nd floor level in the property of the new building, facing the water garden. The shaping with craft technic of Imai who adored Gaudi will continue to attract people's eyes.

全346作品録

[329]

森の霊園・水の納骨堂　進行中
water charnel, cemetery in the woods in progress

1. 台湾 新北市 | new taipei (city), taiwan
2. 設計 | design   2008.6–
4. 鉄筋コンクリート | RC
5. 墓地 | cemetery
6. 敷地 | site   29,157 m²
7. 建築 | building   11,526 m²
8. 延床   total floor   34,975 m²

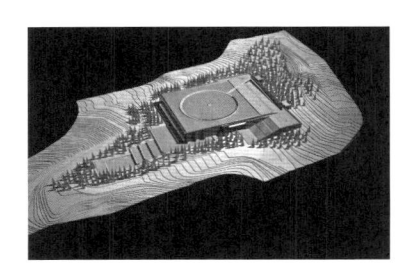

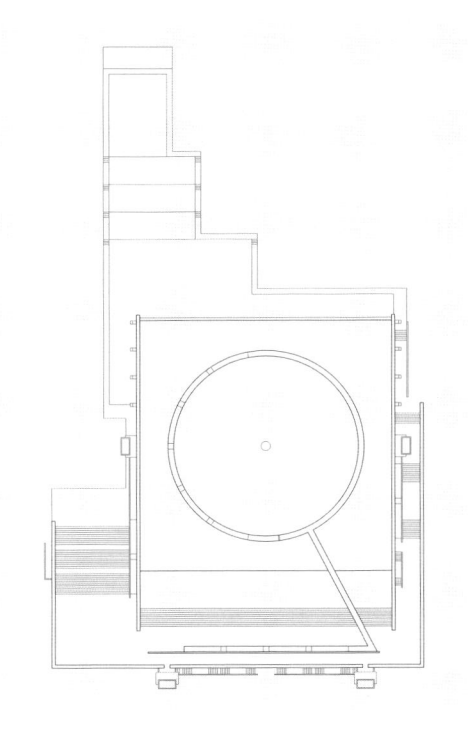

台湾北部の三芝区に計画された霊園の拡張計画。傾斜面の上部に配された納骨堂本体の屋根は一辺81メートルの巨大な水盤になっており、納骨堂内部ではスロープを昇降する。水盤の中央に設けられたトップライトからの光線が時間の移ろいとともに曲面の壁を彩り、人間の生死を熟考させる空間が広がる。納骨堂の足元から斜面を段状で下る人工池があり、水が断えず流れ落ち、悠久の時の流れを彷彿とさせる。一帯はさくらの森として整備される。

An expansion plan of a graveyard planned to be built on the Sanzhi Mountain at north of Taiwan. The roof of the main charnel located on upper area of the slope is a huge circle basin of 81 meters in diameter. A slope inside the cylinder of the charnel is provided to go up and down. The ray from the top light provided at the center of the basin shines depending on the transition of time along the charnel shelf situated on the whole wall expanding the space and it makes people ponder about life and death. The continuous flow of water from an artificial pond on the charnel floor that stream on the stages and it evoke the flow of perpetual time. The whole area will be maintained as a cherry blossom forest.

[330]

ボローニャ ISA　進行中
bologna ISA   in progress

1. イタリア ボローニャ | bologna, italy
2. 設計 | design   2011.7–2015.2
3. 施工 | construction   2015.3–
4. 鉄筋コンクリート、レンガ | RC, brick
5. 私立アカデミー | private academy
6. 敷地 | site   21,000 m²
8. 延床 | total floor   2,100 m²

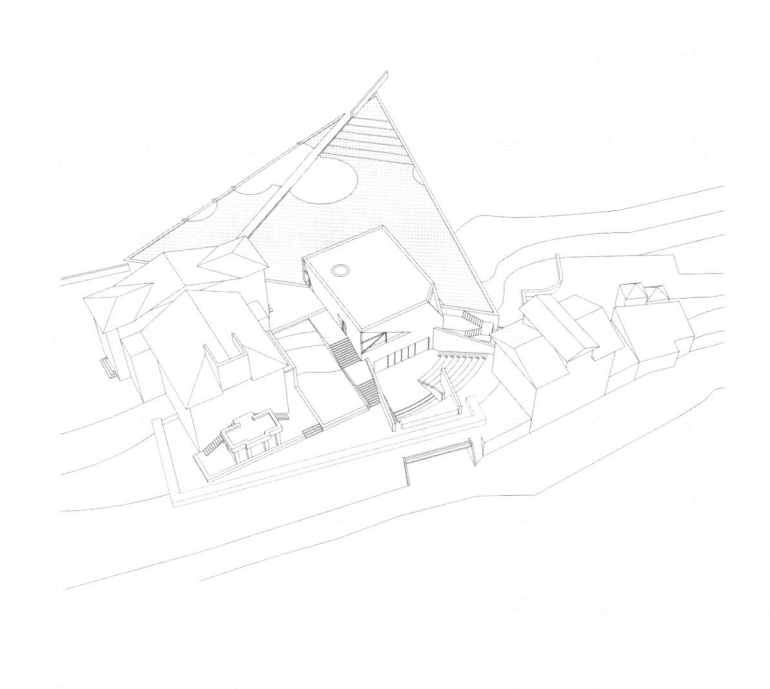

イタリア・ボローニャ郊外の丘陵地に残るヴィラと付属の施設を保存修復し、プライベートな学術機関に再構成する計画。5棟の建築が対象だが、厳しい景観規制もあり、既存のヴィラ、劇場、農家風住宅、森林の小屋の4棟は最小限の変更を加えるだけとなった。ヴィラに講義室、事務室、カフェテリアなどの機能を持たせ、他は宿泊施設とした。家畜小屋のみ撤去する許可があり、コンクリート打ち放しのオーディトリアム棟が新築される。ヴィラとこのオーディトリアム棟の前には正三角形の水庭が新たにつくられ、既存の迷宮庭園と共にランドスケープを再構成する。

A plan for restoring, conserving, and reconstructing a villa and accessory structures at a hill site in a suburb of Bologna, Italy, in order to make a private academic organization. Among five subject buildings, four buildings (the existing villa, theater, farmhouse-like house, and forest hut) had minimal changes partly due to strict landscape regulations. Lecture rooms, offices, and cafeteria functions were added to the villa, while other buildings were converted to accommodation facilities. An as-cast concrete auditorium was newly built since permission was granted to remove the animal shed. An equilateral-triangular-shaped water garden was added in front of the villa and the auditorium building.

[331]
GENESIS MUSEUM　進行中
genesis museum　in progress

1. 中華人民共和国 北京 | beijing, china
2. 設計 | design　2012.4 – 2015.5
3. 施工 | construction　2014.9 –
4. 鉄筋コンクリート | RC
5. 美術館 | museum of art
6. 敷地 | site　27,312 m²
8. 延床 | total floor　9,170 m²

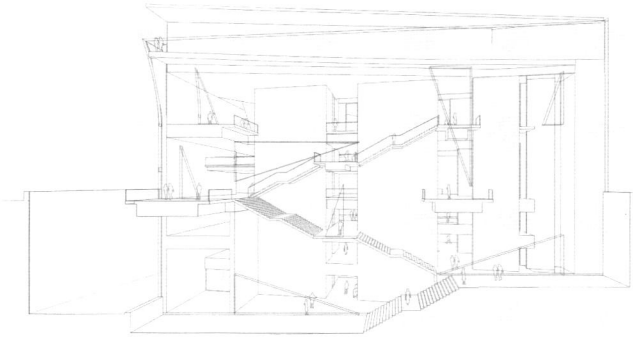

北京の再開発「華都センター」の一角に建設されるアーティスト、曾梵志の現代美術館。周囲に建物が迫り、制約のある台形の敷地に矩形の展示室が配される構成となっている。高さ24メートルのワンルームで、片側の壁際に配した階段を昇降しながら各展示室を巡る。この吹き抜けにはトップライトからの自然光が射し込み、広さに制約のある都心立地のギャラリーに季節の移ろいなどの変化をもたらす効果が託されている。

An art gallery of a contemporary artist, Zeng Fanzhi built at the redevelopment Huadu Center of Beijing. A rectangular exhibition room is placed in the trapezoidal property with certain limitations. A basic exhibition room has a 24-meter high one-room style structure and artworks exhibited on the apron area are observed by going up or down the stairs placed along the wall on one side. Natural light from the top light shines through the open ceiling to provide an effect of seasonal transition to the gallery placed in a city with limited space.

[332]
元祖夢世界　進行中
ganso dream world　in progress

1. 中華人民共和国 上海 | shanghai, china
2. 設計 | design　2013.6 –
3. 施工 | construction　2015.3 –
4. 鉄筋コンクリート | RC
5. 商業施設、ホテル | commercial complex, hotel
6. 敷地 | site　43,653.00 m²
7. 建築 | building　21,827.00 m²
8. 延床 | total floor　148,452.00 m²

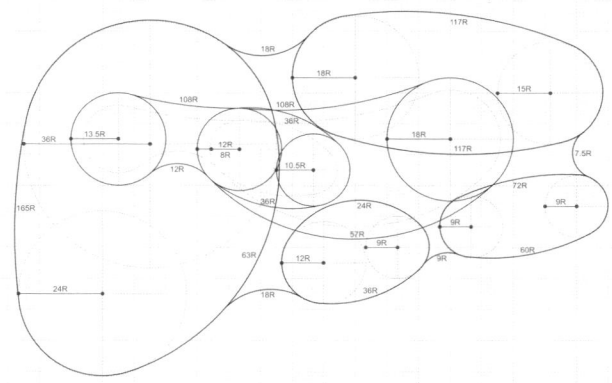

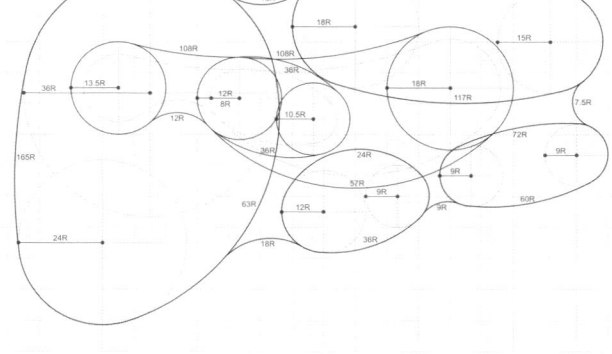

上海の親子向けの体験型商業施設。製造体験などを通して子どもの教育に力を入れてきた「元祖食品」が設ける。卵形のゾーンが連なる流線型の「夢の空」と呼ばれるギャラリー、高さの異なる正方形平面の三つの箱をずらすことによって生まれた立体庭園も楽しめる二つ目のギャラリー「夢の丘」、家族連れ向けのホテル「夢の家」から成る。昼夜で表情が変わるアルミニウムの外装を採用している。

A shopping center in Shanghai mainly for children and their parents. It is sponsored by Ganso Co., Ltd., a food company which has been making efforts for child education through manufacturing workshops. The center consists of a streamline-shaped gallery with oval shaped zones "Ganso's Sky of Dreams", a roof garden-type gallery built by shifting three boxes of square planes with different heights "Ganso's Hill of Dreams", and a family hotel "Ganso's House of Dreams". It adopts aluminum exterior which changes its expression by day and by night.

全346作品録　459

[333]
ライトウッド ギャラリー　進行中
wrightwood gallery   in progress

1. アメリカ シカゴ | chicago, USA
2. 設計 | design   2013.7–2015.8
3. 施工 | construction   2015.8–
4. 鉄骨鉄筋コンクリート | SRC
5. 美術館 | museum of art
7. 建築 | building   721.50 m²
8. 延床 | total floor   2,756.60 m²

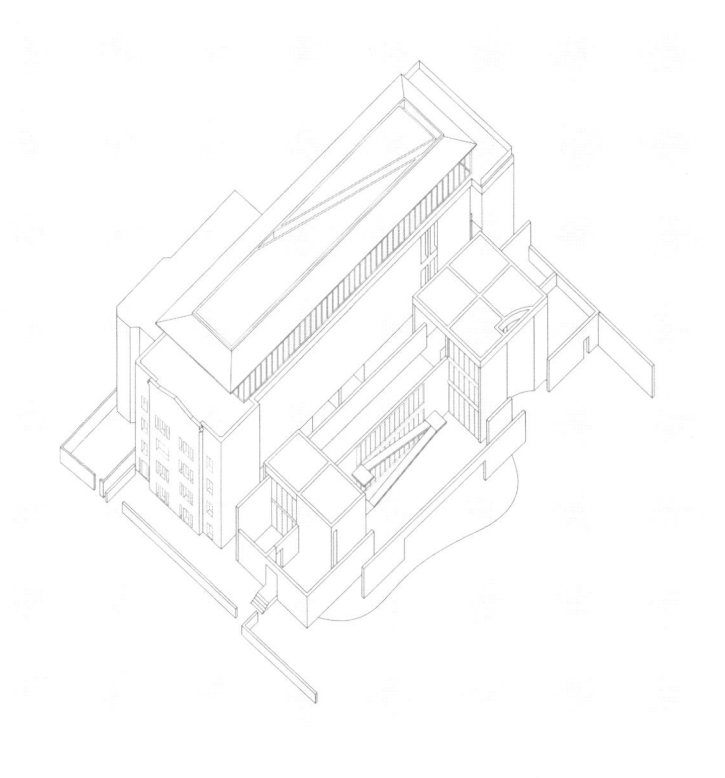

安藤が設計した「シカゴの住宅」の隣地にある煉瓦造の建物を東洋美術品などのギャラリーに改装する。1930年代建設の階高の低い4階建てで、集合住宅だった。展示空間を確保するために大改装した。まず屋内に、鉄筋コンクリートの柱を建て、次に3階建てとする床を張ってから、もとの床を撤去した。屋上にガラスのペントハウスを増築してギャラリーに充てた。外観は維持され、コンクリート打ち放しの「シカゴの住宅」と新旧の対比を示す。→参照 [167]

The objective is to renovate a brick building, in the neighbor of the HOUSE IN CHICAGO Ando designed, into a gallery of oriental art works. A four-story building with low floor height built as a housing complex in the 1930s. A large-scale refurbishment was given to secure space for exhibition. Firstly, reinforced concrete pillars were built. After flooring work to create a three-story building, the original floors were removed. A glass penthouse was extended to the rooftop for additional gallery. The exterior remains the same and expresses a nice contrast of the new and the old with the HOUSE IN CHICAGO built with exposed concrete. → see also [167]

[334]
ヴァルスの広場　進行中
valser path   in progress

1. スイス ヴァルス | vals, switzerland
2. 設計 | design   2013.7–
4. 鉄筋コンクリート | RC
5. 公園、美術館 | park, museum
6. 敷地 | site   28,000.0 m²
7. 建築 | building   7,750.0 m²
8. 延床 | total floor   14,650.00 m²

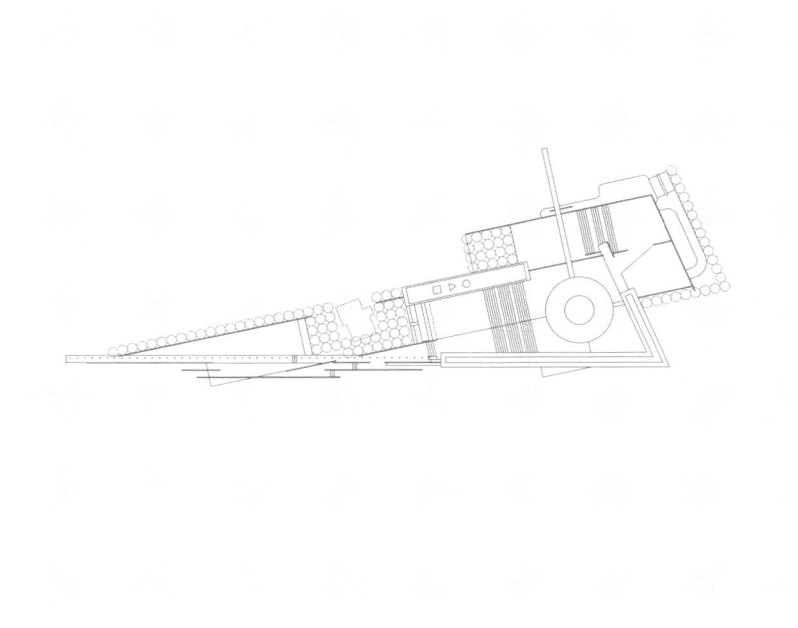

スイスのアルプスに位置するヴァルス村は、ピーター・ズントーの名作「テルメ・ヴァルス」で世界的に知られる。その温泉を起点に、湧水と現地産の石によるランドスケープを構築しようとするプロジェクト。ズントーの温泉は山裾の高台に位置するが、安藤はそこから見おろすヴァルザーライン川の流域に、角柱の連なるプロムナードと水庭、そして、水庭の起点の場所にコンクリートのロトンドを置くことを計画している。開発には、モルフォシスのデザインによる高層ホテルも含まれており、実現すれば山間の温泉地のイメージが一新される。

Vals Village located in the Alps of Switzerland is known internationally by the masterpiece Therme Vals by Peter Zumthor. The project is to build a landscape starting from the hot spring using spring water and locally produced stones. Zumthor's hot spring is located on elevated ground of the mountain skirt. Ando's plan is to place a promenade with series of rectangular columns and a water garden along the Valser Rhine where can be viewed from the hot spring and place a concrete rotunda at the starting point of the promenade. A high-rise hotel designed by Morphosis is included in the development in which the image of the hot spring area in the mountains will completely be renewed.

[335]
マンハッタンのペントハウス III　進行中
penthouse in manhattan III　in progress

1. アメリカ ニューヨーク | new york, USA
2. 設計 | design　2013.9 – 2015.3
3. 施工 | construction　2014.6 –
4. 鉄骨、煉瓦 | steel, brick
5. ペントハウス | penthouse
6. 敷地 | site　775.0 m²
8. 延床 | total floor　235.0 m²

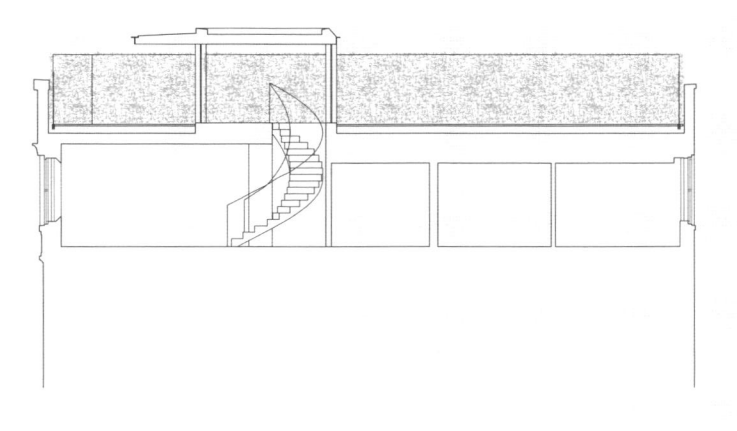

安藤がマンハッタンの中高層ビルに新たな空間を挿入する提案のひとつ。1912年完成の12階建ての集合住宅の最上階を、現代美術の画廊経営者の求めで改装する。シリーズの「II」と同じく屋上にフォリーを新設し、居住の機能が集まる最上階とは、リビングから屋上に伸びる螺旋階段で結ぶ。屋上にはテラスが設えられ、フランスのアーティスト、パトリック・ブランと協同で制作する緑の壁が、アートとしての自然を演出することになっている。

Proposal of Ando to insert a new space among the mid-to-high-rise buildings in Manhattan. A renovation plan of the top floor of the 12-story condominium built in 1912 was requested by the owner of a contemporary art gallery. Same as II of the series, a folly is placed on the rooftop and it is connected with the top floor that has a residential function by a spiral stairway that extends to the rooftop from the living room. A terrace is provided on the rooftop where green walls display fake nature in collaboration with a French artist, Patrick Blanc.

[336]
マンハッタンの集合住宅　進行中
condominium in manhattan　in progress

1. アメリカ ニューヨーク | new york, USA
2. 設計 | design　2013.9 – 2015.8
3. 施工 | construction　2015.1 –
4. 鉄筋コンクリート | RC
5. 集合住宅 | apartment house
6. 敷地 | site　415.0 m²
7. 建築 | building　392.0 m²
8. 延床 | total floor　2,888.0 m²

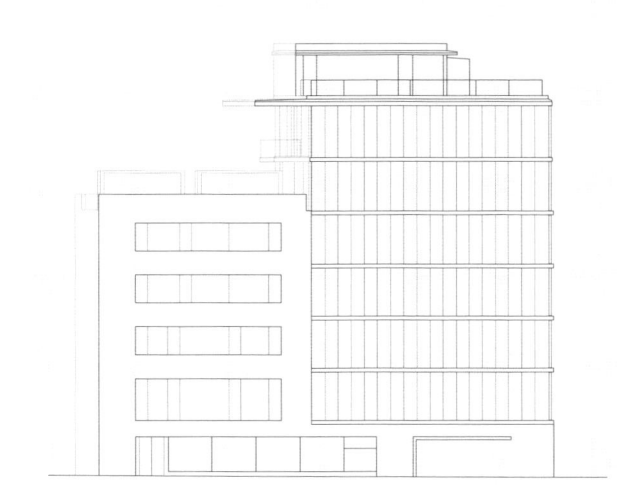

リトル・イタリーやチャイナタウンを控えるニューヨークのダウンタウンのコンドミニアム。全7層の建物は、横長窓を配したコンクリートの基壇部分に、前面ガラスのボックスが載る構成となっている。米大都市の集合住宅の多くが守りの固さを示すのに対して、ガラスの外壁は美しい肢体を惜しげなくさらしているかのようだ。見事な施工の垂直線と水平線の交差が精密感をあふれさせ、隙のない強靭な美が脆弱な印象を斥ける。安藤にとって、ニューヨークでの最初の独立した建築となった。

A condominium in downtown New York containing Little Italy and Chinatown. On the side facing a main street, the seven-story section has an entire glass wall from the 2nd floor to the top, whereas the adjacent five-story part has a concrete wall with horizontal ribbon windows. While many housing complexes in major cities in the U.S. display secure defenses, the glass exterior wall appears as if generously exposing the skin of a beautiful body. A sense of preciseness is given by the excellently constructed intersections of vertical lines and horizontal lines, and its stout and watertight beauty refuses to give a vulnerable impression. This was the first independent architectural work of Ando in New York.

全346作品録

[337]
和美術館　進行中
he art museum   in progress

1. 中華人民共和国　広東省仏山市 | shunde district foshan guangdong, china
2. 設計 | design   2014.4－2017.2
3. 施工 | construction   2017.2－
4. 鉄筋コンクリート | RC
5. 美術館 | museum of art
6. 敷地 | site   8650.48 m²
7. 建築 | building   2780 m²
8. 延床 | total floor   21264 m²

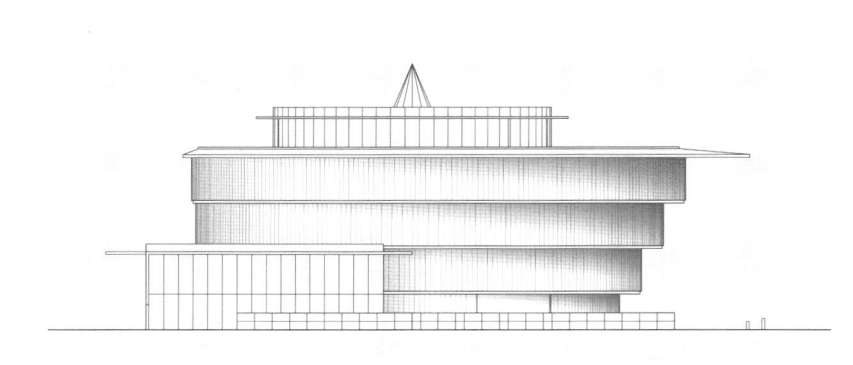

中国広東省仏山市の現代美術館。企業創業者が現代美術のコレクションを展示するために建設する。円形の平面をずらして四層重ねた中心の位置に、二重の螺旋階段が配される。来訪者はそこを伝って展示フロアを昇降する動的なリズム感に包まれながら、現代美術と地元の伝統芸術を鑑賞する。建物を取り巻く外構には円形の水盤を配し、ずれて重なる円形の棟が形作る波紋の広がりのイメージと連動させる。「和」の呼称は、オーナーの目指す「調和」と「平和」に由来する。

A contemporary art museum in Foshan City, Guangdong Province in China. A museum to be built by a founder of a company to display a collection of contemporary arts. A double spiral stairways are placed at the center of four layers of circles formed in an offset position. Visitors will appreciate contemporary arts and local traditional arts being enveloped in a dynamic architectural rhythm when going up or down the spiral stairways to the next exhibition floor. A round water basin is situated on the outside channel that surrounds the building to express an image of an expanding wave pattern together with the round building that is overlapping in an offset position. The name "Wa" is based on harmony (chowa) and peace (heiwa) the owner is pursuing.

[338]
寿長生の郷　点心庵　進行中
sunainosato tenshinan   in progress

1. 滋賀県大津市 | otsu, shiga
2. 設計 | design   2014.5－
4. 鉄骨 | steel
5. 飲食店 | cafe restaurant
6. 敷地 | site   111,890.41 m²
7. 建築 | building   860.78 m²
8. 延床 | total floor   505.90 m²

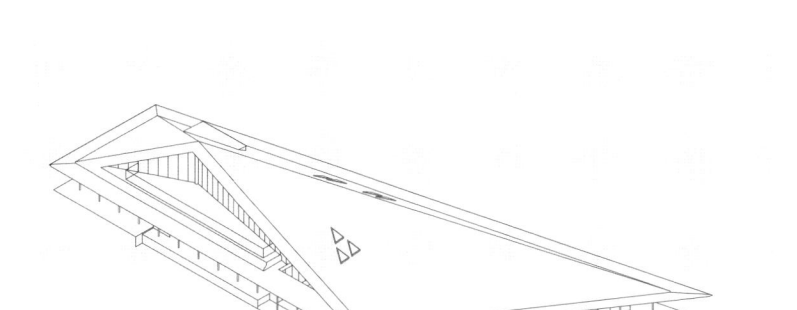

寿長生の郷は、滋賀県大津市の郊外に和菓子メーカーが開設している本社工場と、自然を生かした庭園施設。梅林などを歩きながら環境を堪能するとともに、和食や和菓子を楽しめる。安藤は、その一角にカフェレストラン、料理教室などの機能を持つ「点心庵」を設計した。カフェレストランと料理教室は二つの棟に分かれ、それぞれに深いひさしを持つ傾斜屋根が架かる。屋根が双方の施設を結び、躯体はテラスでわずかに重なり合う。水辺に面した配置で、ひさしの下の屋外空間を現代における縁側と位置づけ、新たな日本建築像を模索している。

SUNAINOSATO is a nature-based eating house established by a Japanese confectionary company in the suburbs of Otsu, Shiga. Guests can appreciate the nature walking through the Japanese apricot grove, while also enjoying the taste of Japanese cuisine and confectionary. Ando designed a café style restaurant and a "Dim Sum Hermitage" which can be used for cooking classes. The café style restaurant and cooking classroom are divided into two buildings, each topped by a sloping roof with deep eaves. The roof connects the two buildings and they slightly overlap each other above the terrace. Arranged to face the waterside, Ando designed the outdoor space beneath the eaves to resemble modern Japanese-style loggia and to seek new image of Japanese architecture.

346 Complete Works

[339]
臥龍山安養院増築計画　進行中
garyozan anyoin temple   in progress

1. 東京都品川区 | shinagawa-ku, tokyo
2. 設計 | design   2015.2 – 2016.4
3. 施工 | construction   2017.2 –
4. 鉄骨鉄筋コンクリート | SRC
5. 仏教寺院 | buddhist temple
6. 敷地 | site   3,576.69 m²
7. 建築 | building   476.92 m²
8. 延床 | total floor   1,543.98 m²

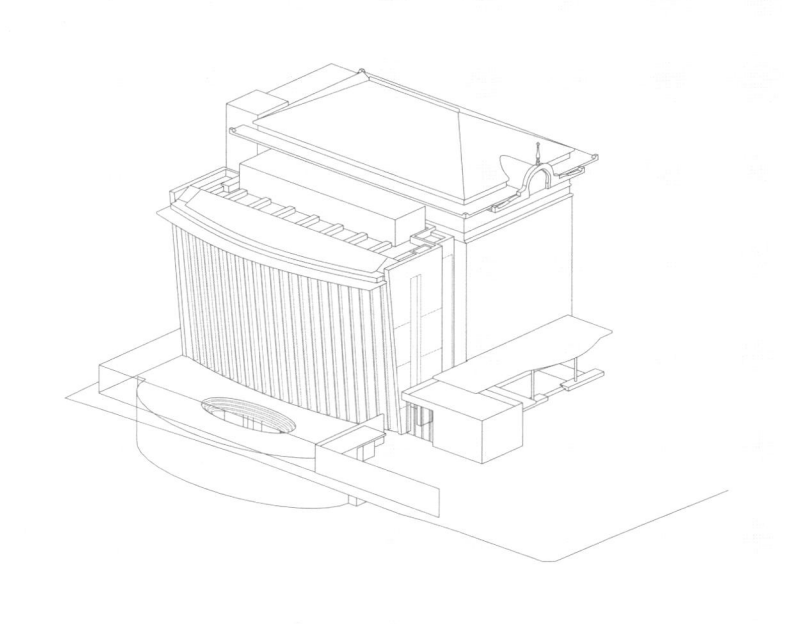

納骨堂の増築。既存の5階建ての納骨堂の背後にあたる四層分に、下すぼまりの斜めのガラス壁で囲われた空間を増築し、足もと地下部分に納骨堂を配する。この納骨堂は、中央が空も望む中庭形式の楕円形平面の空間となっており、床面に水盤が設けられ、仏像を配した木製の納骨棚がそこを囲う。来訪者はこの水を眺めて故人を偲ぶことになる。また、立体広場には屋上緑化を施し、増築部分の建物の上階から緑を見下ろす仕立てにもなっている。

Extension of a charnel house. It is proceeded by adding the space surrounded by narrowing, sloping glass walls to the four-story building behind the existing five-story charnel house and arranging a structural square covered with greenery at the bottom. This three-dimensional square is approximately three meters high and its center is an elliptical open ceiling space. An artificial pond is built on the floor surface and is surrounded by wooden shelves with Buddha statues. Visitors will be gazing at the water of the pond to remember the deceased. Roof greening is given to the structural square where visitors can overlook the greens from the upper floor of the extended part of the building.

[340]
浅草の住宅　進行中
house in asakusa   in progress

1. 東京都台東区 | taito-ku, tokyo
2. 設計 | design   2015.8 – 2017.2
3. 施工 | construction   2017.2 –
4. 鉄筋コンクリート | RC
5. 住宅 | detached house
6. 敷地 | site   140.66 m²
7. 建築 | building   86.32 m²
8. 延床 | total floor   278.24 m²

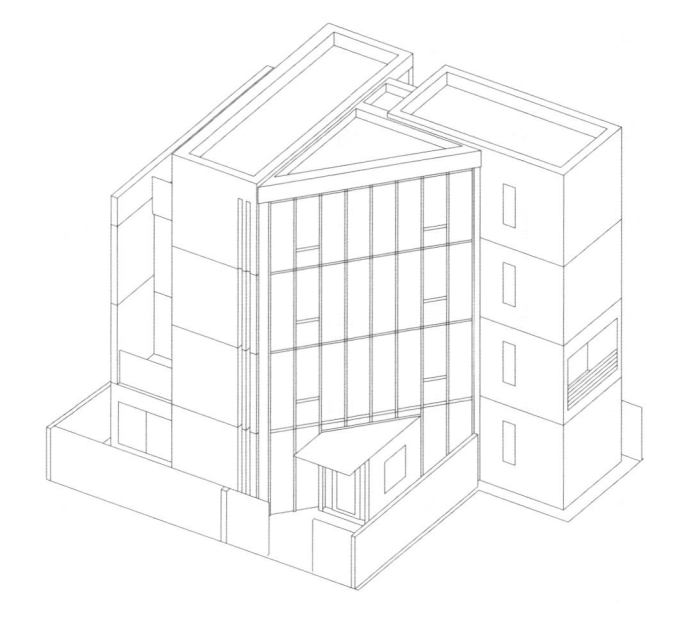

浅草寺の背後に位置する4階建ての戸建て住宅。規則正しく区画された街区の角地を活かして、平面形はL字型を基調にしてまとめられた。Lの角の位置に三角形の床を張り出させ、1階から4階までガラス壁で覆い、密集地では期待できなかったはずの豊かな光が、住居全体に浸透していく。敷地は140平方メートルで決して広くはないが、的確に整理された間取りと相まって、吹き抜けやテラスが空間に刺激を与え、都市の暮らしを彩っていく。

A detached four-story house occupying a corner of Ura-asakusa behind the Sensoji Temple. Utilizing the corner of the regularly divided city block, the plan was based on an "L" shape. The triangle floor was projected at the corner of the L shape and all four floors were covered with glass walls where enough light comes in to fill the entire house, which would have never been possible in this crowded area. Although the size of the site is 140 square meters and is never wide, an accurately organized layout together with an open ceiling space and a terrace spicing up the space brings liveliness to the urban life.

全346作品録

[341]
新華紅星国際広場　進行中
xinhua redstar landmark　in progress

1. 中華人民共和国　上海 | shanghai, china
2. 設計 | design　2015.10–2016.11
3. 施工 | construction　2016.8–
4. 鉄筋コンクリート、鉄骨 | RC, steel
5. 書店、美術館 | book shop, museum
8. 延床 | total floor　3,600.00 m²

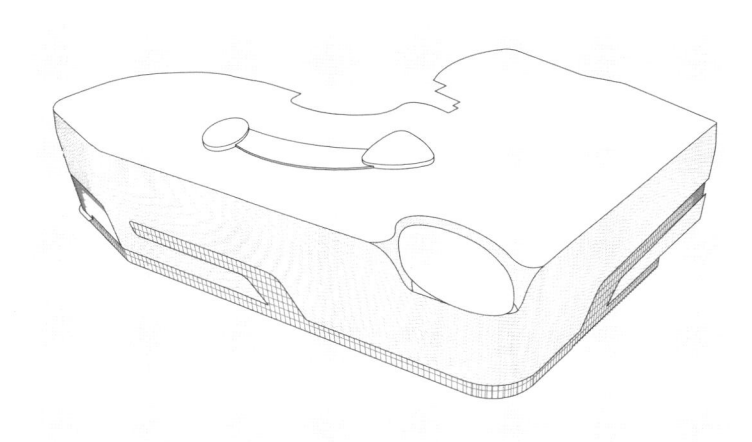

上海に建設中の商業施設の7、8階を占める大規模書店を、カフェ併設の書籍売り場と美術館に仕立てる計画。下階の書籍売り場と上階の美術館を結ぶのは卵形の吹き抜け。そこを囲う二層分の曲面壁は全面が書架に仕立てられ、中央にも円筒形の書架がそびえる。この吹き抜けのブックカフェに集うひとびとは、本に囲まれた空間を味わうことになる。美術館は千平方メートルを超える規模で文化的発信も期待される。この二層分のスペースの外観は、生物的な曲面壁の立体を施設に付加し、ランドマーク性も持たせる。

Large-scale book store occupying seventh and eighth floors of an existing commercial building in Shanghai will be renovated into a book shop with a café and an art gallery. The book shop of the lower floor and the art gallery of the upper floor are connected by the oval-shaped open ceiling. The entire surface of the two layers of the surrounding curved wall is made as a book shelf and a cylindrical book shelf soars in the middle. Guests to this open-ceiling book café will enjoy this space filled with books. The art gallery takes up more than 1,000 square meters and its role as a cultural center is also expected. The exterior of the space of these two layers takes an impressive form, adding the structure of a biological, curved wall to the existing facility.

[342]
ブルス・ドゥ・コメルス　進行中
bourse de commerce　in progress

1. フランス パリ | paris, france
2. 設計 | design　2016.1–2017.4
3. 施工 | construction　2017.5–
4. 鉄筋コンクリート、組積造 | RC, masonry
5. 美術館（再生）| museum of art (renovation)

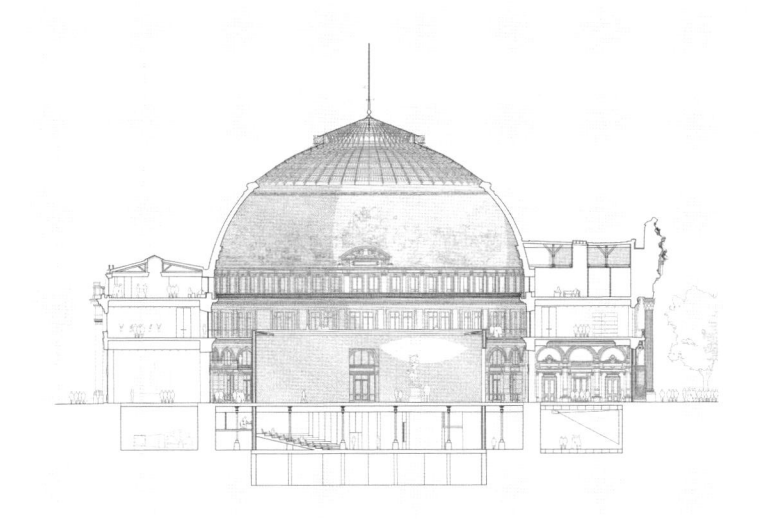

パリの中央市場跡地に隣接する、ドーム屋根とカトリーヌ・ド・メディシス占星術の塔でも知られる「商品取引所」（1898年）を美術館に改装するプロジェクト。安藤と二人三脚でヴェネチアで旧税関などを現代美術のギャラリーに改装した実業家フランソワ・ピノーが19世紀の建築の変身を安藤に委ねた。内部のロトンダに、高さ10メートル、直径30メートルのコンクリートの円筒を構築して、内部を主たる展示空間とする。地下にはオーディトリアムを置く。円筒の外側を巻く階段を設け、壁画の描かれた元の内装と安藤のコンクリートの邂逅が楽しめる。

A project for renovating the "Bourse de commerce (Commodity Exchange)" (1898) — standing next to the former central market site in Paris and known for the dome roof and the astrology tower of Catherine de' Medici — into a museum. Ando was entrusted to transform the 19th century building by businessman François Pinault. A 10m-high concrete cylinder with 30m diameter is made in the rotunda. The inside of the cylinder becomes a main exhibition space and an auditorium is located underground. Stairs wrap around the outside and visitors may enjoy an encounter with history and modern times by walking between the original interiors with fresco paintings and Ando's concrete.

[343]
フォートワース現代美術館
増築計画　進行中
modern art museum of fort worth
expansion project   in progress

1. アメリカ フォートワース｜fort worth, USA
2. 設計｜design 2016.2–
4. 鉄筋コンクリート｜RC
5. 美術館｜museum of art
6. 敷地｜site　44,370.00 m²

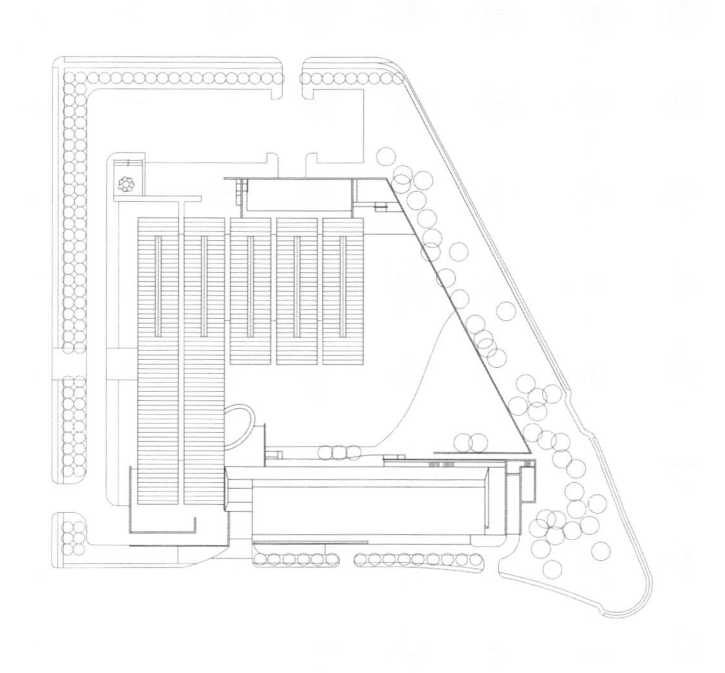

安藤の代表作のひとつ「フォートワース現代美術館」に、低層のギャラリーを新設する。既存の施設と人工池の環境を考慮して、建築は二層に抑制して一層分は地下に置いた。1階はギャラリーとカフェ、地下はサンクンガーデンの彫刻ギャラリーに面した企画展スペース、図書室などが配される。既存のギャラリーからは、池を囲う配置の新棟の屋上植栽された陸屋根が目に入る。広大な郊外地に希有な安寧の場が、さらに定着していく手応えを感じさせる。→参照 [208]

A lower-level gallery will be built as an extension of MODERN ART MUSEUM OF FORT WORTH, one of Ando's masterpieces. Taking into account the existing facility and the environment of the artificial pond, the building was restricted to two layers and one of them was placed underground. The gallery and café will be built on the first floor and a temporary exhibition space facing the sculpture gallery of the sunken garden and a library on the underground floor. From the existing gallery, the flat roof of the new building surrounding the pond comes into view. A rare place of peace and order in this vast suburban area would take a deeper root. → see also [208]

[344]
BIGI青葉台　進行中
bigi aobadai   in progress

1. 東京都目黒区｜meguro-ku, tokyo
2. 設計｜design 2016.9–
4. 鉄筋コンクリート｜RC
5. アトリエ、オフィス｜atelier, office
6. 敷地｜site　332.29 m²

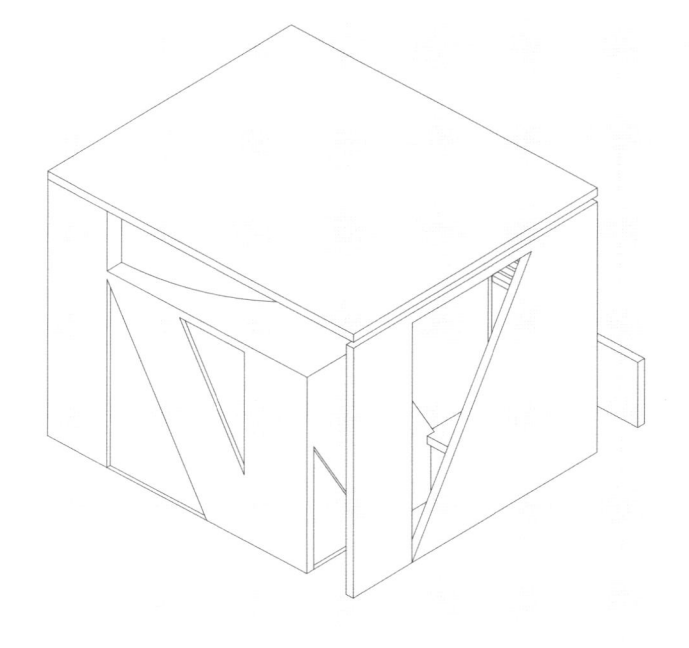

△□〇というユークリッド幾何学でも禅の宇宙観でも「基本原理」とされる形態を、外観、平面配置の基本とする小規模なアトリエ兼オフィス。なにより直角三角形を複数配した外観が安藤の美学を体現している。コンクリート打ち放しのシンプルな力強い外観は、純度の高い幾何学で統御され、都市への大きな刺激となっている。平面形は正方形を基調に構成され、1、2階が店舗、地下がイベントホール、上階は住宅にあてられる。店舗部分には、吹き抜けとテラスが配され、自然光が空間に彩りをもたらす。

A commercial building with its exterior and planar constellation based on the triangle, circle and square that are regarded as the "basic principles" in both Euclidean geometry and Zen cosmology. The exterior ornamented with multiple right triangles embodies Ando's aesthetics. Simple but powerful exterior of exposed concrete is organized with highly-pure geometry and has become a great stimulus to the city. The plan is based on a square, with the first and second floors being the store, the underground floor being the event hall and the upper floors being the houses. An open ceiling space and terrace have been added to the store and natural light spices up the space.

[345]
兵庫県立美術館増築計画　進行中
hyogo prefectural museum of art
expansion project　in progress

1. 神戸市中央区 | chuo-ku, kobe
2. 設計 | design　2016.10 – 2017.12
3. 施工 | construction　2018.1 –
4. 鉄骨 | steel
5. 美術館 | museum of art
6. 敷地 | site　19,000.00 m²
7. 建築 | building　691.22 m²
8. 延床 | total floor　763.89 m²

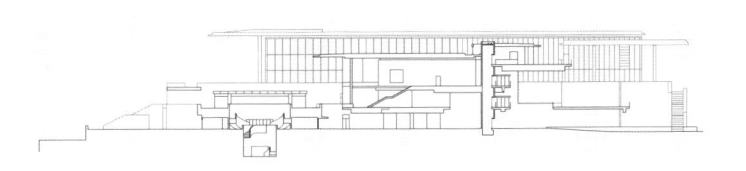

「兵庫県立美術館」の並列する二つの展示棟の間に、安藤の作品の模型や図面のための展示室が創設される。内部は三層構成で、海側は大きなガラスの開口部がとられ、その光があふれる壁際の空間は吹き抜けになっていて、2、3階の展示室を移動する階段が配される。愛着の深い神戸と兵庫県に、震災復興プロジェクトをはじめとする自らの建築模型や図面に加えて、展示室も寄贈することで恩返しがかなえばとの安藤の気持ちが込められている。→参照 [197]

An exhibition room for models and plans of Ando's works will be built in between the two parallel exhibition buildings of the HYOGO PREFECTURAL MUSEUM OF ART. Double-layered structure of the interior has a large glass opening on the seaward side and the space near the window where light comes in has an open ceiling with stairs connecting the exhibition rooms on the first and second floors. By donating an exhibition room in addition to his architectural models and plans, Ando expresses his gratitude to Kobe and Hyogo where he is attached to. → see also [197]

[346]
中之島児童文学館プロジェクト
進行中
nakanoshima children's library project
in progress

1. 大阪市北区 | kita-ku, osaka
2. 設計 | design　2017.2 –
5. 図書館 | library

大阪・中之島の中央公会堂の近傍に構想された児童図書館。安藤は自身の体験を踏まえて、児童期の読書の大切さを認識し、東京・上野の「国際子ども図書館」などの作品を手がけてきた。吹き抜けの閲覧室を囲う曲面壁は、びっしりと書籍の並ぶ書棚で構成される。その光景は、書籍が先人たちの知の集積であり、子どもたちの未来への贈り物であることを問わず語りに伝えている。何らかの形で一般のひとたちも参加でき、社会をあげて知育に取り組む場をつくる仕組みも、あわせて考えている。

A children's library designed to be built in the neighbour of the Central Public Hall in Nakanoshima, Osaka. Based on his own experiences, Ando recognized the importance of reading in childhood years and had been producing works such as THE INTERNATIONAL LIBRARY OF CHILDREN'S LITERATURE in Ueno, Tokyo. The curved wall surrounding the open-ceiling reading room consists of shelves full of books. This wall expresses how books are the collection of our predecessors' wisdom and are the gift for the children's future. The library is planning to call for donations to cover the fund required for its operation and is also expecting to become a center of intellectual education together with society.

資料
・
Appendix

安藤忠雄 経歴

1941年、安藤忠雄が生まれたこの年の暮れ、日本は米国を相手とする太平洋戦争に突入した。そして、4年後の無惨な敗戦。手広く軍関係の仕事をしていた一家は、生活の激変を余儀なくされた。安藤は工業高校に進み、卒業後、建築家になる道を選んだ。多くの日本の建築家と異なり、大学で建築を学び、さらに海外にも勉学の機会を求めるという経路はたどれなかった。建築書を独学で読み解き、名建築を国内外に訪ねる実地の研鑽を重ねた。やがて仕事の場を広げ、斬新な店舗設計などと大胆な論考によって、拠点とする大阪では、30代に入ると、将来を嘱望される若手と目されるに至った。

35歳の時に発表した「住吉の長屋」(1976年完成)は、安藤の建築家としての未来を約束し、活動の舞台を国際的な建築界へと飛躍させる大きなきっかけとなった。おりから建築界では、それまでの支配者だった無装飾のモダニズムへの反感が高まり、コンクリート打ち放しは非難の矢面に立っていた。そのとき安藤の「住吉の長屋」は、鉄筋コンクリートの狭小な庶民住宅に、日本人が古来育んできた自然観を取り込み、国内外の称賛をわがものとした。光や風や雨によって、屋外の自然を抽象化して愛でる伝統的な暮らしの喜びが体現されていたからである。

活動の初期から続く住宅作品は100件を超える。緑の環境に位置する「小篠邸」は、クリティカル・リージョナリズムの典型例として海外からも注目され、安藤はモダニズムの発展的な継承者としての地歩を固めた。その評価は、神戸港の後背地の急斜面に実現した「六甲の集合住宅」でさらに決定的なものとなった。住宅の区画内と棟内のテラスや通路に充てられた「余白」の空間が、住宅の集合体を有機的な存在に仕立てた。4期に及ぶ「六甲の集合住宅」は、万人の認める代表作となった。

40代までの安藤は、住宅作品とともに、神戸の北野町の異人館(明治の開国期に訪日した外国人のための住居)街で、「ローズガーデン」などの複数の商業施設を設計し、「建築家が街にどう貢献できるか」という課題に挑戦した。その試みは日本全国に広がり、建物の中央に配した外部扱いの階段を昇降する香川県高松市の「STEP」、沖縄の風土を活かした「フェスティバル」、京都の高瀬川の水辺を再生させた「TIME'S」は、日本における商業建築の常識を打ち破り、社会的にも大いに注目された。

本来、安藤は「発注者の顔が見えない」として公共建築の設計には自制的だった。それでも作品が単体の建築を超えて、都市や地域へ広がりを見せたことから、安藤に期待する地方自治体の首長は多く、なかでも兵庫県知事の貝原俊民が「兵庫県立こどもの館」をはじめ数々の施設の設計を安藤に依頼した。1995年、安藤が53歳のとき、阪神淡路大震災が起き、その復興をアピールする「淡路花博」の開催をきっかけに「淡路夢舞台」が実現した。広大な斜面地のランドスケープは、安藤の作品のその後の展開を示唆していた。

安藤の活動のもう一つの系譜である美術館建築の始まりは、瀬戸内海の直島をアートによって世界に類のない場にしようと模索していた教育産業の実業家、福武總一郎の来訪だった。1987年、安藤が46歳の時である。「ベネッセハウスミュージアム」(1992年)、「地中美術館」(2004年)など直島の美術関係施設の実現とともに、欧米での美術館などの設計依頼が安藤のもとに殺到した。1992年の「セビリア万博日本館」で、安藤の実作がヨーロッパでお披露目されたことも追い風となった。一国を代表する美術館などの文化施設のコンペ参加者に指名されることが日常化し、海外での評価は美術との関わりのなかで高まっていった。

フランスの実業家フランソワ・ピノーは、2001年、パリ西郊のセガン島で計画した「ピノー現代美術館」の設計者に安藤を選んだ。その計画が挫折を余儀なくされると、イタリア・ヴェネチアで、旧税関を現代美術のギャラリーに改装する「プンタ・デラ・ドガーナ」など複数の施設を安藤に委ねて、代表作の舞台を与えた。ピノーの肝入りで、パリのレ・アール地区の「商品取引所」を現代美術ギャラリーに改装するプロジェクトは、安藤が77歳となる2018年末、完成を予定しており、セガン島に始まる物語は幸福な大団円を迎えることになる。

安藤の最高傑作との呼び声も高い「フォートワース現代美術館」は、2002年、61歳の時の作品。ヨーロッパの「ホンブロイッヒ／ランゲン美術館」などで長年かけて試行したガラス壁の外皮のなかにコンクリートの展示室を入れ子で配する構成が、多様な鑑賞動線を実現した。隣接のルイス・カーンの代表作「キンベル美術館」と比肩する見事な空間への到達だった。これに先立つ「ピューリッツァー美術館」(2001年)をはじめ、米国における美術館建築への挑戦は「クラーク美術館」などに広がりを見せている。

阪神大震災の犠牲者鎮魂のための植樹運動の主導に始まり、社会的活動の牽引者としても大きな成果を上げてきた。それと同時に、現代人の「個」の精神性を主題にした「光の教会」「ユネスコ瞑想空間」などの作品でも成功を収めた。社会のなかでの「個」を視野に入れたうえでの、建築家の既存の枠を超えたところに安藤忠雄の21世紀は展開している。「上海保利大劇場」(2014年)など大空間への大胆な挑戦を目の当たりにすると、世界からの期待に応えながら、さらに密度の高い「建築家の宇宙」を今後完成させるのではと思わせる。

Tadao Ando Career

Japan entered into the Pacific War against the U.S. at the end of 1941, the year Tadao Ando was born. Four years later, Japan was terribly defeated, and Ando's family members—who had worked for a wide range of military-related businesses—were forced to change their lives dramatically. Ando proceeded to the high school of technology and chose an architect career after graduation. Unlike many Japanese architects, he was unable to learn architecture in university or to seek learning opportunities overseas. Ando taught himself by reading architectural literature and continuously visiting excellent architectural works in Japan and overseas. As he earned his standing at work due to his novel shop designs and dynamic discussions, he began to be regarded as a prospective young architect in his home ground of Osaka, when Ando was in his 30s.

ROW HOUSE, SUMIYOSHI (completed in 1976) announced when Ando was 35 brought him a promising future as an architect, and became a major trigger for him to expand his architectural activities abroad. Coincidently, there was more antipathy in the architectural world against dominant non-decorative modernist architecture. As-cast concrete was facing the fire of such criticisms. Ando's ROW HOUSE, SUMIYOSHI—a small house for common people with reinforced concrete construction, integrating traditional Japanese concepts of nature—won domestic and international admiration. It embodied the joy of traditional living, in which people abstracted and cherished outdoor nature through light, wind, rain, etc.

There are more than 100 houses produced by Ando since his early years. KOSHINO HOUSE (1981) is located in a verdant environment. As a typical example of "critical regionalism", the house also attracted attention from overseas, resulting in Ando establishing his position as a progressive successor of modernists. His reputation became even more concrete after materializing ROKKO HOUSING on a steep hill at the back of the Port of Kobe. The "void" spaces were used for terraces and pathways in the housing units and buildings, resulting in making the housing complex an organic existence. The ROKKO HOUSING with four stages became his representative work and was acknowledged on all hands.

Ando tackled the challenge of "how an architect contributes to a town" up until his 40s, by designing several commercial facilities in the Kobe Kitano-cho Ijinkan-gai district (Ijinkan was a dwelling for foreigners that visited Japan after the opening of the country in the Meiji period), in addition to the houses. Such challenges spread all over Japan and other works included: STEP (1980) in Takamatsu City in Kagawa Prefecture, having "exterior" stairs at the center of the building; FESTIVAL (1984) that takes advantage of the climate of Okinawa; and TIME'S (1984) that restored the waterfront of the Takase River in Kyoto. As a result, the works defied Japanese conventions of commercial buildings and drew keen social attention.

Ando tended to restrain himself from designing public buildings, since "it was hard to directly communicate with clients". Yet many leaders of local governments counted on Ando, who designed buildings that became popular at the level of cities or areas, not only architecture. In particular, Hyogo prefectural governor Toshitami Kaihara requested many facility designs from Ando, including CHILDREN'S MUSEUM, HYOGO (1989). In 1995, when Ando was 53, the Great Hanshin Earthquake hit. Japan Flora 2000 (Awaji Flower Expo) exhibition was held to announce rehabilitation from the earthquake, and this became a trigger for realization of AWAJI-YUMEBUTAI (1999). The landscape on a large sloped site indicated the development of Ando's works thereafter.

Museum designs—constituting another portion of Ando's activities—began from a visit from an entrepreneur in the education-related industries, Soichiro Fukutake in 1987, when Ando was 46. Fukutake was attempting to create a unique place in the world on Naoshima Island in the Seto Inland Sea by utilizing art. Many requests from European and American art museums were rushed to Ando, after he had materialized art-related facilities in Naoshima, such as BENESSE HOUSE MUSEUM (1992) and CHICHU ART MUSEUM/NAOSHIMA (2004). Ando's work, Seville Expo '92 JAPAN PAVILION in 1992, was introduced in Europe, and this was favorable for Ando. He was regularly requested to participate in competitions for representative cultural facilities (such as museums) of various nations. His international reputation grew through a relationship with art.

In 2001 French businessman François Pinault designated Ando as a designer for the FRANÇOIS PINAULT FOUNDATION FOR CONTEMPORARY ART on Seguin Island, located in a western suburb of Paris. When the project was forced to discontinue, Pinault requested that Ando design multiple facilities, such as the PUNTA DELLA DOGANA CONTEMPORARY ART CENTER in Venice, Italy, which was a renovation of a former customs building into a contemporary art gallery. Pinault gave Ando opportunities to create his representative works. The renovation project of the commodity exchange BOURSE DE COMMERCE in Les Halles in Paris into a contemporary art gallery, sponsored by Pinault, is scheduled to be completed by the end of 2018, when Ando will turn 77. This will bring a grand finale to the story that started from Seguin Island.

The MODERN ART MUSEUM OF FORT WORTH was created in 2002 when Ando was 61, and is highly renowned as one of his masterpieces. He completed the composition of concrete exhibition rooms nested within a glass-walled outer shell, which had been tested over many years in his designs, including LANGEN FOUNDATION/HOMBROICH (2004) in Europe. The composition materialized various circulation for viewing. Ando created a brilliant space comparable to the adjacent "Kimbell Art Museum", a representative work of Louis Kahn. In addition to the previous work PULITZER FOUNDATION FOR THE ARTS (2001), Ando's challenges for museum designs in the U.S. further developed up to the STERLING AND FRANCINE CLARK ART INSTITUTE.

He has produced successful results as a leader of social activities, such as leading a tree planting campaign for the repose of the souls of the Great Hanshin Earthquake victims. At the same time, he has been successful in his works with a theme of the "individual" spirit of modern humans, such as CHURCH OF THE LIGHT (1989) and MEDITATION SPACE, UNESCO (1995). The 21st century of Tadao Ando has developed beyond the existing activities of an architect, with a perspective of "individuals" in a society. When seeing Ando's adventurous challenges for large spaces, such as SHANGHAI POLY THEATER (2014), it appears to me that he will meet the world's expectations, and he will complete an even denser "universe of an architect" in the future.

安藤忠雄 主要経歴

受賞、叙勲：

- 1979　「住吉の長屋」（1976）で昭和54年度日本建築学会賞
- 1985　第5回アルヴァ・アアルト賞（フィンランド）
- 1989　フランス建築アカデミー大賞（ゴールドメダル）
- 1991　アーノルド・ブルンナー記念賞（米）
- 1992　デンマーク、第1回カールスベルグ建築賞
- 1993　日本芸術院賞
- 1995　プリツカー賞（米）
　　　　フランス芸術文化勲章（シュバリエ）叙勲
- 1996　第8回高松宮殿下記念世界文化賞
　　　　第1回国際教会建築賞「フラテソーレ」（イタリア）
- 1997　王立英国建築家協会（RIBA）ロイヤルゴールドメダル
　　　　フランス芸術文化勲章（オフィシエ）叙勲
- 1998　「大阪府立近つ飛鳥博物館」で第6回公共建築賞
- 2002　アメリカ建築家協会（AIA）ゴールドメダル
　　　　京都賞
　　　　ローマ大学名誉博士号
　　　　同済大学（上海）名誉教授
- 2003　文化功労者
- 2005　国際建築家連合（UIA）ゴールドメダル
　　　　レジオン・ドヌール勲章（シェバリエ）叙勲（仏）
- 2006　環境保全功労者
- 2010　ジョン・F・ケネディーセンター芸術金賞（米）
　　　　第4回後藤新平賞
　　　　文化勲章
- 2012　リチャード・ノイトラ賞（米）
- 2013　フランス芸術文化勲章（コマンドゥール）叙勲
- 2015　イタリア共和国功労勲章グランデ・ウフィチャーレ章
- 2016　イサム・ノグチ賞（米）

名誉会員：

- 1991　アメリカ建築家協会（AIA）名誉会員
- 1993　イギリス、王立英国建築家協会（RIBA）名誉会員
- 1997　ドイツ建築家協会　名誉会員
- 1998　フランス建築アカデミー　名誉会員
　　　　イギリス、王立スコットランド建築家協会　名誉会員
- 2000　中華民国建築師公会全國聯合会　名誉会員
- 2001　アメリカ芸術文芸アカデミー　名誉会員
- 2002　イギリス、ロイヤルアカデミーオブアーツ　名誉会員
- 2005　社団法人　日本建築家協会　名誉会員

教職、公職：

- 1987　イェール大学客員教授
- 1988　コロンビア大学客員教授
- 1990　ハーバード大学客員教授
- 1995　阪神・淡路震災復興支援10年委員会　実行委員長
- 1997　東京大学教授
- 2003　東京大学名誉教授
- 2005　東京大学特別栄誉教授
　　　　カリフォルニア大学バークレー校　客員教授
- 2011　東日本大震災復興構想会議　議長代理

社会貢献活動：

- 1996　ひょうごグリーンネットワーク　呼びかけ人代表
- 2000　瀬戸内オリーブ基金　呼びかけ人
- 2007　海の森募金　実行委員会　実行委員長
- 2011　桃・柿育英会　東日本大震災遺児育英資金　実行委員長

会議：

- 1982　国際建築会議　シャーロッツビル"P3"カンファレンス、アメリカ
- 1986　国際建築会議　シカゴ"P4"カンファレンス、アメリカ
- 1992　〈Anywhere〉カンファレンス、湯布院、大分
- 1996　日仏文化サミット1996、東京
- 1997　日仏文化サミット1997、パリ
- 1999　ルーブル美術館　公開シンポジウム「日本の建築家と美術館」、パリ
　　　　UIA世界大会、北京
- 2000　UTフォーラム2000 イン・ボストン
- 2003　世界経済フォーラム2003（ダボス会議）

展覧会：

- 1979　ハンガリーの建築家協会の招待で作品展
- 1991　ニューヨーク近代美術館で作品展
- 1992　東京、セゾン美術館、大阪、梅田センタービルで作品展
- 1993　パリ、ポンピドゥーセンターで作品展
　　　　ロンドン、王立英国建築家協会で作品展
- 1994　マドリッド、バルセロナで作品展
- 1994　ヴィチェンツァで作品展（–95）
- 1998　ソウル、韓国国立現代美術館で作品展
　　　　ロンドン、ロイヤルアカデミーオブアーツで作品展
- 1999　ベルリン、ギャラリー・アエデスで作品展
- 2001　セントルイス美術館で作品展
- 2002　米クラーク美術館で作品展（–03）
- 2003　東京ステーションギャラリー、兵庫県立美術館で作品展
- 2005　上海美術館で作品展（–06）
- 2008　東京、ギャラリー間（東京）で作品展
- 2009　大阪、サントリーミュージアムで作品展
- 2017　東京、国立新美術館で作品展

国際設計競技参加：

- 1990　ストックホルム現代美術館・建築美術館（–91）
　　　　JR京都駅改築（–91）
- 1992　奈良市民ホール
- 1994　テートギャラリー現代美術館（–95）
- 1996　ローマ司教区教会
- 1997　フォートワース現代美術館　一等当選
　　　　兵庫県立新美術館　一等当選
- 1999　マンチェスター・ピカデリー広場　再開発計画　一等当選
　　　　ネルソン・アトキンス美術館
　　　　レイナ・ソフィア美術館
　　　　ケ・ブランリー美術館
- 2000　セント・ポール聖台　デザインコンペティション
　　　　アントワープ市立美術館
　　　　カルダー美術館　一等当選
- 2001　ピノー現代美術館　一等当選

Tadao Ando Biography

Awards and Conferments:

- 1979 Annual Prize, Architectural Institute of Japan
  for ROW HOUSE, SUMIYOSHI
- 1985 The 5th Alvar Aalto Medal, The Finnish Association of Architects
- 1989 Gold Medal of Architecture (French Academy of Architecture), France
- 1991 Arnold W. Brunner Memorial Prize, U.S.A.
- 1992 Carlsberg Architectural Prize, Denmark
- 1993 Japan Art Academy Prize
- 1995 The Pritzker Architecture Prize, U.S.A.
  Chevalier de l'Ordre des Arts et des Lettres, France
- 1996 The 8th Praemium Imperiale, in Honor of Prince Takamatsu
  First "FRATE SOLE" Award, Italy
- 1997 Royal Gold Medal, Royal Institute of British Architects, U.K.
  Officier de l'Ordre des Arts et des Lettres, France
- 1998 The 6th Public Building Awards
  for CHIKATSU-ASUKA HISTORICAL MUSEUM, OSAKA
- 2002 Gold Medal of the American Institute of Architects, U.S.A.
  The Kyoto Prizes
  Honorary Degree, Università degli Studi di Roma, Italy
  Honorary Degree, Tongji University, Shanghai, China
- 2003 Person of Cultural Merit, Japan
- 2005 Gold Medal of International Union of Architects
  Chevalier de l'Ordre National de la Légion d'Honneur, France
- 2006 Commendation for Contributions in Environmental Conservation
- 2010 The Kennedy Center International Committee
  on the Arts Gold Medal in the Arts, U.S.A.
  The 4th Goto Shinpei Prize
  The Order of Culture, Japan
- 2012 The 2012 Richard Neutra Award for Professional Excellence, U.S.A.
- 2013 Commandeur de l'Ordre des Arts et des Lettres, France
- 2015 Grande Ufficiale dell'Ordine della Stella d'Italia, Italy
- 2016 Isamu Noguchi Award, U.S.A.

Affiliations:

- 1991 Honorary Fellow, The American Institute of Architects
- 1993 International Fellow, The Royal Institute of British Architects
- 1997 Honorary Membership, German Architects Association
- 1998 Honorary Fellow, French Academy of Architecture
  Honorary Fellowship,
    The Royal Incorporation of Architects in Scotland
- 2000 Honorary Fellow, The National Association of Architects,
    Republic of China (Taiwan)
- 2001 Honorary Membership, The American Academy of Arts and Letters
- 2002 Honorary Academician, The Royal Academy of Arts in London
- 2005 Honorary Member, The Japan Institute of Architects

Academic Activities and Public Positions:

- 1987 Yale University, Visiting Professor
- 1988 Columbia University, Visiting Professor
- 1990 Harvard University, Visiting Professor
- 1995 Hanshin Awaji 10 Year Reconstruction Support Committee, Chair Person
- 1997 The University of Tokyo, Professor
- 2003 The University of Tokyo, Emeritus Professor
- 2005 The University of Tokyo, Special University Professor Emeritus
  University of California, Berkeley, Regent Professor
- 2011 The Reconstruction Design Council in Response to
    the Great East Japan Earthquake, Vice Chairman

Civic Activities:

- 1996 Hyogo Green Network, Campaign Leader
- 2000 Setouchi Olive Foundation, Campaign Leader
- 2007 Umi-no-Mori (Sea Forest) Fund-Raising Campaign, Campaign Leader
- 2011 Momo-Kaki Orphans Fund, Great East Japan Earthquake,
    Committee Chairman

Conferences:

- 1982 International Architectural Conference, Charlottesville, "P3", U.S.A.
- 1986 International Architectural Conference, Chicago, "P4", U.S.A.
- 1992 Anywhere Conference, Yufuin, Oita
- 1996 Sommet Culturel Franco-Japonais 1996, Tokyo
- 1997 Sommet Culturel Franco-Japonais 1997, Paris, France
- 1999 Les Architectes Japonais et le Musée, Le Louvre, Paris, France
  The Scientific Committee of
    The 20th UIA Beijing 1999 Congress, China
- 2000 UT Forum 2000 in Boston, U.S.A.
- 2003 World Economic Forum 2003, Davos, Switzerland

Selected Exhibitions:

- 1979 Magyar Epitömuvészek Szövetségének, Budapest, Hungary
- 1991 The Museum of Modern Art, New York, U.S.A.
- 1992 Sezon Museum of Art, Tokyo and Umeda Center Building, Osaka
- 1993 Centre Georges Pompidou, Paris, France
  The Royal Institute of British Architects, London, U.K.
- 1994 Expo MOPT, Madrid, Fundació «la Caixa»,
  Centre Cultural, Barcelona, Spain
- 1994 The Basilica Palladiana, Vicenza, Italy (–95)
- 1998 National Museum of Contemporary Art, Korea, Seoul, Korea
  Royal Academy of Arts, London, U.K.
- 1999 Galerie Aedes Est, Berlin, Germany
- 2001 Saint Louis Art Museum, St. Louis, U.S.A.
- 2002 Clark Art Institute, Williamstown, U.S.A. (–03)
- 2003 Tokyo Station Gallery, and Hyogo Prefectural Museum of Art
- 2005 Shanghai Art Museum, Shanghai, China (–06)
- 2008 TOTO GALLERY-MA, Tokyo
- 2009 Suntory Museum, Osaka
- 2017 The National Art Center, Tokyo

Competitions:

- 1990 The Art Museum in Stockholm, Sweden (–91)
  The Reconstruction of JR Kyoto Station (–91)
- 1992 Nara City Hall, Nara
- 1994 Tate Gallery of Modern Art, London, U.K. (–95)
- 1996 The Church of the Year 2000, Vicariato di Roma, Italy
- 1997 Modern Art Museum of Fort Worth, U.S.A.
  Hyogo Prefectural Museum of Modern Art, Kobe
- 1999 Manchester City Centre Piccadilly Gardens Regeneration, U.K.
  Nelson Atkins Museum of Art, Kansas City, U.S.A.
  Museo Nacional Centro de Arte Reina Sofia, Madrid, Spain
  Musée du Quai Branly, Paris, France
- 2000 A New Font for St. Paul's Cathedral, London, U.K.
  Museum aan de Stroom, Antwerpen, Belgium
  Calder Museum, Philadelphia, U.S.A.
- 2001 Fondation d'Art Contemporain François Pinault,
  Île Seguin, Boulogne-Billancourt, France

書誌 / Bibliography

主な著書:

旅（住まい学大系020）　住まいの図書館出版局
安藤忠雄の都市彷徨　マガジンハウス
家（住まい学大系076）　住まいの図書館出版局
安藤忠雄　建築を語る　東京大学出版会
安藤忠雄　連戦連敗　東京大学出版会
建築に夢をみた　日本放送出版協会
ル・コルビュジェの勇気ある住宅　新潮社
安藤忠雄　建築手法　A.D.A. EDITA Tokyo
建築家　安藤忠雄　新潮社
安藤忠雄　住宅　A.D.A. EDITA Tokyo
安藤忠雄　都市と自然　A.D.A. EDITA Tokyo
私の履歴書　仕事をつくる　日本経済新聞出版社
TADAO ANDO Insight Guide　安藤忠雄とその記憶　講談社ビーシー

主な作品集:

現代の建築家――安藤忠雄　鹿島出版会
GA ARCHITECT 8 TADAO ANDO　A.D.A. EDITA Tokyo
現代の建築家 II――安藤忠雄　鹿島出版会
The Japan Architect 1――TADAO ANDO　新建築社
TADAO ANDO DETAILS　A.D.A. EDITA Tokyo
GA ARCHITECT 12 TADAO ANDO Vol.2　A.D.A. EDITA Tokyo
現代の建築家 III――安藤忠雄　鹿島出版会
TADAO ANDO COMPLETE WORKS, PHAIDON PRESS LIMITED, London
TADAO ANDO DETAILS 2　A.D.A. EDITA Tokyo
淡路夢舞台　千年庭園の記録　新建築社
GA ARCHITECT 16 TADAO ANDO Vol.3　A.D.A. EDITA Tokyo
a+u / Architecture and Urbanism No.378　A+U Publishing
安藤忠雄建築展2003　再生――環境と建築　デルファイ研究所
TADAO ANDO DETAILS 3　A.D.A. EDITA Tokyo
Tadao Ando Light and Water　The Monacelli Press, New York
TADAO ANDO Complete Works　TASCHEN GmbH, Köln
安藤忠雄の建築　1 Houses & Housing　TOTO出版
悪戦苦闘 2006年の現場――21_21 DESIGN SIGHT
　安藤忠雄建築展実行委員会
TADAO ANDO DETAILS 4　A.D.A. EDITA Tokyo
安藤忠雄　ヒューマンスペースの幾何学　TASCHEN GmbH, Köln
安藤忠雄の建築　2 Outside Japan　TOTO出版
安藤忠雄の建築　3 Inside Japan　TOTO出版
Tadao Ando Museums　Skira editore S.p.A., Milan
TADAO ANDO Recent Project　A.D.A. EDITA Tokyo
安藤忠雄の建築　0 Process and Idea　TOTO出版
Tadao Ando 1995–2010　Prestel Verlag, Munich
GA ARCHITECT TADAO ANDO Vol.4 2001–2007
　A.D.A. EDITA Tokyo
TADAO ANDO Recent Project 2　A.D.A. EDITA Tokyo
安藤忠雄の建築　4 New Endeavors　TOTO出版
GA ARCHITECT TADAO ANDO Vol.5 2008–2015　A.D.A. EDITA Tokyo

安藤忠雄論:

挑発する箱　吉増剛造／藤原新也／唐十郎　丸善
壁の探求　古山正雄　鹿島出版会
アンドウ　安藤忠雄・建築家の発想と仕事　松葉一清　講談社
Ando, Architect　松葉一清　講談社インターナショナル（英語）
安藤忠雄　野獣の肖像　古山正雄　新潮社

Major Publications:

Tabi (Sumaigaku Taikei 020), SUMAI Library Publishing Company
Ando Tadao no Toshi Hoko, Magazine House
Ie (Sumaigaku Taikei 076), SUMAI Library Publishing Company
Ando Tadao Kenchiku wo Kataru, University of Tokyo Press
Ando Tadao Rensen Renpai, University of Tokyo Press
Kenchiku ni Yume wo Mita, Japan Broadcast Publishing
Le Corbusier no Yuki aru Jutaku, Shinchosha Publishing
Ando Tadao Kenchiku Shuho, A.D.A. EDITA Tokyo
Kenchikuka Ando Tadao, Shinchosha Publishing
Ando Tadao Jutaku, A.D.A. EDITA Tokyo
Ando Tadao Toshi to Shizen, A.D.A. EDITA Tokyo
Watashi no Rirekisho Shigoto wo Tsukuru, Nikkei Publishing Inc.
TADAO ANDO Insight Guide Ando Tadao to Sono Kioku, KODANSHA BC

Major Collections of Works:

Gendai no Kenchikuka- Ando Tadao, Kajima Institute Publishing
GA ARCHITECT 8 TADAO ANDO, A.D.A. EDITA Tokyo
Gendai no Kenchikuka II — Ando Tadao, Kajima Institute Publishing
The Japan Architect 1 — TADAO ANDO, Shinkenchiku-sha
TADAO ANDO DETAILS, A.D.A. EDITA Tokyo
GA ARCHITECT 12 TADAO ANDO Vol.2, A.D.A. EDITA Tokyo
Gendai no Kenchikuka III — Ando Tadao, Kajima Institute Publishing
TADAO ANDO COMPLETE WORKS, PHAIDON PRESS LIMITED, London
TADAO ANDO DETAILS 2, A.D.A. EDITA Tokyo
Awaji Yumebutai Sennen Teien no Kiroku, Shinkenchiku-sha
GA ARCHITECT 16 TADAO ANDO Vol.3, A.D.A. EDITA Tokyo
a+u / Architecture and Urbanism No.378, A+U Publishing
TADAO ANDO Regeneration — Surroundings and Architecture,
　Ando Tadao Kenchikuten 2003, Delphi Lab, Inc.
TADAO ANDO DETAILS 3, A.D.A. EDITA Tokyo
Tadao Ando Light and Water, The Monacelli Press, New York
TADAO ANDO Complete Works, TASCHEN GmbH, Köln
Ando Tadao no Kenchiku 1 Houses & Housing, TOTO Publishing
Akusenkuto 2006 Nen no Genba—21_21 DESIGN SIGHT,
　Ando Tadao Architectural Exhibition Executive Committee
TADAO ANDO DETAILS 4, A.D.A. EDITA Tokyo
Ando Tadao Human Space no Kikagaku, TASCHEN GmbH, Köln
Ando Tadao no Kenchiku 2 Outside Japan, TOTO Publishing
Ando Tadao no Kenchiku 3 Inside Japan, TOTO Publishing
Tadao Ando Museums, Skira editore S.p.A., Milan
TADAO ANDO Recent Project, A.D.A. EDITA Tokyo
Ando Tadao no Kenchiku 0 Process and Idea, TOTO Publishing
Tadao Ando 1995–2010, Prestel Verlag, Munich
GA ARCHITECT TADAO ANDO Vol.4 2001–2007, A.D.A. EDITA Tokyo
TADAO ANDO Recent Project 2, A.D.A. EDITA Tokyo
Ando Tadao no Kenchiku 4 New Endeavors, TOTO Publishing
GA ARCHITECT TADAO ANDO Vol.5 2008–2015, A.D.A. EDITA Tokyo

Discussions on Tadao Ando:

Chohatsu Suru Hako; Gozo Yoshimasu, Shinya Fujiwara, and Juro Kara,
　MaruzenJunkudo Bookstores
Kabe no Tankyu; Masao Furuyama, Kajima Institute Publishing
ANDO, Ando Tadao, Kenchikuka no Hasso to Shigoto; Kazukiyo Matsuba,
　Kodansha
Ando, architect; Kazukiyo Matsuba, Kodansha (in English)
Ando Tadao, Yaju no Shozo; Masao Furuyama, Shinchosha Publishing

索引

Index of Works

索引

[000] | 全作品録の作品番号
000 | 掲載ページ

あ：

アートギャラリー・コンプレックス［024］	253
アウディジャパン本社ビル［211］	376
青葉台アトリエ［067］	278
赤羽邸［048］	267
秋田県立美術館［295］	436
浅草の住宅［340］	463
アサヒビール神奈川工場ゲストハウス［210］	376
芦屋の住宅［304］	441
亜洲大学 亜洲現代美術館［302］	440
あてま森と水辺の教室〈森のホール〉〈水辺のホール〉［282］	425
アトリエ・ヨシエ・イナバ［065］	277
アブダビ海洋博物館［245］	400
綾部工業団地交流プラザ［152］	335
アルマーニ・テアトロ［202］	369
淡路夢舞台［181］	175, 183, 354, 468
安藤忠雄建築展／Palladian Basilica［147］	331
アントワープ市立博物館国際設計競技案［192］	361

い：

石井邸［045］	265
石河邸［115］	307
石原邸［284］	426
伊豆プロジェクト［090］	291
伊東邸［109］	303
岩佐邸［059］	273

う：

ヴァルスの広場［334］	460
ヴィトラ・セミナーハウス［134］	103, 321
ヴィラ・ブダペスト（旧首相公邸改造計画）［264］	413
植条邸［056］	270
上田邸［032］	257
内田邸［009］	244
靱公園の住宅［279］	057, 423
宇野邸［010］	245
海の集合住宅［157］	338
海の森［253］	020, 205, 405
うめきた広場［303］	441
梅宮邸［052］	269

え：

絵本美術館［225］	387
エリエール松山ゲストハウス［176］	350

お：

老木レディスクリニック［298］	438
青木の集合住宅［171］	347
大楠邸［027］	254
大阪商工信用金庫 新本社ビル［328］	457
大阪府立狭山池博物館［195］	149, 363
大阪府立近つ飛鳥博物館［140］	018, 141, 325
太田邸［057］	272
大谷地下劇場計画［158］	339
大手前大学アートセンター［123］	312
大西邸［030］	256
大山崎山荘美術館［149］	332
大淀のアトリエ［040］	262
大淀のアトリエⅡ［119］	309
大淀のアトリエ・アネックス［156］	338
大淀の茶室（ベニヤ、ブロック、テント）［069］	279
震旦美術館［297］	438
丘の集合住宅［159］	340
岡本ハウジング［019］	125, 250
おかやま信用金庫内山下スクエア［306］	442
沖辺邸［075］	283
小倉邸［095］	295
織田廣喜ミュージアム［178］	352
越知町立横倉山自然の森博物館［168］	346
尾道市立美術館［215］	379
表参道ヒルズ［236］	014, 087, 393

か：

回遊式住宅［234］	392
加賀市立錦城中学校［212］	377
鹿児島大学稲盛会館［143］	327
加子母ふれあいコミュニティセンター［226］	387
片山ハウス［029］	255
金子邸［054］	270
カペラ・ニセコ・リゾートホテル［263］	413
かほく市立金澤小学校［153］	335
上方落語協会会館［300］	439
唐座［086］	289
ガラスブロックウォール――堀内邸［028］	255
ガラスブロックの家――石原邸［026］	254
臥龍山安養院増築計画［339］	463
カルダー美術館［194］	362
カルロス・プレイス「サイレンス」［290］	432
元祖夢世界［332］	459
貫入――平林邸［016］	043, 249

き：

北菓楼札幌本館［325］	456
北野アイビーコート［035］	065, 258
北野アレイ［023］	065, 227, 252
北ヨーロッパの住宅［271］	418
城戸崎邸［072］	014, 053, 281
希望の壁［310］	446
ギャラリー小さい芽（澤田邸）［163］	342
ギャラリー野田［138］	323
京都府立陶板名画の庭［141］	326

く：

九条の町屋――井筒邸［047］	129, 266
熊本県立装飾古墳館［127］	141, 316
クラーク美術館／クラークセンター［312］	124, 447, 468
クラーク美術館／ランダーセンター［255］	124, 406, 468
グラウンド・ゼロ・プロジェクト［204］	371

け：

ゲストハウスOLD／NEW六甲［081］	286
ケ・ブランリー美術館国際設計競技案［187］	357
ゲリラ――加藤邸［003］	027, 241
県立ぐんま昆虫の森 昆虫観察館［220］	382

こ：

甲東アレイ［025］	253
甲南大学スチューデントナークル プロジェクト［122］	312
小海高原美術館［172］	348
ゴールデン・ゲート・ブリッジの住宅［229］	389
コキュ・オフィスビル［214］	378
国際芸術センター青森［201］	368
国際花と緑の博覧会「名画の庭」［110］	304
国立国会図書館 国際子ども図書館（レンガ棟）［207］	018, 373
国立国会図書館 国際子ども図書館アーチ棟［324］	455
小篠邸、小篠邸増築［038］	014, 049, 161, 260, 261, 468
小篠邸ゲストハウス［240］	396
児島の共同住宅――佐藤邸［041］	263

さ：

細工谷の家――野口邸［082］	287
済州島〈石の門〉〈風の門〉［261］	411
坂の上の雲ミュージアム［235］	392
さくら広場［241］	203, 397
佐々木邸［077］	284
佐渡邸［305］	442
砂漠の家・乗馬施設［216］	379
佐用ハウジング［116］	307
サントリーミュージアム＋マーメイド広場［139］	195, 324
サンプレイス［044］	075, 264

し：

シカゴの住宅［167］	345
シカゴ美術館屏風ギャラリー［126］	315
滋賀の住宅［237］	394
四国村ギャラリー［199］	367
芝田邸［008］	244
司馬遼太郎記念館［198］	153, 366
渋谷神社総合開発計画［083］	287
渋谷プロジェクト［071］	101, 280

シャトー・ラ・コスト	115, 428	ち：		の：		ベネッセハウス ミュージアム［125］
アートセンター［287］		地中美術館［223］	097, 385, 468	ノバルティス研究施設棟［275］	420	093, 314, 468
チャペル［287］		チャスカ茶屋町［281］	425	野間自由幼稚園［217］	380	
4 グラス・キューブス・パビリオン［287］		中国太湖博物館［286］	427			ほ：
上海建築文化センター［272］	419			は：		ボスコ・スタジオ＆ハウス［316］ 451
上海デザインセンター［277］	422	つ：		バーレーン考古博物館［250］	403	ポズナニ美術館［252］ 404
上海保利大劇場［313］	014, 233, 448, 468	ツインウォール［013］	247	畑邸［062］	275	ボローニャ ISA［330］ 458
十文字美信仮設劇場［113］	305			服部邸ゲストハウス［070］	280	ポンテ・ミュージアム［296］ 437
ジュン・ポートアイランドビル［063］	275	て：		パラッツォ・グラッシ［242］	107, 398	ホンブロイッヒ／ランゲン美術館［221］
白井邸［162］	342	テアトリーノ［308］	107, 444	播磨高原東小学校、播磨高原東中学校［148］		103, 383, 468
市立五條文化博物館［150］	333	テートギャラリー現代美術館			331	
城尾邸［106］	302	国際設計競技案［155］	018, 337	韓屋のゲストハウス［291］	432	ま：
新華紅星国際広場［341］	464	帝塚山タワープラザ［018］	043, 227, 250	半山半島美術館＋劇場センター［274］	420	真駒内滝野霊園 頭大仏［322］ 454
神宮前の集合住宅［200］	367	帝塚山の家──真鍋邸［021］	251	番匠邸［017］	035, 249	マックスレイ本社ビル［142］ 326
真言宗本福寺水御堂［120］	171, 310	デミアン・ハースト・スタジオ［247］	401	番匠邸増築［042］	263	松谷邸［031］ 256
		デュベティカ ミラノ ショップ		ハンファHRDセンター［260］	411	松村邸［011］ 245
す：		同 ショールーム［315］	450			松本邸［034］ 258
スタジオ・カール・ラガーフェルド［165］		天王寺公園植物温室		ひ：		マリブの住宅［219］ 382
	107, 343	（天王寺博覧会テーマ館）［087］	290	光の教会［102］	014, 165, 299, 468	マリブの住宅 I［317］ 451
ストーン・スカルプチュア・ミュージアム［276］				光の教会／日曜学校［182］	355	マリブの住宅 III［293］ 434
	115, 421	と：		光の美術館［285］	427	マンガロールの住宅［301］ 440
ストックホルム現代美術館・建築美術館		東急大井町線上野毛駅［289］	431	ピノー現代美術館［203］	107, 370, 468	マンチェスター市ピカデリー公園［209］ 375
国際設計競技案［112］	305	東急東横線渋谷駅［258］	014, 409	姫路市立星の子館［129］	317	マンハッタンの集合住宅［336］ 461
寿長生の郷 点心庵［338］	462	東京大学 建築資料館［251］	404	姫路文学館［114］	306	マンハッタンのペントハウス［166］ 344
住吉の長屋──東邸［015］		東京大学情報学環・福武ホール［259］	410	姫路文学館 南館［160］	340	マンハッタンのペントハウス II［254］ 405
	008, 029, 063, 091, 129, 173, 207,	ドールズハウス［049］	267	ピューリッツァー美術館［196］		マンハッタンのペントハウス III［335］ 461
	248, 468	都市の大樹［311］	446		119, 364, 468	
スリランカの住宅［256］	014, 407	冨島邸［005］	029, 242	兵庫県木の殿堂［144］	179, 328	み：
スワン商会ビル──小林邸［002］	240	十和田市教育プラザ［320］	453	兵庫県立大学看護学部・看護研究科［132］		見えない家［222］ 384
					319	三河田原駅［321］ 453
せ：		な：		兵庫県立こどもの館［103］	300, 468	水の教会［093］ 159, 293
聖心女子学院 創立100周年記念ホール［257］		中之島児童文学館プロジェクト［346］	466	兵庫県立美術館＋神戸市水際広場［197］		水の劇場［088］ 290
	408	中之島プロジェクト I（大阪市役所）［037］			103, 197, 365	南寺（直島・家プロジェクト）［184］
セーヌ川橋国際設計競技案［179］	352		018, 201, 259	兵庫県立美術館増築計画［345］	466	097, 356
仙川・安藤ストリート［224］	018, 386	中之島プロジェクト II		平岡邸［006］	243	南林邸［060］ 273
1992年セビリア万国博覧会日本館［124］		（アーバン・エッグ＋地層空間）［099］		平野区の町屋──能見邸［161］	341	ミノルタセミナーハウス［118］ 309
	097, 313, 468		018, 201, 297	広尾の教会［314］	169, 449	みやこ町立伊良原小学校
セント・ポール寺院聖台		中山邸［064］	276			みやこ町立伊良原中学校［323］ 455
デザインコンペティション［193］	362	名古屋の住宅［283］	426	ふ：		宮下邸［128］ 317
		灘浜ガーデンバーデン［213］	378	ファッション・ライブ・シアター［043］	264	ミュージアム SAN［292］ 433
そ：		夏川記念会館［105］	301	フェスティバル［055］	077, 271, 468	ミュゼふくおかカメラ館［191］ 360
双生観──山口邸［012］	043, 246	奈良市民ホール国際設計競技案［130］	318	フォートワース現代美術館［208］		
双生観の茶室──山口邸増築［046］	265	南岳山光明寺［189］	175, 359		103, 119, 374, 468	む：
曹洞宗太岳院［249］	403			フォートワース現代美術館増築計画［343］		ムンク美術館国際設計競技［270］ 418
孫邸［076］	283	に：			465	
		新潟市立豊栄図書館［190］	360	福邸［036］	259	も：
た：		西田幾多郎記念哲学館［206］	179, 372	福原病院［073］	282	茂木邸［053］ 270
ダイコク電機本部ビル［174］	349	西宮市貝類館［183］	355	ブルス・ドゥ・コメルス［342］	018, 464	元麻布の住宅［326］ 456
太陽セメント本社ビル［078］	284	日本橋の家──金森邸［146］	330	プンタ・デラ・ドガーナ［266］		森の教会［230］ 390
高槻の住宅［232］	391	俄本社ビル［269］	417		018, 107, 415, 468	森の教会［319］ 452
高梁市成羽美術館［145］	329					森の中の家 安野光雅館［327］ 457
高橋邸［004］	241	ね：		へ：		森の霊園・水の納骨堂［329］ 458
高松の住宅［299］	439	ネパール子供病院［177］	351	北京紅楼夢ホテル［273］	419	モロゾフP&Pスタジオ［101］ 298
立見邸［007］	043, 243	ネルソン・アトキンス美術館		北京国子監ホテル＋美術館［262］	412	モンテレイ大学RGSセンター［294］
田中山荘［085］	288	国際設計競技案［186］	357	ベネッセハウス オーバル［151］	097, 334	014, 435
谷間の家［246］	401			ベネッセハウス パーク／ビーチ［239］	395	モンテレイの住宅［288］ 014, 430
垂水の教会［136］	322					モン・プティ・シュ［066］ 277

Index of Works　475

や：	
矢尾クリニック［107］	302
八木邸［170］	347
ゆ：	
游庵［243］	399
ユネスコ瞑想空間［154］	101, 179, 336, 468
よ：	
横浜地方気象台［268］	417
吉田邸［097］	296
吉本邸［068］	278
四軒長屋［014］	247
ら：	
ライカ本社ビル［104］	301
ライトウッド ギャラリー［333］	460
ライン世界文化博物館［173］	348
り：	
李禹煥美術館［280］	101, 424
李邸［137］	323
竜王駅＋南北駅前広場［278］	422
良渚村文化芸術センター［318］	452
領壁の家——松本邸［022］	252
リランズゲート［074］	282
リンズギャラリー［039］	065, 261
れ：	
レイナ・ソフィア美術館国際設計競技案［185］	356
ろ：	
ローズガーデン［020］	012, 061, 207, 251, 468
ローマ司教区教会国際設計競技案［164］	343
ロックフィールド神戸ヘッドオフィス／神戸ファクトリー［231］	207, 390
ロックフィールド静岡ファクトリー［117］	207, 308
六甲アイランドプロジェクト［131］	318
六甲の教会［079］	157, 209, 285
六甲の集合住宅 I［050］	018, 125, 268, 468
六甲の集合住宅 II［133］	016, 131, 187, 320
六甲の集合住宅 III［180］	133, 353
六甲プロジェクト IV［265］	135, 414
六甲山バンケットホール［089］	291
わ：	
渡辺淳一記念館［175］	349
和美術館［337］	462
a–z：	
ANDO MUSEUM［309］	101, 445
BIGI青葉台［344］	465
BIGIアトリエ［051］	269
BIGI 3rd［084］	288
B-LOCK神楽岡［096］	295
B-LOCK北山［108］	303
COLLEZIONE［100］	087, 298
FABRICA（ベネトンアートスクール）［188］	097, 103, 358
GALLERIA［akka］［094］	087, 294
GENESIS MUSEUM［331］	459
hhstyle.com/casa［233］	391
I ギャラリー［098］	296
I ハウス［092］	292
I プロジェクト［091］	292
ICED TIME TUNNEL／THE SNOW SHOW 2004［228］	389
IPU環太平洋大学［267］	416
JCCクリエイティブセンター／JCCアートセンター［307］	443
JR大阪駅前プロジェクト'69［001］	240
JR京都駅改築設計競技案［121］	311
MELROSE［058］	272
morimoto nyc（モリモト・ニューヨーク）［238］	395
S ビル［111］	304
STEP［033］	014, 071, 257, 468
TIME'S I, II［061］	014, 081, 274, 468
TOTOセミナーハウス［169］	346
TS ビル［080］	286
YKK津田沼寮［135］	322
0–9：	
2004 サイトウ・キネン・フェスティバル松本・オペラ「ヴォツェック」舞台構成［227］	388
2016年東京オリンピック構想［244］	399
21_21 デザインサイト［248］	402
4×4の住宅［218］	057, 381
4×4の住宅（東京）［205］	372

Index of Works

[000] | Work Number
000 | Page Number

A:

A New Font for St. Paul's Cathedral, International Design Competiton [193] 362
Abu Dhabi Maritime Museum [245] 400
Akabane House [048] 267
Akita Museum of Art [295] 436
Ando Museum [309] 100, 445
Anno Mitsumasa Museum [327] 457
Aobadai Atelier [067] 278
Aomori Contemporary Art Center [201] 368
Architecture and Culture Center, Shanghai [272] 419
Architecture Reference Library, The University of Tokyo [251] 404
Armani Teatro [202] 369
Art Gallery Complex [024] 253
Art Stations Poznan [252] 404
Asia Museum of Modern Art, Asia University [302] 440
Atelier in Oyodo [040] 262
Atelier in Oyodo Annex [156] 338
Atelier in Oyodo II [119] 309
Atelier Yoshie Inaba [065] 277
Atema Project ‹Forest Hall› ‹Waterside Hall› [282] 425
Audi Japan Headquarters [211] 376
Aurora Museum [297] 438
Awaji-Yumebutai [181] 174, 184, 354, 469
Ayabe Community Center [152] 335

B:

Bahrain Archeological Museum [250] 403
Banquet Hall on Mt. Rokko [089] 291
Bansho House [017] 036, 249
Bansho House Addition [042] 263
Beijing Guozijian Hotel [262] 412
Benesse House Museum [125] 096, 314, 469
Benesse House Oval [151] 096, 334
Benesse House Park, Beach [239] 395
BIGI 3rd [084] 288
BIGI Aobadai [344] 465
BIGI Atelier [051] 269
B-Lock Kaguraoka [096] 295
B-Lock Kitayama [108] 303
Bologna ISA [330] 458
Bonte Museum [296] 437
Bosco Studio & House [316] 451
Bourse de Commerce [342] 021, 464

C:

Calder Museum [194] 362
Capella Niseko Resort & Residence [263] 413
Carlos Place "Silence" [290] 432
Chapel in The Woods [230] 390
Chapel on Mt. Rokko [079] 158, 285
Chaska Chayamachi [281] 425
Château La Coste 114, 428
  Art Center [287]
  Chapel [287]
  Four Glass Cubes Pavilion [287]
Chichu Art Museum [223] 100, 385, 469
Chikatsu-Asuka Historical Museum, Osaka [140] 019, 140, 325
Children's Museum, Hyogo [103] 300, 469
Children's Seminar House, Himeji [129] 317
China Taihu Museum, Suzhou [286] 427
Church in Hiroo [314] 168, 449
Church in Tarumi [136] 322
Church in the Forest [319] 452
Church of the Light [102] 015, 166, 299, 469
Church of the Light, Sunday School [182] 355
Church on the Water [093] 162, 293
Clark Art Institute / Clark Center [312] 120, 447, 469
Clark Art Institute / Lunder Center at Stone Hill [255] 120, 406, 469
Cocue Office Building [214] 378
College of Nursing, Art and Science, University of Hyogo [132] 319
Collezione [100] 088, 298
Condominium in Manhattan [336] 461
Crevice House in Manhattan [246] 401

D:

Daikoku Denki Headquarters Building [174] 349
Damien Hirst Studio [247] 401
Daylight Museum [178] 352
Doll's House [049] 267
Duvetica Milano Shop
Duvetica Milano Showroom [315] 450

E:

Elleair Matsuyama Guesthouse [176] 350

F:

Fabrica (Benetton Communication Research Center) [188] 102, 358
Fashion Live Theater [043] 264
Festival [055] 076, 271, 469
François Pinault Foundation for Contemporary Art [203] 108, 370, 469
Fuku House [036] 259
Fukuhara Clinic [073] 282
Fukuoka Camera Museum [191] 360

G:

Galleria [akka] [094] 088, 294
Gallery Chiisaime — Sawada House [163] 342
Gallery for Japanese Screen, The Art Institute of Chicago [126] 315
Gallery Noda [138] 323
Ganso Dream World [332] 459
Garden of Fine Art, Expo'90 / Osaka [110] 304
Garden of Fine Art, Kyoto [141] 326
Garyozan Anyoin Temple [339] 463
Gate of Stone And Gate of Wind in Jeju Island [261] 411
Genesis Museum [331] 459
Glass Block House — Ishihara House [026] 254
Glass Block Wall — Horiuchi House [028] 255
Golden Gate Bridge House [229] 389
Ground Zero Project [204] 371
Guerrilla — Kato House [003] 030, 241
Guest House for Hattori House [070] 280
Guest House for Koshino House [240] 396
Guest House Old / New Rokko [081] 286
Guesthouse, Asahi Kanagawa Brewery [210] 376
Gunma Insect World / Insect Observation Hall [220] 382

H:

Hanwha HRD Center [260] 411
Harima Kogen Higashi Primary School
Harima Kogen Higashi Junior High School [148] 331
Hata House [062] 275
He Art Museum [337] 462
hhstyle.com/casa [233] 391
Hill of the Buddha [322] 454
Hilltop Housing [159] 340
Hiraoka House [006] 243
Hong Lou Meng Hotel [273] 419
House & Stable for Tom Ford and Richard Buckley [216] 379
House in Asakusa [340] 463
House in Ashiya [304] 441
House in Chicago [167] 345
House in Malibu [219] 382
House in Malibu I [317] 451
House in Malibu III [293] 434
House in Mangalore [301] 440
House in Monterrey [288] 015, 430
House In Motoazabu [326] 456
House in Nagoya [283] 426
House in Nipponbashi — Kanamori House [146] 330
House in Northern Europe [271] 418
House in Shiga [237] 394

House in Northern Europe [271] 418	Kitano Alley [023] 064, 227, 252	Museum Aan De Stroom, Antwerp, International Design Competition [192] 361	Passerelle De Bercy-Tolbiac, International Design Competition [179] 352
House in Shiga [237] 394	Kitano Ivy Court [035] 064, 258		
House in Sri Lanka [256] 015, 407	Kojima Housing—Sato House [041] 263	Museum of Gojo Culture [150] 333	Penthouse in Manhattan [166] 344
House in Takamatsu [299] 439	Komyo-Ji Temple [189] 176, 359	Museum of Light [285] 427	Penthouse in Manhattan II [254] 405
House In Takatsuki [232] 391	Konan University Student Circle Project [122] 312	Museum of Literature south annex, Himeji [160] 340	Penthouse in Manhattan III [335] 461
House in Utsubo Park [279] 056, 423			Piccadilly Gardens Regeneration, Manchester [209] 375
House with "Hanok" [291] 432	Koshino House	Museum of Literature, Himeji [114] 306	
Hyogo Prefectural Museum of Art Expansion Project [345] 466	Koshino House Addition [038] 015, 052, 260, 261, 469	Museum of Wood [144] 176, 328	Pulitzer Foundation for the Arts [196] 118, 364, 469
	Koto Alley [025] 253	Museum SAN [292] 433	
Hyogo Prefectural Museum of Art + Kobe Waterfront Plaza [197] 102, 196, 365	Koumi Kogen Museum [172] 348		Punta Della Dogana Contemporary Art Center [266] 019, 110, 415, 469
	Kumamoto Prefectural Ancient Burial Mound Museum [127] 140, 316	**N:**	
		Nadahama Garden Baden [213] 378	
I:		Nakanoshima Children's Library Project [346] 466	**R:**
I Gallery [098] 296			Raika Headquarters Building [104] 301
I House [092] 292	**L:**	Nakanoshima Project I [037] 019, 200, 259	Rin's Gallery [039] 064, 261
I Project [091] 292	Langen Foundation / Hombroich [221] 102, 383, 469		Riran's Gate [074] 282
Iced Time Tunnel / The Snow Show 2004 [228] 389	Lee House [137] 323	Nakanoshima Project II (Urban Egg Space Strata) [099] 019, 200, 297	Roberto Garza Sada Center for Arts, Architecture and Design [294] 015, 435
Inamori Auditorium [143] 327	Lee Ufan Museum [280] 100, 424		
Interfaculty Initiative in Information Studies Fukutake Hall, The University of Tokyo [259] 410	Liangzhu Village Cultural Art Center [318] 452	Nakayama House [064] 276	Rockfield Kobe Headquarters / Kobe Factory [231] 206, 390
		Nara Convention Hall, International Design Competition [130] 318	
	M:		Rockfield Shizuoka Factory [117] 206, 308
International Pacific University [267] 416	Matsumoto House [034] 258	Nariwa Museum [145] 329	Rokko Housing I [050] 019, 126, 186, 268, 469
Interpenetration—Hirabayashi House [016] 044, 249	Matsumura House [011] 245	Natsukawa Memorial Hall [105] 301	
	Matsutani House [031] 256	Nelson Atkins Museum, International Design Competition [186] 357	Rokko Housing II [133] 017, 130, 320
Invisible House [222] 384	Maxray Headquarters Building [142] 326		Rokko Housing III [180] 132, 353
Ishihara House [284] 426	Meditation Space, UNESCO [154] 100, 178, 336, 469		Rokko Island Project [131] 318
Ishii House [045] 265		Niigata City Toyosaka Library [190] 360	Rokko Project IV [265] 134, 414
Ishiko House [115] 307	Melrose [058] 272	Nishida Kitaro Museum of Philosophy [206] 178, 372	Rose Garden [020] 013, 060, 206, 251, 469
Ito House [109] 303	Mikawatahara Station [321] 453		
Iwaki Museum of Picture Books for Children [225] 387	Minamibayashi House [060] 273	Niwaka Headquarters Building [269] 417	Row House, Sumiyoshi —Azuma House [015] 009, 030, 092, 130, 206, 248, 469
	Minamidera (Art House Project in Naoshima) [184] 096, 356	Noma Kindergarten [217] 380	
Iwasa House [059] 273		Novartis WSJ-352 [275] 420	
Izu Project [090] 291			Ryuo Station + Station Square [278] 422
	Minolta Seminar House [118] 309	**O:**	
J:	Miyako Town Irahara Elementary and Junior High School [323] 455	Ogi Housing [171] 347	**S:**
Japan Pavilion, Expo'92 / Seville [124] 100, 313, 469		Ogura House [095] 295	S Building [111] 304
		Oiki Ladies Clinic [298] 438	Sacred Heart School, 100th Anniversary Hall [257] 408
JCC Creative Center	Miyashita House [128] 317	Okamoto Housing Project [019] 126, 250	
JCC Art Center [307] 443	Modern Art Museum of Fort Worth [208] 102, 118, 374, 469	Okayama Shinkin Bank Uchisange Square [306] 442	Sado House [305] 442
Jingumae Housing [200] 367			Saka No Ue No Kumo Museum [235] 392
JR Osaka Station Area Reconstruction Project [001] 240	Modern Art Museum of Fort Worth Expansion Project [343] 465	Okibe House [075] 283	Sakura Hiroba [241] 202, 397
		Okusu House [027] 254	Sasaki House [077] 284
Jun Port Island Building [063] 275	Mon-Petit-Chou [066] 277	Omotesando Hills [236] 015, 088, 393	Sayamaike Historical Museum, Osaka [195] 148, 363
Junichi Watanabe Memorial Hall [175] 349	Morimoto NYC [238] 395	Onishi House [030] 256	
	Morozoff P&P Studio [101] 298	Onomichi City Museum of Art [215] 379	Sayo Housing [116] 307
K:	Motegi House [053] 270	Osaka Shoko Shinkin Bank [328] 457	Sea Forest [253] 021, 204, 405
Kamigata Rakugo House [300] 439	Munch Museum and Stenersen Museum Collections [270] 418	Ota House [057] 272	Seaside Housing [157] 338
Kanadu Primary School, Kahoku [153] 335		Otemae Art Center [123] 312	Sengawa, Ando Street [224] 019, 386
Kaneko House [054] 270	Musée Du Quai Branly, International Design Competiton [187] 357	Oyamazaki Villa Museum [149] 332	Serenity Coast Art Museum + Performing Arts Center [274] 420
Kara-Za [086] 289			
Kashimo Community Center [226] 387	Museo Nacional Centro De Arte Reina Sofia, International Design Competition [185] 356	**P:**	Set Design for 2004 Saito Kinen Festival Matsumoto / Opera "Wozzeck" [227] 388
Katayama Building [029] 255		Palazzo Grassi [242] 108, 398	
Kidosaki House [072] 015, 052, 281			Shanghai Design Center [277] 422
Kinjo Junior High School, Kaga [212] 377			
Kitakaro Sapporo Honkan [325] 456			

索引　478

Shanghai Poly Theater [313]
                               015, 233, 448, 469
Shell Museum of Nishinomiya City [183]   355
Shiba Ryotaro Memorial Museum [198]
                                     152, 366
Shibata House [008]   244
Shibuya Project [071]   280
Shibuya Shrine Redevelopment Project [083]   287
Shiddhartha Children and Women Hospital [177]   351
Shikokumura Gallery [199]   367
Shirai House [162]   342
Shiroo House [106]   302
Son House [076]   283
Soseikan — Yamaguchi House [012]   044, 246
Step [033]   015, 068, 257, 469
Stone Sculpture Museum [276]   114, 421
Studio Karl Lagerfeld [165]   108, 343
Sun Place [044]   074, 264
Sunainosato Tenshinan [338]   462
Suntory Museum + Mermaid Plaza [139]   194, 324
Swan — Kobayashi House [002]   240

T:
Tadao Ando Exhibition in Palladian Basilica [147]   331
Taigakuin Temple [249]   403
Taiyo-Cement Headquarters Building [078]   284
Takahashi House [004]   241
Tanaka Atelier [085]   288
Tate Gallery of Modern Art, International Design Competition [155]   019, 337
Tatsumi House [007]   044, 243
Tea House for Soseikan — Yamaguchi House Addition [046]   265
Tea House in Oyodo (Veneer, Block, Tent) [069]   279
Teatrino [308]   108, 444
Temporary Theater for Bishin Jumonji, Photographer [113]   305
Tenement House with Four Flats [014]   247
Tennoji Park, Greenhouse (Main Pavilion for Tennoji Fair) [087]   290
Tezukayama House — Manabe House [021]   251
Tezukayama Tower Plaza [018]   044, 227, 250
The International Library of Children's Literature [207]   019, 373
The International Library of Children's Literature / Arch Building [324]   455
The Modern Art Museum and Architecture Museum, Stockholm, International Design Competition [112]   305
The Museum of World Cultures on the River Rhine [173]   348
The Reconstruction of JR Kyoto Station, International Design Competition [121]   311
The Tall Green Project [311]   446
The Theater in the Rock, Oya [158]   339
The Yokogurayama Natural Forest Museum, Ochi [168]   346
Theater on the Water [088]   290
Time's I, II [061]   015, 080, 274
Tokyo Oliympic Games 2016 Project [244]   399
Tokyu Oimachi-Line Kaminoge Station [289]   431
Tokyu Toyoko-Line Shibuya Station [258]   015, 409
Tomishima House [005]   030, 242
TOTO Seminar House [169]   346
Towada Education Plaza [320]   453
Town House in Hirano — Nomi House [161]   341
Town House in Kujo — Izutsu House [047]   128, 266
Town House in Saikudani — Noguchi House [082]   287
TS Building [080]   286
Twin Wall [013]   247

U:
Uchida House [009]   244
Ueda House [032]   257
Uejo House [056]   271
Umekita Plaza [303]   441
Umemiya House [052]   269
Uno House [010]   245

V:
Valser Path [334]   460
Vicariato Di Roma — International Design Competition for the Church of the Year 2000 [164]   343
Villa Budapest [264]   413
Vitra Seminar House [134]   102, 321

W:
Walk Around House [234]   392
Wall House — Matsumoto House [022]   252
Wall of Hope [310]   446
Water Charnel, Cemetery in the Woods [329]   458
Water Temple [120]   170, 310
Wrightwood Gallery [333]   460

X:
Xinhua Redstar Landmark [341]   464

Y:
Yagi House [170]   347
Yao Clinic [107]   302
YKK Seminar House [135]   322
Yokohama Local Meteorological Observatory [268]   417
Yoshida House [077]   296
Yoshimoto House [068]   278
Yu-Un (Obayashi Collection) [243]   399

0–9:
21_21 Design Sight [248]   402
4 × 4 House [218]   056, 381
4 × 4 House (Tokyo) [205]   372

著者略歴
Author's Profile

安藤忠雄
1941年大阪生まれ。独学で建築を学び、69年安藤忠雄建築研究所設立。97年から東京大学教授。現在、同名誉教授。イェール、コロンビア、ハーバード大学の客員教授歴任。代表作に「光の教会」「ピューリッツァー美術館」「地中美術館」などがある。日本建築学会賞、日本芸術院賞、プリツカー賞、文化功労者、国際建築家連合ゴールドメダル、文化勲章、フランス芸術文化勲章（コマンドゥール）、イタリア共和国功労勲章グランデ・ウフィチャーレ章など受賞多数。ニューヨーク近代美術館、パリのポンピドー・センターなどで作品展開催。
（詳細は454–458頁参照）

Tadao Ando
Born in 1941 in Osaka. Self-taught in architecture. Established Tadao Ando Architect & Associates in 1969. Professor at the University of Tokyo from 1997 and Professor Emeritus now. Taught as a visiting professor at Yale University, Columbia University and Harvard University. Major works include the Church of the Light, Pulitzer Arts Foundation, and Chichu Art Museum. Awarded the Architectural Institute of Japan (AIJ) Prize, Japan Art Academy Prize, Pritzker Architecture Prize, Person of Cultural Merit (Japan), International Union of Architects (UIA) Gold Medal, Order of Culture (Japan), Commander of the Order of Art and Letters (France) and Grand Officer of the Order of Merit (Italy). Held solo exhibitions at the Museum of Modern Art (MoMA) and Centre Pompidou.
(See 454–458 for details)

松葉一清
1953年神戸生まれ、76年京都大学建築学科卒、朝日新聞社特別編集委員などを経て2008年から武蔵野美術大学教授。主な著書に『近代主義を超えて』（鹿島出版会）、『日本のポスト・モダニズム』（三省堂）、『帝都復興せり！』（平凡社、朝日文庫）、『パリの奇跡』（講談社現代新書、朝日文庫）、『アンドウ　安藤忠雄・建築家の発想と仕事』（講談社、英語版・講談社インターナショナル）、『現代建築のトリセツ』（PHP新書）、『集合住宅——二〇世紀のユートピア』（ちくま新書）などがある。2011年日本建築学会建築文化賞、2017年不動産協会賞。

Kazukiyo Matsuba
Born in 1953 in Kobe. Graduated from the School of Architecture, Faculty of Engineering, Kyoto University in 1976. After working as a special editor at The Asahi Shimbun Company, was appointed Professor at Musashino Art University in 2008. Major publications include "Beyond Modernism" (Kajima Institute Publishing Co., Ltd.), "Post-modernism in Japan" (Sanseido Co., Ltd.), "Reconstruction of the Imperial Capital!" (Heibonsha and Asahi Shimbun Publications Inc.), "Miracle of Paris" (Kodansha Ltd., and Asahi Shimbun Publications Inc.), "ANDO, architect" (Kodansha Ltd.), "Instructions on Contemporary Architecture" (PHP Institute, Inc.), "Apartment Houses — Utopia in the 20th century" (Chikumashobo). Awarded the Appreciation Prize of AIJ in 2011 and The Real Estate Companies Association Prize in 2017.

クレジット
Credits

著者：
安藤忠雄　松葉一清

編集責任者：
川床優

編集担当：
川嶋勝（鹿島出版会）
重政幸治（アイズインク）

編集協力：
森詩麻夫（安藤忠雄建築研究所）
古平知沙都（同）
林田安紀子（同）

ブックデザイン：
渡邉翔

英文翻訳：
牧尾晴喜（フレーズクレーズ）

Author:
Tadao Ando, Kazukiyo Matsuba

Executive Editor:
Yu Kawatoko

Editorial Staff:
Masaru Kawashima
(Kajima Institute Publishing)
Koji Shigemasa
(IZE inc.)

Editing Cooperation:
Shimao Mori
(Tadao Ando Architect & Associates)
Chisato Kodaira
(Tadao Ando Architect & Associates)
Akiko Hayashida
(Tadao Ando Architect & Associates)

Book Design:
Sho Watanabe

Translation into English:
Haruki Makio (Fraze Craze Inc.)

写真（Photography）：
市川かおり（Kaori Ichikawa）
201-2
大橋冨夫（Tomio Ohashi）
107-3, 194, 195
小川重雄（Shigeo Ogawa）
101, 102, 112-117, 168, 169, 200
閑野欣次（Kinji Kanno）
002
白鳥美雄（Yoshio Shiratori）
160
新建築社（Shinkenchiku-sha）
030-2, 032, 034, 048, 049-2, 052, 053,
055-6, 072, 073-4, 078, 079, 084, 085-7,
087-2, 096-3, 097-1, 103 middle & below,
104, 105, 126, 128, 143-3, 148, 149-3,
154-4, 159-3, 163-3, 170, 171-2, 172,
173-5, 197-3, 211
高瀬良夫／GA photographers
（Yoshio Takase／GA photographers）
028
名執一雄（Kazuo Natori）
136-139
藤塚光政（Mitsumasa Fujitsuka）
083, 092, 093, 096-1, 098-100
二川幸夫（Yukio Futagawa）
184-3

松岡満男（Mitsuo Matsuoka）
055-4&5, 056, 057, 088, 089, 094, 095,
103 above, 108, 109-3, 118, 119-1, 120,
121, 123, 132-135, 143-2, 145-6, 149-2,
152, 154-3, 164-166, 173-6, 174-177,
182, 184-2, 185, 187-190, 191-10,
193-13, 196, 197-2, 202, 203, 206, 207-3
松葉一清（Kazukiyo Matsuba）
085-6, 186, 191-9, 193-12
山本糾（Tadasu Yamamoto）
097-2
Andrea Jemolo
111
Jeff Goldberg / Esto
124
Stephane Courtrier
178, 179-3
Palazzo Grassi S.p.A,
ORCH Orsen go-Chemollo
109-1&2, 110
Robert Pettus
119-3

上記以外すべて安藤忠雄建築研究所
Other Photographs: Courtesy of
Tadao Ando Architect & Associates

図版（Drawings）：
安藤忠雄建築研究所
Tadao Ando Architect & Associates

安藤忠雄　建築家と建築作品

2017年10月20日　第1刷発行

著者：安藤忠雄　松葉一清

発行者：坪内文生

発行所：鹿島出版会
〒104-0028　東京都中央区八重洲2-5-14
電話：03-6202-5200
振替：00160-2-180883

印刷：三美印刷

製本：牧製本

©Tadao Ando, Kazukiyo Matsuba 2017,
Printed in Japan
ISBN 978-4-306-04656-6 C3052

落丁・乱丁本はお取り替えいたします。
本書の無断複製（コピー）は
著作権法上での例外を除き禁じられています。
また、代行業者等に依頼して
スキャンやデジタル化することは、
たとえ個人や家庭内の利用を
目的とする場合でも著作権法違反です。

本書の内容に関するご意見・ご感想は
下記までお寄せ下さい。
URL：http://www.kajima-publishing.co.jp/
e-mail：info@kajima-publishing.co.jp

ANDO ARCHITECT AND ARCHITECTURE

© First Published in Japan, October 20, 2017
by Kajima Institute Publishing Co., Ltd.
2-5-14 Yaesu, Chuo-ku, Tokyo
104-0028 Japan
Tel. +81 3 6202 5200

Author: Tadao Ando, Kazukiyo Matsuba
Publisher: Fumio Tsubouchi

All rights reserved.
No parts of this publication may be reproduced,
stored in a retrieval system,
or transmitted in any form or by any means
(electronic, mechanical,
photocopying, recording, or otherwise),
without the prior consent of the publisher.

Printed in Japan

URL: http://www.kajima-publishing.co.jp
e-mail: info@kajima-publishing.co.jp